British Politics in Focus

Roy Bentley
Alan Dobson
Maggie Grant
David Roberts

CPL

To Madeleine, Lise, Zoë, Carol, Wyn, Joan and Ray

The Authors

Roy Bentley is a Senior Lecturer in Social Sciences and Access Coordinator at Oxford College of Further Education.

Alan Dobson is Head of Combined Humanities at Oldham Sixth Form College.

Maggie Grant is a Lecturer in Politics and Sociology at Mid-Warwickshire College.

David Roberts is Head of Continuing Education at Great Yarmouth College.

Cover design by Andrew Allen
Cover illustration provided by The Image Bank
Reader - Richard Holmes
Graphics by Elaine M. Sumner (Waring-Collins partnership)

Acknowledgements

The publishers wish to thank the following for permission to reproduce photographs, cartoons and other illustrations: Advertising Archive p.560; Amnesty International p.280; David Austin p.127, p.141, p.354; Steve Bell p.90, p.96, p.145, p.148, p.219, p.263, p.288, p.352, p.420, p.495, p.545, p.550; Brick p.72 (t), p.78, p.81, p.110, p.132 (bl), p.348, p.428, p.430, p.438, p.543, p.552 (t), p.575, p.584; Sandy Britton-Finnie p.57 (t); British Library p.529 (l), p.559; Dave Burgess p.233 (t); Cartoon Library p.207 (m); Central Office of Information p.61 (b), p.358; CRE p.120; Conservative Central Office p.25, p.62, p.197 (l), p.247; Neil Crossley p.95, p.374 (tl), p.445; Electoral Reform Society p.295 (l); Express newspapers p.267; Lisa Fabry p.470; Farmer's Weekly, p.284; Friends of the Earth p.294; Guardian Newspapers p.333, p.508; Gibbard p.44 (both), p.48 (all), p.318, p.351, p.360; The Howard League p.298 (l); Hulton Deutsch p.200 (Balfour), p.208, p.532, p.552 (b); The Independent p.396, p.458; Independent on Sunday p.340, p.341, 501; IPPR, p.101; John Kent p.256 (b), p.380, p.449; Labour party p.180 (tr), p.197 (r), p.310; Labour Research p.324, p.516; Lancashire County Council p.486; Liberal Democrats p.224, p.336; Liberty p.525; Jenny Matthews p.321; Motorcycle Action Group p.295; Ormskirk Advertiser p.323, p.327; PCA p.520; Ingram Pinn/Financial Times p.399; Political Animal Lobby p.291; Popperfoto, p.179 (b), p.205, p.216, p.301 (r); Press Association p.5 (b), p.57 (b), p.91, p.180 (tl); Punch p.132 (br), p.211, p.222 (t), p.341, p.512; Rex Features p.175 (both), p.180 (b); Saatchi & Saatchi p.45, p.256 (t), p.258; Salvation Army p.19; SCR p.529 (r); Posy Simmonds p.116; David Simonds p.100, p.107, p.124, p.462, p.463, p.501; Ian Traynor p.8, p.171, p.237, p.411; Topham p.92, p.200 (all except Balfour), p.211 (tl), p.222 (b), p.228, p.236, p.297, p.302, p.327 (l), p.423, p.538, p.546; Trog/Observer p.67, p.111; Unison p.285; Universal Pictorial Press p.374 (all except tr), p.375; Weidenfeld and Nicolson p.436; West Lancs District Council p.486, p.490; Tony Winterbottom p.183, p.243, p.402, p.475, p.540.

Every effort has been made to locate the copyright owners of material used in this book. Any omissions brought to the attention of the publisher are regretted and will be credited in subsequent printings.

British Library Cataloguing in Publication Data
A catalogue record for this book is available from the British Library.

ISBN 1 873929 32 3

Causeway Press Limited
PO Box 13, Ormskirk, Lancs, L39 5HP

1st impression, 1995

Graphic origination by Caroline Waring-Collins (Waring-Collins partnership)

Printed and bound by The Bath Press, Lower Bristol Road, Bath.

Contents

Preface

British Politics in Focus has been devised and written by a team of lecturers who teach A level and higher education courses. Its aim is to provide a new approach to the study of British Government and Politics.

Each chapter in **British Politics in Focus** follows the same format. Chapters have the following features:

Introduction	A brief outline of the main subjects to be covered by the chapter as a whole.
Chapter summary	An outline of the material to be covered in each part of the chapter.
Key Issues	At the beginning of each new part of a chapter, Key Issues are raised. A single **part** of a chapter is often broken into several discrete **sections**.
Activities	At the end of each section in a chapter, an activity is provided to apply, reinforce and extend the points made in the preceding text. Activities utilise a wide range of up-to-date primary source material.
Cross referencing	Since many readers will not read the book from beginning to end, cross references are included at frequent intervals to indicate where further information can be found.
References	At the end of each chapter, a list of references is provided. This is not intended to be a comprehensive list. It simply provides further information about the books and articles which are specifically mentioned in the text.

I would like to thank Alan, Maggie and Roy, my fellow authors, who have worked hard through all the stages of the book's preparation and have been willing to revise their work to meet changes and refinements in format and style as the project has developed. Others have also contributed at various stages - notably, John, Philip, Steve, Will and Wyn - and we would like to thank them for their efforts. Thanks are also due to all at Causeway Press who have been associated with the project, especially to Steve Lancaster without whose encouragement and clear-sighted approach to the book as a whole, it may never have reached completion. All mistakes, of course, remain the responsibility of the authors.

Finally, we would welcome any comments you may have about **British Politics in Focus**, whether critical or otherwise.

David Roberts
July 1995

Part 1

What is politics?

1 What is politics?

Introduction

What is the link between the Prime Minister discussing government policy with journalists outside Number 10 Downing Street, a lively debate in Parliament, a local Labour councillor addressing a public meeting about the planned closure of a hospital, and an informal conversation between Conservative backbenchers in a House of Commons bar or tearoom? The answer is that these are all examples of political activity. Political activity, however, is not just activity involving politicians or people who belong to a political party. When, in early 1995, groups of people gathered on the streets to protest against the export of veal calves, for example, many of the demonstrators did not belong to any political party, but their action was still political.

In its broadest sense, politics concerns the way in which people interact - how they make decisions and settle disputes. It is, therefore, concerned with power and the way in which power is distributed in society. Whilst power is most obviously held by the government and its agents, it is not exclusively held by them. Decisions are made at many different levels. Politics therefore operates at many different levels.

This chapter examines what exactly is meant by the terms 'politics' and 'political activity'. More specifically, it considers where political activity takes place in the UK and how power is distributed.

Chapter summary

Part 1 deals with the question **'what is politics?'** It considers two approaches – politics as the study of **conflict resolution** and politics as the study of **power**.

Part 2 considers **different types of political activity**. What is political activity? Who is involved in it? Where does it take place?

Part 3 discusses **where political activity takes place in the UK**. It provides an introduction to the British system of government.

1 Definitions

Key Issues

1. How can politics be defined?
2. What leads to conflict in society and how can it be resolved?
3. What is power and how does it differ from authority?
4. Why is politics necessary?

What is politics?

People are social beings. They choose to live together in groups. Because people live together in groups, there is a need to make decisions - about how the resources available to the group are to be shared out, for example, or how conflicts which arise within the group are to be resolved. The study of politics is the study of how such decisions **are** made. It may also be the study of how such decisions **should be** made.

Since the resources available to any group are limited, questions inevitably arise about how the resources which are available should be distributed. Should everybody have an equal share, for example, or do some people deserve a bigger share than others? Since it is possible to increase the resources available to a group (by conquest, technological advance or better management of existing resources), further questions arise. For example, what (if any) strategy should be employed to increase resources and what is the best way to protect the resources which already exist? Since there is no single correct answer to such questions, different people have different ideas about what is the best action to take. According to some commentators, the conflict which arises from the expression of different views is at the heart of politics. The study of politics is the study of conflict resolution.

a) Politics as the study of conflict resolution

Modern society is highly complex. Individuals argue over many different interests, values and beliefs. Conflict does not just take place between individuals, however. It also exists between larger groups - between countries as well as within them. According to one viewpoint, the aim of politics is to remove conflict so that people can live in reasonable harmony with each other. In other words, the aim of politics is to produce consensus - a broad agreement over what people want and what they believe is right.

In general terms, it can be argued that conflict arises for two main reasons. First, it arises because of conflicting interests. And second, it arises because of conflicting values or beliefs.

Conflicting interests

In a country such as Britain there is a complex web of interests which people want to expand and protect. Many of these interests are economic and financial. People want a job with good pay, a comfortable house, holidays and so on. They want a good education for their children, health care and security against poverty. Miners want a prosperous coal industry. Publishers want people to buy lots of books.

Although many of the interests, such as the desire for a good health system, are common to all people, difficulties and disagreement emerge because resources are limited and different people have different priorities. Some people might want more money to be spent on high-tech machinery in hospitals, for example, whilst others want more nurses to be employed at a better rate of pay. Since there may not be the resources to take both approaches, choices have to be made. It is the necessity of making such choices which leads to conflict.

Conflicting values

When people defend their interests, it does not necessarily mean that they are being selfish. Opponents of a new opencast mine, for example, may be furious that it is close to their homes, but they might also claim with some justification that to open the mine would be an ecological disaster because of the damage it would cause to the wildlife living on the site. Such arguments might produce support from people living miles away who are not personally affected by the project. Political activity, in other words, can spring from a set of values and beliefs as well as from self-interest. Equally, the way in which a conflict is resolved might owe more to the values and beliefs of the decision makers than to their personal interest in the matter.

b) Politics as the study of power

The sociologists Dowse & Hughes (1972), however, argue that politics is about power, claiming that 'politics occurs when there are differentials in power'. This suggests that:

> 'Any social relationship which involves power differentials is political. Political relationships would extend from parents assigning domestic chores to their children to teachers enforcing discipline in the classroom; from a manager organising a workforce to a general ordering troops into battle.' (Haralambos & Holborn, 1995, p.501)

If people have power, it means that they are able to make other people do what they want them to do even if the other people do not want to do it. Power is, therefore, the ability to influence the behaviour of another either by threat, sanctions or through manipulation. In all political situations, those who have power are able to reward those who conform and punish those who do not.

Power cannot be exercised unless there is some way of backing it up. This may be the direct threat of or the use of force, but it does not have to be. Power that is based on the direct threat of or the use of force is usually described as '**coercion**'. But individuals (or governments) often do not have to resort to coercion to get their own way. Rather, some forms of power are accepted as 'legitimate' (as fair and right) and people are obedient because of that. In Britain, for example, most people obey the laws made by the government even if they themselves do not agree with them. They do this because they accept that the system of government is legitimate. Power which is regarded as legitimate is usually described as '**authority**'.

Civil disobedience

There is a fine line between authority and coercion. The British government may gain legitimate power by winning an election, but does it have the right to use coercion if people do not obey laws passed by the government? Should citizens have the right to protest against what they believe are unfair or unjust laws?

When people protest against what they believe are unfair laws, their action is usually described as 'civil disobedience'. According to Heywood (1994), there is an important difference between a criminal act and an act of civil disobedience. Whilst a criminal act is committed for selfish ends, an act of civil disobedience can be justified by reference to 'religious, moral and political principles' (Heywood, 1994, p.216). Civil disobedience is, in other words, political whilst a criminal act is not. This is because civil disobedience uses ethical grounds to question the way in which power is used whilst a criminal act does not.

Activity 1.1

Item A *What is politics?*

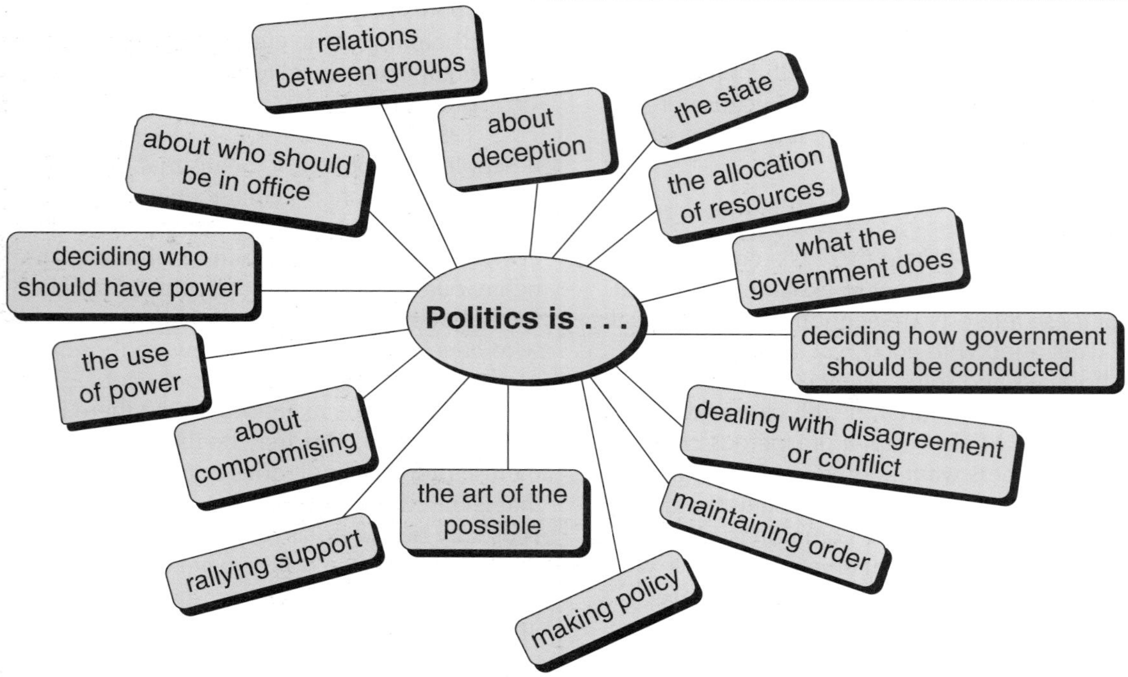

Adapted from Sparkes, 1994.

Item B *Weber's three types of authority*

Max Weber, a German sociologist who lived in the 19th century, distinguished between three different types of authority:

ii) Charismatic authority
Charismatic authority depends upon the special qualities of a leader. People are drawn to follow the leader because of the qualities which they believe that leader to have. Charismatic authority may die with the leader or continue to work through a group of chosen disciples.

i) Traditional authority
Traditional authority depends upon the belief in established customs and traditions. Those in authority expect obedience and loyalty on the grounds that established customs and traditions demand it. For example, the tradition of a hereditary monarchy demands that a new monarch commands as much obedience and loyalty as the previous monarch commanded.

iii) Rational-legal authority
Rational-legal authority depends upon a formal set of rules which gives those who hold authority the right to direct and command others and to take decisions on their behalf. It has a moral dimension in that citizens have freely handed power over to another person (or other people). So, a democratic government can be said to exercise rational-legal authority since the electorate hands over power to it through the ballot box.

It should be noted that Weber regarded these three categories as 'ideal types'. In the real world, authority might come from two or more of the three sources. Second, Weber believed that there was a fixed amount of power in any society. Since the amount of power is constant, power held by any individual or group is power not available to any other individual or group. And third, Weber suggested that power is always used to further the interests of those who hold it.

Adapted from Haralambos & Holborn, 1995.

Item C *Lukes' three faces of power*

In a book published in 1974, Steven Lukes argued that power has three faces or dimensions.

i) Decision making
The first face of power is its open face - the power that can be seen to be exercised when a decision is taken. Suppose the government proposed a law in Britain. This proposal would be debated in Cabinet and in Parliament. Interest groups would lobby MPs. There might be demonstrations for or against the proposal. Eventually, the proposal might pass through Parliament, gain royal assent and become law. In this decision making process, it would be relatively straightforward to identify where power lay.

iii) Manipulating desires
The third face of power goes one step further. Lukes suggests that power can be exercised through manipulation. People with power can persuade others that what is being offered is what is desired. For example, some feminists would argue that men exercise power over women in contemporary Britain by persuading them that being a mother and a housewife are the most desirable roles for women. In reality, feminists claim, women who occupy these roles are exploited by, and for the benefit of, men.

ii) Non-decision making
The second face of power is its secretive face. Power is exercised behind closed doors. Those who have the power to set the political agenda have the power to determine not only what can be discussed, but, more important, what cannot be discussed. Power is, therefore, not just about making decisions. It is also about preventing decisions being taken or about narrowing the choices which are considered. For example, a teacher might offer students the opportunity to decide whether to do a piece of homework that week or the following week. The class appears to have been given the opportunity to reach a decision. In reality, however, power still rests with the teacher who has limited the options open to the students. The students are not free to decide whether or not they do this particular piece of work, nor can they choose to reject doing homework altogether.

Adapted from Haralambos & Holborn, 1995.

Item D *Protest against the export of veal calves*

This photograph shows a protest against the export of live calves in Dover on 20 April 1995. The car has been driven into the road by a demonstrator in an attempt to obstruct lorries carrying live animals.

Questions

1. Using Item A, write a paragraph explaining what is meant by 'politics'.
2. a) Which of Weber's three types of authority in Item B best describes the British political system today? Give reasons for your answer.
   b) Can you think of examples to illustrate the other two types of authority?
3. What does Item C tell us about the way in which politics works in Britain today?
4. a) Explain why what is happening in Item D is political.
   b) What does this picture tell us about the British political system?

2 Political activity

Key Issues

1. What is a political activity?
2. Who gets involved in politics?
3. Where does politics take place?

Types of political activity

When people either belong to or take a side over a particular issue, they are engaged in political activity. The most common political activity in Britain, as in most countries, is voting. In the general election held in April 1992, for example, 77.7% of the electorate turned out to vote. Although a smaller percentage of the electorate tends to vote in local or European elections (just 38% voted in the local elections of May 1995, for example, and only 36.5% voted in the European election of June 1994), these elections involve the political participation of far more people than any other activity.

Apart from voting, people have the opportunity of participating in the political process in a number of other ways. Writing to a local councillor, Member of Parliament (MP) or Member of the European Parliament (MEP), or to a local or national newspaper is one way of participating in the political process. Joining a pressure group or political party is another. But whilst some people feel that paying their membership fee to a pressure group or political party is enough, others are prepared to spend a great deal of their spare time campaigning. There is, in other words, a scale of political participation. This scale ranges from complete inactivity at one end to full-time activity at the other end.

People involved in politics

During election campaigns, activists from the political parties go round from house to house, knocking on doors and canvassing support. On the doorstep, people are often prepared to air their views. When asked what sort of people, in their opinion, are involved in politics, most mention councillors, MPs and MEPs, but few mention themselves. Many say that they are disillusioned with politics and that it is not even worth voting since 'they're all the same'. The fact that they refer to politicians as 'they' rather than 'we' shows that they feel removed from the political process.

In reality, however, political activity covers a much wider area than many people realise. People are involved in political activity whenever they interact with others in any form of social activity. This is because any group, however large or small, involves an element of decision making - and, therefore, involves political activity.

If politics is about decision making, then everybody can be said to be involved in politics through their everyday participation with others. All members of society, after all, are members of groups - either because they are born into them (such as their family or ethnic group) or because they choose to join them (such as a sports club or religious group).

Although everybody participates in political activity in this broad sense, however, far fewer people choose to participate in political activity in the narrower sense of working for a political party or group, or of standing for office.

Those who do choose to get involved in politics in this narrower sense may do so for a number of reasons. First, they may hold a set of beliefs strongly and hope to persuade others to accept them. Second, they may want to bring about change and feel that participation in the political process is the best way to achieve this. Third, they may want to help others. Fourth, they may want to promote their own interests or the interests of their group. And fifth, they may enjoy exercising power over others and want to hold power for its own sake.

Where political activity takes place

If politics is taken in its broadest sense, then it is possible to argue that:

> 'Politics is at the heart of all collective human activity, formal and informal, public and private, in all human groups, institutions and societies, not just some of them, and it always has been and always will be.' (Leftwich, 1984, p.63)

In this sense, political activity can be said to take place wherever one person tries to influence or change the behaviour of another. It takes place in any situation in which decisions have to be made or disagreements sorted out. It takes place wherever there is a power relationship between the participants. It takes place, therefore, at both the micro (small) level and at the macro (large) level.

At the micro level, political activity can be identified, for example, within the family. Take the traditional 'nuclear' family, made up of two parents and two children. In such a family, the roles are clearly defined. The father goes out to work to support the family, whilst the mother stays at home to look after the children and the house. The children are expected to obey the wishes of the parents without question. What the father says, goes. There is, in other words, a power relationship in which the children are at the bottom and the father is at the top. When important decisions have to be made, it is the father who has the final say. But families do not have to work like this, and, indeed, many do not. Many families, for example, have a single parent or, if there are two parents, make decisions jointly rather than allowing the father to have power. The point is that in every family, whether it works as a traditional nuclear family or not, there is a power relationship which determines how decisions are made and disputes are settled. Activity within the family, therefore, can be described as 'political' at the micro level. The same is true of activity which takes place in the workplace or in school or college.

At the macro level, political activity is, perhaps, easier to identify. The work of government ministers, the civil service, opposition MPs or MEPs and local councillors, for example, all comes under the heading of political activity at the macro level. Political activity takes place, therefore, where these people work - at Number 10 Downing Street, in Whitehall, in the British and European Parliaments or in the local council chamber.

It is not only in these places, however, that political activity takes place at the macro level. Since the position of most politicians is dependent on their election to office, it is necessary for them to gain and maintain their electors' support. To do this, they need to communicate with the electorate. As a result, the media is also the centre of a great deal of political activity at the macro level. It is on television or radio, or in the newspapers that politicians try to persuade electors of the validity of their views. Politicians and political activists, therefore, attempt to gain positive exposure of their views in the media and they often stage events for the benefit of the media.

The fact that the media is the focus of a great deal of political activity does not mean, however, that political activity at the macro level is something which only takes place in public. On the contrary, most important decisions are made behind closed doors. Take, for example, the decisions made by the Cabinet. During a parliamentary session, the Cabinet meets each week to discuss what the Prime Minister decides are the key political issues of the day. What is discussed in Cabinet and many of the decisions which are reached, however, remain secret.

Since part or even the whole of the decision making process goes on in secret, it is sometimes difficult to find out exactly how a decision came to be made. It is, therefore, sometimes difficult to be sure exactly where political activity takes place.

Activity 1.2

Item A *The state of the nation (1)*

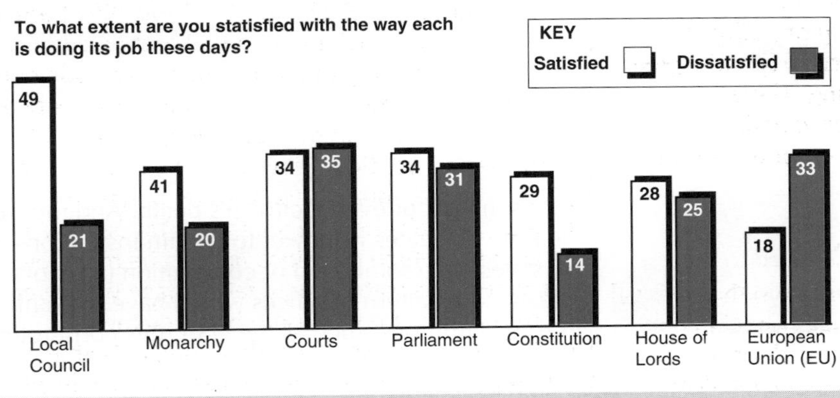

This diagram (left) shows the results of a survey carried out by MORI between 21 April and 8 May 1995. Respondents were asked to say whether they were satisfied with the way each of the political institutions was doing its job. It should be noted, however, that the figures only include those who expressed a preference. For example, 50% of respondents said that they had no opinion about whether the EU was doing a good job.

Adapted from *New Statesman and Society*, 2 June 1995.

Item B *The state of the nation (2)*

The MORI poll carried out between 21 April and 8 May 1995 did not just ask about how satisfied people were with various institutions, it also asked how much people thought they knew about various subjects. Respondents were most confident that they knew about their rights as a citizen - 43% said they knew at least a fair amount about this, although 20% said they knew hardly anything. A third of respondents said that they knew at least a fair amount about the courts and the constitutional role of the monarchy and 32% said the same about their local council. Only 22%, however, said they knew a fair amount about the House of Lords and only 21% said they knew a fair amount about the British constitution. The institution people knew least about was the European Union (EU) - just 19% said they knew a fair amount about the EU, whilst as many as 39% said they knew hardly anything about it.

Adapted from *New Statesman and Society*, 2 June 1995.

Item C *Apathy in the UK*

'I like it! It's a blatant appeal to public apathy.'

Item D *Political activities performed by Conservatives*

How often have you done the following activities during the last FIVE years?

	Never	Rarely	Occasionally	Frequently
Displayed an election poster in a window	51	8	23	18
Signed a petition supported by the party	53	14	26	8
Donated money to Conservative party funds	16	12	45	28
Delivered party leaflets	63	4	13	20
Attended a party meeting	53	13	19	15
Helped at a Conservative party function	58	9	17	16
Canvassed voters	77	6	9	9
Stood for office within the party organisation	89	2	4	5
Stood for office in local government or Parliament	94	1	2	3

This table shows the political activities performed by members of the Conservative party. The survey was carried out in 1992.

Adapted from Whiteley et al., 1994.

Questions

1. Devise a questionnaire to find out the extent to which people participate in political activity. Test your questionnaire on colleagues and friends, and write a short report discussing the findings.
2. What do Items A and B tell us about (a) the political institutions and (b) political activity in the UK?
3. Judging from Item D how politically active is the average member of the Conservative party? What conclusions can be drawn from this information?
4. What point is being made by Item C? Is there any evidence in Items A, B and D to support it?

3 Politics in the UK

Key Issues

1. How is power and authority exercised in the UK?
2. What is the UK's institutional framework?
3. Who exercises power?

3.1 Power and authority in the UK

The institution which exercises power over a defined area is usually described as the **state**. Sovereignty (supreme power) normally lies with the state.

All states have certain characteristics in common. First, they have a territory with clearly defined geographical boundaries. Second, membership is compulsory - all members of the population become citizens at birth. Third, since the state is a sovereign body, it holds the ultimate legal power over its members. The state controls coercive bodies such as the military and the police and it can decide who may use force and to what extent it should be used. Laws made by the state can result in a citizen's imprisonment or even a citizen's death. And fourth, the state delegates its power to certain institutions. All states have some kind of constitution (a set of rules) and a pattern of offices which have to be filled. In some countries, such as the USA, this constitution is written down in a document (codified). In the UK, it is not (see chapter 4).

The UK, like the USA and the other members of the EU, is a 'liberal democracy' (see chapter 7, section 1.1). Three basic types of power are involved in the running of liberal democracies. The first type is **legislative power** - the power to make laws. In the UK, this power has been granted to Parliament. It is the role of Parliament to make new laws and to reform those already in existence. The second type is **executive power** - the power to suggest new laws and to implement existing laws. In the UK, this power has been granted to the government and its departments. The government is helped to fulfill its role by the civil service, a permanent body of supposedly impartial state employees. The third type is **judicial power** - the power to interpret laws and to make judgements about whether or not they have been broken. This power is exercised by the courts. These range from the House of Lords, the highest appeal court, to local courts presided over by magistrates.

In the UK, it is possible to talk of 'parliamentary sovereignty' - the idea that power rests with Parliament. This is because Parliament has the power to make laws which cannot be challenged. Since, however, at regular intervals, Parliament (or, at least the House of Commons) must submit itself to the people in elections, it could be argued that the people are sovereign because they have the power to decide who will rule them.

The institutional framework

The UK is a constitutional monarchy. In former times, the monarch possessed a great deal of political power, but this has now been eroded. Whilst the monarch remains the nominal head of state, the political role played by monarchs in the past is now undertaken by the Prime Minister and other members of government:

> 'The Queen personifies the state. In law, she is head of the executive, an integral part of the legislature, head of the judiciary, the commander-in-chief of the armed forces of the Crown and the "supreme governor" of the established Church of England. As a result of a long process of evolution during which the monarchy's power has been progressively reduced, the Queen acts on the advice of her ministers. Britain is governed by Her Majesty's government in the name of the Queen.' (HMSO, 1994, p.8)

The political power once exercised by the monarch, is now, therefore, exercised by the executive - by the Cabinet, which is chaired by the Prime Minister, and by the government departments. Most government departments are headed by a Cabinet minister chosen by the Prime Minister. The Cabinet meets usually once a week at the Cabinet Room in Number 10 Downing Street, the Prime Minister's official residence.

Most Cabinet ministers are in charge of a government department - such as the Department of Health, the Department of Transport and so on. These ministers are responsible for a particular area of the government's work. Occasionally, however, a Cabinet minister is appointed 'without portfolio'. As well as choosing Cabinet ministers, the Prime Minister also chooses the junior ministers who work in government departments. At any one time, there are around 100 ministers in total. Periodically, the Prime Minister has a 'reshuffle' and sacks, promotes or moves ministers. Whilst ministers are, therefore, political appointees, they work in tandem with permanent civil servants who are state employees.

Legislative power is exercised by Parliament which consists of two Houses, the House of Commons and the House of Lords. Each member of the House of Commons is elected by people living in a constituency (a geographical area). General elections must take place every five years, but they can be called before the five year term has been completed. The vast majority of candidates in general elections belong to a political party and they stand on behalf of that party. The political party which gains the largest number of seats in the House of Commons is usually invited to form a government (it is possible that the combined number of seats held by two or more parties may outnumber the largest party and by making a coalition these smaller parties may be able to form a government). The leader of the party invited to form the government becomes Prime Minister. The largest party outside government forms the official opposition. The leader of the opposition normally chooses a 'shadow Cabinet'.

When a party wins an election and forms a government, it is generally regarded as having a mandate (the authorisation) to put into practice the promises it made in its election manifesto. The British system of government, however, is **adversarial** - it relies on two sides being taken on any issue. It is, therefore, the job of the opposition to oppose proposals made by the government and to criticise them. Since the government usually commands a majority in the House of Commons, it can normally rely on its supporters to pass its proposals regardless of the criticism made by the opposition.

All proposed legislation must pass through a number of stages before it becomes law. Most proposals ('Bills') are first put forward in the House of Commons. They must pass through both the Houses of Parliament, however, before they can be sent to the monarch for royal assent. Once a Bill has received royal assent, it becomes law.

Members of the House of Lords are not elected (see chapter 14, part 3). Most are hereditary Lords (or 'peers') who gained their position by birthright. Life peers may sit in the Lords during their lifetime, but they do not pass on the right to sit in the Lords to their children. Two other groups sit in the House of Lords - the Lords Spiritual (the two Archbishops and other bishops from the Church of England) and the Lords Pastoral (Law Lords who sit in judgement when the House of Lords is used as a court of appeal).

3.2 Who exercises power in the UK?

Three main models have been developed to explain who exercises power in the UK - the pluralist model, the elite model and the Marxist model.

a) The pluralist model

According to the pluralist model, power is exercised

by the mass of the population, rather than by a small, elite group. This conclusion is derived from two main arguments. First, pluralists note that if a majority of people do not like what their representatives are doing, they can vote them out of office at the next election. Representatives, therefore, have to act in a way that is pleasing to the majority. And second, pluralists claim that people are able to exercise power between elections by joining interest groups (such as political parties, trade unions and other pressure groups). Group activity, they argue, is vital to the successful functioning of the political system. Groups constantly compete to gain the attention of decision makers and it is the job of the decision maker to decide between the competing claims made by different groups. It follows from this, therefore, that what matters to pluralists about the distribution of power in society is not that it is uneven, but that it is widely dispersed rather than concentrated into the hands of the few. It also follows that, according to the pluralist model, the state acts impartially, responding to the demands of different popular pressures. No single group can possibly dominate in society since for every force exerted by one group, there is an equal and opposite force exerted by other groups.

Pluralists argue that such a system is healthy because it encourages political participation, it ensures that people can exert influence over decision makers, it ensures that power is dispersed rather than concentrated into the hands of a few and, at the same time, it allows the view of minority groups to be voiced.

b) The elite model

Elite theorists suggest that power in the UK is held by a small minority of people who use it for their own ends. The unequal distribution of power in society, the model suggests, is not necessarily in the best interests of the majority of people. Rather, it benefits a ruling elite.

Classical elite theorists argued that all states are governed by an elite or competing elites and that the majority of the population is basically passive and uninterested in politics. Schumpeter, for example, defined the role of elections in liberal democracies as:

> 'That institutional arrangement for arriving at political decisions in which individuals acquire the power to decide by means of a competitive struggle for the people's vote.' (Schumpeter, 1974, p.269)

The elite model differs from the pluralist model in a number of ways. First, whereas pluralists argue that political parties act as a route through which different interests can be expressed, elite theorists argue that this is not so. Elite theorists point out that political parties often prevent views and opinions being aired if they do not coincide with the particular party's stance. Second, whilst pluralists concentrate on those groups which make an input into decision making, elite theorists point out that a process of non-decision making can operate to prevent certain interests reaching the political agenda. To put this in terms used by Lukes (1974), pluralists concentrate on the first face of power only, whilst elite theorists also consider the second face of power (see above Activity 1.1, Item C). And third, elite theorists point out that interest groups are not equal in status. Some are more powerful than others and any dispute or disagreement is likely to favour the more powerful group. Those with more economic clout or a well-educated and articulate membership, for example, are more likely to shape the political agenda than those representing groups like the homeless, the poor or the elderly. Pluralists, on the other hand, imply that interest groups compete on a level playing field.

Studies of the British political system have led some elite theorists to suggest that there is a cohesive political class which monopolises power. This is sometimes described as the 'Establishment'. Members of the Establishment share the same sort of social and educational background and have a distinct set of values:

> 'A number of researchers have found that the majority of those who occupy elite positions in Britain are recruited from a minority of the population with highly privileged backgrounds. This appears to apply to a wide range of British elites including politicians, judges, higher civil servants, senior military officers and the directors of large companies and major banks...There is also evidence that there may be some degree of cohesion within and between the various elites.' (Haralambos & Holborn, 1995, pp.518-19)

c. The Marxist model

Like most other liberal democracies, the UK is a capitalist country. The vast bulk of its wealth is owned by individuals rather than by the state. In simple terms, those who own and control the wealth are capitalists whilst the people they employ are workers. Although the capitalists are fewer in number than the workers, they tend to acquire political as well as economic power.

Marxists are fundamentally opposed to the capitalist system. They argue that it is responsible for the inequalities in British society and the unevenness of the distribution of power. Marxist studies of the British political system are, therefore, (unlike some pluralist or elitist studies) necessarily critical.

The Marxist model is closer to the elite model than to the pluralist model. Like elite theorists, Marxists argue that a cohesive political elite exists in the UK. Also like some elite theorists, Marxists agree that the democratic institutions in the UK are a sham. It is not, therefore, in their conclusions that elite theorists and Marxists disagree. Rather, it is the arguments they use to reach these conclusions. Marxists argue that the elite - the ruling class - has power because it controls and owns capital. The source of power lies, therefore, in the economic infrastructure (in the way in which the economic system works). Elite theorists, on the other hand, argue that the explanation for the domination of elites is psychological.

Marxists are particularly critical of the pluralist idea that the state is in some way neutral. On the contrary, Marxists argue, the capitalist system developed to protect the interests of those with economic power. Power is distributed in the state to ensure that this happens. One way in which the state does this is to manipulate people's views. The Marxist model, therefore, incorporates Lukes' third face of power (see above, Activity 1.1, Item C).

Activity 1.3

Item A *The British political system*

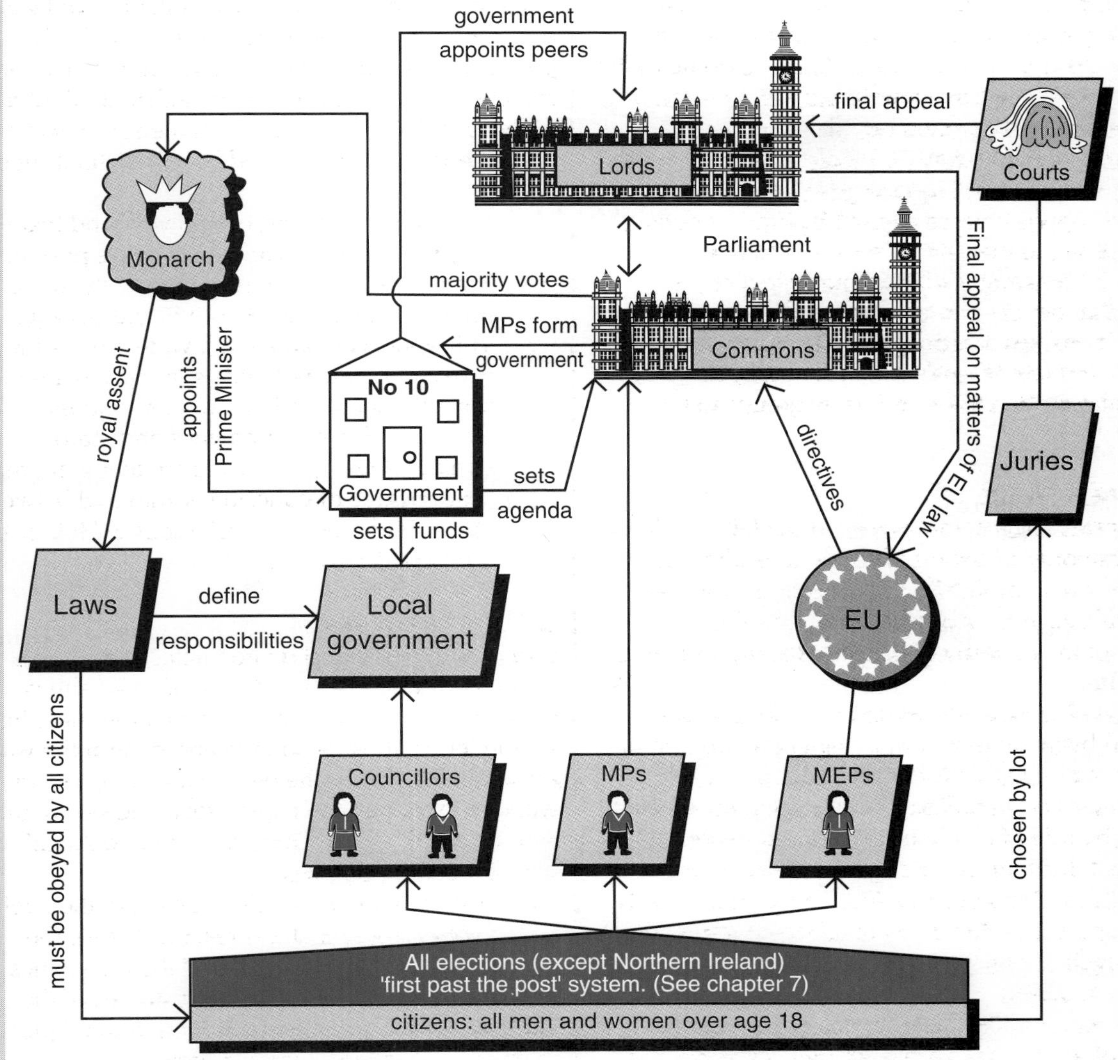

Item B *Political decision making in the UK*

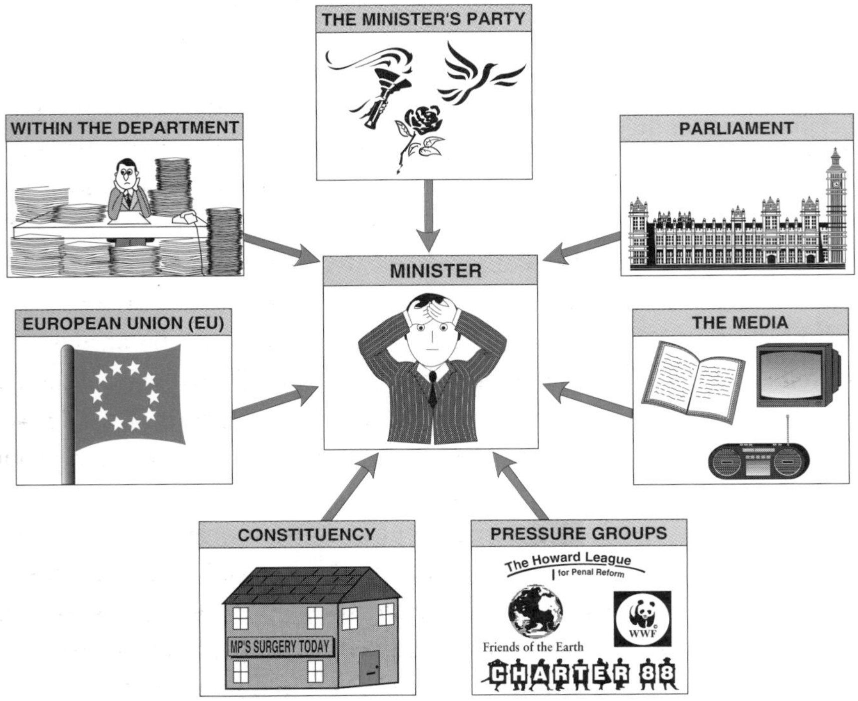

This diagram shows the various pressures on a government minister. Similar diagrams could be drawn for any decision maker.

Questions

1. Use Item A to write a short passage explaining where power is exercised in the UK.

2. a) Which of the three models described in section 3.2 above is illustrated by Item B? Explain how you know.
   b) Design a similar diagram to illustrate one of the other two models.

3. Where does political activity take place in the UK? Use Items A and B and your own diagram from 2b in your answer.

References

Dowse & Hughes (1972) Dowse, R.E. & Hughes, J.A., *Political Sociology*, John Wiley & Sons, 1972.

Haralambos & Holborn (1995) Haralambos, M. & Holborn, M., *Sociology: Themes and Perspectives*, HarperCollins, 1995.

Heywood (1994) Heywood, A., *Political Ideas and Concepts*, Macmillan, 1994.

HMSO (1994) Central Office of Information, *The British System of Government*, HMSO, 1994.

Leftwich (1984) Leftwich, A., *What is Politics?*, Basil Blackwell, 1984.

Lukes (1974) Lukes, S., *Power*, Macmillan, 1974.

Schumpeter (1974) Schumpeter, J.A., *Capitalism, Socialism and Democracy*, Unwin University Books, 1974.

Sparkes (1994) Sparkes, A.W., *Talking Politics: a Wordbook*, Routledge, 1994.

Whiteley et al. (1994) Whiteley, P., Seyd, P. & Richardson, J., *True Blues*, Oxford University Press, 1994.

2 Political ideology

Introduction

Consider the following three statements: 'people are basically selfish and cannot be trusted'; 'the way to reduce crime is to make punishments more severe'; and, 'government should get off our backs'. Do you agree or disagree with each statement? Your answer to this question is important not just because it indicates how you feel about three separate and specific issues but also because it says something about the way in which you view the world. Although everyone views the world in their own, unique way, groups of people hold ideas, beliefs, prejudices, hopes and fears in common. In a group of 10 people, for example, three might agree with all three of the above statements, five might agree with the first two statements but not the third whilst the remaining two might disagree with all three statements. Because groups of people view the world in a similar way, it is possible to identify reasonably coherent structures of thought which are shared by each group. These reasonably coherent structures of thought are known as 'ideologies'.

The identification and analysis of different ideologies is important because it provides explanations of how and why people act as they do and what direction society could or should follow. But such issues are analysed and explained in quite different ways depending on which ideology is used as a guide. It is rather as if each ideology provides us with a pair of glasses which produces its own version of the truth. Change the glasses and the political world is viewed quite differently.

In British politics three key pairs of ideological glasses have been used to view the political landscape: liberalism, conservatism and socialism. This chapter examines the nature of these ideologies, their evolution and the differences between them.

Chapter summary

Part 1 describes the **origin and meaning of the term 'ideology'**. It examines ways in which ideologies can be used as analytical tools.

Part 2 looks at the **core ideas of liberalism**. It focuses on the way in which contemporary progressive liberalism evolved from classical liberalism.

Part 3 considers the **meaning and development of conservatism** - from Burke in the 18th century to the emergence of the New Right and conservatism in the 1990s.

Part 4 explores the **values and beliefs of socialism**, including the impact of Marxism. The differences between democratic socialism and social democracy are analysed.

Part 5 provides an **overview of ideologies** and discusses the role they play in British politics.

1 What is an ideology?

Key Issues

1. How did the term 'ideology' originate and develop?
2. What are political ideologies' concerns?
3. How can ideologies be used as analytical tools?

The origin and definition of the term 'ideology'

The term 'ideology' was first used by the French writer Antoine Destutt de Tracy in his *Elements d'Ideologie*, written between 1801 and 1805. The new term referred to a 'science of ideas' which was to be the basis of a new and better way of conducting politics. This science of ideas was to be free from the kind of prejudice and bias often associated with the intolerance of religious beliefs. In this sense, ideology was not just concerned with ideas but was also a hunt for an objective, scientific and truthful approach to politics.

Since then, the term 'ideology' has been used in a number of ways. Eagleton (1991), for example, provides 16 separate definitions of the term and suggests that:

> 'Nobody has yet come up with a single adequate definition of ideology...This is not because workers in this field are remarkable

> for their low intelligence, but because the term "ideology" has a whole range of useful meanings, not all of which are compatible with each other. To try to compress this wealth of meaning into a single comprehensive definition would thus be unhelpful even if it were possible.' (Eagleton, 1991, p.1)

Whilst it may not be possible to come up with a single, suitable definition, it is possible to identify four distinct ways in which the term 'ideology' has been used.

First, Marx & Engels (1844) suggested that ideology was a set of false and misleading beliefs which provided legitimacy to the existing power structures and prevented the oppressed and exploited masses from seeing and seeking solutions to their oppression.

Second, the philosopher Karl Popper used the term 'ideology' in a negative sense and argued that ideologies were 'closed' systems of political thought:

> 'Ideologies claim a monopoly of truth, they seek to explain everything and in so doing refuse to tolerate rival views or opposing theories. An ideology is thus a "secular religion", which leads to intolerance, censorship and political repression.' (Heywood, 1992, p.7)

Third, when people use the term 'ideology' in ordinary conversation they often use it as a term of abuse. A person who acts 'ideologically' is a person who is extreme, inflexible and intransigent. The implication is that people whose actions are motivated by ideology are completely committed to a set of beliefs which they follow blindly with their minds closed to alternative views. Those who are guided by ideology have a hidden agenda and are, therefore, not to be trusted.

And fourth, an ideology is:

> 'A set of ideas by which men posit, explain and justify the ends and means of organised social action, irrespective of whether such action aims to preserve, amend, uproot or rebuild a given social order.' (Seliger, 1976, p.11)

An ideology is, therefore, a reasonably coherent structure of thought shared by a group of people. It is a means of explaining how society works and of explaining how it ought to work. It is in this sense that the term ideology is most often used by political scientists. Dobson describes this as the 'descriptive' meaning of ideology and argues that an ideology, in this sense, has four elements:

> 'First, it will have a concept of human essence; secondly, an idea about how history has developed and why; thirdly, it will examine the role of the state as it is and ought to be; and, finally, it will have some broad policy prescriptions based on its analysis.' (Dobson, 1992, p.17)

Ideology and human nature

What is the real nature of human beings? Should people be optimists and regard others as essentially trustworthy and able to make their own decisions with a minimum of interference or should they be pessimists who believe that people are flawed and in need of control? How important are people's backgrounds? Does experience shape people's behaviour or is character predetermined?

Such questions may seem to be a long way from what is usually thought of as politics. But that is not so. Take the issue of censorship for example. Those 'optimists' who regard people as essentially trustworthy are likely to oppose censorship because, in their view, people are capable of making up their own minds about what they see, listen to or read. 'Pessimists', on the other hand, believe that people are essentially flawed and so, to them, censorship is necessary to ensure control.

Similarly, different views about human nature are often the basis of disputes about policy towards crime and punishment. Those who believe that experience shapes people's behaviour are likely to argue that crime is caused by poor social conditions and that improving these conditions would reduce crime. But those who believe that people's characters are predetermined are likely to argue that some people are born criminals and it is in society's interest to keep these criminals locked up.

Ideology and the past

How strong a role should tradition play in our lives? Should changes in society be cautious and build on what we know about the past? Or should changes mean a radical break with the past? The answer to these questions depends on how what happened in the past is interpreted. History is not simply a collection of facts or objective truths, it is a matter of judgement. For example, although all historians would agree that it was the Labour government elected in 1945 which set up the welfare state, not all historians would agree that this was a good thing. Indeed, some historians have argued that the setting up of the welfare state exacerbated Britain's economic and political decline whilst others have argued that it was a positive development which led to several decades of social stability. There is no correct answer here. Historians on both sides use the same evidence. The difference lies in their approach and their attitude towards that evidence. In other words, the way in which they interpret the past is determined by their ideological stance. And this is not just the case with professional historians. It is also the case with anyone who formulates an argument which expresses a view of the past or cites an historical precedent.

The individual and the group

What kind of identity do we have or should we have? Should we see ourselves as individuals, members of a class, a community, a nation, a race? People need a sense of place in the world. But what should be the basis for this? Given that people are all members of different groups, which one (if any) should be paramount? The position of an individual in society can cause particular disagreement. Some believe, for example, that the crucial unit is the individual and that individuals should be encouraged to pursue their own self-interest because, in this way, everybody would benefit. Others argue that this simply encourages selfishness and works against the wider interests of the community or against society as a whole. Still others argue that the nation or the race is the supreme unit and individuals only have any importance as part of such a group.

Ideology and the state

Given that the state consists of the government, civil service, police, judiciary, armed forces and so on, it is bound to be of primary significance to all ideologies even though there is considerable disagreement about what its role ought to be. Do we need a strong state or are our interests best served by a much more limited structure with fewer powers? Does the power of the state pose a threat to our freedom or enhance it? What should be the main priority of the state - order, greater equality, freedom? Is 'big government' a positive benefit because it can improve our lives through planning and the provision of social services or does this produce a 'nanny state' where people are reluctant to look after themselves and expect everything to be done for them from the cradle to the grave?

Conclusions

It is useful to unpick an ideology so that the component parts can be identified. But these parts are also interrelated. Views about human nature, for example, influence attitudes towards the role of the state. Those who believe that individuals are well able to manage their own affairs are likely to regard a powerful state as unnecessary and perhaps even a danger to individual freedom. Those who are more dubious about human nature probably prefer a strong state, if only to maintain order. It is this kind of interrelationship which helps to provide coherence and consistency to an ideology and, therefore, gives it a clearer identity.

It should be noted, however, that just because an ideology is called 'liberalism' or 'conservatism' that does not mean that it can only apply to the Liberal party or the Conservative party. It is true that ideologies are often heavily associated with a particular party, but the relationship is not entirely straightforward. Key liberal ideas, for example, have influenced both the Conservative and Labour parties. Similarly, it could be argued that Margaret Thatcher was not really conservative at all when she was leader of the Conservative party. The activity which follows looks at a number of models which have been used to classify ideologies.

Activity 2.1

Item A *The linear model*

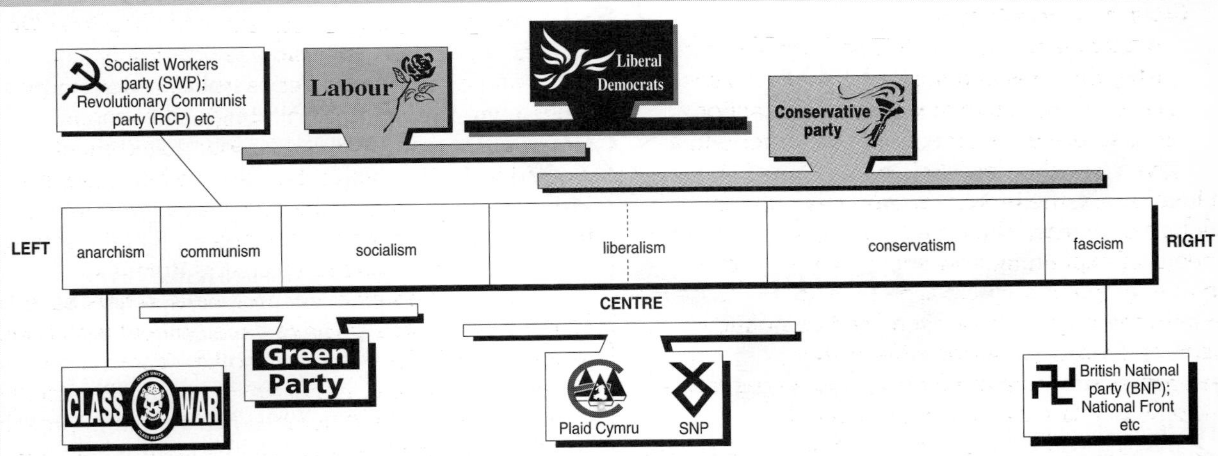

Political scientists who use the left/right linear model of the political spectrum argue that it reflects different political values about economic policy and different attitudes towards equality. Left wingers aim for greater equality and this is reflected in their economic policies. Those on the far left argue for a state-planned economy whilst socialists and liberals support a mixed economy. Right wingers claim that equality is either undesirable or impossible and support free market capitalism and privately owned property. But the model is inconsistent. Some fascist regimes practised state ownership, for example, and anarchists are usually located on the left but they do not support state control.

Adapted from Heywood, 1992.

Item B *Eysenck's model*

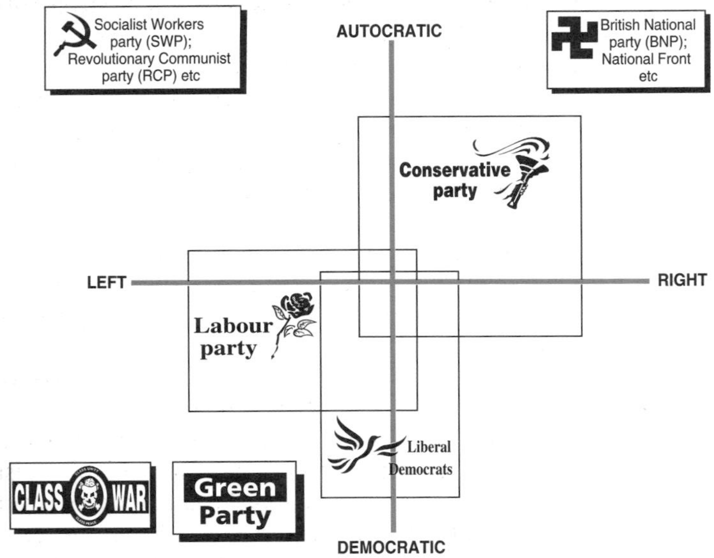

This diagram (left) is based on the model first suggested by Eysenck (1957). He accepted the left/right spectrum, as the horizontal axis of his spectrum, but added a vertical axis. This vertical axis measured political attitudes which were, at one end, democratic (open and accountable) and, at the other end, autocratic (closed and not accountable). This model makes clear the similarities between extreme groups (for example, the fascists and communists), but also indicates the difference between them (for example, by placing the fascists on the extreme right and the communists on the extreme left).

Adapted from Heywood, 1992.

Item C *The 'horseshoe' model*

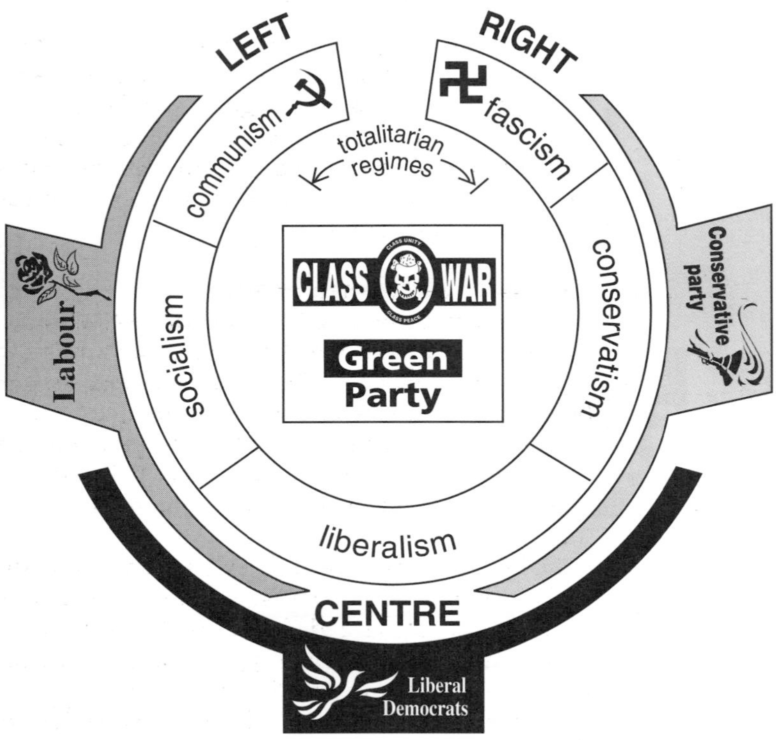

The 'horseshoe' model attempts to overcome the problems of the linear model by emphasising the similarities between the extremes. Both communist and fascist regimes have been described as repressive and authoritarian and so, in this model, they appear side by side. Critics argue that this overplays the similarities. In some respects, for example, Nazi Germany (a fascist state) was very different from the Soviet Union under Stalin (a communist state). For example, capitalism thrived under Nazism whilst it was eradicated by Stalin.

Adapted from Heywood, 1992.

Item D *The political spectrum*

The origin of the terms 'left' and 'right' dates back to the French revolution. Different groups sat in different positions at the first meeting of the Estates General in 1789. Aristocrats who supported the king sat on his right while radicals sat on his left. As a result, 'right' was used of reactionaries (people who opposed change or wanted the old system to remain) whilst 'left' was used of revolutionaries (people who wanted radical change). Today, the left/right divide still exists, but it is complicated. Although some right wingers are reactionaries, others are not. Similarly, although some left wingers are revolutionaries, others resist change.

Adapted from Heywood, 1992.

Questions

1. Using the items in this activity give the arguments for and against pinpointing a person's ideological stance using the terms 'left' and 'right'.
2. Devise a questionnaire that could be used to find out where people fit on the political spectrum.
3. a) What do Items A, B and C tell us about the ideological stance of the three major political parties in Britain?
   b) In your view, which of the three models gives the most realistic account of political debate in Britain today? Give reasons for your answer.

2 Liberalism

Key Issues

1. What is liberalism?
2. How did it develop?
3. What is the difference between 'classical' liberalism and 'progressive' liberalism?

The political roots of liberalism

The political roots of modern liberalism lie in the 17th and 18th centuries when new forces challenged the concentration of political power. The English Civil War of the 1640s led to the execution of Charles I and the creation of a short-lived republic. Although the monarchy was restored in 1660, James II was forced to flee the country in the 'Glorious Revolution' of 1688. It was in this context that the arguments of John Locke (1632-1704) had a considerable impact on the development of liberal ideas.

Locke argued that all people have certain 'natural rights' (the right to life, liberty and property) which cannot be removed except by the agreement of the people themselves. It follows from this that government should be based on the consent of the people as a whole and government should only be tolerated as long as it is prepared to defend the rights of the people. If a government becomes tyrannical and denies its citizens their rights, then it is justifiable for these citizens to withdraw their consent and to rebel against it. To avoid tyranny, Locke argued, there should be limits to the powers of government. For example, the executive (the government) should be separate from the legislature (Parliament) so that power is not overconcentrated.

Locke's arguments made a major impact. For example, the *American Declaration of Independence* of 1776 justified the break with Britain in terms which Locke would have found familiar:

> 'Men are endowed by their creator with certain unalienable rights; that among them are life, liberty and the pursuit of happiness. That to secure these rights, governments are instituted among men, deriving their just powers from the consent of the governed; that whenever any form of government becomes destructive of these ends, it is the right of the people to alter or abolish it and to institute a new government.'

By emphasising the need for consent and for limits on the powers of government, Locke laid the philosophical basis for future liberal reforms.

The economic roots of liberalism

In the 18th and 19th centuries, the old economic order was challenged by the development of new industries and new ways of work in the industrial revolution. The old view was that the state should protect the economy against competition by maintaining high tariffs (a tariff is a tax or a duty placed on goods coming into the country) and by discouraging trade between nations. This view came under attack from liberal economists such as Adam Smith (1723-90). Smith criticised constraints on trade, arguing that the increasing importance of manufacturing and its voracious appetite for raw materials meant that the interests of factory and mine owners lay in widening trade as much as possible. The general prosperity of the country, he claimed, depended on a willingness to accept the forces of the market based on freedom and competition. According to Smith, there was a 'hidden hand of the market' which consisted of thousands of individual decisions made by buyers and sellers. Produce the right goods and profit would follow. Produce the wrong goods and the result was loss and failure. Prosperity depended on allowing people the freedom to make such decisions.

Classical liberalism

Locke, Smith and other writers who challenged the old order and emphasised the importance of freedom, choice and the needs of emerging capitalism, helped to create and develop classical liberalism. Classical liberalism became enormously influential in British politics in the 19th century. Its core ideas can be identified as follows.

Liberalism and human nature

The liberal tradition is to be guardedly optimistic about human nature and about the capacity of people to run their own affairs. This approach stems from the belief that people are rational. Since people know what is in their own interests, they are, therefore, able and willing to make their own choices (whether economic or political) with the minimum of interference.

The individual is at the heart of classical liberalism and the purpose of politics is to enable individuals to develop their talents and abilities so that they can maximise their own happiness. The centrality of the individual is reinforced by the belief that all individuals possess 'inalienable rights' which it is the duty of the state to protect. The liberal philosopher John Stuart Mill (1806-73) argued that individuals should have complete freedom to do whatever they wanted so long as it did not harm others.

Liberalism and the past

Classical liberalism views society as an aggregate of individuals rather than a single body with some kind of collective identity of its own. Reform (which is often equated with 'progress') is seen as both possible and desirable, especially when directed towards maximising the freedom of individuals to make their own choices. According to this view, therefore, social change is the result of individual self-improvement. The liberal view of history is that there is a steady progression towards the formation of a more just and fairer society based on rational principles.

Liberalism and the state

Liberal attitudes towards the state can be illustrated by the comment of the American President Thomas Jefferson who claimed 'that which governs best governs least.' There were two main reasons for such an approach. First, given the stress on the importance of individuals and their capacity for self-government, the role of the state was naturally seen to be minimal. Second, liberals realised that if individuals pursued their self-interest this could mean the emergence of leaders anxious to use their power for their own advantage. The state could become a source of tyranny. Common sense, therefore, dictated that such a possibility could be avoided by both limiting the overall power of the state and by separating the power it was given between different institutions so that it could **not** be concentrated into the hands of one person or group.

At the same time, liberals accepted that some exercise of state power was needed to protect individual interests themselves - for example, by preserving law and order and providing protection from external threats. But, they argued, the state should never be above the law.

The core of liberalism

Liberalism is concerned with three key concepts - freedom, equality and toleration. **Freedom** is important because liberalism is concerned to allow the greatest possible freedom to the individual. The problem is where to draw the line. When are limits on freedom justified? What (if any) constraints should there be on what people can do in pursuit of their own interests?

Equality is closely linked with freedom. For example, by agreeing that all people should have equality before the law and equal political rights, liberals suggest that each individual should have an equal (though restricted) amount of freedom. Similarly, liberals support equality of opportunity but accept that this will not necessarily produce an equal outcome. Even if everybody has an equal opportunity to do something, some people will do it better than others. In this sense, equality, therefore, becomes the right to be unequal.

Linked to the desire for freedom and equality is the liberal's ability to **tolerate** opposing viewpoints. The essence of toleration is for people to accept the people and ideas which they dislike. By believing in the existence of natural rights, such as the freedom to worship, liberals are bound to apply such rights to everyone.

According to Hall (1988), it is because concern about freedom, equality and tolerance is at the heart of classical liberalism that liberals are open-minded, rational, freedom-loving people. Their commitment to individual liberty makes them sceptical of the claims of tradition and prepared to question established authority. But the commitment to individual liberty also means that liberals are often unwilling to interfere in people's private affairs. As a result, in the 19th century liberal politicians advocated minimal interference by the state.

Progressive liberalism

Classical liberalism developed and gained popularity in the late 18th and early 19th century, at the time when Britain's industrial base was becoming established. But industrialisation brought unforeseen social and political changes in its wake. Over time, these social and political changes modified the interpretation and application of classical liberalism.

Perhaps the most important way in which liberalism developed in the 19th century was in relation to the role of the state. Classical liberalism had advocated minimal interference by the state. But the experience of industrialisation raised questions about the legitimacy of this. Despite the Victorian emphasis on the virtue of 'self help', the existence of widespread poverty led to calls for government intervention. Local authorities found that by building schools, hospitals, libraries and houses they could make significant improvements. Besides, surveys carried out at the end of the 19th century found that many people living in poverty simply did not have sufficient means with which to help themselves even if they wanted to. As a result, some liberals began to argue for greater state intervention. T.H. Green, for example, argued that the pursuit of freedom must take into account the practical ability of people to develop their abilities, whilst L. Hobhouse advocated the need to intervene in the market place to secure basic rights such as a living wage. These new ideas, sometimes described as 'progressive liberalism', found their way into the political mainstream in the early part of the 20th century. The Liberal government of 1906 to 1914, for example, intervened in areas of life previously untouched by government when it introduced old age pensions, national health insurance and unemployment insurance.

Progressive liberalism's period of greatest influence, however, came in the first three decades after the Second World War. This was mainly due to the work of two progressive liberals - John Maynard Keynes and William Beveridge. Keynes, an economist, argued that the government should be active in managing or manipulating the nation's economy by using a variety of measures such as the raising or lowering of taxes and the spending of public money on government sponsored projects (see chapter 15, section 1.2). Keynesian economic policies were pursued by both Labour and Conservative governments between 1945 and the mid-1970s. Beveridge produced for the wartime government a report entitled *Social Insurance and Allied Services*. This report, published in 1942, became the blueprint for the welfare state which was set up by the postwar Labour government. The Beveridge Report was concerned with how best to deal with the problems caused by unemployment, sickness and low income. It recommended a system of insurance which would be organised by the state. All those in work would pay insurance to fund benefits for those who were ill or out of work. Health care and education were to be regarded as basic rights and to be provided free by the state (see also, chapter 3, section 1.1).

Activity 2.2

Item A *Classical and progressive liberalism*

(i) The spirit of self help is the root of all genuine growth in the individual. Help from others is often weakening whilst self help is strengthening. Whatever is done for men or groups takes away the incentive and necessity of doing it themselves. And where people are over-guided and over-governed, the inevitable tendency is for them to become comparatively helpless.

Smiles, 1859.

(ii) The working classes have done their best during the past 50 years to make provision without the aid of the state. But it is insufficient. The old man has to bear his own burden while in the case of a young man who is broken down and who has a wife and family to maintain, the suffering is increased and multiplied to that extent. These problems of the sick, of the ill, of the men who cannot find means of earning a living are problems with which it is the business of the state to deal. They are problems which the state has neglected for too long.

David Lloyd George, speech made to Parliament, 15 June 1908.

Item B *Poverty in the early 20th century*

This photo shows a family living in poverty at the beginning of the 20th century.

Item C *Seebohm Rowntree (1)*

Early in 1899, Seebohm Rowntree began an investigation of the working class population of York involving 46,754 people. He found 20,302 people living in poverty - by which he meant that they did not have enough food, fuel or clothing to keep them in good health. About one third did not have a big enough income to live a normal healthy life even if they spent every penny wisely. Rowntree called this 'primary poverty'. All the traditional Victorian 'remedies' like thrift (careful management of money) were no use to these people. You could not be expected to save money when you did not have enough for the basic essentials. Rowntree's figures were very close to those arrived at by Charles Booth who found just over 30% in poverty in East London in the 1890s and early 1900s. It seems likely, therefore, that almost a third of people living in towns in 1900 were forced to go without some of the necessities of a civilised life. Rowntree found two main reasons for 'primary poverty'. In a quarter of cases the chief wage owner of the family was out of action or dead. But in over half the cases, the breadwinner was in regular employment. The wages were simply too low to meet the family's needs. The belief that a man could always provide for his family if he spent carefully and was willing to work hard was shown to be false. However hard he tried, he could not keep out of poverty if he was seriously underpaid.

Adapted from Cootes, 1966.

Item D *Seebohm Rowntree (2)*

(i) The diets of two families interviewed by Rowntree in 1899

FAMILY 1	Breakfast	Dinner	Tea	Supper
Monday	Porridge, fried bacon, toast, butter, treacle, marmalade, tea, coffee.	Boiled mutton, carrots, turnips, potatoes, caper sauce, roly-poly pudding, rice pudding.	Bread, teacake, butter, cake, tea.	Fish, bread, butter, cake, biscuits, cocoa, oranges.
Tuesday	Porridge, fried bacon and eggs, toast, butter, marmalade, coffee, tea.	Mutton, carrots, turnips, caper sauce, potatoes, tapioca pudding.	Bread, cereals, butter, marmalade, tea.	Cutlets, stewed plums, bread, biscuits, cheese, cocoa.
Wednesday	Cereals, fried eggs, bacon, toast, butter, marmalade, coffee, tea.	Rissoles, poached eggs, potatoes, bread pudding.	Bread, butter, teacake, cereals, tea.	Baked haddock, stewed plums, biscuits, hot milk.
FAMILY 2				
Monday	Bacon, bread, tea.	Bacon, bread, tea.	Bacon, bread, tea.	None.
Tuesday	Bread, meat, tea.	Meat, bread, tea.	Meat, bread, tea.	None.
Wednesday	Bread, bacon, tea.	Meat, bread, tea.	Eggs, 'dip', bread, tea.	None.

(ii) The results of Rowntree's first survey were published in 1901. Rowntree conducted two further surveys of York in 1936 and 1951. The results of the three surveys were as follows:

	A	B
1901	43.4	27.8
1936	31.1	18.0
1951	2.8	1.5

Column A shows the percentage of working class families living in poverty.
Column B shows the percentage of the whole population of York living in poverty.

Adapted from Coates & Silburn, 1970.

Item E *Liberal Democrats' constitution*

The Liberal Democrats exist to build and safeguard a fair, free and open society which balances the fundamental values of liberty, equality and community. We champion the freedom, dignity and well-being of individuals. We acknowledge and respect their right of freedom of conscience and their right to develop their talents to the full. We aim to disperse power, to foster diversity and to nurture creativity. We believe that the role of the state is to enable all citizens to attain these ideals, to contribute fully to their communities and to take part in the decisions which affect their lives. We believe people should be involved in running their communities. We are determined to strengthen the democratic process and ensure that there is a just and representative system of government. We will at all times defend the right to speak, write, worship, associate and vote freely and we will protect the right of citizens to enjoy privacy in their own lives and homes. We will foster a strong and sustainable economy which works to the benefit of all with a just distribution of the rewards of success. We want a competitive environment in which the state allows the market to operate freely where possible but intervenes where necessary.

Adapted from Lib Dem, 1994.

Questions

1. Using the passages in Item A write a short passage explaining what classical liberalism and progressive liberalism have in common and how they differ.
2. a) How might it be argued that classical liberalism helped to create the situation illustrated by Items B, C and D?
   b) How do you think information like that in Items B, C and D affected the development of liberalism?
3. 'The principles which lie behind the Liberal Democrats' constitution are liberal principles.' Explain this statement using Item E.

3 Conservatism

Key Issues

1. What is conservatism?
2. How did it develop?
3. What are the different strands of conservatism?

What is conservatism?

The term 'conservative' is used in ordinary conversation to describe a certain state of mind. In general terms, to be conservative is to be cautious, suspicious of change and to prefer to keep things roughly as they are. An extreme conservative may not want any change at all. In this sense 'conservative' can have very wide applications. A football manager may be described as conservative because he is not prepared to experiment with team selection or tactics, for example. The same could be said of someone who finds anything other than meat and two veg for Sunday dinner unacceptably daring.

Using the term 'conservative' in this way can produce some odd results politically. For example, leaders of the old Soviet Union were frequently described as 'conservative' by the mass media in Britain, even though they were all members of the Communist party. In Britain itself, however, membership of the Communist party was regarded as being incompatible with conservatism.

As this example suggests, conservatism in a strict political sense means more than simply having a cautious attitude towards change and a tendency to prefer the status quo (though this is part of its definition). Conservatism as an ideology has distinct views on human nature, for example, and on the role of the state.

Conservatism and human nature

As with all ideologies, views about the nature of human beings underpin a great deal of conservative thinking. Conservatives tend to have few illusions or idealistic hopes about people. It is not just that they see people as being flawed. Rather, conservatives argue that experience shows that people are capable of a whole range of emotions and these different emotions motivate their behaviour in different ways. People are sometimes selfish, sometimes generous, sometimes inconsistent and sometimes quite logical. As a result, conservatives believe that it would be extremely dangerous to base politics on the belief that people are or could be completely rational or predictable in their dealings with one another.

Such views have considerable implications. They mean, for example, that the maintenance of peace and order in society requires a proper framework organised by the state and cannot be left to self-regulation by individuals. Equally, conservatives have little hesitation in blaming human nature for many of the imperfections and problems seen in society.

In addition, conservatives argue that it is a characteristic of human beings that talent and ability are not equally distributed. Therefore, any attempt to impose equality on society is doomed to failure either because natural inequalities are bound to reappear or because the enforcement of equality would require such drastic policies that the result would be a police state. This natural inequality does not, however, lead inevitably to the exploitation of the less privileged since those in a privileged position have a responsibility to use their advantages for the benefit of others.

Conservatism and the past

The conservative view of the past was first set out by Edmund Burke (1729-97) in his *Reflections on the Revolution in France* which was published in 1790, two years after the French Revolution began. Burke saw the French Revolution as a completely undesirable challenge to order, continuity and stability. He believed that society evolves over time and is the product of the gradually accumulated wisdom of the past. It certainly cannot be improved through rapid, especially violent, change. Nor can it be improved by following any kind of abstract idea or blueprint. Reform in society may be desirable sometimes, but it should always be gradual and built on experience. If it is not, the great danger is that a harmonious social fabric, sanctified by tradition, could be recklessly swept away and replaced by chaos.

Burke's arguments are still highly relevant. Modern conservatism emphasises that society should be allowed to develop naturally so that it can reflect the deep needs, values and beliefs which have stood the test of time. Institutions which have evolved (such as Parliament) deserve respect precisely because they have this historic seal of approval. They have proved their worth.

Similar arguments can be used to justify the importance of the ownership of property. Ownership is a reflection of the established rights of individuals and it is a source of stability.

So, if change is necessary, the conservative approach would be to base it on experience and to proceed cautiously. Take the British monarchy for example. This still remains intact, though the monarchy today is very different from that at the beginning of the century (it is less remote from the people than it used to be, for example). Conservatives would argue that it is by responding to changing values and attitudes that the British monarchy has managed to survive in a period when many other monarchies have been discarded.

It is the conservatives' respect for tradition which leads them to criticise the drawing up of idealistic blueprints for social reform. According to conservatives, such reforms are flawed in two ways. They are likely to be based on a lack of understanding of what people really want and, more dangerously, they can destroy something which works. Such a view can be illustrated by the rush to build tower blocks in the 1950s and 1960s. More accommodation was needed at the time, but it can be argued that many of the schemes subsequently failed because they did not take into account the long, established tradition of British people living in houses rather than flats. The result is that, 30 years later, many of these tower blocks are being pulled down.

Conservatism, the individual and the group

Whereas liberalism emphasises the importance of the individual as a basic unit, conservatism stresses the role played by the family and the nation. It is through the family that values can be passed from one generation to the next. This contributes to social harmony. The nation, on the other hand, is typically seen by conservatives as a place where people live in harmony and share deep-seated values and interests. If conflict does occur, it is likely to be blamed on 'troublemakers'. Patriotism, therefore, becomes a source of identity and a stabilising influence because it provides people with a sense of place and a pride in national achievement. To conservatives, the nation is an expression of collective purpose and the symbols of nationhood (such as the flag, the national anthem and celebrations of past achievements or even past defeats) help to weld people together.

Conservatism and the state

Inevitably, to conservatives, the flaws in human nature make a controlling structure necessary. Burke said that good order is the foundation of all good things and conservatism stresses the importance of the rule of law, duty and hierarchy. Here, the state is expected to play an important role. The task of the state, however, is not and cannot be to make people good. Rather, it is to provide a strong framework within which people can be protected while they pursue their own lives.

Conservative attitudes towards the state are also influenced by a traditional respect for the values and virtues of leadership. If human nature is unreliable then it is hardly surprising that mass participation in decision making is treated very cautiously and the importance of leadership is emphasised. Since talents, including leadership talent, are not equally distributed, society needs the guidance of the more able.

Different strands of conservatism

Just as liberalism contains two distinct strands (classical liberalism and progressive liberalism), it is possible to distinguish between a number of different strands of conservatism. In their analysis of the Conservative party, Whiteley and his colleagues (1994) suggest that there are three distinct ideological tendencies within the Conservative party. All three tendencies can be described as variations of conservatism.

1. Traditional conservatism

Whiteley and his colleagues suggest that traditional conservatism is derived from the values and attitudes held in the past by the landowning aristocracy. They categorise it as follows:

> 'It stresses patriotism and authority but often opposes social and political changes such as the emancipation of women, racial integration, the legalisation of abortion and easier divorce...It tends to oppose Britain's closer integration with Europe and is covertly, if not occasionally overtly, racist. Traditionalists are also strong supporters of the idea of social discipline and law and order; they strongly favour capital punishment and emphasise the importance of punishment as a means of dealing with crime...Traditionalists tend to oppose constitutional changes in society, preferring to retain old forms of government...They are strongly attached to the monarchy and to institutions like the House of Lords and would oppose constitutional changes like the introduction of a Bill of Rights.' (Whiteley et al., 1994, pp.130-1)

2. 'One nation' conservatism (see also, p.198)

One nation conservatism was developed in the mid-19th century. This brand of conservatism was first outlined by Benjamin Disraeli (1804-81). Keen to broaden support for the Conservative party, Disraeli argued that, despite class differences, the interests uniting the British people were of far greater significance than those dividing them. It was true that some were more privileged than others, but it was the duty of the more privileged to look after those in need. Heywood (1992) notes that Disraeli's argument had both a pragmatic and a moral strand. On the one hand, Disraeli realised that growing social inequality in Britain had the potential to lead to violent uprisings like those that had taken place in Europe in 1789, 1830 and 1848. Reform was, therefore, necessary on practical grounds because it would protect the long-term interests of the wealthy by ensuring that revolution was avoided. On the other hand, Disraeli argued that reform was necessary on moral grounds. This argument was based on the traditional conservative belief that society was naturally arranged in a hierarchy. Since those at the top of the hierarchy had more wealth and privileges than those at the bottom, those at the top had a greater responsibility to consider the needs of those less fortunate than themselves. In other words, in return for their privileged position, those at the top of the hierarchy had a moral obligation to alleviate the suffering of those at the bottom of the hierarchy. The slogan 'one nation' was given to this type of conservatism because of Disraeli's emphasis on the unity between classes. The British people, the term suggested, all belonged to one happy family, each with a particular role to play and each with a particular place within the family hierarchy.

Whiteley and his colleagues describe one nation conservatives as 'progressives' and argue that:

> '[One nation conservatism] was revived and revitalised by the postwar election defeat of the Conservatives and the perception arising from that defeat that the party needed to modernise itself... Progressives accept and support the Beveridge welfare state and Keynesian methods of macro-economic management...Progressivism stresses the importance of a social safety net to deal with poverty in addition to a limited redistribution of income and wealth. It espouses a paternalistic [father-like] commitment to caring for all members of the community and favours government intervention in the economy to regulate markets.' (Whiteley et al., 1994, p.131)

3. 'Liberal' conservatism

Whilst one nation conservatives accept that the government should play a positive role in economic management and the provision of welfare, 'liberal' conservatives disagree. Liberal conservatism (also called 'libertarian' conservatism) draws on classical liberalism and places it within a conservative framework.

Liberal conservatism is nothing new. Heywood (1992) notes that liberal ideas, especially liberal economic ideas about the free market, have been put forward by conservatives since the 18th century. These ideas are liberal because they support the greatest possible economic liberty and the least possible government regulation of the economy. Liberal conservatism, however, differs from liberalism because liberal conservatives argue that economic liberty is compatible with traditional conservative values such as the belief in authority and duty. Liberal conservatives, therefore, support free market economics and regard state intervention in economic matters as unnecessary and a hindrance. On the other hand, unlike liberals, liberal conservatives do not believe that moral decisions can be left to the individual. They argue that a strong state is required to maintain public order and to ensure that traditional values are upheld.

Whiteley and his colleagues describe liberal conservatives as 'individualists' and categorise them as follows:

> 'Individualism is preoccupied with concerns over private property and the interests of the small businessman. It supports the idea of reduced government intervention in the economy. The most enthusiastic supporters of the Conservative government's privatisation programme can be found among this group. Individualists believe that the welfare state undermines self-reliance and enterprise and that the government should cut taxes and de-regulate business. They also tend to oppose extensions to the welfare state, fearing that this will promote idleness and they are inclined to blame the victim when it comes to explaining the origins of poverty or unemployment.' (Whiteley et al., 1994, p.131)

The New Right

Liberal conservatism has made an important impact on British politics since the mid-1970s. The key event was the election of Margaret Thatcher as leader of the Conservative party. Much of Thatcher's thinking was informed by liberal conservatism and she appointed colleagues with similar views to her own. As a result, liberal conservatism has replaced one nation conservatism as the mainstream ideology in the Conservative party. Since much of liberal conservative thinking fits with attitudes that are generally regarded as being 'right wing' and since the revival of liberal conservatism is a new phenomenon, those who subscribe to liberal conservative thinking are often to be said to belong to the 'New Right'. Like many political movements, the New Right is a loose coalition of writers, politicians and political activists whose views coincide on many, but by no means all, issues. Over the last 20 years, the New Right has made its mark throughout the world - it was, for example, a major influence on American Presidents Ronald Reagan and George Bush during the 1980s.

Activity 2.3

Item A Unemployment

(i) Unemployment 1971-93

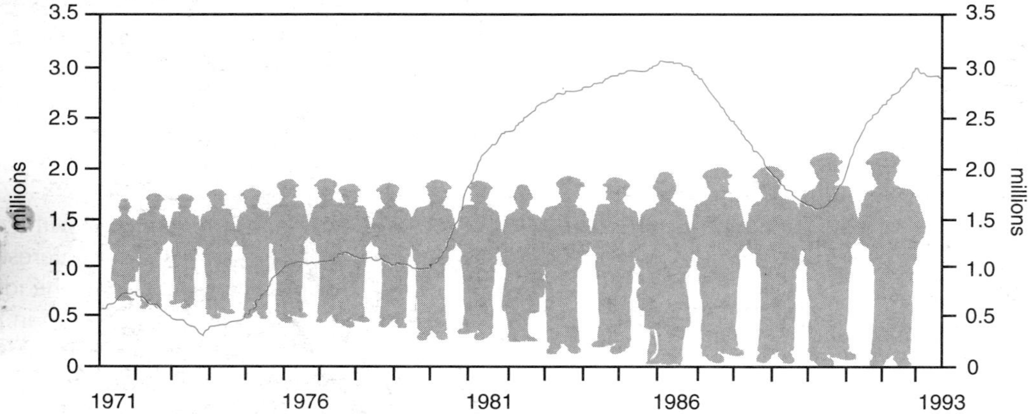

This graph shows the number of people claiming unemployment benefit between 1971 and 1993.

(ii) Frank Monahan says that life on state benefit is stressful. Frank is 40 years old. He is a former sewing machine factory worker but has not been employed since 1981. He lives with his wife Diane who is 35 and their four year old daughter Michelle. They live in a two bedroom council house in Salford. Frank admitted that they do not cope very well. His family lives on £120 a week and it is a struggle to balance the weekly budget. 'If a big gas bill comes in', says Frank, 'I just have to try to pay half and talk them into giving me a bit of time to pay the rest.' Unemployment in Salford is 11.9%.

Adapted from HMSO, 1994 and the *Guardian*, 2 August 1994.

Item B *Survey of members of the Conservative party*

PLEASE TICK ONE BOX FOR EACH STATEMENT

	Strongly agree	Agree	Neither	Disagree	Strongly disagree
The Conservative party should adjust its policies to capture the middle ground of politics	16	54	13	15	2
The next Conservative government should establish a prices and incomes policy as a means of controlling inflation	12	31	12	32	14
A future Conservative government should privatise British Coal	12	44	17	22	5
Income and wealth should be redistributed towards ordinary working people	5	21	20	42	12
A future Conservative government should make abortions more difficult to obtain	12	22	19	35	13
The welfare state undermines individual self-reliance and enterprise	16	46	14	21	3
Unemployment benefit should ensure people a reasonable standard of living	14	60	13	11	2
The death penalty should be reintroduced for murder	36	33	7	17	7
Britain's present electoral system should be replaced by a system of proportional representation	5	17	12	43	24
When it comes to raising a family, a woman's place is in the home	15	41	14	20	11
Restrictions on immigration into Britain are too loose and should be tightened	54	37	5	3	1
Conservatives should resist further moves to integrate the European Community	20	34	16	27	3

This survey of members of the Conservative party was conducted between January and April 1992. In total, there were 2,467 respondents. The figures show the percentage of respondents giving each answer.

Adapted from Whiteley et al., 1994.

Item C *Introducing the Conservative party*

INTRODUCING THE CONSERVATIVE PARTY

WELCOME TO THE CONSERVATIVE PARTY

Joining the Conservative Party means that you become a member of the oldest political grouping in Britain. It started life as the "Tory Party" during the reign of Charles II. By the early 1830s, the name "Conservative Party" had been born. Since then, the Party has produced many of Britain's greatest political leaders: Peel; Disraeli; Winston Churchill; Margaret Thatcher. Now John Major is carrying Conservatism forward through the 1990s.

OUR PRINCIPLES

What are the beliefs that have united and inspired the Party over the decades?

First, the Conservative Party is the party of **FREEDOM**. We believe in the right of each man and woman to use ***their*** initiative and ***their*** effort to better themselves - to be enterprising without a controlling State snatching away the fruits of their achievement.

Second, we believe in **RESPONSIBILITY**. That means a tough stand on law and order; it means upholding our values and our institutions; and it means maintaining a firm stance on the defence of our country. The British people know that you can't have freedom without responsibility.

Third, we believe in **OPPORTUNITY** for all. That means making sure that the chance to do well is within everyone's reach; that ownership is more and more widely spread; that people know that they will be cared for when they are weak - and know that they are part of a society that welcomes their contribution.

These are the values that create a prosperous society, a decent society and a generous society too.

But they are not the values of socialism.

NO TO SOCIALISM

Instead of freedom, Labour believes in crippling taxes so the State can do more - at your expense - at the expense of your freedom and Britain's prosperity.

Instead of responsibility, Labour are soft on crime, soft on defence and hard on Britain - always ready to jettison our traditions and run our country down.

Instead of opportunity, Labour prefer to keep people dependent on the State. That's why they oppose wider ownership of homes and shares, and resent people exercising their choice.

Socialism, all around the world, has been a failure. It left people impoverished and embittered.

But Conservatism works. And we believe it accords with the beliefs of the British people. Four election victories in a row suggest we are right.

This leaflet is part of a recruitment pack produced by the Conservative party

Questions

1. Explain how conservatism differs from liberalism.

2. a) Using Item A write an article which gives a conservative account of the growth of unemployment and provides recommendations for solving this problem.
   b) Would you say that your account conformed more with traditional conservatism, one nation conservatism or liberal conservatism? Give reasons for your answer.

3. a) What do the answers in Item B tell us about the nature of conservatism in the Conservative party in the early 1990s?
   b) Would you say that the majority of members of the Conservative party were traditional conservatives, one nation conservatives or liberal conservatives? Give reasons for your answer.

4. a) 'The principles which lie behind the Conservative party are conservative principles.' Explain this statement using Item C.
   b) How does the definition of freedom in Item C differ from the liberal definition of freedom?

4 Socialism

Key Issues

1. What is socialism?
2. How did it develop?
3. How does it differ from liberalism and conservatism?

The roots of socialism

The changes to British society brought about by the industrial revolution did not just result in the adaptation of existing ideologies such as liberalism and conservatism, they also led to the development of a new ideology - socialism. But whilst liberalism and conservatism accepted and embraced the new capitalist economic order, socialism opposed it, aimed to change it and provided an alternative to it.

Capitalism

An industrial country whose wealth (ie land, raw materials and businesses) is owned mainly by individuals rather than by the state is a capitalist country. In simple terms, those who own and control the wealth are 'capitalists' (they have capital which they invest in businesses). Those who have no capital of their own but rely on being paid for their labour are 'workers'. Although the capitalists are fewer in number than the workers, they tend to acquire political power and social privileges as well as economic power.

Capitalism in Britain

Industrialisation in Britain was piecemeal. It relied upon individual initiative. New industrial enterprises were set up and owned by private individuals. On the whole, central government did not encourage or attempt to organise economic development. It certainly did not attempt to gain ownership of the new industrial enterprises. As a result, it was left to the owners of businesses to decide what conditions their workers should work in and how much they should be paid. Since the aim of these businesses was to make a profit, working conditions were often poor and wages low. In fact, during the early years of the industrial revolution, many working people had to endure appalling working and living conditions. The following two passages indicate the sort of conditions poorly paid working families had to endure. The first passage is an extract from an account written by Lord Shaftesbury who toured poor areas:

> 'In the first house I turned into there was a single room. The window was very small and the light came in through the door. The young woman said, "Look there at that great hole; the landlord will not mend it. Every night I have to sit and watch, or my husband does, because that hole is over a common sewer and the rats come up 20 at a time. If we did not watch for them they would eat the baby up." ' (Shaftesbury, 1847)

The second passage comes from a report written by a parliamentary commission in 1843:

> 'If the statement of the mother be correct, one of her children, four years of age, works twelve hours a day with only an interval of a quarter an hour for each meal at breakfast, dinner and tea, and never going out to play; and two more of her children, one six and the other eight years of age, work in the summer from 6 am til dusk and in winter from 7 in the morning til 10 at night, 15 hours.' (Second Report of the Children's Employment Commissioners, 1843)

It is in this context that socialism first developed.

Writers such as Karl Marx and Friedrich Engels criticised capitalism. They argued that the workers were being exploited by the capitalists and once they realised the extent to which they were being exploited, they would rise up and overthrow the capitalists in a revolution. This revolution would lead to a new way of organising society - socialism. In a socialist society, people would share property and work cooperatively.

By the late 19th century the character of capitalism in Britain had changed. Although there was still a huge divide between rich and poor, living and working conditions had begun to improve. In part, this was due to the more active role taken by government - laws banning child labour and restricting the length of the working week were passed by Parliament, for example, and local councils were given powers to raise local taxes which could be spent on improving local living conditions. But other factors also played a part. The growth and recognition of trade unions provided the workers with the machinery to take collective action. The campaign for greater democracy led to the gradual extension of the franchise and, therefore, wider participation in politics. As a result, there was less alienation amongst the workers. Whilst groups of revolutionary socialists survived, the number of their supporters remained small. More and more socialists supported the idea that socialism could be achieved by peaceful means and by working within the existing system. This split between revolutionary socialists (usually referred to as 'communists') and reformist socialists intensified after the Bolsheviks (Russian communists) seized power in Russia in the revolution of October 1917. In Britain, the influence of revolutionary socialism has remained slight whilst reformist socialism has managed to enter the political mainstream.

The nature of socialism

Socialism has two elements. It is both a criticism of capitalism and a set of ideas for an alternative way of organising society. But these two elements are intertwined. It is through the criticism of capitalism that the alternative way of organising society becomes apparent. This criticism of capitalism can be divided into four areas.

First, the toll on workers in a capitalist system is immense since capitalists compete with each other in the fight for the highest possible profit. Workers are exploited and dehumanised, becoming no more than numbers on a balance sheet. In such circumstances, work has no meaning other than as drudgery which keeps together body and soul.

Second, capitalism produces vast inequalities in society. There is a huge gap between the 'super rich' at the top and the poor at the bottom. The mass of people reap little reward for their labour. Yet it is their labour which actually creates the wealth in the first place. Capitalism by its very nature perpetuates inequalities.

Third, the so-called 'freedoms' which both conservatism and liberalism purport to support are merely a sham and an illusion. 'Freedom' in the conservative or liberal sense is only meaningful for the rich.

Fourth, capitalism is not even an efficient system since it wastes all kinds of limited resources. The emphasis on the market place and the scramble for profit mean that little attention is paid to the interests of society as a whole. The rich, for example, are more likely to spend their money on building a large house for themselves than on building a hospital for the good of the community.

Socialism and human nature

The term 'socialism' itself provides an important clue about attitudes towards human nature. To socialists, people are social beings who thrive best in a close relationship with one another. People are not just motivated by selfish interests, but are capable of living harmoniously and cooperatively together as part of a community with a compassionate attitude towards all. Socialists do not agree that people are inherently flawed. Rather they emphasise that people are largely the product of their upbringing and their environment. If people are selfish, greedy or uncaring, it is likely to be the result of acquiring such characteristics, probably because they are the dominant values in society. It follows from this that, if human capacities are to be developed, then the right environment must be created. This implies that socialists must seek a decisive change in the nature of society.

Socialists explain many types of antisocial behaviour, including crime, by arguing that such behaviour is determined to a large extent by material factors such as unemployment and poverty rather than by weaknesses in human nature. Eliminating these material problems would, therefore, be a major step towards solving many social problems.

If such ideas are taken further, they can lead to socialist utopianism - a belief that a society could be created where better housing, schools and hospitals would produce a more cooperative, compassionate and peaceful society. But not all socialists are utopians. Many socialists accept that Britain is a capitalist society where capitalist values predominate. Since they, as socialists, believe that the environment largely determines political behaviour, they expect people to be seduced by the values portrayed, for example, through advertising and through the media. The onus is on them as socialists to combat such values.

The socialist view of human nature suggests that human happiness depends on reshaping society according to socialist values. There are two main aims. First, the promotion of greater equality by means of a redistribution of resources from the wealthy to the rest. And second, the organisation of society through rational planning rather than by relying on market forces.

Socialism, the individual and the group

If the key unit in liberalism is the individual and in conservatism it is the family and the nation, the key unit in socialism is the group (or class). At the heart of socialism is the belief that people should join together and work collectively. Heywood explains this as follows:

> 'At its heart, socialism possesses a unifying vision of human beings as social creatures capable of overcoming social and economic problems by drawing upon the power of the community rather than simply individual effort. This is a collectivist vision because it stresses the capacity of human beings for collective action, their willingness and ability to pursue goals by working together, as opposed to striving for personal self-interest.' (Heywood, 1992, p.96)

Heywood then goes on to point out that socialists differ from both liberals and conservatives in their attitude towards competition. Liberals and conservatives not only regard competition between people as natural, they also regard it as desirable. Socialists, on the other hand, believe that, by its very nature, competition turns people against each other and, therefore, forces them to suppress or ignore their desire to cooperate. In simple terms, competition encourages selfishness and aggression whilst cooperation makes moral and economic sense. By working together rather than competing, the argument goes, people develop bonds between each other and are able to achieve more than could be achieved by working alone. This belief has led to a great deal of criticism from non-socialists. Socialists have been accused, for example, of ignoring or suppressing individual freedom (by emphasising the needs of the group rather than the individual) and of lacking economic realism (since, it is claimed, economic success relies on competition). It should be noted, however, that socialism, like other ideologies, is ultimately no more than a framework upon which practical policies are based. Since Britain is a capitalist rather than a socialist state, it is perhaps understandable that the policies supported by most British socialists fall short of the ideal. Certainly, the new constitution agreed by Britain's mainstream socialist party, the Labour party, in April 1995 attempts to combine a desire for collective action with an admission that competition is the basis for economic success (see Activity 2.4, Item C).

Socialism and the past

Some socialist historians still subscribe to the view that 'the history of all hitherto existing societies is the history of class struggles.' (Marx & Engels, 1888, p.79) But most accept that:

> 'Capitalism has not appeared to develop as Marx had predicted. Far from becoming more intense, class conflict has gradually been diluted by growing affluence.' (Heywood, 1992, p.101)

Despite this, socialist historians are less likely to analyse developments in terms of individuals than are historians who subscribe to other ideologies. Socialists tend to argue that a 'great man' approach to history (an emphasis on the role of prominent individuals) is not very helpful. What matters is the changing relationship between different groups (classes) in society. By examining the past, socialists are able to understand how capitalism has been able to survive and to suggest ways in which a more just and fairer society, based on rational principles, can be established (it should be noted, however, that 'more just and fairer' has a different meaning for a socialist than it does for a liberal or a conservative).

Socialism and the state

Socialists aim to transform society. Gaining control of the state is, therefore, crucial. Once office has been won, the state becomes the main vehicle of change. A central aim of socialists, for example, is the redistribution of wealth in society. In part, this can be achieved by the exercise of state power. A socialist government, for example, might introduce a system of progressive taxation so that the rich pay a larger proportion of their income in taxation than the poor. The money collected by the state in taxation could then be used to combat poverty and disadvantage. State power might also be used to defend the civil liberties of individuals and groups.

But the role of the state has become a source of considerable debate in British politics and faith in the beneficial effect of state activity has weakened even among socialists. The perceived failure of British nationalised industries in the 1970s (see chapter 3, section 1.2), the experience of the Thatcher revolution in the 1980s (see chapter 3, part 2), the collapse of 'state socialism' in the Soviet Union in 1991 and the fourth successive general election defeat for the Labour party in 1992 have convinced many socialists in Britain that the state is not a neutral entity, simply obeying the wishes of the government of the day. Rather, it is a complex entity with many members and many interests of its own. Some of these interests may be quite unacceptable to socialists. As a result, previous certainties about the beneficial impact of the state as a weapon to achieve socialist objectives are being challenged.

Different strands of socialism

Like liberalism and conservatism, it is possible to identify different strands of socialism. In particular, it is necessary to distinguish between revoltionary socialism and reformist socialism.

Revolutionary socialism

As suggested above (p.26), one strand of socialism is derived from the writing of Marx and Engels. This strand is known as 'revolutionary socialism' because its supporters believe that class conflict will inevitably result in the revolutionary overthrow of the capitalist system. Revolutionary socialists are also described as 'Marxists'. In the UK, revolutionary socialism or Marxism is regarded as an ideology on the extreme of the political spectrum (see p.31 below).

Reformist socialism

Whilst Marxists argue that the irresistible forces of class conflict mean that the revolutionary overthrow of the capitalist system is inevitable, other socialists argue for a more gradual approach. Reformist socialists suggest that even without a revolution socialist parties can achieve socialism - by gaining election to government and then introducing reforms which gradually transform society. It is this path which has been followed by the British Labour party.

Some political commentators distinguish between 'democratic socialism' and 'social democracy'. Whilst both take the reformist rather than the revolutionary path towards socialism, each has different aims.

Democratic socialists hope to use the existing democratic mechanisms in society to gain power and then to introduce a hardline socialist programme which transforms the state. Their aim, in effect, is to alter the balance of power in society to such an extent that the capitalist system ceases to exist. They differ from revolutionary socialists, therefore, in terms of tactics, but not in terms of their aims.

Social democrats, on the other hand, accept that they are living in a capitalist society and do not expect to change the fundamental nature of this society. Rather, they hope to introduce reforms which redistribute resources in such a way that the majority benefit rather than just the few. Whilst social democrats may have similar ideals to democratic socialists, their views about what policies should be pursued are often quite different.

Activity 2.4

Item A *Socialism (1)*

Item B *Socialism (2)*

Socialism is the collective ownership by all the people of the factories, mills, mines, railways, land and all other instruments of production. Socialism means production to satisfy human needs and it means direct control and management of the industries and social services by the workers through a democratic government. Under socialism, all authority will originate from the workers who will be integrally united in socialist trade unions. All persons elected to any post in the socialist government, from the lowest to the highest level, will be directly accountable to the rank and file. Such a system would make possible the fullest democracy and freedom. It would be a system based on the most primary freedom - economic freedom. For individuals, socialism means an end to economic insecurity and exploitation. It means workers cease to be commodities bought and sold on the labour market. It means a chance to develop all individual capacities and potentials within a free community of free individuals. It means a classless society.

Adapted from Levin, 1976.

Item C *Clause IV (1)*

(i) The old clause IV

The Labour party's object is...to secure for the workers by hand or by brain the full fruits of their industry and the most equitable distribution thereof that may be possible upon the basis of the common ownership of the means of production, distribution and exchange, and the best obtainable system of popular administration and control of each industry of service.

Adapted from *Labour*, 1993.

(ii) The new clause IV

The Labour party works for:

- a dynamic economy, serving the public interest, in which the enterprise of the market and the rigour of competition are joined with the forces of partnership and cooperation to produce the wealth the nation needs and the opportunity for all to work and prosper, with a thriving private sector and high quality public services, where those undertakings essential to the common good are either owned by the public or accountable to them;
- a just society, which judges its strength by the condition of the weak as much as the strong, provides security against fear, and justice at work; which nurtures families, promotes equality of opportunity and delivers people from the tyranny of poverty, prejudice and the abuse of power;
- an open democracy, in which government is held to account by the people; decisions are taken as far as practicable by the communities they affect; and where fundamental human rights are guaranteed;
- a healthy environment, which we protect, enhance and hold in trust for future generations.

Adapted from the *Independent*, 14 March 1995.

Item D *Clause IV (2)*

(i) Even though the Conservative party has no equivalent of clause IV, there is little doubt what values Conservatives stand for. Conservatives are and always have been about tradition, the constitution, the minimal state, low taxation and the progress of the individual. The value system laid out in Labour's new clause IV is quite different from this. The only overlap is the belief in individual progress. What the new clause does is to say what it feels like to be on the left rather than the right of British politics. The old clause IV made a commitment to common ownership that no Labour government intended to keep. The new clause replaces hard policy with a broad value system which promotes flexible policies.

Adapted from the *Guardian*, 14 March 1995.

(ii) Beneath the buzzwords which make up Labour's new clause IV, a clear message lurks - there is no intention to bring about fundamental economic change. In its key passage, the new clause praises 'the enterprise of the market and the rigour of competition'. It does not qualify or restrict this 'rigour'. It merely joins it with unspecified 'forces of partnership and cooperation'. The statement goes on to promise both a 'thriving private sector' and 'high quality public services'. But it does not spell out a specific role for the public sector. It says that those undertakings essential to the public good (namely, public utilities, the NHS, education, transport) may be either 'owned by the public or accountable to them'. In other words, Labour has no objection, in principle, to private firms making profits out of the delivery of public services. The new clause also avoids the crucial question about a mixed economy - what is to be the balance between public and private? Nowhere is there any criticism of an economic system governed by the drive for private profit. By ignoring the injustice and inequality at the heart of the present system (ie the monopoly of economic power by a small minority), a future Labour government will be unable to tackle society's injustices and inequalities. By abandoning the commitment to common ownership, the new clause deprives Labour of a distinctive objective and a guiding economic strategy.

Adapted from the *Guardian*, 14 April 1995.

Questions

1. How does socialism differ from (i) liberalism and (ii) conservatism? Use Items A and B in your answer.
2. 'The principles which lie behind the Labour party are socialist principles.' Explain this statement using Item C.
3. At the 1994 Labour party conference, Labour's leader Tony Blair announced that Labour's constitution (including clause IV) was to be rewritten. Why do you think the debate over clause IV was described as a 'battle over Labour's ideological heart'? Use Items C and D in your answer.
4. Herbert Morrison, Labour's deputy leader after World War II, said that socialism is whatever the Labour party happens to be doing at any one time.
   a) What do you think he meant by this?
   b) Do you think this is a sufficient definition of socialism? Give reasons for your answer.

5 Other ideologies

Key Issues

1. What is the nature of ideologies on the extreme of the political spectrum?
2. Have any new ideologies developed since 1945?
3. What impact have ideologies made on British politics?

5.1 Ideologies on the extreme of the political spectrum

Liberalism, conservatism and socialism are all mainstream ideologies. It is these ideologies which determine the parameters of political argument in the UK. Any ideas that fall outside the ideological framework constructed by them are regarded as 'extreme' and unacceptable. In other words, despite their differences, liberals, conservatives and socialists have much in common. Take the system of parliamentary democracy which exists in Britain for example. Most liberals, conservatives and socialists agree that Britain should have a system of parliamentary democracy even if they disagree over exactly how this parliamentary democracy should be organised.

Those who support ideologies on the extreme of the political spectrum, however, reject mainstream politics and support political systems which are fundamentally different. There are three main ideologies on the extreme of the political spectrum - anarchism, Marxism and fascism.

Anarchism

The word anarchy comes from the ancient Greek for 'no rule'. Anarchists are people who oppose all forms of authority. An anarchist state would be a state without any form of government or any laws. People would make decisions amongst themselves within their community without compulsion.

Since anarchists oppose all forms of government, governments and people in authority are bound to feel threatened by the idea of anarchy, especially if (as has sometimes happened) anarchists are prepared to take violent action against them. The result is that in everyday language the term 'anarchy' is often used to mean chaos, disorder and mindless violence. This, most anarchists would argue, is an ugly distortion of the true meaning of the term.

Whilst all anarchists believe that all forms of government and authority should be abolished, there are two distinct types of anarchism. One type can be characterised as an ultra-extreme form of liberalism. It is sometimes called 'anarcho-capitalism'. Anarcho-capitalists take free market economics to their logical conclusion. If a market is to be truly free, they argue, then there is no need for government. People should be free to do anything they like. The success or failure of their actions will be determined by the market. The market will be self-regulatory and so there is no need for regulations to be imposed from outside (by government). Turner suggests that:

> 'In concrete terms this would translate into the modern era as meaning, for example, no taxation, no compulsory education, no protection of minimum rights for workers in areas such as health and safety or redundancy, no regulation of what could or could not be used in the preparation of food or medicines. It is 19th century liberalism pushed to its logical extreme.' (Turner, 1993, p.29)

The second type of anarchism is known as 'left wing anarchism'. This can be characterised as an ultra-extreme form of socialism in that it is based on the premise that people are naturally able and willing to cooperate and work together collectively. If this is the case, then there is no need for government. Left to their own devices, people are perfectly capable of working together and of resolving any differences between them. Turner suggests that there is a series of core principles which are shared by left wing anarchists:

> 'The right to complete individual freedom, a complete rejection of authority of all forms, the establishment of a non-hierarchical society and an abiding belief that human nature is always essentially good. Where it is evidently bad, this is always a consequence of the deleterious [damaging] impact on humans of state exploitation and capitalist influences.' (Turner, 1993, p.29)

Unlike the other major ideologies, anarchism has not been put into practice on a large scale. Heywood suggests that this is because anarchism suffers from three drawbacks:

> 'First, its goal, the overthrow of the state and all forms of political authority, is often considered to be simply unrealistic. Certainly the evidence of modern history from most parts of the world suggests that economic and social development is usually accompanied by a growth in the role of government, rather than its diminution [reduction] or complete abolition. Secondly, in opposing the state and all forms of political authority, anarchists have rejected the conventional means of exercising political influence, forming political parties, standing for elections, seeking public office and so on. Anarchists have, therefore, been forced to rely upon less orthodox methods, often based upon a faith in mass spontaneity rather than political

> organisation. Thirdly, anarchism does not constitute a single, coherent set of political ideas. Although anarchists are united in their opposition to the institutions of the state and indeed other forms of coercive authority, they arrive at this conclusion from very different philosophical perspectives.' (Heywood, 1992, p.195)

Marxism

It has already been noted (part 4 above) that socialism can be divided into two strands. Whilst reformist socialists are able and willing to work within the existing system of parliamentary democracy, revolutionary socialists or Marxists hope to overthrow this system. Marxists may want the same end goal as reformist socialists, but their analysis of the current political situation and their tactics differ from them. For example, many Marxists are internationalists - they believe that a truly socialist society cannot be achieved until the working classes in countries all over the world rise up and overthrow capitalism. Because they are internationalists they are not interested in existing state boundaries. As a result, they discourage patriotism. Because they believe that a revolution is a necessary precondition of socialism, they try to undermine the existing government by encouraging class conflict. Tactics include educating the workers (revealing to them the true nature of their exploitation) and participating in political action designed to alienate workers from the existing political system (in the hope that this will lead the workers to rise up and overthrow the government). Such an analysis and such tactics are not shared by reformist socialists. As a result, Marxists are often branded as the 'enemy within' and tend to be marginalised by mainstream politicians.

Fascism

Whilst Marxism is associated with the extreme left of the political spectrum, fascism is associated with the extreme right. Fascism is notoriously difficult to define. Hunt (1992), however, suggests that fascism is made up of eight separate elements. First, fascists are aggressive nationalists. They believe that their nation is the best, that all citizens should be enthusiastically patriotic and, if necessary, military conquest should be embarked upon to solve struggles between nations. Second, fascists are militarists. They admire organised violence and the military way of life. Third, fascists are racists. This is a particularly important part of modern fascism. Contemporary British fascists, for example, argue that only white people should be allowed to live in the UK. Fourth, fascists believe in charismatic leadership. Fascists place their leader on a pedestal and allow their leader to have absolute authority. They prefer dictatorial rule to democratic rule. Fifth, the key unit to fascists is not the individual or the family, but the state. The state is more important than the individual and, therefore, individuals should be prepared to sacrifice themselves for the good of the state. Sixth, fascists despise Marxism. They despise it because it is internationalist (the opposite of nationalist) and because Marxists encourage class conflict. Class conflict damages the unity of the state. Seventh, fascists are opposed to parliamentary government on the grounds that this type of government's fundamental concern is with the freedom of the individual rather than with the unity of the nation. And finally, fascism revels in the irrational and mystical. Fascists assume that people are irrational and appeal to their irrationality. Fascists also construct myths which are used to bind their supporters together through rituals. For example, fascism often emphasises the idea of rebirth - the idea that fascism will bring economic, political and spiritual renewal. In this sense, fascism has much in common with religion.

5.2 'New' ideologies

Just as liberalism, conservatism and socialism were all shaped by the industrial revolution, two new ideologies have emerged out of the profound socio-economic changes which have taken place since 1945 - feminism and environmentalism. Although the roots of both lie in the prewar world, it is only in recent years that political scientists have begun to accept that they are distinct ideologies rather than tendencies within other ideologies. Significantly, neither ideology fits neatly on the left/right model of the political spectrum. Both aim to influence people on both the left and the right.

Feminism

As with most ideologies, it is difficult to provide a simple, succinct definition of feminism. Bryson, however, argues that:

> 'A starting point for all feminism is the belief that women and men are not equal in society and that women are systematically disadvantaged, subordinated or oppressed. Unlike traditional political thinking which has either defended or ignored gender inequality, feminism sees this as a central issue. As a political theory, feminism tries to understand the nature and causes of women's disadvantage and as a political movement it tries to change it.' (Bryson, 1994, p.31)

Although the term 'feminism' was first used over 100 years ago and the origins of modern feminism can be traced back to the 17th century, it is only since the 1960s that political scientists have begun to take feminism seriously. Heywood points out that:

> 'Until the 1960s, sexual divisions were rarely considered to be politically interesting or

important. If the very different social, economic and political roles of men and women were considered at all, they were usually regarded as 'natural' and, therefore, as inevitable. For example men, and probably most women, accepted that some kind of sexual division of labour was dictated by the simple facts of biology: women were suited to a domestic and household existence by the fact that they could bear and suckle children, while the greater physical strength of men suited them to the outdoor and public world of work...The growth of the women's movement and feminist thought since the 1960s, however, has severely tested such complacency.' (Heywood, 1992, p.216)

Since the 1960s, three distinct strands of feminism have been identified - liberal feminism, socialist (or marxist) feminism and radical feminism.

Liberal feminists argue that women and men have equal moral worth and deserve equal treatment. Women, therefore, should have the same rights as men and the same opportunities. Forbes summarises the key elements of liberal feminism as follows:

> 'Liberal feminists dismiss any talk of essential differences between women and men and are happy to propose changes that introduce formal and legal equality into the relations between the sexes. There is a stress on equal civil and economic rights, the need for education for women (and to change men), full partnership in work and an equal share in the formulation of laws.' (Forbes, 1991, p.63)

According to socialist feminists, however, it is the capitalist system which is responsible for women's oppression. Capitalism ensures that women are exploited either as unpaid workers in the home or as part-time workers on low wages. To combat this, structural change is required:

> 'Socialist feminists believe that the relationship between the sexes is rooted in the social and economic structure itself and that nothing short of profound social change, some would say social revolution, can offer women the prospect of genuine emancipation.' (Heywood, 1992, p.232)

Whilst liberal and socialist feminism owe something to existing ideologies, radical feminism goes beyond them. According to Bryson:

> 'Radical feminism claims that the oppression of women by men is the oldest and most universal form of inequality that there is. It also argues that male domination or 'patriarchy' is not confined to the public worlds of politics and economic life but that it is based upon the most intimate areas of our lives...Many radical feminists reject the idea that women should try to compete with men by becoming like them. They argue, instead, that women are in many ways better than men...For some this means that 'womanly values' should be more powerfully expressed in society as a whole. For others, it leads to the claim that all men are to be seen as 'the enemy' and that lesbian separatism is the only solution. Many, however, reject this conclusion and are careful to distinguish between male power (which they oppose) and individual men (who may be good friends or husbands).' (Bryson, 1994, pp.31-32)

Environmentalism

Worldwide population growth, industrial growth and scientific advance are three factors which, combined, have led to a growing concern about the relationship between human beings and the environment. Until the 1960s, politicians did not really concern themselves with the environment except to consider it as a resource bank to be exploited. Since then, however, there has been a realisation that many of the world's resources are finite and that current practices may be causing long-term, perhaps even irreversible, damage.

The growing concern about the damage that people are or may be doing to the environment is at the heart of the new ideology that has been called 'environmentalism'. The impact of this new ideology is great. Since the late 1980s, for example, all three major political parties in Britain have claimed that they have taken 'green issues' on board. In other words, all three parties admit to having been influenced by environmentalism.

Environmentalism is based upon the principle that there should be a balanced relationship between people and their environment. Whereas other ideologies are only concerned with the relationship between people, environmentalists are concerned about the relationship between people and the natural world. Environmentalists emphasise that people are just one species within a complex ecosystem and that (because of people's ability to manipulate the environment) their behaviour will determine whether or not that ecosystem survives. The implication of this is that people should consider long-term environmental consequences when making political decisions.

Central to environmentalism is the notion of sustainability. Sustainability is:

> 'The capacity of a system, in this case the biosphere [world] itself, to maintain its health and continue in existence. Sustainability sets clear limits upon human ambitions and material dreams because it requires that production does as little damage as possible to the fragile global ecosystem.' (Heywood, 1992, p.267)

Take timber for example. In the world as a whole, an enormous amount of timber is being collected and used. At present, more trees are being cut down than are being planted. As a result, the total number of trees in the world is diminishing. Environmentalists argue that this is shortsighted. To carry on cutting down trees at the present rate is unsustainable since there will come a time when there are no trees left. In the long term, current practice will lead to an ecological disaster. To prevent this happening, there should be a policy of sustainability - for every tree that is chopped down, for example, a new tree should be planted.

This idea has important implications. Whilst other ideologies assume that economic growth is a fundamental aim, environmentalists question whether economic growth is in people's long-term interest. As a result, some environmentalists argue that people should be taught to reject materialism and to look for personal fulfilment in a lifestyle based only on sustainable resources.

Activity 2.5

Item A *Making assumptions*

(i) Every language reflects the prejudices of the society in which it evolved and English evolved through most of its history in a male-centred, patriarchal (male dominated) society. We shouldn't be surprised, therefore, that its vocabulary and grammar reflect attitudes that exclude or demean women. Once we began looking at what the English language had to say at a subliminal level, some things became obvious. What standard usage says about males, for example, is that they are a species whilst females are a sub-species. From this flows a thousand other enhancing and degrading messages all encoded in the language which we in English speaking countries learn when we are born.

(ii) A British Rail advertisement aimed at company executives included the following passage:

'Consider the effects long-distance driving can have on an executive. Chances are when he arrives at his meeting he'll be feeling every inch of that journey. Worse, his tiredness may make him unresponsive and irritable. Would you feel happy about doing business with a man like that.'

(iii) Bill's attempts to interest XYZ company in his products had finally paid off. He was invited to make a presentation and was offered the use of a conference room in a letter signed John Liveridge, assistant to the president. When Bill signalled that he was set up, a woman and a man entered the room. The woman said to Bill, 'I'm Virginia Hancock and this is John Liveridge, my...'. Bill enthusiastically broke in, drowning her last word. 'I'm delighted to meet you, Mr Liveridge, and you too, Ginny.' Ms Hancock owned the company, Mr Liveridge was her assistant and Bill lost a customer.

All passages adapted from Miller & Swift, 1989.

Item B *Class war*

Item C *Living Marxism*

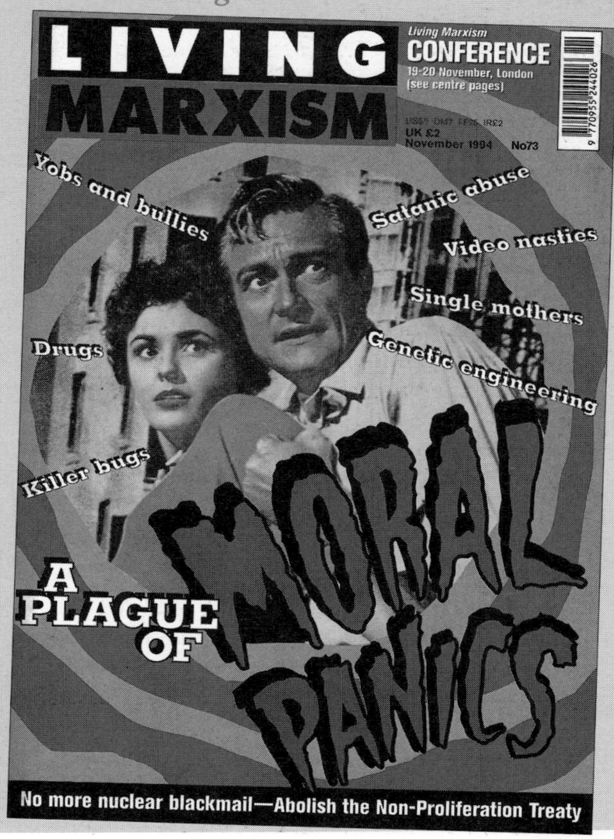

Item D *British Nationalist*

MARCH 1995 30p

British Nationalist

BNP

FOR RACE AND NATION

As uniformed IRA men march through Manchester we say:

BRITAIN BETRAYED TO IRA BY TRAITORS

LEFT-WING MANCHESTER COUNCIL has betrayed Britain for seventy-one pieces of silver. £71 is what they charged the IRA to march through Manchester in full uniform. In one of the greatest betrayals of Britain in post-war history hundreds of IRA men were permitted by the Council, Police, and Government to parade through the centre of one of our greatest cities on January 28 - jeering at our country and at the campaign to free Private Lee Clegg - who was falsely imprisoned to appease the enemies of Britain. Manchester was filled with beret wearing supporters of the people who have murdered and maimed thousands of British people over the last two decades - now the honoured guests of the traitors who run Britain. The three mile procession ended with a speech by Martin McGuinness one of the leaders of the gang which has terrorised our country.

SEVENTY-ONE PIECES OF SILVER - THE PRICE THEY CHARGED TO BETRAY OUR LAND TO THE IRA

Uniformed IRA men march through the centre of Manchester on January 28. They were led by terrorist leader Martin McGuinness. The marchers jeered at the campaign to free Private Lee Clegg. The local Labour Council gave the IRA permission to march through the area for a fee of £71.

SCOTLAND

One band leading the march came from Paisley in Scotland, and wore the insignia of the IRA. The terrorists are poised to renew their campaign of violence the moment the Government fails to give them exactly what they want - with London the prime target for a renewed wave of bombings.

SELL-OUT

The British Government is now cooking up an agreement with the IRA to allow the Irish Government control over the policing of Northern Ireland. Major is also planning to introduce to Ulster the 'race laws', which apply in the rest of Britain - paving the way for a mass of immigrants to flood in.

There is is massive sell-out of Northern Ireland taking place. Now that the IRA have softened up the people of Ulster on Mr. Major's behalf the next stage can go ahead - handing over control progressively to the Irish Government - who in their turn will lose control to the 'Europe of the bankers', and their unelected representatives.

FORCES

Unhappily all too many people still have no grasp of the forces at work in the world today. Our Government shamelessly serves the 'New World Order'. Our society is to be taken apart and turned into an economic unit serving people who have no connection with this country. What is happening in Ulster is simply a small example of the giant deception being practised on us by our leaders.

Venomous attack on Private Clegg

McGuinness launched a venomous attack on the campaign to free Private Lee Clegg - victim of a political prosecution all too familiar to the patriots of the BNP.

The Irish Government has warned the British authorities not to release Private Clegg, or the so-called 'peace process' would be jeopardised. Former Colonel of the Parachute Regiment Sir Michael Gray said recently that he deplored the "sinister propaganda being used against this young man".

Lee Clegg's mother Wynne recently delivered 40,000 letters of protest to 10 Downing Street, demanding his release.

Private Clegg receives hundreds of messages of support every day.

Many people in Britain still believe that there are no such things as politically conceived prosecutions in this country. There are, in fact, two laws in Britain, one for patriots who stand up for the British people and another for anyone who assists in the destruction of our country.

No one, for example, has been prosecuted for the quite public calls to murder Salman Rushdie within our territory. Nationalists, on the other hand, were dragged through the courts on trumped up charges in the furore which followed the election of Derek Beackon in 1993.

Private Lee Clegg's mother, Wynne Johnson, hears one of the countless messages of public support

Hounded from job by 'race police' - Page 3	The face they tried to hide - Page 4	Newham Election result - Page 8

Item E *The three main political parties and the environment*

(i) **We will create a cleaner, safer environment**

The greatest challenge we face is the responsibility to ensure the survival of the planet. Economic progress goes hand in hand with environmental responsibility. Labour will embrace the goal of sustainable development, with environmental modernisation an integral part of our industrial strategy.

Adapted from the Labour party manifesto, 1992.

(ii) Liberal Democrats are determined to ensure that Britain changes its ways so that it becomes a leader, not a laggard, in facing the environmental challenge. Polluters will pay and conservers will be rewarded. Taxation will be gradually shifted from the things we want more of - income, savings and value added - to the things we want less of - pollution and resource depletion.

Adapted from the Liberal Democrats' manifesto, 1992.

(iii) **THE ENVIRONMENT**

The Conservative Party's commitment to the environment is beyond doubt. Other parties promise the earth. We have taken action - both nationally and internationally - to preserve it. Environmental protection can impose financial costs on producers, consumers and taxpayers, so we must make sure the threat of damage is a real one. But we also accept the precautionary principle - the need to act, where there is significant risk of damage, before the scientific evidence is conclusive. And we recognise that higher environmental standards can offer new opportunities for business.

Adapted from the Conservative party manifesto, 1992.

Questions

1. Look at Item A.
   a) What evidence is there in passage (ii) to support the view expressed in passage (i)?
   b) Why do you think some feminists argue that the way in which people use language is important?
   c) What does passage (iii) tell us about the impact of feminism?
2. What are the main differences between anarchism, Marxism and fascism? Use Items B-D in your answer.
3. The major chains of newsagents refuse to stock *Class War*, *Living Marxism* and *British Nationalist*. Why do you think this is so?
4. a) Judging from Item E, what is the evidence that the main political parties have been influenced by environmentalism?
   b) Why do you think these parties might find it difficult to adopt some elements of environmentalism?

References

Bryson (1994) Bryson, V., 'Feminism', *Politics Review*, Vol.4, No.1, September 1994.

Coates & Silburn (1970) Coates, K. & Silburn, R. *Poverty: The Forgotten Englishmen*, Penguin, 1970.

Cootes (1966) Cootes, R.J., *The Making of the Welfare State*, Longman, 1966.

Dobson (1992) Dobson, A., 'Ideology', *Politics Review*, Vol.1, No.4, April 1992.

Eagleton (1991) Eagleton, T., *Ideology*, Verso, 1991.

Forbes (1991) Forbes, I., 'The politics of gender' in *Wale (1991)*.

Hall (1988) Hall, J., *Liberalism: Politics, Ideology and the Market*, Paladin, 1988.

Heywood (1992) Heywood, A., *Political Ideologies: an Introduction*, Macmillan, 1992.

HMSO (1994) Central Statistical Office, *Social Trends*, Vol.24, HMSO, 1994.

Hunt (1992) Hunt, S., 'Fascism and the race issue in Britain', *Talking Politics*, Vol.5, No.1, Autumn 1992.

Levin (1976) Levin, J., 'Levin speaks for socialism', *Weekly People*, 9 October 1976.

Labour (1993) *Labour Party Rule Book 1993-94*, Labour Party, 1993.

Lib Dem (1994) *The Liberal Democrats' Constitution*, Liberal Democrat Publications, 1994.

Marx & Engels (1844) Marx, K. & Engels, F., 'The German ideology' in *McLellan (1977)*.

Marx & Engels (1888) Marx, K. & Engels, F., *The Communist Manifesto*, Pelican, 1967.

McLellan (1977) McLellan, D., *Karl Marx: Selected Writings*, Oxford University Press, 1977.

Miller & Swift (1989) Miller, C. & Swift, K., *The Handbook Of Non-sexist Writing*, The Women's Press, 1989.

Smiles (1859) Smiles, S., *Self Help*, Penguin, 1986.

Seliger (1976) Seliger, M., *Politics And Ideology*, Allen & Unwin, 1976.

Shaftesbury (1847) Lord Shaftesbury, *Description Of Frying Pan Alley*, 1847.

Turner (1993) Turner, R., 'Anarchism: what is it?', *Politics Review*, Vol.3, No.1, September 1993.

Wale (1991) Wale, W. (ed.), *Developments in Politics*, Vol. 2, Causeway Press, 1991.

Whiteley et al. (1994) Whiteley, P., Seyd, P. & Richardson, J., *True Blues: the Politics of Conservative Party Membership*, Oxford University Press, 1994.

Part 2

British politics in context

3 Thatcherism and its legacy

Introduction

For 15 years Margaret Thatcher was a central figure in British politics. In 1975, she became the first woman to become leader of the Conservative party. In 1979, she became the first woman Prime Minister in the UK. Under her leadership, the Conservative party went on to win general elections in 1983 and 1987. It was only when a leadership struggle broke out within the Conservative party itself that her position became insecure and she was finally forced to resign in November 1990. By then, she had remained in office for nearly 12 years, the longest period of continuous office served by any Prime Minister this century.

But Thatcher's importance as a political figure is not due only to the fact that she managed to stay in power for so long. When people use the term 'Thatcherism', they are not just thinking of the personality of Margaret Thatcher and her time in office. They are also thinking of a particular style of leadership and a distinctive set of ideas and policies. Whether or not this leadership style and this set of ideas and policies is anything new, however, is open to debate. Some argue that the Thatcher years were a time of fundamental change, whilst others argue that this was a period in which old ideas were dressed in new clothes.

This chapter examines the impact made by Margaret Thatcher on British politics and considers three main questions. First, to what extent did the Thatcher years mean a break with the political consensus which had dominated postwar Britain? Second, how important was Margaret Thatcher's individual contribution to what happened during the 1980s? And third, to what extent did her successor, John Major, follow in her footsteps?

Chapter summary

Part 1 provides the **political context** in which 'Thatcherism' developed. It describes the development of a **postwar consensus** and the attack on it mounted by the New Right in the 1970s.

Part 2 considers whether **Thatcherism** is a distinct phenomenon. To what extent did the Thatcher governments change British politics?

Part 3 looks at **opposition to Thatcherism**. What light does this cast on Thatcherism itself? How did the Thatcher governments deal with this opposition?

Part 4 discusses the career of **John Major** and his programme as Prime Minister. To what extent have Major's policies represented **continuity with** the Thatcher years or **deviation away** from them?

1. The postwar consensus

Key Issues

1. What is the 'welfare state' and why was it set up?
2. What was the 'postwar consensus'?
3. Why did the postwar consensus break down?

1.1 The founding of the welfare state

Although the postwar Labour government was responsible for taking the actual measures which set up the welfare state, the principles which underlay these measures were established by a liberal, William Beveridge. Beveridge was a senior civil servant who had worked on social policy for many years before the outbreak of the Second World War. In 1941, he was commissioned by the Prime Minister, Churchill, to examine existing welfare schemes and to suggest ways of improving them. The Beveridge Report, entitled *Social Insurance and Allied Services*, was published in 1942 and became an instant bestseller (it sold more than 100,000 copies in December 1942 alone). In his report, Beveridge explained that social problems were all linked:

> 'Social insurance should be treated as one part only of a comprehensive policy of social progress. Social insurance, fully developed, may provide income security; it is an attack on Want. But Want is only one of the five giants on

the road to reconstruction and in some ways is the easiest to attack. The others are disease, ignorance, squalor and idleness.' (Beveridge, 1942)

By arguing that the 'five giants' were all linked, Beveridge suggested a new role for government. Whereas government had previously been reluctant to intervene in the affairs of individuals, the Beveridge Report gave government the philosophical justification for intervention. For the first time, it was conceded that poverty and underachievement might be the result of material, social conditions rather than individual failings. As a result, the ground was cleared for the state to set up institutions designed to help all, regardless of their ability to pay. Beveridge argued that there should be a single national insurance scheme to finance welfare provisions. Every worker would make a weekly contribution to this government-run scheme and this would protect them and their family 'from the cradle to the grave'. The scheme would provide benefits for the unemployed, sick and disabled, pensions for the old and widowed, funeral grants and maternity benefits. Beveridge also expected the government to provide family allowances, create a national health service and maintain full employment.

Despite the popular reception of the Beveridge Report, Churchill put it on ice, arguing that the main priority must be winning the war. Whether the Conservatives would have implemented the measures recommended in the report is a matter of speculation. To many commentators' surprise, Labour won the 1945 general election convincingly (with 393 seats to the Conservatives' 213). Having won its first overall majority, the Labour leadership considered that it had a mandate (the political authority) to implement its programme.

The main elements of the welfare state

The programme carried out by the postwar Labour government was an ambitious attempt to conquer Beveridge's 'five giants' of want, disease, ignorance, squalor and idleness.

Some of the ground had already been prepared. For example, one of the giants - ignorance - had already been tackled by Butler's 1944 Education Act. This made secondary schooling compulsory and free for all children to the age of 15. It also created the tripartite system of grammar, secondary modern and technical schools (which in practice became a two tier system since very few technical schools were built). Although the provisions of this Act later came under attack, at the time the Act was, generally, regarded as an attempt to create an educational system which would suit the needs of all. The incoming government, therefore, decided that further educational reforms were not necessary.

Education, however, was an exception. In other areas, the incoming government was prepared to introduce reforms which transformed the relationship between the state and the individual. Perhaps the most significant reform was the setting up of a national health service. Before the 1946 National Health Act was passed, most people had to arrange their own medical insurance or relied on charity. Only workers who paid into the state health insurance scheme set up by the Liberal government of 1906-14 could receive free treatment. Before 1946, therefore, the principle that the state should look after the individual had not been established. Hospitals were all privately funded, for example, and doctors charged fees for visiting or treating their patients. The 1946 National Health Act, however, brought the nation's hospitals and doctors under state control. For the first time, every British citizen was entitled to free health care. This new, universal service was financed by new National Insurance contributions automatically deducted from every pay packet.

Whilst the new National Health Service was designed to combat disease, the government took other measures to combat want, squalor and idleness. First, perhaps the most significant reform in this regard was the 1946 National Insurance Act. This Act created a full system of benefits covering unemployment, sickness, maternity and death. Although a national insurance scheme had been set up by the reforming Liberal government of 1906-14, it was by no means universal (it only covered some groups of workers). Besides, the prewar insurance scheme had incurred hatred when the dreaded 'means test' had been introduced (this took the earnings of the whole family into account when deciding whether a worker was eligible for benefit after exhausting insurance entitlement). The National Insurance Act 1946 extended the existing scheme and committed the state to provide a safety net to all who fell on hard times, whatever their background or previous contribution. It was this commitment to universal provision that was its most important innovation.

Second, in addition to setting up this safety net, the Labour government embarked on a house building programme. By 1951, over one million houses had been built using government funds. This demonstrated a commitment to the view that the state had a role to play in ensuring a basic human need was satisfied - the need for shelter.

Third, a number of key industries and services were 'nationalised'- transferred from private to state ownership. Two main arguments were put forward for nationalisation. It was argued that nationalised industries and services would not exploit workers or make decisions only in the hope of making a quick profit (a characteristic of privately owned industries, it was alleged). Also, it was claimed that the nationalisation of basic utilities such as gas and electricity was crucial in establishing the welfare state since it enabled the price of such basics to be governed by social considerations rather than by a desire to make a profit.

And finally, the postwar government pursued economic policies whose primary aim was to ensure that full employment was maintained. In this, the government was successful. Between 1945 and 1955 the number of unemployed workers did not exceed 320,000.

The postwar consensus

The postwar Labour government retained power until 1951. By then, the foundations of the welfare state had been laid. But these foundations would not have come to anything if the Conservative government which took office in 1951 had immediately begun to dismantle them. That it chose not to do so, indicates the extent to which the principles behind the welfare state had been accepted by both the public at large and by the political elite. Indeed, not only did the Conservative government elected in 1951 not attempt to dismantle the new welfare state, but every government elected between 1945 and 1979, whether Labour or Conservative, pledged to maintain and improve its main institutions and practices (the only exception being the first two years of the Heath government elected in 1970).

It is because there was substantial agreement between the two main political parties over the direction which foreign and domestic policy should follow that the term 'postwar consensus' was coined. During the period of postwar consensus, the main parties agreed about aims and principles but differed in emphasis and style. That does not mean that there was no conflict. Debates in the House of Commons were as heated as at any time in the past, for example. Rather, it means that the parameters within which conflict took place were clear and both main parties pursued similar policies. As Kavanagh remarks:

> 'The package of policies on the domestic front is familiar: full employment budgets; the greater acceptance, even conciliation, of the trade unions; public ownership of the basic monopoly services and industries; state provision of social welfare requiring in turn high public expenditure and taxation; and economic management of a sort via a large public sector and a reduced role for the market.'
> (Kavanagh, 1990, p.34)

If substantial agreement exists as to what the postwar consensus was, however, far less agreement is to be found as to why this consensus came about. Middlemass (1979) and others have argued that the period of consensus had its origins in the 1920s and 1930s when Conservative politicians were able to introduce Labour politicians to the highest echelons of the British political system, thereby incorporating their aspirations within this system. Writers on the left, such as Miliband (1961), on the other hand, have maintained that members of the Labour party and trade unions did not need to be incorporated since they already had a constitutional and parliamentary orientation and sought to contain working class objectives within these bounds. Rather, Miliband argues, the postwar consensus was achieved by the deradicalisation of working class demands. Others argue that it was cooperation between the two main parties in the wartime coalition government, together with the collective effort of the nation in defeating the Nazis, which laid the basis for consensus. Still others have argued that the growth of public expenditure and controls during the war prepared both the public and politicians for the growth of the public sector when the welfare state was established after the war.

All these interpretations emphasise the different elements of a complex process in which, for a relatively short period, a common view was held about how best to ensure political stability, prosperity and security for Britain's citizens. The consensus did not last, however. Depending on which line is followed, either in the mid-1960s or in the 1970s, the consensus began to break down in the face of economic and political developments which appeared to show that stability and prosperity could not be guaranteed by the policies adopted during the years of consensus.

Activity 3.1

Item A *The welfare state*

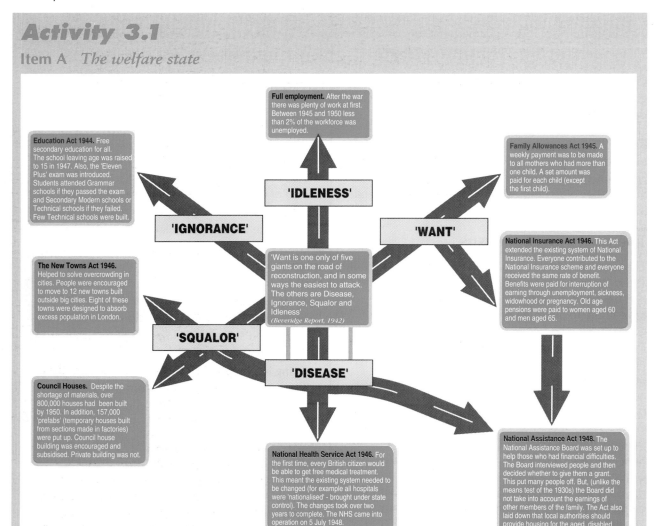

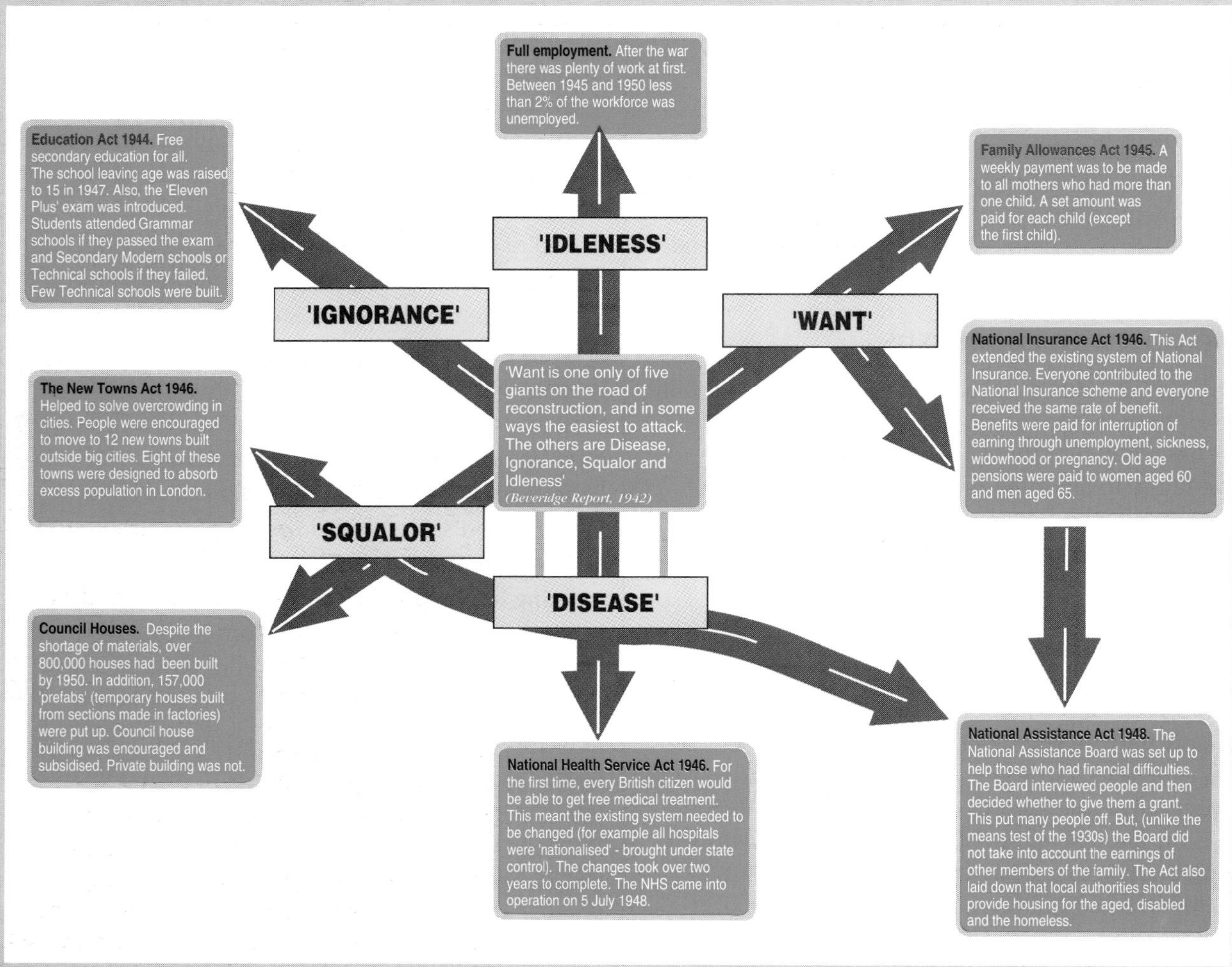

Full employment. After the war there was plenty of work at first. Between 1945 and 1950 less than 2% of the workforce was unemployed.
Education Act 1944. Free secondary education for all. The school leaving age was raised to 15 in 1947. Also, the 'Eleven Plus' exam was introduced. Students attended Grammar schools if they passed the exam and Secondary Modern schools or Technical schools if they failed. Few Technical schools were built.
Family Allowances Act 1945. A weekly payment was to be made to all mothers who had more than one child. A set amount was paid for each child (except the first child).
'IDLENESS'
'IGNORANCE'
'WANT'
National Insurance Act 1946. This Act extended the existing system of National Insurance. Everyone contributed to the National Insurance scheme and everyone received the same rate of benefit. Benefits were paid for interruption of earning through unemployment, sickness, widowhood or pregnancy. Old age pensions were paid to women aged 60 and men aged 65.
The New Towns Act 1946. Helped to solve overcrowding in cities. People were encouraged to move to 12 new towns built outside big cities. Eight of these towns were designed to absorb excess population in London.
'Want is one only of five giants on the road of reconstruction, and in some ways the easiest to attack. The others are Disease, Ignorance, Squalor and Idleness' (Beveridge Report, 1942)
'SQUALOR'
'DISEASE'
Council Houses. Despite the shortage of materials, over 800,000 houses had been built by 1950. In addition, 157,000 'prefabs' (temporary houses built from sections made in factories) were put up. Council house building was encouraged and subsidised. Private building was not.
National Health Service Act 1946. For the first time, every British citizen would be able to get free medical treatment. This meant the existing system needed to be changed (for example all hospitals were 'nationalised' - brought under state control). The changes took over two years to complete. The NHS came into operation on 5 July 1948.
National Assistance Act 1948. The National Assistance Board was set up to help those who had financial difficulties. The Board interviewed people and then decided whether to give them a grant. This put many people off. But, (unlike the means test of the 1930s) the Board did not take into account the earnings of other members of the family. The Act also laid down that local authorities should provide housing for the aged, disabled and the homeless.

Item B *The general election of 1950*

i) This is the Road - Conservative manifesto, 1950

The Labour party has imposed a crushing burden of taxation. Enterprise and extra effort have been stifled. Success has been penalised. A vote for Labour is a vote to continue the policy which has endangered our present economic independence. The social services were born of Parliaments with Conservative and Liberal majorities. They rest on the productive effort of British industry and agriculture. The Labour party has by inflation reduced their value and compromised their future. By energetic action they can be saved and their value maintained. We are prepared to give a solid base of social security below which none shall fall and above which each must be encouraged to rise. We pledge ourselves to maintain and improve the Health Service. Every year the estimates laid before Parliament have been greatly exceeded. Administrative efficiency and correct priorities throughout the whole system must be assured so that the proper balance is maintained.

ii) Let Us Win Through Together - Labour manifesto, 1950

The task now is to carry the nation through to complete recovery. The choice for the electors is between the Labour party - the party of positive action, of constructive progress, the true party of the nation - and the Conservative party - the party of outdated ideas, of unemployment, of privilege. Labour has honoured the pledge it made in 1945 to make social security the birthright of every citizen. Today destitution has been banished. The best medical care is available to everybody in the land. Great Acts of Parliament have been placed on the statute book. This social legislation has benefited all sections of the community, including members of the middle class. Professional families have been relieved of one of their worst anxieties - the fear of sudden illness, the expensive operation, the doctors' crippling bills. What is needed now is not so much new legislation as the wise development of the services now provided.

Item C *Differences between the two main parties, 1951-79*

Date	1951	1955	1959	1964	1966	1970	Feb 1974	Oct 1974	1977	1979
Important differences	71	74	66	59	55	54	57	54	34	54
Very little difference	20	20	29	32	37	41	38	41	60	41
Don't know	9	6	5	9	8	5	5	5	6	5

This table shows voters' perceptions of differences or similarities between the major political parties, 1951-79. The figures show the percentage of people who, at that time, believed there were important differences or very little difference.

Adapted from Kavanagh, 1993.

Questions

1. a) Judging from Item A what are the main aims and elements of the welfare state?
2. a) What evidence is there in Item B to suggest that a consensus developed after the war?
   b) Explain the link between the establishment of the welfare state and the development of the postwar consensus
3. What does Item C tell us about the development and decline of the postwar consensus?

1.2 The breakdown of the consensus

Whilst governments continued to act within the framework of the postwar consensus until the general election of 1979, outside government criticism of the consensus became more and more strident, especially amongst groups on the right. Within the Conservative party, splits began to appear between those who supported the consensus (the one nation Conservatives) and those who wanted to end it (the New Right). By the mid-1970s the New Right had grown in strength. When a leadership election was called in 1975 it was a member of the New Right - Margaret Thatcher - who gained victory.

The New Right

During the 1970s, the political movement known as the New Right emerged in the USA and in Britain (see also chapter 2, p.23). It was from this movement that Margaret Thatcher drew her inspiration. The birth of the New Right in Britain can be traced to three major intellectual sources.

The first of these sources was the work of the academics Milton Friedman and Friedrich Hayek. Although the two men disagreed over some fundamental issues, they made common cause in their support of the importance of free markets. A free market is a market in which the laws of supply and demand can operate without interference from any external source. Friedman and Hayek maintained that markets played a crucial role in ensuring the maximum level of human freedom, that markets were better at distributing resources than planned economies and that inflation was the primary economic and political evil - an evil which, they argued, could only be defeated by control of the money supply (see chapter 15, section 1.3).

The second major source of New Right ideas was the ex-Conservative MP and minister Enoch Powell. During the 1960s, Powell articulated a coherent critique of the consensus politics which had dominated postwar Britain. He argued against incomes policies, economic planning and high levels of public expenditure. Like Friedman and Hayek, Powell argued in favour of a free market economy, claiming that a free market was the basis upon which individual freedom was built and was the best way of distributing resources. Indeed, as early as 1958, Powell had argued that inflation was a consequence of the growth of the money supply and public expenditure. He was also a nationalist. He resisted Britain's entry into the European Economic Community in 1973 (see chapter 6, section 1.1) and he made a number of interventions on the issue of immigration (he was forced to resign as a minister after making a speech which was condemned as promoting racism). Ironically, by the time Powell's views entered the Conservative mainstream, he had broken with the party.

The third major source of New Right ideas was a number of think tanks which gained importance in the 1970s and early 1980s. In particular, the Institute of Economic Affairs (set up in 1955), the Centre for Policy Studies (set up in 1974) and the Adam Smith Institute (set up in 1978) all set out to promote the ideas of New Right thinkers such as Hayek and Friedman (see also chapter 10, section 1.6).

The debate over the term 'New Right'

Whilst the intellectual sources of the New Right are not in dispute, the term 'New Right' has aroused controversy. Doubts about the applicability of the term centre upon two objections. First, some commentators argue that to describe the movement as 'right wing' ignores the fact that much of its impetus came from liberal ideas about reducing the role of government and the state. Barry (1987), for example, argues that 'New Liberals' would be a more accurate description (though it should be noted that this would not be entirely accurate since it would ignore the stress that the movement places on the restoration of the authority of the state and the family). The second objection is that the groups on the right which emerged in the 1970s were so diverse that they do not fit any one label.

Whilst it may be true that the New Right is not a formally constituted entity and there is indeed a degree of diversity between the aims and emphases of different groups withing the movement, it is possible to identify a common goal shared by them all:

> 'What all strands within the New Right share...is the rejection of many of the ideas, practices and institutions which have been characteristic of social democratic regimes in Europe and of the New Deal and Great Society programmes in the United States. The New Right is radical because it seeks to undo much that has been constructed in the last 60 years.' (Gamble, 1988, p.27)

In other words, the New Right is unified in its attack on the postwar consensus - on Keynesian economics, on the welfare state and on state provision more generally. Indeed, it is this which defines it as a distinct movement.

That there should be a degree of diversity between the different groups which fall under the umbrella term 'New Right' is understandable since different groups place different emphases on the best way to break down the postwar consensus and to replace it with a new consensus. Some New Right groups, for example, place emphasis on the importance of market solutions to economic problems. These groups might be described as the liberal New Right. Other groups, on the other hand, tend to attack the postwar consensus for the way it has undermined social order and the authority of the state and family. These groups might be described as the conservative New Right. Whilst the conservative New Right supports the liberal New Right's call for market solutions, it believes that such solutions are not ends in themselves, but should buttress social order. Clearly, both versions of New Right theory have priorities which may come into conflict. But they are also capable of being fused to form two aspects of a single New Right doctrine - what Gamble (1988) calls 'the free economy and the strong state'.

New Right doctrine

According to the New Right, during the period of postwar consensus the government intervened in economic affairs when it should not. This resulted in economic decline and a loss of individual freedom and choice. At the same time, the government acted too timidly in areas where it alone can act - in law and order, in defence and in encouraging respect for authority. The solution to these problems was twofold. First, the government should intervene less. It should reduce its involvement in social affairs and nurture individual freedom, choice and responsibility. And second, the government should be more rigorous in enforcing law and protecting Britain's interests.

The Conservative leadership election 1975

The views of the New Right might have remained on the margins of British politics if Margaret Thatcher had not been elected leader of the Conservative party in 1975. According to Young (1991), Thatcher owed her election to two mistakes made by her opponents, a piece of luck and two positive factors.

The first mistake was Edward Heath's refusal to resign after the Conservatives were defeated in the 1974 general elections. Young (1991) suggests that Thatcher probably would not have stood as a candidate if a contest had been held soon after the general election in October 1974.

The piece of luck was Keith Joseph's decision to drop out of the leadership contest. After the general election in October 1974, the Conservative party was divided about what might be the best course for the party to follow in the future. Whilst most Conservative MPs agreed that a new leader was desirable, they were divided about the direction the new leader should take. A minority supported the New Right agenda. This group was supported by Margaret Thatcher, but it was led by Keith Joseph. As soon as the result of the general election in October 1974 was announced, Keith Joseph declared that he would stand in a leadership contest against Edward Heath. But, before a leadership contest took place, Joseph was forced to withdraw his candidature after suggesting that lower class parents should be prevented from having children since their offspring were undermining the quality of the British population. As soon as Joseph stood down, Thatcher put herself forward as a candidate. Had Joseph stood in a contest, Thatcher would not have done so.

The second mistake made by Thatcher's opponents was Edward Heath's refusal to permit any of his close allies to stand against him. This meant that in the first ballot (which involved only Heath, Thatcher and an outsider), all those who wished to see change but were not necessarily committed to the ideas of the New Right had to vote for Thatcher.

In addition, two positive factors contributed to Thatcher's victory. The first positive factor was the campaign waged on her behalf by Airey Neave who used his skills to persuade opponents of Heath (who were not natural supporters of Thatcher), to vote for her. The second positive factor was Thatcher's skilled performance in the Commons as opposition Treasury spokesperson. This won her considerable respect from many Conservative backbenchers.

In the first ballot, Thatcher won 130 votes to Heath's 119. Heath immediately resigned. In the second ballot, Thatcher was challenged by four Heathites, but her bandwagon was unstoppable. She received 146 votes, whilst her nearest challenger, William Whitelaw, received 79.

It should be noted that, although Thatcher was the right wing candidate in the leadership election, it was not because of this that she was elected leader. It was mainly because she was not Heath or one of his followers. It may be because of this that she proceeded cautiously in her first years as leader. For example, her shadow Cabinet was by no means dominated by right wingers, though it did include Keith Joseph and Airey Neave. Between 1974 and 1979, however, a debate took place within the party about its future direction. Gamble argues that:

> 'The Conservatives were not committed to a radical Thatcherite programme by the 1979 election. Yet by that date the main outlines of Thatcherism were clearly established. A new political agenda had been mapped out.' (Gamble, 1988, p.86)

The Labour government 1974-79

According to the mythology which developed after Thatcher's general election victory in 1979, the Labour government of 1974-79 lurched from crisis to crisis until it was eventually undone by the so-called 'winter of discontent'. Whatever the truth behind this interpretation of events, it is important to be aware of it since it was used by the Thatcher governments to justify their attacks on the postwar consensus. By pointing to the mistakes made in the past, the Thatcher governments were able to present their policies as fresh and necessary. The Thatcherite view of the 1970s, therefore, highlights themes that set the agenda in the 1980s.

The first of these themes was that the management of the economy under the terms of the postwar consensus directly led to high inflation. According to this view the Labour government of 1974-79 had been unable to control inflation and this was a major cause of Britain's economic decline. In fact, the Labour government had been relatively successful in dealing with inflation. Following the doubling of oil prices in 1973, inflation grew rapidly throughout the industrialised West and in Britain it reached 23% by the end of 1974 (it rose to 26% in 1975). By the time of the general election of 1979, however, a range of deflationary measures had brought inflation down to 9.5%. Of course, inflation at 9.5% was still relatively high. But the idea that inflation spiralled out of control in the late 1970s is an exaggeration. Those on the New Right, however, had good cause to make this claim since they argued that defeating inflation should be the government's priority rather than, for example, maintaining full employment.

The second theme was that public spending in the 1970s led to a balance of payments crisis which also hastened Britain's economic decline. Again, whilst it is true that the Labour government inherited a large deficit in 1974 and in 1976 was forced to ask for a loan from the International Monetary Fund (IMF), from 1976 the Labour government imposed strict limits on public expenditure with the result that the balance of payments problem had begun to ease by 1979. The Thatcherites made much of the deficit and the IMF loan. They blamed the inefficiency of nationalised industries (industries under public ownership) for the balance of payments problems and thus paved the way for their programme of privatisation and tighter controls on public spending.

The third theme was that the country had been held to ransom by the trade unions. According to this view, by including the unions in the decision making process and by attempting to work out an incomes policy with them, the Labour government had, in effect, handed power over to unelected union leaders. The result was that when the union leaders did not get their own way, they seriously damaged Britain's industry by calling workers out on strike. This view was bolstered by evidence from the so-called 'winter of discontent'. When, in 1978, the unions refused Prime Minister Callaghan's call for a 5% wage ceiling, a rash of strikes in the public sector broke out. These strikes dominated the winter of 1978-79 and damaged Labour's chances at the 1979 election. Whilst the New Right could claim that the 'winter of discontent' showed that the power of the unions must be curbed, supporters of the unions could claim, with some justification, that the close relationship between the government and the unions between 1974 and 1978 had laid the foundations for economic recovery.

Activity 3.2

Item A *Nationalised industries*

Discovering the Loss World

By the mid-1970s the nationalised industries were making a loss.

Item C *The IMF loan, 1976*

In November 1976, Britain applied for a £3 billion loan from the IMF. In return for the loan, the IMF demanded £5 billion in public spending cuts. The man in the water is the Prime Minister, James Callaghan.

Item B *Thatcher, the conviction politician*

When asked whether she felt she was offering something that was different from what Edward Heath had stood for, Margaret Thatcher said: 'I felt, and the Conservatives who elected me presumably felt, that the next leader of the party must clearly stand up against the direction in which the country was moving under both previous governments. We had moved too much to a society controlled by government. My aim was and is not the extension but limitation of government. At the time of the leadership contest which began in November 1974, we were coming to the stage when there really wasn't a party which was clearly standing for the limitation of government.' She added: 'I'm not a consensus politician or a pragmatic politician: I'm a conviction politician. And I believe in the politics of persuasion: it's my job to put forward what I believe and try to get people to agree with me.' When asked about forming a Cabinet, she said: 'There are two ways of making a Cabinet. One way is to have in it people who represent all the different viewpoints within the party, within the broad philosophy. The other way is to have in it only the people who want to go in the direction in which every instinct tells me we have to go. Clearly, steadily, firmly, with resolution. We've got to go in an agreed and clear direction. As Prime Minister I couldn't waste time having any internal arguments.'

Adapted from an interview in the *Observer*, 25 February 1979.

Item D *Labour isn't working*

This poster was produced during the 1979 general election campaign.

Questions

1. Why might the point being made in Item A appeal to members of the New Right?
2. What evidence is there in Item B to suggest that (a) Margaret Thatcher was a member of the New Right and (b) that she aimed to break down the postwar consensus?
3. a) What point is being made in Item C?
   b) How would you expect a member of the New Right to respond to the news that Britain was seeking a loan from the IMF? Explain your answer.
4. Can you think of reasons why the poster in Item D was effective in the 1979 general election campaign?
5. Write an article entitled 'Why the postwar consensus broke down'. Use Items A-D in your answer.

2. Thatcherism

Key Issues

1. What is 'Thatcherism'?
2. Was there a coherent Thatcherite programme?
3. What impact did the Thatcher government make on Britain?

2.1 What is Thatcherism?

Criticisms of the use of the term 'Thatcherism' have been made on two grounds. First, critics on the left (notably Tony Benn MP) have argued that the term personalises the politics of the post-1979 period and, therefore, conceals its true nature. In other words, the term acted as a smokescreen, encouraging opponents to concentrate on the personality of Margaret Thatcher rather than on the policies she promoted. And second, it has been argued (for example by Riddell, 1985) that use of the term grants to the Thatcher project a much higher level of ideological and political consistency than it actually ever had. It should be noted, however, that even Riddell, despite his reservations, decided to use the term since:

> 'However difficult it is to define, Thatcherism does have a meaning for those in the political world.' (Riddell, 1985, p.6)

In a general sense, Thatcherism was an attempt to establish a new political and ideological framework which was based on a mixture of liberal and authoritarian New Right ideas. More specifically, a number of different strands can be identified.

First, most writers agree that Thatcher's personality and leadership style is a part of what is meant by 'Thatcherism'. How important this personal role was, however, is the subject of debate. Riddell, for example, says:

> 'Mrs Thatcher's views, prejudice and style have determined government actions more than any other single factor.' (Riddell, 1985, p.6)

Gamble, on the other hand, argues that:

> 'Thatcherism cannot be reduced to the personal project of a single individual.' (Gamble, 1988, p.22)

If controversy rages over Thatcher's personal role, greater agreement exists over the other strands which comprise Thatcherism. Most writers agree that ideology is an important component of Thatcherism. Equally, most writers agree that specific political circumstances (the apparent failure of the postwar consensus) provided the context in which Thatcherism could flourish. And finally, most writers agree that Thatcherism is associated with a specific set of policies and positions - in particular, a degree of authoritarianism new in postwar British politics, a particular style of government and a number of key policy elements.

The key elements of Thatcherism

With hindsight, it is possible to identify a number of key elements which, together, can be grouped under the term 'Thatcherism'. It should be emphasised, however, that there was no blueprint. These policies developed over time.

1. Monetarism (see chapter 15, section 1.3)

In the early years of Thatcher's first administration a new way of managing the economy - 'monetarism' - was tried. Monetarism is an economic theory which completely rejects the aims and techniques of economic management proposed by Keynes. Whilst the primary goal of Keynesianism is to maintain full employment, the primary goal of monetarism is to keep inflation under control - even if that means maintaining a high level of unemployment. Whereas Keynesian economists argue that the government should play an active role by managing demand, monetarists argue that the government's only role should be to control the money supply (the money supply is the total amount of money circulating in the economy). By adopting monetarism, the first Thatcher government took an important step in breaking with the postwar consensus.

2. Privatisation

If, as monetarist economists argued, the main cause of inflation was government borrowing, there was a need to reduce this borrowing. One way of doing this was to raise income and a way of raising income was to sell government owned assets - in particular the nationalised industries and services. Privatisation would bring three benefits, according to the Thatcherites. First, it would raise government funds and, therefore, help to stem inflation. Second, it would improve the efficiency of the formerly nationalised industries since they would no longer enjoy monopoly status, but would be subject to the rigours of the market. And third, since the money from privatisation would be raised by selling shares to the public, privatisation would encourage wider share ownership. This was considered desirable on the grounds that it encouraged people to participate in the economic and political life of the country. By the late 1980s, the government was using the term 'popular capitalism' to describe the society it was trying to create.

At first, government receipts from privatisation were small. But the sales of British Telecom and British Gas after 1983 were lucrative and generated a great deal of public enthusiasm. Privatisation also occurred in other fields - most notably, tenants were able to buy their council houses at discounted prices after the Housing Act of 1980 was passed.

By privatising nationalised industries and services, the Thatcher government broke with the postwar consensus.

3. Curbing the unions

During the years of postwar consensus, the relationship between government and unions was close even when the Conservatives were in power. The New Right, however, was hostile towards trade unions. This hostility was due to three main factors. First, there was an element of fear of the unions. The miners' strike of 1974 led to the downfall of the Heath government. Similarly, the rash of strikes in the winter of 1978-79 discredited the Callaghan government. By the late 1970s, it seemed to those on the right that the unions had become a threat to the authority of government. Second, the New Right argued that the activities of trade unions distorted the working of the market by allowing the growth in wages to outstrip growth in productivity. Unions, in other words, were responsible for reducing the competitiveness of British industry and should be blamed for Britain's economic decline. And third, the New Right believed that incomes policies were a cause of inflation rather than a cure for it. Inflation could be reduced by controlling the money supply, not by making agreements with trade unions. There was, therefore, no need for government to have any contacts with union leaders. For these reasons, the Thatcher governments decided that it was necessary to draw up legislation which would curb the power of the unions. This had been attempted once before in 1971 when the Industrial Relations Act had been passed. But, by refusing to cooperate, the unions had made this Act unworkable and it had been repealed in 1974. To avoid this happening again, the Thatcher governments took a step by step approach. Legislation affecting trade unions was passed in 1980, 1982, 1984 and 1988. In addition, the government planned for the expected union backlash. When confrontation came in 1984 with the miners' strike, the government was able to force the unions into submission.

4. Centralisation

That policies involving the centralisation of power should be at the heart of Thatcherism may seem strange since the New Right places great emphasis on individual freedom and the severing of the relationship between the state and the economy. But the need to centralise power arises from a paradox which lies at the heart of New Right thought. As Gamble put it:

> 'The New Right would like to be conservatives but they are forced to be radicals. They have to struggle against the forces which have gravely undermined the market order and which, if left unchecked, will destroy it.'
> (Gamble, 1988, p.32)

So, to achieve the changes to the postwar consensus which they wished to secure, the Thatcherites needed to concentrate as much power into their hands as possible whilst ensuring that alternative, opposition sources of power were controlled or removed. The struggle against the trade unions is one example of how power was removed from a source of opposition. The changes made to the structure and finance of local government (for example the abolition of the Greater London Council (GLC) and the metropolitan counties - see chapter 16, p.470) is a second example. The GLC, especially, was seen as a potent source of opposition to Thatcherism.

5. Authoritarianism

An authoritarian stance is central to Thatcherite ideology. One of the criticisms levelled at government policies during the postwar consensus was that by involving the state in activities it should play no part in, the credibility of the state had been undermined. A key plank of the Thatcher strategy, therefore, was to restore the authority of the state and to increase it. Authority was to be restored by removing the state from activity in areas where it ought not to have a role (for example by privatising nationalised industries). But where the state should be strong, for example in the areas of law and order and defence, it was to be strengthened. As a result, the phrase 'free economy, strong state' has been applied to the Thatcherite project.

The Thatcher style of government

It was noted above that even those commentators concerned to minimise the personal role of Margaret Thatcher do not seek to deny that her personal style of leadership made an impact. One commentator, Kavanagh (1990), argues that Thatcher's individual contribution to British politics can be described under four headings. First, she had an unusually decisive and confrontational style and forceful personality. Second, she was an activist in the Cabinet. She saw herself as the leading participant in Cabinet discussion and pushed ministers into what she believed was right rather than what was expedient. Third, she was an excellent parliamentarian who was determined never to be bettered either at Question Time or in debate. And finally, there was her public image. Polls show that she rated low on compassion but very high on decisiveness, resolution and principle. She was not a leader about whom people were ambivalent. People tended to like her or loathe her with great passion.

Was Thatcherism a coherent programme?

Whether or not Thatcherism constituted a coherent programme is debatable. There seems to be considerable agreement amongst writers that before the 1979 general election there was no Thatcherite blueprint which she went on to implement during her three terms of office. But, with hindsight, it is possible to trace back a number of coherent themes. First, the three terms were based on an identifiable set of philosophical and political ideas which, although they were not always rigidly adhered to, provided a framework of thought within which Thatcher and her colleagues worked. Second, key policies were either in accord with this philosophical framework or were justified in terms of it. Third, the personality and style of Thatcher herself ensured that there was a certain continuity throughout the period. And finally, Thatcherism was a project which saw itself as an attempt to save Britain from the mess caused by the policies of the period of postwar consensus. It was supposed to bring a new golden age which would be characterised by freedom, obedience to the law, prosperity and national pride. It was also a strategy for restoring the profitability of industry and the power of owners and managers to discipline their workforces.

Thatcherism was not coherent, therefore, in the sense that it was a pre-established plan. But it was coherent in the sense that it was a reasonably consistent overall strategy which aimed to solve a specific set of problems. The term 'Thatcherism' is, therefore, a useful one, but it must be used carefully and with appropriate qualification, not as a crude label to be applied to a supposedly fixed set of ideas.

Activity 3.3

Item A *Margaret Thatcher's memoirs*

In her memoirs, Margaret Thatcher argues that her background and experience were not those of a traditional Conservative Prime Minister. She could not rely on the automatic deference that other Prime Ministers enjoyed, but she was less afraid of change than some previous Prime Ministers. She argues that many of her senior colleagues were too ready to accept that the Labour party and trade unions were in touch with the desires of the mass of the people. On the contrary, she was convinced that she was in tune with the mood of the people. Also, she argues that her experience of life had prepared her well for the battles she had to face. For example, 40 years before becoming Prime Minister, her father had taught her about the benefits of the free market and how it is blind to a person's status. The next 40 years had proved that he had been correct in all that he had said. It was because of him, she claimed, that she knew what had to be done to rebuild an economy ruined by socialism. Once she had been elected as Conservative party leader, she urged the party to put its faith in freedom and free markets, limited government and strong national defence. This programme, she knew, would keep the party united when the general election campaign began. Until then, it was a matter of holding firm. If she failed to win at her first attempt, she knew there would never be another chance.

Adapted from Thatcher, 1993.

Item B *Aspects of Thatcherism*

(i) The cartoon to the left was produced in August 1980, just over a year after the Thatcher government was elected. In that year, the number of unemployed people rose by more than 500,000, the highest annual rise since 1930. In August 1980, the inflation rate was 16.3%. In 1980 as a whole, the inflation rate was 18%.

(ii) The cartoon above was produced in October 1980. It shows the leaders of the major trade unions hitching a ride.

(iii) The cartoon above was produced in November 1988 just after it had been announced that the water industry would be privatised.

Questions

1. Give arguments for and against the use of the term 'Thatcherism' in analysing British politics since 1979.
2. What does each cartoon in Item A tell us about the nature of Thatcherism?
3. 'The heart of Thatcherism was the desire to end the postwar consensus.' Explain this statement using Items A and B.
4. How much do you think we can learn about Thatcherism from Margaret Thatcher's memoirs? Use Item B in your answer.

2.2 The record of the Thatcher governments

It is clear that Margaret Thatcher and her supporters aimed to bring fundamental and lasting change to the UK. But, does the record of the Thatcher governments indicate that they achieved this? This section will look at the impact of the Thatcher governments in the following areas - the economy, welfare, defence, law and order, foreign policy and the world beyond Whitehall. It will also consider the extent to which Thatcherism has affected the attitudes of the British people in general and Conservative party supporters in particular.

The economy (see also chapter 15)

It has already been noted that when the Labour government approached the IMF in 1976, a loan was only secured when the government agreed to adopt economic policies which were monetarist in orientation if not in name. Before Margaret Thatcher became Prime Minister, therefore, the notion that inflation could be controlled by cutting public expenditure had already been established. What was new about the first Thatcher government was that the theoretical foundations of such policies were promoted. It was claimed, for example, that such policies would lead to the regeneration of the economy as a whole.

When the Conservatives came to power in 1979, they made it clear that dealing with inflation was their most important objective. This was, they argued, the key to economic stability and growth in the medium term. Casting inflation as public enemy number one was a substantial break with the past.

The fight against inflation was successful. Between 1961 and 1982, the rate of inflation in Britain was higher than average for industrialised countries. Indeed, after 1970 it was substantially higher - 13.7% a year on average compared to 9% in other industrialised countries. But, after three years in power, the Conservatives managed to reduce inflation to a rate comparable to that in other industrialised countries. By 1986, inflation was down to 2.5%. Although it then began to rise again, government policy was altered to ensure that it remained at a low level.

The second plank upon which Thatcherite economic policy was based was control of public expenditure. This was a key means of controlling the money supply and a necessary prelude to cutting taxation. But the Thatcher governments, despite their pledges, were unable to reduce public expenditure. Indeed, it rose. Only by 1988-89 had the proportion of public expenditure in relation to GDP fallen back to its 1979 level. In practice, therefore, there was continuity here rather than change. The picture is, however, more complex than this suggests. Public spending grew because some areas were expanded deliberately (especially defence and law and order) whilst other areas expanded as a consequence of economic strategy (for example, social security expenditure grew massively as a result of a large increase in unemployment). Attempts to control public spending were concentrated in a few areas such as housing, support for trade and industry and contributions to Europe. The novel aspect of the Thatcher years was not the attempt to control public spending, but the way in which it was targeted.

The third key economic area was taxation. Beginning in 1979, income tax rates were cut whilst indirect taxes, such as VAT, were raised. This is a clear break with past policies. The shift to indirect taxation was justified by the argument that this enhances choice since income tax is levied automatically whilst people have the choice whether or not to pay for items or services whose price includes indirect taxes. But the result has been the widening of the gap between high earners and those on low incomes since indirect taxes hit those on small incomes harder than those on high incomes. This happens because the lower the income of a family, the greater the proportion of that income which is spent on goods and services which charge indirect taxes (see chapter 15, part 5).

Whilst it had been a priority of previous governments to maintain full employment, this was not the case with the Thatcher governments. They were prepared to accept high levels of unemployment in the hope that this would bring greater efficiency. The number of unemployed people rose from 1.5 million in 1979 to 3 million in late 1983. It reached 3.2 million in mid-1985. After this, it fell, gradually dipping below 2 million at the start of 1989. But from late 1989, it began to rise again. It should be noted, however, that between 1979 and 1990 the way in which unemployed figures are calculated was altered more than 20 times. On all but one of these occasions, the number of people unemployed fell after the adjustment. As a result, the official figures are likely to underestimate, considerably, the rise in unemployment during the Thatcher years.

A further break with the past was the privatisation programme which began slowly with the government reducing its holding in BP in 1979 and selling off its holding in Cable and Wireless in 1981. The first major sale was that of British Telecom in 1984. This was followed by a rash of sales. Between 1979 and 1990, the government raised £32.9 billion from privatisation.

Welfare

In her memoirs, Margaret Thatcher writes:

> 'Welfare benefits, distributed with little or no consideration of their effects on behaviour,

> encouraged illegitimacy, facilitated the breakdown of families and replaced incentives favouring work and self reliance with perverse encouragement for idleness and cheating.' (Thatcher, 1993, p.8)

This passage suggests that Margaret Thatcher was hostile to the very notion of a welfare state. It might be expected, therefore, that the record of her governments would be one of cutting back on welfare spending by reducing or abolishing benefits. There is evidence that this did happen, but, in practice, the Thatcher governments found it much more difficult to curb welfare spending than they imagined it would be.

Some areas of welfare expenditure were severely cut back. For example, public expenditure on housing suffered a 74% cut in real terms between 1978 and 1989. Child benefit was frozen. Students' income was eroded by preventing them from claiming supplementary benefit and housing benefit and by massively reducing student grants in real terms. One-off payments for items such as cookers were abolished and replaced with loans from a 'Social Fund'. These loans are repaid by the automatic deduction of a weekly sum from a person's benefit.

Other areas of welfare expenditure, however, expanded rapidly. The problem, from the government's point of view, was that their economic policies resulted in a massive rise in the amount of unemployment benefit, supplementary benefit and housing benefit that was claimed. In addition, the British population was ageing. As more people reached retirement age, expenditure on the state pension rose. The result was that while the government clawed back money in some areas, it was forced to spend a great deal more in others.

In relation to welfare benefits, therefore, there was both continuity and change. The state remained the main welfare provider and continued to see people through times of economic hardship. Overall, spending on benefits increased. But, on the other hand, some welfare benefits were reduced and a powerful anti-welfarism culture was fostered.

Likewise, there was both continuity and change in relation to the NHS. Spending on the NHS, for example, increased by nearly one third between 1979 and 1990, an increase from 14% to 16% of overall public spending. In this respect, there was continuity. But, critics argued, the NHS was not expensive by international standards (5.6% of GNP in 1989 compared with an average of 7.6% in countries which belonged to the Organisation of Economic Cooperation and Development). An ageing population and the huge cost of modern medicine meant that a greater increase in spending on the NHS was necessary just to maintain the existing quality of service. Although there was an overall increase in expenditure on the NHS, there was no corresponding improvement in NHS provision. In this respect, therefore, there was a change in attitude. The Thatcher governments were less willing than previous governments to accept that ever greater amounts of public money should be spent on health care. In addition, it was whilst Thatcher was still Prime Minister that the review of the NHS began which was to lead to the most fundamental reform of the NHS for a generation. The 1991 health reforms, notably the creation of an internal market within the NHS, mark an important break with the past.

Defence

In defence policy, the Thatcher governments adopted policies which broke with the past. First, unlike most governments after the 1960s, the Thatcher governments increased defence expenditure even when they cut other public spending programmes. Between 1978 and 1986, defence spending increased by 27%.

In addition, the Thatcher governments' nuclear policy was distinctive. In 1983, American Cruise and Pershing missiles were stationed in Britain. Also, it was decided that Britain's ageing Polaris nuclear weapons system would be replaced by the American Trident system. The maintenance of an independent nuclear deterrent and the fostering of a close relationship with the USA were central to the Thatcher governments' defence policy. In a sense, however, this meant little change with the past. Previous governments had developed and maintained Britain's independent nuclear deterrent. Britain's 'special relationship' with the USA had a long history.

Law and order (see also chapter 18)

Until 1994, when poll evidence suggested that opinion was shifting, the Conservatives had always been regarded as the party of law and order, a traditional connection which Margaret Thatcher was keen to develop. At the 1977 party conference, for example, she said:

> 'People have asked me whether I am going to make the fight against crime an issue at the next election. No, I am not going to make it an issue. It is the people of Britain who are going to make it an issue.' (quoted in Hall & Jacques, 1983, p.216)

There were four law and order commitments in the 1979 election manifesto - to hold a free parliamentary debate on the reintroduction of the death penalty; to introduce a tougher regime in detention centres; to develop a wider range of centres, especially for young offenders; and, to tighten immigration laws. All four pledges were fulfilled, but the outcome of the fulfilment of the first three was not, perhaps, what the Thatcherites expected. The hanging vote was lost in the Commons, despite Thatcher's support for hanging.

Similarly, the tougher regime and wider range of centres were introduced, but proved incapable of significantly reducing crime, especially by young males.

In addition, the first Thatcher government made the police a priority. Police officers were given a pay rise shortly after the 1979 election and 9,500 officers were recruited in England and Wales between 1979 and 1983. Also, a process of re-equipment took place. The result was a 20% increase in expenditure on the police between 1979 and 1983. In addition to financial support, the police were given overwhelming political support. For example, the police were given uncritical support by the government during the miners' strike of 1984-85 and criminal justice legislation strengthened the police's position.

The Thatcher governments' law and order policy was certainly less equivocal than that of previous governments. It showed a greater emphasis on the establishment of a strong state.

Foreign policy

The cornerstone of the Thatcher governments' foreign policy was the development of Britain's 'special relationship' with the USA. This was facilitated by the election of Ronald Reagan and then George Bush. Reagan's ideological stance was close to Thatcher's. Both agreed that the Soviet Union posed an increasing threat to the West and that a resolute response was needed if this was to be counteracted. Although a special relationship with the USA was not new, the intensity of Thatcher's pro-American stance was unusual.

Whereas the Thatcher governments cultivated a close relationship with the USA, they remained frosty towards the European Community (EC), especially after 1988. In 1979, the Conservatives were thought to be far more pro-European than Labour. By 1990, however, the position had been reversed. In the early 1980s, the main government aim was to reduce the size of Britain's contribution to the EC budget. Thatcher made much of the fact that she was able to secure £3 billion in rebates from the EC between 1980 and 1984. By 1990, however, there was a major change in approach. Until then, Thatcher argued that her aim was to apply her own vision of financial prudence to the EC and to protect Britain's interests. In 1988, however, Jacques Delors' proposals for European monetary and political union were vehemently opposed by Thatcher. In the summer of 1988, she delivered her 'Bruges speech' in which she outlined her vision of Europe as a union of sovereign states cooperating together but preserving their own economic interests and cultural and historical diversity. This was a stance which Thatcher retained until her resignation. It was manifested in her refusal to join the European Exchange Rate Mechanism until October 1990 (see chapter 15, section 2.2).

The Falklands War

According to Thatcher herself, the high point of her career came in the field of foreign policy:

> 'Nothing remains more vividly in my mind, looking back on my years in Number 10 than the 11 weeks in the spring of 1982 when Britain fought and won the Falklands War.' (Thatcher, 1993, p.173)

Thatcher devotes two whole chapters of her memoirs to the Falklands War, a measure of its importance in her eyes. Indeed, there are a number of reasons why the war can be termed as an important event. First, it was a military success and, therefore, helped to erase the memories of the failure of Suez (in 1956, American pressure had forced the British government to withdraw its troops after they had invaded Egypt in an attempt to seize the Suez canal and overthrow the Egyptian leader Colonel Nasser). Second, it marked a departure from the line taken by other postwar governments which had been shy of military intervention. Third, there is little doubt that the war won prestige for Britain amongst its allies. And fourth (and perhaps most important), it helped to restore Margaret Thatcher's popularity at a time when it had reached an all-time low.

Beyond Whitehall (see also chapter 16)

The Thatcher governments were determined to break with the relationship which had persisted in the past between local and central government. Local government gains its powers by Act of Parliament. This places power squarely in the hands of the centre. But, by convention, although central government set the financial and organisational framework for local government, it allowed local government considerable freedom to act in the interests of local citizens. Conflict between local and central government was not new in 1979, but it reached a new pitch during the Thatcher years. This was due to two factors. First, the Thatcher governments' commitment to bringing down inflation meant that they wanted to reduce public expenditure. Since local government is substantially financed by central government grants, there was a powerful incentive for the Thatcher governments to exercise greater control over local finances. Second, the Thatcher governments were committed to a reduction in state provision. Active, high spending and taxing local authorities stood in the way of the Thatcherite vision. The result was conflict over finance and over organisation.

On the financial front, four key pieces of legislation were passed. The 1980 Local Government Planning and Land Act altered the way in which central government grants were allocated to local government (making them easier for central government to control). The 1982 Local Government

Finance Act removed the power of local authorities to raise supplementary rates. The 1983 Rates Act provided central government with the power to limit (or 'cap') the spending of local authorities. And the introduction of the poll tax in Scotland in 1989 and in Wales and England a year later changed the way in which local taxation was raised.

The organisational changes to local government were politically controversial. Most important was the abolition of the GLC and the metropolitan counties (see chapter 16, p.470). Central government argued that the services provided by these bodies could be devolved to lower tier authorities, saving considerable sums of money. These authorities were all Labour controlled. The abolition of the GLC left London without an overall elected authority for the first time in nearly 100 years. It remains the only capital in western Europe without such an authority. In addition, organisational changes which took place in the Thatcher years resulted in the growth of quangos - unelected bodies with the power to distribute public funds (see chapter 16, part 4).

Activity 3.4

Item A *Has the electorate become Thatcherite (1)?*

(i) Should the government aim (column A) to curb inflation or (column B) to reduce unemployment?

Date	A	B	Don't know
Oct 1976	54	36	10
Jun 1980	52	42	7
Nov 1980	30	62	8
Jan 1982	23	70	8
Nov 1982	21	73	6
May 1983	22	69	9
Jul 1984	18	75	7
Aug 1985	16	77	7
Feb 1986	15	78	7

(ii) Which is more to blame if people are poor? Lack of effort on their part (column A)? Circumstances beyond their control (column B)? Or, both (column C)?

Date	A	B	C
Jan 1977	35	32	33
Mar 1985	22	50	28

(iii) Do you approve or disapprove of the following government policies?

Policy	Approve	Disapprove
Abolition of GLC	21	79
Banning of trade unions at GCHQ.	31	69
Privatisation of British Gas	43	57
Privatisation of British Telecom	44	56
Poll tax	29	71
Privatisation of electricity and water	28	72

(iv) Do you agree that when someone is unemployed it is usually his or her fault?

Date	Agree	Disagree
May 1986	10	90
Nov 1987	13	87

All figures are percentages.

Adapted from Crewe, 1986.

Item B *Has the electorate become Thatcherite (2)?*

Was there an ideological shift in Britain during the Thatcher period? Were the attitudes of the population transformed? Certainly, there is empirical evidence which shows that the electorate became less respectful of authority and more liberal on issues like pornography, abortion, capital punishment and equality for women between 1979 and 1987. In addition, the electorate came to reject both Thatcherite economic priorities and the idea that there was no alternative to government policies. There was little support for Victorian values and significant opposition to a wide variety of specific government decisions. Overall, Thatcher's missionary preaching fell on deaf ears. It is clear that anti-Thatcherite trends in social attitudes have continued. The British Social Attitudes Report published at the end of 1992 shows, for example, a clear trend in public opinion against free enterprise and towards intervention in the economy. Only a third of the population believes that private enterprise is the best way to solve economic problems. Only 29% agree that 'the less government intervenes the better it is for the economy'. There is growing support for price control and for state subsidy to industry and 87% of respondents support government funding of job-creating projects. At the same time, 65% favoured higher taxes rather than lower spending - just 3% favoured cuts in taxes and in public spending.

Adapted from Marsh & Tant, 1994.

Item C *Has the Conservative party become Thatcherite?*

(i)

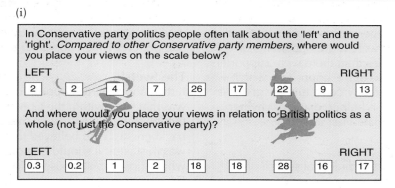

In Conservative party politics people often talk about the 'left' and the 'right'. *Compared to other Conservative party members,* where would you place your views on the scale below?

LEFT								RIGHT
2	2	4	7	26	17	22	9	13

And where would you place your views in relation to British politics as a whole (not just the Conservative party)?

LEFT								RIGHT
0.3	0.2	1	2	18	18	28	16	17

(ii)

Please indicate whether you think the government should or should not do the following things, or doesn't it matter either way?

	Definitely should	Probably should	Doesn't matter	Probably should not	Definitely should not
Encourage private education	29	36	20	12	3
Spend more money to get rid of poverty	29	52	8	9	2
Encourage the growth of private medicine	17	35	16	25	7
Put more money into the NHS	31	49	8	11	2
Reduce government spending generally	14	46	9	27	4
Introduce stricter laws to regulate the trade unions	28	38	12	19	3

(iii)

	Strongly agree	Agree	Neither	Diasgree	Strongly disagree
The Conservative party should adjust its policies to capture the middle ground of politics	16	54	13	15	2
The public enterprises privatised by the Conservative government should be subject to stricter regulation	24	48	12	14	1
A future Conservative government should privatise British Coal	12	44	17	22	5
The welfare state undermines individual self-reliance and enterprise	16	46	14	21	3
When somebody is unemployed, it is usually their fault	2	5	15	56	22
The next Conservative government should establish a prices and incomes policy as a means of controlling inflation	12	31	12	32	14

The information above comes from a survey of Conservative party members carried out in early 1992. Overall, 3,066 Conservatives responded to the survey - 78% of those approached. All figures are percentages.

Adapted from Whiteley et al., 1994.

Questions

1. 'The Thatcher governments transformed British society.' Give arguments for and against this view.
2. 'Thatcherism will live. It will live long after Thatcher has died.' Judging from Items A-C do you agree with this statement? Give reasons for your answer.
3. What evidence is there in Item A to support the arguments made in Item B?
4. Judging from Item C would you say that Margaret Thatcher transformed the Conservative party? Give reasons for your answer.

3. The opponents of Thatcherism

Key Issues

1. Who opposed the Thatcher governments?
2. What was the nature of this opposition?
3. How did the Thatcherites deal with this opposition?
4. What light does the opposition cast on Thatcherism?

The opposition

When considering the Thatcher years, it is often easy to think of them as a period in which the political scene was so dominated by Margaret Thatcher and her ideas that there was no worthwhile opposition. This would, however, be far too simplistic a view. Throughout the Thatcher years, there was a significant opposition to the policies that the government pursued. Nor, as is sometimes thought, did Thatcher and her allies sweep all before them at elections. Although the Conservatives under Margaret Thatcher won three elections in a row, they never gained more than the 43.9% of the vote which they won in 1979. In other words, at each of the three general elections there were more opponents of Thatcher and her policies than there were supporters. Paradoxically, the extent of the opposition which was ranged against Thatcher may constitute the greatest tribute to her. It may also help to explain why her achievements did not match her ideology.

The Labour party

Perhaps the least important practical source of opposition to the Conservatives during the Thatcher years was the Labour party. Although it remained the official opposition to the government in Parliament, the party spent much of the 1980s engaged in internal struggles over constitutional and policy issues. These internal struggles were motivated by the realisation that the party was in crisis. In part, this crisis was the consequence of electoral defeat, but there were a number of additional factors. First, there was the realisation that the party had not performed well in government in the 1970s. Second, there was fear that the party was losing its core support (the manual working class) or, at least, fear that the manual working class was shrinking. And third, there was the awareness that Thatcherism provided an alternative ideological perspective. To survive and prosper, the Labour party needed to counter the challenge presented by Thatcherism and to present the electorate with a convincing programme of its own.

It was the response of the left within the party to these problems which precipitated the internal struggles. Led by Tony Benn, many on the left argued that the reason for the difficulties experienced in government after 1974 and the electoral defeat in 1979 was that the party leadership had betrayed its socialist principles. Based upon this analysis, the left argued that more radical socialist policies were required in order to counteract Thatcherism. In addition, changes to the party constitution were demanded, to make the leadership more accountable to the members. By 1981, a leftward shift in policy had been achieved. The party was committed to unilateral nuclear disarmament, the closure of American nuclear bases in Britain, withdrawal from the EC, the repurchase of council houses sold to their tenants, the abolition of public schools and subsidised low fares for public transport. The *Alternative Economic Strategy* had been adopted which called for reflation, import controls, the 35 hour week, more public ownership, planning agreements and industrial democracy.

This leftward shift resulted in a split in the Labour party. Several prominent MPs on Labour's right wing broke away to form their own party - the Social Democratic Party (SDP). The Labour party was vilified in the media for being out of touch and disunited. This image of impotence grew stronger after the Conservatives won the 1983 general election. It was only after the election of Neil Kinnock as leader in 1983 that Labour began to rebuild itself as a credible opposition party with an internal cohesion and policies which appealed to the electorate.

The 'wets'

If the Labour party's opposition was ineffective, so too was that from within the Conservative party, even though there were those in the Cabinet and on the backbenches who believed that government policy was mistaken. It should be noted, however, that whilst those who opposed Thatcher within the Conservative party were known collectively as 'wets', the wets were by no means a unified group. The term was applied to all those who were suspicious and fearful of the consequences of pursuing a monetarist economic policy. Also, since the government had a large overall majority, it was able to whip up sufficient support to avoid defeat.

Thatcher herself was aware that the wets inside the Cabinet could cause problems, but she did not make a concerted effort to root them out until September 1981. By then she had concluded that:

> 'The differences between Cabinet ministers over the economic strategy - and myself and Jim Prior over trade union reform - were not just ones of emphasis but of fundamentals.' (Thatcher, 1993, p.150)

The Employment Secretary, Jim Prior was moved to the Northern Ireland Office and replaced with the 'dry' Norman Tebbit whilst two other wets, Ian Gilmour and Christopher Soames, were both sacked.

Although Gilmour in particular mounted a campaign against the government from the backbenches, three factors tended to undermine the wets' opposition to the Thatcherites. First, they had no coherent strategy. The only policies they suggested as alternatives were those which were perceived to have failed in the past. Second, from autumn 1981, the first signs of economic recovery appeared and undermined the pessimistic predictions of those who opposed the monetarist economic strategy. And third, in 1982, the Falklands War broke out. British success in the war was equated with growing economic success. Both were seen as evidence of the value of the resolute approach.

So, by the end of 1982, the wets' opposition had been marginalised substantially. There is no doubt that this diverse group of Conservatives did raise some difficult questions, but their rebellion was not sufficient to undermine the assurance of the Prime Minister that the course the government was following was the right one.

The trade unions

It was a key principle of the New Right that unions were undemocratic, disruptive of free markets and acted against the national, and often their own members' interest. Previous governments had attempted to control the power of trade unions, with a notable lack of success. The Thatcher governments adopted a gradualist approach and, most important, made changes to the civil law, not to the criminal law (see chapter 17, section 2.1 for an explanation of these terms). This encouraged individual trade unionists and employers (rather than the government) to take action against strikes. Three pieces of legislation passed in 1980, 1982 and 1984 altered the framework in which unions operated. First, limits were placed upon the 'closed shop' (an agreement between an employer and union that all employees must belong to a single union). Second, picketing was only allowed at the place of the dispute and secondary action (sympathy strikes) were made illegal. Third, secret ballots became compulsory before strike action could be called. Elections for senior union officials also became compulsory. In all these cases, if a civil action was brought before the courts and the courts then found the union to be in breach of the law, the union would be fined and required to change its behaviour. Failure to do so would be contempt of court, giving the judge the right to impose an unlimited fine and to take control of a union's assets.

Between 1979 and 1985, the unions campaigned against these changes and challenged the government through a number of industrial disputes. The first strike took place in the steel industry over issues surrounding pay and redundancy. It lasted from December 1980 to April 1981 with the government refusing to intervene to force the board of the then nationalised steel industry to review its pay offer. When the strike was settled, the union had not secured the pay offer it wanted. This was regarded as a victory for the government. Later in 1981, workers at British Leyland went on strike over pay. Then, in 1982, a succession of strikes by rail workers, NHS workers and water workers caused considerable disruption. It was clear, however, that the showdown between the government and the unions would involve the miners (NUM).

From the time when he had been appointed Energy Secretary in 1981, Nigel Lawson had built up supplies of coal at power stations and encouraged the electricity generating board to ensure that as much capacity as possible could be run using oil or nuclear fuel. Ian McGregor was appointed chair of the National Coal Board in September 1983. He formulated a plan to bring the coal industry into profit, but this required pits to be closed and jobs lost. The implementation of this plan was the immediate cause of the miners' strike which began in March 1984. In the year-long dispute which followed, all the means at the state's disposal were deployed to ensure the miners were defeated (see also chapter 18, Activity 18.7), whilst the NUM laid itself open to public hostility and court action by failing to call a ballot before the strike began. As a result, the NUM's funds were sequestrated by the courts.

The strike ended in March 1985 with defeat for the miners. For Thatcher and her supporters, this was a major victory:

> 'The coal strike was always about more than uneconomic pits. It was a political strike. And so its outcome had a significance far beyond the economic sphere. From 1972 to 1985, the conventional wisdom was that Britain could only be governed with the consent of the trade unions. No government could really resist, still less defeat, a major strike; in particular a strike by the miners' union. Even as we were reforming trade union law and overcoming lesser disputes, such as the steel strike, many on the left and outside it used to believe that the miners had the ultimate veto and would one day use it. That day had come and gone.'
> (Thatcher, 1993, pp.377-78)

After the miners' strike, trade union opposition to Thatcherism was no longer a major issue.

Pressure groups

Three pressure groups were of particular significance - the Campaign for Nuclear Disarmament (CND), the Greenham Common women's protest against nuclear missiles and the anti-poll tax campaign.

The first Thatcher government aimed to improve Britain's independent nuclear deterrent and agreed to allow new American nuclear missiles to be stationed on British soil. This, combined with renewed fears of a nuclear war, led to a substantial revival of CND (which had lain dormant since the early 1960s). Estimates vary, but Young (1991) suggests that membership of CND rose from 2,000 in 1979 to 100,000 in 1981. Optimism that popular pressure would result in unilateral disarmament grew when the Labour party adopted a unilateralist position at its 1982 conference.

Despite the evidence of popular support for CND (rallies were regularly attended by 250,000 people in the early 1980s), the government remained firm. Michael Heseltine, Secretary of State for Defence, waged a vigorous campaign against CND. But it was probably the Falklands War and the general election which followed it that really undermined CND. With a unilateralist platform, the Labour party suffered a humiliating electoral defeat in 1983. This suggested that, despite CND's popularity, wide support remained for the government's nuclear policy. The rise to power of Mikhail Gorbachev in the Soviet Union in February 1984, moreover, signalled the start of a process which defused international tension and, thereby, removed the basis for much of CND's campaigning.

It was at the time of CND's revival that the Greenham and other peace camps were established by women who were opposed to the siting of American nuclear missiles at air bases in Britain. The women developed a new type of protest with a specifically female focus. The Greenham women in particular attracted a great deal of attention in the mid-1980s. Although they became less significant as the decade wore on, the peace camps remained until the weapons were removed as a consequence of arms control agreements.

If nuclear disarmament was the focus of protest in the early Thatcher years, the poll tax (see chapter 16, section 2.5) was the focus later. Unlike CND, however, the anti-poll tax campaign was a success. Indeed, it played an important part in Thatcher's downfall. Although the campaign did use traditional means of protest such as rallies, public meetings and letter writing campaigns, its main strength was that huge numbers of people simply refused to pay. The bureaucratic chaos that non-payment brought not only revealed the depth of opposition to the tax, it demonstrated that the tax was unworkable.

Local government

Opposition to the Thatcher regime from local government was based on the principle that local authorities not controlled by Conservatives had a mandate to pursue policies different from those initiated by central government. In practical terms, this opposition took several forms. First, in the early Thatcher years, non-Conservative local authorities defied central government by ignoring demands for reduced expenditure. For example, South Yorkshire Council continued to operate a cheap fares policy. Second, after 1984, local authorities attempted to get round the budget cuts forced on them initially by raising the rates and then by 'creative accountancy'. Third, local authorities initiated campaigns against central government's plans to abolish the GLC and metropolitan counties. Later, they campaigned against the introduction of the poll tax. In addition, some councils (for example, Liverpool) mounted ideologically inspired fights with central government.

In general, these tactics were unsuccessful. Local authority spending was capped. The GLC and metropolitan counties were abolished. The poll tax was introduced. Council houses were sold and building programmes cut.

Urban unrest

The final major source of opposition to Thatcherism was less focused but nonetheless important. On a number of occasions in the 1980s, violence flared up in the inner cities. The first major outbreak of urban unrest was the Brixton riot of April 1981. This was followed by a week of rioting in July 1981 in Liverpool, London, Birmingham and eight other inner city areas. Although peace was restored and the government promised to examine and provide solutions to the people living in inner city areas, riots again broke out in October 1985. Benyon (1986) notes:

> 'It does seem that in 1985, as in 1981, the areas in which disorder occurred share certain common characteristics. In addition, it seems that the riots themselves began in 1985, again as four years earlier, after similar events. The immediate precipitants or trigger events in each case involved police officers and black people, as they did in 1981. The trigger events are the sparks which ignite the tinder, the tinder being the underlying causes which give rise to the potential for disorder. There seem to be five characteristics which are common to the areas where rioting occurred in 1985.' (Benyon, 1986, p.7)

These five characteristics were as follows. First, unemployment was high. Second, deprivation was widespread. Third, racial disadvantage and discrimination were common. Fourth, there was a feeling of political exclusion and powerlessness. And fifth, there was mistrust and hostility towards the police.

Although the opposition to the government expressed by these outbreaks of urban unrest was sporadic and short-lived, it focused attention on those who, because of their colour or economic position, had been left behind by the Thatcherite enterprise economy.

Activity 3.5

Item A *Election results 1983 and 1987*

1983 general election

Party	Votes	%	No. seats
Con	13,012,316	42.4	397
Lab	8,456,934	27.6	209
Lib/SDP	7,780,949	25.4	23
Others	1,418,938	4.6	21

Con overall majority of 144

1987 general election

Party	Votes	%	No. seats
Con	13,760,583	42.3	376
Lab	10,029,807	30.8	229
Lib/SDP	7,341,633	22.5	22
Others	1,397,555	4.4	23

Con overall majority of 102

Adapted from Craig, 1989.

Item B *The Conservative and Labour parties in the 1980s*

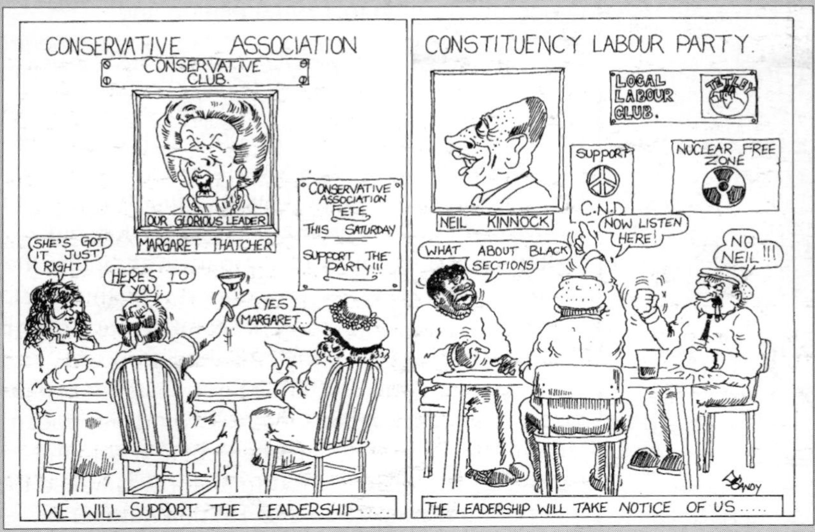

Item D *CND demonstration*

More than 250,000 people attended this CND march through London in October 1981.

Item C *The opposition*

Again and again, attempts to reform or redefine the old consensus on 'one nation' lines failed. Those who hoped that the new Social Democratic Party (SDP) would break the mould were disappointed. Internal divisions followed electoral disaster in 1987. By 1989, the centre in British politics was split between the Liberal Democrats (a merger of the Liberal party and the SDP), the Democrats (ex-SDP members whose leader David Owen opposed the merger), the Liberal party (Liberals who opposed the merger) and the Green Party. The Labour party, too, was damaged by internal division and self-doubt. It seemed in long-term decline for sociological as well as ideological reasons. Large sections of the community, especially blacks in the urban ghettos, young unemployed in urban areas in the North and large numbers of people in Scotland, seemed almost to contract-out from traditional forms of participation and civic involvement.

Adapted from Morgan, 1992.

Questions

1. a) What do Items A-D tell us about the nature of the opposition faced by the Thatcher governments?
   b) Why do you think this opposition failed to make an impact on government policy?
2. Judging from Items A-C why do you think the opposition parties were ineffective during the Thatcher years?
3. 'There is no point in going on demonstrations when conviction politicians are in power.' Give arguments for and against this view, using Item D in your answer.

4. The British government under John Major

Key Issues

1. What led to the appointment of John Major as Prime Minister?
2. What continuity, if any, is there between the governments of John Major and Margaret Thatcher?
3. What policies have been pursued since 1992?

4.1 The rise to power of John Major

When Margaret Thatcher resigned as Prime Minister and leader of the Conservative party in November 1990, she made it clear that John Major was her favoured successor.

Like Thatcher, whose background was modest (she was the daughter of a greengrocer), Major did not come from a rich family. His parents had been vaudeville performers when they were young. But by the time John was born, his father ran a small business manufacturing garden ornaments. Unlike Thatcher, however, Major did not owe his rise to his education. Whereas Thatcher went to Oxford University to study Chemistry, Major left school at 16 with just three 'O' levels. Major had several jobs and a spell of unemployment before starting a successful career with a merchant bank. His first political experience came when he was elected as a local councillor in the borough of Lambeth in 1968. In 1970, he was chosen to chair the Housing Committee.

It was not until 1976 that John Major was selected to stand for Parliament. He beat more than 300 prospective candidates to the safe seat of Huntingdon. Once elected as an MP in 1979, his rise to power was swift. In 1983, he became Minister for Social Security. Immediately following the 1987 general election, he entered the Cabinet as Chief Secretary to the Treasury. In June 1989, after Geoffrey Howe was sacked, Major became Foreign Secretary. But he only remained at the Foreign Office for three months. In October 1989, Nigel Lawson resigned as Chancellor and Major moved to Number 11 Downing Street. Just over a year later, he was able to move next door after being chosen to be leader of the Conservative party and Prime Minister. Benyon points out:

> 'Extraordinarily, in the space of 16 months Mr Major had been Foreign Secretary, Chancellor and, now, Prime Minister. This was indeed a meteoric rise.' (Benyon, 1991, p. 148)

The fall of Margaret Thatcher

Five factors combined to bring about Margaret Thatcher's downfall. The first factor was Britain's economic position in 1990. Inflation and unemployment were rising whilst consumer spending and manufacturing output were falling. Coxall (1991) notes that such developments, in the face of nearly twelve years of Thatcherite economic policy, were not treated sympathetically by the electorate. The second factor was the poll tax. Popular hatred of this tax was particularly pronounced with widespread protests and anti-payment campaigns attracting the headlines and considerable support. The third factor was Europe. By 1990, the Conservative party was in disarray over its policy towards the European Community. From 1988, Margaret Thatcher began to take a strong line against moves towards European federalism. This led to a fierce debate within the Conservative party. The fourth factor was linked to the third. Between 1989 and 1990, a number of senior Cabinet ministers resigned, giving the impression that all was not well within the Conservative leadership.

The problems within the Conservative leadership began in June 1989 when Thatcher refused, at a meeting of the European Council, to commit Britain to membership of the European Exchange Rate Mechanism (ERM). By threatening to resign, Chancellor Lawson and Foreign Secretary Howe persuaded Thatcher to change her mind and to make this commitment. But a Cabinet reshuffle in July 1989 moved Howe from the Foreign Office to the post of Deputy Prime Minister and Leader of the House, a move he resented. Then, three months later, Lawson resigned as Chancellor. Again, Britain's commitment to the ERM was the catalyst. Thatcher gave the impression that she supported her adviser Alan Walters who strongly opposed Britain's entry into the ERM. Lawson argued that public disagreement between the Chancellor and the Prime Minister made his position untenable. Nine months later, Europe was again the source of a Cabinet resignation. Nicholas Ridley, Trade and Industry Secretary, claimed in an outspoken interview that the European commissioners were Nazis and that the European Community was a conspiracy by the Germans to take over Europe. Hostile reactions to this interview forced his resignation. And finally, on 30 October 1990, Europe sparked a third Cabinet resignation. On that day, Margaret Thatcher made a fiercely anti-European speech in the Commons. Two days later Geoffrey Howe resigned in protest.

The fifth and final factor was a series of election results which indicated that the unpopularity of the third Thatcher government was not just reflected in opinion polls. In 1989, the Conservatives lost 13 seats to Labour in the European elections. In March 1990, Labour won the mid-Staffordshire by-election with a swing of 21.4% from the Conservatives. And in October 1990, the Liberal Democrats won the Eastbourne by-election with a swing of over 20% from the Conservatives. Together with the results of the European election, these by-elections demonstrated that the government was deeply unpopular. This brought added pressure. As Coxall (1991) notes, with a leader who was lagging in the opinion polls and who was unwilling to alter her policy, many Conservative MPs were beginning to worry about their seats at the next election.

Geoffrey Howe's resignation

Many commentators played down the importance of Geoffrey Howe's resignation on the grounds that Howe was not a vindictive man and, anyway, his political influence was already on the decline. But, on 13 November, Howe made a resignation speech in the Commons in which he revealed his worries about the way in which government was being conducted. The speech was greeted by stunned silence. Its impact was sufficient to convince Michael Heseltine that he should mount a leadership challenge and the next day he announced his candidature.

The contest (see also, Activity 8.4)

Heseltine based his appeal upon an alternative policy framework and personality. He promised an immediate review of the poll tax, a more interventionist stance in economic and industrial policy and a pro-European approach. He argued that he had the right personality to arrest the Conservatives' decline and to deliver victory at the next general election. Opinion polls found that Heseltine was the person found most appealing by those who would not vote Conservative again without a change of leader.

In the first ballot, Conservative MPs had a straight choice between Margaret Thatcher and Michael Heseltine. As the leadership campaign progressed, it became more bitter. Thatcher said that Heseltine's policies were the same as the Labour party's. Heseltine revived the Westland Affair which had resulted in his resignation from Cabinet in 1986 (Westland, Britain's only helicopter manufacturer, was in financial difficulties. Heseltine supported a European takeover bid whilst Thatcher supported an American bid. When Thatcher refused to back down, Heseltine resigned). Heseltine attacked Thatcher for her authoritarian style of leadership.

Although Thatcher won more votes than Heseltine in the first ballot on 20 November, she was four votes short of the number needed to prevent a second ballot. At first, she said she would stand in that ballot. But when she had interviewed members of the Cabinet and found that about 12 of them did not believe she would win, she decided to resign.

Thatcher's resignation allowed Douglas Hurd and John Major to enter the contest. Without intervening directly in the campaign, Thatcher made it clear that Major was her favoured candidate and this undoubtedly affected his chances of success. Heseltine's decision to challenge Thatcher was resented by a large number of Conservative MPs and Heseltine's supporters may have damaged his chances by 'talking up' his support. Hurd's chances were damaged by media reports which made much of his education at Eton and his privileged background. The second ballot was held on 27 November. Major won 185 votes, Heseltine 131 and Hurd 56. Although Major failed by two votes to gain a technical victory (50% of the vote plus one), the other candidates withdrew, leaving Major as leader and Prime Minister.

4.2 John Major's premiership 1990-92

Although few questioned the constitutional legitimacy of the way in which Major became Prime Minister, many did question whether it was right that a Prime Minister should come to power not as a result of a general election, but as the result of a ballot within a party. Despite these criticisms, John Major waited until April 1992 before calling a general election.

John Major's first Cabinet

In choosing his Cabinet, Major demonstrated a desire to heal the wounds which had split the Conservative party over the previous months. He did fail, however, to appoint a woman to the Cabinet, an omission for which he was criticised. Also, a high proportion of the Cabinet had served in Thatcher's last Cabinet. Major did, however, reward colleagues who had helped in his campaign - Norman Lamont (Chancellor), David Mellor (Chief Secretary to the Treasury) and Chris Patten (Conservative party chairman). Most important, perhaps, was his inclusion of Michael Heseltine as Environment Secretary. Not only was this a senior post in its own right. It had added importance since the Environment Secretary was charged with dealing with the poll tax.

John Major's programme

The policies which emerged in Major's first two years as Prime Minister demonstrated both a degree of change and considerable continuity. The impression that resulted was that, in many ways, Major remained committed to the fundamentals of Thatcherism, but he was keen to mitigate some of its more unpleasant side effects.

The new regime was determined to present the image of 'capitalism with a caring face'. Kelly (1993) notes that within weeks of taking power, the Major government announced £200 million of extra spending on hospitals, AIDS, London's homeless and social housing. The freeze on child benefit was removed and public sector pay increases above the rate of inflation were announced. Significantly, the government moved quickly to announce the end of the poll tax (in March 1991). It was to be replaced by the council tax (see chapter 16, section 2.5).

The main theme, until the 1992 general election, was the establishment of a nation 'at ease with itself'. The implication was that the radical changes of the Thatcher years had been necessary, but the time for consolidation had arrived. This was symbolised by an initiative launched in the summer of 1991 - the Citizen's Charter (see chapter 17, part 1). The Charter initiative was meant to encapsulate a continuation of the Thatcherite insistence on high standards in public service and a new emphasis on partnership and cooperation, combined with recognition of achievement.

But not every initiative was characterised by a softening of the Thatcherite approach. Kelly points out:

> 'The most important comparison between Major and his predecessor naturally comes in respect of inflation. For Major, defeating inflation became the kernel of economic policy in much the same way it had been for Thatcher ten years earlier.' (Kelly, 1993, p.142)

In addition, Major maintained a commitment to further privatisation, notably of the coal industry and railways. He also maintained a commitment to a basic rate of income tax of 20p in the pound, a long cherished Thatcherite dream. Moreover, the contracting-out of public services to the private sector was to be continued and extended. Here again, the Citizen's Charter had a role to play. But, in this case, by laying out the standards which had to be maintained, the charters put pressure on public bodies to meet those standards or suffer the consequences:

> 'Some on the left blissfully imagine that...the innocuous sounding Citizen's Charter will just copy the toothless but well meaning measures of Labour-run York City Council. In fact, it will be the public sector's worst nightmare. If a range of services, including health care, is not carried out by the public sector according to a specified standard and timescale, the citizen can use private sector alternatives and send the bill to the public sector bureaucrats. The bill will have to be paid within the existing fixed budget and so savings will be needed to finance it. There will be sackings and pay cuts.' (Phibbs, 1991)

In overall terms, the policies pursued during the first two years of Major's premiership aimed to score two, perhaps contradictory, goals. The first was to establish Major as a Prime Minister in his own right with a distinctive perspective and direction of his own. His early policy pronouncements and his more conciliatory and cooperative style were indications of this. Second, at the same time, it was crucial for Major's credibility within his party that he establish a degree of continuity between his own regime and that of his predecessor. This was necessary to satisfy the needs and expectations of two groups - those on the backbenches who considered Thatcher as the bringer of a golden age and those in the Conservative constituency parties around the country who still adored the Thatcher policies and the Thatcher style.

Activity 3.6

Item A *A Major effect?*

(i) Images of the party leaders 1987 and 1992

Image	1987 Thatcher %	1987 Kinnock %	1992 Major %	1992 Kinnock %
Extreme	68	35	16	40
Moderate	24	56	78	52
Don't know	8	9	6	8
Looks after one class	59	48	43	47
Looks after all classes	36	42	51	44
Don't know	6	10	6	9
Caring	50	78	73	75
Uncaring	42	13	21	18
Don't know	9	9	7	8
Capable of being a strong leader	96	51	69	44
Not capable of being a strong leader	2	42	26	51
Don't know	1	8	5	5

Figures do not add up to 100% because of rounding.

Adapted from Heath et al., 1994.

(ii) Voting intentions August 1989 to February 1992

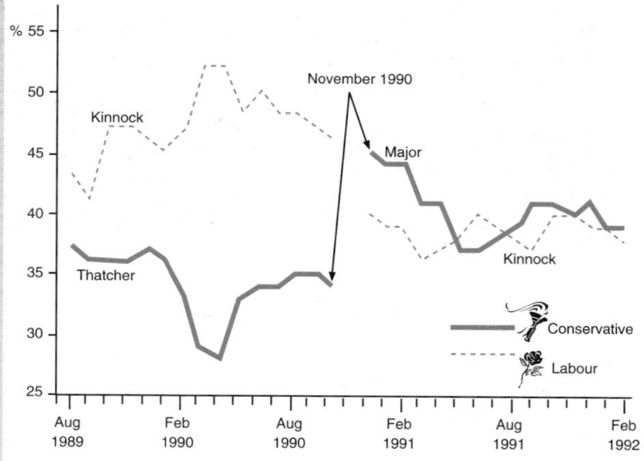

This graph shows how voting intention changed after John Major became Prime Minister in November 1990.

Adapted from Heath et al., 1994.

Item B *The Cabinet*

(i) Margaret Thatcher's Cabinet, November 1990

Prime Minister	Margaret Thatcher	**Health Secretary**	Kenneth Clarke
Leader of the House of Commons	Geoffrey Howe	**Education Secretary**	John MacGregor
Lord Chancellor	Lord MacKay	**Scottish Secretary**	Malcolm Rifkind
Foreign Secretary	Douglas Hurd	**Transport Secretary**	Cecil Parkinson
Chancellor of the Exchequer	John Major	**Energy Secretary**	John Wakeham
Home Secretary	David Waddington	**Leader of the House of Lords**	Lord Belstead
Welsh Secretary	Peter Walker	**Social Security Secretary**	Tony Newton
Employment Secretary	Norman Fowler	**Environment Secretary**	Chris Patten
Defence Secretary	Tom King	**Northern Ireland Secretary**	Peter Brooke
President of the Board of Trade	Nicholas Ridley	**Minister of Agriculture**	John Gummer
Chancellor of the Duchy of Lancaster	Kenneth Baker	**Chief Secretary to the Treasury**	Norman Lamont

(ii) John Major's Cabinet, April 1991

Back row (from left): Richard Ryder (chief whip), Ian Lang (Scottish Secretary), Peter Lilley (President of the Board of Trade), Michael Howard (Employment Secretary), Peter Brooke (Northern Ireland Secretary), Tony Newton (Social Security Secretary), John Wakeham (Energy Secretary), Chris Patten (Chancellor of the Duchy of Lancaster), John Gummer (Minister of Agriculture), David Hunt (Welsh Secretary), William Waldgrave (Health Secretary), David Mellor (Chief Secretary to the Treasury), Sir Robin Butler (Head of civil service) **Front row** (from left): John MacGregor (Leader of the House of Commons), Tom King (Defence Secretary), Norman Lamont (Chancellor of the Exchequer), Lord Waddington (Leader of the House of Lords), Lord MacKay (Lord Chancellor), John Major (Prime Minister), Douglas Hurd (Foreign Secretary), Kenneth Baker (Home Secretary), Michael Heseltine (Environment Secretary), Kenneth Clarke (Education Secretary), Malcolm Rifkind (Transport Secretary).

Item C *John Major's style*

John Major's managerial style is different from Thatcher's. He is less assertive. Rather, he attempted to heal the splits in the Conservative party by bringing the various factions together. Certainly, his style in Cabinet appears to be collegial. Similarly, he is happy to cultivate the idea that he is dull and ordinary - like his grey Spitting Image puppet. In the 1992 general election campaign he aimed to appear as a 'man of the people'. Hence, the first Conservative election broadcast entitled 'The Journey' which concentrated upon his rise from humble origins to Prime Minister. His image as a Prime Minister who was more willing to listen to people was, therefore, accompanied by a softer, more compassionate approach. As might be expected, the key decisions of the first two years - on the poll tax and the Maastricht treaty - were the result of extensive discussion in the Cabinet.

Adapted from Marsh & Tant, 1994.

Item D *John Major's address in the 1992 election manifesto*

THE BEST FUTURE FOR BRITAIN

I believe in a responsible society. Government's duties are clear: to protect Britain in a dangerous world; to look after those who cannot look after themselves; to protect law-abiding people from crime and disorder; and to protect the value of our currency - without which all spending pledges are worthless and all savings at risk.

But I believe also in a society in which government doesn't try to take responsibility away from people. Politicians must never make the mistake of thinking the state always knows best, or that it is entitled to the lion's share of people's money. I believe in low taxes not just because they ignite enterprise - the spark of economic growth - but because they put power and choice where it belongs: in your hands.

I do not believe the answer to every problem is simply for government to dig deeper in your pocket. I believe it often lies in changing the way government works; in making it respond to you. Government should look outwards. It should listen. It should put you in the know, not keep you in the dark.

You know I believe in choice. And in this election, as always, there is another choice. You can vote for our opponents, and watch them take Britain back to the 1970s. Back to socialism. Back to strikes. Back to strife. Back to the world's pity, or worse still, contempt. I don't believe Britain wants that. I know the world doesn't want that for Britain.

I hope you will choose a different path - to go forward, not back; to go for the best, knowing that Britain can be the best and do it best. My belief is clear. Only the best is good enough for Britain.

John Major

Item E *Nice guys do finish first*

Daily Mail

FRIDAY, APRIL 10, 1992

30p

BRITAIN DECIDES 92

UNRIVALLED ELECTION COVERAGE IN THE MAIL. NATIONAL NEWSPAPER OF THE YEAR

Premier John Major is staying on at No. 10

NICE GUYS DO FINISH FIRST

By GORDON GREIG, Political Editor

JOHN MAJOR, the quiet man of British politics, goes back into 10, Downing Street this morning.

He is the Prime Minister who not only defeated Neil Kinnock and his Labour Party — but also the combined polling organisations of Great Britain.

Feared

Turn to Page 2, Col 1

JOHN MAJOR . . . Winning despite all the poll results

The front page of the *Daily Mail* on 10 April 1992, the day after the general election.

Questions

1. 'Thatcherism with a human face'. Is this a fair description of Major's first 18 months in power? Use evidence from Items A-E in your answer.
2. Judging from Items A, B and D what changed when John Major became Prime Minister and what stayed the same?
3. Judging from Item D would you say that John Major's ideology differed substantially from that of Margaret Thatcher? Give reasons for your answer.
4. What do Items C and E tell us about the image that John Major projected after he became Prime Minister? Why do you think he chose to project this image?

4.3 The Major government since 1992

When John Major announced the date of the 1992 general election, most commentators predicted a Labour victory or a hung Parliament. These predictions were based upon two main factors. First, most opinion polls showed the Conservatives lagging. And second, the economy remained in recession. In practice, however, such predictions proved to be wrong. The Conservative party did lose 39 seats and its share of the vote fell to its fourth lowest since 1945. Despite this, however, the result was a Conservative victory and a fairly comfortable overall majority of 21.

According to Crewe (1992), there were five main reasons for a Conservative victory in 1992. First, the size and distribution of the swing to Labour favoured the Conservatives. Second, many people did not believe that Neil Kinnock had the leadership qualities to be Prime Minister. Third, the Conservatives' negative campaigning made an impact - especially their assertion that a Labour government would raise taxation and allow inflation to rise. Fourth, there was a general fear that Labour was not competent to govern. And fifth, there was a last minute swing to the Conservatives amongst the middle classes and skilled working class voters, especially in marginal seats in England.

Once he had secured electoral victory, John Major could claim to have a mandate from the people. The question that he had to address, therefore, was whether he should use this mandate to take the government in a new direction or whether his aim should be to continue along the path which had already been established.

The Major government's record

By winning the 1992 general election, John Major vindicated those Conservatives who had argued that a change of leader was a necessary prerequisite if the Conservative party was to retain power. But John Major's post-election honeymoon was short-lived. By late 1994, for example, David McKie could write:

> 'No government since polling began had fallen as fast and as far from public favour as John Major's did between its election and its second anniversary in April 1994. Major himself was the least popular Prime Minister ever, yet his government's ratings were even worse than his own. On the issues where the Conservatives, even in bad times, had dominated Labour - their superior capacity for managing the British economy, their greater command in the fight against crime - Labour had taken the lead and showed no sign of relinquishing it.' (McKie, 1994, p.3)

The problems which beset the Major government came thick and fast. They can, perhaps, be categorised under five headings.

1. Black Wednesday (see also chapter 15, section 2.2)

In September 1990, Britain finally agreed to join the Exchange Rate Mechanism (ERM) of the European Monetary System (EMS). It did so when the pound's exchange rate was high. As Chancellor, and then as Prime Minister, John Major made his support for Britain's participation in the membership of the ERM clear. In the 1992 Conservative election manifesto, for example, membership of the ERM in the long term was to be a central plank in government economic policy:

> 'Membership of the ERM is now central to our counter-inflation discipline...In due course we will move to the narrow bands of the ERM.'
> (CCO, 1992, p.6)

But in the summer of 1992, the money markets began to exert pressure on the pound. Despite promising that the government would not pull out of the ERM and despite spending as much as £10 billion trying to protect the pound, the Chancellor Norman Lamont was forced to take the pound out of the ERM and to devalue it. This was not just a reversal of government policy, it was also a humiliation. McKie argues:

> 'Britain's forced retreat from the ERM, only days after stern reassurances from the Prime Minister and the Chancellor that it must not and would not happen, had left wounds behind that would not heal. The government's credibility crumbled and did not recover. The impression left behind by these events - that John Major and friends said one thing but did another - was repeatedly reinforced in subsequent misadventures.'
> (McKie, 1994, p.3)

2. Taxation

It is generally agreed that the crucial issue in the 1992 general election campaign was taxation. The Conservatives made a great deal of political capital by portraying Labour as a high tax party. Conservatives, they argued, cut taxes. They did not put them up. As late as 1 January 1994, John Major said:

> 'The Conservative party remains the party of the lowest possible tax, the party of low income tax and the only party whose instinct is to cut tax and leave money with individuals and families and not take it for the state.' (John Major's New Year Message, 1994)

Despite these words, Britain's budget deficit was around £50 billion in 1993. To reduce this debt, more money had to be raised. As a result, the Chancellor, Norman Lamont, announced in his March 1993 Budget that indirect taxes would be raised over the following three years. When Lamont was replaced by

Kenneth Clarke in May 1993, Clarke continued the policy set in place by Lamont. By January 1994, the Labour party was able to claim for the first time in 15 years that tax levels under a Conservative government exceeded the tax levels of the last Labour government. This embarrassment for the Conservatives turned into humiliation in November 1994 when the government's plans to raise VAT on fuel were defeated by a backbench revolt.

3. Euroscepticism

The third blow to the Major government was the split which developed within the Conservative party over Europe. Although the government was able to secure a parliamentary majority in support of the Maastricht Treaty, arguments within the Conservative party over the role which Britain should play in the EU were not solved at that time. A stubborn group of anti-Europeans (the 'Eurosceptics') remained at odds with the government and finally voted against the government on a confidence issue in late November 1994. As a result, the Conservative whip was withdrawn from eight Conservative MPs. Due to by-election losses, the government at that point technically became a minority government. Although the whip was restored in April 1995, the Conservative party's reputation for avoiding schisms and in-fighting was severely damaged.

4. The 'sleaze' factor

In addition to the other problems facing the Major government, a number of sexual and financial scandals involving members of the government or Conservative backbenchers provided critics with the ammunition to accuse the government of sleaze. A number of these scandals took on added importance because they were exposed whilst the Conservatives were in the midst of the 'Back to Basics' campaign. This campaign was launched by John Major at the 1993 Conservative party conference when he talked of the need to go back:

> 'To self discipline and respect for the law, to consideration for others, to accepting responsibility for yourself and your family - and not shuffling it off on other people and the state.' (Speech made on 8 October 1993).

Although John Major did not intend it, 'Back to Basics' was taken to mean that the government supported old-fashioned family values and disapproved of permissiveness and the growth of single parent families. As a result, when a number of sexual and financial improprieties involving Conservative MPs came to light, the government appeared to be hypocritical.

In addition, the opposition parties pointed to the huge growth in unelected posts which, they claimed, tended to be filled by Conservative supporters. This, it was alleged, was symptomatic of a government whose only concern was to look after its own.

5. The Labour party

Following Labour's defeat in the 1992 general election, the Labour leader Neil Kinnock resigned and John Smith was elected in his place. John Smith, it was generally agreed, had suitable credentials to pose a formidable threat to John Major at the next election, but he suffered a heart attack and died in May 1994. After Tony Blair was elected in John Smith's place in July 1994, Labour's opinion poll ratings reached record highs. This was due in part to the image projected by Blair and his colleagues. They presented the Labour party as united, modern and progressive and they attacked the Conservatives for being disunited, complacent and stale. Whilst John Smith's death worked to John Major's advantage in the short term since it meant that no challenge was made to his leadership later in 1994, in the longer term the Labour party's revival has been responsible for and added to the problems facing the Major government.

Policies pursued by the Major government since 1992

It is possible that history will not judge the Major government by the problems it faced, but by its achievement in certain policy areas. After all, in 1981-82, opinion polls suggested that Margaret Thatcher was the most unpopular Prime Minister since polls began. Yet, in 1983 she went on to win an overall majority of well over 100 seats. If John Major were to win a second general election in a row, it is likely that the problems outlined above would be regarded as of minor importance.

Personnel

Since 1992, the Major government has shown a remarkable degree of continuity with its Thatcherite predecessors. A high proportion of ministers served under Margaret Thatcher. In 1994, for example, almost half the Cabinet was made up of ministers who had served in Margaret Thatcher's last Cabinet. Also, most of the 'new faces' came from the Thatcherite wing of the party.

Economic policy

The main principles behind the management of the economy since 1992 have been very much the same as those which were adhered to before. The main priority has been the maintenance of low inflation, a priority which may even have been assisted by withdrawal from the ERM. Withdrawal allowed interest rates to fall and a period of economic growth to begin. By early 1995, the problem faced by the government was not recession. On the contrary, most economic figures suggested that the economy had recovered. Instead, the problem facing the government was a lack of confidence and a general unwillingness to believe that the recovery would prove beneficial to ordinary voters. Most commentators, in early 1995, agreed that the 'feel-good' factor was missing from the recovery.

Another area of continuity with the past was the Major government's desire to continue with a privatisation programme. But, whereas there is evidence of support for (or at least indifference towards) the major privatisations which took place under Thatcher, the Major government's proposals to privatise the railways and the Post Office provoked a great deal of public hostility.

Welfare

As with the Thatcher governments, reform of the welfare state under John Major has stopped short of outright privatisation. Nevertheless, the Major government has been perturbed at the cost of maintaining the welfare state and has considered ways in which to reduce it. In the name of efficiency, a number of changes have been introduced, most of them consistent with the reforms begun under Thatcher:

> 'Having rejected privatisation of health and education, John Major's task has been to import the best of private sector practice as a means of improving the performance of these services. This includes performance pay, audit, competition and more information about performance. The government has tried to mobilise consumers to expect and demand a level of performance comparable to what they would expect from say, Marks and Spencer. In health, the devices have been internal markets, hospital trusts and fund-holding doctors, in schools, core curriculum, opting out and local budgets. These were all set in train by 1990 but John Major has implemented them energetically.' (Kavanagh, 1994, p.10)

It is not just in health and education that there have been moves towards the contracting-out of services. The welfare benefit system has also moved in that direction. Unemployment offices are now run by a Next Steps agency (an autonomous agency given a contract to do a specific job by a government department - see chapter 13, p.389) and the provision of all benefits is to be handled by an agency rather than directly by government. In addition, benefits themselves have been reformed. Unemployment benefit and income support, for example, have been replaced by the new 'job seekers allowance'. As with reforms in this area under Thatcher, the aim is to attack the culture of dependency which, the Conservatives claim, is one result of the development of a welfare state.

Defence policy

Since the end of the Cold War, defence policy has been dominated by the question of how to make cuts in expenditure whilst preserving Britain's influence in the world. The government has struggled to make cuts in the face of opposition from its own backbenches, the defence establishment and the defence industry. The result is that cuts have been made, but these cuts were not as substantial as those envisaged in the much revised *Options for Change* document issued just before the Gulf War and Margaret Thatcher's downfall.

Law and order

A full five pages of the Conservative 1992 election manifesto were devoted to law and order. But since the 1992 general election, public confidence in the government's policies on law and order has not been high. Indeed, in 1994, for the first time in living memory, the Conservatives fell behind Labour in opinion polls taken on this issue. This was in part due to the success of Labour's work in this area. But it was also a reflection of public discontent. This discontent was the product of several factors. First, the media gave the impression that crime was soaring in Britain. Whatever the actual statistics, there was evidence that people were more worried about crime than used to be the case. Second, the freeing of a number of prisoners falsely accused of serious crimes (for example, the Guildford four, freed in 1989, and the Birmingham six, freed in 1991) seriously undermined the public's faith in the British system of justice. Although the Major government was not responsible for these miscarriages of justice, they produced a climate of mistrust. Third, the government faced a great deal of opposition over its policies to combat crime. And fourth, the government's credibility on law and order was undermined by a number of escapes and prison riots. Especially embarrassing was the early record of Group 4, a private security company which took over the running of Wolds prison in April 1992. In the first week of Group 4's administration there were no less than four escapes from custody.

At the 1993 Conservative party conference, the Home Secretary, Michael Howard, promised a package of 27 measures to combat crime. But he then found it hard to deliver these promises. Two major pieces of legislation were drawn up - the Police and Magistrates Bill and the Criminal Justice and Public Order Bill. But both Bills faced opposition within Parliament (especially in the House of Lords). Although the two Bills had become law by the end of 1994, the Police and Magistrates Bill had been considerably watered down and the Criminal Justice Bill had provoked a wave of public demonstrations.

Northern Ireland

Perhaps the biggest breakthrough to be made since 1992 came over Northern Ireland. The spark appears to have been the *Downing Street Declaration* issued by John Major and Albert Reynolds in December 1993 (see chapter 4, p.89). After secret negotiations and semi-public manoeuvring, the IRA declared a ceasefire on 31 August 1994. The Loyalist paramilitaries quickly followed suit. As a result, for the first time since 1969, there seemed to be a real possibility of a negotiated settlement. By the end of 1994, preliminary talks had been held between government officials and the IRA. Expectations of further progress were consequently high.

Foreign policy

After the 1992 general election, the 'special relationship' with the USA, which Thatcher had regarded as the cornerstone of foreign policy, came under strain following the election of the Democrat Bill Clinton in November 1992. Conservative party strategists had helped to plan the election campaign of his opponent, George Bush. This, unsurprisingly, strained relations. In the autumn of 1994, disagreements between Britain and the USA again broke out over the precise extent to which military action should be taken in Serbia.

Government beyond Whitehall

The Major government's local government policy has continued on the path laid down during the Thatcher years. This policy has three main strands. First, the independence of local authorities has been further eroded. The council tax (which replaced the poll tax) has a smaller yield than its predecessor and local authorities are, therefore, more dependent on grants from central government. This dependence has restricted their freedom of movement since central government has continued to place strict limits on local authority spending.

The second strand is the continuation of the process of altering the internal management of local authorities. More and more Compulsory Competitive Tendering (CCT) has been introduced (see chapter 16, section 2.5). The idea behind these changes is that local authorities should, increasingly, be service commissioners rather than service providers.

The third strand is local government reorganisation. Although the government hoped that the Local Government Commission set up in 1992 would recommend the replacement of two tier local authorities with unitary authorities, public opinion in many areas was opposed to this. As a result, by the end of 1994, the Commission agreed that many counties should retain their existing structure. Unitary authorities would only be introduced in those areas where there was strong evidence that people were in favour of them. The area of government beyond Whitehall which has really sparked controversy since 1992, however, is the growth of quangos - non-elected bodies responsible for the spending of public funds (see chapter 16, part 4).

Activity 3.7

Item A *John Major's public image (1)*

(i) Percentage of people satisfied with John Major

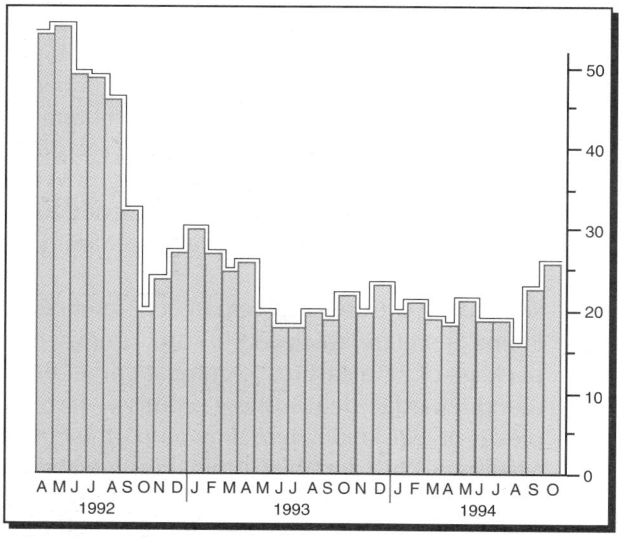

This table shows the respondents who said that they were satisfied with the way John Major was doing his job as Prime Minister between April 1992 and October 1994.

(ii) Voting intentions 1994-95

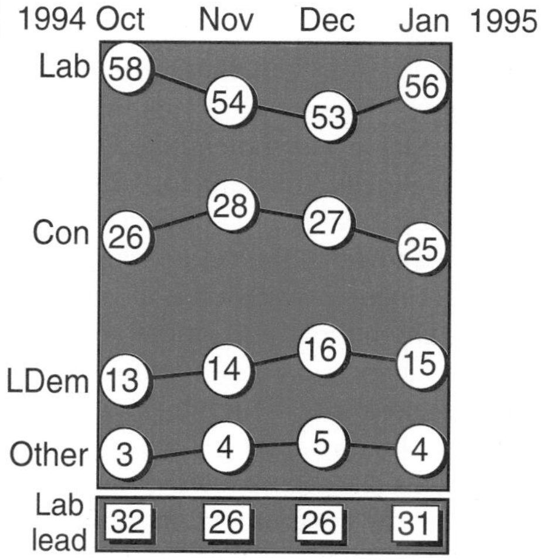

This graph shows the results of opinion polls between October 1994 and January 1995. Respondents were asked who they would vote for if there was a general election on that day.

Adapted from the *Times*, 28 October 1994, and the *Guardian*, 18 January 1995.

Item B *John Major's public image (2)*

Following a series of sexual and financial scandals involving Conservative MPs in the autumn of 1994, this was one of the more polite cartoons to suggest the damage being done to John Major's reputation.

Item C *The Major effect*

It is difficult to recall any other Prime Minister in the postwar period who has been subject to such a bitter and sustained media attack as John Major. Since Britain's withdrawal from the ERM in September 1992, criticism of his leadership has been unrelenting. But there is a case for saying that any leader who came to power in November 1990 would have faced considerable difficulties, not least because they would have been taking over from Margaret Thatcher. There is an argument that no matter who was Conservative leader, Europe would have been an issue which split the party and that the economic recession would have restricted their options. In addition, it should be noted that the Conservatives have remained in power without a break for longer than any other party this century and this is bound to have taken its toll. Besides, John Major has not had the luxury of a large overall majority in the Commons. After the Eastleigh by-election in June 1994 his overall majority was cut to just 15. But, despite these handicaps, by the time of his fourth anniversary in office, John Major will have served as Prime Minister for longer than eight other Prime Ministers this century and there is no doubt that John Major's Britain is very different from that of Margaret Thatcher.

Adapted from Kavanagh & Seldon, 1994.

Item D *Election results, 1993-94*

(i) By-elections 1993-94

	Con	Labour	Lib Dem	Swing
Newbury	-29.0	-4.0	+27.8	28.4 Con to Lib
Christchurch	-32.2	-9.4	+38.6	35.4 Con to Lib
Rotherham	-13.9	-8.3	+17.4	12.9 Lab to Lib
Barking	-23.5	+20.5	-2.5	22.0 Con to Lab
Eastleigh	-26.5	+6.8	+16.3	21.4 Con to Lib
Newham NE	-16.0	+16.6	-7.0	16.3 Con to Lab
Bradford S	-20.6	+7.7	+10.2	14.1 Con to Lab
Dagenham	-26.4	+19.7	-3.1	23.1 Con to Lab

All figures are percentages. The swing is the change in the vote since the 1992 general election.

(ii) Local elections May 1994

Party	% vote	seats * gained	Councils controlled
Lab	41	+88	+4
Con	27	-429	-18
Lib Dem	27	-388	+9

*** Compared to 1990 when these seats were last fought**

(iii) European elections June 1994*

Party	% vote	No. seats
Lab	44	62
Con	27	18
Lib Dem	16	2
Others	13	2

*** Does not include Northern Ireland**

Questions

1. Judging from Items A and B above and Item E in activity 3.6 how did John Major's public image change between 1992 and 1994? Give reasons to explain this change.
2. a) Do the figures in Items A and D suggest that John Major's government was suffering from 'mid-term blues' at the end of 1994 or from something more serious? Suggest reasons to back up your argument.

   b) What part has hindsight played in your answer? What does this tell us about the difficulty of interpreting contemporary events?
3. Would you agree with the assertion in Item C that 'there is no doubt that John Major's Britain is very different from that of Margaret Thatcher'? Give reasons for your answer.

References

Barry (1987) Barry, N., *The New Right*, Croom Helm, 1987.

Benyon (1986) Benyon, J., 'Turmoil in the cities', *Social Studies Review*, Vol.1, No.3, January 1986.

Benyon (1991) Benyon, J., 'The fall of Margaret Thatcher: the end of an era' in *Wale (1991)*.

Benyon & Denver (1990) Benyon, J. & Denver, D., 'Mrs Thatcher's Electoral Success', *Social Studies Review*, Vol.5, No.3, January 1990.

Beveridge (1942) Beveridge, W., *Social Insurance and Allied Services*, Cmd 6404, HMSO, 1942.

CCO (1992) *The Conservative Manifesto 1992*, Conservative Central Office, 1992.

Coxall (1991) Coxall, B., 'The struggle for the Conservative leadership in 1990', *Talking Politics*, Vol.4, No.1, autumn 1991.

Craig (1989) Craig, F.W.S., *British Electoral Facts 1832-1987*, Dartmouth, 1989.

Crewe (1986) Crewe, I., 'Has the electorate become Thatcherite?' in *Skidelsky (1986)*.

Crewe (1992) Crewe, I., 'Why did Labour lose (yet again?)', *Politics Review*, Vol.2, No.1, September 1992.

Gamble (1988) Gamble, A., *Free Economy, Strong State*, Macmillan, 1988.

Hall & Jacques (1983) Hall, S. & Jacques, M., *The Politics of Thatcherism*, Lawrence and Wisehart, 1983.

Heath et al. (1994) Heath, A., Jowell, R. & Curtice, J., *Labour's Last Chance*, Dartmouth, 1994.

Kavanagh (1990) Kavanagh, D., *Thatcherism and British Politics: an End to Consensus?*, Oxford University Press, 1990.

Kavanagh (1994) Kavanagh, D., 'A Major agenda?' in *Kavanagh & Seldon (1994)*.

Kavanagh & Seldon (1994) Kavanagh, D. & Seldon, A. (eds), *The Major Effect*, Macmillan, 1994.

Kelly (1993) Kelly, R., 'After Margaret: the Conservative party after 1990', *Talking Politics*, Vol.5, No.3, Summer 1993.

Marsh & Tant (1994) Marsh, D. & Tant, T., 'British politics post Thatcher: a minor Major effect' in *Wale (1994)*.

McKie (1994) McKie, D., *The Guardian Political Almanac 1994/5*, Fourth Estate, 1994.

Middlemass (1979) Middlemass, K., *Politics in an Industrial Society*, Andre Deutsch, 1979.

Miliband (1961) Miliband, R., *Parliamentary Socialism*, Merlin, 1961.

Morgan (1992) Morgan, K.O., *The People's Peace*, Oxford University Press, 1992.

Phibbs (1991) Phibbs, H., 'Iron man', *New Statesman and Society*, 7 June 1991.

Riddell (1985) Riddell, P., *The Thatcher Government*, Basil Blackwell, 1985.

Skidelsky (1986) Skidelsky, R. (ed.), *Thatcherism*, Chatto & Windus, 1986.

Thatcher (1993) Thatcher, M., *The Downing Street Years*, HarperCollins, 1993.

Wale (1991) Wale, W. (ed.), *Developments in Politics*, Vol.2, Causeway Press, 1991.

Wale (1994) Wale, W. (ed.), *Developments in Politics*, Vol.5, Causeway Press, 1994.

Whiteley et al. (1994) Whiteley, P., Seyd, P. & Richardson, J., *True Blues: the Politics of Conservative Party Membership*, Oxford University Press, 1994.

Young (1991) Young, H., *One of Us*, Macmillan, 1991.

4 The British constitution

Introduction

A constitution is a system of rules which describes the structure and powers of government, the relationship between different parts of government and the relationship between government and citizen. The constitution is, therefore, an essential starting point for uncovering the structure and processes of government and the location of power in the political system. In many countries, the constitution has been codified (written down in a single document) and copies are widely available. The constitution of the USA, for example, is inexpensive and relatively short. It can be purchased in any decent bookshop in the USA. But a comparable rule book cannot be purchased in the UK. This is not because the UK does not have a constitution. It is because the rules which describe the structure and power of government and the relationship between government and citizen are not found in any single document. The British constitution remains uncodified. Instead, the fundamental rules and principles underlying the operation of government in the UK are scattered among a variety of different sources.

Supporters of the British constitution argue that its great strength is its capacity for evolution. The British constitution should not be written down in a single document, they argue, because it is constantly changing. Written, codified constitutions lack flexibility. Against this, a growing number of people argue for constitutional reform. They claim that the British constitution is out of date and undemocratic, drawbacks which could be remedied by producing a new written constitution. This chapter begins by examining the British constitution as it is and then goes on to consider the arguments for and against reform.

Chapter summary

Part 1 attempts to define the British constitution by examining the **six main sources** from which the constitution is derived. It also looks at the **evolution of the constitution**.

Part 2 analyses **parliamentary sovereignty** and the **rule of law**.

Part 3 asks what is meant by the term **'unitary state'** and considers arguments for and against **devolution**. It also discusses the place of **Northern Ireland** in the UK.

Part 4 considers the **role of the monarchy**.

Part 5 presents the arguments for and against **constitutional reform** .

1 Defining the British constitution

Key Issues

1. What do we mean by 'separation of the powers'?
2. From what sources is the British constitution derived?
3. Which is better a codified or an uncodified constitution?
4. How did the British constitution evolve into its present form?

1.1 The different parts of government

Government involves three main tasks. First, there is the **legislative function**, the process of making laws. Second, there is the **executive role** of implementing the law and ensuring that legislative requirements are carried out. Third, there is the **judicial task** of law enforcement, of deciding whether laws have been broken and, if they have, of dispensing punishment.

Constitutions usually define which people or institutions have the power to carry out these tasks. Some constitutions stipulate that legislative, executive and judicial powers should each be exercised by a different person or group. This is known as the principle of the **separation of the powers**. The object of such a principle is to avoid the concentration of power into the hands of a single person or group. Defining the different parts or branches of government (and the relationships between them) is, therefore, of central constitutional significance. It is a crucial element in establishing how a particular political system should work.

Sources of the British constitution

The six main sources from which the British constitution is derived are statute law, common law, royal prerogative, constitutional conventions, various 'works of authority' and the treaties and law of the European Union.

a) Statute law

A statute is an Act of Parliament. It is a written law which has been passed (approved) by Parliament and is enforceable by the law courts. Over time, some statutes have come to be regarded as having special significance because they contain rules relating to constitutional rights or duties of the citizen or to how the government of the country should be organised.

The Habeas Corpus Act of 1679 is an example of a statute of constitutional significance because it affords some protection for the citizen against wrongful imprisonment. The Act enables anyone who has been confined to demand to be brought before a court for a just trial. In the past, this Act was used to free slaves, to free apprentices from cruel owners and to prevent husbands confining their wives without their consent.

Other examples of statute law are the Representation of the People Acts which stipulate the rules under which elections may take place and the Parliament Acts of 1911 and 1949 which place limits on the powers of the House of Lords.

Because (at least in theory) Parliament can pass any law it wishes, statute law takes precedence over the other sources of the constitution. But that does not mean that it is all-powerful. In 1972, for example, Parliament passed the European Communities Act and Britain joined the European Union (EU) - see chapter 6, section 1.1. One of the conditions of membership of the EU is that European law is binding on all member states and, therefore, takes precedence over domestic law. Despite this, it is possible to argue that statute law still takes precedence over European law since Parliament has the power to repeal the 1972 European Communities Act.

b) Common law

Common law is law made by judges. Common law arises out of the custom that a decision made by one court of law must be followed by other courts facing similar facts. Judges are, in this way, bound by legal precedents. Much of the original law of civil liberties, for example, as well as the procedures to be followed by the courts in reviewing the actions of public bodies, is based on common law.

c) Royal prerogative

The royal prerogative is a set of privileges or powers held by the monarch. The royal prerogative includes the powers to:

> 'Declare war, make treaties (recently the Anglo-Irish Agreement and the Maastricht Treaty), to annex and cede territory (Hong Kong), to determine the disposition and use of the armed forces (Northern Ireland, Falklands, the Gulf and Bosnia), to do anything reasonably necessary to defend the realm and maintain the "Queen's Peace", the emergency powers to requisition and destroy property, conscript into the Crown Service (possibly) and intern aliens, as well as the prerogatives relating to the power of patronage and control and management of the civil service.' (Carroll, 1994, p.54)

Although these powers are still exercised in the name of the monarch, in practice they have passed to the Prime Minister and Cabinet:

> 'With rare exceptions (such as appointing the Prime Minister), acts involving the use of "royal prerogative" powers are nowadays performed by government ministers who are responsible to Parliament and can be questioned about particular policies. Parliamentary authority is not required for the exercise of these prerogative powers, although Parliament may restrict or abolish such rights.' (HMSO, 1994, p.9)

Since parliamentary authority is not required for the exercise of prerogative powers, these powers provide the executive (the government) with a means of bypassing the legislature (Parliament). Critics argue that this permits profoundly undemocratic government:

> 'The prerogative derives from the time when Britain was ruled according to the divine right of kings. Government ministers have inherited its powers which allow them to rule virtually by decree in many areas not covered by statute. These powers...lie behind the near absence in our constitutional arrangements of the kind of citizens' rights that exist in the United States. The prerogative is all about the power of government over the people and virtually nothing to do with the power of the people over government.' (*Independent on Sunday*, 17 July 1994)

d) Constitutional conventions

A convention is a practice which, through custom, is considered to be the appropriate or proper behaviour or procedure to follow in given circumstances. Constitutional conventions are, therefore, rules related to the exercise of governmental powers which, through precedent, are considered binding by and on those concerned, even though they are not enforced by the law courts. Examples include the doctrines of individual and collective ministerial responsibility (see chapter 12, section 2.2 and chapter 13, section 1.4) and the rule that the assent of the monarch is required before Bills passed by the two Houses of Parliament can become law.

e) Works of authority

Certain books written by constitutional theorists are sometimes cited by politicians and others to establish appropriate procedures. Two major sources are Erskine May's *Parliamentary Practice*, first published in 1844, and *An Introduction to the Study of the Law of the Constitution* by A.V. Dicey, first published in 1885. Although these works have no definitive legal standing, appeals to them can be persuasive in settling disputes or uncertainties arising from interpretations of aspects of the constitution.

f) Treaties and laws of the European Union

As was suggested above, in practice, the treaties and law of the European Union now form a significant additional source of the British constitution. The implications of this are explored in section 2.1 below.

Flexibility or rigidity?

Since the British constitution is uncodified and is derived from sources of varying status (statute law has greater weight than conventions or works of authority, for example), it does not provide an accessible and easily understood reference point for students of government or for the ordinary citizen. At least in theory, elements of the constitution can easily be changed. For example, even those constitutional rules laid down in statute law can be altered by the same processes which apply to any other piece of legislation. To some people, this is a major disadvantage since it means that, for example, hard won civil rights could be abolished over night by a political party which temporarily wins power. Written, or codified, constitutions often contain sections which outline the basic rights of citizens and these usually have a special status preventing easy or quick alterations to them.

On the other hand, the British constitution's capacity to change can be seen as an advantage. The constitution can adapt to political changes and developments and is, therefore, less likely to contain rules and obligations which are out of date. Written constitutions tend to be much less flexible. They contain special, rigid, often lengthy procedures which must be followed before any constitutional changes can be introduced. As a result, such changes may be rare. The USA's constitution, for example, has been altered only 26 times and the first ten amendments were made together in 1791, just four years after the constitution had been drawn up.

Activity 4.1

Item A *The sources of the British constitution*

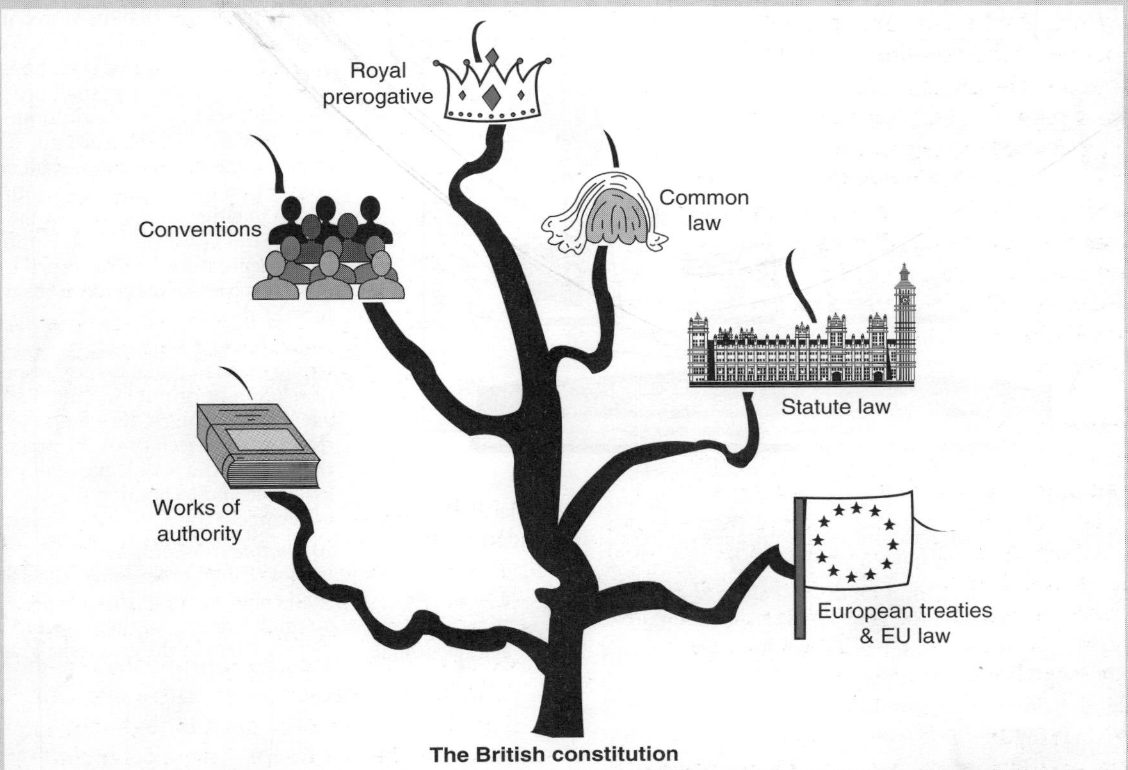

Item B *The British and American constitutions compared*

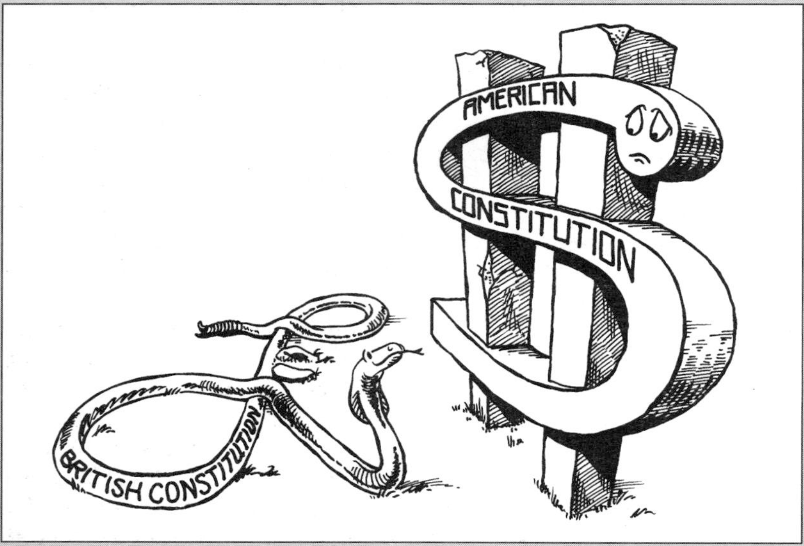

Item D *The British constitution*

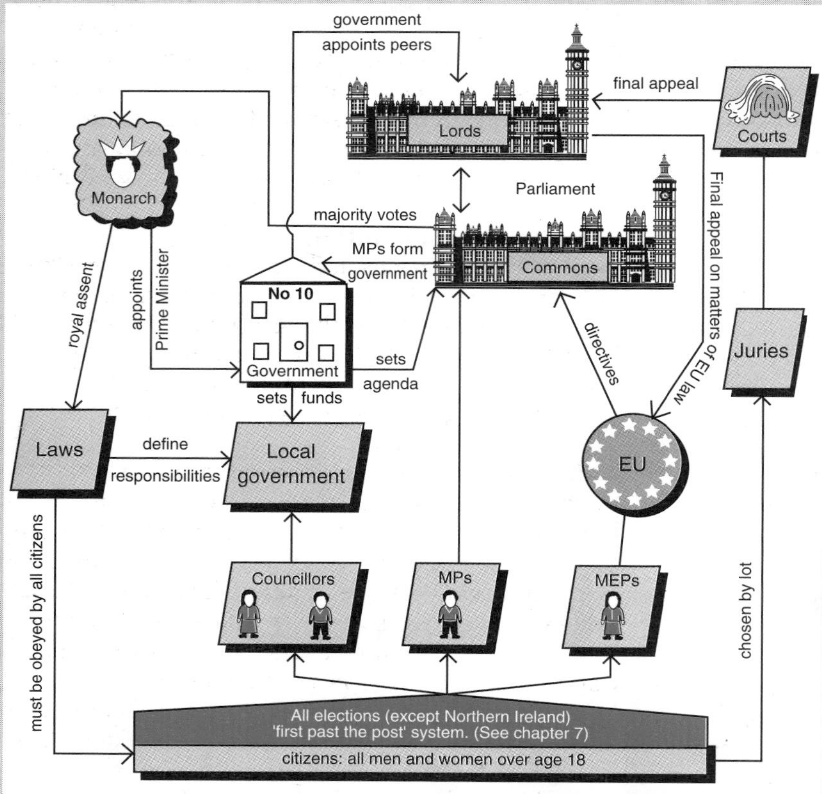

Questions

1. What are the advantages and disadvantages of a constitution derived from the sources shown in Item A?
2. Judging from Items C and D, do you agree with the point being made by Item B? Give reasons for your answer.
3. Using Item C draw a diagram of the American constitution in a style similar to that used in Item D.
4. Judging from Item D, would you say that the principle of separation of the powers is put into practice in the UK? Give reasons for your anwer.

Item C *The American constitution*

Articles 1-5 (adapted)

All legislative powers herein granted shall be vested in a Congress of the United States which shall consist of a Senate and a House of Representatives. The House of Representatives shall be composed of members chosen every second year by the people. The Senate shall be composed of two senators from each state chosen for six years. All Bills for raising revenue shall originate in the House of Representatives. Every Bill which shall have passed the House of Representatives and the Senate shall, before it becomes law, be presented to the President of the United States. If he approve, he shall sign it, but if not, he shall return it with his objections. If after reconsideration two thirds of the House of Representatives shall agree to pass the Bill, it shall be sent, together with the objections, to the other house [the Senate], by which it shall likewise be reconsidered; and if approved by two thirds of that house, it shall become a law. The executive power shall be vested in a President of the United States of America. He shall hold his office during the term of four years. The President shall be commander in chief of the Army and Navy of the United States. He shall from time to time give to the Congress information on the state of the Union, and recommend to their consideration such measures as he shall judge necessary and expedient. The judicial power of the United States shall be vested in one Supreme Court. The Congress, whenever two thirds of both houses shall deem it necessary, shall propose amendments to this constitution, or, on the application of the legislatures of two thirds of the several states, shall call a convention for proposing amendments, which in either case shall be valid as part of this constitution when ratified by the legislature of three fourths of the several states or by conventions in three fourths thereof.

Amendment 1 (adapted)

Congress shall make no law respecting of religion or prohibiting the free exercise thereof; or abridging the freedom of speech or of the press; or the right of the people peaceably to assemble and to petition the government for a redress of grievances.

Amendment 6 (adapted)

In all criminal proceedings the accused shall enjoy the right to a speedy trial by an impartial jury of the state and district wherein the crime shall have been committed.

1.2 The evolution of the British constitution

One of the reasons why Britain does not have a codified constitution is that British political history over the past three centuries has followed an evolutionary rather than a revolutionary path. In other countries, written constitutions have been introduced following sudden and total changes to their political system. The French revolution of 1789, for example, led to the introduction of a written constitution, as did the Russian revolution of 1917. Similarly, new written constitutions were introduced in Germany after defeat in 1918 and 1945 and India drew up a written constitution when British rule ended in 1947.

Until the 17th century, there was no real separation of powers in the British system of government. Rather, there was a system of absolute monarchy. The monarch could overrule decisions made by Parliament. Ministers were merely personal advisers. Judges were appointed and removed by the monarch. It was only after the English Civil War of 1642-52 and the short period of republican government (Charles I was executed in 1649 and the monarchy was restored in 1660) that the power of the monarch was curtailed. When the monarchy was restored, the new king, James II attempted to reassert royal power. But this resulted in his exile (the so-called 'Glorious Revolution' of 1688) and the introduction of a Bill of Rights which granted Parliament protection against royal absolutism.

From the beginning of the 18th century, therefore, Britain was no longer governed by an absolute monarch. Constitutionally, although monarchs still exercised considerable power, they needed the support of Parliament. The monarch's business was carried out by the Cabinet (the monarch's ministers). The Cabinet brought matters before Parliament for its approval. This system became known as a constitutional monarchy. Britain remains a constitutional monarchy today.

Development of the British constitution since 1700

Dearlove & Saunders (1991) argue that it is necessary to see how the 20th century notion of a liberal-democratic constitution emerged from the liberal model of the 19th century which itself evolved from the theory of a balanced constitution of the 18th century.

The balanced constitution

The authoritative work detailing the theory of the 18th century constitution was Sir William Blackstone's *Commentaries upon the Laws of England*. Blackstone saw the principal institutions of government as providing a set of mutual checks and balances. The House of Commons could reject what the nobility (the Lords) had decided and vice versa. The monarch could act as a check on both Houses, whilst they, in turn, had sanctions which could be used to check the executive power of the monarch's ministers.

According to Dearlove & Saunders, this theory was to some extent borne out in practice. But, the practice of checks and balances was based largely on the patronage and corruption that a very small electorate permitted (even by the end of the 18th century less than 5% of adult men and no women were permitted to vote - see chapter 7, section 1.2). The constitution, therefore, operated essentially in the interests of the aristocracy:

> '[The constitution provided] state power to a narrow group of substantial landowners in loose alliance with merchants and the small towns which were able to return members to the Commons.' (Dearlove & Saunders, 1991, p.24)

This constitutional set-up was workable so long as the feudal system, which supported it, remained in place. But, by the late 18th century, the erosion of the old feudal system had been accelerated by the industrial revolution. Industrialisation produced a new class of wealthy factory owners who had considerable economic power but no direct political power since their interests were not represented in Parliament or by members of the government. Economic and social developments, therefore, gave rise to political pressure which challenged the existing constitution.

The liberal constitution

Whilst the main constitutional concern in the 18th century was the balance of governmental powers within Parliament, the changes which occurred in the 19th century shifted the constitutional focus to divisions outside Parliament. For a while, this produced a 'golden period' of dominance for the House of Commons.

The principal, division in the 19th century was between the aristocratic class (predominantly landowners who wanted to preserve the status quo) and the new middle classes (predominantly industrial capitalists who were resentful of the power of landed interests and were eager for political representation and power for themselves). Both groups wished to avoid granting any representation or power to the working class (the majority of the population). But the middle classes needed the support of working class reformers to push through any extension of the franchise and reform of the House of Commons.

This political conflict culminated in the Great Reform Act of 1832 which extended the vote to the new middle classes (see chapter 7, section 1.2). This meant that it was no longer possible for the Lords, through patronage, to control the composition of the House of Commons. The Act also redistributed the seats in the House of Commons to allow the newly developed industrial areas to be represented in Parliament. In addition, the powers of the monarch were further limited as the choice of Prime Minister and senior Cabinet members now passed to the Commons.

These developments increased the independence of the House of Commons and, effectively, ended the relevance of the theory of the 'balanced constitution'. This was noted by Walter Bagehot whose *The English Constitution*, published in 1867, provided an account of the relationships between the institutions of the state in the post-1832 period, a period in which the power of the new propertied middle classes grew substantially. According to Bagehot, the middle classes defined their interests in terms of 'liberty' and they wanted a 'liberal' constitution in which the role of the state would be restricted in order to protect individual freedom.

Bagehot argued that this liberal constitution contained two separate parts - the **dignified** and the **efficient**. The dignified part of the constitution was the House of Lords and the monarchy. Although these institutions were still publicly regarded as powerful (and thereby provided legitimacy to the constitution as a whole) their real powers had diminished. In reality, they had been taken over by the efficient parts - the House of Commons and the Prime Minister and Cabinet. It was with these efficient parts that power now lay. Bagehot claimed that the secret of the constitution was the very close relationship between the legislature and the executive. It was particularly significant that the Cabinet (the centre of executive power) was (after 1832) chosen by the House of Commons (the locus of legislative power).

The liberal-democratic constitution

The liberal constitution described by Bagehot, however, was not a democratic constitution. The vast majority of the adult population was still denied the vote, though this began to change in 1867, the year in which Bagehot's work was first published. Those in power grudgingly came to realise that some form of working class political representation would need to be introduced to avoid threats to the existing political and social order posed by the growth in ideas about equality and socialism. The 1867 Electoral Reform Act (see chapter 7, section 1.2) gave the vote to some workers and, therefore, began the process of creating a mass electorate. The growth of a mass electorate was of great importance constitutionally. It encouraged the development of mass parties. These parties came to dominate Parliament and government. The result was a constitutional shift. The brief period of the House of Common's predominance began to draw to a close. Power shifted to the Prime Minister and Cabinet who were chosen from the party with the majority in the House of Commons. At the same time, the growth of a mass electorate meant that parties could only govern if they gained the support of the electorate at election times. The need to consider public opinion added a new dimension to the constitution.

Eighteen years after the 1867 Act, the first edition of A.V. Dicey's *An Introduction to the Study of the Law of the Constitution* was published. This book remains one of the most influential works of authority on the British constitution. Although Dicey himself was no democrat, his account was able to accommodate some of the changes which had been taking place. According to Dicey, the 'twin pillars' of the British constitution are **parliamentary sovereignty** (the supremacy of Parliament in making the law) and the **rule of law** (the law as the ultimate source of authority to which all, including the organs of state, are subject). To this legalistic interpretation, Dicey added a further dimension to the notion of sovereignty. He argued that if **legal** sovereignty resided in Parliament, **political** sovereignty rested with the electorate because the electorate chooses parliamentary representatives. Dicey added that because of the constitutional convention of **ministerial responsibility** (the principle that ministers are accountable to Parliament for the actions of government), the executive is also brought under the influence of the political sovereignty of the electorate.

According to Birch (1964), Dicey's interpretation of the constitution represents an idealised view. It is based on the assumption of a one-directional flow of power from the electorate to Parliament to government. It, therefore, ignores the possibility that power also flows in the reverse direction. Birch also argues that Dicey's model fails to recognise the significant influences that parties and the Cabinet have exercised on Parliament since the Electoral Reform Act of 1867. In general, 20th century interpretations of the British constitution have acknowledged the proactive role of the executive in the policy making process (especially the role of the Prime Minister and Cabinet). Parliament is, thus, presented in a more diminished reactive role and the electorate largely viewed as passive.

But the ideological hold of the liberal view (that there is a need for restricted government and the safeguarding of individual freedoms) remained (and remains) strong. In 1929, for example, the Lord Chief Justice, Lord Hewart, in *The New Despotism*, bitterly criticised the inflated powers of the executive and argued that parliamentary sovereignty and the rule of law (Dicey's twin pillars) had been eroded. Against this, however, it can be argued that the developments in the late 19th century (the extension of the franchise and the change in the balance of power between the legislature and the executive) were achieved without fundamentally altering the structures of power or class in British society. A democratic element (a mass electorate) was added to the existing liberal constitution without altering the dominance of the ruling classes and without threatening the continuation of the existing capitalist economic system. The result was a liberal-democratic constitution and it is this which has formed the basis of the British political system in the 20th century.

Activity 4.2

Item A *The liberal constitution*

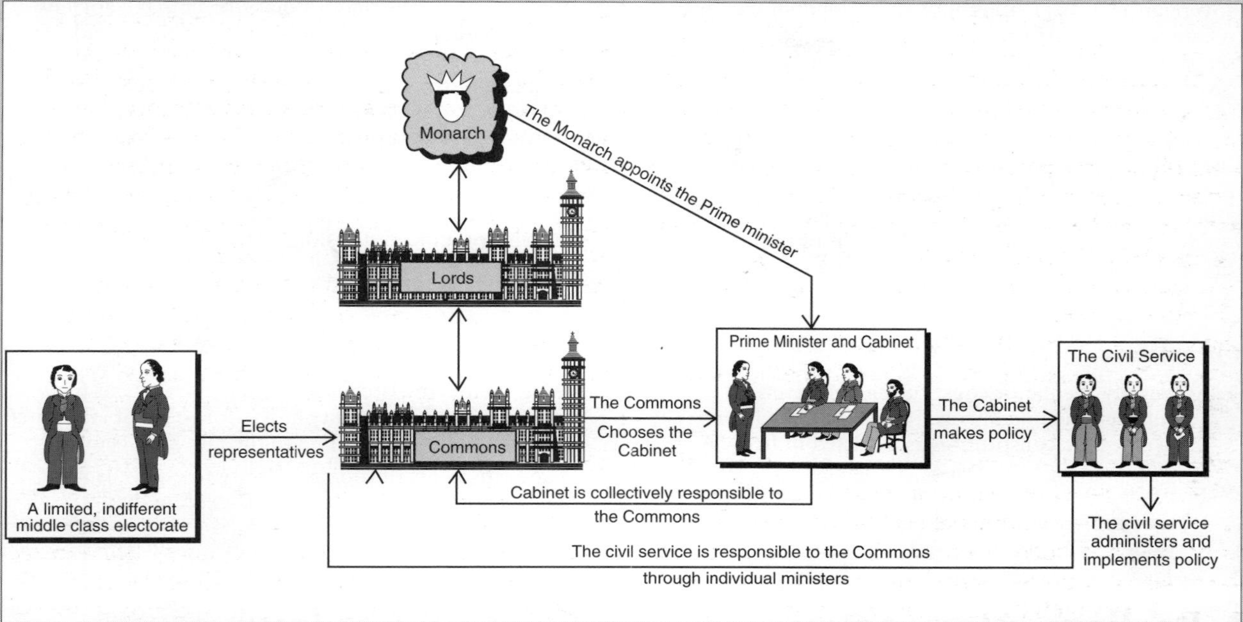

Adapted from Dearlove & Saunders, 1991.

Item B *The liberal-democratic constitution*

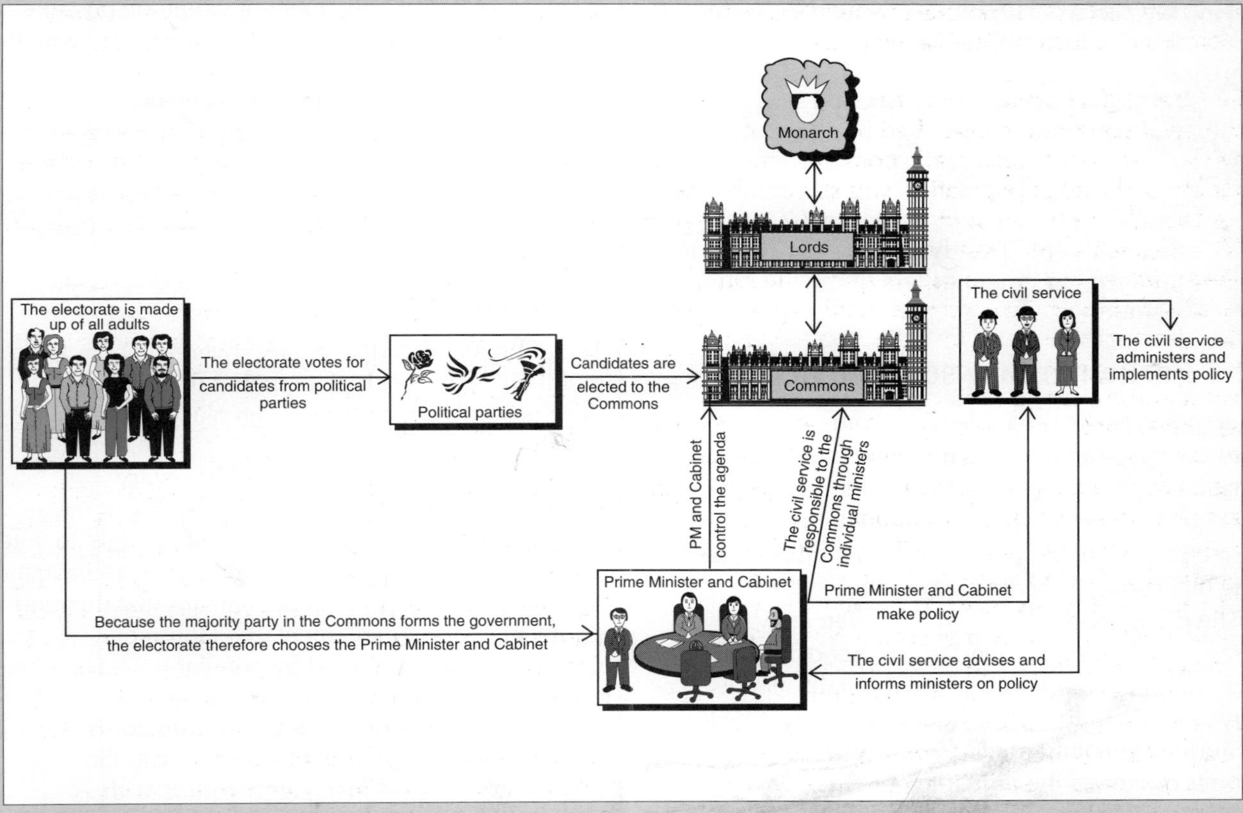

Adapted from Dearlove & Saunders, 1991.

Item C *Dicey's two pillars of the constitution*

Two features have, at all times since the Norman Conquest, characterised the political institutions of England. The first of these features - royal supremacy - has now passed into the sovereignty of Parliament. The principle of parliamentary sovereignty means neither more nor less than this, namely, that Parliament has the right to make or unmake any law whatever; and, further, that no person or body is recognised by the law of England as having the right to override or set aside the legislation of Parliament. The second of these features, which is closely connected with the first, is the rule or supremacy of law. When we say that the rule of law is a characteristic of the English constitution, we generally include, under one expression at least three distinct though kindred conceptions. We mean, in the first place, that no man is punishable or can be lawfully made to suffer in body or goods except for a distinct breach of law established in the ordinary legal manner before the ordinary courts of the land. We mean, in the second place, not only that no man is above the law, but that every man, whatever be his rank or condition, is subject to the ordinary law of the realm and amenable to the jurisdiction of the ordinary tribunals. Third, the general principles of the constitution (as, for example, the right to personal liberty or the right of public meeting) are the result of judicial decisions determining the rights of private persons in particular cases brought before the courts.

Adapted from Dicey, 1885.

Questions

1. a) Identify the major constitutional differences between the liberal constitution and the liberal-democratic constitution as depicted in Items A and B.
   b) Explain when and how the liberal constitution changed into the liberal-democratic constitution.
2. Using Item C rewrite Dicey's interpretations of (i) parliamentary sovereignty and (ii) the rule of law using language more appropriate to the late 20th century.
3. 'The British constitution's capacity to evolve is its major strength.' Using Items A-C explain this statement.

2. Parliamentary sovereignty and the rule of law

Key Issues

1. What does parliamentary sovereignty mean in theory and in practice?

2. To what extent does parliamentary sovereignty remain one of the two main pillars of the constitution?

3. What does the rule of law mean in theory and in practice?

4. To what extent does the rule of law remain one of the two main pillars of the constitution?

2.1 Parliamentary sovereignty

According to the principle of parliamentary sovereignty, Parliament is the only body that can make law for the UK. No other authority can overrule or change the laws which Parliament has made. This principle, therefore, gives statute law precedence over the other sources of the constitution.

The principle of parliamentary sovereignty, however, cannot be found in any Act of Parliament. It is a part of common law which established itself as judicial rule in the late 17th century, following the 'Glorious Revolution' of 1688. Norton (1982 & 1988) points out that if the principle of parliamentary sovereignty were to be part of statute law, it could not have the pre-eminence claimed for it. This is because parliamentary sovereignty implies that Parliament can pass, change or repeal any law it likes and is not bound by the laws made by previous Parliaments. If the principle of parliamentary sovereignty was found in an Act of Parliament, it would be possible for Parliament to repeal this Act and do away with the principle.

As it stands, the principle of parliamentary sovereignty means that British courts are obliged to enforce any law passed by Parliament. This is very different from the USA, for example, where the Supreme Court can declare a law passed by Congress to be unconstitutional.

Modifications

The principle of parliamentary sovereignty has been modified as the result of a number of political developments which have taken place in the 19th and 20th centuries.

First, when the principle of parliamentary sovereignty was established, less than 5% of the adult male population and no women had the right to vote. Today, virtually all adults over the age of 18 have the right to vote. This development means that the most significant part of Parliament, the House of Commons, is now elected by popular vote. So, where does sovereignty now lie - with Parliament or with the electorate? Dicey's answer was to distinguish between **political** sovereignty resting with the electorate and **legal** sovereignty resting with Parliament. But this, as Norton has recognised, raises a problem:

> 'If one accepts that sovereignty is indivisible, how can one have two distinct bodies (the

> electorate and Parliament) each exercising sovereignty?' (Norton, 1982, p.13)

This duality is further reflected in the assumption that government ministers are **legally** responsible to the monarch (strictly they are 'Ministers of the Crown') but, **by convention**, they are responsible to Parliament.

Second, the use of referendums on three occasions in the 1970s also seems to have affected the notion of a sovereign Parliament. Referendums, it can be argued, remove decision making (or at least the confirmation of decisions) from Parliament. It could be argued, therefore, that referendums and parliamentary sovereignty are incompatible.

Third, the growth of a mass electorate in the late 19th century led to the development of the party system. This, in turn, altered the balance of power between Parliament and the executive (in favour of the executive). Since the government is now generally formed from the largest party in the House of Commons, it can usually rely on its majority to secure parliamentary approval for its proposals. Most laws are, therefore, now initiated not by Parliament but by government. This may have affected parliamentary sovereignty.

Fourth, the principle of parliamentary sovereignty implies no theory about the location of political power. If, in the final resort, political power rests on the use or threat of force, then the principle has little relevance. If, however, power depends on popular consent, then what if this consent is withdrawn? What would that withdrawal of consent tell us about where sovereignty lies? Erskine May, writing in 1844, noted:

> 'The legislative authority of Parliament extends over the United Kingdom and all its colonies and foreign possessions; and there are no other limits to its power of making laws for the whole empire than those which are incident to all sovereign authority - the willingness of the people to obey or their power to resist.' (quoted in Silk, 1989, p.37)

This serves as a reminder that the sovereignty of Parliament has always been limited by the need to take account of political realities.

Other limitations

In addition to the modifications outlined above, more recent developments can be seen to place practical limitations on the principle of parliamentary sovereignty.

First, there have been occasions when powerful pressure groups have been able to frustrate attempts to implement legal measures. In other words, extra-parliamentary action has sometimes forced Parliament to revise or repeal laws it has made. In the 1970s, for example, trade unions forced Parliament to amend the 1971 Industrial Relations Act and in the late 1980s extra-parliamentary action forced the government to replace the poll tax with the council tax. These examples suggest that, in practice, the principle of parliamentary sovereignty is limited.

Second, the UK has, at various times, committed itself to international agreements and treaties which place upon it certain obligations. For example, in 1949 the UK joined NATO and, as a result, ceded some control over defence policy and foreign policy. Theoretically, of course, commitments like this do not infringe parliamentary sovereignty since Parliament could decide to ignore or cancel its commitments. But in practice the political and often economic consequences of so doing make such actions unlikely. This point can be demonstrated most clearly by reference to Britain's membership of the European Union (EU).

Britain and the EU

Britain's membership of the EU has raised important questions about the limitations on the sovereignty of the British Parliament. Under the terms of membership, the UK is a member of the EU 'in perpetuity'. EU law is binding on all member states and, therefore, takes precedence over British domestic law. The British Parliament can express its disapproval in the case of amendments to the Treaty of Rome (the founding treaty signed by all members of the EU), but otherwise EU legislation automatically becomes law within the UK, irrespective of what the British Parliament thinks about it.

On the face of it, this seems to breach the principle of the sovereignty of Parliament. But (despite the enormous economic and political consequences of so doing), Parliament could agree to repeal previous legislation, withdraw from the EU and thereby demonstrate that parliamentary sovereignty still exists.

Complete withdrawal from the EU, however, seems increasingly unlikely. Despite resistance from 'Euro-sceptics', the continuing movement in Europe as a whole towards greater European integration is pulling the UK along this route too. Nugent (1993) argues that the 1986 Single European Act and the Maastricht Treaty (see chapter 6, section 3.2) can be seen as further reducing Britain's sovereignty since they have extended the range of policy areas on which the EU can legislate.

Activity 4.3

Item A *The Factortame Case*

Following the signing of the 1986 Single European Act, Spanish fishing vessels registered in Britain in order to qualify for a share of the fishing quota awarded to the UK. Two years later, however, the British government passed the Merchant Fishing Act 1988 ordering vessels to re-register and to satisfy additional nationality requirements. The vessels owned by Factortame Ltd and other Spanish companies failed to qualify and were prevented from fishing after 1 April 1989. These companies applied to the High Court for a ruling that the 1988 Act was incompatible with European law and, therefore, inoperable. The High Court referred the case to the European Court of Justice (ECJ) and ordered the Transport Secretary not to apply certain parts of the 1988 Act. The Transport Secretary, however, successfully appealed against this on the grounds that no UK court had the power to suspend an Act of Parliament. On further appeal to the House of Lords, it was agreed that under existing English law no court could suspend an Act of Parliament. But the case was referred to the ECJ on the question of whether or not EC laws confer on national courts the power and/or the obligation to restrain the government during the period taken for a final judgement to be made by the ECJ. In 1990, the ECJ ruled that British courts do indeed have power to suspend Acts which appear to breach a European law. Meanwhile, the European Commission had initiated an action against the British Government. The ECJ ruling on this was that the requirements made in the 1988 Act contravened the 1986 Single European Act - they were discriminatory and contrary to article 52 of the EEC Treaty. The Spanish-owned fishing companies have lodged a claim for up to £20 million compensation for loss of profits during the 18 months they were unable to fish.

Adapted from Dowdle, 1994.

Item B *Two horses*

'The UK government has seated Parliament on two horses, one straining towards the preservation of parliamentary sovereignty, the other galloping in the general direction of Community [EU] law supremacy.' (De Smith in Street & Brazier, 1981, p.91)

Item C *The EU and sovereignty*

Membership of the EU has brought a new role for the British courts. Under the terms of EU membership, if there is a clash between the provisions of European law and domestic UK law, then the European law must win out. Under the provisions of the Treaty of Rome, cases which reach the highest domestic court of appeal (in Britain, the House of Lords) must be referred to the European Court of Justice. In 1990, the European Court of Justice in the Factortame case ruled that courts in the UK had the power to suspend an Act of Parliament which appeared to breach an EU law. The House of Lords then restrained the minister from enforcing the Act. The effect of this was to challenge the principle of parliamentary sovereignty because it challenged the idea that the decisions of Parliament are binding and can be set aside by no body other than Parliament. The European Court's ruling meant that British courts could now set aside Acts passed by Parliament. This does not mean, however, that the principle of parliamentary sovereignty is dead. Parliament retains the power to repeal the 1972 European Communities Act. Furthermore, if Parliament passed an Act explicitly overriding European law it is likely that the British courts would enforce the Act. Whilst the principle of parliamentary sovereignty may not be dead, it is clearly under challenge. The power of government is no longer concentrated in the Cabinet, but is shared with the European institutions. As a result, the constitution is not what it used to be.

Adapted from Norton, 1994.

Questions

1. Using Items A and C explain how the Factortame case challenges the principle of parliamentary sovereignty.
2. At the time you are reading this chapter, which horse in Item B appears to be gaining the most ground? Explain your answer.
3. Has the doctrine of parliamentary sovereignty outlived its usefulness? Give arguments for and against.

2.2 The rule of law

According to Dicey, writing in 1885, the rule of law has three main elements. First, nobody can be punished unless convicted of an offence by a court of law. Second, the law applies equally to everybody. Third, the general principles of the constitution (such as the right to personal liberty) do not stem from declarations made by rulers, they arise out of decisions made in individual cases by an independent judiciary. Writing more than 100 years later, Grant describes the rule of law as follows:

> 'Essentially the concept of the rule of law seeks to equate law and justice, ie it seeks to ensure that the law and the legal system are fair and equitable. This is an idea which is hard, perhaps impossible, to achieve in practice.' (Grant, 1994, p.51)

Whilst Dicey argued that the rule of law had three main elements, Grant has identified five. By examining these five elements, she suggests, it is possible to see both the strengths and weaknesses of a constitution which relies on the rule of law.

The first element identified by Grant is legal equality, the idea that:

> 'Everyone, including governments should be equally subject to the same laws, and should have equal access to the law.' (Grant, 1994, p.51)

Grant argues that, in reality, this ideal is not attained. Only the very rich or the very poor (who are eligible for legal aid) can afford to go to court. The majority of people cannot afford to take legal action. Also, some people are, in some sense, above the law. For example, MPs have parliamentary privilege which makes them immune from prosecution for libel or slander and the monarch is above the law.

The second element is the 'just law', the idea that under the rule of law, justice and the law are the same thing. There is, in other words, no such thing as an unjust law. The trouble with this idea is that there are occasions when the majority of people simply do not agree that a law is just. This happened with the poll tax. Although people were legally obliged to pay the tax, many simply refused to do so on the grounds that it was unjust. Grant also points out that the idea of the just law requires consistent legal practice. When judges give completely different sentences for the same crime or when miscarriages of justice are discovered, this undermines the rule of law.

The third element is 'legal certainty', the idea that the law:

> 'Should amount to a clear statement of rights, obligations and limits to power, especially the power of state and government. It should not be uncertain, arbitrary, ambiguous or contradictory.' (Grant, 1994, p.52)

The problem with this idea is that the law often relies, to some extent, on interpretation and is, therefore, uncertain. Grant cites the example of public order laws. On some occasions, the term 'offensive weapons' has been interpreted to mean articles such as keys and combs, whilst on other occasions these, articles would not fall under this heading. In addition, if the government is taken to court and found to have broken the law, it may choose to change the law rather than to follow the court ruling.

The fourth element is the idea that everybody is innocent until proven guilty. Grant notes two problems with this. First, the Criminal Justice Act passed in November 1994 has eroded the accused person's right of silence. And second, media coverage may prejudice the attitudes of jurors before a trial has taken place.

The final element is the independence and impartiality of the judiciary (see also chapter 17, section 2.2). Grant notes that:

> 'Judges are largely separate from the executive and the legislature; they should be appointed on a non-political basis; senior judges can only be removed from office by a majority vote in both Houses of Parliament; their salaries are not subject to party debate; their decisions should not be questioned in Parliament; and their remarks in court are not subject to the laws of libel and slander.' (Grant, 1994, p.53)

She adds, however, that, despite this, senior judges are also members of the House of Lords and thus part of the legislature as well as the judiciary. Also the Lord Chancellor is a member of the judiciary, a member of the Cabinet and a member of the House of Lords. In other words, the Lord Chancellor is a member of all three branches of government and this can lead to a conflict of interest.

The rule of law as a constitutional check

As a general principle, the notion of the rule of law reflects the liberal fear of arbitrary and excessive government. In those societies which have a written, codified constitution, protection against arbitrary government may be built in and overseen by the courts. In the USA, for example, the constitution provides the Supreme Court with the power to declare 'unconstitutional' laws passed by Congress. But no such check applies in the UK. This explains why Dicey regarded the rule of law as one of the twin pillars of the constitution. He claimed that the rule of law was an important balancing mechanism which kept in check parliamentary sovereignty. So, although the courts in the UK have no power to decide upon the content of laws passed by Parliament (because of parliamentary sovereignty), they may be called upon to review allegations that government ministers or officials have acted illegally.

McAuslan & McEldowney (1985), however, doubt the effectiveness of the rule of law as a check. They argue that parliamentary sovereignty, which in practice means the wishes of the government of the day, has now taken precedence over the political and legal constraints embodied in constitutional conventions and in the rule of law. Since 1979, they claim, governments have taken a cavalier attitude to what Dicey understood as the rule of law. To back up this claim they provide a list of examples of ministerial actions which, they allege, amount to 'abuse and excess of power'. In short, they argue that there has been:

> 'A general pattern of contempt for...the constraints on power imposed by the checks and balances...involved in a constitution based upon the concept of limited government.' (McAuslan & McEldowney, 1985, p.32)

Similar concerns were expressed by a senior Conservative politician during the period of Labour government in the 1970s. In a lecture delivered in 1976, Lord Hailsham claimed that the British system of government had become an 'elective dictatorship'. According to Hailsham, because governments in Britain are usually formed from the largest party represented in the House of Commons, the power arising from parliamentary sovereignty now effectively rests with the government. Yet, the checks on this power, such as the rule of law, are weak.

A somewhat different view is provided by Jowell (1989). He argues that the courts have become more prepared to uphold the rule of law against actions of the executive which appear either to go beyond the powers granted by legislation or which may involve the bypassing of appropriate legal procedures. To Dicey and other 19th century liberals who supported limited government, the rule of law was a way of excluding discretionary action by ministers and officials. But the greater scope of government activity in the 20th century, for example the administration of the welfare state, has necessitated wide discretionary powers. The rule of law is, therefore, not now seen so much as a way of precluding official discretion, but as a protection against the abuse of discretion. It is in this sense that Jowell refers to the rule of law as a 'principle of institutional morality'. The rule of law, in this sense, provides limits and restricts the abuses of power which can occur under any government in modern times.

Activity 4.4

Item A *The Tameside dispute (1)*

Section 68 of the 1944 Education Act states that if the Secretary of State for Education is satisfied that any local education authority has acted or is proposing to act unreasonably, then the Secretary of State may give whatever directions seem expedient. In March 1975, Tameside Council (a Labour council) drew up plans to convert secondary schools into comprehensives. The proposals were approved by the Secretary of State in November 1975 and the plans were due to come into operation in September 1976. But, at the local elections in May 1976, the Conservatives won control of the council and in June they informed the Secretary of State that the plans would not be carried out. On 11 June, the Secretary of State gave a direction under section 68 requiring the council to implement their predecessors' plans. On 18 June, the High Court ordered the council to do this. But on 26 July, the Court of Appeal overruled the High Court and on 2 August the House of Lords agreed with the Court of Appeal. The basis of this final decision was that the minister could give a valid direction only if he was satisfied that no **reasonable** local authority could have decided as the Conservative majority did. Since the minister could not be satisfied, he could not issue a valid direction.

Adapted from Griffith, 1985.

Item B *The Tameside dispute (2)*

Of course, judges may pass judgements on the acts of ministers, as they have recently done in the Tameside dispute. To this extent, the rule of law applies and prevails here as in other free countries. But once the courts are confronted with an Act of Parliament, all they can do is to ascertain its meaning if they can, and then apply it justly and mercifully as the language of the law permits. So, of the two pillars of our constitution, it is the sovereignty of Parliament which is paramount in every case.

Adapted from Hailsham, 1976.

Item C *The British constitution*

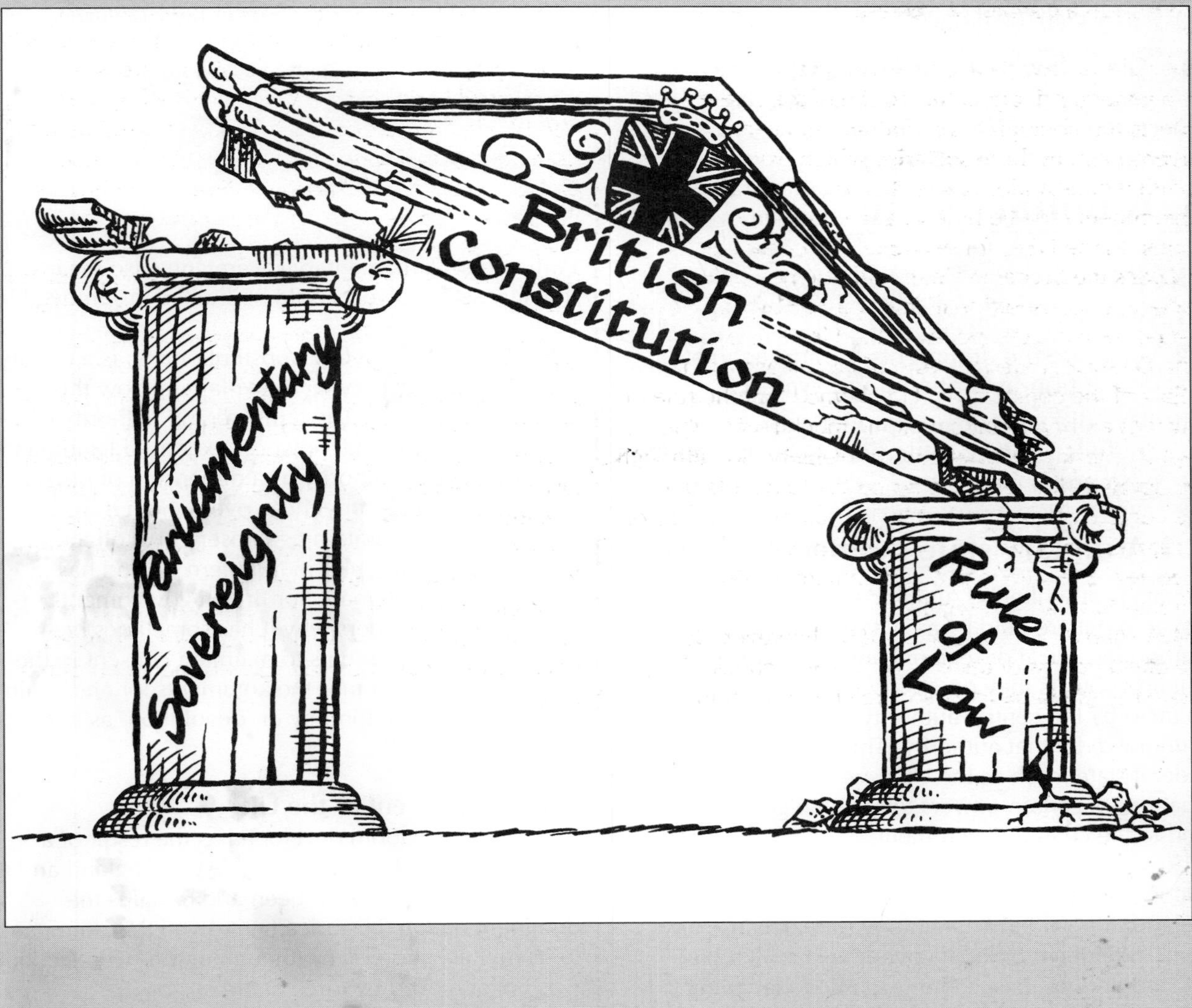

Item D *Lord Taylor and the rule of law*

Last week something very unusual in British constitutional history happened. Lord Taylor, the Lord Chief Justice, publicly attacked two Bills currently before Parliament. He spoke against parts of the Police and Magistrates Courts Bill and also against proposals to place restrictions on the right of defendants to remain silent. Lord Taylor's concerns are important because the proposed legislation represents a serious threat to civil liberties. They take away rights that have been part of the system of justice for centuries. They bring the police under direct control of politicians. And they put judicial independence at risk. The judicial system is the only power in the constitution which can help to limit the power of the state. If it is prevented from doing this, the ordinary citizen is left with no protection. At worst, Britain could become a society dominated by a Home Secretary who has personal control of the courts and law enforcement and who deals with social decline and inequality by imprisonment - something approaching a police state. Lord Taylor's concerns come on top of the Master of the Rolls' comments a year ago. He argued that judges had an increasing role to play as a balancing mechanism. Fourteen years of one party government had reduced Parliament's ability to act as a check on the executive. Parliamentary absolutism had replaced parliamentary sovereignty.

Adapted from the *Observer*, 23 January 1994.

Item E *Ministers acting illegally*

Within the space of a few days in November 1994, the courts ruled that Michael Howard, the Home Secretary, and Douglas Hurd, the Foreign Secretary, had each acted unlawfully. The Court of Appeal declared that Michael Howard had abused his powers in implementing changes to the compensation scheme for victims of violent crime. It was argued that the new scheme would leave many of those with severe injuries in financial difficulties. Douglas Hurd was found by the High Court to have contravened the law in sanctioning a deal with Malaysia that involved linking part of the overseas budget with the sale of armaments in what has become known as the Pergau Dam affair.

Adapted from reports in the *Independent*, 10 November 1994 and the *Observer*, 13 November 1994.

Questions

1. In what way do Items A,B and E support Jowell's argument about the willingness of courts to uphold the rule of law?
2. How accurate is the view of the constitution presented in Item C?
3. a) Using Item D explain the connection between the rule of law and the principle of the separation of powers.
   b) How might the concept of an 'elective dictatorship' be used to express the fears of Lord Taylor?
4. Judging from Items A-E to what extent do you think the rule of law is (i) applicable and (ii) desirable?

3. A unitary state

Key Issues

1. What is a unitary state?
2. What are the arguments for and against devolution in Scotland and Wales?
3. Why did violence erupt in Northern Ireland and what sort of settlement is likely to bring permanent peace?

3.1 A unitary state defined

A state is described as 'unitary' when the powers of government are held by a central authority, or set of authorities. Local or regional authorities may exist, but any powers they possess will have been granted to them by the central authority and could be withdrawn by that authority. This differs from a federal state, such as the USA, where the constitution guarantees certain powers to regional governments and to the central government.

Through various statutes, the United Kingdom is a union of England, Wales, Scotland and Northern Ireland. It is said to be a unitary state because any form of regional or local government which has existed or does exist cannot legally do anything unless it has been empowered to do so by Acts of Parliament. Parliamentary sovereignty also means, that any such powers could be limited or removed by future statutes.

But, to say that the UK, constitutionally, is a unitary state does not go very far in explaining how this operates politically. The term 'central authority of the state' suggests that power is exercised legitimately whilst the term 'authority' is a dimension of power that implies consent by those over whom it is exercised. But, maintaining consent in Scotland, Wales and in particular in Northern Ireland has, at times, been problematic for British governments. This section considers why it has sometimes been difficult for governments to maintain consent in the regions and it examines the arguments for and against greater regional autonomy or 'devolution' as it is known .

The development of the UK

The United Kingdom developed as the result of a series of Acts of Union made between England and its neighbours. England has been and remains the dominant nation. Historically, it owed this dominance to its military supremacy (though union with Scotland was not achieved by force of arms).

Wales had been conquered by England as early as

1282, but it was not until the 16th century that it was brought into union with England - by Acts passed in 1536 and 1542. An indication of English supremacy was the decision enshrined in the Acts to forbid the use of the Welsh language in the administration of the country. In addition, in 1746 Parliament decided that the term 'England' in any Act of Parliament automatically included Wales, a provision which did not change until 1967.

In 1907, Wales began to be viewed as a distinctive entity by the government - a separate Welsh Secretary of Education was created. In 1957, the new post of Minister of State for Wales was established. This was upgraded to Cabinet rank in 1964. There is a Welsh Office in Cardiff. But, in practice, much administration is based in Whitehall.

Scotland was brought into union with England in two stages. In 1603 James VI of Scotland became James I of England. But complete political union did not occur until the Act of Union in 1707 which disbanded the Scottish Parliament and led to government from London. Unlike Wales, Scotland was not incorporated into the UK by conquest. It negotiated the terms of its entry into the union. As a result, it retains its own legal and educational system as well as a distinctive form of local government and its own established church.

Scotland began to be viewed as a distinctive entity earlier than Wales. The position of Secretary of State for Scotland was established in 1885. Since 1892, the Secretary of State for Scotland has been a member of the Cabinet. A separate government department, the Scottish Office, was set up to deal with Scottish affairs in 1928. The Scottish House of Commons Grand Committee is open to all 72 Scottish MPs and meets in Edinburgh.

The completion of the conquest of Ireland was achieved in Tudor times. But opposition to British rule has continued to the present day. An Act of Union passed in 1800 brought the whole of Ireland into the UK and it remained part of the UK until the end of 1921. Nationalist opposition to control from Westminster led to the Irish Treaty of 1921 which divided Ireland into two. The south of Ireland became a dominion (a self-governing territory belonging to the British Commonwealth) and then, in 1949, an independent republic. The six counties of Ulster in the north of Ireland have remained as part of the UK. Between 1922 and 1972 Northern Ireland was self-governing. But in 1972 direct rule from Westminster was imposed and a Secretary of State of Cabinet rank was created.

3.2 Devolution

Devolution has been defined as follows:

> 'The process of devolution involves the dispersal of power from a superior to an inferior political authority. More precisely it consists of three elements: the transfer to a **subordinate elected body** on a **geographical basis** of **functions at present exercised by Parliament**...Devolution involves the creation of an elected body, subordinate to Parliament. It therefore seeks to preserve intact the supremacy of Parliament, a central feature of the British constitution.' (Bogdanor, 1979, p.2)

In practical terms, therefore, devolution involves the setting up of an elected regional assembly whose powers and responsibilities are carefully defined. Normally these powers would not include the control of defence or foreign policy (areas which would still be dealt with by the central government). The new elected regional assembly may or may not have tax raising powers. Whether it does or not, a devolved assembly is by no means independent. It is still bound by decisions made by central government.

Devolution is, therefore, different from federalism and separatism. Federalism involves the division of sovereignty between two levels of government which then become (in theory at least) autonomous. Separatism, on the other hand, refers to the creation of a self-governing independent state with complete control over its internal and external affairs.

Scottish and Welsh nationalism

Mitchell points out that:

> 'The formation of the United Kingdom occurred over a long period of time during which special measures were taken to permit a degree of distinctiveness to its component parts. Little effort was made, unlike in France for example, to impose uniformity throughout the state. The United Kingdom was a unified state rather than a unitary or uniform state. It responded to pressures.' (Mitchell, 1994, p.128)

It is the 'degree of distinctiveness' in the component parts of the UK which led to the growth of nationalism in Scotland and Wales and the demand for devolution or 'home rule'.

Scottish nationalism arises from the fact that Scotland negotiated the terms of union in 1707:

> 'As a result, it was able to retain its own distinctive institutions - a separate legal system, church, schools and universities - which have helped to nurture the strong sense of national identity in Scotland. Scots are well aware that they were once an independent nation and could be so again. The union with England, which was considered so advantageous at one time, could be broken if it ceased to work to Scotland's benefit.' (Gamble, 1993, p.75)

Gamble goes on to point out that Britain's economic decline, the development of the EU and the discovery of North Sea oil have all contributed to Scottish discontent with rule from Westminster. This discontent was exacerbated by the fact that four successive general elections between 1979 and 1992 resulted in a Conservative government even though the vast majority of Scottish people did not vote Conservative. According to Mitchell (1994), since 1945 about 75% of people living in Scotland have supported some measure of home rule.

Welsh nationalism, however, is centred on the Welsh language and traditional Welsh culture. As a result, it has a less widespread appeal than Scottish nationalism since it tends to alienate non-Welsh speakers who make up a large part of the Welsh population:

> 'Many of the modern battles of Welsh nationalism have been around the status of the Welsh language. Wales has an estimated 500,000 Welsh speakers out of a total population of 2.7 million. Much of the effort of Welsh nationalists has been to ensure that the Welsh language is protected and that its official status is recognised...Apart from these expressions of cultural nationalism, Wales has been affected only to a small extent by nationalist movements.' (Gamble, 1993, p.82)

The struggle for devolution

The electoral success of the nationalist parties in the general election of 1974 brought devolution onto the political agenda. The Labour government's weak position in Parliament led to a deal in which referendums were conceded. These referendums were held on 1 March 1979 (see chapter 7, section 3.3). Whilst the result of the Welsh referendum was conclusive (there was clearly little popular support for devolution), the Scottish result was inconclusive. A majority voted in favour of devolution, but the majority was not large enough for devolution to be implemented.

In the short term, the result of these referendums was a major blow for the nationalists. But the issue of home rule in Scotland has gradually re-emerged. Since the general election of 1987 (when the Conservatives received their lowest share of the vote in Scotland since mass enfranchisement was introduced), there has been growing support for some degree of home rule. Two main camps have emerged. On the one hand, the Scottish National party (SNP) has rejected devolution because it does not go far enough. Instead, it has adopted a new position - independence within the EU. On the other hand, the Labour party and Liberal Democrats are committed to devolution and they have joined together in the Scottish Constitutional Convention (SCC). The SCC is a forum for all Scottish groups committed to devolution. It was set up in 1989:

> 'To reach agreement on how Scotland ought to be governed.' (SCC, 1989, p.1)

During the 1992 general election campaign, hopes were high that the Conservatives would suffer further losses and the case for devolution would then become irresistible. In fact, the Conservatives gained one seat and 1.7% in their vote. Although this was a minor gain, it was interpreted by the media as a victory for the unionist cause. Following the election, the Conservative government published a re-evaluation of its position on devolution. This document made it clear that the government favoured the status quo:

> 'Since the Act of Union and, in particular over the last 100 years or so, there has evolved the framework for the governance of Scotland which is basically sound and which has shown itself adaptable to changing circumstances.' (HMSO, 1993, p.11)

The 1995 local election results in Scotland, however, suggested that the Conservatives may have underestimated support for devolution. The Conservatives (the only party opposed to constitutional change) attracted just 11% of the vote and failed to gain control of any council (*Guardian*, 8 April 1995).

Arguments for and against devolution

Supporters of devolution argue that if devolution took place, power would be dispersed more fairly, government would be more efficient and local people's loyalties would be served:

> 'Giving power to new assemblies, it is claimed, would relieve a major burden on central government. By allowing decisions to be taken close to the local area affected by them, they would also be more efficient - targeted on the area's needs and probably taken more quickly than at national level. By being closer to the people and being seen to be closer...the assemblies would engage the attention and loyalties of citizens; they would be 'their' assemblies. That support would also be an important dynamic in encouraging cooperation and support in the implementation of policies.' (Norton, 1994, pp.9-10)

Arguments against devolution tend to emphasise the cost of establishing a new tier of government and the difficulties of administering this extra tier:

> 'By interposing a new layer between central and local government, the potential for delay would be increased, as would the potential for clashes between central and regional government. Another layer of government may also produce greater confusion as to the responsibilities of the different layers. Who should the citizen complain to? Who should be held responsible if the dustbins aren't emptied?' (Norton, 1994, p.10)

Opponents of devolution also argue that devolution is

the first step on the road to complete independence and it should, therefore, be resisted. The 1992 Conservative election manifesto, for example, claimed that devolution proposals:

> 'Do not intend to bring about separation, but run that risk. They could feed, not resolve, grievances that arise in different parts of Britain. They would deprive Scotland and Wales of their rightful seats in the United Kingdom Cabinet, seats the Conservatives are determined to preserve...The plans for devolution put forward by the other parties would have a grave impact, not just on Scotland and Wales, but also on England. They propose new and costly regional assemblies in England for which there is no demand.' (CCO, 1992, p.47)

Activity 4.5

Item A *Independence, devolution or status quo in Scotland?*

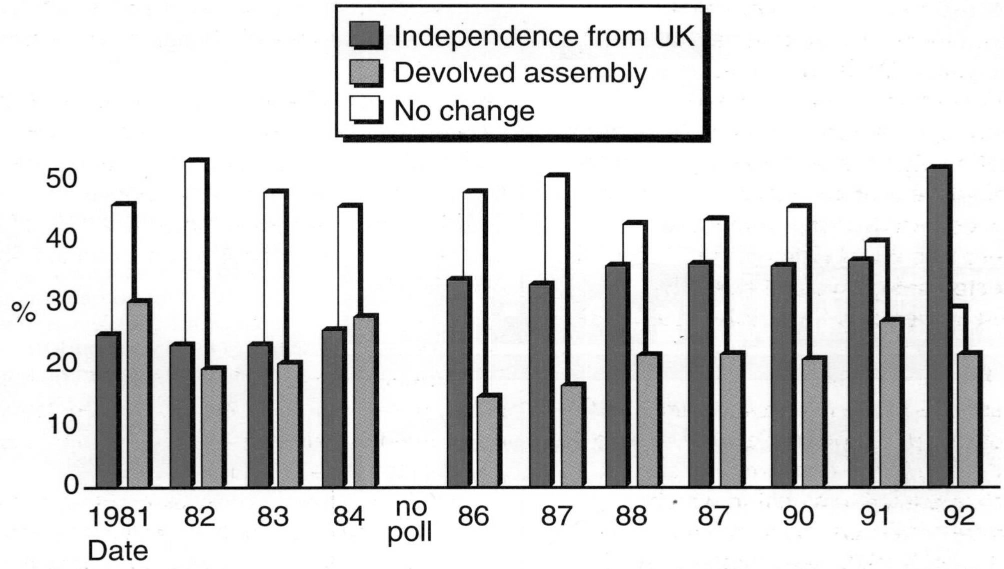

This table shows the results of opinion polls conducted between 1981 and 1992 in Scotland. Respondents were asked whether they wanted: (a) Scotland to become independent from the UK; (b) Scotland to remain within the UK but to have a devolved assembly with some taxation or spending power; or (c) no change from the present system.

Adapted from the *Guardian*, 18 February 1992.

Item B *The 1992 general election result, April 1992*

	Scotland						England			
	Total votes cast	% of vote 1992	Change from 1987	Number of MPs 1992	% of seats 1992	Change from 1987	% of vote 1992	Change from 1987	Number of MPs 1992	Change from 1987
Con	751,954	25.7	+1.7	11	15.3	+1	45.5	-0.7	319	-39
Lab	1,142,866	39.0	-3.4	49	68.1	-1	33.9	+4.4	195	+40
Lib Dem	383,856	13.1	-6.1	9	12.5	0	19.2	-4.6	10	0
SNP	629,552	21.5	+7.5	3	4.2	0	–	–	–	–

In the 1992 general election, the Conservative party was the only one of the main parties not to support some degree of home rule for Scotland.

Adapted from Kellas, 1992 and *The Independent*, 11 April 1994.

Item C *Proposals made by the Scottish Constitutional Convention*

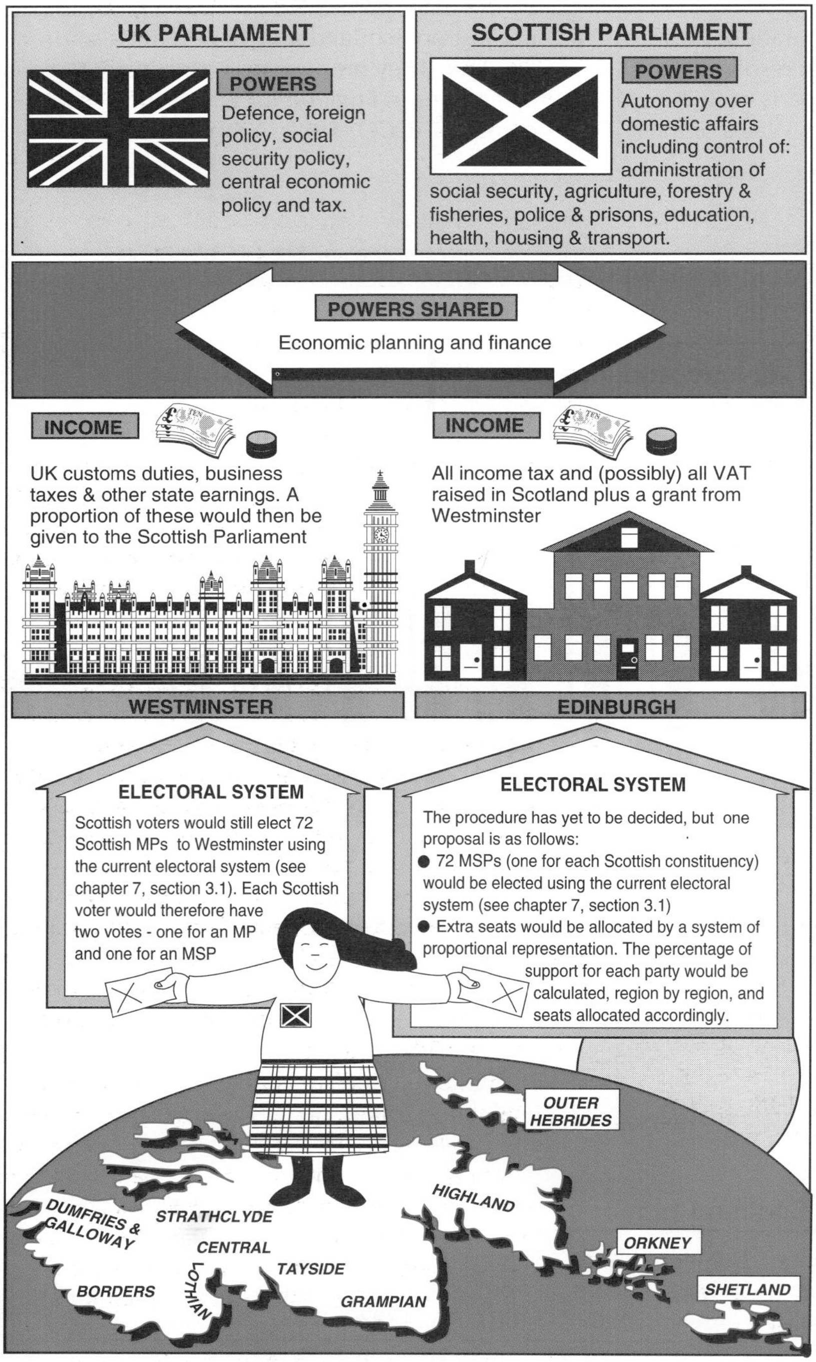

UK PARLIAMENT
POWERS
Defence, foreign policy, social security policy, central economic policy and tax.
SCOTTISH PARLIAMENT
POWERS
Autonomy over domestic affairs including control of: administration of social security, agriculture, forestry & fisheries, police & prisons, education, health, housing & transport.
POWERS SHARED
Economic planning and finance
INCOME
UK customs duties, business taxes & other state earnings. A proportion of these would then be given to the Scottish Parliament
INCOME
All income tax and (possibly) all VAT raised in Scotland plus a grant from Westminster
WESTMINSTER
EDINBURGH
ELECTORAL SYSTEM
Scottish voters would still elect 72 Scottish MPs to Westminster using the current electoral system (see chapter 7, section 3.1). Each Scottish voter would therefore have two votes - one for an MP and one for an MSP
ELECTORAL SYSTEM
The procedure has yet to be decided, but one proposal is as follows:
● 72 MSPs (one for each Scottish constituency) would be elected using the current electoral system (see chapter 7, section 3.1)
● Extra seats would be allocated by a system of proportional representation. The percentage of support for each party would be calculated, region by region, and seats allocated accordingly.
OUTER HEBRIDES
HIGHLAND
DUMFRIES & GALLOWAY
STRATHCLYDE
CENTRAL
ORKNEY
TAYSIDE
LOTHIAN
BORDERS
GRAMPIAN
SHETLAND

This diagram shows the plans for a Scottish Parliament drawn up by the Scottish Constitutional Convention in 1992. These proposals were supported by the Labour party and Liberal Democrats.

Adapted from the *Guardian*, 18 February 1992.

Item D *Two steps to English home rule*

The opposition parties (both dominated by Celts) are suggesting that, after the next election, Wales and Scotland should have national assemblies whilst England is divided into regions. This is divide and rule by the Celts and must be fought. We, the English, must insist on home rule. The first advantage is that we will be able to see where our taxes are going - to the Celtic fringes. When they realise this, the English will struggle for the power to raise and spend their own revenue in England. An English assembly with powers to raise and spend taxes will be a properly devolved Parliament. The next step will be to leave the UK altogether. By doing this we will be able to get rid of our crazy military expenditure and our world commitments. England will be able to revert to a happier, bygone role. We shall become a nimble and talented mercantile nation which enjoys the opportunities of an unashamedly second rank power. In two steps we will be free. You think this is a joke? You wait.

Adapted from the *Times*, 26 September 1994.

Questions

1. a) Suppose the poll whose results are shown in Item A was brought up to date and you were asked for your opinion. How would you have replied? Give reasons for your answer.
   b) What does the table in Item A reveal about changing attitudes towards constitutional change in Scotland?
   c) How does the information in Item A relate to that in Item B?
2. a) Give arguments for and against the specific proposals laid out in Item C.
   b) What consequences would the setting up of a Scottish Parliament have on the UK?
3. Do you agree with the author of Item D that home rule would bring greater freedom for England? Give reasons for your answer.

3.3 Northern Ireland

From the standpoint of the Westminster government, the problem of legitimacy, of maintaining consent to the central authority of the British state, appears at its most critical in the case of Northern Ireland.

Britain's relations with Ireland have been troubled ever since the first English landing in 1169. The roots of the current conflict lie in the 17th century when, after a period of conquest, some 170,000 settlers (Protestants, mainly from Scotland) made the journey to Ireland and were given parcels of land which had been snatched from the indigenous Catholics. From this time onwards, the population of Ireland has been politically divided along religious lines. It is these divisions which have given rise to the constitutional problem of securing consent from all sections of the population. Put simply, a majority in Northern Ireland (mainly Protestant) remain loyal to Britain whilst a substantial minority (mainly Catholic) does not willingly give its consent to rule by Westminster. For British governments, the long-term problem is how to achieve a constitutional settlement which is acceptable to both communities.

Ireland before partition

Following the British occupation of Ireland in the early 17th century the indigenous Catholic population suffered great oppression. In 1649, Cromwell brought an army to Ireland to take revenge for the 'great rebellion' of 1641 in which Catholic rebels killed 12,000 Protestant settlers. Not only did this lead to even greater loss of life, also:

> 'The percentage of the land of Ireland owned by Catholics which had shrunk by the time of the great rebellion to 59% was reduced by Cromwellian land settlement to a mere 22%. After further Catholic humiliation in great events to come it was to shrink by 1695 to 14% and by 1714 still further to 7%.' (Kee, 1980, p.48)

Perhaps the most important of the 'great events' to which Kee refers was the Battle of the Boyne in 1690. This battle was fought between the forces of the Protestant William of Orange and the Catholic James II. The victory of William is still celebrated by the Protestant 'Orange lodges' in Ulster on 12 July each year. William of Orange's victory established a Protestant ascendancy which:

> 'Proceeded to consolidate its position by enacting a penal code against the Catholics designed essentially, not to punish the Catholics for their beliefs nor to convert them to any form of Protestantism, but to prevent them from obtaining, as a group, property, position, influence or power. The penal laws ratified, as it were, the identification of opposed classes in terms of religion. They secured the privileges of planters, settlers, speculators and adventurers in land and ensured that the great mass of the native stock of the country should be deprived of land, property, education and the prospects of advancement.' (De Paor, 1970, p.17)

The penal code ensured that divisions between the Catholic and Protestant communities widened. It helps to explain why, in the long term, demands for Irish self-rule have tended to come from Catholics, whilst the Protestants have tended to favour close ties with Britain.

Not that this was always the case. For example, in 1791, Wolfe Tone set up the Society of United Irishmen, an organisation whose aim was to unite Protestants and Catholics and to remove British rule from Ireland. But Tone's attempt to bring over French troops failed in 1796 and the 'rebellion' of May 1798 only led to brutal reprisals.

The rebellion of 1798 was the catalyst for the abolition of the Irish Parliament and the passing of the Act of Union 1800. The whole of Ireland remained part of the UK from 1801 (when the Act came into force) until the end of 1921. But a significant number of Irish people never accepted the legitimacy of the union.

Throughout the 19th century, politicians in Parliament struggled to solve the 'Irish Question'. The problem was that there were deep divisions within Irish society. The majority of Catholics were nationalists who wanted some degree of home rule (devolution) whilst the majority of Protestants (most of whom lived in Ulster in the north) were unionists who supported the status quo. In part, this was a religious and a geographical divide. In part, it was a divide which reflected the relative status of Catholics and Protestants (in general, Catholics remained second class citizens). And in part, this was a divide which deepened because of changes which took place in the 19th century:

> 'Protestant unionism (support for unity with mainland Britain, under the English crown) was the product of 19th century economic change. Unionism in its modern form was a response to the integration of industrial Ulster into the economy of mainland Britain and to the threat to that integration which was posed by the prospect of political separation.' (Moran, 1985, p.50)

By the end of the 19th century, politicians in Westminster had failed to find a compromise. Two Home Rule Bills had been defeated (in 1886 and 1893), but the very fact that they had been proposed meant that nationalists had high expectations and unionists felt under threat. In 1912, matters came to the boil. The general election of 1910 resulted in Irish Nationalist MPs holding the balance of power in the British Parliament. The Irish Nationalists made a deal with the Liberals. In return for a Home Rule Bill, they would support the Liberals in Parliament. In 1912, this

Bill was passed in the Commons, but rejected by the Lords. Due to the Parliament Act of 1911 (which meant the Lords had only the power of delay, not of rejection - chapter 14, p.406), rejection by the Lords was only temporary. By the summer of 1914, the Bill would be law.

Outside Parliament, opposition to the Home Rule Bill was formidable. The Ulster Unionists set up an armed force to resist home rule (the Ulster Volunteer Force) and the Conservative party, including the leader Andrew Bonar Law, argued that the use of force would be justified to resist home rule. In response, nationalists set up their own armed groups (the Irish Citizen Army and the Irish Volunteers). Civil war seemed inevitable. The government agreed that Ulster could opt out of home rule for six years.

The outbreak of the First World War had a profound effect upon the development of Irish politics. First, it ensured that the threatened civil war did not break out. Second, in 1916, a group of republicans (nationalists who wanted Ireland to become an independent republic) staged a rebellion against British rule on Easter Sunday. The rebellion was easily crushed by British troops and the leading rebels were executed. Although this rebellion failed, it was a turning point. The rebels showed that they were prepared to die for their beliefs and this made a deep impression. Before 1916, the majority of people in Ireland wanted home rule rather than independence. But after 1916, the mood changed. People began to support and vote for republicans. The main beneficiary was the republican party Sinn Fein which had been set up in 1905. In the general election of 1918, Sinn Fein won three quarters of the Irish seats. Instead of going to Westminster, these MPs set up their own Irish Parliament, the Dail Eireann. The Dail issued a declaration of independence and began recruiting an army - the Irish Republican Army (IRA). The aim was to provoke the British government into fighting a war:

> 'The sooner fighting is forced and a general state of disorder is created throughout the country, the better it will be for the country.' (part of a speech made to the Sinn Fein Executive by Michael Collins, Head of the IRA and Minister of Finance in the Dail, in February 1919)

Michael Collins' wish was granted. Between 1919 and 1921, a war was fought between Irish and British troops. In 1921, the British government finally agreed to negotiate with Sinn Fein. A ceasefire was agreed in July and in December a treaty was signed. This treaty was a compromise. Southern Ireland would be a self-governing dominion (the Irish Free State) whilst Ulster (Northern Ireland) would remain part of the UK. Ireland, therefore, was to be partitioned.

Northern Ireland

Following the signing of the treaty in December 1921 British troops were withdrawn from the new Irish Free State and it was left to its own devices. It was no longer part of the UK. Over the years, the Irish Free State gradually loosened its ties with the UK. In 1937, it renounced the oath of loyalty to the British monarch. In 1949, it became a republic and left the British Commonwealth.

The six counties of Ulster, however, remained part of the UK. The British Parliament remained in overall charge. But the Northern Irish Parliament, set up in 1921, looked after day-to-day affairs. Between 1921 and 1972 the British government did not interfere in the running of Northern Ireland. Downing notes that:

> 'The characteristics of successive Northern Ireland Cabinets show remarkable consistency. Up to 1969, every member of the Cabinet was a Protestant and a member of the Unionist party and all but three were members of the Orange Order [a society set up in 1795 to defend Protestant privilege]. Of the six members of the first Cabinet in 1921, four of them were still in office fourteen years later. Twenty years tenure of office was not unusual...All the ministers shared a common vision and political stance; they tended to view all questions about the constitution, the administration of justice and the role of government in the economy from a narrow Ulster Unionist perspective. They all shared the same fears of Catholicism and Socialism. After all, they had gone into Ulster politics to protect and maintain the union with Britain...Anything that threatened this union was a threat to the state itself.' (Downing, 1989, p.103)

Although there was a large Catholic minority in Northern Ireland (c.33% of the population in 1921), the Protestant majority ensured that Protestants maintained their privileged position. One way of doing this was by ensuring that electoral boundaries were set in such a way that the Catholic electorate would have minimal representation:

> 'The population of the city of Londonderry is roughly three fifths Catholics and nationalists...and two fifths Protestants and unionist. This population distribution has remained more or less constant ever since the foundation of the state. For the state's first 50 years, the Corporation of Londonderry was composed the other way round: three fifths Protestant and unionist and two fifths Catholic and nationalist. This effect was achieved by 'gerrymandering' or concentrating large numbers of people with majority political views in overlarge political districts and their opponents in smaller ones, so that, in representation district by district, the latter are bound to win. Thus, in Londonderry, 87% of the large Catholic population were placed in one ward which

> returned eight seats while 87% of the much smaller Protestant population were placed in two wards which returned 12 seats. Year after year there was a Protestant and unionist majority of 12 to eight.' (Kee, 1980, p.229)

Lack of political representation ensured that the Catholic population remained socially disadvantaged. Catholics formed a disproportionately large percentage of those in low paid, unskilled jobs. They were under-represented in the police force, higher grades of the civil service and universities, but over-represented in terms of unemployment. Although this was not entirely due to discrimination (for example, most Catholics would not have wanted to take a job in the police force even if it was offered to them), there was a direct link between the Protestants' political control and the Catholics' lack of opportunity:

> 'Key localities with Catholic majorities were gerrymandered to produce Protestant councils: these councils in turn gave jobs and houses to Protestants in preference to Catholics.' (O'Brien & O'Brien, 1985, pp.168-9)

The turning point was the setting up of the Civil Rights Association (CRA) in 1967. The aim of the CRA was to win civil rights for Catholics by peaceful mass demonstration, but Protestant politicians saw the marches organised by the CRA as a direct challenge to Protestant dominance. Heavy-handed tactics were used by the police to break up the marches. The atmosphere became tense and, following the annual Orange parades in July 1969, violent clashes between Catholics and Protestants broke out. These clashes culminated in the 'battle of the Bogside' which began on 12 August. The Bogside is a Catholic area in Londonderry ('Derry' to nationalists). When police tried to take control of the Bogside, Catholics set up barricades and fought them off, declaring the area 'free Derry'. Since the police appeared to have lost control, the British government agreed to intervene and sent in British troops to restore order. These troops arrived on 14 August 1969.

The British troops soon lost the support of the Catholic community - especially when 'internment' (imprisonment without trial) was introduced in August 1971 (see chapter 18, section 2.2). By then, paramilitary groups on both sides had begun a campaign of bombing and shooting.

On 20 January 1972, 'Bloody Sunday', British troops killed 13 men taking part in a Civil Rights march. Although troops claimed that they had been fired upon first, the march was shown on television and it shocked many people in Britain. It seemed that civil war was about to break out. On 24 March 1972, the British government suspended the Northern Ireland Parliament and direct rule from Britain began. Between 1969 and 1994, over 3,000 people were killed in violent incidents in Northern Ireland.

Peace initiatives since 1969

Since 1969, the response of the British government to events in Northern Ireland has moved through a number of phases. Generally, there has been bipartisan agreement between Labour and the Conservatives and so policies have reflected different approaches rather than party political divisions.

McCullagh & O'Dowd (1986) suggest that, between 1969 and 1975, British policy was incoherent and at the level of crisis management. But, between 1975 and 1985, containment and stabilisation became paramount and the British government pursued a policy of 'criminalisation' (see chapter 18, section 2.2). Although the policy of criminalisation remained in place, a new phase began in 1985 with the signing of the Anglo Irish Agreement. Crucially, this agreement established that the Republic of Ireland had the right to be consulted over policy formulation in Northern Ireland, though executive responsibility remained with Westminster. In other words, by establishing, for the first time, structures by which the Republic of Ireland might participate in the government of Northern Ireland, the agreement meant the first change in the constitutional status of Northern Ireland since 1921. In Northern Ireland, the unionists opposed the agreement on the grounds that it was the first step towards a united Ireland and Sinn Fein (the political wing of the IRA) opposed the agreement on the grounds that it strengthened partition. In 1991, the Northern Ireland Secretary, Peter Brooke, suspended the Anglo Irish agreement to allow for constitutional talks. These talks finally broke down in November 1992. Just over a year later, in December 1993, the British and Irish governments issued what has become known as the 'Downing Street Declaration', an attempt to pull together the different positions. In this declaration the following statement was made:

> 'The British government agree that it is for the people of Ireland alone, by agreement between the two parts respectively to exercise their rights of self-determination on the basis of consent freely and concurrently given, North and South, to bring about a united Ireland if that is their wish...The British and Irish governments reiterate that the achievement of peace must involve a permanent end to the use of, or support for, paramilitary violence. They confirm that, in these circumstances, democratically mandated parties which establish a commitment to exclusively peaceful methods and which have shown that they abide by the democratic process are free...to join in dialogue in due course.' (*Guardian*, 16 December 1993)

Although, in the short term, the terms of this declaration were rejected by both the unionists and by Sinn Fein, it was this declaration which paved the way for the IRA ceasefire which was declared on 31

August 1994. Once this ceasefire had been declared, it made a lasting peaceful settlement more likely than at any time since the violence began in 1969 since it provided the opportunity for political discussions between the different parties and interest groups.
As part of the peace process, the British and Irish governments issued the *Framework Document* (see Activity 18.3, Items D and E) in February 1995. This document emphasised that the key to any progress in the peace process is agreement by the political parties of Northern Ireland and then by the people. It proposed cross border bodies, a parliamentary forum with representatives from the north and south, a new 90 strong Northern Ireland Assembly elected by proportional representation with devolved powers, and a three member panel also elected by proportional representation to advise the Assembly. Although the document states that the Irish government will end its constitutional claim to jurisdiction over Northern Ireland, Unionists reacted with anger to the proposals which they see as a first step towards a united Ireland.

Activity 4.6

Item A *The IRA's ceasefire statement*

Recognising the potential of the current situation and in order to enhance the democratic process and underlying our definitive commitment to its success, the leadership of the IRA have decided that as of midnight, 31 August 1994 there will be a complete cessation of military operations. All our units have been instructed accordingly. At this historic crossroads, the leadership of the IRA salutes and commends our volunteers, other activists, our supporters and the political prisoners who have sustained the struggle against all the odds for the past 25 years. Your courage, determination and sacrifice have demonstrated that the freedom and the desire for peace, based on a just and lasting settlement, cannot be crushed. We remember all those who have died for Irish freedom and we reiterate our commitment to our republican objectives. Our struggle has seen many gains and advances made by nationalists and for the democratic position. We believe that an opportunity to secure a just and lasting settlement has been created. We are, therefore, entering into a new situation in a spirit of determination and confidence, determined that the injustices which created this conflict will be removed and confident in the strength and justice of our struggle to achieve this. We note that the Downing Street Declaration is not a solution.

This statement was issued on 31 August 1994.

Item B *The IRA ceasefire - a cartoonist's view*

John Hume (left) and Gerry Adams tattoo a member of the IRA whilst a unionist looks on. Hume, leader of the Social Democratic and Labour party (SDLP - the party representing moderate nationalist opinion) and Adams (leader of Sinn Fein) conducted talks in 1993 and presented proposals to the Irish government. These proposals were soon followed by the Downing Street Declaration and then the IRA ceasefire.

This cartoon appeared in the Guardian, 2 September 1994.

Item C *Comment on the IRA's ceasefire statement*

The IRA's ceasefire statement cannot be taken at face value. It should be read as a message to the IRA's supporters as well as a public response to the Downing Street Declaration (DSD). There are three key passages. First, the statement announces, 'a complete cessation of military operations'. Whilst this fulfils one requirement of the DSD by stating that the ceasefire will be 'complete', it fails to meet another requirement by not using the word 'permanent'. Whilst some politicians argue that the statement implies the ceasefire will be permanent, others argue that the countdown to talks cannot begin until this is made explicit, since talks cannot begin under the threat of renewed violence. The second important passage is the section praising IRA supporters. The IRA leadership needs to make it clear that the IRA is not surrendering, but has gained something. This section, therefore, is for internal consumption. The third key passage is the final sentence. This is included as a negotiating tactic. By stating that the DSD is a starting point, the IRA leadership makes it clear that it expects concessions to be made in return for its decision to call the ceasefire.

Adapted from the *Times*, 1 September 1994.

Item D *The IRA ceasefire - the unionist reaction*

This mural shows how 'loyalists' (as fervent unionists call themselves) viewed the declaration of the IRA ceasefire.

Item E *Proposals for political settlement*

1. Joint authority
A federal arrangement for the whole of Ireland. Joint authority in Northern Ireland would be exercised by London and Dublin equally. One proposal is for a six member commission to run Northern Ireland comprising three locally elected representatives and one commissioner from London, Dublin and the EU.

2. Power sharing
The devolution of power to a Northern Irish assembly. Northern Ireland would remain part of the UK. One plan is to have a 78 member assembly elected by proportional representation. Ministerial posts would be shared out between parties.

3. Re-partition
A plan to hand some of the border counties which have Catholic majorities back to the Republic, leaving unionists in firm control of counties in which they have a majority.

4. United Ireland
A plan to unite Northern Ireland with the Republic to create a unitary state. With some groups this is a long-term objective rather than a short-term goal.

5. Independence
Northern Ireland would be granted complete independence. The most popular model suggests a 100 member assembly elected by proportional representation with power sharing at all levels.

6. Euro-federalism
Northern Ireland would be an independent state within the EU. This plan assumes that European integration proceeds at a fast pace.

7. Integration
This plan involves the complete absorption of Northern Ireland into the UK without any regional self-government. Britain's mainstream political parties would all organise in Northern Ireland (at present, only the Conservative party puts up candidates for election).

8. The Opsahl Commission
A regional government model based on the principle that each community has an equal voice in making and executing laws or a veto on their execution. Any constitutional change would require the consent of the government and people of Northern Ireland.

Adapted from the *Guardian*, 4 November 1993.

Item F *The IRA ceasefire - Sinn Fein's HQ*

This photo was taken on 30 August, the day before the IRA declared its ceasefire. The mural was painted on the side of Sinn Fein's headquarters building in the Falls Road, Belfast.

Questions

1. Using Items A-F explain why the IRA's declaration of a ceasefire was an important step towards a new constitutional settlement in Northern Ireland.
2. What point is the cartoonist (Item B) making about the position in Ireland after the IRA ceasefire was declared?
3. Judging from Items D and F what was the difference in the way in which nationalists and unionists viewed the declaration of the IRA ceasefire?
4. a) Which of the possible constitutional arrangements outlined in Item E would alter the UK's status as a unitary state? Give reasons for your answer.
   b) Which of the solutions would you choose? Assess its likelihood of success (i) in the short term and (ii) in the long term.

4. The monarchy

Key Issues
1. What is the monarch's constitutional position?
2. What are the actual powers of the monarch?
3. Is the monarchy under threat?

A constitutional monarchy

The formal way of describing British government is to say that the UK has a parliamentary government under a constitutional monarchy. Norton (1992) points out that this has resulted in the development of a whole series of institutions whose relationships are governed by convention rather than embodied in statute. The term 'parliamentary government under a constitutional monarchy', says Norton:

> 'Refers to government **through** rather than **by** Parliament, with the system being presided over by a largely ceremonial monarch. Government is elected through Parliament and is expected to formulate - to 'make' - public policy. The role of Parliament is to scrutinise and, if necessary, modify that policy before giving its assent. The monarch - as a neutral figure representing the unity of the nation - then formally gives the final seal of approval.' (Norton, 1992, pp.30-31)

The constitutional position

Apart from the period 1649-60, England has had a monarchy based on the hereditary principle since the 10th century. Today it is commonly thought that the monarch is a symbolic head of state only, performing primarily ceremonial functions such as visiting or entertaining leaders of foreign countries or opening new buildings. In Bagehot's terms (see p 74 above), it is thought that the monarch carries out some of the 'dignified', as opposed to the 'efficient', parts of the constitution.

The official view of the monarch's constitutional position, however, is as follows:

> 'The Queen personifies the state. In law, she is head of the executive, an integral part of the legislature, head of the judiciary, the commander-in-chief of the armed forces of the Crown and the 'supreme governor' of the established Church of England. As a result of a long process of evolution, during which the monarchy's absolute power has been progressively reduced, the Queen acts on the advice of her ministers. Britain is governed by Her Majesty's government in the name of the Queen. Within this framework, and in spite of a trend during the past 100 years towards giving powers directly to ministers, the Queen still takes part in some important acts of government. These include summoning, proroguing (discontinuing until the next session without dissolution) and dissolving Parliament; and giving Royal Assent to Bills passed by Parliament. The Queen also formally appoints many important office holders.' (HMSO, 1994, p.8)

Although, as this passage indicates, the monarch does have an important political role to play, in practice power has, substantially, been removed from the **personal** control of the monarch. A formal link remains and is reflected in official titles such as 'Her Majesty's government', but executive power has come to be employed by ministers or their agents even though it is still nominally vested in the Crown. As Norton puts it:

> 'Ministers remain legally responsible to the Queen for their actions, but by convention are responsible to Parliament.' (Norton, 1982, p.14)

In addition, membership of the EU has made an impact. Since EU law takes precedence over UK law, it is therefore no longer the case that all laws effective in the UK receive Royal Assent.

There are, however, two areas where there is at least the potential for the personal exercise of power by the monarch. First, the monarch has the power to appoint the Prime Minister. By convention, the monarch invites the leader of the largest party in the House of Commons to form a new government after a general election has been held. There is, however, always the possibility of a hung Parliament - a Parliament in which no single party has an overall majority of seats in the House. If this was to happen, the choice of Prime Minister and, thereby, the choice of the party or parties from which the government could be drawn, might not be obvious. In such a case, the monarch would play a decisive political role in determining the nature of the government.

Second, the power of the monarch to dissolve Parliament could also lead to the monarch's personal involvement in politics. Suppose, for example, that a newly formed minority government wished to call a general election in an attempt to strengthen its position. The monarch could decide not to dissolve Parliament and invite the leader of another party to form a coalition government. Constitutional precedents offer no clear guidance in such a case.

Is the monarchy under threat?

An opinion poll carried out by NOP in August 1994 found that 66% of respondents thought that the monarchy should continue indefinitely. Just 26% of respondents wanted the monarchy to be abolished at some point - 9% said that the monarchy should end now, 12% said that the monarchy should end when the Queen died and 5% said that the monarchy should end some time after the Queen died. But David McKie, writing in the *Guardian*, argued that a closer examination of the figures in this survey showed that support for the monarchy was by no means overwhelming amongst all sections of the population:

> 'People who are aged 55 plus respect the institution in copious numbers: 74% in favour, 25% against. But among the under 35s, 48% respect the monarchy but 51% don't.' (*Guardian*, 19 September 1994)

This suggests that attitudes towards the monarchy may be changing. Certainly, it seems that the monarchy in the 1990s is not as popular an institution as it once was. In the 1950s, for example, the monarchy was seemingly above criticism. When the broadcaster and journalist Malcolm Muggeridge wrote an article which asked whether Britain really needed a Queen, for example, he was sacked by a Sunday newspaper and by the BBC. Not only does this indicate the strength of support for the monarchy in the 1950s, it also suggests how deferential people were towards the royal family. Even in the 1980s, 85% plus of people told opinion pollsters that they supported the monarchy.

In recent years, however, the royal family has been criticised on two fronts. First, the behaviour of individual members of the royal family has been criticised on the grounds that it has failed to set the standards expected of prominent public figures. The well-publicised break-up of a number of marriages, including that of the heir to the throne, and other personal scandals, have given the impression that the royal family is in crisis. And second, there has been increasing concern about the cost of maintaining the royal family. The Queen has great private wealth, but when part of Windsor castle burned down in November 1992, the government promised to use public funds to repair it. This provoked a storm of criticism, not least because, at the time, the Queen did not pay income tax. In response to this criticism, it was announced at the end of November 1992 that the Queen would, in future, pay income tax. In addition, the civil list - the list of members of the royal family who receive public funds to pay for their expenses in performing public duties - would be cut to just the Queen herself, the Duke of Edinburgh and the Queen mother. Although this announcement met with approval, the role of the monarchy has remained high on the political agenda. In November 1994, for example, Labour proposed that the royal family should be slimmed down and 'a more Scandinavian style' of monarchy introduced.

Although Labour's proposal fell far short of abolition of the monarchy, there has been increasing speculation about what would happen if Britain was to become a republic (a republic is a state whose head is not a monarch). Most British republicans argue that the monarchy should be replaced by an elected President with limited powers, rather than a strong executive President like that in the USA or France:

> 'A British President would be a figurehead and honest broker, chosen by a college of politicians, as in Germany, or elected directly by the people, as in Ireland. Members of the royal family would be free to stay in Britain, just as members of the Hapsburg royal family are free to live in the Republic of Austria. But the wealth and buildings they held in the public name would be taken away.' (*Independent on Sunday*, 28 October 1994)

The monarchy - arguments for

Those in favour of retaining the monarchy more or less in its present form put forward the following arguments. First, despite some bad publicity, it is still a popular public institution. Second, the monarchy symbolises national unity and purpose both to the outside world and to people living in Britain. It helps to integrate British society. Third, through its maintenance of British traditions, the monarchy provides continuity in an otherwise rapidly changing society. Fourth, the cost of sustaining the monarchy (according to Norton (1994), £60 million per year) is less than the income it generates through tourism and trade. It is also a great deal less than the cost of supporting a presidency in some countries (for example the USA). Fifth, the hereditary principle keeps the royal family above party politics. A disassociation from party politics would be essential in the event of a hung Parliament since the monarch would need to make decisions about the formation of a new government. Any alternative (such as a presidency) would involve elections and, thereby, automatically introduce a party political element.

The monarchy - arguments against

Arguments against a monarchy include the following. First, the hereditary principle is not acceptable in a democratic society. People should gain positions on merit, not because they happen to be born into a particular family. Second, far from uniting the nation, the privileges enjoyed by the extended royal family emphasise to ordinary people just how great a divide there is from top to bottom in British society. Third, the popularity of the monarchy has declined and no longer commands universal support. Fourth, because of the behaviour of individual members of the royal family, the monarchy no longer provides a model of idealised family life. Fifth, the cost of maintaining a monarchy is too great. It is an unnecessary burden on the taxpayer. Income generated by tourism does not directly feed back into the public purse and, in any case, abolishing the monarchy would not necessarily reduce tourism. And finally, there is no reason why the functions of Head of State could not be performed by an elected President or even by the holder of an existing post. The Labour MP Tony Benn, for example, has suggested that the Speaker of the House of Commons could be given the power to dissolve Parliament and to choose the Prime Minister (see chapter 14, p.407 for a description of the Speaker's role).

It should be noted that, traditionally, republicanism has been associated with those on the political left. But, more recently, calls for a major rethink on the future of the monarchy have come from the radical right, too. When considering the arguments for and against the monarchy it is advisable, in taking a long-term view, to distinguish between the formal, constitutional position and role of the monarchy on the one hand and the activities and public perception of members of the royal family on the other.

Activity 4.7

Item A *Respect for the monarchy*

Item B *The new republicans*

In the last few months, judging from a number of opinion polls, there has been a sea change in attitudes towards republicanism. Just five years ago, pollsters who asked people if they were in favour of the abolition of the monarchy could expect just 5% to say yes. But in January 1994, 53% said that Britain should follow Australia's example by considering whether to abolish the monarchy. In February 1994, 44% in a TV poll said that the monarchy should be abolished. And in March 1994, only 40% said that Prince Charles was doing a good job. Whilst these polls were not subject to the normal safeguards used by professional polling organisations, they do confirm a significant shift in public attitudes. According to opinion pollsters MORI, one in five of the public are republicans which was not the case ten years ago. And whilst a firm majority exists in favour of the monarchy (including a 25% hard core of unshakable loyalists), once the Queen's reign ends, many would be hostile to the idea of Charles III. Symptomatic of the change in attitudes is the growth of the pressure group Republic. This group was set up in 1983 to oppose the monarchy, Lords and all hereditary office. Until 1991, membership of Republic was tiny. But since then, it has grown to over 1,000.

Adapted from the *Guardian*, 28 March 1994.

Item C *A model family?*

Item D *In defence of the monarchy*

Tonight Jack Straw, shadow Home Secretary, will reveal Labour's proposal to reform the monarchy along Scandinavian lines. Many voters have begun to think it was safe to vote Labour again. But the party's promise of a constitutional revolution is likely to scare them away. In particular, Mr Straw's remarks about the royal family will surely backfire. The Queen has already responded to public criticism by removing most of her relations from the civil list, by agreeing to pay income tax and by agreeing to publish accounts of her expenditure. The style of her monarchy is her concern. By interfering, Mr Straw insults the monarchy and miscalculates. The personal scandals and breakdown of royal marriages may be embarrassing for the Queen but they have no bearing on the status of the monarch nor on the public duties which the royal family perform. Britain is extremely fortunate to have an institution which is politically neutral, which has deep historical roots and which has made such a large contribution to its nationhood. Countries are defined by their institutions. If Labour attacks the monarchy, it risks undermining people's sense of Britishness and it risks losing support.

Adapted from the leading article in the *Times*, 5 December 1994.

Questions

1. Should the monarchy be abolished? Use Items A-D in your answer.
2. How accurate is the view of the monarchy portrayed in Item A? Use Items B-D in your answer.
3. Judging from Items B and C why do you think that there has been a growth of republicanism over the last few years? Can you think of reasons not mentioned in these two items?
4. a) Why do you think none of the main political parties supports the abolition of the monarchy? Use Item D in your answer.
   b) How convincing do you find the arguments made in defence of the monarchy in Item D? Give reasons for your answer.

5. Constitutional reform

Key Issues

1. Why has pressure for constitutional reform developed?
2. What are the arguments for and against a written constitution?
3. What would a reformed constitution look like?

Pressure for reform

According to Norton, the British constitution:

> 'Used to be a subject of praise but little discussion. Today it is a subject of discussion but little praise.' (Norton, 1989, p.10)

It is Norton's thesis that debate about constitutional reform has only developed since the 1960s. It was during the 1960s and 1970s that governments first appeared ineffectual in the face of rising unemployment and inflation. This apparent weakness, he argues, led not just to criticism of individual politicians but to criticism of the system of government itself.

At first, the call for constitutional reform came from a small number of outspoken critics. Lord Hailsham's warning in 1976 that Britain was becoming an elective dictatorship, for example, received attention because it was a view not often heard in public.

It is only since the late 1980s that support for constitutional reform has begun to reach the political mainstream. This is due to two main factors. First, the formation of the constitutional reform group Charter 88 in 1988. And second, the Conservative party's electoral success. These two factors are, of course, interlinked. Charter 88 was set up in 1988 partly because this was the tricentenary of the Glorious Revolution (supporters of Charter 88 argued that it was time that a new constitutional settlement replaced that made in 1688). But, 1988 was also the year after the Conservative party had won its third general election victory in a row. In that election just 32% of the total electorate voted Conservative - 68% either voted for another party or did not vote at all. Frustration with the electoral system led many people to question it. By 1991, Charter 88 had over 25,000 signatories.

Frustration, however, is not in itself enough to explain why constitutional reform has risen up the political agenda. Norton points out that:

> 'The constitution of the UK is ever changing. Some changes are essentially at the margins (the creation of a new parliamentary committee, for example), others are more fundamental (the passage of the 1972 European Communities Act, for example). The constitution of 1991 is markedly different to that of 1961.' (Norton, 1992, p.38)

Although the constitution changed in some ways between 1961 and 1991, supporters of constitutional reform argue that these changes were inadequate:

> 'For critics of the constitution, the existing arrangements were no longer adequate to cope with the challenges now facing the United Kingdom. The UK, it was argued, was out of step with the rest of Europe, with rights and liberties being curtailed by an antiquated system of government which relied for its existence on tradition and apathy. Power, it was argued, was too centralised, engendering inefficiency in decision making as well as alienation, citizens having little say in decisions that affected them. Given this, radical surgery was needed.' (Norton, 1992, p.39)

This 'radical surgery' includes demands for:

1. **The abolition of the monarchy.** Reformers aim to replace the monarchy with an elected President (see part 4 above).
2. **Reform of the House of Lords.** Reformers aim to replace the Lords with an elected second chamber (see chapter 14, section 3.2).
3. **Reform of the House of Commons.** Demands include the introduction of a fixed term of office and changes in hours and procedures.
4. **Electoral reform.** Reformers aim to introduce proportional representation in place of the current 'first past the post' electoral system (see chapter 7, part 4).
5. **A Bill of Rights.** Reformers hope to protect citizens from arbitrary government by enshrining individual rights in an entrenched Bill of Rights (see chapter 17, part 4).
6. **Devolution.** Reformers argue that regions of the UK, especially Wales, Scotland and Northern Ireland should be given greater autonomy (see part 3 above.)
7. **A written constitution.** Reformers would like to see the reforms they envisage codified in a single document. Such a document would enable citizens to understand the relationships between different parts of government and between government and themselves (see below).

All the demands mentioned above are made by Charter 88.

A written constitution - arguments against

When people talk of a 'written constitution' what they mean, more precisely, is a constitution that has been codified (drawn up in a single document). Although part of the British constitution is written (statute law, for example), part is not. Supporters of the current system argue that this is its strength. Since the constitution is not cast in stone, it is able to evolve and develop according to circumstances. It has a flexibility which codified constitutions do not have.

Norton (1988) points out that three main arguments are used against the introduction of a written constitution. The first is that a written constitution is unnecessary. Not only is the current system flexible, it has a number of checks and balances built into it. For example, there is a degree of balance between the executive, legislature and judiciary. The executive does not always manage to win the day. Opposition within Parliament or outside pressures sometimes force the government's hand (as, for example, over the poll tax). Also, judgements in the courts may curb government excesses.

The second main argument is that a written constitution is undesirable. A written constitution would mean that any dispute over the structure and powers of government, the relationship between different parts of government and the relationship between government and citizen would be settled by a court. Power would, therefore, be transferred from the executive (which is an elected body) to the judiciary (which is an unelected body). Also, in its role of interpreting the constitution, the judiciary would have the power to declare laws and actions unconstitutional, thus involving judges in political decisions. Political decisions, supporters of this point of view argue, should be left to politicians.

The third argument is that a written constitution is unachievable. There are two main reasons for this. First, it would be difficult to gain a consensus about what exactly should be written down in the constitution. And second, under the existing constitution there is no way of introducing a new constitution. Norton explains that:

> 'There is no body that can authorise or legitimise it. An Act of Parliament creating a new constitution or stipulating the procedures for creating one would derive its legitimacy from the doctrine which it sought to destroy. The one thing that Parliament cannot do is use its power under the doctrine of parliamentary sovereignty to destroy that doctrine, because its legitimacy to do so derives from the very power which it seeks to destroy. Hence, to create a new, written constitution we would have to start from scratch, disavow, by some means, our existing constitution. And that would cause constitutional and political turmoil that would not be worth enduring.' (Norton, 1988, pp.12-13)

A written constitution - arguments for

According to Norton:

> 'The principal argument for change derives from the perception that power in Britain has become too centralised. The old checks and balances identified by Dicey have been eroded, leaving the executive pre-eminent in the political system and able to get enacted, as Acts of Parliament, whatever measures it wants.'
> (Norton, 1988, p.10)

Those who support a written constitution, therefore, tend to argue that there is a need to limit government in Britain and that codifying the constitution is the best means to achieve this end. A written constitution would describe and entrench the structure and powers of government, the relationship between different parts of government and the relationship between government and citizen. It would, therefore, prevent arbitrary government since any disputes would be solved by (new) constitutional judicial procedures. The argument is similar to that made by Lord Hailsham in 1976 - namely that Britain has, in effect, become an elective dictatorship and the only way to curb the power of the executive is to write down precisely where its powers lie.

Linked to the above argument is the idea that citizens' rights can only be properly protected if they are entrenched in a written constitution. At present a government with an overall majority can add or remove citizens' rights simply by introducing a Bill and relying on its parliamentary majority to pass it. Take, for example, the Criminal Justice Act which became law in November 1994. This law restricts the right of people to protest and specifically targets minorities such as squatters and hunt saboteurs. Under a written constitution, the government would not be able to introduce legislation targeting minorities in this way or restricting citizens' rights. The only way to do this would be to amend the constitution - which would be a deliberately difficult and lengthy process.

There are three further arguments for constitutional change. First, parliamentary sovereignty has been profoundly affected by Britain's membership of the EU (see above, section 2.1). Since parliamentary sovereignty is no longer fully intact, there is therefore a need for a new constitutional settlement. Second, all political parties in the Commons, with the exception of the Conservatives and Ulster Unionists, support some form of devolution of power to the regions. Should this be enacted, then the UK would no longer be a unitary state and the constitutional relationship between the centre and the regions would need to be redefined. Again, this would require a new constitutional settlement. And third, the UK is the only country in the EU without a written constitution. It, therefore, needs a written constitution to bring it into line with its European partners.

Activity 4.8

Item A *A reformed British constitution*

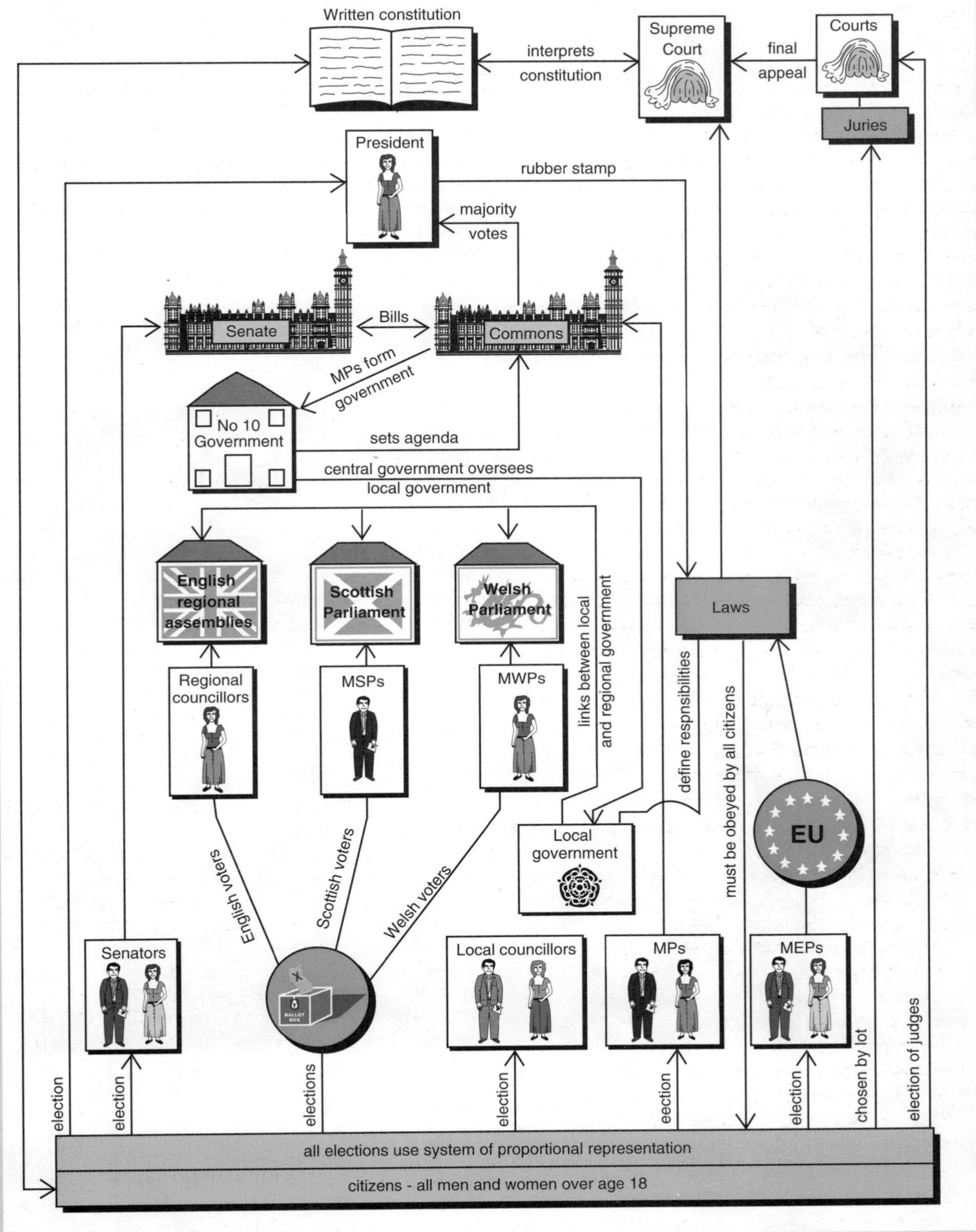

Item B *The problems facing the reformers*

The two main opposition parties generally accept the case for constitutional reform put by Charter 88. They want the European Convention on Human Rights to have the same status in British law as it has in European law. They want legal limits on the royal prerogative. They want power to be shifted from Whitehall departments and unelected public bodies to new regional assemblies. They want a more representative House of Lords. And they want the machinery of justice to be modernised. But, assuming that the Conservatives lose the next general election, constitutional change will not be easy. Past efforts show that officials will be obstructive and little will be achieved if the new government attempts constitutional reform by introducing piecemeal legislation. This is what happened in Harold Wilson's first government. A Bill was introduced to reform the House of Lords. But the Commons was divided between those who wanted abolition, those who wanted no change, or other changes, and those who supported the Bill. Eventually the Bill had to be abandoned. Similarly, in 1974, Home Office officials were so obstructive to Labour's commitment to sexual and racial discrimination legislation that the author of the white paper was sent home to rewrite it. Constitutional reform could easily suffer similar opposition next time. To bring about a new constitutional settlement, it is necessary to introduce a new way of law making. Rather than introducing separate laws for each area of change, the new government should set up a non-partisan Constitutional Convention. This would draw up a package of measures which would then be submitted to the people in a referendum.

Adapted from the *Observer*, 20 November 1994.

Item C *The Labour party and constitutional reform*

This cartoon shows members of the Labour party's leadership contemplating constitutional reform. Depicted (from left to right) are John Prescott, Margaret Beckett, Tony Blair and Robin Cook. Robin Cook has made public statements in favour of constitutional reform.

Item D *The constitution of the United Kingdom*

1

THE CONSTITUTION OF THE UNITED KINGDOM
TABLE OF ARTICLES

Preamble

CHAPTER 1
THE CONSTITUTION

1. Constitution as foundation of power in United Kingdom

CHAPTER 2
RIGHTS AND FREEDOMS

Part 1: Fundamental Rights and Freedoms

Division 1 : The Bill of Rights

2. Right to life
3. Freedom from torture
4. Freedom from slavery and forced labour
5. Right to liberty and security
6. Right to fair and public hearing
7. Retrospective offences prohibited
8. Respect for private and family life
9. Freedom of thought
10. Right to education
11. Freedom of expression
12. Freedom of assembly and association
13. Rights in respect of marriage
14. Right to enjoyment of possessions
15. Right to participate in public life and service
16. Freedom of movement
17. Freedom from expulsion from United Kingdom
18. Right of asylum
19. Equality

2 CONSTITUTION

Division 2 : Application and interpretation

20. Application of Bill of Rights
21. Scope of exceptions
22. Interpretation
23. Rights under other agreements
24. Abuse of freedoms

Division 3 : Remedies

25. Remedies
26. Human Rights Commission

Part 2: Social and Economic Rights

27. Social and economic rights

Part 3: Freedom of Information

28. Access to official information
29. Use of information by public authorities

CHAPTER 3
NATIONALITY

30. British nationality
31. Acquisition and loss of British nationality
32. Allegiance and dual nationality
33. Civic rights of non-nationals

CHAPTER 4
THE HEAD OF STATE

34. The Head of State
35. Functions of the Head of State
36. Duties of the Head of State
37. Personal powers of the Head of State
38. The power of mercy
39. The Privy Council

In 1991, the Institute for Public Policy Research (IPPR, 1991) drew up a draft written constitution for the UK. The first two pages of its contents are reproduced here.

Questions

1. a) Would you say that the reformed constitution shown in Item A was an improvement on the existing British constitution? Give reasons for your answer.
   b) Judging from Items B and C how likely are these constitutional reforms to be implemented?
2. Look at Item C. Suppose you had been asked to provide the Labour leadership with advice about constitutional reform. What advice would you give? Prepare a document outlining what, if any, constitutional reforms should be promised in a future Labour party general election manifesto.
3. Item D shows part of the content covered by the IPPR's written constitution. What other content would you expect to be covered? Give reasons for your answer.
4. Does Britain need a written constitution? Give reasons for your answer.

References

Barnett et al. (1993) Barnett, A., Ellis, E. & Hirst, P. (eds), *Debating the Constitution*, Polity Press, 1993.

Benn & Hood (1993) Benn, T. & Hood, A., 'Constitutional reform and radical change' in *Barnett et al., (1993).*

Birch (1964) Birch, A.H., *Representative and Responsible Government,* Allen & Unwin, 1964.

Bogdanor (1979) Bogdanor, V., *Devolution,* Oxford University Press, 1979.

Carroll (1994) Carroll, A.J., 'Judicial control of prerogative power', *Talking Politics*, Vol.7, No.1, autumn 1994.

CCO (1992) *The Conservative Manifesto*, Conservative Central Office, 1992.

Dearlove & Saunders (1991) Dearlove, J. & Saunders, P., *Introduction to British Politics: Analysing a Capitalist Democracy,* Polity Press, 1991.

De Paor (1970) De Paor, L., *Divided Ulster*, Penguin, 1970.

Street & Brazier (1981) Street, H & Brazier R., *Constitutional and Administrative Law*, Penguin, 1981.

Dicey (1885) Dicey, A.V., An *Introduction to the Study of the Law of the Constitution*, Macmillan, 1959.

Dowdle (1994) Dowdle, J.L., 'The Glomar explorer, the common fisheries policy and the Factortame case', *Talking Politics,* Vol.6, No.3, summer 1994.

Downing (1980) Downing, T. (ed.), *The Troubles*, Thames Macdonald, 1989.

Dunleavy et al. (1993) Dunleavy, P., Gamble, A., Holliday, I. & Peele, G., *Developments in British Politics 4*, Macmillan, 1993.

Gamble (1993) Gamble, A., 'Territorial Politics' in *Dunleavy et al.*, (1993).

Grant (1994) Grant, M., 'The rule of law - theory and practice', *Talking Politics*, Vol.7, No.1, autumn 1994.

Griffith (1985) Griffith, J.A.G., *The Politics of the Judiciary*, Fontana, 1985.

Hailsham (1976) Lord Hailsham, 'Elective dictatorship', the 1976 Dimbleby Lecture reprinted in *The Listener*, 21 October 1976.

HMSO (1993) *Scotland in the Union: a Partnership for Good*, HMSO, Cmnd 2225, 1993.

HMSO (1994) Central Office of Information, *The British System of Government,* HMSO, 1994.

IPPR (1991) Institute for Public Policy Research, *The Constitution of the United Kingdom*, IPPR, 1991.

Jowell (1989) Jowell, J., 'The rule of law today' in *Jowell & Oliver (1989).*

Jowell & Oliver (1989) Jowell, J. & Oliver, D., *The Changing Constitution*, Clarendon Press, 1989.

Kee (1980) Kee, R., *Ireland: a History, Abacus*, 1980.

Kellas (1992) Kellas, J., 'The general election in Scotland', *Politics Review*, Vol.2, No. 2, November 1992.

McAulsan & McEldowney (1985) McAuslan, P. & McEldowney, J.F. (eds), *Law, Legitimacy and the Constitution*, Sweet & Maxwell, 1985.

McCullagh & O'Dowd (1986) McCullagh, M. & O'Dowd, L., 'Northern Ireland: the search for a solution', *Social Studies Review*, March 1986.

Mitchell (1994) Mitchell, J., 'Devolution' in *Wale, (1994).*

Moran (1985) Moran, M., *Politics and Society in Britain. An Introduction*, Macmillan, 1985.

Norton (1982) Norton, P., *The Constitution in Flux,* Martin Robertson, 1982.

Norton (1988) Norton, P, 'Should Britain have a written constitution?', *Talking Politics*, Vol.1, No.1, autumn 1988.

Norton (1989) Norton, P., 'The changing constitution - part 2', *Contemporary Record*, Vol.3, No.2, November 1989.

Norton (1992) Norton, P, 'The Constitution' in *Wale (1992).*

Norton (1994) Norton, P., 'The constitution in question', *Politics Review*, Vol.3, No.4, April 1994.

Norton (1994a) Norton, P., 'Europe and the constitution', *Talking Politics*, Vol.6, No.3, summer 1994.

Nugent (1993) Nugent, N., 'The European dimension' in *Dunleavy et al.*, (1993).

O'Brien & O'Brien (1985) O'Brien, M. & O'Brien, C.C., *Ireland: a Concise History*, Thames and Hudson, 1985.

SCC (1989) Scottish Constitutional Convention, *Towards a Scottish Parliament*, Scottish Constitutional Convention, 1989.

Silk (1989) Silk, P., *How Parliament Works*, Longman, 1989.

Wale (1992) Wale, W. (ed.), *Developments in Politics*, Vol.3, Causeway Press, 1992.

Wale (1994) Wale, W. (ed.), *Developments in Politics*, Vol.5, Causeway Press, 1994.

5 The social context

Introduction

Politics in the United Kingdom does not function in a vacuum. It operates in a context which is the product of historical, geographical, social and economic factors. There is, in other words, a distinct political culture. This political culture is passed on from generation to generation, but it is not static. The political culture changes as society changes.

Since 1945, British society has changed in many important ways. Take class, gender and ethnicity, for example. Not only have there been objective changes since the 1940s (for example, it is now unlawful to pay a woman less than a man for the same work), but also attitudes have changed. People in public positions now talk the language of equal opportunities, even if their actions do not always live up to their rhetoric. As a result, the contemporary way of life is very different from that which existed after the Second World War. This chapter examines these social changes.

Social changes are closely intertwined with economic changes. Since 1945, Britain's industrial base has changed dramatically. Whilst the old manufacturing industries have declined, service industries and new industries have grown up. The growth of service industries and new industries has meant that old ways of work are no longer appropriate. In particular, the role of trade unions has been challenged and reappraised. This chapter considers how economic change has affected the way in which people live their lives and it assesses the developing role of the trade unions.

Chapter summary

Part 1 defines and examines the key political terms **political socialisation** and **political culture**.

Part 2 considers the importance of **class, gender and ethnicity**. To what extent do these social factors determine the nature of British political culture?

Part 3 describes the **social impact of economic change** since 1945. The impact of **de-industrialisation** and the changing role of **trade unions** are analysed.

1 What is the 'social context'?

Key Issues

1. What is 'political socialisation' and how does it take place?
2. What do we mean by 'political culture'?
3. Is there cultural diversity or uniformity?

1.1 Political socialisation

The term 'socialisation' refers to the way in which people, through interaction with members of their family and other social groups, learn how to become members of society. Political socialisation is the process by which people acquire their attitude towards politics. People are not born with political dispositions. They have to acquire them as children and then as adults. Two models have been developed to explain the process of political socialisation - the primacy and recency models.

The primacy model

Some studies of political socialisation focus on childhood on the grounds that this is a time when people are particularly susceptible to the influence of others. This emphasis on childhood has been described as the 'primacy model'. Research has found that children acquire political attitudes quite early on in their lives, mainly from their parents. There is, for example, some continuity of voting patterns between parents and children (see, for example, Butler & Stokes, 1971). Research suggests that by the age of 10 or 11 children have acquired party loyalties, a sense of national identity and a rudimentary knowledge of their country's main political institutions.

The recency model

Other studies have suggested that political socialisation is a lifelong process. This idea has been described as the 'recency model'. According to this model:

> 'Socialisation experiences have a greater impact the closer in time they are to the political context.' (Kavanagh, 1983, p.45)

So, experiences in adulthood are likely to be more important than childhood experiences because they are closer in time to the occasion when an adult performs a political action. The recency model also draws attention to 'zeitgeist effects' - the impact of personalities, issues and events associated with certain periods in adults' lives. For example, the 1960s is often seen as a period which affected a whole generation.

Agencies of socialisation

According to Rush (1992), the main agencies of political socialisation are the family, peer groups, the Church, the education system, the mass media and political parties. Only political parties within this list are overtly and consciously intent on political socialisation as a main aim. The other items on the list can be defined as agencies of political socialisation for the following reasons.

The family is a small, intimate group that, in the early years, has a near monopoly of a child's cognitive, emotional and physical development. Through socialisation, the child learns attitudes, values and ways of looking at the world. Also, the family is located within the class and social structure of this country and this influences the life of the child in profound ways. The family can be seen as a power structure in miniature. Families can operate in authoritarian or democratic styles and, in so doing, can influence the way in which children think.

Peer groups are people who associate with each other on the basis of equal status. Children's peer groups are usually thought to have a particular significance, but friendship groups and work groups are important throughout people's lives. Peer groups act as reference points for individuals and, in so doing, influence the attitudes and behaviour of individuals.

As Britain has become increasingly secular, the influence of the Church has declined. Nevertheless, the Church is still afforded a special place in social and political life and it does seek to influence the attitudes and behaviour of people. In the past, the Church of England was described as 'the Tory party at prayer'. But in the 1980s and early 1990s, leading figures in the Church were highly critical of the Conservative government and provided an alternative vision of society.

The education system provides a place in school for all children aged five to 16. So, for some 15,000 hours, the education system is responsible for each child's development. Ironically, little (and in some schools none) of that time is spent learning about contemporary politics. Yet, schools play an important part in political socialisation since children learn how to survive in a hierarchical, bureaucratic organisation which provides a framework for the bulk of their waking lives.

Finally, the mass media provides a view of the world beyond an individual's immediate experience. Newspapers, radio, film and television reach millions of people and they undoubtedly make some impact on people's attitudes and behaviour. Precisely what impact they make is the subject of debate. This is discussed more fully in chapter 19.

Imitation, instruction and motivation

Political scientists argue that socialisation takes place through imitation, instruction and motivation. According to Rush, these terms can be defined as follows:

> '[Imitation is] the copying of the behaviour of other individuals or groups of individuals and is generally most important in childhood...[Instruction is] the more or less intended learning of appropriate behaviour through formal education and less formally through discussion groups and other activities such as vocational training...[Motivation is] the learning of appropriate behaviour by experience, by a process of trial and error.' (Rush, 1992, p.104)

Political socialisation - problems

The very concept of political socialisation is problematic. One difficulty is that no satisfactory way has been devised to find out how far early experiences in a child's life compare with later experiences as an adult when it comes to determining political behaviour. Behaviour is not just determined by socialisation alone. Personal and situational factors operating at the time affect how an individual responds to events. A second difficulty is that no satisfactory way has been devised to judge the effects of socialisation, particularly when much socialisation is not overt, but is simply part of a pattern of everyday assumptions. Even when socialisation is overt, individuals can appear to be impervious to the process. In other words, a sophisticated model of political socialisation is necessary or there is a danger of ending up with an 'over-socialised' view which simply regards people as puppets waiting to be manipulated.

1.2 Political culture

'Political culture' is a difficult term to define. According to Kavanagh, it is:

> 'A shorthand expression to denote the set of values within which the political system operates.' (Kavanagh, 1983, p.49)

This set of values is the product of historical, geographical, social and economic factors. Since these factors change over time, political culture is not static. It changes as society changes.

Since the values within which the political system operates vary from country to country, each country has its own political culture. For example, not only does the USA's political system differ from the British system institutionally, it also differs culturally. American citizens have different expectations of their government from British citizens. They expect their politicians to behave in ways which would seem alien to British citizens. In other words, a different set of values pervades political life in the USA and it is this different set of values which distinguishes it culturally from political life in Britain.

Of course, not all citizens can be expected to accept the same set of values and so, within a single country, it is possible for different political cultures to coexist. Take, for example, attitudes towards the settlement of political disputes, by the use of violence. The vast majority of British people oppose the use of violence to settle disputes, but a small minority dissent from this view. In some cases, a dissenting minority, whose members share similar values, may be said to belong to a subculture. When people talk of 'the political culture', what they usually mean, more precisely, is the **dominant** political culture.

The civic culture

In their seminal study of political culture in five different countries, Almond & Verba (1963) classified differences in political involvement and awareness and found three broad types of political culture: **parochial** cultures where people only had a limited awareness of government and did not feel affected by its policies; **subject** cultures where individuals knew about their government and might even express strong support for it, but did not expect to have any influence over it; and **participant** cultures where people knew about their government and expected to act in ways which influenced it.

Almond & Verba argued that Britain was a prime example of a fourth type of political culture - a **civic culture**. A civic culture is a hybrid which mixes elements of a subject culture with elements of a participant culture. It is, they argued, because it is a hybrid that it is the most appropriate culture for a stable democracy. According to Kavanagh, a civic culture can be defined as follows:

> 'It is a mixed culture in which the subject orientations allow the elites the initiative and freedom to take decisions, while the participant orientations make the elites sensitive to popular preferences.' (Kavanagh, 1983, p.60)

So, in a country with a civic culture, ordinary citizens (the 'subjects') allow decision makers (the 'elite') the freedom to make any decisions they feel appropriate, so long as these decisions take into account public opinion.

Central to this view of British political culture is the notion of 'deference'. As early as 1867, the writer Walter Bagehot argued that a key characteristic of British people was their tendency to defer to those in authority. It was this, he argued, which explained why, on the whole, the British people were law abiding and there was little support for radical change. Almond & Verba agreed with Bagehot's view and incorporated it into their civic culture ('civility') model. Moran points out that:

> 'The deference component of the civility model can take three forms: it may assert that the British defer to the high born, defer to all figures in public authority or defer to social and economic hierarchies.' (Moran, 1989, p.36)

The point is that the tendency of British people to accept decisions made by those in authority has resulted in peace and stability.

Almond & Verba's view of political culture in the UK has been criticised for its emphasis on consensus and homogeneity (uniformity) where none exists. Critics (for example, Pimlott, 1989) have pointed out that, even during the period of so-called 'postwar consensus' between 1945 and 1979 (see chapter 3, section1.1), there was considerable political conflict. And the idea that the UK is homogenous is simplistic. The revival of nationalism in Scotland and Wales in the 1970s and the 'Troubles' in Northern Ireland indicated that there were important regional variations in political culture. Writing in 1981, Kavanagh argued that Almond & Verba's civic culture was in decline:

> 'There is no great confidence in the political institutions, though there is also no desire for radical changes...[There is] more dissatisfaction with the specific performance of government than the system as a whole. The recent years of slow economic growth have led to greater social tensions, group rivalries and growing dissatisfaction with the incumbent authorities...What does seem clear is that the traditional bonds of social class, party and common nationality are waning and with them the restraints of hierarchy and deference.' (Kavanagh, 1981, p.73)

The Marxist view

Marxists such as Miliband (1972) have argued that the ruling class, which has economic and political power, has developed a strong degree of control over British society. The ruling class has successfully promoted a dominant value system which endorses the status quo and, therefore, consolidates the position of the rich and powerful. This promotion of dominant values takes place through institutions such as the education system, the mass media and the main political parties. So, while consensus might be a feature of political life, it is a consensus imposed by the ruling class to facilitate its interests. But, while the ruling class might appear to be successful in imposing its view of the world, there is always the potential for the working class to resist and for class conflict to break out.

A cultural revolution?

During the 1980s, the Thatcher governments set out to alter fundamentally the political culture. The dominant political culture of the 1970s was regarded as a reason for Britain's poor economic performance and the Thatcher governments aimed to create a new culture of self-reliance, enterprise and market values. There is little evidence, however, to suggest that the Thatcher governments achieved this aim. In reviewing the eighth *British Social Attitudes Survey*, published in 1991 and covering the Thatcher years, the *Guardian* commented:

> 'Its consistent conclusion is not how much of a mark but how little Mrs Thatcher's radicalism has left on British society. The people's devotion to state provision of welfare, especially the NHS, survives undiminished. The preference for maintaining public spending rather than cutting taxes has grown. And as Mrs Thatcher's government, in its search for growth and for tax incentives, widened the gap between rich and poor, support has swelled for redistribution of wealth to help the have-nots.' (*Guardian*, 20 November 1991)

However, recent research into British political culture tends to suggest that there is now a fragmentation in society and a cultural diversity which pervades all aspects of social and political life (see, for example, Lash & Urry, 1987). This diversity has developed as traditional class divisions have changed and new important divisions in society, based on gender, race and region, have emerged.

Activity 5.1

Item A *Political socialisation*

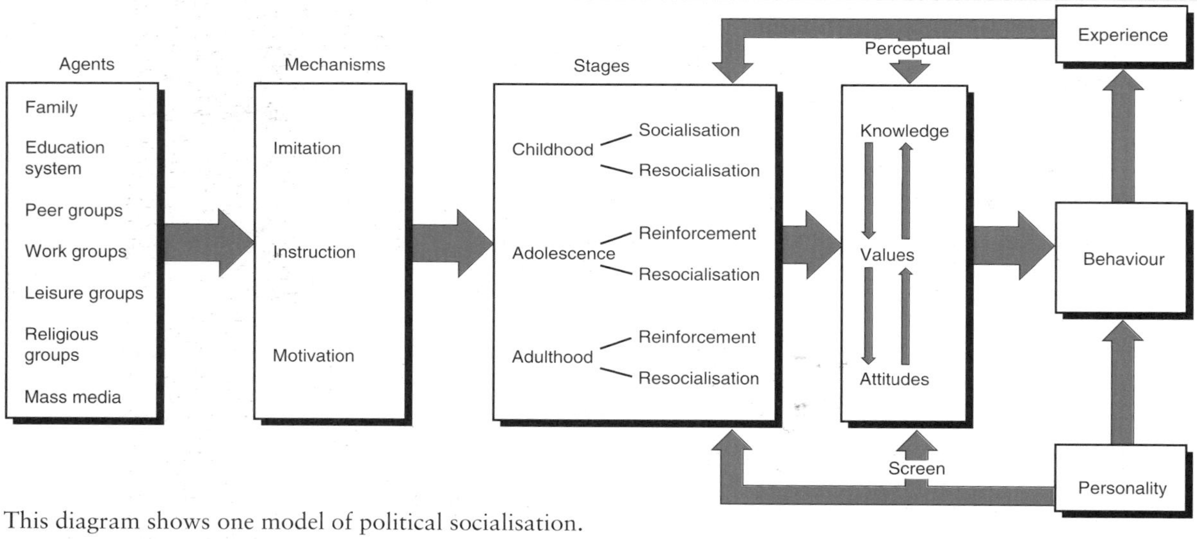

This diagram shows one model of political socialisation.

Adapted from Rush, 1992.

Item B *The British political culture (1)*

The minute the news reached the press room at the Liberal Democrats' conference that the vote to decriminalise cannabis had been carried, joy filled the air. It was 'Dopes! Paddy goes potty' for the tabloids whilst the serious papers filled column inches with head-shaking and mumbling about a 'blow to leadership'. And there was more of the same to come. Yesterday, there was the 'embarrassment' of a conference debate on the abolition of the monarchy. What a timid, grey, prissy, introverted, anally retentive, miserable and generally joyless political culture we have. It is a world of self-censoring politicians and tooth-sucking hacks. In the real world, there has been a national conversation going on for many years about whether to legalise soft drugs. It is a difficult issue. But when politicians try to join in, they are immediately branded as 'irresponsible'. The same is true of the monarchy. It is apparently unacceptable to have a serious conversation about the current constitutional position. Say anything negative and you get the full force of the Establishment. This Establishment includes newspaper editors who find it acceptable to report in toe-curling detail the unhappy sex lives of these same royals. What a funny country. These may be small examples, but there is a wider point. The political classes are becoming gutless. In private, many of them are interesting and thoughtful, as always. But, in public, they stick with the safe, old stories. And, not surprisingly, voters are turning off.

Adapted from the *Independent*, 21 September 1994.

Item C *The British political culture (2)*

Tonight, I am going to discuss one of the greatest threats ever to have confronted the British nation - the New British Disease, the self-destructive sickness of national cynicism. Too many politicians, academics, churchmen and journalists suffer from this disease. We Britons are famous for self-mocking humour, a tendency to understatement and, above all, for tolerance. But, something's changed. Until the 1970s, despite our shrunken role in the world, we took for granted the value of a constitutional monarchy, our parliamentary democracy and an established Church. People 'knew' that we did things best in Britain. But, Britain is very different today. It is not that the average Briton feels less British or less proud of our country. Read the newspapers or watch television and you see it: leading citizens telling us how much worse we do things in Britain. For decades, we have allowed ourselves to fall prey to cynics and socialists. And this breakdown in respect for our institutions matters because the relations which hold society together stretch from top to bottom. If Crown, Parliament and Church are not respected, there will be no respect for the law or judges or the police or teachers or bosses. Social disorder follows when respect breaks down.

Adapted from a speech made by Michael Portillo, then Chief Secretary to the Treasury, quoted in the *Guardian*, 16 January 1994.

Item D *Who do the British people trust?*

Group	1983	1993	Change
Teachers	79	84	+5
Doctors	82	84	+2
Clergy	85	80	-5
Newsreaders	63	72	+9
Judges	77	68	-9
Ordinary people	57	64	+7
The police	61	63	+2
Civil servants	25	37	+12
Trade union officials	18	32	+14
Business leaders	25	32	+7
Politicians generally	18	14	-4
Government ministers	16	11	-5
Journalists	19	10	-9

All figures are percentages

This table shows the results of a survey carried out by MORI in 1993. Respondents were asked whether or not they trusted each of the different types of people in the list to tell the truth.

Item E *A cartoonist's view of British political culture*

This cartoon presents a critical view of British political culture in the 1990s.

Questions

1. a) Using Item A make a list of people, groups and institutions that have helped to shape your attitudes towards politics.
   b) Put the items on your list in order of priority.
   c) Why is it difficult to produce an adequate model of political socialisation?
2. a) What do Items B and C tell us about British political culture in the 1990s?
   b) Explain why political culture is a difficult term to define.
3. Using Items B-D give arguments for and against the view that Almond & Verba's civic culture model is an adequate explanation of political culture in Britain.
4. Write a passage explaining how the cartoon (Item E) relates to British political culture. How accurate would you say it was?

2 Social factors

Key Issues

1. How important is class as a means of analysing British society?
2. To what extent do gender and ethnicity determine the status and lifestyle of people living in Britain?
3. How has British society changed since 1945?

2.1 Social class

According to Pulzer who wrote an analysis of British politics in the 1960s:

> 'Class is the basis of British party politics; all else is embellishment and detail.' (Pulzer, 1967, p.98)

Today, most British people are aware of social class. If they were asked, most people would be willing to locate themselves within the class structure. Yet, John Major has said that we now live in a classless society and he claims that his own background demonstrates that class is no longer of any real significance in Britain (he did not come from a privileged background and never went to university, yet he managed to become Prime Minister). This section will consider what exactly is meant by social class and how the class structure has changed since 1945.

Definitions of class

One of the difficulties with determining the importance of social class is that class is defined in many different ways. Income, wealth, education, accent, dress, work, lifestyle, and housing may all be taken into account when discussing class. Most definitions of social class, though, are economic in origin and are derived from the work of the political philosopher Karl Marx.

Marx and class

Writing in the 19th century, Marx defined social class in terms of economic relationships. He argued that in a capitalist society there are two main social classes - the **capitalist class** (or bourgeoisie) and the **working class** (or proletariat). The capitalist class is a relatively small group made up of those who own and control land and businesses. They are the 'capitalists' because they have capital (money) to invest. The working class, on the other hand, is a large group - the majority of the population - made up of people who only have their labour to sell. Members of the working class hire out their labour in return for wages.

Marx claimed that, in a capitalist society, the capitalist class derives its wealth and income from the exploitation of the working class. In a factory, for example, it is the workers who produce wealth by actually making the manufactured goods. But much of the wealth created by the workers is taken away by the owners in the form of profits (the capitalist class is a non-producing class. It does not actually produce anything). Marx argued that since the workers receive scant reward for their labour, they are being exploited. Over time, he said, this exploitation was bound to alienate the working class and bring the workers into conflict with the capitalists. In short, it was inevitable that a struggle between the classes would arise, with the workers struggling to improve their pay and conditions whilst the capitalists struggled to maintain and improve the size of their profits.

Marx also pointed out that, in a capitalist society, the capitalist class was able to control the state in accordance with its broad overall interests. The capitalist class was, therefore, also the ruling class. Those in power in a capitalist society would inevitably protect the interests of the capitalists rather than the workers. Although Marx recognised that there was an intermediate stratum (the middle class, as it would be called today) he regarded this group as a temporary phenomenon.

Later definitions

Most subsequent definitions of social class have taken issue with the model proposed by Marx. The German sociologist Max Weber, for example, argued that Marx's division of society into two classes was too simple. Although Weber agreed with Marx that class should be seen in economic terms and that the major class division is between those who owned land and businesses and those who did not, he argued that other factors, such as differing skills, should be taken into account.

As a result, Weber's model of social class includes four categories - the **propertied upper class, propertyless white collar workers** (managers, administrators and professionals), the **petty bourgeoisie** (small property owners) and the **manual working class.** The manual working class is divided into two groups - skilled workers and unskilled workers. This division reflects the fact that skilled workers tend to be paid more than unskilled workers. Weber also introduced the notion of an expanding middle class. He argued that, by developing skills, it is possible, for example, for unskilled manual workers or (more often) their children to change class.

Weber's distinction between skilled and unskilled workers has been taken further in the Registrar

General's occupational definition of social class, the definition normally used in government reports and surveys. The Registrar General divides the British population into five classes according to occupation. These five classes are described as follows:

The Registrar General's definition of class

Class 1 Professional	Accountant, doctor, dentist, solicitor, university lecturer.
Class 2 Managerial and technical	Manager, teacher, librarian, farmer.
Class 3 (Non-manual) Clerical and minor supervisory	Clerk, shop assistant, police officer, sales representative.
Class 3 (Manual) Skilled manual	Electrician, tailor, bus driver, printer, cook.
Class 4 Semi-skilled manual	Agricultural worker, postal worker telephone operator, builder.
Class 5 Unskilled manual	Railway porter, labourer, window cleaner, office cleaner.

It is important to note that the Registrar General does not just take economic rewards into account when deciding which occupation fits into which class. The prestige of an occupation is also taken into account. This explains why, for example, a relatively low paying occupation such as university lecturer is included in class 1.

By way of contrast, the Oxford Mobility Study (a survey of 10,000 men conducted in 1972), identified seven separate classes. These classes were identified on the basis of the economic reward gained from each person's occupation. For convenience, these seven classes were then amalgamated into three. So, the top paid people were classified as members of the **Service Class**, middle income earners were classified as members of the **Intermediate Class** and low income earners were classified as members of the **Working Class**.

One further definition of class should be described since it is commonly used by the media. This is the division of society into six classes by the Institute of Practitioners in Advertising (IPA). Advertisers use the sixfold division to work out where to place an advert and which groups to target when selling a particular product. The IPA's definition has been adopted by political commentators not least because political parties have to 'sell' their image and policies in much the same way that a company has to sell its brand name and products. The six classes are defined as follows:

The IPA's definition of class

Class A	Higher managerial, administrative or professional
Class B	Intermediate managerial, administrative, or professional
Class C1	Supervisory or clerical, and junior managerial, administrative or professional
Class C2	Skilled manual workers
Class D	Semi-skilled and unskilled manual workers
Class E	State pensioners or widows (no other earnings), casual or lowest grade workers, or long-term unemployed.

It should be clear from the different ways of defining class described above that different researchers use different criteria when undertaking their research. This means that it is important to be clear exactly what criteria have been used because the results of two studies using two different sets of criteria are not strictly comparable.

Class and politics in Britain

For the first 20 years after the Second World War, most political commentators agreed that social class was the driving force behind British politics. Studies were conducted to show that people voted on a class basis (see chapter 9, section 1.1). The two party system was seen as a reflection of the British class system - the Conservative party represented the capitalist class whilst the Labour party represented the working class. This attitude was summed up by Butler & Stokes in 1971:

> 'Our findings on the strength of links between class and partisanship in Britain echo broadly those of every other opinion poll or voting study...the pre-eminent role [of class] can hardly be questioned.' (Butler & Stokes, 1971, p.102)

This conclusion was also supported by those who wrote from a Marxist perspective. For example, Westergaard & Resler argued that voting Labour was:

> 'The outcome of a general sense of class identity: of common interests to be protected or advanced. Asked why they vote as they do, manual working class Labour supporters usually refer to the fact that the party is - or is supposed to be - the party of the working class.' (Westergaard & Resler, 1976, p.364)

Similarly, Miliband claimed that the Conservative party's function was:

> 'To aggregate the different interests of the dominant class.' (Miliband, 1972, p.187)

More recently, however, the claim has been made that the class structure has changed fundamentally. Saunders (1990), for example, notes that social mobility between the classes has increased and divisions between the classes are more fluid. Inequalities in income and wealth, he claims, are less marked than used to be the case and there has been a major expansion of middle class occupations. He describes the spread of share ownership and house ownership and the growing consumption of consumer durables. Ownership and control of industry, he argues, are no longer in the hands of a capitalist class, but in the hands of millions of shareholders and professional managers. The upper class no longer has the power and privileges that it once had. Traditional working class communities have disappeared as heavy industries such as shipbuilding and mining have declined. New industries have developed without the traditional lines of demarcation between the classes. Bonnett (1994) pursues this theme and claims that Britain's industrial structure has changed dramatically. There has been a shift away from the mass production of standardised products to flexible specialisation in production and products. There has also been a shift away from the old centres of capitalism (in Europe) to a new, global system of capitalism. One result of these changes is a decline of class-based politics and institutions.

The decline in class-based politics and institutions, it is claimed, is reflected in changing voting patterns (see chapter 9, section 1.1). Fewer working class people vote Labour in the 1990s than used to be the case in the 1950s and a growing number of the middle classes vote for third parties rather than for the Conservative party. This, it is argued, has forced the political parties to change their image. Labour has worked hard to rid itself of the 'cloth cap' image whilst the 'hunting, shooting and fishing' image of the Conservative leadership has been replaced by claims of classlessness. All the parties now claim to represent the national interest rather than a particular section of society. Some commentators even argue that political behaviour can be better explained by reference to new social movements - such as feminism or environmentalism - rather than to class.

Against this view, however, other commentators have argued that class is still an important political phenomenon. Benyon (1994), for example, notes the major inequalities of income and wealth in Britain. These inequalities, together with disparities in educational opportunities and housing patterns and the other measures of class differences, he claims, provide sufficient evidence to show that class is still an important means of analysing British society. Miliband sums up this viewpoint as follows:

> 'Notwithstanding a torrent of propaganda to the contrary, advanced capitalist countries are now and will remain highly structured and hierarchical societies...The substance of life experience for everyone in these societies remains utterly shaped by the fact of class and class inequality.' (Miliband, 1989, pp.203-4)

Activity 5.2

Item A *The class structure*

Item B *Case studies*

1. **Ned** is aged 44. He works on the production line in the car assembly plant at Ford Dagenham. He has worked there for 16 years. He earns £6.50 an hour and works a 39 hour week. If he is five minutes late he loses five minutes' pay. He lives in Bexleyheath, South London, in a house which he owns. He is married with two children. He left school at 16.

2. **Anna** is aged 31. She works as a gardener and for her husband's computer consultancy. She was brought up on a council estate and went to a Roman Catholic girls' comprehensive school. She says that the school was responsible for ensuring that she is well-spoken. If she had enough money, she would send her children to a private school. Both her parents were Irish and working class. She lives in the village of Botesdale, near Diss in Norfolk, with her husband and two children. She is a member of the Conservative party.

3. **Charles** is aged 37. He is a banking director at a merchant bank. He lives with his wife in a large old house in Cornwall and commutes weekly to a London flat. He was educated at a private school and at Exeter University. His father was in the army and his mother trained as a painter. Charles earns between £60,000 and £150,000 a year. He says he is unusual in the City because he has only voted once. He describes himself as 'essentially conservative'. He says that he would send his children to state schools.

4. **Andrew** is aged 73. He is the 11th Duke of Devonshire and lives at the family home, Chatsworth in Derbyshire. Chatsworth is owned by a family charitable trust and is open to the public for seven months of the year. It has 175 rooms and a garden of 100 acres. It is surrounded by an estate of 11,000 acres. A total of 175 people work at Chatsworth and on its estate.

Adapted from the *Observer*, 12 December 1993.

Item C *The classless society (1)*

This cartoon appeared in the *Observer* on 1 February, 1991.

Item D *The classless society (2)*

Nobody has confused us more than John Major with his talk of a classless society. Major, with his placeless drone of a voice and drab suits, likes to suggest he is classless. He is careful to stress his time living in Brixton and his short periods of unemployment. But how many of Major's Cabinet colleagues would have got there if there really was a classless society? Seventeen went to Oxbridge. Nearly all of them are educating their children privately. Anyone who believes that Britain has a classless society should look at who enters higher education. The number of students from working class backgrounds is minute. The root of our confusion is our equation of class with money. As people have become able to buy more consumer durables, obvious class differences have faded. Everyone has moved up. Cappuccino, fresh pasta and good wine are available almost everywhere. We are all middle class now - or, at least, that is the myth. The truth, however, is rather different. The gap between the classes is, in fact, growing. Between 1980 and 1985, the top 20% of the population's share of national income grew from 40% to 45% whilst the number of people on below average incomes doubled. Time and again, statistics show up class differences. Members of the working class are far more likely, for example, to die of heart disease, lung cancer and strokes than the middle class. Babies born to middle class families have a better chance of survival than those born to working class families. In the end, class is not just a question of lifestyle but a question of life itself.

Adapted from the *Observer*, 6 October 1991.

Item E *Changing views on the class struggle 1975-93*

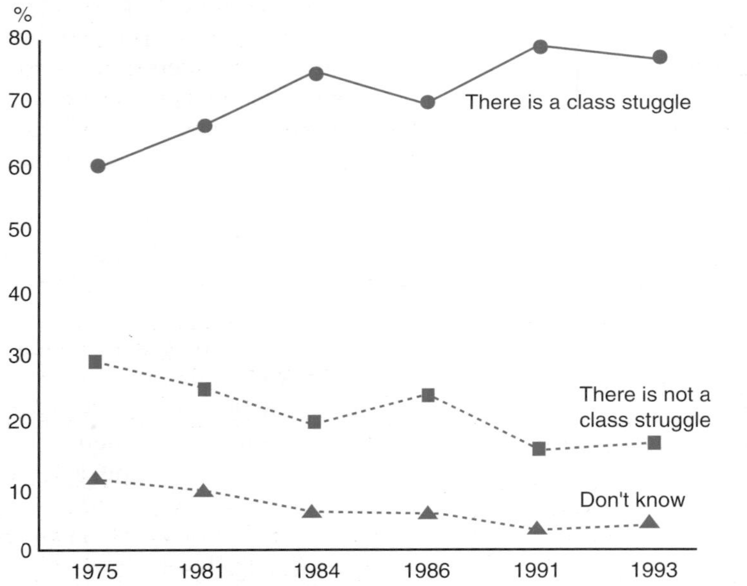

This graph shows the result of surveys conducted between 1975 and 1993. Respondents were asked whether or not they thought there was a class struggle.

Adapted from Allan, 1994.

Questions

1. Suppose you had been asked to conduct a survey to find out the class background of your colleagues. Write down the criteria you would use. Devise a questionnaire, conduct the survey and write a report.
2. Describe your own class using (i) the Registrar General's classification (ii) the Oxford Mobility Study's definition and (iii) the IPA's definition. Give reasons for your choices.
3. How accurate are the class differences portrayed in Item A?
4. Identify the class of each person profiled in Item B. Explain how you reached your conclusion.
5. Give the arguments for and against the view that Britain is becoming a classless society. Use Items C-E in your answer.

2.2 Gender

It is not just class that determines the position and role of people in British society. Other social factors are important. Take gender, for example. Although there is some evidence to suggest that in Britain there is less discrimination against women today than was once the case, there is overwhelming evidence that women have less chance of achieving high status and high earnings than men. Women may have won equality in the eyes of the law, but they have yet to win equality of opportunity. This section considers the importance of gender in British society.

First and second wave feminism

Feminists are supporters of and campaigners for equality between women and men. Although commentators talk about two 'waves' of feminism, it is only since the 1960s that the term feminist has gained common usage (see chapter 2, section 5).

'First wave' feminism refers to the period beginning in the late 19th century when women in Britain (and other countries) mobilised and campaigned to win the right to vote (see chapter 7, section 1.2). But, although the right to vote was the focus of the campaign, the goal of many 'first wave' feminists was much wider. They hoped to eradicate inequalities between men and women. For example, when women finally won equal voting rights with men in 1928, Ray Strachey pointed out:

> 'There are aspects of equality which cannot be won by law. These are changes of thought and outlook which even yet have not arrived. Above all, economic equality with men is still a distant dream. The struggle for these things goes on and must go on. But the main fight is over and the main victory is won.' (Strachey, 1928, pp.384-5)

The problem (from the feminists' point of view) was that winning the right to vote did not automatically mean that the problems outlined by Strachey were tackled. In fact, rather than encouraging women to campaign for further changes, electoral reform led to a period of 40 years in which feminism was marginalised. Bouchier suggests reasons for this:

> 'After several years of being nervously sensitive to women's issues, politicians realised that women were simply not voting on such issues as a group; nor did they have an effective political party of their own; nor were women entering politics in significant numbers. All three conditions are necessary before a group can begin to turn the democratic system to its own advantage.' (Bouchier, 1983, p.16)

The result was that it was not until the late 1960s that a 'second wave' of feminism began. Its origins lie in the USA, but it soon spread to Britain. Mitchell (1971) suggests three reasons for the resurgence of feminism in the 1960s. First, the late 1960s was a time of political turbulence. Many young people joined groups which aimed to change or upset the Establishment. Women who participated in these groups gained political experience and, at the same time, encountered a great deal of sexism (prejudice against them because of their sex). Women were expected to make the tea, for example, and to follow the lead of male leaders. As a result, some women began to argue that there was a need to struggle against male domination. Second, the contradictions in many women's lives led to the need for them to get together to reconsider their role. For example, the 1960s was the age of sexual liberation, yet women were often treated as little more than sex objects. A growing number of married women went out to work, yet it was commonly argued that a woman's place was in the home. These contradictions encouraged women to challenge the status quo. And third, the 1960s presented women with new opportunities which raised their awareness of their position in society. The number of women who entered higher education and embarked on careers grew rapidly. The development of the contraceptive pill gave women greater freedom to choose when and whether to have children. This greater awareness encouraged women to take political action.

The development of the new wave of feminism was sparked by a number of influential books, including Germaine Greer's *The Female Eunuch* and Betty Freidan's *The Feminine Mystique*. The latter was published in 1963 and summed up what Freidan described as the 'problem that has no name':

> 'The problems lay buried, unspoken for many years in the minds of American women. It was a strange stirring, a sense of dissatisfaction, a yearning that women suffered in the middle of the 20th century in the United States. Each suburban housewife struggled with it alone. As she made the beds, shopped for groceries, matched slip cover material, ate peanut butter sandwiches, chauffeured Cub Scouts and Brownies, lay beside her husband at night, she was afraid to ask even of herself, the silent question: is this all?' (Freidan, 1963, p.1)

In order to challenge the view that women should be satisfied with domestic life, especially when it served to restrict their opportunities in employment, politics and public life, Freidan helped to set up NOW (the National Organisation of Women), a group which served as a blueprint for many British feminists. Women's groups began to spring up throughout Britain:

> 'Here women began to explore the ways that

> their lives were constrained in the private realm of home and the social forces forced upon girls and then women. In these man-free meetings, women discovered a new confidence. They began to name the male practices which contributed to their lack of freedom and attempted to devise alternative ways of behaving to escape the traps of male logic, language and power games.' (Forbes, 1991, p.62)

Collectively, the women's groups which sprung up in Britain were known, at first, as the Women's Liberation Movement. In the 1970s, the Women's Liberation Movement agreed on seven demands which must be met before equality with men could be achieved (see Item D in Activity 5.3).

The position of women in Britain in the 1990s

Examination of five areas should clarify the position of women in Britain in the 1990s. These areas are as follows: women's legal status; women at work; women at home; women and education; and, women and politics.

Women's legal status

The Prime Minister, Stanley Baldwin, argued in 1928, after the Electoral Reform Bill was passed:

> 'The inequality of women, if there be such a thing, will not now depend on any creation of the law. It will never again be possible to blame the state for any position of inequality. Women will have, with us, the fullest rights.' (Speech in the House of Commons, 29 March 1928)

But it was not until 1975 that the Equal Pay Act 1970 came into force. Before then, the law allowed employers to pay women a lower rate of pay for doing the same job as a man. Similarly, it was not until 1975 that the Sexual Discrimination Act was passed. Before then, the law did not allow the idea that a woman might be discriminated against because of her sex.

Although the Equal Pay Act and Sexual Discrimination Acts mean that, in theory, men and women are now equal before the law, in reality this legislation has lacked teeth. Bassnett, for example, argues that:

> 'The vagueness of the Sex Discrimination Act which came into force with the Equal Pay Act left so many legal loopholes that anyone set against implementing the Act could manage to do so with regular impunity, a fact borne out by the difficulty women have had in winning cases of sexual discrimination in employment.' (Bassnett, 1986, p.141)

Women in work

The number of women in work is growing whilst the number of working men is declining. According to Edward Balls, between 1970 and 1994, female employment rose by a fifth whilst male employment fell by the same amount (*Guardian*, 5 September 1994). At the start of 1994, women made up 48% of the workforce.

Although these figures may suggest that women have been making progress towards equality at work, Forbes argues:

> 'It would be wrong to assume that women have gained a more equal footing in employment, because fully 4.6 million of the 10.1 million jobs occupied by women in 1993 were part-time. Moreover, after nearly 20 years of the operation of the Equal Pay and Sex Discrimination Acts, women received, on average, 75% of men's salaries for the same work. This compounded the inequalities of status, employment protection and pension rights and the lack of career advancement opportunities associated with part-time employment.' (Forbes, 1994, p.194)

In addition, women have to confront the 'male culture' which dominates many workplaces. Women often find that employers assume that, because they are women, they are suited to particular kinds of work (usually caring, non-competitive roles) and not suited to other kinds of work (such as management, engineering or scientific research). Because an invisible barrier (sexual discrimination) prevents women breaking into these areas of work, commentators have talked of a 'glass wall' blocking women's way forward. Similarly, even when women are allowed into what were previously regarded as male occupations, they often find that they are not promoted as often as men or that they are not promoted at all. Again, an invisible barrier - a 'glass ceiling' - blocks their way upwards. These tendencies are often compounded by the fact that many women have career breaks to look after children and find that, when they return, they have been left behind.

Women at home

Although the traditional attitude that women (especially married women) should stay at home and tend to the needs of their children and husband is changing, women still do most of the domestic work in Britain. This was graphically illustrated by market research carried out by Mintel in July 1993:

> 'Mintel tried to interview couples who equally shared grocery shopping, cooking and doing the laundry, but had to abandon the search after finding only one man in 100 did his fair share of housework. Fewer than one woman in ten thinks her partner shares

> cooking equally, while nearly two men in ten think they do...Only 20% of working women report that their male partner equally shares any single domestic task, whereas 85% say they almost always do all the laundry, ironing and a similar number say they are entirely responsible for cooking the main meal.' (*Guardian*, 21 December 1993)

A major reason why 80% of part-time jobs are taken by women is that women are expected to combine work with their domestic responsibilities. Since few employers make any provision for childcare and few men are prepared to leave their jobs to look after their children, it is women who generally break their careers to look after their family. Whilst the other 11 members of the EU agreed in September 1994 to allow all fathers three months unpaid paternity leave to look after each newborn child, Britain refused to give fathers this right. As a result, whilst mothers in Britain are entitled to 40 weeks leave (including 15 weeks on the equivalent of sick pay), fathers are not entitled to any leave.

Women and education

Some feminists argue that girls are disadvantaged at school because of the sexist attitudes of some teachers and because of social conditioning which encourages boys to be assertive and competitive whilst girls are quiet and non-competitive. But even if girls do have to overcome such obstacles, figures compiled by the government show that, between 1975 and 1991, a larger percentage of girls than boys gained grades A-C in GCSE exams or their equivalents and whilst a slightly smaller percentage of girls than boys achieved one or more A levels in 1976, since 1987 this position has been reversed. Although it is more than 100 years since the first women students were allowed to take a degree, there are still more male than female students in higher education. Nevertheless the gap is narrowing fast. Whereas in 1970 there were 274,000 male students in higher education compared to 182,000 female students, in 1991 there were 442,000 male students compared to 400,000 female students (HMSO, 1994).

Women and politics

Although women have been able to stand as candidates in parliamentary elections since 1918, women are still under-represented in Parliament and on local councils. The evidence to support these assertions and possible reasons are considered in chapter 11.

Activity 5.3

Item A *Women at work (1)*

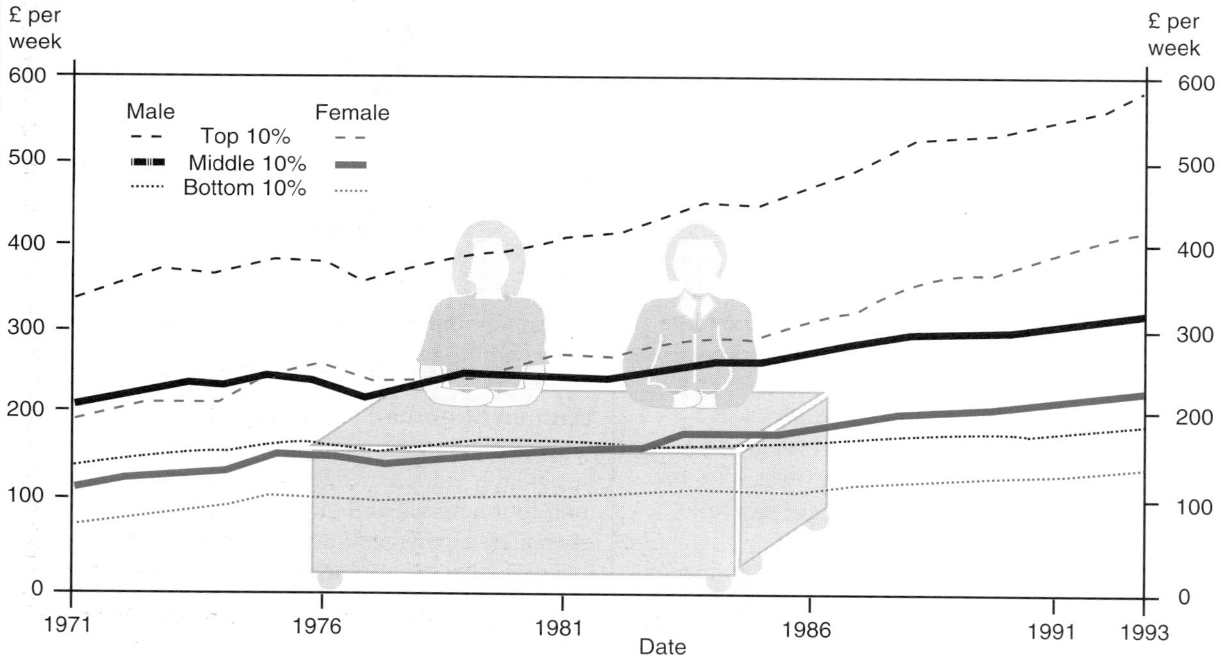

This graph shows a comparison between the weekly earnings of men and women between 1971 and 1993.

Adapted from HMSO, 1994.

Item B *Women at work (2)*

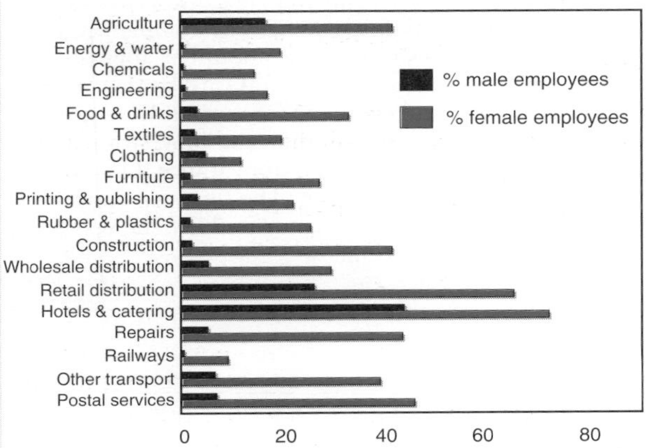

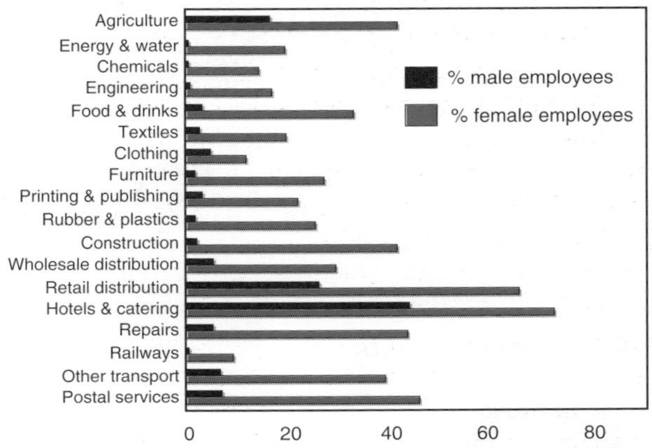

This table shows the percentage of men and women working part time in selected industries in 1993.

Adapted from *Labour Research*, July 1994.

Item C *Women at work (3)*

According to a survey published today by the Institute of Management, the number of female managers has fallen at almost every level for the first time since 1973. In total, the number of female managers has fallen from 10.2% in 1993 to 9.5% in 1994 (in 1983 the figure was 3.3%). The survey also shows that female managers have fewer perks and lower salaries than their male colleagues. Female managers earn, on average, £27,862 compared to £32,303 for men. Only 51.6% of female managers have company cars compared to 61.1% of men. Also, women are more likely to be managers in areas like marketing and personnel rather than research and development, manufacturing and production. According to Claire Austin of the Institute of Management, women find it difficult to work for firms that have a male culture. Companies, she said, should realise that many women are responsible for their home, children and elderly parents and have to contend with all that on top of their career. So, it is no good companies organising meetings at 5.30 and expecting women to work late. They should be more flexible.

Adapted from the *Times*, 3 May 1994.

Item D *The seven demands*

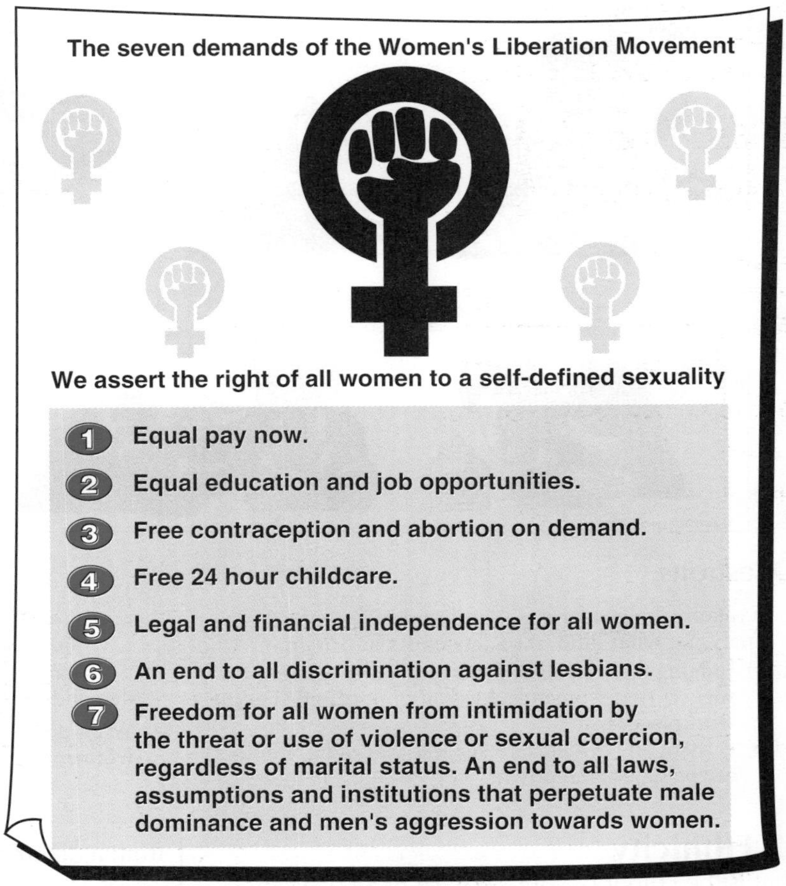

These seven demands were made by the Women's Liberation Movement in the 1970s.

Item E *Women at work (4)*

A woman aged 31 who worked as a financial consultant in Glasgow told an industrial tribunal yesterday of the constant stream of sexual harassment she had been subjected to. Every day she ended up in tears because of the taunts and sexual remarks made by her male colleagues and eventually she suffered a breakdown. When she complained to a director because he called her 'darling', he began calling her 'you old bag'. Remarks were made about her appearance, her underwear and what she had been doing the previous night. Male colleagues altered her dental card so that instead of reading 'oral surgery' it read 'oral sex'. They told disgusting stories every day and claimed that women were good for only two things - one of them in the kitchen. One male colleague would phone a sex chatline and look straight at her while giving a running commentary. Women visitors were given marks out of ten for their appearance. On a coach trip to a business meeting the men refused to turn off a pornographic video they were playing. The financial consultant said that she felt totally humiliated and demeaned. When she complained, the managing director told her she was being petty. The company, her former director and branch manager all deny sex discrimination.

Adapted from the *Times*, 21 September 1994.

Item F *Superwoman*

Questions

1. Explain why gender is a useful tool to use when analysing what kind of society exists in Britain.
2. a) Judging from Items A-E what evidence is there to suggest that women lack equal opportunities in the workplace?
   b) Is there any evidence to suggest that old prejudices are being broken down?
3. a) Take any of the demands in Item D and explain why feminists want change in that area.
   b) What progress has been made in meeting these demands?
4. What does Item F tell us about the pressures that women face in contemporary Britain?

2.3 Ethnicity

What is the colour of your skin? Think of ways in which your life might have been different if your skin had been a different colour. Where were your parents and grandparents born? Think of ways in which your life has been shaped by your family and how your family environment would have been different if your parents or grandparents had come from a different culture.

Along with class and gender, sociologists argue that ethnicity is a key social factor. 'Ethnicity', however, is a difficult term to define. According to a House of Lords ruling in 1983, an ethnic group is a group in society which has a distinct cultural identity, a long, shared history, a common geographical origin or common descent, a common language, a common literature peculiar to the group and a common religion. Using these criteria it is possible to divide the British population into a number of ethnic groups. The majority of the population belongs to a single, dominant ethnic group (white Britons descended from white Britons), whilst the remainder of the population belongs to a number of ethnic minority groups - for example, white Britons descended from Irish immigrants, black Britons descended from West Indian immigrants or black Britons descended from Pakistani immigrants. Although, as these examples indicate, some ethnic minority groups are white, all black Britons belong to ethnic minority groups. As a result, the issues of skin colour (race) and racism (prejudice against people because of their skin colour) are closely linked to any discussion of ethnicity.

In the past, many studies failed to distinguish between different ethnic groups, lumping people together as 'blacks' and 'whites'. There were a number of problems with this. First, 'black' took on a dual meaning, sometimes referring to all black people and sometimes referring only to Afro-Caribbean groups. Second, this classification did not take account of the way in which black people see themselves. Modood (1988), for example, argues that people from the Indian subcontinent do not define themselves as 'black'. Third, some critics argue that the black-white distinction is unlikely to improve race relations since it encourages polarisation. Despite these problems, however, 'black' is still a widely used term.

By dividing up society along ethnic lines, sociologists are able to target groups in society and find out how different ethnic backgrounds affect the life chances of different groups of people. This means of classification includes consideration of cultural factors as well as skin colour and, therefore, provides a more complex model than that based on skin colour alone. For example, a study showing that Indian Britons do better at school than both Bangladeshi Britons and Afro-Caribbean Britons, but not as well as white Britons, may be of greater use than a study which simply shows that, overall, white Britons do better at school than black Britons since it allows politicians to target resources at areas which need it (areas where Bangladeshi Britons live, for example). Having said this, however, it should not be assumed that each ethnic culture is uniform. Gilroy (1987) warns against 'ethnic absolutism' - the idea that once a researcher has identified which ethnic group a person belongs to, then that person's behaviour can be predicted. Ethnicity is dynamic and flexible. It is not fixed.

Historical background

British history has been shaped by waves of immigration. Romans, Saxons, Angles, Vikings and Normans all settled in Britain and helped to shape British culture. In the 19th century, thousands of Irish people fled the famine and settled in Britain. During the 1930s and 1940s, Jews and others fled to Britain to escape Nazi persecution.

Records of black people in Britain stretch back to the period of Roman occupation (there is evidence that soldiers recruited in Africa served in Britain and some are known to have settled here). Walvin (1984) notes that there has been a small but continuous black presence in Britain for the last 500 years. The growth of the British Empire played a part in this. As British contact with black people grew, small black communities established themselves in Britain. It was, however, only after 1945 that substantial numbers of black people settled in Britain.

During the 1950s and early 1960s, Britain experienced an economic boom which led to an acute labour shortage. This shortage was met, in part, by encouraging the immigration of workers, mainly from the New Commonwealth countries (countries which had formed part of the British Empire). In the 1950s, most of these workers came from the West Indies and, in the 1960s, most came from the Indian subcontinent. Many of these immigrants were employed in unskilled and low paid jobs which the indigenous white population were unwilling to take. This had immediate and serious consequences:

> 'Partly because of low pay, partly because of their relative newness and partly because of implicit discriminatory practices on the part of both public and private authorities, black people found themselves forced into cheap rented housing, much of it located in the already decaying inner areas of Britain's cities. So, from their arrival, black people suffered from economic and housing disadvantage, to which was added other forms of disadvantage resulting from lack of attention to their needs, particularly with regard to education. Finally, in terms of social interaction, black people suffered from the hostility of their erstwhile hosts. Centuries of colonialism had left their mark in terms of popular stereotypes of black people as being pagan, uncivilised, inherently inferior to Europeans and ignorant. These images were reflected in white attitudes and behaviour.'
> (Taylor, 1993, p.146, slightly adapted)

Throughout the 1950s, immigration remained unchecked. Between 1955 and 1957, for example, more than 40,000 people each year emigrated from New Commonwealth countries into Britain. In the early 1960s, however, increasingly strident calls began to be made in favour of immigration control. The Notting Hill riots in 1958 drew attention to growing racial tension (white youths shouting racist slogans clashed with black youths in the Notting Hill area of London over several days). And, in 1962, the government passed the first of what was to become a string of Immigration Acts designed to restrict the influx of immigrants. Further Acts were passed in 1968, 1971 and 1981. According to Wilson (1984), each Act was designed to shut the door on black immigration whilst leaving it open for white immigrants, with the result that:

> 'The most brutal and wide-ranging racism which occurs day after day is not the work of fascist minority parties but of Her Majesty's government. It is the racism written into and demanded by Britain's immigration laws.' (Wilson, 1984, p.72)

Although tighter immigration controls have restricted the number of new immigrants (especially black immigrants) settling in Britain, a number of measures have been taken to combat racism within Britain. Race Relations Acts were passed in 1965, 1968 and 1976. Since 1976, racial discrimination has been outlawed (both 'direct' or intentional discrimination and 'indirect' or unintentional discrimination) and the Commission for Racial Equality (CRE) has been given investigative and legal powers to counter racism. But whilst restrictions on immigration have been effective, measures to combat racism have not:

> 'Despite three Race Relations Acts (in 1965, 1968 and 1976) and over 20 years of inner city policy initiatives, black people in Britain still suffer widely from racial discrimination and racial disadvantage. While a few have broken through to public prominence...black people are generally under-represented in high status occupations. They find it much more difficult to secure jobs and...live disproportionately in the poorest, most neglected and most deprived parts of the country.' (Taylor, 1993, pp.162-3)

A measure of this deprivation and discontent was the outbreak of a number of serious riots in inner cities during the 1980s. Although the government denied that racial tension explained the outbreak of these riots, Lord Scarman, who was appointed to investigate the causes of the rioting in Brixton, felt able to conclude:

> 'The evidence which I have received...leaves no doubt in my mind that racial disadvantage is a fact of current British life. It was, I am sure, a significant factor in the causation of the Brixton disorders. Urgent action is needed if it is not to become an endemic, ineradicable disease threatening the very survival of our society.' (Scarman, 1981, p.209)

Racism in the 1990s

The 1991 population census revealed that out of a total population of 54.811 million, 51.8 million people were white whilst 3.011 million were black. The three largest groups of black Britons were Indian Britons (840,000), Caribbean Britons (500,000) and Pakistani Britons (467,000). In 1991, therefore, 5.5% of the total population was black. This was a rise from 2.3% in 1971 and 3.9% in 1981.

The Runnymede Trust (Runnymede, 1991) notes that white people often overestimate how many black people live in Britain. In 1978, for example, Margaret Thatcher warned that Britain might be 'swamped' with immigrants, a warning repeated by the Conservative MP Nicholas Fairbairn in the 1992 general election campaign. In May 1993, the Conservative MP Winston Churchill went even further:

> 'Tory backbencher Winston Churchill ignited a blazing row last night by demanding an end to the 'relentless flow' of immigrants. In some of the most inflammatory remarks made in years on the race issue, Mr Churchill, grandson of the wartime leader, said that unless urgent action was taken, the British way of life was under threat.' (*Daily Mail*, 29 May 1993)

It is clear from the 1991 census figures that comments such as these are deliberately provocative. But, the fact that politicians still choose to 'play the race card' in the 1990s is significant. It suggests that they feel there is popular support for such attitudes, a feeling which is confirmed by surveys of public attitudes and by figures such as the number of recorded racial attacks (which rose from 4,383 in 1988 to 7,780 in 1993), the 1992 Crime Survey from the Home Office which recorded 140,000 episodes of racial harassment or attack (*Guardian*, 25 January 1994) and the London Housing Survey which reported in March 1993 that 10% of ethnic minority households had been subjected to racial abuse or attack in 1992.

Ethnic minority groups suffer in other ways too. Figures from the Employment Department (HMSO, 1994) revealed that unemployment rates were higher than average for certain ethnic minority groups, especially amongst Afro-Caribbean Britons, Bangladeshi Britons and Pakistani Britons. And even when people from ethnic minority groups do find jobs, they are unlikely to find high status jobs:

> 'Ethnic and racial minority groups make up some 6% of the population of Great Britain and 4.7% of its working population. They make up 2% of the teaching profession, less than 2% of solicitors, 1.0% of police officers; they are virtually absent from the top levels of the civil service and the armed forces; there are no black judges and very few barristers; and there are none at the top levels of our major financial institutions.' (Edwards, 1992, p.23)

One reason why people from ethnic minority groups are under-represented in the professions is because they have been educationally disadvantaged. But there are signs that this is changing. The Labour Force Surveys carried out between 1988 and 1990 show that some ethnic minority groups have begun to outperform white students. For example, whilst 9% of white Britons aged 16-24 have achieved an A level pass, 11% of African-Asian Britons, 12% of Indian Britons and 13% of Chinese Britons have achieved an A level pass. This trend was confirmed by a study published by the Policy Studies Institute in July 1993. This study showed that 37% of Afro-Caribbean female students gained at least one A level pass compared to 31% of white female students. But, whereas 23% of the white female students with at least one A level pass found professional or managerial jobs, only 16% of the Afro-Caribbean female students with the same qualification were recruited to such jobs.

Activity 5.4

Item A *Racism in Britain (1)*

I first understood the meaning of the term 'racism' when I was a guest of an Asian family in the East End of London. I listened to bricks crashing against the door and heard bellowed abuse. The arrival of the police did not bring this to an end. It was only when the attackers grew tired that they ambled away, each booting the door one last time as he went. The daughter of my hosts kept a diary. It was often written by candlelight because she dared not turn on the light. This is a typical entry: 'When the trouble started, we phoned the police, but they never came. Then my father went to the police station to get the police. We had a witness. The police said they didn't need a witness.' She wrote to her local MP as follows: 'We are an Asian family under attack. My mother has not slept for two months and has had to go to hospital. We cannot furnish or decorate our home because we are too busy looking out through the window day and night.' The letter was quoted in Question Time and the Prime Minister said that the matter would be 'taken up'. It wasn't.

Adapted from Pilger, 1994.

Item B *Racism in Britain (2)*

Race and Prejudice

	1983	1987	1991
Racial prejudice in Britain is now:			
Worse than in the past	43	48	23
Same as in the past	36	34	49
Better than in the past	16	12	24
Prejudice compared to 5 years ago is:			
More	45	50	24
Less	16	13	24
About the same	36	35	50
In 5 years time it is likely to be:			
More	42	46	21
Less	17	12	25
About the same	36	37	50
How would you describe yourself?			
Very prejudiced	4	4	2
A little prejudiced	31	34	29
Not prejudiced at all	64	60	68
How much prejudice is there against Asians?			
A lot	54	62	58
A little	37	30	35
Hardly any	6	6	4
Don't know	3	2	3
How much prejudice is there against blacks?			
A lot	50	57	50
A little	40	33	41
Hardly any	7	7	7
Don't know	3	2	3

This table is based on a Social Attitudes Survey carried out in 1992.

Item C *Education and ethnicity*

Students whose highest qualification is:	Ethnic group (figures in %)								
	White	Afro Caribbean	African - Asian	Indian	Pakistani	Bangladeshi	Chinese	African	Other
A level or higher	33	30	41	36	18	5	44	40	28
Just A level (or equivalent)	26	26	26	27	15	3	24	30	18
Just GCSE (or equivalent)	30	28	20	25	18	16	31	30	31
No qualification	20	21	18	22	48	54	15	7	20

This table is based on information provided by the Labour Force Surveys, 1988-90.

Item D *Racism in Britain (3)*

This poster was produced by the Commission for Racial Equality (CRE) as part of a three year campaign to combat racism.

Item E *Ethnic minority groups*

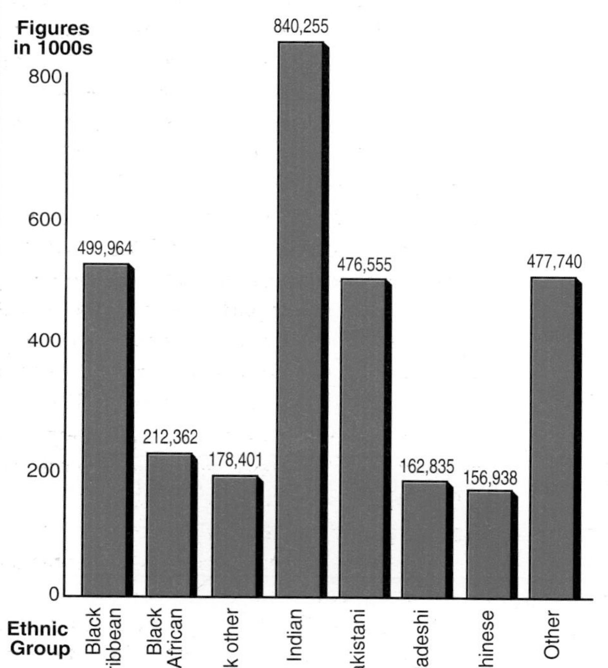

This graph is based on data collected in the 1991 census.

Item F *Racism in Britain (4)*

One of the largest car hire firms in Northern England has been accused of crude racial discrimination by the Commission for Racial Equality (CRE). The company, Salford Van Hire, charged customers different deposits according to the colour of their skin. White customers were asked to pay £50, but black and Asian customers were asked for £100. The CRE has ordered the company to cease this practice. It will monitor the company's procedures for five years. The CRE's inquiry was launched after former employees made allegations to the CRE. The allegations were confirmed when white and Asian CRE investigators made a series of undercover visits. They received written quotations with different deposit rates. The company denied the accusation but cooperated with the investigation and agreed to take measures to prevent accusations being made in the future. A company spokesman said: 'We have disputed this but have to accept their findings. We suggested that discrimination over deposits was not connected with race but with the age and record of drivers. We now charge all drivers over the age of 25 the same deposit. Our reception staff at Leeds have been told that there must be no discrimination on the basis of religion or race and we have introduced staff training to ensure that we are never accused of this sort of thing again.'

Adapted from the *Guardian*, 4 June 1994.

Questions

1. Using Items A-F, give arguments for and against the view that Britain is moving towards racial harmony.
2. What conclusions about British people's attitudes can you draw from Item B?
3. a) 'Ethnicity is an important social factor.' Explain this statement using Items C and E.
   b) What use should politicians make of the information in Item C?
4. a) What is the point being made by the poster in Item D?
   b) Explain why a three year campaign is necessary.

3 The social impact of economic change

Key Issues

1. How has de-industrialisation affected Britain's workforce?
2. How has the role of trade unions developed?

3.1 De-industrialisation

In the 19th century, Britain's wealth was primarily derived from its manufacturing base. The majority of the working population was employed in the extraction of raw materials and in manufacturing industries rather than in service industries. But today, the position is the reverse. Manufacturing industries have declined whilst service industries have grown.

The decline of Britain's manufacturing base has been described as 'de-industrialisation' (see chapter 15, section 3.1 for a more detailed account of this process). Although de-industrialisation began before 1979, since then the process has accelerated. Between 1979 and 1991, for example, one in three manufacturing jobs was lost. In 1994, manufacturing jobs accounted for just 20% of those in employment, whilst service industries accounted for 75% of jobs.

The consequences of de-industrialisation

The traditional view of British working practices can be summarised as follows. In the years following the Second World War, the labour force was predominantly male. Men expected to work full-time in a single job for many years, even for the whole of their working lives. Unmarried women might work, but they would be expected to stop work once they were married. There was a general expectation that there would be 'full' employment.

This traditional view has been challenged by the process of de-industrialisation which has led to a changed labour force, new working practices and new employment levels.

The first point to make is that, in the 1990s, the labour force is no longer predominantly male. According to Victor Keegan:

> 'Since the start of the 1970s, the size of the male labour force has risen by barely more than 300,000 to 15.4 million while the female labour force has increased by 3.1 million to 11.7 million. But these figures conceal what is happening underneath because the "labour force" is a portmanteau total which includes the self-employed, the unemployed, the armed forces and people on training and related schemes. All of these are disproportionately male preserves. Strip them out and you find that in the latest month in which figures are available (December 1993) the actual number of women with jobs was 10.53 million compared with 10.85 million men with jobs.' (*Guardian*, 9 April 1994)

This growing number of women in work is both a reflection of and a consequence of the process of de-industrialisation. Traditionally, many men had jobs in manufacturing industries. But these jobs have disappeared as Britain's manufacturing base has declined. Whilst jobs in the manufacturing industries have disappeared, jobs in service industries have been created. Many of these new jobs have been taken by women rather than by men.

One reason why many jobs in service industries have been taken by women rather than by men is that many of these jobs are part-time (and low paid). Recent research has shown that the number of part-time jobs has risen dramatically since 1979:

> 'The number of part-timers in Britain has risen by a third since the Conservatives came to office [in 1979]. There are now just under 21 million employees of which 5.88 million (28%) work part-time. Fifteen years ago, when unemployment was lower and manufacturing played a more decisive role in the economy, there were more than 22 million employees of which 4.4 million (19.7%) worked part-time. The extent of part-time working, however, varies greatly between the sexes. While employees are now divided almost equally between men and women, only 10.5% of men work part-time compared with 46.4% women. Put another way, four in five part-timers are women. There is also a major variation between industries with 7.3% of production industry employees working part-time and 35.6% of service industry workers.' (*Labour Research*, July 1994, p.6)

Many employers prefer to take on part-timers because part-timers do not make the same demands on employers as full-time workers. Part-timers can be sacked more easily than full-timers, they can be paid lower rates of pay and employers often do not have to pay part-timers' national insurance or pension contributions. At the same time, surveys show that 80% of women are prepared to take part-time work because it is possible to combine part-time work with domestic responsibilities. Men, on the other hand, are often reluctant to take part-time work:

> 'There are now 2.1 million unemployed males (against 630,000 women) many of whom are still locked into a culture shock. They still think of jobs in terms of a Golden Age (not that it seemed golden at the time) which may have vanished for good. They

> can't take the full-time "men's" jobs in industry because there simply aren't enough of them and they are culturally - and financially - unprepared to apply for part-time "women's" jobs.' (*Guardian*, 9 April 1994)

De-industrialisation, therefore, has changed not just the composition of the labour force but the way in which people work. Increasingly, there is a move away from the old style, 'nine to five', full-time jobs to new ways of work. More and more people are job sharing, on 'flexitime' (flexible working hours) or on short-term contracts. In 1993, 1.2 million people were using their homes as an office, thus saving their employers costs such as light, heat and office rent. Some companies have introduced practices such as 'hot desking':

> '[Hot desking] works like this: you check into the office and request a workstation, like checking into a hotel and requesting a room. You are allocated a free desk for a set time and you take your possessions out of a locker and wheel them in a golf caddie to the allotted space. When you have finished, you store them away and relinquish the space to the next user.' (*Guardian*, 3 December 1993)

The advantage for the employer is that hot desking reduces office space costs. Whilst the employee may not like the practice, if the choice is between hot desking and unemployment, then it is likely that the employee will choose to hot desk.

That the choice for many is between unsatisfactory employment or unemployment is a further consequence of de-industrialisation. The decline of Britain's manufacturing base has led to a net loss in the number of jobs available. Whilst the unemployment rate between 1945 and 1979 never rose above one million, since 1979 it has soared. For much of the 1980s, more than 3 million people were unemployed.

High rates of unemployment have resulted in a realignment of the labour force. On the top level, there is the core group of workers with secure, full-time jobs. This group is continually shrinking. Below the core, is the peripheral labour force which consists of part-time employees and employees on temporary contracts. These workers are generally less skilled and receive lower pay than the core group and they can be taken on or laid off according to demand. Below the periphery are the short-term unemployed (people unemployed for less than a year). When demand is high, people in this group move into the periphery. When demand is reduced, people from the periphery join the ranks of the short-term unemployed. And finally, at the bottom, is a large and growing group of long-term unemployed. Members of this group find it incredibly hard to find a job. Many have never had a job. They exist on state benefits and the 'black economy'.

Some authors (for example, Dahrendorf, 1992) have described this group as a separate 'underclass' with a distinct culture - a 'dependency culture' - of its own. Members of this underclass, it is argued, are responsible for their own plight:

> 'When I use the term "underclass" I am indeed focusing on a certain type of poor person defined not by his condition eg long-term unemployed, but by his deplorable behaviour in response to that condition, eg unwilling to take the jobs that are available to him.' (Murray, 1990, p.68)

According to this view from the New Right, members of the underclass choose to live in a cycle of deprivation. Other authors (for example, Walker & Walker, 1994), however, argue that this cycle of deprivation could be broken simply by providing more jobs and a higher level of income.

Activity 5.5

Item A *Unemployment*

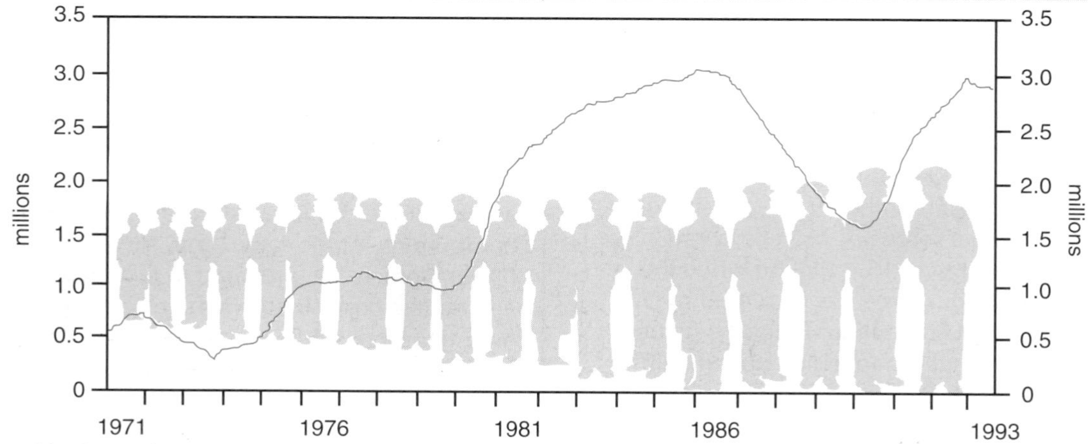

This table shows the number of people claiming unemployment benefit between 1971 and 1993. Between 1979 and 1994, the government changed the way in which unemployment figures were calculated on 23 occasions. On all but one of these occasions the number of people unemployed fell after the adjustment.

Adapted from HMSO, 1994.

Item B *De-industrialisation*

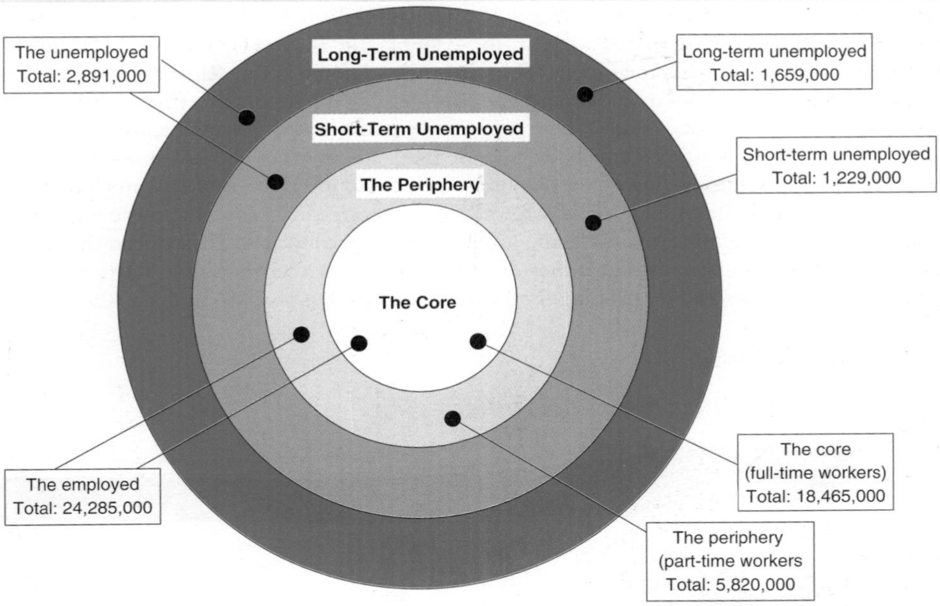

This diagram shows the effect of de-industrialisation on the labour force. All figures are for Spring, 1993.

Adapted from HMSO 1994 and *Employment Gazette*, October 1994.

Item C *The rich and the poor (1)*

Natalie Upperton, aged 24, and her partner Michael Peckett, aged 35 are both unemployed. They have three children aged three, six and ten. They live in a three bedroom house in East Grinstead. They receive £200 a week in state benefits, barely enough to cover their bills and run their battered 14 year old car. East Grinstead is one of the wealthiest areas in the country. 'We're an island surrounded by all that money', said Natalie, 'It costs £2 for a cup of coffee in the high street. We never go there.' Just over an hour's drive from East Grinstead is seriously poor Newham. Every social problem is there: rampant crime, drug dealing, drug taking, unemployment over 20%, poor housing. The Duncombe family (Marina aged 39, Michael aged 52 and their two children aged eight and 11), however, choose to live there even though their income is more than £50,000 a year. Marina explains that you get a lot more house for your money in Newham. Their four bedroomed Victorian house cost £38,000 13 years ago and is now worth about £120,000. Also, Newham is convenient for the City where Michael works. The Duncombes did consider moving to another area to find better schools for their children but in the end they sent them to a private school in East London. The Duncombes have no plans to leave Newham. They certainly would not want to swap with the Uppertons of East Grinstead.

Adapted from the *Observer*, 3 June 1994.

Item D *The rich and the poor (2)*

(i) Growing poverty, 1961-91

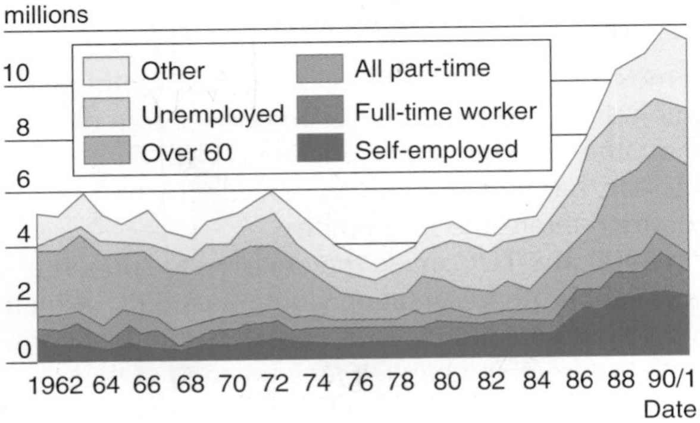

This table shows the number of individuals receiving below half the national income 1961-91.

Adapted from the *Financial Times*, 3 June 1994

(ii) The distribution of wealth, 1979-92

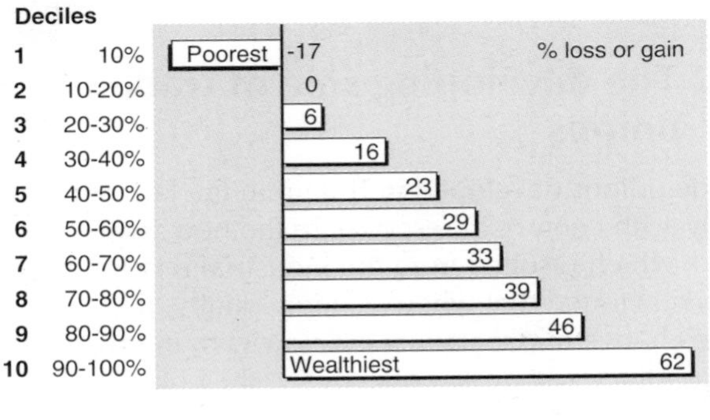

In this table, the population is divided into deciles (10% blocks). The table shows how the distribution of wealth changed between 1979 and 1992

Item E *Part-time Britain*

Part-time and casual jobs are usually among the lowest paid and least skilled. All too often a part-time job is a last resort for people displaced from full-time jobs. Last year, for example, the Burton Group, one of Britain's biggest retailers, decided that too many shop assistants spent too much time standing about when business was slack. To overcome this, it made 2,800 shop assistants redundant and took on 7,000 part-time staff. This has been resented by some members of staff. One shop manager said, 'There is a definite management policy to cut staff hours to 20 hours or below. Half the staff, mainly youngsters, came back because they had no other choice. As soon as they see a full-time job, they're off. Quality of service is down and the job is more difficult. There is not as much training, no continuity, no loyalty and not the same standards of service to the customers.' Usdaw, the trade union for shop assistants, says that some shop assistants are now being given 'zero hour' contracts. These mean that the assistant has to wait to be called to work in busy periods. But if they are not called, they receive no pay. Staff also complain of no overtime, poor promotion prospects and no training. Employees working less than 16 hours a week are not entitled to most fringe benefits.

Adapted from the *Observer*, 17 April 1994.

Item F *De-industrialised Britain - a cartoonist's view*

This cartoon appeared in the *Guardian* on 13 June, 1994.

Questions

1. Judging from the items in this Activity what have been the social consequences of economic change?
2. What do Items A-D tell us about the distribution of wealth in Britain in the 1990s? What changes have taken place?
3. What is the social impact of growing numbers of part-time jobs likely to be? Use Item E in your answer.
4. What point is Item F making about the social consequences of economic change?

3.2 The developing role of trade unions

Trade unions developed in Britain in the late 18th and early 19th century in response to the new ways of work which resulted from the industrial revolution. Workers found that whereas, individually, they had little chance of persuading employers to improve pay or conditions at work, collectively, they had a great deal of bargaining power. As a result, workers in the same industry set up organisations whose function was to represent them in disputes with their employers. These organisations became known as trade unions. By the end of the 19th century, workers in most industries had the opportunity of joining a union. In 1868, a number of unions set up a national body, the Trades Union Congress (TUC). Since 1868, the TUC has met annually to consider matters of common interest to its members.

In 1900, the TUC made the decision to support a new Labour Representation Committee (LRC) which would put up candidates in parliamentary elections. Unions agreed to charge a levy on each of their members to help fund the election of these candidates. In 1906, the LRC changed its name to the Labour party. The Labour party and the trade unions have maintained close ties ever since (see chapter 8, sections 3.1 and 3.2).

Although the first unions encountered a great deal of opposition from employers and governments, by the end of the 19th century, they had managed to gain legal recognition and over two million members. Trade union membership had grown to 7.8 million by 1945 and reached its peak of 13.4 million in 1979.

The unions and politics

Although the main role of trade unions is to protect and improve the pay and conditions of the workers whom they represent (an industrial and economic function), there is an underlying political element in their work. By organising and representing the workers, the unions ensure that employers cannot hire and fire at will and that the interests of the workers must be taken into account. A union's ultimate weapon is to call a strike. By withdrawing their labour, the workforce ensures that the employer loses profits. A strike or a threat of a strike, therefore, puts pressure on the employer to meet the union's demands. On a large scale, this can have important political implications. Since unions represent many different groups of workers, it is possible that if one group is in dispute, then unions representing other groups will take action in support of this group. There is, in short, the possibility that the workers, rather than the employers or the politicians, will use their collective power to dictate what industrial policy should be. It is because this is a possibility that many employers and politicians have been or remain hostile to trade unions.

On occasion, the reaction to union action has been dramatic. In 1926, for example, when the unions called for a general strike (a strike by all union members), the Conservative government was convinced that the unions intended to overthrow the government. A national emergency was declared and troops and volunteers used to break the strike. In fact, the General Strike lasted for just 13 days. Its defeat was followed by the passing of anti-union legislation (just as anti-union legislation was passed by the government after the miners' strike of 1984-85). Despite enduring hostility from the government on occasions, however, trade union links with the Labour party have ensured that the point of view of the unions is represented in Parliament.

The decline of unions since 1979

Governments and employers have not always been hostile to unions. During the Second World War and for the following 30 years, unions were tolerated and even involved in policy making at government level. This was the period of 'corporatism' (see chapter 10, section 3.1). The setting up of the welfare state after 1945 meant a huge growth in the public sector. Since the government was responsible for setting the wages and working conditions of public sector employees, it was imperative for it to maintain good relations with the unions (since strikes in the public sector could be politically damaging). Besides, the successful management of the public sector would ensure national economic success. Between 1945 and 1979, Labour and Conservative governments alike included trade unionists in policy making as a matter of course.

The involvement of unions in government policy making did not, however, prevent significant industrial disputes from taking place. In the 1970s, for example, a number of major strikes were called. A miners' strike in 1974 significantly contributed to the downfall of Edward Heath's government and the so-called 'winter of discontent' of 1978-79 saw widespread strike action amongst public sector employees. As a result, by 1979 unions were being blamed by opponents for Britain's economic decline and polls showed that a majority of the population agreed that unions had too much power (see also, chapter 3, p.46). Since then, not only have unions been excluded from government policy making, they have also been the subject of a number of hostile laws (see below, Activity 5.6, Item A).

Throughout the 1980s, union membership declined rapidly. This was, in part, due to public disaffection with the unions and, in part, due to the rapid decline of manufacturing and other strongly unionised industries (such as the coal industry). This combination of government hostility to unions and de-industrialisation has forced unions to reconsider their role, as John Monks, General Secretary of the TUC, makes clear in the following passage:

> 'The re-awakening of trade unions as a central force in public life will depend on our efforts to convince workers, especially those in newly developing industries and services, that it is in their interests to join and play an active part in the movement. Equally, it is up to unions to show to employers, politicians and the community that we have a positive contribution to make to the development of public policy. The new trade unionism will not be the same as that of the 1960s or 1970s...We are determined to focus our resources on the key issues, such as jobs, the rights of people at work and developing a union response to new management styles.'
> (*Guardian*, 31 August 1994)

Activity 5.6

Item A *Trade union legislation 1979-93*

A. Employment Act 1980
1. No new closed shop agreements to be made unless at least 80% of workers vote for them in a ballot.
2. Employees who lose their jobs through refusal to join a union on principle to be eligible for compensation.
3. Government to fund union ballots.
4. Picketing and secondary action severely limited.

B. Employment Act 1982
1. Existing closed shop agreements to be put to the vote and only to remain if at least 80% of workers vote in favour.
2. Compensation (See A.2 above) to be increased.
3. Sympathy action, 'political' strikes and action against non-unionised companies made illegal.

C. Trade Union Act 1984
1. Strikes only lawful if majority vote for them in a ballot.
2. Union leaders to be elected if members request it.
3. Unions obliged to hold ballot every 10 years on whether members want to continue to pay into the political fund (which goes to the Labour party).

D. Employment Act 1988
1. Illegal to dismiss worker for not joining union, even if 80%+ have voted for closed shop.
2. Illegal to strike in support of closed shop agreement.
3. Illegal for union to discipline a member who refuses to join in strike action.

E. Employment Act 1990
1. Illegal for employer to refuse job on grounds that applicant does not belong to a union.
2. All secondary or sympathy action illegal.

F. Trade Union Reform Act 1993
1. Unions prevented from poaching each other's members.
2. Union members must write to employer every three years if they want employer to deduct union dues from their pay.

Adapted from Dorey, 1991 and Allan et al., 1994.

Item B *Trade union membership*

(i) Number of unions and members, 1896-1986

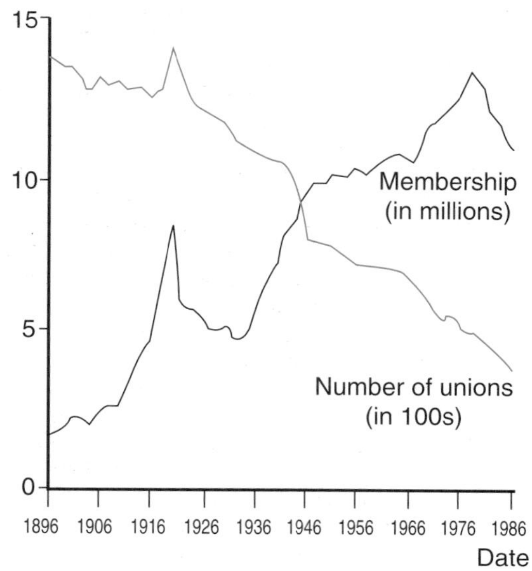

This graph shows the number of trade unions and the number of union members between 1896 and 1986.

Adapted from Pelling, 1987 and the *Times*. 5 September 1994.

(ii) Union membership, 1979-93

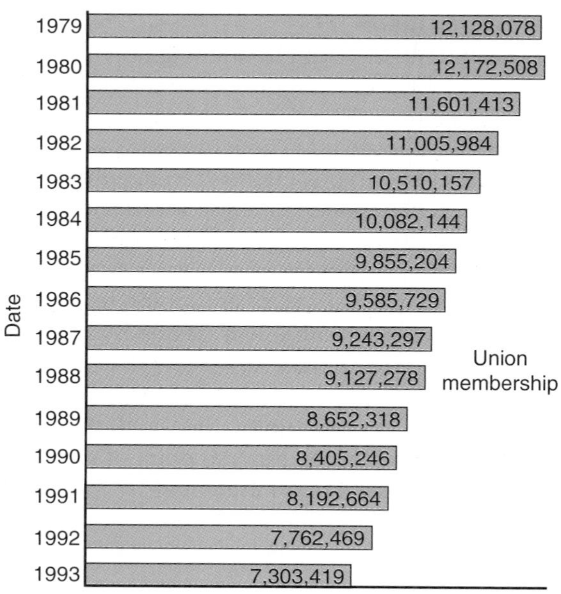

This table shows the decline in union membership between 1979 and 1993.

Item C *Strike action*

Number of working days lost through strikes (in millions)			
1900-09	35.46	1950-59	32.51
1910-19	132.50	1960-69	35.55
1920-29	332.41	1970-79	128.69
1930-39	29.79	1980-89	70.11
1940-49	20.24	1990-94	3.80

Adapted from Pelling, 1987 and HMSO, 1994.

Item D *Unions in the 1990s*

This cartoon was produced in November 1992 when London Underground considered going on strike

Item E *The need for unions*

There are two worlds of work in Britain. On the one hand, there are the backstreet sweatshops - dirty, noisy, smelly, with an atmosphere of fear. One wrong word can lead to the sack. Working conditions are poor and wages as low as £1 an hour. On the other hand, there are world class companies where union officials and managers are proud of the changes they have made. In these companies, managers treat workers with respect. They invest in training. They solve problems together. I am sure that it is no coincidence that out of Britain's top 50 companies, 47 recognise trade unions. But what depresses me is the government's attitude towards these two worlds of work. Certainly, the government praises our top companies. But everything else it does, encourages employers to exploit their workers. For example, in 1993 it abolished the wages councils that set minimums for pay in areas such as catering. The message to employers was clear - pay as little as you like, it doesn't matter to us. The result is that people who might expect a living wage are forced to turn to the state for income support. And the taxpayer ends up subsidising employers who are too mean or inefficient to pay a decent wage. Then, there is the emphasis on 'flexibility' and 'deregulation'. These words have a sour taste for workers who know that 'flexibility' means a short-term contract when they want long-term security and 'deregulation' means the removal of redress against exploitation. My job is to make the case that Britain works better when workers are treated well and when the role of trade unions is recognised by employers. But I also believe that what happens at work has wider consequences. If society is to be stable and secure, people need to feel secure about their jobs.

Adapted from an article by John Monks, General Secretary of the TUC, the *Daily Telegraph*, 2 March 1994.

Item F *Trade unions and new working practices*

Margaret Prosser, chair of the TUC women's committee, recently visited a school where the cleaners (who were all women) had just suffered a pay cut from £3.50 an hour to £3. At the same time, their hours were cut, but they were still expected to clean the same school to the same high standard. One of the women asked her what membership of a union could do to help her. Prosser suggests that, in order to encourage her and women like her to join a union, it is necessary for unions to get their own house in order. For example, unions should argue for equal pay for work of equal value in pay negotiations. They should consider maternity rights, rights for part-time workers, childcare provision and sexual harassment. They should, in short, offer women what they want rather than what they think they want. Prosser identifies two main priorities. The first arises from the recent House of Lords ruling which established that part-timers should enjoy the same employment rights as full-timers. Prosser suggests that unions identify the women workers who have suffered discrimination on this and ensure they take advantage of the ruling. The second priority should be a campaign for a comprehensive network of affordable childcare. Prosser argues that childcare provision makes the difference as to what sort of job millions of women can have or even whether or not they can work. But, Britain lags behind the rest of Europe.

Adapted from the *Guardian*, 24 May 1994.

Questions

1. a) Judging from Items B and C what were the consequences of the legislation outlined in Item A?
   b) Can you think of any other reasons to explain the trends shown in Items B and C?
2. Look at Item D. What point is the cartoonist making about the image of trade unions in the 1990s?
3. Do trade unions have a role to play in the future? Use Items E and F in your answer.

References

Allan et al. (1994) Allan, P., Benyon J. & McCormick B., *Focus on Britain 1994*, Perennial Publications, 1994.

Almond & Verba (1963) Almond, G. & Verba, S. (eds), *The Civic Culture: Political Attitudes and Democracy in Five Nations*, Princeton University Press, 1963.

Almond & Verba (1981) Almond, G. & Verba, S. (eds), *The Civic Culture Revisited*, Little Brown (Boston, USA), 1981.

Bassnett (1986) Bassnett, S., *Feminist Experiences*, Allen & Unwin, 1986.

Benyon (1994) Benyon, J., 'Profile of society' in *Allan et al. (1994)*.

Bonnet (1994) Bonnet, K., 'Power and politics' in *Haralambos (1994)*.

Bouchier (1983) Bouchier, D., *The Feminist Challenge*, Macmillan, 1983.

Butler & Stokes (1971) Butler, D. & Stokes, D., *Political Change in Britain*, Penguin, 1971.

Dahrendorf (1992) Dahrendorf, R., 'Footnotes to the discussion' in *Smith, 1992*.

Dorey (1991) Dorey, P. 'Politics and the trade unions', *Politics Review*, Vol. 1, September 1991.

Edwards (1992) Edwards, J., 'The politics of racial equality', *Politics Review*, Vol.2, No.2, November 1992.

Forbes (1991) Forbes, I., 'The politics of gender' in *Wale (1991)*.

Forbes (1994) Forbes, I., 'Gender and politics in the 1990s' in *Wale (1994)*.

Freidan (1963) Freidan, B., *The Feminine Mystique*, Norton (New York), 1963.

Gilroy (1987) Gilroy, P., *There Ain't No Black in the Union Jack*, Hutchinson, 1987.

Haralambos (1994) Haralambos, M. (ed.), *Developments in Sociology*, Vol. 10, Causeway Press, 1994.

HMSO (1994) Central Statistical Office, *Social Trends*, Vol.24, HMSO, 1994.

Kavanagh (1981) Kavanagh, D., 'Political culture in Great Britain: the decline of the civic culture?' in *Almond & Verba (1981)*.

Kavanagh (1983) Kavanagh, D., *British Politics. Continuities and Change*, Oxford University Press, 1983.

Lash & Urry (1987) Lash, S. & Urry, J., *The End of Organised Capitalism*, Polity, 1987.

Miliband (1972) Miliband, R., *The State in Capitalist Society*, Weidenfeld and Nicholson, 1972.

Miliband (1989) Miliband, R., *Divided Societies*, Oxford University Press, 1989.

Mitchell (1971) Mitchell, J., *Woman's Estate*, Penguin, 1971.

Modood (1988) Modood, T., 'Black, racial equality and Asian identity', *New Community*, Vol.14, No.3, 1988.

Moran (1989) Moran, M., *Politics and Society in Britain. An Introduction*, Macmillan, 1989.

Murray (1990) Murray, C., *The Emerging British Underclass*, Institute of Economic Affairs, 1990.

Pelling (1987) Pelling, H., *'A History of British Trade Unionism'*, Pelican, 1987.

Pilger (1994) Pilger, J., 'The rise of respectable fascism', *New Statesman and Society*, 15 April 1994.

Pimlott (1989) Pimlott, B., 'Is the postwar consensus a myth?', *Contemporary Record*, Summer 1989.

Pulzer (1967) Pulzer, P.G., *Political Representation and Elections*, Allen & Unwin, 1967.

Runnymede (1991) Runnymede Trust Bulletin, No.247, July/August 1991.

Rush (1992) Rush, M., *Politics and Society. An Introduction to Political Sociology*, Harvester Wheatsheaf, 1992.

Saunders (1990) Saunders, P., *Social Class and Stratification*, Routledge, 1990.

Scarman (1981) Lord Scarman, *The Scarman Report*, Penguin, 1981.

Smith (1992) Smith, D. (ed.), *Understanding the Underclass*, Policy Studies Institute, 1992.

Strachey (1928) Strachey, R., *The Cause*, Virago, 1979.

Taylor (1993) Taylor, S., 'The politics of immigration and race in Britain' in *Wale (1993)*.

Wale (1991) Wale, W. (ed.), *Developments in Politics*, Vol.2, Causeway Press, 1991.

Wale (1993) Wale, W. (ed.), *Developments in Politics*, Vol.4, Causeway Press, 1993.

Wale (1994) Wale, W. (ed.), *Developments in Politics*, Vol.5, Causeway Press, 1994.

Walker & Walker (1994) Walker, C. & Walker, A., 'Poverty and the poor' in *Haralambos*, 1994.

Walvin (1984) Walvin, J., *Passage to Britain*, Penguin, 1984.

Westergaard & Resler (1976) Westergaard, J. & Resler, H., *Class in a Capitalist Society*, Penguin, 1976.

Wilson (1984) Wilson, A., *Finding a Voice*, Virago, 1984.

6 Europe and the international context

Introduction

All too often, Europe has been portrayed as something out there - just another factor in Britain's external relations, albeit a factor which can influence domestic decisions. Such a picture is misleading. The European Union (EU) is far more significant than any other international organisation to which Britain belongs.

When Britain decided to join the European Economic Community (as it then was) in 1972, the government signed a number of treaties. These treaties have all the characteristics of a written constitution and are binding within the UK. The treaties set out the powers and responsibilities of the European Union's institutions and their decision making procedures. They also provide the means of settling disputes through the European Court. Since 1973, membership of the European Union has made an impact on a wide range of domestic policies - including trade policy, agricultural policy, environmental policy and social policy, to give just a few examples.

With the passing of the Single European Act in 1986 and the ratification of the Maastricht Treaty in 1993, the ties between member states have become closer and there is pressure to make them closer still. Some member states want to move towards political and economic union. Others (including Britain) are concerned that this would mean an unacceptable loss of sovereignty. In Britain, there is intense debate over the exact role that Britain should be playing within the European Union. Some politicians have even argued that Britain should withdraw from the EU altogether.

This chapter concentrates on the European Union, but it also looks at how Britain's role and status in the world has changed since 1945. In particular, it examines the international organisations to which Britain belongs (such as Nato, the United Nations and the Commonwealth) and considers the role which Britain plays within these organisations.

Chapter summary

Part 1 looks at the **development of the European Union**. Why was it first set up and how has it developed since then?

Part 2 focuses on the **organisation of the EU**. It looks at how decisions are made and the balance of power between the various institutions.

Part 3 analyses the present **debate over the direction which the EU should take**. Should it cement ties and become a federation or loosen ties and become a confederation of nation states?

Part 4 examines **Britain's changing role and status in the world since 1945**. How has Britain's role changed? What is Britain's relationship with the international organisations to which it belongs?

1 The development of the European Union

Key Issues

1. What led to the foundation of the European Economic Community in 1958?
2. Why was Britain not one of the founder members of the EEC?
3. Why did Britain decide to join the EEC after refusing to join at first?

Historical background

The term 'European Union' has evolved as the organisation has evolved. At first, the organisation was known as the 'European Economic Community' (EEC) or 'Common Market', but after the Single European Act was passed in 1986, the name changed to 'European Community' (EC). In 1993, after the ratification of the Maastricht Treaty, the name changed again from European Community to 'European Union' (EU). The evolution of the name reflects changes in the structure and nature of the organisation.

Three factors are central to the origins of the EEC. First, at the end of the Second World War, European politicians were very aware that both world wars had followed a similar pattern. Twice, Germany had invaded France through Belgium, Luxembourg and the Netherlands (the 'Benelux' countries).

It seemed to some politicians, therefore, that the best way of avoiding a third war was for European countries to work together politically, economically and perhaps even militarily. Second, the vast majority of countries in Europe had been involved in the Second World War. Not only had a great deal of fighting taken place in these countries, the economies in many of them had been stretched to breaking point. As a result, European countries did not have the resources to rebuild their economies on their own. Economic necessity led them towards cooperation. And third, the end of the Second World War was soon followed by the outbreak of the Cold War. Europe quickly became divided between the East (dominated by the Soviet Union) and the West (dominated by the USA). The Cold War encouraged Western European countries to cooperate with each other.

First moves towards union

The idea of a united Europe was first put forward in public by the British Prime Minister, Winston Churchill, in a speech made on 19 September 1946. Churchill advocated the building of a 'United States of Europe'. It is ironic that a British politician should have been the first to suggest European union since Britain refused to become a founding member of the EEC.

The first step towards a united Europe was made by the Benelux countries when they joined together to establish the Benelux customs union which came into effect in January 1948.

This was soon followed by the setting up of the Organisation for European Economic Cooperation (OEEC). The OEEC was set up to administer 'Marshall Aid' - a massive programme of financial aid set up by the USA to encourage economic recovery in Europe ($13 billion was distributed in four years). Although Marshall Aid (named after American Secretary of State, George Marshall) was offered to East European countries, they refused it on the grounds that it would lead to American interference in their domestic affairs (see p.153). Consequently, members of the OEEC all came from Western Europe.

The Schuman plan

The next important step on the road to European union came in 1950 when Jean Monnet, a French civil servant, and Robert Schuman, French Foreign Secretary, formulated what became known as the Schuman plan. Their aim was twofold. First, they wanted to promote economic recovery in both France and West Germany by pooling both countries' coal and steel industries. And second, they hoped to make war between the two countries impossible by placing their key industries under joint authority.

The Schuman plan was announced in 1950 and led to the creation of the European Coal and Steel Community (ECSC). The ECSC came into operation in 1952 after six countries (France, West Germany, Italy and the Benelux countries) signed the Treaty of Paris in 1951. The aim of the ECSC was to:

> 'Establish a common market for coal and steel, to ensure supplies, to promote expansion and modernisation of production and to provide better employment conditions.' (HMSO, 1992, p.3)

In addition, the ECSC was the first European organisation to have a **supranational** structure. A supranational organisation is one in which institutions are created which have powers above that of any individual nation's government. The supranational structure of the ECSC became the blueprint for the structure of the EEC.

By the time the ECSC was set up, disagreements over the future shape of Europe had begun to emerge. The British government was particularly suspicious of supranational organisations, favouring instead intergovernmental organisations (in which each member state has the right to veto any measure, to protect its national interests). Geddes notes that:

> 'Tension between supranationalists and intergovernmentalists became apparent at the May 1948 Congress of Europe in the Hague, where over 700 prominent Europeans met to discuss the future of the continent. The outcome of the meeting was the creation of the Council of Europe in May 1949...Britain's preference for intergovernmentalism prevailed in the Council of Europe: decisions in its Council of Ministers are taken on the basis of unanimity.' (Geddes, 1993, p.21)

Whilst the Council of Europe represented a triumph for intergovernmentalists, the creation of the ECSC represented a triumph for supranationalists.

The Messina conference and the creation of the EEC

In 1955, the foreign ministers of the ECSC member states met at Messina in Italy and agreed to set up a committee to consider further progress towards European integration. This committee's report led to the drawing up of the two Treaties of Rome which were signed by the six ECSC members in March 1957. One Treaty established the European Atomic Energy Community (Euratom) to coordinate members' development of nuclear energy. The second set up the European Economic Community:

> 'Its founding Treaty was premised on an "ever closer union of the peoples of Europe". It abolished trade barriers and customs duties and established a common external tariff, thereby making the EEC a customs union. The EEC was also designed to promote the free movement of people, goods, services and capital within a common market. The member states transferred to the EEC powers to conclude trading agreements with international organisations on

their behalf.' (Geddes, 1993, p.24)

The EEC formally came into existence on 1 January 1958.

Britain's early relations with Europe

Although the British government was invited to join the negotiations which led to the foundation of the EEC, it refused to become involved, on the grounds that joining a supranational organisation would endanger national sovereignty. It was argued that if Britain joined the EEC, it would lose the right to follow independent economic and defence policies. There were a number of reasons for Britain's aloofness. Britain was geographically separate from mainland Europe and, unlike its neighbours, had not been subject to conquest in recent times. In addition, Britain still had strong ties with countries outside Europe. Although the British Empire broke up after 1945, Britain still retained trading links with former colonies, especially those in the British Commonwealth. And third, the British government believed that it had a 'special relationship' with the USA.

In response to the creation of the EEC, Britain attempted to establish a free trade area which covered all members of the OEEC (including the six members of the EEC). France, however, rejected this idea and negotiations failed. Instead, Britain and six countries which belonged to the OEEC but not to the EEC (Austria, Norway, Sweden, Denmark, Portugal and Switzerland) formed the European Free Trade Association (EFTA) in 1960. The aim of EFTA was to dismantle barriers to trade between members (so that trade would increase amongst members) and to provide a base from which to negotiate with the EEC over the creation of a single European market. During the l960s, however, it became apparent that Britain's trade was growing faster with the EEC than it was with EFTA.

Britain's attempts to join the EEC

When the British government realised that the EEC was becoming a powerful trading bloc, it applied to join the EEC. Britain's first application was made in 1961. Negotiations continued until 1963 when the French President, Charles de Gaulle, vetoed Britain's application. Britain reapplied in 1967, but again this application was vetoed by de Gaulle. It was only after de Gaulle retired in 1969 that the British government was able to negotiate its entry into the EEC. In 1971, the Prime Minister, Edward Heath, held talks with de Gaulle's successor Pompidou. The following year, Heath signed the Treaty of Accession and on 1 January 1973, Britain became a member of the EEC (together with two other new members - Ireland and Denmark).

The EEC referendum, 1975

When Britain joined the EEC in 1973, it was confronted by a number of problems. First, most British politicians did not share the vision of those Euro-enthusiasts who looked forward to the creation of a European superstate. Although the British government, by joining the EEC, had accepted the EEC's supranational structure, many politicians accepted this only reluctantly. Second, friction arose because Britain had not been a member from the start. As a result, Britain had to accept existing policies and regulations which it had played no part in developing. Third, there was a price to pay for membership, in the short term at least. Since Britain had substantial trading links with non-EEC countries (especially Commonwealth countries) its contribution to EEC funds was particularly high (trading with non-EEC countries was penalised). On the other hand, because Britain's agricultural sector was highly efficient, it did not benefit from the EEC's Common Agricultural Policy (CAP) as much as other member states.

Rather than addressing each of these problems and tackling them head-on:

> 'British membership of the EC was advocated on pragmatic economic grounds. Britain thought it was joining a common market - an economic organisation - and played down the political consequences of membership.' (Geddes, 1993, p.33)

Concern about membership of the EEC came to a head after the general election of 1974. The new Labour government came to office with the pledge to renegotiate Britain's terms of membership and to hold a referendum. This referendum was held in June 1975. There was a 64% turnout and 67% voted in favour of remaining in the EEC.

Margaret Thatcher and the EEC

On becoming Prime Minister in 1979, Margaret Thatcher launched an attack on the EEC because Britain's contribution to the EEC budget was too high (Britain was the second largest contributor to the EEC budget even though it had the third lowest GDP per capita of all members). The result was a long and acrimonious battle over Britain's contribution. The issue was not settled until 1984 when a rebate was agreed.

The second major development in the Thatcher years was the passing of the Single European Act in 1986. This Act was supported by Thatcher and her allies on the grounds that a free, single market would mean greater deregulation and less governmental intervention (and, therefore, greater economic growth). It was also supported by the President of the European Commission, Jacques Delors, however, on the grounds that it would restart the move towards greater European integration. The result has been an ongoing debate about the future direction of Europe. This debate has yet to be resolved.

Activity 6.1

Item A *The evolution of the EEC*

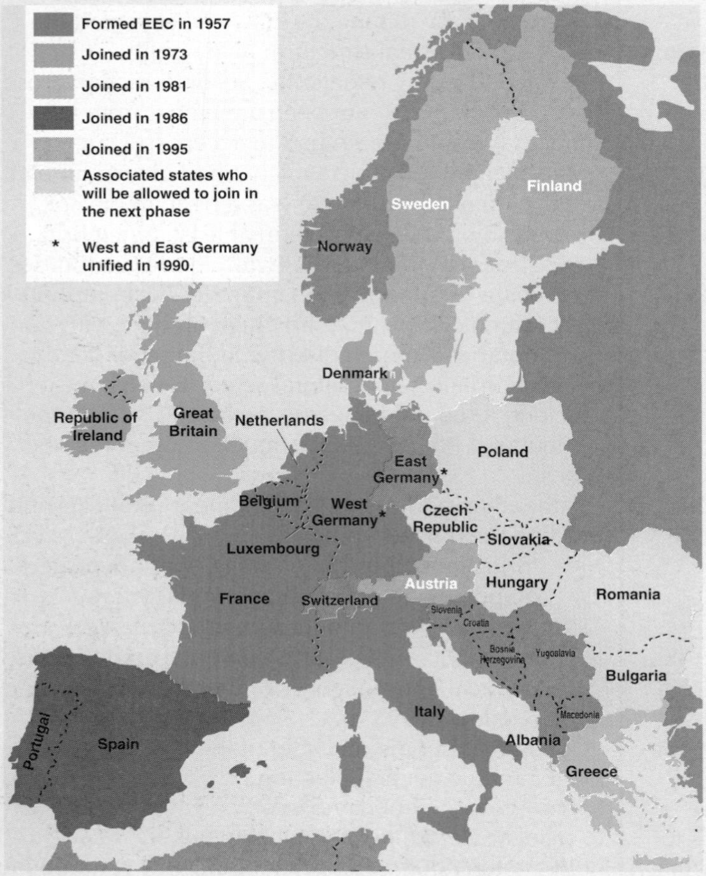

Item B *De Gaulle's veto (1)*

(i) After refusing to join the community we are building, after creating a free trade area with six other states (EFTA) and after trying to prevent a real beginning for the Common Market, Britain has now applied for membership - on its own terms. But, Britain is insular, maritime, linked by trade, markets and food supply to very different and often very distant lands. How can Britain be brought into this system? How far is it possible for Britain to accept a truly common tariff? For this would involve giving up all Commonwealth preferences and treating as null and void obligations entered into with the Free Trade Area. It is possible that one day Britain might manage to transform itself sufficiently to become part of the EEC. In that case, the Six would open their door and France would raise no obstacle.

Adapted from a speech made by President de Gaulle in January 1963.

(ii) To tell the truth, Britain's attitude is easy to explain. Having seen more clearly the great changes sweeping the world - the enormous power of the USA, the growing power of the Soviet Union, the revitalised power of the EEC, the new power of China and the growing independence of Commonwealth countries, its future is at stake. Moreover, financial difficulties and social problems force Britain to seek a framework both to safeguard itself and to play a leading role in the world.

Adapted from a speech made by President de Gaulle in September 1967.

Item C *A common tariff*

Trade between the EEC and the rest of the world was regulated so that every EEC member charged the same tariff (tax on imported goods) when trading with non-members. This had two advantages. It encouraged trade within the EEC and it prevented non-members from selling goods to the member with the lowest tariff on the understanding that this member would then sell on the goods to the other members. This common external tariff had been achieved by 1968.

Item D *De Gaulle's veto (2)*

"I suspect you of driving under the influence of America"

This cartoon was produced in 1967. It shows De Gaulle (left) and the British Prime Minister, Harold Wilson.

Item E *Britain's economy*

(i)

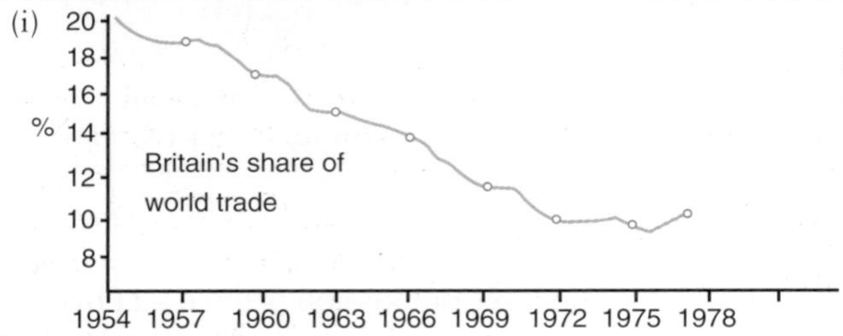

(ii)

Industrial production 1959-67			
	1959	**1963**	**1967**
Britain	105	119	133
W. Germany	107	137	158
France	101	129	155
Italy	112	166	212
USA	113	133	168
Japan	120	212	347

This table gives comparisons with industrial production in 1958 (=100)

(iii)

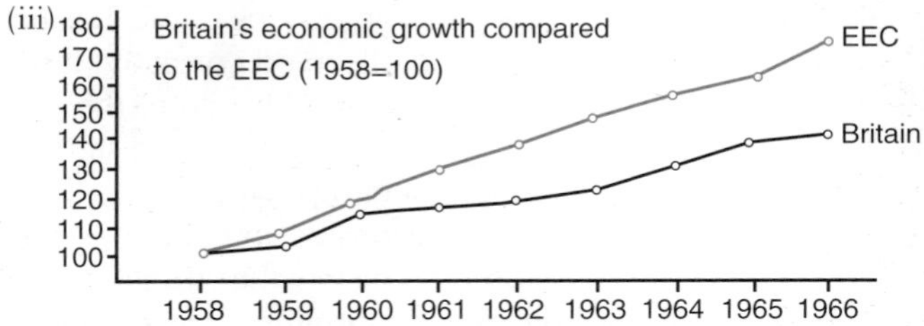

Adapted from Coates, 1994.

Questions

1. Suppose Items A and C were used to illustrate an article entitled: 'The evolution of the EEC, 1958-95'. Write the article to accompany the pictures.
2. Using Items B, D and E explain why Britain was not one of the founding members of the EEC and why it applied to join the EEC in the 1960s.
3. Judging from Items B and D, why did President de Gaulle veto Britain's two applications to join the EEC in the 1960s?

2 The organisation of the European Union

Key Issues

1. How are decisions made in the EU?
2. What is the role of the different institutions?
3. Where is power located?

How the EU works

An important characteristic of the EU is its mixture of supranational and intergovernmental institutions. This mixture ensures that, in some areas, member states are able to veto proposals which they feel are disadvantageous whilst in other areas decisions are made at the European level and must be implemented by members regardless of their reservations. Decisions in the EU are made by five main institutions - the Council of Ministers, the European Commission, the European Parliament, the European Court of Justice and the European Council of Heads of Government.

a. The Council of Ministers

The Council of Ministers is the EU's ultimate decision making body. Its job is to discuss and approve (or reject) proposals drawn up by the Commission. Unlike other EU institutions, members of the Council of Ministers directly represent the interests of their member state. The Council has the power to issue regulations, directives, decisions, recommendations or resolutions:

> 'The Council has the power to make **regulations** (or Community laws) which are binding on member states and directly applicable. **Directives** are equally binding as to the aims to be achieved but leave national authorities to decide on the methods of carrying them out. In addition, the Council can issue **decisions** binding those to whom they are addressed, whether member states, firms or private individuals. **Recommendations** and **opinions** are not binding. The Council can also indicate a general policy direction through **resolutions**.' (HMSO, 1992, pp.17-18)

The Council of Ministers is, in reality, not a single council. It is a series of councils. The ministers responsible for the matter under discussion attend. So, if, for example, an environmental matter is under discussion, then the environment minister from each member state attends. The member state holding the presidency of the EU (which changes every six months) chairs the Council. The office of President is allocated on a rota basis. The three areas most commonly discussed by the Council are foreign affairs, economics and finance, and agriculture. The Council of Foreign Ministers has a coordinating role.

Before proposals are put before the Council, they are considered by the Committee of Permanent Representatives (COREPER) which is made up of senior civil servants from the member states. This committee is able to resolve many of the issues under discussion and, often, the meeting of the Council of Ministers which follows acts merely as a rubber stamp. The Council of Ministers has its own staff of 2,000.

The voting procedure used by the Council of Ministers depends on the matter under discussion. Some matters require **unanimity**. Some matters are decided by a **simple majority**. And some matters are decided by **qualified majority voting**. Under the qualified majority voting system, each member state is allocated a certain number of votes (Britain has 10, for example, whilst Luxembourg has two). Each member state is given roughly one vote for every four million people in its population, but the system is designed to favour the smaller states (to prevent their views always being swamped). Larger states, therefore, do not always have one vote for every four million people (Britain has 10 votes, for example, even though its population is over 50 million). The system ensures that no single member state can block a proposal. At least three member states (including two of the big states) must vote against a proposal for it to fail. The number of matters decided by the qualified voting system increased after the passing of the Single European Act in 1986.

b. The European Commission

The Commission is the permanent bureaucracy of the EU. It is headed by a college of commissioners appointed from the member states. As a result of the enlargement of the EU, the number of commissioners appointed from January 1995 was 20 (two from the five largest members Britain, Germany, France, Italy and Spain and one each from the others). These commissioners are chosen by the heads of government of each member state.

The Commission's primary responsibility is to initiate European legislation. Each commissioner has responsibility for a particular sector which is allocated by the President of the Commission - for example, the two British commissioners appointed in 1995, Leon Brittan and Neil Kinnock, were given responsibility for trade relations with developed countries and transport respectively. Commissioners have to disavow any national allegiance. Since 1995, the length of tenure of office has been set at five years.

The Commission has a large administrative staff of around 15,000 people, based in both Brussels and Luxembourg. The Commission works, in theory, in all the members' languages, though, in practice, English and French predominate. Around 15% of the Commission's staff are employed in linguistic work (translating and interpreting). It should be noted that, although the Commission is often criticised for being over-bureaucratic, in fact:

> 'The Commission employs fewer people than the French Ministry of Culture and the British Lord Chancellor's office, neither of which is a major department of state. It is smaller than the governments of cities like Amsterdam and Madrid.' (Geddes, 1993, pp.43-4)

Civil servants working for the Commission must be completely neutral and objective. They must act in the interests of the EU as a whole, rather than for their individual member states.

The role of the Commission has been described by a British government pamphlet as follows:

> 'The European Commission is the executive organ of the Community, ensuring that Community rules and provisions of the Treaties are implemented and observed correctly. It puts forward policy proposals and executes the decisions taken by the Council [of Ministers]. It attends all Council meetings, where it participates in discussions as an equal partner. The Commission administers the structural funds established by the Community, prepares a draft budget which must be approved by the Council and the European Parliament and negotiates international agreements on behalf of the Community.' (HMSO, 1992, p.18)

The Commission can investigate any complaint that the principles laid down in the Treaties signed by member states have been breached and impose fines if it finds that rules have been broken or disregarded. When requested by an individual state, it can consider whether there is a case for a temporary waiving of rules. If a member state does not fulfil its obligations, the Commission can take it to the European Court of Justice (see below).

c. The European Parliament

The European Parliament is located in Strasbourg. Since 1979, its members (Members of the European Parliament - MEPS) have been directly elected every five years. The number of MEPs has risen from 518 in 1989 to 626 in 1995. This reflects the growth of the EU (in 1990, for example, East and West Germany were unified and in 1995 three new member states joined the EU). The number of MEPs elected by each member state is determined roughly by population. Germany returns 99 MEPs whilst the UK and France return 87 and Luxembourg returns six. Members sit in Parliament according to party group rather than nationality.

The power of the European Parliament has been restricted by the fact that the final decision on legislation remains with the Council of Ministers. For this reason, the Parliament has often been accused of being little more than a talking shop. Since the late 1980s, however, the Parliament's formal and informal influence has been growing.

Before 1987, Parliament's powers were limited. The so-called **consultation procedure** ensured that Parliament was consulted during the decision making process, but, in practice, made it easy for the

Commission and Council of Ministers to ignore the views of Parliament:

> 'Under this procedure, Parliament is asked for an opinion on Commission proposals for Council legislation on only one occasion. Once that opinion is given, the Council may take a decision. What use the EP [European Parliament] is able to make of this single referral depends, in part at least, on its own subject competence and its tactical skills.' (Nugent, 1994, p.176)

Since the Single European Act came into operation in 1987, however, the so-called **cooperation procedure** has given the Parliament new powers. The cooperation procedure allows the Parliament to become involved in the decision making process at a number of different stages:

> 'Whereas under the consultation...procedure the Council can take final decisions after the EP [European Parliament] has issued its opinions, under the cooperation procedure there is a second reading process. On first reading, the Council is confined to adopting 'common positions' which must be referred back to the EP. In making the reference back, the Council is obliged to provide the EP with explanations for common positions - including giving reasons for any EP amendments which have been rejected - and if the EP is dissatisfied, it can exert further pressure at its second reading by amending or rejecting common positions by votes that include an absolute majority of its members.' (Nugent, 1994, p.176-77)

Although, under the cooperative procedure, the European Parliament cannot veto measures outright, it can put considerable pressure on the Commission and the Council:

> 'If the Parliament rejects the Council's position, then unanimity by the Council is required for the proposal to come into force as Community law. If the Parliament proposes amendments, the Council votes by qualified majority where the Commission endorses them and unanimously where the Commission has been unable to do so.' (HMSO, 1992, p.21).

The Maastricht Treaty has given the Parliament further powers by introducing the **codecision procedure**. This works as follows:

> '[The codecision procedure] is similar to the cooperation procedure up to the point when the EP [European Parliament] issues its second reading position. The procedure then changes, for if the Council cannot accept the EP's position as indicated by a vote of the majority of its component members, and if the differences between the two institutions cannot be resolved in a Conciliation Committee composed of an equal number of representatives from
> and the Parliament, the EP can pr
> from being adopted (again by a vo
> majority of its members) if the Coun
> press ahead. In other words, the EP h
> veto on legislative proposals which are
> this procedure.' (Nugent, 1994, p.177)

The Maastricht Treaty also requires the Parliament to approve international treaties and gives it the power **to ask the Commission** to propose new laws. Whether or not this will mean that the Parliament can initiate legislation will depend on how the word 'ask' is interpreted.

d. The European Court of Justice

The Court of Justice has 15 judges - one from each member state. Judges are appointed by member states for a period of six years. There are six advocates general who assist the judges by analysing the arguments of those in dispute. The Court sits in Luxembourg.

The role of the European Court is to interpret European law and to make decisions which are binding on member states. It rules on the interpretation and application of EU laws and sorts out disputes between member states. Given the scope of the Treaties, a very wide range of matters can be brought before the Court. It is, in effect, the Supreme Court of the European Union.

Due to the increasing workload of the Court of Justice, the Single European Act provided for a Court of First Instance to be set up. This court listens to and makes judgements on points of law only. There is the right of appeal from this court to the Court of Justice.

Norton notes:

> 'Under the terms of EU membership, if there is a conflict between the provisions of European law and domestic UK law, then the European law is to prevail. The 1972 European Communities Act provided that any dispute over the interpretation of Community Treaties (and the laws made under them) was to be treated as a matter of law. Under the provisions of the Treaty of Rome, cases which reach the highest domestic court of appeal (in the case of the UK, that means the House of Lords) must be referred to the Court of Justice...for a definitive ruling. Lower courts may also request a ruling from the Court of Justice on the meaning and interpretation of the Treaties. There is no appeal from a decision of the Court of Justice.' (Norton, 1995, p.30)

The European Court of Justice should not be confused with the European Court of Human Rights. This was established by the Council of Europe which has twice as many members as the EU. The European Court of Human Rights examines violations of the 1950 European Convention on Human Rights.

e European Council of Heads of Government

tablished in 1974, the European Council was set up to try to break the log-jam in Community policy making. The European Council brings together all the heads of member governments, their foreign ministers and the President of the Commission. Meetings of the European Council are held twice a year (though extra meetings may be called in exceptional circumstances). They are always held in the country of the member state holding the EU presidency (the presidency is held for six months on a rota basis). The aim of these meetings is to discuss major policy issues. Geddes claims that:

> 'In the 1980s and 1990s, international summitry has been a key feature of world politics. The European variant - the European Council - has been the scene of many landmark decisions in recent community history. The pace of Community development is strongly influenced by decisions taken by the European Council which is the dominant political forum within the EC.' (Geddes, 1993, p.53)

Activity 6.2

Item A *The EU decision making process*

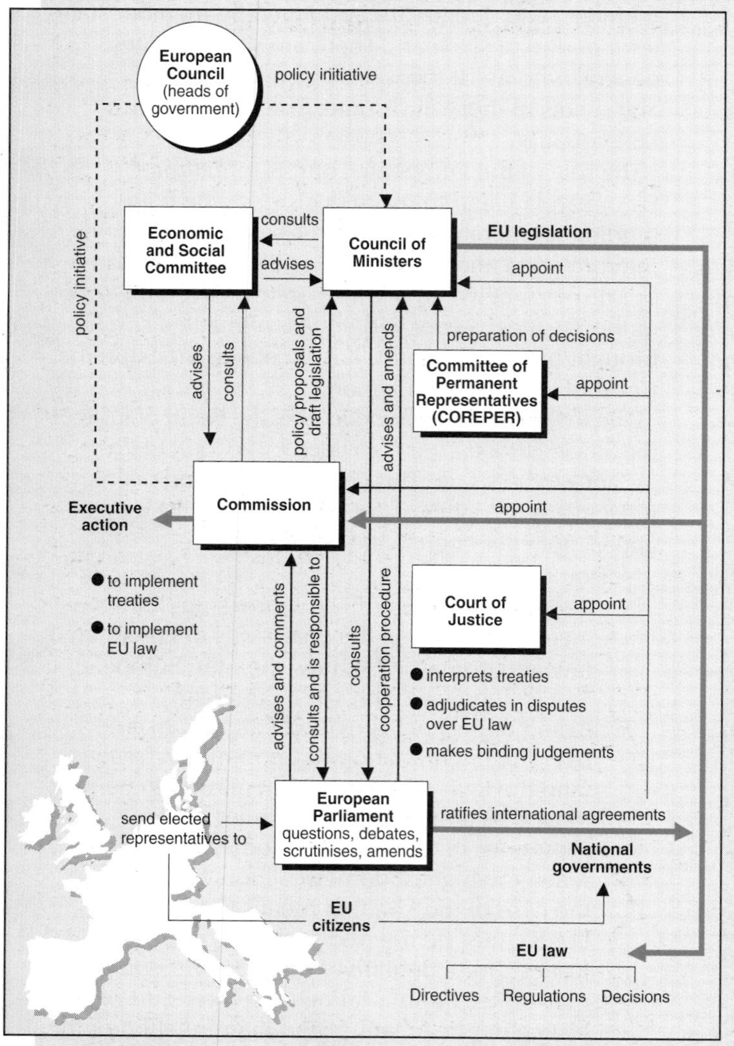

Adapted from Mazey & Richardson, 1993.

Item B *The qualified majority voting system (1)*

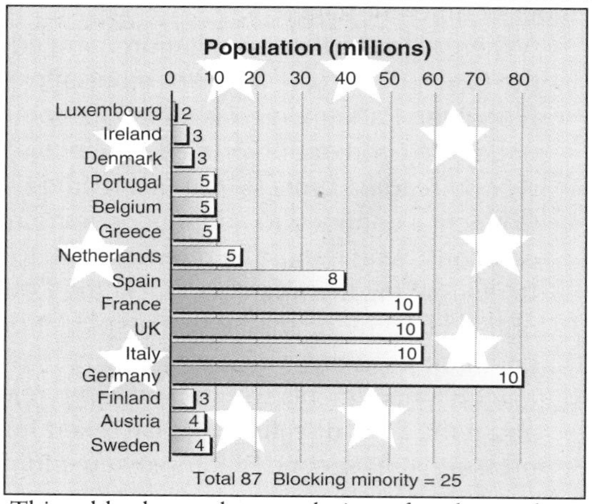

This table shows the population of each member state of the EU and the number of votes each member state has in the Council of Ministers.

Adapted from the *Guardian*, 16 March 1994.

Item C *The qualified majority voting system (2)*

In 1994, the British government used the forthcoming enlargement of the EU as an opportunity to press for greater influence in the Council of Ministers. Before 1995, the 12 members of the EU had a total of 76 votes in the Council and a measure could be blocked by 23 (or more) votes - a minimum of two large states and one small state voting against the measure. In March 1994, the British government proposed that the blocking threshold should remain at 23 votes even after the new members joined the EU in January 1995. The main argument was that this would prevent the big states being swamped by the wishes of the smaller states. It was a question of protecting national sovereignty, especially since the number of decisions which required qualified majority voting had grown and was likely to grow. Most other members argued against Britain's proposal on the grounds that retaining the 23 vote blocking mechanism would make it too easy to reject proposals and EU business would grind to a halt. It was eventually agreed that there should be a 25 vote blocking mechanism.

Adapted from the *Guardian*, 20 March 1994 and 30 January 1995.

Item D *The European Parliament*

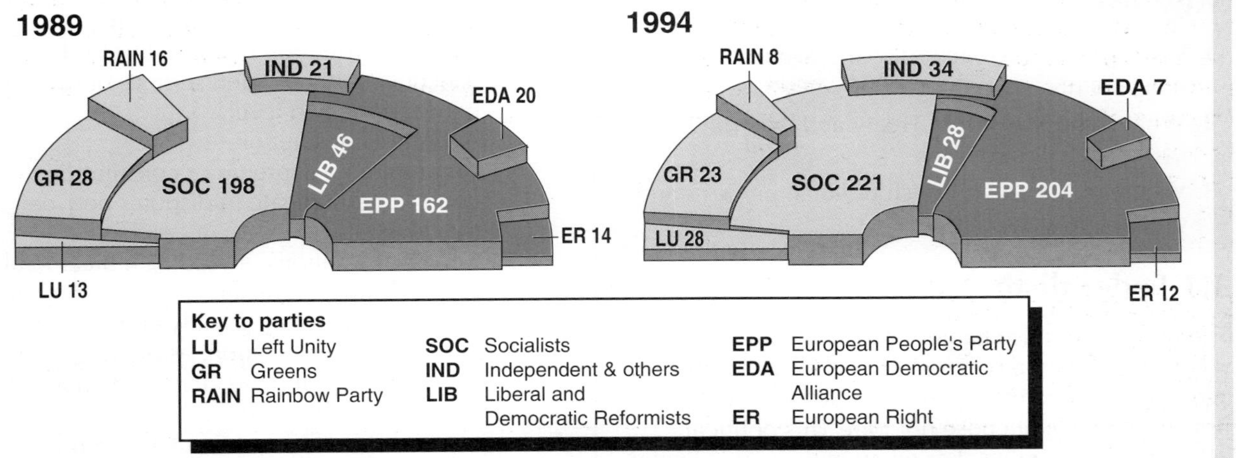

In April 1995, the former Chancellor, Norman Lamont, made a speech in which he gave five reasons for the abolition of the European Parliament (EP). First, he argued that the EP is not a truly representative body. In the 1994 European elections, for example, only 36% of people bothered to vote. This suggests that most people do not believe that participation in such elections is worthwhile. It also means that MEPs cannot claim with any justification to have a mandate for their vision of Europe. Second, the EP is expensive. In 1994, it cost over £500 million to run it. The cost of maintaining an MEP is much greater than maintaining an MP. Third, the EP is not a proper Parliament. MEPs from different countries belong to different political parties which are only linked by a system of weak alliances. Parliamentary democracy cannot function properly without political parties being organised on a Europe-wide basis. Fourth, the continued existence of the EP only makes sense if there are plans for its power to continue to evolve. This assumes that an EP with greater powers is desirable. If it is not, then the EP should be abolished immediately. And fifth, British MEPs are in a minority in the EP and, therefore, cannot protect Britain's interests. The work of the EP should be confined to consultation and MEPs should be nominated or elected from national Parliaments. The existing system is inconsistent with the idea of a Europe of nation states.

Adapted from the *Times*, 13 April 1995.

Item E *Euro-myths*

Fishermen will have to wear hairnets. Cheddar cheese will have to be renamed unless it actually comes from Cheddar. Home-made jam is to be banned. Firefighters will have to wear blue trousers. Prawn cocktail crisps are doomed. These are all examples of Euro-myths. Many contain a grain of truth. After all, to create and maintain a common market, Brussels has to regulate. Otherwise, every country would cheat to gain a competitive advantage. Myths may arise when a country argues against a particular regulation. A politician from that country takes the argument to its logical extreme. The press picks up the politician's argument. Even if the argument is taken into account before the final directive is issued, the damage has been done. Sometimes mistakes are made in the drafting of a directive - as with prawn cocktail crisps (the mistake was rectified). Sometimes, wires are crossed - as with fishermen and hairnets (health rules require staff in fish processing factories, not on fishing boats, to wear headgear). Besides, people want to believe these myths. In the 17th century, people in Britain were just as suspicious of London as people today are suspicious of Brussels. London in the 17th century was the home of bullies and smart alecs. If Londoners could be caught out, everybody else was delighted. Britain's resentment of Brussels has an extra edge because the UK entered the European Community late and it joined because it felt it ought to, not because it wanted to. It helps if, occasionally, Brussels actually does go over the top. The examples above are all myths, but there really is a maximum noise level for lawn mowers.

Adapted from the *Independent on Sunday*, 25 September 1994.

Questions

1. a) Using Item A describe the different stages that a proposal has to go through before becoming law.
   b) Where is power located in the EU?
   c) Isolate the intergovernmental and supranational elements in the decision making process. Would you say that the balance is right? Give reasons for your answer.
2. 'The European Parliament plays an important role now and it should play an even more important role in the future.' Do you agree with this statement? Use Item D in your answer.
3. Judging from Items B and C why do you think the British government attempted to retain the 23 vote blocking threshold in the Council of Ministers? Do you think its arguments were justified? Give reasons for your answer.
4. Give arguments for and against the view that the EU decision making process is over-bureaucratic. Use Item E in your answer

3 The debate over federalism

Key Issues

1. What are the arguments for and against greater federalism?

2. What is the Maastricht Treaty and why did it cause such controversy?

3. Where do the main British political parties stand on the European question?

3.1 Federalism

The first part of this chapter noted that when the EEC was set up, it had a political as well as an economic agenda. That was the reason why, to begin with, the British government chose not join. This political agenda was ambitious. For many of those involved in the setting up of the EEC, the hope was that one day the organisation would evolve into a kind of United States of Europe. Although, after it joined, the British government played down the political consequences of membership, they have already been extensive:

> 'The British constitution has changed significantly over the past 25 years. It has undergone its most dramatic change as a result of British membership of the European Community. That has limited the role of government and Parliament in policy making, injecting new supranational bodies into the process (supranational bodies which enjoy supremacy over the national institutions). The effect has been to undermine and potentially destroy the basic tenets, and consequences, of the traditional constitution.' (Norton, 1995, p.40)

Since the mid-1980s, the future direction of the European Union has been the subject of debate. The Single European Act and Maastricht Treaty have raised questions about the direction in which the EU should head. Central to this debate is the question of federalism. Should the EU continue in the direction of a federal system or should it become a loose confederation of nation states?

A federal system of government is a system where different levels of government coexist and remain autonomous. If, for example, a federal state has a national government and regional governments, the regional governments are not subordinate to the national government. Rather, the two layers of government have their own areas of responsibility and they have control over these areas. The aim of a federal system is to ensure that decisions are made at an appropriate level. Matters concerning everyone are dealt with by national government, whilst matters concerning a particular region only are dealt with by regional government. Geddes claims that federal systems of government share five main features:

> '1. Two levels of government, a general and regional.
> 2. Formal distribution of legislative and executive authority and sources of revenue between the two levels.
> 3. A written constitution.
> 4. An umpire - a supreme or constitutional court - to adjudicate in disputes between the two levels.
> 5. Central institutions, including a bicameral [two chamber] legislature within which the upper chamber will usually embody territorial representation, as in the case with the US Senate and the German Bundesrat.' (Geddes, 1993, p.12)

The opposite to a federal system of government is a unitary system of government. The British system of government is unitary (see chapter 4, section 3.1). The powers of government in the UK are held by a central authority. Local authorities exist, but any powers they possess have been granted to them by central government and could be withdrawn by central government.

Since the end of the Second World War when plans to create a united Europe were first laid, there has been a great deal of scepticism amongst British politicians about the desirability of political union at the European level. Geddes notes that Eurosceptics in Britain use the term 'federalism' in a distinct way:

> 'In Britain, opponents of a "federal Europe" use the term in a way markedly different to the meaning given to it by most federalists. For its opponents, a "federal Europe" means a European superstate with a huge, centralised Brussels bureaucracy limiting the sovereign authority of member states. Advocates, on the other hand, see federation as a way of combining the political virtues of unity and diversity. For them, federalism is a means of decentralising power, not centralising it.' (Geddes, 1993, p.13)

It is necessary to bear in mind these different ways in which the term 'federalism' is used when considering the arguments used for and against a federal Europe below.

Arguments for a federal Europe

According to Pinder:

> 'The essence of the federal case is this: it is time to replace relations among states based on their relative power by relations among people based on law...The European nation state is too small a polity to cope with the needs of society in the age of modern technology. We must complement it with a wider polity to do the things that our states can no longer do separately.' (Pinder, 1991, p.5)

Pinder goes on to argue that a number of steps have been taken towards a federal Europe and a number of other steps could easily be taken. For example, two layers of government already exist (government at national and at European level). A written constitution could easily be drawn up from the Treaty of Rome and the other Treaties signed by the member states. The European Court of Justice can be seen as a kind of supreme court. The European Parliament and Council of Ministers can be seen as a nascent two chamber legislature, with the Commission as an executive. Certainly, if member states have the political will, the framework for a federal Europe is in place.

The main argument used against a federal Europe is that it inevitably leads to a loss of national sovereignty (see below). There are a number of ways of countering this argument. First, there is the argument that national sovereignty is compromised as soon as a country joins the EU:

> 'The United Kingdom became a member of the EC on 1 January 1973. Under the terms of membership, policy making competence in certain sectors of public policy moved upwards from the institution of the British state to the institutions of the EC, principally the Commission and the Council of Ministers... Once a measure of EC law has been approved by the Council of Ministers, it has legal force. This is a condition of membership...The assent of the British Parliament is not required.'
> (Norton, 1995, pp.26-7)

Second, there is the argument that, in practice, a nation's sovereignty was by no means absolute before it entered the EU. Britain's 'special relationship' with the USA, for example, meant that informal pressures determined Britain's foreign policy. Similarly, on a number of occasions, pressure from the money markets (rather than Parliament) has determined economic policy. And third, there is the argument that, in fact, federalism does not lead to a loss of national sovereignty at all. In a federal Europe, decisions that affected the whole of the EU would be made at European level whilst decisions affecting an individual nation would be made by that nation's government. The advantage of making decisions at the European level would be that there would be a degree of harmony amongst member states, whilst regional differences could be preserved.

Some federalists argue that the logic of the development of the EU up to now suggests that, in time, the remaining barriers between members will be broken down. The Single European Act, for example, has already created a single market within the EU in which the free movement of goods, persons, services and capital is ensured. Since goods, persons, services and capital can now move freely around the EU, it is argued, there is no good reason to have 15 different national currencies. It would be far better to have a single European currency (see chapter 15, section 2.2). Similarly, it makes sense for the EU to negotiate on behalf of its members (as happened during the Uruguay round of the GATT negotiations, for example - see chapter 15, p.461 for information on GATT) rather than each member to negotiate on its own behalf. There is a tendency for the world to form bigger interest blocs and the EU is a formidable interest group in international negotiations.

It is, perhaps, no surprise to find that the most committed federalists are found in the Benelux countries. Before the EU was formed, small countries like these had very little international clout, but membership of the EU has provided them with a significant voice in deciding matters which affect them. It has also provided them with a degree of security - both politically and economically. Such benefits, federalists argue, would be greater in a truly federal Europe.

A number of other arguments are used in favour of European federalism. First, it is argued that federalism would bring great social benefits to citizens of the EU. Workers, for example, could expect to find the same basic minimum standards of health and safety in the workplace throughout the EU. Second, it is argued that federalism would help to combat the ultra-nationalism that has led to the growth of neo-Nazi movements and it would ensure that political instability (like that which led to civil war in Yugoslavia) would be unthinkable. Third, there is the argument that greater harmonisation would mean less regulation and less bureaucracy. The result would be greater economic prosperity as well as political stability.

Many federalists are opposed to further enlargement of the EU in the near future for two main reasons. First, they argue that enlargement would drain off resources from the stronger states since they would have to subsidise the new, weaker members. And second, new coalitions would be formed, changing the balance of power in the EU and possibly preventing greater political union.

Arguments against federalism

The main argument used by those opposed to a federal Europe is that federalism is a threat to national sovereignty. Sovereignty requires autonomy, but the existence of supranational institutions, by definition, restricts a nation's freedom of manoeuvre:

> 'Opponents of the EC argue that a loss of sovereignty in a democratic political system reduces the rights of citizens to exercise control over the decision making authority. The ultimate recourse of the British electorate is to "kick the rascals out" by voting for a change of government at a general election. However, if national government is no longer the sovereign

> authority then national elections and policy preferences expressed in them may make little difference if they run counter to preferences agreed at Community level.' (Geddes, 1993, p.11)

Whilst most Eurosceptics in the UK accept that membership of the EU brings benefits to trade and the economy, they are reluctant to agree to moves which might further restrict national sovereignty. For many, the EU should be a free trade area and no more.

The second main argument against a federal Europe is that there is too great a diversity between the member states for a United States of Europe to be a practical possibility. There are different cultures, different languages, different standards of living and different types of economy. Imposing uniformity is not the solution. The differences between member states should be recognised and accommodated.

Again, the question of enlargement (or 'widening') is important in this context. If, in the near future, the EU was to expand to an organisation of 20 to 30 states, there would be even greater diversity. Harmonisation would be proportionately more difficult and less practical. A larger EU is, therefore, likely to be a less federal-minded EU.

A third argument against a federal Europe has been suggested above. Many Eurosceptics are hostile towards EU institutions. They accuse the Commission of being over-bureaucratic and the Parliament of being an expensive burden. They note that there is, at present, only one chamber in the Parliament and that the Commission takes on both a legislative and an executive role. Commissioners are not elected and MEPs are not really accountable to the electorate. EU institutions are remote from ordinary people and to transfer more power to them would be to transfer power to unknown bureaucrats. In short, there is a democratic deficit that would be exacerbated in a federal Europe.

Linked to the above argument is the Eurosceptics' claim that the march towards a federal Europe is taking place without the consent of the majority of people living in the EU:

> 'It is now abundantly clear that a strong federalist current is carrying the European Community towards a destination which has never been approved or even discerned by a majority of our fellow citizens. Almost daily, speeches are made, conferences held or proposals put forward which reflect this trend.' (Vander Elst, 1991, p.11)

Other arguments against a federal Europe include the following. First, Eurosceptics argue that nationalism (or 'patriotism') is a virtue:

> 'Nationalism has many advantages: it reconciles classes; smooths over regional differences; and gives ordinary people a sense of community, pride and history.' (Sked, 1989)

Replacing the nation state with a supranational superstate would destroy this valuable motivating force. Second, Eurosceptics argue that a federal Europe is an idealistic dream rather than a practical reality. It would cause more problems than it solved. And third, they argue that in a federal Europe the will of the small nations would swamp that of the larger nations. Inevitably, therefore, Britain would end up losing out.

Enlargement

In its first 30 years, the EU doubled in size from six members in 1958 to 12 by 1988. By 1995, it had increased in size to 15 and a large number of applications are pending. Thus far, enlargement has been a slow and relatively painless process. EU institutions have managed to evolve in line with increased membership, without changing the decision making process in a fundamental way. In particular, member states have retained their vetoes over certain issues. Commentators and politicians agree, however, that an EU with, for example, 30 members would have to be a very different organisation from that which now exists. With the end of the Cold War and the break-up of the Soviet Union, many states in eastern Europe are aiming to gain membership of the EU and an EU of 30 members is not beyond the bounds of possibility. The question is whether existing members will allow the EU to be widened in this way.

A two tier or multi-speed Europe?

The question of enlargement has raised the possibility of a two tier or multi-speed Europe. Within the EU, there is a division between those members who are keen to speed up the process towards political and economic union (most of the original six members have been especially keen to speed up the process) and those who are reluctant to move in this direction (the British government has been especially reluctant). A possible consequence of this division within the EU is the development of two tiers, with one tier accepting a single currency and moving towards greater political cooperation at the European level and the second tier opting out of such arrangements. Enlargement is likely to exacerbate this process since new members will come into the EU with different expectations. Some will be better equipped to move towards political and economic union than others. As a result, a multi-speed Europe is a possibility with different members working towards 'ever closer union' at different rates.

Activity 6.3

Item A *Enlargement (1)*

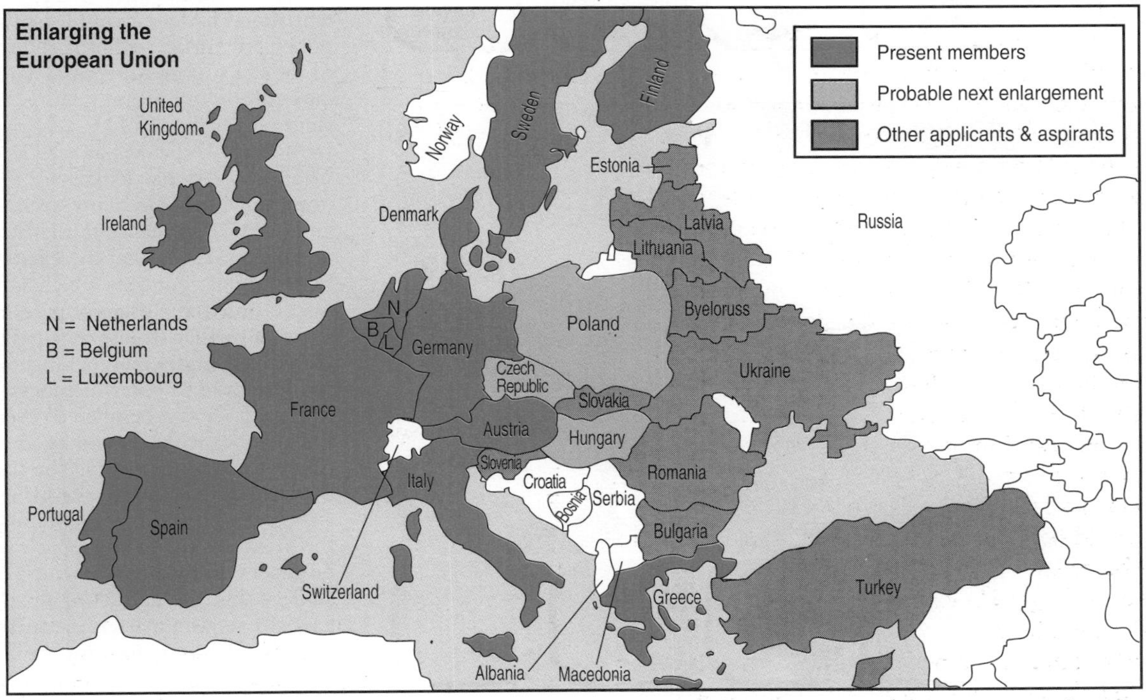

This map shows existing members of the EU and those countries which have expressed a desire to join the EU.

Adapted from Church, 1992.

Item B *Enlargement (2)*

The EU's present rules were devised when it had only six members and they can hardly cope now that it has 15. The problem is that the EU is growing in diversity as much as in unity. At present, it is split between rich and poor, north and south, big and small. In addition, it is split between those proud of their independence (such as Britain and France) and those ready and eager to cooperate supranationally. These trends will be exacerbated by enlargement. There is no doubt that the EU will have to make further changes to its institutional structure to cope with bigger numbers. Getting unanimity with more members, for example, would be increasingly difficult and so national vetoes would have to be restricted. There will also be policy and financial costs. How would the Common Agricultural Policy cope if countries like Poland and Hungary were to join? Behind all this lies, a debate on the future shape of the EU. Should the widening or the deepening of the EU be a priority? Would enlargement drain off resources and energies by introducing members who are not committed to 'ever closer union'? Would enlargement result in a new balance of power within the EU which halted the march towards integration? How can members ensure that enlargement will not make the EU less stable and less democratic?

Adapted from Church, 1992 and the *Economist*, 21 January 1995.

Item C *Enlargement (3)*

I CAN'T SLEEP. TELL ME ABOUT THE E.U. ENLARGEMENT DEBATE AGAIN.

This cartoon was published in the *Guardian* on 21 March 1994.

Item D *The emergence of a two tier Europe (1)*

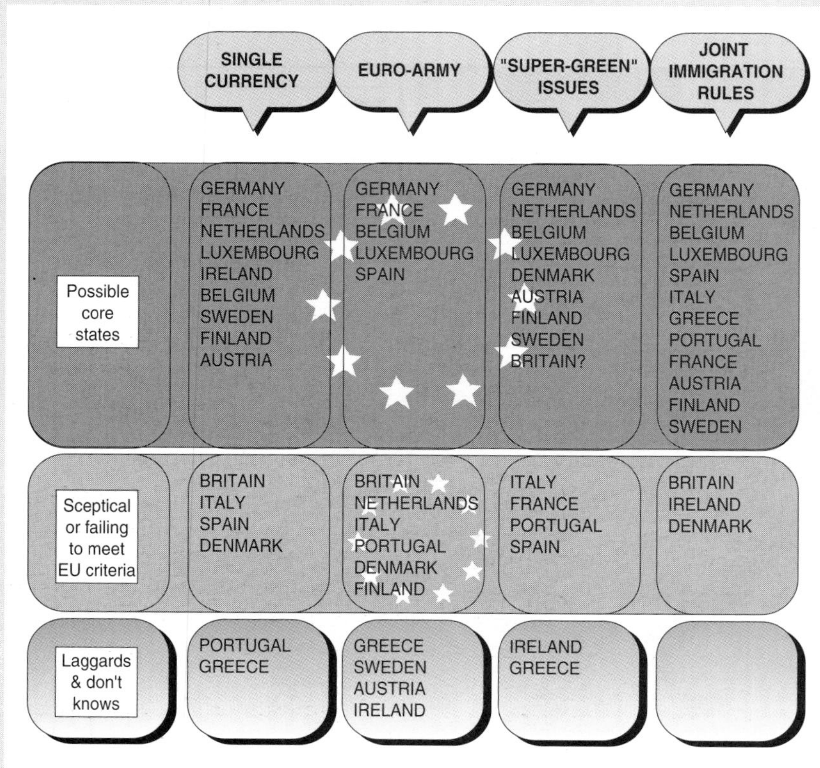

Adapted from the *Times*, 2 June 1994.

Item E *The emergence of a two tier Europe (2)*

In September 1994, Germany's Christian Democrats published a policy document outlining their view of the EU's future direction. This is a particularly important document since Chancellor Kohl is a Christian Democrat. The views of the German Chancellor are particularly important since Germany exercises a great deal of influence in the EU. The document argued that the existing hard core of countries which support integration and closer cooperation must be further strengthened. This core (the founder members) should not be closed to other members. Rather, it should be open to every EU member which is willing and able to meet its requirements. The task of the hard core is to give the EU a strong centre which will counteract the pressures to splinter which will be generated by enlargement. To achieve this, the hard core must participate, as a matter of course, in all policy fields and it must be recognisably more community spirited than other members. The document notes that there are strong signs of a hard core emerging in the monetary field. Monetary union will only be achieved if this hard core works towards ever closer cooperation in the fields of monetary, fiscal and budgetary, and economic and social policy. By so doing, they will lay the foundations for monetary union, irrespective of the formal decisions which are made in 1997 and 1999.

Adapted from the *Guardian*, 7 September 1994.

Questions

1. Is a federal Europe a realistic possibility? Use Items A-E in your answer.
2. a) Should the EU should continue to enlarge? Give reasons for your answer.
   b) What are the likely consequences of enlargement?
3. What does Item C tell us about British attitudes towards the enlargement debate? Why might such attitudes be misguided?
4. a) Is a two tier Europe emerging? Use Items D and E in your answer.
   b) What are the advantages and disadvantages of a two tier Europe?

3.2 The Maastricht Treaty

At the Maastricht summit in December 1991, the 12 heads of state of the European Community agreed on a Treaty on European Union which changed the provisions laid down by the Treaty of Rome and made new commitments. The Maastricht Treaty, as it is usually known, set out to strengthen political and economic ties between member states:

> 'The effect of the Treaty was to form a European Union, to enlarge the area of policy competence of this Union beyond that enjoyed by the European Community and to strengthen further the European Parliament. It laid down a timetable for economic and monetary union. The final stage of the process will involve the introduction of a single currency and the establishment of a Committee of the Regions. The Treaty also contained a protocol (the Social Chapter) giving force to the Social Charter, previously agreed by heads of government in 1989.' (Norton, 1995, p.29)

By the end of 1993, all member states had ratified the Treaty, though a number of opt-out clauses were agreed with Britain and Denmark. As a result of these opt-outs, the Treaty will not have the same effect throughout the Union. Members are due to review the provisions of the treaty at an intergovernmental conference to be held in 1996.

What does the Maastricht Treaty aim to achieve?

The Maastricht Treaty is a long and complicated document. Its passage through the British Parliament was painfully slow even though it had the backing of the government and the main opposition parties. This was due to the opposition of backbench Conservatives who were concerned about the implications of some provisions in the Treaty.

By ratifying the Maastricht Treaty, member states created a European Union (hence the name-change from EC to EU) with three main pillars. The European Community forms one pillar, foreign and security policy forms a second pillar and justice and home affairs forms the third pillar. Whilst the European Community functions by means of a mix of supranational and intergovernmental institutions (described in part 2 above), members agreed that in the spheres of foreign affairs, defence, home affairs and justice they should proceed through intergovernmental cooperation.

Although some member states wanted a commitment to greater federalism to be explicitly stated in the text of the Treaty, the British government vehemently opposed the use of the word 'federal'. Instead, the text of the Treaty uses the term 'ever closer union':

> 'This Treaty marks a new stage in the process of creating an ever closer union among the peoples of Europe, in which decisions are taken as closely as possible to the citizen.' (quoted in Nugent, 1994, p.65)

Provisions of the Treaty and controversies

A government pamphlet suggests that the main features of the Maastricht Treaty can be summarised as follows:

> '1. It embodies the principle of subsidiarity, whereby action should be taken at Community level only if its objectives cannot be sufficiently achieved by the member states acting alone.
> 2. It introduces the concept of Union citizenship, complementing existing national citizenship and conferring new rights for citizens of the Union to vote in elections to the European Parliament and local elections in whichever member state they live.
> 3. It introduces measures of institutional reform, including new powers for the European Parliament, some extension of qualified majority voting in the Council of Ministers and the establishment of a new advisory Committee of the Regions.
> 4. It strengthens control of the Community's finances...
> 5. It provides for the establishment of a common foreign and security policy conducted on an intergovernmental basis rather than within the existing framework of Community law.
> 6. It endorses a commitment stepping up intergovernmental cooperation on interior and judicial issues, such as asylum and immigration policy and fighting international crime, terrorism and drug trafficking...
> 7. It provides for moves towards economic and monetary union.'
>
> (HMSO, 1992, pp.14-15, adapted)

The commitment to economic and monetary union (EMU) is one of the most controversial parts of the Treaty. The Treaty lays down provisions which are intended to ensure both the disappearance of national currencies (they would be replaced by a single European currency, the ECU) and the setting up of a European central bank (with powers to set interest rates for the whole EU). But, Britain withdrew from the Exchange Rate Mechanism in 1992 (see chapter 15, section 2.2) and some members have faced difficulties in meeting the convergence criteria laid down by the Treaty. As a result, economic and monetary union has been delayed and possibly even derailed. France, Germany and the Benelux countries remain keen to push ahead, but both Denmark and Britain have negotiated opt-out clauses until after 1997.

Another controversial provision in the Treaty is the protocol (the Social Chapter) giving force to the Social Charter previously agreed by heads of government in 1989. The aim of this protocol is to harmonise laws on the social rights of workers to prevent unfair competition between member states through the exploitation of the workforce. Health and safety regulations, a common minimum wage and an agreed maximum number of working hours are all examples of measures covered by the Social Chapter. The British government negotiated an opt-out from the Social Chapter, claiming that it is an unnecessary intervention which will significantly increase the costs faced by employers.

A third area which has caused controversy is the commitment to apply the principle of subsidiarity - the principle that decisions should be taken at the lowest appropriate level. The problem is that different people use the term in different ways and it is, therefore, unclear exactly what sort of future is implied by making a commitment to apply the principle. As in so many other areas, the debate over the term 'subsidiarity' boils down to a debate about whether or not the EU should move towards federalism. Carr & Cope, for example, point out that:

> 'The Major government sees the principle of subsidiarity as a way of trimming the powers of the European Commission, while other member states regard the principle as providing a federal basis for the development of the EU.' (Carr & Cope, 1994, p.167)

Activity 6.4

Item A *The Maastricht Treaty and federalism (1)*

(i)

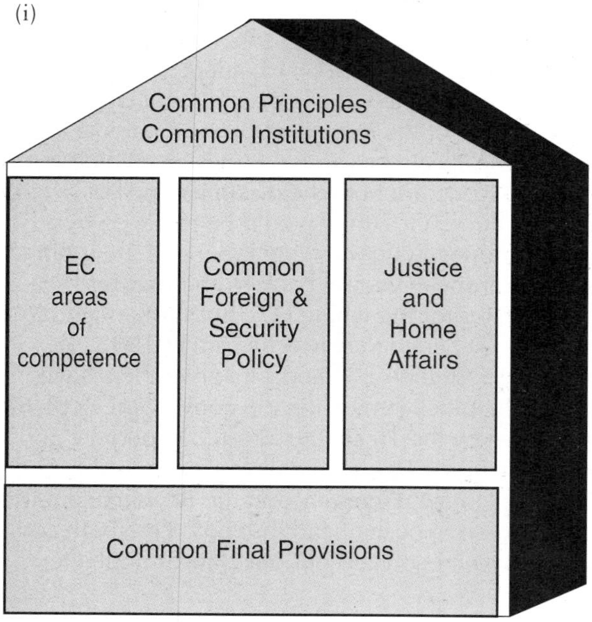

(ii) The negotiation of the Maastricht Treaty was marked by a clash between two rival views of the future of the EU. One, shared by Germany and the federalist smaller states, saw the EU as a tree with all its activities brought together in one set of institutions, eventually creating a single federal state. According to this view, the EU is a single, growing, living organism with one trunk, its roots sunk in the rich European soil. The rival metaphor, backed by France and Britain, was that of the temple. Supporters of this view wanted different policy areas split off from each other in separate pillars. Unity was provided by the 'pediment' - the part of the Treaty which covered policy areas common to all members. It was this architectural version which won out.

Adapted from Lodge, 1993 and the *Independent on Sunday*, 11 September 1994.

Item B *The Maastricht Treaty and federalism (2)*

The Maastricht Treaty was derided by its opponents as heralding a federal superstate. Like the Single European Act, however, it simply amends, refines and extends key provisions of the existing Treaties. It is paradoxical that the most centralised of the EU member states, the UK, should have drawn this conclusion from a treaty geared towards decentralised, devolved and regionalised decision making. Indeed, it is the provisions for decisions to be taken at levels lower than that of national governments which annoyed the British government. The Maastricht Treaty set up a new Committee of the Regions to achieve this. Only the British government wanted to appoint national government nominees to this new body. The federal and non-federal characteristics of the EU, post-Maastricht, can be listed as follows:

Federal characteristics

1. Important policy responsibilities are exercised at both the central (EU) and the regional (member state) levels.
2. Well developed institutions exist at both levels.
3. The Court of Justice is a central judicial body with the authority to rule on disputes between the two levels.
4. There is common citizenship.

Non-federal characteristics

1. Although the power of the centre (EU) has grown, the balance between the two levels is tipped very much in favour of the regional (member state) level.
2. Control of financial resources remains with the regional level. The EU budget is just 3% of total national budgets.
3. The EU's political structure is not well ordered or based on established and shared principles.
4. The rights of EU citizenship are extremely limited.

Adapted from Lodge, 1993 and Nugent, 1994.

Item C *Subsidiarity (1)*

The subsidiarity principle means that decisions made by Parliaments, governments and other authorities are to be taken as close as possible to the citizen. In other words, decisions are taken at the lowest possible level (preferably by the local or regional authority). Decisions are taken at a higher level only if there is a good reason. Article 3b of the Maastricht Treaty defines subsidiarity as follows: 'The Community shall act within the limits of the powers conferred upon it by this Treaty and of the objectives assigned to it therein. In areas which do not fall within its exclusive competence, the Community shall take action, in accordance with the principle of subsidiarity, only if and in so far as the objectives of the proposed action cannot be sufficiently achieved by the member states and can, therefore, by reason of the scale or effects of the proposed action, be better achieved by the Community. Any action of the Community shall not go beyond what is necessary to achieve the objectives of this Treaty.' But subsidiarity does not just apply to legislative powers. The Treaty claims to mark: 'A new stage in the process of creating an ever closer union among the peoples of Europe, in which decisions are taken as closely as possible to the citizen.' Subsidiarity is, therefore, one of the fundamental characteristics of the EU and expresses the principle that member states preserve their individual identities.

Adapted from OOPEC, 1992.

Item D *Subsidiarity (2)*

These cartoons appeared in the *Guardian* in 1992. In the top cartoon, Prime Minister John Major is talking to the former Heritage Secretary, David Mellor. In the bottom cartoon, John Major is talking to the former Education Secretary, John Patten.

Questions

1. Why was the acceptance of the Maastricht Treaty such an important event in the history of the European Community?
2. 'Once the Maastricht Treaty was ratified, a federal Europe became an inevitability.' Using Items A-C give arguments for and against this view.
3. Using Items C and D explain why the principle of subsidiarity is supported by (a) politicians who support a federal Europe and (b) politicians who oppose a federal Europe. Given that the principle is supported by these different groups, how useful is it?

3.3 Where British political parties stand on Europe

The British government's policy towards the EU is one of the most contentious issues in British politics in the 1990s. Whilst feelings about the EU are strong in all parties, neither the Conservative nor the Labour party has been able to remain fully united over the issue. Divisions over Europe, however, are nothing new. Ever since the formation of the EEC, British politicians have been divided about the extent to which Britain should become involved in the European project. The positions adopted by the Conservative and Labour parties have fluctuated so much that at different times both have been predominantly pro-European and predominantly anti-European. With the exception, perhaps, of the Heath government which negotiated Britain's entry into the EEC, no British government has adopted an unreservedly pro-European stance. As a result, Britain has earned the reputation of being a semi-detached member of the EU.

Ashford (1992) claims that three factors affect the attitudes towards the EU adopted by the main parties. First, he contrasts the adversarial nature of the British system with that of other European countries, such as Germany, which have a more consensual style of politics. Regardless of which party has been in power in Britain, criticism has been made of the government's stance on Europe by the opposition parties. This has led to governments being reluctant to accept moves towards greater integration and, in turn, it has led to a lack of enthusiasm towards the EU amongst the British electorate. Second, due to inter-party divisions, there have never been clear-cut proposals over Britain's future role in Europe. And third, both main parties are concerned that their ideological self-image is under threat from further European integration. Many Conservative supporters can see the advantage of a single market, for example, but oppose giving up economic sovereignty to achieve this. Similarly, although most Labour supporters agree with the provisions of the Social Chapter, some regard the EU as a capitalist club which is incompatible with socialism.

The Conservative party and Europe

With hindsight, it is possible to see mainstream Conservative thinking over Europe going through four distinct phases in the period since 1945.

The first phase was dominated by Churchill's view of what Britain's relationship with Europe should be. In one sense, Churchill was a supporter of European integration. He said in 1946:

> 'If Europe is to be saved from infinite misery and indeed from final doom, there must be an act of faith in the European family. We must build a kind of United States of Europe.' (quoted in Lipgens, 1981, p.319)

But, Churchill's 'United States of Europe' did not include Britain. Britain was to encourage its European neighbours to unite, but it was to remain aloof. This reflected Churchill's view that Britain was still a great power with worldwide obligations (to the Empire, for example). Britain, in other words, was not just geographically detached from Europe, it should remain politically detached as well. When Churchill became Prime Minister in 1955, the decision was taken not to participate in the Messina Conference (see above, p.130). Although Britain was invited to become a founder member of the EEC, the invitation was turned down.

The second phase began when Harold Macmillan, Conservative Prime Minister, applied to the EEC for entry in 1961. This phase lasted from 1961 to 1975. It is characterised by the pro-European stance adopted by the Conservative leadership. Justifying his party's apparent U-turn, Macmillan said in 1961:

> 'Most of us recognise that in a changing world, if we are not to be left behind and to drop out of the mainstream of the world's life, we must be prepared to change and adapt our methods. All through history this has been one of the main sources of our strength.' (Hansard, 2 August 1961)

Macmillan, therefore, supported membership of the EEC on the grounds of pragmatism. Although Britain's application to join the EEC was vetoed in 1963 and again in 1967, the Conservative leadership continued to press for membership. Edward Heath, a pro-European, became leader of the Conservative party in 1965 and it was he who finally signed the Treaty of Accession in 1972. Having negotiated Britain's entry into the EEC, the Conservative party leadership then supported continued membership when the referendum on this issue was held in 1975.

The third phase began in 1975 when Margaret Thatcher was elected leader of the Conservative party and lasted until 1987. Whilst in opposition between 1975 and 1979, Thatcher began to criticise the over-bureaucratisation of the EEC and she complained about the amount Britain contributed to the EEC budget. When she became Prime Minister in 1979, her attitude was markedly different from that of Edward Heath. Although she remained committed to membership of the EEC, she made it clear that her aim was to get the best deal for Britain (regardless of what that meant for the other members). Between 1979 and 1984, the EEC agenda was dominated by the question of how much members (especially Britain) should contribute to the EEC budget. This was finally resolved when it was agreed that Britain should receive a rebate. Then, between 1984 and 1987 the British government was at the heart of plans to create a single market in Europe. This idea clearly reflected the deregulatory policies which the Thatcher government pursued in Britain. Ironically, however, it was the Single European Act which became the root of conflict in the Conservative party.

The fourth phase began after the Single European Act came into operation in 1987 and still continues. Whilst the majority of Conservatives approved the idea of a single European market, the full implications of the Single European Act took many of them by surprise and alienated them. By 1988, Margaret Thatcher had joined the ranks of the disaffected. In her Bruges speech of September 1988, she criticised what she saw as growing federalism, arguing instead that:

> 'My first guiding principle is this: willing and active cooperation between independent and sovereign states is the best way to build a European Community.' (Thatcher, 1988)

The Bruges speech was a turning point since Thatcher's Euroscepticism was not shared by some of her Cabinet colleagues. Divisions over Europe were instrumental in Thatcher's downfall. And they soon reappeared when John Major became Prime Minister. Although in the run up to the Maastricht Treaty Major's negotiation of opt-outs appeased the majority of Conservatives, hard-line Eurosceptics began to emerge. After the 1992 general election, Major's small majority ensured that backbench rebellion could have serious consequences. The Eurosceptics took advantage of this and put pressure on the government. This culminated in the withdrawal of the whip from eight backbench MPs in November 1994. Although the whip was restored in April 1995, the Conservative party remained deeply divided on Europe. Geddes argues that it is now possible to identify six different groups within the Conservative party:

> '1. **Tory traditionalists** would like to see the Community operate along intergovernmental lines...
> 2. **Neo-liberals** favour a free market EC and are willing to cede some sovereignty in order to secure success for the single market...
> 3. **Modernisers** believe EC membership can help Britain cast off the burdens of the past and recast itself as a modern and dynamic European power...
> 4. **Federalists**...would like to see a wholehearted endorsement of the integrative process. They are small in number...
> 5. **Anti-marketeers**...espouse an endemic hostility to European integration which they see as a threat to national identity...
> 6. **Pragmatists** are the biggest Conservative group. They adhere to "common sense Europeanism" and accept membership on pragmatic grounds. They can be characterised as neither enthusiasts nor sceptics.' (Geddes, 1993, pp.95-6)

The Labour party and Europe

As with the Conservative party, mainstream Labour thinking was hostile towards the EEC at first. It was not until Labour won power in 1964 that the pro-European wing of the party managed to gain an ascendancy. The party voted in support of an application to join the EEC in 1967, but 36 Labour backbenchers voted against their party. The split in the party between pro-and anti-Europeans remained festering until Labour formed the government again in 1974. Most commentators agree that the split was the main reason why Harold Wilson agreed to a referendum in 1975.

Although the electorate voted in the 1975 referendum by a substantial majority to remain in the EEC, a significant minority of Labour MPs and supporters remained opposed to membership on the grounds that the EEC was a capitalist club which would hinder rather than foster socialism. After Labour's general election defeat in 1979, this faction gained the upper hand in the Labour party. The anti-European direction in which the Labour party seemed to be heading was one reason why several senior Labour MPs left the party to form the SDP (see pp.220-21) in 1981.

Labour fought and lost the 1983 general election on an anti-European platform - its 1983 manifesto committed a Labour government to withdraw from the EEC. The scale of the defeat, however, was so great that the party was forced to re-evaluate its policies. Under the leadership of Neil Kinnock, the Labour party was transformed into an overwhelmingly pro-European party. This transformation came about for a number of reasons. First, the Labour party remained in opposition throughout the 1980s. This frustrated the party's supporters who felt helpless in the face of the Thatcher 'revolution'. Many began to look to Europe to ameliorate the worst excesses of Thatcherism. Second, the pro-European Liberal/SDP Alliance had taken away votes from Labour in the 1983 general election. Third, the Social Charter and the social dimension of changes agreed by the EC appealed ideologically to Labour supporters. And fourth, a pro-European stance made sense tactically in the late 1980s since it became clear that the Conservative party was moving gradually towards an anti-European position.

Although divisions over Europe in the Labour party are less overt than those in the Conservative party, they do still exist. There is, for example, a small core of Labour MPs who support withdrawal from the EU. Geddes claims that it is possible to identify five different groups within the Labour party:

> '1. **Modernisers** are enthusiastic advocates of European integration...
> 2. **Bennites** see the EC as a capitalist club which offers little to working people and would frustrate the actions of a Labour government. Tony Benn was a leader of the 'No' campaign in the 1975 referendum on British membership of the EC and has remained hostile to the Community ever since.
> 3. **Nationalists**...are fearful of the implications of EC membership for national sovereignty...
> 4. The **"new left"** believes that the failure of the French Socialist government's attempted economic reflation in the early 1980s demonstrates that nation states can no longer act alone in the face of transnational capitalism. It sees a reformed EC as the best route to socialism.
> 5. **Pragmatists** are a large group in the Labour party. They espouse a 'common sense Europeanism' which accepts Britain's EC membership but without real enthusiasm.'
> (Geddes, 1993, pp.96-7)

It should be noted that Tony Blair's election as leader was widely regarded as a victory for the modernisers. His deputy, John Prescott, also has a long record of support for greater European integration. Certainly there is little evidence to suggest that a Labour government would suffer from the same degree of dissent from within its party as that suffered by the Conservative government since 1990.

The other parties and Europe

The Liberal Democrats are organised on federal lines (see chapter 8, section 4.2) and so it is no surprise to learn that they are enthusiastic supporters of greater European integration. As early as 1951, Liberals were arguing that Britain should join the European Steel and Coal Community, and the Liberal party was the only mainstream party to support Britain's entry into the EEC in 1957. The Liberal Democrats can, therefore, claim to have a long tradition of pro-Europeanism. Their long-term aim is for a federal Britain within a federal Europe.

Both the Scottish Nationalist party (SNP) and Plaid Cymru (the Welsh nationalists) were originally opposed to Britain's entry into the EEC. But since 1988, the SNP has adopted a pro-European stance. The SNP now calls for an independent Scotland within a federal EU. Plaid Cymru remains suspicious of the EU, not least because it has been heavily influenced by green politics. Like the Green party, Plaid Cymru is critical of an organisation whose priority is economic growth rather than environmental protection.

In Northern Ireland, the Social and Democratic Labour party (SDLP - a moderate nationalist party) is a keen supporter of greater European integration, on the grounds that it will help to heal divisions in Northern Ireland. The official Unionists are opposed to Britain's membership of the EU, but accept that withdrawal is unlikely. The Democratic Unionist party fears domination by Catholics in the EU and its leader, Ian Paisley, has denounced what he sees as 'Popish influences' in the European Parliament.

Activity 6.5

Item A *The Conservative Cabinet and Europe, February 1995*

The following remarks were made in public by members of the Conservative Cabinet in 1994 and early 1995:

(i) It is quite possible to have a monetary union without political union. It is a mistake to believe that monetary union need be a huge step on the path to a federal Europe.

Kenneth Clarke, Chancellor of the Exchequer

(ii) A single currency would mean giving up the government of the UK. No British government can give up the government of the UK. That is impossible.

Michael Portillo, Secretary of State for Employment

(iii) To say either yes or no now to the option which might occur in, say, 1999 would be unnecessary. 'Never' is as foolish a word as 'now' in this context.

Douglas Hurd, Foreign Secretary

(iv) If Britain does not take part in work on a single currency, the French and Germans will design arrangements in their interests and not in ours.

Michael Heseltine, President of the Board of Trade

(v) I don't want to see a single currency, period, for as far as I can possibly foresee. I would hesitate for an eternity before I came out and said I would vote for a single currency.

Jonathan Aitken, Chief Secretary to the Treasury

Adapted from the *Independent*, 11 February 1995.

Item B *John Major and Europe (1)*

(i) My aims for Britain in the Community can be simply stated. I want us to be where we belong - at the very heart of Europe, working with our partners in building the future. That is a challenge we take up with enthusiasm.

Part of a speech made on 11 March 1991

(ii) I make no secret of my view that we want a Europe that is a community of nation states. I do not want a United States of Europe. Such a concept would never be in the interests of the British people.

Part of a speech made on 28 April 1992

(iii) Have your reservations by all means. Nobody says Europe is perfect. But, since we joined, our exports to the EU have grown nearly 50% faster than those of our old European Free Trade Area partners.

Part of a speech made on 23 April 1993

(iv) Our vision is a strong one. We want a strong Britain in a strong Europe. We want a prosperous Europe; a Europe with more jobs; a competitive Europe; a Europe built on free trade; a Europe of independent nation states; a wider Europe, spreading peace and prosperity across our continent.

Part of a speech made on 18 February 1994

(v) I will tell you my fear: unless economic conditions are right, a single currency would tear the European Union apart. And by the right economic conditions, the government does not only mean the Maastricht criteria - they are a necessary, but not a sufficient condition to justify a single currency.

Part of a speech made on 3 February 1995

Adapted from the *Independent on Sunday*, 12 February 1995.

Item C *John Major and Europe (2)*

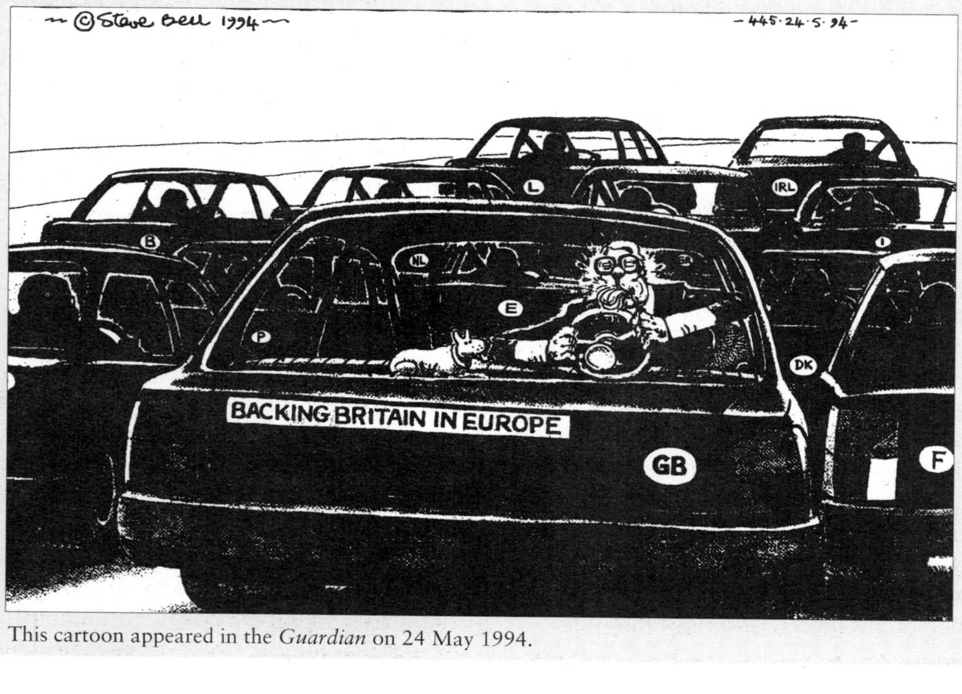

This cartoon appeared in the *Guardian* on 24 May 1994.

Item D *Where the main parties stand on Europe*

Where the parties stand	CON	LAB
Trading bloc	Yes	Yes
Single currency	Decide in 1999	Decide in 1999
Single market	Yes	Yes
Veto	No change	Retain for vital issues
CAP	Fundamental reform	Fundamental reform
Referendum	If justified	Not ruled out
Enlargement	Yes	Yes
Change qualified majority voting	Yes, more weight for UK	Yes, details unclear
Federalism	No	No
Common foreign and security policy	No	No
Common defence policy	No	No
Social Chapter	No	Yes
European Parliament	No more power	Powers shared with national Parliaments

Adapted from the *Financial Times*, 12 February 1995.

Questions

1. a) What evidence is there in Items A and B to suggest that John Major's Cabinet was split over policy towards the EU?
   b) Geddes (1993) identifies six different viewpoints towards Europe within the Conservative party. Which group does each Cabinet member mentioned in Items A and B belong to? Give reasons for your answer.
2. a) 'John Major has played his cards just right over Europe.' Using Items B and C give arguments for and against this statement.
   b) What evidence is there in Item B to support the point being made by Item C?
3. What does Item D tell us about the policies of the two main political parties towards Europe? Explain the limitations of this table.
4. Why do you think divisions over Europe affect the Conservative party more than other political parties in Britain?

4 Britain and the world

Key Issues

1. How has Britain's role in the world changed since 1945?
2. What is Britain's relationship with the Commonwealth, NATO and the United Nations?
3. How does membership of these organisations affect decision making in the UK?

4.1 Britain and the Commonwealth

In 1945, Britain was an imperial power. The British Empire covered 11.5 million square miles and included over 400 million inhabitants. This vast empire was controlled by imperial staff in the colonies and by staff in London where three departments of state had imperial responsibility (the Dominions Office, Colonial Office and India Office).

By 1945, the British Parliament had granted independence to a number of former colonies, such as Canada, Australia and South Africa. These former colonies (or 'dominions' as they were known) were self-governing, but the British government retained ties with them and some influence over them. In 1914, for example, the British government declared war on behalf of the whole Empire (including the dominions) without consultation. During the war, however, the dominions were consulted on an equal basis and in 1919 they signed the peace treaties individually and joined the League of Nations individually. In the interwar period, these dominions gained further autonomy:

> 'At the 1926 Imperial Conference, the dominions were described as: "autonomous communities within the British Empire, equal in status, in no way subordinate one to another in any respect of their domestic or external affairs, though unified by a common allegiance to the Crown and freely associated as members of the British Commonwealth of Nations." This principle was legally formulated in the Statute of Westminster, an Act passed by the British Parliament in 1931.' (HMSO, 1992a, p.5)

It was the Statute of Westminster which laid the legal foundations of the Commonwealth.

The dominions affected by the Statute were Australia, Canada, Newfoundland (which became a province of Canada in 1949), the Irish Free State, New Zealand and South Africa. All had a number of characteristics in common. First, they all had a developed economy. Second, all (except South Africa) had majority populations descended from white settlers. Third, all (except South Africa) had universal suffrage and a parliamentary system based on that of Britain. And fourth, all agreed to continued allegiance to the British monarch (who was represented in each dominion by a Governor General).

Decolonisation

Although some colonies had pressed for the end of British rule before 1945, it was only after the Second World War was over that the process of decolonisation began in earnest (see Item A in activity 6.6). This was due to a number of factors. First, during the war, the British government raised expectations in the colonies and, after the war was over, people in the colonies pressed for these expectations to be realised. Many colonies had sent troops to fight for the Allied cause, for example. After the war was over, there were hopes that their contribution would be rewarded by freedom from imperial control. Similarly, in 1941, Britain had signed the Atlantic Charter which committed it to 'uphold the rights of all people to choose the form of government under which they will live.' But people in the colonies had no choice over the form of government under which they lived. They hoped that British government propaganda which had claimed that the Allies were fighting to preserve freedom of choice and the right to self-determination would mean an end to imperial rule once the war was over. Second, the war drained Britain economically. The Empire had become simply too expensive to maintain. It was only after the war that the British government realised that this was the case. Third, decolonisation gained a momentum of its own. Once independence had been granted to one colony, it was harder to argue against independence for other colonies. The result was a 'domino effect' - the colonies fell like a stack of dominos, one after another. Fourth, it should be noted that no imperial power was able to resist the pressure to decolonise after the war. This suggests that support for independence in the colonies did not depend upon the type of imperial rule (different imperial powers ruled in different ways). Rather, it suggests that the pressure to decolonise became irresistible. And fifth, pressure to decolonise did not just come from the colonies. There was a change of attitude in Britain. Although some people advocated fighting to preserve the Empire, most British politicians took the pragmatic view that decolonisation was inevitable and should, therefore, be put into practice in as painless a manner as possible.

According to Simpson (1986), official policy towards the Empire in the 1940s and 1950s had two elements. First, there was the desire to protect strategic interests in order to maintain Britain's position as a world power. And second, there was a desire to promote the welfare of people living in the colonies and to prepare them for self-government when Britain withdrew.

The process of decolonisation was spectacular. By 1980, only 15 dependent territories remained under British control and most of these were small islands with small populations (such as the Falkland Islands, the Cayman Islands and the British Virgin Islands). The loss of its Empire undoubtedly affected Britain's status. Before the Second World War, Britain was regarded as a major power. The postwar world, however, was dominated by two superpowers, the Soviet Union and the USA. Britain's loss in status led the American Secretary of State, Dean Acheson, to comment in a speech made in December 1962, 'Great Britain has lost an Empire and has not yet found a role.'

The Commonwealth

The Commonwealth is a free association of 51 sovereign independent states which evolved from the former British Empire. It is an international organisation which contains both developing and developed countries working in cooperation together. Membership of the Commonwealth is voluntary. Although the British monarch is the head of the Commonwealth, the position is only ceremonial. In 1949, it was decided that allegiance to the Crown was not a necessary criterion for Commonwealth membership. This allowed former colonies to become republics (states without a monarch at their head), but to retain membership of the Commonwealth. Many current members of the Commonwealth are republics.

Those countries which were members of the Commonwealth before 1949 still (in theory at least) accept the British monarch as their head of state and are often referred to as the 'Old Commonwealth', whilst those members who gained independence from British rule after 1945 are often referred to as the 'New Commonwealth'.

From the British point of view, membership of the Commonwealth is important because:

> 'The Commonwealth enables Britain to play a responsible part alongside other nations in aiding the development and stability of the Third World. Britain participates fully in all Commonwealth activities (most of Britain's aid to developing countries goes to Commonwealth member states) and welcomes it as a means of consulting and cooperating with people of widely differing cultures.' (HMSO, 1992a, p.1)

Close cultural, educational, sporting and some economic links exist between Commonwealth countries. But members find it difficult to make political decisions together. The members have very different types of government and often very different policy aims.

The character of the Commonwealth has altered as new members have joined. Before 1960, it was dominated by white nations. Since then, black nations have been in the majority. By 1968, 12 of the 28 members were from Africa.

The changing nature of the Commonwealth has led to a number of political conflicts - notably over white rule in Rhodesia (now Zimbabwe) in the late 1960s and over the system of apartheid in South Africa that remained in place between 1948 and 1994. Following South Africa's withdrawal from the Commonwealth in 1961, there was growing division and tension within the Commonwealth along racial lines. In 1971, Commonwealth heads of government met in Singapore and drew up a code of ethics, known as the 'Singapore Declaration'. It was signed by all members and covered human rights, racial equality, economic freedom and support for the United Nations. Tension within the Commonwealth over South Africa continued, however. In the 1980s, the main issue was whether or not Commonwealth countries should impose economic sanctions on South Africa as a means of protesting about the continuation of repression of the black majority population under the apartheid regime. The British government argued against sanctions, whilst most other Commonwealth countries supported them. Following the release from prison of Nelson Mandela in 1990, sanctions were lifted. In April 1994, the first ever democratic elections were held in South Africa and Nelson Mandela became President. Shortly after the elections, South Africa rejoined the Commonwealth.

Organisation of the Commonwealth

The Commonwealth Secretariat was established in London in 1965. Its duties are to promote Commonwealth cooperation and to provide the central organisation for joint consultation between member states. In 1976, it was granted observer status at the United Nations. Meetings take place regularly between member states at various levels - from heads of government down to officials concerned with individual projects. The Secretariat provides information and policy advice to member governments on a wide range of issues. Since it is neutral, the Secretariat can also provide arbitration in the event of dispute.

The Commonwealth Secretary-General is head of the Secretariat and has access to all heads of governments. The Secretary-General is elected by Commonwealth heads of government. The Secretariat is based in London and staffed by over 400 officials from 30 countries. It is financed through contributions from member governments. Contributions are related to capacity to pay and are based on population and national income. In 1992, Britain paid 30%, Canada 19%, Australia 9.7%, India 3.3% and New Zealand 2.2%. Other members paid between 1.7% and 0.3%. The Secretariat provides technical assistance through the separately funded Commonwealth Fund for Technical Cooperation (CFTC).

Activity 6.6

Item A *Decolonisation 1945-95*

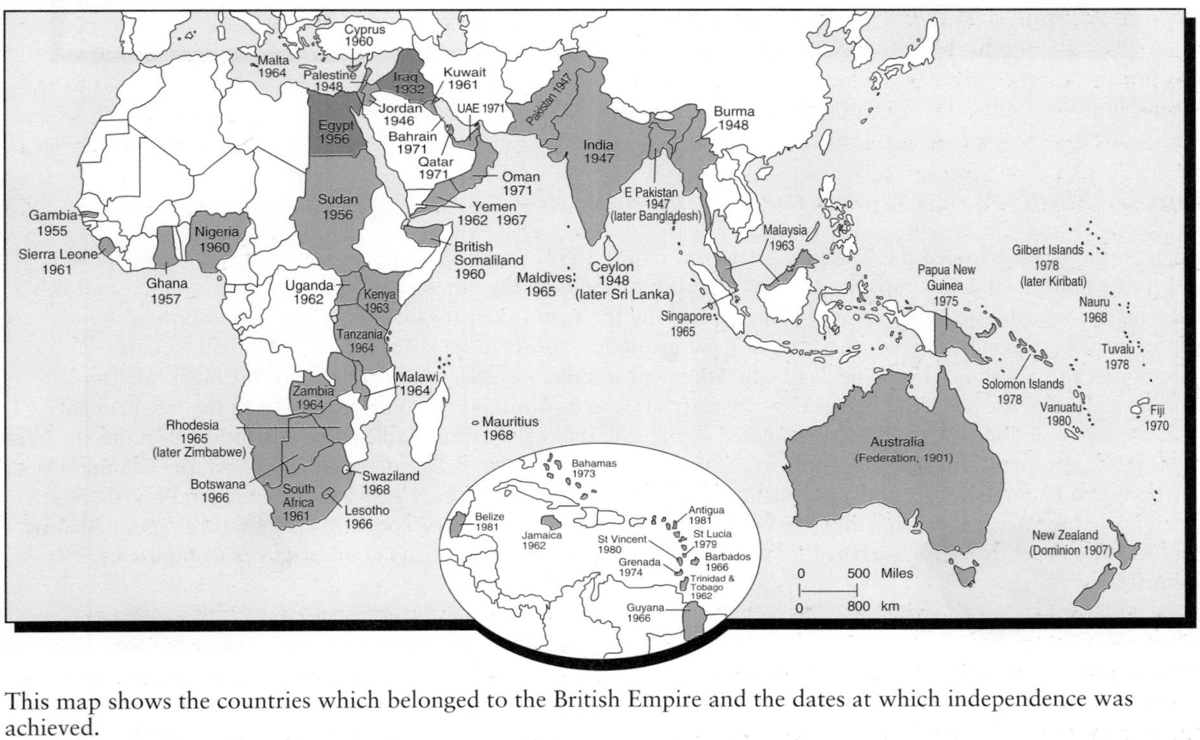

This map shows the countries which belonged to the British Empire and the dates at which independence was achieved.

Item B *The Commonwealth Fund for Technical Cooperation (CFTC)*

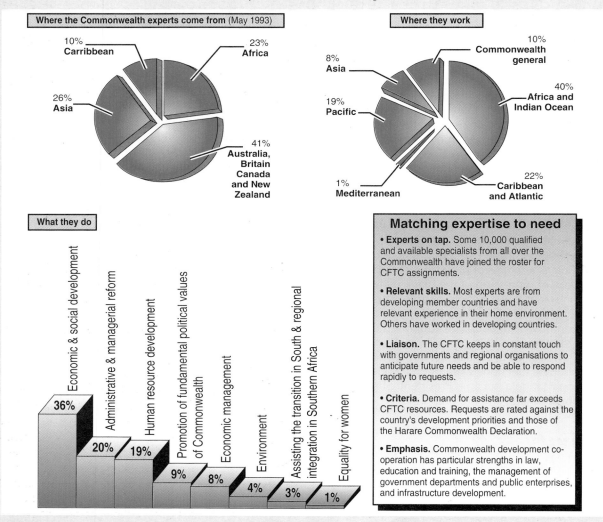

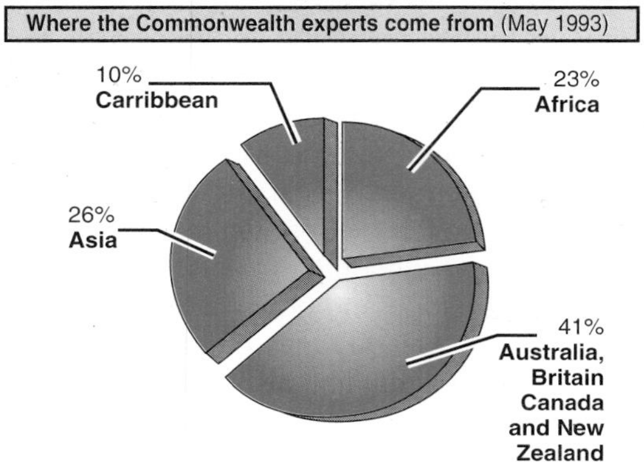

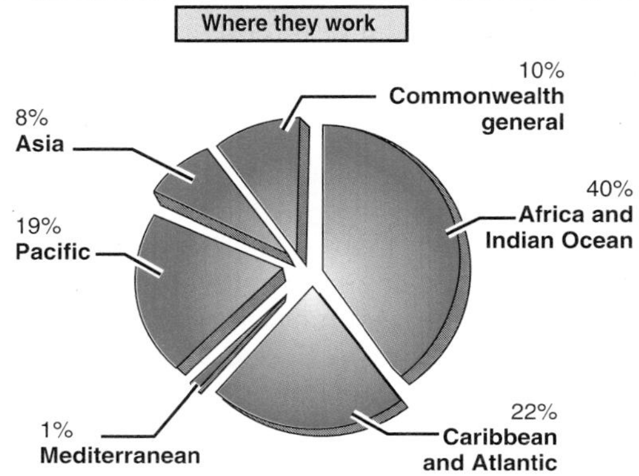

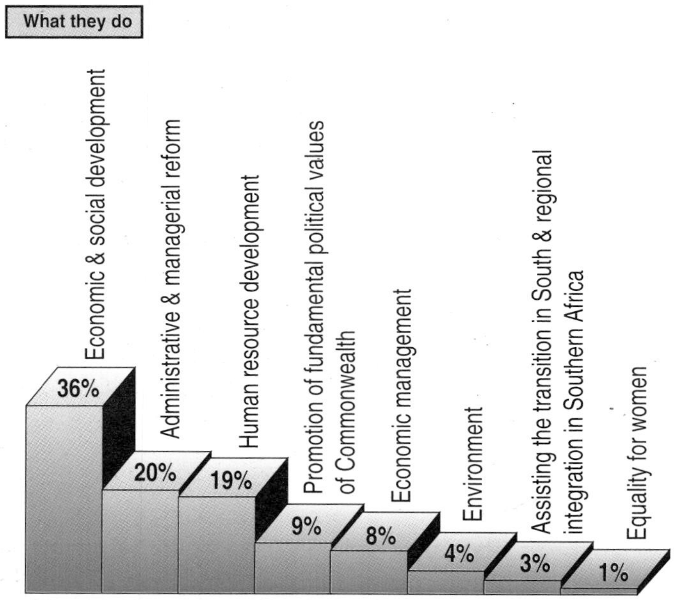

Matching expertise to need

- **Experts on tap.** Some 10,000 qualified and available specialists from all over the Commonwealth have joined the roster for CFTC assignments.
- **Relevant skills.** Most experts are from developing member countries and have relevant experience in their home environment. Others have worked in developing countries.
- **Liaison.** The CFTC keeps in constant touch with governments and regional organisations to anticipate future needs and be able to respond rapidly to requests.
- **Criteria.** Demand for assistance far exceeds CFTC resources. Requests are rated against the country's development priorities and those of the Harare Commonwealth Declaration.
- **Emphasis.** Commonwealth development co-operation has particular strengths in law, education and training, the management of government departments and public enterprises, and infrastructure development.

Adapted from the report of the Commonwealth Secretary-General, 1993.

Item C *South Africa rejoins the Commonwealth*

When South Africa rejoined the Commonwealth on 1 June 1994, Secretary-General, Chief Emeka Anyaoku, said: 'The return of a non-racial democratic South Africa, working alongside the other 50 members of the Commonwealth is a boost for the association, not least in the task of making the world safer for diversity.' The Commonwealth hopes to help in its newest member's reconstruction and reconciliation efforts in four ways. First, there will be more Commonwealth assistance in the fields of education and training - especially the training of the black African professionals who are needed if national reconstruction is to be a success. Second, assistance to the Independent Electoral Commission (IEC) is being considered so that the IEC will be better able to handle future elections (in April 1994, the Commonwealth sent 56 people to South Africa to offer their electoral expertise). Third, the Commonwealth is expected to help the integration and restructuring of South African military and police forces. And fourth, South Africa can expect to benefit from all Commonwealth political, economic and sporting links. In turn, South African technical and other expertise, such as that in mining technology, will now be available to other Commonwealth countries.

Adapted from Commonwealth, 1994.

Item D *The Singapore Declaration, 1971*

1. We believe that international peace and order are essential to the security and prosperity of mankind. We support the United Nations in its efforts to remove the causes of tensions between nations.
2. We believe in the liberty of the individual - in equal rights for all regardless of race, colour, creed, political belief.
3. We recognise racial prejudice as a dangerous sickness - we will each combat this evil within our own nations.
4. We oppose all forms of colonial domination. We are committed to furthering the principle of self-determination.
5. We believe that the wide disparities of wealth now existing between different sections of mankind are too great to be tolerated. We seek to overcome poverty, ignorance and disease and to achieve a more equitable society.
6. We believe that international cooperation is essential to remove the causes of war.

Adapted from an information sheet produced by the Commonwealth Secretariat in 1993.

Questions

1. Using Item A describe the process of decolonisation. What evidence is there of a domino effect?
2. Judging from Items B-D what is the role and the purpose of the Commonwealth?
3. 'For Britain, it is an expensive burden.' Is this a fair assessment of the Commonwealth? Give reasons for your answer.

4.2 Other international organisations

In addition to the European Union and the Commonwealth, the UK is a member of the North Atlantic Treaty Organisation (NATO) and the United Nations Organisation (UNO). Membership of both influences and, to some extent, determines the direction of Britain's foreign policy.

The Cold War

The North Atlantic Treaty Organisation (NATO) is a product of the Cold War which broke out shortly after the end of the Second World War and lasted until the collapse of Soviet Communism in 1991.

The Second World War broke Europe's domination of world affairs and resulted in the emergence of the USA and the Soviet Union (USSR) as 'superpowers'. Even as the Americans and Soviets cooperated to defeat Hitler, they saw each other as rivals. Within a few years of the end of the war, the world had been divided into two competing areas of influence - the American dominated West which supported capitalism and the Soviet dominated East which supported communism. The conflict between the two blocs became known as the 'Cold War' because, although there was a massive build-up of weapons, actual war did not break out directly between the superpowers. The fact that both sides had nuclear weapons, it has been argued, made them stop short of direct fighting. It is, however, slightly misleading to talk of a 'cold' war since this implies that there was no real combat. In fact, both superpowers backed or fought wars in countries outside Europe (such as Korea, Vietnam and Afghanistan) and millions died as a result.

The Cold War developed out of what happened in the final stages of the Second World War. Soviet troops pushed the Nazis back through Eastern Europe into Germany whilst the troops of the Western Allies (the USA, Britain and France) crossed the Channel and pushed the Nazis back though France and the Benelux countries. Soviet troops occupied Eastern Europe, therefore, and the troops of the Western Allies occupied Western Europe.

Suspicions between the two superpowers stretched right back to the Russian revolution of 1917 and beyond. The USA was as fierce a champion of capitalism as the Soviet Union was a champion of communism. Suspicions remained throughout the Second World War and were exacerbated by the American announcement of the Marshall Plan in June 1947 (see p.130). Under this plan, the USA promised a massive programme of financial aid to rebuild the stricken European economy. Although this aid was offered to Eastern European countries, they rejected it. Stalin claimed that the Marshall Plan was a plot to spread American control by economic rather than military means. In reply, the USSR set up the 'Molotov plan' in July 1947. This tied Eastern Europe to the USSR in a series of trade agreements.

When Germany finally surrendered in 1945, the country was divided into four zones, each zone occupied by one of the victorious Allies - the USA, Britain, France and the Soviet Union. Berlin, the capital, was also divided into four zones. Suspicion between the Soviet Union and the other three Allies led to these temporary zones becoming pawns in the early phase of the Cold War. Whilst cooperation between the Western Allies led to the removal of barriers between their zones, the Soviet Union kept its zone separate. When, in 1948, the Soviet Union tried to prevent the other allies crossing Soviet controlled territory to bring goods into their zones in Berlin, the Western Allies sent in supplies by air for more than a year until the Soviets finally relented. This, the 'Berlin Airlift', was typical of a Cold War confrontation.

The confrontation over Berlin had two main consequences. First, the division of Germany into East

Germany (the Soviet zone) and West Germany (the other three zones) became fixed. In 1949, the American, British and French zones were amalgamated and the area became the Federal Republic of Germany (West Germany) with its own Western style government and constitution. In response to this, the Soviet Union set up the German Democratic Republic (East Germany) with a Soviet style government and constitution. And second, the Berlin airlift revealed that the Western Allies could force the Soviets to back down if they combined their forces. The result was the formation of a military alliance - the North Atlantic Treaty Organisation (NATO).

The North Atlantic Treaty Organisation (NATO)

The origins of NATO are closely linked to the signing of the Brussels Treaty in March 1948. This Treaty bound Britain, France and the three Benelux countries to assist each other in the event of armed aggression against any one of them from the Communist East. It was drawn up in response to a British initiative.

The Canadian Secretary of State for Foreign Affairs picked up on this initiative and suggested that the idea of a mutual defence system be extended to include Canada and the USA. The result was the development of a single defence system for the North Atlantic and Western Europe. On 4 April 1949, the North Atlantic Treaty was signed by the foreign ministers of 12 states - the original five members plus Canada, Denmark, Iceland, Norway, Italy, Portugal and the USA.

The need for a mutual defence organisation was (it was argued) immediately underlined when, in July 1949, news reached the West that the Soviet Union had successfully test-exploded an atom bomb for the first time. Until then, the USA had been the only country with nuclear capability in the world (the first atom bomb was test-exploded in the USA in July 1945). Once both superpowers had nuclear capability, an arms race began with huge amounts of money being poured into projects designed to build more and bigger nuclear weapons with more and more sophisticated delivery systems. NATO (like its counterpart, the Warsaw Pact) soon became a nuclear umbrella behind which its members sought protection. Greece and Turkey joined NATO in 1952, West Germany joined in 1955 and Spain joined in 1982.

NATO's main aim was to safeguard its members against aggression from the Soviet bloc. To achieve this, a great deal of political cooperation and joint defence planning was necessary. In theory, all members were to be equal, but, in practice, NATO was dominated by the USA from the start. There were two main reasons for this. First, the USA was the only state capable of matching the might of a potential Soviet attack. And second, the European members were more concerned with economic recovery than possible rearmament.

The USA's domination of NATO is particularly significant when considering Britain's changing role since 1945. During the war, Britain was a major player and Churchill helped to shape the postwar world, along with Roosevelt and Stalin. But after the war was over, Britain's desperate economic position ensured that it quickly lost ground to the two emerging superpowers. Although the British government prided itself on its 'special relationship' with the USA, in reality, the relationship was not one of equals. Where the USA led, Britain followed. This disparity was particularly obvious in the military sphere. Although the British government prided itself on its independent nuclear deterrent, in reality, Britain's nuclear stockpile was soon minuscule compared with that of the USA. Consequently, the USA's military dominance ensured that it dominated NATO policy.

Since the collapse of Soviet Communism in 1991, NATO has been searching for a new role. When a NATO summit was held in November 1991:

> 'A new strategy called Strategic Concept was adopted, by which Britain and its allies acknowledged that the threat of a full-scale attack on all NATO's European fronts has been removed. At the same time, there are other possible risks - notably ethnic rivalries and territorial disputes - which could involve outside powers or spill over into NATO countries. In addition, account has to be taken of a substantial nuclear arsenal held in the republics of the former Soviet Union; Russia in particular remains the largest military power in Europe. There are other dangers outside Europe where developing states have modern weapons of mass destruction that could reach NATO territory.' (HMSO, 1993, p.51)

As a result of these concerns, NATO members agreed that NATO should remain as the bastion of defence and security in Europe and that smaller, more flexible reaction forces should be deployed. These reaction forces should have a more multinational nature than was the case in the past (when the USA provided the majority of personnel). In addition, NATO has sought to promote closer relations with former members of the Eastern bloc via the North Atlantic Cooperation Council (NACC):

> 'The NACC was established by NATO as a sort of sop to those states - especially Poland, Hungary and Czechoslovakia - which sought membership of NATO as the best guarantee of their long-term security against a renewed threat from Russia or from instability arising in eastern

> Europe...The NACC has expanded to include all the former members of the Warsaw Pact and the European states of the former Soviet Union. It has developed a particular role in arms control and in confidence-building measures...NATO finally offered a 'Partnership for Peace' rather than full membership to the states of the east.' (Byrd, 1994, pp.146-7)

The United Nations

The first truly international organisation was the League of Nations, established after the First World War. The idea was that all countries in the world would join the League and if there was a dispute between two countries, the League would decide which country was in the right. If one country broke international law (for example, by invading another country), the other members of the League would join together and take action against that country. The League of Nations suffered from the start because the USA refused to join it. It was then discredited when Japan invaded Manchuria in 1931 and Italy invaded Ethiopia in 1935, and it proved unable to prevent the outbreak of the Second World War.

The idea of a United Nations Organisation was developed during the Second World War. Churchill, Roosevelt and Stalin agreed at the Tehran conference in 1943 that a new international organisation should be set up to replace the League of Nations. Between August and October 1944, a conference was held in Washington DC to work out the final plans. The result was the United Nations Charter. This Charter was signed by 51 states in San Francisco in June 1945. The main aim of the UN is to secure peace throughout the world. It also works to eradicate suffering and poverty.

Membership of the UN is open to all states which accept the aims of the Charter. The main institutions of the UN are the Security Council, the General Assembly, the Secretariat and the International Court of Justice (see Activity 6.7, Item B).

The Security Council consists of five permanent members (Britain, France, China, Russia and the USA - the victors in the Second World War) and 10 other members elected every two years by the General Assembly. The permanent members have the power to veto draft resolutions. During the Cold War, this power was often used to block resolutions because it was felt that one side or the other was trying to manipulate the UN to its own advantage. As a result, it was difficult for the UN to function properly. Since the end of the Cold War, however, there has been a degree of optimism that the UN will be able to play a more positive role in international affairs. A British government pamphlet reflects this sentiment:

> 'Because of the Cold War, the Security Council was for many years unable to function fully in the ways intended by the Charter. Now that the Cold War has ended, Britain believes that the UN has the chance to revive its authority and to seek to resolve disputes which threaten international peace and stability.' (HMSO, 1993, p.8)

UN peacekeeping since the collapse of Soviet Communism in 1991 has had mixed fortunes. Military action against Iraq in 1990-91 had full UN backing and achieved its aim of forcing the Iraqis out of Kuwait, but this was achieved only at the cost of great loss of life. Similarly, UN intervention in the former Yugoslavia has failed to bring about permanent peace.

Although UN peacekeeping operations capture most public attention, the UN's aid agencies carry out work that helps to prevent war breaking out in the first place. The best known of these agencies are the World Health Organisation (WHO) and UNICEF (the UN's children fund). As a result of UNICEF's immunisation programme, the number of children in the developing world who have been immunised has risen from less than 5% in 1974 to 80% in 1991. A third agency, the UN Educational, Scientific and Cultural Organisation (UNESCO) aims to change people and politics through education. Its activities range from literacy programmes to campaigns to preserve ancient monuments. However, because it deals in ideas and culture, it is the most controversial UN agency. In 1985, Britain withdrew from UNESCO because:

> 'Although Britain supports the ideals and objectives contained in UNESCO's constitution, it had doubts about the effectiveness with which the organisation pursued them.' (HMSO, 1993, p.11)

After a review of UNESCO's activities in 1990, the British government decided not to rejoin UNESCO.

Most of the UN aid agencies' work takes place in underdeveloped countries. Long-term projects are designed to improve the local economy, whilst short-term projects help to provide food and medical relief. Despite the work of the UN agencies, however, the gap between the rich and poor nations has widened.

Activity 6.7

Item A *The UN Charter*

The preamble to the United Nations Charter states that: 'We are determined to save succeeding generations from the scourge of war which twice in our lifetime has brought untold misery to mankind.' The aims of the UN can be summarised as follows:

1. To maintain international peace and security.
2. To settle international disputes in conformity with justice and international law.
3. To achieve cooperation in solving international problems and to promote respect for human rights and fundamental freedoms for all without distinction as to race, sex, language or religion.

UN members are committed:

1. To refrain from the threat or use of force against the territory or political independence of any state.
2. To seek solutions to disputes by peaceful means.

The Charter recognises and permits the right of the individual or collective defence against armed attack and the existence of regional arrangements designed to maintain peace and security.

Adapted from an information sheet produced by the UN's London office, 1995.

Item B *How the UN works*

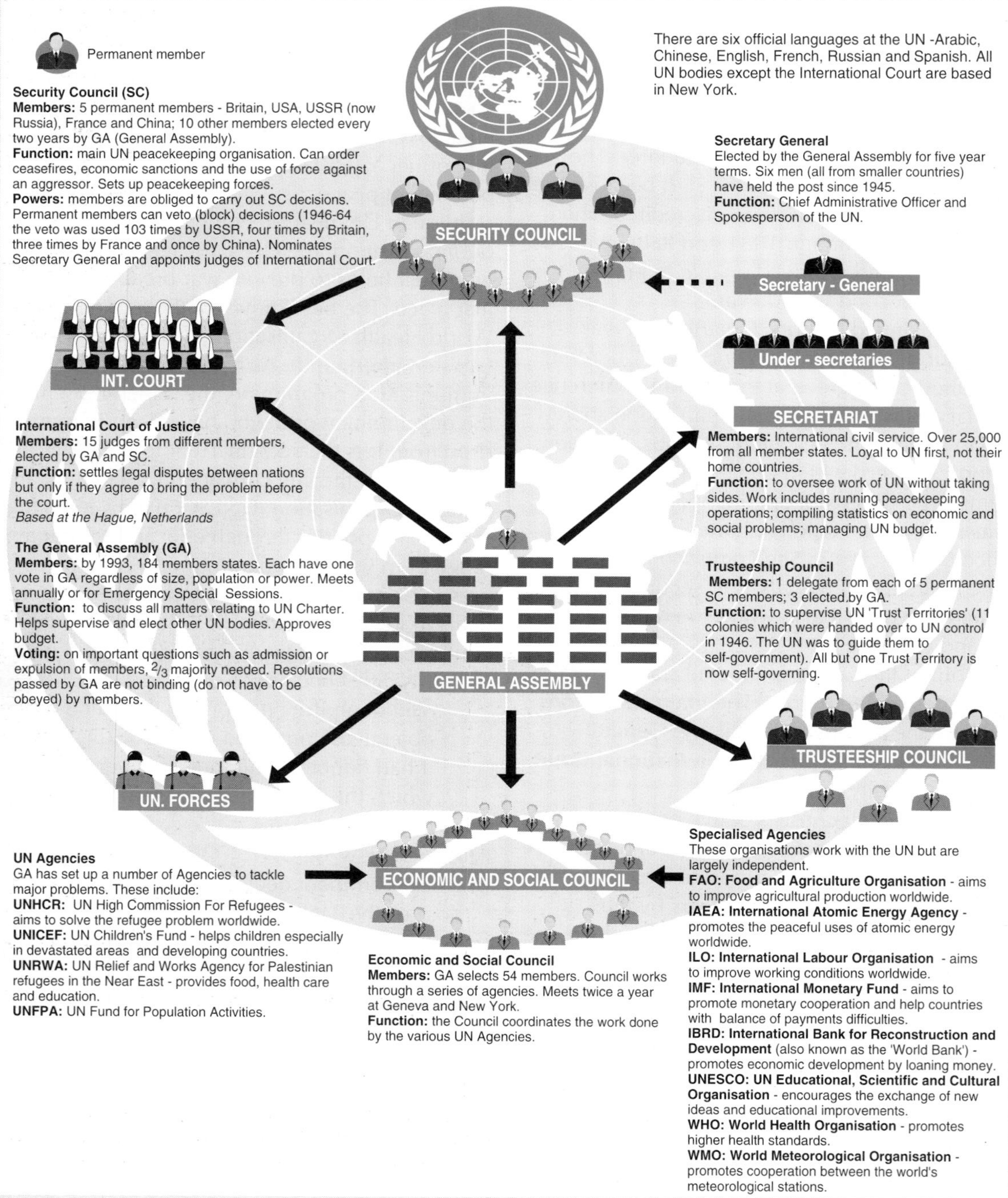

Permanent member
Security Council (SC)
Members: 5 permanent members - Britain, USA, USSR (now Russia), France and China; 10 other members elected every two years by GA (General Assembly).
Function: main UN peacekeeping organisation. Can order ceasefires, economic sanctions and the use of force against an aggressor. Sets up peacekeeping forces.
Powers: members are obliged to carry out SC decisions. Permanent members can veto (block) decisions (1946-64 the veto was used 103 times by USSR, four times by Britain, three times by France and once by China). Nominates Secretary General and appoints judges of International Court.
There are six official languages at the UN -Arabic, Chinese, English, French, Russian and Spanish. All UN bodies except the International Court are based in New York.
Secretary General
Elected by the General Assembly for five year terms. Six men (all from smaller countries) have held the post since 1945.
Function: Chief Administrative Officer and Spokesperson of the UN.
SECURITY COUNCIL
Secretary - General
Under - secretaries
INT. COURT
SECRETARIAT
International Court of Justice
Members: 15 judges from different members, elected by GA and SC.
Function: settles legal disputes between nations but only if they agree to bring the problem before the court.
Based at the Hague, Netherlands
Members: International civil service. Over 25,000 from all member states. Loyal to UN first, not their home countries.
Function: to oversee work of UN without taking sides. Work includes running peacekeeping operations; compiling statistics on economic and social problems; managing UN budget.
The General Assembly (GA)
Members: by 1993, 184 members states. Each have one vote in GA regardless of size, population or power. Meets annually or for Emergency Special Sessions.
Function: to discuss all matters relating to UN Charter. Helps supervise and elect other UN bodies. Approves budget.
Voting: on important questions such as admission or expulsion of members, 2/3 majority needed. Resolutions passed by GA are not binding (do not have to be obeyed) by members.
Trusteeship Council
Members: 1 delegate from each of 5 permanent SC members; 3 elected by GA.
Function: to supervise UN 'Trust Territories' (11 colonies which were handed over to UN control in 1946. The UN was to guide them to self-government). All but one Trust Territory is now self-governing.
GENERAL ASSEMBLY
TRUSTEESHIP COUNCIL
UN. FORCES
ECONOMIC AND SOCIAL COUNCIL
UN Agencies
GA has set up a number of Agencies to tackle major problems. These include:
UNHCR: UN High Commission For Refugees - aims to solve the refugee problem worldwide.
UNICEF: UN Children's Fund - helps children especially in devastated areas and developing countries.
UNRWA: UN Relief and Works Agency for Palestinian refugees in the Near East - provides food, health care and education.
UNFPA: UN Fund for Population Activities.
Economic and Social Council
Members: GA selects 54 members. Council works through a series of agencies. Meets twice a year at Geneva and New York.
Function: the Council coordinates the work done by the various UN Agencies.
Specialised Agencies
These organisations work with the UN but are largely independent.
FAO: Food and Agriculture Organisation - aims to improve agricultural production worldwide.
IAEA: International Atomic Energy Agency - promotes the peaceful uses of atomic energy worldwide.
ILO: International Labour Organisation - aims to improve working conditions worldwide.
IMF: International Monetary Fund - aims to promote monetary cooperation and help countries with balance of payments difficulties.
IBRD: International Bank for Reconstruction and Development (also known as the 'World Bank') - promotes economic development by loaning money.
UNESCO: UN Educational, Scientific and Cultural Organisation - encourages the exchange of new ideas and educational improvements.
WHO: World Health Organisation - promotes higher health standards.
WMO: World Meteorological Organisation - promotes cooperation between the world's meteorological stations.

Item C *Peacekeeping*

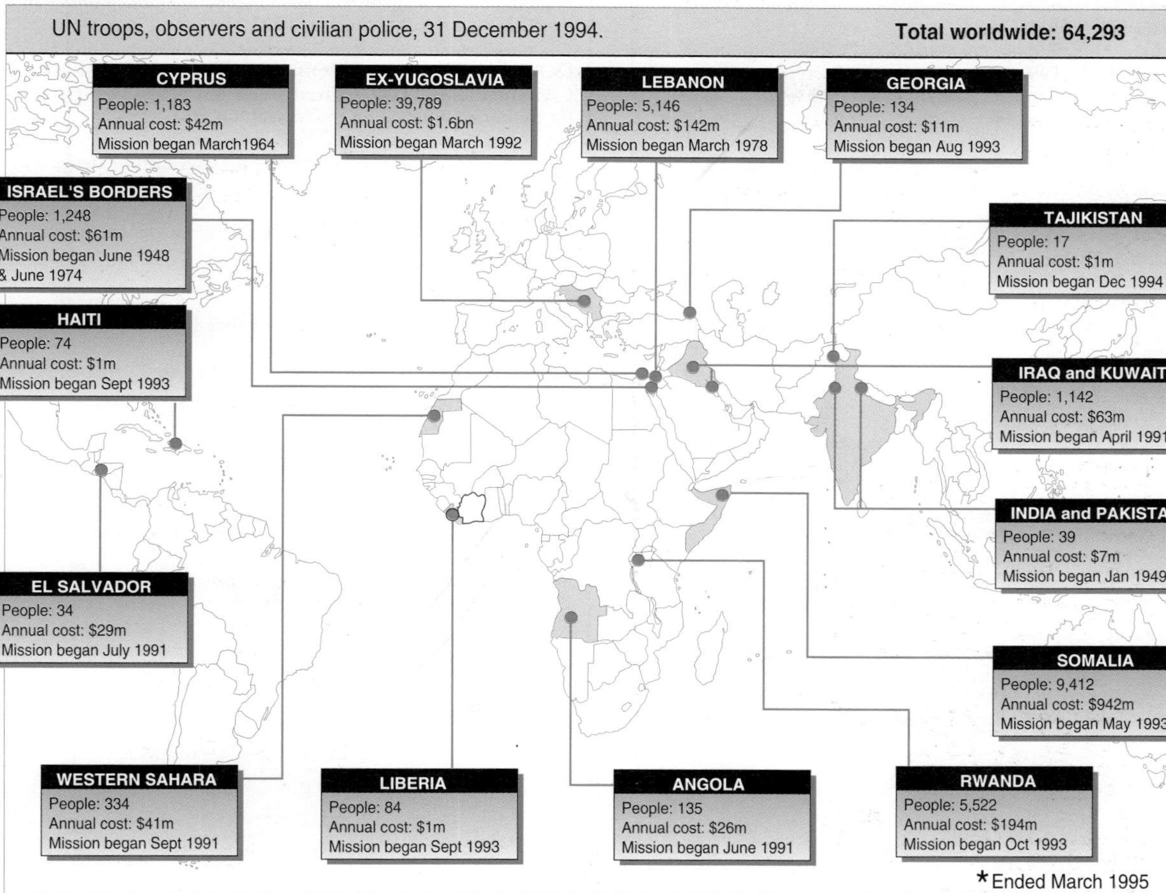

Adapted from the *Economist*, 11 February 1995.

Item D *The post-Cold War world*

The West has not yet developed a clear foreign policy direction for the 21st century, but it needs one rather urgently. The world is in the early stages of what promises to be one of its most tumultuous periods. Gone are the certainties of the Cold War world. By going back to a multi-power system, there is greater risk. Now, policy makers have to calculate the reactions of a number of other powers before formulating any major policies. There is, therefore, a risk that the reactions of the various powers will collide over any policy. The probable main contenders for power in the 21st century are the USA, Russia, China, the EU and some new Muslim entity. These powers have little in common and are likely to misunderstand each other and miscalculate each other's reactions. They will inhabit a world which is ever more dangerous since technologically it will be a world capable of doing more damage by nuclear and other means.

Adapted from the *Economist*, 24 December 1994 and 6 January 1995.

Questions

1. Judging from Items B and C how does the UN attempt to achieve the aims set out in Item A? Why do you think the UN had difficulties fulfilling its role during the Cold War?
2. 'The world has become a safer place since the end of the Cold War.' Using Items C and D give arguments for and against this view.
3. Why do you suppose Britain joined both the UN and NATO? Is there still any reason to belong to both organisations?

References

Ashford (1992) Ashford, N., 'The political parties' in *George (1992).*

Byrd (1994) Byrd, P., 'Defence policy since 1990' in *Wale (1994).*

Carr & Cope (1994) Carr, F. & Cope, S., 'Implementing Maastricht: the limits of European Union', *Talking Politics,* Vol.6, No.3, summer 1994.

Church (1992) Church, C.H., 'Widening the European Community', *Politics Review*, Vol.2, No.1, September 1992.

Coates (1994) Coates, D., *The Question of UK Decline*, Harvester Wheatsheaf, 1994.

Commonwealth (1994) Commonwealth Secretariat, 'South Africa is welcomed back into the family', *Commonwealth Currents*, June/July 1994.

Geddes (1993) Geddes, A., *Britain in the European Community*, Baseline Books, 1993.

George (1992) George, S. (ed.), *Britain and the European Community*, Clarendon, 1992.

HMSO (1992) Central Office of Information, *Britain in the European Community*, HMSO, 1992.

HMSO (1992a) Central Office of Information, *Britain and the Commonwealth*, HMSO, 1992.

HMSO (1993) Central Office of Information, *Overseas Relations and Defence*, HMSO, 1993.

Lancaster (1995) Lancaster, S. (ed.), *Developments in Politics*, Vol.6., Causeway Press, 1995.

Lipgens (1981) Lipgens, W., *European Integration*, Vol.1, Oxford University Press, 1981.

Lodge (1993) Lodge, J., *'Europe'* in *Wale (1993)*.

Mazey & Richardson (1993) Mazey, S. & Richardson, J., 'Pressure groups and the EC', *Politics Review*, Vol.3, No.1, September 1993.

Norton (1995) Norton, P., 'The constitution' in *Lancaster (1995)*.

Nugent (1994) Nugent, N., *The Government and Politics of the European Union*, Macmillan, 1994.

OOPEC (1992) Office for Official Publication of the European Communities (OOPEC), *From Single Market to European Union* (in the series, Europe on the Move), OOPEC, 1992.

Pinder (1991) Pinder, J., *The Federal Case*, European Movement, 1991.

Simpson (1986) Simpson, W., *Changing Horizons*, Stanley Thornes, 1986.

Sked (1989) Sked, A., *Good Europeans?, An occasional paper*, The Bruges Group, 4 November 1989.

Thatcher (1988) Thatcher, M., *Britain in the European Community*, Conservative Political Centre, 1988.

Vander Elst (1991) Vander Elst, P., *Resisting Leviathan: the Case Against a European State*, The Claridge Press, 1991.

Wale (1993), Wale, W (ed.), *Developments in Politics*, Vol. 4, Causeway Press, 1993.

Wale (1994), Wale, W (ed.), *Developments in Politics*, Vol. 5, Causeway Press, 1994.

Part 3

Representation

7 Democracy and elections

Introduction

If there is one thing that all politicians from the main political parties in Britain can agree on, it is that democracy is the best form of government. It is only when they are asked what exactly they mean by 'democracy' and how it should be delivered that the differences between them become apparent. In Britain, it is assumed that everyone supports democracy and that the British system of government is democratic. The trouble is that the term 'democracy' (which comes from two ancient Greek words - **demos** meaning 'the people' and **cratos** meaning 'power') covers a wide range of meanings. For example, Communist East Germany used to describe itself as 'democratic'. Yet, the system of government there was very different from the system of government in Britain.

This chapter describes the main characteristics of democratic political systems and examines the development of democracy in Britain. Since one of the features of a smoothly functioning democracy is that the majority of people participate in some way in decision making, the chapter considers to what extent people in Britain participate in politics. Perhaps the most obvious way in which people participate in politics is by voting in elections. This chapter examines the electoral system in Britain in some detail and considers alternative electoral systems. This raises the question of electoral reform. What are the arguments for and against electoral reform in Britain and why has the debate over electoral reform risen up the political agenda in recent years?

Chapter summary

Part 1 defines the term 'democracy' and examines the **development of democracy** in Britain.

Part 2 looks at **political participation** in Britain. Who participates and why? In what different ways do people participate in politics?

Part 3 describes the **current electoral system** in Britain. It considers the range of different types of election and includes a case study of an election campaign.

Part 4 evaluates **alternative electoral systems**. What alternative systems are available? How do they work? What are the **arguments for and against electoral reform** in Britain?

1 Democracy

Key Issues

1. What are the main characteristics of a democratic political system?
2. What different forms can a democratic political system take?
3. How did democracy develop in Britain?

1.1 The main characteristics of democratic political systems

The distinction between democracy and other political systems had already been established by the 4th century BC when the Greek philosopher Aristotle wrote his *Politics*, the earliest surviving attempt to catalogue different political systems. Aristotle distinguishes between **democracy** (rule by the many), **oligarchy** (rule by the few) and **monarchy** (rule by one).

Aristotle was aware that there is an important difference between how political systems work ideally and how they work in practice. In the *Politics*, he claimed that all existing political systems were imperfect because their rulers aimed at their own interests rather than at the interests of all. Oligarchs, for example, promoted their own interests (the interests of the rich) at the expense of poor. Democrats promoted their own interests (the interests of the poor) at the expense of the rich. By associating oligarchy with the rich and democracy with the poor, Aristotle adds an economic dimension to his definition of these political systems. Indeed, he argues that in a state where there are only a few poor people, but these few poor people are the rulers, that state should be defined as a democracy.

Aristotle's line of argument indicates that a simple definition of democracy as 'rule by the many' is not sufficient. Most modern political scientists would agree with the following conclusion:

> 'Democracy is the most valued and also the vaguest of political terms in the modern world...The ancient Greek word 'democracy' means rule by the *demos* which can be translated as either rule by 'the people' or by 'the mob', depending upon one's ideological preference. By itself, democracy means little more than that, in some undefined sense, political power is ultimately in the hands of the whole adult population and that no smaller group has the right to rule. Democracy only takes on a more useful meaning when qualified by one of the other words with which it is associated, for example, liberal democracy, representative democracy...or direct democracy.'
> (Robertson, 1986, p.80)

Direct democracy

According to the traditional view, the birthplace of democracy was ancient Athens. By the 5th century BC, a form of 'direct democracy' had developed in Athens. Athens at that time was an independent self-governing city state. Due to the survival of the writing of the ancient Greeks and the rediscovery of this writing during the Renaissance, Athens' experiment with democracy became an important influence on the development of political culture in Western Europe. The popularity of democracy in Britain today is due, in part, to the fact that Athenian democracy was admired so much in the past.

The city state of Athens in the 5th century BC had a total population in the region of 250,000 people. This figure, however, includes women, children and slaves, none of whom were full citizens and none of whom, therefore, had a right to vote or to participate in the democratic process. Historians estimate that Athens had around 40,000 (male) citizens when its democracy was at its height in the years following the battle of Marathon in 490 BC.

Every Athenian citizen had the right to attend meetings of the assembly, a meeting of the citizen body which was called more than 40 times per year. Decisions at the assembly were taken on the basis of a majority vote and any proposals which were passed by a majority became law. Because every citizen had the right to speak and to vote at the assembly, every citizen had the chance of directly determining what the laws should be. It is because of this that the system is known as **direct democracy**.

Each citizen belonged to one of ten 'tribes' and each year 50 members of each tribe were chosen by lot to serve on the council. It was the council which prepared the agenda for each meeting of the assembly. Also, the council chose a rotating presiding committee which, in turn, chose a presiding officer by lot. The presiding officer held office for a single day and no citizen was allowed to hold this office more than once. All roles concerned with government were, therefore, shared out between citizens who were chosen by lot. Citizens held office for one year and were then replaced by others. The only exception was the election of ten generals. These generals were chosen by direct election and they could stand for election more than once.

The Athenian system established a number of democratic principles or ideals, some of which have survived in modern democracies. One of the basic principles behind the Athenian system was that every citizen should have the right to vote and to hold office. A second principle was that it was the duty of all citizens to participate actively in the system. And, a third principle was that decisions should be made by majority vote.

Some elements of the Athenian system have not proved as long lasting. The idea that the presiding officer should be chosen randomly by lot and should only serve for a day, for example, has found few supporters since the 5th century BC. Most modern democrats would disapprove of the idea that people in executive positions should be untrained and unelected. And, whilst most modern democrats would embrace the idea that every citizen should be allowed to participate in the political system, their definition of citizenship would normally be wider than that of the Athenians (by including women). But, perhaps the most obvious way in which modern democracies differ from the Athenian model is in the lack of direct involvement of most citizens in decision making. Obviously, the size of the citizen body is important. Whereas it is possible to accommodate 40,000 citizens in one place for a meeting, it is not so easy to accommodate 40 million citizens. Besides, direct democracy requires time and commitment. In a direct democracy, citizens need to be informed of what issues need to be resolved and the arguments for and against a particular decision. Not only does this beg the question of who should inform them, it also means that people have to be prepared to spend a large amount of their time preparing for and taking decisions.

Since the 5th century BC, there have been a few experiments with direct democracy. For example, the Swiss constitution incorporates elements of direct democracy by allowing frequent referendums. And, it is possible that, in the future, given the rapid development of communications technology, direct democracy will be possible in a large society (every citizen could vote for or against a new law by pressing a button on their home computer, for example).
But, in general, apart from decisions made on a very small scale where direct democracy is sometimes employed, representative democracy is the norm.

Representative democracy

Whereas, in a direct democracy, every citizen is able to participate directly in decision making, in a representative democracy, citizens elect representatives to make decisions for them. In Britain, for example, voters elect Members of Parliament (MPs) to represent them. These MPs meet in an assembly (the House of Commons) which is responsible for making laws. Every MP has the right to speak and vote for or against proposed laws. Proposals normally become law if a majority of MPs vote in favour of them.

By voting for a representative, citizens hand over the responsibility for making decisions to someone else. This has important implications. First, although the voters have handed over responsibility for making decisions to their representative, that does not necessarily mean that they have no further part to play in the political process. A key to representative government is that the representatives are, in some way, accountable to the electorate. Or, to put it the other way round, the electorate, in some way, exercises control over the representatives. Unless representatives act in a way that meets with the approval of the majority of the electorate, for example, they (or their party) will not be re-elected. The fear of this affects the representatives' behaviour. On the other hand, by handing over responsibility for making decisions to someone else, citizens hand over the opportunity to make a personal contribution to the formation of legislation.

Second, the exact role played by the representative becomes crucially important. Whereas some representatives might argue that it is their duty only to do what their electors have mandated (instructed) them to do, others might argue that, once elected, it is their duty to act according to their conscience. It is the latter view which was famously put forward by Edward Burke in a speech to his constituents in Bristol in 1774:

> 'Your representative owes you not his industry only but his judgements; and he betrays, instead of serving you, if he sacrifices to your opinion.'

Burke's view has made a lasting impression on British politicians and it is often used by MPs to justify their behaviour. The problem is that it is a licence for MPs to ignore the wishes of their constituents.

On the other hand, the view that representatives should only do what they are mandated to do is equally difficult to sustain. How can representatives know what the majority of their electors think about a particular issue? And even if they do know, adhering only to the wishes of the majority can, on occasion, lead to tyranny for the minority (something which democracy is supposed to prevent). In other words, representative democracy raises a whole range of problems which do not arise in a direct democracy.

Liberal democracy (see also chapter 4, section 1.2)

Britain and other industrialised countries in the West are often described as 'liberal democracies'. According to Heywood:

> 'The liberal element in liberal democracy is a belief in limited government, the idea that the individual should enjoy some protection from arbitrary government. The second element, democratic government, reflects the idea that government should in some way be tied to the will of the people.' (Heywood, 1991, p.57)

Ideas about liberal democracy evolved in the 19th century in Britain and they can be summarised as follows. Government should be limited and its purpose should be the removal of obstacles to individual wellbeing. The market should have a paramount role and state interference should be minimal. The state should play a 'nightwatchman role'. The franchise should be gradually extended from men with property to members of the working class. Central to a liberal democracy is the existence of civil liberties - for example, freedom of speech, freedom of assembly and freedom to dissent. In Britain, these civil liberties are safeguarded by the 'rule of law' (a 19th century concept) and the separation of the powers (the maintenance of a separate executive and judiciary). The rule of law guarantees equality before the law and ensures that the powers of rulers can be curtailed by laws enforceable in courts (see chapter 4, section 2.2). The separation of the powers ensures that independence is maintained and that power is fragmented.

As ideas about liberal democracy evolved, Dearlove & Saunders argue:

> 'Its radical and egalitarian ideals were softened so that, in practice, democratic politics worked within the prevailing system of power in economy and society. Democracy ceased to embody the cry from below for the overthrow of the limited liberal state and the competitive market society to which it was connected. Instead, democracy came to embody the more limited claim that the working class had the right to compete within the established state institutions and within the established society, with the clear expectation that they would not use the state to intervene to effect fundamental change.' Dearlove & Saunders, 1984, p.26)

In the 20th century, liberal democracies have come to have a number of defining characteristics. First, they are representative democracies. Political authority is based on popular consent. Second, popular consent must be given by the whole adult population, with no groups excluded. Third, elections must be free and fair. And fourth, there must be open competition for power and a real choice between the individuals, groups and parties which put up candidates for election.

Parliamentary democracy

There are different ways in which liberal democracies work. The two main ways are through a parliamentary system or through a presidential system. According to Norton, the term 'parliamentary democracy':

> 'Distinguishes the system from those in which the executive and legislature are elected independently of one another and in which one does not depend for its continuance in office on the confidence of the other.' (Norton, 1991, p.22)

So, in the USA, which has a presidential form of democracy, the elections for President and for Congress are held separately and the President forms a separate administration. In contrast, the UK is a parliamentary democracy and the government is formed from whichever party can command a majority in the House of Commons.

Criticisms of parliamentary democracy

Marxists are critical of parliamentary democracy on the grounds that it is a sham in which the democratic parliamentary institutions provide a smokescreen for the exploitation of the majority of the population. Raymond Williams, for example, argued that parliamentary democracy can be defined as:

> 'The coexistence of political representation and participation within an economic system which admits no such rights, procedures or claims.' (Williams, 1981, p.3)

So, for Marxists, parliamentary elections merely serve to permit competing political elites, all of whom fundamentally represent ruling class interests, to alternate in positions of power. Parliamentary democracy conceals the location of real power which is based on wealth and capital. This is even true when the Labour party forms the government since the power of capital still predominates. In support of this argument, Marxists point to the growth in power of capitalist organisations outside and beyond the state - such as multinational companies, the International Monetary Fund and the European Union. The growing power of these institutions exposes the limitations of parliamentary democracy.

Criticism of parliamentary democracy also comes from the right. For example, Lord Hailsham, a former Conservative minister, suggested in 1976 that parliamentary democracy brought the danger of an 'elective dictatorship'. Writing in 1978, when Labour was in power, he said:

> 'It is only now that men and women are beginning to realise that representative institutions are not necessarily guardians of freedom but can themselves become engines of tyranny. They can be manipulated by minorities, taken over by extremists, motivated by the self-interest of organised millions. We need to be protected from our representatives no less than our former masters.' (Hailsham, 1978, p.13)

Hailsham feared that an elected government had few checks on its power and, therefore, parliamentary democracy should be contained. This would be achieved by returning to limited government, a period of stability, legislative restraint and constitutional reform.

It should be noted that Parliament itself has only one democratic element, the House of Commons. The House of Lords is an unelected second chamber and the monarch retains certain prerogative powers.

Activity 7.1

Item A *What is democracy? (1)*

Democracy is a simple idea based on two principles - popular control and political equality. Democracy requires that the rules and policies of any group should be subject to control by all its members. Also, the members of the group should have equal influence over the framing of its rules and policies. In a small group, these two principles can be realised directly. In a larger group, they can only be realised indirectly through the agency of chosen representatives. In a representative democracy, popular control means exercising control over the decision makers. It should be noted that democracy is not an all or nothing affair. It is a matter of degree - of the extent to which the two principles of popular control and political equality are realised in practice. The answer to the following four questions can be used to measure the level of democracy in a country. First, what kind of electoral system is used - is it free and fair? Second, how open and accountable is the government? Third, what civil and political rights exist (for example, is there freedom of speech)? And fourth, does the political and social culture encourage democracy to flourish at all levels in society?

Adapted from Beetham, 1994.

Item B *Athenian democracy - 5th century BC*

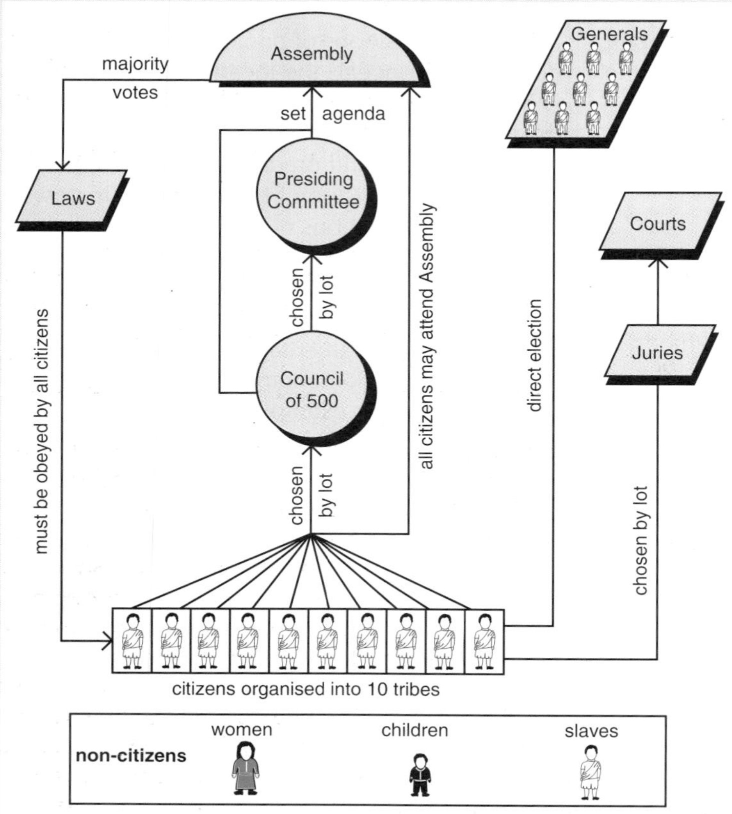

Item C *What is democracy? (2)*

Quality	%
Living in a free country	*64*
An equal society	*38*
Voting for a government in elections	*31*
Strong and effective government	*27*
Popular control over government	*17*
A free market economy	*13*

A survey carried out in 1994 asked people to choose two qualities out of a list of six that they felt were most important about democracy'. The results of this survey are shown above.

Adapted from Weir, 1994.

Item D *British democracy - 1990s*

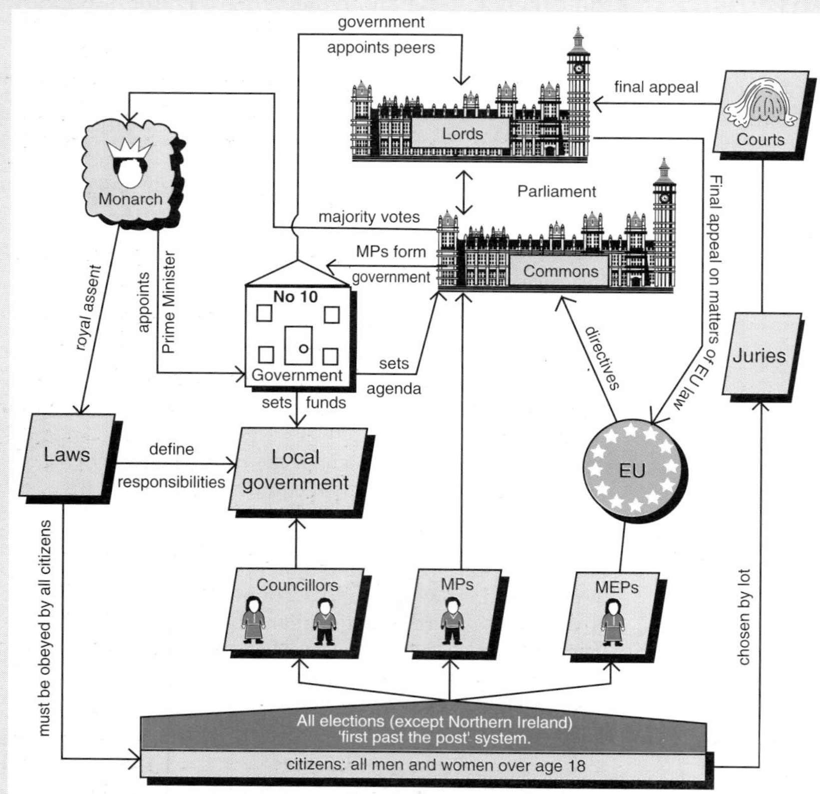

Questions

1. a) Judging from Items A and C what is democracy?
   b) Would you say that there is a high level of democracy in the UK? Give reasons for your answer.
2. Using Items B and D explain how direct democracy differs from representative democracy.
3. a) Using Item D describe the ways in which the principles of popular control and political equality are realised in the UK.
   b) Are there any elements in the British political system which could be described as undemocratic? Explain your answer.

1.2 The development of democracy in Britain

In Britain, the evolution from absolute monarchy to representative democracy was a slow and complex process. Gradually, the power of the monarchy was handed over to elected representatives and democratic mechanisms and controls developed. Unlike in France where the revolution of 1789 swept away the monarchy for good, in Britain civil war in the 17th century was followed by the restoration of the monarchy. It is the lack of a decisive break in the past which explains the survival of undemocratic elements (such as the unelected monarchy and the House of Lords) in the British political system today.

Although Parliament's control of public finance and law making has been guaranteed since the Glorious Revolution of 1688, other democratic elements are much more recent. In 1688, for example, less than 5% of the adult population had the right to vote. This was still the case in 1830. Given that the provision of fair and free elections is a basic component of representative democracy, it seems reasonable to argue that Britain should not be regarded as a legitimate democracy until fair and free elections were established. The struggle for the universal right to vote (also known as the 'franchise' or 'suffrage') and the development of fair electoral practice occurred during the 19th and early 20th centuries.

The electoral system in the early 19th century

At the beginning of the 19th century, the British electoral system was far from democratic. It was not just that less than 5% of adults had the right to vote or that bribery and corruption were prevalent. The electoral system did not provide the means for fair and equal representation. The right to vote (and to stand for election) was restricted to men and was dependent on a property qualification - only those who owned property worth a certain value were eligible to vote. These voters were able to vote in two types of constituencies - counties and boroughs (boroughs were towns which had at some time been granted a royal charter). Voters elected two MPs in each county and two MPs in each borough. But the number of voters in each county and borough varied widely. Some boroughs had several thousand voters whilst some had less than 50. As the industrial revolution gained momentum and new towns began to develop, the populations of these new towns found themselves without any representation at all. Thomas Paine, writing in 1791, noted:

> 'The county of Yorkshire, which contains nearly a million of souls, sends two county members [MPs]; and so does the county of Rutland which contains not a hundredth part of that number. The town of Old Sarum which contains not three houses sends two members [MPs]; and the town of Manchester, which contains upwards of sixty thousand of souls, is not admitted to send any.' (Paine, 1791, p.51)

Constituencies with populations small enough for each voter to be bribed were known as 'pocket boroughs' because the MP who bribed the voters had them 'in his pocket'. Constituencies with only a handful of voters were known as 'rotten boroughs' - their population had once been large but, due to demographic changes, had dwindled.

Elections at the beginning of the 19th century were not conducted by secret ballot. They were 'open'. When an election was announced, a large wooden platform (the 'hustings') was built in a public place. Candidates made speeches from the platform and then the voters were asked to vote by a show of hands. If the vote between two candidates was close, then a 'poll' could be demanded. Each voter would have to go up onto the platform and prove that he had a vote. He would then have to state publicly which candidate he supported. This system was a recipe for corruption and intimidation. Bribery was rife and it was common, for example, for landlords to threaten to evict their tenants unless they voted for the candidate supported by the landlord.

A variety of social and political factors combined to produce reform. The development of new ways of work and living conditions, the growth of population and towns and the formation of the working and capitalist classes, for example, combined to produce a new set of relations in Britain. In addition, the lessons of the French revolution, the spreading of new, radical ideas and growing popular discontent piled pressure on the legislators. The result was gradual reform which gained a momentum of its own. The first Reform Act was passed in 1832, but it was not until 1928 that universal suffrage was achieved.

The extension of the franchise in the 19th century

During the 19th century, three Electoral Reform Acts and a number of other Acts affecting electoral procedure were passed. The first Reform Act (also known as the 'Great' Reform Act) was passed in 1832. This Act abolished 56 rotten boroughs (which had elected a total of 112 MPs) and changed the law so that 30 boroughs with a population of under 4,000 elected one rather than two MPs. This meant that there were 142 'spare' MPs. These 142 MPs were now to be elected by voters who lived in the new industrial towns. The Act also reduced the property qualification with the result that the total number of voters rose by 200,000. In addition, an electoral register was established for the first time. Although the net result was that still just 7% of the adult population had the right to vote, this Act was of immense importance because it established the principle that there should be fair and equal representation. It also conceded that the franchise could be broadened.

Despite the efforts of the Chartists, a mass movement

of mainly working people who demanded universal suffrage in the late 1830s and 1840s, it was not until 1867 that the second Reform Act was passed. Like the first Reform Act, the distribution of MPs was changed - 45 boroughs with a population under 10,000 were to elect one MP rather than two and the 45 'spare' MPs were to be elected by voters in the new industrial towns and in London. Again, the property qualification was lowered in the boroughs, with the result that all male householders living in boroughs could vote. The property qualification in the counties was not lowered. The result of these changes was that a million new voters were added to the register. For the first time, therefore, it was possible to talk of a 'mass' electorate. This had important consequences. For example, it forced the political parties to set up national organisations and it encouraged MPs to consider working class interests for the first time (since many of their constituents belonged to the working class). Nevertheless, still just 16% of the adult population was enfranchised after the second Reform Act was passed.

The second Reform Act was followed shortly by the Secret Ballot Act of 1872. This Act put an end to open elections by introducing the secret ballot. Its aim was to stamp out electoral corruption and it was strengthened, in 1883, by the Corrupt and Illegal Practices Act. This Act standardised the amount candidates were allowed to spend on election expenses and made it an offence to attempt to bribe voters. These two Acts went a long way to ensuring that elections became free and fair.

The third Reform Act of 1884-85 was, in fact, made up of two separate Acts - the Franchise Act of 1884 and the Redistribution of Seats Act of 1885. The Franchise Act lowered the property qualification in the counties so that all male householders were allowed to vote. This added another 2.5 million voters to the register. The Redistribution of Seats Act abolished boroughs with a population of under 15,000 and changed the law so that boroughs with fewer than 50,000 inhabitants were to return one MP, not two as before. This meant that, for the first time, single member constituencies became the rule. Although more than five million men had the right to vote after the third Reform Act was passed, this was only around 28% of the total adult population.

By the end of the 19th century, therefore, it is possible to argue that, in relative terms, some progress had been made towards free and fair elections. But the majority of the adult population remained disenfranchised.

Electoral reform in the 20th century

By the beginning of the 20th century, most disenfranchised men could expect to gain the vote in the near future. Looking back over the previous 30 years, they could see that there was a tendency to reduce the property qualification slowly. It seemed only a matter of time, therefore, before all men had the right to vote.

The same, however, could not be said of women. Although a small number of women had argued for the vote before 1867, it was only after the second Reform Act had been passed that large numbers of women began to mobilise and to campaign for the vote. By then, it seemed that the principle that there should be universal suffrage had been conceded by Parliament. Women began to argue that if the vote was to be extended to more and more men, there was no reason why they should be excluded. It is, perhaps, no accident that, at first, this campaign was mainly waged by middle class women. They saw that less educated men of lower social status were being given the vote, but they remained disenfranchised. Whilst their campaign in the late 19th century was conventional and muted, at the beginning of the 20th century it boiled up into a major confrontation with the patriarchal (male dominated) state.

The suffragists and suffragettes

Women who campaigned to win the vote became known as suffragists or suffragettes. The term 'suffragist' is usually used of those women who were members of the National Union of Women's Suffrage Societies (NUWSS) whilst the term 'suffragette' is usually used of those women who were members of the Women's Social and Political Union (WSPU).

The NUWSS was founded in 1897 when suffragist groups from all over Britain joined together to form a single campaigning organisation. The NUWSS used peaceful, moderate, law-abiding tactics. By 1914, over 600 local groups had joined the NUWSS and it had over 100,000 members. Throughout the period 1897 to 1914, the NUWSS continued to lobby MPs, gather petitions and organise peaceful rallies.

The WSPU was set up by Emmeline Pankhurst and her daughters in 1903. Unlike the NUWSS, the WSPU believed that because peaceful, law-abiding tactics had not won women the vote, more forceful action was necessary. Members of the WSPU began a campaign of direct action to draw attention to their cause. Suffragettes made public protests and, if arrested, always chose prison rather than paying a fine. From 1909, imprisoned suffragettes began to go on hunger strike and were subsequently force-fed by the authorities. These tactics certainly brought great publicity, but opponents argued that the publicity was damaging to the cause.

When war broke out in 1914, despite the efforts of the suffragists and suffragettes, women still did not have the right to vote. As soon as war was declared, however, the WSPU called a truce and redirected its efforts into helping the war effort. During the First World War, women made an important contribution by taking over the work that had previously been done by men. This allowed men to go and fight. When the war was over, the government promised to support the extension of the franchise to women.

Historians are divided as to whether the earlier campaign for women's suffrage speeded up or slowed down the granting of the right to vote to women. Without doubt, it ensured that the issue remained close to the top of the political agenda.

Representation of the People Act 1918

More new voters were added to the register in 1918 than had been added in all previous Electoral Reform Acts combined. The Representation of the People Act which was passed in 1918 raised the number of voters from 7.7 million in the 1910 general election (the last general election to be held before the outbreak of the First World War) to 21.4 million in the general election held in 1918.

During the debate over this Act in Parliament, MPs argued that it was wrong that men who had served in the British army during the First World War should not have the vote. They also agreed that women should be rewarded for their contribution to the war effort. As a result, all men over the age of 21 and all women over the age of 30 were given the right to vote. Women under the age of 30 remained disenfranchised on the grounds that they lacked maturity. In reality, MPs feared that women under the age of 30 were more radical than older women and were worried that they would lose their seats if younger women were given the right to vote. A separate Act in 1918 gave women over the age of 30 the right to stand for election as MPs.

Electoral reform since 1918

By the mid-1920s, most people agreed that it was ridiculous to allow men aged 21 the vote, but not women. Since fashionable young women in the 1920s were known as 'flappers', people talked of the 'flapper vote'. The Equal Franchise Act of 1928 at last gave women the vote on the same terms as men. The historian A.J.P. Taylor notes:

> 'The British electoral system reached theoretical democracy only in April 1928. An Act promoted by the government for no particular reason then lowered the voting age for women from 30 to 21. Joynson-Hicks, a Conservative MP, promised the 'flapper' vote in the excitement of a public meeting and the government felt that they must honour this promise. The Act of 1928 added about five million new voters to the register.' (Taylor, 1965, p.332)

Since 1928, several further Acts have been passed. The Representation of the People Act 1949 abolished additional votes for university graduates and for those owning business premises and land in constituencies other than those in which they lived. It also removed the six month residence qualification. In 1969, the minimum voting age was lowered from 21 to 18. The Representation of the People Act 1985 gave British citizens living abroad the right to vote for a period of five years after they had left Britain. In 1989, this period was extended to 20 years and those who were too young to register as voters before they left Britain became eligible to vote.

Activity 7.2

Item A *The six points of the people's charter*

The Chartist movement in the 1830s and 1840s was the first nationwide protest movement. It attracted the support of many thousands of people, but the government refused to listen to Chartist demands. Although the Chartists failed to achieve their demands in the short term, five out of the six points were achieved in the long term. The second point refers to the introduction of a secret ballot. The fourth point - the payment of MPs - was introduced in 1911. Before 1911, MPs were unpaid and this made it very difficult for members of the working class to gain representation in Parliament. The sixth point is the only one not to have been put into practice.

The Six Points

OF THE

PEOPLE'S

CHARTER.

1. A VOTE for every man twenty-one years of age, of sound mind, and not undergoing punishment for crime.

2. THE BALLOT.—To protect the elector in the exercise of his vote.

3. NO PROPERTY QUALIFICATION for Members of Parliament —thus enabling the constituencies to return the man of their choice, be he rich or poor.

4. PAYMENT OF MEMBERS, thus enabling an honest tradesman, working man, or other person, to serve a constituency, when taken from his business to attend to the interests of the country.

5. EQUAL CONSTITUENCIES, securing the same amount of representation for the same number of electors, instead of allowing small constituencies to swamp the votes of large ones.

6. ANNUAL PARLIAMENTS, thus presenting the most effectual check to bribery and intimidation, since though a constituency might be bought once in seven years (even with the ballot), no purse could buy a constituency (under a system of universal suffrage) in each ensuing twelvemonth; and since members, when elected for a year only, would not be able to defy and betray their constituents as now.

Item B *Extension of the franchise*

(i) Electorate and population

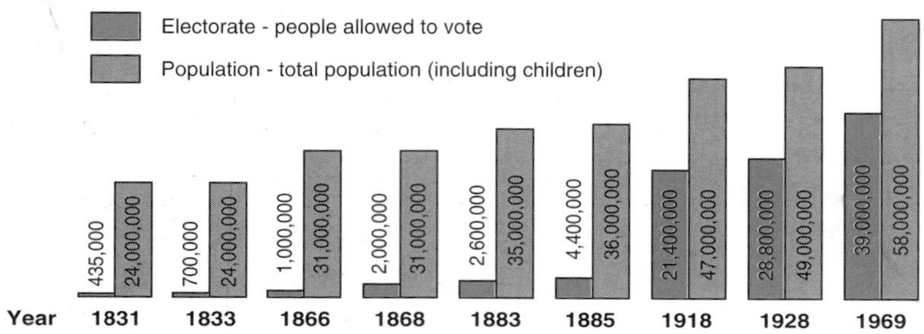

(ii) Percentage of adults (18 years and over) allowed to vote

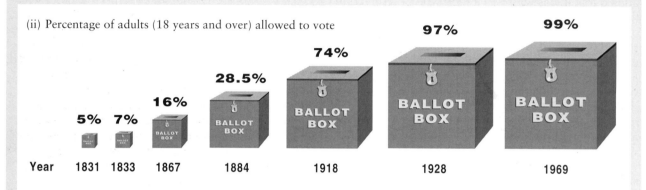

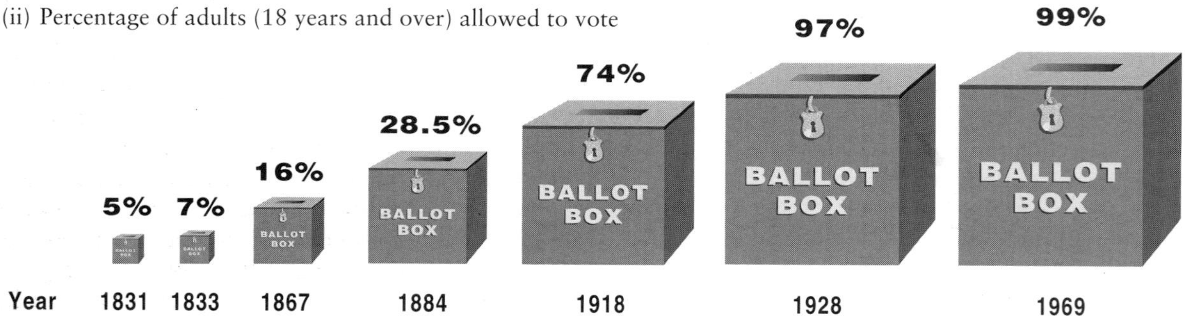

Item C

The channels of democracy in our society - trade unions, political parties, local councils, Parliament - were set up by men, for men. They are not designed to allow women's participation. They ignore important areas of women's lives. They must be forced to change. We have grown used to the idea that we are living in a democracy. But we women are still, in effect, fighting for the franchise. We will not be the silent majority.

Adapted from Coote & Campbell, 1982.

Item D *Suffragette banner*

This banner was produced in the early 20th century.

Questions

1. 'Britain has a long tradition of democratic government.' Give arguments for and against this statement.
2. a) What does Item A tell us about democracy in Britain in the 1830s?
   b) Give arguments for and against the view that annual elections (point 6) would strengthen democracy in Britain.
3. What do Items B and D tell us about the development of democracy in Britain?
4. a) Explain why the extension of the franchise, on its own, is not sufficient to guarantee democracy. Use Item C in your answer.
   b) How might the extension of the franchise lead to greater democracy?

2 Political participation

Key Issues

1. Why is the level of political participation important?
2. How do people participate?
3. What factors determine the level of participation?

Political participation and democracy

In a direct democracy, every citizen has the chance to make an impact on every decision put before the citizen body. There is, therefore, a great deal of incentive to participate in political decision making. By participating, citizens make sure that their views are heard and taken into account. If they do not participate, those citizens with opposing views might be able to gain a majority. Citizens, therefore, have a direct and vested interest in participating.

In a representative democracy, however, the mass of citizens do not have a direct input into political decision making. Representatives are elected to make decisions on their behalf. As a result, the question of political participation is rather different. Some commentators argue that there is no need for citizens to become involved in politics, other than to vote at elections. After all, those who are elected as representatives have the time, the skills and the access to information that ordinary citizens do not have and are, therefore, in a far better position to make decisions (see, for example, Held, 1987 for a discussion of this viewpoint). Others, however, argue that a high level of political participation is important because it ensures that popular control is exerted on decision makers. Decision makers, they claim, take into account the views of those who are politically active. Activists constantly monitor the work of decision makers and hold them accountable for their actions (see, for example, Beetham, 1993).

The debate over participation is, therefore, similar to that over representation (see above, section 1.1). Those who subscribe to Burke's view that representatives should act according to the dictates of their conscience, rather than to the wishes of their constituents, imply that, once representatives are elected, they have no obligation to listen to anyone else. Therefore, ordinary citizens should leave their representatives alone so that they can get on with decision making without interference. On the other hand, those who argue that representatives should act in accordance with the wishes of the majority of their constituents imply that political participation should be encouraged. Ordinary citizens should be constantly informing their representatives of their views so that the representative has firm guidance about what view is held by the majority.

It is clear, therefore, that the level of political participation can determine, to some extent, the behaviour of decision makers. In states with low levels of political participation, decision makers have greater leeway to impose their will than they do in states with high levels of political participation. But, this does not necessarily mean that a state with a high level of political participation is more democratic than a state with a low level. Beetham points out that:

> 'We should be careful not to confuse democracy with participation, or to define it in terms of the level of citizen participation. To do this would produce the bizarre conclusion that the societies under Communist rule were the most democratic because they had the highest levels of voter turnout and the most active and widespread involvement of citizens in party life and public affairs. The problem with such 'participation' from a democratic point of view was that it delivered very little control over the agenda or personnel of government for the citizen body because it was largely subject to control by the government itself.' (Beetham, 1993, pp.8-9)

Different types of political participation

Apart from voting in local, general, European and by-elections, ordinary people in Britain have the opportunity of participating in the political process in a number of other ways. Writing a letter to a local councillor, MP or MEP, for example, is one type of political participation. Joining a pressure group or a political party is another. But whilst some people feel that paying their membership fee to a pressure group or political party is enough, others are prepared to spend a great deal of their spare time campaigning. There is, in other words, a scale of political participation. This scale ranges from complete inactivity at one end to full-time activity at the other end.

Since political participation in a representative democracy is a means by which popular control can be exerted on decision makers, it is understandable that people should act collectively. By demonstrating that a large number of people have the same viewpoint, individual supporters of that viewpoint increase the pressure on decision makers to act in their favour. That is why activities such as collecting and signing petitions, mass lobbies of MPs at Westminster and marches and rallies are organised. Linked to this type of activity are the publicity stunts and other forms of direct action that are reported in the media. People and groups are well aware that the mass media plays a part in setting the political agenda and they design their political activity accordingly.

In their study of political participation in Britain, Parry and his colleagues (Parry et al., 1991) identified 23 political actions (see below Activity 7.3, Items D and E).

How active are people in Britain?

It is easy to measure the level of participation in elections since the turnout is measured as a matter of course. It is less easy to measure the other ways in which people participate in the political process. Nevertheless, a survey carried out by Parry and his colleagues in 1984-85 attempted to measure the extent to which people in Britain participate in the political process (Parry et al., 1991). This survey found that whilst the vast majority of people participate in general elections, only a minority of people participate beyond general elections. In terms of elections, 82.5% of respondents said that they had voted in the previous general election but only 27.7% said that they had voted in most local elections. In addition:

> 'Outside of elections when the individual has to put in more effort, the rate of political participation declines even further. In contacting politicians or decision makers where one might simply write a letter or leave a telephone message, those who had managed to do so 'at least once in the last five years' were few - 20.7% in the case of a local councillor and only 9.7% for a Member of Parliament. A similar pattern applies to involvement in groups. Not more than about one in ten had been active in an informal or formal group to raise an issue. For party campaigning numbers shrank to single digits.' (Parry & Moyser, 1993, p.20)

In the survey, respondents were asked which of the 23 different political actions identified by Parry and his colleagues they had performed in the last five years. Those who answered that they had performed more than four of these actions made up just 23% of the respondents. In other words, only a quarter of people in Britain can, in any sense, be described as 'political activists'. Britain, it seems, is a country with a low level of political participation. But, according to Parry and his colleagues, this is not unusual:

> '[People] may be aware of politics and even have an interest in it, but they tend not to speak out all that much beyond the confines of the voting booth. In this, however, they are not perhaps atypical of ordinary people in other West European democracies.' (Parry et al., 1991, p.47)

Who are the activists?

Parry and his colleagues (1991) discovered that the minority of the population which is politically active is not typical of the nation as whole. This conclusion was reached by examining four characteristics - class, gender, party identification (which political party a person supports) and political outlook (whether a person holds 'moderate' or 'extreme' views).

In terms of class, it was found that the majority of activists came from the 'salariat' - people who are relatively wealthy and who have professional and managerial occupations. Parry & Moyser argue that:

> 'This arises because class is associated with the possession of social and economic resources like education and wealth. These are the resources that ease the entry of the individual into the political arena.' (Parry & Moyser, 1993, p.21)

Gender and party identification, however, seem to play little part in determining how active people are. Activists are no more likely to be men than women and, whilst people who support different political parties may differ in the type of activities they choose, there is little difference in the level of participation between supporters of the main parties. Although party identification does not seem to determine how active people are, political outlook does. Those with more 'extreme' views on both the right and the left tend to be more active than those with more moderate views.

These findings suggest that the average activist is well educated, earns more than the average wage and holds views which are more radical than the views of most people.

Further information on activists can be found in chapter 11.

Activity 7.3

Item A *Turnout at general elections 1945-92*

Year	% turnout
1945	72.8
1950	83.9
1951	82.6
1955	76.8
1959	78.7
1964	77.1
1966	75.8
1970	72.0
1974 (Feb)	78.8
1974 (Oct)	72.8
1979	76.0
1983	72.7
1987	75.3
1992	77.7

Adapted from Craig, 1989 and Wood & Wood, 1992.

Item B *The Channel 4 democracy poll*

According to a poll commissioned by Channel 4 in 1994, the public wants more control over government. The table shows that there is a huge gulf between people's aspirations and their sense of the realities of political power.

Between elections, how much power	should voters have? %	do voters have? %
A great deal	31	2
A fair amount	47	14
A little	12	53
None at all	4	26
Don't know	6	6

Adapted from Weir, 1994.

Item C *Apathy*

'All you apathetic non-voters stay at home and don't vote, because according to the latest polls I'm going to win.'

This cartoon was produced in 1989.

Item D *The level of political activity in Britain (1)*

Action	%
Voting in elections	
1 Local	68.8
2 General	82.5
3 European	47.3
Party campaigning	
4 Fund raising	5.2
5 Canvassed	3.5
6 Clerical work	3.5
7 Attended rally	8.6

Action	%
Group activity	
8 Informal group	13.8
9 Organised group	11.2
10 Issue in group	4.7
Contacting	
11 MP	9.7
12 Civil servant	7.3
13 Councillor	20.7
14 Town Hall	17.4
15 Media	3.8

Action	%
Protesting	
16 Attended protest meeting	14.6
17 Organised petition	8.0
18 Signed petition	63.3
19 Blocked traffic	1.1
20 Protest march	5.2
21 Political strike	6.5
22 Political boycott	4.3
23 Physical force	0.2

This table shows the 23 political actions identified in the survey carried out by Parry and his colleagues in 1984-85. The figures show the percentage of respondents who had performed these activities in the last five years.

Adapted from Parry et al., 1991 and Parry & Moyser, 1993.

Item E *The level of political activity in Britain (2)*

The level of participation was measured by finding out how many of the 23 activities listed in Item D had been performed by individuals over the past five years. Seven categories were produced.

Category	Proportion of the population (%)	Average number of actions
1 Almost inactives	25.8	2.05
2 Just voters	51.0	3.53
3 Contacting activists	7.7	6.54
4 Direct activists	3.1	6.96
5 Collective activists	8.7	7.13
6 Party campaign activists	2.2	10.03
7 Complete activists	1.5	15.75
Whole population	100.0	4.21

(1) **Almost inactives** - people who barely 'spoke out' on anything even at election time. (2) **Just voters** - people who vote but do not participate in other ways. (3) **Contacting activists** - people who take part in contacting activities. (4) **Collective activists** - people who participate by working through pressure groups. (5) **Direct activists** - people who participate in protests. (6) **Party campaign activists** - people who actively work for a political party. (7) **Complete activists** - people who were involved in most of the 23 activities.

Adapted from Parry et al., 1991 and Parry & Moyser, 1993.

Questions

1. Why is the level of political participation in the UK important?
2. a) Using Items A-E give arguments for and against the view that most British people do not care about politics.
   b) What factors would you say determine the level of political participation in the UK?
3. What point is being made by the cartoon in Item C? How accurate is its message?
4. Draw up a questionnaire and find out the level of political activity of your colleagues. Are the results above or below average? Suggest reasons for the results.
5. Would you expect the level of political participation to have grown since the survey mentioned in Items D and E was carried out? Give reasons for your answer.

3 The British electoral system

Key Issues

1. What kind of electoral system operates in the UK?
2. How do local, general, European and by-elections differ?
3. What happened in the 1992 election campaign?
4. When and why are referendums called?

3.1 The British electoral system

The system of voting for all elections in Britain and for general elections in Northern Ireland is often described as a 'first past the post' or 'simple majority' system. Both terms are slightly inaccurate. Cowley & Dowding point out:

> 'Britain has a plurality system, sometimes misleadingly called 'first past the post'. In order to win a constituency, a candidate requires a plurality of the votes; that is, he or she needs more votes than any other single candidate. A majority system (which Britain is also sometimes incorrectly called) is where a candidate requires more votes than all the other candidates put together.' (Cowley & Dowding, 1994, p.19)

The British system works as follows. Each elector has one vote which is used to elect a candidate. The candidate with the most votes in a constituency wins the seat. Candidates can win seats with less than 50% of the vote. For example, suppose there was a constituency with three candidates standing. It is possible for one candidate to win 34% of the vote and the other two to win 33% of the vote. In this case, the candidate with 34% of the vote would win the seat.

Whilst most plurality systems operate with single seat constituencies, it is possible to have multi-seat constituencies. These fall into two main categories. The first is the system which operated in Britain after the Great Reform Act of 1832 and lasted until 1945 in some seats. It is exactly the same as the single seat constituency system except that there are two or more seats. Voters have as many votes as there are seats but can only vote once for a single candidate. If there are two seats in the constituency then the two candidates to have accumulated the highest number of votes win. The second kind of multi-seat constituency permits voters to have just one vote. Again, the seats are allocated to the candidates who receive the highest number of votes. This system is used in Japan and is known as the single non-transferable vote system. The aim is to reduce the bias towards major parties which tends to be a feature of plurality systems.

All British citizens are entitled to vote at parliamentary elections provided that they are aged 18 or over and are not disqualified. Citizens of other Commonwealth countries and citizens of the Republic of Ireland who are resident in Britain are also eligible to vote so long as they are aged 18 or over and not disqualified. Further, British citizens living abroad are eligible to vote for up to 20 years after they have left Britain. Those who were too young to vote when they left Britain are able to register when they reach the age of 18. The following people are disqualified from voting in parliamentary elections: members of the House of Lords; patients detained under mental health legislation; sentenced prisoners and people convicted within the last five years of corrupt or illegal electoral practices. Those eligible to vote are only able to vote if they are registered in a constituency (British citizens living abroad register in the constituency in which they were living before they went abroad). Electoral registers are updated annually. Voters in England, Scotland and Wales must have registered by 10 October and voters in Northern Ireland must have registered by 15 September or their names will not appear on the register. The new register comes into operation on 16 February each year. Voting in elections in Britain is voluntary (in some countries it is compulsory and those who fail to vote can be fined).

Since the movement of people within Britain results in some areas gaining and some areas losing population, the area covered by constituencies is periodically altered so that the size of population within each constituency is roughly equal. The exact location of each constituency's borders is determined by the Boundary Commission - an independent body chaired by the Speaker of the House of Commons. The Boundary Commission recommends new constituency boundaries every 10 to 15 years. These changes can have important political consequences and MPs monitor the work of the Boundary Commission closely.

Electoral procedures - general elections

A government's term of office is subject to a five year maximum. But, the government can decide to call a general election at any time within that five year period. That means that, unless the government loses a vote of confidence in the House of Commons or the full term has run, the Prime Minister can call a general election at the time when there is maximum party advantage to be gained.

Formally speaking, a general election is called when Parliament is dissolved by the monarch on the advice of the Prime Minister. When a decision has been made to dissolve Parliament, the monarch directs the Lord Chancellor to fix the Great Seal to the royal proclamation which dissolves the old Parliament and calls the new one. The Lord Chancellor and Secretary of State for Northern Ireland are then directed to issue the Writs of Election. Polling takes place within 17 days of the dissolution of Parliament, not including weekends, bank holidays and days of public thanksgiving or mourning. If the monarch were to die after Parliament was dissolved, then polling would be delayed for two weeks. Whilst the general election campaign is in progress, senior civil servants take over the day to day running of the country - though the Cabinet can be reassembled if there is a crisis.

The five formal stages of general elections are as follows:

> '1. Royal proclamation.
> 2. Issue of writs, as soon as possible after the royal proclamation - usually the same day.
> 3. Publication of the notice of election, not later than the second day after the writ is received.
> 4. Delivery of nomination papers, not later than the sixth day after the royal proclamation.
> 5. Polling day, on the eleventh day after the last day for delivery of nomination papers (that is, about three to four weeks after the election is announced).' (HMSO, 1991, p.19)

By convention, polling day is a Thursday. But there is nothing to prevent the Prime Minister choosing another day.

Candidates for parliamentary elections must be aged 21 or over. They must be British citizens, citizens of another Commonwealth country or citizens of the Republic of Ireland. Those disqualified from standing for election include the following:

> 'Undischarged bankrupts; people sentenced to more than one year in prison; clergy of the Church of England, Church of Scotland, Church of Ireland and Roman Catholic Church; members of the House of Lords; and people holding offices listed in the House of Commons Disqualification Act 1975. This includes judges, civil servants, some local government officers, members of the regular armed forces or the police service, some members of public corporations and government commissions and members of Parliaments or assemblies of countries outside the Commonwealth.' (HMSO, 1991, pp.12-13)

Candidates must return nomination papers to their local Returning Officer during the period between the publication of the notice of election and six days after the proclamation summoning the new Parliament. Nomination papers must be signed by 10 electors from the constituency and must state the candidate's full name, address and description (six words maximum). Candidates must also put down a deposit of £500. This is returned to candidates who receive

5% or more of the votes cast. In the 1992 election, there were 901 lost deposit. The Liberal Democrats only lost 11 deposits, the Conservative party only lost four and the Labour party only lost one.

There are strict limits on how much each candidate can spend in their constituency. During the 1992 general election campaign, in borough constituencies (the more densely populated urban areas) candidates could spend £4,144 plus 3.5p per elector. This amounted to around £6,600 in an average urban constituency. In county constituencies (less densely populated rural areas) candidates could spend £4,144 plus 4.7p per elector. This amounted to about £7,400 on average.

During the campaign, candidates may post one communication to each household free of charge. All other expenses are subject to the limit. After the election, the candidate's agent must declare all election expenses within 35 days. But, the amount spent by national party organisations is not limited. They may spend what they like on party political broadcasts and other publicity.

Electoral procedures - by-elections

By-elections are called when a sitting MP dies or retires from the Commons before Parliament is dissolved. The formal procedure for calling a by-election is as follows:

> 'When a by-election is to be held the Speaker of the House of Commons issues a warrant to the Clerk of the Crown directing the Clerk to issue a Writ of Election. The writ is usually issued on the same day as the Speaker's warrant. If a vacancy occurs while Parliament is meeting, the motion for a new writ is usually moved by the party to which the former MP belonged. If the House is not meeting, the Speaker can issue a warrant if two MPs certify that a seat is vacant and notice is given in the *London Gazette*.'
> (HMSO, 1991, pp.14-15)

Once a by-election has been called, the same procedural rules apply as in a general election with the exception that candidates are allowed a higher rate of expenses. National interest in by-elections tends to be high as they are regarded as barometers of public opinion between general elections. Because of this, the Representation of the People Act 1989 set the maximum level of expenses in by-elections at £16,577 plus 14.1p per elector in borough constituencies and £16,577 plus 18.6p per elector in county constituencies.

Until the 1970s, by-elections tended to have a low turnout and it was assumed that there was less interest in them than in general elections because the formation of a government was not at stake. Since 1970, however, media attention and active campaigning by the major political parties have boosted turnout to levels nearer to those found in general elections. Governments find it very hard to maintain support in by-elections as many voters use the opportunity to register a protest vote. They can do this knowing that, generally, this will not mean defeat for the government since only one seat is at stake (see chapter 9, section 5.3).

Electoral procedure - local elections

Councillors are elected to serve four year terms. They are elected using the same plurality system that is used in parliamentary elections. But, different councils (see chapter 16, section 1.2 for a description of the different types of council) elect councillors at different times. County councils, for example, hold a 'clean sweep' election every four years. At the end of a four year term, all county councillors resign at the same time and an election is fought to fill the seats. Once elected, the councillors keep their seats for the following four years. Metropolitan district councils, on the other hand, use a system of partial renewal. Metropolitan district councils are divided into multi-seat wards (a ward is an administrative area) and elections take place every year. So, suppose a ward has three seats held by councillors A, B and C. In the first year, councillor A's seat comes up for election. In the second year, councillor B's seat comes up. And in the third year, councillor C's seat comes up. In the fourth year, there is no district election, but county councillors are elected in a clean sweep election. If a ward has two rather than three seats, then there is no election in one of the four years. If a ward has four seats, then two seats come up for election in one of the three years in which there are district council elections.

When local government was reorganised in the 1970s, a third type of council was established - the rural (or 'shire') district council. Rural district councils were able to select either system. As a result, one third of rural districts use the partial renewal system whilst the other two thirds hold a clean sweep election in the year midway between county council elections.

One advantage of the partial renewal system is that it means there is an election most years. This encourages participation and keeps local parties active. A disadvantage is that a party might become very unpopular and lose seats all over the country, but that party could still retain control of councils for the forthcoming two or three years because not all representatives in a ward come up for election at once.

Local elections are usually held on the first Thursday in May. Turnout in local elections is, generally, much lower than in general elections.

Electoral procedure - European elections

Since 1979, voters have had the opportunity to vote in the elections for the European Parliament once every five years. In the European election of 1994, voters in the UK elected 87 Members of the European Parliament (MEPs). Of the 87 MEPs, 71 were elected in England, eight in Scotland, five in Wales and three in Northern Ireland. In England, Scotland and Wales the same plurality system is used as in parliamentary elections. In Northern Ireland, however, a system of proportional representation is used - the single transferable vote system (see section 4.1 below for a description of this voting system).

In the UK, the electoral procedure for European elections is very similar to that used in parliamentary elections. Those qualified to vote in parliamentary elections are qualified to vote in European elections. In addition, members of the House of Lords are allowed to vote in European elections. Similarly, those qualified to stand as candidates in parliamentary elections are qualified to stand in European elections. In addition, peers and members of the clergy of the Church of England, the Church of Scotland, the Church of Ireland and the Roman Catholic Church may stand. Candidates must be nominated by 30 electors and must put down a deposit of £1,000. This is returned if the candidate receives 5% of the vote in England, Scotland and Wales or one quarter of the electoral quota at any stage in the electoral process carried out in Northern Ireland. The election expenses for Euro-candidates are a maximum of £10,000 plus 4.3p per elector.

Activity 7.4

Item A *A polling station*

Most polling stations are in schools, but other buildings are used. A presiding officer is responsible for ensuring that secrecy is maintained and there is no electoral malpractice.

Item C *The count*

Sealed ballot boxes are taken to the count together with unused and spoilt ballot papers. The count is presided over by the returning officer.

Item B *Tidying up the electoral mess*

The Labour MP Jeff Rooker thinks that the way in which we run elections is old-fashioned and should be modernised. Take, for example, the count. Current electoral practice is to count every one of the thousands of ballot papers by hand. This means that election results are almost always modestly wrong. Jeff Rooker proposes in a Bill (which has no chance of reaching the statute book) that voting machines should be introduced. His Bill also suggests that there should be fixed-term elections. Since the present system allows the Prime Minister to choose the election date, it argues, this gives too great an advantage to the party in power. Other proposals in the Bill include an end to the practice of holding elections on Thursday (allowing polling on Saturday and Sunday morning, as happens in other European countries), the introduction of controls over national, as well as constituency, spending in British elections and the setting up of an independent Electoral Commission. An Electoral Commission would ensure fair play and listen to complaints. Since 1867, this has been the job of the courts, but using the courts is slow and costly. At the last election, for example, allegations were made of malpractice at an old people's home in a marginal constituency, but the Crown Prosecution Service decided not to take up the matter. If there was an independent Electoral Commission, allegations like this would be taken up as a matter of course.

Adapted from the *Guardian*, 25 April 1994.

Item D *Border skirmishes*

Why should it take 85,000 electors to send an MP to Parliament from Wiltshire but only 47,000 to send an MP from Glasgow? The answer, of course, is that it should not. But, at the general election in April 1992, it did. That is what happens when an election is fought on the basis of boundaries set a decade ago. Since the last time constituency boundaries were changed, the number of voters in Wiltshire's five constituencies has grown by 10% to 428,935 whilst the number of voters in Glasgow's 11 constituencies has shrunk by 10% to 518,716. In other words,Glasgow had c.90,000 more voters than Wiltshire but six more MPs. If nothing was done before the 1996-97 general election, then discrepancies like this will have grown. Although Labour is supposed to be the party of equality, it has little enthusiasm for the work of the Boundary Commission. That is because, historically, Labour has lost out. The work of the Boundary Commission could give the Conservatives an extra 15 seats, making Labour's struggle to win an overall majority at the next general election even harder. These extra seats do not go to the Conservatives because the Boundary Commission is anything less than impartial, but because it is bound to create new seats in fast growing areas like Wiltshire (which is overwhelmingly Conservative) and to liquidate seats in declining areas like Glasgow (which is predominately Labour). Rather than complaining about the Boundary Commission, a better course might be to concentrate on demanding drastic improvements in the state of the electoral register from which something like a million voters are missing - many because they feared being caught by the poll tax, but others because of the ramshackle way the system works. The Boundary Commissioners themselves will be using these defective registers.

Adapted from the *Guardian*, 9 May 1992.

Item E *The announcement of the result*

The returning officer announces the election result in public.

Questions

1. a) You have been given Items A,C and E as illustrations to accompany an article entitled, 'Electoral procedure at British general elections'. Write the article.
   b) How would your account differ if it looked at (i) local elections, (ii) European elections or (iii) by-elections?
2. 'Britain has a fair electoral system'. Give arguments for and against this statement using Items B and D in your answer.
3. Do you think Britain should have fixed-term elections? Explain your answer.
4. Using Item D explain why the work of the Boundary Commission is important.

3.2 General election campaigns

Although some people claim that a fresh general election campaign begins the day after an election result is declared, it is only once the Prime Minister has asked the monarch to dissolve Parliament that the political parties begin to campaign in earnest. General election campaigns proper last from three to four weeks and are perhaps the most intense three to four weeks that politicians have to face in the political cycle. Before the development of the mass media, party leaders travelled round the country addressing election rallies and meeting ordinary voters. Today, they use the television and radio to communicate their ideas. They still make speeches and meet ordinary voters but this is done in front of the cameras. As a result, their words and actions are not just designed to appeal to the audience at the meeting they are attending. They are also intended to appeal to the wider audience at home.

Every general election campaign has its own characteristics, but there are some factors which all general election campaigns have in common. This section looks at campaigning in general and then at a particular campaign - the 1992 general election campaign. The influence that general election campaigns have on the result of elections is considered in chapter 9, section 5.4.

Campaigning in general

All general election campaigns are run on two levels -

the national level and the local level. At the national level, the party leadership decides upon the themes and tactics which it feels will project the best image for the party throughout the nation and it outlines the party's policies in a manifesto. Leading members of the main parties become the focus of intense media coverage and they attempt to use this to persuade wavering voters to vote for their party. In addition, the national parties organise nationwide advertising campaigns and party election broadcasts and they may organise rallies or other political meetings or events.

At the local level, parliamentary candidates and their agents run campaigns in their constituency. Again, a high public profile is important and much time and effort is spent on generating publicity. All parties rely on volunteers to deliver leaflets and to knock on doors and canvass support.

Party election broadcasts

Although parties are permitted to pay for political adverts in the press or on billboards, they are not allowed to pay for political adverts on television or radio. Instead, free airtime is allocated to parties by the Committee on Party Political Broadcasting (CPPB), a committee first set up in 1947. This committee is made up of representatives from the main political parties, the BBC, the Independent Television Commission (ITC) and the Radio Authority. It decides how many party election broadcasts are permitted for each party and when they can be broadcast. The criteria for allocating party election broadcasts have been consistent since 1947. The amount of time each party is allowed is determined, in part, by the number of candidates it puts up for election and, in part, by its strength in the previous Parliament. Parties which lack parliamentary representation (such as the Green party) are allocated a five minute broadcast if they contest at least 50 seats. For parties with MPs in Parliament, between 1964 and 1979, party election broadcasts were allocated to the Conservatives, Labour and Liberal parties on a ratio of 5:5:3. The creation of the Alliance brought a revision to 5:5:4 in 1983 and 5:5:5 in 1987. In 1992, the ratio reverted to 5:5:4.

The 1992 general election campaign

The timing of a general election can be crucial. It is generally agreed, for example, that if James Callaghan had called an election in the summer or autumn of 1978, Labour would have won. But, Callaghan waited until May 1979. By then, the mood of the electorate had changed and Labour was defeated by the Conservatives.

Given that John Major had only taken over as Prime Minister in November 1990, it was, perhaps, inevitable that he would delay before announcing a general election since he needed time to establish his reputation with the electorate. Few people, therefore, expected an early election. But, the previous general election had been held in June 1987 and so the latest an election could be held was June 1992. John Major avoided giving the impression that he was hanging on right to the very end by choosing to hold an election on 9 April 1992. He announced this date on 11 March, the day after the Chancellor made the Budget statement. The timing was deliberate. The Chancellor, Norman Lamont, had announced tax cuts in the Budget and taxation was to prove to be a major issue in the election campaign. On the day when the date of the election was announced, opinion polls suggested that Labour and the Conservatives were neck and neck.

For the next 28 days, the words and actions of leading politicians were reported and discussed in great detail. Opinion polls were taken almost every day. And party workers throughout the country set out to mobilise support. One political commentator, Robin Oakley, described the different tactics used by the two main parties as follows:

> 'The Tory leadership decided to run several risks. The first was a largely negative campaign based on highlighting the fears about Labour's likely tax burden and on contrasting the experience and approach of Mr Major and Mr Kinnock, an already proven election fighter. Secondly, against a stack of opinion polls suggesting a hung Parliament, the Prime Minister decided on an all or nothing strategy. He insisted on every opportunity that he would do no deals or contemplate PR [proportional representation]. Thirdly, in spite of the urgings of many within his own party that it was time for a concession to the rising tide for Scottish devolution, he and his advisers took the view that there was nothing for the Tories in being the fourth best devolution party. Instead he played the union card for all it was worth, insisting that any concession to devolution would threaten the strength of the whole UK. Labour's strategy, by contrast, was a safety first one of leaving the government to lose the election. Labour's press conferences were polished, drilled and regimented, with supplementary questions ruthlessly ruled out. The aim was to drive to the top of the agenda the 'caring' issues of health, education and pensions. Mr Kinnock and his team also pushed home the idea that only a Labour government would take action to counter the recession with jobs, training and investment packages. And then there was their one

> big risk: they decided to tackle head-on fears about their taxation policies.' (*Times*, 11 April 1992)

There is a consensus amongst commentators that, with hindsight, a number of events during the election campaign made an impression on the voters. First, Labour's decision to announce their own shadow Budget proposals (after Norman Lamont had announced the real Budget) may have backfired. Certainly, it set the agenda in the early part of the election campaign and allowed the Conservatives to claim (unfairly, the Labour party argued) that a Labour government would introduce higher levels of taxation for most people. By focusing on Labour's tax policies, the Conservatives were able to deflect attention away from the recession and their own economic record.

Second, there was the battle over 'Jennifer's ear'. This refers to a Labour party election broadcast which went out on 24 March. The broadcast looked at two small girls with the same problem - blocked ears. Whilst one girl's NHS operation was repeatedly delayed, the other girl quickly had a private operation. Labour made it clear that this broadcast was based on real case histories and the name of one of the girls - Jennifer - was leaked to the press. Labour blamed the Conservatives for the leak. The Conservatives accused Labour of bad judgement and irresponsibility. The result was a heated argument. This detracted from the main issue which was meant to be how the NHS was being run by the Conservatives.

Third, about halfway through the campaign, John Major attempted to seize the initiative by addressing voters standing on a soapbox. This had a number of purposes. It indicated that Major was a 'man of the people'. It gave the impression that the Conservative campaign was not just a slick, stage-managed media circus. It answered media criticism that Major was on the defensive. And it suggested a criticism of Labour's highly polished and professional campaign.

Fourth, on 1 April, Labour held an American-style rally in Sheffield which was immediately criticised by the media for being overconfident and triumphalist. Although it is unlikely that the rally made a huge impact on votes, it is also unlikely to have won over many voters. After the election, Labour party members were highly critical of it:

> 'Labour's private polls suggested that the public did not much notice it - and it was far down in the 9 o'clock news. But it was to acquire a mythic status as one of the key mistakes in the campaign. Many Labour candidates replying to our post-election questionnaire commented on the counter-productive impact of its razzmatazz and its triumphalism.' (Butler & Kavanagh, 1992, p.126)

And fifth, there is a consensus amongst commentators that the turning point in the campaign came in the last week. According to Colin Brown:

> 'The Major camp was to suffer a further shock on Wednesday 1 April. Mr Major was about to board his BAe jet back to RAF Northolt at Manchester airport when he received news of an opinion poll giving Labour a seven point lead, partly due to a loss of Tory votes to the Liberal Democrats. He found it difficult to believe. From the Battlebus he agreed with Chris Patten [Conservative party chairman] to unleash an attack on the Liberal Democrats, warning they would put Neil Kinnock into No. 10. This was the turning point towards victory for the Tories.' (*Independent*, 11 April 1992)

Whilst the Conservatives decided to attack the Liberal Democrats, Labour was attempting to woo Liberal Democrat support and to prevent Tory switchers to the Liberal Democrats returning to the Tories. Patrick Wintour explains that:

> 'The chosen technique was to reassure these groups over the tone of a Labour government. Fortunately, Labour had planned to use Thursday 2 April - Charter 88's democracy day - to pitch for the middle class vote with Roy Hattersley holding a press conference on constitutional reform...But the agenda took hold too effectively and sidetracked Labour, a group of internal critics claims. With the polls pointing to a hung Parliament, the issue ran on for more than four days. The critics say this prevented Labour from campaigning effectively on its key issues of health and the recession in the final days.' (*Guardian*, 11 April 1992)

Activity 7.5

Item A *1992 election campaign diary*

1992 Election Campaign Diary

Major issue	Date	Event
Tax = major issue	March 10	Budget.
	11	Date of election announced.
	12	Liberal Democrats announce that they will put 1p on income tax to pay for education if they form the next government.
	16	Labour's shadow Budget. Liberal Democrats' manifesto launch.
	17	Conservatives' manifesto launch.
	18	Labour's manifesto launch.
	19	Government damaged by highest unemployment figures in four years.
	22	Kinnock convinced Labour have won battle over taxation.
Health = major issue	March 24	'Jennifer's ear' broadcast.
	27	Editor of *Daily Mail* meets Major and tells him to buck up his ideas or he will lose election.
	28	Major uses soap box for first time, in Luton.
Hung Parliament = major issue	April 1	Labour seven points ahead in polls. Sheffield rally.
	2	Conservatives attack Liberal Democrats, describing them as a Trojan Horse which will let Labour into Number 10 Downing Street.
	2-6	Labour gets bogged down over electoral reform and what would happen if there was a hung Parliament.
	4	Major says he will surprise the nation.
	7	Conservatives' final Wembley rally.
	9	Election day.

Item B *Launch of the Conservative party manifesto*

This photograph shows John Major, surrounded by members of his Cabinet, at the launch of the Conservative party manifesto on 17 March 1992.

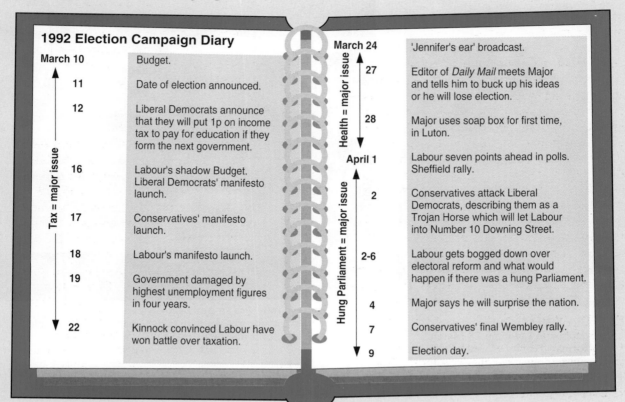

Item C *John Major on his soapbox*

After John Major first used the soapbox in Luton on 28 March, Norman Tebbit (a former Cabinet minister) remarked 'they've stopped putting sedatives in his tea.'

Item D *Labour's Sheffield rally*

Labour's Sheffield rally was an American-style show intended to demonstrate that Labour was ready to take power. To many people, however, it seemed 'over the top'.

Item E *A lacklustre campaign but a Conservative victory*

The Conservatives' campaign was criticised for being lacklustre, ill-conceived and lacking in direction. But the Conservatives still won. Although some Conservative strategists yesterday tried to claim that it had all gone according to a secret masterplan, an equal number (including Chris Patten) conceded that the election had only been won in the last few days as wavering Tory voters were frightened back into the fold by the Conservatives' intensive negative campaigning. This view was summed up by John Wakeham who said: 'It was trench warfare. We came through in the end.' Before the result was known, there were misgivings about the success of Mr Major's campaign style during his lacklustre three and a half week tour through 90 constituencies, starting in Grantham and finishing in Dulwich. This suggests that, as in 1987, the Conservatives lost the election campaign but won the election.

Adapted from the *Guardian*, 11 April 1992.

Item F *Jennifer's ear*

This picture shows Jennifer Bennett with her parents. Jennifer was identified as the girl in the Labour party election broadcast whose NHS operation had been delayed.

Questions

1. Collect newspaper cuttings and keep a diary during a local election campaign. At the end of the campaign:
   a) explain in what ways the campaign was different from a general election campaign and in what ways it was the same.
   b) describe the techniques used by party members to win votes during the campaign.
2. a) Write an analysis of the 1992 general election campaign using Items A- F.
   b) How do you think your analysis would have differed if Labour had won the election?
3. Describe the different techniques used by the political parties to win support during the 1992 general election campaign. Which techniques were most and which were least successful? Why?

3.3 Referendums

One of the problems with representative democracy is that when a party is elected to govern the country, there is no way of knowing whether the electorate supported all, or only some parts, of the party's programme. It is possible, for example, that voters for a particular party liked that party's economic policies but did not like its policies on education. Elections are not fought on a single question and so it is never clear which parts of a government's programme have popular support.

One way of finding out whether voters support a particular policy is to ask them to vote 'yes' or 'no' to a single question on that policy. A vote on a single issue is known as a referendum (the plural is either 'referendums' or 'referenda'). Since the electorate is asked to vote directly on a particular issue, holding a referendum is a way of exercising direct democracy within a system of representative democracy.

Although referendums have not been held often in Britain, they are common in some other countries. Batchelor notes that:

> 'In Australia, for example, eight constitutional amendments were approved in referendums between 1901 and 1988...From 1950 to 1986, Switzerland held no fewer than 190 referendums, which resulted in decisions such as permitting women to vote in elections, agreeing free trade with the EC and rejecting limits on the number of foreign resident workers. Many states in the USA permit initiatives (proposals put forward by voters) and referendums. In 1986, voters in 43 states faced referendums or initiatives with Oregan having an astonishing 16 on the ballot paper. The people of Rhode Island, Massachussetts and Oregan declined to forbid state-financed abortions but in Arkansas the proposal was approved.' (Batchelor, 1992, p.21)

As the above examples suggest, referendums are commonly held to answer questions of a constitutional or moral nature. Indeed, Bogdanor argues that:

> 'The main function of the referendum is to offer constitutional protection, to prevent laws being changed without the consent of the people.' (*Guardian*, 22 November 1991)

Against this, however, opponents of referendums have argued that their use undermines the sovereignty of Parliament. After all (so the argument goes) the people vote for their representatives at elections and by so doing they pass responsibility for decision making on to these representatives. Since the people's consent is given to the party of government at election time, there is no need to hold referendums between elections.

Other problems over the use of referendums can arise. First, if the government alone decides whether or not to hold a referendum, it is likely that referendums will essentially be a conservative weapon. Governments will only hold them for pragmatic reasons. Second, the phrasing of the question is very important. If the government chooses the wording, it might well be able to determine the outcome it desires. Third, voters may lack sufficient information to give a considered judgement. Therefore, there is a need for them to be provided with information before the referendum takes place. The question of who provides this information and how it is provided is a thorny one. Fourth, it is possible that an issue may be too complex to allow a 'yes' or 'no' answer to a simple question. And finally, there is the problem of public apathy. Low turnout might mean that the result of a referendum lacks credibility. The more referendums that are held, the lower the turnout is likely to be since people tend to suffer from voting fatigue.

Referendums in the UK

It was not until 1973 that a referendum was held in the UK for the first time. The electorate for this referendum was confined to people living in Northern Ireland. Voters were asked in this referendum (held on 8 March 1973) whether they wished to remain in the UK or to join the Republic of Ireland. The result was a large majority in favour of remaining in the UK. But, the referendum was boycotted by all shades of nationalist opinion, including supporters of Sinn Fein and the SDLP.

The government decided to hold this referendum in the hope that, by clearly demonstrating the views of the population of Northern Ireland, it would be easier to encourage politicians on all sides to discuss, in a constructive manner, how to resolve the conflict in the province. But, the size of the electorate became a contentious issue. Republicans and nationalists argued that the population of the whole of Ireland should be allowed to vote in the referendum, rather than only the people of Northern Ireland. Because of the boycott, the voting figures became rather meaningless and government intentions were undermined.

Two years later, in 1975, the whole of the UK participated in a referendum held on the issue of whether Britain should remain a member of the European Economic Community (see also, chapter 6, p.131). The UK had entered the EEC in 1973 when the Conservative party under Edward Heath was in power. But in the vote in Parliament on this issue in 1973, 69 Labour MPs had defied the Labour whip and voted with the Conservatives. When Labour won the general election in 1974, the party was still divided over the issue and the Labour leader, Harold Wilson, promised a referendum to test public opinion. Batchelor argues that this referendum was called for reasons of political expediency:

> 'When Harold Wilson found that he could

not unite the 1974 Labour government on the issue of the UK's membership of the EEC, he found it expedient to call a referendum so that the electorate could decide - and thus let the Labour party off the hook. Labour's zeal for such participatory exercises might have been regarded with less cynicism if the 1983 manifesto, which advocated the UK's withdrawal from the EC, had suggested a similar consultation exercise.' (Batchelor, 1992, p.22)

In the House of Commons, a free vote was held and 396 MPs voted to stay in the EEC whilst 170 voted to leave. As a result, the government issued a simplified white paper arguing in favour of continued membership. All those entitled to vote in the referendum were then provided with a statement for and a statement against membership drawn up by the pro-EEC and anti-EEC campaigning organisations. It should be noted that in the run-up to the referendum, the pro-EEC campaigning group collected ten times as much money in donations as the anti-EEC group. Also, most of the press supported the pro-EEC campaign. The referendum was held on 5 June 1975 and the following question appeared on ballot papers:

> 'The government have announced the results of re-negotiation of the UK's terms of membership of the European Community. Do you think that the UK should remain in the EEC?' (Keesings, 16-22 June 1975)

A large majority of voters voted in favour of remaining in the EEC.

The third occasion on which a referendum was held in the UK came on 1 March 1979 when the people of Scotland and Wales voted on whether or not they wished to accept the devolution proposals passed by Parliament in the Scotland Act 1978 and the Wales Act 1978. The vote was complicated by the fact that Labour backbenchers managed to secure in the Acts the need for 40% of the electorate as a whole to vote in favour of devolution. If 40% of the electorate as a whole did not vote in favour of devolution, then the Act would be repealed.

In Scotland a majority of those voting voted in favour of the devolution proposals. But, because there was a relatively low turnout, the total voting in favour of devolution was less than 40% of the electorate as a whole. As a result, the Scotland Act 1978 was repealed. In Wales there was little support for devolution and the Wales Act 1978 was also repealed. It should be noted that, even if large enough majorities had been obtained in favour of devolution, there was no guarantee that the provisions of the two Acts would be implemented. Bruce Millan, Secretary of State for Scotland at the time when the referendums were held, said:

> 'Obviously the House, as well as the Secretary of State, will take full account of the referendum. Nevertheless, it is ultimately an advisory referendum in the sense that the House will make the final decision.' (Keesings, 20 April 1979)

Since 1979, there have been a number of occasions when referendums have been called for but none has been held. The most vociferous demands for a referendum were made at the time when the Maastricht Treaty was being debated by the House of Commons in 1992 (see chapter 6, section 3.2). Other members of the EU - namely, Denmark, France and the Republic of Ireland - held referendums on whether or not to accept the terms of this treaty. But, the leaders of the Conservative and Labour parties opposed a referendum in Britain. Although the Maastricht Treaty was ratified without a referendum, John Major refused to rule out a referendum on proposed 1996 changes in EU institutions.

Activity 7.6

Item A *Referendums in the UK*

Date	Electorate	Issue	'Yes' vote	%	'No' vote	%	Turnout (%)
8 March 1973	Northern Ireland	Should Northern Ireland remain part of the UK?	591,820	98.9	6,463	1.1	58.1
5 June 1975	United Kingdom	Do you think that the UK should remain in the EEC?	17,378,581	67.2	8,470,073	32.8	63.2
1 March 1979	Scotland	Devolution for Scotland	1,230,937	51.5	1,153,500	48.3	62.9
1 March 1979	Wales	Devolution for Wales	243,048	20.3	956,330	79.7	58.3

This table shows the results of the four referendums held in the UK. Although 51.5% of voters in the referendum in Scotland in 1979 voted for devolution, this came to just 32.8% of the total electorate. The Scotland Act 1978 was, therefore, repealed. In Wales, the 20.3% who voted in favour of devolution came to just 11.9% of the total electorate and so the Wales Act 1978 was repealed.

Adapted from Batchelor, 1992.

Item B *Demands for a referendum (1)*

A referendum on Europe moved to centre stage in the battle for Tory unity yesterday when Home Secretary, Michael Howard, refused to rule out a referendum on proposed 1996 changes in European Union institutions. Instead of ruling out a referendum - in line with government policy - Mr Howard left the question open, saying: 'We can talk in due course about whether there should be a referendum and all these other interesting questions that are for the longer term.' Whilst John Major and the party chairman, Norman Fowler, appealed for unity, two senior MPs from opposite wings of the party debate on Europe united in their agreement over the need for a referendum. Teddy Taylor, a leading Eurosceptic said: 'It's 1996 before the next treaty and if people were to say in advance "We will consult the people before this happens", I think it would unite the party.' This view was supported by Peter Temple-Morris a pro-European.

Adapted from the *Observer*, 8 May 1994.

Item D *Should referendums be held?*

Item C *Demands for a referendum (2)*

For Mr Major to promise a referendum in 1996 might seem an embarrassing turnround given his opposition to a referendum on the Maastricht Treaty. But he could argue that because of the opt-outs negotiated by Britain during the build-up to Maastricht, the Maastricht Treaty did not mean profound constitutional changes that would justify a referendum. His promise of a referendum in 1997 might then be conditional on constitutional changes being proposed at the intergovernmental conference which is due to be held in 1996. In fact, a referendum would almost certainly be justifiable in 1997, even if the intergovernmental conference was confined to apparently technical matters such as EU voting rules. For, after the large extension of the EU's potential powers at Maastricht, even small administrative reforms could, over time, make a big impact on Britain's sovereignty. If Britain's sovereignty is affected then that is justification for holding a referendum. It is likely that Britain will be faced with a serious choice in 1997. Suppose, for example, that a small group of European countries wanted to move towards federalism. Britain would have to decide whether to join them. If the EU as a whole continued to evolve in a federalist direction, Britain would have to decide whether or not to remain a member of the EU.

Adapted from the *Times*' leading article, 10 May 1994.

Questions

1. In what circumstances, if at all, do you think referendums should be held? Give reasons for your answer.
2. Look at Item A.
   a) Why do you think these referendums were held?
   b) Would you agree that these referendums were a useful exercise in democracy? Give reasons for your answer.
3. a) What do Items B and C tell us about why governments might choose to call a referendum?
   b) Do you think a referendum on Europe should be held in 1997? Give reasons for your answer.
   c) Supposing a referendum was to be held. What question should be asked?
4. How would you answer the question posed in Item D? Explain why. What arguments might opponents use against you?

4 Electoral reform

Key Issues

1. What types of electoral systems are available and how do they work?
2. What is the difference between majority and proportional systems?
3. What are the arguments for and against electoral reform in Britain?

4.1 Different voting systems

A Royal Commission appointed in 1911 to examine voting systems claimed that there were over 300 voting systems either actually in existence or potentially available. In other words, every country in the world could have a different voting system and there would still be systems that remained unused.

Despite this great diversity, many of these 300 or more voting systems have much in common - they differ in terms of practical details. For convenience, it is possible to distinguish between two main groups: majority systems and proportional systems. In addition, one hybrid system will be described - the additional member system.

Majority systems

Majority systems include mechanisms to ensure that the winning candidate achieves more than 50% of the vote in a constituency. The three best known of these systems are the alternative vote system, the supplementary vote system and the second ballot system. All three systems assume that the country is divided into single member constituencies. None of the systems is proportional because none ensures that, overall, the results of general elections reflect the number of votes cast for each party.

1. The alternative vote system

Under the alternative vote system, voters have the opportunity of ranking all the candidates whose names appear on the ballot paper in order of preference. As in the British plurality system, candidates stand for election in a constituency and one member is elected in each constituency.

If any candidate receives more than 50% of first preferences in the initial ballot, then that candidate is elected. If, however, no candidate receives more than 50% of first preferences, then the candidate with the lowest number of first preferences is eliminated and that candidate's second preferences are redistributed to the other candidates. If no candidate has reached 50% of the vote after this redistribution, then the candidate with the lowest number of votes after the redistribution is eliminated and that candidate's second preferences are redistributed. This process is continued until a candidate gains more than 50% of the vote.

Voters are not obliged to indicate preferences on their ballot paper. They may vote for a single candidate because they do not want to support another candidate, should their candidate be eliminated. In safe seats, there may be little point in indicating preferences since it is likely that a candidate will gain more than 50% of the vote without the need for any redistribution of votes. In marginal seats, however, second preferences may be crucial. Indeed, the system may encourage electoral pacts between two parties at the expense of a third since the two parties which made the pact could then recommend to their supporters which party to nominate as their second preference.

Supporters of this system emphasise that it retains constituency representation and it ensures that the winning candidate has more than 50% of the vote. Critics argue that the system leads to disproportional support for the centre parties because, while they are not voters' first choice, they are nearly always voters' second choice. The alternative vote system is used in elections to the Australian House of Representatives.

2. The supplementary vote system

A variation on the alternative vote system has been proposed by the Labour MP Dale Campbell Savours. This is called the supplementary vote system. Under this system, candidates with more than 50% of first preferences in the initial ballot are automatically elected. But if no candidate gains more than 50% of the vote, only two candidates remain in the race - the two candidates with the highest number of first preferences. The second preferences from the losing candidates are then redistributed and, following the redistribution, whichever of the two remaining candidates has the largest total wins the seat.

3. The second ballot system

As the name implies, the second ballot system includes the provision for voting to take place on two separate occasions. In the first ballot, voters vote for their favourite candidate. If any candidate wins more than 50% of the vote in a constituency, then that candidate is elected. But, if no candidate wins more than 50%, a second ballot is held, usually a week or two later. In some variations of this system, only the two candidates with the highest number of votes in the first ballot are allowed to stand in the second ballot. This ensures that the successful candidate in the second ballot achieves an absolute majority.
In other variations, either all the earlier candidates are allowed to stand or there is a threshold in the first

ballot (10% of the vote, for example) and only those who crossed the threshold (by winning more than 10% of the vote, for example) are allowed to stand in the second ballot. Some variations even allow newcomers to stand in the second ballot.

This system is in no sense proportional and does nothing to ensure a fair representation for small parties. It does, however, allow genuine choice since voters can vote for their favourite party in the first ballot, knowing that their vote will not be wasted since they will probably be able to cast a second vote in the second ballot. The system also encourages pacts between parties - parties which put up candidates in the first ballot agree not to stand in the second ballot to ensure that their allies have a better chance of being elected.

A version of the second ballot system is used in France. Only those candidates who win more than 12.5% of the vote in the first ballot are allowed to stand in the second ballot. In the 1993 election in France, 90 of the 577 seats were elected in the first ballot and in virtually every case only two challengers remained to contest the second ballot.

Proportional systems

Majority voting systems do not ensure that, overall, the results of general elections reflect the number of votes cast for each party. After all, a successful candidate in a majority system might have won just 51% of the vote. That means that, in a sense, 49% of votes in that constituency have been wasted. In the country as a whole, a party might have won many thousands of votes but not have won even one seat. This is what happened in the European elections in Britain in 1989. The Green party won 15% of the vote nationally. But it did not win a single seat. In a system which was truly proportional, the Green party would have won 15% of the seats.

Proportional systems - systems of proportional representation (PR) - do not work on a single member constituency basis. In fact, the bigger the number of representatives elected in a single constituency, the more proportional the result because the election of a large number of representatives means that smaller parties have a greater chance of winning seats. Ideally (for those who support PR), a whole country should be a single multi-member constituency. The voters can then vote for their favourite party and seats can be allocated to the parties on the basis of the number of votes each has secured.

Urwin (1987) argues that PR has two conflicting aims. First, it attempts to ensure that party representation mirrors, as closely as possible, the level of support for various parties over the country as a whole. And second, PR aims to provide voters with some degree of choice, not only between the parties but also between individual candidates. There are two main systems of PR: the list system and the single transferable vote system. The list system comes closer to achieving the first aim whilst the single transferable vote system comes closer to achieving the second aim.

1. The list system

The list system involves multi-member constituencies in which voters vote for political parties rather than for individual candidates. Seats in each constituency are divided according to the proportion of votes won by each party.

In its most basic form, a whole country is a single constituency (this is the case in Israel and the Netherlands). Each party presents a list of candidates (which may, in some variations of the system, consist of a single name - thus allowing an individual to stand). Voters throughout the country then vote for one or other of these party lists and seats are shared out on a proportional basis. So, suppose that a country had 100 seats in its Parliament and three parties - party A, party B and party C - put up lists for an election. If party A won 45% of the vote, party B won 40% of the vote and party C won 15% of the vote, then the top 45 candidates on party A's list would be elected. Similarly, the top 40 candidates on party B's list and the top 15 on party C's list would be elected.

The list system is used in many countries including Sweden, Norway, Belgium, Spain and Finland. The exact details of how it works vary from country to country. Catt & Shaw (1990) explain how the list system works in Sweden:

> 'Sweden is divided into constituencies which each return a number of representatives (averaging 11). Parties put forward a slate of candidates in each area. Voters vote for one list and may alter the order in which the party has placed the candidates. Seats are allocated by the use of quota to the parties according to the strength of their support. Parties then allocate these seats to their candidates according to the preferences marked by the voters (no alteration means voters accept the order given by the party). A few extra seats (11% of the total) are used to give national proportionality if this has not been achieved by the constituency results. Before it wins any seats, a party must pass a 'threshold'; it must gain 12% of the vote in a constituency or 4% of the national vote. Any mid-term vacancy is filled by the next most popular candidate on that party's list.' (Catt & Shaw, 1990, pp.15-16)

Critics of the list system argue that since the lists of candidates are drawn up by party headquarters, voters have no real choice over individual candidates. In addition, the size of constituencies means that the links between a representative and the local community are broken. MPs do not individually have a constituency and so there is no sense of local MPs being accountable to their electors.

2. The single transferable vote system

The single transferable vote system (STV) was created in the 19th century and is based upon the idea that votes should be given to candidates rather than parties. The country is divided into multi-member constituencies and parties may put up as many candidates in each constituency as there are seats. Voters have the opportunity of ranking all the candidates whose names appear on the ballot paper in order of preference. But they can vote for just one or two candidates if they choose to do so.

Seats are allocated according to a quota system. If a candidate reaches the quota on first preferences, then that candidate is elected. If the candidate receives more first preferences than are required by the quota, then the surplus votes are redistributed to that candidate's second preferences on a proportional basis (in other words, all that candidate's second preferences are counted and the surplus votes redistributed proportionally amongst the other candidates). This redistribution may allow other candidates to reach the quota. If candidates thereby manage to gain more votes than are needed for the quota, their votes are redistributed in the same way. But if seats still remain unfilled, the candidate with the least number of votes is eliminated and that candidate's second preferences are redistributed. This process is continued until all the seats are filled. As a result, third, fourth and even fifth placed preferences may be brought into the calculation.

The formula most often used for calculating the quota is as follows. The number of votes cast is divided by the number of seats in the constituency plus one. When this is calculated, one is added to the answer.

It is difficult in a multi-member constituency to hold by-elections and different versions of STV use different methods. Some versions hold a ballot of the whole constituency using the alternative vote system since only one seat is to be filled. Some versions ballot only part of the constituency. And still others do not hold a ballot at all. They elect the candidate who, according to the original ballot, would have been next to win a seat.

The STV system is currently used in the Republic of Ireland, in Australia (for the Senate) and in Northern Ireland (for European elections).

The additional member system

After the Second World War the Allies created the additional member system in West Germany. It remains the system used in Germany and has been adopted in Hungary. Of the four wartime Allies, Britain and the USA used a plurality system whilst France and the Soviet Union used proportional systems. As a result, the additional member system combines a regional list system with a single member constituency plurality system. The Allies were aware that the Nazis had gained power through their electoral success in the early 1930s. As a result, the main aim of the additional member system was to prevent extremists from being able to gain power in the future. The idea was that the new system would combine all that was best in the Allies' various electoral systems in such a way that democratic stability could be assured.

Under the additional member system, the country is divided into single member constituencies and into regions. Voters have two votes - one for a constituency candidate and one for a party. In each constituency, a candidate is elected by simple majority. The remaining seats are then allocated from regional party lists of candidates on a proportional basis. The share of seats won by a party in the constituency election is compared to the proportion of the vote won by the party overall. If there is a discrepancy, this is corrected by the allocation of seats from the regional party lists. Parties which won fewer constituency seats than was merited by their proportion of the party vote gain extra regional seats and vice versa. By this means, the overall result is proportional. To qualify for this redistribution of seats in Germany, parties need to cross a 'threshold'. They must win either at least three constituency seats or 5% of the party vote.

Supporters of this system claim that it retains the best feature of plurality and majority systems, namely the fact that everyone has a local MP, and removes the worst feature, namely the fact that some parties are grossly over-represented in Parliament. Critics argue that two classes of representative are created - those who have to fight for re-election in their constituency and those whose re-election is ensured if they remain at the top of the party list. Also, since constituencies elect only half of the representatives, they are very large and the representatives are correspondingly more remote.

Activity 7.7

Item A *The alternative vote system*

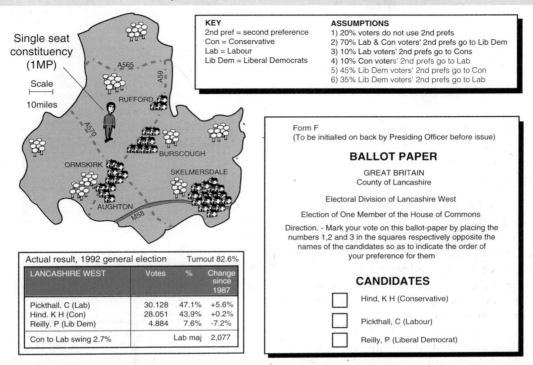

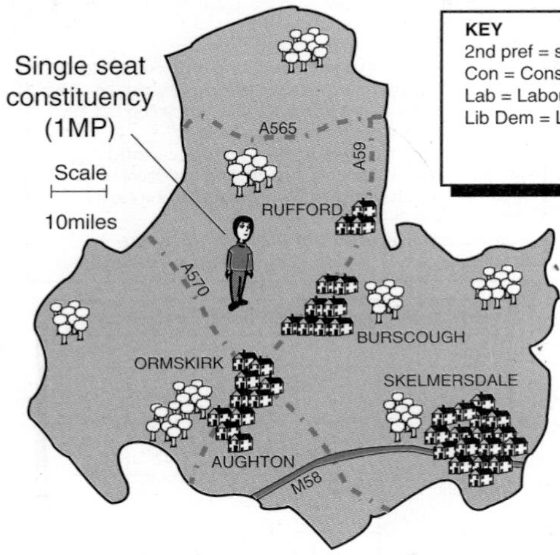

KEY
2nd pref = second preference
Con = Conservative
Lab = Labour
Lib Dem = Liberal Democrats

ASSUMPTIONS
1) 20% voters do not use 2nd prefs
2) 70% Lab & Con voters' 2nd prefs go to Lib Dem
3) 10% Lab voters' 2nd prefs go to Cons
4) 10% Con voters' 2nd prefs go to Lab
5) 45% Lib Dem voters' 2nd prefs go to Con
6) 35% Lib Dem voters' 2nd prefs go to Lab

Form F
(To be initialled on back by Presiding Officer before issue)

BALLOT PAPER

GREAT BRITAIN
County of Lancashire

Electoral Division of Lancashire West

Election of One Member of the House of Commons

Direction. - Mark your vote on this ballot-paper by placing the numbers 1,2 and 3 in the squares respectively opposite the names of the candidates so as to indicate the order of your preference for them

CANDIDATES

☐ Hind, K H (Conservative)

☐ Pickthall, C (Labour)

☐ Reilly, P (Liberal Democrat)

Actual result, 1992 general election — Turnout 82.6%

LANCASHIRE WEST	Votes	%	Change since 1987
Pickthall. C (Lab)	30.128	47.1%	+5.6%
Hind. K H (Con)	28.051	43.9%	+0.2%
Reilly. P (Lib Dem)	4.884	7.6%	-7.2%
Con to Lab swing 2.7%	Lab maj		2,077

The diagram above shows the actual parliamentary constituency of Lancashire West and the result in the 1992 general election. It also shows what a ballot paper would look like if the alternative vote system had been used. The assumptions are based on evidence from opinion polls. Using the 1992 election results and these assumptions, it is possible to work out what would have happened if the alternative vote system had been used.

Item B *The single transferable vote system*

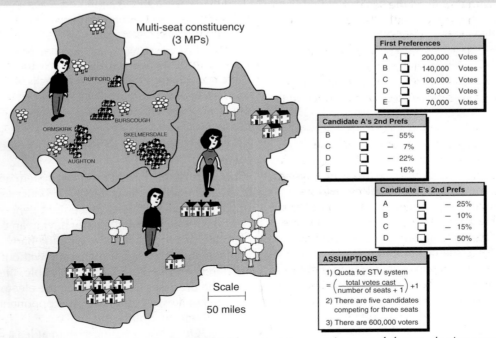

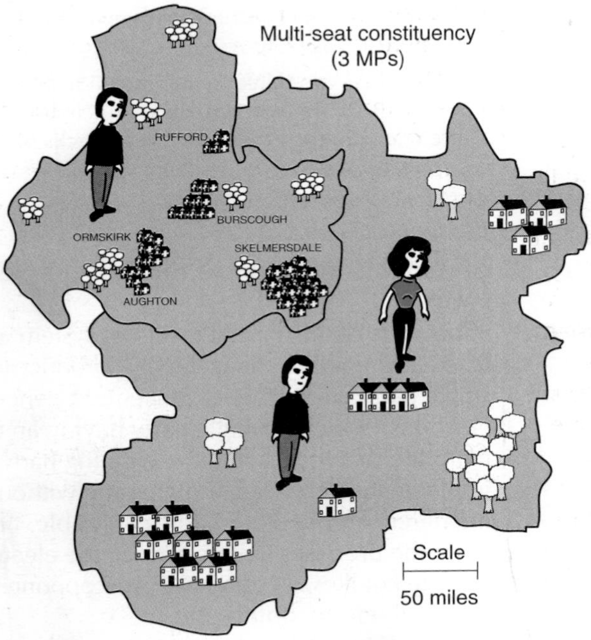

First Preferences

A	☐	200,000	Votes
B	☐	140,000	Votes
C	☐	100,000	Votes
D	☐	90,000	Votes
E	☐	70,000	Votes

Candidate A's 2nd Prefs

B	☐	– 55%
C	☐	– 7%
D	☐	– 22%
E	☐	– 16%

Candidate E's 2nd Prefs

A	☐	– 25%
B	☐	– 10%
C	☐	– 15%
D	☐	– 50%

ASSUMPTIONS
1) Quota for STV system
$$= \left(\frac{\text{total votes cast}}{\text{number of seats} + 1}\right) + 1$$
2) There are five candidates competing for three seats
3) There are 600,000 voters

The diagram above assumes that the single transferable vote system was in use and that an election was fought in a constituency which elected three MPs. The constituency is shown on the left, the election result on the right. It is assumed there are five candidates (candidates A-E) and 600,000 voters.

Item C *The additional member system*

Table 1 Result of constituency election

Party	Votes	Seats
A	184,000	5
B	116,000	3
C	55,000	1
D	50,000	0

Table 2 Final overall result

Party	Constituency results	Additional seats	Total seats
A	5	1	6
B	3	1	4
C	1	0	1
D	0	1	1

ASSUMPTIONS

1. The region is made up of 9 single seat constituencies and 3 additional seats. The electorate in the region, therefore, elects a total of 12 members.
2. Additional seats are allocated as follows:
a) The total number of votes for each party is divided by the number of single seat constituencies already won, plus one. The first additional seat is allocated to the party which now has the highest number of votes (ie party D in table 3).
b) The party's original total number of votes is re-divided by its new total number of seats plus one. The next additional seat is then allocated to the party with the highest total of votes (ie party A in table 3).
c) The process is repeated until all additional seats are allocated (ie party B in table 3 also receives an additional seat).

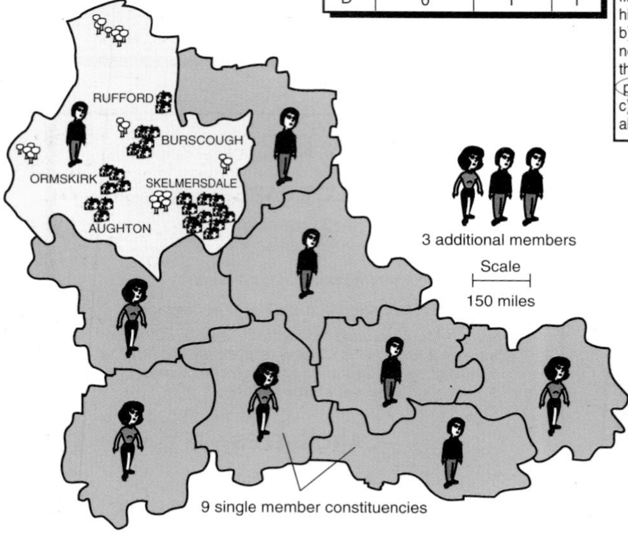

Table 3 Allocation of Additional Seats

Party:	A	B	C	D
Directly elected seats	5	3	1	0
Number of votes	184,000	116,000	55,000	50,000
Divide by: 1				50,000
2			27,500	25,000
3				
4		29,000		
5				
6	30,667			
7	26,286			

The diagram above shows how the additional member system would work in an area divided into nine constituencies with three additional members. In Germany a region with nine constituencies would elect nine additional members. It is assumed that four parties (A-D) won enough votes to cross the threshold and that each party in the region won the national average.

Adapted from Watts, 1994.

Questions

1. a) Look at Item A and suppose the 1992 election had been fought using the alternative vote system. Which candidate would have won?
   b) How would the result have differed if the supplementary vote system had been used?
   c) What are the benefits and drawbacks of (i) the alternative vote system and (ii) the supplementary vote system?
2. a) Using the information in Item B work out which candidates were elected.
   b) What are the benefits and drawbacks of the single transferable vote system?
3. a) Why do you think the additional member system (Item C) has been described as a 'hybrid system'?
   b) What are the benefits and drawbacks of the additional member system?

4.2 The debate over electoral reform in Britain

In recent years, the debate over electoral reform in Britain has risen up the political agenda, not least because between 1979 and 1992 the Conservatives won an overall majority in four general elections in a row. Critics point to the fact that in none of these elections did the Conservatives receive more than 50% of the vote. In fact, the highest share of the vote they achieved was 43.9% in 1979. In other words, for four terms a majority of voters have been governed by a party which they did not vote for. This, critics say, is the fault of the British electoral system and so the system should be changed. This section considers arguments for and against electoral reform. It begins with a critique of the current system.

Arguments in favour of the current electoral system

Supporters of the current electoral system argue that its great strength is the fact that it produces strong single party governments. Since most general elections result in a single party having an overall majority, that means that the winning party is able to implement its proposed programme without interference from other parties. It is able, therefore, to fulfill the promises that it made to the electorate. As George Foulkes, a Labour MP and opponent of electoral reform, points out:

> 'Our present voting system at least ensures that government decisions are made by the party which has the most votes - admittedly usually the largest minority. However, experience elsewhere has shown that PR

> often puts crucial government decisions in the hands of very small minorities, possibly extremists, who hold the balance of power.' (Foulkes, 1992, p.9)

It is also the case that coalition governments (which other electoral systems are likely to produce) are the result of compromise deals between parties after a general election. So, the programme of such governments has not been directly voted on by the electorate.

A second argument in favour of the present electoral system is that it ensures that there are strong links between an MP and the local community. Small single member constituencies mean that local people can air their grievances directly with their MP. Foulkes argues that:

> 'It is an historic and essential part of our democracy that all constituents know that they have an MP who has a duty to pursue individual problems and constituency issues on their behalf, either individually or collectively.' (Foulkes, 1992, p.8)

Watts (1994) points out that MPs have sole responsibility for the area which they represent and, once elected, they represent all those who live in the area not just those who voted for them.

A third argument in favour of the current electoral system is that it is based on a readily understood principle - everyone has a vote and the candidate with the most votes is the winner. Watts notes that:

> 'The system is easy to understand, especially for the voter who marks an X on the ballot paper. It has the alleged merits of simplicity and familiarity and, as such, is widely accepted. The demand for change comes especially from those who have something to gain from it and the alternatives they propose can, in most cases, be said to be more complex and not without other problems.' (Watts, 1994, p.7)

A further argument in favour of the current system is that by providing an outright winner (most of the time) the current system ensures that a single party is provided with a mandate to carry out its programme. There is (usually) no need for post-election trade-offs and coalitions. The party with the most seats normally has an overall majority and is, therefore, able to carry out its programme without having to be compromised by the smaller parties. This allows strong government and maintains the principle that a party in government should be elected on the strength of its proposed programme and then judged on its actions. Coalitions with other parties would give undue influence to small parties which do not represent the opinion of a large section of the population.

Finally, it can be argued that the current electoral system should be preserved simply because it works and has been proved to work over many years. All other electoral systems are flawed and so there is little point in replacing one flawed system with another.

Arguments against the current electoral system

Perhaps the greatest drawback of the current electoral system is that in each constituency up to 70% of the votes are wasted. Votes cast for the losing candidates are wasted in the sense that they are ignored in seat allocation. Votes that add to the winning candidate's majority are wasted in the sense that they give no extra benefit to the party whose candidate has won. As a result, the number of seats won by each party nationally is in no way proportional to the number of votes cast for each party. For example, in the 1992 general election the Liberal Democrats won 17.9% of the vote nationally but they won just 3.1% of the seats. Indeed, under the current system it is possible for a party to win fewer votes than another party but more seats. This happened in February 1974 when Labour won 301 seats with 37.2% of the vote whilst the Conservatives won just 297 seats with 37.9% of the vote.

A second drawback with the current electoral system is that the winning party rarely wins a majority of votes. In fact, this century there have only been two occasions when, nationally, a single party has won more than 50% of the vote in a general election - in 1900 when the Conservative and Liberal Unionists won 50.3% of the vote and in 1931 when the Conservatives won 55% of the vote. In 1935, candidates standing for the National government won a total of 53.3% of the vote, but the National government was a coalition and the biggest party within the coalition (the Conservatives) won just 47.8% of the vote. The fact that the government is normally formed by a party which has only won a minority of the total vote means that more people voted against it than for it.

A third drawback is that the current electoral system has resulted in regional imbalance. Labour MP Jeff Rooker points out that:

> 'The current system is also polarising the country into a 'Labour' north and a 'Tory' south. Even under the current system there are 1.5 million Labour voters in the south of England outside London compared to 1.3 million in the whole of Scotland. Yet there are only two Labour MPs in the South and there are now 48 in Scotland.' (Rooker, 1992, p.7)

Britain's 'electoral geography' means that some parties gain an electoral advantage:

> 'It is frequently observed that the relative success of the three parties which contest and win seats throughout Great Britain is a function not only of the number of votes that

> they win but also of where those votes are. The Labour party is said to be particularly disadvantaged, for example, because it wins by very large majorities in its 'safe' seats, though that disadvantage is somewhat countered because the constituencies where it is successful are on average smaller than those won by the Tories. The Liberals, on the other hand, are disadvantaged by the dispersion of their votes: they have too few in enough places to win many seats. The Conservative party, meanwhile, is said to have the 'best' geography of voting, in terms of potential seat winning.' (Heath et al., 1994, p.261)

Critics of the current system also point out that general elections are decided by what happens in a small number of marginal constituencies. In other words, some votes matter more than others. Around 500 seats are 'safe' seats. In these seats, the result is almost a foregone conclusion. The winning party gains many more votes than it needs to win. Votes for the other parties count for little. In marginal seats, however, every vote is important. The result in marginals determines the complexion of the government. If just 11 marginal seats had gone to Labour rather than to the Conservatives in the 1992 general election, then the Conservatives would not have won an overall majority and there would have been a hung Parliament. In other words, the vote of a few hundred thousand voters in marginal seats can determine the fate of the country as a whole.

Whilst supporters of the current system argue that the link between an MP and the local community is important, some critics argue that this is a weak argument. In reality, MPs cannot possibly represent all those who live in the area. According to Plant:

> 'The critic will point out that within many existing constituencies there are very significant social, political, economic, ethnic and religious cleavages which undermine the idea constituencies are in some sense natural communities.' (Plant, 1992, p.47)

And, besides, it is possible to look at the concept of representation rather differently. Plant suggests that supporters of PR believe that Parliament should not be made up of individuals who each claim to speak on behalf of a particular area. Rather:

> '[It] should be seen as a microcosm of society. That is to say, the Parliament should represent all shades of opinion if they are numerically significant. The Parliament should reflect in proportion these shades of opinion. The root idea of the microcosmic view is that of the representative sample. On this understanding of representation, a representative is a person whose characteristics and opinions reflect those of a wider group of people. When we say that a committee is representative, we mean it reflects the composition of some wider groupings which are believed to have an interest in the work or the outcomes of the committee. In this sense, we can say that a Parliament is representative when it reflects, in a proportionate way, wider society.' (Plant, 1992, p.47)

In other words, according to this view, a system which divides the country into small single seat constituencies is likely to produce a Parliament which is less representative than a system which divides the country into large multi-seat constituencies.

In addition, whilst supporters of the current system argue that it encourages strong government which does not rely on coalitions, critics point to the danger of a single party becoming entrenched in power. They also point out that the political parties themselves are, in effect, coalitions. A single party in government has to make deals with members of its own party in the same way that coalition governments have to make deals. The difference is that in a coalition government these deals are made openly. Besides, PR does not necessarily lead to coalition government:

> 'There are plenty of other countries that have PR which have majority or one party governments. Spain elected its third majority socialist government on PR in 1989. Sweden has had a left majority in Parliament and a one party Labour government for 28 out of the last 34 years - with PR.' (Rooker, 1992, p.8)

Finally, it should be pointed out that, although systems such as the single transferable vote are mathematically complex, all voters have to do on the ballot paper is to indicate their order of preference. It is the returning officer who is responsible for working out the result. There is, therefore, no reason why voters should not be able to cope with other voting systems.

Prospects for change

The only major political party definitely committed to the current electoral system for the foreseeable future is the Conservative party. The Liberal Democrats are committed to the introduction of a single transferable vote system for all elections. The Labour party set up a Commission under Raymond Plant in 1990 to investigate electoral reform. The Plant Commission's final report was published in April 1993. It recommended a regional list system for European elections and elections to Labour's proposed second chamber and it recommended the supplementary vote system for elections to the House of Commons. In 1993, the Labour leader John Smith made a pledge that the Labour party would hold a referendum on electoral reform if it won the next election. The referendum would be similar to that held in 1992 in New Zealand when voters were asked first whether they wished to abandon the current system and then which of several systems they wanted to replace it. However, Tony Blair who was elected Labour leader after John Smith's death is reported to be 'luke warm' about electoral reform and did not refer to it in his acceptance speech after winning the Labour leadership election in July 1994.

Activity 7.8

Item A *The 1992 general election (1)*

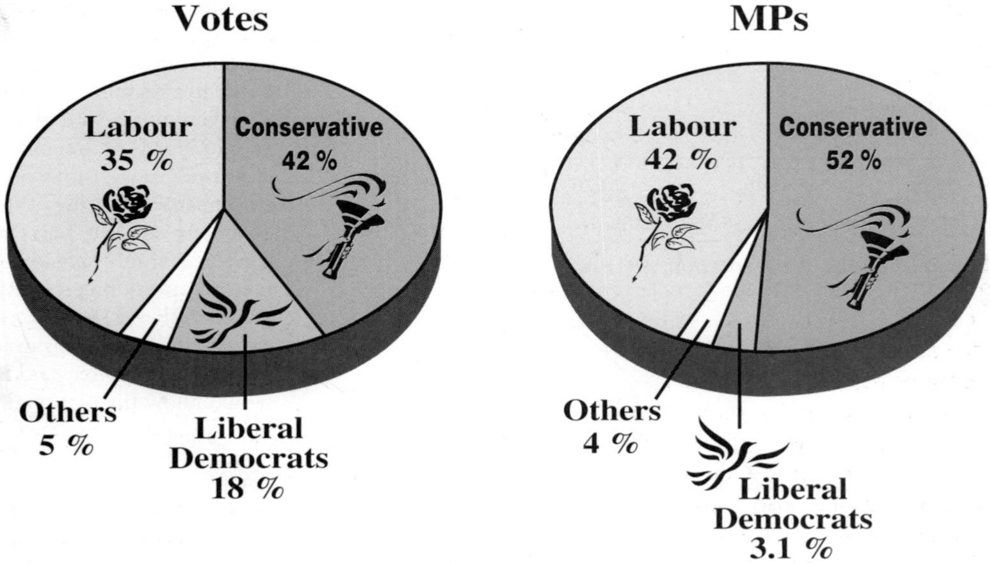

These pie charts show the percentage of votes and the percentage of seats won by parties in the 1992 general election.

Adapted from Wood & Wood, 1992.

Item B *The 1992 general election (2)*

Party	Actual votes, 1992 general election	Actual seats, 1992 general election		Using **alternative vote** system		Using **single transferable vote** system		Using **additional member** system	
	%	Seats	%	Seats	%	Seats	%	Seats	%
Conservative	**42.0**	**336**	(51.6)	**323**	(49.6)	**275**	(42.2)	**346**	(45.9)
Labour	**35.4**	**271**	(41.6)	**261**	(40.1)	**237**	(36.4)	**283**	(37.7)
Liberal Democrats	**17.9**	**20**	(3.1)	**39**	(6.0)	**102**	(15.7)	**89**	(11.9)
Scottish Nationalists	**2.1**	**3**	(0.5)	**6**	(0.9)	**17**	(2.6)	**10**	(1.3)
Plaid Cymru	**0.4**	**4**	(0.6)	**5**	(0.8)	**3**	(0.5)	**4**	(0.5)
Ulster parties	**2.2**	**17**	(2.6)	**17**	(2.6)	**17**	(2.6)	**19**	(2.5)

After the 1992 general election, the *Independent on Sunday* examined ways in which the election result would have changed if Britain had used different electoral systems. A number of assumptions were made. First, for the alternative vote system, it was assumed that 80% of voters voted for just one candidate, 70% of second preferences went to the Liberal Democrats from Labour and Conservative voters and Liberal Democrats' second preferences were split 45%-35% between the Conservatives and Labour. For the single transferable vote system, it was assumed that there were multi-member seats and voters voted on a party ticket basis. For the additional member system, it was assumed that an additional 100 MPs would be allocated in proportion to the votes cast for the existing 651 seats.

Item C *Representation of MPs in Parliament 1918-87*

(i) Conservative over-representation, 1918-87

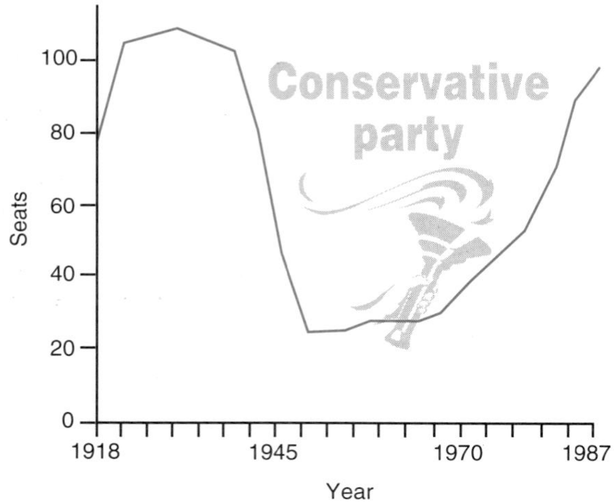

(ii) Labour under- and over-representation, 1918-87

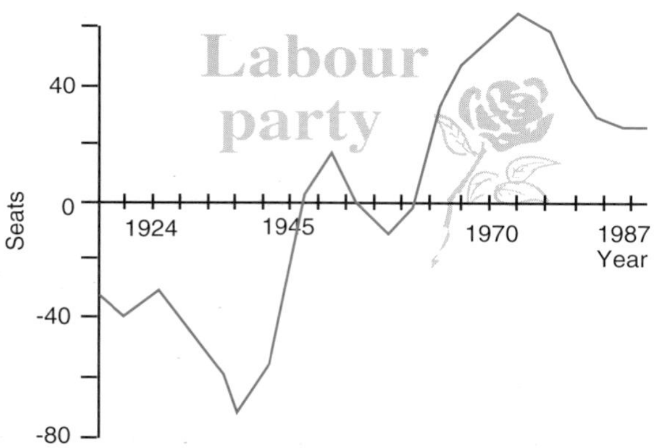

(iii) Liberal under-representation, 1918-87

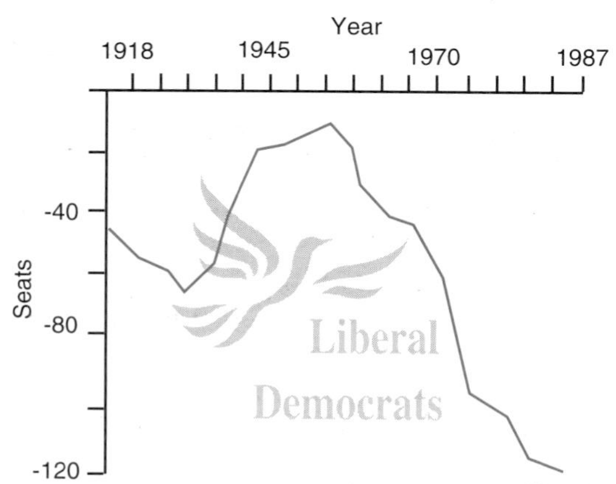

By comparing the number of votes cast for a political party with the seats gained, it is possible to work out by how many seats a party is over- or under-represented in Parliament.

Adapted from Plant, 1992.

Item D *PR and extremism (1)*

During the 1992 election campaign, Kenneth Baker said that PR had helped Fascists to gain support in Europe again. PR is often accused of allowing extremists to gain power. But such a charge has little substance. It is true that PR can help minorities. But, so can plurality systems. The two types of system favour different kinds of minorities. A plurality system, for example, favours a geographically concentrated minority like Plaid Cymru in north west Wales or Sinn Fein in Northern Ireland. Such minorities may or may not be extremist. PR, on the other hand, benefits a minority party whose support is thinly spread. Such a minority party might be moderate like the Liberal Democrats or extreme like the Nazis in interwar Germany. It is often said that PR would allow the National Front into Parliament. But even if a National Front MP was elected, would this really endanger the political system? After all, a Communist MP was elected in 1935 and two more in 1945 but they made little impact. Besides, PR would greatly increase the representation of ethnic minorities. In a single member constituency, it is the presence of a candidate deviating from the white Anglo-Saxon male norm which is noticed. But in a multi-member constituency, the lack of a balanced ticket would cause comment. Better ethnic minority representation would counterbalance the possibility of a National Front MP. Anyway, PR registers the strength of tendencies in society. So, if racist tendencies are present, PR will reflect them. But if one does not like what one sees in the mirror, does it make sense to blame the mirror?

Adapted from the *Guardian*, 17 April 1992.

Item E *PR and extremism (2)*

If there had been PR in the 1992 general election, then no party would have had an overall majority. The result would have been a political impasse until either Labour or the Conservatives managed to do a deal with the Liberal Democrats. The same would have happened in other recent elections. The largest party would have been unable to enact any legislation without the blessing of a much smaller centre party. The small centre party could, in effect, hold the bigger parties to ransom. This is what happens in Israel where a handful of MPs regularly threaten to bring the government down unless their policies are implemented. Government coalitions held together by political protection rackets are notoriously weak and unstable. They tend to produce either paralysis or upheaval. The introduction of PR in Britain might result in weak and unstable government based on opportunistic pacts and cynical horse-trading.

Adapted from Colman, 1992.

Questions

1. a) Using the items in this activity give the arguments for and against electoral reform in Britain.
   b) Why do you think the Conservative party is the only major party to support the current system?
2. a) Write an analysis of the evidence which appears in Items A-C.
   b) Which electoral system in Item B would have produced the fairest result? Explain your answer.
3. Describe the attitude of the authors of Items D and E towards electoral reform. Which phrases reveal their attitudes?
4. Do you think a referendum should be held on the subject of electoral reform in Britain? Give reasons for your answer.

References

Batchelor (1992) Batchelor, A., 'Referendums and initiatives', *Politics Review*, Vol.1, No.3, February 1992.

Beetham (1993) Beetham, D., *Auditing Democracy in Britain*, The Charter 88 Trust, 1993.

Beetham (1994) Beetham D 'Are we really free?' in *Bite the Ballot*, a supplement in *New Statesman and Society*, 29 April 1994

Butler & Kavanagh (1992) Butler, D. & Kavanagh, D., *The British General Election of 1992*, Macmillan, 1992.

Catt & Shaw (1990) Catt, H. & Shaw, A., 'The intelligent person's guide to electoral reform', *New Statesman and Society/Common Voice,* April 1990.

Colman (1992) Colman, A.M., 'Polemic: arguments against proportional representation', *Politics Review*, Vol.2, No.2, November 1992.

Coote & Campbell (1982) Coote, A. & Campbell, B., *Sweet Freedom: The Struggle for Women's Liberation*, Blackwell, 1982.

Cowley & Dowding (1994) Cowley, P. & Dowding, K., 'Electoral systems and parliamentary representation', *Politics Review*, Vol.4, No.1, September 1994.

Craig (1989) Craig, F.W.S., *British Electoral Facts* 1832-1987, Parliamentary Research Services, 1989.

Dearlove & Saunders (1984) Dearlove, J. & Saunders, P., *Introduction to British Politics*, Polity Press, 1984.

Foulkes (1992) Foulkes, G., 'Face to face', *Politics Review*, Vol.1, No.4, April 1992.

Hailsham (1978) Hailsham, Lord, *The Dilemma of Democracy*, Collins, 1978.

Haralambos (1994) Haralambos, M. (ed.), *Developments in Sociology*, Vol.10, Causeway Press, 1994.

Heath et al. (1994) Heath, A., Jowell, R. & Curtice, J. (eds), *Labour's Last Chance?*, Dartmouth, 1994.

Held (1987) Held, D., *Models of Democracy*, Polity Press, 1987

Heywood (1991) Heywood, A., 'Liberal democracy', *Talking Politics*, Vol.3, No.2, winter 1990/91.

HMSO (1991) Central Office of Information, '*Parliamentary Elections*' in the *Aspects of Britain* series, HMSO, 1991.

Norton (1991) Norton, P., 'Parliamentary democracy', *Modern History Review*, Vol.2, No.3, 1991.

Paine (1791) Paine, T., *The Rights of Man*, Everyman's Library, Dent Dutton, 1979.

Parry & Moyser (1993) Parry, G. & Moyser, G., 'Political participation in Britain', *Politics Review*, Vol.3, No.2, November 1993.

Parry et al. (1991) Parry, G., Moyser, G. & Day, N., *Political Participation In Britain*, Cambridge University Press, 1991.

Plant (1992) Plant R., 'Electoral reform and electoral systems' in *Wale (1992)*.

Robertson (1986) Robertson, D., *The Penguin Dictionary of Politics*, Penguin, 1986.

Rooker (1992) Rooker, J., 'Face to face', *Politics Review*, Vol.1, No.4, April 1992.

Taylor (1965) Taylor, A.J.P., *English History 1914-45*, Penguin, 1965.

Urwin (1987) Urwin, D., 'Electing representatives: proportional systems', *Social Studies Review*, Vol.2, No.5, May 1987.

Wale (1992) Wale, W. (ed.), *Developments In Politics*, Vol.3, Causeway Press, 1992.

Watts (1994) Watts, D., *Electoral Reform: Achieving a Sense of Proportion*, PAVIC Publications, Sheffield Hallam University, 1994.

Weir (1994) Weir, S., 'Crisis of confidence' in *Bite the Ballot*, a supplement in *New Statesman and Society*, 29 April 1994.

Williams (1981) Williams, R., *Parliamentary Democracy*, Spokesman Press, 1981.

Wood & Wood (1992) Wood, A.H. & Wood, R. *The Times Guide to the House of Commons April 1992*, HarperCollins, 1992.

8 Political parties

Introduction

Which political party do you belong to? The chances are that the answer to this question is 'none'. Party membership of all three main parties over the last 20 years has been in decline. But, that does not mean that political parties are any less important than they were 20 years ago. The British political system has developed in such a way that political parties are at its heart.

A political party is a group of like-minded people who agree to abide by a set of rules and set out to win political power in order to achieve their common goals. Normally this means that the party puts up candidates for election, though some parties choose to attempt to win power in other ways. That political parties aim to win power and to govern (rather than just to influence the government) is important. It is one of the factors which distinguishes them from pressure groups. Another factor is that, unlike most pressure groups which concentrate on a single issue, political parties formulate and try to implement a broad range of policies.

Most people, no matter how little interest they have in politics, could name the current Conservative, Liberal Democrat and Labour leaders because they see all three regularly on the television, hear them on the radio and read about them in the newspapers. Fewer people could identify the main policies of these parties. Fewer still would feel able to discuss the parties' history, ideology or internal structure. This chapter looks in general at the evolution of the British party system since the 19th century and examines, in detail, the development and internal structure of the three main political parties.

Chapter summary

Part 1 looks at the **history of British political parties** and their **role and functions** within the British political system. It asks why political parties are necessary.

Part 2 focuses on the **Conservative party**. The development and organisation of the party are examined. Sections discuss the **selection of the leader** and the **role of the leader** and the **party conference.**

Part 3 focuses on the **Labour party**. It follows the same pattern as part 2.

Part 4 focuses on the **Liberal Democrats**. It follows the same pattern as parts 2 and 3.

Part 5 provides a survey of the **minor parties**.

Part 6 considers the arguments for and against the view that Britain has a **two party system**.

1 The development of political parties in Britain

Key Issues

1. Why did political parties first develop?

2. What are the functions of political parties?

Why did political parties first develop?

Before the 19th century, political parties did exist but they were very different from modern political parties. The first political parties - the Whigs and the Tories - existed only within Parliament. These parties were rather loose groups of MPs who were drawn together by family ties or who shared similar views. It was not until the mid-19th century that mass political parties with organisations and members outside Parliament began to develop.

The key to the growth of mass political parties was the extension of the franchise (see chapter 7, section 1.2). Before there was a mass electorate, participation in politics was confined to a small and wealthy elite. As a result, political parties were unnecessary outside Parliament. There were so few voters that candidates could canvass their vote individually - they did not need a party machine behind them.

The Great Reform Act of 1832 was the catalyst for change. Although the electorate remained tiny after 1832, one of the requirements of the Act was that voters must be registered. The political parties quickly realised that it was essential to get their supporters registered. To ensure that the registration process was carried out efficiently, the parties saw the need for some central control over the activities of groups of local supporters. The Tories, therefore, established the Carlton Club as their headquarters in 1832 and the Whigs established the Reform Club as their headquarters in 1836. Once this central organisation had been established, political parties began to take on new roles. The Great Reform Act, therefore, led the parties to establish links between politicians and voters via a central organisation. These links are a characteristic of modern political parties.

Further electoral reform, later in the 19th century, led to a truly mass electorate and to the establishment of more rigorously democratic electoral procedures. For a party to win the support of a mass electorate it became necessary for the party to have a reasonably clear set of policies and ideas which could be articulated to the electorate. It also became necessary for a party which hoped to govern the country to have representatives and supporters in every constituency. So, the growth of the mass electorate led directly to the growth of the mass party. To survive, parties had to adapt to the new conditions. Not only did they have to ensure that party supporters actually went to the polls and voted on election day, they had to ensure that the government (when they formed it) was able to remain in office and implement its programme. This required discipline and tight organisation both in Parliament and in the constituencies.

By the early 20th century, the fundamental features of modern political parties were in place. By then, the two main parties - the Liberal party (which evolved from the Whigs) and the Conservative party (which evolved from the Tories) - fulfilled the same key functions which are exhibited by political parties today.

The functions of political parties

As Ball (1987) and Garner & Kelly (1993) point out, political parties exist because they perform functions which are essential to the working of the political system. It is possible to classify these functions under the following headings.

The governing function. The British government is formed by the political party with an overall majority in the House of Commons or (more rarely) by the largest single party. The Prime Minister is the leader of the governing party and the Cabinet is drawn from its senior members (or, in a coalition government, from the senior members of the governing parties). In this sense, therefore, political parties are central to the process of government.

The electoral function. The electoral process is dependent upon political parties. Parties choose candidates at local and national elections. They provide funds and facilities for election campaigns. They devise policies which the electorate is asked to support. They provide a label with which voters can identify. They provide a means of accountability since the electorate is able to hold them responsible for policy successes or failures.

The representative function. Political parties enable the views of people to be heard and they ensure that matters of public concern reach the political agenda. Some parties allow the views of key sectional interests to be represented. For example, the Labour party has traditionally represented the views of trade unions. But, to win the support of the majority of the population, parties need to represent interests which go beyond these sectional concerns.

The policy function. In performing their representative function, political parties are led to formulate policies which relate to the sectional and more broadly based interests which they seek to articulate. By formulating policies, they ensure that the electorate has a choice between different approaches at election time. This lends clarity to the political process. Parties are supposed to implement these policies if they form the government and they are held responsible by the electorate at the next election for the successes or failures of the policies.

The recruitment and participation function. Political parties play a key role in encouraging people to become political activists. Most political activists are members of political parties. Once people have joined a political party, the party provides a continuing means of political participation.

The communicative and ideological function. Political parties provide their leaders with the means to communicate with their members and vice versa. Parties also allow the debate to take place between competing principles. For example, the 1980s were dominated by the debate between the ruling Conservatives, whose main economic goal was low inflation, and the opposition parties, whose main concern was the high level of unemployment that this entailed.

Political parties are often criticised for a number of reasons. First, parties are accused of imposing a uniformity of views upon their members. Since party members are encouraged to 'toe the party line', important debate can be stifled. Second, it is argued that the existence of parties perpetuates social divisions. Since the essence of the party system is that the different parties compete against each other, it is necessary for them to emphasise their differences and, sometimes, to maintain them artificially. And third, it is claimed that parties prevent new ideas from emerging. Since the British political system is dominated by the three main parties, it is very hard for new ideas to break through into the mainstream.

Activity 8.1

Item A *The role of political parties*

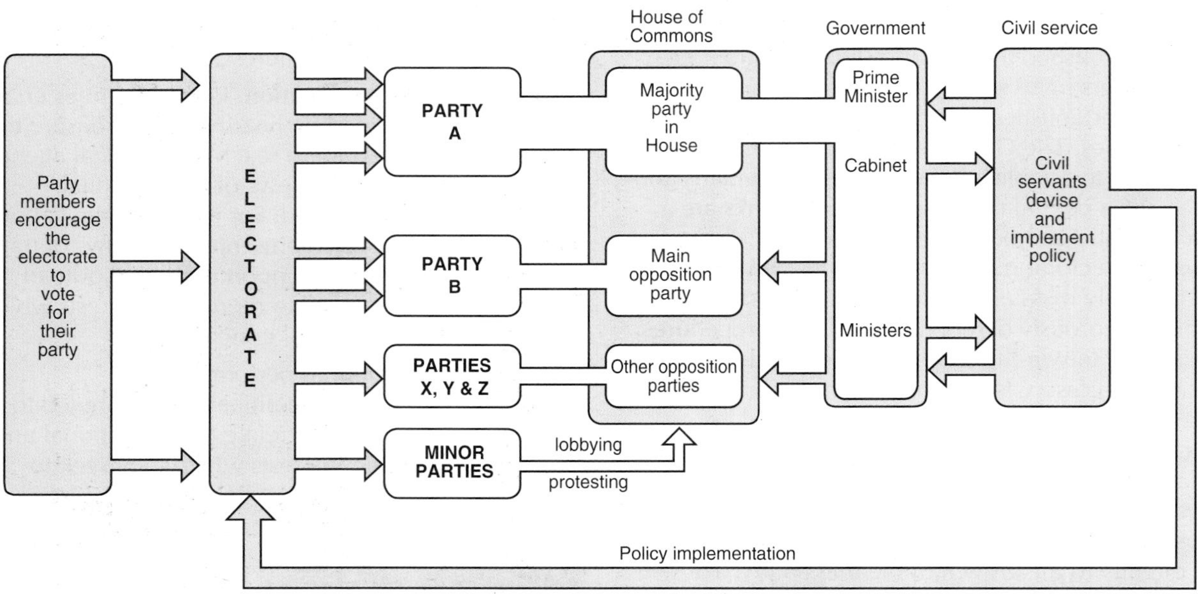

This diagram shows the role of political parties in the British political system.

Item B *The changing role of political parties*

The following examples indicate that the role of political parties in Britain has been changing over recent years. First, at the 1992 general election, all three main parties and the nationalist parties supported greater participation in the EU. The voters were simply not offered a choice. Second, in 1992, Labour suffered its fourth election defeat in a row. For the last 14 years, Britain has been governed by a single party. Third, throughout this period of Conservative rule, the opposition parties have been unable to put to the test their alternative sets of policies. The only effective opposition has come from the Conservative backbenches and the House of Lords. Fourth, in its 1992 election manifesto, the Conservative party's central economic commitment was to the exchange rate mechanism (ERM) of the European Monetary System. Yet within five months of the election, Britain had left the ERM. But nobody in the Cabinet resigned. This manifesto commitment was simply reversed. And, fifth, in the general election of 1992, about 75% of Scottish voters voted for parties which supported constitutional change, but they continue to be governed by a party which rejected this and which won just 11 out of the 72 Scottish seats. In fact, in Britain as a whole, a majority of voters voted for parties other than the Conservative party. In other words, the party system has been unable to prevent the country being run by a government which is representative of only a minority of the voters.

Adapted from Ingle, 1993.

Item C *Party loyalty 1979-92*

Party	1979	1983	1987	1992	Change 1979-92
Con	37	40	38	39	+2
Lab	38	34	33	35	-3
Lib Dem	13	15	16	12	-1
Other	3	2	2	2	-1
None	10	9	12	12	+2

This table shows the percentage of people who have shown long-term loyalty to a particular political party. The figures include people who did not vote. The columns do not all add up to 100% since figures have been rounded up.

Adapted from Crewe, 1993.

Item D *Joining a party*

WELCOME TO THE CONSERVATIVE PARTY
THE BEST FUTURE FOR BRITAIN

"Now Labour needs YOU"
"As Labour's new leader, I invite you to play your part in this time of change and renewal...
Labour's vision for Britain is founded on opportunity for all. We will rebuild our country with an agenda which combines social justice and economic prosperity. Through education, training and the goal of full employment, a Labour Government will create a Britain in which we all have the chance to achieve our potential.
Members help to create and sustain this vision and make it a reality. A great task lies ahead of us, which is why I ask for your support.
If you share this commitment to rebuilding Britain, join us by becoming a member today."
Tony Blair
YES, I want to join Labour
3P
Please tick as appropriate:
I enclose £15 standard rate to join Labour
£3 trade union rate (levy-paying affiliated trade union members)
£5 student/unwaged/part-time worker/retired/on a government training scheme (delete as appropriate)
I enclose an additional donation of £
Please make cheques/postal orders payable to The Labour Party.
Full Name
M F
(BLOCK CAPITALS)
Address
Postcode
Date of birth / /
Trade Union
Signature
Date
I agree to abide by the rules of The Labour Party.
Labour
Please send to: Tony Blair, Room 416, The Labour Party, 150 Walworth Road, FREEPOST, London SE17 1BR.

Questions

1. 'Political parties are at the heart of the British political system.' Explain this statement using Items A-C.
2. Use Item A to explain how parties 'provide the means for peaceful resolutions of political tensions' (Ball, 1987).
3. How has the role played by political parties changed since 1979? Use Items B and C in your answer.
4. Look at Item D. How would you answer the charge that all political parties are as bad as each other and it's not worth joining any of them?

2 The Conservative party

Key Issues

1. How did the modern Conservative party evolve?
2. What is the structure and organisation of the Conservative party?
3. How powerful is the leader of the Conservative party?

2.1 The roots of the modern Conservative party

If a political party is judged by its ability to win elections and form governments, then the Conservative party has been by far the most successful party in Britain throughout the 20th century.

The roots of this success were laid in the 19th century. Although there is no firm date to mark the transition from Tory party to Conservative party, most commentators date this transition to 1834, the year in which Robert Peel became leader (see, for example, Garner & Kelly, 1993).

At the general election of 1832, the first to be held after the Great Reform Act was passed, the Tories won just 185 seats out of 658. Before 1832, the Tories had been able to appeal to the interests of the landed gentry and win sufficient seats to form a government.

But, the 1832 Act enfranchised those who had become wealthy through business rather than inheritance and their interests were very different from those of the landed gentry. The 1832 Act provoked a crisis in the Tory party. This crisis was only overcome when Peel became leader.

Robert Peel's great achievement was to develop a political party which could represent the interests of all people of wealth whether that wealth was derived from property or land, industry or the professions. He managed to create this new voting alliance by advancing a new political creed - conservatism. Peel argued that social, economic and political change should not automatically be opposed. It should be welcomed, but only if it occurred slowly and if it built upon established institutions rather than sweeping them away. By encouraging change, Peel appealed to entrepreneurs and those who had become wealthy through the changes brought by the industrial revolution. By emphasising respect for established institutions such as the monarchy and the Church, Peel appealed to the ancient traditions of the landed aristocracy.

The crisis over the Corn Laws

In the short term, Peel was successful. The Conservatives won the general election of 1841. In the longer term, however, this new voting alliance was uneasy. In 1846, the party split over the Corn Laws or, more accurately, it split between those who supported free trade and those who supported protectionism (see chapter 15, section 1.1). The Corn Laws placed duty on imported grain. They were, therefore, protective tariffs which kept the price of grain artificially high. Whilst the landed gentry benefited from these laws (since their wealth came from agriculture), those whose wealth came from manufacturing argued for their abolition.

Manufacturers argued that the Corn Laws kept the price of food artificially high. High food prices led to demands for high wages. If the Corn Laws were abolished, they argued, the price of food would come down and wages could then be reduced to enable profits to grow. Peel pushed through legislation for the abolition of the Corn Laws and in so doing divided his party. Although it was a Conservative government which abolished the Corn Laws, many Conservatives who supported free trade left to join the Whigs, whilst the Conservative party returned to its pre-Peelite position as the party of the landed gentry.

One nation conservatism (see also, chapter 2 p.22)

Conservative fortunes were revived by the practical and ideological contribution of Benjamin Disraeli (Conservative Prime Minister in 1868 and between 1874 and 1880). Not only was Disraeli responsible for organisational changes (Conservative Central Office was set up in 1870, for example), it was Disraeli who created 'one nation' conservatism.

Like Peel, Disraeli's concern was to broaden the electoral appeal of the Conservative party. But, Disraeli did not restrict this appeal just to the wealthy. He aimed to unite the interests of both the wealthy and the underprivileged. Despite class differences, Disraeli maintained, the interests uniting the British people were of far greater significance than those dividing them. True, he argued, rich and poor sections in society did exist. But the rich, because they held a pre-eminent position in society, had a duty to look after the welfare of their inferiors. The Conservative party, he claimed, was, therefore, the party of both rich and poor. It stood for the interests of the wealthy and, at the same time, favoured measures to support the poor.

This ideological strategy was a great success. Between 1830 and 1865, the Conservatives had an effective parliamentary majority for only five years. But, from 1865 to 1900, the Conservatives had overall majorities for 17 years. It should be noted, however, that Conservative fortunes were aided during this latter period by a split in the Liberal party in 1886 over home rule for Ireland (the formation of the Liberal party is usually dated to 1859 when Whigs, Peelites and Radicals joined together to set up a new party - see section 4.1 below). This split in the Liberal party brought back to the Conservative party some of those with manufacturing backgrounds who had left in 1846. By 1900, therefore, the Conservatives had been able to forge an alliance of forces which included landed and industrial wealth and whose aim was to preserve the power of property whilst maintaining social stability through paternalistic measures intended to ease the suffering of the poor.

The one nation strand of conservatism has remained a key aspect of Conservative party ideology and practice in the 20th century. It underpinned, for example, the long period of rule under Harold Macmillan whose governments demonstrated an ability to come to terms with the postwar welfare state and Keynesian economics.

Liberal conservatism (see also chapter 2, p.23)

Like most political parties the Conservative party is a broad alliance. Not all Conservatives are one nation Conservatives. Indeed, in the 1990s, the one nation Conservatives are in the minority. Since the election of Margaret Thatcher to the Conservative party leadership in 1975, the Conservative party has been dominated by those who subscribe to a different tradition - 'liberal' conservatism. Those within the Conservative party who support liberal conservatism are often said to belong to the 'New Right'.

Liberal conservatism also has its origins in the 19th century and it is mainly derived from those supporters of the Conservative party whose basis of wealth was manufacturing and finance rather than land. Such people had always championed the individual as well as the nation and they believed in free enterprise, individual initiative and in limited government intervention in the running of the economy. Whilst some of these liberal Conservatives came from the Liberal party when it split over home rule in 1886, many more came from the Liberal party when it fell into deep decline after the First World War. The emphasis placed on individual initiative and free market economics by liberal Conservatives has informed debate within the Conservative party throughout the 20th century. Whilst the one nation Conservatives held sway for 30 years after the Second World War, since 1975 the pendulum has swung towards the New Right.

Tendencies and factions within the Conservative party

Today, few people would argue that the Conservative party does not have an ideology. Yet, that used to be the prevailing view. Ingle argues that the Thatcher governments changed this:

> 'Thatcherism could be said to have brought ideology into Conservative party politics and in doing so destroyed the basis of unity, trust and loyalty which had been the party's most reliable weapon. Thus, one of the party's abiding myths, that it was not an ideological party, [has] been destroyed.' (Ingle, 1993, p.3)

An examination of the various groups that have grown up within the Conservative party, however, indicates that the myth that the Conservative party was not an ideological party is just that. Most of these groups existed before Margaret Thatcher became party leader. Their different aims reflect the different ideological tendencies within the Conservative party. The following groups have emerged since the Second World War.

1. The Bow Group was set up in 1951. Its ideas are broadly social democratic, though since 1979 it has moved towards economic liberalism. It publishes a journal called *Crossbow*.

2. The Monday Club was set up in 1961 to protect right wing authoritarian Conservative principles against what was seen at the time as the left wing policies of Harold Macmillan. The Monday Club champions the fight against 'moral decline', immigration and Europe.

3. The Tory Reform Group was set up to encourage support for the principles of one nation conservatism. It has resisted economic liberalism and maintained a social democratic approach to the management of the economy. It supports the involvement of the state in industrial policy and welfare provision.

4. The No Turning Back Group was set up in 1983 to protect and extend the policies supported and implemented by Margaret Thatcher. It has been particularly active since Thatcher's downfall in 1990.

5. Conservative Way Forward is a group whose membership includes a number of ministers who served in the Thatcher governments. It has similar objectives to the No Turning Back Group.

6. The Liberation Alliance is, perhaps, the most extreme group within the Conservative party. Its opposition to state interference in people's lives goes so far that it supports the legalisation of incest and heroin.

7. The Bruges Group was set up in 1988 after Margaret Thatcher made a speech in Bruges which opposed the plan of the President of the European Commission, Jacques Delors, to move to greater European unity. Although this group is not drawn entirely from Conservatives, it is dominated by them. The Bruges Group is the focal point for those Conservatives who oppose greater European integration - the Eurosceptics.

In addition to the groups mentioned above, there are informal groupings of Conservative MPs. The division of Conservatives into Europhiles and Eurosceptics is one such informal grouping. The division of Conservatives into 'wets' (opponents of Thatcherism) and 'dries' (Thatcherites) is another.

Activity 8.2

Item A *Conservative Prime Ministers and general election victories since 1900*

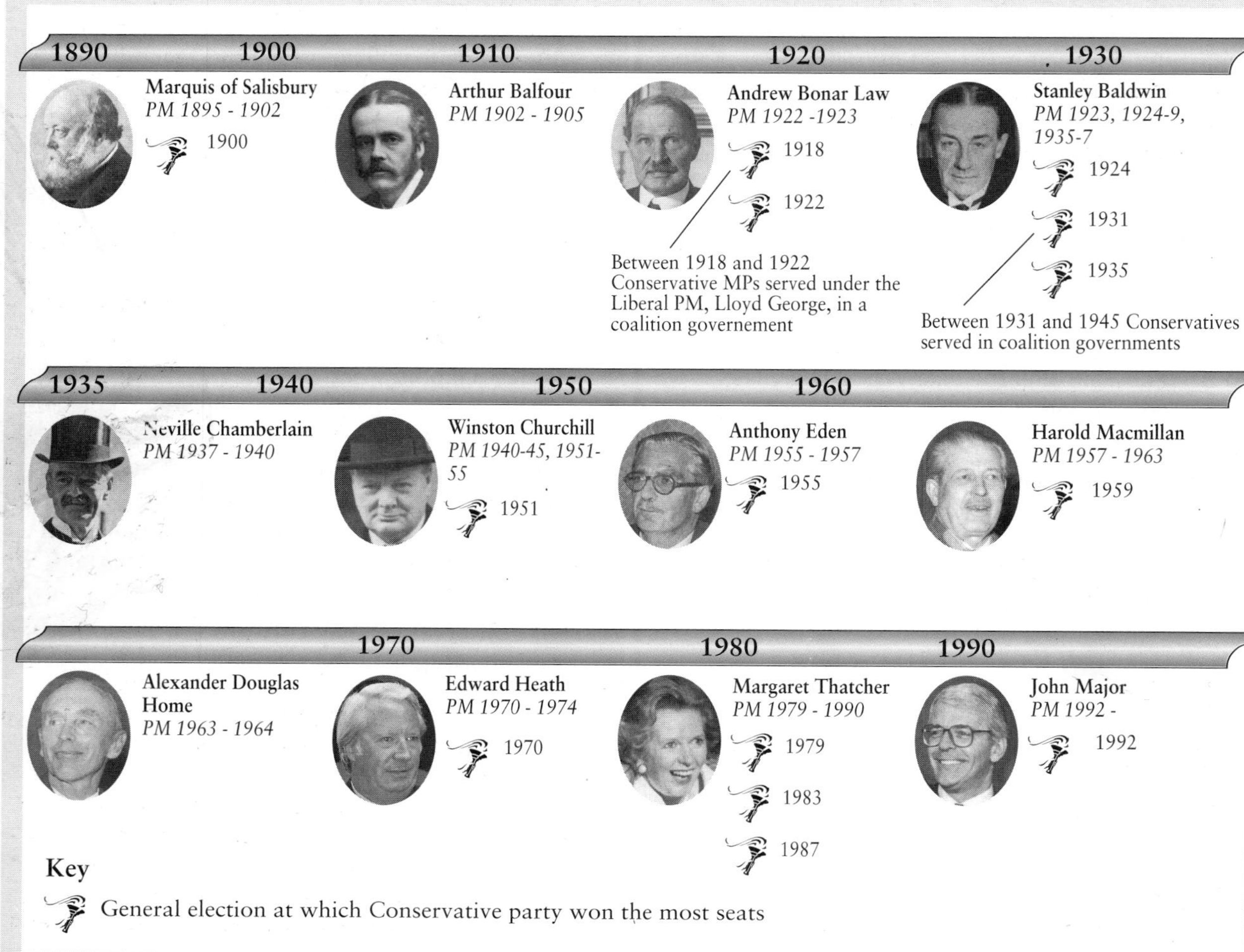

Item B *The secret of Conservative success (1)*

During the interwar years the Conservatives relied mainly on their natural advantages. Prominent local figures were nearly always on the Conservative side. Most of the national press supported it. In 1929, for example, seven daily papers out of 10 and all the Sunday papers but one supported the Conservative party. The Conservatives claimed patriotism for themselves. The Union Jack draped the table at their meetings. The British Empire was their private estate. Universities, chambers of commerce, the civil service, the armed forces, Women's Institutes and, to a great extent, the Church of England were all pillars of Conservatism in thin disguise.

Adapted from Taylor, 1965.

Item C *The secret of Conservative success (2)*

A political party has two main problems: how to obtain power and what to do with it once obtained. In the interwar years, the Conservatives solved the first problem more successfully than the second. They won five out of seven general elections and were in office either on their own or as dominant partners in a coalition for 18 out of 21 years. In two of their five electoral victories (1922 and 1924), the Conservatives won the election because the vote was split between the Liberals and Labour. In two more elections (1918 and 1935), the Conservatives won less than half the popular vote (though on both occasions they would have scored a higher total if they had not made an electoral pact with a section of the Liberal party to win seats for a coalition). Only in 1931, did the Conservatives win more than half of the votes cast.

Adapted from Blake, 1985.

Item D *Conservative party values in the 1990s*

Freedom, responsibility and opportunity are the bases of Conservative philosophy. By freedom, we mean the right of each man and woman to use their initiative and their effort to better themselves without the state interfering and snatching away the fruits of their achievement. By responsibility, we mean a tough stand on law and order, we mean being loyal to the constitution, and we mean maintaining a firm stance on the defence of our country. By opportunity, we mean making sure that everyone has the chance to do well, we mean ensuring that ownership is more and more widely spread, and we mean caring for people in need. The Conservative party is a national party. It represents all the people of Britain without regard to religion, sex, race or background.

Adapted from CCO, 1994.

Questions

1. 'The natural party of government.' Is this a fair description of the Conservative party? Give reasons for your answer.
2. Judging from Items A-C:
   a) what evidence is there to suggest that the Conservative party was a successful political party before the Second World War?
   b) how would you account for this success?
3. What evidence is there in Item D to suggest that 'one nation' conservatism still influences the Conservative party?

2.2 The structure and organisation of the Conservative party

As Kelly points out, for such a successful organisation, surprisingly little is known about the internal workings of the Conservative party. This is due, in part, to the fact that Conservative party has no official constitution:

> 'The arcane nature of Tory organisation owes much to the lack of any grand constitution outlining the powers and functions of its various organs. Indeed, a legal inquiry in 1982, involving Conservative Central Office and the Inland Revenue, found that the Conservative party did not even exist as "a compact, legally recognised organisation". It concluded that the party consisted instead of "three separate components" operating mainly on the basis of convention.' (Kelly, 1994, p.52)

The three components referred to by Kelly are: the volunteers in the constituency associations; the party professionals at the regional headquarters and at Central Office and the parliamentary party.

One reason why the Conservative party does not exist as a 'compact, legally recognised organisation' is that, historically, the party only existed in Parliament as a parliamentary group. The extension of the franchise in the 19th century produced the pressure to build up popular support, but the real power in the party remained with the parliamentary leadership. To a large extent, this remains true today. Ingle notes that:

> 'Properly speaking the Conservative party is that body of MPs and peers who take the Conservative whip and the function of the constituency associations and regional and national structures is to support and sustain that body.' (Ingle, 1993, p.3)

Constituency associations

Like all political parties, the Conservative party relies on volunteers to work on its behalf locally. These volunteers join their local constituency association, the key organisation at local level.

Constituency associations are run by an executive committee which is elected at the annual general meeting (AGM). Unlike their Labour equivalent, Conservative constituency associations do not have a policy making role and meetings are attended by ordinary members rather than delegates.

Each constituency association is divided into branches. These branches are based on local council polling districts and exist to fight local elections. According to a Conservative party leaflet:

> 'Every local area should have a branch which is responsible for building up membership, raising money, communicating with the electorate and campaigning to win elections. Each branch should be run by a committee.' (CCO, 1994)

The executive committee of the constituency association is made up of representatives from the branches.

According to Pinto-Duschinsky (1990), Conservative constituency associations have greater autonomy than their Labour counterparts because they are financially self-sufficient. Constituency associations are responsible for raising two thirds of total Conservative party revenue.

The functions of constituency associations

In addition to the general function outlined by Ingle above (that the function of constituency associations is to support and sustain the body of MPs and peers who take the Conservative whip), Conservative constituency associations have three specific functions. Their primary role is to provide the local organisation necessary to win elections. To this end, the local party organisation plays a vital part in the process of recruiting members, publicising party policy and running local and national election campaigns in its locality. This involves liaising with the media, organising public meetings, canvassing and getting people to the polls. Many associations employ a full-time agent whose job is to ensure that these functions are performed efficiently. The second function of the constituency associations is to play a part in the selection of candidates for local and national elections (see chapter 11, section 2.1 for a description of the selection process). The third function of Conservative constituency associations is to provide a place for like-minded people to meet and socialise. Recent studies have shown that the majority of members of the Conservative party do not attend party meetings or participate in party activities. They join so that they can use the party's social facilities (see, for example, Whiteley et al., 1994).

The National Union (NU)

The National Union of Conservative and Unionist Associations (NU) was founded after the passing of the electoral reform Act of 1867. It was set up to encourage the spread of Conservatism nationally by organising the formation of new constituency associations and coordinating those which already existed. Today, the NU is responsible for supervising all aspects of unpaid party activity throughout the country. All constituency associations belong to the NU. But the NU's powers are limited. The NU is subservient to the parliamentary party and its decisions are purely advisory.

The NU's key decision making body is the National Union General Purposes Committee which has 65 members. Most of the members of this committee are not elected. They are appointed by the party leader or party chairman. Less than a fifth are elected by a ballot of ordinary members.

The NU's most important job is to organise conferences for party members. Not only does the NU organise the annual party conference, it also organises 12 area conferences and six sectional conferences (for young Conservatives, Conservative councillors, Conservative women, Conservative trade unionists, Conservatives in higher education and for the Conservative political centre).

The annual party conference

The annual party conference has no formal powers to make party policy. Decisions made at conference are advisory only. The party leadership may choose to ignore them. It is, therefore, no surprise that the traditional view of the annual party conference is that it has little political importance. Rather, it has been seen as a rally of the party faithful where dedicated party members meet together, reinforce each other's views and enjoy an exciting social occasion. In support of this view, it should be noted that, until 1965, the party leader only attended the conference on the final afternoon. Although party leaders have always attended the whole conference since then (which may suggest that the conference has grown in importance), they are automatically given a standing ovation regardless of their popularity or the content of their speech. This suggests that the purpose of the conference is to rubber stamp the decisions made by the party leadership.

Annual party conferences may be carefully stage managed public relations exercises, but that does not necessarily mean that they do not have any political importance. It has long been known, for example, that a poor speech from a frontbencher can dash their hopes of promotion or even (in the case of Reginald Maudling in 1965) their hopes of party leadership. Besides, the polite surface may conceal underlying currents. Journalists often make a great deal of the length of time that standing ovations last and they attempt to 'decode' the 'mood' of the conference. A cool response to a senior figure's speech may be a sign of widespread grass roots discontent. The 1992 annual party conference provides an example of this. Norman Tebbit's anti-Maastricht speech on the conference fringe won enthusiastic support from ordinary members whilst the pro-Maastricht line adopted by the party leadership was coolly received (see chapter 6 section 3.2 for a discussion of the Maastricht Treaty). The 'coded' message to the leadership was that ordinary members were unhappy with the pro-European policies favoured by the leadership.

Despite the fact that the annual party conference does not have a formal role in policy making, senior Conservatives often use it as a forum either to 'test the water' before devising concrete proposals or actually to announce new policies. It was at the 1993 annual conference, for example, that the Home Secretary, Michael Howard, announced his 27 measures to combat crime and it was at the same conference that the Conservatives' ill-fated 'Back to Basics' campaign was launched. That senior party figures use the conference for this purpose suggests that they consider conference to be an important body.

In addition, it has been suggested that, in fact, the regional and sectional conferences have a bigger influence over policy development than is generally realised. Kelly (1989) has argued that much of the ground work for the annual party conference is done at these regional and sectional conferences.
He notes that debates at these conferences are much more critical and frank than those at the annual party conference, and they are encouraged to be so by senior Conservatives. Kelly suggests that the annual party conference:

> 'Is, in a sense, the climax of an oblique conference system where ministers earn their

ovations only by showing some accommodation of the advice rendered by Tory activists at previous conferences held that year.' (Kelly, 1992, p.27).

Conservative Central Office

The Conservative party employs a full-time bureaucracy which has its headquarters in Smith Square, London. Conservative Central Office was set up in 1870 by Disraeli as his private office and it owes its allegiance to the party leader, not to the party as a whole. The party chairman (the Conservatives refuse to use the gender-neutral term 'chairperson') and other party officials are appointed by the party leader and are answerable to the party leader alone. The party chairman is in charge of Central Office.

Central Office has 250 staff and is divided into three departments - organisation, research and publicity. Until 1993, it was supported by 11 area offices and a Scottish Central Office. These area offices have now been replaced by a smaller number of regional offices (see below). Central Office is responsible for the party's finances and for membership policy. It also has a coordinating role at election time. It is responsible for national campaigning, liaising with the media and for ensuring satisfactory resources are available in the constituencies.

Central Office provides an important bridge between ordinary party members and the parliamentary party. It provides constituency associations with information and advice and trains the professional agents employed by constituencies. Whilst candidates for election are selected locally, this takes place under the supervision of Central Office.

Although the Conservative party has always been the wealthiest party, in recent years it has been suffering from a severe shortage of funds. In 1992, the party's debt was around £20 million. In part, this is a reflection of the growing expense of modern elections, though the expensive refurbishment of Smith Square in the early 1990s has also been blamed. This shortage of funds has led to calls for greater democracy within the party. According to Ingle:

> 'In October 1991 the reformist constituency organisation the Charter Movement mounted a scathing attack on the organisation's "stunningly incompetent" financial stewardship...The Charter Movement urged proper democratic control of the voluntary donations that had come to provide the lion's share of income.' (Ingle, 1993, p.4)

In addition, after both the 1987 and the 1992 general elections, Central Office was criticised for delivering unconvincing campaigns. Again, critics argued that there would only be improvements if there was greater democracy within the party.

In response to this criticism, a working party was set up under the party chairman, Norman Fowler, to improve managerial efficiency and to reduce the party's debt. This working party reported in February 1993. The result was that the old area offices were replaced by a smaller number of regional offices (with the loss of 60 jobs) and a new Board of Party Management was set up. The director general of this Board is appointed by the party chairman and just three of the 13 members of the Board have any connection with the constituency associations. Kelly (1994) argues that Fowler's 1993 report ignored the important changes in attitude that have taken place since 1979. Party activists are no longer prepared to accept instructions from on high. They want to participate in their party's decision making process. Kelly suggests that:

> 'Fowler's 1993 report, by signally ignoring such shifts in attitude, perpetuates a profoundly undemocratic party structure, apparently in conflict with a new, questioning generation of Tory activists, fortified in their self-belief by the party's electoral triumphs. This may be a recipe for grave internal conflict in the years ahead, especially if the party were to lose its knack of winning general elections.' (Kelly, 1994, p.62).

The party chairman

The Conservative party chairman and vice chairman or chairmen are appointed by the party leader. The party chairman has a dual role - to run Central Office and to publicise Conservative party policies. Since the party chairman is responsible for publicising party policy, it is the party chairman who is responsible for running the party's national election campaigns.

Although the chairman performs both a managerial and a political role, appointments to this post are decidedly political. Senior party figures, normally ex-Cabinet ministers, are appointed. Michael White the *Guardian's* political editor, suggests that a pattern has emerged in the appointments made since 1979:

> 'Recent tradition tends to appoint a caretaker manager for the first half of Parliament (to sack surplus staff and pay off the debts) and a star to help win next time. John Gummer (1983-85) minded the shop between Parkinson [1981-83] and Tebbit (1985-87). Peter Brooke stood in from 1987-89 when Mr Baker took over, only to be replaced by Chris Patten (1990-92) after The Fall [the resignation of Margaret Thatcher]. Norman Fowler [1992-94], and he knows it, is a B-team man, though he got the accounts solvent and the overdraft down to £16.5 million.' (*Guardian*, 21 June 1994).

In July 1994, Norman Fowler was replaced by Jeremy Hanley as chairman of the Conservative party. This was a surprise to many commentators since Hanley had only served as a junior minister before his appointment. Three vice chairmen were appointed to assist Hanley - Michael Dobbs, John Maples and Angela Rumbold.

Activity 8.3

Item A *The structure and organisation of the Conservative party*

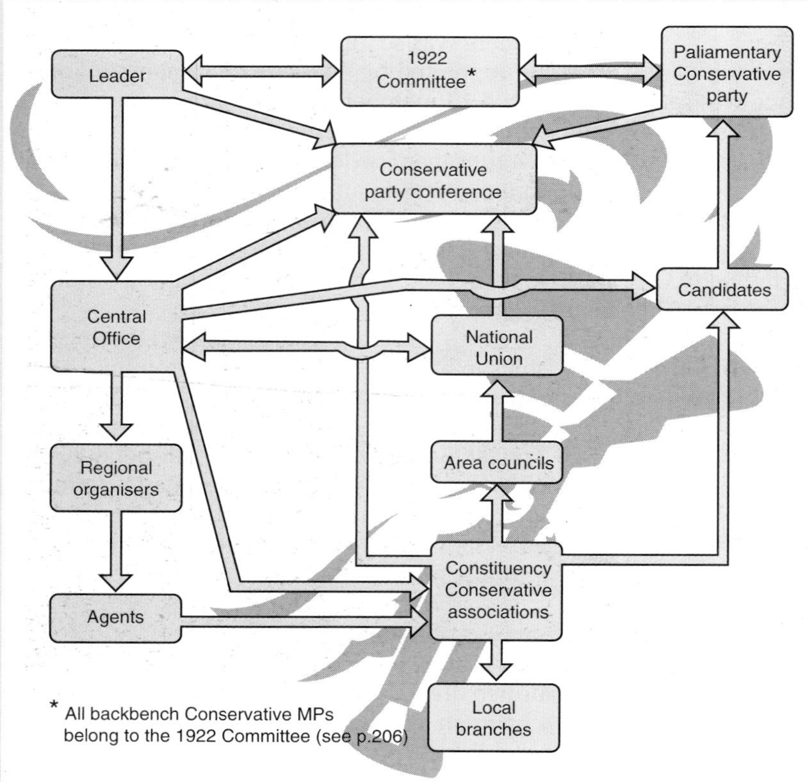

Item B *Internal reform*

The Conservative party chairman, Norman Fowler, has blocked efforts made by Conservative members who want to know who finances their party and how its finances are managed. Relations have deteriorated so much that legal advice has been sought by each side. Norman Fowler refused to allow a special meeting of the party's Central Council to discuss reforms, even though 50 constituencies (the number required by the rules) have demanded it. In turn, the constituencies have blocked the party chairman's attempts to change the rules of the National Union (Fowler hoped to gain access to the estimated £8 million of assets held by local parties). The Party Reform Steering Committee, which represents the dissidents, has described Central Office as remote, out of touch and sometimes in conflict with constituencies. It wrote in a letter: 'The employees of the party at national and area level should be governed by elected party members. There is nothing novel in this, merely a belated recognition that the members of the Conservative party need democratic institutions just as much as members of other organisations.'

Adapted from the *Guardian*, 29 April 1994.

Item C *The party chairman*

After the European elections held in June 1994, Norman Fowler, the Conservative party chairman, announced that he would be retiring from his post. His job description might be as follows: *Wanted: part-time non-executive chair to front ramshackle organisation with dodgy legal status and a falling market share. Would be required to tackle brand loyalty problems among those who the advertising companies classify as As, Bs and C1s. Debts well in excess of assets will need attention. Staff cuts already made, but boardroom shake-up still pending. Previous experience with hostile media an advantage. Must have valid passport for fundraising work. Short-term contract only. Salary by negotiation, but preferably nil. For details write to N. Fowler, 32 Smith Square, London.*

Adapted from the *Guardian*, 21 June 1994.

Item D *Party members*

Judging from a recently completed survey, the successor to Norman Fowler will have a tough job. Morale amongst ordinary Conservative party members is very low and there are signs that activism is declining. The survey shows that a quarter of members are less active than they were five years ago. Three quarters devote no time at all to party activities. The new party chairman will also be worried by the finding that 43% of members believe that the leadership 'does not pay a lot of attention to the views of the ordinary party member'. Theresa Gorman, MP for Billericay, has called for the party chairman to be elected whilst Eric Chalker, a member of the Charter Movement (Conservative party members committed to greater party openness) warned that: 'If the Conservative party refuses to care for its members, they will cease to care for it.' He added that, in the Conservative party, nobody who has any real authority is elected.

Adapted from the *Independent on Sunday*, 26 June 1994.

Item E *Party finances*

During a fund raising tour this year, a Chinese billionaire, Peter Woo, gave £200,000 to the Conservative party. One of Mr Woo's colleagues said that he had made his donation to boost his standing in Peking by showing he has influence with the British government. Since making the donation, Mr Woo's colleague said, Mr Woo has met both John Major and the Chancellor, Kenneth Clarke. By concentrating on its fund raising and reducing costs, the Conservative party has managed its first operational surplus since the mid-1980s. Cheques were collected, for example, from foreign tycoons who were invited to attend fund raising meetings hosted by John Major at Downing Street. A source close to the Prime Minister said: 'John Major has never been comfortable with fund raising or with businesspeople, but this is a sign of the seriousness of the debt.' The party is so short of funds that it has considered privatising its own research department.

Adapted from the *Observer*, 5 June 1994.

Item F *The annual party conference*

This photo shows John Major surrounded by members of the Cabinet after addressing the 1994 Conservative party conference.

Questions

1. 'The organisation of the Conservative party reflects its ideology.' Consider the arguments for and against this view in light of the items presented above.
2. a) Judging from Item A where does power lie in the Conservative party?
   b) Which structures might campaigners for internal party reform want to alter? What obstacles are they likely to encounter?
3. a) How accurate is the job description of the party chairman which appears in Item C?
   b) Using Items B-E describe the problems faced by the Conservative party chairman in 1994. What solutions would you suggest?
4. What do Items B-E tell us about the way in which the Conservative party is organised and run?
5. Suppose you were a reporter covering the Conservative annual party conference. Write a report to accompany the picture in Item F. The report should explain what role the annual party conference plays.

2.3 The power of the Conservative leader

Until the resignation of Margaret Thatcher in November 1990, there was a general consensus amongst political scientists that Conservative leaders enjoyed almost unrestrained power so long as they were able to bring electoral success (see, for example, McKenzie, 1955 and Garner & Kelly, 1993).

The powers of the Conservative leader are indeed considerable. First, in theory at least, the leader alone is responsible for choosing the Cabinet or shadow Cabinet. Second, unlike the Labour leader, the Conservative leader does not have to work with an elected deputy. Third, the Conservative leader has sole responsibility for the formulation of the party's election manifestos (which tend to be written with the help of only a few senior colleagues). And fourth, the Conservative leader chooses the party chairman. These powers allow Conservative leaders the opportunity of introducing the policies and style of their own choosing.

The pre-eminent role of the Conservative leader can be explained by a number of factors. The first factor is the belief in hierarchy and leadership which is embodied in Conservative ideology. The second factor is the importance of electoral success to the party - an objective which appears to be best served in the British system by a party unified behind a strong leader. And the third factor is the lack of a written party constitution. This enables an effective leader to exercise great power.

But, the leader's freedom of movement is restricted by the need to consider the views of two groups -

senior colleagues and backbench MPs. Whether in government or in opposition, it is vital that the leader retains the support and loyalty of senior colleagues. Without their support it would be impossible for the leader to continue in office. In addition, the leader has to consider the views of backbenchers. These views are channelled through the chair and officers of the 1922 Committee, the semi-official representative of Conservative backbenchers. The 1922 Committee meets weekly and has regular contact with the party whips. Although its main official role is to conduct the ballot in the event of a leadership contest, it also plays the unofficial role of conveying information about backbench feeling to the party leader.

In considering their support or otherwise for the leader, both senior party members and backbenchers regard not just electoral failure but the prospect of it as the litmus test of the leader's credibility. The speedy downfall of Margaret Thatcher indicates just how quickly support can crumble once senior colleagues and backbenchers become convinced that the leader is an electoral liability. This suggests that the concept of the all-powerful leader is short of the mark.

The selection of the party leader

Until 1965, the Conservative leader was chosen by what has been called 'emergence'. New party leaders were not selected by any formal system. Rather, the new leader would 'emerge' from meetings held between senior party members, influential backbenchers and others considered to be of importance within the Conservative party. It is, perhaps, no surprise to learn that those senior Conservatives involved in the choice of leader were known as the 'magic circle'.

After the resignation of Harold Macmillan in 1963, this system proved itself inadequate. There was no clear successor to Macmillan and the 'magic circle' chose Lord Home as leader. Many Conservatives considered Home to be an inappropriate choice. This view seemed to be confirmed when Home lost the 1964 general election. Before Home resigned, however, he set up an inquiry to establish a new way of choosing the Conservative leader.

The result of the inquiry was that a new system for electing the Conservative leader was set up. From 1965, a candidate for the leadership needed a nominator and a seconder. There would then be a maximum of three ballots in which Conservative MPs would be allowed to vote. In the first ballot, a successful candidate needed to gain **more than 50% of votes cast** and to have 15% more votes than any other candidate. Later this was changed. A successful candidate needed **more than 50% of the votes of those entitled to vote** and 15% more votes than any other candidate. If the first ballot was inconclusive, a second would be held. In the second ballot a successful candidate simply needed to win more than 50% of the votes cast. If that did not produce a winner, a third round would be held. In this ballot, the three most popular candidates (according to the results of the second round) would contest the post. The winner was the candidate who had the majority using an alternative vote system. Candidates could withdraw from the contest at any stage.

The first contest to be held under this system took place in 1965. It was won by Edward Heath. Heath failed to gain the required majority in the first round, but he led his opponents by such a margin that they all withdrew. Subsequent contests took place in 1975, 1989 and 1990. In 1975, Margaret Thatcher won on the second ballot. In 1989, Margaret Thatcher won on the first ballot. And in 1990, despite having a majority, Margaret Thatcher withdrew after the first ballot because she had failed to win an outright victory. Her withdrawal was followed by the victory of John Major (see chapter 3, pp.58-9).

Since the leadership contest of 1990, changes have been made to the leadership election system. The contest must now take place within 14 days of a new Commons session or within three months of a new Parliament (unless a contest is called by the current leader - as happened in June 1995 when John Major resigned as party leader and called a leadership election). Also, any challenger must have the backing of 10% of Conservative MPs. These new arrangements were made in response to the 'frivolous' challenge of Anthony Meyer in 1989. Anthony Meyer took advantage of a rule change in 1974 which stipulated that there should be a leadership election every year whether or not the Conservatives were in power (Margaret Thatcher was elected unopposed every year between 1975 and 1989). Although Anthony Meyer had no hope of winning himself, he hoped that other more serious challengers would come forward. His actions, therefore, put the leader under pressure. Although the new rules, introduced in 1991, appear to strengthen the position of the leader, since they make it more difficult to mount a challenge, they do mean that when a challenge comes, it is bound to be a serious threat to the leader's position.

Activity 8.4

Item A *The downfall of Margaret Thatcher (1)*

The need for party support was demonstrated with dramatic force when Margaret Thatcher was challenged in a leadership election in November 1990. The drama was, in part, a product of Thatcher's personality. She was Britain's first woman Prime Minister. She held office for $11^1/_2$ years, more than any other Prime Minister this century. She won three general elections and lost none. Her views and policies were so distinct that the term 'Thatcherism' was coined to describe them. But, there was more to her downfall than her personality. The Conservative party was struggling in the polls. Some MPs were afraid they would lose their seats if another election was held whilst Thatcher remained leader. Also, the Conservatives were deeply divided over Europe. These divisions led to the resignation of Nigel Lawson and Geoffrey Howe, both of whom were senior Cabinet members. It was Howe's resignation speech in the Commons in November 1990 which triggered off Michael Heseltine's leadership challenge.

Adapted from Barber, 1991.

Item B *The Ides of March*

This cartoon shows Margaret Thatcher as Julius Caesar, surrounded by assassins.

Item C *Results of the November 1990 leadership election*

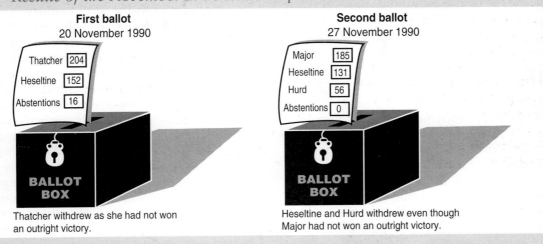

First ballot
20 November 1990

Thatcher withdrew as she had not won an outright victory.

Second ballot
27 November 1990

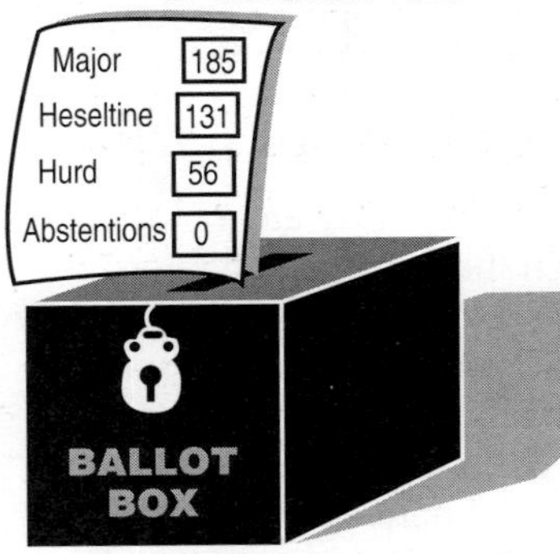

Heseltine and Hurd withdrew even though Major had not won an outright victory.

Item D *The downfall of Margaret Thatcher (2)*

The day after the first ballot, Margaret Thatcher announced: 'I fight on. I fight on to win.' But, there was intense speculation about whether she would be forced to withdraw. Later that day, she met individual members of the Cabinet to discuss her position. It appears that a majority said that they did not believe that she could win and there were reports of threatened resignations unless she stepped down. The next day, supporters described this as the time when 'the rats got at her'. They also claimed that after the first ballot, a number of MPs who had voted for Heseltine lied to journalists and fellow MPs. They said that they had, in fact, voted for Thatcher, but were switching their vote in the next round. This gave the impression that support for Thatcher was falling away. Two days after the first ballot, Margaret Thatcher informed the Cabinet that she would stand down as soon as a successor had been chosen.

Adapted from Benyon, 1991.

Item E *Margaret Thatcher resigns*

This photograph was taken as Margaret Thatcher drove away from No. 10 Downing Street after her resignation on 28 November 1990.

Questions

1. a) Why do you think the downfall of Margaret Thatcher changed the way in which political scientists have assessed the power of the Conservative leader?
   b) Where would you say power is located within the Conservative party? Give reasons for your answer.
2. Using Items A-E say why you think Margaret Thatcher decided not to stay on as Conservative leader after the result of the first ballot was announced.
3. Item C provides the ballot results from the 1990 leadership election. Use this as the basis for a full explanation of the procedure used to choose a Conservative leader.
4. Judging from the items in this activity what measures is it necessary for the Conservative leader to take to avoid a leadership challenge?

3 The Labour party

Key Issues

1. How did the modern Labour party evolve?
2. What is the structure and organisation of the Labour party?
3. How powerful is the leader of the Labour party?

3.1 The roots of the Labour party

Electoral reform in the 19th century gave more and more working class men the vote (see chapter 7, section 1.2). At first, this made little difference to the party system. The Conservative and Liberal parties both claimed that they could represent the new voters. It was not until the beginning of the 20th century that a new political party was set up specifically to represent the interest of the newly enfranchised working class in Parliament. This party - the Labour party - owed its existence to the support of the trade union movement. Links between the Labour party and the trade unions have remained ever since.

Socialist groups in the 19th century

Although socialist groups existed in the 19th century, they had little electoral success. Not only did they face competition from the established parties, they faced a number of other difficulties. First, even by the end of the 19th century, less than 70% of adult men and no women had the vote. Most working class people were, therefore, still disenfranchised in 1900. Second, the traditional way of protesting against the system was to use extra-parliamentary techniques such as demonstrations and marches. There seemed no place for working class people within the parliamentary system and socialists felt more comfortable campaigning outside the system. Third, working class people did not have the resources to become MPs. In 1900, MPs were unpaid and so candidates needed another source of income if they were to be able to carry out their duties as an MP. And fourth, opponents of socialism were very successful in promoting the idea that socialism would lead to bloody revolution and should, therefore, be opposed (see chapter 2, part 4 for an explanation of the term 'socialism').

Trade unions in the 19th century

Although socialist groups did not gain much success by 1900, the same is not true of the trade union movement. In 1850, the trade union movement was of little consequence. But, by 1900, several million workers had joined unions, the TUC (Trades Union Congress - the national body for all trade unions) had been established, unions had won some legal rights and a number of union leaders had become MPs. The first union leaders to be elected as MPs were elected in 1874. Alexander Macdonald and Thomas Burt were miners sponsored by their union and recruited to stand for their local Liberal party (a few local Liberal parties decided to put up working class candidates after the extension of the franchise in 1867 because they realised that working class people would make up the majority of voters in their constituencies). By 1884, there were nine 'Lib-Lab' MPs, as these working class Liberals became known. The Liberal Prime Minister, Gladstone, promoted one of these Lib-Lab MPs, Henry Broadhurst, to the Cabinet in 1886. Gladstone was convinced that Lib-Lab MPs should be concerned with trade union matters alone. They should not put forward the working class view on other issues.

Keir Hardie and the ILP

At the TUC conference held in 1887, Broadhurst came under attack from Keir Hardie. Hardie argued that working people should not join a political party which supported the employers against the workers. He urged workers to set up their own independent political party. Although Hardie failed to convince delegates at the conference in 1887, he continued to argue his case and brought up the question at every TUC conference in the 1890s. In 1892, Keir Hardie was invited to stand as an independent candidate in West Ham and he won the election. Hardie shocked his fellow MPs by refusing to conform to their dress code. Whilst the other MPs wore top hats and morning dress, Hardie wore a deerstalker and a checked suit. This symbolised the difference in class and ideology between Hardie and the other MPs.

In Parliament, Hardie attacked the Liberal and Conservative parties for their lack of concern for working people. Outside Parliament, he helped to set up the Independent Labour Party (ILP). At a conference in Bradford in January 1893, a group of socialists agreed to stand as ILP candidates in the forthcoming election. In the 1895 election, 28 ILP candidates stood, but all, including Hardie, were defeated. Despite this setback, support for a working class party which would work within the existing political system began to grow. In 1898, the ILP won a majority on West Ham's borough council.

The Labour Representation Committee (LRC)

At the TUC conference in 1899, the Amalgamated Society of Railway Servants (ASRS) put forward a proposal that a conference be organised between the ILP, the Fabians (an early socialist think tank - see chapter 10, section 1.6), the SDF (a Marxist group) and the unions. The aim of the conference was to devise ways of securing the return of a group of working class (labour) MPs in the next Parliament. The ASRS could not get the railway companies to recognise it as an official union and it blamed this on the number of MPs who had shares in the railways. This suggested to the ASRS the advantage of having a distinct group of working class MPs in Parliament. The ASRS managed to persuade a majority of delegates at the TUC conference to support its proposal.

The conference was held in London in February 1900 and it was attended by seven unions (representing a membership of 353,070), a member of the ILP, a member of the Fabian society and a member of the SDF. None of the major unions attended. At the conference, the Labour Representation Committee (LRC) was set up. The purpose of the LRC, on a motion proposed by Keir Hardie, was to create a distinct Labour group in Parliament which would be subject to its own whips. The LRC was, therefore, to be a new political party. Six months after the LRC was set up, a general election was called. The LRC managed to put up 15 candidates. Two - Keir Hardie and Richard Bell (secretary of the ASRS) - were elected. Although this was a modest start, it had immense consequences. Six years later the LRC was renamed the Labour party. The first person to act as secretary to the LRC was Ramsay MacDonald. In 1924, he became the first Labour Prime Minister.

The Taff Vale case

In August 1900, workers on the Taff Vale railway in South Wales went on strike. The railway company sued the union, claiming damage for loss of profits. In July 1901, the House of Lords ruled in favour of the company and the union was forced to pay £23,000 in damages. This meant that any union could now be sued if it organised a strike - a disaster for unions since they would no longer be able to use their main weapon. All unions, therefore, realised that their funds would be in danger unless a new law was passed to protect them. The Conservative government, however, refused to intervene and unions could not be sure what priority would be given to this issue by the Liberals. As a result, the idea of an independent party representing working class interests began to gain wider support from the unions. By 1904, the number of union members affiliated to the LRC had more than doubled to 956,025 and the affiliated unions had agreed to charge a levy of one penny on every member to raise the funds necessary to pay Labour MPs' salaries. So, the Taff Vale case not only provided the LRC with a clear issue on which to campaign (the right to strike), it also brought an increased membership and greater funds.

The Lib-Lab pact, 1903

In 1903, Ramsay MacDonald, secretary of the LRC, made a secret pact with the Liberal chief whip, Herbert Gladstone. The deal was as follows. After the next election, LRC MPs would support the Liberals in Parliament if the Liberals agreed not to put up candidates in a number of constituencies during the election itself. When the 1906 general election was called, no Liberal candidates were put up in 30 constituencies. This allowed LRC candidates in these constituencies to have a clear run against the Conservatives. Of the 50 LRC candidates who stood in the 1906 general election, 29 were successful. Most of these owed their success to the secret Lib-Lab pact.

Winning 29 seats was a major achievement. The LRC MPs elected Keir Hardie as their leader and decided to take a new name - the Labour Party. The gains made in 1906 provided the platform for the new Labour party to develop into a major party.

The Labour party 1906-24

Between 1906 and 1916, Labour did not appear to be a great threat to the Liberal party. The Liberals won a large overall majority in the election of 1906, so the new Labour MPs could make little impact. Between 1906 and 1916 the Labour party failed to win any new seats. The number of Labour MPs rose to 40 in 1910 because the Miners' Federation had joined the Labour party and its Lib-Lab MPs were instructed to take the Labour whip. It was not until the Liberal party split in 1916 (see section 4.1 below) that Labour's fortunes began to improve. Between 1916 and 1924, four factors combined to change Labour from a small, opposition party into a major party of government. First, the Liberal split in 1916 and its continuation after the war undoubtedly boosted Labour's support. Second, Labour MPs served in Lloyd George's wartime coalition government thus providing Labour with experience of government and bolstering the party's credibility. Third, the Representation of the People Act of 1918 enfranchised a huge number of people (see chapter 7, p.167). Many of the newly enfranchised came from the working classes. And fourth, in 1918 the Labour party adopted a new constitution and its structure and organisation was shaken up. This provided it with a political platform and the organisation necessary for it to become a mass party.

The Labour party in power

It is a measure of the Labour party's initial success that in 1924, just 24 years after its first two MPs were elected, the Labour party was able to form a government, albeit a minority government which relied on Liberal support to survive. The first Labour government lasted just 10 months and is, perhaps, most notable for the way in which Labour ministers tried desperately to convince the public that, whatever their opponents might claim, the Labour party was a party of moderation and respectability. Since the government relied on Liberal support, there was no chance of implementing a socialist programme even if ministers had wanted to do so.

The same points can be made about the second Labour government of 1929-31. This was also a minority government and it contained many of the same faces - for example, Ramsay MacDonald was Prime Minister and Philip Snowden Chancellor in both administrations. But the second government ended with the Labour party in disarray. In August 1931, Ramsay MacDonald, convinced that there was a major economic crisis, dissolved the Labour government and agreed to form a 'national' government (a coalition government containing members of all three main parties). MacDonald failed to consult with his colleagues before agreeing this course of action and it is unlikely he would have gained their agreement if he had done so. The result was a split in the party. MacDonald and seven other MPs joined the National government whilst the Labour party went into opposition (in the subsequent election the number of Labour MPs was reduced from 288 to 46). MacDonald and his colleagues were expelled from the party.

The Labour party remained in opposition until it won its first overall majority in 1945. This was the first time that a Labour government had been able to set its own agenda. Despite the economic difficulties facing Britain after the war, the Labour government under Attlee embarked on an ambitious programme of nationalisation and set in place the main elements of the welfare state.

In the 34 years between 1945 and 1979, the Labour party held power for 17 years - the same number of years as the Conservatives. It is only since 1979 that questions have been raised about the ability of the Labour party to mobilise enough support to regain a majority in the House of Commons.

Activity 8.5

Item A *Labour Prime Ministers and general election victories since 1900*

1920

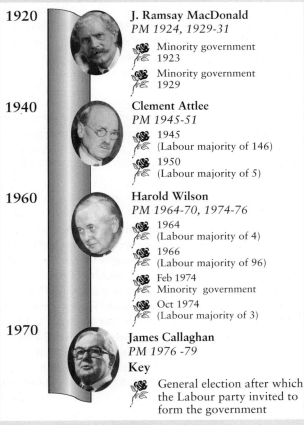

J. Ramsay MacDonald
PM 1924, 1929-31

- Minority government 1923
- Minority government 1929

1940

Clement Attlee
PM 1945-51

- 1945 (Labour majority of 146)
- 1950 (Labour majority of 5)

1960

Harold Wilson
PM 1964-70, 1974-76

- 1964 (Labour majority of 4)
- 1966 (Labour majority of 96)
- Feb 1974 Minority government
- Oct 1974 (Labour majority of 3)

1970

James Callaghan
PM 1976 -79

Key

General election after which the Labour party invited to form the government

Item B *The development of the Labour party*

Date	Seats contested	MPs elected	Total votes polled
1900	15	2	63,304
1906	50	29	323,195
1910 (Jan)	78	40	505,657
1910 (Dec)	56	42	371,772
1918	361	57	2,244,945
1922	411	142	4,241,383
1923	422	191	4,438,508
1924	512	151	5,489,077
1929	571	288	8,389,512
1931	491	46	6,362,561
1935	552	154	8,325,491
1945	604	393	11,995,152
1950	617	315	13,266,592
1951	617	295	13,948,605
1955	620	277	12,404,970
1959	621	258	12,215,538
1964	628	317	12,205,606
1966	621	364	13,064,951
1970	624	288	12,179,341
1974 (Feb)	623	301	11,639,243
1974 (Oct)	623	319	11,457,079
1979	623	269	11,532,148
1983	633	209	8,457,124
1987	633	229	10,029,270
1992	634	271	11,559,735

Adapted from Pelling, 1991.

Item C *Labour and the Liberal party*

Then and Now.

LIBERAL PARTY: My dear sir, I am delighted to give you a lift. It is quite a pleasure to have your company.

LIBERAL PARTY: Dear me! If he grows much bigger, I shall be crowded out of the trap altogether.

It has been resolved that the Miners' Federation shall join the Labour Party.

This cartoon was produced in 1909.

Item D *Labour's election manifesto, 1906*

The House of Commons is supposed to be the people's House and yet the people are not there. Landlords, employers, lawyers, brewers and financiers are there. Why not labour? The trade unions ask for the same freedom that capital enjoys. They are refused. The aged poor are neglected. The slums remain. Overcrowding continues whilst the land goes to waste. Shopkeepers and traders are overburdened with rates and taxation. Wars are fought to make the rich richer and underfed children are still neglected. You have it in your power to see that Parliament carries out your wishes. The Labour Representation Executive appeals to you in the name of a million trade unionists to forget all the political differences which have kept you apart in the past and to vote for.......(signed by the Labour candidate).

Adapted from the Labour Party election manifesto, 1906.

Questions

1. 'The natural party of government.' Is this a fair description of the Labour party? Give reasons for your answer.
2. Using Items A and B isolate the key dates in the development of the Labour party and write a short piece explaining why these dates are important.
3. Suppose you had chosen the cartoon in Item C to illustrate an article entitled: 'The Liberal and Labour parties 1900-25'. Write the text to accompany the picture.
4. What does Item D tell us about the nature of the early Labour party?

3.2 Reform in the Labour party since 1979

Since the Labour party lost power in 1979, there has been extensive reform of the structure and organisation of the party. In part, this is a reflection of the party's electoral failures in the 1980s. In part, it is a reflection of an ideological struggle between different factions within the party. Since 1979, there have been two distinct phases.

Phase 1. The Bennite challenge 1979-83

Following Labour's 1979 general election defeat, a group of Labour party activists led by Tony Benn attempted to change the balance of power within the party. According to Kelly these reformers argued that:

> 'By ignoring the wishes of Labour's activists, its parliamentary leaders had lost touch with the wishes of its natural working class electorate, which paved the way for Mrs Thatcher's victory in 1979. Benn thus contested that organisational reform had become necessary, not just to satisfy abstract theories of party democracy, but to ensure that future Labour governments would not "betray" the socialist ideas developed in opposition.' (Kelly, 1994, p.40)

According to Kelly, therefore, the internal party reforms supported by Tony Benn and his colleagues after 1979 were designed not just to ensure that the Labour party became electable once again, they were also designed to ensure that a distinct ideological standpoint was reflected in the way in which the party worked.

The pressure for reform exerted by this group produced two main changes. First, as a result of a rule change made at the 1980 party conference, it became mandatory (compulsory) for Labour MPs to be reselected by their constituency Labour parties (CLPs) before each general election (see chapter 11, section 2.1). And second, the right to elect Labour's leader and deputy leader was no longer the responsibility of the parliamentary party (PLP) alone. From 1981, the leader and deputy leader were to be elected by an electoral college (an electoral college is a mathematical device for measuring votes). This electoral college was made up of the PLP (which had 30% of the vote), CLPs (which had 30% of the vote) and trade unions (which had 40% of the vote). For the first time, it became possible to challenge the leader and deputy leader whether they were in government or in opposition. Prior to this, it had not been possible to challenge the leader and deputy leader whilst they were in government.

The aim of these reforms was to give greater power to Labour activists in the CLPs who (it was assumed) were more radical than the party's leadership and, therefore, more likely to support socialist measures. There is little doubt that these reforms encouraged the damaging split which resulted in the departure of 30 Labour MPs to the SDP (see section 4.1 below). The culmination of this phase was the adoption of a radical manifesto for the 1983 general election.

Phase 2. 'Modernisation' since 1983

Labour's poor showing in the 1983 general election resulted in a backlash against the ideas and strategy of Benn and his colleagues. Since 1983, the party leadership has reasserted its authority and introduced organisational reforms which have both broadened and centralised the decision making process within the party.

Whilst Benn and his colleagues aimed to extend the power of CLPs because that is where party activists were to be found, the Labour leadership since 1983 has sought to extend power beyond the CLPs to ordinary members. The introduction of 'one member, one vote' (OMOV) is an important part of the party's modernisation programme. OMOV extends democracy within the party by encouraging the participation not just of activists, but of every ordinary member.

The debate over OMOV has also, most importantly, raised the question of the Labour party's relationship with the trade unions. The unions were instrumental in the setting up of the Labour party (see above, section 3.1) and since then have provided the Labour party with most of its funds and most of its members. Traditionally, the unions have enjoyed an important role in the party's decision making. But, since 1979, this role has increasingly been attacked from within as well as from outside the party. During the 1980s, many union leaders joined the Labour leadership's demand for greater democratisation of the party. It is true that some union leaders argued that:

> 'While we continue to fund the party, we'll have a say - it's as crude as that...No say, no pay' (Tom Sawyer, deputy general secretary of NUPE in the *Independent*, 2 June 1992)

But, others agreed that the unions' say in determining party policy and in internal party elections should be curbed. Since 1993, although the unions still have an important role in decision making in the Labour party, the principle of OMOV has been conceded.

Equally important has been the reassertion of the authority of the Labour party leadership. Neil Kinnock's determined efforts to expel members of the Militant Tendency in the mid-1980s suggested that the party was changing direction (Militant Tendency is a Trotskyist group whose members joined the Labour party in the hope of moving Labour policies to the left - see part 5 below). Also, the united front presented by the shadow Cabinet (even during the potentially divisive leadership struggles of 1992 and 1994) has promoted the idea that the organisational reforms carried out since 1983 have resulted in a united party.

Although the reforms introduced since 1983 have been branded as 'centralist' by some critics (see, for example, Kelly, 1991), it is noticeable that the candidates for the leadership in 1994 avoided the old division between left and right (with the centralists in between) just as they objected to being branded as 'modernisers' or 'traditionalists'. In public, at least, the ideological battles of the early 1980s have been replaced by an image of unity and electability.

3.3 The structure and organisation of the Labour party

The Labour party differs from the Conservative party in two important ways. First, unlike the Conservative party, the Labour party is a 'compact legally recognised organisation' with a written constitution. This written constitution was first drawn up in 1918 but it has been amended since then. Second, whilst the Conservative party originated as a grouping within Parliament, the Labour party was created by a number of groups which functioned outside Parliament. It is, therefore, no surprise that the structure and organisation of the Labour party should be markedly different from that of the Conservative party.

Labour party branches and constituencies

Ordinary members of the Labour party belong to a local branch. They are invited to attend branch meetings and can stand for election to the branch's executive committee at the branch's annual general meeting. Individual branches are responsible for looking after their own members and finance and branches choose candidates for local elections. Branch rules are laid down in the Labour party constitution.

Each branch is able to elect a number of delegates to the CLP's general committee (GC) and to the CLP's executive committee (EC). The number of delegates is determined by the number of paid-up members in the branch. In addition, a number of delegates are appointed to the CLP's GC by trade unions which are affiliated to the Labour party. Ordinary branch members and union members can attend meetings of the CLP's GC, but only delegates are allowed to vote. Delegates to the CLP can stand for election to the CLP's general management committee. Rules governing the CLP are laid down in the Labour party constitution.

In the early 1980s, the power of the CLP was a matter of great concern (see above). Until 1987, one of the key functions of the CLP was to select parliamentary candidates. But since 1993 every ordinary member of the Labour party has been able to vote in the selection process (see chapter 11, section 2.1). Local and national election campaigns are organised at constituency level. Delegates are elected by the CLP to attend regional and annual conferences.

The National Executive Committee (NEC)

According to the Labour Party constitution, the National Executive Committee (NEC) is the 'administrative authority of the party' (Labour Party, 1993, p.14). The NEC contains 29 members who are elected as follows: 12 members are elected by trade union delegates at the annual conference (four members must be women); one member is elected by delegates of socialist, cooperative and other affiliated organisations at the annual conference; seven members are nominated by CLPs and are elected by ordinary members in a ballot (three members must be women); five members are women nominated by any organisation affiliated to the Labour party and are elected by a ballot of ordinary members. In addition, the party leader, party deputy leader, party treasurer and one youth member elected at the national youth conference automatically have a place on the NEC.

The duties and powers of the NEC are laid down in the constitution. The NEC oversees the work of the extra-parliamentary party between conferences. It is the responsibility of the NEC to ensure that the party machinery runs smoothly at all levels (at constituency, district, county and regional level). In addition, the NEC plays an important role in the formulation of Labour policy (for example, it participates with the Cabinet or shadow Cabinet in writing the party's election manifesto) and it is charged with ensuring that the rules laid down by the constitution are followed. It has the power of discipline if rules are breached and can expel individuals or groups (subject to final authority by annual conference). The NEC is responsible for the financial affairs of the party and for running its headquarters. It is the NEC which organises the annual party conference. The NEC also plays an important part in the selection of parliamentary candidates, especially at by-elections (see chapter 11, section 2.1).

John Smith House, Walworth Road

The Labour party's national office is John Smith House, in Walworth Road, London. It is here that the national party bureaucracy is based (it was named John Smith House in 1994, after the former leader's sudden death). The head of the national party bureaucracy is the party's general secretary, who is elected by the annual party conference on the recommendation of the NEC. There is no time limit on the general secretary's tenure of office.

Following the disappointing general election result in 1983, Neil Kinnock and his NEC allies brought changes to the organisation of the party's national bureaucracy at Walworth Road. A new general secretary, Larry Whitty, was appointed and a new post, director of communications, set up. By gaining the assistance of pollsters, marketing specialists and media experts, the general secretary and director of communications were able (with the support of Neil Kinnock) to rejuvenate Labour's national bureaucracy and give the party a new image. Most commentators agreed that Labour's election campaigns in 1987 and 1992 were highly slick and professional, though some party members have remained critical of this new 'designer socialism'.

The annual party conference

Labour's annual party conference bears many outward similarities to the Conservative annual party conference. Both conferences, for example, provide the chance for a morale boosting visit to the seaside. Both provide the opportunity for ordinary members to air their views in public. Both debate issues and, at both, the leaders expect to win a standing ovation. But, unlike the Conservative annual party conference, Labour's annual party conference has the power to make policy. In theory at least, the annual party conference is the sovereign body of the Labour party. This power is laid out in Clause five of the constitution:

> 'The party conference shall decide from time to time what specific proposals of legislative, financial or administrative reform shall be included in the party programme. No proposal shall be included in the party programme unless it has been adopted by the party conference by a majority of not less than two thirds of the votes recorded on a card vote.' (Labour Party, 1993, p.11)

On some occasions, the party conference has exercised this right against the wishes of the party leadership - for example, by approving the policy of unilateral nuclear disarmament in 1992, though such examples are relatively rare.

Examples of delegates defying the wishes of the party leadership have been rare largely because of the voting system used at conference. Until 1993, voting at conference was dominated by the trade unions. Trade unions affiliated to the Labour party had one conference vote for every registered affiliated member (affiliated members are union members who pay the political levy as part of their union subscription). Before 1993, a union was able to cast all of its votes in a single block (hence the term 'block vote'). How the union's block vote was cast was usually decided by the union's leadership. As a result, provided the Labour leadership had the support of union leaders, it was able to guarantee a majority at conference. In fact, the leadership could simply ignore the wishes of constituency delegates since they had so few votes relative to the unions. In 1993, however, an electoral college was introduced. This divided conference into a union section with 70% of the vote and a constituency section with 30% of the vote. Moreover, for every 30,000 new individual members, the constituency section gains an extra 1% of the vote (whilst the union section loses 1%).

Although conference has the constitutional power to decide policy, this power has been somewhat diluted since the setting up of the National Policy Forum in 1990. The National Policy Forum is split into policy commissions which produce reports for the NEC and, ultimately, conference to approve. According to Kelly:

> 'It looks as if this system, due to be fully operational by 1997, will enhance the leader's control over detailed policy making; all the commissions will be coordinated by the appropriate frontbench MP, affiliated bodies will not be able to submit policy resolutions while the commissions are deliberating and conference itself will only be able to vote on the commissions' reports en bloc rather than on specific items.' (Kelly, 1994, p.49)

Activity 8.6

Item A *The structure and organisation of the Labour party*

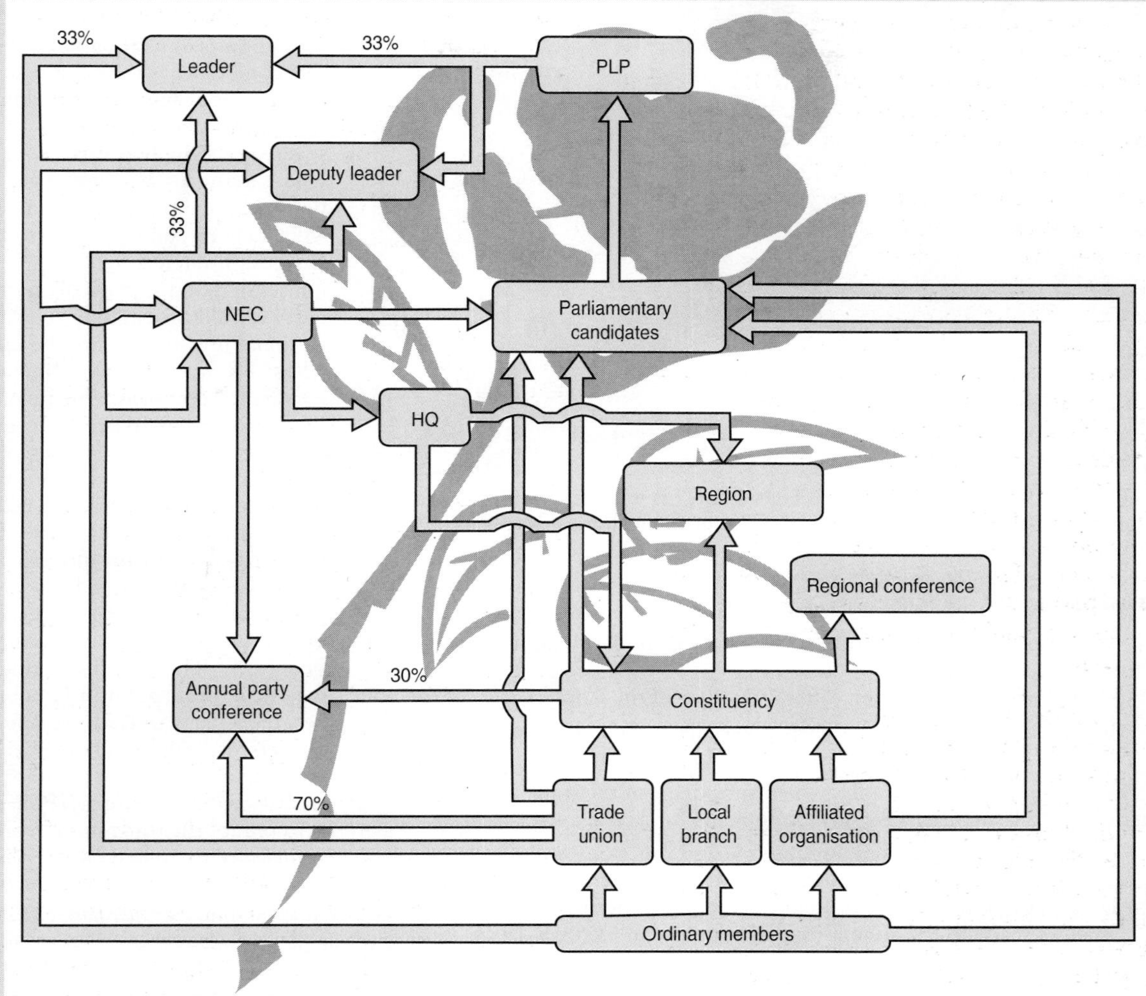

Item B *Labour and the unions (1)*

Despite all the rhetoric and arm twisting at Labour's 1993 annual conference, the party remains a wholly owned subsidiary of the trade union movement. The OMOV debate left the position unchanged. First, the unions will still decide Labour's policy since they will cast the lion's share (70%) of votes at conference. Even though the votes will not be cast in a block, delegates from a particular union will all vote the same way since they will have been mandated to do so by their union's annual conference. Second, the unions continue to sponsor every MP in the shadow Cabinet and they sponsor 163 of Labour's 269 MPs. Third, the unions will continue to play an important part in the election of the party's leader and deputy leader. Fourth, the unions will continue to manage the party since 12 members of the NEC must be trade unionists.

Adapted from *CRD*, 1994.

Item C *Labour and the unions (2)*

Brothers, we formed the Labour party in 1900. We helped to develop and strengthen it. Some of our finest people achieved great office in the party. But now, after four successive election defeats, our political leaders are less and less interested in us. All they want is our money. Without it they couldn't survive. So, why not dump the Labour party? After all, the unions could get better value for their cash by investing it in their own members, in education recruitment and in improving their services. This would be better than throwing it down the bottomless pit which is Walworth Road. This does not necessarily mean the end of a beautiful relationship. The unions founded the Labour party because they required a political voice. They still do, but one which is effective. They could still sponsor MPs and maintain political funds. But, the Labour party should not automatically think it has a right to them. With 8 million members the unions would remain an important pressure group and have growing access to backbench Liberal and Tory MPs. They cannot be ignored but they should not be taken for granted.

Adapted from the *Guardian*, 14 May 1993.

Item D *The annual party conference*

This photo shows Labour's leader Tony Blair, his wife, Cherie Booth, and senior members of the Labour party just after the leader's address to the 1994 party conference.

Questions

1. a) To what extent does the organisation of the modern Labour party reflect its historical origins?
   b) How does its organisation differ from that of the Conservative party?
2. a) Judging from Item A where does power lie in the Labour party?
   b) Explain how decisions are made in the Labour party.
3. 'The Labour party is a wholly owned subsidiary of the trade union movement.' Using Items B-E give arguments for and against this view.
4. a) Using Items D and E compare the role and functions of Labour's annual conference with the Conservatives' annual conference.
   b) Do you think the author of Item E would have been satisfied with the changes made to the annual party conference in October 1993? Give reasons for your answer.

Item E *Reforming the annual party conference*

There is a need for a new structure for Labour's annual party conference. The conference is the great assembly of the Labour movement and has traditionally been seen as its sovereign body. But, it is a sovereign whose authority has often been flouted by Labour governments and MPs. One reason why the sovereign has been flouted is that it is a nonsense that a supposedly national party should be dictated to by a sectional pressure group (the unions) whose block votes have dominated conference decisions. One possible remedy is simply to break the ties between the party and the unions and hope for the friendly relations which, for example, the Democrats usually enjoy with the American unions. This might free Labour for modernisation whilst killing the union bogy in public image terms. But, it might also kill the golden goose - and not just financially. The British working class may be in decline, but if Labour became a party of lecturers and lawyers without union members, working class voters would not identify with it for long. The solution is to reduce the trade union vote at conference to 50% whilst abolishing the block vote in its existing form.

Adapted from the *Guardian*, 22 February 1993.

3.4 The selection and role of the Labour leader

Until 1922, the Labour party's main spokesperson was known as 'Chairman of the Party'. It was only after 1922 that the term 'leader of the Labour party' came into common usage.

The parliamentary Labour party (PLP)

All MPs who take the Labour whip belong to the parliamentary Labour party (PLP). Until 1980, the PLP alone chose the leader in a series of ballots. The last Labour leader to be elected in this way was Michael Foot in 1980. He defeated Denis Healey in the second ballot.

The PLP is still responsible for choosing the composition of the shadow Cabinet when the party is in opposition. Each MP has 18 votes and, since 1989, must cast at least three votes for women candidates. Those elected form a pool from which the party leader, deputy leader, chief whip and chair of the party select the shadow Cabinet. Since 1980, the Labour leader has been obliged, following a general election victory, to form the first Cabinet from those who had served in the existing shadow Cabinet. But, the leader is unrestricted in any future reshuffles.

Selecting the leader and deputy leader

Candidates for the posts of leader and deputy leader of the Labour party must be MPs. Between 1981 and 1988 candidates had to secure the support of 5% of the PLP before they could be nominated. Following Tony Benn's abortive challenge to Neil Kinnock in 1988, however, the rules were changed. Candidates now have to secure the support of 12.5% of the PLP if there is a vacancy or 20% of the PLP if there is no vacancy to the positions whilst Labour is in opposition. If Labour is in government, then, whether there is a vacancy or not, challengers have to secure the support of 20% of the PLP and they also have to gain the backing of two thirds of those who can vote at annual conference. Before 1981, challenges to the leadership whilst the Labour party was in government were not allowed.

Since 1981, the Labour leader and deputy leader have been chosen by an electoral college. Between 1981 and 1993, this electoral college was split as follows: the trade unions had 40% of the vote; the CLPs had 30% of the vote; and the PLP (including MEPs) had 30% of the vote. Since 1993, this electoral college has been divided equally between trade unions, CLPs and the PLP (including MEPs). Also since 1993, one member, one vote has been introduced. So, every paid up member of the Labour party is able to vote in the constituency section and every trade union member who pays the political levy and whose trade union is affiliated to the Labour party is able to vote in the trade union section (the block vote, therefore, no longer has a place in the selection of Labour leaders).

To win, a candidate for the leadership or deputy leadership has to gain more than 50% of the vote. If no candidate wins more than 50% of the vote outright, the candidate with the least number of votes is excluded and their second preference votes redistributed (this is known as the alternative vote system - see chapter 7, p.184).

Under the rules laid down in the constitution, the election for leader and deputy leader should take place at the time of the annual party conference unless for some reason the leader or deputy leader becomes 'unavailable' (ie becomes ill, resigns or dies). If that happens, then the NEC can arrange for a ballot before the next annual conference is held. This happened when John Smith died in May 1994. The results of the leadership election were announced in July 1994, more than two months before the annual party conference was held.

Role of the Labour leader

The role of the Labour leader is not easy to determine. In theory, the leader is responsible only for directing the party in Parliament and is, therefore, subordinate to the annual party conference and to the NEC. In practice, however, the leader has a much broader role. First, the leader is the party's main spokesperson and the public nature of the position ensures that the leader has considerable influence. Second, although, in theory, the wishes of the leader are subordinate to the wishes of the annual party conference, in practice, on most occasions leaders are able to manufacture the decisions they want at conference. Third, it has been regular practice for Labour leaders to ignore or to manipulate the NEC. And fourth, although conference policy is meant to be included in the party election manifesto, leaders are usually able (if they so desire) to dilute or to alter it in such a way that its original intentions are lost.

So, the leader performs a powerful role but a role lacking in clarity. Determined leaders with clear intentions are able to wield as much power as their Conservative counterparts and can do so with a greater degree of security (between 1961 and 1994 the only time that a sitting leader was challenged was in 1988). A weak leader, however, will be bound by the decisions of a variety of other party institutions.

The location of power in the Labour party

In his classic analysis of the organisation of the Labour party, McKenzie (1955) argued that real power in the Labour party rested with the Labour leadership. There was, he argued, a fundamental gap between the party's constitutional theory, which suggested that real power lay with extra-parliamentary bodies such as the annual conference, and party political practice which resulted in the party leadership taking all the key decisions. McKenzie suggested that this was a consequence of the fact that the party leadership always has to perform the role of government or government in waiting. The government is accountable to Parliament, not to bodies outside Parliament. Equally, the government is expected to represent the wishes of the people as a whole and not just the wishes of a narrow section. In other words, members of the government have a wider responsibility than to the annual Labour party conference and, to demonstrate that it is capable of government (ie to win general elections), the Labour leadership has to be prepared to ignore or act against the wishes of the majority of ordinary party members.

The fact that Labour leaders have continued to ignore or act against the wishes of the majority of ordinary members since McKenzie wrote his book in 1955, suggests that power has remained with the Labour leadership and there is still little real democracy within the party. The moves towards centralisation, undertaken by Neil Kinnock after 1983, strengthen this view. But two points can be made against it. First, even if it is not all-powerful, the annual party conference does restrict the Labour leadership's freedom of manoeuvre. Neil Kinnock could not have abandoned the policy of unilateralism without the support of conference, for example. It may be true that Labour leaders usually get their own way, but they are always aware that failure to carry the majority of conference with them will lead to a public fight and unsightly shows of disunity. And second, in recent years there have been genuine attempts to democratise the party. The unions' block vote has been reduced, for example, and OMOV has given ordinary members the chance to participate in internal party elections.

Activity 8.7

Item A *Labour leadership and deputy leadership contests 1976-94*

(i) Leadership election, 1976

Candidate	Ballot 1	Ballot 2	Result
Callaghan	84	141	176
Foot	90	133	137
Healey	30	38	
Jenkins	56		
Benn	37		
Crosland	17		
100% votes cast by PLP			

(ii) Leadership election, 1983

Candidate	PLP	Constituency	Trade unions	Total
Kinnock	14.8	27.5	29.0	71.3
Hattersley	7.8	0.6	10.9	19.3
Heffer	4.3	2.0	0.1	6.3
Shore	3.1	0.0	0.1	3.1
PLP section = 30%; constituency section = 30%; trade union section = 40%				

(iii) Leadership and deputy leadership election, 1994

Leader	MPs/MEPs	Ordinary members	Trade unions	Total
Blair	60.5	58.2	52.3	57.0
Prescott	19.6	24.4	28.4	24.1
Beckett	19.9	17.4	19.3	18.9
Deputy leader	**MPs/MEPs**	**Ordinary members**	**Trade unions**	**Total**
Prescott	53.7	59.4	56.6	56.5
Beckett	46.3	40.6	43.4	43.5
MPs' & MEPs' section = 33.3 %; ordinary members' section = 33.3%; trade union section = 33.3%				

Item B *Electing a Labour leader in 1994 (1)*

Here are a number of things you need to know to understand Labour's 1994 leadership election. First, an electoral college is something which does not actually exist. It is a mathematical device for measuring the votes. Second, the most important votes are cast by Labour MPs and MEPs (not union barons). Suppose 332 MPs and MEPs vote, each of their votes will amount to 0.1004% of the electoral college (332 times 0.1004 equals 33.3%). Third, anyone whose party membership was paid up by 25 May gets one vote. Suppose that 220,000 members vote, each will be worth 0.0001666%. Fourth, anyone who belongs to one of the 36 trade unions or other organisations affiliated to the party and has paid a political levy will also be entitled to vote. Each levy payer has to sign a declaration stating that they support the principles of the Labour party and are not a supporter of any organisation opposed to it. That amounts to about 4 million members. But suppose a mere 1 million vote. Each of their votes will be worth 0.0000333%. So the vote of one MP will equal that of 3,125 union voters. Fifth, the union barons have lost their power in this election. In 1992, Bill Morris cast about 8% of the total vote by filling in the TGWU's ballot paper. Then, he was worth 84 MPs. Now, one MP is worth 625 Bill Morrises. And sixth, with so many taking part in the election it is no use fixing deals in smoke filled rooms. It doesn't even help much to be the sort of speaker who rouses a party conference or a first rate parliamentary operator. You have to come over well on TV.

Adapted from the *Observer*, 29 May 1994.

Item C *Electing a Labour leader in 1994 (2)*

This cartoon shows from left to right: Tony Blair, John Prescott, Gordon Brown, Margaret Beckett and Robin Cook. It appeared in the *Guardian* on 26 May 1994. At that point, none of the Labour leadership contenders had formally declared that they would be standing. By the time nominations closed, both Gordon Brown and Robin Cook had dropped out of the race. Brown, a close ally of Blair, stood aside to give Blair a greater chance. Cook's image was criticised in the media and he scored low ratings in several opinion polls.

Item D *Electing a Labour leader in 1994 (3)*

The contest for the Labour leadership is developing into the most surreal political event of recent times. There will be a massive process engaging perhaps 4 million voters and lasting for over two months. Yet, the conclusion looks foregone. It is true that there needs to be a contest. For Tony Blair to sweep in unopposed would be ridiculous after the years spent battling over internal democracy. The trouble is that the process (unlike the block vote manipulations that produced Neil Kinnock or the solely parliamentary vote that produced Jim Callaghan and every earlier leader) requires the open taking of positions and the spelling out of manifestos to millions. The theory is that there are grand disagreements which need democratic decision. But, actually, there are no important disagreements. And meanwhile, the man who is laughing is John Major. Under the old method, there would have been a few respectful days of mourning and then the contestants would have entered the race. They would have got in before the opinion polls showed that they lacked support. So, the choice would have been wider, perhaps much wider. It would have been no more and no less a personality contest than the one starting on Friday. The result would almost certainly have been the same. And, Mr Major would not have had two months to recoup his miserable fortunes.

Adapted from the *Guardian*, 7 June 1994.

Item E *Electing a Labour leader in 1994 (4)*

Although Tony Blair's vote was highest among MPs and MEPs and lowest among the unions, the margin of victory was clear in each section. Considering that, in the past, Blair has fought against the unions over the closed shop, union immunities and OMOV, it was a particularly impressive achievement to beat Prescott who was thought to be the friend of unions. In the parliamentary section (for the leadership election), Beckett had the support of 48 MPs and 17 MEPs, Prescott had the support of 50 MPs and 14 MEPs and Blair had the support of 169 MPs and 29 MEPs. Three MPs and two MEPs did not vote. In the party membership section, the turnout of 69.1% members (172,356 votes) was very respectable. The only concern in what has been a well managed 10 week election is the low turnout in the unions. Only 19.5% of the union levy payers cast a vote (779,426 votes in total). Also, many union members' votes were ruled out of order because the voter had inadvertently failed to tick the box on the ballot form stating that they supported the Labour party. In one union, more than 8,000 votes were ruled out of order. This put spoilt papers into second place behind Blair.

Adapted from the *Guardian*, 22 July 1994.

Questions

1. a) Look at Item A and explain how the Labour leader was selected in 1976 and 1983 and how the system had changed by 1994.
   b) 'Despite the changing selection system, there have been few surprises in leadership elections since 1981.' What evidence is there to support this statement? Why do you think this has been the case?
2. Using Items A-E:
   a) write an account of the 1994 Labour leadership election.
   b) how did the election of Tony Blair differ from previous leadership elections?
   c) what were the advantages and disadvantages of using the system of selection employed in 1994?
3. a) In your view what is the best way to choose a Labour leader? Explain why.
   b) How might your view differ if you were: a Labour MP; a member of a trade union executive; chair of your local constituency party; a floating voter?

4 The Liberal Democrats

Key Issues
1. How did the Liberal Democrats evolve?
2. What is the structure and organisation of the Liberal Democrats?
3. How powerful is the leader of the Liberal Democrats?

4.1 Origins and history of the Liberal Democrats

The Liberal Democrats came into being in March 1988 when the Liberal party formally merged with the Social Democratic Party (SDP) to form a new party. At first, this new party was known as the Social and Liberal Democrats (SLD), but, after a ballot of the members in October 1989, Liberal Democrats was adopted as the common name of the party. Although the party is, therefore, the youngest of the three main parties, its roots reach back way beyond 1988. Whilst the SDP was formed after a split in the Labour party in 1981, the foundation of the Liberal party is generally dated to June 1859.

The rise and fall of the Liberal party

Like the Conservative party, the Liberal party emerged from an existing parliamentary group - the Whigs. Whigs supported free trade, religious tolerance and the power of Parliament over that of the monarch. At first, the Liberal party was a loose coalition of Whigs, Peelites (Conservatives who had broken from their party in 1846 because they supported free trade) and Radicals (MPs who supported reform, especially religious reform). Support for free trade and individual freedom were the main areas of agreement. But under the leadership of Gladstone (Prime Minister 1868-74, 1880-85 and 1892-94), the Liberal party developed into a modern political party with a mass membership and nationwide extra-parliamentary organisation.

Between 1860 and 1914, the Liberal party was the main alternative to the Conservative party. The two parties alternated in power and dominated Parliament. But, in the early 20th century, the Liberal party went into rapid decline. Although the Liberals won an overall majority in the general election of 1906 and remained the party with the largest number of seats after the general election of 1910, within 20 years the party was only able to win a handful of seats and it had been replaced as the main party of opposition by the Labour party.

Historians do not agree about when the decline of the Liberal party started nor why it happened. But, most would agree that the following factors made an impact. First, the Liberal party suffered from internal divisions before and during the First World War and this affected its credibility. In 1916, for example, David Lloyd George replaced Herbert Asquith as Prime Minister and in so doing split the party. In the 1918 election, Lloyd George Liberals remained in coalition with the Conservatives and they fought seats against Asquith Liberals. Second, the extension of the franchise, following the Representation of the People Act of 1918, trebled the number of voters (from around seven to 21 million). It soon became clear that the majority of these new voters were not prepared to vote Liberal. Third, the war brought changed social and economic circumstances. Fourth, in the early years of the 20th century the Labour party was becoming established and, although it had not made a significant breakthrough before 1914, the foundations for electoral success had been laid. It is significant that the Labour party was set up specifically to provide a voice for the working class. Although the Liberal government of 1906-11 had introduced reforms which were designed to ease the suffering of the disadvantaged, the Liberal party could not claim to represent the working class in the way that the new Labour party could. And finally, Liberal support was evenly spread rather than concentrated in dense pockets. As a result, the first past the post system (see chapter 7, p.172) ensured that the Liberals gained far fewer seats than the number of votes for them would suggest they should receive.

The general election of 1923 was the last time when the number of Liberal MPs reached three figures. In 1935, the number of Liberal MPs fell to a low of 21. Between 1935 and 1988 (when the Liberal party was formally disbanded), it never managed to win more than 23 seats in a general election. These figures show that the decline of the Liberal party was not just sudden and deep, it was also long lasting. By the time the Second World War broke out, the idea that the Liberal party was a minor party was well established.

Although the Liberal party was never able to return the significant number of MPs that it returned up until the early 1920s, the party always managed to retain a toehold in Parliament and it always managed to win votes in the millions. From the 1950s, periodically, there were signs that a significant revival in the fortunes of the party was about to happen. But despite winning 19% of the vote in February 1974, 25% of the vote in 1983 and 22.5% of the vote in 1987, the party was unable to shake the hold that the two other major parties had on the electoral system.

The SDP

In November 1979, shortly after Margaret Thatcher's election victory, Roy Jenkins (a former Labour Home Secretary and Chancellor) delivered the annual Dimbleby lecture. In his speech, he lamented the drift of Conservatives to the right and Labour to the left and called for a realignment of British politics to enable the majority of moderate voters to be represented. Jenkins allowed his Labour party membership to lapse.

It was the organisational changes won by Tony Benn and his colleagues at the special Labour conference in 1981 (see above, section 3.2), however, which were the catalyst for the formation of the Social Democratic Party (SDP). Shortly after the conference, three senior Labour MPs, Bill Rodgers, David Owen and Shirley Williams, together with Roy Jenkins, issued the 'Limehouse Declaration'. This was a statement which attacked the Labour party for heading towards extremism and set up a Council for Social Democracy. Rodgers, Owen, Williams and Jenkins (who became known as the 'gang of four') set up the SDP in March 1981 and, the following autumn, formed a formal alliance with the Liberal party.

Initially, the prospects for the Alliance seemed excellent. By the end of 1981, the SDP was able to claim 27 former Labour MPs and one former Conservative. It received a great deal of money and many offers of support. Opinion polls suggested that the Alliance would win a majority of votes. The findings of these polls seemed to be confirmed when the Alliance won three by-election victories. But this early enthusiasm was not translated into general election success. In the 1983 general election, although the Alliance came close to pushing Labour into third place in terms of votes cast, it won only 23 seats. Of these 23 seats, 17 were won by Liberals and six by members of the SDP. The general election of 1987 was even more of a disappointment. The number of seats and the percentage of the vote won by the Alliance dropped.

From Alliance to merger

After the 1987 general election, David Steel, the Liberal leader, called for a complete merger of the two parties. He argued that voters had been confused about the exact nature of the Alliance. The fact that there were two leaders (David Steel and David Owen) particularly caused problems in the 1987 election campaign. The debate over merger was fierce with both parties divided on the issue. But after balloting the membership, merger was agreed.

Within the SDP, however, the leader, David Owen, and a group of supporters refused to accept this majority decision and they set up a rival party which retained the name SDP. Owen and two other MPs fought on until 1990 when successive electoral defeats demonstrated clearly that the party had little support. Similarly, disenchanted Liberals continued to struggle on under the banner of the Liberal party until they too found that they were marginalised by the electorate.

Since merger, the Liberal Democrats have regularly scored 20% of the vote in local elections and higher in council by-elections. But in national elections they have been less successful. Although they have won some spectacular by-election victories, they only won 17.8% of the vote and 20 seats in the 1992 general election and 16% of the vote and two seats in the 1994 European elections. This suggests that the Liberal Democrats have yet to bring about the change in voting behaviour that will mean an end to the domination of the two main parties.

Two activities follow. The first examines the decline of the Liberal party. The second looks at the record of the Liberal Democrats.

Activity 8.8

Item A *Liberal and Labour performance at general elections 1900-45*

	Labour vote	Labour % of vote	Labour MPs	Liberal vote	Liberal % of vote	Liberal MPs
1900	63,304	1.8	2	1,568,141	44.6	184
1906	528,797	9.4	30	2,583,132	45.9	377
1910 (June)	505,657	7.6	40	2,880,581	43.2	275
1910 (December)	371,772	7.1	42	2,295,888	43.9	272
1918	2,398,773	22.2	60	2,754,448	25.6	161
1922	4,237,769	29.4	142	4,183,982	29.1	116
1923	4,438,508	30.5	191	4,311,147	29.6	159
1924	5,489,077	33.3	151	2,928,747	17.6	40
1929	8,389,512	37.1	288	5,308,510	23.4	59
1931	6,649,630	30.7	52	2,318,510	10.7	72
1935	8,325,491	37.8	154	1,422,116	6.5	21
1945	11,967,985	48.2	394	2,227,400	8.9	12

Item B *Punch cartoon, 1909*

FORCED FELLOWSHIP

SUSPICIOUS-LOOKING PARTY. "ANY OBJECTION TO MY COMPANY, GUVNOR' I'M AGOIN' YOUR WAY"- *(aside)* " AND FURTHER."

Item C *Decline of the Liberal party*

(i) The year 1910 marks the beginning of the decline of Liberal England. That was the year when the old Liberal values of toleration, moderation and reason were damaged by the House of Lords (which blocked the People's budget of 1909), the suffragettes (women who campaigned for the vote) and socialists (supporters of the new Labour party).

Adapted from Dangerfield, 1935.

(ii) The year 1914 marks the beginning of the Liberals' decline. Asquith, Prime Minister when war broke out, soon proved to be unequal to the task and was overthrown by Lloyd George. Lloyd George formed a new coalition with the Conservatives in the majority and this inflicted a grievous wound on his party. For Labour, war provided a taste of office in the coalition and a chance to demonstrate patriotic qualities.

Adapted from Kingdom, 1991.

(iii) Between 1910 and 1914 the Liberals lost 15 seats in by-elections to the Conservatives and won two from Labour. In 11 constituencies, Labour put up third party candidates and it was because of this that five of the Liberal seats were lost. The Lib-Lab alliance was breaking down. But it is difficult to find evidence that Labour was taking the working class vote away from the Liberals. Labour finished bottom in all the by-elections it fought between December 1910 and July 1914.

Adapted from Adelman, 1981.

(iv) The Representation of the People Act of 1918 was of immense importance in Labour's replacing the Liberal Party as the principal party of progress. It trebled the electorate from seven to 21 million voters. The industrial working classes became, for the first time, the majority in a new mass electorate. Until 1918, many working class men (as well as all women) did not have the vote. It seems probable that it was from the new voters that Labour drew its electoral strength in the postwar world.

Adapted from Adelman, 1981.

Item D *Liberal Prime Ministers and general election victories since 1900*

1900

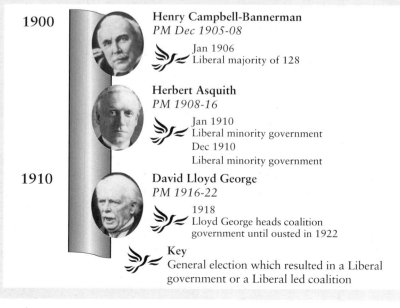

Henry Campbell-Bannerman
PM Dec 1905-08

Jan 1906
Liberal majority of 128

Herbert Asquith
PM 1908-16

Jan 1910
Liberal minority government
Dec 1910
Liberal minority government

1910

David Lloyd George
PM 1916-22

1918
Lloyd George heads coalition government until ousted in 1922

Key
General election which resulted in a Liberal government or a Liberal led coalition

Item E *Decline of the Liberal party (2)*

(i) Broadly speaking, in the 1920s, the Conservatives could count on more cars with which to drive voters to the polls at general elections. Labour could count on more canvassers. In both cases, local organisation was not created for a general election. It already existed. The Liberals failed to transform themselves in this way. They were confused by the feuds between their leaders which began in 1916. Their central fund was usually short of money. But, their greatest handicap was that they ceased to make a distinctive contribution in local affairs. Liberalism became a national cause increasingly cut off from its local roots.

Adapted from Taylor, 1965.

(ii) There was still an unmistakable upper class after the First World War. One per cent of the population owned two thirds of the national wealth. Three quarters of the population owned less than £100. The political governing class was largely drawn from a few hereditary families. Most were educated at Eton. Nearly all went to Oxford or Cambridge. The war brought some changes. The rich, though still rich, became less idle. They earned their living. The old split between landowners and capitalists almost disappeared - hence in part the decline of the Liberal Party. The Conservatives caught up with the modern world and their leaders added wider experience to their traditional toughness.

Adapted from Taylor, 1965.

Questions

1. 'By the time the Second World War broke out the idea that the Liberal party was a minor party was well established'. What evidence is there to support this statement in Items A and D?
2. Using the other items write a caption to explain the point being made in Item B.
3. When and why did the Liberal party fall into decline? Use Items A-E in your answer.

Activity 8.9

Item A *The Liberal Democrats since 1992 (1)*

On 6 May 1993, the first by-election since the 1992 general election took place in Newbury. This was a safe Conservative seat. But, the result stunned the government. David Rendel, the Liberal Democrat candidate, took the seat with a massive 22,055 majority. This represented a swing of 28% from the Conservatives. Labour saw its worst result in a parliamentary election since 1918. The county council elections held the same night completed the story of disaster for the Conservatives. They lost 490 seats and control of all but one county council. The Liberal Democrats were the main beneficiaries. They gained 397 seats and two councils. The spectacular swing in Newbury was derided by some as a one-off. But less than three months later Diana Maddock surpassed it with a 35% swing at the Christchurch by-election. This record breaking result brought talk of a sea change in British politics.

Adapted from Lib Dems, 1993.

Item B *The Liberal party's performance in general elections, 1945-92*

Election	No of candidates	MPs elected	Forfeited deposits	Total votes	% of UK total
1945	306	12	76	2,252,430	9.0
1950	475	9	319	2,621,487	9.1
1951	109	6	66	730,546	2.6
1955	110	6	60	722,402	2.7
1959	216	6	55	1,640,760	5.9
1964	365	9	52	3,099,283	11.2
1966	311	12	104	2,327,457	8.6
1970	332	6	184	2,117,035	7.5
1974 (Feb)	517	14	23	6,059,519	19.3
1974 (Oct)	619	13	125	5,346,704	18.3
1979	577	11	303	4,313,804	13.8
1983	633	23	11	7,780,949	25.4
1987	633	22	1	7,341,633	22.5
1992	632	20	11	5,998,446	17.8

Adapted from Craig, 1989 and the *Guardian*, 11 April 1992.

Item C *The Liberal Democrats since 1992 (2)*

Remember Graham Tope? Or Michael Hancock? Or William Pitt the very youngest? They were three of the Liberal/SDP/Alliance/Liberal Democrats whose by-election victories in safe Conservative seats between 1962 and 1991 had (so we were told) once and for all broken the mould of British politics. But where are they now? All but David Steel and Alan Beith have gone to their political graveyards. Hardly any survived the following general election. This time, of course, we're told that the Liberal triumph in Newbury was different - different because the Liberals did well in the county council elections as well. But that was no surprise. The Liberals do well in most local elections and by-elections held mid-term. What is baffling is that, whenever one of these electoral upsets happens, we are assured that it is irreversible. Not only politicians, but press commentators seem to have learned nothing and forgotten everything. Yet, experience teaches that Tory governments come back repeatedly from the depths of electoral unpopularity. Most Liberal voters vote Liberal as a protest.

Adapted from an article by Gerald Kaufman (a Labour MP) in the *Guardian*, 10 May 1993.

Item D *The Newbury by-election, 6 May 1993 (1)*

Paddy Ashdown (right), the Liberal Democrat leader, celebrates the by-election win at Newbury with the successful candidate, David Rendel.

Item E *The Newbury by-election, 6 May 1993 (2)*

1987 Turnout 78%	1992 Turnout 82.8%	1993 Turnout 71.25%
Con 35,266 **60.1 %***	Con 37,135 **55.9 %***	Lib Dem 37,590 **65.0 %***
Lib Dem 18,608 **31.7%**	Lib Dem 24,778 **37.3%**	Con 15,535 **26.8%**
Lab 4,765 **8.1%**	Lab 3,962 **6.0%**	Lab 1,151 **1.9%**
Con majority 16,658	Con majority 12,357	Lib Dem majority 22,055

* Figures do not add up to 100% since other candidates also received a percentage of the vote.

This table shows the election results in the constituency of Newbury in the 1987 and 1992 general elections and the 1993 by-election.

Adapted from Wood & Wood, 1992 and the *Guardian*, 8 May 1993.

Item F *Liberal/Alliance/Lib Dem by-election results 1958-94*

Constituency	Result	Swing
1958 Torrington	Gain from Con	*
1962 Orpington	Gain from Con	26.8
1969 Ladywood	Gain from Lab	32.0
1972 Sutton	Gain from Con	32.7
1973 Isle of Ely	Gain from Con	*
1973 Ripon	Gain from Con	25.3
1979 Edge Hill	Gain from Lab	32.5
1981 Warrington	Lab hold	22.4
1981 Croydon NW	Gain from Con	24.2
1981 Crosby	Gain from Con	25.6
1983 Bermondsey	Gain from Lab	44.2
1988 Epping Forest	Con hold	20.1
1989 Richmond	Con hold	25.6
1990 Eastbourne	Gain from Con	20.1
1991 Ribble Valley	Gain from Con	24.8
1993 Newbury	Gain from Con	28.4
1994 Eastleigh	Gain from Con	21.5

* Liberals won these seats despite not putting up candidates in the previous general election. In Torrington, they won 38.0% of the vote. In the Isle of Ely, they won 38.3% of the vote.

Adapted from the *Guardian*, 8 May 1993 and the *Guardian*, 11 June 1994.

Questions

1. 'In British politics there are three, not two, main parties.' Argue the case in favour of this statement.
2. Why do you think the Liberals failed to win more than 23 seats in the general elections held between 1945 and 1992?
3. Give the arguments for and against the view that Liberal Democrat by-election victories since 1992 have produced a sea change in British politics.
4. Using Items D-F write an analysis of the Newbury by-election explaining its significance for the Liberal Democrats.

4.2 The structure and organisation of the Liberal Democrats

When the members of the Liberal party and the SDP agreed to merge in 1988, one of the key issues that had to be resolved was the structure and organisation of the new party. The result was a compromise between the centralised structure of the SDP and the federal structure of the Liberal party. Like the Labour party, the structure and organisation of the Liberal Democrats is laid down in a written constitution.

The federal structure

A federal party is a party in which the central decision making body of the party (the federal party) is not all-powerful. Power is devolved to area and local parties. The area and local parties remain independent with regard to local and internal affairs. Any matter of national concern is dealt with by the federal party. The federal principle survived the merger of the two parties and, as a result, considerable autonomy is granted to area and local party organisations.

In Wales and Scotland, the party has three tiers. In England there are four. At the national level, there is the federal party. This is responsible for the preparation of policy for the UK as a whole. It also has overall responsibility for parliamentary elections and national fund raising. All other matters are delegated to the three 'state' parties - one each for England, Scotland and Wales. Scotland and Wales are then subdivided into constituency parties (known officially as 'local' parties) whilst England is subdivided into 12 regional parties and then into local parties.

The state parties are responsible for the operation of local parties, selection procedures for parliamentary candidates, the arrangements for collecting and renewing party membership and local policy matters. In England, each regional party appoints representatives to the English Council, the state party's governing body. For its own convenience the English state party has delegated policy making powers to the federal party. In Scotland and Wales, members of the local parties elect representatives to the Scottish Conference and the Welsh Council, their governing bodies. The Scottish and Welsh state parties have policy making powers.

Every member who joins the Liberal Democrats automatically becomes a member of the federal party, the relevant state party and the relevant local party. Their membership fees are divided between these three levels in the way determined by the federal conference and the relevant state conference.

Party headquarters

The Liberal Democrats' federal party headquarters is based in Cowley Street in London. In 1994, 24 full-time staff were employed there. The main tasks carried out by this staff are the organisation of campaigns and elections, the management of the national membership list and national finances, and the organisation of federal conferences. Because of the party's federal structure, party headquarters is not the focal point of the party in the way in which the party headquarters of the Labour and Conservative parties are the focal points. Each state party has its own headquarters and employs its own administrative staff. If ordinary members have a query, they approach their regional party headquarters (in England) and their state party headquarters (in Scotland and Wales) in the first instance.

Advantages and disadvantages of the federal system

The Liberal Democrats' federal structure means that

considerable autonomy is given to the party in the English regions, Scotland and Wales. This reflects the Liberal Democrat emphasis on community politics. The party argues that flexibility is needed to respond to the needs of a particular locality and this is best achieved by giving the local party power to respond to local needs as it sees fit.

But giving such autonomy to local parties can also create difficulties. This can be demonstrated by reference to the actions of the Liberal Democrats in Tower Hamlets, East London. Tower Hamlets hit the headlines in 1993 when a British National party (BNP) candidate was elected to the local council. This shocked the major parties and highlighted the racial tension that existed in the area. Following this election, an internal Liberal Democrat inquiry revealed that the local party had issued an election leaflet in 1991 which encouraged racism. The inquiry's report suggested that the local Liberal Democrats had deliberately contributed to the growth of racist sentiments during the time when they had been the largest party on the local council. In addition to criticising the behaviour of local activists, the report blamed the federal nature of the party. Lack of central control, the report suggested, had resulted in inadequate supervision and discipline in the local party.

The federal conference

Twice a year (in March and September) delegates from every local party are elected on a system of one member, one vote to attend the federal conference (local parties with less than 30 members have to combine with neighbouring parties to obtain representation). The federal conference is the final decision making body of the party. Like the annual Labour party conference, the Liberal Democrat federal conference is sovereign.

The federal conference is responsible for making policy decisions at the federal level. In other words, it takes policy decisions which affect the country as a whole. For example, the federal conference would take decisions about foreign policy or about transport in the UK as a whole. It would not take decisions about transport in Scotland. That and other Scottish issues would be decided at the conferences organised by the Scottish conference. But since the English state party has delegated policy making powers to the federal party, the federal conference does make policy decisions which only affect England.

The federal conference is also responsible for electing members to the three federal committees (the executive, policy and conference committees).

The three federal committees

Each of the three federal committees contains, in addition to representatives elected by the federal conference, members of the parliamentary party, councillors and representatives from the Scottish and Welsh state parties. At least a third of each committee must be women and at least a third must be men.

The **federal executive** is chaired by the president of the party. The president is elected for a two year term by all members of the party on a one member, one vote basis. The executive committee has 14 elected members. In addition, the party leader, president, three vice presidents, two other MPs, one peer, two councillors and one representative from each state party have the right to vote (Lib Dems, 1994). The executive committee is responsible for overseeing and implementing the decisions made by the federal party. It has the right to initiate a ballot of all members on any issue it considers important.

The **policy committee** contains 29 members: the party leader, four MPs, one peer, the president, three councillors, two representatives from the Welsh and two from the Scottish state parties and 15 people elected by federal conference (Lib Dems, 1994). This committee is responsible for drawing up and developing policy proposals. Most of the policy proposals debated at conference are put forward by the policy committee.

The **conference committee** is responsible for organising the two annual conferences and for drawing up the agenda for the conferences. This committee contains 21 voting members: 12 people elected by the federal conference, two members elected by the federal executive, two elected by the federal policy committee, a representative from each state party, the party's chief whip and the party president (Lib Dems, 1994).

Policy making

It is the federal principle which determines Liberal Democrat policy making. Policy decisions which affect a particular locality are made locally, whilst those affecting the country as a whole are made by the federal institutions. The Liberal Democrat constitution explains that:

> 'The federal party shall determine the policy of the party in those areas which might reasonably be expected to fall within the remit of the federal institutions in the context of a federal United Kingdom.' (Lib Dems, 1994, p.16)

In a federal United Kingdom, there would probably be a federal Parliament, a Scottish Parliament, a Welsh Parliament and regional assemblies in England. Whilst the federal Parliament would make decisions about matters which affected the country as a whole, each of the state and regional assemblies would be responsible for making decisions about local issues. The Liberal Democrat policy making system reflects this division of responsibility.

The supreme policy making body is the federal conference. If conference accepts the motions proposed by the federal policy committee, local, regional and state parties, then they become party policy. But policy proposals concerning, for example, Scottish affairs would not be put forward to the federal conference. They would be proposed and debated at a conference organised by the Scottish state party and, if the proposals were passed, they would become party policy in Scotland.

Although the federal conference is supposedly the sovereign body and it must give its formal approval to policy, the party leadership retains a great deal of control over the formulation of policy. Most major policy proposals are initiated by the federal policy committee (see above) which is dominated by the party leadership. This committee sets up working groups to study subjects in depth and, after consultation, submits these papers to federal conference for approval. Conference can amend these papers, but if that happens the policy committee must review them once more before they return to conference. Although delegates at conference are able to propose motions on policy issues for debate, the policy committee has the power to insist that a final decision is postponed. Also, the policy committee, together with the parliamentary party, is responsible for drawing up the party's election manifestos. So, again, the system ensures that the party leadership retains control of the policy making process. In addition, the federal conference committee (see above) determines which motions are debated at conference. As with the policy committee, composition of this committee is such that the party leadership is able to keep a firm grip on its decisions.

Selecting the Liberal Democrat leader

The Liberal party was the first of the major parties in Britain to involve its ordinary members in the choice of the leader. A system of weighted votes was first adopted in 1976. This early attempt to involve the broad range of party members was a response to the increasing emphasis that the Liberal party placed on grassroots involvement at the local level. In 1981, the weighted votes system was replaced by a full one member, one vote system.

Unlike the Liberal party, the SDP had a leadership selection system which placed much more power in the hands of the leader and the parliamentary party. Although the leader was elected by the whole membership, a challenge could be mounted only if the leader was not also Prime Minister and if more than half the parliamentary party passed a motion calling for a contest within one month of a new parliamentary session.

The system adopted by the Liberal Democrats stipulates that a contest, using the single transferable vote system (see chapter 7, p.186) must take place two years after every general election. A leadership election can also be called either when the current leader resigns or is incapacitated, or when a majority of MPs or 75 local parties demand it. Every paid-up member is entitled to vote in the election on a one member, one vote basis. Candidates for the leadership must be MPs, they must be proposed and seconded by other MPs and they must be nominated by no less than 200 members in at least 20 different local parties.

Activity 8.10

Item A *The structure and organisation of the Liberal Democrats*

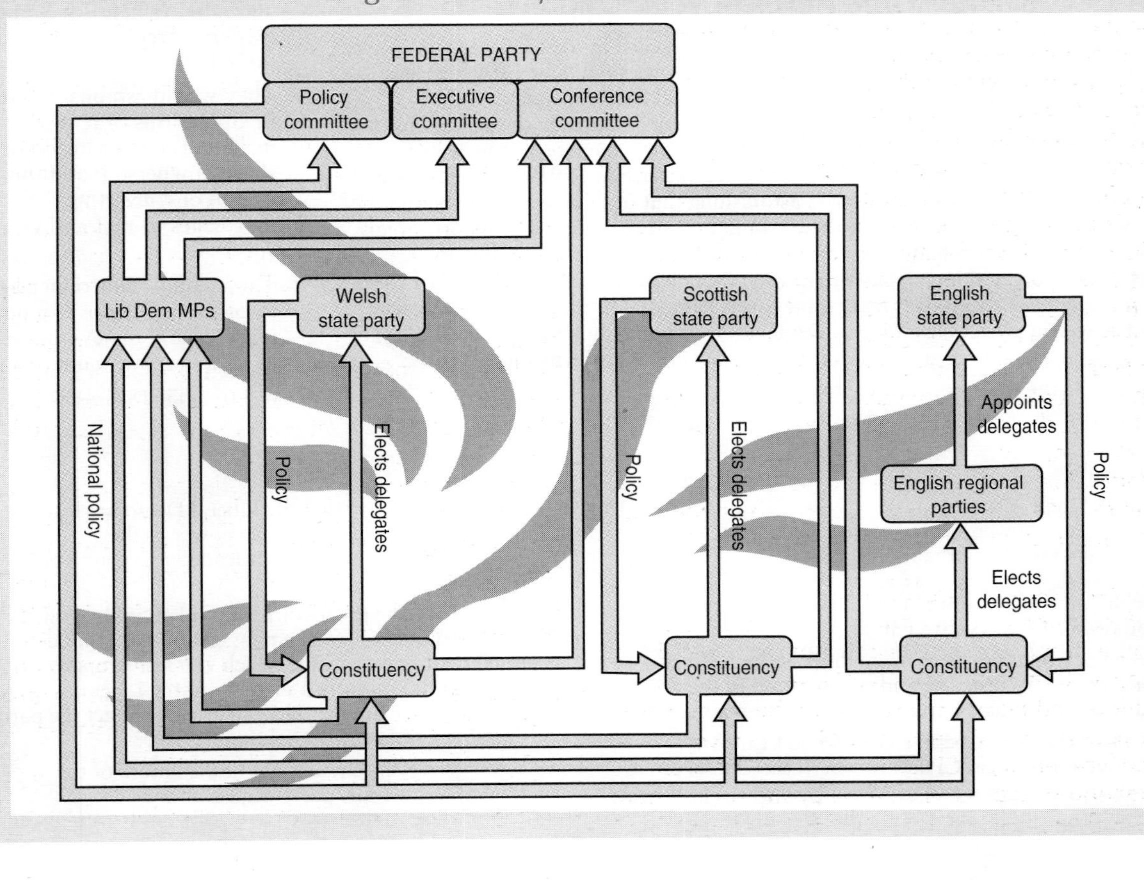

Item B *The Liberal Democrats' constitution*

The Liberal Democrats exist to build and safeguard a fair, free and open society in which they seek to balance the fundamental values of liberty, equality and community. They aim to disperse power and to foster diversity. They believe that the role of the state is to enable all citizens to contribute fully to their communities and to take part in decisions which affect their lives. They believe that people should be involved in running their communities. They are determined to strengthen the democratic process. They believe that sovereignty rests with the people and that authority in a democracy derives from the people. The people should, therefore, determine what form of government best suits their needs. They believe that as much power as possible should be exercised by the nations and regions of the United Kingdom. They also believe that decisions should be taken and services delivered at the most local level which is viable.

Adapted from Lib Dems, 1994.

Item C *The federal party conference*

This photo shows Paddy Ashdown, leader of the Liberal Democrats, addressing the federal conference in September 1994.

Item E *The inquiry into events in Tower Hamlets*

The Liberal Democrat internal inquiry into alleged racism in the local party in Tower Hamlets criticises the party leadership. The report states that: 'Since 1990, at least, there is ample evidence that the party at national level has been aware of the problems in Tower Hamlets. It is also clear that despite a number of suggestions, no effective action has been taken at any time to ensure that these problems were resolved.' The report claims that, following a hearing over a 1991 party leaflet which encouraged the growth of racism: 'It is astonishing that nothing was done within the local party or above to ensure that there would be no repetition.' The report reveals that many other leaflets had to be changed by the national leadership due to offensive wording and it concludes that, even though the three people expelled from the party were not themselves racists, they were prepared to play on people's racial prejudice to win power. The Liberal Democrats nationally hope that by mounting such an open and thorough inquiry, they will gain credit in the medium term.

Adapted from the *Guardian*, 18 December 1993.

Item D *Liberal Democrats' housing policy*

Liberal Democrats are committed to the provision of affordable homes for all citizens as a fundamental right, whether they rent or buy. If they were in government, the Liberal Democrats would take the following steps:

1. They would create a new 'partnership housing' sector financed by a combination of private investment and public spending to increase the availability of high quality, affordable rented housing.
2. They would create an independent Bank of England to ensure interest rate stability so that mortgage payers can plan ahead.
3. They would introduce a new and fairer benefit for home owners to replace mortgage tax relief.
4. They would establish more flexible forms of tenure including the expansion of shared ownership and the option of converting mortgages to rent and vice versa.
5. They would reintroduce loans to cover rent deposits paid in advance and review rent levels in temporary accommodation.

Adapted from Lib Dems, 1993.

Questions

1. Look at Item A.
   a) Where is power located within the Liberal Democrat party organisation?
   b) How does the organisation of the Liberal Democrats differ from that of (i) the Labour party and (ii) the Conservative party?
2. To what extent are the aims outlined in Item B reflected in the structure and organisation of the Liberal Democrats? Explain how they are connected.
3. a) How does the Liberal Democrat federal party conference (Item C) differ from (i) the Conservative party conference and (ii) the Labour party conference?
   b) Would you say that the Liberal Democrat leader has less, more or the same power as the Conservative and Labour leaders? Explain your answer.
4. a) Describe the process which resulted in the policies described in Item D becoming official party policies.
   b) Think of a local issue which you feel strongly about. If you were a member of the Liberal Democrats how would you attempt to get the party to adopt a policy proposal on this issue?
5. What does Item E tell us about the nature of the Liberal Democrats' party organisation?

5 The minor parties

Key Issues

1. What is the significance of the minor parties?
2. What are the aims of the minor parties?
3. How much success have they had?
4. What are the main characteristics of the minor parties?

The significance of the minor parties

Throughout the 20th century new parties have been set up in the hope that they would attract sufficient support to break the mould of British politics. But, with the exception of the Labour party which was itself a minor party in the early years of the 20th century, no party has managed to achieve nationwide success. Since 1918, British politics has been dominated by the three main parties and there is little sign that this will change, certainly whilst the current electoral system survives.

But, although the three main parties dominate the political arena, that does not mean that the minor parties do not have any significance. In Wales and Scotland, for example, the nationalist parties are an important force and they regularly win seats in Parliament. Despite the small number of MPs from these parties, they can still play a crucial role in certain circumstances. In the October 1974 general election, for example, Labour won an overall majority of three whilst 11 Scottish National party (SNP) MPs and three Plaid Cymru (Welsh nationalist) MPs were elected. Once the Labour government's overall majority of three disappeared as a result of by-election losses, it was forced to do a deal with the nationalist parties. In return for their support in Parliament, the government promised to hold referendums on devolution in Scotland and Wales (see chapter 4, p. section 3.2). This shows that, even within the existing electoral system, it is possible for minor parties to exert influence and to play an important political role.

Whilst parliamentary success is unusual for the minor parties, they have found it easier to make an impact in local politics. The number of Green councillors has grown over the last decade and even the Monster Raving Loony party has won seats on local councils. It should be noted that success, even at local level, has been far harder to achieve for minor parties whose ideology is located on the extreme right or the extreme left than it has been for the nationalist parties or Greens. The nationalists and Greens are generally perceived as being within the mainstream, whilst the parties on the extreme left and right are generally perceived as being a threat to the system.

On the few occasions when groups on the extreme right or left have achieved electoral success (winning a substantial percentage of the vote may be regarded as an electoral success, even if the candidate is not elected), this has been greeted with considerable popular concern. Again, this suggests that minor parties do have a significance, even if they are unable to win seats in elections. Their role is, perhaps, to be barometers of public opinion. When people are generally content with the existing party system the minor parties do badly. A significant vote for a minor party can suggest that people are discontented with the existing party system. The ebb and flow of support for minor parties provides a judgement on the party system and provides a legitimate avenue for the expression of views beyond the mainstream.

The Scottish National party (SNP)

The SNP was founded in 1934 when two small nationalist parties merged. Its aim is the creation of an independent Scotland. At present, there are two distinct viewpoints within the SNP. Whilst the right wing (which has generally maintained control of the party) stresses traditional values and a variety of nostalgic nationalism, the left wing has pressed the case for a socialist Scotland as an independent country within the EU.

The SNP won its first seat in Parliament in a by-election in Motherwell in April 1945, but lost the seat in the following general election. It was not until a by-election held in 1967 that the SNP won another seat. But again, it lost the seat in the next general election in 1970. The 1970 general election was, however, the first general election in which the SNP managed to win a seat. This was a turning point in the party's fortunes. It has won seats in every general election since then.

The SNP's best general election result came in October 1974 when it won 30.4% of the vote in Scotland and 11 seats. Although it was unable to sustain this level of support (especially in the years following the referendum in 1979), the SNP has established itself as the third party in Scotland (and in many Scottish constituencies in the 1990s it has become the main challenger to the Labour party). Voters who are disaffected with the Conservatives or Labour tend to register their protest with the SNP. The SNP, therefore, plays a role similar to that played by the Liberal Democrats in England. This was graphically illustrated in the by-election in the constituency of Monklands East which was held on 30 June 1994 following the death of Labour's leader, John Smith. Whilst Labour won a majority of 15,712 in the 1992 general election, this majority was cut to just 1,640 in the by-election. The SNP vote went up from 6,554 to 15,320, a gain of 27%. This is just the sort of by-election result achieved by the Liberal Democrats in England.

Plaid Cymru

Plaid Cymru was founded in 1925. The term Plaid Cymru means 'free Wales'. Its aim is an independent Wales. Like the SNP, Plaid Cymru supports the setting up of an elective assembly as the first step towards independence. But Plaid Cymru has always laid more stress on cultural and linguistic identity than the SNP (partly because there are many more Welsh speakers than Gaelic speakers). Plaid Cymru aims for a completely bilingual Wales and it works hard at increasing the use of Welsh in schools, broadcasting and in public administration. The problem that Plaid Cymru faces with insisting on bilingualism is that it does tend to alienate people living in Wales who do not speak Welsh. Most party members are Welsh speaking and most of the party's support comes from areas where Welsh is the first language.

Plaid Cymru won its first seat in a by-election in 1966. It lost this seat in the subsequent general election. Its best performance in terms of size of vote then came in the 1970 general election when it won 11.5% of the vote in Wales (175,016 votes). But it did not win any seats in that election. Like the SNP, Plaid Cymru did well in October 1974. It won 10.8% of the vote and three seats. But, the disappointing referendum result in 1979 led to a decline in votes which continued until the 1992 general election. Despite this, Plaid Cymru managed to hold onto two seats in the 1979 and 1983 general elections. It won three seats in 1987 and four in 1992.

The Green party

The Green party's origins lie in the protest movements of the 1960s and the growing environmental concerns of the 1970s and 1980s. The birth of the party can be traced back to 1973 when an environmental pressure group was formed, named 'People'. As this group began to explore the connections between environmental concerns and began to formulate policies to deal with them, it transformed itself into the Ecology party. It changed its name to the Green party in 1985. The Green party is committed to the broad aims of other European Green parties, namely the decentralisation of political power and the placing of environmental issues at the top of the political agenda.

Although the Greens have not enjoyed any electoral success in parliamentary elections, they have enjoyed some success in local elections. By 1994, the Green party had won over 100 council seats (Hutchings, 1994). The party's greatest electoral success, however, came in 1989 when it won 15% of the vote in the European election. Although it did not win any seats, Greens polled more of the vote nationally than the Liberal Democrats. Since 1989, support for the Greens has dropped rapidly, not least because of the internal divisions which have dogged the party (see Carter, 1995).

Fascist groups

Fascist politics emerged in Britain, as in most other West European countries, in the years between the two world wars. After sitting as a Conservative MP between 1918 and 1922 and as a Labour MP between 1926 and 1931, Oswald Mosley opted out of mainstream politics and set up the British Union of Fascists (BUF) in 1932. At its peak in 1934, the BUF had around 35,000 members. It contested elections but never won a seat. Like other Fascist groups, the BUF was racist, militaristic and violently nationalistic. Modern Fascist groups trace their ancestry back to Mosely's group through a complex web of splits and schisms.

Perhaps the most influential postwar Fascist group is the National Front (NF), founded in 1967. In the mid-1970s the NF had a membership of around 20,000. Although the NF contests elections, it also maintains links with neo-Nazi paramilitary groups both at home and abroad. The NF has never won a seat, but it has polled well in some constituencies. In the London boroughs of Hackney, Newham and Tower Hamlets, for example, it gained 10% of the vote in 1977. Its support dwindled in the late 1970s and had fallen to around 6,000 by 1980. It has been argued that support for the NF fell because Margaret Thatcher's government promoted policies which attracted the support of many who had shown an interest in the far right (Ball, 1987).

In the 1980s, the NF split and from this split the British National Party (BNP) emerged. The BNP hit the headlines in September 1993 when a BNP candidate won a local seat in a ward by-election in Tower Hamlets, East London. Although this seat was subsequently won back by Labour in the local elections of May 1994, the support given to the BNP in this part of London was a source of great concern to many people.

Marxist groups

Like the Fascist groups, Marxist groups have, on the whole, been on the periphery of British politics, though there have been periods when their influence has appeared to be growing. In the 1945 general election, for example, the Communist party of Great Britain (CPGB), founded in 1920, won two seats and polled over 100,000 votes. Since 1950, however, no Communist MP has been elected and by 1964 the CPGB won just 0.8% of the vote in the constituencies it contested. Although the CPGB remained an important lobbying group (especially within the trade union movement), it split in the 1980s between those who followed the line laid down by the Communist government in the USSR and the 'Eurocommunists' (who aimed to promote a new, independent and progressive form of Marxism). Following the collapse of Communism in Eastern Europe, the CPGB collapsed and dispersed.

In the 1980s, the Trotskyist left received more publicity than the CPGB. Perhaps the most publicised Trotskyist group is Militant Tendency. The activities of Militant Tendency were the subject of considerable media interest in the mid-1980s because it was revealed that members of Militant had joined the Labour party in the hope of influencing Labour party policy. This led Neil Kinnock to conduct a purge of Militant members from the Labour party with the result that there was a wave of expulsions, including several MPs.

Other Trotskyist groups include the Socialist Workers party (SWP) which was prominent in the anti-Nazi League of the 1970s (set up to combat the NF). The SWP rejects the parliamentary system, though it does sometimes put up candidates for election. Members of the SWP are expert at ensuring that their flags and posters are prominent at any demonstration or protest organised for a left wing cause.

Other minor parties

The above survey of minor parties is by no means exhaustive. It does not include, for example, the Monster Raving Loony party or the Natural Law party, both of which put up candidates around the country in national and local elections. Those standing for the Monster Raving Loony party are literally joke candidates. Like those who stand for the Natural Law party, they use elections to promote their ideas rather than to mount a serious challenge against the main parties. The Natural Law party is a semi-religious party which advocates a variety of transcendental policies to right the wrongs of the world.

Political parties in Northern Ireland

Between 1972, when direct rule from Britain was imposed on Northern Ireland, and 1992, none of the three main political parties fielded any candidates in Northern Ireland. In the 1992 general election, however, the Conservative party did put up candidates in Northern Ireland, but none was elected. Since 1972, therefore, the people of Northern Ireland have elected MPs from what, in terms of the UK as a whole, are minor parties. In the 1992 general election, the 17 MPs from Northern Ireland were divided as follows: 9 MPs from the Official Unionist party; 4 MPs from the Social Democratic and Labour party (SDLP); 3 MPs from the Democratic Unionist party; and one MP from the Ulster Popular Unionist party. In addition, Sinn Fein and the Alliance put up candidates, but none was elected. Unlike in the rest of the UK, almost all of the political parties in Northern Ireland are clearly divided between those supported by the Protestant community and those supported by Catholics.

The two main Protestant parties in Northern Ireland are the Official Unionist party (OUP) and the Democratic Unionist party (DUP). Both oppose power sharing with the Catholic community. The aim of both parties is to maintain the constitutional link with Britain on the grounds that it is the union which has allowed continued Protestant domination in Northern Ireland. The OUP's formal name is the Ulster Unionist party. It was this party which ruled Northern Ireland from the time when it was set up as a province in 1922 until direct rule was imposed in 1972 (see chapter 4, section 3.3). Before 1972, the Ulster Unionists were closely associated with the Conservative party, but they broke with them over direct rule. Despite this, in Parliament the Ulster Unionist MPs tend to vote with the Conservatives on most issues. The same is true of the Democratic Unionist Party (DUP). The DUP is an offshoot of the OUP, founded in 1971 by Ian Paisley. The DUP takes a more extreme position than the OUP on Northern Irish affairs. It refuses any concessions to the Catholic population of Northern Ireland.

The importance of the OUP and DUP to a Conservative government with a small majority was demonstrated during the debates over the Maastricht Treaty in 1993. By voting with the government, the OUP and DUP (12 MPs in all) ensured that the government had a majority. In return, John Major invited the leaders of the two parties to Downing Street and agreed to set up a special parliamentary select committee on Northern Ireland.

The main nationalist party in Northern Ireland is the Social Democratic and Labour party (SDLP), founded in 1970. Although the SDLP was not set up to represent just Catholics, the vast majority of its support comes from the Catholic community. The SDLP supports a united Ireland, but only if this is achieved by agreement. The party supports power sharing between Catholics and Protestants. In the 1980s, the SDLP's grip on the Catholic vote was challenged by Sinn Fein. Sinn Fein is the Republican party whose military wing is the IRA. Before the early 1980s, Sinn Fein boycotted elections, but the popular support for the hunger strikers (see chapter 18, section 2.2) encouraged them to stand for election. In the 1983 general election, Gerry Adams won Belfast West for Sinn Fein and he held the seat until 1992. Throughout this period he refused to take his seat in Parliament. Sinn Fein's aim is a united Ireland. It has close links with the IRA, acting as the IRA's public mouthpiece. Since the IRA declared a ceasefire in August 1994, the Sinn Fein leadership (with Gerry Adams as Sinn Fein President) has worked towards peace talks with the British and Irish governments.

Whilst almost all political parties in Northern Ireland appeal to either Protestants or Catholics, the Alliance party, founded in 1970, is an exception. This party manages to gain around 10% of the vote mainly from middle class people in both communities. The party supports a devolved Northern Irish government which would share power between Protestants and Catholics and govern with the Republic of Ireland as an equal partner.

Activity 8.11

Item A General election result 1992 - the minor parties

Party	Total votes	Candidates	MPs	%**
SNP	629,564	72	3	1.9
PLAID CYMRU	156,796	28	4	0.5
GREEN	170,047	253	0	0.5
LIBERAL*	64,744	73	0	0.2
NATURAL LAW	62,888	309	0	0.2
OTHERS	138,462	220	0	0.4

* The Liberal party is a splinter group formed when the Liberal/SDP Alliance merged in 1988.

** This column shows the percentage of the total number of votes cast in the UK.

Item B The SNP and Plaid Cymru's performance in general elections, 1945-92

(i) The SNP's electoral record

Election	Candidates	MPs	Total votes	% *
1945	8	0	30,595	1.2
1950	3	0	9,708	0.4
1951	2	0	7,299	0.3
1955	2	0	12,112	0.5
1959	5	0	21,738	0.8
1964	15	0	64,044	2.4
1966	23	0	128,474	5.0
1970	65	1	306,802	11.4
1974 (Feb)	70	7	633,180	21.9
1974 (Oct)	71	11	839,617	30.4
1979	71	2	504,259	17.3
1983	72	2	331,975	11.8
1987	71	3	416,473	14.0
1992	72	3	629,564	21.5

* This column shows the number of votes won by the SNP as a percentage of the total votes cast in Scotland.

(ii) Plaid Cymru's electoral record

Election	Candidates	MPs	Total votes	%*
1945	7	0	16,017	1.2
1950	7	0	17,580	1.2
1951	4	0	10,920	0.7
1955	11	0	45,119	3.1
1959	20	0	77,571	5.2
1964	23	0	69,507	4.8
1966	20	0	61,071	4.3
1970	36	0	175,016	11.5
1974 (Feb)	36	2	171,374	10.7
1974 (Oct)	36	3	166,321	10.8
1979	36	2	132,544	8.1
1983	38	2	125,309	7.8
1987	38	3	123,599	7.3
1992	38	4	156,796	11.1

* This column shows the number of votes won by Plaid Cymru as a percentage of the total votes cast in Wales.

Item C Interview with the Green party's press office

In the European election of 1989, the Green party polled 15% of the vote. This made it the third biggest party for a while. But, that only exacerbated the party's problems. In an interview, a press officer explained: 'We used to draw up strategies for the day every morning, but then the phone started ringing and we never got to do any of it. Our members are always complaining we are not in the news any more, but quite honestly if we are going to react to events as Britain's third largest party, we've got to have some money.' Greater freedom in Communist countries has brought East European diplomats beating a path down to Balham to find out how Europe's most successful Green party is organised. But, often, they have left bewildered. How on earth, they keep asking, can the party survive on a full-time staff of four and a phone? 'I feel so awful giving them coffee in this chipped mug,' says a volunteer helping out in the office.

Adapted from the *Guardian*, 14 February 1990.

Item D *Raving loonies in 1992*

Item E *Oswald Mosely and the BUF*

This photograph shows Oswald Mosley inspecting BUF volunteers.

Questions

1. a) Why is it difficult for minor parties to win support in elections? Use Items A-E in your answer.
   b) Why do you think people vote for the minor parties?
2. 'The minor parties face problems which the major parties do not have to face.' Explain this statement using Items A-C.
3. What do Items D and E tell us about the political climate at the time when they were produced? Would you say that they provide a representative view of Britain at that time? Give reasons for your answer.
4. 'The Liberal Democrats should be added to the list of minor parties.' Give arguments for and against this view.

6 The party system

Key Issues

1. How are party systems classified?
2. What are the advantages and disadvantages of the two party system?
3. Does Britain have a two party system?
4. Has the party system in Britain changed since 1945?

The nature of party systems

Most political scientists would accept that party systems can be divided into four categories: the single party system; the dominant party system; the two party system; and the multi-party system (see, for example, Ball, 1987).

In a **single party system,** only one party puts up candidates for election. Other parties are banned. The single party system is often, therefore, described as undemocratic and authoritarian. Nazi Germany and the Soviet Union under Communism are two examples of the single party system.

The **dominant party system** is a system where many parties may exist and fight elections, but only one party tends to win power - either on its own or as the dominant member of a coalition. Political scientists have often cited Japan as the classic example of the dominant party system. Japan's Liberal Democratic party (LDP) remained in government from its foundation in 1955 until August 1993.

In a **two party system,** two parties compete for power on an equal or near equal basis. Other parties may stand against the two dominant parties, but, in a two party system, these other parties win few seats and exercise little power. It has often been argued that Britain has a two party system, though some political scientists deny that this is the case.

A **multi-party system** is one in which more than two parties compete on an equal or near equal basis. In such a system, power may alternate between the various parties or it may be shared in coalitions. Political scientists often used to cite Italy as the classic example of the multi-party system because proportional representation in Italy continually produced multi-party coalition governments. In April 1993, however, a large majority of Italians voted to change their electoral system to a first past the post system.

Britain as a two party system

The idea that Britain has a two party system was given great currency by Robert McKenzie's 1955 study of British political parties (McKenzie, 1955). In this study, McKenzie spent 595 out of the 597 pages discussing the Conservative and Labour parties. By dismissing the Liberal party and the minor parties in two pages, McKenzie suggested that they were all but irrelevant to the British party system. Since 1955, political scientists have periodically returned to Mckenzie's ideas and tested them in light of what happened later (see, for example, Kelly, 1994).

In the two party system described by McKenzie and his followers, the two main parties compete in elections for an absolute majority of seats. Whilst one party forms the government, the role of the other is to form an opposition which exposes government policy to scrutiny and develops its own policies. The opposition party works on the assumption that it will take over the reins of government at the next election and, more often than not, that is what happens.

Advantages of the two party system

According to this model, the two party system is integral to the success of Britain as a democracy. It is the two party system which ensures that the democratic process works smoothly. It does this in three ways. First, by choosing one party to govern and then another, the electorate exercises choice and choice is a vital element of democracy. Second, since the vast majority of the electorate votes for the two main parties and it is in the interest of neither of the main parties to upset a system which favours them, the system ensures that legitimacy is maintained and political conflict is kept within limits (see chapter 18, section 2.1 for a definition of legitimacy). And third, the need to win an overall majority ensures that both parties shape their policies to appeal to the needs of the majority.

Another way of looking at this is to consider what would happen if the system broke down. Suppose that a single party found itself being elected time after time. Then, the ruling party would have few checks on its power since a government with an overall majority can ensure that legislation is passed even if the opposition parties are vehemently opposed to it. The party in opposition would have no opportunity to put its programme into operation or to change the direction in which the government was going. In short, there would be a good case for arguing that the country's democratic process was in danger of decay.

A number of other advantages in a two party system have been identified (see, for example, Padfield, 1981). First, the two party system presents voters with a clear choice between two rivals. Two different programmes are presented during the election campaign and it is up to the voters to choose between them. Second, the two party system produces stable and strong government. Since the party in government normally has an overall majority in Parliament, it is able to implement the pledges made during the election campaign and the electorate can check the actions of the government against its election pledges. This may not be possible in a system which allows a coalition government to be formed after an election. Third, the seating arrangements in the House of Commons and the debates for and against a motion encourage a two party system. British politics has an adversarial nature (the opposition is expected to criticise and make arguments against the government and vice versa). This is facilitated by the two party system. Fourth, if the government fails or loses its way there is always a ready-made government waiting in the wings. And fifth, supporters of the two party system would argue that the system has been proven to work and, therefore, it should not be changed.

Disadvantages of the two party system

Critics of the two party system have argued that it suffers from a number of disadvantages (see, for example, Ball, 1987). First, critics question whether adversarial politics are constructive and desirable. In a two party system it is the job of the opposition party to criticise the government on all counts. But this results in an unnecessary and harmful exaggeration of the differences between the two parties. The opposition opposes virtually all government policies, regardless of their merits. That makes it difficult for the public to judge whether policies are being opposed because they are genuinely harmful or simply because that is what politicians do. In addition, the adversarial nature of politics leads to a tendency for extremists to gain control of the two main parties. The system encourages polarisation rather than consensus. Second, the two main parties are not really representative of the majority of the electorate (most governments this century have won less than 50% of the votes) and, therefore, the party in power does not really have a mandate to govern. Third, a two party system is wasteful because it produces huge swings in government policy. Since the two parties alternate in power and since they are diametrically opposed on many issues, there is a tendency for a new government to repeal many of the decisions made by the previous government. And fourth, the two party system undermines the importance of the House of Commons. The government can rely on its overall majority to pass legislation, regardless of criticisms made by the opposition. Debates in the Commons rarely change anything.

Does Britain have a two party system?

Having surveyed the historical development of British political parties between 1689 and 1989, Ingle concludes:

> 'Our historical survey indicates that the British political system has been dominated on and off, over the past 300 years, by two parties, but it also shows the nature of this domination and of the parties themselves to have been subject to constant and considerable change. The pattern of party politics, moreover, has changed just as dramatically, with long spells of dominance by one party and with parties constantly breaking up and regrouping.' (Ingle, 1992, p.3)

This passage shows how important a historical perspective is in considering whether or not Britain has a two party system. If someone is living through a period in which two parties have been alternating in power for the previous 30 years, then it appears that Britain has a two party system. Conversely if someone has lived through a long period of government by a single party, it appears that a dominant party system has replaced the old two party system. Similarly, if someone chooses to examine the party system in Britain between 1945 and 1979, that will probably lead them to different conclusions from someone who looks at trends over the last 150 years.

At the time when McKenzie was writing (1955), it did indeed seem that a two party system had established itself after the Second World War. Labour governed from 1945 to 1951 and then the Conservatives took over. And for a while after 1955 it seemed that McKenzie's analysis was faultless. Between 1945 and 1979 - a period of 34 years - both Labour and the Conservatives held power for exactly the same number of years.

But, even this period of seeming two party rule is open to reinterpretation. Between 1951 and 1964, Labour lost three general elections in a row. For those who, by 1964, had lived through 13 years of Conservative rule, it probably did not seem much like a two party system. And if a wider perspective is taken, the idea that the two party system is the norm loses some of its credence. According to Heywood:

> 'Taking a longer perspective, it could be argued that Britain has had a dominant party system through much of the 20th century and certainly since the old Liberal-Conservative two party system collapsed after the First World War. The Conservatives have been in government, either alone or as the dominant member of a coalition, for 51 of the last 70 years. Two party politics undoubtedly took place during this period, but was largely confined to the 1964-79 period when Labour won four out of five general elections. The important point is that Labour has only twice, in 1945 and 1966, recorded decisive election victories and at no time has the party managed to serve two consecutive full terms in office.' (Heywood, 1993, pp.86-87)

If this is the case, then the four Conservative election victories between 1979 and 1992 merely confirm the trend (that the Conservative party is the single dominant party) rather than indicate a turning point (from a two party to a dominant party system).

A further point needs to be examined - namely that Britain is or is becoming a multi-party system. Since the early 1970s, the Liberals (now, the Liberal Democrats) have won a considerable number of votes, if only a small number of seats. Between 1945 and 1974, the combined share of the vote for the two main parties never fell below 80%. But, between 1970 and 1992, the two main parties' share of the vote declined markedly. In 1983, the Alliance scored the most votes won by a third party since the 1920s. Although the SDP failed to 'break the mould' of British politics by forming a government, the Liberal Democrats have become an important force in British politics. So, how do they fit in the British party system?

One way of answering this question is to consider how representative the British party system is (or is not). It is significant to note that only in the elections of 1931 and 1935 have the parties which took over the reins of government scored more than 50% of the vote. And, in both 1931 and 1935, a National government (a coalition government formed in response to a national emergency) was elected rather than a single party. If Britain had a different electoral system which allowed the size of a party's vote to be reflected in the number of seats it won, then, after the 1992 general election, the Liberal Democrats would probably have become partners in a governing coalition. Considerations such as these led Dearlove & Saunders to suggest:

> 'Britain can be characterised as a two party system (in the Commons); as a multi-party system (in the country); and as a dominant party system (in the corridors of power) because the electoral system and multi-party politics have together enabled the Conservatives to monopolise the control of the state for more than a decade in a way that has mocked the close competition in the country at large.' (Dearlove & Saunders, 1991, p.55)

Activity 8.12

Item A *The House of Commons*

Item B *Labour's electoral mountain*

The simple fact is that the Conservative party has held power alone since 1979. Following its fourth election victory in a row in 1992, it can expect to stay in power at least until 1996. Moreover, there are good reasons to believe that Conservative dominance may be extended. In the 1992 general election, support for the Labour party remained below the level that the party achieved in 1979. In each of the elections in 1987 and 1992 Labour improved by 3.5%. But even if it gained another 3.5% in 1996, this would not necessarily be enough to win an overall majority. In the 1992 general election, the Conservatives won by 7%. To overcome this lead, Labour needs the biggest swing since 1945. In addition, Labour's task will be made harder by the boundary changes which will have come into place by 1996. Apart from all this, social and demographic trends point to further Conservative success. Labour has been damaged by the shrinking of the manual working class, the decline of public sector employees and the shift of the population from urban to rural areas. All the evidence suggests that these trends are set to continue.

Adapted from Heywood, 1993.

Item C *General election results 1945-92*

General Election	Seats			Prime Minister
	Lab.	Con.	Lib.	
1945	393	210	12	C. Attlee (Lab)
1950	315	298	9	C. Attlee (Lab)
1951	295	321	6	W. Churchill (Con)
1955	277	345	6	A. Eden (Con) **1**
1959	258	365	6	H. Macmillan (Con)
1964	317	304	9	H. Wilson (Lab)
1966	364	253	12	H. Wilson (Lab)
1970	288	330	6	E. Heath (Con)
1974 (Feb)	301	297	14	H. Wilson (Lab)
1974 (Oct)	319	277	13	H. Wilson (Lab) **2**
1979	269	339	11	M. Thatcher (Con)
1983	209	397	23	M. Thatcher (Con)
1987	229	376	22	M. Thatcher (Con) **3**
1992	271	336	20	J. Major (Con)

1. Eden resigned Jan. 1957 and replaced by Macmillan
2. Wilson resigned Mar. 1976 and replaced by Callaghan
3. Thatcher resigned Nov. 1990 and replaced by Major

Adapted from Craig, 1989 and the *Guardian*, 11 April 1992.

Item D *A dominant party?*

After the general election in 1992, many commentators confidently proclaimed the arrival of the dominant party system. Anthony King, for example, wrote: 'Britain no longer has two major parties. It has one major party, the Conservatives, one minor party, Labour, and one peripheral party, the Liberal Democrats.' But within six months of the election, the Conservatives' grip on power seemed highly fragile and Conservative party internal divisions seemed very serious. The *Financial Times* reported just before the Maastricht vote: 'It is now clear that what was elected on 9 April 1992 was not a Conservative government with a majority of 21, but a hung Parliament in which the parties that most loathe one another, the Thatcherites and the Majorites, stand beneath the Tory flag.' The government's survival by three votes in the Commons debate over Maastricht, the threatened backbench rebellion over pit closures and the reversal of its economic strategy by withdrawing from the ERM all point to a much more conditional Conservative dominance than was previously expected to be the case.

Adapted from Dunleavy, 1993.

Item E *A two party system?*

Questions

1. a) Give arguments for and against the view that Britain has a two party system.
   b) Why is it important to know whether Britain has a two party system or some other system?
2. Use Items A and E to support the case that Britain has a two party system.
3. a) 'By 1993 the two party system had been replaced by a dominant party system.' Explain this statement using Items B-D.
   b) Do you agree with the statement? Give reasons for your answer.
4. What conclusions can be drawn about the British party system using Item C?

References

Adelman (1981) Adelman, P., *The Decline of the Liberal Party 1910-1931*, Longman, 1981.

Ball (1987) Ball, A., *British Political Parties*, Macmillan, 1987.

Barber (1991) Barber, J., 'Finding the leader', *Politics Review*, Vol.1, No.2, November 1991.

Benyon (1991) Benyon, J., 'The fall of a Prime Minister', *Social Studies Review*, Vol.6, No.3, January 1991.

Blake (1985) Blake, R., *The Conservative Party from Peel to Thatcher*, Fontana, 1985.

Carter (1995) Carter, N., 'The environment' in *Lancaster (1995)*.

CCO (1994) Conservative Central Office, *Welcome to the Conservative Party* (a leaflet), Conservative Central Office, 1994.

Craig (1989) Craig, FWS (ed.), *British Electoral Facts*, Dartmouth, 1989.

CRD (1994) Conservative Research Department, 'Left Stranded. The Labour party today', *Politics Today*, 28 February 1992.

Crewe (1993) Crewe, I., 'The changing basis of party choice', *Politics Review*, Vol.3, No.2, February 1993.

Dangerfield (1935) Dangerfield, G., *The Strange Death of Liberal England*, Constable, 1935.

Dearlove & Saunders (1991) Dearlove, J. & Saunders, P., *Introduction to British Politics*, Polity Press, 1991.

Dunleavy (1993) Dunleavy, P., 'The political parties' in *Dunleavy et al. (1993)*.

Dunleavy et al.. (1993) Dunleavy P., Gamble A., Holliday I. & Peele G. (eds), *Developments in British Politics 4*, Macmillan, 1993.

Garner & Kelly (1993) Garner, R. & Kelly, R., *British Political Parties Today*, Manchester University Press, 1993.

Heywood (1993) Heywood, A., 'The dominant party system', *Talking Politics*, Vol.5, No.2, winter 1993.

Hutchings (1994) Hutchings, V., 'Support Your Village Green', *New Statesman and Society*, 11 March 1994.

Ingle (1992) Ingle, S., 'The Glorious Revolution and the party system', *Politics Review*, Vol.1, No.3, February 1992.

Ingle (1993) Ingle, S., 'Political parties in the nineties', *Talking Politics*, Vol.6, No.1, autumn 1993.

Kelly (1989) Kelly, R., *Conservative Party Conferences*, Manchester University Press, 1989.

Kelly (1991) Kelly, R., 'British political parties: developments in the 1980s and prospects for the 1990s' in *Wale (1991)*.

Kelly (1992) Kelly, R., 'Power in the Conservative party', *Politics Review*, Vol.1, No.4, April 1992.

Kelly (1994) Kelly, R., 'British political parties: organisation, leadership and democracy' in *Wale (1994)*.

Kingdom (1991) Kingdom, J., *Government and Politics in Britain*, Polity Press, 1991.

Labour Party (1993) *Labour Party Rule Book 1993-4*, Labour Party, 1993.

Lancaster (1995) Lancaster, S. (ed.), *Developments in Politics*, Vol. 6, Causeway Press, 1995.

Lib Dems (1993) Liberal Democrat Policy Unit, *Liberal Democrat Policy Briefing*, August 1993.

Lib Dems (1994) *Constitution of the Liberal Democrats*, Liberal Democrat Publications, 1994.

McKenzie (1955) McKenzie, R.T., *British Political Parties*, Heinemann, 1955.

Padfield (1981) Padfield, C.F., *British Constitution Made Simple*, Heinemann, 1981.

Pelling (1991) Pelling, H., *A Short History of the Labour Party*, Macmillan, 1991.

Pinto-Duschinsky (1990) Pinto-Duschinsky, M., 'The funding of political parties since 1945' in *Seldon (1990)*.

Seldon (1990) Seldon, A. (ed.), *UK Political Parties Since 1945*, Philip Allan, 1990.

Taylor (1965) Taylor, A.J.P., *English History 1914-45*, Penguin, 1965.

Wale (1991) Wale, W. (ed.), *Developments in Politics*, Vol.2, Causeway Press, 1991.

Wale (1994) Wale, W. (ed.), *Developments in Politics*, Vol.5, Causeway Press, 1994.

Whiteley et al. (1994) Whiteley, P., Seyd, P. & Richardson, J., *True Blues: the Politics of Conservative Party Membership*, Oxford University Press, 1994.

Wood & Wood (1992) Wood, A.H. & Wood, R., *The Times Guide to the House of Commons April 1992*, HarperCollins, 1992.

9 Voting behaviour

Introduction

On the face of it, any attempt to explain voting behaviour is an impossible task. The system for electing politicians in Britain involves a secret ballot. Voting is a very individual act which takes place in the privacy of the voting booth. Voters have free choice. There is no legal obligation to vote and no compulsion to vote for one candidate rather than another.

Although voting is an individual act, it does not take place in isolation. Voters are constrained and influenced by a whole host of factors. Some of the constraints are obvious. If the voter's name is omitted from the electoral register, for example, then that voter is unable to cast a vote. Similarly, illness may prevent a visit to the polls or a voter's favoured party may not put up a candidate in that constituency. Other limitations and influences on voters may be more complex, but they are equally potent. The role of the television and the press, the economic performance of the government, the policies and promises of the parties competing for power, the social origins and circumstances of the voter, the voter's family and friends - all these factors and more may help to predefine the context in which the voter carries out the seemingly solitary act of voting.

It is the task of political scientists to discover patterns and trends in political behaviour. As a result, various theories or models have been devised to make sense of voting behaviour. This chapter looks at a number of these models. Each model offers a different explanation of voting behaviour. But, although each model examines voting behaviour from a different perspective, not all the models are necessarily competing with each other.

Chapter summary

Part 1 looks at the **social structures model**. To what extent is voting determined by **occupational class** and other social factors?

Part 2 examines the **party identification model** . How important is **party loyalty** in explaining voting behaviour?

Part 3 focuses on the **rational choice model** . Do people make **rational decisions** rather than **emotional decisions** when they vote? If so, what determines which candidate or party they choose?

Part 4 investigates the **dominant ideology model** . How do powerful groups attempt to set the political agenda via the media? What impact do **messages in the media** have on voting behaviour? What is the role and importance of **opinion polls**?

Part 5 analyses the **voting context model**. How do **perceptions** about the purpose of an election and the **particular context** in which voting takes place affect voting behaviour?

Part 6 uses a **general model of voting** to suggest ways in which the various models outlined earlier in the chapter are connected.

1 The social structures model

Key Issues

1. What connection is there between voting behaviour and social groups?
2. To what extent is class a factor in voting behaviour?
3. Do studies of voting behaviour reveal variations according to religion, age, sex, ethnicity and religion?

1.1 Class and class dealignment

One explanation for voting behaviour is that most people vote according to their objective class interests. Traditionally, class is seen in occupational terms. Those in manual jobs (the working class) are expected to vote for the Labour party whilst those in non-manual jobs (the middle class) are expected to vote for the Conservatives (see chapter 5, section 2.1 for the different definitions of class).

Although the figures depend on the criteria used for

measurement, between 1945 and 1970 a majority of people belonged to the working class. So, if people always voted according to their occupational class position, the Labour party would have won every general election during this period. As this did not happen, either a considerable proportion of the working class did not bother to vote or there was some degree of cross-class voting with more manual workers not voting Labour than non-manual workers not voting Conservative (or both). In fact, survey results show, that at some general elections since 1945, a third or even more of the working class vote has gone to the Conservatives.

Embourgeoisement

In the decades following the Second World War, various explanations were offered for working class Conservative voting. One argument concerned people's perceptions of their own status or class position in society. If they viewed themselves as middle class rather than working class, they were more likely to vote Conservative. This argument is associated with the theory of embourgeoisement - the idea that, because of rising pay levels and living standards, the attitudes and behaviour of better-off manual workers become more like those of the middle class (including a willingness to vote Conservative).

A study in the 1960s (Goldthorpe et al., 1969), however, found no systematic evidence to support this theory. Instead, the authors found a more significant correlation: non-Labour support of manual workers was higher amongst those who had friends or family connections with non-manual ('white collar') employees. Consistent with this finding is the argument that manual workers living outside the more traditional, single industry, working class communities are more exposed to what Frank Parkin described as the 'dominant value system' and, therefore, less likely to vote Labour (Parkin, 1972).

The string of Conservative general election victories after 1979 led to the revival of the theory of embourgeoisement as an explanation of the decline in the working class Labour vote. But, the theory has few supporters since it fails to account for the fall in middle class Conservative support that has also occurred during this period.

Deferential and secular Conservatives

In another study of cross-class voting, McKenzie & Silver distinguished between deferential and secular working class Conservative voters. Deferential voters look up to Conservative politicians and believe that it is their duty to support traditional authority which is represented by Conservative leaders. Deferential voters, therefore, see Conservatives as Britain's 'natural rulers'. Secular voters vote Conservative not because they are enthusiastic supporters of Conservative values, but because they believe they will be better off, particularly financially, with a Conservative government. They are secular Conservatives because they are not true believers in Conservative ideology (McKenzie & Silver, 1968).

Class dealignment

Despite a significant degree of working class Conservative voting, the voting patterns between 1945 and the 1970s seemed to indicate quite strong class alignment. In the 1945-70 period, nearly two thirds of all voters voted for their 'natural' class party. In other words, most manual workers did vote Labour and most non-manual workers voted Conservative. But, since the mid-1970s, a number of political scientists have claimed that a process of class dealignment has been taking place. They argue that the link between occupational class and party preference at election times has diminished. This argument was first fully developed in 1977 (Crewe et al., 1977). Further studies have concluded that the process of class dealignment has continued in later elections (for example, Benyon and Denver, 1990). It should be noted, however, that although these commentators argue that the link between class and party preference has diminished, they still consider class to be important. As Crewe put it:

> 'In the 1945-70 period, nearly two thirds of all voters voted for their class party. From February 1974 the link slowly and fitfully weakened and since 1983 the proportion has been under half (44-47%) with a majority voting for either the 'class enemy' or for the non-class centre or nationalist parties. This trend should not be exaggerated, however: class remains the single most important social factor underlying the vote.' (Crewe, 1993a, pp.99-100).

The Heath thesis

In 1985, the theory of class dealignment came under attack. The sociologist Anthony Heath and his colleagues published a book which claimed that there was no evidence that there had been a fall in working class loyalty to the Labour party or that the proportion of members of the working class voting Labour had fallen. Rather, the overall decline in the Labour vote reflected a reduction of the size of the working class as a whole. Class alignment was still important, but the balance of the classes had changed. The long-term pattern in class voting is one of 'trendless fluctuation' rather than inevitable decline (Heath et al., 1985). This thesis was further explored in 1991 (Heath et al., 1991).

At the heart of the debate between those who support and those who oppose the theory of class dealignment is the definition of the term 'class'.

Whereas conventional accounts used a simple manual/non-manual definition, Heath and his colleagues split the electorate into five categories:

> 'Distinguished according to their degree of economic security, their authority in the workplace, their prospects of economic advancement and their sources as well as their level of income.' (Heath et al., 1991, p.66).

Other writers, however, do not accept the measures of class alignment used by Heath and his colleagues (see, for example, Denver, 1993). Although most would go along with the proposition that the working class as a whole has been shrinking, they argue that Labour's declining share of the vote has been exacerbated by the process of class dealignment.

Explanations of class dealignment

A number of explanations, often interconnected, have been suggested for the process of class dealignment.

a) Party dealignment

Some explanations of class dealignment are associated with the related phenomenon of party dealignment (a decline in party identification) and require consideration of, for example, the role of education, media coverage, ideological changes and dissatisfaction with party performance. These issues are examined in part 2 of this chapter.

b) Changes in the occupational structure

Since the 1960s, there have been important changes in the structure and pattern of employment in Britain. A process of 'de-industrialisation' - a decline in the traditional manufacturing industries such as mining, shipbuilding and steel manufacture - has taken place (see chapter 5, section 3.1 and chapter 15, section 3.1). De-industrialisation has gathered pace since 1979 and it is, perhaps, no surprise that it has affected the way in which people vote.

In the traditional manufacturing industries, the workforce exhibited a strong, collective trade union identity. Historically, these unions had close links with the Labour party and the vast majority of workers voted Labour. But, since the 1960s, several million of these workers have either lost their jobs or they have found work in new high-tech or service industries. High-tech and service industries are not organised in the same way that traditional industries were organised. For example, the role of trade unions (if trade unions are tolerated) is reduced. As a result, the old ties between workers and the Labour party have been broken (the number of trade union members, for example, fell from 13.3 million (53% of the workforce) in 1979 to 10.2 million (38% of the workforce) in 1990. This has led to class dealignment.

But, class dealignment has not only affected the Labour vote. There has also been some falling away of middle class support for the Conservatives. This too can be explained by reference to the changing occupational structure. Many workers have managed to gain promotion to non-manual jobs. They have, in other words, moved from the working class to the middle class. There is evidence that an increase in non-Conservative voting among the middle class is due to the fact that some of the 'newer recruits' to the middle class have retained their allegiance to Labour (see, for example, Benyon & Denver, 1990).

c) Production and consumption cleavages

Dunleavy & Husbands (1985) argue that the significance of the old manual/non-manual class divisions is being replaced by new sectoral cleavages based on public-private splits. They distinguish between production sector cleavages and consumption sector cleavages (see Item C in Activity 9.1 below).

Production sector cleavages refer to the real or assumed conflicts of interest between employees in the public sector and those in the private sector. It is argued that these cleavages have resulted in the development of new political alignments, largely irrespective of whether employees are in manual or non-manual occupations.

Consumption sector cleavages refer to the ways in which certain services are purchased and provided. Two important examples are housing and transport. Together, these constitute a significant proportion of most people's disposable incomes. A trend to privately owned (as opposed to publicly rented) housing and a greater emphasis on personal rather than public transport are likely to affect a large section of the population significantly. Indeed, the policies of the Conservative governments since 1979 have brought about such changes from public to private provision. Dunleavy & Husbands argue that new alignments have been developing which relate party choice to patterns of consumption. These new alignments, they argue, cut across the manual/non-manual class alignments.

d) The traditional and new working classes

There are some similarities between the ideas of Dunleavy & Husbands and those of Ivor Crewe. Following the major defeat of Labour at the 1983 general election, Crewe focused on what he saw as divisions within the working class (*Guardian*, 13 June 1983). Elaborating on a survey which found that only 38% of manual workers voted Labour, he claimed that the party could only rely on the shrinking traditional working class and it was losing the support of the new working class. Those who belonged to the traditional working class were predominantly people who lived in Scotland and the North of England and those in other areas who lived in council houses or worked in the public sector. Those who belonged to the new working class were manual workers employed by private firms who lived mainly in the South and owned their own homes.

Following the 1987 general election, Crewe pursued his theory of a divided working class and he brought union membership into the equation (Crewe, 1987). But, although the Conservatives still won the 1992 general election, the overall swing to Labour from 1987 seemed to have reversed any polarisation between the new and the traditional working classes. Crewe admitted that the gap between the two groups was 'much narrower' than previously (Crewe, 1992). He attributed this change to the differential effects of the recession in the early 1990s - by the 1992 general election, the high-tech and service industries in the South of England had been hit by recession harder than the public sector and the North.

Activity 9.1

Item A *Occupational class and party choice 1964-92*

N/M = non-manual M = manual All figures in percentages

	1964		1966		1970		1974 (Feb)		1974 (Oct)		1979		1983		1987		1992	
	N/M	M	N/M	M	N/M	M	N/M	M	N/M	M	N/M	M	N/M	M	N/M	M	N/M	M
Con	62	28	60	25	64	33	53	24	51	24	55	36	51	35	49	37	49	35
Lib	16	8	14	6	11	9	25	19	24	20	19	17	31	28	31	23	25	20
Lab	22	64	26	69	25	58	22	57	25	57	26	46	18	37	20	40	26	45
class voters	63		66		60		55		54		51		45		44		47	

This table shows the percentage of non-manual and manual workers who voted for each of the three main parties between 1964 and 1992. The bottom row shows the percentage of manual workers voting Labour and non-manual workers voting Conservative.

Adapted from Benyon & Denver, 1990 and Crewe, 1993b.

Item B *The 1987 general election*

(i) Voting according to class (1)

Party	Class 1	Class 2	Class 3	Class 4	Class 5
Conservative	56	52	65	39	31
Labour	15	26	16	36	48
Liberal & SDP	29	23	20	24	21

All figures in percentages

This table shows the way in which people voted in the 1987 general election according to the Registrar General's definition of class (see p.109).

Adapted from Heath et al., 1991.

(i) Voting according to class (2)

Social class	Con	Lab	Lib
A/B professional	54	13	30
C1 white collar	47	24	26
C2 skilled manual	42	35	21
D/E semi & unskilled	31	46	20

All figures in percentages

This table shows the way in which people voted in the 1987 general election according to the IPA's definition of class (see p.109).

Adapted from the *Independent*, 13 June 1987.

Item C *Production and consumption sector cleavages*

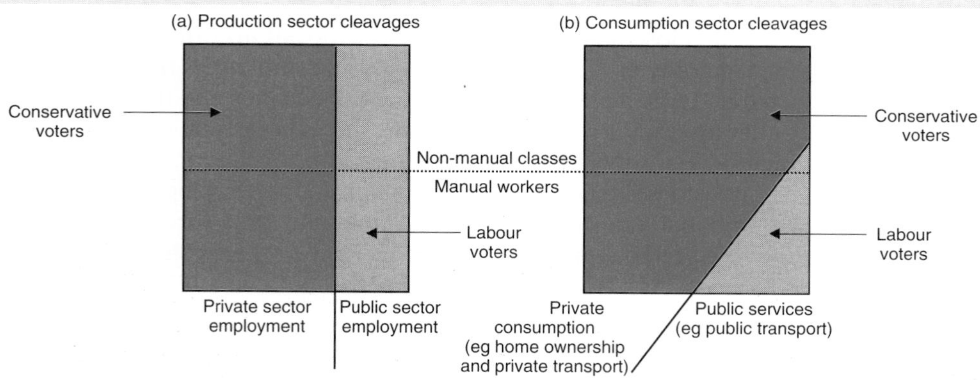

The diagrams above show how sectoral cleavages translate into support for the Labour and Conservative parties. Since the Labour party is associated with the public sector, their support is indicated to the right of the dividing line. Support for the Conservatives is indicated to the left of the dividing line. In employment terms, about 30% of the total working population is employed in the public sector. But, in consumption terms, most non-manual people are involved in private consumption (for example, home ownership and private transport).

Adapted from Dunleary & Husbands, 1985.

Item D *The traditional and the new working class*

(i) 1987 general election

The new working class

Party	Lives in South	Home owner	Non-union member	Private sector worker
Con	46	44	40	38
Lab	28	32	38	39
Lib/SDP	26	24	22	23

The traditional working class

Party	Lives in Scotland or North	Council tenant	Union member	Public sector worker
Con	29	25	30	32
Lab	57	57	48	49
Lib/SDP	15	18	22	19

(ii) 1992 general election

The new working class

Party	Lives in South	Home owner	Non-union member	Private sector worker
Con	40	40	37	32
Lab	38	41	46	50
Lib Dem	23	19	17	18

The traditional working class

Party	Lives in Scotland or North	Council tenant	Union member	Public sector worker
Con	26	22	29	36
Lab	59	64	55	48
Lib Dem	15	13	16	16

These tables show how different groups of people voted in the 1987 and 1992 general elections. Some columns do not add up to 100% since the figures have been rounded up or down.

Adapted from Crewe, 1987a and Crewe, 1992.

Item E *The problem faced by political scientists*

Questions

1. a) What evidence is there to suggest that 'class remains the single most important social factor underlying the vote'?
   b) What problems arise when political commentators attempt to explain voting behaviour on the basis of class?
2. a) Judging from Item A what is the evidence to support the view that class dealignment has taken place?
   b) Different surveys produce different figures because sampling techniques and sample sizes vary. Does this matter? Explain your answer.
3. What do Items B-D add to our understanding of voting behaviour?
4. Judging from Item E what is the problem faced by political scientists who attempt to explain voting behaviour by reference to class?

1.2 Other social factors

Class is just one of a number of social factors which influence voting behaviour. Regional differences, age, gender, religion and ethnicity must also be taken into account. This section looks at how each of these social factors influence the way in which people vote.

Regional differences

During the 1980s, political commentators increasingly used the term 'North/South divide' to describe the geographical polarisation of support for the Labour and Conservative parties. In general terms, support for the Conservatives appeared to be declining in the North of England, Scotland and Wales whilst support for Labour declined in the South of England.

Although regional differences existed before the 1980s, two new developments have come to light. First, whereas before 1970 the changes in party support from one election to another tended to be similar across most regions of Britain, since 1970 this has changed. Swings vary from region to region. Second, a further spatial divide has been revealed. Since 1959, electoral support for the Conservatives in general elections has shown a relative decline in urban areas whilst the vote for Labour has declined in rural areas.

Explanations of regional differences

Explanations of regional differences in voting behaviour have been related to class differences; cultural variations, economic circumstances, and levels of third party support.

a) Class differences

Although most political scientists agree that there has been a degree of class dealignment (see above, section 1.1), they still accept that the relationship between occupational class and party support is important. Likewise, some relationship between class and region is to be expected. For example, the South of England contains a higher proportion of middle class home owners than the North. This could partly account for the Conservative predominance in the South and Labour strongholds in the North. But, it should be noted that geographical differences in voting behaviour still show up when the class variables are held constant.

b) Cultural differences

Research carried out by Miller (1984, 1990) on constituency voting trends has shown that, since the 1960s, class polarisation between constituencies has increased as class polarisation between individuals has declined. In other words, there is an increasingly powerful 'locality effect'. People tend to adopt the dominant political norms of their locality. So, people living in predominantly middle class areas are more likely to vote Conservative, whatever their own class might be, whilst people living in working class areas are more likely to vote Labour. Put another way, local culture has an important influence on voting behaviour because:

> 'If almost everyone whom a voter meets at work, in shops, in pubs and clubs, at church or on the housing estate appears to support the same party, then there is strong pressure on the individual to support that party too.'
> (Denver, 1993, p.66)

This cultural dimension is emphasised by Johnston & Pattie (1989) who argue that geographical variations in voting behaviour suggest that there is a growing local and regional consciousness in Britain. They argue that geographical variations in voting behaviour contradict the idea that there is a uniform British political culture - even though the parties themselves increasingly rely on the **national** mass media to project their images.

c) Economic circumstances

Since the 1970s, it has been possible to demonstrate a relationship between the economic fortunes of the regions and variations in party support - particularly in terms of a broad North/South divide.

Johnston & Pattie (1989) have emphasised the connection between regional voting patterns and regional economic factors. They argue that those areas of Britain that have experienced economic decline have seen the Conservative vote fall and those faring better have shown a drop in the Labour vote. Furthermore, this pattern seems to have been produced not just by people who have been affected personally by the relative economic fortunes. It seems that the influence of regional economic prosperity or decline is more general than this. These findings, again, suggest the cultural significance of the social and economic context in which people live.

d) Support for third parties

Geographical variations in electoral support for the Labour and Conservative parties may be intensified where third parties do well. The rise of support for the Scottish and Welsh Nationalist parties in the 1970s and the Liberal/SDP Alliance in the 1980s accounts, in part, for the regional variations in support for Labour and the Conservatives. If Labour is weak in the South overall, for example, it is likely to do even worse in southern constituencies where the third party vote is substantial. Similarly, greater support for a third party in Scotland is more likely to be at the expense of the Conservatives than Labour. Tactical voting (see section 5.3 below) intensifies this phenomenon.

Age

Survey data from general elections usually shows a tendency for younger people to vote Labour and older people to vote Conservative. In the October 1974 election, for example, 42% of new voters voted Labour compared to 24% who voted Conservative. Although in 1983 and 1987 the Conservatives obtained clear majorities from the youngest voters, by 1992 the traditional pattern seemed to have reasserted itself with Labour once again winning a majority of first-time votes.

Studies have shown that swings within the 18-22 age group can be quite marked and, therefore, no party can afford to take their support for granted. Anthony Heath and his colleagues have remarked:

> 'The young elector tends to be rather less interested in politics, somewhat less likely to turn out and vote, less committed to any political party and somewhat more volatile.' (Heath et al., 1991, p.212).

Gender

Writing in 1967 one political scientist stated:

> 'There is overwhelming evidence that women are more conservatively inclined than men.' (Pulzer, 1967, p.107)

Pulzer argued that, between 1945 and 1966, whilst men had given the Labour party a victory at every general election, women had done so only twice. In the four general elections held between 1979 and 1992, more women voted for the Conservatives than for the other parties (see Activity 9.2, Item C).

So, why do more women vote for the Conservative party than for other parties? One reason might be that women have experienced lower levels of exposure to pro-Labour ideas and influences. According to this argument, a common source of exposure to pro-Labour ideas is the workplace. It is through work, for example, that people are likely to come into contact with the trade union movement. Traditionally, fewer women than men have been in work (it was only in 1994 that the number of women in paid employment reached the number of men). In addition, the majority of women in work have tended to take part-time non-unionised jobs. As a result, (the argument goes) many women have simply not been exposed to pro-Labour ideas. A second suggestion is that because women's traditional role has been in the home, they are more likely to be influenced by traditional values relating to the family and religion - values which tend to form the basis of Conservative election campaigns. A third suggestion is that it is age and not gender which is important. The life expectancy of women is higher and there are, therefore, more older women than older men. Since older voters are more likely to vote Conservative than the young, this explains the higher Conservative vote amongst women as a whole. Whatever the reasons, it should be remembered that the differences in party choice between men and women overall are not great.

Religion

Historically, there have been close links between religion and politics in Britain. In the 19th century, for example, the Church of England was described as 'the Tory party at prayer' and was closely identified with the political Establishment. Non-conformist sects such as the Methodists and Baptists, on the other hand, were associated with support for the Liberal party. But, although links between religion and politics are still important determinants of party choice in some parts of Western Europe (including Northern Ireland), it is generally agreed that their significance in most parts of Britain has disappeared. Denver (1989) points out that religious affiliation is now rarely examined in major works on voting behaviour.

An exception to this is the work of Anthony Heath and his colleagues (Heath et al., 1991 and Heath, 1992). In the 1960s, the assumption was made that the connection between voting preference and religious affiliation would continue to weaken. Heath and his colleagues, however, have uncovered evidence which suggests that this has not necessarily been the case. Although they have found evidence of a general decline in religion, their comparison of voting patterns in 1964 and 1987 indicates that the connection between Church of England attendance and Conservative voting still persists (at least amongst the middle class) as does the connection between non-conformist sect attendance and Liberal voting. Heath and his colleagues acknowledge, however, that the reasons for any connections between religious groups and party choice may not be due to religion itself. For example, the high Labour vote among British Catholics, many of whom are of Irish descent, may be related historically to the policies of the main parties on the 'Irish question'. Similarly, the voting preferences of Sikhs and Muslims in Britain may have more to do with ethnicity than with religion.

Ethnicity

The more recent analyses of the relationship between voting behaviour and ethnicity have focused on the voting patterns of different black ethnic groups (see chapter 5, section 2.3 for an examination of the term 'ethnicity'). Although studies show that, overall, the majority of black people vote Labour, different levels of party support have been noted between Asians and Afro-Caribbean voters as well as differences within each of these groups. Using unpublished data from 1987, Saggar (1993) reports a difference of nearly 20% between Asian support for the Labour party (which stood at 67%) and Afro-Caribbean support (which stood at 86%). Fitzgerald (1988), using data from the same year, notes markedly higher levels of support for the Conservative party among East African Asians than among those from the Indian subcontinent. It should be noted that such variations may have a differential effect if turnout levels also vary. Layton-Henry (1990) reports a lower turnout at elections of Afro-Caribbeans compared to Asians. He attributes this not to political apathy, but to a greater degree of alienation from British politics.

Three main factors have been suggested to explain why the Labour party attracts the votes of immigrants and their descendants: class, race and political geography.

a) Class

The most common reason given by black respondents to survey questions about why they vote for the Labour party is that Labour is for the working class (see, for example, Saggar, 1993a). But, further analysis of the evidence leads Heath and his colleagues (1991) away from a simple class explanation. By itself, it would not explain, for example, why the black working class Labour vote is much higher the working class Labour vote in general. Fitzgerald (1988) also doubts the validity of a simple class explanation. She claims there is no clear evidence that black people especially perceive themselves to be working class.

Also, she points to the variety of socio-economic positions occupied by black people, particularly Asians. A major survey in the 1980s showed that 22% of East African Asian men, 20% of Hindus, 11% of Muslims and 4% of Seiks were employed in professional or managerial jobs. The comparable figure for whites was 19%.

b) Race

The Labour party is usually seen as more liberal than the Conservative party on issues related to race and immigration. According to Denver (1989), this is one reason for the high black Labour vote. But the majority of evidence suggests that black voters are not predominantly concerned with 'race' issues. Most surveys reveal a high similarity between blacks and whites. Differences among black voters are likely to be as significant as differences between blacks and whites.

c) Political geography

Although Asians and Afro-Caribbeans, together, constitute under 4% of the electorate, residential concentration of some black communities means that in some constituencies the black vote is large enough to make a significant impact. The concentration of black voters in constituencies which have become Labour strongholds has been historically significant in forging the close two-way relationship between black communities and Labour (a link which has not developed with other political parties). Fitzgerald (1988) points out that from the early days of postwar black immigration, black people have relied on their local Labour MPs for political support. At the same time, the most obvious and accessible route for black people who wish to play a role in public life has been through the Labour party. Political geography has, therefore, functioned to strengthen the links between black people and the Labour party.

Activity 9.2

Item A *Vote by age in the 1979, 1987 and 1992 general elections*

	Con	Lab	Lib Dem	Con lead over Lab	Swing to Labour
FIRST-TIME VOTERS					
Vote in 1992	35	40	25	-5	+9.5
Change from 1987	-10	+9	+2	-19	
Change from 1979	-11	+3	+8	-14	+7.0
PEOPLE AGED 22-29					
Vote in 1992	43	41	16	+2	-1.5
Change from 1987	+7	+4	-11	+3	
Change from 1979	+7	-4	-3	+11	-5.5
PEOPLE AGED 30-44					
Vote in 1992	39	39	21	0	+5.0
Change from 1987	-3	+7	-6	-10	
Change from 1979	-9	+3	+5	-12	+6.0
PEOPLE AGED 45-64					
Vote in 1992	44	35	21	+9	+2.0
Change from 1987	-1	+3	-2	-4	
Change from 1979	-3	-6	+8	+3	-1.5
PEOPLE AGED 65 AND OVER					
Vote in 1992	48	37	14	+11	+2.5
Change from 1987	0	+5	-6	-5	
Change from 1979	+2	0	-3	+2	-1.0

This diagram shows how different age groups voted in the 1979, 1987 and 1992 general elections. All figures are percentages.

Adapted from Crewe, 1992.

Item B *Britain after the 1992 election*

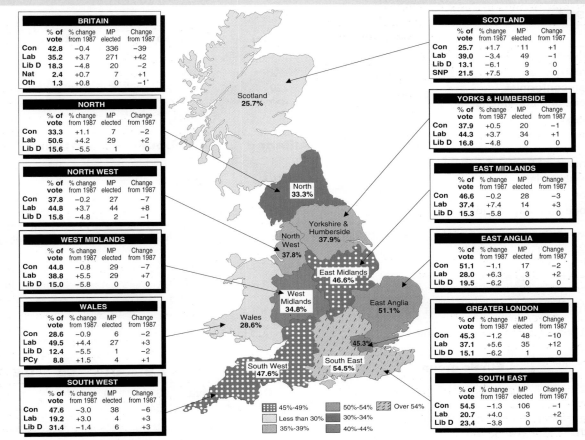

BRITAIN

	% of vote	% change from 1987	MP elected	Change from 1987
Con	42.8	−0.4	336	−39
Lab	35.2	+3.7	271	+42
Lib D	18.3	−4.8	20	−2
Nat	2.4	+0.7	7	+1
Oth	1.3	+0.8	0	−1

NORTH

	% of vote	% change from 1987	MP elected	Change from 1987
Con	33.3	+1.1	7	−2
Lab	50.6	+4.2	29	+2
Lib D	15.6	−5.5	1	0

NORTH WEST

	% of vote	% change from 1987	MP elected	Change from 1987
Con	37.8	−0.2	27	−7
Lab	44.8	+3.7	44	+8
Lib D	15.8	−4.8	2	−1

WEST MIDLANDS

	% of vote	% change from 1987	MP elected	Change from 1987
Con	44.8	−0.8	29	−7
Lab	38.8	+5.5	29	+7
Lib D	15.0	−5.8	0	0

WALES

	% of vote	% change from 1987	MP elected	Change from 1987
Con	28.6	−0.9	6	−2
Lab	49.5	+4.4	27	+3
Lib D	12.4	−5.5	1	−2
PCy	8.8	+1.5	4	+1

SOUTH WEST

	% of vote	% change from 1987	MP elected	Change from 1987
Con	47.6	−3.0	38	−6
Lab	19.2	+3.0	4	+3
Lib D	31.4	−1.4	6	+3

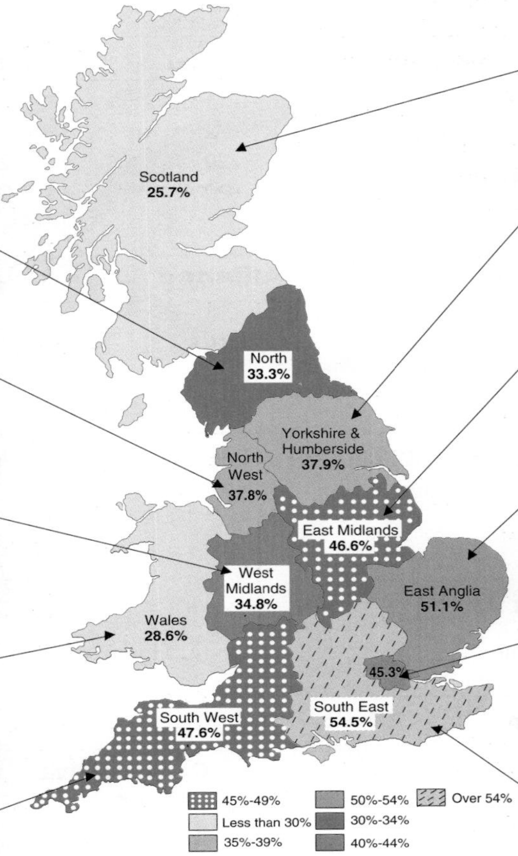

SCOTLAND

	% of vote	% change from 1987	MP elected	Change from 1987
Con	25.7	+1.7	11	+1
Lab	39.0	−3.4	49	−1
Lib D	13.1	−6.1	9	0
SNP	21.5	+7.5	3	0

YORKS & HUMBERSIDE

	% of vote	% change from 1987	MP elected	Change from 1987
Con	37.9	+0.5	20	−1
Lab	44.3	+3.7	34	+1
Lib D	16.8	−4.8	0	0

EAST MIDLANDS

	% of vote	% change from 1987	MP elected	Change from 1987
Con	46.6	−0.2	28	−3
Lab	37.4	+7.4	14	+3
Lib D	15.3	−5.8	0	0

EAST ANGLIA

	% of vote	% change from 1987	MP elected	Change from 1987
Con	51.1	−1.1	17	−2
Lab	28.0	+6.3	3	+2
Lib D	19.5	−6.2	0	0

GREATER LONDON

	% of vote	% change from 1987	MP elected	Change from 1987
Con	45.3	−1.2	48	−10
Lab	37.1	+5.6	35	+12
Lib D	15.1	−6.2	1	0

SOUTH EAST

	% of vote	% change from 1987	MP elected	Change from 1987
Con	54.5	−1.3	106	−1
Lab	20.7	+4.0	3	+2
Lib D	23.4	−3.8	0	0

This diagram shows the share of the vote in Britain region by region following the 1992 general election.

Adapted from Benyon, 1993.

Item C *Gender and party choice 1964-92*

Year		Con	Lab	Lib Dem
1964	Men	40	48	11
	Women	46	42	12
1966	Men	38	53	8
	Women	45	46	9
1970	Men	44	49	8
	Women	51	41	8
1974 (Feb)	Men	40	41	19
	Women	40	38	22
1974 (Oct)	Men	34	46	19
	Women	40	39	21
1979	Men	47	39	13
	Women	46	39	14
1983	Men	46	30	24
	Women	43	28	28
1987	Men	44	33	22
	Women	44	31	25
1992	Men	41	40	19
	Women	45	36	19

This table shows voting according to gender 1964-92. All figures are percentages.

Adapted from Denver & Hands, 1990 and Crewe, 1992.

Item D *Conservative party poster*

LABOUR SAYS HE'S BLACK.
TORIES SAY HE'S BRITISH.
CONSERVATIVE

This poster was produced for the 1983 general election campaign.

Item E *Christianity and voting patterns in the middle class, 1964 and 1987*

1964

	Conservative	Liberal	Labour	Other
Church of England	72	11	16	1
Presbyterian	74	22	4	0
Non-conformist	51	29	20	0
None and non-attenders	47	20	30	3

1987

	Conservative	Alliance	Labour	Other
Church of England	67	25	8	0
Presbyterian	63	19	13	6
Non-conformist	40	46	13	2
None and non-attenders	50	30	19	2

This table shows the result of the 1964 and 1987 general elections according to religious affiliation. Rows do not always add up to 100% because of rounding.

Adapted from Heath, 1992.

Item F *Voting and ethnicity, 1987*

(i) Voting intentions by ethnic group

	Ethnic group			Ethnic Concentration	
	All	Asian	Afro-Caribbean	High	Low
Con	18	23	6	15	39
Lab	72	67	86	77	43
Alliance	10	10	7	8	17

This table shows voting intentions in general and how they varied according to whether voters came from an area with a high or low ethnic population. All figures are in percentages

(ii) How black people voted, by class

	A,B	C1	C2	D,E
Conservative	33	30	14	10
Labour	54	52	78	84
Alliance	13	17	9	5

This table shows how all black people voted according to class. All figures are in percentages.

Adapted from Sewell, 1993.

Questions

1. You have been asked to explain why people voted as they did in the 1992 general election. Write an account using the social structures model of voting behaviour.
2. a) Judging from Item B what is the evidence of a North/South divide in voting behaviour? Why do you think this has developed? Did this divide become wider or narrower between 1987 and 1992? Give reasons for the change.
   b) Identify regions where the Liberal Democrat vote was (i) higher and (ii) lower than average. To what extent does this information lend support to the idea that a growing vote for third parties intensifies the North/South divide?
3. What conclusions can you draw from Items A, and C-F about the importance of age, gender and ethnicity as determinants of voting behaviour?
4. Do you think the Conservatives would benefit electorally if they used a poster similar to that in Item D in their next general election campaign? Use the information in Item F in your answer.
5. What does Item E tell us about the relationship between religious affiliation and voting behaviour?

2 The party identification model

Key Issues

1. Why do people identify themselves as supporters of a political party?
2. Why do people form long-term attachments to a political party?
3. How does the support for a political party affect people's attitudes towards issues, personalities and government performance?

2.1 Principal elements of the model

Party identification (or partisanship) refers to the attachment, over a period of time, to a particular political party. According to Miller (1990), the basic claims of this model are as follows:

1. Many voters identify themselves as supporters of a political party.
2. The party identification of these voters is relatively stable and enduring.
3. The party identification of these voters influences their attitudes towards issues, personalities and government performance.
4. Party identification directly affects these voters' voting behaviour.

The party identification model is derived from studies in the USA in the 1950s. By party identification, political scientists mean psychological attachment to a party, rather than a rational choice based on an instrumental assessment of the party's aims, promises or practices. Party identification, therefore, has much to do with a party's public image and it should be seen as one of the long-term influences on voting behaviour. Although the assumption is that most people who identify with a party (partisans) would normally vote for the party with which they identify, the model does not claim that this is always the case. For example, some people vote tactically.

Work on the party identification model in Britain in the 1960s emphasised the effects of 'political socialisation' - the term used to mean the process by which people acquire their political attitudes, values and ways of behaving (see chapter 5, section 1.1). Most theories of political socialisation assume that the majority of people retain the party preferences and voting habits formed when they first become politically aware. The influences of childhood and early adulthood are, therefore, considered important. Family (especially parents), friends and work colleagues are regarded as the main agencies of political socialisation (although with each of these, the class connection is frequently seen as central). Today, political socialisation has become less important in most explanations of voting behaviour.

Over recent years, research has focused on three areas of party identification - its extent, its direction and its intensity. Extent (or incidence) refers to the proportion of the electorate that self-consciously identifies with a particular political party. Do more or less people identify with a party than did so 20 years ago? Direction refers to the choice of party. How many voters are attached to the Conservative party, for example, and has the percentage changed over time? Intensity refers to the strength of an individual's support for a party. Why do some people feel strongly attached to a party whilst others do not?

If the extent and intensity of party identification are high then political scientists refer to high degrees of party alignment. If the extent and/or the intensity of party identification are low or falling, then a process of party dealignment is said to be taking place.

Variations in the extent and intensity of party identification may determine the degree of electoral stability and volatility. High levels of strong party identification are likely to mean that few people switch their vote from one election to another - with the result that there is a period of electoral stability. Weak or low levels of party identification, on the other hand, are likely to mean that voters are less predictable in their party choices and so voting behaviour is more volatile. Short-term factors (such as current issues, the personalities of party leaders and the role of the media) tend to have a greater influence on electoral outcomes when party identification is low since party loyalty has less of a role to play.

2.2 Party dealignment

Whilst there has been a debate about the extent or even existence of class dealignment (see above, section 1), there is general agreement that party dealignment has been taking place since the early 1970s.

Before 1970, the postwar period had been characterised electorally by extensive and intensive party identification with the Conservative and Labour parties. In the 1950s and 1960s, although there had been changes in government, electoral outcome varied little. Partisan (and class) alignment supported a stable two party system. This electoral stability then started to give way to a greater volatility. The two party system came under attack from other parties. The Liberal party began to attract votes in greater numbers. The Scottish and Welsh Nationalist parties also gained support.

But, to what extent have Labour and the Conservatives lost support? Have they suffered equally? These questions can be answered in two ways - by examining the changes in the parties' share of the actual vote at election times and by analysing survey data related to party identification.

Share of the vote

Between 1950 and 1983, there was a marked decline in the share of the actual vote won by Labour and the Conservatives combined. This trend showed signs of reversal in 1987 and 1992:

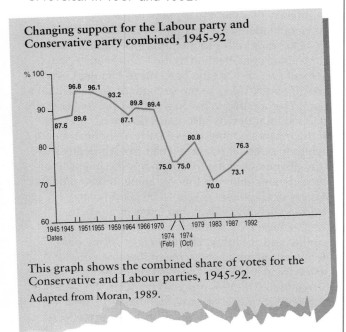

Changing support for the Labour party and Conservative party combined, 1945-92

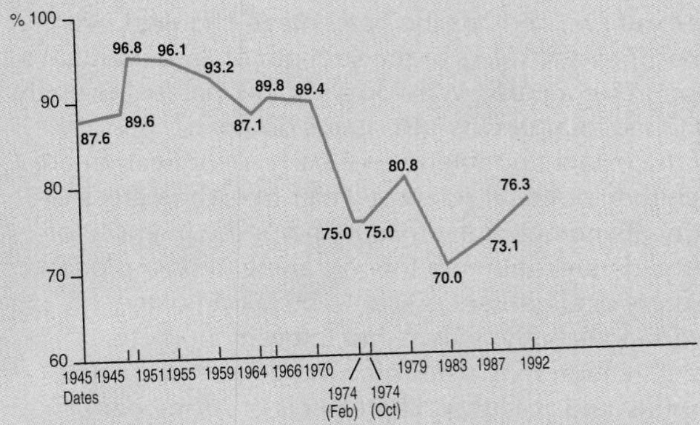

This graph shows the combined share of votes for the Conservative and Labour parties, 1945-92.

Adapted from Moran, 1989.

The fall in the combined Conservative-Labour share of the vote can be explained by the growth in fortunes of other parties, especially the Liberals. It may be significant, for example, that the Liberals fielded just 109 candidates in 1951 but 523 in 1979. Moran (1989), however, argues that the willingness of third parties to field more candidates may itself be a reflection of the decline in support for the two major parties. It should be noted that in terms of loss of voting support, Labour has suffered more than the Conservatives.

Party identification

Voting for a party is not the same as identifying with it. It is, therefore, necessary to add other information about party support to knowledge of the actual share of the vote. Crewe (1993a) has provided evidence to suggest that the percentage of Conservative identifiers has held up better than the percentage of Labour identifiers.

But if, among the identifiers, intensity of identification is measured, then according to Denver (1989) both major parties have suffered from partisan dealignment since the 1960s. In 1964, 48% of Conservative and 51% of Labour voters identified 'very strongly' with their party. By 1987, the corresponding figures were 23% for Conservative voters and 26% for Labour voters.

Denver also found that, between 1964 and 1987, the number of Liberal voters who identified 'very strongly' with their party fell from 32% to 10%. This suggests that partisan dealignment is not confined to the two major parties. It also suggests that the electoral fortunes of the Liberal Democrats can be expected to fluctuate more than the other main parties since it has fewer identifiers. One explanation for this is that the Liberal Democrats gain the votes of disaffected voters from the Conservative and Labour parties. The Liberal Democrats' record at by-elections would seem to confirm this. Their gains at by-elections are almost invariably wiped out in general elections.

The extent of party dealignment

Writing after the 1987 general election, Crewe conceded that declining party identification should not be overemphasised:

> 'Long-term allegiance to the Conservative and Labour parties remains the dominant fact about the British electorate, the psychological anchor of a stable, slow moving party system.' (Crewe, 1988, p.3)

Indeed, there may even be signs that party identification is beginning to strengthen again. One analysis of data from a post-1992 election survey argues that although there was little change from the 1987 general election in terms of the overall proportion of respondents identifying with different parties, there had been a noticeable increase in the proportions of voters identifying 'very' or 'fairly' strongly (Sanders, 1993).

The causes of party dealignment

Political scientists have suggested a number of factors which may have contributed to party dealignment. Taken individually, however, it is unlikely that any single factor could provide a definitive and undisputed case. The reason for this is that correlative evidence (evidence which shows a connection between two variables) does not prove the existence of a causal relationship.

a) Class dealignment (see above, section 1)

Most commentators recognise a connection between partisan dealignment and class dealignment. Crewe and his colleagues, for example, suggested that the decline in the links between class and party may have helped to weaken party identification. They claimed that:

> 'Partisan decline reflected a continuing erosion of the class-party tie.' (Crewe et al., 1977, p.183)

b) The generation effect

The electorate does change from one general election to the next. New (usually young) voters enter the register for the first time whilst others (generally older) have died. But, the idea that a generational effect explains party dealignment has been dismissed by some political analysts. Evidence analysed by Crewe and his colleagues, and later by Clarke & Stewart (1984), for example, indicated that a decrease in party identification was not confined to young voters but spanned the range of age groups in the electorate.

c) Education

There is an argument that partisan dealignment has followed a period during which the electorate became better educated. According to this view, a better educated electorate is better able to make rational political decisions. Voters are, therefore, less reliant on an unthinking psychological attachment to a particular party.

d) Television

As well as more formal education, some commentators suspect that party dealignment is linked to the growing and changing television coverage of political events. It was not until the 1960s that the majority of households in Britain had a television set. Since then, coverage has changed. Interviews are much less deferential today than they were in the early 1960s, for example. It has been suggested that developments in television broadcasting and a better educated electorate have heightened political awareness and led to the questioning of traditional party loyalties. The political balance of programmes and the treatment of politics as a series of events rather than a struggle between ideologies may encourage the belief that partisan positions are unreasonable. Satirical programmes, like *Spitting Image*, may contribute to, as well as merely reflect, a greater cynicism about politics and reduce party loyalty.

e) Ideological disjuncture

Party loyalty is likely to be adversely affected if the attitudes, beliefs or wishes of a party's supporters become out of step with some of the basic principles or policies of the party. There is some evidence that such an ideological disjuncture affected the Labour party in the 1960s and 1970s - over the issues of public ownership, trade union power and welfare expenditure. If Labour has suffered more from party dealignment than the Conservatives (the evidence is inconclusive), then ideological disjuncture may have played a part.

f) Performance of the parties

It is sometimes argued that voters have become increasingly dissatisfied with the performance of their preferred party, particularly when that party has formed the government. Denver (1989, 1990) argues that this has been the case since the mid-1960s. High levels of satisfaction with party performance tend to go together with high levels of party identification. A decreasing faith in parties and politicians, on the other hand, is likely to accompany falling levels of partisan loyalty. What is debatable is whether growing dissatisfaction in the performance of parties is a cause or an effect of party dealignment.

Party dealignment and electoral volatility

A common argument is that party dealignment produces greater volatility in voting behaviour. But, this argument is not accepted by all political scientists. Some argue that, although party dealignment has taken place, volatility has increased very little (see, for example, Heath et al., 1991). The different conclusions reflect the different ways in which electoral volatility is measured.

Measurements are able to distinguish between overall and net volatility. **Net volatility** refers to changes in the parties' share of the vote from one election to another. **Overall volatility** refers to the total amount of vote switching which takes place. It is possible to have high overall volatility and low net volatility if, for instance, votes which have switched from Labour to Conservative are matched in number by votes which have switched from Conservative to Labour. The changes cancel themselves out in terms of their net effect.

Denver (1992) draws attention to the example of the Conservative share of the vote since 1979. The relatively small decline in the Conservative vote, from 43.9% in 1979 to 41.9% in 1992, appears to indicate stability rather than volatility. But these figures only show the net effect of switches in the vote between parties. According to Denver, these figures conceal a degree of overall volatility which indicates that the Conservatives as well as Labour have suffered from party dealignment.

As well as differing interpretations about the extent of electoral volatility, there is also disagreement about the nature of its connection to party dealignment. Since party identification is a psychological attachment to a political party, those who support the idea of a causal link between party dealignment and electoral volatility explain any upsurge in electoral volatility by reference to changes in the social psychology of voters. But Heath and his colleagues (1991) doubt the necessity to do this. They argue that changing political circumstances (for example, an increased tendency for a party to change its policies) might themselves be sufficient to lead to greater volatility. In other words, they see no reason why increased volatility and party dealignment should be linked. In fact, Heath and his colleagues (1988) doubt that party identification has become significantly less influential in determining voter choice. Miller (1990) also concedes that a decline in intensity of party identification may have accompanied electoral volatility and not necessarily caused it.

Activity 9.3

Item A *Party identification*

At election time, there is an interplay between a voter's long-term party identification and short-term influences such as current political issues and campaign events. Out of this interplay comes a voting decision. A person's party identification will determine how issues and events are interpreted and evaluated. In other words, identification can serve as a filter through which political messages pass to the individual voter and it can provide a framework within which political events are understood and evaluated. But, identifying with a party is not the same as voting for it. Voting is a behavioural act whereas party identification is psychological - it exists only in the head. Voting is also time-specific (taking place only when there is an election) whilst identification can be ongoing and continuous. Unlike voting, party identification varies in intensity.

Adapted from Denver, 1990.

Item B *Party identification 1964-92*

(i) Party identification 1964-87

	1964	1966	1970	1974 Feb	1974 Oct	1979	1983	1987
% With identification	92	90	89	98	88	85	86	86
% With Con or Lab identification	81	80	81	75	74	74	67	67
% 'Very strong' identifiers	43	43	41	29	26	21	20	19
% 'Fairly strong' Con or Lab	40	39	40	27	23	19	18	16

This table shows the results of surveys held between 1964 and 1987. People were asked whether they identified with one of the two main parties and, if so, how strongly.

Adapted from Benyon & Denver, 1990.

(ii) Party identification 1979-92

	1979	1983	1987	1992	Change 1979-92
Con	37	40	38	39	+2
Lab	38	34	33	35	-3
Lib Dem	13	15	16	12	-1
Other	3	2	2	2	-1
None	10	9	12	12	+2

This table shows the percentage of people who identified with a particular party. The figures have been rounded, so they do not always add up to 100%.

Adapted from Crewe, 1993a.

Item C *Gallup poll survey, 1993*

This survey was published in the *Daily Telegraph*, 13 September 1993.

Item D *Intra-election volatility, April 1992*

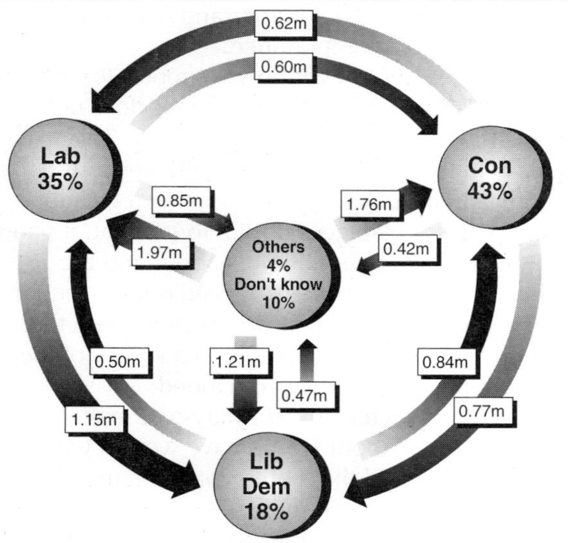

Net voter movement during the campaign

	Con	Lab	Lib Dem	Others & Don't know
+	+3.20 m	+3.09 m	+3.13 m	+1.74 m
-	-1.81 m	-2.60 m	-1.81 m	-4.94 m
Net	**+1.39 m**	**+0.49 m**	**+1.32 m**	**-3.20 m**

Note: Width of arrows represents number of voters. Percentages represent the standing of the parties after reallocating the don't knows.

Intra-election volatility is a measure of electoral volatility within a single election. This table shows the results of a panel survey conducted after the 1992 general election. It shows that 11 million votes changed their minds during the 1992 general election campaign.

Adapted from Game, 1995.

Item E *Inter-election volatility, 1959-92*

	1959-64	66-70	70-74 Feb	74-79 Oct	79-83	83-87	87-92
1. % Switched parties	18	16	24	22	23	19	22
2. % Switched parties (including non-voters)	35	34	42	37	40	37	37

Inter-election volatility is a measure of electoral volatility between successive elections. Row 1 in this table shows the percentage of voters who switched parties in successive elections. Row 2 includes those who did not vote in one election but did so in the next or vice versa.

Adapted from Heath et al., 1994.

Questions

1. Using the party identification model write a short passage describing the major trends in voting behaviour between 1960 and 1992.
2. Judging from Item A how does the party identification model differ from the social structures model?
3. a) Using Item B what are the trends in (i) the direction (ii) the extent and (iii) the intensity of party identification?
   b) What is the evidence of party dealignment and to what extent has it taken place?
4. How would you explain the results of the survey in Item C using the party identification model?
5. a) Judging from Item D what impact did intra-election volatility make on the 1992 general election?
   b) Judging from Item E what evidence is there of inter-electoral volatility? Explain your answer.

3 The rational choice model

Key Issues

1. Is there evidence to suggest that people vote according to rational criteria rather than class or party loyalty?
2. How important are issues and values in determining how people vote?
3. To what extent do perceptions of the competence of parties determine whether voters will vote for them?
4. How important is the personality of party leaders?

3.1 Principal elements of the model

The rational choice model suggests that political parties cannot rely simply on the loyalty of their supporters or on particular social classes to win elections. They have to compete for votes on the basis of their policies, their past records and the credibility of their leaders.

The rational choice model focuses on the connection between the attitudes of voters and their decision to vote for a particular party. It does not concern itself with the origins or sources of these attitudes, but adopts a supermarket or consumer choice view of voting behaviour. Voters are seen as shopping around for the best deal and then voting accordingly. This model, therefore, emphasises the significance of **instrumental voting** (making rational decisions) rather than the **expressive voting** (making emotional decisions) portrayed in the social structures and party identification models discussed in sections 1 and 2 above.

Since the rational choice model can encompass a number of variations according to the type of attitudes that are thought to lead to voting choice, various labels are used to indicate the possible connections. These include: the issue voting (or policy preference) model, the value (or ideological voting) model, the prospective (or investment) model, the retrospective model and the leader personality model. Each of these models is examined in turn in this section.

3.2 Issue voting

Supporters of the issue voting (or policy preference) model argue that class and party dealignment have been accompanied by a greater willingness on the part of the electorate to be more rational and less emotional in their voting choices. A study by Franklin (1985), attempted to measure this change statistically by analysing a collection of influences upon party preferences. The study concluded that there had been an increase in the contribution which issue opinions make in determining party preference - from 25% in the 1964 election to about 40% in the elections of 1979 and 1983. Referring to the 1979 election, Ivor Crewe remarked:

> 'It was issues that won the election for the Conservatives...The Conservatives' success came from saying the right things about the right issues.' (quoted in Benyon & Denver, 1990, p.93)

Supporters of the issue voting model agree with this analysis and argue that the Conservatives won and Labour lost the general elections in 1983, 1987 and 1992 because voters supported Conservative policies which promoted individualism and self-interest (such as extending share ownership, reducing income tax rates and the sale of council houses), whilst they were scared by Labour's left wing programme (such as its support for the trade unions, nationalisation and unilateral nuclear disarmament). Although, by 1992, Labour had discarded or radically altered many of its left wing policies, the memory of them, so the argument goes, lingered in the minds of the electorate.

But, the problem with the issue voting model is that whilst most people would agree that issues do have some effect on voting behaviour, it is difficult to find an exact link. According to Crewe (1992), the significance of an issue in contributing to electoral swing depends upon three factors. First, how important the issue is to the voters. Second, which party is preferred and by how much. And third, how these factors have changed since the last election. This, however, assumes that voters are able to match specific policies with particular parties - an assumption which has been questioned (for example by Conley, 1990). Also, for a particular issue to be influential in affecting the outcome of an election, one party must have substantially greater support on that issue than the other parties and that issue must be considered of great importance.

Even then, studies have shown, support for a party's stance on an issue or a range of issues does not necessarily result in a vote for that party. This was the case in the 1983, 1987 and 1992 general elections. In a study of the 1983 general election, Heath and his colleagues (1985) found that, if people had voted on the issues alone, Labour and the Conservatives would have received roughly equal numbers of votes, but the Conservatives won the election by a very large margin. In a survey of the 1987 election, Ivor Crewe concluded:

> 'Had electors voted solely on the main issues, Labour would have won. It was considered the more capable party on three of the four leading issues - jobs, health and education - among those for whom the issue was important.' (*Guardian*, 16 June 1987)

Yet, again the Conservatives won an overall majority. And, in a study of the 1992 general election, Crewe (1992) concluded that if electors had voted on the issues, the Conservatives would still have won, but their lead over Labour would have been 5% rather than 8%. Using data from the same post-election (after the election) Gallup survey used by Crewe in 1992, Sanders (1993) concluded that if voters had voted on the issues alone, Labour would have won the election with 44% of the vote compared to 33% for the Conservatives. The discrepancy between Crewe's account and that of Sanders indicates how difficult it is to measure the effect that support for particular issues has on a person's vote. The fact that both accounts conclude that Labour's support would have increased if issue voting had taken place suggests that it was not issues which led voters to vote Conservative. It must have been other factors.

There are two further problems with the issue voting model. First, it ignores the way in which the choices confronting voters are limited or manipulated by the media. Media effects may help to produce contradictory opinions on related issues within the same voter. If this occurs, then the vote itself may not be the outcome of careful, rationally thought out decision making. Second, (as with other explanations of voting behaviour) there is the danger of confusing a correlation with a cause. Rose & McAllister (1986) point out, for example, that the attempt to explain a connection between issues and voting choice through post-election analyses is unsatisfactory since only a correlation can be shown. This problem is summed up by Benyon & Denver as follows:

> 'Does the voter pick the party because of its policies or choose the policy positions because they are favoured by the party he or

she supports?' (Benyon & Denver, 1990, p.93)

3.3 Ideological voting

Problems with the issue voting model have led to the development of a variant - the ideological voting model. Heath and his colleagues (1985), for example, are not convinced that issue voting has increased, particularly if the term implies that voters make their choice after weighing up the parties' detailed policy proposals. They do, however, argue that there is a connection (a fit) between voters' general values or ideologies and their overall perception of what parties stand for. The closer the fit, they argue, the stronger the attachment to the party concerned.

According to Rose & McAllister (1986 and 1990) durable political values outweigh issues by more than 10 to one in their importance in explaining voting behaviour. Issues on their own, they argue, are not that significant because voters' evaluation of the parties are made within the context of 'a lifetime of political learning' (Rose & McAllister, 1990, p.141). At election times, a number of different influences are operating simultaneously. Family loyalties, socio-economic interests, the social and political context and the current and recent performance of political parties and leaders all play a part in determining a person's voting behaviour. The most important part, however, is played by the person's political values.

One problem with the ideological model is that, since 1979, opinion polls have consistently indicated that a majority of people are prepared to pay higher taxes to maintain or improve standards of public service, but this support has not been translated into votes. This suggests that there is a gap between people's values and their actions. Ivor Crewe (*Guardian*, 15 & 16 June 1987), however, explains away this gap by arguing that responses to opinion polls are constructed in terms of 'public problems' whilst, at the time of voting, 'family concerns' are uppermost in voters' minds.

Activity 9.4

Item A *Issues and the 1992 general election*

Issue	All voters	Change since 1987	Party advantage 1992	Party advantage 1987
NHS/Hospitals	41	+8	Lab +34	*Lab +49*
Unemployment	36	-13	Lab +26	*Lab +34*
Education	23	+4	Lab +24	*Lab +15*
Prices	11	+5	Con +59	–
Taxation	10	+3	Con +72	*Con +68*
Defence	3	-32	Con +86	*Con + 63*

This table shows the percentage of people who described the above issues as one of the two most important facing the country at the time of the general election in 1992. 'Party advantage' refers to the lead of the party chosen as the best on that issue among respondents for whom the issue was important.

Adapted from Crewe, 1992.

Item B *The issue voting model and the general election of 1992*

On the dominant campaign issues (health, unemployment and education) Labour's policies were clearly preferred to those of the Conservatives. Since the Conservatives won an overall majority, this suggests that people did not vote on the issues. But three points should be taken into account. First, on some issues the Conservatives were the preferred party by a large margin - for example on taxation policy and on their general ability to handle the economy. The Harris exit poll found that 49% of voters cited taxation as the most important issue affecting their vote. Second, the exit polls and Gallup post-election survey found that there had been a significant shift towards the Conservatives on the issues towards the end of the campaign. It seems likely that this reflects a good deal of rationalisation after the election was over. Third and most important, issue voting should not be too narrowly defined. It should include voters' judgements about the party leaders and more general perceptions of the parties.

Adapted from Denver, 1992.

Item C *Poster from the 1992 election campaign*

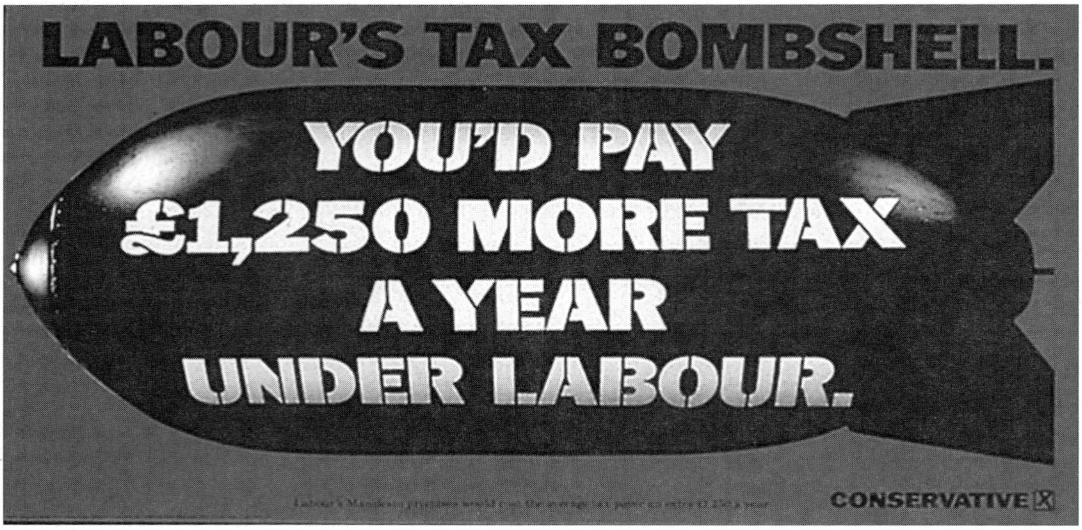

This poster was produced by the Conservative party in the 1992 general election campaign.

Item D *Ideology and voting behaviour*

When voters were asked in the 1987 election campaign which policies they supported, most preferred Labour on unemployment, health, housing and education - the welfare issues. During the campaign, these remained the most important issues for voters. Yet, if voters were asked about image - questions like: 'who is doing a good job?' or 'who is making it feel good to be British again?' - the majority consistently said, ' Maggie'. Given that the Conservatives won the election, it seems that, increasingly, the electorate is thinking in terms of images rather than policies. This does not mean that policies do not matter. It means that policies do not capture people's imaginations unless thay are constructed into an image with which people can identify. Some people argue that this trivialises politics. But, images are not trivial things. It is through images that political questions are being posed and argued through. Political imagery is not a matter of presentation, but of ideology - which is a different and altogether more serious matter.

Adapted from Hall, 1987.

Item E *Issues and elections*

This cartoon appeared in *Private Eye*, 26 June 1987.

Questions

1. a) How does the rational choice model differ from the social structures and party identification models?
   b) Give arguments for and against the view that voting is a rational act.

2 Look at Items A-C.
   a) How do Items A and B help us to explain the result of the 1992 election?
   b) Would you say that Item C was an example of effective campaigning? Give reasons for your answer.

3. Using Item D explain how the ideological voting model differs from the issue voting model.

4. What does Item E tell us about the issue voting model?

3.4 Perceptions of competence

To what extent do perceptions of the competence of parties determine whether voters will vote for them? The answer to this question depends on how voters evaluate two factors - the past performance of the parties (the retrospective model) and their likely future performance (the prospective model).

The prospective model

According to the prospective model, people vote for the party which they judge most likely to raise (or at least to protect) their standard of living. For some voters, this judgement depends not just on considerations of their personal economic wellbeing, it also depends on a wider perception of the competence of a party to manage the economy in general.

This model fits with Stuart Hall's idea that the electorate thinks in terms of images rather than policies (see Item D in Activity 9.4 above). If a party manages to project the image of economic competence, he suggests, then it will attract voters regardless of their existing economic circumstances. This is what happened in the 1987 general election. The Conservative party attracted votes not only from those who had prospered in the 1980s, but also from those who believed that they might prosper in the future.

Hall (1992) also used this model (which he terms 'the sociology of aspirations') to explain the Conservatives' election win in 1992. He claimed that the Conservatives (but not Labour) were aware of the importance of the perception of economic competence during the 1992 election campaign, and this explains their emphasis on taxation as an issue. British voters now tend to calculate their tax liabilities not so much on their current earnings, but on the income they aspire to in the near future. By mounting a relentless attack on Labour's taxation plans, the Conservatives made it difficult for Labour to shake off its image as the party of high taxation.

Hall's analysis of the 1992 election implies that it was fear of Labour, rather than faith in the Conservatives, which led to a Conservative victory. This is the other side of the prospective model - the idea that voters choose the party which they consider will be the least incompetent. Crewe (1992) argued that two pieces of evidence suggest that this is what happened in the 1992 general election. First, there was the 'feel good' factor (which is measured by deducting the percentage of those who expect their financial prospects to deteriorate in the following year from the percentage of those who expect their financial prospects to improve). Just before the 1987 general election the feel good score was +12. But, immediately before the 1992 election, the feel good score was -3. Since the Conservatives retained power, this suggests that they were considered the least incompetent. Second, there were the polls. Only 47% of those polled thought that the Conservatives were competent to manage the economy, but this figure was 7% higher than that scored by Labour.

The retrospective model

Whereas the prospective model examines ways in which forecasts of party performance affect voting behaviour, the retrospective model focuses on voters' perceptions of the parties' past records and especially on the past record of the incumbent government. As such, the retrospective model fits more closely into a purely rational choice model since voters can base their decisions on concrete evidence.

As with the prospective model, the retrospective model suggests that voting behaviour is primarily determined by economic factors. What counts is the voters' perception of the past economic record of the government and the policies supported by the opposition parties. Although, on occasion, non-economic factors can influence voting behaviour (for example, the Falklands War was a significant factor in the Conservative election victory of 1983), this model suggests that management of the economy and economic issues determine the outcomes of most elections.

Like the prospective model, the retrospective model can be used to explain the result of the 1992 general election. The parties entered the 1992 election campaign with the economy in recession. Businesses were going bankrupt, workers were losing their jobs and many house buyers were unable to keep up with their mortgage repayments. More voters claimed that their living standards had fallen over the previous year than those who believed they had risen (Crewe, 1992). On the basis of recent past performance, therefore, it might be expected that the government would lose the election. But, it did not. Somehow, it managed to deflect the blame for the poor economic circumstances which prevailed at the time. The Harris exit poll indicated that voters (including some Labour and Liberal Democrat supporters) were much more likely to blame 'world economic conditions' or even 'Mrs Thatcher's government' than they were to blame John Major's government. Only 5% of Conservative voters and 7% of other voters gave 'John Major's government' as the reason for the poor state of the economy - despite the fact that most of John Major's Cabinet ministers had served in the Thatcher government, including Major himself as Chancellor. These figures suggest that the past record of the government was important, but people separated the past performance of the Thatcher government from the performance of the Major government. In addition, there is evidence that voters were afraid of Labour's economic policies, especially their policies on taxation. One reason for this was that Labour had a reputation as a party of high taxation. Whatever the truth behind this reputation, it was a reputation built on Labour's past performance in government. In other words, enough voters to ensure a Conservative victory were prepared to look kindly on the past performance of the Major government, but looked unkindly on the past performance of the Labour party.

3.5 Leadership and personality

Between 1945 and 1994, the Labour party chose eight leaders whilst the Conservatives chose seven. In other words, the two major parties chose a new leader, on average, every six or seven years. Although some party leaders retained their position for considerably longer than the average (for example, Margaret Thatcher was Conservative party leader for 15 years and Harold Wilson was Labour leader for 13 years), these leaders were not typical. On the whole, party leaders change fairly frequently. As a result, voter perceptions of the personality or competence of a party leader can be classed as a short-term factor in accounting for voting behaviour. If it is correct to assume that, as a result of class and party dealignment , long-term factors have decreased in significance, then perceptions of leadership may be one of the factors which has come to play a greater role in party choice at election times.

In their observations of pre-1974 elections, Butler & Stokes (1971) recognised that leadership could be an issue in voting behaviour, but it was only one of a number of influences and usually only became a factor if one party leader stood out as being particularly more popular than another. Since 1974, the extent and style of media coverage of election campaigns has changed. Media attention on personalities, rather than on policies, is nothing new. But, in recent general elections, the media has focused attention on the party leaders much more than used to be the case. By 1983, studies suggest, leadership had become crucial. Miller (1984), for example, argued that Labour lost the 1983 election not primarily because of unpopular policies, but because its divided leadership failed to give the impression that Labour was competent to rule. When asked which leader would make the best Prime Minister, respondents to opinion polls in 1983 gave Labour's leader, Michael Foot, very low ratings.

These findings raise a number of questions. First, if the personalities of the party leaders do have some effect on party choice, is the impact positive or negative - do voters tend to vote for parties whose leaders they like most or dislike least? Second, can voters' attitudes towards party leaders be separated successfully from their views of the parties in general? And third, do voters tend to draw a distinction between the personality of a leader and the leader's leadership qualities - what is it about the leader (if anything) which determines voting behaviour?

It is difficult to answer these questions. It may, for example, simply not be possible to disentangle voters' perceptions about personality from those concerning leadership qualities. As Benyon & Denver (1990) have noted, it may be that voters are more likely to operate in terms of generalised images which involve a combination of views on and perceptions of personalities, policies, competence and ideology. But, given that most people obtain the bulk of their information about policies and politicians from television and newspapers, media coverage is likely to feature significantly in the formation of such images.

Activity 9.5

Item A *Election poster, 1992*

This poster was produced by the Conservative party in the 1992 general election campaign.

Item B *The Labour party and the 1992 general election*

(i) Labour's fatal error in the 1992 election campaign was to base its economic strategy on higher taxes for the rich. Labour decided that it could afford to alienate the champagne socialists of central London and the leafy suburbs as long as it didn't hurt the lower middle class voters. But, it forgot about the aspirations of the lower middle class. Consequently, Labour not only forced the champagne socialists to vote Tory with their wallets, it also lost the hearts of aspiring Basildon voters. Labour MP Ken Livingstone clearly recognised this when he said: 'We threw it away by watering down true socialism and scaring the voters with high taxes at the same time.'

Adapted from the *Times*, 11 April 1992.

(ii) The idea that the Conservatives won the 1992 general election because voters were frightened by Labour's tax plans has been shown to be a myth. What mattered was voters' judgement about the overall competence of the two parties. Perceptions of economic competence form only part of that judgement. Leadership, unity and other components of the capacity to govern are also important. That, perhaps, is why the current economic recovery has not been accompanied by any signs of a revival in the government's popularity. The polls show that voters know that unemployment is coming down and that inflation is low. In last month's Gallup poll the feel good factor improved sharply, but the Conservative vote in the local elections fell to the lowest ever recorded. Just as the government escaped blame for the recession in 1992, it is not now being given credit for the recovery.

Adapted from an article by Ivor Crewe in the *Observer*, 12 June 1994.

(iii) Voters' economic perceptions are based on the answers to three main questions. First, who do the voters hold responsible for current economic successes or failures? Second, do voters think that the main opposition party is likely to manage the economy more effectively than the incumbent government? And third, do voters believe their own financial interests are likely to be maximised if they support the incumbent government?

Adapted from Sanders, 1993.

Item C *Policies, competence and leadership*

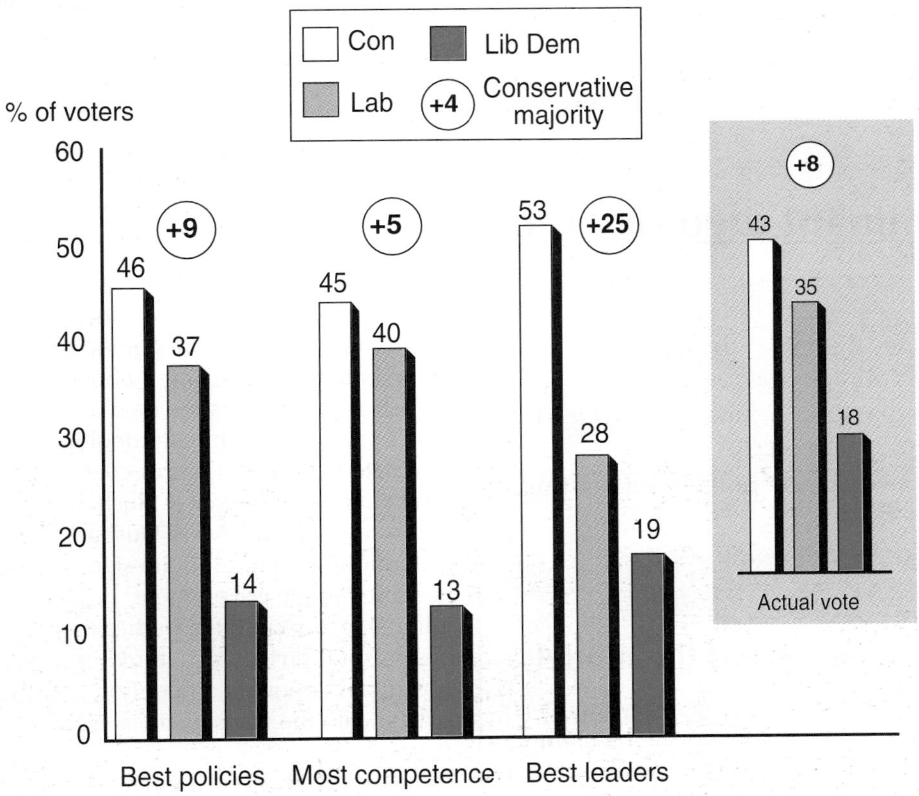

This table shows the result of a post-election poll in which voters were asked to say which party had the best policies, which party could best handle the two issues voters considered most important and which party had the best leaders. The actual vote in the 1992 general election is shown on the right.

Adapted from Crewe, 1992.

Item D *Appraising party leaders*

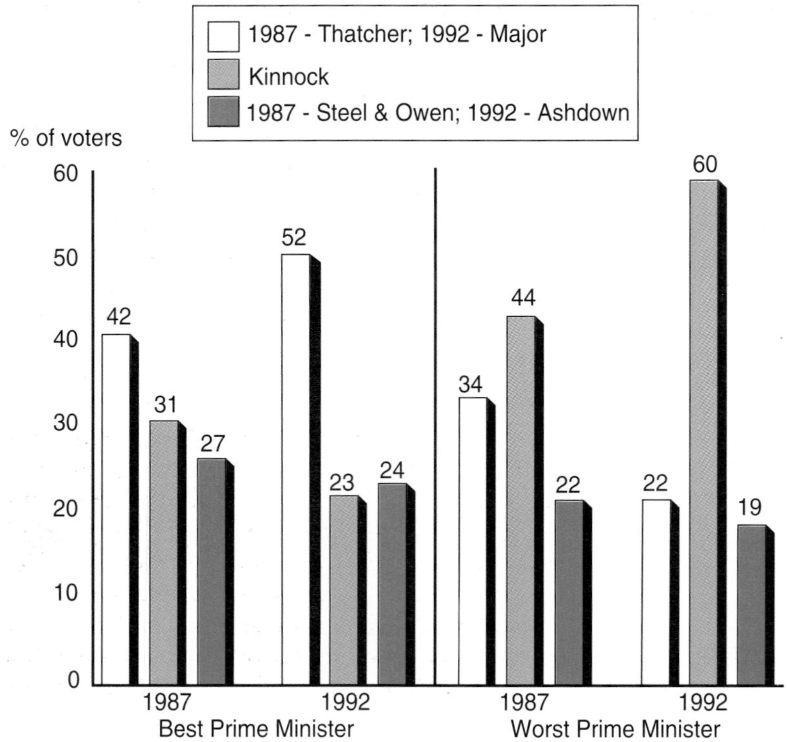

This table shows the results of a post-election poll in which voters were asked who would make the best Prime Minister and who would make the worst.

Adapted from Crewe, 1992.

Questions

1. a) Describe the various elements which make up the rational choice model.
   b) Using this model and Items A-D explain the outcome of the 1992 general election.
2. Judging from Items A-C how did perceptions of the competence of the main parties affect the way in which voters voted in the 1992 general election?
3. Which of the three questions asked in Item B (iii) relates to the prospective model and which to the retrospective model of voting behaviour? Explain your answer.
4. Judging from Items C and D what impact do you think voter perceptions of party leaders had on the outcome of the 1992 general election? Explain how you reached your answer.

4 The dominant ideology model

Key Issues

1. What role does the mass media play in determining voting behaviour?
2. Does the media affect voting behaviour in the short term or long term?
3. How useful are opinion polls in forecasting voting behaviour?
4. Do opinion polls determine voting behaviour?

4.1 Principal elements of the model

The central claim of the dominant ideology model is that powerful groups in society influence the attitudes and behaviour (including the voting behaviour) of the public. This influence is exerted by the control that these groups exercise over public institutions and through the mass media.

Dunleavy & Husbands (1985) suggest that an analysis of voting behaviour cannot be reduced to the level of the individual voter. Instead, analysis should focus on shifts of party support in the electorate as a whole. The way in which society is organised (the social structure) and people's locations within that organisation may well be significant influences on voting behaviour (see part 1 above), but the effects of such structural factors are mediated in many complex ways by 'a set of dominant ideological messages formulated by institutions of central social significance' (Dunleavy & Husbands, 1985, p.19). According to Dunleavy & Husbands, these 'institutions of central social significance' include the mass media, the government, business interests, political leaders and the parties themselves. Together, these institutions are structured in such a way as to provide an unequal competition between the political parties, with the Conservatives at an advantage.

The dominant ideology model in practice

Although Crewe (1992) has doubts about the dominant ideology model, he recognises the existence of institutional inequalities in some areas. For example, he has examined the phenomenon of under-registration (see also section 5.2 below). By the time of the 1992 general election, around one million adults were not registered to vote. This was a large increase compared to previous elections - an increase mainly due to concerns about the poll tax. Since under-registration is more common amongst groups more likely to vote Labour (such as the unemployed, the geographically mobile young and those living in inner cities), the Labour party was disproportionately affected. It was estimated that differential under-registration was worth about eight seats to the Conservatives at the 1992 general election (Crewe, 1993a). Since the poll tax was the product of the dominant ideology in the late 1980s, it could be argued, therefore, that the dominant ideology directly affected voting behaviour.

4.2 The mass media

Central to the dominant ideology model is the role of the mass media. It is through the mass media that groups attempt to set the political agenda and influence public opinion (see also, chapter 19).

The party bias of the press

Most adults in Britain read a national daily and a Sunday newspaper. The vast majority of these newspapers actively support the Conservative party and urge their readers, on election days, to vote Conservative. The tabloid newspapers tend to be highly partisan, with news, opinion and party propaganda mixed together. According to Crewe (1993), 75% of voters, including a majority of working class and a majority of Labour voters, regularly read a Conservative newspaper.

The relationship between the political persuasion of a newspaper and its readers' party preference or voting behaviour is not, however, a straightforward one. A significant minority of *Sun* readers, for example, mistakenly believes that the *Sun* supports the Labour party. Besides, even newspapers which support the Conservatives sometimes turn against their preferred party between elections, particularly if the owner or editor wishes to exert pressure for change. An example of this was the sustained attack made by some sections of the Conservative press on John Major's 'Back to Basics' campaign during the winter of 1993-4.

Broadcasting

Unlike the press, news and current affairs broadcasts on the television and radio operate under legal obligations to be neutral on party political matters. Broadcasters go to great lengths at election times to attempt an almost arithmetic balance in their coverage of the three main parties. Since most voters gain most of their political information from television rather than from newspapers, it could be argued that such a balance is a political necessity.

Whether such a balance is actually achieved, however, is open to debate. It has been suggested, for example, that newspapers are significant in setting the agenda for television news coverage. If most of the newspapers concentrate on issues which are more favourable to the Conservative party and ignore those which are favourable to Labour, then television might well reflect this in its coverage of the issues. A study of the 1987 general election campaign confirms this view (Miller et al., 1990). Television coverage in the 1987 general election campaign focused on defence and law and order (issues more favourable to the Conservatives), rather than on those issues which favoured Labour - such as unemployment, education and health.

The apparent neutrality of radio and television broadcasting might also conceal another factor contributing to what Miller and his colleagues have described as 'a massive bias towards the government' (Miller et al., 1990, p.57). Although the parties might well receive equal campaign coverage, the party in power gets a good deal of additional attention through the reporting of the activities and pronouncements of the government of the day. Crewe (1993) has pointed out, however, that this additional coverage could be a two-edged sword since news reports discuss government failures as well as government successes.

Does bias matter?

It is one thing to show that the mass media is biased and quite another to show that this bias does, in fact, influence voters. The traditional view is that whilst newspapers are probably responsible for few conversions from one party to another, they do have a reinforcing effect on voting behaviour. At most, they play a role in persuading the previously uncommitted to vote for a particular party.

The problem facing all social scientists in attempting to assess the degree of media influence on any aspect of behaviour is how to isolate the effects of all the other possible variables such as family, class, age and a whole range of other factors. But recent attempts to do this (for example, Miller, 1991 and Newton, 1992) have suggested that newspapers do exert some influence over the results of elections.

Short-term and long-term effects

When Neil Kinnock resigned as Labour leader following the 1992 general election, he blamed the election result on the anti-Labour attacks during the campaign made by the Conservative tabloid newspapers. Evidence of a noticeable swing to the Conservatives among *Sun* readers during the later stages of the campaign lends some support to Kinnock's claim. But, the late swing was not just confined to *Sun* readers (Crewe, 1993).

Although short-term effects of media bias cannot be

ruled out, the traditional view that the media has limited influence is challenged more strongly by approaches and studies that take a longer-term view. The traditional claim has been that people's choice of newspaper depends on their political preference rather than vice versa and so newspapers reinforce rather than convert. But, continual reinforcement over a long period may well be significant. The long-term drip-by-drip effect of the media may be more important than any short-term story or campaign run by a newspaper. Miller attempted to look beyond the short-term effects of newspaper coverage during general elections by interviewing the same panel of respondents on a number of occasions over a 12 month period preceding the 1987 general election (Miller, 1991). The results of this survey indicate that newspapers do influence their readers over the long term.

Even more influential in helping to produce or confirm a 'world view' among voters could be those things which the media choose to omit. In their urge to convey news, the mass media are more likely to focus on short-term, trivial issues and events rather than on longer-term, larger and more underlying questions. The range of issues, beliefs and arguments projected by the media forms the context in which voters make their choices. This context also affects the behaviour of the parties. It has been argued, for example, that a Conservative dominated press has forced Labour to be extra cautious to avoid tabloid accusations of 'loony leftism' (Newton, 1992).

Media effects and party dealignment

Most commentators agree that there has been party dealignment over the past 20 years (see above section 2.2). It has been suggested that one cause of this is the balanced, non-partisan and non-ideological style of television coverage. This style, it is argued, has contributed to the decline of party identification (Denver, 1989). At the same time, party dealignment may have resulted in a more influential role for the mass media. Since (due to party dealignment) there are now fewer committed voters, more voters should be open to persuasion and there should, therefore, be greater scope for media influence.

Political advertising and the manipulation of news

All political parties attempt to manipulate the ways in which political affairs are reported and presented in the media. But, since most of the press is sympathetic to the Conservative party, this process of manipulation is more easily managed by the Conservatives (at least as far as newspapers are concerned). There is evidence, for example, of particularly close collaboration at election times between leading Conservatives and the editors of newspapers which support the Conservatives (see, for example, Benyon & Denver, 1990).

The Conservatives' advantage is heightened if they are also the party of government. Miller (1990), for example, has drawn attention to the way in which Conservative governments in the 1980s altered the way in which unemployment figures were calculated. These altered figures were then reported uncritically by sympathetic elements in the media. In addition, during the 1980s, Conservative governments ran advertising campaigns to publicise certain policies even before Parliament had granted legal approval for their implementation.

It is at election time, however, that party advertising is most common. All the major parties spend a great deal of effort and money on their pre-election advertising campaigns. There are legal ceilings on the amount that can be spent by parliamentary candidates at constituency level, but no such restrictions apply to the parties nationally and this is where most of the spending occurs. Here again, the Conservatives have an advantage. Not only does the Conservative party have access to more funds than the other main parties, it also gets help in kind. For example, during the 1992 election campaign, tobacco companies allowed Conservative party adverts to be pasted up on billboards in place of cigarette adverts, free of charge.

Not infrequently, party election broadcasts and adverts are exercises in negative propaganda which criticise the policies or leadership of opposing parties. Negative campaigning often leads to charges of media manipulation. After the 1992 general election campaign, for example, complaints were made that elements of Conservative party advertising so distorted Labour's taxation policies that they amounted to a major misrepresentation and to an unfair electoral advantage.

It is not only the political parties which engage in political advertising at election times. Professional associations, trade unions and groups representing business interests use elections to campaign on issues on which there are clear policy differences between the parties. In 1992, for example, NALGO (the local government officers' union) paid for an advert which referred to government training schemes as 'half baked', whilst the Institute of Directors ran full page anti-Labour adverts in the press. Such adverts are designed to influence voting behaviour.

Media manipulation and the dominant ideology model

Supporters of the dominant ideology model see some of the activities described above not so much as isolated attempts to secure support for or against particular policies, but as part of a wider network of control through which powerful groups, with the aid of the mass media, are able to influence the attitudes and behaviour of the public. Divorced from other factors, the claims of those who detect bias in the media may seem to be exaggerated. But, viewed in combination with other factors affecting voting behaviour, their claims may have greater substance. It has been suggested by some writers that rising economic optimism was a significant factor in the Conservative election victory of 1987. Miller (1990), however, asks what it was that encouraged such optimism during the election campaign. If there is evidence that the Conservative government manipulated both the media and the economy, he argues, then the dominant ideology model rather than a rational choice model provides a better explanation of voting behaviour.

Activity 9.6

Item A *The political system*

Item B *Headlines from the 1992 election campaign*

Daily Mail 23 March
Labour to ration mortgages

Daily Express *7 April*
BAKER'S MIGRANT FLOOD WARNINGS; LABOUR SET TO OPEN DOORS

Sun 24 March
Threat of return to picket terror

Daily Express 9 April
A vote for Ashdown will let Kinnock into No. 10, Vote Conservative

Sun 9 April
If Kinnock wins today will the last person to leave Britain please turn out the lights?

Daily Mail 9 April
The winter of shame: this was the face of Britain the last time Labour ruled

Sun 11 April 1992
IT'S THE SUN WOT WON IT.

Item C *The press and the 1992 general election*

(i) The last minute swing at the 1992 general election is unlikely to have been created by short-term events. It is the long term which counts. If the press plays a role in determining voting behaviour, it is because day after day people read a newspaper which supports a particular party. If the Tory tabloids did swing the campaign in the last few days they did so by reawakening fears and memories sustained over a long period. For example, the myth of the 'winter of discontent' in 1979 was created by the tabloids and has been nurtured by them ever since. If the tabloids' reference to the 'winter of discontent' had an effect on voting, it was because the folk memory, created over the years, was triggered just before election day.

Adapted from Newton, 1992.

(ii) It is estimated that 7.5% of *Sun* readers swung to the Conservatives during the last few days of the 1992 election campaign. But, the same estimate shows a 7% swing to the Conservatives amongst readers of the *Independent* and a 5.5% swing amongst readers of the *Daily Mirror*. These figures all show an above average swing. But, the swing amongst readers of the *Daily Express*, *Daily Mail* and the *Times* was 2.5%, 4% and 0% respectively - a below average swing. The most decisive conclusion that can be drawn is that some Conservative tabloids gave an extra push to the Conservative bandwagon which was already rolling. An analysis of constituencies with large *Sun* readerships suggests that, at most, the *Sun* may have saved six marginal seats for the Conservatives. The Conservatives won an overall majority of 21 seats.

Adapted from Crewe, 1992.

(iii) There is no evidence for the theory that the press was responsible for the Conservatives' general election victory in 1992. Among readers of pro-Tory tabloids, support for the Conservatives fell by 3% during the election campaign. It also fell by 1% amongst readers of the quality newspapers which support the Conservative party. On the other hand, support for the Conservatives rose amongst readers of the pro-Labour *Daily Mirror*. It also rose among people who did not read any newspaper. This may seem to be good news for Labour, but it is not necessarily so. Since 1992, much of the traditional Tory press has begun to attack John Major's government. Some Labour supporters welcome this as a decisive change. But, if the press did not help the Conservatives in 1992, it is equally unlikely to help Labour in 1996 or 1997.

Adapted from Heath et al., 1994.

Item D *National newspaper circulation and party support, 1992*

	Circulation (000)	% of total	Party support
Dailies			
Mirror/Record	3,618.9	25.5	Labour
Sun	3,587.7	25.3	Conservative
Mail	1,667.6	11.8	Conservative
Express	1,517.7	10.7	Conservative
Telegraph	1,046.4	7.4	Conservative
Star	803.7	5.7	Conservative
Today	483.5	3.4	Conservative
Guardian	418.3	2.9	Labour
Times	389.4	2.7	Conservative
Independent	374.2	2.6	Independent
Financial Times•	290.7	2.1	Labour
Sundays			
News of the World	4,716.8	29.6	Conservative
Sunday Mirror	2,782.4	17.4	Labour
People	2,141.2	13.4	Labour
Sunday Mail	1,974.7	12.4	Conservative
Sunday Express	1,679.3	10.5	Conservative
Sunday Times	1,173.9	7.4	Conservative
Sunday Telegraph	560.1	3.5	Conservative
Observer	542.4	3.4	Labour
Independent on Sunday	386.7	2.4	Independent

• The Financial Times surprised its readers by advising them on election day to vote Labour

Adapted from Newton, 1992.

Questions

1. The cartoon in Item A illustrates the dominant ideology model. Use it to explain how the dominant ideology model works and how it differs from other models used to explain voting behaviour.
2. Give the arguments for and against the view that the *Sun* newspaper won the 1992 general election for the Conservatives.
3. How important is the media in determining voting behaviour (a) in the short term and (b) in the long term?

4.3 Opinion polls

Opinion polls on political matters are not only carried out at election times, nor are their questions confined to voting intentions. But, it is during election campaigns that polls attract the greatest attention and scrutiny. The first British general election campaign in which opinion polls were conducted was the general election of 1945. At that time, only one polling organisation existed. Since the 1970s, the number of polls published in the media has increased sharply. Indeed, most polls are commissioned by the media. During the four week general election campaign in 1992, over 50 sets of national poll results were published. Most used samples of about 1,000 adults chosen from between 50 and 100 constituencies. An exception to this was a late poll carried out by ICM in which 10,000 electors from 300 constituencies were interviewed. Almost all polls are carried out by just five agencies - ICM, Gallup, NOP, Harris and MORI.

Strictly speaking, questions designed to discover how people will vote are not polls of opinion but surveys of intended behaviour. Nor are poll results predictions of election results. What they provide is a snapshot of voting intentions on a certain day (or over a period if the poll is conducted over number of days). But, the media often does present poll data as forecasts (as do the polling organisations when they present their final pre-election polls). As a result, comparisons are made with the actual election results to assess the polls' accuracy. As Conley (1993) points out, because those who study voting trends - 'psephologists' - rely heavily on data from opinion polls, the validity of psephology depends to a large extent on the accuracy of poll data.

Accuracy

According to Kavanagh (1992), the polls had a reasonably good record of accuracy at general elections up to 1970, but after 1970 polls were inaccurate in five of the following seven elections. Even so, Eatwell (1993) has calculated that the average error of the final polls between 1945 and 1987 was only 1.3%. This is an impressive record, especially given that the polling organisations themselves stress that in general elections with a sample of around 1,000 respondents there is a margin of error of plus or minus 3%. It should be noted that polls conducted during by-elections are usually less accurate because there is often a greater degree of volatility in voting behaviour compared to that in a general election.

Despite this record of accuracy, the reputation of the polling organisations suffered a great deal after the 1992 general election (see Game, 1995). Throughout the election campaign, the polls suggested a narrow Labour lead. Even most of those polls conducted during the final two days of the campaign either gave Labour a marginal lead or had Labour and the Conservatives even. A hung Parliament was regarded as the most likely electoral outcome. Overall, the five major polling organisations, on average, gave Labour a 1.3% lead over the Conservatives, but the actual result was a 7.6% win for the Conservatives. The verdict afterwards was that this was the pollsters' worst ever election performance and there was the suspicion that polls had been overestimating Labour support for a long time. Complaints about the inaccuracy of the polls intensified because the polls themselves had been a major item of news throughout the campaign - perhaps because they suggested such a close-run contest between the two main parties.

Reasons for polling errors

According to Ivor Crewe, there were two reasons why the polls failed to forecast the result of the 1992 general election accurately:

> 'Either voters swung in massive and unprecedented numbers on the eve and day of polling or the polls systematically underestimated Conservative support and overestimated Labour - or both. It is highly implausible that a last minute swing (of the order of 4%) can account for all the polls' error.' (Crewe, 1992, p.2).

Although there is some evidence of a late swing - mainly Liberal Democrat to Conservative according to Eatwell (1993), most psephologists would agree that the swing was not big enough, of itself, to explain the polls' inaccuracy. Rather, a number of explanations have been considered. First, it has been suggested that, as a result of the poll tax, the proportion of adults who did not appear on the electoral register was much higher than before and this under-registration adversely affected the Labour vote (see above, pp.260-61). Second, it has been argued that the Conservatives benefited from a change in electoral regulations which permitted a greater number of expatriates (people who had emigrated from Britain) to vote. Most expatriates were considered likely to vote Conservative, but they were not sampled by the pollsters.

Growing under-registration and a larger number of voting expatriates, however, are not in themselves sufficient to explain the disparity between the polls and the final result. A third argument is that people did not provide the polls with accurate information. As Sanders (1993) has noted, the question of the accuracy of the polls boils down to one or both of the following - either the polls were correct at the time they were conducted (and late switching took place) or the polls unconsciously misrepresented 'true' public opinion. It is the latter idea which has presented pollsters with a major problem. Much of the work of psephology involves the construction of ideas and theories about what people think and what they do, but opinion polls only measure what people say. They cannot be expected, therefore, to take account of discrepancies that might arise between these different facets of human behaviour. That people might say one thing, yet think or do another is a possibility at any election. The 1992 election campaign was marked by the high moral tone taken by the opposition parties and by an appeal to self-interest by the Conservatives. If, as some studies suggest (for example, Kavanagh 1992), people tend to give what they feel are 'politically correct' answers to opinion poll questions, whilst voting according to what they perceive to be their economic self-interest, this might account for the discrepancy between the polls and the actual election result.

The idea that some respondents did not tell the truth could also explain why the exit polls (the polls taken as people come out of the polling station) underestimated the Conservative vote in 1992. Exit polls do not ask people how they intend to vote, but how they have just voted. The samples of voters questioned in exit polls are considerably larger than pre-election polls. Since samples are larger and polling takes place after voters have voted, exit polls should be more accurate than pre-election polls. It is only after the 1992 election that their use as an accurate forecast of the election result has been seriously challenged.

Do polls influence voting behaviour?

In addition to the three arguments mentioned above, there is a long running debate about whether or not the publication of opinion poll results influences voting behaviour. One view is that polls have a bandwagon effect and encourage some voters to vote for the party which appears to be the most popular. An opposite view is the idea of a 'boomerang' effect - a party trailing in the polls picks up sympathy votes as the 'underdog' or supporters of the leading party become complacent and fail to turn out to vote. According to Denver (1989), however, research has found little evidence to support either view.

Although it is difficult to find evidence to support the bandwagon or boomerang effects, Crewe suggests that the publication of the polls did have a marked effect on voting behaviour in the 1992 general election. He suggests that because the opinion polls put Labour ahead, people became afraid of a Labour government and ended up voting Conservative. He adds:

> 'There is an irony here. Had the campaign polls consistently shown the Conservatives to be ahead, as they probably were, the government might not have mobilised the anti-Labour vote so effectively and hence might not have survived in office.' (Crewe, 1992, p.11)

There are two other ways in which opinion polls may influence voting behaviour. First, it is possible that opinion poll results are used by some people who vote tactically (see section 5.3 below). Since, however, effective tactical voting at a general election needs to be based on information about relative party support at constituency level, the publication of national opinion poll results is not much of a guide (though this is not to say that polls are not used by tactical voters). Certainly, in by-elections it is easier for people to vote tactically since opinion polls are conducted locally as well as nationally.

Second, whatever they may say in public, opinion polls are taken seriously by politicians. Not only do parties commission private polls, they base their campaigns on information gained from polls. The results of polls can have a marked effect on morale. Newton (1992) explains how the Labour lead in the polls during the 1992 election campaign seems to have contributed to the widely criticised triumphalist style of the party's pre-election rally in Sheffield.

The future of opinion polls

Because of the possible influence of opinion polls, there are those who would like to see restrictions placed on the publication of opinion poll results. The publication of poll results is banned in France and Germany during the final week of an election campaign. In 1967, the Speaker's Conference on Electoral Reform advocated a similar ban in the UK over the final three days of an election campaign. Although Parliament rejected this recommendation, the question is still raised from time to time in Parliament.

The poor performance of the polls in 1992 resulted in immediate changes in the way in which the media reports poll findings and in the way polling was to be conducted. The BBC issued guidelines on the reporting of poll findings and its *Newsnight* programme announced a ban on exit polls until improved methods of polling were announced. The polling organisations themselves undertook to review their methods and to make greater use in the future of panel studies. Panel studies involve repeated interviews with the same sample of respondents at different stages during (and sometimes after) an election campaign. In addition, polling organisations have begun to adjust their figures to take account of factors which were ignored in the past. For example, some polls now take account of former Conservatives who are now 'don't knows' or 'won't says', but might revert at a general election. Some polls are adjusted to make sure that the sample includes the right proportion of Conservative, Labour or Liberal Democrat voters according to the number of votes each party received in the last general election.

Activity 9.7

Item A *Opinion polls held during 1992 general election campaign*

	March																					April							
	11	12	13	14	15	16	17	18	19	20	21	22	23	24	25	26	27	28	29	30	31	1	2	3	4	5	6	7	8
Con	38	40	39	39	39	39	39	39	39	39	38	39	39	39	39	39	38	38	38	37	37	36	36	37	37	37	37	37	38
Lab	40	40	40	40	40	41	41	41	41	41	41	40	40	40	41	41	39	39	39	40	41	40	40	39	40	40	40	40	39
Lib Dem	17	15	17	16	16	15	16	17	17	17	17	16	16	16	17	17	18	18	18	18	18	19	19	19	19	19	19	19	19
Others	5	4	5	5	5	4	4	3	3	3	4	5	4	4	4	4	4	4	4	5	4	5	5	4	4	4	4	4	3
Lab Lead	**2**	**-**	**1**	**1**	**1**	**2**	**2**	**2**	**2**	**2**	**3**	**1**	**1**	**1**	**2**	**2**	**1**	**1**	**1**	**3**	**4**	**4**	**4**	**2**	**3**	**3**	**3**	**3**	**1**
Maj	Lab	Con	nil	nil	nil	Lab	Lab	Lab	Lab	Lab	Lab	nil	nil	nil	Lab	Lab	nil	nil	nil	Lab	Lab	Lab	Lab	Lab	Lab	Lab	Lab	Lab	nil

This table shows the result of opinion polls held during the 1992 general election campaign. The bottom line shows which (if any) party would gain an overall majority if the result of the poll was the result of the actual election.

Adapted from the *Guardian* 9 April 1992 (the day of the general election).

Item B *The 1992 exit polls*

(i) Exit polls

Poll by	Sample size	Con %	Lab %	LibDem %	Other %	Con Lead %
ICM	25,300	38	41	18	3	-3
Harris	4,701	41	37	18	4	5
NOP National	4,719	40	36	18	5	6
NOP Marginals	18,747	43	39	16	2	4
Actual result		**42.8**	**35.2**	**18.3**	**3.7**	**7.6**

This table shows the result of exit polls held on the day of the 1992 general election.

(ii) Projected seats (10 pm)

Poll by	Con	Lab	LibDem	Other	Con lead over Labour
ICM	302	307	18	24	-5
Harris	305	294	25	27	+21
NOP	301	298	25	27	+3
Actual result	**336**	**271**	**20**	**24**	**+65**

This table shows the projections made as a result of the exit polls held on the day of the 1992 general election.

Adapted from Game, 1994

Item C *The pollsters and the 1992 general election*

This cartoon was published in the *Daily Express* after the 1992 election. John Major stands on the left and Neil Kinnock walks off on the right.

Item D *The problem with polls*

A key error in the pollsters' method is that they fail to take into account the huge number of people (sometimes 45% of a sample) who refuse to answer questions when approached by an interviewer. The 1992 British General Election Study shows that these 'refusers' are more likely to vote Conservative than Labour or Liberal Democrat. The 'don't knows' or 'won't says' recorded in opinion poll results are the replies given by people who cooperate with the interviewer. Until now, opinion polls have simply ignored the refusers who simply will not cooperate at all. So, if a middle class, middle aged man refuses to answer, the interviewer goes off and finds another middle class, middle aged man who will answer. Polling organisations hope that by asking quotas of people from different classes, ages and sexes they will produce a representative sample. But the 1992 British General Election Study did not use quotas. It selected 2,800 people at random. If the people were out or said they were too busy to talk, the interviewers went back again and again until they got answers. The study found that amongst those who would not or could not answer first time, the Conservatives gained 6% more support than they had amongst those who did answer. This means that the Conservatives may not be as far behind as recent polls claim. Also, it means that results showing a one or two point gap between the parties are pretty meaningless.

Adapted from the *Independent On Sunday*, 17 April 1994.

Item E *Injecting 'realism' into the polls*

Table A Raw poll results

	May	Apr	Mar	Feb	1992*
Con	26	26	24	26	43
Lab	44	48	49	51	35
LibDem	26	22	22	20	18
Others	5	4	5	4	4
Lab lead	+18	+22	+25	+25	-8

* Actual result in the 1992 general election

Table B Adjustment (1)

	May	Loc*	Apr	Mar
Con	27	27	29	28
Lab	43	42	46	47
LibDem	25	27	22	21
Others	4	4	4	4
Lab lead	+16	+15	+17	+19

* Local election result in May 1994

Table C Adjustment (2)

	May	Loc*	Apr
Con	28	27	28
Lab	41	42	43
LibDem	26	27	23
Others	5	4	5
Lab lead	+13	+15	+15

* Local election result in May 1994

Table D Both adjustments

	May	Loc*	Apr
Con	30	27	32
Lab	40	42	41
LibDem	26	27	23
Others	4	4	4
Lab lead	+10	+15	+9

* Local election result in May 1994

In May 1994 the *Guardian*'s ICM poll began to include adjustments to give a more realistic picture of voting intentions. Table A shows the raw poll results. Table B shows the raw data adjusted to take account of former Conservative voters who are now 'don't knows' or 'won't says'. Table C shows the raw data adjusted so that the respondents contained the right proportion of people who voted Labour or Conservative at the last general election. Table D shows what happens if both adjustments are applied together. ICM's director argues that the double adjustment is necessary before it is possible to show how people would vote if there was a general election today.

Adapted from the *Guardian*, 11 May 1994.

Questions

1. a) Use Items A and B to give arguments for and against the view expressed in Item C.
   b) Suppose you worked for a polling organisation. Write an article explaining why the 1992 general election was particularly difficult to forecast.
2. Look at Items B and D.
   a) What could account for the degree of inaccuracy in the exit polls at the 1992 general election?
   b) How does the accuracy of the exit polls compare with that of the pre-election polls (Item A)? Explain why this is so.
3. Would you say that the adjustments described in Item E are sufficient to restore people's faith in opinion polls? Explain your answer.
4. a) Do you think that the publication of opinion poll results should be banned in the week before a general election? Give reasons for your answer.
   b) How would you respond to those who argue the opposite view to yours?

5 The voting context model

Key Issues

1. How do the perceptions that voters have about an election and the range of options available to them affect their voting behaviour?
2. Why do some people choose not to vote?
3. Why do some people vote tactically?
4. How important is the election campaign in determining how people vote?

5.1 Principal elements of the model

Miller (1990) claims that, unlike journalists, political scientists have paid little attention to voters' assessments of the context in which they vote. By 'voting context', Miller has in mind the perceptions that voters have about the purpose of the election and the range of options available to them. These options may include not voting (abstention), using the vote as a protest (which is more common in by-elections) or voting tactically. The range of options may be influenced by what the voter perceives to be the purpose of the election. This, in turn, may be related to the type of election. Voting behaviour varies according to whether it is a local, general, European or by-election. By emphasising the context, Miller suggests that voting is not always limited to a straightforward expression of personal preference. Voters, in considering these options, are also weighing up the likely consequences of their vote.

5.2 Turnout

Turnout is an important factor in explaining voting behaviour since it is, in a sense, a measure of abstention. The number of people turning out to vote at an election is expressed as a percentage of those whose names appear on the electoral register. This register is compiled by local authorities every October, comes into operation from the following February and remains in force for one year. It can, therefore, never be completely accurate. Apart from bureaucratic errors, some households do not complete the registration forms. According to Platt & Smyth (1994) the numbers not registered are increasing and include 20% of young people, 24% of black people and 15% of Asians. In addition, some people die or move house in the period between registering and election day.

When allowances have been made for some of these factors, turnout trends have been fairly consistent since 1966. Platt & Smyth (1994) compare the 73-75% turnout at general elections in the 1980s unfavourably with the 84% recorded in 1950. But, over a longer timespan, the 1950 turnout (together with 82.5% in 1951) appears as a high point. The average between 1922 and 1945 was 74%. Turnout at the 1992 general election was 77.7%. This was 2.4% up on the 1987 general election and was also the highest since 1974. Butler & Kavanagh (1992) suggest that this was because the 1992 general election was the first election since February 1974 whose outcome, according to the opinion polls, was in doubt.

Differential turnout

Overall rates of turnout mask quite marked variations among different sections of the electorate. Considerable differences are found when turnout is compared constituency by constituency. For example, Denver (1989) reports that constituencies with a higher level of owner occupiers tend to show higher turnouts. Inner city areas, on the other hand, tend to have more transient populations and a lower turnout rate. At the 1992 general election, turnout rose most in safe Conservative seats, but rose hardly at all in constituencies which Labour was defending. Investigations into districts within constituencies can also show important variations. For example, Platt & Smyth (1994) noted that there was a turnout of just 20% in the West End of Newcastle Upon Tyne in the 1992 election, but a turnout of 71.3% in the constituency as a whole.

Although there appears to be little in the way of variation according to gender, class, income level or education, Denver (1989) points to four factors associated with low turnout. People who are young, single, live in privately rented accommodation or are residentially mobile are less likely to vote. These four factors are frequently interrelated. Denver suggests that the lower the degree of social involvement in a stable community, the less inclined people are to vote.

As might be expected, the stronger people's party identification, the more likely they are to vote. This connection is most clearly seen in local elections where overall turnout is usually substantially lower than at a general election. Party dealignment could, therefore, be a factor in any decline in turnout at local elections.

Abstention

As with many other aspects of voting behaviour, explanations of non-voting may focus on individual motivation or on social groups. For example, at the level of the individual, a distinction can be made between **passive** and **active** abstainers (passive abstainers are also sometimes described as accidental, negative or apathetic non-voters). Whilst passive abstainers have no or very little interest in politics, active abstainers are those who refuse to vote on principle or as a protest. They may disagree with the electoral system (or indeed with the entire political system) or they may simply not be attracted to any of the parties or candidates standing in their constituency. Platt & Smyth argue that one reason for a growing number of positive abstainers is the falling number of marginal constituencies:

> 'There is a growing sense of an individual's vote being unimportant. The results of the next general election will be determined in perhaps as few as 40 to 50 "swing" constituencies. Barring some unforeseen sea-change in voting behaviour, the results in over 600 others can already be predicted. The feeling - why vote if it makes no difference to the outcome? - fuels the increasing cynicism about politics as a whole. It merges into the idea that there is no real difference between the parties or politicians. "They're all the same. Why vote? It only encourages them" has become the justificatory cry of disengagement.' (Platt & Smyth, 1994, p.5)

5.3 Tactical voting

Tactical voters can be defined as those voters who, rather than voting for their preferred party, choose to vote for another party in the hope that this will help to prevent their least favoured party from winning the seat.

Tactical voting has been particularly significant at by-elections for many years. In recent years, however, evidence has come to light that tactical voting has influenced the outcome of local elections too. In the 1994 local elections, for example, the Labour party attracted by far the largest share of the votes. The Conservatives were beaten, just, into third place behind the Liberal Democrats. Although the total number of votes cast for the Liberal Democrats was only marginally higher than their share in the 1992 local elections, on this occasion their proportion of the vote delivered a large increase in the number of seats. According to Crewe (*Observer*, 8 May 1994) this was the result of tactical voting.

Miller (1990) records a study of data from by-elections which shows that tactical voting is of great importance. This study suggests that the electorate can be divided into four groups. The largest group is that of core voters. Core voters already know at the start of the campaign how they will vote, and they would not change their minds even if their preferred candidates had no chance of winning. This group makes up about 39% of the electorate at by-elections. The second largest group is that of tactical voters. They make up about 37% of the electorate at by-elections. The third largest group is that of the abstainers - people with no intention of voting. They make up about 15% of the electorate at by-elections. And the smallest group is that of the floating voters - voters who are unsure about who they will vote for until the last minute. They make up about 9% of the electorate at by-elections.

There is also evidence to suggest that tactical voting has been growing in general elections. In fact, political analysts have argued that tactical voting at the 1992 general election had a greater impact than at any previous general election. Butler & Kavanagh (1992), for example, claim that it reduced the Conservative majority by half. Certainly, the swing to Labour in Conservative/Labour marginals was higher than elsewhere (3.5% compared with 2% overall). This suggests tactical voting by Liberal Democrat supporters.

To be effective, tactical voting needs to be based on good information about likely voting support for the different parties in that constituency. This is not always available and decisions about whether or not to vote tactically may in some cases be made on the basis of the standing of the parties nationally - a poor guide to the standing of the parties locally. Alternatively, voter perceptions about party support in their own constituency may be based on the results of recent local elections - which also may be misleading.

Protest voting

A protest vote is a negative vote. It is a vote against a policy or against the current direction of the government, rather than a vote for one of the opposition parties. Tactical voting can be seen as a form of protest voting in the sense that it is based on voters' dislikes rather than on what they like.

Protest voting is more common in by-elections and in local or Euro-elections than in general elections. Since 1979, especially, protest voting has produced some spectacular results. No matter how large the government majority at the previous general election, this majority can be eroded at a by-election. For example, in June 1994 a Conservative majority of 17,702 was overthrown in the Eastleigh by-election, a clear sign that the voters of Eastleigh wanted to protest about the government's recent behaviour. Similarly, one reason why Conservative governments have fared badly in local elections since 1979 is that people who vote Conservative in general elections are prepared to register a protest vote against the government in local elections.

Governments, however, can afford not to be too worried by protest voting. It is often short-lived and many voters revert to their usual preferences at the next general election. In 1987, for example, a general election was held only five weeks after local elections, yet only 71% of those who voted in both elections chose the same party both times. Similarly, at the 1992 election, the Liberal Democrats did not retain any of the seats which they had won in by-elections during the course of the previous Parliament.

5.4 Election campaigns

It is difficult to measure exactly how much of an impact the election campaign makes on voting behaviour. What is clear, however, is that politicians and party workers from all parties behave as if election results are solely determined by the success or failure of the campaign.

One argument is that if class and party dealignment has taken place, then fewer voters should have made firm voting choices before the election date is announced. So, more voters should be open to persuasion and, therefore, influenced by the election campaign. An examination of late deciders (voters who make up their minds during the election campaign) and waverers (voters who seriously consider voting for a party other than the one they finally choose) in general elections between 1964 and 1987 shows that around a quarter of voters make up their minds during the election campaign.

Late deciders and waverers 1964-92

	1964	1966	1970	Feb. 1974	Oct. 1974	1979	1983	1987	1992
Late deciders	12	11	12	23	22	28	22	21	24
Waverers	24	22	21	25	21	31	25	27	26

Adapted from Heath et al.,1988 and Heath et al.,1994.

The figures in the table above suggest, first, that election campaigns are an important determining factor for a significant number of voters and, second, that the proportion of hesitant voters has varied only slightly since the 1960s. It should be noted, however, that the accuracy of the above figures has been questioned. Denver (1989), for example, records the results of a panel study of voters during the 1987 general election. This found that just 13% of panellists voted for a party other than the one chosen at the start of the campaign (compared to 27% in the table above). But, even if the lower figure is correct, it still translates into a significant number of voters. This helps to explain why the main parties are prepared to spend so much money and effort ensuring that their campaigns are run professionally.

The 1992 general election campaign has come under great scrutiny because opinion polls showed Labour and the Conservatives to be neck and neck, but the Conservatives ended up with a 7.6% lead. The immediate reaction of some commentators was to suggest that the campaign was decisive. This was the conclusion of Butler & Kavanagh:

> 'The 1992 campaign presents a challenge. The Conservatives' lead was so clear that the events of the final three weeks could not have altered the outcome. However, a mere one per cent swing nationwide would have reduced the Conservatives to 312 seats, not enough for them to have carried on as a government. Their victory was a near-run thing. The Conservatives, with a mistake or two, could have forfeited their triumph; the Opposition, acting differently, could have won. The campaign is worthy of scrutiny because it was, perhaps, decisive.' (Butler & Kavanagh, 1992, p.247)

In their study of the 1992 general election Heath and his colleagues (1994) agreed that the election campaign may have been decisive in ensuring that the Conservatives won an overall majority. They point out that no matter how good an election campaign Labour had fought, it would not have been enough to win Labour an overall majority:

> 'Butler & Kavanagh were almost certainly right in suggesting that the campaign was decisive. An error-free Labour campaign might have pushed their share of the vote up from 35% to 36% - nowhere near enough to have made them the largest party, but probably enough to deprive the Conservatives of their overall majority...It is very unlikely, however, that Labour could have done anything in the campaign to have generated enough votes for an overall majority or even to have made it the largest party in a hung Parliament.' (Heath et al., 1994, p.20)

Activity 9.8

Item A *Turnout at elections*

(i) Turnout in the 1992 general election

Five seats with the highest increase in turnout

Turnout	increase	seat	result	
75.1	+9.3	Hendon North	Con maj	7,122
81.3	+8.8	Horsham	Con maj	25,072
73.3	+8.6	Kensington	Con maj	3,548
72.4	+8.6	Hendon South	Con maj	12,047
78.6	+8.6	Chipping Barnet	Con maj	13,951

Five seats with the highest decrease in turnout

Turnout	decrease	seat	result	
54.6	-10.7	Liverpool Riverside	Lab maj	17,437
60.8	-9.6	Manchester Gorton	Lab maj	16,279
56.9	-7.0	Manchester Central	Lab maj	18,037
68.5	-6.6	L/pool Mossley Hill	Lib maj	2,606
56.1	-6.3	Sheffield Central	Lab maj	17,294

This table shows the five seats with the highest increase in turnout and the five seats with the greatest decrease in turnout in the 1992 general election.

(ii) Turnout at different types of election 1992-94

April 1992	General election	77.7%
May 1994	Local elections	43.0%
June 1994	European election	36.5%
June 1994	By-elections*	42.8%

* Five by-elections were held on 9 June 1994, the same day on which the European election was held.

Adapted from Wood & Wood, 1992.

Item B *Three marginal constituencies*

(i) VALE OF GLAMORGAN		No change from 1987
Electorate % Turnout	66.672 81.9% 1992	65.310 79.3% **1987**
Sweeney , W E (Con)	24,220 44.2% -2.4%	24,229 46.8% Con
Smith JWP (Lab)	24,201 44.3% +9.6%	17,978 34.7% Lab
Davies K (Lib)	5,045 9.2% -7.4%	8.633 16.7% Lib
Con to Lab swing 6.0%	**Con maj 19**	**Con maj 6,251**

(ii) BRECON AND RADNOR		Con gain
Electorate % Turnout	51,509 85.95 1992	49,394 84.4% **1987**
Evans, JP (con)	15,977 36.1% +1.4%	14,509 34.8% Lib
Livsey, R A L (Lib)	15,847 35.8% +1.0%	14,453 34.7% Con
Mann, C J (Lab)	11,634 26.3% -2.9%	12,180 29.2% Lab
Lib to Con swing 0.2%	**Con maj 130**	**Lib maj 56**

(iii) CORBY		No change from 1987
Electorate % Turnout	68,333 82.95 1992	66,119 79.6% **1987**
Powell, W R (Con)	25,203 44.5% +0.2%	23,323 44.3% Con
Feather, H A (Lab)	24,861 43.9% +3.0%	25,518 40.9% Lab
Roffe, M W (Lab)	5,792 10.2% -4.6%	7,805 14.8% Lib
Con to Lab swing 1.4%	**Con maj 342**	**Con maj 1,805**

Adapted from Wood & Wood, 1992.

Item C *Tactical voting*

(i) Under Britain's first past the post system, constituency boundaries are crucial since they define the local level of support for each party. A voter may live in an extremely safe Labour local government ward which is situated within a marginal Labour/Conservative parliamentary constituency which is part of a marginal Conservative/Liberal Democrat Euro-constituency. Clearly, the tactical voting pressures on voters depend upon what sort of election is being held. The tactical voter who wants to prevent the Conservatives winning seats will vote Labour at local and general or by-elections and Liberal Democrat at Euro-elections.

Adapted from Miller, 1990.

This photograph was taken in Oxford in March 1992, a month before the general election was held.

(ii) What the tactical voters don't understand is that without a Labour government millions of us are simply defenceless. We don't vote Labour because we think a Labour government will bring socialism or because we think it will end the recession or even because we particularly like its policies. We vote Labour because it's our party. It's on our side as it was on the side of our forefathers. When times are good, under Labour they will be good for us. When times are bad, under Labour they will be less bad for us. I would rather die than not vote Labour.

Adapted from Coward, 1992.

Item D *The general election campaigns of 1987 and 1992*

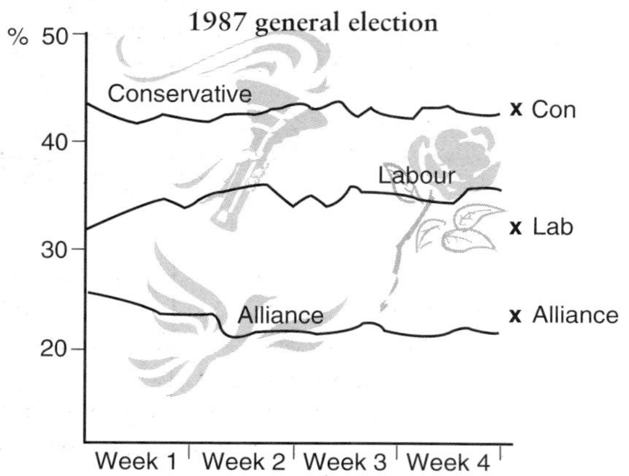

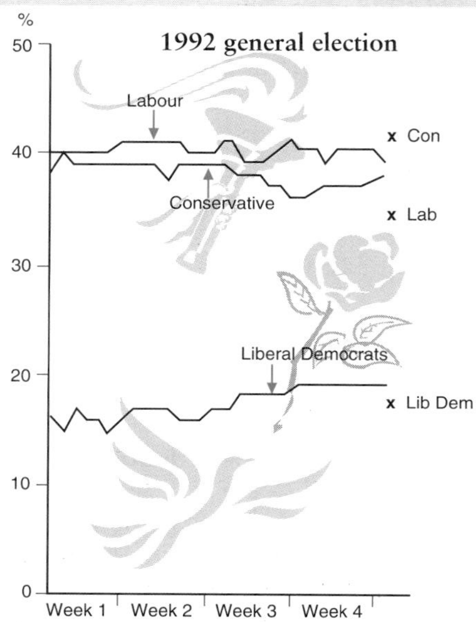

These graphs show the average daily support for each party during the 1987 and 1992 general elections (the data comes from the opinion polls held during the campaign). The X shows the actual share of votes.

Item E *The 1992 election campaign*

The Conservatives' campaign was run by young and inexperienced officials, whilst Labour's was organised by veterans of the 1987 campaign. Throughout the campaign, voters identified the 'caring' issues promoted by Labour as those most important in determining their vote. On these issues, Labour retained a comfortable lead throughout the campaign. Generally, Labour's campaign was regarded as professional and effective, the Liberal Democrats' as fresh and energetic and the Conservatives' as uninspired and defensive. Asked at the NOP/BBC exit poll which party's campaign was most impressive, 32% said Labour, 27% said the Liberal Democrats and only 19% chose the Conservatives.

Adapted from Crewe, 1992.

Questions

1. How would you explain Labour's defeat in the 1992 general election using the voting context model of voting behaviour?
2. What does Items A tell us about voting behaviour in elections held between 1992 and 1994?
3. Suppose you are a Liberal Democrat supporter who has decided to vote tactically. How would you cast your vote in each of the three marginal seats in Item B if you were living there when the next general election was called? Explain your choices.
4. a) Why do you think none of the main parties supports tactical voting?
   b) What are the advantages and disadvantages of voting tactically? Use Item C in your answer
5. Judging from Items D and E would you say that the main parties are justified in spending large amounts of money and effort on their election campaigns? Give reasons for your answer.

6 A general model of voting

Key Issues

1. What does a general model of voting behaviour look like?
2. What are the links between the models of voting behaviour which were described earlier?

6.1 A general model of voting

Each of the five models of voting behaviour discussed in this chapter focuses on particular aspects of why people vote as they do. Political scientists disagree about which are the most useful or appropriate. However, not all the models necessarily compete with each other, nor do the different models necessarily claim to provide a full or exhaustive explanation of why people vote as they do. On the contrary, it is possible to find links between the different models and elements within them which complement each other.

Some political scientists make a distinction between short-term and long-term influences on how people vote. Long-term influences include factors such as social class, age, gender, occupation and region. Short-term factors may be those which determine the result of a single election - specific events, issues or policies, the style of party leaders or the attitude of the media during the campaign, for example. It has been suggested that if long-term factors predominate, then changes in voting patterns from one election to another are likely to be slight. If short-term factors predominate, electoral outcomes are likely to be less predictable and more volatile. Such a distinction, however, should not be exaggerated. Policies and issues do not occur in a political vacuum. They may well be related to longer-term party strategy or ideology. Similarly, changes in the class or age structure of the population may occur over time and result in significant alterations in the distribution of votes to the main parties.

William Miller (1990) has constructed a general model of voting which summarises and synthesises the models of voting behaviour discussed earlier in this chapter. His model suggests some of the possible links between the different models. It also suggests a way in which political scientists might attempt a full explanation of why people vote as they do. This model can be depicted as follows. Miller explains how the various elements in the diagram are connected:

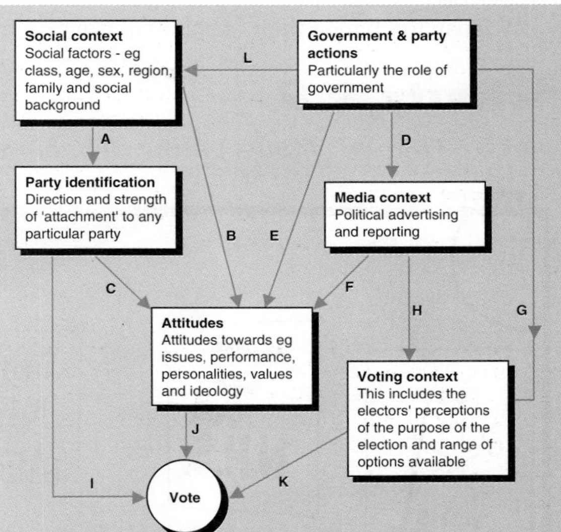

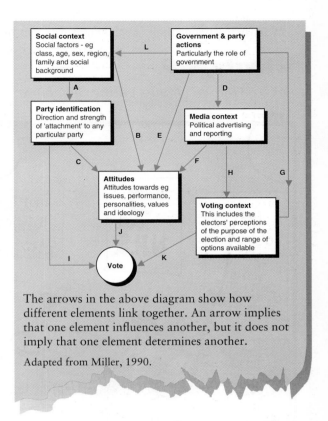

The arrows in the above diagram show how different elements link together. An arrow implies that one element influences another, but it does not imply that one element determines another.

Adapted from Miller, 1990.

'Arrow A says that voters' social and family backgrounds influence their sense of party identification. For example, working class children with working class, Labour voting parents who grow up in a working class neighbourhood are more likely to identify themselves with the Labour party than those who come from a different background. Links B and C suggest that voters' attitudes are influenced by their background and by this pre-existing sense of party identification. Link D suggests that the content and style of the mass media is influenced by the actions of government and the parties...The actions of government and parties influence voters' attitudes directly through personal experience (eg of inflation or unemployment) shown by link E; and indirectly through mass media reports (eg about defence policy) represented by link F. Similarly, voters' perceptions of party credibility are influenced by direct experience (eg the availability of candidates, whether they have been leafleted or canvassed) shown by link G; and by media reports (eg opinion poll projections of the parties' chances) represented by link H. The voter's ultimate decision about which way to vote is based upon a mix of influences from party loyalty (link I), political attitudes (link J) and the voting context (link K)...Governments can also influence social background (link L). Obviously, nothing can be done to change voters' family backgrounds, but it is quite easy to change their...social circumstances by selling them council houses, privatising their employers and encouraging them to rely on private health care organisations instead of the NHS.' (Miller, 1990, pp.43-5)

Activity 9.9

Item A *How to change voting behaviour*

'Your husband's had an injection to cure his allergy and a tiny frontal lobotomy to cure his nasty voting habits'

This cartoon appeared in the *Daily Mail* on April 1989.

Item B *Why I can't vote Liberal*

On reaching Cambridge University aged 19, I joined both the Liberal party and a group called Pressure for Economic and Social Toryism (PEST). This would allow me to hear the best speakers from both sides. After a few meetings, I still saw much to recommend them both. Then came the local elections. I read the manifestos. The Liberals seemed fresh and well-meaning. The Tories seemed like placemen. I entered the polling station to vote for the first time. Uncertain of the procedure, I found my way to the ballot paper and voting booth. Pencil poised above the ballot paper, I prepared to select and mark the Liberal candidates. Then something extraordinary happened. I saw a name which was attached to the words - the Conservative party candidate. I never knew how it happened or why. The only thing I knew was that I placed a faltering cross in the box next to that name. Thus began a lifetime of voting Conservative.

Ever since then, I've supposed there was a suppressed idealist within and that he was a Liberal. So, it was with a clear conscience that I decided to vote Liberal in the local elections last Thursday. The Lib Dems narrowly controlled the council, Labour were challengers and the Tories had no chance. To keep Labour out, you had to vote Lib Dem. Besides, the Liberals had canvassed and sent an election address. The Tories had not bothered. I approached the polling station clutching a little leaflet with the Lib Dem names on it. I held my pencil above the ballot paper. And again it happened. I saw the words - the Conservative party candidate - and, as if gripped by some higher force, wrote a cross in the box next to that name. It was a wasted vote. The Lib Dems lost and Labour won. I was a fool, I know. But there's no saving me.

Adapted from the *Times*, 9 May 1994.

Item C *View from the Tory heartlands*

David Leach, 23, a computer programmer from Norwich, was a first time voter in 1992 and voted Conservative, but events over the last two years have left him disillusioned. He said that the biggest blow to him was news of the imposition of VAT on fuel. The new taxes, he argued, had been introduced through the back door. He would not have minded paying an extra penny or two on income tax. Mr Leach also criticised the government for moving Department of Health workers to Leeds. He argued that the government had got its priorities wrong because it spent so much on this when the money was needed for hospital beds. Mr Leach is a supporter of the Prime Minister, John Major, however. 'Personally', he said, 'I think he's a decent man with a good style.' Mr Leach comes from a family which has traditionally voted Labour. He and his mother, who set up her own business some years ago, both voted Conservative in 1992. Neither of them are as committed to voting Conservative as they were before.

Adapted from the *Daily Telegraph*, 21 March 1994.

Item D *Voting behaviour in Eastleigh 1987-1994*

(i) General election 1987

Con	35,584	51.3%
Lib	22,229	32.0%
Lab	11,599	16.7%

Con maj 13,355. Turnout 79.3%

(ii) General election 1992

Con	38,998	51.3 %
Lib Dem	21,296	28.0%
Lab	15,768	20.7%

Con maj 17,702. Swing to Con 2.0%. Turnout 82.9%

(iii) By-election 1994

Lib Dem	24,473	44.3%
Lab	22,229	27.6%
Con	11,599	24.7%

Lib Dem maj 9,239. Swing to Lib Dem 21.5%. Turnout 58.9%

Questions

1. You have been asked to explain why the 1992 general election resulted in a Conservative overall majority of 21 seats. Go back through the chapter and collect information relevant to each element in the general model. Use this information as the basis of a newspaper article entitled: 'How did Labour lose in 1992'?
2. Item A suggests that voting behaviour can be scientifically analysed. Do you agree that this is the case? Give reasons for your answer.
3. How would you explain the voting behaviour of the author of Item B? Is there any evidence in this passage which could be used to link the voting behaviour of the author with any of the models which make up the general model of voting?
4. How useful are interviews like that in Item C for political scientists trying to explain voting behaviour?
5. Using your knowledge of voting behaviour, how would you explain the election results in Item D?

References

Benyon (1993) Benyon, J., 'Britain's political divisions', *Politics Review*, Vol.2, No.3, February 1993.

Benyon & Denver (1990) Benyon, J. & Denver, D., 'Mrs Thatcher's electoral success', *Social Studies Review*, Vol.5, No.3, January 1990.

Butler & Kavanagh (1992) Butler, D. & Kavanagh, D., *The British General Election of 1992*, Macmillan, 1992.

Butler & Stokes (1971) Butler, D. & Stokes, D., *Political Change in Britain*, Penguin, 1971.

Clarke & Stewart (1984) Clarke, H.D. & Stewart, M.C., 'Partisan change in Britain, 1974-83' in *Denver & Hands (1992)*.

Conley (1990) Conley, F., *General Elections Today*, Manchester University Press, 1990.

Conley (1993) Conley, F., 'The 1992 general election: the end of psephology?', *Talking Politics*, Vol.5, No.3, summer 1993.

Coward (1992) Coward, M., 'Campaign trail diary', *New Statesman & Society*, 10 April 1992.

Crewe et al. (1977) Crewe, I., Sarlik, B. & Alt, J., 1977, 'Partisan dealignment in Britain 1964-1974', *British Journal of Political Science*, Vol.7, No.2, 1977.

Crewe (1987) Crewe, I., 'The 1987 general election' in *Denver & Hands (1992)*.

Crewe (1987a) Crewe, I., 'Why Mrs Thatcher was returned with a landslide', *Social Studies Review*, Vol.3, No.1, September 1987.

Crewe (1988) Crewe, I., 'Voting patterns since 1959', *Contemporary Record*, Vol.4, No.2, winter 1988.

Crewe (1992) Crewe, I., 'Why did Labour lose (yet again)?', *Politics Review*, Vol.2, No.1, September 1992.

Crewe (1993) Crewe, I., 'Voting and the Electorate' in *Dunleavy et al.* (1993).

Crewe (1993a) Crewe, I., 'The changing basis of party choice, 1979-1992', *Politics Review*, Vol.2, No.3, February 1993.

Denver (1989) Denver, D., *Elections and Voting Behaviour in Britain*, Philip Allen, 1989.

Denver (1990) Denver, D., 'Elections and voting behaviour' in *Wale (1990)*.

Denver (1992) Denver, D., 'The 1992 general election: in defence of psephology' in *Talking Politics*, Vol.5, No.1, autumn 1992.

Denver (1993) Denver, D., 'Elections and voting behaviour' in *Wale (1993)*.

Denver & Hands (1990) Denver, D. & Hands, G., 'A new gender gap...', *Talking Politics*, Vol.2, No.3, 1990.

Denver & Hands (1992) Denver, D. & Hands, G. (eds), *Issues and Controversies in British Electoral Behaviour*, Harvester Wheatsheaf, 1992.

Dunleavy & Husbands (1985) Dunleavy, P. & Husbands, C.T., *British Democracy at the Crossroads*, Allen & Unwin, 1985.

Dunleavy et al. (1990) Dunleavy P., Gamble A., & Peele G. (eds), *Developments in British Politics* 3, Macmillan, 1990.

Dunleavy et al. (1993) Dunleavy P. , Gamble A., Holliday I. & Peele G. (eds), *Developments in British Politics 4*, Macmillan, 1993.

Eatwell (1993) Eatwell, R., 'Opinion poll accuracy: the case of the 1992 general election', *Talking Politics*, Vol.5, No.2, winter 1993.

Fitzgerald (1988) Fitzgerald, M., 'There is no alternative...black people and the Labour party', *Social Studies Review*, Vol.4, No.1, September 1988.

Franklin (1985) Franklin, M., *The Decline of Class Voting in Britain*, Oxford University Press, 1988.

Game (1994) Game, C., 'Snapshots of public opinion', *Politics Review*, Vol.3, No.3, February 1994.

Game (1995) Game, C., 'Opinion polls: the lessons of 1992' in *Lancaster (1995)*.

Goldthorpe et al. (1969) Goldthorpe, J.H., Lockwood, D., Bechoffer, F. & Platt, J. (1969) *The Affluent Worker in the Class Structure*, Cambridge University Press, 1969.

Hall (1987) Hall, S., 'Blue election, election blues', *Marxism Today*, July 1987.

Hall (1992) Hall, S., 'No new vision, no new votes', *New Statesman & Society*, 17 April 1992

Heath (1992) Heath, A., 'Social class and voting in Britain', *Sociology Review*, Vol.1, No.4, April 1992.

Heath et al. (1985) Heath, A., Jowell, R & Curtice, J. *How Britain Votes*, Pergamon, 1985.

Heath et al. (1988) Heath, A., Jowell, R. & Curtice, J., 'Partisan dealignment revisited' in *Denver & Hands (1992)*.

Heath et al. (1991) Heath, A., Jowell, R & Curtice, J., Evans, G., Field, J. & Witherspoon, S., *Understanding Political Change: the British Voter* 1964-1987, Pergamon, 1991.

Heath et al. (1994) Heath, A., Jowell, R. & Curtice, J., *Labour's Last Chance*, Dartmouth, 1994.

Johnston & Pattie (1989) Johnston, R.J. & Pattie, C.J., 'The changing electoral geography of Great Britain' in *Denver & Hands* (1992).

Kavanagh (1992) Kavanagh, D., 'Polls, predictions and politics', *Politics Review*, Vol.2, No.2, November 1992.

King et al. (1993) King, A., Crewe, I., Denver D., Newton, K., Norton P., Sanders, D. & Seyd, P., *Britain at the Polls 1992*, Chatham, 1993.

Lancaster (1995) Lancaster, S. (ed.) *Developments in Politics*, Vol. 6, Causeway Press, 1995.

Layton-Henry (1990) Layton-Henry, Z., 'The black electorate', *Contemporary Record*, Vol.3, No.3, February 1990.

McKenzie & Silver (1968) McKenzie, R. & Silver, A., *Angels in Marble*, Heinemann, 1968.

Miller (1984) Miller, W.L., 'There was no alternative...' in *Denver & Hands (1992)*.

Miller (1990) Miller, W.L., 'Voting and the electorate' in *Dunleavy et al. (1990)*.

Miller (1991) Miller, W.L., *Media and Voters: the Audience, Content and Influence of Press and Television at the 1987 General Election*, Clarendon Press, 1991.

Miller et al. (1990) Miller, W.L., Clarke, H.D., Harrop, M., Leduc, L. & Whiteley, P.F., *How Voters Change: the 1987 British Election Campaign in Perspective*, Clarendon Press, 1990.

Moran (1989) Moran, M., *Politics and Society in Britain* (2nd edn), Macmillan, 1989

Newton (1992) Newton, K., 'Caring and competence: the long, long campaign' in *King et al. (1992)*.

Parkin (1972) Parkin, F., *Class, Inequality and Political Order*, Paladin, 1972.

Platt & Smyth (1994) Platt, S. & Smyth, G. 'Bite the ballot', *New Statesman & Society*, 29 April 1994.

Pulzer (1967) Pulzer, P.G.J., *Political Representation and Elections in Britain*, Allen & Unwin, 1967.

Rose & McAllister (1986) Rose, R. & McAllister, I., *Voters Begin to Choose*, Sage, 1986.

Rose & McAllister (1990) Rose, R. & McAllister, I., *The Loyalties of Voters*, Sage, 1990.

Saggar (1993) Saggar, S., 'Analysing race and voting', *Politics Review*, Vol.2, No.3, February 1993.

Saggar (1993a) Saggar, S., 'Competing for the black vote', *Politics Review*, Vol.2, No.4, April 1993.

Sanders (1993) Sanders, D. in *King et al. (1992)*.

Sewell (1993) Sewell, T., *Black Tribunes: Black Political Particpation in Britain*, Lawrence & Wishart, 1993.

Wale (1990) Wale, W. (ed.), *Developments in Politics*, Vol.1, Causeway Press, 1990.

Wale (1993) Wale, W. (ed.), *Developments in Politics*, Vol.4, Causeway Press, 1993.

Wood & Wood (1992) Wood, A.H. & Wood, R. (eds), *The Times Guide to the House of Commons 1992*, Times Books, 1992.

Worcester (1992) Worcester, R., 'The polls' in *Wood & Wood (1992)*.

10 Pressure groups

Introduction

Farmers facing riot police on the streets of Brussels; mass lobbies of Parliament; letter writing campaigns; publicity stunts; meetings between ministers and members of the Adam Smith Institute. These are all examples of pressure group activity, a form of political action that has been growing in importance in Britain.

As the membership of political parties has fallen, that of pressure groups has increased. This may indicate a fundamental shift in the British political system. Like political parties, pressure groups want to affect the outcome of the political decision making process. Unlike political parties, however, they do not contest elections.

As membership of pressure groups has grown, so has their professionalism. It is not uncommon today for people concerned about an issue to employ paid, professional lobbyists to promote their cause. Not that all pressure groups act or would want to act in this way. The problem with the term 'pressure groups' is that it encompasses a huge variety of organisations - from ad hoc local protest movements based in a single village to huge, international organisations. These groups promote their interests in a variety of ways, with a varying degree of success. How they do this and how it is possible to distinguish between them are the two main subjects of this chapter.

Chapter summary

Part 1 asks the question, **what is a pressure group?** It examines the different ways in which this question has been answered.

Part 2 considers **the ways in which pressure groups achieve their aims.** How can we measure their success?

Part 3 examines the way in which **the role of pressure groups has changed** since the early 1970s.

Part 4 considers **the European dimension.** How has membership of the EU affected pressure groups in Britain?

1 What is a pressure group?

Key Issues

1. What exactly is a pressure group?
2. What are the differences between different groups? What problems are encountered in categorising them?
3. How do the aims and functions of pressure groups differ?

1.1 A definition

Amnesty International, the Confederation of British Industry (CBI), the Worldwide Fund for Nature (WWF), the Centre for Policy Studies (CPS), the Campaign for Nuclear Disarmament (CND), the National Union of Students (NUS), Charter 88 - these are all examples of pressure groups. Whereas the number of political parties in Britain is very small (fewer than double figures if minor parties like 'Lord' Sutch's Official Monster Raving Loony party are excluded), the number of pressure groups runs into the thousands - tens of thousands if local groups are counted. In fact, any organised group that does not put up candidates for election, but seeks to influence government policy can be described as a pressure group.

Pressure groups are also sometimes described as 'interest groups', 'lobby groups' or 'protest groups'. Some writers avoid the term 'pressure groups' because it implies that such groups use coercion to achieve their ends. This does not necessarily happen.

Clearly, the definition above is far too loose to be of use for most writers. It does not distinguish between a huge organisation like the CBI (which represents 150,000 businesses) and a single issue locally based organisation like the Save Audley Campaign (Audley is a small village in Staffordshire. The Save Audley Campaign was set up in the 1970s to fight planning proposals to build factories on local farm land. The group had around 50 members and disbanded as soon as the plans were dropped). Nor does such a definition distinguish between groups on the fringes of society such as the Animal Liberation Front (whose campaigns include illegal activities such as planting bombs) and those at the very heart of the Establishment such as the Adam Smith Institute (some of whose proposals have formed the basis of government legislation and some of whose members have enjoyed regular contact with Cabinet ministers).

Despite this, such a definition does indicate how pressure groups differ from established political parties and how they differ from groups which make no attempt to influence government policy. Therefore, it is an adequate starting point.

1.2 Sectional groups and cause groups

One of the earliest attempts to classify pressure groups produced the division between sectional groups and cause groups (Stewart, 1958). Later writers have sometimes used the same criteria but different terms - sectional groups are called 'interest groups' (which is confusing because other writers use interest groups to mean all pressure groups) and cause groups are called 'promotional groups.'

Sectional groups

Sectional groups seek to represent the common interests of a particular section of society. As a result, members of sectional groups are directly and personally concerned with the outcome of the campaigns fought by the group because (usually) they stand to gain professionally and/or economically. Trade unions, employers' associations and professional bodies are all sectional groups. The National Union of Teachers (NUT), the Society of Motor Manufacturers and Traders and the British Medical Association (BMA) are three examples of sectional groups.

Because sectional groups are solely concerned with a particular section of society, membership is usually restricted. Since the aim is to look after the interests of all people in that section of society, sectional groups tend to aim to get as many eligible members as possible to join the group.

Cause groups

Cause groups pursue a particular set of objectives (a cause), the achievement of which is not necessarily of direct professional or economic benefit to the members of the group. Shelter (whose cause is helping the homeless), CND (whose cause is nuclear disarmament) and the Society for the Protection of the Unborn Child (whose cause is the prevention of abortions) are three of the myriad of cause groups.

Because cause groups aim to promote a cause (which might potentially be supported by everybody, regardless of their profession or economic position), membership is not usually restricted. However, that does not mean that cause groups have or want to have a large membership.

Some cause groups have influence out of proportion to their size. For example, the British Field Sports Society, which had 80,000 members in 1992, was able to persuade enough MPs to defeat the Wild Mammals (Protection) Bill in February of that year, even though a Gallup poll had shown that 79% of the population was in favour of legislation to ban hunting. Other cause groups, on the other hand, have many members but little influence. For example, in the early 1980s, CND had over a quarter of a million members, but it was unable to persuade the government to change its defence policy.

Cause groups can be subdivided according to the aims they pursue:

Sectional cause groups aim to protect the interests of a section of society. For example, members of Shelter work on behalf of the homeless. The Child Poverty Action Group works on behalf of children who live in poverty. The group MIND works to protect and fight for the rights of those suffering from mental illness.

Attitude cause groups aim to change people's attitudes about a particular issue or policy. For example, Greenpeace, Friends of the Earth (FoE) and the Worldwide Fund for Nature (WWF) aim to change people's attitudes towards the environment.

Political cause groups aim to change the political system or political process in some way. For example, Charter 88 argues that, because our political system does not have a written constitution, strong governments can pass laws which erode civil liberties. As a result, Charter 88 campaigns for a written Bill of Rights and other constitutional changes.

Problems with this classification

The first problem with this method of classification is that many groups cut across the two categories. For example, many trade unions campaign for causes, such as equal opportunities in society as a whole or a cleaner environment, as well as pursuing sectional interests, such as better pay and conditions in a specific industry. Equally, some cause groups pursue sectional interests. For example, many members of the Campaign for the Advancement of State Education are teachers in state schools and thus have a vested interest in the success of this organisation.

Second, people using this method of classification often assume that sectional groups are generally more influential and better resourced than cause groups. In fact, a major trend over the last 30 years has been the growth in membership, income and expertise of many cause groups. Besides, some sectional groups are poorly resourced and lack substantial influence.

A third problem is the use of the terms 'sectional' and 'cause'. Some people argue that these terms are sometimes used to suggest an ideological preference, namely that sectional groups are in some sense 'bad' whilst cause groups are in some sense 'good'. The fact that some writers do use the terms in this way suggests that the distinction between the two types of groups is rather vague and it might be better to search for a different method of classification.

1.3 Insider groups and outsider groups

Rather than classifying pressure groups in terms of what motivates their members, some authors classify them in terms of their strategies and the way in which decision makers react to those strategies. The distinction here is between insider and outsider groups.

Insider groups

Insider groups are the groups which the government considers to be legitimate and are, thus, given access to decision makers. For example, insider groups might be involved in regular meetings with ministers or civil servants and they might be included on lists for circulation of new government proposals.

Insider groups are similar in one respect. Generally, they abide by the 'rules of the game'. For example, they tend to respect confidences and do not make public attacks on ministers.

Insider groups can be further divided into two categories:

Institutions within the state apparatus. This category includes organisations such as the Church of England and the police force. They can be described as insider groups because they are included in the consultation process as a matter of course when government proposals relevant to their activities are discussed. For example, when the government was drawing up plans for educational reform in the mid-1980s, the Department of Education and Science consulted representatives of the Church of England about the place of religious studies in the new curriculum. Similarly, representatives of the police force are consulted when matters of law and order are under discussion.

External groups. Groups in this category are in a different position from institutions within the state apparatus. Whilst institutions within the state apparatus are consulted as a matter of course when government proposals relevant to their activities are discussed, the same is not true of external groups with insider status. External groups with insider status are the independent organisations such as charities, trade unions or pressure groups which are called upon by the government to provide expertise when it is needed. The type of groups selected for consultation varies according to the government's ideological orientation and other factors such as public opinion. So, the type of external groups given insider status varies from government to government. For example, Labour governments in the 1970s often included trade union representatives in the consultative process, whereas trade unions certainly did not have insider status during the 1980s when Margaret Thatcher was Prime Minister.

Outsider groups

Outsider groups have none of the advantages of insider groups. They cannot expect to be consulted during the policy making process, nor can they expect to gain access to ministers and civil servants. Rather, they have to work outside the governmental decision making process and thus have fewer opportunities to determine the direction of policy.

Outsider groups adopt a wide range of strategies and can be further subdivided accordingly. They can be divided into groups which aim for insider status and groups which do not.

Groups aiming for insider status. Those outsider groups which do aim for insider status may be waiting for a different political climate, such as a change in government. If such a climate materialises, they immediately gain insider status (as, for example, the Adam Smith Institute did during the 1980s). Such groups may already work closely with the opposition in Parliament and, generally, like existing insider groups, their strategy is to abide by 'the rules of the game'. Alternatively, groups seeking insider status may be new groups with little experience, resources and expertise. Decision makers might support the aims of such organisations, but do not consult them because they are perceived as having little to offer.

Groups not aiming for insider status. Those outsider groups which do not aim for insider status may do so out of necessity. For example, the Save Audley Campaign was set up by villagers on a temporary basis to fight a particular planning proposal. It never aimed for or was likely to get insider status. There are many small single issue pressure groups like this. Equally, there are larger outsider groups which do not aim for insider status out of necessity. CND is a good example. Since 1987, none of the major political parties has supported CND's aims. Out of necessity, therefore, CND has not been able to aim for insider status. In addition, there is a category of outsider groups which do not aim for insider status because they are ideologically opposed to the political system. By definition, such groups have no interest in gaining access to governmental decision makers.

Problems with this classification

One problem with this method of classification is that it does not concede that some groups described as insiders adopt strategies that are the same as those adopted by some groups described as outsiders. For example, is WWF an insider group or an outsider group?

WWF has considerable resources and expertise and its officers are sometimes invited to consult with members of government. In 1991, for example, WWF was invited to a series of meetings with Lynda Chalker, the Minister for Overseas Development. As a result of these meetings, the government's policy concerning the World Bank and deforestation was substantially altered. This suggests that WWF is an insider group.

But, in other ways, WWF behaves more like an outsider group. For example, Lynda Chalker only approached WWF after a mass card writing campaign had proved successful (over 30,000 people signed cards produced by WWF and sent them to their MPs, a number sufficiently large to put pressure on the government). Without such a campaign, it is unlikely that WWF would have been included in the consultation process. That WWF is not automatically consulted suggests that it is an outsider group.

A second problem with this method of classification is its fluidity. Today's outsider group may be tomorrow's insider group and vice versa. That means it is difficult to generalise about the nature of insider and outsider groups. Groups and strategies which were successful in the 1970s are not necessarily the groups and strategies which are successful today.

Activity 10.1

Item A *REPUBLIC*

REPUBLIC is a non-party political pressure group committed to the modernisation of the British constitution by abolishing all forms of hereditary public office. This leaflet contains twelve of the most common claims made in support of the monarchy together with REPUBLIC's responses. If you are among the growing number of people who favour a democratically elected head of state and second chamber and would like to join REPUBLIC, please complete and return the reply slip overleaf.

Adapted from a leaflet produced by *REPUBLIC* in 1993.

Item B *Advert produced by Amnesty International*

Item C *CBI postpones 'putting the boot in'*

The Confederation of British Industry (CBI) assembles tomorrow in Harrogate, sagging under the weight of recession, but with high expectations that the government is about to put the flesh on the bones of its strategy for growth.

As a string of Cabinet ministers take their turn on the CBI platform, they will be left in no doubt that business leaders are not interested in hearing more political platitudes. Mr Howard Davies, who will be addressing his first CBI conference as director general says: 'We have told the Prime Minister and the Chancellor that we are not yet in a slump, but that we soon could be. We have reached a critical point. Perhaps now is not the time to put the boot in, but we have to make clear we expect immediate action.' The CBI will use the conference to announce its plan for reviving the manufacturing sector, the outline of which was put to the Prime Minister last week.

Adapted from the *Financial Times*, 8 November 1992.

Item D *The aims, income and resources of selected pressure groups*

Group	Aims	Members	Income	Staff
British Road	Pro-road lobby group which centres on the need for more roads	150 businesses	£500,000	15 F/T
Charter 88	Campaigns for a written constitution and a Bill of Rights	54,000	£600,000	13 F/T
Central Area Leamington Residents Association (CLARA)	Campaigns to preserve and improve the town of Leamington Spa and its surrounding area	20 families	£400	relies on volunteers
Friends of the Earth (FoE)	Campaigns to preserve and protect the environment	200,000	£1,930,000	122 F/T
League Against Cruel Sports	Campaigns to end blood sports	30,000	£1,400,000	21 F/T
Liberty	Campaigns to defend and extend human rights and civil liberties in the UK	5,270	£540,000	17 F/T;19 P/T
Motor Cycle Action Group	Campaigns on behalf of motorcyclists	22,000	£150,000	2 F/T
National Farmers Union (NFU)	Looks after the interests of farmers	150,000	£21,414,658	108 F/T
Royal Society for the Protection of Birds (RSPB)	Campaigns to conserve and protect birds and their environment	850,493	£30,835,000	620 F/T
Worldwide Fund for Nature (WWF)	Campaigns to preserve and protect wildlife species and their habitat	200,000	£19,230,000	197 F/T

This table shows the aims, income and resources of a number of pressure groups. F/T stands for full time and P/T stands for part time.

Item E *Insider and outsider groups*

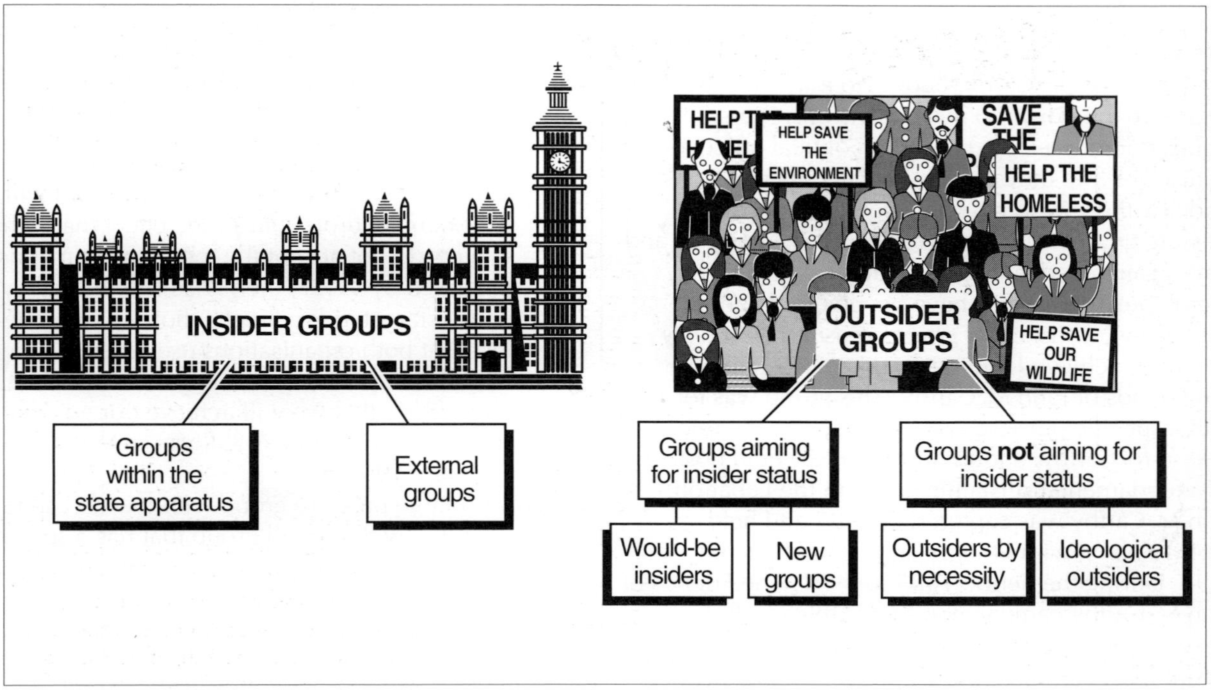

Item F *Sectional and cause groups*

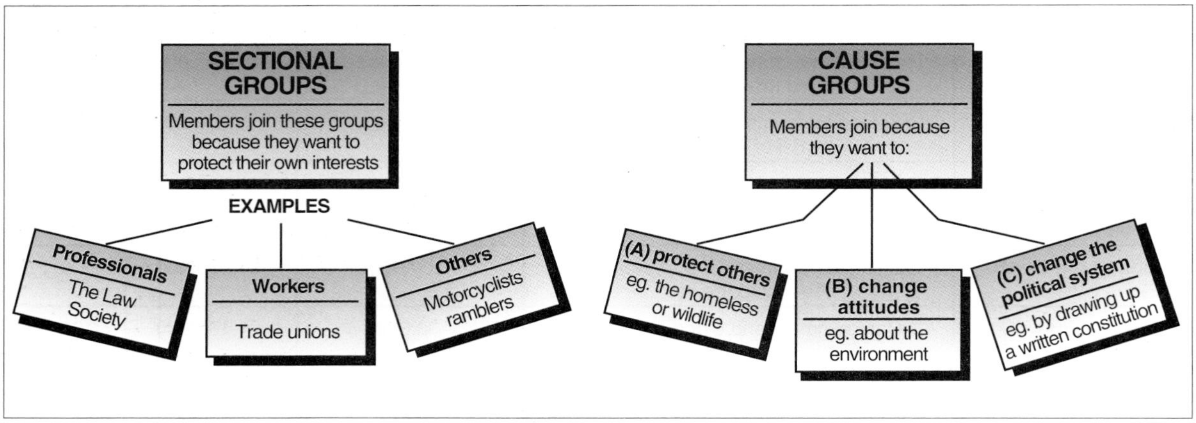

Questions

1. a) How would you classify each of the three pressure groups mentioned in Items A-C? Give reasons for your answers.
   b) Which is the better method of classification - sectional/cause or insider/outsider? Explain your answer.
2. a) Which, if any, of the groups in Item D would fit under the following headings: sectional cause group, attitude cause group, political cause group?
   b) Which of the groups in Item D are insider groups and which are outsider groups? Explain how you know.
3. a) Look at Items E and F and find a group mentioned in Item D which fits each separate category.
   b) How useful would you say these separate categories are?
   c) Why do you think people writing about pressure groups attempt to classify them?

1.4 The aims and functions of pressure groups

The aims of pressure groups

The aim of all pressure groups is to influence those who have the power to make decisions. Pressure groups do not seek the power of political office for themselves, but they do aim to affect the decisions made by those who have this power. If necessary, pressure groups will compete against rival groups and aim to gain an advantage over them.

Some pressure groups have become permanent institutions, whilst other groups cease to exist once they have achieved their aim. Take, for example, The Friends of John McCarthy. This group was formed with a specific purpose - to campaign for the release of John McCarthy, a journalist who was held hostage by a fundamentalist Islamic group in the Lebanon. John McCarthy was captured in 1985 and held captive, along with other hostages, until his release in 1991. During the period 1985 to 1991, The Friends of John McCarthy campaigned for his release. But, when this was achieved in 1991, the group no longer had a reason for continuing and was, therefore, disbanded.

The aims of one pressure group may coincide with another and, sometimes, this can result in two or more groups working together. For example, Friends of the Earth (FoE) and WWF have a similar aim - the protection of the environment. Often, they work together using their different methods to complement each other's campaigns. One of WWF's conservation officers said:

> 'My concern is with sustainable forestry. WWF, like FoE, aims to stop the destruction of the world's forests by promoting sustainable forest management. When I am negotiating with logging companies, I often exploit the different reputations of the two groups. I will, for example, drop hints to the effect that if the loggers do not accept the moderate demands proposed by WWF, then it is likely that they will be targeted for direct action by FoE. The fact that both organisations use different methods in pursuing the same aims makes it more likely that we will achieve our goals.' (interview with Francis Sullivan of WWF, February 1994)

Similarly, a large pressure group with a wide agenda may join forces with a small group that has a specific aim. For example, FoE joined forces with a local action group, the Twyford Down Association, to oppose an extension of the M3 motorway through a Site of Special Scientific Interest. The Twyford Down Association was set up in 1990 specifically to campaign against this extension.

On other occasions, pressure groups may find themselves in direct conflict with each other. For example when the Wild Mammals (Protection)

Bill was introduced by Labour MP Kevin McNamara in February 1992, the RSPCA and the League Against Cruel Sports campaigned in favour of the Bill, whilst the British Field Sports Society campaigned against it.

The functions of pressure groups

Although it is difficult to generalise because of the diversity of pressure groups, it is possible to identify three separate functions.

First, pressure groups provide a means of popular participation in national politics between elections. It is true that a government with an absolute majority can be sure of passing legislation regardless of popular opinion, but pressure groups are sometimes able to mobilise sufficient support to force the government to amend or even to scrap legislation. An example of this was the poll tax. A MORI poll, taken in September 1988, showed that 70% of people (including 32% of Conservative voters) were opposed to this new tax, and, as soon as it was introduced, a pressure group (the Anti-Poll Tax Federation) was set up to campaign for its abolition. Due to public pressure, the government was forced to rethink the issue. In 1991, the poll tax was replaced with the council tax.

Second, pressure groups provide a means of popular participation in local politics between elections. Just as national campaigns can affect the decisions made by Parliament, local campaigns can affect decisions that affect a locality - whether these decisions are made by local or by central government. For example, the Save Audley Campaign was set up after developers had approached the district council with proposals to build factories on farmland. The group's aim was to pressurise the district council into refusing planning permission. It did this by organising public meetings and encouraging local people to voice their complaints to the council. In other words, the group's function was to encourage and to coordinate popular participation in local politics. Similarly, it was the function of each local branch of the Anti-Poll Tax Federation to mobilise and coordinate opposition to the poll tax in that branch's locality.

Third, it is a function of pressure groups to act as a source of specialist knowledge. Since most pressure groups are concerned with a single issue or a narrow policy area, they often develop expert knowledge of that issue or area. Many groups attract and bring together specialists. Some of the better resourced groups are able to employ a team of specialists. As a result, pressure groups often have access to information which is highly valued by decision makers. Sometimes, this specialist knowledge provides groups with direct access to the decision making process. For example, specialists who work for MENCAP and MIND (groups which campaign on behalf of people with mental disabilities) are often invited to give briefings to government departments. In return, not only do these groups have an important input into the making of decisions, they also receive financial contributions. About one fifth of MIND's total funds comes direct from the government.

1.5 Pressure groups and pluralism

In a representative democracy, representatives are chosen infrequently and they are voted in by a majority. In theory, that means that the extent of most people's political participation is to cast a vote every few years. It also means that people have little or no influence over decision makers between elections and that the views of minorities may not be represented or supported by the elected decision makers. It means, in short, that there is a democratic deficit.

According to the pluralist view of politics, the operation of pressure groups remedies these shortcomings. The pluralist view has four main strands.

First, pressure groups are an important means of political participation. Casting a vote does not express the strength of feelings that people may have about a specific issue. By joining a pressure group, people can express their strength of feeling and they can take active steps to influence decisions relating to the matter about which they feel so strongly. Also, joining a pressure group is a way for ordinary individuals to take part in political activity between elections.

Second, the work of pressure groups complements that of political parties. Individuals with strong views on a particular issue may support a political party in general terms, but be unhappy about a policy on a particular issue or the lack of priority given to it. By joining a pressure group, such individuals can put pressure on decision makers in political parties. Also, pressure groups often raise questions that are not addressed in party manifestos and they ensure that issues which are of importance to people who do not belong to political parties appear on the political agenda.

Third, members of pressure groups ensure that a group's views (especially a minority group's views) are heard by decision makers. This is particularly important in a democracy since the majority view tends to prevail. Without pressure groups, it would be very difficult for the rights of minorities to be protected.

Fourth, pressure groups help to disperse power away from central institutions. Decision makers are continually confronted by groups competing for their attention and for every policy there are groups for and groups against a particular point of view. Since this is the case, decisions are reached as a result of bargaining and compromise. It is the role of decision makers to arbitrate between the views presented to them.

Criticisms of the pluralist view

Pluralism is a political model, a theoretical construct.

But, how well does this model translate into practice? Although few people would deny that pressure groups play an important role in British politics, critics have argued that this role may not be the one suggested by the pluralist model.

First, the idea that it is the role of decision makers to arbitrate between different interest groups is unrealistic. Decision makers have their own agenda. Although the views of pressure groups may sometimes be considered, they are likely to be ignored if they do not conform with the ideology or agenda of the decision makers.

Second, pressure groups themselves may not be representative of their members. Their officers are not usually elected. Few groups have procedures for consulting their members. As a result, the views expressed by group officials may not be those shared by the group's members.

Third, Marxists argue that the pluralist view is a convenient justification used by the ruling class to disguise the true nature of its power. By claiming that decision makers merely arbitrate between the views presented by competing groups, supporters of pluralism give the impression that decision makers are somehow neutral when, actually, their primary concern is maintenance of the capitalist system. In practice, Marxists argue, there are elite pressure groups whose function is to maintain the status quo and it is these groups which gain access to decision makers. Pressure group activity gives people hope that they can make a difference. This hope is a distraction. The ruling class would rather that people put their energies into pressure group activities which do not question the fundamentals of the system than into political activity which seriously challenges the right of the elite to govern.

Activity 10.2

Item A *United against an unfair system*

The Child Support Agency was set up in April 1992 to assess and collect children's maintenance. But, it has proved to be so shambolic that more than 20 pressure groups and charities have joined together to set up a monitoring group. Mary Honeyball, a spokeswoman for Gingerbread (a support group for lone parents) and a member of the monitoring group says: 'All our worst fears are coming true. Right from the beginning it is not working efficiently. It could all have been done under the old system.' Emma Knights, a spokeswoman for the Child Poverty Action Group (CPAG), says: 'When the Child Support Act was introduced, it was promoted by the government as making absent fathers pay, which everyone thought a good thing. If people had realised what it was all about, I am sure it would never have been passed.' The CPAG is pressing for reform and is swapping complaints with other organisations. Roger Smith, a spokesman for the Children's Society, is lobbying on two fronts - to get legislative change and to deal with injustices.

Adapted from the *Independent*, 18 September 1993.

Item B *The Ramblers Association (1)*

Predator at large: The Ramblers Association's "footpath fighter" finds tracks you never knew existed.

This picture appeared in *Farmer's Weekly* on 11 September 1992. Most of those who read Farmer's Weekly are members of the National Farmers Union (NFU).

Item C *The Ramblers Association (2)*

For almost every yard of its 65 mile journey, the Oxfordshire Way rambles through the beautiful English countryside. Except, that is, where it reaches the brow of Lobbersdown Hill near Thame which used to offer one of the finest views on the route. There, walkers have to pick up a hard hat, walk into a half completed building, clamber down breeze block steps and emerge through the cellars. This building is going to be the clubhouse of a new luxury golf course. It is built across the line of a long distance footpath. Today, members of the 89,000 strong Ramblers' Association will stomp through this bizarre obstacle course as part of Forbidden Britain Day, a nationwide protest against the wilful blocking of tens of thousands of miles of Britain's footpaths and bridleways.

Adapted from an article in the *Observer*, 27 September 1992.

Item D *Parents misled over opt-outs*

According to leaders of a new parents' campaign against opting out, parents are being hoodwinked by heads, governors and the government in battles over school opt-outs. The group, Parents Opposed to Opting Out, is demanding money from John Patten, the Secretary of State for Education, to fund a campaign that will ensure that parents receive fair play when a school ballots on opting out. The group says that the government has spent £3 million in the past five years promoting its opt-out policy, whilst parents have had difficulties in obtaining unbiased information. The group has collected evidence of unfair actions. For example, pro-opting out campaigners in Devon stapled leaflets in favour of opting out over a local authority leaflet giving both sides of the case. Parents in Sussex were misled into thinking they had signed a petition for more information instead of one requesting a ballot. And, governors in Essex waited four weeks before telling parents of their decision to hold a ballot. Parents Opposed to Opting Out is funded by voluntary contributions and contains members of all political parties.

Adapted from the *Independent*, 28 September 1993.

Item E *Advert produced by Unison*

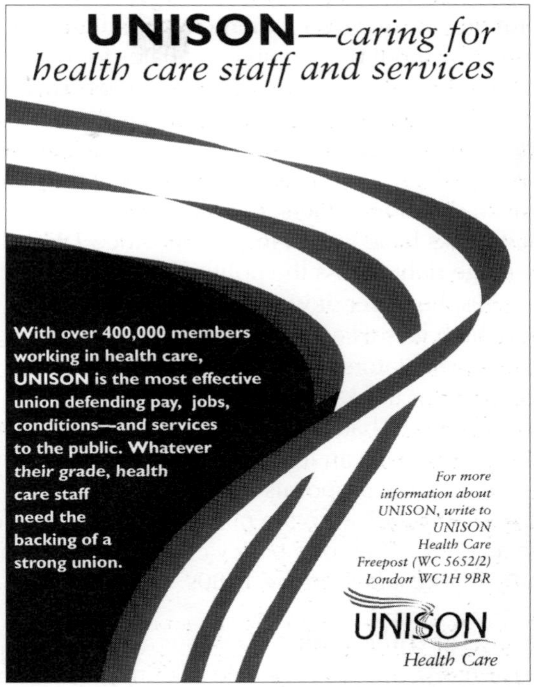

This advert was produced by UNISON, the trade union for workers in the public service and essential industries, in 1994.

Questions

1. a) Make a list of the pressure groups mentioned in Items A-E and classify them using the criteria laid down in sections 1.1-1.3 above.
   b) What evidence is there in Items A-E to support the points made about the aims and functions of pressure groups in section 1.4 above?
2. Using the information in Items A-E give arguments for and against the role of pressure groups suggested by the pluralist model.
3. a) Would you say that the pressure groups mentioned in Item A all have the same functions and aims? Explain your answer.
   b) Why do you think so many pressure groups were involved in this matter?
4. Look at Items B and C.
   a) Why do you think people join the Ramblers' Association?
   b) How would you expect the NFU's aims to differ from those of the Ramblers' Association?
5. a) What are the aims of Parents Opposed to Opting Out in Item D?
   b) Would you say that creating a pressure group was the best way of achieving the aims of Parents Opposed to Opting Out? Explain your answer.

1.6 Think tanks

Think tanks are organisations set up to undertake research and to formulate policy ideas which (they hope) will be adopted by those who have the power to make decisions. 'Think tank' is an American term that was first used in Britain in 1970 when Edward Heath's Conservative government set up the Central Policy Review Staff (CPRS). The CPRS was a small unit in the Cabinet Office (the civil service department in charge of administrative and secretarial work within the Cabinet system). Its aim was to serve the Cabinet as a whole by providing stategic advice on policy and by promoting interdepartmental cooperation. To achieve this aim, it undertook research and presented papers which were free from a departmental perspective. Although the CPRS survived the downfall of Edward Heath, it fell out of favour with Margaret Thatcher and was disbanded in 1983.

Think tanks are different from other pressure groups in three respects. First, most think tanks aim to influence the policy decisions made by a particular political party (most other pressure groups are careful not to be too closely tied to a particular political party). Second, think tanks are interested in a whole political programme not just a single issue or narrow policy area. Third, think tanks are overtly ideological. Their ideas come from a carefully considered ideological standpoint and there is, usually, little concern with 'balance'. Think tanks often compete with each other to win over the ideological soul of a political party. Sometimes that means that they get involved in public debates about internal party matters.

These differences have led some critics to question whether think tanks are in fact pressure groups at all. But, if the definition of a pressure group is an institution whose aim is to influence political decisions without putting up candidates for election, then think tanks qualify as pressure groups. They do not put up candidates at elections. They certainly try to influence political decisions. And, like all pressure groups, they can only exert an influence if they are in line with decision makers' current thinking.

Think tanks have grown in number since 1970. They now range right across the political spectrum. During the 1980s, however, it was the New Right's think tanks which gained access to government. Although some commentators claim that the 1980s was a golden age for think tanks which came to an end when Margaret Thatcher resigned, think tanks have continued to make an impact on the political agenda. For example, the proposals made by John Major's government to privatise the railways and Post Office were a continuation of a policy championed by the Adam Smith Institute in the 1980s.

The role of think tanks

As their name suggests, the role of think tanks is to employ people to do the thinking which many of the people actively involved in decision making simply do not have the time to do. It is usual, therefore, for think tanks to hold seminars, to publish research and discussion documents and to draw up policy recommendations. Political parties rely on think tanks to come up with fresh and original ideas. They also expect them to produce the relevant data and support material which will enable them to package these policy ideas in an appealing manner.

Since think tanks are influenced by current concerns, this can often lead to contradictory reports. In June 1992, for example, the right wing Institute of Economic Affairs published a report claiming that gender roles are genetically determined, not learned, and so women are unsuited for management. At the same time, the left wing Institute of Employment Rights published a report claiming the opposite.

Like many of the well established pressure groups, some think tanks have become sophisticated institutions. According to Graham Mather who recently set up a new think tank called the European Policy Forum (see below), a think tank needs to raise a minimum of £100,000 before it has any chance of making an impact (*Independent on Sunday*, 24 June 1993).

The Fabian Society

The Fabian Society was founded in 1884 by Sidney Webb, Beatrice Webb and George Bernard Shaw. It is upon the Fabian Society that other think tanks have been modelled (in terms of organisation, if not in terms of ideology). The Fabian Society was set up to promote the gradual path to socialism. It was named after the Roman general Fabius Cunctator who defeated Hannibal by delaying and avoiding a direct confrontation. The early Fabians tried to win a wide audience for their ideas by organising debates and seminars and by publishing pamphlets. Perhaps the Fabians' period of greatest influence was during the years 1900-14 when they helped to shape the new Labour party and provided ideas which were incorporated into the Liberal government's social reforms. The Fabian Society remains an important source of ideas for the Labour party today.

The Institute of Economic Affairs (IEA)

The IEA was founded in 1955. Its aim was to do for free market economics what the Fabians did for socialism. Keith Joseph, Geoffrey Howe and Margaret Thatcher all learned their economic theory through the IEA. According to Grant, the IEA has had:

> 'A significant influence on the way in which the intellectual climate has changed from favouring the interventionist, neo-Keynesian ideal to support for more market orientated approaches. (Grant, 1989, p.50)

In the 1990s, its key areas of concern are the European Union and constitutional reform.

The Centre for Policy Studies (CPS)

This think tank has been described as 'the engine room of Thatcherism'. It was founded by Margaret Thatcher and Keith Joseph shortly after the Conservatives' defeat in February 1974 and quickly became one of the main vehicles for policies favoured by the New Right (see chapter 3, section 1.2). The CPS recruited non-political specialists such as the economist Alan Walters. Margaret Thatcher was more inclined to take notice of Alan Walters' opinions on the economy than those of her Chancellor Nigel Lawson. This was a major factor in Lawson's decision to resign in 1989. Young says that when Margaret Thatcher became leader of the Conservative party the CPS:

> 'Effectively eclipsed the official Conservative Research Department as the source of approved intellectual activity.' (Young, 1989, p.113)

The CPS is, therefore, an excellent example of just how much influence a think tank can have.

The Adam Smith Institute

The Adam Smith Institutute was founded in the USA in 1978 and set up in Britain in 1981. Like the CPS, the Adam Smith Institute's ideology is that favoured by the New Right. Also, like the CPS, the Adam Smith Institute made an important contribution to the policies adopted by the Thatcher governments, especially privatisation. For example, Norman

Fowler's proposals for privatising the NHS ancillary services came direct from the Adam Smith Institute (*Labour Research*, February 1984).

The Institute for Public Policy Research (IPPR)

The IPPR was founded in 1988 by a group of Labour party supporters. It was set up to do for the Labour party what the IEA and CPS did for the Conservative party. Its intellectual mission is to make the idea of **collectivism** respectable again.

The Social Market Foundation (SMF)

The SMF was set up in 1989 by supporters of David Owen after the SDP was disbanded. Its aim is to perpetuate David Owen's ideological vision of the **social market**. The ideas generated by the SMF are popular with some members of the Conservative party.

The European Policy Forum (EPF)

In 1992, the CPS and Adam Smith Institute were joined by a third New Right think tank - the European Policy Forum (EPF). The EPF was set up by Graham Mather and Frank Vibert, the former director and deputy director of the IEA. They left the IEA after a bitter dispute over policy and aims. The EPF's aim is to promote a free market and anti-federalist Europe. Senior Conservatives, such as Douglas Hurd and John Major, support the aims of the EPF and have spoken at EPF meetings.

Demos

Demos (ancient Greek for 'the people') was launched in March 1993. Unlike the other think tanks mentioned above, Demos claims to be an independent, non-partisan organisation. It has three main aims:

> 'To enrich the culture of political debate that has become narrow and self-referential; to develop strategic approaches to the fundamental problems faced by both the UK and other advanced societies; and to encourage radical thinking that helps to harness the inventiveness and motivation of citizens alienated from the existing political mainstream.' (Demos Briefing, spring 1994)

The work of Demos is overseen by an advisory council of 23 people drawn from business, academia, the media and the public and voluntary sectors. None of the 23 members of this council is a professional politician and their political affiliation is diverse. For example the council is chaired by Martin Jacques, an ex-Communist. But John Ashworth, director of the London School of Economics, is also a member. He was once described as Margaret Thatcher's favourite academic. Demos, therefore, has close ties with no one political party and aims to appeal not just to government and opposition parties but to:

> 'Change makers in the public, private and voluntary sectors, at whatever level.' (Demos 1993, p.7)

Activity 10.3

Item A *The ideas industry (1)*

Think tanks used to be where people went for big ideas. It was think tanks such as the Adam Smith Institute and the Centre for Policy Studies that honed and propagated Thatcherite ideology. But, the new consensus means that think tanks of the right and left are now converging as they seek to influence the centre ground occupied by the two main parties. There might be a bit more emphasis on Europe here, a bit more enthusiasm for proportional representation there, but the ability to shock and disturb is little more than a memory.

Adapted from the *Independent on Sunday*, 24 January 1993.

Item B *The ideas industry (2)*

One business at least has survived the 1980s intact - the political think tank. There may be a growing number of think tanks, but they are increasingly competing for impact with multinationals, consultancies and even cooperatives. How best to encourage the flow of ideas within parties from the grass roots remains a key question. As Geoff Mulgan, director of Demos, has put it, 'The next generation of useful ideas will not come from reading off policy answers from ideological templates, whether Marxist or monetarist: on the majority of issues they have nothing to say.' The traditional think tanks have recently had to rethink their roles. In its third annual report, the Institute for Public Policy Research (IPPR) admitted that its efforts to devise 'practical policy proposals' for an incoming Labour government ran out of steam. The IPPR's David Miliband believes, however, that think tanks still have a valid role to play. 'There's a political vacuum in Britain and people are dissatisfied with the old ideologies', he says. 'Think tanks have an important role to play in filling this gap.'

Adapted from *BTM*, 1993

Item C *The ideas industry (3)*

These cartoons appeared in the *Guardian* in May 1992.

Item D *Demos' mission*

Serious new ideas need the contribution of doers as well as thinkers. We will draw on people from across the political spectrum in the belief that the best ideas have no preordained political home. The traditional think tank is organised as a pyramid with a group of the 'great and good' or an intellectual guru at the top. Demos will organise itself as a network of partners working both full- and part-time to encourage flexibility and openness. These partners will, in turn, form the hubs of much larger networks of thinkers and doers. The traditional think tanks target government and Parliament. They have no contact with people who make things and provide services. Demos will seek a close relationship with doers. Demos will not be confined to the narrow world of politicians and civil servants. Of course we will seek to influence both government and opposition parties. But public policy can no longer be made in charmed circles. Our primary audience will be change makers in the public, private and voluntary sectors, at whatever level. Demos will address unexpected subjects. Research will be carried out on issues that cut across professional divides and on broader issues that are ignored by the over-specialisation of policy analysis. Our work will range from the future of Parliaments to parks, from the role of religion to fiscal regimes.

Adapted from *Demos*, 1993.

Questions

1. a) How would you classify think tanks using the criteria laid out in sections 1.1-1.3 above?
   b) What are the aims and functions of think tanks? Use Items A-D in your answer.
2. Using Items A, B and C explain how (if at all) the role of think tanks has changed since the resignation of Margaret Thatcher in 1990?
3. What does Item C tell us about think tanks?
4. Judging from Item D what are the aims of Demos? How does Demos differ from other think tanks?

2 How do pressure groups achieve their aims?

Key Issues

1. What tactics are used by pressure groups which campaign within the governmental system?
2. What tactics are used by pressure groups which campaign outside the governmental system?
3. What are the most effective ways for pressure groups to achieve their aims?

2.1 Campaigning within the governmental system

How do pressure groups make contact with decision makers? In an ideal world, perhaps, members of a pressure group would approach decision makers and ask them directly to incorporate their demands. In reality, of course, this rarely happens. It is often difficult to pinpoint who exactly makes a decision - most decisions are the outcome of a process rather than the work of an individual - and, therefore, it is difficult to know who to approach. And besides, decision makers do not have the time (and sometimes the inclination) to meet all the interested parties before making their decisions. As a result, pressure groups have to adopt other tactics to make sure that their voice is heard. What tactics they adopt is determined, to some extent, by the status of the pressure group. Some groups are able to get their voice heard within the governmental system. It is with these groups that this section is concerned.

Influencing ministers and civil servants

Ministers and civil servants are involved at all stages in the formation of government policy and the making of legislation. Many pressure groups, therefore, aim to gain access to ministers and civil servants at the earliest possible stage in the decision making process.

Ministers and civil servants invite interested parties for consultation as a matter of course. Insider groups have a close and secretive relationship with the government. Consultation is, therefore, frequent and private. Outsider groups may also be invited for consultation, but their effectiveness will be determined by the point at which they enter the decision making process. There are three main stages at which consultation occurs. The earlier a group is included, the greater its chance of success.

The earliest stage is the point at which government is working out new policy, but has not made any public statement about it. Since the government will not lose face by retreating from a publicly announced position, this is the stage at which pressure groups can exert most influence. At this point, thinking is more fluid and decision makers are open to advice.

The second stage is the period after governmental intentions reach the public domain, but before a proposal becomes law. This stage might begin with the publication of a green paper (a consultative document setting out policy options for discussion). Once the green paper has been circulated, civil servants invite interested groups to give their views on the matters raised in it. Large numbers of groups can become involved in the consultation process. Some are taken more seriously than others.

The chances of success recede as this stage progresses. Once a white paper (a document outlining proposals for legislation) has been published, it is much more difficult to secure fundamental changes since the white paper contains firm proposals backed by the government. Nevertheless, change is possible and it is worthwhile for groups to continue to lobby MPs or civil servants right up to the point at which a proposal becomes law.

The third stage concerns the implementation of the policy. Parliament has only a limited time in which to instigate new legislation. Many Acts of Parliament are brought into force and the details of policy filled in later through secondary legislation. This means that the implementation of policy is delegated to a minister who sets out the powers, rights and duties. The timing and the detail of these proposals can be very important to pressure groups.

Why do civil servants listen to pressure groups?

There are three main reasons why civil servants take the policy proposals made by pressure groups seriously.

First, consultation is regarded as an accepted and important part of the democratic process. Therefore, civil servants are obliged to consult.

Second, Britain has a generalist civil service. Although the civil service does employ all kinds of specialists, pressure groups often know more about a subject than the civil servants and can help them to make informed decisions. This trend towards a specialist dialogue has been seen as part of a professionalisation of policy making in which civil servants see themselves as talking to fellow professionals who staff pressure groups (Richardson, 1990).

Third, pressure groups can help put policies into practice. For example, they might ask their members to follow a voluntary code of practice or ask them to cooperate with a new government policy on training.

Influencing Parliament

Pressure groups expend less energy trying to influence Parliament than they expend upon influencing ministers and civil servants. According to one survey, the overwhelming majority of pressure groups are clear in their perception that ministers and civil servants are the key actors in the policy process (Rush, 1990). In another study, Miller gives MPs as a group an influence score of four out of ten, rising to six if there is a small majority or an obvious public issue. Individual MPs get a score of one. This compares with eight for civil servants and seven for ministers (Miller, 1990).

Despite this, a knowledge of parliamentary procedure allows a group to act at the right time and it is, perhaps, no surprise to learn that insider groups place a higher emphasis on influencing Parliament than outsider groups. There are three areas in which parliamentary influence on the decision making process can be seen at work.

First, MPs who win a high place in the ballot for private members' Bills are likely to be approached by pressure groups. Some pressure groups have achieved their objectives through such Bills. For example, the Abortion Reform Bill brought forward by David Steel (with pressure group backing) was legalised by a 1967 Act.

Second, backbench committees can exert some influence over decisions - Miller gives them a six on his influence grid (Miller, 1990). As a result, pressure groups may approach these committees in the hope that their demands will be adopted by the committee and presented to government.

Third, pressure groups are sometimes invited to appear before select committees (see chapter 14, section 2.1). Since 1979 these committees have enjoyed greater powers and their reports are often seriously considered by government. If pressure groups appear before these committees, their views may find their way into the committee's report and, by appearing there, influence government policy.

Influencing political parties

Perhaps the most obvious link between pressure groups and political parties is the link between trade unions and the Labour party. Despite the decision at the 1993 Labour party conference to introduce OMOV (one member, one vote), trade unions still retain financial and organisational ties with the Labour party. Labour MPs sponsored by a union are expected to support the interests of that union in Parliament and union delegates still have a voice in the formulation of Labour policy at every level. Relatively speaking, however, the unions have much less influence over Labour policy than used to be the case (see chapter 8, part 3).

Other pressure groups do have links with political parties, but on a more casual basis. Although most pressure groups are careful to maintain a non-partisan approach, some can only realistically expect to exert influence if a particular party is in power. For example, the Electoral Reform Society can only expect to achieve its goals if Labour or the Liberal Democrats are in power because the Conservatives are firmly opposed to electoral reform. As a result, groups like this often target their resources accordingly.

It should be emphasised, however, that it is not always pressure groups that approach political parties. Political parties sometimes approach pressure groups in the hope that they will support a policy or a campaign. Many pressure groups are widely respected and so their endorsement of a policy or a campaign can bring a political party great credibility. In cases like this, pressure groups have to consider carefully whether they are prepared to risk the charge of abandoning their political neutrality.

Using the courts

One way in which pressure groups can challenge and sometimes overturn a government decision is to take action in the courts. Legal actions, however, are often expensive and lengthy. A study of the poverty lobby, published in 1987, found that most groups have not seen the judicial process as a significant focus of their activities, though legal action can be useful as a way of politicising an issue and exerting pressure for changes in the law (Whitely & Winyard, 1987).

Most of the larger pressure groups now have a legal representative or department. Dr Simon Lyster, environmental lawyer for WWF, for example, says that it is important for his organisation to have legal expertise because international treaties are being increasingly used by governments as a means of setting environmental policies. He says that, today, WWF goes to court more often to seek better enforcement of these treaties (WWF, 1991).

British membership of the European Union has widened the scope of legal action through use of the European Court of Justice. For example:

> 'In recent years, environmental organisations and women's groups, especially, have used the Court...as a means of forcing recalcitrant national governments to implement EC legislation concerning the quality of drinking water and equality between working women and men.' (Mazey & Richardson, 1993a, p.15)

Sometimes, winning a case is not important. The publicity surrounding a case can be sufficient for the decision makers to back down. On other occasions, however, a public outcry can be ignored by decision makers. Besides, the cost of taking legal action means that, in general, the courts are only used as a last resort when all other methods have been unsuccessful.

Using professional lobbyists

Over recent years, there has been a rapid expansion of paid political consultants who offer to act as intermediaries between pressure groups and Parliament. Although lobbyists are used mainly by sectional groups and commercial clients, some cause groups do make use of them.

Most professional lobbyists concentrate their efforts on Parliament. This is a little surprising given that political power is concentrated in the executive. But, civil servants are more cautious than politicians about dealing with lobbyists. MPs have few support services from which they can gain information. So, material supplied by lobbyists may be of use to them. The ethical issues raised by MPs' connections with professional lobbyists are explored in chapter 11, section 3.3.

In most cases, the job of the lobbyist is to advise the client how to organise and put their case across to decision makers, not to make their case for them. According to Barney Holbeche, lobbyist for the National Farmers Union, it is essential to have regular contact with politicians, including members of the House of Lords. Lords are particularly important when the government has a large majority since they can amend a Bill passed by the Commons. Holbeche sees professional lobbying as a long-term process. He argues that lobbyists have an intelligence role. They find out what initiatives are being proposed, with the object of influencing them from the outset (Smith, 1991).

It should be noted that for every lobbying success, there is a similar story of failure, not least because consultants are frequently hired on both sides of a dispute. There are some cases, however, which suggest that lobbyists have achieved for their clients outcomes that otherwise were unlikely to have been achieved. For example, lobbyists successfully persuaded the government to drop a proposed levy on blank audio cassette tapes in 1985.

The fee for altering a major piece of legislation was thought to be around £40,000 in 1990 (Grantham & Seymour Ure, 1990).

Activity 10.4

Item A *The tape tax*

In 1985, green and white papers were published proposing the introduction of a tax or levy on blank audio cassette tapes. The main debate centred on who should pay it - the manufacturers or the consumers? Civil servants listened to the manufacturers who claimed that, because large numbers of people illegally recorded records or copied tapes at home, consumers should pay the levy. Opponents of the levy claimed that civil servants had only taken into account the record industry's statistics and had ignored other evidence. They pointed out that it was in the manufacturers' interest to prove that there was a considerable amount of home recording going on. Eventually, the proposal was dropped.

Adapted from Miller, 1990.

Item B *Blood sport*

Four weeks ago the Campaign for Hunting feared that the Bill introduced by Labour MP Kevin McNamara, vice chair of the League Against Cruel Sport, would get its second reading. Even though the Bill could not have reached the statute book, because there are only a few weeks to go before the general election, this would have set an awkward precedent. As a result, the Campaign for Hunting lobbied hard against the second reading. Having succeeded in preventing the second reading going ahead, Colin Cullimore, director of the Campaign for Hunting, said: 'The great triumph has been making people aware of the problem that exists and the fact that so many people showed an interest in this.' But, the Conservative MP, Sir Nicholas Bonsor, chairman of the British Field Sports Society (a group which supports hunting), warned: 'This is the first battle in what will undoubtedly be a prolonged war.'

Adapted from the *Independent*, 15 February 1992

Item C *Mailshot produced by the Political Animal Lobby*

This mailshot was distributed in October 1993.

Item D *Influencing the government*

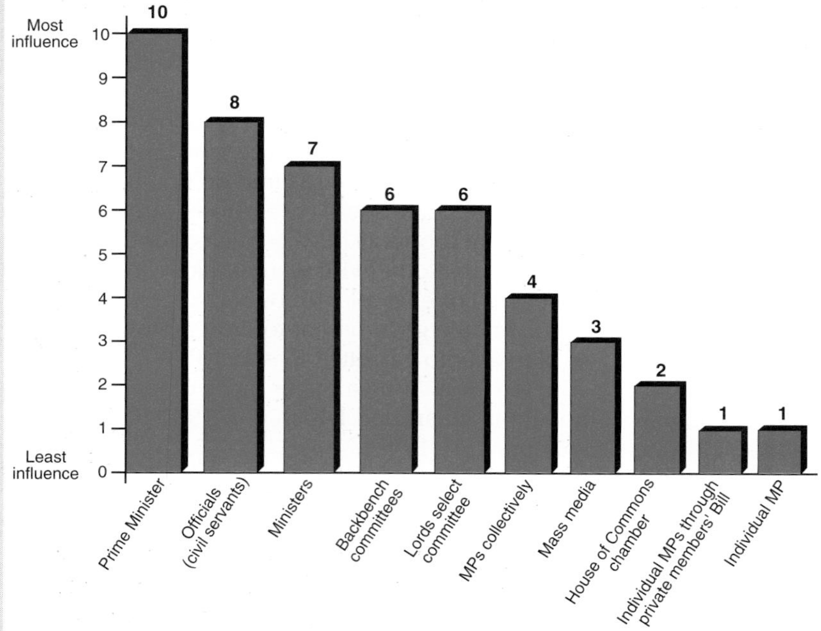

This table shows how much influence each person or group has in the decision making process.

Adapted from Miller, 1990.

Questions

1. Using Items A, B, C and E explain how pressure groups can achieve their aims by campaigning within the governmental system.
2. a) What does Item D tell us about the location of power in the governmental system?
   b) How might a pressure group use the information in Item D when planning a campaign?
3. What factors determine whether a pressure group which tries to influence governmental policy will be successful?
4. Think of an area of government policy which you feel strongly about. How would you organise a campaign to make sure that your views are heard by decision makers? Which elements of your campaign would you expect to have most clout? What problems would you expect to encounter?

Item E *The law and the environment*

The Wildlife and Countryside Act is the main piece of legislation designed to protect the environment of the UK. Under this Act 5,000 Sites of Special Scientific Interest (SSSI) have been designated. Theoretically, these sites are protected. But, in practice, this protection can be overruled by local authority planning departments granting permission for development. WWF has been campaigning through the courts to try to stop housing being built on part of an SSSI heathland near Poole in Dorset. By means of this legal action, WWF is testing the effectiveness of the Wildlife and Countryside Act. Victory would save the site. But, win or lose, WWF will be lobbying hard to get the law changed to improve protection for the UK's countryside and its marine environment. Apart from testing existing legislation, WWF is concerned about the use of parliamentary procedures to circumvent conservation efforts. WWF is supporting a consortium of local conservation groups which aims to defeat the Cardiff Bay Barrage Bill. In addition, WWF constantly monitors European legislation for its effect on UK wildlife and habitats.

Adapted from WWF, 1990.

2.2 Campaigning outside the governmental system

All pressure groups need to attract public support. They do this by using the media, by appealing to members of the public directly, by organising demonstrations or by other forms of direct action. There are two types of campaign - long-term educational and propaganda campaigns designed to produce significant shifts in public opinion and short-term campaigns aimed at warning the public about a specific problem and trying to solve it. Attracting public support is particularly important for outsider groups because outsider groups cannot expect to have direct contact with decision makers. Insider groups are, generally, reluctant to become involved in campaigns that involve direct action.

Using the media

The media plays a central role in modern politics and is used by all pressure groups. Television, radio and newspapers are particularly important in determining which issues appear on the political agenda both nationally and locally. They can also help to create a climate of public opinion which puts pressure on decision makers. It is for these reasons that pressure groups issue press releases and cultivate contacts with the media.

The relationship between pressure groups and the media, however, does not flow one way. People working in the news media are always looking for story ideas, just as pressure groups are looking for media exposure. In fact, pressure groups often do journalists' ground work for them. Suppose, for example, that an editor received a press release from a pressure group. This might be passed onto a journalist. The journalist's first action would then be to contact the pressure group. In this way, pressure groups can set the agenda. If the story is run, it is more likely that the pressure group's aims will become of concern to decision makers.

Grant (1989) suggests that there are six ways in which pressure groups can make use of the media. First, the media can provide visibility. References to a new group establish a presence in the audience's mind, making it easier to recruit new members. Constant exposure reassures a group's supporters that the group is active and helps the retention and recruitment of members. Second, the media acts as a source of information for pressure groups. Pressure groups often scrutinise the media for relevant information and are able to build campaigns around issues that are in the news or which have a local relevance. Third, the media plays a part in changing the political climate and this can have a direct effect on pressure group popularity. For example, the Abortion Reform Association was set up in 1936, but its views were ignored until a new liberal outlook emerged in the 1960s. Fourth, pressure groups may need to react to a news item. For example, when, in December 1988, Edwina Currie announced that most of Britain's egg production was contaminated with salmonella, the National Farmers Union had to react quickly to defend its members. Fifth, media coverage can demonstrate that a matter is of public concern. This is especially useful when pressure groups are presenting their case to decision makers since the decision makers are more likely to take notice of issues of public concern. And sixth, information provided by pressure groups may directly influence the content of articles or programmes.

Sometimes, it is advantageous for pressure groups to try and reach the largest possible audience. On other occasions, it is better to target certain strands of the media. No matter how large or small, pressure groups have to make tactical decisions about how best to achieve the publicity they desire.

The main problem with basing a campaign around media attention is that it is difficult to sustain. It may be difficult to keep a story in the news for the length of time that it takes to bring about effective change.

Resources also determine effectiveness. The Women's Environmental Network (WEN), for example, could only afford to employ four members of staff in 1994 to cover all aspects of WEN's work, whilst WWF employed three press officers and two assistants in the press office alone. Some groups have even started to charge journalists for talking to campaign staff or for the use of their libraries. But, this may be counterproductive since it might cut off the publicity upon which the groups depend not just to influence decision makers but also to gain new members and donations.

Finally, there are the problems that arise if the media takes a negative attitude towards a group. This makes it more difficult for the group to get its message across and the group may lose members or find it more difficult to recruit them in the future.

The timing of publicity campaigns

Publicity campaigns may be organised for the following reasons.

First, publicity campaigns are often launched to take advantage of the fact that a particular issue is in the news. For example, the Anti Apartheid Movement launched a publicity campaign around the time when Nelson Mandela was released from prison. Mandela's release was the focus of a great deal of media attention.

Second, publicity campaigns are designed to coincide with pre-planned summits or conferences relevant to the interests of the group. For example, Friends of the Earth (FoE) ran an extensive advertising campaign to coincide with the 1992 Earth Summit in Rio, Brazil.

Third, publicity campaigns are designed to draw attention to new pieces of legislation. The Anti-Poll Tax Federation, for example, began to campaign against the poll tax as soon as it became law.

In practice, two or more of these reasons may coincide. Karen Talbot, campaign organiser of The Friends of John McCarthy (see above, p.282), for example, said:

> 'We rely on Joe and Joanna public. We don't have a large, structured, national organisation. Supporters were asked to write when news of the hostages hit the headlines or when there was an anniversary of a kidnapping. People were then urged to lobby or to write to their MP.' (*Independent*, 20 April 1991).

Campaigning techniques

There are a number of ways in which a campaign can be conducted.

First, a group might pay for adverts in newspapers. The aim of this is twofold. The group hopes to attract support for its cause and it hopes for donations and new members. Advertising is expensive and so only groups with large funds can afford to use this technique. Methods of presentation vary. Some groups use shock tactics to gain support. Others focus on a success which shows that the group is able to achieve its aims.

Second, some economically powerful pressure groups pay for the services of professional advertising agencies. For example the RSPCA uses professional lobbyists and a PR consultancy to run its campaigns.

Third, groups may produce mailshots which are posted direct to members of the public. This is a way of reaching a large number of people relatively cheaply. Some mailshots are designed to recruit new members. Others are designed to inform people about important developments or to ask them to take action. Greenpeace, for example, has managed to persuade nearly half a million people to write letters protesting about whaling.

Fourth, some groups are not viewed in a sympathetic light by the media and, therefore, cannot expect to receive publicity as a matter of course. Other groups may find that their press releases are ignored because other issues are given a higher priority. As a result, groups often organise events that are designed to gain publicity. These events might be marches or demonstrations or they might be other forms of direct action. Some groups even use violence as a means of publicising their cause.

Activity 10.5

Item A *Eco-radicals warn of violence*

Earth First! members gathered in Brighton to discuss tactics for their first conference this weekend. Harry [not his real name] said: 'People are getting angrier. Bombs have been used in the USA and Europe and we're bound to see desperate acts here. There's a frustration. Nobody talked about the environment during the election campaign. Industry and government are just not listening.' Members of Earth First! have been arrested for getting in the way of bulldozers preparing the M3 extension across Twyford Down in Hampshire and they have occupied docks importing tropical timber. But, last Sunday, Earth First! took its first step over the line that divides civil disobedience from criminal damage. Members raided a Fisons compound in South Yorkshire. FoE and nine other organisations have been campaigning for two years against Fisons' practice of stripping peat from the few lowland peat bogs in England. In a few hours, Earth First! members caused £100,000 worth of damage by cutting wires and pouring sand into the engines of nine tractors and earthmovers and wrecking pumps and fire fighting equipment. Jerry, a northern member, said, 'You'll talk to a lot of people in Earth First! who will condemn what happened to Fisons, but I think it was great. People like Fisons have got to be physically stopped and the only way is by hitting them where it hurts - in their pocket. Even if we've only put their insurance premiums up, we've caused them bother.'

Adapted from the *Independent on Sunday*, 19 April 1992.

Item B *Leaflets produced by FoE in 1995*

Item C *The Electoral Reform Society*

A travesty of democracy

As usual, the number of Parliamentary seats won by each party in the Election bears little or no resemblance to their share of the popular vote.

Some parties are grossly over-represented, others iniquitously under-represented.

In other words all voters are equal but some are more equal than others.

It's a travesty of democracy.

Our electoral system was designed at a time when transportation was arduous and communications were painfully slow.

It was never a perfect system, made in Heaven and carved in stone. It was the best system that could be devised at the time.

And over the last century or so it has become one of the worst.

Now it is as antiquated as an old gramophone, muffling and distorting the voice of the people.

Throughout the world other countries survive and thrive with electoral systems that are both more democratic and more efficient than ours.

In Europe we are now the only country that still clings to the outmoded first-past-the-post system.

The Electoral Reform Society is committed to changing things.

We want a system that is both fair and efficient - a system based on proportional representation.

And every single opinion poll on the subject shows that the majority of the public agrees with us.

If you, too, believe that our ludicrously unreasonable system can't be allowed to continue, why don't you support us?

It is no good waiting until the next election. By then it will be too late. We need to get going now.

To: The Electoral Reform Society
6 Chancel Street, London, SE1 0UU

I would like to make a donation to the ERS:
☐ £50 ☐ £25 ☐ £15 ☐ Other

☐ I would like more information.

ers

Name ______
Address ______
______
______
Postcode ______

This advert appeared in the *Guardian* on 14 April 1992, in the week after the general election.

Item D *The Motorcycle Action Group (MAG)*

Join the leading Riders' Rights organisation!

Motorcycle Action Group

TACTICS

MAG has been closely identified with demonstrations since it was founded. The demos represent only a small part of MAGs activities these days, but they still have a role to play. It is very difficult for a minority pressure group to get anywhere without a public profile. MAG demos ensure that motorcyclists, the media and politicians are aware of riders' rights issues.

It is important when communicating with politicians that they appreciate that we represent the views of a significant number of people. The high profile demonstrations fulfil this objective and have not, as critics feared, engendered public antipathy.

While national media attention has been sparse, regional newspapers consistently devote considerable space to MAG demos. It is to be remembered that all MPs read papers local to their constituencies, taking note of anything of a political nature.

Increasingly, MAG groups are employing stunts to draw media attention. These require less people and, if novel, may earn more media attention than a huge cavalcade of bikes.

KEEP THEM OFF YOUR BACK!

Questions

1. a) Using Items A and B explain how the tactics used by FoE and Earth First! differ.
   b) Why do you think each group has chosen to use these tactics?
   c) Suppose you could interview a member of FoE and a member of Earth First! What would you expect each to say about the tactics used by the other group?
2. Why do you think the Electoral Reform Society (Item C) chose to buy an advert in the *Guardian*? Would you say it was money well spent? Explain your answer.
3. 'Demonstrations are pointless.' Give arguments for and against this view. Use Item D in your answer.
4. Think of an issue you feel strongly about. Suppose you were a member of a pressure group which campaigned on this issue. What tactics would you use? Explain why you could not or would not use certain tactics.

2.3 Factors affecting pressure group success

It is not easy to measure the success of a pressure group. Although there are some cause groups which have a single objective, most pressure groups have multiple objectives and it is difficult to know which has priority. Objectives may vary over time according to what is on the political agenda or there may be different factions within a group which have to be considered. Besides, even in the case of groups with a single objective, it is difficult to be sure to what extent the achievement of the objective was due to the work of the pressure group. Take, for example, The Friends of John McCarthy (see above p.282). This group had the single objective of securing the release of John McCarthy and in 1991 he was released. But, how far was his release due to the work of the pressure group and how far was it due to other factors such as pressure from the American and British governments, negotiations between the Iranians and the hostage takers and a change in the political climate?

It is clear from this example that factors other than the pressure groups' objectives need to be taken into account when evaluating their success. For example, it is important to consider whether or not decision makers are responsive to a pressure group's message. If a pressure group's message fits with the decision makers' ideology, it is much more likely to be accepted and the group is, therefore, much more likely to be effective.

Second, the fact that much of the discussion about a decision often takes place in private is also important since later it may not be clear from the records whether a pressure group's actions have been influential.

Third, the fact that, sometimes, several pressure groups campaign for the same outcome means that it can be unclear which particular group, if any, influenced the decision makers.

Fourth, even if decision makers do not appear to be receptive, this does not mean that they have taken no notice of a pressure group's campaign. Pressure group demands may be taken on board quietly to avoid a loss of face.

Fifth, it may not always be obvious what the decision makers' policy really is. They may take a tough line in the beginning for tactical reasons so that they can give ground and appear more generous later, for example.

And sixth, although a pressure group may occasionally achieve exactly what it wanted, it should be emphasised that, generally, a degree of compromise is involved. In fact, policy often emerges as a series of compromises and it is difficult to unravel who or what exactly was responsible at each stage of the process.

Grant's classification of pressure group effectiveness

Grant (1989) argues that there are three main factors which affect pressure group effectiveness. These factors are domain organisation, resources and features of the external economic and political environment.

Domain organisation

The characteristics of the membership of a pressure group, to some extent, determine the effectiveness of the pressure group. A group whose membership is drawn from a disadvantaged section of the population, for example, is less likely to be effective than a group whose membership comes from the middle classes. This is because middle class members tend to be educated and articulate, have organisational ability and know how the political system works. By definition, these qualities tend to be lacking in the disadvantaged sections of the population. So, WWF with its mass membership and middle class activists is more likely to be effective than the Claimants Union, the bulk of whose membership are unemployed.

The attractiveness of a group in terms of its electoral influence may also play a part in determining effectiveness. It is easier to arouse public concern and, therefore, the support of decision makers for the elderly than for, say, offenders or the low paid.

In addition, competition for members can lead to groups becoming less effective. Rather than presenting a united front, groups representing the same interests may be fragmented by their differing ideologies and strategies. If this is the case, then decision makers are likely to adopt a 'divide and rule' policy which reduces the chance of any of the pressure groups fulfilling their objectives. This is a tactic often used by the government when dealing with unions. For example, in the late 1980s, the government was willing to negotiate with the moderate Royal College of Nursing, but refused to meet officials from COHSE and NUPE.

Resources

The finance, number of staff and the organisational structure of a pressure group has a bearing on its effectiveness.

Financial resources not only affect what campaigning techniques a group can use, they also determine how many members of staff a group can employ. A group which is able to employ 100 people full-time is almost certainly going to be more effective than a group with the same objectives which can only afford to employ one person full-time. Employees have the time and expertise to ensure that campaigns are organised in a professional, effective manner. Not that size in itself is a guarantee of success. Many trade unions have large financial reserves and employ many full-time officials. But the anti-union attitude adopted by the Conservative government during the 1980s meant that unions had little chance of achieving their objectives.

Financial uncertainty can also effect a group's effectiveness. Most groups rely on membership subscriptions and donations. But these sources of funds can easily dry up. Between 1989 and 1992, for example, WWF's income fell by more than £3 million because it lost a tenth of its members. This drop in membership was due both to the depth of the economic recession and the fact that the environment had slipped down the political agenda (Carter, 1995).

A group's organisational structure also has a bearing on its effectiveness. Sectional groups tend to have a centralised structure consisting of a council which is the ultimate policy making body and smaller specialised groups which look after individual areas or campaigns. Cause groups, on the other hand, tend to have a more decentralised structure. The advantage of a decentralised structure is that local groups and members feel they are intimately involved in the group's decision making process. Also, information can easily be fed back from the grassroots to the centre. The disadvantage is that local groups may decide to take action without fully consulting the rest of the organisation. Such action could embarrass the group and might lead to relations with decision makers being soured.

Every group has finite resources, but the way in which a group chooses to use these resources helps to determine that group's effectiveness. A bad choice of tactics can mean a long-term setback. Overuse of the strike tactic in the 1970s, for example, led to the anti-union legislation of the 1980s.

The external environment

Public opinion can be an important factor in determining a pressure group's effectiveness. Attitudes tend to change slowly, but a series of events or a crisis may lead to the expression of new views. Often these new views are first expressed in the media. Decision makers tend to be concerned with what the media sees as important and give priority to these issues. That is one reason why pressure groups cultivate contacts with the media.

The importance of public opinion can be seen in the way in which the environmental movement grew in the 1980s. Much media coverage was given to environmental problems such as the depletion of the ozone layer, global warming and acid rain. Public concern about environmental issues led not only to an increase in membership of environmental groups (their combined membership was around four million in the 1980s), it also led to greater emphasis being placed on the environment by decision makers. As Friends of the Earth pointed out, politicians rarely act until public pressure forces them to do so (FoE 1992).

But, public opinion can change and it did so during the recession of the early 1990s. By June 1993, the public was tired of the gloomy messages put over by environmental groups and had begun to suffer from 'doom fatigue'. This forced environmental groups to respond to the public mood. They changed tactics and began to emphasise the solutions being delivered rather than the problems that they faced (*Observer*, 27 June 1993).

Rose's classification of pressure group values

According to Richard Rose there are six types of relationship between pressure groups and public attitudes (Rose, 1974). The more acceptable that a pressure group's values are to the general public, the more chance a group has of achieving its objectives.

The first, and ideal relationship is one in which the values of a pressure group are in harmony with general cultural norms. For example, the vast majority of people agree with the RSPCA that people should not be cruel to animals. As a result, the RSPCA has a good chance of achieving its objectives.

Second, a group may support values which are becoming increasingly acceptable. Fifty years ago, for example, homosexuality was illegal. In the 1960s, homosexuality became lawful over the age of 21. In 1994, the age of consent for homosexuals was lowered to the age of 18. Homosexuality is, therefore, becoming more acceptable and pressure groups campaigning for an equal age of consent between homosexuals and heterosexuals have a reasonable chance of success in the near future.

Third, some attitudes fluctuate. Whereas most people, at all times, think it is wrong to be cruel to animals, the population is divided about trade unions. Some people support their objectives, whilst others do not. Because attitudes fluctuate, at different times unions have have been more or less effective. In the 1970s, for example, public opinion was in favour of union involvement in decision making whereas in the 1980s it was not.

Fourth, some pressure groups meet with cultural indifference. The Pedestrian Association is an example. It only has 600 members nationally and attracts little attention from a car loving public.

Fifth, some pressure groups have goals which aim to halt or reverse long-term cultural trends. Since the tide is moving against them, these groups have difficulty in achieving their aims. An example of this is the Lord's Day Observance Society which opposes work on Sunday. The growth of Sunday trading and the recent legislation on this issue mean that this group has little chance of achieving its aim.

And sixth, there is sometimes conflict between the cultural values of the public and the tactics adopted by pressure groups. Some groups are not prepared to compromise in any way and they use tactics which alienate potential supporters. For example, even if they share the objectives of Earth First! or the Animal Liberation Front, most people do not agree with their use of violence. Lack of public support hinders the effectiveness of such groups.

Activity 10.6

Item A *The anti-poll tax movement*

The anti-poll tax movement was at its most enthusiastic in Spring 1990. All sorts of stunts were tried. In Nottingham, for example, protesters dressed like Robin Hood tried to invade the council chamber and in Exeter councillors were pelted with cornish pasties. But, these efforts were in vain. The legislation was in place and millions of bills were being prepared. Non-payment was a better tactic. It tapped into an old tradition of civil disobedience and it had the rare advantage of combining strong, moral anger with material self-interest. Non-payment is also passive. The number of non-payers was probably ten times the number of people involved in the anti-poll tax movement. Without cooperation from the public, it became clear that the tax would never work.

Adapted from Barr, 1992.

Anti-poll tax demonstration, 1991.

Item B *The Howard League*

the Howard League

- The Howard League was established in 1866, named after John Howard who had been the very first prison reformer.
- Over the years we have achieved many changes. We led the campaigns to abolish capital and corporal punishments, and helped establish probation.We cherish our independence. The Howard League has never accepted any Government funding, and we therefore rely on voluntary contributions from individuals and trusts.

The Howard League quarterly magazine Criminal Justice

We Run Vigorous Public Education Campaigns:

- Children in prison. The Howard League believes that 15 year old boys and girls are too young to be locked up in prisons. They can be managed effectively in the community using the very wide range of schemes available. We absolutely oppose the new secure training centres for children aged 12, 13 and 14.
- Suicides in prison. We first raised the issue of people committing suicide in prisons. We have conducted research, published reports and factsheets, held conferences and meetings with MPs and Ministers, and kept in contact with the families.
- Over-use of prison. We believe over-crowding is a symptom of a more profound problem: Too many people are sent to prison on remand and under sentence. It is not possible, or desirable, to build our way out of this. We should reduce the use of prison in the first place. We examined who goes to prison, published factsheets on imprisonment for debt and other trivial offences, raised it in Parliament.
- Developing alternatives. Most people can be managed effectively in the community. We work closely alongside probation, social services, police, magistrates and voluntary agencies to encourage the development of alternatives.
- Prisoners' Families. Children and families have a right to keep in close contact, and this gives prisoners the best chance of resettling. We produced the first ever guide to visiting prisons for families. We held 10 workshops inside prisons to open them up to the community and families. We published a report called Families Matter which generated a great deal of local media coverage. As a result, many prisons are improving their visiting facilities.

Our many activities include:

- Original research on a wide range of issues of public concern: commercial prisons, mothers behind bars, prison conditions, racial discrimination, foreign nationals in prison, are just a few recent titles. We also publish briefings on legislation, and set up working groups to consider aspects of penal policy and practice.
- Conferences for professionals and anyone interested in the criminal justice system, on issues like young people and crime, race, violence, minorities, or European prisons.
- A public information service, for schools, students, the media and MPs. We publish factsheets on 30 different topics, a video and teachers' notes on the prison system, booklets and briefings.
- Political briefing. We work closely with politicians by providing factual information, holding fringe meetings, and organising events.
- The Howard League was one of the first voluntary agencies in the world to be granted Consultative Status with the United Nations. We participate in international debates and conferences, advising on penal reform worldwide.
- All members receive a quarterly magazine **Criminal Justice**, and full members receive the **Howard Journal of Criminal Justice** which provides rigorous academic analysis. You will also be sent regular mailings advertising our latest publications and forthcoming events.
- Membership of the Howard League is a real contribution towards changing the way people are treated by the penal system. Your support is greatly valued and ensures that the Howard League can continue to campaign for reform.

The Howard League for Penal Reform

Item C *Final message from the Friends of John McCarthy*

Don't forget the British Hostages in Beirut.

FRIENDS OF JOHN McCARTHY

November 1991

Dear Friends

We are writing for the last time to all supporters of the Friends of John McCarthy. We are now planning to wind down the campaign, with the office closing at the end of the year, although as you will see below we are suggesting some ways in which you could if you wish continue to support work that is similar to ours. Perhaps the most important thing we must say first is that we cannot adequately express our appreciation for all your efforts, nor emphasise enough how much it was all your work and support that enabled the Friends of John McCarthy to keep going when there was no news and little hope: you showed that the hostages were not forgotten men and that so many people cared and wanted them home.

John's release obviously saw us achieve the main object of our work: however, after 8 August we did not want to close down immediately when other hostages remained behind. We have now seen the release of Edward Tracy, Jesse Turner and of course, Jackie Mann and the start of a political process that was absent for so many long years. With the United Nations seeking to broker the release of hostages and others unjustly held in the region, there has been a major breakthrough: for the first time there is neither the same need for us to remind politicians to act, nor are the remaining hostages forgotten.

We obviously remain cautious and recognise that many problems can still occur before all the hostages are free. We hope that everyone will continue to remember and to pray for Terry Waite, his family and all his fellow captives. One important gesture we hope everybody will continue with until Terry is home is to keep displaying the yellow ribbons as visibly as possible. We still have supplies in the office should you need more.

Item D *The Officers' Pensions Society campaign*

The Officers' Pensions Society protects the interests of war widows (women whose husbands have died on active service). Their recent campaign aimed to achieve equal pensions for all. Until the campaign's successful conclusion, women whose husbands died prior to 1973 were paid half the amount of those whose husbands had died since then. The campaign had five stages.

STAGE ONE

A public relations specialist, Citigate Communications, contacted.

STAGE TWO

Preparation for the campaign (behind the scenes):

(1) Research - revealed precedents for the government paying higher amounts.
(2) Lobbying - Citigate's lobbyist sounded out opinion in Westminster and Whitehall and found strong backbench support.
(3) Other groups - Royal British Legion and other service organisations contacted and asked to support the campaign.
(4) Interested individuals - contacted and asked to lobby local MPs.

STAGE THREE

Influencing public opinion:

(1) Advertising - a full page display was placed in several newspapers stating the case for equal pensions and appealing for donations.
(2) Mass media - ITN picked up on the story for early evening news.
(3) Personalities - Dame Vera Lynn offered her support.

STAGE FOUR

The campaign:

(1) Launch date set for 30 November (close to Remembrance Sunday).
(2) 100 parliamentary questions placed by MPs.
(3) Sympathetic MPs briefed and journalists alerted.
(4) Vera Lynn launches campaign at press conference.
(5) Provincial newspapers print stories from local sources.
(6) Campaign featured by national TV news and national papers.
(7) Ex-chiefs of staff write letters to the *Times*.

STAGE FIVE

Further action:

(1) Demands for action come from the Lords.
(2) Armed Forces minister jeered in House.
(3) Prime Minister shows signs of second thoughts at Question Time.

Success was achieved six weeks after the launch of the campaign. The Defence Secretary announced pension concessions after a meeting of the Cabinet.

Adapted from the *Financial Times*, January 1990.

Questions

1. Using Items A-D describe the range of tactics used by pressure groups.
2. a) Why was each of the campaigns described in Items A, C and D successful? Were there any common elements in the three campaigns which explain their success?
   b) To what extent did the success of these campaigns depend upon factors referred to in Grant's classification of pressure group effectiveness and Rose's classification of pressure group values?
3. Suppose you had been asked to decide whether the work of the Howard League had been effective (Item B). What criteria would you use?

3 How the role of pressure groups has changed

Key Issues

1. What is corporatism and why did it fail?
2. How did the role of pressure groups change in the 1980s?
3. What are the current trends?

Corporatism

When the major pressure groups in a society are incorporated into the state machinery, this is known as corporatism. Corporatism was a feature of British politics in the 1960s and 1970s. According to Dorey, corporatism in Britain worked as follows:

> 'Major economic or producer groups such as the Trade Union Congress (TUC) and the Confederation of British Industry (CBI) [participated] in discussions and decision making with the government (or bodies appointed by the government) to decide on industrial or economic policies. Once agreement was reached, the groups would then share responsibility for making sure that the agreed policies were actually implemented and adhered to by their members. Government and major economic groups would thus work together in mutual interdependency, in order to formulate and administer public policy.'
> (Dorey, 1993, p.24)

Since corporatism in Britain involved three parties (the TUC, the CBI and the government), it is also known as **Tripartism**.

Corporatism in Britain is usually dated from 1961 when the National Economic Development Council (NEDC) was set up. The NEDC was a forum where civil servants, members of the government, employers and trade unions could meet regularly to consider ways of promoting economic growth. This was the first time that the government had invited both employers and trade unionists into the heart of the decision making process. It set the pattern for the next 15 years.

Throughout the 1940s and 1950s Britain managed only slow economic growth compared to its competitors. It was to remedy this that governments sought a corporatist solution. The assumption which was shared by Labour and Conservative governments alike was that if both employers' representatives and trade unionists agreed to cooperate with the government over prices and wages, then the economy as a whole would grow more quickly. Clearly, then, corporatism was very much a product of the postwar consensus. It was also closely associated with the incomes policies which were the centrepiece of government economic policies in the 1960s and 1970s.

The failure of corporatism

The drift towards corporatism stopped when the Conservatives, under Margaret Thatcher, were elected in 1979. By then, a number of criticisms had been levelled at this method of governing.

First, critics complained because tripartite decision making bypassed Parliament. Important decisions were made in private by ministers with the help of pressure group officials. This, it was argued, was harmful to parliamentary democracy.

Second, critics argued that corporatism simply did not work. Neither the CBI nor the TUC had sufficient control over their members to ensure that any decision they made with the government would be implemented. It seemed that the government was continually making concessions in return for assurances on prices and incomes policies which then turned out to have no lasting value. Employers became less enthusiastic about such policies when profits were eroded by the rules to which they had agreed. Government concessions to the unions were not sufficient to prevent strikes.

Third, some critics argued that the system was bound not to work because it was so exclusive. Only some groups were invited to participate in the decision making process. Many were excluded. Those which were included did not necessarily represent the true interests of their members.

Fourth, the New Right argued that corporatism was damaging because it stifled the free market and granted far too much power to trade unions. The New Right's antipathy towards corporatism is closely tied to its determination to break with the postwar consensus.

Fifth, critics on the left argued that far from enhancing the power of the unions, corporatism weakened them. By including the TUC in tripartite negotiations, the government and CBI were able to extract greater concessions than they would otherwise have achieved.

According to Grant, the problems with corporatism can be summarised as follows:

> 'In the 1970s, concerns were expressed that organised interests, particularly the bigger producer lobbies, were gaining too much influence in the political process. There were fears that Parliament was being bypassed, and that the interests of the ordinary citizen who was not a member of that powerful lobby were being brushed aside. The interests of doctors often seemed to come before those of patients; of farmers before consumers of food and recreational users of the countryside.' (Grant, 1991, p.16)

Changes in the 1980s

The antagonism of Margaret Thatcher towards large organised interest groups ensured that contact with both the CBI and the TUC ceased after 1979. By 1988, Lord Young, Trade and Industry Minister, could claim:

> 'We have rejected the TUC. We have rejected the CBI. We do not see them coming back again. We gave up the corporate state.' (*Financial Times*, 9 November 1988)

But the rhetoric of the Conservatives in the 1980s did not always live up to the reality. Reviewing the experience of pressure groups under Prime Minister Thatcher, Richardson (1990) claims that, although the Thatcher governments sometimes excluded groups from major policy decisions, they then brought them in to discussions on implementation. Although some groups lost out (especially local authorities and trade unions), others did not. Richardson also notes that the Thatcher governments' confrontational style was often not well thought through. Radical changes to existing policy were often proposed but not implemented swiftly enough. By the time the government got round to implementation, pressure groups had managed to organise themselves. The result was a traditional round of bargaining and consultation.

Baggot (1992) in a statistical survey of pressure group activity during the 1980s confirms that there was a reduction of contact between labour groups and the government, but there was also a growth in parliamentary lobbying, especially amongst labour groups.

Two other phenomena must be taken into account when assessing the role of pressure groups in the 1980s. First, think tanks have grown in importance (see section 1.6 above). And second, the huge growth in numbers and significance of cause groups has made an impact. Membership increases were huge in the 1980s. For example, FoE had 1,000 members in 1971, 55,000 members by 1980 and 110,000 by 1990. Similarly the RSPB grew from 98,000 members in 1971 to 561,000 in 1987 and 880,000 in 1992. Although some groups with large memberships were clearly unsuccessful in the 1980s (CND is an obvious example), others made a substantial impact (environmental groups, for example). As the unexpected success of the 'Live Aid' concert in 1985 indicates, it seems that people began to look for new ways in which to participate in politics during the 1980s.

Current trends

Since 1990, hostility towards corporatism has continued. This was made quite clear when the NEDC was finally abolished after the general election in 1992. Despite this, however, there have been some signs that John Major's government is prepared to take a less hostile view towards organised interest groups.

First, in 1991, the new Secretary of State for Health, William Waldegrave, offered to discuss proposed changes to GPs' contracts with the British Medical Association (BMA). The BMA had been ignored prior to this.

Second, in July 1992, Michael Heseltine announced that he intended to reorganise the Department of Trade and Industry so that it related more closely to individual sectors of industry. This reversed the arrangements made by Lord Young in 1988 which had been designed to reduce contacts between the Department and pressure groups.

And third, in March 1994, Stephen Dorrell (Treasury Financial Secretary) became the first Conservative minister for more than 20 years to address the TUC. According to Grant, however, successive governments' hostility towards corporatism may, ironically, have produced a power vacuum which ushers in a whole new set of problems:

> 'The prospect of a corporatist democracy, in which a few economic interest groups would

be very powerful, has receded. This modernist nightmare may, however, have been replaced by a postmodernist one in which a large number of fragmented and fractured pressure groups defend their own particular interests or their own pet causes. Particularly when government appears to lack a coherent vision or overall policy, a political vacuum may arise which is then filled by a number of competing groups with their own vision for parts of society, but not for society as a whole. Although there is considerable dispersal of power, there may also be an inability to take effective political decisions. In its way, that is as great a danger as the concentration of power that could have arisen under a functioning corporatist arrangement.' (Grant, 1993, p.76)

Activity 10.7

Item A *The dual state model*

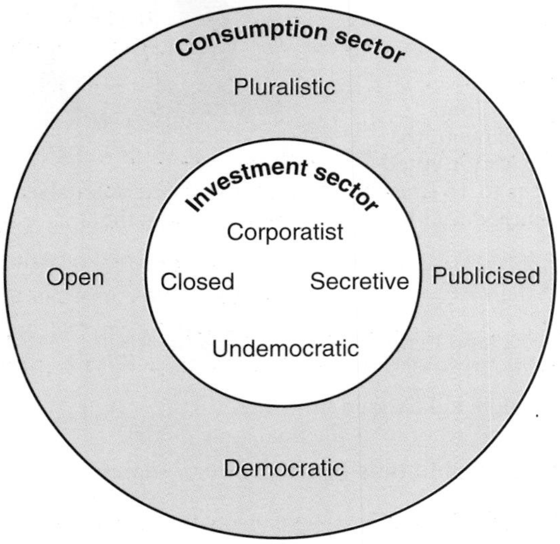

According to the dual state model, decisions made about production (in the investment sector) tend to be settled in a corporatist style (by a small number of large, organised interest groups in secret), whilst those concerning the consumption sector (welfare and moral issues) are settled by a pluralistic process (by a large number of groups of varying sizes openly competing for government attention).

Item B *The CBI and the government*

A decade ago, the CBI promised the government a bare knuckle fight. But, in recent months, CBI officials have begun to wear the doormats thin at 10 and 11 Downing Street. So, why the improved relationship? The director general of the CBI argues that the CBI's success in getting the government to listen to its viewpoint is a direct result of the CBI's lobbying skills. But, one of the Chancellor's advisers admitted that when the promise of economic recovery aborted for the third time, the pressure on the government became intense.

Adapted from the *Independent*, 1 December 1992.

Howard Davies, director general of the CBI at a press conference in 1994.

Item C *The TUC and the government*

Yesterday, Stephen Dorrell, the Treasury's Financial Secretary, became the first Conservative minister to deliver a speech to a TUC meeting for more than 20 years. More than 300 trade unionists listened in silence as Dorrell used his platform to emphasise the government's determination to make the public sector pay freeze stick. At the end of the speech, there was lukewarm applause. The atmosphere was one of strained politeness. John Monks, TUC general secretary, welcomed Dorrell's decision to attend the meeting, but admitted that there had been no meeting of minds. Even those on the far left, however, agreed that if the TUC was to regain any of its influence, it had to hold out an olive branch to the government.

Adapted from an article in the *Daily Telegraph*, 4 March 1994.

Item D *Doctors and Ministers*

When William Waldegrave replaced Kenneth Clarke as Health Secretary in November 1990, he brought a climate of change. Formal negotiations between the Department of Health and the BMA which Clarke had halted, for example, have now resumed. But there are reasons for change other than Waldegraves's less combative personality. Whilst Clarke battled his way to the statute book, Waldegrave has inherited the task of making the reforms work. To be fully effective, next April's changes require cooperation from the medical profession. Doctors' leaders hope that the better relationship with the government will enable them to influence details of the reforms as they are implemented.

Adapted from the *Financial Times*, 8 February 1991.

Item E *John Major and gay rights*

Six weeks ago, the door of 10 Downing Street opened to admit a man who had come to discuss homosexual affairs, the actor Ian McKellen. Was the meeting a genuine attempt by John Major to undo the damage done to gays and lesbians by his predecessor, or was he just making a token gesture aimed at mopping up votes at the next election? Although John Major did not seem overly enthusiastic about the issues raised by Ian McKellen, he agreed to receive a copy of the proposed Homosexual Law Reform Bill drafted by the pressure group *Stonewall*. He also assured him that he would be seeking further advice on the issues raised. Ian McKellen said John Major was prepared to listen, but he remains highly sceptical of the Prime Minister's commitment to legislative reform. He said: 'I won't believe it until I see it.' Still, this was a start. It was something that even two years ago would have been thought astonishing: the reappearance on the political agenda of gay and lesbian issues in a positive form for the first time in 25 years.

Adapted from the *Independent on Sunday*, 10 November 1991.

This photo (right) shows Ian McKellen on his way to a meeting with John Major in September, 1991. In February 1994, in a free vote in Parliament, the age of consent for homosexuals was lowered from 21 to 18. John Major voted for this reduction, but he voted against lowering the age of consent to 16 (the age of consent for heterosexuals). The Bill proposing a lower age of consent for homosexuals was introduced by a backbencher, not by the government (see chapter 14, p.410).

Questions

1. 'The announcement of the death of corporatism was premature.' Using Items A-D give arguments for and against this statement.
2. a) What evidence is there in Items B-E to support the dual state model illustrated in Item A?
   b) Judging from your knowledge of pressure groups, how useful and accurate is the dual state model?
3. Judging from Items B-E would you say that pressure groups have a significantly better chance of success under John Major than they had under Margaret Thatcher?

4 The European dimension

Key Issues

1. Why has the European Union become an important focus for British pressure groups?
2. How can pressure groups influence policy making in the EU?

The 1986 Single European Act (SEA)

Like most aspects of British politics, the role of pressure groups has changed since Britain joined the EU. Pressure groups go where the power goes. As more and more power has shifted towards Brussels, pressure groups have begun to place increasing emphasis on lobbying EU decision makers.

This has particularly been the case since the Single European Act (SEA) was passed in 1986. The SEA resulted in two major changes, both of which have encouraged greater pressure group activity in Brussels.

First, the SEA changed the voting procedure in the Council of Ministers. Whereas a single member state had previously had the power to veto a proposal, the SEA allowed for the introduction of qualified majority voting on some matters:

> 'The Act extended the provision for weighted majority voting in the Council of Ministers. Each country is allocated a number of votes, depending on size. The big four, the UK, Germany, Italy and France, have 10 votes each. Each of the remaining countries have fewer. However, the votes of one country alone are not enough to veto a measure...Ministers from at least three countries have to combine in order to prevent it going through.' (Norton, 1995, p.28)

Second, the range of policies covered by the EU has been extended. Policies which had previously been decided by national governments are now decided by the EU. As a result, pressure groups have been forced to lobby the EU to have any hope of influencing decisions.

The net result of these changes is that any pressure group which continues to rely exclusively on lobbying Whitehall and Westminster is adopting a high risk strategy. The trend is to put pressure on EU decision makers. By 1993, over 3,000 lobbyists worked full-time in Brussels.

Lobbying the EU

It is more difficult for groups to influence EU decisions

than it is to influence decisions made in the UK because the decision making process within the EU is more complicated and more unpredictable. According to Grant (1990), there are four main channels through which pressure groups can work.

First, a pressure group may decide to work through contacts with the British government in the hope of persuading the government to adopt the position favoured by the group in discussions at European level. This tactic is often favoured by insider groups since they can make use of contacts with the government which are already established. Those outsider groups, however, which support issues that can be presented as being in the national interest may also be able to persuade the government to adopt their point of view. The advantage with this method is that a group's position may be presented direct to the ultimate EU decision making body, the Council of Ministers. The disadvantage is that the group relinquishes control. The group's proposals may be altered, watered down or even abandoned during the bargaining process.

A further reason for adopting this method is that even though the EU passes the legislation, it is up to the member states to implement it. By working with the national government, groups may gain the opportunity to influence the way in which EU legislation is implemented.

Second, a pressure group may choose to work through a federation made up of representative groups from each of the 15 members - the so-called Eurogroups. Although they are more common among sectional groups, some cause groups are also organised into federations. For example, the Motorcycle Action Group is the UK representative of the Federation of European Motorcyclists. The number of Eurogroups doubled from around 250 in 1970 to over 500 in 1993.

Eurogroups are recognised by the European Commission as being representative of European-wide interests. As a result, their officials are able to cultivate close ties with EU bureaucrats. Although the EU has a reputation for being over-bureaucratic, the number of civil servants is small. Less than 4,000 civil servants work for the European Commission, for example. As a result, the Commission relies upon outside groups to supply expertise. Pressure groups are positively welcomed into the decision making process.

Eurogroups, however, often lack sufficient resources. This makes it difficult for them to respond quickly to changing events. They also suffer from the problem of gaining agreement between organisations from 15 different member states. It has been argued that their impact on EU policy is minimal because, by trying to reconcile national differences, they tend to end up with the lowest common denominator.

Third, a pressure group may choose to join a direct membership association. That is, rather than joining a national organisation affiliated to a federation, members join a Brussels based organisation. For example, 40 of the largest firms in Western Europe have formed the European Round Table of Industrialists. The advantage of this is that members have direct contact with the organisation rather than going through an intermediate level or national body. Not only can a direct membership association respond quickly to changing events, it also has the authority to develop effective policies. For example, the European Round Table of Industrialists was instrumental in persuading the EU to introduce a single market policy. It has access to heads of national governments and to commissioners. Although few such organisations exist at present, the number is likely to grow as the EU develops.

Fourth, a pressure group might choose to set up office in Brussels and lobby directly. This option is only open to large, well-established groups, such as the CBI, as it is very expensive. It has the advantage of providing direct access to decision makers.

The three laws of Euro-lobbying

In an article written in 1993, Mazey & Richardson identified three laws of lobbying. It is by observing these laws that pressure groups have the best chance of influencing decisions made by the EU.

The first law of Euro-lobbying is to discover exactly where the power lies. Although the Council of Ministers is the ultimate EU decision making body, much of the power actually lies with the Commission. It is the Commission which draws up policy proposals for the Council of Ministers and it is the Commission which is responsible for policy implementation. As a result, it is the Commission which is targeted by most pressure groups based in Brussels.

The second law of Euro-lobbying is to be willing to compromise. Since so many different interests are at stake, it is rare for any single party to get its own way completely. Pressure groups need to be willing to make deals. They often have to make a concession over one clause in the hope that the favour will be returned later. Mazey and Richardson say that EU policies are:

> 'as much peace treaties between competing interests and nations as they are **rational decisions'**. (Mazey & Richardson, 1993, p. 21)

The third law of Euro-lobbying is that the most effective time to influence a decision is at the earliest possible stage. Ideally, a pressure group should be there at the start. The further along the road a policy has travelled the less chance groups have to change it. One EU official told Mazey and Richardson that, in general, probably 80% of the initial proposal remains in a directive's final draft. That indicates just how important it is to be involved in drawing up the initial proposal. It also indicates how important advance information can be. It may be expensive to maintain an office in Brussels, but groups which do so are likely to have earlier access to the decision making process than other groups.

Activity 10.8

Item A *Oxleas Wood (1)*

This photo shows members of PARC and the EU flag flying from Severndroog castle

Seven environmental groups yesterday formed an alliance to fight government plans to build a road through the last ancient woodland in London, Oxleas Wood. To celebrate the new alliance, a giant EU flag was raised at Severndroog castle in the wood. Dr Barry Gray, chair of the protest group People Against The River Crossing (PARC) said: 'We have gone to great lengths to make the government see reason and halt this road scheme. The European Commission's action has vindicated PARC's complaint that the British government has not carried out a proper environmental assessment of this scheme.' The government says it has not broken EC rules on the environment and all correct procedures have been followed.

Adapted from the *Independent*, 11 May 1993.

Item B *Oxleas Wood (2)*

The European Commission yesterday responded to complaints that the British government had breached an EC directive when it put forward plans to build a road through Oxleas Wood. After meeting protesters the Commission announced that if, in two months time, it is still not satisfied with the British government's explanation, it will take the government to the European Court of Justice. The key issue for protesters is whether there will be a judgement before a large part of the woodland is destroyed. Britain is highly unlikely to act in defiance of a court ruling, but several years can elapse before a final judgement is made. Protesters have been disappointed at the pace with which the Commission has handled their complaint. Peter Price, a Conservative MEP who was at the meeting with the Commission said: 'I'll be keeping up the pressure on the Commission to go ahead quickly with their action in the European Court.'

Adapted from the *Independent*, 28 April 1993.

Item C *Motorcylists and the EU*

MAG (Motorcycle Action Group) stresses that many of those making the legislation, whether in London or Brussels, have little real knowledge of motorbikes. For example, legislation has been proposed to make leg protectors compulsory. But MAG argues that leg protectors increase rather than decrease accidents. Tory MEPs who had previously supported compulsory leg protectors changed their minds after MAG officials presented them with evidence. MAG has now secured almost 100% support from MEPs. But the British government is still intent on getting them into European law.

Adapted from *Magnews*, February/March 1992.

Item D *CBI successes in Europe 1992*

- The CBI helped to shape the agenda for the British Presidency of the EC.
- The CBI produced a briefing paper in support of the Maastricht Treaty and distributed it before the debate in the Commons. The debate was won by three votes.
- The CBI and UNICE (the Union of Industrial and Employers' Confederations of Europe, the official representative of business in the EU) played a key role in shaping the Sutherland Committee Report on making the Single Market work.

Adapted from the CBI's Annual Report, 1992.

Item E *Decision making in the EU (see also chapter 6, section 2.1)*

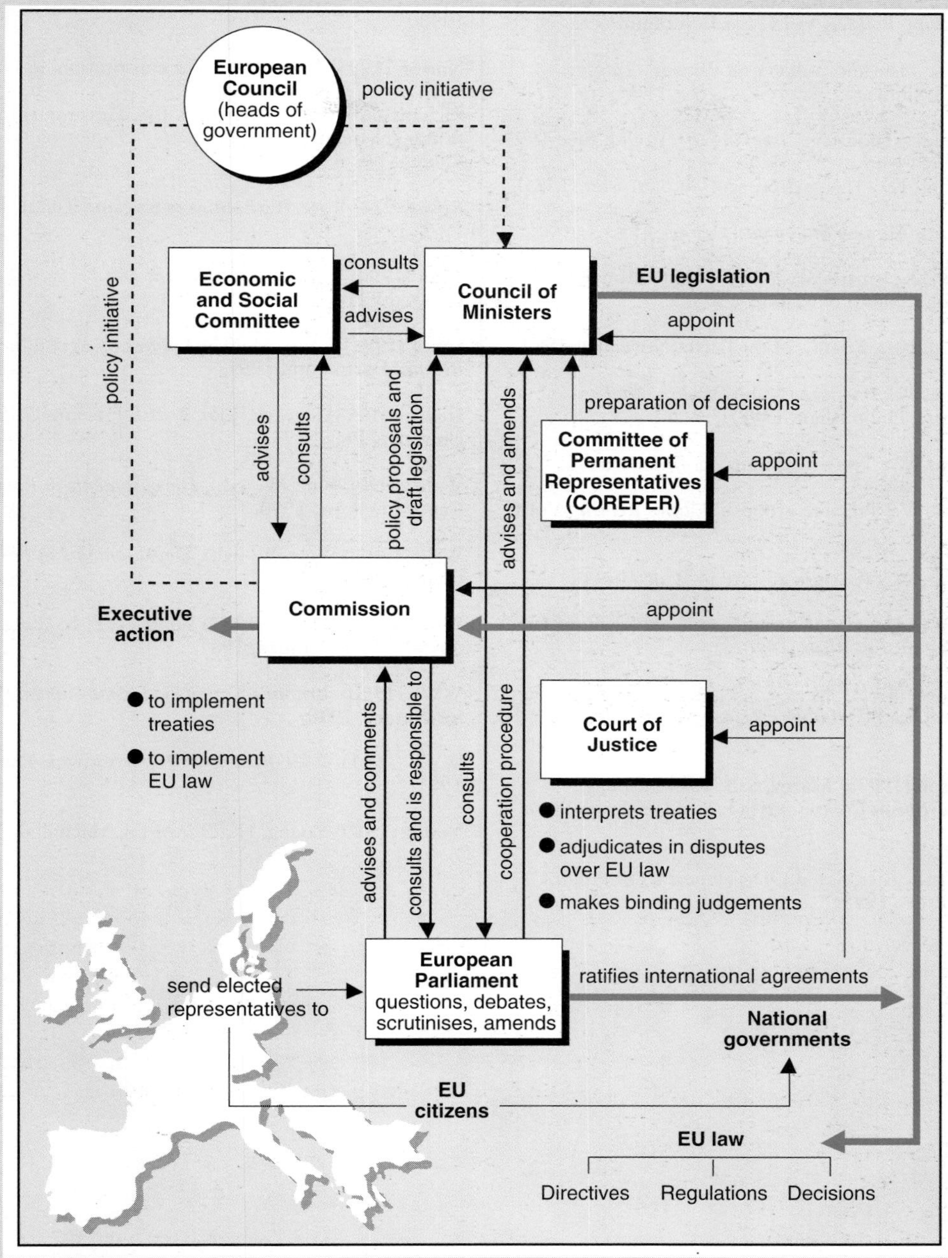

Adapted from Mazey & Richardson, 1993.

Questions

1. a) What do Items A, B, and C tell us about the different methods pressure groups use to influence decisions made by the EU?
   b) Evaluate the effectiveness of each method.
   c) What evidence is there to suggest that lobbying the EU will become increasingly important for pressure groups?
2. What methods do you think the CBI would have used to achieve the successes outlined in Item D?
3. Suppose you had been asked to organise a Euro-lobby on an issue which you feel strongly about. Using Item E:
   a) describe the tactics you would use.
   b) explain which points in the EU decision making process you would target.
   c) what factors do you think would determine the success or failure of your campaign?
4. Using Items A-E, describe the problems that pressure groups face when attempting to influence EU decisions. Suggest ways in which these problems might be overcome.

References

Baggot (1992) Baggot, R., 'The measurement of change in pressure group politics', *Talking Politics*, Vol.5, No.1, autumn 1992.

Barr (1992) Barr, G., 'The anti-poll tax movement', *Talking Politics*,Vol.4, No.3, summer 1992.

BTM (1993) 'The ideas industry', *Breaking the Mould*, June 1993.

Carter (1995) 'Carter, N., 'The environment' in *Lancaster (1995).*

Demos (1993) *Demos Mission Statement*, Demos, 1993.

Dorey (1993) Dorey, P., 'Corporatism in the United Kingdom', *Politics Review*, Vol.3, No.2, November 1993.

FoE (1992) *Earth Matters*, Friends of the Earth, November 1992.

Grant (1989) Grant, W., *Pressure Groups, Politics and Democracy in Britain*, Philip Allan, 1989.

Grant (1990) Grant, W., 'Pressure groups' in *Wale (1990).*

Grant (1991) Grant, W., 'Pressure groups', *Politics Review*, Vol.1, No.1, September 1991.

Grant (1993) Grant, W., 'Pressure groups' in *Wale (1993).*

Grantham & Seymour Ure (1990) Grantham, C. & Seymour Ure, C., 'Political Consultants' in *Rush (1990).*

Mazey, & Richardson (1993) Mazey, S. & Richardson, J., 'Pressure groups and the EC', *Politics Review*, Vol.3, No.1, September 1993.

Mazey & Richardson (1993a) Mazey, S. & Richardson, J., *Lobbying in the European Community*, Oxford University Press, 1993.

Lancaster (1995) Lancaster, S. (ed.), *Developments in Politics*, Vol. 6, Causeway Press, 1995.

Miller (1990) Miller, C., *Lobbying* (2nd edn), Basil Blackwell, 1990.

Norton (1995) Norton, P., 'The constitution' in *Lancaster (1995).*

Richardson (1990) Richardson, J.J., 'Government and groups in Britain: changing styles', *Strathclyde Papers on Government and Politics*, No. 69, 1990.

Rose (1974) Rose, R., *Politics in England Today*, Faber and Faber, 1974.

Rush (1990) Rush, M., *Parliament and Pressure Politics*, Oxford University Press, 1990.

Smith (1991) Smith, M., *The Politics of Agricultural Support in Britain*, Dartmouth, 1991.

Stewart (1958) Stewart, J.D., *British Pressure Groups*, Oxford University Press, 1958.

Wale (1990) Wale, W. (ed.), *Developments in Politics*, Vol.1, Causeway Press, 1990.

Wale (1993) Wale, W. (ed.), *Developments in Politics*, Vol.4, Causeway Press, 1993.

Whiteley & Winyard (1987) Whiteley, P. & Winyard, S., *Pressure for the Poor*, Methuen, 1987.

WWF (1990) *Britain's Threatened Environment*, Worldwide Fund for Nature, 1990.

WWF (1991) *WWF Review 1991*, Worldwide Fund for Nature, 1991.

Young (1989) Young, H., *One of Us*, Macmillan, 1989.

11 Political recruitment

Introduction

It is difficult to establish accurate figures for the number of people who are politically active. The results of a survey published in 1994 (Whiteley et al., 1994) suggested that membership of the Conservative party is around 750,000. But, this includes the 'drinking membership' - people who join the party to use Conservative Clubs socially and never participate in Conservative party politics. The Labour party, on the other hand, claimed to have a membership of about 300,000 at the end of 1994. But, an internal Labour party report admitted that only about a third of these members were fully paid up. The Liberal Democrats claimed a membership of around 87,000 for 1993 and the Greens 10,000. But, again, it is difficult to say how many of these members simply pay their subscriptions and never attend meetings or other events organised by their party.

If the number of political activists is small, then the number of activists who seek to become candidates for local, national and European elections is even smaller. This chapter examines the type of people who stand as candidates and the procedures that are used to select them. It also considers whether councillors, MPs and MEPs are representative of the population as a whole and how the pressures on them affect the extent to which they can claim to be accountable to their constituents.

In addition to the recruitment of elected representatives, this chapter examines the recruitment of people whose work is political but who are not elected - people who are appointed to serve on quangos. What sort of people are appointed to do these jobs and why? To whom are they accountable? What does their appointment tell us about the British political system?

Chapter summary

Part 1 examines **the selection and role of local councillors**. Who stands for office? How representative are they? What rewards do they get from office? What sacrifices do they have to make?

Part 2 looks at **the selection of parliamentary candidates**. How do selection procedures differ in the main parties? What qualities are sought?

Part 3 considers in detail **whether or not MPs are representative of their constituents**. What background do they have? How accountable are they? What pressures are put upon them? What rewards do they get from office?

Part 4 looks at **who stands for the European Parliament and how they are selected**. It also considers MEPs' pay and conditions and factors affecting their accountability.

Part 5 focuses on **people whose work is political but who are not elected**. It examines the criteria used for the appointment of people to quangos. What sort of people are appointed to these posts? To whom are they accountable?

1 The selection of local councillors

Key Issues

1. Who stands for office and why?
2. How are candidates selected?
3. What are councillors' hours and rewards?
4. What role do councillors play?
5. How representative are councillors?

Who stands for office?

Each year thousands of individuals make the decision to stand as candidates in local elections. Their reasons for standing may vary, but it is possible to group them under the following headings: ideology; power; personal satisfaction; specific policy interest; and ambition (Kingdom, 1991).

The level and type of commitment required from candidates depends on whether they are standing at parish, district or county level. At parish level, seats are usually contested by individuals who avoid a party political label. As parish councils have little power and are responsible for only small amounts of money, often little interest is shown in the elections. As a result, it may be difficult to persuade people to stand for office. At district and county level, most elections are party political contests, but independents do stand, especially in rural areas.

For some who join a political party, becoming a candidate for a local council election is the climax of years of political activity in their local branch. For others, it is a first step on a planned political career. All those who stand have a wish to represent their fellow citizens in some way.

The selection and election of candidates

Independent candidates make their own choice to stand and then have to find friends and supporters to help them if they decide to run an election campaign. The number of independent candidates standing in district and county council elections has fallen since 1974. Before the 1974 local government reorganisation, only 46% of councils were classed as 'party authorities' (where the three main parties make up more than 50% of council membership). Immediately after the 1974 local government reorganisation, this rose to 64%. By 1987, only 34 of the 369 councils where elections were held had a majority of independent councillors.

Candidates who stand on behalf of political parties are selected at a special selection meeting. Even when there is a shortage of candidates or the seat is impossible to win and only one person agrees to stand, a selection meeting is generally held. Candidates are selected by the local branch of the party, though the party tier at district level often has an input into the process, perhaps by having an approved list of candidates.

At the selection meeting, party members listen to potential candidates and ask them questions. Voting then takes place and a single candidate is selected. The local party then supports their candidate in the election campaign. Election campaigns vary from an active campaign in which votes are canvassed on the doorstep to a 'paper' campaign where the candidate does no canvassing.

Candidates supported by political parties have the advantage of access to money (for leaflets and so on) and personnel. But, even though the major political parties try to fight every seat, some council seats are still uncontested (the number in this category is falling). Once elected, on average, a councillor in the UK represents a population of 1, 800.

Hours and rewards

Being a councillor is a time consuming business. The Widdicombe Report (Widdicombe, 1986) found that councillors spent, on average, 74 hours per month on council business (though this figure conceals considerable variation between the more and the less active councillors). Council leaders and chairs of committees are likely to spend much longer on council business than ordinary councillors. The time spent shows a small decrease compared to a study in 1976, but is considerably more than the Maud study in 1965. A study by the Joseph Rowntree Foundation found that 74 hours per month remained the average in 1993.

There is some evidence that time and commitment given to council work varies according to political party. Wood & Crawley show that Labour and Liberal Democrat councillors, on average, spend more time on council work than others. Conservative councillors often define their role in more limited terms than others. They tend to see council work as one of a number of leisure interests and certainly no more than a voluntary activity, requiring only limited commitment (Wood & Crawley, 1987).

Councillors in the key positions on district and county councils have the task of spending millions of pounds and are responsible for the delivery of efficient services to their community. As a result, meetings often have to be held during the day. This is a problem for many councillors who find it difficult to combine a full-time job with their council work. If they work in the private sector, they are dependent on the generosity of their employer to release them from work. The Widdicombe Report recommended that public sector employees be allowed up to 26 days a year leave to undertake council work. It is, therefore, not too surprising that the majority of councillors are either self-employed, working in the public sector, retired or not in full-time work.

The large majority of councillors undertake their council work on a voluntary basis, not for financial reward. Since 1991, all councillors have been able to claim a small basic allowance. Those with special responsibilities are eligible for an allowance and councils usually pay an 'attendance allowance' to councillors. According to the Audit Commission's 1990 study, the average amount claimed by councillors per year was £2,000.

For a small minority of councillors, council activities in the 1980s evolved into a full-time job (though no councillor was paid a full-time salary). This happened because committee chairs or party leaders were expected to attend council meetings on a daily basis. They then simply claimed the attendance allowance due to them for the large number of meetings they attended and the special responsibility allowance available for senior councillors. Councillors such as Ken Livingstone and David Blunkett found the demands of council work such that it required their full-time attention. In both cases, they also found that their service as a councillor was a useful stepping stone to becoming an MP.

This evolution of full-time councillors met with the disapproval of the Department of the Environment (the ministry responsible for local government). In the 1980s, the Department of Environment favoured the voluntary principle. To deter would-be full-time councillors, the special responsibility allowance was frozen. As a result, little has been heard about full-time councillors in the 1990s.

Although the Department of the Environment favoured the voluntary principle in the 1980s and early 1990s, there are signs that this policy may be about to change. In an effort to attract higher quality councillors, there are plans to make the role of councillors more demanding and to offer payments of up to £20,000. Ministers have begun to argue that, in the future councillors will need different skills. According to the *Guardian*:

> 'The ability to manage large numbers of directly employed staff is becoming less important than the ability to oversee contracts, set standards, award contracts fairly, monitor performance and act if it falls short of the required level.' (*Guardian*, 10 April 1993)

How representative are councillors?

It is clear from the Widdicombe Report of 1986 that councillors tend not to mirror the electorate they represent socially (see below, Activity 11.1, Item C). Despite this, they often claim to represent the view of their constituents politically. The degree to which councillors can be said to represent their constituents is, to some extent, determined by the way in which they themselves perceive their role since that determines the extent to which they consult with and take on board the views of constituents. Kingdom (1991) has suggested that the ways in which councillors perceive their role can be divided into four categories. First, councillors may act as delegates, directly reporting the views of their constituents to the council. Because of the small size of local government electoral units, it is possible for councillors to work in this way. Second, councillors may claim a mandate if they have presented a manifesto to the electorate and won the election. Third, councillors may see themselves as leaders who should exercise personal judgement. And fourth, councillors may be self-seeking and have minimal interest in the local community.

One difficulty that all councillors face in claiming to represent the community politically is the low proportion of the electorate which turns out to vote in local elections. Given that few councillors in contested seats are likely to receive much more than 20% of the total electorate's vote, they cannot easily be confident that they have the support of the public for any policy initiatives.

Activity 11.1

Item A *The amount of time spent on council duties, 1964-85*

Average number of hours in a typical month	1964	1976	1985	1993
Attending council meetings (including committee meetings)	11	23	21	22
Preparation for meetings and travelling	18	26	25	24
Attending party meetings related to council activities	-	5	5	5
Dealing with electors' problems, surgeries, pressure groups	8	13	13	13
Meeting external organisations	5	8	8	7
Public consultation meetings	-	-	2	3
Other	10	4	-	-
Total average	**52**	**79**	**74**	**74**

This table shows how much time councillors spent on the same duties between 1964 and 1993.

Adapted from Widdicombe, 1986 and Rowntree, 1995.

Item B *Candidates who fear the price of victory*

Adrian Slade served for five years as the only Liberal member of the Greater London Council. He found that he was spending up to three days a week on council business and earned from this less than £3,000 before tax. He argues that: 'You have to be either very rich or self-employed or unemployed or retired unless you work for someone who will give you as much time off as you want.' All parties face difficulties recruiting the candidates they would like for council seats. Off the record, one candidate fighting a hopeless seat said: 'If I'm elected it will be a catastrophe. I would have to resign immediately.'

Adapted from the *Guardian*, 5 May 1986.

Item C *The Widdicombe Report*

Compared to Britain's population as a whole, councillors tend to be:

1. Older - most are aged 55 or over. The number of councillors under the age of 45 is small.
2. Male - less than one councillor in five is female.
3. Owner occupiers - 85% of councillors own their house compared to 57% of the general population.
4. White collar - 41% of councillors are managers or professionals (or their last job was in those categories) compared to 14% of the general population. Just 5% of councillors have a manual job compared to 25% of the general population.
5. Better educated - 25% of councillors have a degree compared to 5% of the general population.
6. Better paid - councillors with jobs, on average, earn more than the average wage.

Adapted from Widdicombe, 1986.

Questions

1. Using Items A, C and D explain what the Widdicombe Report tells us about who stands in local elections and why they stand.
2. Judging from Items A-C what factors might deter people from standing as candidates in local elections?
3. a) Would you say that the councillor profiled in Item E was typical? Give reasons for your answer.
   b) How might you expect the councillor's profile to differ if she belonged to a different political party?

Item D *Who becomes a local councillor?*

All figures are in percentages.		Con	Lab	Lib	Ind	Other	All
Age	60+	37	32	22	52	30	**36**
	45-59	42	33	30	36	33	**37**
	18-44	19	33	49	11	33	**26**
Gender	Male	78	83	79	81	81	**81**
	Female	21	17	21	19	19	**19**
Activity	Employed	64	59	74	47	67	**60**
	Unemployed	2	8	3	1	2	**4**
	Retired	24	22	13	40	30	**25**
Socio-economic group	Professional	75	59	81	62	63	**69**
	Manual*	11	33	12	19	14	**20**
	Other	12	8	8	16	5	**11**

This table shows the social characteristics of local councillors. The figures may not add up to 100 because they have been rounded up or down.
* includes those unemployed or retired

Adapted from Widdicombe, 1986.

Item E *Profile of a district councillor*

Name Cynthia Derelli

Age 47

Job Lecturer in English at Edge Hill College, Lancs

Salary £19,000

Hours Full time (18 hours teaching per week + at least 18hrs preparation, research and student consultation)

Home owner? Yes

Party affiliation Member of the Labour party for 15 years.

Positions in local government District councillor for 3 years. First elected in 1991. Member of Development & Amenities Committee and Policy & Resources Committee. Also on Ormskirk town centre working party, Housing Approval sub-committee, New Technology working party and the Environment working party.

Why did you become a councillor? 'Because I wanted a useful role in the community. Having seen the needs of people locally, I wanted to be able to participate in decision making at a local level and to bring people's wishes and needs to the attention of the council.'

Hours Approximately 16 hours per week - though it varies considerably.

Rewards 'Ours has been a hung council so it is difficult for the policies of the Labour Group to come to fruition. When policy goals are achieved it is very rewarding.'

Allowances £14 per meeting and petrol allowance for travel on council business (taxed).

How do you see your role? 'My role is to represent people at local level and to liaise between local people and the council. When an issue arises in my ward I always try to consult local people before making a decision. I then try to present the majority view to the council.'

Adapted from an interview conducted in January 1994.

2 The selection of parliamentary candidates

Key Issues

1. How are parliamentary candidates selected by the major political parties?
2. What qualities should a parliamentary candidate have?
3. Why are so few parliamentary candidates women or from the ethnic minorities?

2.1 Selecting candidates

In the general election of 1992, there were 2,946 candidates fighting for the 651 parliamentary seats - an average of five per constituency.

A minority of candidates are either individuals who want publicity for a particular cause or are from small political parties. Most candidates are members of the three main parties. The three main parties expect to fight every seat in mainland Britain. Only the Conservatives put up candidates in Northern Ireland in 1992. Since the 1960s, Scottish and Welsh Nationalists, the Green Party and other small parties have gradually increased the number of seats which they contest.

Becoming a candidate for any of the parties fighting the election seriously is a competitive process. Even in a seat which a party has little chance of winning, several potential candidates invariably put themselves forward. For some political activists, fighting the election campaign as the party's official candidate is the peak of their political career. For others, an election campaign in an unwinnable seat is seen as a first step towards fighting a winnable seat later. In most parliamentary seats, there is already an incumbent MP who was elected in the previous general election and who is standing in the same seat for the same party in the subsequent general election. Generally, incumbent MPs can expect to be selected as their party's candidate for subsequent general elections and a high proportion can expect to be re-elected - 92% of incumbent MPs who stood again were re-elected in 1992. Candidates who inherit a 'safe' seat, where their party's sitting MP has retired, also have a very good chance of being elected. But, challengers who are fighting a seat held by another party have a very low rate of success. The process has been described as 'one where many run but few succeed'. (Norris & Lovenduski, 1995, p.25)

The process of selecting candidates varies from party to party. There are, however, certain common features. The process combines local political choice with an element of central control. Candidates must present themselves to the relevant local party organisations and attempt to win support for their candidature. Endorsement by the party headquarters is also necessary. Since, in safe seats, the choice of candidate by party members (the 'selectorate') is tantamount to choosing an MP, how the process works is of considerable importance.

Labour's selection procedure before 1993

The selection of parliamentary candidates in the Labour party has been a controversial procedure. It has undergone a number of changes since 1980.

In 1980, a rule change passed at party conference meant that a system of mandatory (compulsory) reselection should occur for all sitting Labour MPs between general elections. Before that, sitting Labour MPs could not be challenged. Although mandatory reselection has survived into the 1990s, a shortlist of only one candidate is permitted. If a sitting MP is nominated by two thirds of all organisations from which nominations are received, that MP is selected without a ballot.

In 1987, a second change was made to procedure. Before 1987, the parliamentary candidate was selected by the constituency general committee (GC). Ordinary party members had no direct vote in the proceedings (though they did vote for the delegates to the GC). After the 1987 general election, an electoral college was introduced. This consisted of 60% of votes for individual party members and 40% for affiliated organisations (including trade union branches). Members were able to cast their votes at ballots held in the branch or by postal vote.

Labour's selection procedure since 1993

The Labour party conference in 1993 brought further changes to the selection procedure. Most noticeably, the franchise was extended further so that the principle of one member, one vote was secured.

The choice of parliamentary candidate is made from a shortlist. The names on this shortlist may come from a number of sources. First, there are the national lists held by the national executive committee (NEC). There are four of these lists: the 'A' list of trade union sponsored candidates; the 'B' list of constituency nominated candidates; the 'C' list of candidates sponsored by the Cooperative party; and the 'W' list of women candidates. These lists are circulated to constituencies.

In addition, the local party, through its branches and affiliated organisations, can nominate candidates (usually from the locality). Each branch and affiliated organisation is allowed to nominate one candidate. The constituency party executive committee (EC) is also allowed to make one nomination.

Those nominated are placed on a list which is presented to the GC. If a sitting Labour MP is nominated by two thirds of all organisations from which nominations are received, that MP is selected without a ballot. Otherwise, the GC draws up a shortlist which must observe the following criteria. First, if the constituency party or NEC has determined that there shall be an all women shortlist, only women nominees can be validated. Second, any nominee receiving 25% of nominations (including at least one from a party branch) must be automatically placed on the shortlist. Third, any nominee receiving 50% of nominations from affiliated organisations must be automatically placed on the shortlist. Fourth, any sitting MP who chooses to stand must be included (if that MP represents a constituency that is wholly or substantially within the area covered by the constituency Labour party). Fifth, if no sitting MP stands, there should be at least four nominees (including at least one woman).

Once the shortlist has been agreed, each successful candidate is invited to produce an address of 500 words (maximum) by a set date. Selection meetings are then arranged as follows:

> '(a) one members' meeting for the whole constituency.
> (b) members' meetings for each branch.
> (c) joint branch members' meetings...' (Labour Party, 1993, p.57)

At meetings, shortlisted candidates are invited to speak and to answer questions. After hearing all the candidates, members make their selection by secret ballot. Members who cannot attend their selection meeting are able to apply for a postal ballot. The selection ballot is conducted using the single transferable vote (STV) method (see chapter 7, p.186).

The Labour leadership has claimed that these changes will broaden party democracy at local level. Individual party members now decide who should be the candidate, rather than delegates elected to the constituency GC and local trade union branches. Critics from the left have argued that democracy will be reduced because the new rules encourage 'armchair' involvement, prevent the participation of the unions and reduce the power of reselection.

Throughout this period of change at local level, the NEC has retained power at national level. Endorsement by the NEC is required once the vote has been taken at local level. This power, which includes, ultimately, the power to impose a candidate on a local constituency, ensures that party headquarters can keep control of events and weed out what the party leadership regards as unsuitable candidates. It is in by-elections that this power has proved particularly important. In by-elections, an unusual degree of attention is focused on individual candidates. By reserving the right to reject the shortlist drawn up by the local party and to draw up its own shortlist, the NEC (so the argument goes) ensures that only candidates capable of withstanding intense media pressure are selected.

Selection procedure in the Conservative party

Since 1969, the Conservative party's parliamentary selection procedure has been based on a system of 'model rules'. These model rules have been adopted by most local Conservative parties.

Like the Labour NEC, Conservative party headquarters (Central Office) also draws up a list of approved candidates. It is not easy to get onto this list. First of all, references from influential party figures are required. Once these have been accepted, potential candidates are interviewed by the regional agent and by the vice chair at national level who has responsibility for selecting candidates. The interviews are followed by a residential weekend where all-round abilities are assessed. Finally, recommendations are made to the standing advisory committee on selection. Only half of those attending the residential weekend are placed on the list. This list usually contains around 800 names before a general election (Norris & Lovenduski, 1989).

Evidence suggests that the competition to get onto the approved list has increased and the hurdles which potential candidates have to overcome have become more formidable (Rush,1987). Whilst local Conservative parties still have the right to choose candidates not on the list, only 7% did so in the 1987 general election. Ratification is still required by Central Office.

At the constituency level, the local party informs Central Office when a vacancy becomes available. Unlike in the Labour party, there is no system of mandatory reselection of MPs though, on occasions, local MPs do lose the confidence of their local party members. In that case, a ballot of all local party members is held. For example, Sir Anthony Meyer, the challenger to Margaret Thatcher's leadership in 1989, found that his constituency association voted by 206 votes to 107 that they had lost confidence in him.

Candidates on the approved list are informed of vacancies. If they are interested in standing, they inform Central Office which, in turn, passes on their details to the local party. Other candidates may also apply. A shortlist is then drawn up by the constituency selection committee and interviews are held by the constituency executive committee. After the choice has been made, all members of the local party are invited to a general meeting to endorse the decision. In recent years, there has been a move to present up to three candidates to the general meeting (unless a candidate has a clear majority of votes in the constituency executive committee vote) so that all the local party members can be involved in the final selection process. (Norris and Lovenduski, 1995).

The Liberal Democrats' selection procedure

Like the Labour and Conservative parties, the Liberal Democrats keep a national list of approved candidates. At the party's 1989 conference, there were only 50 names on this list and an appeal was made for more candidates to come forward so that the party could fight all 632 seats. Local constituency parties before the 1992 election were free to make local nominations as well as making use of the national list. As a result, candidates were found for all 632 seats in the 1992 election. But, according to Butler & Kavanagh, the vetting procedure was not rigorous. A senior party spokesperson observed that:

> 'Of the candidates fielded in the election, the top third were good, the middle third adequate and the bottom third weak' (Butler & Kavanagh, 1992, p.219)

After the 1992 election, a new system was set up. Now, all candidates must be on a national list and they are not eligible for selection until they are. Selection procedure is as follows. When a vacancy arises, the local constituency party invites applications. Usually an advert is placed in *Liberal Democratic News*. A shortlist is then made of potential candidates (any members who want to be placed on the shortlist must ensure that their names appear on the national list) and all constituency members are invited to a selection meeting. After each candidate has spoken and answered any questions, a ballot is held. Absent members can only have a postal vote if they make a special application (to encourage as many members as possible to be present at the meeting). The person with the majority vote is duly selected as parliamentary candidate.

Conclusions

According to Geddes and colleagues there are four general criteria which can be applied to the selection procedure in any party. The procedure should be:

> 'Explicit - so that applicants know the rules; fair - so that the participants feel that there has been no undue influence; thorough - so that the qualifications, experience and abilities of candidates are closely scrutinised; and open - to attract a good range of candidates (Geddes et al., 1991, p.19)

If there are agreed procedures which meet these four criteria, then it is more likely that there will be an internal consensus within the party. This will encourage party members to work collectively for victory at the polls.

It can also be argued, however, that the base for choosing candidates should be widened so that it is not only party members who are involved, but also people who vote for the party. This could be achieved by introducing a system of primary elections similar to the system in the USA. People who regularly vote for a party could register as a party supporter and then be invited to vote in a primary election to choose the candidate.

Activity 11.2

Item A *Selection by OMOV*

Labour's new one member, one vote (OMOV) system raises new concerns. These were highlighted by the recent selection of a candidate for the Rotherham by-election following the death of the Labour MP Jimmy Boyce. First, early in the selection process a popular local nominee was taken off the shortlist by the national leadership because he buckled under the kind of questioning which by-election candidates have to endure. This upset local activists. Second, observers wondered whether outsiders skilled in the world of media manipulation - ie the Geneva based journalist and trade unionist Denis McShane - would gain an unfair advantage simply by being better known. The same question was asked of Barbara Boyce, Jimmy Boyce's widow, who was able to announce her candidacy on television. Third, there was the worry that OMOV would prevent talented outsiders (people like Tony Blair who came from London to win Sedgefield in 1983) from beating well known local candidates. As it happened, the selectorate chose the cosmopolitan Mr McShane, close runner up to Mr Boyce in 1992.

Adapted from the *Guardian*, 8 March 1994.

Item B *Labour reforms*

Labour reforms of candidate selection have been designed to achieve four specific goals: devolving control of the process from left wing activists on the constituency GC to grass roots members; reducing the potential for intra-party conflict; diluting the influence of the trade unions in the process; and producing parliamentary candidates from a wider range of social backgrounds.

Adapted from Geddes et al., 1991.

Item C *Labour's selection system since 1980*

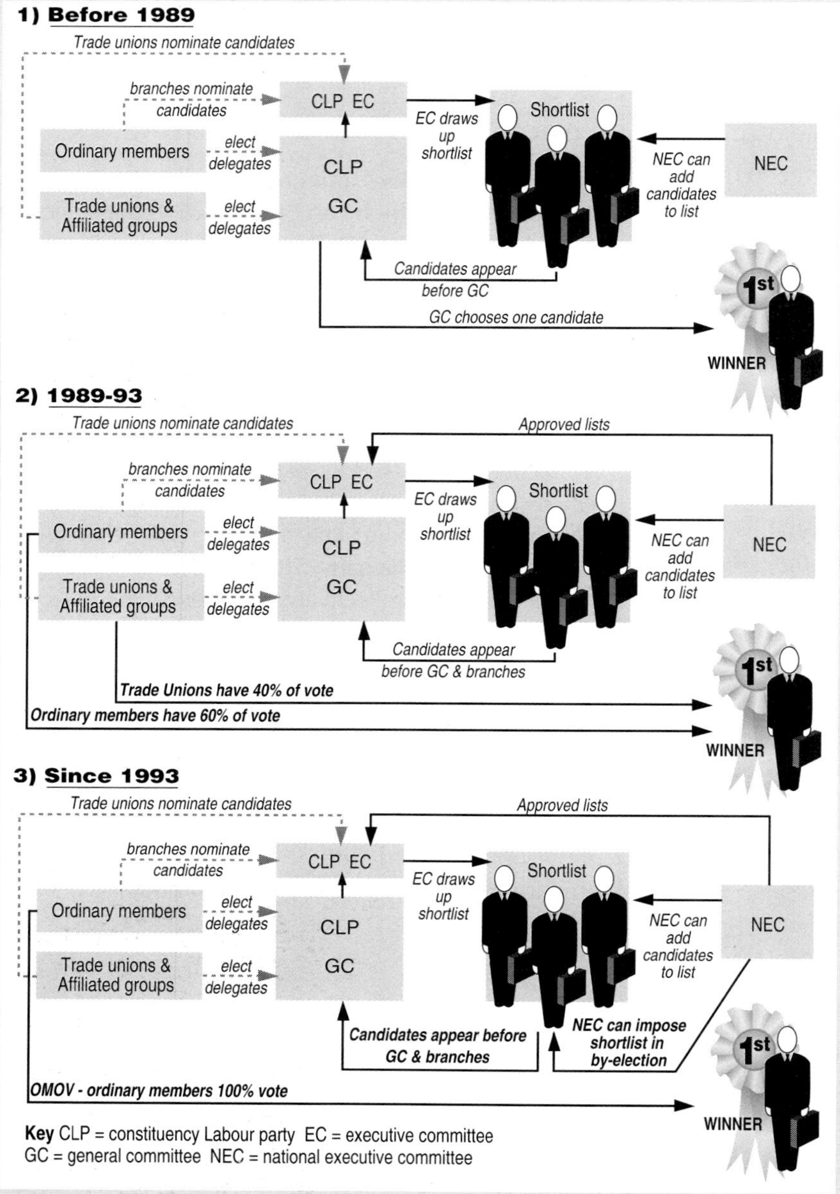

Item D *The selection process in the Conservative party.*

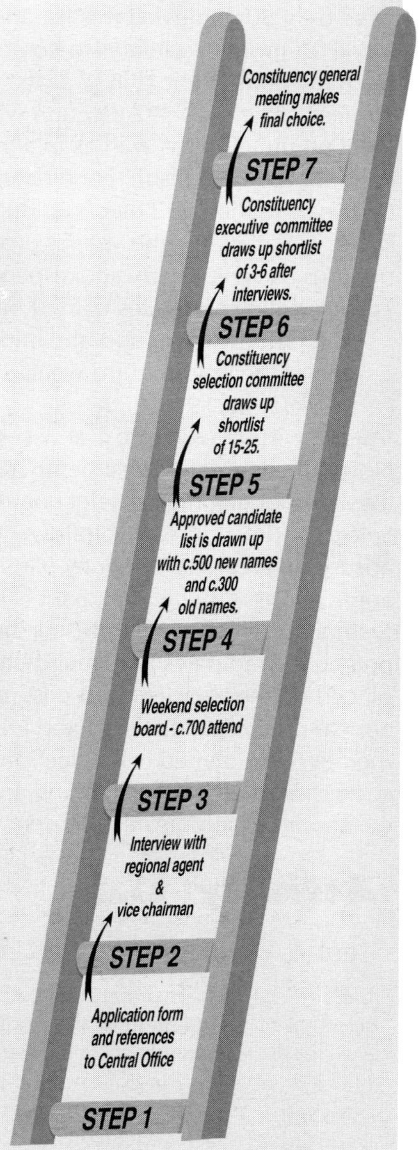

Item E *Welsh Tories mobilise to unseat silent knight*

Disgruntled constituents in the Welsh Tory stronghold of Monmouth want to replace the MP who has represented them for 20 years. They claim that Sir John Stadling Thomas, who faces a reselection ballot of Conservative members in April, has not been sufficiently active, that he is slow to reply to letters and unreliable in attending to his constituency surgery duties. The reselection ballot brings into conflict local Tories' personal loyalty to their MP and their loyalty to their party. Sir John's fate will be decided by the secret ballot of 1,700 paid up constituency members.

Adapted from the *Guardian*, 5 February 1990.

Questions

1. Look at Items A-C
   a) Describe how Labour's selection procedure has changed since 1980.
   b) Would you say that the goals outlined in Item B have been achieved?
   c) What are the advantages and disadvantages of selection by OMOV?
2. Judging from Items D and E would you agree that ordinary members of the Conservative party play a sufficiently active part in the selection of parliamentary candidates? Explain your answer.
3. a) Would you describe the selection procedures adopted by the three main parties as 'democratic'? Give reasons for your answer.
   b) In what circumstances do you think a sitting MP should be deselected?

2.2 Parliamentary candidates

The qualities sought in a parliamentary candidate

The local party members who choose the parliamentary candidate seek to select the best candidate to win the seat for their party. Their choice is based, fundamentally, on two criteria - the personal qualities of the candidate and the candidate's political views.

A survey carried out in 1987 (the British Candidates Survey - see Norris & Lovenduski, 1989) revealed the personal qualities which the selectorate regarded as important. The findings of this survey are shown in Item A in Activity 11.3. It should be noted that, although there are some differences between the political parties, there are also a number of similarities. For example, all parties regard a candidate's speaking ability as important. In general terms, this means that more highly educated candidates are likely to be chosen since a higher education often gives people both the confidence and the ability to express their views in public.

It is not just personal qualities that are important, however, during the selection process. The political views of both the candidate and the selectorate can affect the outcome. In all the major parties there is, commonly, a divide between left and right with a large centre ground which encompasses the majority. During their campaigns, candidates can be expected to temper their views to the political complexion of the particular members they are addressing. They need to exercise some care, however, to avoid the charge of political opportunism.

Data gathered for the British Candidates Survey makes it clear that social and economic policy issues dominate the questioning at interviews. Local issues and the candidates' political and personal experience generate fewer questions. Foreign policy and the candidates' family life are usually of least concern. Particular circumstances, however, may mean exceptions to these findings. For example, the Conservative party's 'Back to Basics' campaign brought an unusual amount of attention to MPs' family affairs during the winter of 1993-94.

Activity 11.3

Item A *Qualities sought by selectors in a parliamentary candidate*

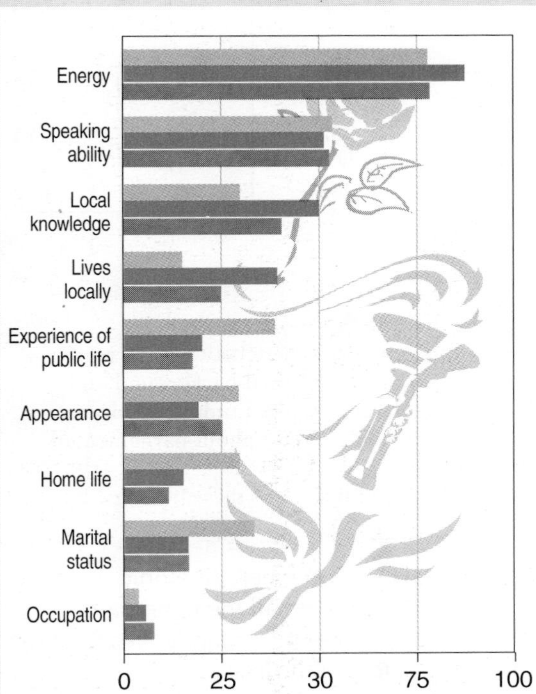

This chart shows which qualities selectors find important when choosing a parliamentary candidate.

Adapted from Norris & Lovenduski, 1989.

Item B *The educational background of parliamentary candidates in 1992*

Type of education	Con *E	Con D	Lab *E	Lab D	Lib Dem *E	Lib Dem D
State school	19	40	34	60	2	79
State school + poly/college	28	53	61	93	2	152
State school + university	81	100	127	173	6	257
Public school	28	11	-	3	-	11
Public school + poly/college	16	11	2	3	1	12
Public school + university	164	83	38	31	9	100
Total	**336**	**298**	**271**	**363**	**20**	**612**
Oxford	83	24	28	23	4	40
Cambridge	68	23	16	9	2	31
Other universities	94	136	122	172	9	286
All universities	**245**	**183**	**166**	**204**	**15**	**357**
	(73%)	(61%)	(61%)	(56%)	(75%)	(58%)
Eton	34	9	2	-	-	5
Harrow	7	2	-	-	-	3
Winchester	3	-	1	-	-	-
Other public schools	164	94	37	37	10	115
All public schools	**208**	**105**	**40**	**37**	**10**	**123**
	(62%)	(35%)	(14%)	(10%)	(50%)	(20%)

*E = elected in the 1992 general election and D = defeated

This table shows the different educational backgrounds of candidates in the 1992 general election. 'Poly' stands for Polytechnic.

Adapted from Butler & Kavanagh, 1992.

Item C *The occupation of parliamentary candidates in 1992*

Occupation	Conservative elected	Conservative defeated	Labour elected	Labour defeated	Liberal Democrats elected	Liberal Democrats defeated
Professions						
Barrister	39	26	9	9	5	13
Solicitor	21	18	8	11	1	18
Doctor/dentist	4	6	2	5	-	13
Architect/surveyor	3	6	-	6	-	9
Civil/chartered engineer	3	4	-	9	-	23
Civil servant/local government	10	5	16	21	-	20
Armed services	14	3	-	-	1	1
University teachers	4	3	14	6	1	13
Polytechnic/college teachers	2	4	24	33	-	46
School teachers	16	16	38	73	3	103
Other consultants	2	2	-	1	1	3
Scientific/research	1	-	2	8	-	12
Total	**131**	**107**	**115**	**188**	**12**	**303**
	(39%)	**(36%)**	**(42%)**	**(52%)**	**(60%)**	**(50%)**
Business						
Company director	37	30	1	-	-	20
Company executive	75	73	8	13	2	88
Commerce/insurance	9	15	1	5	-	22
Management/clerical	4	5	11	14	-	20
General business	3	8	1	12	-	22
Total	**128**	**131**	**22**	**44**	**2**	**172**
	(38%)	**(44%)**	**(8%)**	**(12%)**	**(10%)**	**(28%)**
Miscellaneous						
White collar	9	11	36	64	1	69
Politician/political organiser	20	17	24	17	2	10
Publisher/journalist	28	9	13	14	3	19
Farmer	10	15	2	-	-	8
Housewife	6	7	-	4	-	9
Student	-	-	-	-	-	6
Total	**73**	**59**	**75**	**99**	**6**	**121**
	(22%)	**(20%)**	**(28%)**	**(27%)**	**(30%)**	**(20%)**
Manual workers						
Miner	1	-	12	1	-	-
Skilled worker	3	1	43	27	-	15
Semi/unskilled worker	-	-	4	4	-	1
Total	**4**	**1**	**59**	**32**	**0**	**16**
	(1%)	**(-)**	**(22%)**	**(9%)**	**(-)**	**(2%)**
Grand total	**336**	**298**	**271**	**363**	**20**	**612**

Adapted from Butler & Kavanagh 1992.

Questions

1. a) Using Items A-C write a profile of the ideal parliamentary candidate for the Conservative party.
   b) How would your profile differ for the Labour party and Liberal Democrats?
   c) Can you think of negative qualities which might persuade the selectorate not to choose someone?

2. Look at Items B and C.
   a) What differences are there between the parties in terms of (i) the educational background and (ii) the occupations of the candidates selected?
   b) What do the tables tell us about parliamentary candidates in general?
   c) What is the significance of these findings?

2.3 Ethnic minority parliamentary candidates

Although all the major parties claim that the ethnicity of a potential candidate has no bearing on the outcome of the selection process, the small number of ethnic minority candidates selected suggests that this is not so. In 1992, just 23 ethnic minority candidates were selected to fight seats for the three main parties - nine for Labour, eight for the Conservatives and six for the Liberal Democrats. This figure is lower than in the 1987 general election when 28 ethnic minority candidates stood. Although all the main parties claimed that they wanted more candidates from the ethnic minorities, few of those selected stood for safe or winnable seats. In 1987, however, four black MPs were elected - the first to be elected since 1929. In 1992, all four retained their seats and the total number of black MPs rose to six.

This raises two questions. Why are so few ethnic minority candidates selected? And, are there any grounds to expect more ethnic minority candidates to be selected in the future? According to Terri Sewell:

> 'The most pernicious factor working against the selection of black candidates remains the popular perception that black candidates lose votes.' (Sewell, 1993, p.136)

Sewell cites a 1983 study of the selection process in the Labour party which revealed that:

> '23% of white selectors thought that a black candidate would be a great disadvantage; 48% thought they would be some disadvantage; 25% thought it would make no difference and only 2% believed it would actually be some advantage...The reality is that black candidates seeking support for their nomination are greatly dependent on white support, but there are no guarantees that even black selectors will prefer a black candidate.' (Sewell, 1993, p.137)

Despite the prevalence of this attitude, the general election results of 1987 and 1992 have shown that black candidates are not necessarily electoral liabilities. The election and re-election of black candidates may provide the impetus for a growing number of ethnic minority candidates to be selected. On the other hand, the drop in the number of ethnic minority candidates from 28 in 1987 to 23 in 1992, combined with the lack of public debate on this issue, may suggest that the struggle for greater ethnic minority representation in the House of Commons is far from over.

Black Sections and the Labour party

Traditionally, the Labour party has attracted more support from black people than any other party. A study carried out by the Commission for Racial Equality, for example, shows that around 81% of black voters voted for Labour in the 1983 election (see also chapter 9, pp. 245-48).

The Black Sections movement began in the 1980s as an attempt to increase black representation at all levels in the Labour party. The aim was to create a group within the Labour party which would promote black issues and which would enjoy the same status as the existing Women's and Youth Sections. In particular, supporters of the Black Sections movement demanded the right to nominate and select their own candidates for council and parliamentary seats.

These demands were perceived as a threat by the Labour leadership and, from July 1984, a battle began within the Labour party. At all Labour party conferences between 1984 and 1988, motions in support of the setting up of Black Sections were defeated. But, by 1990, both sides felt able to compromise. In October 1990, the Labour party adopted a proposal which allowed:

> 'The setting up of a single affiliated organisation for members of African, Caribbean and Asian descent with local and regional groups and direct representation on the National Executive Committee.'
> (*Composite 8*, Labour party conference, 1990).

Although this did not create the Black Sections that had been sought, it was a formal recognition of black involvement in the party. Besides, the struggle for Black Sections had in itself ensured that the issue of black representation was placed on the political agenda within the Labour party.

Activity 11.4

Item A *Black, hopeful but not stereotypes*

In the early hours of 12 June, a result will be flashed on the television screens that will make little difference to the outcome of the election as a whole, but might make history in another way. 'Labour holds Brent South' will mean, if it appears, that Britain has its first black MP for 58 years and its first ever MP of Afro-Caribbean origin. Paul Boetang recognises that his election (or the election of any of the 28 black candidates) would have a great symbolic significance for black people, but he insists that it is not and must not be seen as an issue in his campaign. He has the largest Labour majority and the highest proportion of black voters of any of the black candidates. Bernie Grant ought to have almost as solid a chance in Tottenham where the Labour majority is 9,396 and the electorate is 37% black. So should Diana Abbot in Hackney North where the Labour majority is 8,545 and the electorate is 31% black. The Conservatives have six black candidates, all of them in Labour held seats where they have little hope of winning unless the polls turn strongly in Margaret Thatcher's favour.

Adapted from the *Guardian*, 2 June 1987.

Item B *Cheltenham (1)*

The Cheltenham Conservative who racially abused the Tory party's first black candidate to be selected to fight a winnable seat was unrepentent yesterday, despite being told publicly by the Prime Minister, John Major, that there was no place for such sentiments in the party. Bill Galbraith, who was involved in attempts last week to overturn the decision to select John Taylor as the Conservative parliamentary candidate for Cheltenham, claimed that his remarks had been spoken in private amongst friends and he had been misquoted. However, he added: 'I did say we would not let bloody niggers into this town.'

Adapted from the *Guardian*, 5 December 1990.

Item C *Cheltenham (2)*

This cartoon was published in the *Guardian* on 5 December 1990.

Item D *Black tribunes*

The riots of the 1980s served as a catalyst to black political participation in Britain. However unwelcome, they did raise the awareness of the nation to the needs and demands of black people. Diana Abbot specifically attributed her election to this effect. Similarly, the campaign for Black Sections in the Labour party has been cited by many black candidates as a factor in their selection. The best known example was the selection of Russell Profitt in Lewisham East. As a result of the involvement of Black Sections, his candidacy was nullified by the NEC. Profitt, however, was reselected by his constituency party in opposition to the NEC ruling and his candidacy was allowed to stand. He asserted: 'Black Sections provided a well organised group of people involved at grassroots level. Lewisham East was the first place where this tactic was successfully used to bring about the selection of someone who was black. I saw my selection as very much part of this campaign.' While it is difficult to know the extent to which black under-representation was considered by selectors in some constituencies which chose black candidates in 1987, the impact was clearly evident. This appears to have been a major consideration in the selection of Paul Boetang in Brent South, for example. 'It was very natural to choose a black candidate', confirmed one member of Brent South Labour party. 'There was a general acceptance that Brent South should be represented by someone who truly reflected the multiracial nature of the community.'

Adapted from Sewell, 1993.

Item E *Ethnic minority candidates in the 1992 election*

Party	Name	Constituency	Place	No of votes	% of vote	Loss/gain
Lab	Diana Abbot*	London	1	20,083	57.8	+9.1
Lab	Kingsley Abrams	London	2	11,570	23.3	+1.7
Lab	Claude Ajith Moares	London	2	12,343	22.5	+5.3
Lab	Mohammed Akhbar Ali	Liverpool	2	2,498	9.2	-2.0
Lab	Paul Boateng*	London	1	20,662	57.5	+5.6
Lab	Doreen Cameroon	Ashford, Kent	3	11,365	20.0	+5.3
Con	Lurline Champagnie	London	2	8,958	23.7	-1.6
Con	Abdul Qayyum Chaudhary	Birmingham	2	8,686	25.0	+3.8
Con	Nirj Joseph Deva	London	1	24,752	45.8	-1.9
Lib	Zerbanoo Gifford	London	3	10,681	18.9	-4.9
Lab	Bernie Grant*	London	1	25,309	56.5	+12.9
Lab	Piara Khabra	London	1	23,476	47.4	-3.3
Con	Mohammed Khamisa	Birmingham	2	8,544	24.8	-0.9
**Lab	Askhok Kumar*	Langbaugh, E. Yorks	2	28,454	43.1	+4.7
Lib Dem	Pash Nadhra	London	4	3,790	7.7	-5.7
Con	Andrew Popat	Bradford	2	20,283	38.4	-2.4
Con	Mohammed Riaz	Bradford	2	15,756	32.2	-7.3
Con	Mohammed Rizvi	Edinburgh	3	8,496	21.1	-1.8
Lib Dem	Vin Sharma	Stourbridge, W. Midlands	3	7,941	12.4	-9.6
Con	John Taylor	Cheltenham	2	28,683	44.7	-5.4
Lab	Keith Vaz*	Leicester	1	28,123	56.5	+10.4
Lib Dem	Marcello Verma	Cynon Valley, Wales	4	2,667	7.0	-5.2
Lib Dem	Peter Verma	Cardiff	3	3,707	7.8	-7.6

* sitting MPs ** Ashkok Kumar was elected in a by-election in 1991

Adapted from Sewell, 1993.

Questions

1. Judging from Items A-E:
   a) What problems do ethnic minority candidates have to overcome before they are selected?
   b) How have potential candidates attempted to overcome these problems?
   c) Why might the selectorate be less likely to select black candidates than white?
2. 'A significant breakthrough was made by ethnic minority candidates in the 1987 election.' Using Items A-E give arguments for and against this view.
3. Use Item B to explain the point being made by the cartoon (Item C).

2.4 Women parliamentary candidates

In recent years, there has been a growing concern that the number of women parliamentary candidates is very unrepresentative of the number of women in the population as a whole and is even unrepresentative of the number of womens who are members of political parties. There has been a slight improvement in the number of women selected in recent elections. The three main parties fielded 341 women candidates in 1992, for example, compared to 243 in 1987. The Liberal Democrats had the largest number of women candidates with 144, followed by Labour with 138 and the Conservatives with 59. In the 1992 election, 60 women candidates were elected, compared to 41 in 1987 and 23 in 1983.

Between 1918 and 1992, just 1,721 women have stood as parliamentary candidates (around 2,000 candidates stand in a general election and there were 21 general elections between 1918 and 1992). During this period there have been 166 women MPs. All three main parties claim that they are taking active steps to encourage the selection and election of more women, but it is only in the Labour party that structural changes have been made in recent years to ensure that this happens (it was written into the Liberal Democrats' original constitution that at least one woman must be included in shortlists of two to four candidates and at least two in larger shortlists).

Women parliamentary candidates and the Labour party

It is only in the 1990s that the Labour party has begun to take positive action to increase the number of women MPs. To do this, efforts are being made to provide women with experience at every level of the party. At branch and constituency level, for example, it is now compulsory for members to ensure that two of the four main officers on the executive (Chair, Vice Chair, Secretary and Treasurer) are women. Similarly, whenever delegates are appointed, 50% must be women. If only one delegate is appointed, then it must be a woman every other year.

These new rules at branch and constituency level are designed to encourage more women to gain experience which will help them to climb the party ladder. The same is true of the rule making it compulsory to include at least one woman on each constituency shortlist when selecting parliamentary candidates. The more women who gain experience of the selection process, the argument goes, the more women who will eventually be selected.

At its 1989 conference, the Labour party took the decision to implement a programme designed to ensure that half the PLP would be composed of women by the year 2000. The conference agreed that the NEC should consider the possibility of a women's panel and a proportion of constituency parties selecting from women only shortlists. It is this decision that has led to the following rule:

> 'In pursuance of the party's objective of considerably increasing the number of women candidates in winnable seats, the regional secretary shall convene 'consensus' meetings of constituency Labour parties from vacant Labour seats and the most winnable seats to agree which constituencies will comprise the 50% quota of all women shortlists.' (Labour Party , 1993, p.52)

Despite these rule changes, women in the Labour party face an uphill task. In the 1992 general election, women were selected in only 10% of the safe Labour seats that became vacant. Although 20 Labour MPs retired in safe seats only two of them were replaced by women. The rule change (quoted above) which introduces all-women shortlists applies only to target seats and vacant Labour seats where sitting MPs are retiring. According to Labour Women's Network, this rule is unlikely to affect more than 55 seats (LWN, 1993).

EMILY's List UK

Campaigning to be a parliamentary candidate can be an expensive business. It often runs into several thousand pounds. Potential candidates have to bear the cost of transport, loss of earnings, childcare and accommodation. They often have to campaign for selection in several constituencies before they are chosen. This adds to the cost. In addition, many potential candidates would benefit from training (in public speaking, media management and so on). This, too, can be costly.

There is little doubt, therefore, that some people who would make excellent candidates (especially women who are on low incomes or have young families) are deterred by considerations of expense. To combat this, a group of Labour women launched a campaign on 6 February 1993 to raise money to support women who want to become candidates for the British or European Parliament but cannot afford to put their names forward. This campaign (EMILY's List UK) is for women who belong to the Labour party only. The idea came from a successful campaign in the USA (EMILY's List USA), but there are no formal links between the two organisations.

EMILY is an acronym for 'Early Money Is Like Yeast' (that is, it makes the 'dough' rise). In Britain, the name also conjures up memories of two of the best known suffragettes - Emmeline Pankhurst and Emily Wilding Davison.

In the USA, the campaign began in 1986. The aim was to raise money to fund the election campaign of women standing for Congress as Democrats. In its first year, $350,000 was raised and Barbara Mikulski became the first woman Democrat to be elected to the Senate. In 1992, EMILY's List USA raised $6.2 million. This money helped to triple the number of Democrat women in the House of Representatives (from 12 to 36) and it helped to raise the number of women in the Senate from one to five.

EMILY's List UK was launched on the 75th anniversary of the day on which women first won the right to vote. Its aim is to raise £30,000 annually (even before its launch more than £28,000 had been pledged). This money is used to sponsor women in much the same way that trade unions sponsor their candidates. Sponsored women are given grants to cover the cost of training, travel, accommodation and childcare during their campaign to gain selection.Then, once selected, EMILY'S List UK sponsored candidates can apply for funds to help cover their election expenses.

The organisers of EMILY'S List UK believe that £30,000 is sufficient to provide backing for 10 women candidates each year. Any woman belonging to the Labour party can apply for EMILY'S List UK sponsorship. The organisation has set up a panel of 25 Labour members to interview applicants and decide which to sponsor. The only political stipulation is that applicants must support a woman's right to choose whether to have an abortion.

Activity 11.5

Item A *Number of women candidates and MPs, 1945-1992*

Year	Women candidates	Women MPs				
		Con	Lab	Lib Dems*	Others	Total
1945	87	1	21	1	1	24
1950	126	6	14	1	-	21
1951	74	6	11	-	-	17
1955	87	9	14	-	1	24
1959	75	12	13	-	-	25
1964	89	11	17	-	-	28
1966	80	7	19	-	-	26
1970	97	15	10	-	1	26
1974 (Feb)	143	9	13	-	1	23
1974 (Oct)	150	7	18	-	2	27
1979	206	8	11	-	-	19
1983	276	13	10	-	-	23
1987	327	17	21	2	1	41
1992	568	20	37	2	1	60

This table shows the number of women who have stood for Parliament and the number elected between 1945 and 1992.

* Includes all women MPs elected for Liberal and SDP parties.

Adapted from Wood & Wood 1992.

Item B *An uphill task (1)*

Out of the 14 new women Labour MPs elected in 1992, 11 had to win their seats off the Tories and only three have majorities of more than 2,500. Three have majorities of less than 600. A vast majority of the Labour women MPs with majorities over 5,000 owe their seats to special circumstances such as a by-election, a sudden retirement or an expulsion. This strengthens the idea that men have usually stitched up the best seats in advance. If men are not already entrenched locally, they tend to be freer to travel around the country looking for vacancies because they, generally, have more money and less responsibility for childcare. At the next general election, Labour needs to win an extra 55 seats in order to form a majority government. If half of these seats are contested and won by women, an extra 28 will be elected. Add to these the 12 women who may replace retiring members and there will be a total of 40 women MPs. Add the existing 37 Labour women MPs and there will be a total of 77 women. If Labour wins an overall majority, there will be at least 326 Labour MPs in Parliament. So, that means 77 women out of 326 Labour MPs - fewer than one in four. And that assumes that they all make it. Most people reckon that, at best, there will be no more than 65 Labour women MPs after the next election.

Adapted from Baxter, 1993.

Item C *Raising the dough*

Janet Anderson, aged 43, who won her seat for Labour by a mere 120 votes at the 1992 general election, is a founder member of EMILY's List UK. She spent six years fighting a seat whilst bringing up three children. She had to take out a second mortgage. 'Money is the biggest hurdle for female candidates. It is for men, too. But, women also have to think about getting childcare and cleaning and are more concerned about using valuable housekeeping money for travel expenses and accommodation', she says. 'In the USA they need $10 million to run a presidential campaign. Here, a little would go a long way.'

Adapted from the *Times*, 1 February 1993.

Item D *An uphill task (2)*

Janet Anderson estimates that she made at least 20 return trips from her London home to local party branches, trade union groups and full constituency party before she was selected. Her constituency is Rossendale and Darwin, near Chorley in Lancashire. There was one day in the middle of the party conference in Bournemouth when one of the 15 branch committees and half a dozen trade union groups, which each had the right to vet her selection, demanded her attendance. The trip cost £80.

Adapted from *Today*, 2 February 1993.

Item E *The launch of EMILY's List UK*

This photograph was taken in Westminster on 6 February 1993 at the launch of EMILY's List UK.

Item F *Criticisms of EMILY's List UK*

There are a number of worrying points about EMILY's List UK. First, as one of two women who managed to appear on the ballot paper in the Labour party's Glasgow European selection, I am convinced that no amount of money would have made any difference to either of the women prospective candidates. To assume that initiatives directed at American political conditions can be relied on to deliver for women in Britain is simplistic. Second, it appears that a very select group is following the traditional male way of organising. Third, it absolves the party of any responsibility to deal with the lack of women MPs. Fourth, why isn't this money going to the party centrally, to be accessed by all women prospective candidates? Fifth, the proposed secrecy of the steering committee to 'avoid lobbying' means that its decisions on who is to receive funding remains closed to challenge.

Adapted from a letter by Rosina McCrae in the *Guardian*, 2 February 1993.

Questions

1. a) Using Items A-F give the arguments for and against the view that there are likely to be substantially more women MPs by the year 2000.
   b) Suppose you were a woman who wanted to be selected as a parliamentary candidate in a safe Labour seat. What problems do you think you would face?
2. Look at Items A and B.
   a) Make a list of the conclusions that you can draw from examining Item A.
   b) How does Item B help you to explain the conclusions that you have drawn from Item A?
   c) How useful would you expect Items A and B to be if you wanted to predict the number of women MPs there are likely to be (i) in the short term and (ii) in the long term? Give reasons for your answer.
3. 'EMILY's List UK should be welcomed by all women in the UK.' Using Items C-F give arguments for and against this view.
4 Using Items C-E design a leaflet which could be used to promote EMILY's List UK. Make sure that you appeal to (a) potential donors and (b) potential candidates. Apart from producing a leaflet, how else would you promote the campaign?

3 How representative are MPs?

Key Issues

1. What is the socio-economic background of MPs?
2. How do MPs' working conditions affect their ability to do their job effectively?
3. What pressures are there on MPs?
4. What rewards can MPs expect?

3.1 The socio-economic background of MPs

The verdict of the voters translates a minority of parliamentary candidates into MPs. After each general election a significant number of new faces appear in the House of Commons. But, these new faces tend to look very much like those which they have replaced. If the criticism of parliamentary candidates is that they are predominantly white, male and middle class, this criticism is even more apt for MPs.

The fact that most MPs come from a relatively narrow stratum in society is a cause of concern for those who argue that the House of Commons should be a microcosm of the nation. It patently is not. MPs are, on the whole, older and more highly educated than the general population. If the House of Commons was truly representative, 29 black MPs would have been elected in 1992 (rather than 6) and 332 women would have been elected (rather than 60).

The class background of MPs

In class terms (as judged by occupation), MPs are, generally, drawn from a narrow segment of society. The Conservatives tend to have many bankers, barristers and company directors amongst their MPs. According to a survey, 135 Conservative backbench MPs held a total of 287 directorships in 1992-3 (*Labour Research*, March 1993). Farming, consultants and professional lobbyists are other favourite professions of Conservative MPs. Many continue to fit their professions around their parliamentary duties. For example, barristers can appear in court in the morning and still be available to attend the House for afternoon sittings. Only a tiny proportion of Conservative MPs claim to have a manual working class background.

The Labour party tends to have many more lecturers and teachers amongst its ranks. There is also a spread of white collar occupations. A significant minority generally has a manual working class background.

For the Liberal Democrats, the legal profession has predominated and none of their 20 MPs elected in 1992 had a manual working class background.

In the 19th century, one of the major criticisms of Parliament was that the House of Commons was made up entirely of people from the middle and upper classes. In the early part of the 20th century, this began to change as the franchise was extended and the Labour party grew in popularity. Before the Second World War, a high proportion of Labour MPs had working class backgrounds. Now, however, the parliamentary Labour party (PLP) is increasingly dominated by members of the public sector middle class.

The educational background of MPs

MPs' educational experiences are also not typical of the electorate as a whole. Conservative MPs in particular tend to have experienced an exclusive education in public schools. The 1992 general election, for example, produced 35 Conservative MPs who had been educated at Eton, nine who had been educated at Rugby and seven who had been educated at Harrow. Until 1992, the majority of Conservative MPs had been to public school, but after that election a small majority (53%) of Conservative MPs were educated in state schools. A large majority of Conservative MPs elected in 1992 (73%) had attended university and 61% of those who had attended university had been to Oxford or Cambridge.

Relatively few Labour MPs elected in 1992 had attended public school (5%), but most had attended university (73%). Of those who attended university, 22% went to Oxford or Cambridge universities.

Nearly half of the Liberal Democrat MPs elected in 1992 had been educated in a public school and four fifths had attended university.

Although fewer Conservative MPs went to public schools than was the case in the past, only the Labour party can claim that a large proportion of its MPs have experienced state education in common with the overwhelming majority of the population.

The age of MPs

Generally, MPs are middle aged. The proportion of MPs aged over 60 has fallen as the work of MPs has increased. Although the voting age was reduced from 21 to 18 in 1969, the minimum age at which a person can stand as an MP remains 21, but only one MP under the age of 30 was elected in 1992 (the Liberal Democrat MP, Matthew Taylor). This may well be a reflection of the attitudes of the selectorate as much as reluctance on the part of young people to stand. The result, however, is that many young people feel very remote from the typical MP who is a white man in his late 40s.

Why are most MPs middle aged, white, middle class men?

The selection process is likely to lead to the selection of candidates who are replicas of the selectorate. If most people involved in the selection process are middle aged, white, middle class men, then it is likely that they will choose someone like them. Besides, the selectorate is often reluctant to choose candidates who do not conform to the stereotype supposedly popular with the voters. There are fears, often not openly expressed, that such candidates will be electoral liabilities. It is no surprise, therefore, that potential candidates who are untypical in some way often do not feel that it is worth pursuing their candidature.

In safe and marginal seats, competition is usually intense and the selectorate looks for a candidate of exceptional ability. In such circumstances, previous political experience (service as a local councillor or previous nominations as a parliamentary candidate) is often a prerequisite. Such experience is almost inevitably linked to age. Young candidates have little chance of competing against more experienced colleagues.

Similarly, a university education is often regarded as a sign of a trained mind and is, therefore, taken as an indication that a person would be capable of handling the complexities of the work of an MP. Since much of that work requires communication skills, it is, perhaps, little wonder that occupations such as barrister, solicitor, teacher and lecturer are often seen as suitable training.

Finally, the political complexion and class background of the parties at local and national level inevitably affects the make-up of the House of Commons. Given that the Conservatives won overall majorities in all general elections between 1979 and 1992, it is, perhaps, no surprise that most MPs during that period were middle aged, white, middle class men.

Activity 11.6

Item A *Profile of a backbench MP*

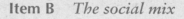

Name: Colin Pickthall

Date of birth: 13 September 1944

Party: Labour

First elected: April 1992

Constituency: Lancashire West

Schools: Broughton Road County Primary 1952-56 (state school)
Ulverston Grammar 1956-63 (state school)

University: University of Wales 1963-66 (BA-English & History)
University of Lancaster 1966-67 (MA-Socialism and English poetry in the 1930s &1950s)

Former employment:
Labourer in shipyards
Teacher at Ruffwood Comprehensive School, Kirkby 1967-70
Lecturer Edge Hill College 1970-92

Previous political experience:
County councillor 1989-93
Chair of governors, Skelmersdale FE College

Parents: Father worked in shipyards in Barrow-in-Furness
Mother was a housewife

Adapted from an interview held in November 1994.

Item B *The social mix*

In social, if not political terms, Conservative and Labour MPs have more in common with each other than with the party members who selected them or the voters who elected them. The social distance between the parties has gradually narrowed, mainly because the PLP has ceased to be working class: the proportion of manual workers on the Labour benches has steadily fallen from 72% between the wars to 36% in the 1950s to 29% in 1987. Over the same period, the proportion of graduates has risen from 17% between the wars to 40% in the 1950s and 56% in 1987. In 1987, twice as many Labour MPs were teachers as miners. The Conservative party has also lost some of its patrician element, although only very gradually. In the 1950s, 75% went to public schools and 22% to Eton alone; in 1987 the figures were 68% and 11%.

Adapted from Crewe, 1993.

Item C *Social composition of MPs, members and voters of the Conservative and Labour parties, 1987*

	Conservative party			Labour party		
	MPs	Members	Voters	MPs	Members	Voters
	%	%	%	%	%	%
Classes 1 & 2	90	46	31	66	56	14
Class 3	9	41	39	15	18	23
Classes 4 & 5	1	12	31	19	26	63
Public schools	68	na	9	14	na	3
Further education	82	14	13	79	32	10
University	70	na	11	56	na	6
Oxbridge	44	na	na	15	na	na
Women	5	58	52	9	41	52
Ethnic minorities	0	na	2	2	na	9

This table uses the Registrar General's definition of class (see p.109). na stands for not available.

Adapted from Crewe, 1993

Item D *The 'Cambridge mafia'*

Of the 336 victorious Tory MPs in the last election, 149 were Oxbridge graduates. In John Major's first cabinet, 16 of 22 were Oxbridge graduates. Out of those 16, five were contemporaries at Cambridge. Four of these five were, and remain, close friends. Widen the circle slightly to include former Cabinet ministers and other prominent Conservatives and the number of close friends from Cambridge in the early 1960s who rose to high positions in the party rises to nearly a dozen. What was it that made that time and that place so significant? Twenty years earlier it would have been easy: the British disease of reproducing the elite through public school, Oxbridge and connections. But, most of those who rose to Cabinet level from early 1960s Cambridge were not the sons of the elite. They were not boys who owed their advancement to their family connections. They were the product of a particular moment in postwar social history. For the first time, bright children from modest backgrounds could attend selective state schools free and state grants would take them to university. The grammar schools were able to compete with the public schools in training students for university entrance. Smart universities, even Oxford and Cambridge, began to recruit them.

Adapted from the *Independent on Sunday*, 7 March 1993.

Item E *The parliamentary privileged*

THE CONSERVATIVE MP WHO WENT TO A COMPREHENSIVE

This cartoon appeared in *Labour Research*, July 1987.

Questions

1. Look at Items A-C.
   a) Would you describe Colin Pickthall as a typical Labour MP? Explain your answer.
   b) How would you expect his profile to differ if he was (i) a Liberal Democrat MP or (ii) a Conservative MP?
   c) 'In social, if not political, terms Conservative and Labour MPs have more in common with each other than with the party members who selected them or the voters who elected them.' Is there evidence in Items A-C to support this comment?
2. 'Over the last 20 years, the type of person becoming a Conservative MP has changed'. Give arguments for and against this view using Items B-E.
3. What does the cartoon in Item E tell us about the background of MPs in 1987? Could the same point be made today?
4. 'It is misleading to list MPs' characteristics as if they are a single species because Labour and Conservative members differ significantly along most dimensions.' Would you agree with this statement? Explain your answer.

3.2 How accountable are MPs?

Theories of representation

Section 3.1 above established that most MPs are not representative of their constituents in terms of their class, gender, ethnicity and age. But this does not mean that MPs cannot represent their constituents in some other way. There are two main theories of representation.

First, there is the theory articulated by Edmund Burke (who lived between 1729 and 1797). In a speech to his constituents in Bristol, Burke argued that, if they elected him as their MP, they should expect not a slavish concern to please them, but the exercise of his own judgement and conscience. According to this theory of representation, although MPs have a duty to consult and to take into account the opinions of their constituents, their primary duty is to act according to their own consciences. The prevalence of this view amongst British MPs explains why, for example, the House of Commons has consistently voted against the reintroduction of the death penalty even though surveys have shown that a majority of voters support it.

The second theory is that MPs are given a mandate by the voters. They are the voters' delegates whose job is to do what they promised to do in their electoral manifesto and to act as a mouthpiece through which the voters' concerns are voiced. The MPs' personal views on a matter are not relevant and should be suppressed. If MPs subscribe to this theory, therefore, they will vote according to the dictates of their constituents rather than according to the dictates of conscience. In practice, it is difficult for MPs to adhere strictly to this theory because issues might arise upon which the MP has been given no clear mandate by the voters.

Accountability

These two contradictory views of the role of a representative, in turn, help to determine views about the accountability of MPs.

MPs who subscribe to the Burkean view of representation do not have to account for their actions, other than to explain that they voted according to their conscience. Of course, if they choose to ignore the views of their constituents completely, there is the chance that they will not be elected next time. Also, there is usually great pressure from the party whips to conform to the party line. But, if MPs are allowed a free vote, there is, in theory, no reason for those who follow the Burkean line to worry about accountability.

MPs who see themselves as delegates, however, are much more directly accountable. It is their duty to carry out a mandate and they must, therefore, be able to show that they have exercised their powers and discharged their duties properly.

In practice, politicians will claim to be either delegates or subscribers of the Burkean view depending on what seems expedient at the time. Understandably, therefore, it is difficult to determine a hard and fast rule about just how accountable MPs are or to whom they are accountable. Are they accountable to all their constituents, for example, or just to those constituents who voted for them? Are they accountable to their local party or to their colleagues in Parliament? Is it possible that they are accountable to all these elements and more?

MPs' work - backbench MPs

The answer to the questions posed above may become clearer after examining the work of backbench MPs and ministers. During the 20th century, the work of backbench MPs has increased both at Westminster and in the constituencies. Boundaries are set so that there are 65,000 constituents in the average constituency. On average, constituencies cover 150 square miles. Most are a long way away from Westminster and so the time travelled to and from London is a significant addition to the hours worked by MPs each week.

Most MPs claim that their constituency workload is growing. This is due to the growing amount of casework undertaken on behalf of constituents. MPs also have to be seen to be active in their constituency to maintain the support of party members and their electorate.

The volume of MPs' work at Westminster has grown as the activities of government have grown. There is evidence that parliamentary sessions last longer and more legislation is passed than was the case at the beginning of the century. In 1900, the average length of a Public Act was 200 pages. By the 1970s, 2,000 pages was the average. Similarly, the length of the parliamentary session has risen from 129 days before 1914 to 163 days since 1945. In addition, the advent of select committees (see chapter 14, section 2.1) has resulted in more work for the 25% of MPs who sit on them. Some MPs spend 20 hours per week preparing for and attending these committees.

An article, published in 1988, suggested that many MPs work for more than 70 hours per week when the House is sitting (Vallence, 1988). Most do much of this work in cramped and overcrowded conditions, lacking office space and even a phone of their own. Only about 270 MPs have a room to themselves in the House of Commons and about 60 have to share with four or more others. A year after his election in 1987, Ken Livingstone, Labour MP and ex-leader of the Greater London Council, walked out of the House claiming that he would not return until he had the facilities to do the job properly. His frustration is not at all uncommon. Many MPs have been accustomed to far higher standards of office support before they came to Westminster.

It is clear from the above that MPs' hours and working conditions make it difficult for them to perform their duties adequately. This must necessarily affect any assessment of how representative and how accountable they are.

The growth of 'career' MPs

In 1981, Anthony King wrote an article identifying a new breed of 'professional' or 'career' politicians. These were MPs who had entered Parliament at a relatively young age and whose aim was to retain their seats for the whole of their working lives. These MPs look upon their work as a career with the same promotional prospects and the same insecurity that can be found in any profession (King, 1981). By 1994, Philip Norton was able to find further evidence of this trend. He identified a growing number of MPs who had already made their name in the world of politics either by serving as advisers to ministers, professional lobbyists or party officials (Norton, 1994). These MPs were 'professional' politicians in the sense that it was through paid political work that they were noticed and selected as candidates. Like those MPs identified by King, once elected these MPs hoped for continuous re-election and promotion to ministerial post and the Cabinet. Greater professionalism is also suggested by longer-term trends. In 1945, the average length of service as an MP was just over five years. In 1974, it was 10 years (Vallence, 1988).

If there is a trend towards professional politicians, there is still a large number of MPs who do not expect Parliament to be their sole provider. Until 1911, MPs were not paid and when pay was introduced it was meant to be a minimum payment. David Lloyd George (the Chancellor of the Exchequer) made this quite clear:

> 'When we offer £400 a year as payment to members of Parliament, it is not a recognition of the magnitude of the service, it is not a remuneration, it is not a recompense, it is not even a salary. It is just an allowance, and I think a minimum allowance, to enable men to come here, men who would render incalculable loss to the state not to have here, but who cannot be here because their means do not allow it.' (Hansard, 1911)

Today, many MPs still see their pay as no more than an allowance. Some claim that they need to have other sources of income in order to maintain an adequate standard of living (see chapter 14, pp. 419-20 for the consequences of this) and they combine other jobs with their parliamentary duties. This has led to the charge from the Labour MP Dennis Skinner (amongst others) that those who do this are merely part-time MPs. In mitigation, some MPs argue that poor facilities and poor pay make it impossible to represent their constituents adequately.

Clearly, the degree of professionalism within the House of Commons has a bearing upon how representative and how accountable MPs are.

MPs' work - ministers

A large minority of MPs who belong to the governing party achieve ministerial office. On joining the government, ministers are expected to resign from any directorships that they might hold and to make sure that any investments are placed into the hands of independent advisers. If the investments are likely to impinge directly on their work, they are encouraged to dispose of them. This procedure is designed to protect ministers from conflicts of interest and possible corruption. But in the Register of Members Interests examined by Labour Research in 1993, only 43 out of the 83 ministers declared that they had nil interest (*Labour Research*, March 1993).

Government ministers are obliged to take individual ministerial responsibility for the work undertaken in their departments (see chapter 13, section 1.4) and collective responsibility for the work of government (see chapter 12, section 2.2). As a result, ministers are bound by collective decision making. This automatically reduces their leeway as representatives.

Ministers work long hours and have heavy workloads. As well as their ministerial duties, they also have the normal parliamentary and constituency duties to perform. The sheer volume of work makes it difficult for a minister to be an efficient representative.

Activity 11.7

Item A *Career politicians - a cause for concern?*

The number of career politicians elected in the general election of 1992 was 105, just under a sixth of the 651 MPs (64 are Conservatives, 36 Labour and five Liberal Democrats). This figure excludes those who had a career in local government and those who had been trade union officials or journalists. Of the 105, most were first returned to the House in one of the past three elections: 22 in the 1983 election; 22 in 1987; and 26 in 1992. Some commentators (and MPs) take the view that it is unhealthy for the House to have members whose knowledge is confined essentially to the world of Westminster. There are two potential problems. One is that the party background (and the ambition to achieve promotion) might ensure slavish obedience to the whips in the House. The other is that constituents may come to see the House as an essentially closed institution, full of career politicians driven by ambition for office rather than by a desire to serve their constituents. This perception may serve to undermine trust in Parliament.

Adapted from Norton, 1994.

Item B *Career politicians - not a cause for concern?*

Of the 105 career politicians, the vast majority have worked outside the field of politics. The late Judith Chaplin (head of John Major's Political Office), for example, was a head teacher before entering Parliament. Indeed, only nine of the 105 appear to have had a pre-parliamentary career that was exclusively in the political domain. Having some knowledge of the political world ensures that some new members know how to use parliamentary procedures. Given the demands now made on members by constituents and pressure groups, the capacity to hit the ground running is a valuable one. The rise of the career politician over the past 20 years has coincided with a rise in backbench dissension. For the career politician, it is essential to be re-elected. Volatility in voting intentions (more pronounced since the mid-1960s) ensures that MPs are aware of their electoral vulnerability. To try to bolster support, tremendous effort is put into constituency activity and casework.

Adapted from Norton, 1994.

Item C *A minister's workload in 1977*

Name: Tony Benn
Status: Labour MP for Bristol SE & Secretary of State for Energy

TOTAL WORKLOAD IN 1977

1. ***MP for Bristol SE***
   50 public engagements; 12 speeches in the city; 16 surgeries; 5,000 letters to be dealt with.
2. ***Member of Bristol SE CLP***
   4 general meetings; 20 branch meetings; a membership drive; 5 Labour Group meetings.
3. ***MP in House of Commons***
   129 votes registered; the House sat for 149 days.
4. ***Member of PLP***
   12 PLP meetings; 14 speeches to subcommittees.
5. ***Secretary of State for Energy***
   3 energy Bills; 8 speeches to House; 5 parliamentary statements; 154 meetings with non-government organisations; 8 meetings of energy subcommittees; 1-3 hours per night work on government papers.
6. ***Member of the Cabinet***
   42 Cabinet meetings; 106 Cabinet committee meetings; 4 Cabinet papers submitted; 45 Cabinet subcommittee papers submitted; 1,750 Cabinet papers received.
7. ***Member of Labour party NEC***
   15 NEC meetings; 62 NEC committee meetings.
8. ***International Work***
   19 visits abroad; 32 meetings with foreign ministers; 6 EC Council meetings.
9. ***General political works***
   80 speeches; 83 radio interviews; 57 television interviews; 34 press conferences; 16 articles; 30 interviews with individual journalists; 1,000 letters received or answered which did not involve constituency work.

Adapted from the *Guardian*, 11 February 1978.

Item D *An MP's workload in 1993*

Name: Colin Pickthall
Status: Labour MP for Lancashire West (backbencher)

TOTAL WORKLOAD IN ONE WEEK IN 1994

1. I spent 14 hours in the House of Commons (less than an average week).
2. I spent 13 hours on select committee duties.
3. I met 68 constituents in four different groups.
4. I received 280 items of correspondence - 120 needed at least one letter in reply.
5. I had two advice centres with 25 constituents which generated 62 items of correspondence.
6. I spent eight hours in a local hospital studying the financial problems involved with hip replacements.
7. I participated in a TV programme (4½ hours).
8. I made four constituency visits (4 hours).
9. I spent a great deal of time on the phone.

Adapted from an interview held in November 1994.

Questions

1. a) Using Items A and B give the arguments for and against the view that the growth of career politicians is a cause for concern.
   b) Would you say that the growth of career politicians is likely to result in MPs becoming more or less accountable to (i) their constituents (ii) their local party and (iii) their parliamentary colleagues? Give reasons for your answer.
2. Look back at Colin Pickthall's profile (Item A on page 323). Would you say that Colin Pickthall was a career politician? Give reasons for your answer.
3. a) 'A minister and a backbench MP are accountable to different groups of people.' Explain this statement using Items C and D.
   b) How would you attempt to hold your own MP accountable?

3.3 Pressures on MPs - who pulls the strings?

MPs are not just elected to represent parliamentary constituencies. They also represent their political party. In addition, they may be sponsored by a trade union or have business connections. They may be members of pressure groups. They are certainly members of their parliamentary party and they all have their own personal and financial interests.

All these factors exert pressures on MPs, but they do not necessarily pull in the same direction. In fact, an MP can often face pressure to act in one way from one side and in the opposite way from another side. On every occasion when a decision is made, an MP has to make a choice between competing views.

Links with the community

Most MPs claim, when they have been elected, that they intend to represent all their constituents even though it was probably a minority who voted for them. In practice, however, MPs cannot possibly know the views of all their constituents. In any case, their constituents' views are likely to be divided.

Individuals do lobby their MPs by writing letters and attending constituency surgeries. Occasionally, they go to Westminster to lobby their MP in person at the House of Commons.

MPs usually try to meet local organisations and local pressure groups to show that they are concerned about the views they hold. It is easier for them to promise to represent these views either when the views are in line with broad party policy or when the issues are not party political. On occasion, very strong local feelings can present a dilemma for the MP if those feelings do not accord with party policy.

Parliamentary pressures

At Westminster, nearly all MPs are subject to a party whip. The whips are key figures in the political parties. Not only do they work to maintain party discipline and loyalty amongst MPs, they also serve as a communication line along which views can be carried between backbenchers and the party leadership. An article in the *Guardian* in 1992 described the government's chief whip as:

> 'A personnel manager whose job it is to keep the legislative production line running to prevent strikes at minimum expense.'
> (*Guardian*, 19 October 1992)

This is achieved through an elaborate network of information which includes information on MPs' strengths and weaknesses, their vanities, ambitions and drinking habits.

The 1992 election resulted in a small overall majority for the Conservatives (21 seats). A small overall majority can lead to government defeats if backbenchers rebel. But MPs are well aware of the costs of such rebellions. Defeat for the government could lead to a vote of no confidence. This, in turn, could lead to a general election. In such a general election, many MPs from the government's party might well lose their seats. These conditions influence backbench MPs' behaviour.

The 1993 pit closure programme, for example, brought the real threat of defeat for the government. The government whips had the task of preventing this by offering concessions and threats. In the end, only six Conservatives voted with Labour, though as many as 21 had publicly threatened not to support the government. Even when the whip was withdrawn from eight Conservative MPs between November 1994 and April 1995 and the government technically became a minority government (see also chapter 3, p.64), it still managed to secure enough support on the backbenches not to be defeated on a confidence motion.

As well as the formal pressures from the whips there are informal pressures from colleagues and the knowledge that disloyalty could end the chance of promotion.

Trade union sponsorship

The Labour party operates a system of trade union sponsorship. This practice stems from the early days of the Labour party when MPs were unpaid and Labour parliamentary candidates would have been unable to support themselves if elected.

Today, unions which are affiliated to the Labour party provide limited financial assistance to help with an MP's election expenses and general costs in the constituency. This money is paid to the constituency party and not to the individual. In 1992, the level of financial sponsorship typically stood at £2,000 to £3,000 towards an MP's election expenses plus £150 per quarter paid direct to the MP's constituency party. In 1992, sponsorship was at an all time high with 152 out of the 271 Labour MPs receiving financial aid.

Originally, the unions sponsored members of their union who stood for Parliament. But today, they sponsor MPs who have little or no link with that union through work. Two thirds of union sponsored MPs in 1987, for example, had no experience of manual work.

The unions expect their sponsored MPs to promote the interests of the union in a general sense as well as taking up particular causes in which the union has an interest.

Members' interests

In 1965, James Callaghan commented in the House of Commons:

> 'When I look at some members discussing the Finance Bill I do not think of them as the hon. member for X, Y or Z. I look at them and say

> "investment trusts", "capital speculators" or "that fellow who is the stock exchange man who makes a profit on gilt edged".'

The concern expressed in 1965 has grown in succeeding years. Many MPs, especially Conservatives, have business interests which they maintain whilst serving as MPs.

Because of the fear of corruption and the fact that MPs might be concealing vested interests when they take part in parliamentary activities, Parliament established a Register of Members Interests in 1975. But, although MPs have to declare an interest when speaking in debates in the House, they do not have to do so when asking parliamentary questions, signing Early Day Motions or voting - so long as they have declared their interests in the Register.

In 1990, nearly 400 MPs had outside interests and more than 1,200 directorships, consultancies, trades, professions, employments, clients, gifts, free trips, property holdings and share holdings were declared in the Register.

There is growing evidence that the Register is inadequate, does not provide enough information and leaves questions unanswered. MPs are left to provide information which they think is appropriate. Also, MPs do not have to disclose how much they are paid by outside interests and lobbyists. The 'cash for questions' scandal (see chapter 14, pp.419-20) and Nolan Report (submitted in May 1995) may result in tighter control being exerted over MPs' outside interests.

Lobby firms and consultancies

There is a growing concern about the development of lobby firms, especially those which are run by MPs or employ MPs to do the work for them. There are more than 60 of these specialised companies and their turnover is worth over £10 million a year. In addition, major public relations companies engage in lobbying.

Parliamentary consultants or 'lobbyists' who claim to have inside knowledge of the ways in which ministers, civil servants and Parliament work, sell their services to whoever can afford to pay them. They represent the views of their clients to those making political and administrative decisions and seek to influence the outcome.

The inside knowledge that these companies claim is based partly on the fact that many of them employ or are run by MPs. According to Vandermark whose information comes from the House of Commons Register of Members' Interests, 1993:

> 'In the 1992-93 session, 430 out of 650 MPs were sponsored from outside interests, with 29 consultancy firms making direct payments to MPs. In particular, 25 of the 38 new Conservative MPs took up paid consultancies [and] 20 MPs were directors of consultancy related businesses.' (Vandermark, 1994, p.40)

In 1995, there were 167 MPs with more than 350 consultancies between them. Of these 167 MPs, 145 were Conservative MPs, 15 were Labour MPs and 6 were Liberal Democrats (*Observer*, 21 May 1995). MPs are employed in this way because it is assumed that they have inside knowledge of how the system works and important contacts. Although it is not illegal for an MP to be a paid consultant for a company, the proliferation of consultancies over recent years and the links between MPs and lobby firms have become a cause for concern both within Parliament and outside:

> 'Some MPs allege that a number of their colleagues' financial links with these firms, in the form of an executive directorship or a monthly sponsorship payment, is tantamount to being "bought". Political commentators have shared their anxiety, believing the many lobbyists who claim to be able to "sell influence" are achieving this by effectively paying MPs to take account of their concerns first.' (Vandermark, 1994, p.34)

The result is that public perception of the work done by MPs has suffered. In a survey conducted by Gallup in 1995, for example, almost two thirds of respondents agreed that 'most MPs make a lot of money by using public office improperly'. It was to counter this public cynicism that the Nolan Report recommended that MPs should be banned from working for lobbying firms that have more than one client and that MPs should disclose their employment contract and earnings from outside interests (*Independent*, 12 May 1995).

Activity 11.8

Item A *Backbenchers' response to the Nolan Report*

The Nolan Committee argued that it is crucial to know how much cash is being paid to MPs for outside consultancies. While the Conservatives are in office, however, that will not happen. Resistance on the Conservative backbenches is strong. Some MPs are muttering about resigning their seats immediately if they are stripped of their consultancies. It is argued that if middle class Conservatives were expected to stand for Parliament on a salary of £33,189 with no extras, they would not stand at all. Those who oppose the Nolan Report argue that the House of Commons has always dealt robustly with its own transgressors and there is no need for external regulation. The former Prime Minster, Edward Heath, said that in his 45 years as an MP he could only recall two occasions when MPs had broken the rules and, on each occasion, the House dealt with the cases swiftly and effectively. 'There is', he said, 'such a thing as the privacy of the individual.'

Adapted from the *Independent*, 19 May 1995 and the *Observer*, 21 May 1995.

Item B *Members' interests*

The Nolan Report of May 1995 recommends that MPs be banned from working for lobbying firms that have more than one client. In addition, although it does not suggest MPs be banned from working for outside interests, it recommends that, if they are hired for their parliamentary services, they must disclose their contract and earnings. The Register of Members' Interests, the report says, should be improved to make it clearer what MPs have been doing. According to an opinion poll published on 31 May 1995, most people agree with the recommendations. Although people would allow MPs to carry on their professions, huge majorities were opposed to them working for lobbying firms, speaking or voting on issues where they have a financial interest or asking questions for money. The table (right) shows the result of a MORI poll published on 30 May 1995.

MPs should be allowed to:	Yes	No
1. Carry on trade or profession (eg farmer, lawyer, dentist etc) while being MP	45	33
2. Be paid to write articles for papers	35	43
3. Have any paid job outside Parliament	28	48
4. Be paid to represent non-commercial interest group, (eg Police Federation)	21	44
5. Be sponsored by trade unions	21	48
6. Speak or vote where they stand to gain	4	77
7. Receive fees for lobbying	3	78
8. Ask questions for money	8	83

Who should enforce rules of MPs' conduct?	
MPs as now	8
MPs but tightened up	19
Law - civil courts & independent commission	38
Law - Police & criminal courts	29

Who should investigate accusations of ministerial misconduct?	
Prime Minister	11
House of Commons	12
Independent commission	47
Police	31

All figures are percentages.

Adapted from the *Times*, 12 May 1995 and the *Guardian*, 31 May 1995.

Item C *Extract from Register of Members' Interests.*

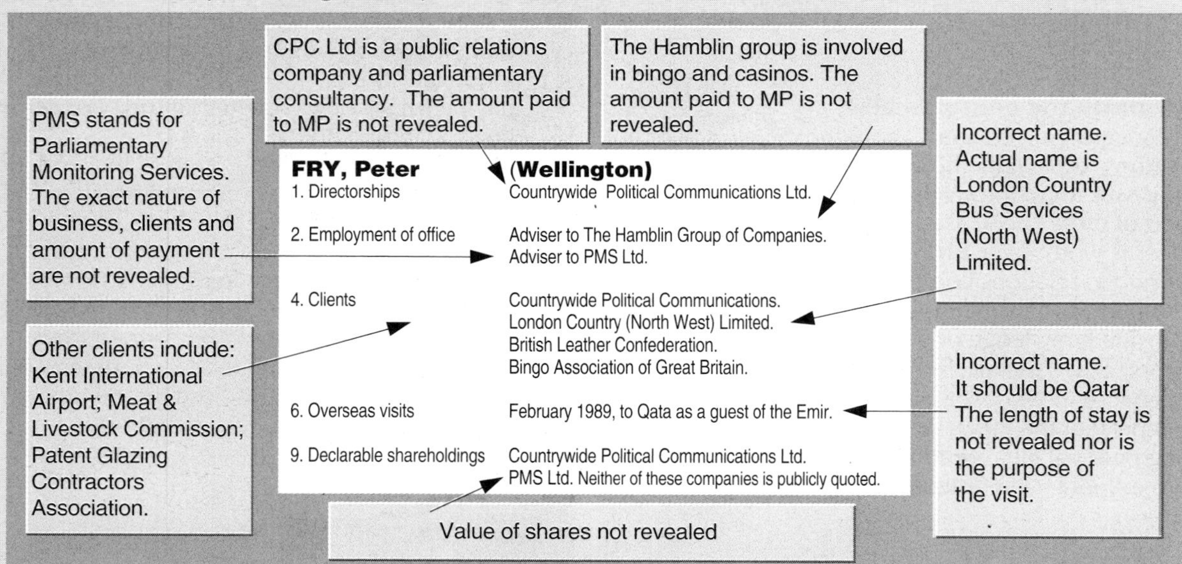

Adapted from the *Observer*, 14 October 1990.

Item D *Lobbying*

It would be naive to argue that lobbyists never have any influence over Parliament. During the 1980s, the Conservatives enjoyed large and impregnable majorities in Parliament. But, even so, lobbyists were able to achieve a number of successes through campaigns and activity aimed at ordinary backbench MPs. For example, in 1986 there was a concerted campaign to defeat the government's proposed Sunday trading reforms. The success of this campaign was due, in part, to the efforts lobbyists made to influence backbench opinion. Lobbyists also played a crucial role on technical Bills in the 1980s. Often they provided their clients with information or demystifed pieces of complex and highly detailed legislation for them. Many City interests actively lobbied the standing committee considering the Financial Services Act, for example. They were influential in securing a number of technical amendments. But, such examples may be the exception rather than the rule.

Adapted from Berry, 1993.

Item E *Influencing parliamentary decisions*

1.	Contacting members of the House of Lords	77.3
2.	Circulating documents to all or many MPs	65.4
3.	Circulating documents to Standing Committee	58.3
4.	Asking MPs to propose an amendment	53.6
5.	Asking MPs to ask parliamentary questions	53.6
6.	Asking MPs to speak in second reading debate	52.6
7.	Arranging to meet MPs or hold seminar for them	49.3
8.	Asking MPs to arrange meeting with minister	31.3
9.	Direct contact with ministers or civil servants	17.5
10.	Organising lobby or letter writing campaign	7.6
11.	Using the media	1.9
12.	Cooperating with other pressure groups	1.4
13.	Not specified	0.5

This table shows the result of a 1989 survey. Lobbyists were asked which techniques they used to influence the outcome of parliamentary decisions (the figures show the percentage of those questioned who used the technique).

Adapted from Berry, 1993.

Questions

1. 'The Register of Members Interests seeks to balance the public interest against the privacy of individual MPs and their families.' Judging from Items A-C does it succeed? Give arguments for and against.
2. a) Using Items D and E explain what factors determine the effectiveness of lobbyists.
   b) Do you agree with the Nolan Report's recommendation that MPs be banned from lobby firms? Give arguments for and against.
3. a) Describe the different pressures that are exerted on an MP.
   b) How do these pressures affect an MP's accountability?

3.4 The rewards of office

Backbench MPs' pay

Backbench MPs were paid a basic salary of £31,687 in 1994. In addition, they were able to claim a number of allowances: up to £40,380 to pay for secretarial and support services; up to £10,958 to pay for accommodation in London if their constituencies were outside Inner London (and up to £1,222 if their constituencies were inside Inner London); between 28.8p and 68.2p per mile for the first 20,000 miles depending on engine size (and between 15.1 and 34.1p per mile for miles above 20,000) to cover the cost of car travel on parliamentary business (including travel between the MP's constituency and Westminster). In addition, MPs receive travel warrants if they need to travel on parliamentary business by air, sea or rail and they receive free stationery and phone calls for all parliamentary business conducted from the Palace of Westminster. All claims have to be submitted for approval to the Fees Office in the House of Commons.

Compared to legislators in other countries, however, British MPs are not well paid and they lack adequate support. The Top Salaries Review Body in 1987 concluded that, in terms of services and facilities, British MPs lagged behind legislators in Canada, West Germany, France and MEPs (TSRB, 1987).

Ministers' pay

Ministers are paid more than MPs. In 1994, the Lord Chancellor received £110,940; the Prime Minister received £78,292; Cabinet ministers received £64,749 if they were members of the House of Commons or £52,260 if they were members of the House of Lords; ministers of state received £52,790 if from the Commons or £46,333 if from the Lords; under secretaries received £45,815 if from the Commons or £38,894 if from the Lords. Ministers have the luxury of chauffeur driven cars and special residences come with some ministerial posts. Otherwise, ministers are eligible for the same allowances as MPs and no more.

Some ministers argue that the pay they receive is poor recompense for the degree of responsibility they have and that it compares very badly with pay in the private sector. One minister, Lord Gowrie, resigned in 1985 because, he claimed, he could not live on his salary. He promptly found work which gave him a much higher financial reward.

Ex-ministers and ex-MPs

After ministers leave the government there are no restrictions on their activities (though the Nolan Report published in May 1995 recommended that ex-ministers should seek clearance for jobs taken in private industry within two years of office and Cabinet Ministers should automatically have to wait three months before taking up outside employment). Since 1979, there has been a growing trend for ex-ministers to join companies as directors. For example, after resigning as Chancellor of the Exchequer in 1989, Nigel Lawson immediately joined Barclays Bank as a part-time consultant non-executive director. He earned £100,000 a year for this, doubling his ministerial salary. Lawson was just one of many ministers who left Margaret Thatcher's government and immediately found highly paid posts. Margaret Thatcher herself accepted a three year consultancy for a reported £550,000 with the American company Philip Morris (maker of Marlboro cigarettes), shortly after resigning.

Ex-MPs can also find that their parliamentary experience has proved useful. Two days after losing his seat in the general election of 1992, Roger King (ex-MP for Birmingham Northfield) found a job as the public affairs director for the Society of Motor Manufacturers. Whilst an MP, Roger King had spoken extensively on the car industry.

Patronage

The exercise of patronage is an important part of the Prime Minister's job. On appointment to the office of Prime Minister, the incumbent has the constitutional right to choose the Cabinet and to make all other ministerial appointments. In addition, further appointments during the lifetime of Parliament are anticipated by backbenchers and their behaviour is shaped accordingly. It is the job of the party whips to identify potential talent and to make recommendations to the Prime Minister. Julian Critchley, a longstanding Conservative backbench MP, has commented on this process:

> 'What is it the whips are looking for? It could be "bottom", whatever that might mean. It will certainly be loyalty, the cement that keeps a broad church together. It could be ability, although intelligence is not enough on its own. It might even be expertise. But what are civil servants for? What I think they are looking for above everything else is predictability.'
> (Critchley, 1989, p.60)

Predictability is found in loyal votes and speeches and hard, unstinting work on committees. But even that may not be enough. At any one time, only around 100 MPs can be chosen for ministerial office.

The Prime Minister also has the power to appoint or influence the selection of other posts. The Prime Minister can create peers and appoint people to the following posts: top civil servants at the permanent secretary level, chairs of nationalised industries, heads of the security services and chairs of Royal Commissions. In addition, the Prime Minister has the ultimate responsibility for recommendations of knighthoods, MBEs and so on in the various honours lists (see also, chapter 12, section 1.2).

Honours

In March 1993, the Prime Minister, John Major, announced a reform of the honours system as part of his drive towards a 'classless' society. Since then, members of the public have been able to nominate candidates for awards simply by filling in a form and sending it to the Honours Secretariat at 10 Downing Street. In addition, it was announced that the award of honours to senior civil servants and high ranking military officers solely on the grounds of seniority or status would be stopped after the Queen's birthday honours list in 1993. The differentiation of military medals according to the rank of the recipient was also abolished after that date.

Despite the changes outlined above, secrecy still surrounds the procedure which results in a shortlist of candidates being presented to the Prime Minister. Also, John Major's reform did not address the most controversial aspect of the honours system - the practice of giving honours as rewards for party or political services.

During the 1980s, there was growing concern about the use of the honours system to reward those who had provided political support to the Conservative party (or even, more personally, to the Prime Minister), especially if they worked in the media. The knighthoods given to David English, editor of the *Daily Mail*, and Larry Lamb, editor of the *Sun*, for example, were said to have been rewards both for the support that these papers had given to the Conservative party during the 1979 and 1983 general elections and for the advice these men had given at face-to-face meetings with Margaret Thatcher. Similarly, Margaret Thatcher's resignation honours list was seen as rewarding those who had remained loyal to her. The editor of the *Daily Express* received a knighthood for keeping his newspaper 'sound'. Five leading businessmen who offered Margaret Thatcher advice and support in the 1980s received peerages. In addition, 37 other people (mainly from her personal staff) were rewarded.

According to research conducted by the Labour party, 25 private sector industrialists were nominated by the Conservative party for peerages between 1979 and 1990. Of these, 17 were connected to companies which had donated large sums to the Conservative party. The same research shows that John Major has continued this tradition. By April 1993, he had awarded 17 knighthoods to private sector industrialists. Of these, 13 were connected to companies which had donated, together, £3 million to the Conservative party since 1979 (*Labour Research*, April 1993).

Activity 11.9

Item A *Ex-ministers in the money*

This graphic appeared in the *Guardian*, 27 August 1990.

Item B *MPs' Pay*

In the early 1980s, Margaret Thatcher had a habit of announcing a pay rise for ministers and simultaneously informing the public that she had no intention of taking the extra money herself. This annoyed some ministers who, unlike her, could not rely on a rich husband to pay the bills. Amongst those who were annoyed was Norman Lamont, the current Chancellor. As Chancellor, he struggles to get by on £63,000 a year. Poverty amongst politicians (as elsewhere in society) is relative. For some Labour newcomers, a backbencher's £30,000 plus office and travel expenses is a step into middle class comfort. For a Tory ex-merchant banker like Norman Lamont, promotion may represent a 50% pay cut. It helps having a £200,000-a-year wife as other ministers, like Michael Portillo and John Patten, have wisely arranged to do. But Norman Lamont's wife does not work. Rent from their Notting Hill house probably covers the mortgage and tax. School fees for their two children cost around £20,000. No wonder he feels poor, juggling his credit cards on £63,000.

Adapted from the *Guardian*, 1 December 1992.

Item C *Honours (1)*

The public will be able to nominate candidates for awards such as MBEs under reforms of the honours system outlined by the Prime Minister yesterday. This announcement drew widespread Conservative support, but derision from the Labour benches because the Prime Minister repeatedly declined to end awards for political service - particularly knighthoods to long serving Conservative MPs and wealthy supporters of the party. More than 100 knighthoods have been awarded to the government's backbench supporters since 1979.
Regular rebels or those perceived to be insufficiently supportive do not receive a knighthood. John Smith, the Labour leader, asked: 'Why do Conservative governments and only Conservative governments wish to use the honours system for the reward of political services? It is a shocking misuse of a system set up to reward public service.' Paddy Ashdown, Liberal Democrat leader, claimed that honours should be awarded by an independent commission and there should only be one graduated honour for all recipients. Mr Major said that it was open to all parties to nominate supporters for knighthoods and accused Labour sceptics of sour grapes.

Adapted from the *Guardian*, 5 March 1993.

Item D *Honours (2)*

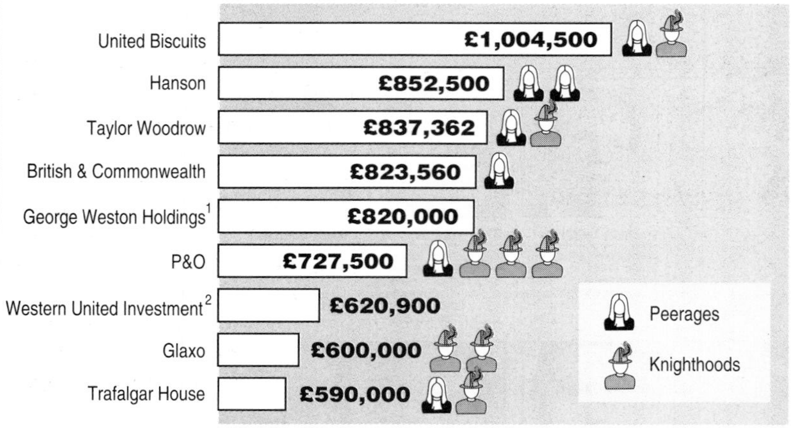

1 Headed by a Canadian
2 One of its two directors is hereditary peer Lord Vestey

This diagram shows the amount of money nine companies donated to the Conservative party and the honours their directors received between 1979 and 1992.

Adapted from the *Guardian*, 14 April, 1994.

Item E *Honours (3)*

Five Labour MPs on the Home Affairs Select Committee yesterday published a minority report on party funding. This report alleges links between donations to the Conservative party and government policy. For example, it suggests the government's refusal to ban tobacco advertising is due to the fact that the tobacco industry makes large donations to the Conservative party. It also notes that between 1979 and 1993, 18 life peerages and 82 knighthoods were given to 76 business people whose companies between them donated £17.4 million to the Conservative party. The report makes the following recommendations:

1. An electoral commission be set up to oversee parties' finances.
2. No honour to be given to any industrialist whose company has donated to a party in the past five years.
3. The awarding of honours to be removed from the hands of serving politicians.
4. Fund raising by ministers on trips paid for by taxpayers to be banned (ministers found time to fund raise on 14 trips to Hong Kong between 1988 and 1991).
5. Access to poster sites at election time to be controlled (tobacco advertisers donated all their sites to the Conservatives in the 1992 election).

Adapted from the *Guardian*, 14 April 1994.

Questions

1. a) What rewards can MPs expect?
   b) Do you think these rewards are sufficient to attract people of high calibre to serve as MPs?
   c) How do you think the desire for reward might affect the performance of an MP?
2. Look at Items A and B.
   a) What objections could there be to ex-ministers joining the boards of companies?
   b) Give the arguments for and against the view that ministers earn too little.
3. a) Judging from Items C-E why do you think honours are given?
   b) 'There is absolutely no need to alter the honour system.' Using Items C-E give arguments for and against this view.

4 The recruitment of MEPs

Key Issues

1. Who stands for office and why?
2. How are candidates selected?
3. What are the pay and conditions of MEPs
4. How representative are MEPs?

Who stands for office?

Since 1979 when the first direct elections to the European Parliament were held, elections have taken place every five years. At the election held in June 1994, the Parliament had a total of 567 seats. These seats are allocated to ensure a degree of equality between the number of people per seat in each member country, balanced by the need for smaller countries to have adequate representation. In June 1994, 87 MEPs were elected in the UK. Since there are just 87 seats for the whole of the UK, that means that the size of the average constituency (and the number of voters in the average constituency) is much larger than the average parliamentary constituency. Roughly, each Euro-constituency incorporates seven parliamentary constituencies (and includes, on average, 550,000 voters). In the UK, the electoral system used for Euro-elections is the same as that for general elections - the first past the post system.

Since 1979, the three main parties have put up candidates for all the Euro-seats that have been contested in mainland Britain. In addition, a large number of fringe candidates have stood, often seeking to draw attention to a particular cause. All candidates must be over the age of 21 and they must not be bankrupt. People holding certain posts are not allowed to stand, namely judges, members of the armed forces, police officers, members of national governments and members of the European Commission. But, peers and religious ministers are allowed to stand even though they are disqualified from elections to the House of Commons.

There is a certain amount of interchange between the European Parliament and the House of Commons. In the 1994 European election, for example, Edwina Currie, a Conservative backbench MP, stood for election to the European Parliament, whilst three sitting Labour MEPs did not stand for re-election because they had become MPs in the 1992 general election. There is no rule preventing a politician sitting as both an MP and an MEP. But, obviously, it is difficult for one person to perform both roles adequately.

The selection of Euro-candidates

Candidates must complete a nomination paper with the signatures of a proposer, a seconder and 28 other voters in the constituency in which they wish to stand. Candidates can stand in countries other than their home state (for example, the British businessman James Goldsmith stood as a candidate in France in June 1994), but candidates can only stand in one seat. A £1,000 election deposit must be paid. It is returned if the candidate receives 5% or more of the votes cast.

Although any individual can put themselves forward, the only candidates with a serious chance of being elected in a British Euro-election are candidates from the three main parties. It is highly unlikely, given the size of the Euro-constituencies and the fact that a first past the post system is used, that any of the fringe candidates will be elected. Candidates for the major parties are selected in the same way that parliamentary candidates are elected. The only difference is the scale of the operation. The qualities sought in candidates are similar to those required of MPs.

MEPs' pay and working conditions

MEPs are paid the equivalent of their national parliamentary salary. So, there are considerable discrepancies between salaries received by members from different countries. In 1994, British MEPs earned £31,687 a year. By comparison, the lowest salary was £21,436 (paid to Spanish MEPs) and the highest salary was £73,051 (paid to Italian MEPs). The salary, however, is by no means the only money that MEPs receive. The *Guardian* has claimed that British MEPs can earn up to another £10,000 a year in profit just by claiming expenses on their weekly business flights to Brussels or Strasbourg. This is due to the fact that MEPs are paid a flat rate mileage allowance for air travel which is well in excess of the price of even the most expensive air ticket. In addition, MEPs can claim further generous expenses. They can claim a daily subsistence allowance (of £159 in 1994) every time they attend an official meeting of a European parliamentary body. There is a monthly expenditure allowance of £2,196 to cover the costs of running an office and £6,004 a month to employ secretaries and research assistants. There are allowances for computer equipment, language courses, extra travel, free taxis, life assurance and insurance. The EU budget estimates £106.5 million for MEPs expenses and allowances. This works out at £180,000 a member (*Guardian*, 1 June 1994).

Working conditions at Brussels and Strasbourg are far superior to those at Westminster. MEPs have their own desks and telephones as well as reserved seats in the European Parliament. There are no late night sittings. But, there are the strains of the long absences from home and an interminable round of meetings conducted in a multiplicity of European languages. A working month usually consists of three weeks in Brussels (two weeks working on parliamentary committees and one week working for political groups) followed by a mass upheaval to Strasbourg where the Parliament sits for one week.

How representative are MEPs?

MEPs are not typical of the electorate as a whole. Of the Conservative candidates in 1994, 52% attended public school, 34% went to Oxford or Cambridge universities, 23% were company directors, there were no manual workers and only 16% were women. Of the Labour candidates only 2% attended public school, 12% went to Oxford or Cambridge universities, 6% were manual workers, there were no company directors and 29% were women (*Labour Research*, June 1994).

The first past the post system used in Britain means that Labour and the Conservatives secure the vast majority of seats. In the 1994 Euro-election, for example, Labour won 44% of the vote and 62 seats, the Conservatives won 28% of the vote and 18 seats whilst the Liberal Democrats won 17% of the vote, but just two seats (the Liberal Democrats had not won a single seat before 1994). No minor party has ever won a seat. Even though the Green party won 15% of the vote in 1989, it did not win a single seat. In Northern Ireland, on the other hand, the single transferable vote system is used (see chapter 7, p.186). This system was introduced on the grounds that it would prevent Protestant domination. It could be argued, therefore, that the adoption of the first past the post system in Britain ensures that MEPs are unrepresentative of the broad range of opinion in the country.

The turnout in Euro-elections also raises questions about how representative MEPs are. In 1994, 38% of the electorate voted, compared to 36% in 1989. These figures suggest a degree of apathy and indifference among the voters which MEPs do not seem able to counter. The ability of MEPs to represent their constituents is further restricted by the nature of party discipline which operates in the same way as at Westminster. It is also restricted by the large geographical and population sizes of their constituencies. Most of the electorate do not know the name of their local MEP and MEPs have direct contact with very few of their constituents.

Activity 11.10

Item A Profile of a Euro candidate

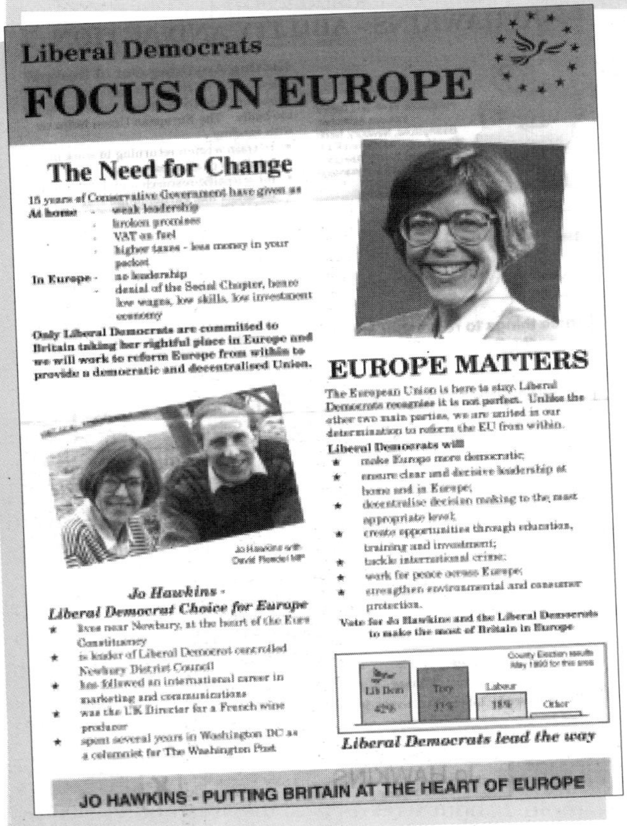
Liberal Democrats
FOCUS ON EUROPE

The Need for Change

15 years of Conservative Government have given us

At home - weak leadership
- broken promises
- VAT on fuel
- higher taxes - less money in your pocket

In Europe - no leadership
- denial of the Social Chapter, hence low wages, low skills, low investment economy

Only Liberal Democrats are committed to Britain taking her rightful place in Europe and we will work to reform Europe from within to provide a democratic and decentralised Union.

Jo Hawkins with David Rendel MP

Jo Hawkins - Liberal Democrat Choice for Europe

- ★ lives near Newbury, at the heart of the Euro Constituency
- ★ is leader of Liberal Democrat controlled Newbury District Council
- ★ has followed an international career in marketing and communications
- ★ was the UK Director for a French wine producer
- ★ spent several years in Washington DC as a columnist for The Washington Post

EUROPE MATTERS

The European Union is here to stay. Liberal Democrats recognise it is not perfect. Unlike the other two main parties, we are united in our determination to reform the EU from within.

Liberal Democrats will

- ★ make Europe more democratic;
- ★ ensure clear and decisive leadership at home and in Europe;
- ★ decentralise decision making to the most appropriate level;
- ★ create opportunities through education, training and investment;
- ★ tackle international crime;
- ★ work for peace across Europe;
- ★ strengthen environmental and consumer protection.

Vote for Jo Hawkins and the Liberal Democrats to make the most of Britain in Europe

County Election results May 1993 for this area

Lib Dem 42% | Tory | Labour 18% | Other

Liberal Democrats lead the way

JO HAWKINS - PUTTING BRITAIN AT THE HEART OF EUROPE

This leaflet was produced by the Liberal Democrats in the Hampshire North and Oxford Euro-constituency for the 1994 Euro-election.

Item B The youngest MEP

Only three months ago Eluned Morgan was a £17,000-a-year researcher at BBC Wales, sharing digs with two others in the terraced house in Cardiff which she bought last year. Now she is the youngest member of the European Parliament - she won Mid and West Wales for Labour with a majority of 30,000. So, she is busy setting up four offices in Brussels, Strasbourg, Aberystwyth and Carmarthen. She needs to find an apartment to rent in Brussels. And she needs to hire at least three full-time staff/researchers and some secretaries. Her £35,000 salary will be magnified by up to a million pounds a year by expenses. As to whether this is appealing, she says: 'I've never had these opportunities before. But I'm not terribly impressed. Money has never been that important to me.' Eluned was born a vicar's daughter and lived on a council estate in Cardiff. Both her parents were local councillors. Her passion for things European grew from her time at Atlantic college, the Prince of Wales' pet project, to which she won a scholarship. She joined a Cardiff Labour supporters trip to Strasbourg and then studied for a year at the University of Strasbourg. She now speaks French, Spanish, German and Welsh. After reading European Studies at Hull University, she worked for five months in Brussels as a researcher on regional policy for the socialist group in the European Parliament. It was after this that she worked for BBC Wales. In a sense, much of her life has been a preparation for Brussels. 'I'll be able to use all my skills', she says.

Adapted from the *Times*, 22 June 1994

Item C How representative are MEPs?

(i) MEPs elected, June 1994

Party	Men	Women	Total	Total, 1989
Con	16	2	18	32
Lab	49	13	62	45
Lib Dem	2	0	2	0
SNP	1	1	2	1
Others	3	0	3	3
Total	**71**	**16**	**87**	**81**

This table shows the gender of the MEPs elected in June 1994.

(ii) Share of the votes at Euro-elections 1984-94

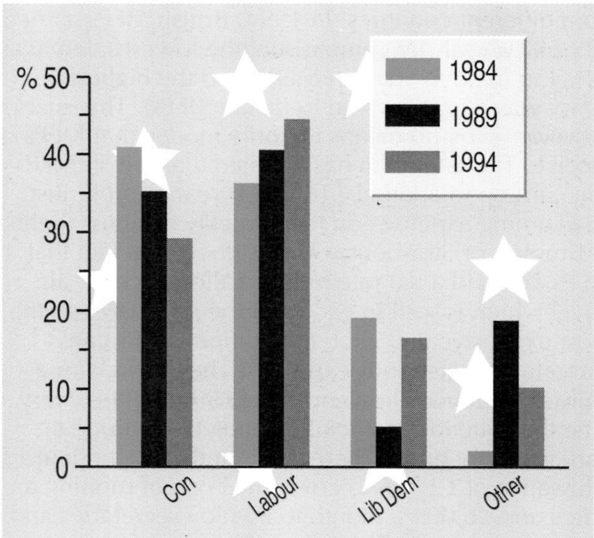

This table shows the share of the vote received by parties in Euro-elections 1984-94.

Item D *Strasbopoly - a month in the life of an MEP*

Adapted from the *Guardian*, 1 June 1994.

Item E *The occupations of Euro-candidates, 1994*

Conservative		***Labour***	
Occupation	**No.**	**Occupation**	**No.**
Company director	19	Lecturer	14
Consultant	9	Teacher	13
Lawyer	9	Voluntary sector	11
Journalist	7	Council officer	7
Manager	7	Party employee	5
Party employee	6	Manual worker	5
Farmer	6	Journalist	5
Banker	4	Lawyer	2
Lecturer	4	Trade union employee	1
Other	10	Other	19
Unknown	2	Unknown	1

This table shows the occupations of candidates who stood for the Labour and Conservative parties in the European election of June 1994.

Questions

1. Using the information in Items A, B and E what similarities and differences are there in the background of candidates in the three main parties?
2. How typical a candidate would you say Eluned Morgan was (Item B)? Give reasons for your answer.
3. Judging from the information in Item C would you say that MEPs are representative of the electorate as a whole? Explain how you reached your conclusions.
4. Look at Item D. What do you think MEPs should receive in pay and allowances? Make out a case justifying the amount and also consider whether MEPs should be paid the same amount regardless of the country they come from.

5 Quangocrats

Key Issues

1. What sort of people are appointed to serve on quangos?
2. What criteria are used for their appointment?
3. What are their pay and hours?
4. To whom are they accountable?

What is a quangocrat?

The preceding sections in this chapter have considered the recruitment of elected politicians. But the chapter would be incomplete if it did not also consider the recruitment of political appointees - people who have political responsibilities even though they have not been elected. In the early 1990s, the number of political appointees has grown rapidly, reflecting a growing number of unelected agencies or quangos (for a full definition and description of the work of quangos, see chapter 16, part 5). Quangos are set up by central government and staffed by appointees rather than by elected representatives. A quangocrat, therefore, is quite simply a person who is appointed to serve on a quango.

What sort of people are appointed to serve on quangos?

According to recent surveys, the typical quangocrat is a middle class, white male who works in business and finance and votes for the Conservative party (see, for example, Jones, 1994). This profile is derived from the following information.

First, in 1993 there were three times as many male quangocrats as female and just 2% of quangocrats came from the ethnic minorities. Only 15% of quangos are chaired by women. These figures account for the white and male elements of the typical quangocrat (Jones, 1994).

Second, a Labour party survey of 372 NHS trusts in England and Wales found that 54% of trust board members came from business and finance (NHS trust boards are quangos). Other surveys confirm that the majority of quangocrats are middle aged and middle class with backgrounds in business or finance.

Third, allegations that ministers are deliberately packing quangos with Conservative party supporters have been supported by a growing body of evidence. That this could be government practice was suggested by Baroness Denton in June 1993. She had been responsible for 804 public appointments when she confessed publicly that she had never knowingly appointed a Labour supporter (*Guardian*, 21 June 1993). A report in the *Observer* the following month showed that of the 38 largest quangos (which are responsible for dispensing billions of pounds of public funds), in 14 instances the chair or chief executive was either involved in businesses that contributed to Conservative party funds or had been a Conservative party activist. Since then, further evidence of this sort has continued to emerge. The following extract is typical:

> The chairman of the [Funding Agency for Schools] is Sir Christopher Benson. He is also chairman of the Sun Alliance Group (which has given £280,000 to the Conservative party in the past six years), director of MEPC property group (£25,000 to the Tories in 1992) and chairman of the Costain property group (another contributor to party funds). Joining him is Stanley Kalms, chairman of Dixons (£25,000 to the Tories in 1992); Edward Lister, the Conservative leader of Wandsworth council; and Sir Robert Balchin, chairman of the South East Conservative party.'
> (*Independent on Sunday*, 3 April 1994)

Although it has been the case for many years that most quangocrats are white, middle class, middle aged males, it is only in recent years that party affiliation appears to have become important. As with many other changes, this development has been ascribed to Thatcherism:

> 'In pre-Thatcher days, quangos were assembled in much the same way as a royal commission, a committee of inquiry or the board of a public corporation. There would be a trade unionist, a local councillor, a professor, a lawyer, an accountant, a Welshman, a Scotsman and a housewife. Undoubtedly, politics played a part in these appointments to these bodies. In periods of Labour government, trade unionists and councillors would be rewarded while, under Conservative governments, councillors and industrialists might find their services to the party modestly acknowledged. But, no previous Prime Minister had asked "Is he one of us?" with the persistence or the intensity which Lady Thatcher was to demonstrate.'
> (*Independent on Sunday*, 30 January1994)

According to a survey published in 1994 (Weir & Hall, 1994), in 1993 over 73,000 appointments were made to quangos. At local level, there are between 57,296 and 63,120 non-elected quangocrats, more than twice the number of elected councillors (there were 25,093 councillors in 1993).

What criteria are used for the appointment of quangocrats?

Until July 1994, it was thought that people who wanted to serve on quangos applied to central government and, if they managed a successful interview, their names were placed on a central register from which appointments were made. But, by following up the replies given to parliamentary questions asked by Labour MP Peter Kilfoyle on 8 July 1994, the *Observer* newspaper was able to establish that, although a list of people who might be considered for appointment is compiled by central government, it is only 'suggestive'. The Cabinet Office said that ministers are able to:

> 'Maintain their own lists, consult interested bodies, make personal suggestions or use headhunters.' (quoted in the *Observer*, 10 July 1994)

In other words, ministers are free to use or to ignore the central register and there is no formal appointment procedure that has to be followed. That informal methods of recruitment are commonplace is suggested by Sir Derek Barber, chair of a quango called the Countryside Commission:

> 'I became Chairman...as a consequence of sharing a cab with a stranger. Another quango chairman was appointed following a pheasant shoot at which a Secretary of State was a fellow gun; the subsequent chairman of a water authority bumped into a Cabinet minister while birding on a Greek Island. It is a splendidly capricious and British way of doing things. I am advised that the success/failure rate is about the same as when headhunters are engaged. And look at the thousands of guineas you save?' (an extract from the Countryside Commission's 1991 newsletter quoted in *Labour Research*, August 1994)

In 1994, 73,000 people were appointed to serve on quangos (Democratic Audit, 1994). In general, appointments are made by the minister in charge of the department responsible for sponsoring the quango. Often the minister is only responsible for appointing the chair of a quango. The chair is then responsible for appointing other members of the board. The board will then employ other staff. In 1991, for example, the Welsh Secretary was responsible for 1,400 appointments to quangos. Altogether these quangos employed 57,311 people.

Although there are no published guidelines laying down the criteria that ministers must apply when making appointments, support for the government's stance on the issue for which the quango is responsible is obviously important. For example, the Funding Agency for Schools is a quango which was set up in April 1994 to control the funds and monitor the performance of schools which have opted out of local authority control (Grant Maintained Schools). Clearly, there was little incentive for the then Secretary of State for Education, John Patten, to appoint people who did not support the policy of opting out. Indeed, according to Sir Robert Balchin who was appointed to serve on the board:

> 'John Patten [the Education Secretary] told me that the first criterion for membership of the board was that you must be supportive of the concept of Grant Maintained Schools.' (quoted in the *Independent on Sunday*, 3 April 1994)

This stipulation immediately ruled out virtually all members of the Labour party and Liberal Democrats since, at the time, these parties had policies which were opposed to Grant Maintained Schools. As a result, the division between government and party interests became hopelessly blurred and the minister left himself open to the charge that the appointments had been made entirely for party political gain.

Charges of this sort are not uncommon and they are not just directed at ministers. For example, in 1994 it was revealed that Ian Byatt, the head of Ofwat (a quango responsible for regulating the newly privatised water authorities), appointed an old school friend, the wife of a former colleague and a director of a firm with £10 million contracts with a water authority to chair Ofwat's regional consumer services committees (*Guardian*, 13 April 1994). Although Ian Byatt argued that all these appointments could be justified on the grounds of merit, critics argued that this was a blatant example of favouritism.

Pay and hours

Many quangos are organised so that policy decisions are made by a board of directors which meets infrequently whilst the day-to-day work is undertaken by a full-time chief executive and staff. In general, the payment of board members and chief executives is generous. Certainly, it is much more than any local councillor can hope to earn. Take the Higher Education Funding Council, for example. The figures refer to the year 1993-94. Its chair, Brandon Gough, received £33,170 for working part-time. Its chief executive, Graeme Davies, received £82,925 for working full-time. Board members were paid £4,000 and allowed to claim subsistence and travel allowances at standard civil service rates. They also only worked part-time. (*TES*, 22 April 1994).

These figures are not unusual or confined to education. Membership of a district health authority board, for example, involves one day's work a month and means payment of £5,000 a year. Since membership of a quango board is often not very time consuming, some individuals are able to hold multiple appointments. In 1993, Sir Geoffrey Inkin chaired both the Cardiff Bay Development Corporation and the Land Authority for Wales, for example. Each paid £30,000 per year (*Guardian*, 19 November 1993).

To whom are quangocrats accountable?

Although quangocrats are appointed by ministers or ministerial appointees, ministers have no control over the day-to-day running of quangos. Quangocrats are not, therefore, directly accountable to them. Also, unlike elected representatives, quangocrats are not obliged to explain or justify their actions to the public. Quangos can meet behind closed doors. There are no formal mechanisms that concerned members of the public can use to take quangocrats to task if they feel that they have acted improperly. Whereas, in an elected council, there are members of opposition parties who do their best to seek out corruption and inefficiency, quangos are not challenged in this way. In short, quangocrats are not accountable through the ballot box to the people who elected them (since nobody elected them). They are not obliged to respond to criticisms made by members of the public. And, they are only indirectly accountable to the minister who appointed them.

Whilst critics argue that the growth of quangos means a growing 'democratic deficit', supporters of quangos argue that quangocrats are, in fact, accountable for their actions. It is just that they are accountable in a different way from elected representatives. According to William Waldegrave, when he was Citizen's Charter minister, quangocrats are accountable to the consumers of the public services they administer in the same way that the people who manage a shop are accountable to their customers (*Observer*, 20 March 1994). This is the view adopted by Malcolm Nothard, the former Conservative leader of Dartford council and board member of the Dartford and Gravesham NHS trust. In an interview, he justified his appointment by saying:

> 'If you walk into your local store, you'll find that the management are only accountable to their customers, not to the people who live in the area. The public can't elect people to do everything. Are we going down the American route of electing everyone but the local dog catcher? That's not the British way.'
> (*Independent on Sunday*, 3 April 1994)

In a separate interview, Christopher Thomas, chair of the Bristol Development Corporation, added further justifications for political appointments. He argued that it was actually an advantage that quangocrats were appointees and not elected representatives because that ensured that they acted independently of any political party. He also said that he was accountable to the local community because he was a local and had to live in the local community. If the board of the quango made bad decisions then the board members would lose respect in the eyes of the local community. This, he suggested, was enough to ensure that board members acted in the best interests of the community (Jones,1994).

Activity 11.11

Item A *Lord Wade of Chorlton*

According to his official biography, Lord Wade of Chorlton is: 'A farmer and cheesemaster who, having developed a number of cheese companies and holding a number of directorships, became chairman of the Cheese Export Council.' These, it appears, are perfect credentials for a role in today's National Health Service. Lord Wade is a non-executive director of the Countess of Chester hospital NHS trust. By April 1994 there will be 2,000 other 'non-execs' of NHS trusts. Like them, Lord Wade will receive £5,000 a year for his trouble. The Countess of Chester trust says that its non-execs were chosen for a variety of reasons. These include: commitment to health care; residence within the hospital's catchment area; ability to devote sufficient time to trust matters; and specific expertise and experience to complement that of the five executive directors. Lord Wade is indeed a local resident. He lives just outside Chester. According to *Who's Who*, his interests include 'politics, reading, shooting, food, travel'. There is also a further clue to his selection in *Who's Who*. He was joint treasurer of the Conservative party from 1982 to 1990.

Adapted from an article in the *Guardian*, 19 November 1993.

Item B *Quangowatch*

Quangowatch

A new guide to those unelected quasi-autonomous non-governmental organisations that run our lives

No 1: Scottish Enterprise Tayside

What does it do? Spends £24.3m of taxpayers' money each year on training, business development and environmental improvement in Dundee and Tayside.

Links to the Conservative Party? Its board is appointed by the national directors of Scottish Enterprise who are appointed by Ian Lang, Secretary of State for Scotland.

Chairman designate Jimmy Millar was at a fund-raising dinner organised by the Scottish Conservative Central Office last month at the Invercarse Hotel, Dundee. Also on the guest list were other Dundee quangocrats, J Stuart Fair, a solicitor and chairman of the Dundee Port Authority and Dundee Teaching Hospitals Trust, Dr Donald Grant, former chairman of the Tayside Health Board, and John Beaton, the head of a local engineering firm, recently awarded an the MBE by John Major.

Conflicts of interest: Charles Fairley, who was the chief executive, was and is non-executive chairman of Medical Laser Technologies. He resigned from his £58,000-a-year job with Scottish Enterprise Tayside on 27 January after a two-month inquiry into his business connections. A co-director of Medical Laser Technologies had been hired as a consultant by the quango to investigate Laser Ecosse, an ailing local firm. "Nothing illegal happened but there was thought to be a potential conflict of interest," said a Scottish Enterprise Tayside spokesman.

Meanwhile, Mr Millar, the chairman designate, said 10 days ago he would not take over as chairman in April. He is chairman of the Scottish supermarket chain William Low. The quango had announced it would help rival retailers J Sainsbury set up on the outskirts of Dundee, and Mr Millar said this was "too much of a contradiction."

Accountability? Just one of the 12-member board is a local councillor. Press and public are barred from its meetings. Details of the companies and individuals that receive public money from Scottish Enterprise Tayside are not published.

Annoyed by the collapse in accountability in local government? Call us on 071-415 1396

Quangowatch was a weekly series which appeared in the *Independent on Sunday* in 1994

Item C *Jobs for the boys and girls*

Sir Robin Buchanan, a former Tory councillor resigned as chair of Wessex regional health authority in August 1993 after it was revealed that computer contract losses had cost the authority £63 million. But, despite this, Health Secretary Virginia Bottomley allowed Sir Robin to keep his other part-time job (with a salary of £21,000) chairing the NHS Supplies Authority, the biggest quango in the NHS with a staff of 4,500. Most dual roles were banned by health authority regulations introduced in 1990. But the NHS Supplies Authority was set up in 1991 and is exempt. This was the second recent case of Tory 'jobs for boys and girls'. Last Thursday, Anne-Marie Nelson, a Tory party member, was forced to resign as chair of West Kent health district after it became clear it was illegal for her to chair that body and the Special Hospital Services Authority.

Adapted from the *Observer*, 17 April 1994.

Item D *Quangocrats*

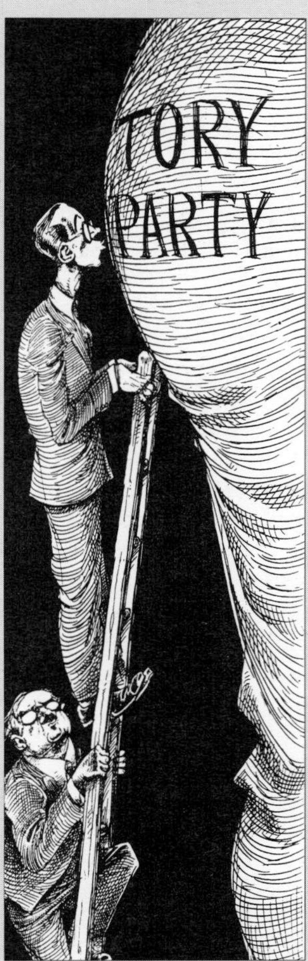

This cartoon appeared in the *Independent on Sunday*, 3 April 1994.

Item E *The committee on women's rights*

"The committee on women's rights will now come to order.

Questions

1. Look at Item A. Why do you think Lord Wade was chosen to serve on a quango? What does his appointment tell us about the system of recruitment to quangos?
2. a) Judging from Items A-E how does the recruitment of quangocrats differ from the recruitment of elected representatives?
   b) Would you agree that the appointment of quangocrats results in a 'democratic deficit'? Explain your answer.
3. Using the information in Items A-E write a report on the recruitment of quangocrats which answers the following questions: (a) What sort of people are appointed to serve on quangos? (b) What criteria are used for their appointment? (c) To whom are quangocrats accountable? (d) What are the advantages and disadvantages of this recruitment system?

References

Baxter (1993) Baxter, S., 'The nimbies in the Labour party', *New Statesman and Society*, 26 November 1993.

Berry (1993) Berry, S., 'Lobbying - a need to regulate?', *Politics Review*, Vol. 2, No. 3, February 1993.

Budge & McKay (1993) Budge, I. & McKay, D. (eds), *The Developing Political System: the 1990s*, Longman, 1993.

Butler & Kavanagh (1992) Butler, D. & Kavanagh, D., *The British General Election 1992*, Macmillan, 1992.

Crewe (1993) Crewe, I., 'Parties and electors' in *Budge & McKay (1993).*

Critchley (1989) Critchley, J., *Palace of Varieties,* John Murray, 1989.

Geddes et al. (1991) Geddes, A., Lovenduski, J. & Norris, P. (1991) 'Candidate Selection', *Contemporary Record*, April 1991.

Jones (1994) Jones, B., 'The unknown government: government by quango', *Talking Politics,* Vol.6, No.2, winter 1994.

King (1981) King, A., 'The rise of the career politician in Britain - and its consequences', *British Journal of Political Science*, Vol. 11, 1981.

Kingdom (1991) Kingdom, J., *Local Government and Politics in Britain*, Philip Allan, 1991.

Labour Party (1993) , *Labour Party Rule Book 1993-4*, Labour Party, 1993.

LWN (1993) *Labour Women's Network Newsletter 15*, winter 1993-4.

Norris & Lovenduski (1989) Norris, P. & Lovenduski, J., 'Pathways to Parliament', *Talking Politics*, Vol.1 No.3, summer 1989.

Norris & Lovenduski (1995) Norris P. & Lovenduski J., *Political Recruitment: Gender, Race and Class in the British Parliament*, Cambridge University Press, 1995.

Norton (1994) Norton, P., 'A 'new breed' of MP?', *Politics Review*, Vol. 3, No.3, February 1994.

Robins (1987) Robins L. (ed.), *Political Institutions in Britain,* Longman, 1987.

Rush (1987) Rush, M., 'The selectorate revisited.' in *Robins (1987).*

Rush (1990) Rush, M., *Parliament and Pressure Politics*, Oxford University Press, 1990.

Sewell (1993) Sewell, T., *Black Tribunes: Black Political Participation in Britain*, Lawrence & Wishart, 1993.

TSRB (1987) Top Salaries Review Body, *Report No.24*, HMSO, 1987.

Vallence (1988) Vallence, E., 'The job of a backbencher', *Contemporary Record*, Vol. 2, No. 3, 1988.

Vandermark (1994) Vandermark, A., 'Lobbying and registration: biting the bullet or shifting the focus?', *Talking Politics*, Vol. 7, No. 2, autumn 1994.

Weir & Hall (1994) Weir, S. & Hall, W., *Ego Trip*, Democratic Audit, The Charter 88 Trust, 1994.

Widdicombe (1986) Widdicombe, D., *The Conduct of Local Authority Business*, Cmnd 9797, HMSO, 1986.

Whiteley et al. (1994) Whiteley, P., Seyd, P. & Richardson, J., *True Blues: the Politics of Conservative Party Membership*, Oxford University Press, 1994.

Wood & Crawley (1987) Wood, T. & Crawley, G., 'Equal access to political power - a principle in danger', *Local Government Chronicle*, 21 August 1987.

Wood & Wood (1992) Wood, A.H. & Wood, R. (eds), *The Times Guide to the House of Commons 1992*, Times Books, 1992.

Part 4

Decision making

12 Prime Minister and Cabinet

Introduction

Most people would agree that the most powerful individual in the British system of government is the Prime Minister. The exact extent of the power exercised by the Prime Minister, however, is not easy to calculate since Prime Ministers do not govern alone. Strategic policy decisions, for example, are made by the Cabinet, a group of senior ministers appointed by the Prime Minister. Since most matters of substance are discussed in the Cabinet, it is possible to argue that power is exercised collectively, by the Cabinet as a whole. On the other hand, since the Prime Minister appoints (and sacks) members of the Cabinet and since many policies are initiated outside the Cabinet, it is also possible to argue that the Cabinet has little real power.

To some extent, of course, the exact relationship between the Prime Minister and the Cabinet is determined by the personalities of those involved. A Prime Minister with a forceful, authoritarian character, for example, is less likely to listen to and take note of the views of Cabinet colleagues than a Prime Minister with a passive, cooperative character. In addition, it should be noted that power is not necessarily static. The location of power in one government may be very different from its location in another government.

This chapter looks at the role played by the Prime Minister and the Cabinet and examines the relationship between them. In particular, it considers who has the central position in decision making - the Prime Minister, the Cabinet or other groups? This is an important question since its answer may reveal a great deal about the way in which British government functions.

Chapter summary

Part 1 looks at the **role played by the Prime Minister**. What **powers** does the Prime Minister have? What limits these **powers**? How does the **leadership style** of Prime Ministers vary? Is there a need for a **Prime Minister's department**?

Part 2 considers the **role of the Cabinet**. How much **power** does the Cabinet have? What is **collective responsibility**? What is the purpose of **Cabinet committees**?

Part 3 discusses the idea of a **core executive**. What is meant by such a term? Why is it useful? Where does **power** lie within the core executive?

1 The Prime Minister

Key Issues

1. How did the post of Prime Minister develop and what is the Prime Minister's role today?
2. What are the sources and limitations of prime ministerial power?
3. How does the leadership style of different Prime Ministers vary and what impact does this make?
4. Is there a need for a Prime Minister's department?

1.1 The development of the post of Prime Minister

Following the Glorious Revolution of 1688 (see chapter 14, p.406), Parliament passed the Bill of Rights in 1689. The Bill of Rights curbed the powers of the monarch by making it illegal to raise money through taxation or to dispense or execute laws without the consent of Parliament. The monarch, however, remained the head of the executive and appointed a group of ministers (the Cabinet) to govern the country. These ministers, however, had to have the support of a majority in the House of Commons or they would be unable to pass legislation or raise taxation.

It was not until the reign of George I (1714-27) that the monarch stopped attending meetings of the Cabinet. When the monarch did stop attending Cabinet meetings, they were chaired by the First Lord of the Treasury who was later to become known as the Prime Minister. 'First Lord of the Treasury' remains one of the Prime Minister's official titles.

Historians have, traditionally, agreed that Robert Walpole, who was First Lord of the Treasury from

1721 to 1742, was Britain's first Prime Minister. But, Wilson (1977) notes that, at that time, the departments of state were still individually answerable to the monarch and, in this sense, the monarch could still be regarded as head of the executive. In addition, the term 'Prime Minister' was applied to Walpole as a term of abuse, implying that he was the monarch's favourite. It may have been true that Walpole was 'first minister' and enjoyed predominance over other heads of department, but he was not a Prime Minister in the modern sense.

By the beginning of the 19th century, William Pitt the Younger was arguing that there was:

> 'An absolute necessity...that there should be an avowed and real minister possessing the chief weight in the Council and the principal confidence of the king.' (quoted in Wilson, 1976, p.17)

It was not until 1878, however, that the term 'Prime Minister' was used in an official document for the first time (by Disraeli) and it was not until 1917 that the office was recognised for the first time in statute.

Although the term 'Prime Minister' was not established until late in the 19th century, it has been argued that the first Prime Minister, in the modern sense, was Robert Peel, who held office from 1841 to 1846. By then, it was Parliament rather than the monarch which chose the government. Wilson (1976) argues that the Great Reform Act of 1832 (see chapter 7, p.165) was the turning point since the widened franchise meant that the monarch's patronage, which was exercised through the First Lord of the Treasury, could no longer be decisive in buying seats. After 1832, the House of Commons could more legitimately claim to represent the voice of the people and, as a result, it was the Commons rather than the monarch which determined the composition of government and whether or not the government should stay in office. When the franchise was widened further in 1867, political parties became established on a national basis and elections came to be fought as much on the personality of the party leader as on the government's or the party's policies. The leader of the party with a majority in the Commons automatically became Prime Minister with the rights of appointment previously held by the Crown.

1.2 The role and powers of the Prime Minister

What role does the Prime Minister play in the British system of government and how has this role changed? Have recent Prime Ministers exercised more power than their predecessors? Would it be reasonable to say that the British Prime Minister had presidential powers? These are the questions addressed in the section which follows.

Prime ministerial duties

The role played by the Prime Minister is governed far more by convention than by law or by rules and regulations. It is, for example, by convention that the Prime Minister always sits in the House of Commons. Similarly, a number of formal duties have evolved:

> 'The Prime Minister presides over the Cabinet, is responsible for the allocation of functions among ministers and informs the Queen, at regular meetings, of the general business of the government. The Prime Minister's other responsibilities include recommending a number of appointments to the Queen. These include:
>
> - Church of England archbishops, bishops and other Church appointments;
> - senior judges, such as the Lord Chief Justice;
> - privy counsellors;
> - and, Lord Lieutenants.
>
> They also include certain civil appointments, such as...Poet Laureate, Constable of the Tower and some university posts; and appointments to various public boards and institutions, such as the BBC.' (HMSO, 1994, p.37)

The way in which particular Prime Ministers carry out the job depends to some extent on their leadership style and personality, but, as James (1992) points out, it is also likely to be significantly determined by the day-to-day events and problems facing the government and by the capabilities of and relationships with political colleagues.

Prime ministerial powers

According to the former Cabinet minister Tony Benn, the powers enjoyed by the British Prime Minister can be classified into 10 separate categories. The first of these is the power to appoint, reshuffle or dismiss ministers. Benn argues that this is the Prime Minister's most important power:

> 'The authority to appoint and dismiss ministers, without any constitutional requirement to get these changes approved by Parliament or the party, is the most decisive [power]. For, by the use, or threat of use, of this authority, all the other powers described below fall into the hands of the Prime Minister alone; to exercise as he or she thinks best.' (Benn, 1981, p.26)

The other nine categories are as follows:

2. Power to create peers.
3. Power to give out honours.
4. Power to appoint chairs of nationalised industries.
5. Power to make other appointments (eg top civil servants, ambassadors, bishops, judges).
6. Power over ministerial conduct (rules are laid out in *Questions of Procedure for Ministers* - see p.359).

7. Powers relating to government business (eg setting agenda for Cabinet meetings, setting up Cabinet committees and choosing whether or not to circulate minutes or papers).
8. Powers over information (eg deciding whether or not to inform Parliament about government activities and using lobby system to inform the media - see p.567).
9. Powers in international relations.
10. The power to terminate a Parliament or government.

Adapted from Benn, 1981.

During the late 1980s, it became increasingly common for political commentators to argue that the Prime Minister had accrued power at the expense of the Cabinet. This was not a new argument. Indeed, the classic case for this view was provided by Richard Crossman in his introduction to Bagehot's *The English Constitution*, published in the 1960s. In this introduction, Crossman traced the changes in the way in which the UK was governed between the time when the Second Reform Act was passed in 1867 to the end of the Second World War. There had, he argued, been a shift from Cabinet government to prime ministerial government which came about for two main reasons. First, the party system had developed in such a way that the party machinery had been centralised under the control of the Prime Minister. And second, the civil service had grown too large to be controlled by the Cabinet and, instead, had developed into a centralised bureaucracy with the Prime Minister ultimately in control. The combined effect of these changes, Crossman argued, was that the Prime Minister came to stand at the apex of the administrative and the political arms of government. As a result, the role played by Prime Ministers was complicated by the fact that they were both head of government and leader of the dominant party in Parliament.

In addition, other developments may suggest that the UK now has prime ministerial government. Prime Ministers are now closely involved in foreign and economic affairs. The electorate, through the mass media, is, now more than ever, encouraged to identify parties, governments and their policies with party leaders. The formal structure of Cabinet and its committees has been downgraded by the practice of 'pre-cooking' policy in informal meetings between the Prime Minister and one or two other ministers (see section 2.5 below). Business tends to flow through the Prime Minister's office at least as much as through the Cabinet Secretariat.

Presidential powers?

Some commentators have argued that the British Prime Minister is becoming 'presidential' and, as in many other areas of British political life, this development is associated with Margaret Thatcher's premiership. Johnson, for example, argued that:

> 'It is hardly exaggerating to describe Thatcher's premiership as not merely presidential, but quasi-monarchical. This is not just a matter of verbal usage - the royal "we are a grandmother" or "I as government" (both things even monarchs would blench to say), or Thatcher's habit of making policy on the hoof, or the record reduction in the number, duration and documentation of Cabinet meetings, or even the fact that, last year, for the first time, the cost of the PM's department was higher than the Queen's household. It is all these things and more: the huge devotional pictures of Thatcher at Tory meetings, her endless taking of the salute on military occasions, the overt tensions with the palace, the mother-of-the-nation act at national tragedies, and so on.' (Johnson, 1990, p.8)

In his analysis of 'presidential' politics in Britain, Foley explains that Thatcher's perceived domination of government revived interest in the traditional debate between prime ministerial and Cabinet power:

> 'In order to maximise the point of executive centralism, references were often made to the comparability of the British Prime Minister with the American Presidency. The association of the personal authority of the Prime Minister as the "focal point of the modern Cabinet" and the evident individual stature of an American President proved too close and too appealing a linkage to ignore.' (Foley, 1994, p.137)

Some writers, however, are sceptical about such a comparison. Burch (1990), for example, notes that there are practical restrictions on the Prime Minister's formal power to hire and fire ministers, there are limits on the involvement of a Prime Minister in the initiation of policy and there are constraints on the capacity of the Prime Minister to control government business. Jones (1965 and 1990) concedes that Prime Ministers can be in a powerful position, but only so long as they can carry their colleagues with them - they are only as strong as their colleagues allow them to be. The significance of this statement was underlined by the downfall of Margaret Thatcher in November 1990 (see chapter 3, section 4.1), especially as she was regarded as the most powerful postwar Prime Minister. The point is that the conventional debate about the move towards prime ministerial government or towards a presidential premiership has been based on the assumption that the power of the Prime Minister has increased whilst that of the Cabinet has declined. But, this may ignore other, perhaps wider, analytical frameworks through which the location of power might be explored (see part 3 below). Furthermore, the presidential analogy glosses over the very different constitutional position of an American President compared to a British Prime Minister. The American President, for example, has a much weaker hold on the legislature.

Nevertheless, Foley (1994) argues that some features of the American presidency can be employed to analyse some of the changes in the role of the Prime Minister which have taken place since the late 1970s. He isolates four features of the American presidency which, he claims, have been adopted by British Prime Ministers.

The first of these is **spatial leadership** - the attempts made by American Presidents to distance themselves politically from the presidency when it is expedient to do so. John Major's Citizen's Charter initiative is a good example of the way in which this idea has been adopted in the UK. By publicly criticising bureaucratic elements of government, Major gave the impression that he was on the side of the ordinary citizen, battling against oppressive bureaucracy.

Linked to this is the **cult of the outsider**. Just as Presidents Nixon, Carter, Reagan and Clinton all claimed to be outsiders (both politically and socially), and, therefore, not to have the vested interests of government insiders, this has also been the stance of Prime Ministers from Callaghan onwards. Thatcher, in particular, maintained close ties with the party rank and file and engaged in populist politics which circumvented the Whitehall machine.

Third, American Presidents have increasingly appealed for support directly to the public over the heads of Congress:

> 'Presidents exploit the individuality of office to project themselves as the focal embodiments of popular concern and the public interest.' (Foley, 1994, p.139)

Foley describes this as **public leadership** and argues that British political leadership has developed in a similar way:

> 'With the emergence of a much less hierarchical social order and with the establishment of television as the primary medium of news information and political exchange, a leader's relationship with the public is now central and decisive.' (Foley, 1994, p.139)

Linked to this is reliance on the **personal factor**. As in the USA, an integrated image of a party and its programme is being routed through its leader. In this way, differences between parties tend to become personalised. It is assumed that the personal qualities of the Prime Minister and other party leaders are central to public evaluations of political leadership and performance.

Together, Foley argues, these developments have resulted in a new kind of British Prime Ministership. He concludes that:

> 'Given the scale, depth and implications of these largely unacknowledged changes, it is no exaggeration to declare that, British premiership has to all intents and purposes turned not into a British version of the American presidency, but into an authentically British presidency.' (Foley, 1994, p.141)

Activity 12.1

Item A *A Prime Minister's diary*

1975	
Audiences with the Queen	8
Cabinet meetings	11
Cabinet committees	24
Other ministerial meetings	43
State visits	1
Other head of government visits	5
Other foreign VIP visits	8
Visits abroad	2
Visits to Northern Ireland	1
Meetings with industry, prominent industrialists, etc	28
Official meetings	27
Ministerial speeches	17
Political speeches	9
Visits within Britain	13
Official lunches and dinners	20
Political meetings - no speech	11
TV or radio broadcasts	8

This diagram shows an analysis of Harold Wilson's diary for the last three months of 1975. Wilson noted that, apart from Christmas day, he was not able to record a single private or social engagement.

Adapted from Wilson, 1976.

Item B *Constraints on the Prime Minister (1)*

In 1990, Martin Burch argued that the idea of prime ministerial government can easily be overstated. In reality, he claimed, there are a number of constraints on the Prime Minister. First, ministerial appointments have to be made with some recognition of the need for political balance and administrative competence. The Prime Minister may be under pressure (from colleagues or the media) to appoint certain people to the Cabinet. All Prime Ministers at least listen to advice from senior colleagues before making appointments. Second, the Prime Minister's ability to control the flow of business is restricted. Much is determined by the pressure of business flowing through the Cabinet. It would simply be impractical for a Prime Minister to intervene constantly in the drawing up of agendas or the composition of Cabinet minutes. Third, apart from the drawing up of the party manifesto, most Prime Ministers have taken a limited part in the initiation of policy. In part, this is because they have a small staff. It is also due to the fact that most expertise and detailed information is located in individual departments and it is difficult for Prime Ministers to interfere constantly in the work of a department. According to Burch, the main point is this: it is simply beyond the ability of a single person, no matter how self-assured or single-minded, to be everywhere and to know everything.

Adapted from Burch, 1990.

Item C *Constraints on the Prime Minister (2)*

In 1994, Martin Burch returned to the subject of prime ministerial power and made a comparison between the premierships of Margaret Thatcher and John Major. Major, he argued, had made much less use of the powers of direction and management vested in his office. For example, Major was much more reluctant to hire and fire ministers than Thatcher. While Thatcher's Cabinet had a large turnover, Major sacked very few ministers and those he did sack were often dismissed with reluctance and in response to outside pressure. Burch argued that Major could be described as a 'constrained' Prime Minister and that the sources of this constraint were political and economic. The political constraints are derived from the ideological divisions in the Conservative party (divisions which are very deep and are found at all levels, including Cabinet level). As a result of these divisions, the parliamentary party is difficult to manage, especially as the government has a small and dwindling majority. The economic constraints are derived from the overheating of the economy which took place in the late 1980s. This made severe deflation necessary, with the result that, for its first three years, the Major government was operating in the worst economic recession since 1945. Economic downturn leads to falling popularity which, in turn, exacerbates the political constraints.

Adapted from Burch, 1994.

Item D *A presidential Prime Minister?*

Questions

1. 'The office of Prime Minister has long been overrated.' In what ways and to what extent are the powers of the Prime Minister limited? Use Items A-C in your answer.
2. Using Items B and C explain why there is much more to the role played by Prime Ministers than the performance of their formal duties.
3. Does the British Prime Minister have presidential powers? Use Item D in your answer.

1.3 Prime ministerial styles

As Norton (1987) has noted, the formal powers of a Prime Minister are a necessary, but not a sufficient, condition for the effective application of prime ministerial power. Other variables come into play - such as the political circumstances of the time and relationships with Cabinet colleagues. How these variables are handled depends to some extent upon the political skills and personality of the Prime Minister. It depends, in other words, on the style of leadership which the Prime Minister chooses to adopt.

Most commentators would agree that prime ministerial style is important, but to what extent does it account for the variations in the role which Prime Ministers play in the policy making process? Although there have been studies of the style adopted by individual Prime Ministers (for example, King (1985a) examines the style of Margaret Thatcher), the subject has not been examined systematically. Burch (1994) suggests that attempts to analyse prime ministerial power and style purely in terms of the personality types of those who hold the office are severely limited. There is no single, generally accepted method of classifying personalities and few political analysts, commentators or psychologists are sufficiently close to a Prime Minister to be able to build up an accurate personality profile. This limitation is all the stronger since during the time Prime Ministers are in office, personal aspects and characteristics are filtered through, and probably distorted by, the party image makers and organs of the mass media.

Norton's fourfold typology of prime ministerial style

Despite the drawbacks mentioned above, Norton

(1987) argues that it is possible to classify Prime Ministers according to a fourfold typology. He argues that different Prime Ministers seek or end up in office for different reasons and these different reasons then have a bearing on how they behave in office. The four categories he suggests are: innovators, reformers, egoists and balancers.

Innovators seek power in order to achieve some future goal (they are, in other words, ideologically motivated). They are prepared to risk unpopularity in order to achieve that goal. The goal is not necessarily formulated and agreed by their party. It bears the personal imprint of the innovator.

Reformers also seek power in order to achieve some future goal (they are also ideologically motivated). But, this goal has been previously formulated and agreed by their party. The goal does not necessarily bear their personal imprint.

Egoists seek power simply in order to exercise and retain power. They are, in other words, motivated by self-regard, not by ideology. Since their main aim is to retain power for themselves, they are principally concerned with the present and not with some future goal.

Balancers seek power to ensure that peace and stability are maintained - both within their party and within society as a whole. Balancers fall into two subcategories - those who actively seek office and those who do not. Those who do not actively seek office tend to be compromise candidates in leadership elections. Norton describes them as 'conscripts'.

Whilst Norton's four categories are not mutually exclusive, he argues that their value is that all Prime Ministers exhibit a preponderance of characteristics of a particular type. For example, he describes Margaret Thatcher as an innovator, citing her address to the 1979 Conservative conference when she said:

> 'We have to move this country in a new direction - to change the way we look at things, to create a wholly new attitude of mind.'

Thatcher had a radical vision and she was prepared to lead from the front, hoping that her party would follow. In this, she was very different from other radical Prime Ministers. Norton contrasts Thatcher's style with that of the postwar Labour Prime Minister Clement Attlee. Like Thatcher, Attlee had a radical vision, but he was careful to ensure that he had the backing of the party before agreeing on a course of action.

Norton is careful to point out that this typology must be used carefully. He emphasises in particular two qualifications. First, Prime Ministers cannot be rigorously 'boxed' - an individual may straddle two or more types. And second, even though most individuals do fall preponderantly within a category, there is no rule that they must remain there. Norton describes Churchill, for example, as an innovator in wartime and a balancer in peacetime.

Despite these qualifications, Norton claims that his typology provides a focus for enquiry. By looking at 'purpose' (the reason why Prime Ministers seek power), it is possible to go beyond a study of prime ministerial powers themselves and towards an examination of the 'why of prime ministerial power' (Norton, 1987, p.345).

Political skills

Most analyses of prime ministerial styles, however, have focused on the political skills required by Prime Ministers and the effectiveness with which different Prime Ministers have selected and applied such skills. In the article mentioned above, for example, Norton (1987) identifies a number of skills which a Prime Minister may need, depending on political circumstances.

First, at a general level, Prime Ministers need to develop the skill of 'impression management'. They need to give the appearance that they are suited to the role of Prime Minister. Second, they should have and sustain a 'feel for the office' - an intuitive grasp of when to deploy and when not to deploy the specific skills that they need in order to achieve their purpose in office. Third, they need to know when to lead and when to react. To do this, a successful Prime Minister knows when to command, when to persuade, when to manipulate and when to 'hide' (to keep a distance from a crisis).

Margaret Thatcher's style of leadership

The idea that Britain had prime ministerial government gained support in the 1980s because of Margaret Thatcher's style of leadership. In particular, Thatcher gained the reputation of being a Prime Minister with a dominant personality (see chapter 3, part 2). She described herself as follows:

> 'I'm not a consensus politician or a pragmatic politician: I'm a conviction politician. And I believe in the politics of persuasion: it's my job to put forward what I believe and try to get people to agree with me.' (Interview in the *Observer*, 25 February 1979)

As such, she appeared to meet with some success in pushing through innovative policies in the face of some opposition from members of her government and party.

In terms of political skills, Thatcher seems to have deployed a number of those identified by Norton above. Certainly she knew how to 'hide'. King (1985a), for example, notes that she sometimes distanced herself from her own government by referring to it as 'they' rather than the more usual 'we'. In addition, she was, generally, effective in getting her own way when the government appeared to be enjoying popular support, though the reverse applied when popular support ebbed, as it did on a number of occasions between general elections. This suggests that Burch was right to state that:

> 'While Prime Ministers may increasingly be given more of the credit for the success of a government, they must also take more of the blame for its failure.' (Burch, 1985, p.356)

John Major's style of leadership

Every Prime Minister brings their own style to the job or develops it during the course of their premiership. Since this is the case, there is no reason to assume that any radical alterations in the way in which one Prime Minister carries out the role will have an impact beyond the term in which that individual holds office. Thatcher's style was very different from that of her immediate predecessors, but did the job of Prime Minister change as a result of that? Have any of the innovations made by Thatcher been institutionalised or, at least, did her successor John Major attempt to emulate elements of her style or to incorporate her skills into his way of working?

As early as 1985, King pointed to the possibility that future Prime Ministers might follow Thatcher's example:

> 'We now know what we did not before: that the job of Prime Minister can be done in Thatcher's way. The repertory of available styles has been extended.' (King, 1985a, p.137)

The circumstances of Thatcher's downfall (see chapter 3, section 4.1), however, dictated that Major needed to adopt a different style. It is no surprise, therefore, that Major's first months as Prime Minister were characterised by consensus-seeking and a less strident, less decisive and more pragmatic approach than that exhibited by his predecessor. At the time of the 1992 general election, Major was described in the newspapers as 'honest John' whose government had shown the 'caring face of capitalism'. The contrast with the style of Thatcher was quite deliberate.

Yet, on an organisational level, Major did formalise some of the practices introduced or developed by his predecessor. For example, according to Burch (1994), Major introduced a 'political' session after most Cabinet meetings (a meeting of Cabinet ministers and other senior party members without the presence of civil servants). Meetings like this had been held informally under Thatcher, but under Major they became a regular event. In addition, when Major became Prime Minister, the chief whip, Leaders of both Houses and the party chairman met the Prime Minister regularly at the beginning of each week to review the political and parliamentary developments expected in the week ahead. This way of bringing party management more closely into the formal structure of the Cabinet system had been practised by Thatcher, but in a less formal way.

It can also be argued that in terms of policy direction and executive action, there has been little change under Major. Thain (1993), for example, argues that the moves towards the privatisation of public services and the infusion of private sector ideas and techniques into the remaining areas of the public sector indicate that changes under Major have been a matter of style rather than substance.

The impact of prime ministerial style on decision making

Any examination of variation in styles should not be taken in isolation from the political structures and the political context within which Prime Ministers operate. Margaret Thatcher's downfall demonstrates the need for Prime Ministers to maintain the support of their Cabinet colleagues. It is partly this requirement which leads King (1985b) to argue that, although British Prime Ministers are often described as political 'leaders', most, in fact, rarely lead. It is, in other words, not often that Prime Ministers make decisions entirely on their own and not often that they are able to steer Cabinet colleagues in directions that they do not want to take. This observation suggests that the power of Prime Ministers to make an impact on decision making is limited.

Activity 12.2

Item A *Margaret Thatcher's style (1)*

In 1985, Anthony King argued that Margaret Thatcher's prime ministerial style was very different from that of her predecessors. She was very much an activist who was in politics not 'to be' but 'to do'. Since she was elected Conservative leader not because of her economic views, but despite them, she had to lead from the front if she was to achieve her goals. In part, this was a matter of personality. But, it was also a reflection of the political situation in which she found herself. She was forced to act as an outsider because she was an outsider. The style she adopted can be seen most clearly in her dealings with the Cabinet. According to King, most Prime Ministers play a waiting game, only intervening in a discussion at a fairly late stage. Their aim in acting this way is to see whether a consensus emerges. If it does, then that usually settles the matter. If there is no consensus, then the Prime Minister's intervention may sway feelings one way or another. Thatcher's style, however, was very different. She stated her views at the outset, often thought aloud and interrupted ministers with whom she disagreed. In other words, she did not simply chair Cabinet meetings, she actively participated in them and often dominated them. The result was twofold. On the one hand, she got her own way more often than is normally the case with Prime Ministers. On the other hand, she was sometimes defeated in the Cabinet and was seen to be defeated.

Adapted from King, 1985a.

Item B *Margaret Thatcher and John Major compared*

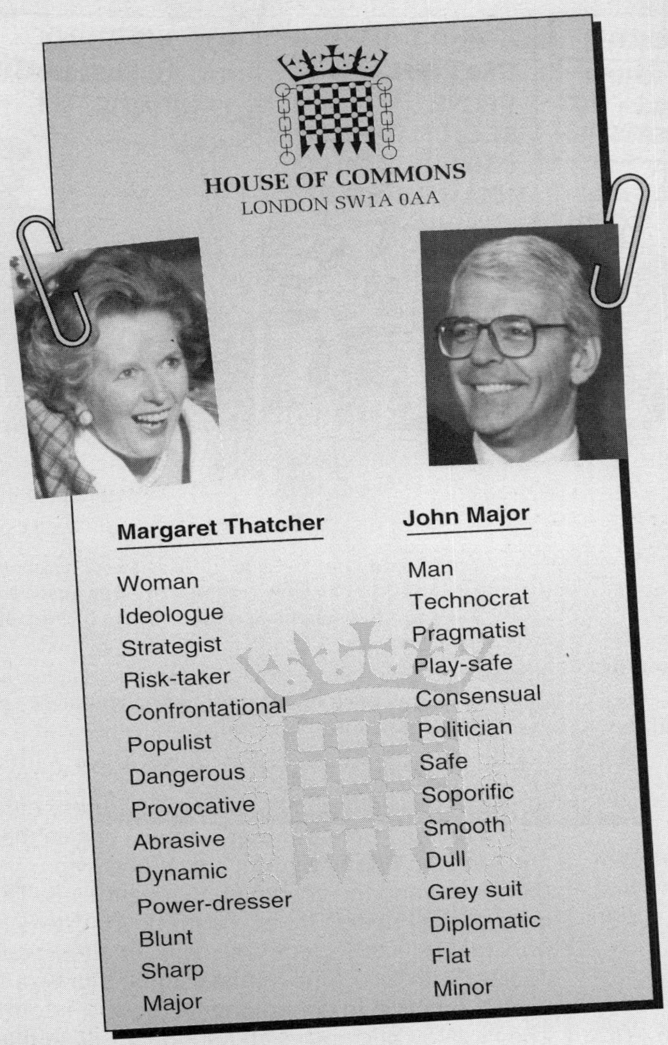

HOUSE OF COMMONS
LONDON SW1A 0AA
Margaret Thatcher
Woman
Ideologue
Strategist
Risk-taker
Confrontational
Populist
Dangerous
Provocative
Abrasive
Dynamic
Power-dresser
Blunt
Sharp
Major
John Major
Man
Technocrat
Pragmatist
Play-safe
Consensual
Politician
Safe
Soporific
Smooth
Dull
Grey suit
Diplomatic
Flat
Minor

Item C *John Major's style (1)*

In an article written in April 1994, Hugo Young argued that whilst John Major's prime ministerial style was a source of strength when he was first elected, by 1994 it had become a source of weakness. Major's rise to power, Young claimed, was due to his ability to soothe very many and enrage very few members of his party. He did this by being neither opinionated nor autocratic. He gave the impression that he was prepared to listen and to proceed by consensus. Whilst this was just the contrast that was needed in 1990, by 1994 it had come to be seen as weak leadership personified. By then, it seemed that Major's attempts to subcontract decision making to the Cabinet were evidence of his indecisive nature. Hence the frequent complaints that Major lacks charisma. As an example of the problems created by Major's style of leadership, Young cites Major's stand against the EU (and subsequent backdown) over the qualified voting majority. At no point was Major prepared to describe his own position on the matter. He refused to take a stand and lead from the front. Rather, the Foreign Secretary was sent to the Commons to say that he could not give his opinion until the Cabinet had met. This, says Young, is collegiate leadership at its worst - the leader invites others to push him and the views of those who push hardest prevail.

Adapted from the *Guardian*, 29 April 1994.

Item D *Margaret Thatcher's style (2)*

Changing the orchestra won't affect the tune - they're only there for appearances.

This cartoon was published in the *Guardian* on 26 July 1989.

Item E *John Major's style (2)*

This cartoon appeared in the *Guardian* in November 1992.

Questions

1. a) Judging from Items A-E how do the prime ministerial styles of Margaret Thatcher and John Major differ?
   b) To what extent would you say that a difference in style means a difference in substance? Give reasons for your answer.
2. a) Using Norton's typology of prime ministerial styles, how would you describe (i) MargaretThatcher and (ii) John Major? Give reasons for your answer.
   b) What are the benefits and drawbacks of Norton's typology?
3. Compared to other factors affecting the exercise of power, how much importance would you place on the question of prime ministerial style?

1.4 Prime Minister's staff

There is no Prime Minister's department. Unlike most ministers in the Cabinet, Prime Ministers do not have their own ministry to run. There is, however, a Prime Minister's Office. This Office includes political appointees and advisers (some of whom are employed as 'temporary civil servants') as well as permanent civil servants. All are there, primarily, to serve the Prime Minister. In June 1995, according to the Prime Minister's Press Office, the total number of staff working in the Prime Minister's Office was 35. By contrast, the Department of Employment employed 52,408 civil servants in 1993 and even a small government department like the Department of National Heritage employed 965 civil servants. Similarly, Blondel (1993) notes that the American President has a staff of 400 and the German Chancellor a staff of 450.

Since 1974, there have been at least four identifiable functional groups within the Prime Minister's Office. Although, in practice, the dividing lines between their respective functions are not always clear-cut, these groups are: the Prime Minister's Private Office, the Political Office, the Press Office and the Policy Unit. In addition, Prime Ministers sometimes make use of external advisers.

The Private Office

The Prime Minister's Private Office is staffed by permanent civil servants 'on loan' from other government departments. In June 1995, seven civil servants worked in the Private Office. These officials deal with the Prime Minister's official engagements and with the Prime Minister's relations with Parliament and the government departments. The head of the Private Office, the Prime Minister's principal private secretary, remains in almost constant contact with the Prime Minister and performs a central function in controlling the flow of information. The Private Office plays an important role in filtering the mass of information which converges on the Prime Minister's Office from all branches of the Cabinet system, including all the government departments. If its job is done properly, the Prime Minister should have sight of all important policy initiatives at an early stage in their development. Such knowledge should, therefore, aid the potentially powerful position of the Prime Minister at the centre of the government apparatus.

The Political Office

The Prime Minister's Political Office often contains young politicians who later progress to ministerial careers. For example, Nigel Lawson worked in the Political Office when Alec Douglas Home was Prime Minister (1963-64) and Douglas Hurd worked in the Political Office when Edward Heath was Prime Minister (1970-74). In June 1995, four members of staff worked in the Political Office - two officers and two support staff.

The main function of the Office is party liaison. It deals with the Prime Minister's party and constituency affairs and is, therefore, in close contact with the headquarters of the party in power as well as with the party's supporters and MPs. The office also assists with the Prime Minister's speeches and offers general advice of a political nature. According to James (1992), however, such advice is frequently ignored and the Political Office has little influence on policy.

The Press Office

The Prime Minister's Press Office looks after the Prime Minister's relations with the media. During Margaret Thatcher's premiership, Bernard Ingham, the press secretary, gave the Press Office a formidable 'up-front' role - particularly in his handling of lobby correspondents (see chapter 19, pp.567-68). With the occasional exception (such as Harold Wilson's press secretary Joe Haines who is said to have exercised considerable influence over incomes policy in the mid-1970s), the staff of the Press Office are more likely to affect the presentation rather than the content of policy. In June 1995, six press officers and four support staff worked in the Press Office.

The Policy Unit

The most recent addition to the Prime Minister's Office is the Policy Unit. Created by Harold Wilson in 1974, it has been used by Prime Ministers ever since. The Unit is usually made up of outside specialists taken on as temporary civil servants, though Margaret Thatcher brought in officials from government departments. A complete change of staff occurs with each new Prime Minister. In June 1995, nine policy advisers and five support staff worked in the Policy Unit. The function of the Policy Unit is to advise the Prime Minister on particular aspects of government policy - mainly to provide medium and long-term forward policy analysis, but also to provide more immediate policy advice, if required.

The Policy Unit can strengthen Prime Ministers in their dealings with other ministers because it is somewhat distanced from the civil service machine (which operates on a departmental basis, providing advice to individual government ministers). As a result, it can provide Prime Ministers with an alternative source of policy advice. According to James, the job of the Policy Unit under John Major has been:

> 'To alert the Prime Minister to dangers, drawbacks and omissions in departments' policies and to give him the ammunition to argue back effectively.' (James, 1992, p.230)

The Unit has also put forward its own policy initiatives, sometimes promoting ideas from outside specialist advisers, from think tanks and from other countries. James (1992) notes, for example, that the notion of an 'internal market' for the NHS was apparently suggested to Prime Minister Thatcher by her head of the Policy Unit, John Redwood. His suggestion was, in turn, based on an idea proposed by an American academic.

Although Prime Ministers often reject Policy Unit advice, acceptance of an idea by the Prime Minister means that government ministers and their departments can sometimes be persuaded to develop an initiative made by the Unit.

Burch (1994) reports that under John Major the Policy Unit has taken a less proactive direction. It has not been so concerned with policy initiatives or even with the close monitoring of departmental developments. Rather, its job has been to provide advice directly to the Prime Minister. Nonetheless, it is a measure of the Unit's continued importance that Major allocated it a significant role in the writing of the Conservative manifesto for the 1992 general election.

Political advisers

Prime Ministers sometimes appoint political advisers on specific policy areas who are not placed formally in one of the four groups in the Prime Minister's Office mentioned above. Although she did not initiate this practice, Margaret Thatcher made considerable use of specialist advisers. Most famously, she appointed Professor Alan Walters as her economic adviser (policy differences between Walters and Nigel Lawson, the Chancellor, were a major factor in Lawson's decision to resign in 1989 - see chapter 3, p.58). Thatcher also appointed specialist advisers for foreign affairs and defence. In addition, she took advice from external bodies, such as the Centre for Policy Studies, and she used public relations specialists and speech writers to assist with her own image presentation. These moves, combined with the abolition of the Central Policy Review Staff (see chapter 10, p.285), strengthened the office of Prime Minister at the expense of the Cabinet.

A Prime Minister's department?

Although John Major seems to rely less on external advisers than his predecessor did, it is doubtful whether the Cabinet has retrieved the full extent of the power once attributed to it. Major, for example, significantly increased the number of staff employed in the Prime Minister's Office. There is even the argument that, taken together, the Prime Minister's Office and the Cabinet Office (the civil service department in charge of administrative and secretarial work within the Cabinet system) now constitute a formidable alternative power base to that of the Cabinet. Bearing in mind that the Prime Minister and the Cabinet Secretary (the head of the Cabinet Office) have a close working relationship, this implies that in effect, if not in name, a Prime Minister's department has emerged.

Against this, however, is the view that most Cabinet ministers have the administrative support of vast government departments and receive advice from their senior permanent officials. The sources of advice and support to a Prime Minister, on the other hand, are more transitory and more difficult to control. For these and other reasons (see Item A in Activity 12.3 below), it is still sometimes suggested that Prime Ministers need their own department of state.

Activity 12.3

Item A *The case for a Prime Minister's department*

In 1980, Kenneth Berrill, a former head of the Central Policy Review Staff, gave a lecture in which he argued in favour of a Prime Minister's department. His central argument in this lecture was that the powers and duties of the Prime Minister have grown and will continue to do so. As a result, it is necessary for the Prime Minister to have an adequate support system. Prime Ministers, after all, may have to intervene in any field at any time. They have to be able to strike a balance between departmental and wider strategic objectives. They have to be able to provide Parliament and the media with a ready answer to almost any aspect of government action. And, the globalisation of political affairs means that modern Prime Ministers need to be well briefed on issues in their international context. Yet, despite these growing pressures, the Prime Minister's Office remains very small compared to the departments at the disposal of Prime Ministers in other countries with a similar political system to that in Britain. British Prime Ministers, Berrill concluded, need an advice system of their own and one which has the time and the personnel to provide advice based on knowledge and study at a reasonable depth across the range of government activities. This could only be provided by a department set up to serve the Prime Minister.

Adapted from Berrill, 1985.

Item B *The case against a Prime Minister's department*

In an article published in 1980, Professor George Jones argued against the setting up of a Prime Minister's department. His main argument was that a Prime Minister's department would be a revolution in the constitution, a move from a ministerial and Cabinet system to prime ministerial government. Yet, he argued, the existence of such a department might weaken the powers of the Prime Minister because what Prime Ministers need are flexible arrangements rather than a rigid bureaucratic structure. Jones notes that, over the years, the basic structure of the Prime Minister's Office at Number 10 Downing Street has adapted easily to what Prime Ministers have required. The current system is responsive to the political control and direction taken by the Prime Minister. If it became a bureaucratic structure, it would develop a momentum of its own, have a view of its own and put to the Prime Minister a certain line. In addition, a strength of the current system is its ability to prevent the emergence of one person who has the Prime Minister's ear. Under the current system, there is a group of people who are in constant daily touch with the Prime Minister. In the early 1980s, this group numbered about nine. The Prime Minister was, therefore, able to pick and choose between these nine or so people and to counterbalance one view against another. A further argument against a department is that it would generate a large amount of paperwork. The Prime Minister would find it difficult to keep on top of this paperwork. Far better is the current informal system which allows the Prime Minister to keep abreast of events by having a word here, a chat there or dropping in for drinks at the end of the day.

Adapted from Jones, 1980.

Item C *The schools inspection service*

IT'S JUNK MAIL. INSURANCE, DOUBLE-GLAZING, SCHOOL INSPECTORS....

Evidence has emerged that the Education Secretary Kenneth Clarke's review of the 152 year old schools inspectorate was ambushed by the Prime Minister's Office with the result that the reduction in the inspectorate's activities went further than originally planned. Lobbying by the Centre for Policy Studies, a right wing think tank, for the complete privatisation of the service was met with scepticism by ministers in the Department of Science and Education, but was backed by prime ministerial advisers. As a result, Kenneth Clarke was forced to cut the number of inspectors from 480 to 175 and the inspectorate will lose most of its traditional role in inspecting individual schools and advising ministers on trends in the service. Instead, schools will be obliged to employ independent teams, including lay members such as parents or local businessmen, to carry out inspections. Everybody will be able to apply to work as a school inspector. The government will supply successful applicants with the necessary training.

Adapted from the *Guardian*, 3 October 1991.

Questions

1. 'The establishment of a Prime Minister's department is unnecessary.' Using Items A and B give arguments for and against this view.
2. How would the establishment of a Prime Minister's department affect the way in which Prime Ministers do their job?
3. a) What does Item C tell us about the location of power in the executive?
   b) Would the Education Secretary's position have been strengthened or weakened by the existence of a Prime Minister's department? Explain your answer.

2 The Cabinet

Key Issues
1. What role is played by the Cabinet?
2. What is 'collective responsibility' and how does it work?
3. What role is played by Cabinet committees?

2.1 The Cabinet

The element of the executive now known as the Cabinet first emerged at the end of the 17th century, following the curbing of the powers of the monarch after the Glorious Revolution. After the Bill of Rights was passed in 1689, the monarch at first remained at the centre of the executive:

> 'To enable the Sovereign and Parliament to work together to carry on the government of the country, a group of ministers, or Cabinet, became the link between the executive and the legislature. Although the ministers were appointed by the Sovereign, they had to have sufficient support in the House of Commons to enable them to persuade Parliament to pass legislation and vote for taxation.' (HMSO, 1994, p.3)

From the reign of George I, however, the monarch ceased to attend meetings of the Cabinet. Instead, the Cabinet was chaired by the First Lord of the Treasury, later known as the Prime Minister. The Cabinet developed into its modern form during the 19th century when the extension of the franchise and the evolution of the party system resulted in governments (and hence the Cabinet) relying on the support of the House of Commons. From this requirement grew the convention of collective responsibility (see below, section 2.2).

The role played by the Cabinet

Although the Cabinet may have developed into its modern form in the 19th century, the role played by the Cabinet then was very different from that which it plays today. James notes that:

> 'Many studies explore the Cabinet's genesis and evolution in past centuries. This can be unhelpful and even misleading. The post-1945 Cabinet is very different from its ancestors... [After the Second World War], the character of Cabinet government changed markedly. The volume of work grew enormously, this work became complex and detailed, and departments' problems became more closely interrelated, particularly in the economic and social fields. Ministerial life became frantic and high-pressured...A huge network of Cabinet committees developed to cope with the load. It became less easy for the Cabinet to exercise full control over the government's main policies. Inevitably, the Cabinet's role was eroded.' (James, 1992, p.2)

Despite this, the Cabinet is still typically seen as one of the central institutions of the British political system. Although its methods of operating have changed over time, the Cabinet is normally portrayed as occupying the apex of the executive arm of government. The Cabinet's functions have been described as follows:

> 'The functions of the Cabinet are policy making, the supreme control of government and the coordination of government departments.' (HMSO, 1994, p.39)

The Cabinet, therefore, has a dual role - to propose legislation and to supervise administration. Full meetings of the Cabinet, however, take place only once or twice a week and usually last for only a couple of hours. It is simply not feasible for the full Cabinet, therefore, to carry out detailed policy making over all areas covered by government policy.

In any case, the Cabinet's dual role rests upon the party system. Elections are party contests. The outcome of elections determines the party balance in the House of Commons and, therefore, which party (or parties, if there is a coalition) forms the government. In so far as the government then has a mandate to implement party policy as presented in its election manifesto, the Cabinet's policy making role clearly has a party political dimension. The Cabinet also depends on party support in the House of Commons for its continued existence.

The size and structure of the Cabinet

In the period since 1945, Cabinets have, generally, consisted of around 20 ministers, chaired by the Prime Minister. Most Cabinet ministers are responsible for particular government departments. Since they are expected to explain and defend their policies in Parliament, most Cabinet ministers are MPs, though a few sit in the House of Lords. Outsiders may be appointed to the Cabinet, but they would normally be made a peer or would be expected to fight and to win a by-election. For example, the businessman David Young was made a life peer when he was appointed as Employment Secretary under Margaret Thatcher, whilst the trade unionist Frank Cousins fought and won a by-election in 1964 after being appointed Minister for Technology.

The structure and size of the Cabinet, therefore, are prime ministerial decisions. But the fact that the number of Cabinet ministers at any one time has varied so little since 1945 suggests that there are practical limitations on prime ministerial discretion.

Certain departments, because of their centrality to

key areas of government policy, are now always represented - the Treasury, Home Office and Foreign Office, for example. The fact that the ministers representing these three departments are usually placed at the top of the list published when a new Cabinet is formed suggests that there is a hierarchy within the Cabinet. But, the order of ministers in the hierarchy is not fixed. The exact positioning in the list is likely to reflect the relative political status of the holder of the post as well as the post itself. Ministers new to the Cabinet are normally first appointed to junior positions within the hierarchy.

The Prime Minister's choice of Cabinet ministers may be influenced by the expectations of the parliamentary party, though this constraint is often exaggerated. There are numerous examples of senior party figures who have been left out of Cabinets. The former Prime Minister, Edward Heath, for example, never served in a Cabinet under Margaret Thatcher or John Major.

Is the Cabinet too big?

It has been suggested that a Cabinet of 20 or more members is too large a decision making body to operate effectively. Also, it has been argued that if most of the Cabinet's members have departmental responsibilities, there is a danger that departmental concerns, rather than overall matters of policy planning, tend to dominate proceedings. As a result, it is sometimes argued that a much smaller Cabinet, composed of perhaps six to eight ministers who have no departmental responsibilities, would be more effective. Members of such a Cabinet would be free from the administrative workload current heads of departments have to undertake and would, therefore, be able to give their full-time attention to overall matters of policy planning and its coordination.

Experiments this century with much smaller Cabinets have largely been confined to the emergency conditions of wartime. During the second half of the First World War, for example, Lloyd George headed a Cabinet that varied in size from five to nine members. Similarly, in 1940, Churchill's War Cabinet initially contained only five members, though it was soon expanded to eight. Churchill's experiment with 'overlords' (coordinating ministers) in 1951 reduced the size of the Cabinet to 16, but within two years it had grown to 19 and the experiment was abandoned.

Those who argue against the idea of small Cabinets say that it is based on the false assumption that policy and administration can be separated. They claim that the two are closely enmeshed, with the details of policy merging with matters of administration so that it is not practical to exclude heads of major government departments from the Cabinet. Attempts to separate policy making from administration could also interfere with the principle of individual ministerial responsibility (see chapter 13, section 1.4) - which minister would be answerable to Parliament for which matter might become less clear.

Whatever the validity of the arguments for and against smaller or larger Cabinets, the fact remains that, for most of the 20th century, Prime Ministers have looked to other ways to facilitate coordination or otherwise improve the efficiency of the decision making process. Rather than focusing on Cabinet size, they have, for example, sought to expand the Cabinet Secretariat (see below, section 2.4), amalgamated government departments (or, on occasions, split them) and made greater use of Cabinet committees (see below, section 2.3).

Reshuffles

From time to time, Prime Ministers reshuffle their Cabinets. This may be necessitated by a death, illness or resignation from government. In such cases, the changes may be slight, involving only one or two alterations to the team. Alternatively, the Prime Minister may wish to alter the balance of views reflecting different sections or wings of the parliamentary party, or to discourage the formation of alternative power bases. In such cases, new members may be appointed, with some Cabinet ministers being promoted, moved sideways or dropped. In the biggest reshuffle of recent times, Harold Macmillan sacked a third of his Cabinet in a single reshuffle in 1962. This reshuffle became known as the 'night of the long knives' after Hitler's purge of the SA (the military wing of the Nazi party) in 1934.

The place of the Cabinet within the government structure

The Cabinet does not operate in isolation. It forms part of a wider system involving a large number of Cabinet committees and government departments. The work of the Cabinet is supported by the Cabinet Office which is staffed by civil servants, headed by the Secretary to the Cabinet (see below, section 2.4).

This broader 'Cabinet system' functions within a political environment in which pressure is constantly exerted from Parliament, political parties, the media, interest groups and a whole series of central and local government agencies.

Where does power lie?

It is one thing to identify the key formal elements and wider context of the Cabinet system. It is another to examine and evaluate its operation. As Burch (1990a) has observed, this is subject to great variety. Cabinet government can operate in a number of ways, depending on:

1. The approach of the particular Prime Minister.

2. The complexion of government.
3. The nature of the policy issues under consideration.
4. The prevailing political circumstances.

These and other factors need to be taken into account when dealing with the question of where power lies within the Cabinet system.

The traditional view is that the Cabinet is the seat of power in terms of policy initiation and decision making. It is not just that the Cabinet decides all important issues, it also coordinates and controls government policy as a whole. In this way, it plans overall strategy. Rush notes that the 19th century political commentator Walter Bagehot regarded the Cabinet as the crucial institution of government, describing it as the 'efficient secret':

> 'What he meant by this was that government was still carried on in the name of the monarch - a role to which he assigned the term "dignified" - but that in reality it was the Cabinet that made political decisions. He described its role as "secret" because of the monarchical facade by which it operated, and "efficient" because, having the support of a majority in the House of Commons, it could provide firm and effective government and yet remain sensitive to criticism through its constitutional responsibility to Parliament. Bagehot was writing just as the modern party system was beginning to emerge, however, and he did not fully anticipate the strong, disciplined parties that would come to dominate the political system.' (Rush, 1984, pp.15-16)

The assumption behind the traditional view (which also underlies the principle of collective responsibility, see below, section 2.2) is that Cabinet ministers meet together to thrash out all major issues of policy before coming to a collective decision which then binds all members of government. Burch summarises this view as follows:

> 'Cabinet does not make all the decisions, but it does make all the major ones and it sets the broad framework within which more detailed policies are initiated and developed.' (Burch, 1990, p.103)

Whether 20 or so people, meeting together only once or twice a week, can really control, collectively, the policy and decision making process of large-scale, modern government, however, is open to debate. Most Cabinet ministers are already fully stretched in their roles as political head of a specialist government department. As Sir John Hoskyns, former head of the Downing Street Policy Unit, notes:

> 'The crippling workload will frequently impair health and marriage, for the minister must do it all - Cabinet and its committees, the department, public appearances, attendance in the House - on top of his work as a constituency MP.' (quoted in Hennessy, 1986, p.187)

Not only are Cabinet ministers overworked, the limited time they spend together may not always be used constructively. Anthony Crosland, Secretary of State for Education between 1965 and 1967, for example, complained that:

> 'There isn't much correlation between how important an issue is and how much time is spent on this in Cabinet...The issues that take up Cabinet time are those which are controversial within the government...it's not their intrinsic importance, but their political context, that puts them on the Cabinet agenda.' (quoted in Hennessy, 1986, pp.185-6)

If the traditional view is wrong and power does not lie with the Cabinet, where then does it lie? Burch (1990) puts forward five possibilities:

1. Ministers and officials in their departments (see chapter 13).
2. Ministers in Cabinet committees (see below, section 2.3).
3. The Cabinet Secretariat (see below, section 2.4).
4. Informal groups of ministers and others (see below, section 2.5).
5. The Prime Minister (see above, part 1).

The shadow Cabinet

Although it is not part of the structure of government, a shadow Cabinet operates in the British political system. In a predominantly two party system, the shadow Cabinet is composed of frontbench politicians from the official opposition party (the leading opposition party in Parliament). Though not necessarily identical, the posts of the shadow Cabinet normally mirror those in the Cabinet itself. So, for example, there is a shadow Chancellor, a shadow Home Secretary and so on.

Not only does the existence of a shadow Cabinet ensure that an opposition spokesperson is available to put the opposition's side in any political debate, it also means that a team of opposition politicians gains some expertise across the range of policy areas. Since the shadow Cabinet is a government in waiting, the performance of its members is closely scrutinised by political commentators and the public.

The key difference between the Cabinet and shadow Cabinet is that, although the shadow Cabinet formulates policies, it is unable to implement them. The shadow Cabinet, therefore, has no executive support in the form of a shadow civil service.

Activity 12.4

Item A *The Cabinet room (1)*

This photograph shows the Cabinet room which is located at 10 Downing Street.

Item B *The Cabinet room (2)*

Writing in 1992, Simon James argued that the physical layout of a meeting room often affects the quality of discussion, and the layout of the Cabinet room is particularly unhelpful. Ministers sit around a long table with the Prime Minister at the centre of one of the long sides. The Cabinet Secretary sits to the right of the Prime Minister and the most senior colleagues sit to the left and opposite. Other ministers are allocated seats by the Cabinet Office in such a way that the more senior a minister, the closer that minister's seat is to the centre. Junior ministers, therefore, sit at the far extremities of the table. The acoustics of the Cabinet room are bad. There is a constant rustling of papers and murmuring between ministers. When ministers speak, they naturally turn their heads to face the Prime Minister. The result is that those at the end of the table can hear little. In addition, the style of proceedings is unhelpfully formal. For example, remarks are addressed to the Prime Minister and ministers refer to each other by their formal titles. This ensures a rather stilted atmosphere. In the 1970s, Labour Cabinets allowed ministers to use first names and this changed the whole atmosphere. Since 1979, however, Conservative Cabinets have revived the more formal conventions.

Adapted from James, 1992.

Item C *A Cabinet minister's working week*

Activity	Time in hours
Cabinet	4
Cabinet committees	4
Parliament	14
Party meetings	3
Visits, inspections	6
Interviews, deputations and the press	5
Formal receptions	8
Constituency matters	2
Paperwork, office meetings	15
Total hours	**61**

This table shows how a Cabinet minister filled up a week in 1974.

Item D *Meetings of the full Cabinet*

Sir Douglas Wass, a top civil servant, claims that ministers in Cabinet rarely look at the totality of their responsibilities, at the balance of policy or at the progress of government towards its overall objectives. Rather, Cabinet's staple diet consists either of a selection of individually important one-off cases or of issues about which those ministers whose departments are affected are unable to agree. Wass argues that the form and structure of the Cabinet, combined with the matters it chooses to discuss, ensure that it functions as a group of individuals and not as a unity. It is significant that ministers do not win political distinction by their performance in Cabinet or by their contribution to collective decision making. As far as the public and the House of Commons are concerned, a minister is the head of a particular department. The only Cabinet member who is not seen in this way is the Prime Minister.

Adapted from Hennessy, 1986.

Questions

1. Judging from Items A-D why might Cabinet ministers find it difficult to perform their role satisfactorily?
2. 'The ideal Cabinet would consist of five or six ministers who do not have departmental responsibility.' Give arguments for and against this statement.
3. Would you agree that the Cabinet is the seat of power in terms of policy initiation and decision making? Use Items A-D in your answer.

2.2 Cabinet collective responsibility

One of the first documents given to new ministers on their appointment is *Questions of Procedure for Ministers* (QPM), a document first made public in May 1992. Over the years, this document has been changed and added to, but there is always a section on collective responsibility. According to Woodhouse:

> 'QPM states in paragraphs 17 and 18: "Decisions reached by the Cabinet or ministerial committees are binding on all members of the government" and ministers should maintain "a united front when decisions have been reached". It follows, therefore, that (paragraph 87): "Ministers cannot speak publicly for themselves alone. In all cases they speak as ministers and the principle of collective responsibility applies. They should ensure that their statements are consistent with collective government policy and should not anticipate decisions not yet made public. Ministers should exercise special care in referring to subjects which are the responsibility of other ministers." ' (Woodhouse, 1995, p.26)

Within Cabinet and its committees, therefore, ministers can express their own views and disagree with each other. The doctrine of collective responsibility, however, requires that, once a decision has been reached, all ministers must accept it and must not publicly disagree with it.

According to the traditional interpretation of this doctrine, any minister either unable or unwilling to support a Cabinet decision publicly must resign from government. This has important implications. Some commentators, for example, argue that since ministers only resign as a last resort, the doctrine of collective responsibility strengthens the hand of Prime Ministers. Prime Ministers can push a line knowing, first, that dissenting ministers are unlikely to resign when it is accepted and, second, that, once it has been agreed, no minister will be able to criticise it in public. Other commentators, however, argue that the doctrine encourages constructive collective decision making. Under the doctrine, views expressed within Cabinet and its committees are completely confidential. That means that even if ministers vehemently oppose measures in Cabinet meetings, that opposition remains unknown to everyone except those present at the meeting (who are themselves obliged to keep silent). As a result, when dissenting ministers are later asked to defend the measures they have criticised, they can do so without losing face. Also, since confidentiality is ensured, ministers are more likely to be critical and this, in theory at least, should have the effect of improving the quality of the decisions made.

According to Dorey (1995), the application of the doctrine of collective responsibility has been subject to two trends in recent years - it has been applied more widely and it has been applied less stringently. The result is that the traditional interpretation needs to be updated.

Wider application of the doctrine of collective responsibility

Dorey (1995) notes that when the Prime Minister Lord Salisbury described the doctrine of collective responsibility in 1878, he was referring only to collective responsibility within the Cabinet. Other ministers were exempt. During the 20th century, however, the doctrine has come to be more widely applicable. Today, *Questions of Procedure for Ministers* makes it quite clear that the doctrine applies not just to Cabinet ministers, but also to all junior ministers and even to parliamentary private secretaries (those just below ministerial level - see chapter 13, p.372). The result of this development is that junior ministers are asked to support, without question, decisions which are made without consulting them. From the executive's point of view, this is clearly desirable since it means that the government can present a united face in public and dissent can be minimised. From the point of view of the individuals concerned, however, it may mean that they feel obliged to go along with decisions about which, in private, they have grave reservations. This, it seems, is what happened with the poll tax. Privately, ministers had grave reservations, but publicly they presented a united front.

Further evidence of wider application of the doctrine of collective responsibility is the fact that the doctrine is now adopted by the shadow Cabinet. Just as the government wants to present a united front, so too does the government-in-waiting. It is, therefore, no surprise that public dissent is prohibited on the opposition frontbench.

Less stringent application of the doctrine of collective responsibility

Whilst ministers do still, on occasion, resign because they feel unable to toe the government line, there is some evidence that the traditional assumption that a dissenting minister must resign (or be sacked) is weakening. Indeed, Dorey (1995) argues that, on a number of occasions, ministers who have resigned on the grounds that they could no longer maintain collective responsibility have used this as a pretext to cover ulterior motives.

Dorey (1995) cites Michael Heseltine's resignation over the Westland Affair in 1986 as a prime example of this tendency. In January 1986, Heseltine, the Defence Secretary, stormed out of a meeting of the Cabinet, claiming that he was unable to support the government's policy over Westland helicopters.

Heseltine wanted the company (which was in financial trouble) to be taken over by a European consortium, whilst the official Cabinet line was one of neutrality between the European consortium and an American bid (it was well known that the Prime Minister and Secretary of State for Trade and Industry favoured the American bid). Dorey argues that, although Heseltine claimed he was forced to resign because he was unable to support government policy, this was really a pretext. Heseltine aimed to make a bid for the leadership of the Conservative party and realised he would be unable to do so while he remained as part of the government team. Similarly, Dorey argues, Geoffrey Howe said that he was resigning from the Cabinet in November 1990 because he could no longer support the government's policy on Europe. The timing of his resignation, however, suggests that his real reason was to ensure that a serious leadership contest took place that year (he resigned in time for a leadership challenge to be mounted at the beginning of the parliamentary session, the only time it can be done under Conservative party rules). Dorey's argument is, therefore, that:

> 'Some of the recent resignations by ministers, ostensibly in accordance with the doctrine, have raised doubts about whether such resignations were primarily concerned with policy disagreements or whether they were really manifestations of personality and power struggles within the government, with collective responsibility being invoked in order to legitimise and give credence to the actions of resigning ministers.' (Dorey, 1995, p.105)

Dorey goes on to provide three further indications of the weakening of the doctrine of collective responsibility. First, he claims that the publication of a growing number of ministerial diaries and memoirs suggests that confidentiality is no longer as secure as was once the case. Second, he notes that on three occasions this century, Prime Ministers have suspended the doctrine of collective responsibility, allowing members of the Cabinet to talk against and vote against government policy. The first occasion was in 1932. The second and third occasions took place in 1975 and 1977 and both concerned Britain's membership of the EC. In 1975, the Prime Minister allowed members of the Cabinet to support both sides in the referendum over membership of the EC. In 1977, the Prime Minister allowed a free vote over the type of electoral system to be used in European elections. And, the third indication of the weakening of the doctrine of collective responsibility is the growing tolerance of public dissent from Cabinet members which has been permitted by John Major since the 1992 general election. In 1994, for example, Michael Portillo made a number of speeches which appeared to criticise the official government line. Although Major appealed to his ministers to avoid the public airing of differences over policy, no member of the Cabinet resigned or was dismissed.

Activity 12.5

Item A *The Westland affair (1)*

This cartoon shows Michael Heseltine storming out of the Cabinet room after failing to convince the Prime Minister and the rest of the Cabinet to follow his line. It was first published in the *Guardian* on 10 January 1986.

Item B *The Westland affair (2)*

Margaret Thatcher is very clear about her views, very much a leader. Because of that, she doesn't need or want to resolve things by collective discussion. She knows what she wants to do about almost everything. But, it is a collective machine because they must all sink or swim with her. She uses the Cabinet as a sort of sounding board. It restrains her when restraint is necessary. She has her own instinct when she cannot carry her colleagues with her. She lets them know what she thinks. Then they try to adapt and mould it. She has very acute antennae. She's very quick to take the signals if she can't carry it.

Senior civil servant quoted anonymously in Hennessy, 1986.

Item C *The Westland affair (3)*

(i) There was a period when the Cabinet did not seem and, in fact, was not acting with collective responsibility because one person [Michael Heseltine] was not playing as a member of the team. The press was very critical of me in many ways before that. Some said that I should have asked Mr Heseltine to go earlier.

Margaret Thatcher quoted in Hennessy, 1986.

(ii) Ministers who feel unable to overcome personal doubts about the nature of government policy, as agreed in full Cabinet or in one of its committees, should, under normal circumstances, resign if they wish to criticise such policy. Concerning the Westland affair, Thatcher's argument was that she had stretched the doctrine of collective responsibility to its absolute limit in an attempt to accommodate Heseltine. She claimed that the government policy of neutrality was the result of collective discussion between ministers on nine occasions whilst Heseltine was in the Cabinet. Heseltine's view was completely different. He believed that the majority of his colleagues might well have supported the bid by the European consortium if he had been given a chance to explain it properly. Neutrality, he claimed, was a sham used by the Prime Minister and her allies to subvert the collective policy of Cabinet.

Adapted from Pyper, 1987.

Item D *Cabinet splits*

The Conservatives were struggling last night to prevent the ideological Cabinet split between Michael Portillo and Michael Heseltine breaking into open party warfare. The confrontation between the two men became public yesterday when the *Guardian* published a leaked letter from Portillo, the then Chief Secretary to the Treasury. This letter criticised Heseltine for failing to cut public spending and introduce free market policies at the Department of Trade and Industry. Seething right wing backbenchers blamed the DTI and Heseltine for the leaking of the letter and claimed that Heseltine was trying to discredit Portillo, one of his chief rivals for the party leadership. Industrialists, opposition MPs and some Tory backbenchers, however, were dismayed at the patronising tone of Portillo's letter. Some argued that the scale of government withdrawal from industrial support demanded by Portillo would leave British industry at a great disadvantage. Portillo responded by defending his letter, saying that it: 'Reflected an appropriate and healthy tone of debate about the proper role of government.' Robin Cook, shadow Industry Secretary, pointed out that the root of the row is an ideological dispute about the role of government in aiding industry. He said: 'It shows up a divergence between Mr Heseltine and Mr Portillo so sharp that it cannot be accommodated in one Cabinet.'

Adapted from the *Guardian*, 2 August 1994.

Questions

1. 'Collective responsibility is absolutely essential for good government.' Do you agree with this statement? Use Items A-D in your answer.
2. Why was the Westland affair an important milestone in the history of collective responsibility? Use Item A-C in your answer.
3. Is there any evidence in Item D to suggest that collective responsibility was breached? Give reasons for your answer.

2.3 Cabinet committees

Officially, the term 'Cabinet' embraces the full Cabinet and its committees. From this perspective, it would, therefore, be inappropriate to suggest that there is any conflict between the two. But, for the purposes of analysing where power lies, the official view does not have to be followed. It is, in other words, worth investigating the extent to which policy decisions are reached in Cabinet committees, with or without reference to the full Cabinet.

Evolution of the Cabinet committee system

Although Cabinet committees were in use in the 19th century, primarily on an ad hoc basis, their existence on something like their present scale only dates back to the 1940s. During the Second World War, Cabinet committees took on much of the work usually done by the Cabinet, thus allowing the small wartime Cabinet to concentrate on matters concerning the war effort. After the war, the system of Cabinet committees was developed further in response to the expansion of government activity arising out of the setting up of the welfare state and the interventionist economic and social policies pursued by the Labour government (see chapter 3, section 1.1).

The current system

All Cabinet committees are composed of ministers. Some comprise ministers of Cabinet rank. Some include junior ministers. Some include senior civil servants and some do not. Ministerial committees are usually mirrored by so-called 'official' committees composed entirely of civil servants. Official committees are significant because they often meet in advance to prepare the ground for ministerial meetings.

There are two main types of Cabinet committee - standing and ad hoc. **Standing committees** are referred to by code names or letters (see Item C in

Activity 12.6 below). They deal with a specific policy area and are relatively permanent. **Ad hoc committees** are set up to deal with specific short-term problems and issues or are committees which meet irregularly. For example, Dorey (1991) notes that, while Margaret Thatcher was Prime Minister, ad hoc committees were set up to prepare for the 1984 miners' strike, to prepare for the abolition of the Greater London Council and to investigate the replacement of Polaris nuclear submarines by Trident.

The extent to which Cabinet committees are used

The composition and even the existence of Cabinet committees was supposed to be secret until 1992 when, for the first time, a list of all Cabinet standing committees (together with their membership and terms of reference) was made public. Before 1992, editions of *Questions of Procedure for Ministers* argued that such secrecy was a necessary part of collective responsibility. Despite the secrecy, however, political commentators made educated guesses about the number and type of committees which existed under different governments. These educated guesses suggest a great deal of variation under different Prime Ministers. From the information available, it seems that Margaret Thatcher made less use of the formal Cabinet committee system than did her predecessors. For example, Burch (1994) notes that 941 meetings of Cabinet committees were recorded in 1978, compared to 340 in 1989. Similarly, he notes that although Thatcher was Prime Minister for much longer than Attlee, she set up less than half the number of ad hoc Cabinet committees and only one sixth of the standing committees he set up in the immediate postwar era. John Major is reported to have made more use of the committee system, though Burch (1994) claims that the number of meetings is lower than that in the 1970s.

The shape of the Cabinet committee system, therefore, appears to depend on the particular style of the Prime Minister. It is the Prime Minister who decides which committees should be set up, what their terms of reference should be, who should chair them and who should sit on them. There may be practical and political restrictions on the Prime Minister's choice - the nature of an issue may require the inclusion of ministers from certain departments, for example. But, there is still considerable room for manoeuvre.

Burch notes that under John Major:

> 'There has been a streamlining of the standing committees of Cabinet. An important innovation has been the creation of a new overarching committee, chaired by the Prime Minister, to cover the whole range of domestic policy - EDP. This follows on from the closer amalgamation of economic and home affairs secretariats which took place under Thatcher. In addition, under Major, the designated membership of ministerial standing committees has tended to be smaller, especially so far as those chaired by him are concerned...In effect, he only chairs one substantive domestic committee, the aforementioned EDP. Whereas, Thatcher chaired at least four standing committees on the domestic side. Moreover, under Major, standing committees tend to have a more strategic, wide-ranging remit than under Thatcher.' (Burch, 1994, p.29)

Cabinet committees and policy making

Although the shape of the Cabinet system varies according to the particular style of the Prime Minister, it has now become common practice for many important decisions to be reached in Cabinet committee, particularly in the key areas of defence and economic and domestic affairs where the Prime Minister is in the chair. Decisions made in these committees are not necessarily discussed further in, or even reported to, meetings of the full Cabinet. The same is true of decisions made by some ad hoc committees:

> 'The decision to prohibit trade union membership at the government communications headquarters (GCHQ) in Cheltenham was taken by an ad hoc Cabinet committee comprising the Prime Minister, the Defence Secretary, the Employment Secretary, the Foreign Secretary and the Deputy Prime Minister, at that time William Whitelaw. The rest of the Cabinet first heard of the decision when it was announced in the House of Commons.' (Dorey, 1991, p.13)

Despite the variations in the way in which different Prime Ministers use the system, there appears to be considerable scope for the exercise of power by the ministers chairing the committees and by any minister who is a member of several different committees. But, although decisions may often be reached in Cabinet committees and they may, therefore, represent what Burch (1990) describes as 'the points at which major policies are determined and decided', these committees may not so frequently initiate policy.

2.4 The Cabinet Secretariat

The administrative and secretarial work connected with the flow of policy business within the Cabinet system is carried out by the Cabinet Secretariat. The Secretariat forms a major part of the Cabinet Office which is headed by the Cabinet Secretary, one of the top posts in the civil service. The Cabinet Office has a total staff of around 1,500.

The job of the Cabinet Secretariat is to arrange the times of meetings and, in conjunction with the chairs of Cabinet committees, to prepare agendas. The Secretariat also briefs committee chairs and records and circulates the minutes of the meetings of the Cabinet and its committees. It contains around 40 senior officials and is divided into five smaller secretariats - Economic and Domestic, Overseas and Defence, European (EU), Security and Intelligence, and Telecommunications.

Because of the pressure of business flowing into the Cabinet system, Burch (1990) argues that the Economic and Domestic and the Overseas and Defence secretariats (which are engaged in the work of the two key policy Cabinet standing committees) probably do little in the way of initiating policy. They do, however, set the pace of dealing with business. This, in itself, gives them the potential to influence policy, albeit in a negative fashion by slowing down proposals it does not favour or speeding up proposals it does favour. The European and Telecommunications secretariats, Burch argues, have more scope for policy initiation. The European secretariat played an active role in the formation of policy initiatives concerning the then European Community in the early 1980s, for example. The work of the Security and Intelligence secretariat is too cloaked in secrecy for a clear picture of its operations to emerge, though it probably does not play a significant policy making role in the work of central government as a whole.

The drawing up of minutes

One aspect of the work of the Cabinet Secretariat which concerns some politicians and political analysts is the task of recording the minutes of Cabinet and its committees. In his diaries, for example, the former Cabinet minister Richard Crossman claimed that Cabinet minutes bore little relationship to what actually went on in Cabinet meetings. According to Crossman's biographer, the Labour MP Tam Dalyell:

> 'I was not in Cabinet, but from March 1965 until 1970 I saw a great many Cabinet minutes. From what other members of the Cabinet said, the minutes did not tally with what had occurred in Cabinet. They were an amalgam of the official brief which a minister took along to Cabinet, the official papers on the original policy, and the official conclusions. The minutes anaesthetised the ministers' contributions and usually did not identify who said what. This had the effect of enormously strengthening the civil service against politicians.' (Dalyell, 1989, p.235)

Dalyell argues that the publication of Crossman's diaries exposed the inaccuracy of the way in which minutes were made. Indeed, it has been argued that the publication of Crossman's diaries encouraged later governments (notably the Thatcher governments) to take measures to ensure that a more accurate record was made.

The power of the Cabinet Secretariat

Through interviews with serving and retired ministers and civil servants, Seldon (1990) has pieced together a picture of the way in which the Cabinet Secretariat worked between 1979 and 1987. For virtually all of this period, the Cabinet Secretary was Robert Armstrong. Seldon's study plays down the power exerted by Armstrong, though it does recognise that he had 'considerable potential influence' through his daily contact with the Prime Minister and other senior ministers and through his attendance of meetings of the Cabinet and its committees. Seldon argues, however, that the power of the Cabinet Secretariat was muted during the early 1980s because of the personality of the Cabinet Secretary. Armstrong, he claims, was 'always more in the faithful servant mould' than was his predecessor.

Referring to the role of the Secretariat in general, rather than to the performance of its head, Burch also concludes that the power of the Cabinet Secretariat was muted. He describes its part in the policy making process as 'marginal' and adds:

> 'It is mainly concerned with the smooth running of business and if it has any influence, it is exercised through shaping and handling rather than the content of policy and through briefing committee chairmen and the Prime Minister.' (Burch, 1990, p.106)

Other writers are more equivocal. For example, whilst acknowledging that policy is initiated elsewhere, Madgwick (1991) notes that, as the policy process is 'confused and circular', it is not always easy to distinguish policy initiation from the process of policy development and management which is more clearly the official role of the Cabinet Secretariat.

2.5 Informal groups

Whilst the Cabinet, its committees and the Cabinet Secretariat constitute the Cabinet system in formal terms, the system also involves many meetings and contacts of a less formal nature. Informal groups are not necessarily subject to the same procedures of official agenda setting and minute taking as formal groups, though some informal meetings are more organised than others. Informal meetings may range from the casual chat in the corridor to the regular gathering of an inner circle of senior colleagues. Such inner circles are by no means uncommon. James argues that some Prime Ministers rely upon them:

> 'To discuss the main issues of the day, do some of the fixing and dealing necessary to keep any government working and...to give some

strategic steering.' (James, 1992, p.194)

Informal groups are by no means confined to ministers. They may include advisers or civil servants. They may be bilateral - an informal discussion between the Prime Minister and one other minister, official or adviser, for example. Or, they may be multilateral - an informal discussion between several ministers, officials or advisers, for example.

Policies may be initiated or at least shaped by informal meetings. This suggests that power is exercised by informal groups. But, to what extent has power within the Cabinet system come to reside in informal groups and what changes have been taking place?

The use of groups outside the formal structure is not a particularly recent development. There is, however, little doubt that informal meetings of groups of ministers outside the formal Cabinet committee system increased substantially during Margaret Thatcher's premiership. Burch (1990a), for example, notes that this way of conducting business was actively encouraged, with many matters being decided interdepartmentally, outside the formal Cabinet structures, often by ministerial correspondence. In addition, Thatcher herself made extensive use of such informal networks. Seldon, for example, explains that:

> 'When there was a particularly sensitive issue, or one which gave rise to a good deal of controversy, Margaret Thatcher liked to have a multilateral (non-Cabinet committee) meeting with small groups of ministers...to allow her to clarify her mind. It also allowed her to prepare a caucus ahead of full Cabinet or Cabinet committees. Another reason why she often favoured discussing business in non-Cabinet committee meetings, undoubtedly, was fear of leaking...A multi- or bilateral meeting with the PM would usually have an official from the Cabinet Office in attendance, but Number 10 would take and circulate minutes in the form of a private secretary letter to the offices of the ministers present at the meeting.' (Seldon, 1990, p.115)

In general, it is the informal groups centring on or involving the Prime Minister which exercise the most influence on policy formation. Burch (1990) notes, for example, that, under Thatcher, links between the Treasury and the Prime Minister's Office were strengthened because of the greater emphasis placed on restraining public expenditure.

When John Major became Prime Minister, there was some movement back towards the greater use of formal structures, but Burch argues that this has not resulted in a restoration of fully collective government. Rather, there has been a formalisation of some of the practices initiated by Thatcher. Under Major there has still been extensive use of informal networks, even if not all the strands centre on the Prime Minister:

> 'Under Major, the informal structure is still used extensively, though its complexion is quite different from that which operated under his predecessor. Its most noticeable feature is that it is less singular, less focused solely on the Prime Minister. Major has a tendency to rely on an informal inner group of senior ministers and confidants whom he may call upon for advice and to clear particular decisions. This varies according to the task and issue at hand... Moreover, Cabinet and key committee meetings are often still a bit of a fix, with tricky issues being dealt with on a one-to-one basis beforehand.' (Burch, 1994, p.30)

The trend towards dealing with business in smaller, less formal groups at the centre of government cannot, therefore, be explained simply by reference to the style of an individual Prime Minister. Other factors are also significant. The trend may be the result of greater concern about secrecy, for example, exacerbated by an increased likelihood, or fear, of leaks. It may be because the formal structure of the Cabinet system has proved to be too unwieldy to handle many of the sensitive or urgent issues facing modern governments. Or, it may be a reflection of, as well as a contribution to, the centralisation of power around the office of the Prime Minister.

Whatever the reasons for the increased use of informal groups, one conclusion is clear. The formal structure of the Cabinet system now plays less of a policy formulating and policy coordinating role than used to be the case. The formal structure may still be used to ratify or confirm decisions, but policies are determined elsewhere:

> 'Informal groups may both initiate policy and, in effect, decide its content for they often predetermine what is later discussed and decided within the more formal structure.' (Burch, 1990, p.107)

Activity 12.6

Item A *The Cabinet system*

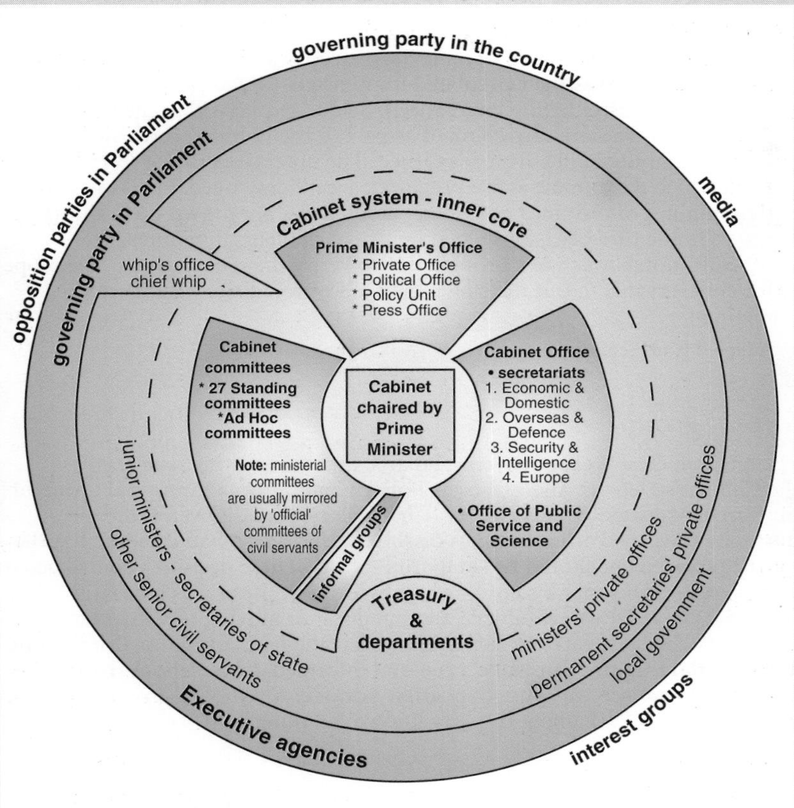

Adapted from Pyper & Robins, 1995.

Item B *Cabinet committees - for and against*

(i) Cabinet committees are the most private and well protected parts of our democracy. Power ought to reside where the public can see it in Parliament, but, in fact, it hides in these committees. The Prime Minister appoints their members and is, therefore, able to pack them to achieve a desired result. Cabinet committees often present the full Cabinet with a fait accompli.

Adapted from Cockerell et al., 1984.

(ii) Some critics have argued that Cabinet committees enhance the power of the Prime Minister, but, to Harold Wilson, this was a facile view - Cabinet committees make government more effective and prevent the Cabinet being bogged down in detail. Wilson claimed that the role of the Prime Minister is to ensure that the Cabinet committee system works smoothly by delegating authority to the committees and by being sufficiently sensitive to know when to respond to an appeal by a dissatisfied minority or to spot a case which should go straight to Cabinet. He said that it did not increase prime ministerial power since it would be difficult even for a megalomaniac Prime Minister to ignore a decision made by a committee of Cabinet colleagues.

Adapted from Wilson, 1976.

Item C *Cabinet committees*

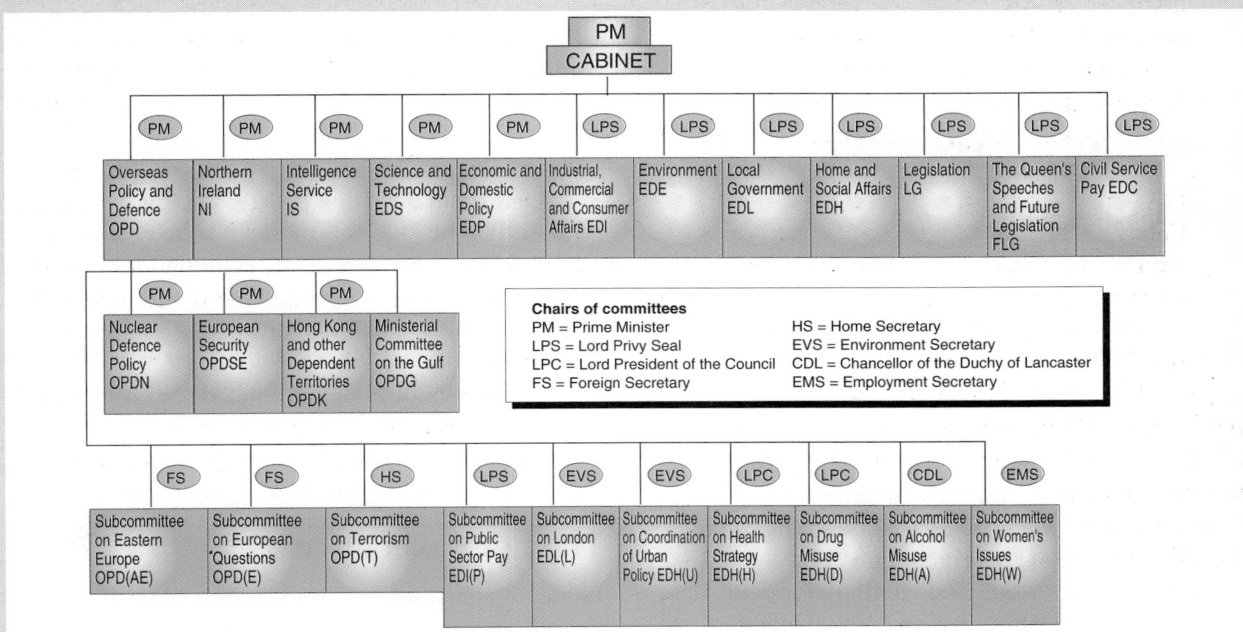

This diagram shows the Cabinet committees in existence in 1992.

Adapted from Pyper & Robins, 1995.

Item D *Cabinet minutes*

(i) In 1940, at the age of 24, Harold Wilson (who worked as a civil servant) was asked by the Cabinet Secretary to write the Cabinet minutes. When Wilson pointed out that he had not been there and had not heard what was said, the Cabinet Secretary said that even if he had been present, he would not have been any better informed. He ordered Wilson to produce the minutes in one hour, saying: 'This is your subject. You know what they ought to have decided, presumably. Write the minutes on those lines and nobody will ever question it.' Wilson says that he was right. Nobody did question the minutes.

Adapted from Wilson, 1976.

(ii) Anthony Seldon claims that, during Margaret Thatcher's premiership, the Cabinet Secretary and at least one member of the secretariat most directly responsible made a full record of the discussion in their notebooks. From their notes, officials compiled draft minutes. These were collated and edited by the Cabinet Secretary who produced a final copy. This final copy was then circulated to ministers (it was never cleared with the Prime Minister before circulation). Seldon explains that the Cabinet Secretary's own notes are counted as part of the public record and preserved in the Public Records Office. The notebooks of the secretariats, from which draft minutes are prepared, are all destroyed. He also explains that minutes of meetings of Cabinet committees are drawn up in the same way. On the rare occasions when ministers challenged minutes, the officials' notebooks were brought out to verify the record given. The scope for civil servants to put their own gloss on proceedings was, therefore, minimal.

Adapted from Seldon, 1990.

Item E *Decision making by informal group*

In January 1978, the question of replacing Britain's nuclear weapon system, Polaris, arose. Since the issue was regarded as too sensitive to be put before the Cabinet's Defence and Overseas Policy Committee, an informal group of four was set up comprising James Callaghan (Prime Minister), Denis Healey (Chancellor), David Owen (Foreign Secretary) and Fred Mulley (Defence Secretary). By the time Parliament was dissolved, this group had decided that the Polaris weapons should be replaced and that the replacement should be submarine-borne. These decisions contradicted the promise made in Labour's 1974 election manifesto. The only sign of this highly secret decision was a passage inserted in the 1979 election manifesto which read: 'In 1974 we renounced any intention of moving towards the production of a new generation of nuclear weapons...We reiterate our belief that this is the best course for Britain. But many great issues are involved. We think it is essential that there must be a full and informed debate about these issues in the country before any decision is taken.' The last sentence was pure hypocrisy. For over a year, the group of four had been engaged in private government, without people, Parliament or party knowing a thing.

Adapted from Cockerell et al., 1984.

Questions

1. Using Item A explain where power lies in the Cabinet system.
2. What are the benefits and drawbacks of the use of a system of Cabinet committees? Use Items B and C in your answer.
3. What conclusions can be drawn about the taking of Cabinet minutes from Item D?
4. What are the advantages and disadvantages of policy formulation by informal groups? Use Item E in your answer.

3 The core executive

Key Issues

1. What is the core executive?
2. Where does power lie in the core executive?

The traditional view

According to the traditional view, Britain has Cabinet government. The executive is, in other words, centred on the Cabinet. Leadership is collective rather than singular. There are certain key features:

> 'That the Cabinet is the main steering organ of British central government and has general oversight over policy; that all major decisions are reached with the active involvement or at least full awareness of all its members; and that the Prime Minister, who chairs the Cabinet is "first among equals": dominant but not predominant.' (Burch, 1995, p.15)

As Burch points out, this model has been unsustainable for many years. Although it became popular to argue that Thatcher's authoritarian style was responsible for the decline of Cabinet government, in fact, the evidence suggests that it has been in decline for a much longer period. The fact that Cabinet government is in decline, however, does not necessarily mean that prime ministerial government has taken its place.

The core executive

In recent years, some commentators have argued that the old debate over Cabinet government versus prime ministerial government is too simplistic. It is not sufficient, they argue, merely to examine the relationship between the Prime Minister and the

Cabinet and to decide which of the two has most power. Such an approach, it is claimed, is subject to a number of limitations.

First, compared to the amount written about the other institutions of government (such as Parliament) there is not a great deal of academic literature on the Prime Minister and Cabinet. King notes:

> 'Biographies and memoirs abound, but works by academic political scientists are few and far between. All of the books on the prime ministership can easily be held in one hand; the books on the prime ministership and Cabinet together can easily be held in two hands' (King, 1985, p:1)

This is due, in part, King argues, to research difficulties (few academics have access to the Prime Minister or Cabinet ministers and, therefore, few studies are based on primary source material). It is also due to the limited resources of British political science (in 1985 there were around 1,000 political science teachers in the UK and of this total only a few were engaged in original research into the relationship between the Prime Minister and Cabinet). The net result is that little progress has been made in this area of study.

Second, despite some small moves towards openness during John Major's premiership, the operations of the Prime Minister and the Cabinet remain surrounded by secrecy. It is difficult to provide up-to-date information about the inner workings of government when, for example, all Cabinet records are subject to the 30 year rule. The traditional reluctance of senior civil servants to discuss their work also helps to preserve a remoteness and inaccessibility.

Third, the limitations may also be due to the wrong questions being asked. Nobody would deny that a study of the Prime Minister and Cabinet is essential to an understanding of British government and politics. The traditional debate between Cabinet government versus prime ministerial government, however, tended to ignore the wider economic and political context. This context goes some way to determining the degrees of freedom within which a Prime Minister or Cabinet can act. The traditional debate also tended to oversimplify the distribution of power and the nature of decision making within the structure of British government. Rather than comparing the powers of Prime Minister and Cabinet and asking which is dominant, it has been argued, the focus of inquiry should be wider. Dunleavy & Rhodes, in an influential article published in 1990, suggested that the focus should be broadened to include the whole of the core executive which they define as:

> 'A complex web of institutions, networks and practices surrounding the Prime Minister, Cabinet, Cabinet committees and their official counterparts, less formalised ministerial "clubs" or meetings, bilateral negotiations and interdepartmental committees. It also includes some major coordinating departments - chiefly the Cabinet Office, the Treasury, the Foreign Office, the law officers and the security and intelligence services...All those organisations and structures which primarily serve to pull together and integrate central government policies or act as final arbiters within the executive of conflicts between different elements of the government machine.' (Dunleavy & Rhodes, 1990, pp.3-4)

Instead of continually rehearsing the unresolvable institutional question of Cabinet government versus prime ministerial government, Dunleavy & Rhodes argue for 'core executive studies', hoping that this will shift the ground not only on what is studied, but also on how it is studied. They want to see, for example, more case studies of top level decision making. They also suggest that greater attention be paid to influences such as the variations of leadership styles and personalities. This was attempted by Dunleavy and colleagues in a comparative study of Prime Ministers (see Dunleavy et al., 1990). They suggested that previous attempts to compare the performance of Prime Ministers have been vague and judgemental and, therefore, what was needed was 'systematic and reasonable quantitative measures'. The result is shown in Item C, Activity 12.7 below.

Where does power lie in the core executive?

This chapter has examined the location of power in the various elements which, together, make up the core executive. By bringing the various elements of the chapter together, it should be clear that power is not located in any single place. It can be found throughout the core executive, though it is not found in equal measure at its various locations. It should also be clear that not only does power not lie in a single place, its nature varies. Burch notes, for example, that:

> 'There are clear variations in the operation of power according to whether the task is one of initiating or determining policy. As far as the determination of policy is concerned, it would seem that the key elements in the system are ministers meeting formally in committee and, increasingly in recent years, informal groupings centring on the Prime Minister.' (Burch, 1990, p.108)

And finally, it should be clear that where power does exist, it varies over time and according to the particular environment which prevails at a particular time.

By focusing on the core executive as a whole rather than on the Cabinet or on the Prime Minister (or the relationship between the two), it is possible to construct new models to explain how the complex machinery of the executive works. A number of these models are explored in Activity 12.7.

Activity 12.7

Item A *Models of core executive decision making*

Type	Characteristics/issues
1. PM government	- PM has virtual monopoly of power. - PM able to decide on policy in any area or in key strategic areas, or by determining the ideological direction. - Most associated with Thatcher. - Limited value as a model.
2. PM clique	- PM's power derived from inner group of advisers. - Fits with reality of difficulty of one person running big government. - Recent emphasis on degree to which news management by PM's Press Office is key to power of clique.
3. Cabinet government	- Traditional notion of how UK system works. - In reality, Cabinet can't take all decisions. - Even under Thatcher, Cabinet was a court of appeal, means of holding PM in check constitutionally and a final authoritative forum for the resolution of policy.
4. Ministerial government	- Political and administrative departmentalism, a federation of more or less equal agencies which marks out UK government. - PM and Cabinet government limited by this constraint. - Ministers have their own power resources and are deemed to be responsible for activities in their domain.
5. Segmented decisions	- PM and Cabinet operate in different policy areas. - PM control strong on defence, foreign and important economic issues. - Cabinet and ministers dominate in all other areas of domestic policy. - Implies that the core executive has limited control over government.
6. Bureaucratic coordination	- Core executive has very limited control. - PM, Cabinet and ministers minimal role. - Emphasis here on civil servants as a power elite (left wing view) or as monopoly suppliers of information and maximisers of budgets (New Right view).

Adapted from Thain, 1993.

Item B *A model of prime ministerial power*

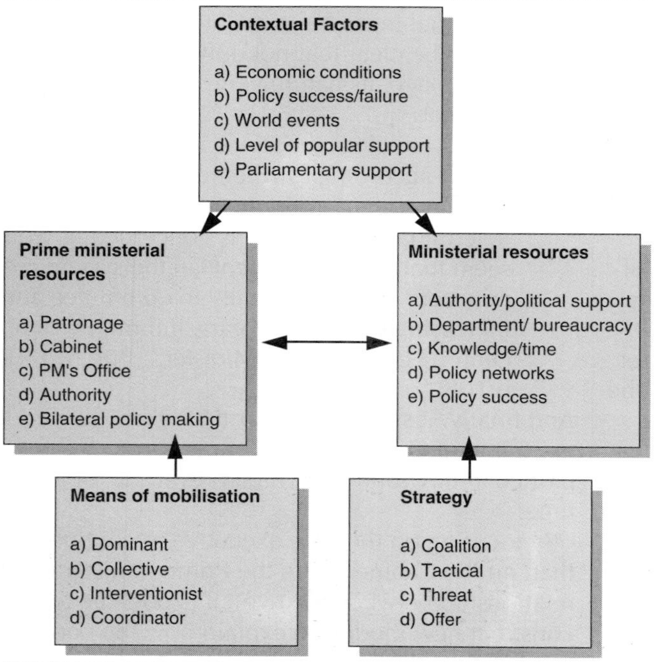

The diagram (left) is an attempt to draw up a model of prime ministerial power which is aware of the complexities of power and of the need to place the relations between Prime Ministers and Cabinet in context. In this model, both Prime Ministers and the Cabinet have resources. The authority of a Prime Minister derives from the Cabinet. Ministers owe their positions to a Prime Minister. The freedom to use these resources, however, depends on external circumstances and policy area. In making a decision, the Prime Minister has to exchange resources with one or more ministers. Prime Ministers have a range of different strategies of exchange - they may be dominant, collective, interventionist or coordinators (or a mixture). They are constrained, however, by the resources of ministers. Ministers have specialist skills or political authority which makes it difficult for the Prime Minister to override them. Also, ministers may build coalitions or threaten to resign. By mobilising their resources like this, they can defeat the Prime Minister.

Adapted from Smith, 1994.

Item C *Prime ministers compared*

(a) Parliamentary days between questions

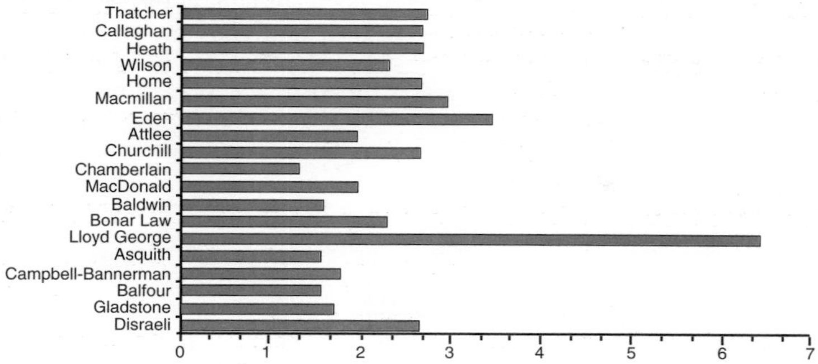

(b) Parliamentary days between statements

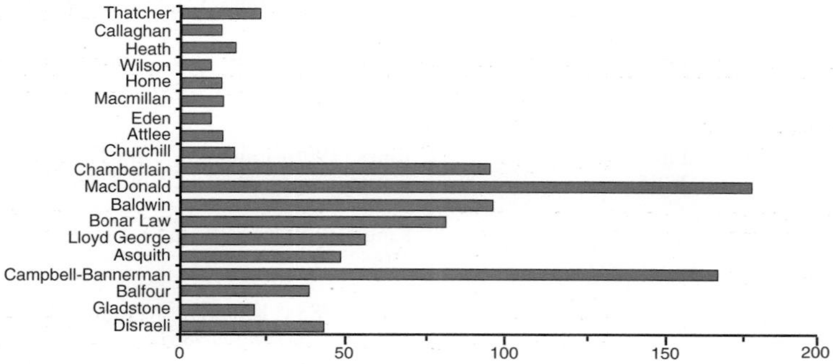

(c) Parliamentary days between speeches

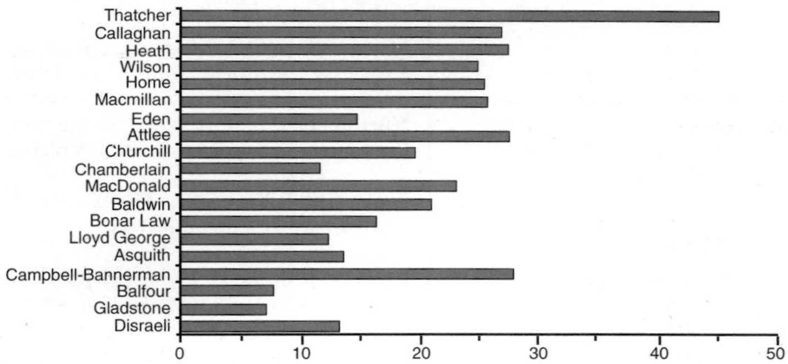

(d) Parliamentary days between debating interventions

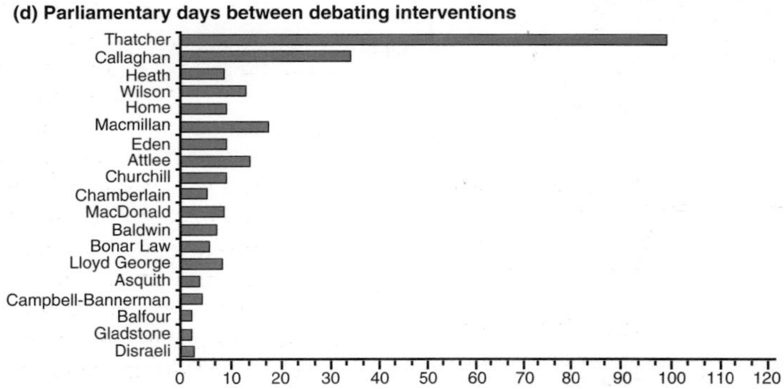

The above data provides a means for a comparative and quantitative analysis of the patterns of behaviour in the House of Commons of Prime Ministers from 1868 to 1987 (the dates of the Prime Ministers can be found in chapter 8, pages 200, 211 and 222). Each chart gives the number of parliamentary days between the occurrence of the particular activity under consideration. This was calculated by dividing the total number of parliamentary session days for each Prime Minister by the number of days on which they carried out the activity.

Adapted from Dunleavy et al., 1990.

Questions

1. a) Which of the models outlined in Item A best explains the way in which John Major's government worked after the 1992 general election? Give reasons for your answer.
   b) What are the benefits and drawbacks of each model?
2. a) What advantages does the model in Item B have over more traditional approaches to the study of decision making?
   b) Apply the model to what you know about the functioning of the government under John Major.
3. a) What trends and changes in prime ministerial behaviour can be identified from Item C? Suggest possible explanations.
   b) What value (if any) do you think the study has? Give reasons for your answer.

References

Benn (1981) Benn, T., *Arguments for Democracy*, Jonathan Cape, 1981.

Berrill (1985) Berrill, K., 'Strength at the centre - the case for a Prime Minister's department', in *King (1985)*.

Blondel (1993) Blondel, J. (ed.), *Governing Together*, Macmillan, 1993.

Burch (1985) Burch, M., 'The demise of Cabinet government?', *Teaching Politics*, Vol.14, No.3, September 1985.

Burch (1990) Burch, M., 'Power in the Cabinet system', *Talking Politics,* Vol.2, No.3, spring 1990.

Burch (1990a) Burch, M., 'Cabinet government', *Contemporary Record,* Vol.4, No.1, September 1990.

Burch (1994) Burch, M., 'The Prime Minister and Cabinet from Thatcher to Major', *Talking Politics,* Vol.7, No.1, autumn 1994.

Burch (1995) Burch, M., 'Prime Minister and Cabinet: an executive in transition?' in *Pyper & Robins (1995)*.

Cockerell et al. (1984) Cockerell, M., Hennessy, P. & Walker, D., *Sources Close to the Prime Minister*, Macmillan, 1984.

Dalyell (1989) Dalyell, T., *Dick Crossman: a Portrait*, Weidenfeld & Nicolson, 1989.

Dorey (1991) Dorey, P., 'The Cabinet committee system in British government', *Talking Politics,* Vol.4, No.1, autumn 1991.

Dorey (1995) Dorey, P., 'Widened, yet weakened: the changing character of collective responsibility', *Talking Politics,* Vol.7, No.2, winter 1994/95.

Dunleavy et al. (1990) Dunleavy, P., Jones, G.W. & O'Leary, B., 'Prime Ministers and the Commons: patterns of behaviour, 1868-1987', *Public Administration,* Vol.68, No.1, spring 1990.

Dunleavy & Rhodes (1990) Dunleavy, P. & Rhodes, R.A.W., 'Core executive studies in Britain', *Public Administration,* Vol.68, No.1, spring 1990.

Foley (1994) Foley, M., 'Presidential politics in Britain', *Talking Politics,* Vol.6, No.3, summer 1994.

Hennessy (1986) Hennessy, P., *Cabinet*, Blackwell, 1986.

HMSO (1994) Central Office of Information, *The British System of Government*, HMSO, 1994.

James (1992) James, S., *British Cabinet Government*, Routledge, 1992.

Johnson (1990) Johnson, R.W., 'The president has landed', *New Statesman and Society*, 30 November 1990.

Jones (1965) Jones, G., 'The Prime Minister's power' in *King (1985)*.

Jones (1980) Jones, G., 'The Prime Minister's aides' in *King (1985)*.

Jones (1990) Jones, G., 'Mrs Thatcher and the power of the PM', *Contemporary Record,* Vol.3, No.4, April 1990.

King (1985) King, A. (ed.), *The British Prime Minister*, Macmillan, 1985.

King (1985a) King, A., 'Margaret Thatcher: the style of a Prime Minister' in *King (1985)*.

King (1985b) King, A., 'Introduction: the textbook prime ministership' in *King (1985)*.

Madgwick (1991) Madgwick, P., *British Government: the Central Executive Territory*, Philip Allan, 1991.

Norton (1987) Norton, P., 'Prime ministerial power: a framework for analysis', *Teaching Politics,* Vol.16, No.3, September 1987.

Pyper (1987) Pyper, R., 'The Westland affair', *Teaching Politics,* Vol.16, No.3, September 1987.

Pyper & Robins (1995) Pyper R. & Robins, L. (eds), *Governing the UK in the 1990s*, Macmillan, 1995.

Rush (1984) Rush, M., *The Cabinet and Policy Formation,* Longman, 1984.

Seldon (1990) Seldon, A., 'The Cabinet Office and coordination', *Public Administration,* Vol.68, No.1, spring 1990.

Smith (1994) Smith, M.J., 'Reassessing Mrs Thatcher's resignation', *Politics Review,* Vol.3, No.4, April 1994.

Thain (1993) Thain, C., 'The core executive' in *Wale (1993)*.

Wale (1993) Wale, W. (ed.), *Development in Politics, Vol.4*, Causeway Press, 1993.

Wilson (1976) Wilson, H., *The Governance of Britain*, Michael Joseph and Weidenfeld & Nicholson, 1976.

Wilson (1977) Wilson, H., *A Prime Minister on Prime Ministers*, Michael Joseph and Weidenfeld & Nicholson, 1977.

Woodhouse (1995) Woodhouse, D., 'Questions of procedure for ministers', *Politics Review,* Vol.4, No.3, February 1995.

13 Ministers and civil servants

Introduction

Although all members of the Cabinet are ministers, not all ministers are members of the Cabinet. There is a ministerial hierarchy with the Cabinet at its apex. By convention, ministers are drawn from Parliament, with the vast majority of ministers being drawn from the Commons. Each minister is appointed by the Prime Minister and may be replaced at any time. Ministerial appointments, therefore, lack security.

Ministers play both a political and an administrative role. Politically, all ministers are members of the government team and each is responsible for an area of government policy both in Parliament and in public. Administratively, ministers are responsible for overseeing the implementation of government policy. The administration of government takes place through government departments. Ministers instruct their departmental officials (civil servants) who then deal with the day-to-day running of each department. Ministers are also responsible for building links between their own department or, when necessary, defending their departments against attacks from outside. This chapter examines the career structure and role of ministers.

The civil service also consists of a hierarchy. But, unlike ministers who rely on the good will of the Prime Minister to retain their position, civil servants are permanent officials. The range of jobs performed by civil servants is immense. Whilst a small number of high ranking civil servants work closely with ministers, many thousands of civil servants are employed to process claims and deal with administrative matters which arise from government decisions. Since 1979, the structure of the civil service and the scope of its activities have changed fundamentally.

The group of civil servants which is of most interest to political scientists is that at the very top of the hierarchy. This is because it is this small group (sometimes referred to as the 'mandarins') which is closely involved with ministers on policy issues. This chapter examines the characteristics of mandarins and the role they perform.

Chapter summary

Part 1 examines the **qualities** that a person needs to be chosen for ministerial office and the **duties performed by ministers**. It considers the reasons why ministers resign and examines the convention of **ministerial responsibility**.

Part 2 focuses on the **structure of the civil service** and the **impact of recent reforms**. To what extent are civil servants involved in policy making? Can they be described as '**neutral**'? How is policy implemented?

Part 3 analyses the **relationship between ministers and high ranking civil servants**.

1 Ministerial careers

Key Issues

1. What special qualities are required to become a minister and what makes a successful minister?
2. Who is held responsible if a mistake is made in a government department and who has to take the blame? For what reasons does a minister have to resign?
3. What duties do ministers perform? How does a minister's personality affect the way in which a department is run?

1.1 The ministerial hierarchy

The administration of government takes place through departments. Each department is responsible for a particular area of government policy and is headed by a Secretary of State who is a Cabinet minister. Ministers are responsible for the work of their departments. The role of the department is to prepare future legislation and, when passed, to put that legislation into effect.

Departments vary in size. The most important department is the Treasury. Madgwick (1991) describes the Treasury as a 'super department' and the Chancellor as the 'super minister'. This is because the Treasury manages the economy and controls public expenditure. All other departments depend on the Treasury for approval of their spending plans (see chapter 15, section 4.1).

From time to time, changes are made in the organisation of departments. For example, the Department of Trade was amalgamated with the Department of Industry in 1983, the Department of Health was split from the Department of Health and Social Security in 1988 and the Department of Employment was split between the Department of Education, the Department of Trade and Industry and the Department of the Environment in July 1995. Similarly, John Major created a new National Heritage Department in 1992. If government departments are amalgamated, this may reduce the number of ministers in Cabinet.

The route to the top

There is a hierarchy of ministers ranging from the Prime Minister at the top to (unpaid) private parliamentary secretaries at the bottom. Senior ministers, secretaries of state, are those who have a place in Cabinet. All other ministers below that level hold junior non-Cabinet posts.

Most departments are headed by a Cabinet minister (it is up to the Prime Minister to decide which departments are represented in Cabinet). The Treasury (since it is regarded as the most important department) has two ministers in Cabinet - the Chancellor of the Exchequer who is head of the department and the Chief Secretary who is responsible for the control of public expenditure (see chapter 15, section 4.1).

The private parliamentary secretary (PPS)

Strictly speaking, PPSs are not ministers. But, many MPs begin their ministerial careers as PPSs. The role of the PPS is to act as a general assistant to a minister in parliamentary matters and to serve as the minister's eyes and ears. At one time, only Cabinet ministers were entitled to have a PPS, but now any minister can, except for the lowest rung of the ministerial ladder (the parliamentary under secretary of state). The whips like to have large numbers of PPSs because they need to be aware of the opinions and feelings of MPs over an issue before an important vote takes place. Also, party loyalty is important and PPSs are obliged always to vote with the government or risk being dismissed. The government document *Questions of Procedure for Ministers* which outlines ministerial duties (and was published on the Prime Minister's authority in 1992) states that:

> 'No parliamentary private secretary who votes against the government may retain his or her position.' (Cabinet, 1992, section 3.47)

One of the functions of the PPS is to find a 'pair' for the minister. If a member of the government is unable to attend Parliament for an important vote, then a backbencher from the opposition must be found who will also be absent. They then form a 'pair' cancelling out each other's vote. One former member of Margaret Thatcher's government remembers his role and responsibilities as a PPS as rather a miserable one:

> 'The task [of the PPS] is to act as the private bagman of his minister, [by] listening to his critics among the troops at Westminster and finding him a pair from the opposition parties...In return, he is allowed to sit in on meetings at his boss's department (as long as nothing significant or confidential is under discussion). He is unpaid and mostly unconsulted.' (Bruce-Gardyne, 1986, p.14)

Despite this, the job is regarded as a route to ministerial office (the job of PPS to the Prime Minister is regarded as particularly desirable). Most PPSs hope to be promoted to parliamentary under secretary of state.

Junior ministers

The post of parliamentary under secretary of state (or 'pussy' as it sometimes called) is usually an 'up or out' post. That is, successful parliamentary under secretaries of state are likely to be promoted within a few years, whilst those not regarded as a success return to the backbenches with the hope of a knighthood. About half of those who serve as parliamentary under secretaries of state go no further. The number of parliamentary under secretaries of state in each department varies. For example, in June 1995, the Ministry of Defence and Home Office had only one each whilst the Department of Education and the Department of Health both had three.

The next rung up is the post of minister of state. The post dates back to the 1830s, but has only existed in its modern form since 1955. It was first confined to those departments where senior ministers were likely to be away from London for some time due to wider geographical commitments and, therefore, needed someone to stand in for them. Today, most departments have ministers of state because of the increasing workload and wider range of responsibilities of many departments. For example, in June 1995, the Department of Trade and Industry had four ministers of state, each being responsible for a particular area (industry, trade, consumer affairs and small firms, and energy).

A quarter of ministers of state go no further. Sideways movements are more common at this level, but the 'up or out' principle usually prevails eventually. Around 20% of all junior ministers eventually become Cabinet ministers (see chapter 12, part 2 for further information on Cabinet ministers).

1.2 What makes a successful minister?

In theory, the qualifications for becoming a minister are minimal. Any MP or peer who is prepared to support the government can be appointed. In practice, however, there are a number of qualifications which help a person to succeed as a minister.

Probably, the most important qualification for all ministers at any level is a considerable capacity for hard work. Theakston (1987) notes that for a junior minister:

> 'A 12 to 15 hour working day is common. Often starting in the office or leaving on a visit before nine o'clock in the morning and not finishing until well after 10 o'clock at night if there is a vote in the House of Commons.' (Theakston, 1987, p.77)

Nor can ministers who are MPs relax at the weekend since, like all MPs, they have to look after their constituency affairs. Joel Barnett, Chief Secretary to the Treasury in the 1970s, recalled:

> 'I soon found that good health and an ability to manage on little sleep - I am fortunate in only needing five or six hours - were invaluable assets in my new job. Having always been accustomed to working seven days a week, I was not troubled by the actual volume of work, although it was soon clear that not only would I be working seven days, but also much of the evenings and nights too.' (Barnett, 1982, p.16)

Second, a talent for good organisation and the ability to put over a good argument in public are advantageous. A good performance in the Commons is important, particularly in the early stages of a minister's career. An impressive speech can help make a junior minister's reputation and a poor performance can help to break it. The chances of success (especially for Conservative ministers) are improved if junior ministers keep in touch with specialist backbench committees since junior ministers are more likely to gain support if they are putting over what backbenchers want to hear. Also, at a more senior level, the reception given to a speech at the party conference can do much to boost or undermine a minister's reputation.

Third, ministers' reputations are judged on how well they handle pieces of legislation (this is particularly so at Cabinet level) and how well they fight for their corner in interdepartmental battles. If legislation passes through Parliament smoothly and seems to be working well, a minister's reputation tends to be enhanced. Similarly, ministers with a reputation for being tough fighters for their departments tend to be promoted.

Fourth, ministers need to show loyalty if they are to advance their career. Ministers are often appointed as a reward for their loyalty to the party leader. For example, Sir Keith Joseph was promoted to Industry Secretary by Margaret Thatcher in 1979, following his public displays of loyalty to her. Similarly, Norman Lamont was appointed as Chancellor in 1990 after playing a prominent role in John Major's leadership campaign.

Fifth, it can be advantageous for junior ministers to gain the backing of formal and informal groups of backbenchers, especially if these groups do not represent mainstream opinion. For example, there is little doubt that the promotion to the Cabinet of Michael Portillo in 1992 and John Redwood in 1993 was due, in part, to the backing of right wing Conservative MPs. These MPs put pressure on John Major to include representatives from the right in his Cabinet.

And finally, ministers at any level need to build a good working relationship with other members of their department. Since ministers tend to be in post for a relatively short time, they cannot possibly know all the answers. As a result, they need to be able to listen to their civil servants and yet to be decisive when they have heard what options are available. They need to be able to draw a fine balance between what their government wants, what their department wants and what other interests want.

Activity 13.1

Item A *The need for fewer ministers*

In Attlee's government there were 33 junior ministers. In Major's there are 64. But, Attlee's government was responsible for setting up the health service, for running the Empire and for running much of industry. Major's aim is for ministers to subcontract government to others. The premise behind the reforms that have taken place since 1979 is that departments and their ministers are not as good as devolved chief executives at running prisons, controlling health authorities, organising defence research and so on. There is, for example, still a minister in charge of prisons, but he no longer does the heavy work. The decisions are made by the director general of the prison service whose duties also include responding to the public and answering parliamentary questions. In such a world, ministers (especially junior ministers) increasingly appear to be little more than public relations agents for a service someone else is providing. So, why has the number of junior ministers not declined? The answer has to do with party management. Unless one third of the parliamentary party is in government and another third has expectations, the condition of the final third (mainly sour and disillusioned) might take over the party as a whole. The government is bloated because patronage is the only way to keep it afloat.

Adapted from the *Guardian*, 11 January and 13 January 1994.

Item B *The ministerial hierarchy*

This cartoon shows the number of each type of minister. The figures were provided by the House of Commons Information Department on 14 February 1995.

Item C *Fast and slow track careers*

(i) John Major - fast track

1979 Elected to Parliament.
1981-83 PPS to ministers of state in the Home Office.
1983-84 Assistant government whip.
1985-86 Under Secretary of State in the Department of Health and Social Security.
1987-89 Chief Secretary to the Treasury (joins Cabinet)
1989 Foreign Secretary
1989-90 Chancellor of the Exchequer
1990- Prime Minister

(ii) Norman Lamont - slow track

1972 Elected to Parliament.
1974 PPS to the Minister for the Arts.
1975-79 Opposition spokesperson.
1979-81 Under Secretary of State for the Department of Energy.
1981-85 Minister of State in the Department of Trade and Industry.
1985-86 Minister of State for Defence Procurement.
1986-89 Financial Secretary to the Treasury.
1989-90 Chief Secretary to the Treasury (joins Cabinet).
1990 Helps to runs John Major's leadership campaign.
1990-93 Chancellor of the Exchequer.
1993 Offered the post of Secretary of State for the Environment in a reshuffle, he chooses instead to return to the backbenches.

Adapted from Wood & Wood, 1992 and the *Guardian*, 22 January 1995.

Item D *Michael Portillo*

(i) When, in 1992, Michael Portillo was promoted to the Cabinet as Chief Secretary to the Treasury, he was, at the age of 39, the youngest Cabinet entrant since David Owen. Portillo is the rising star of the Tory right wing and has been tipped as a future party leader. Initially, he worked in the Tory research department and as a special adviser to the Secretary of State for Trade and Industry and the Chancellor of the Exchequer. He was elected to Parliament in 1984 after the death of Anthony Berry in the Brighton bombing. He became a PPS to the Minister of Transport in 1986 and was then appointed as assistant government whip (1986-87). His first ministerial post was Under Secretary of State in the Department of Health and Social Security (1987-88), the first post held by Thatcher and Major. He displayed there a fearsome grasp of detail and political implication. He was then promoted to the post of Minister for Public Transport (1988-90) and Minister for Local Government (1990-92). Portillo is personable, charming, amusing and very able. He lacks the sour edge which infects some other Thatcherites. His main handicap is the 'future Prime Minister' tag.

Adapted from the *Guardian*, 24 May 1993 and Wood & Wood, 1992.

Item E *Stephen Dorrell*

(ii) In the late 1970s, Stephen Dorrell worked as the personal assistant of Peter Walker, a Cabinet minister in the Heath government and, later, the longest surviving 'wet' in Margaret Thatcher's Cabinet. When Dorrell won Loughborough from Labour in 1979, Walker spoke of him as a future Prime Minister and did so again when he finally stood down in 1992. It was a burden Dorrell bore throughout the 1980s when he remained on the backbenches. He served as PPS to Peter Walker when he was Secretary of State for Energy (1983-87). He became an assistant whip in 1987 and was a whip between 1988 and 1990. When John Major became Prime Minister in 1990 he was promoted to the post of Under Secretary of Health (1990-92). After the 1992 general election, he was appointed Financial Secretary in the Treasury. When Norman Lamont's resignation created a Cabinet vacancy in 1993, John Redwood's right wing credentials made the vital difference over Dorrell's claims. Dorrell finally entered the Cabinet as Secretary of State for National Heritage in July 1994.

Adapted from the *Guardian*, 31 January 1994, the *Times*, 25 July 1994 and *Wood & Wood*, 1992.

Questions

1. a) Using Items A and B explain why the number of junior ministers has grown since 1945.
   b) Give arguments for and against the view that the existing ministerial system is satisfactory.
2. Judging from Item C would you say that the ministerial careers described in Item D were fast or slow track careers? Give reasons for your answer.
3. Judging from Items C-E what factors determine a successful ministerial career?

1.3 Ministerial turnover

Ministers may move or be moved for a number of reasons. They may lose their seat at a general election (as happened to Chris Patten who was Conservative party chairman at the time of the 1992 general election, for example). They may choose to resign for personal reasons or out of principle. They may resign in connection with individual or ministerial responsibility. But, as Pyper (1993) found in a study of ministerial moves since 1964, by far the most common reason for moving is a reshuffle by the Prime Minister. In reshuffles, ministers may find that they have been moved to another post or that they have been dropped altogether.

Ministerial reshuffles

A great deal of secrecy surrounds a ministerial reshuffle. Although ministers are aware that a reshuffle is in the offing, most are not informed of the actual date. The Prime Minister usually seeks opinions over particular appointments. The chief whip is normally consulted, as is the Leader of the House and the Chancellor (if the appointments affect economic departments). But, it is the personality of the Prime Minister which determines procedure. Both Richard Crossman and Barbara Castle (former Labour ministers) record in their diaries, for example, that Harold Wilson sounded out opinions before finalising changes, whereas James Callaghan tended to keep his plans to himself. Margaret Thatcher refers to conversations she had with William Whitelaw and John Wakeham before her 1985 reshuffle and observes:

> 'They were both shrewd and party to the gossip which constitutes parliamentary opinion.' (Thatcher, 1993, p.418)

A minor reshuffle may only involve a small number of ministers. A large reshuffle, however, may radically alter the complexion of the government. In 1962, Harold Macmillan removed a third of his Cabinet colleagues in what came to be called 'the night of the long knives'. This was the biggest change of the Cabinet in modern times. Margaret Thatcher's reshuffle in July 1989 is a good example of a large reshuffle. It involved the shuffling of 62 people, leaving only three departments unaffected.

Reshuffles may also result in structural reorganisation. For example, Margaret Thatcher, initially, had two separate Cabinet ministers for Trade and for Industry, but, in 1983, the two departments were merged. Conversely, the Department of Health and Social Security was divided into two separate departments in 1988. Similarly, in July 1995, the Department of Employment was split between the Department of Education (to link training and employment), the Department of Trade and Industry (whose role was to look after industrial relations and pay) and the Department of the Environment (whose role was to deal with health and safety issues). The Employment Secretary at the time of this reorganisation was Michael Portillo. He remained in the Cabinet since he was given a new job - Defence Secretary.

Are British ministers reshuffled too much?

Compared to other ministers in Europe, British ministers have relatively short periods in a particular job. Rose (1991) found that, since 1964, the average length of tenure of office was two years, regardless of which party was in government. Junior ministers are more likely to be reshuffled than senior ministers. Turnover also differs between departments. Chancellors last longest (on average $4^1/_2$ years) whilst:

> 'Since the 1983 election there have been seven Environment Secretaries: that means on average a new one every 19 months. It's a huge and complex department, and if sometimes they don't seem to be on top of every aspect of it, no wonder.' (David McKie writing in the *Guardian*, 25 July 1994)

Rose (1991) argues that this rapid turnover has important implications. First, rapid ministerial turnover is an important factor when considering the balance of power between ministers and civil servants. Permanent secretaries (the chief civil servants in government departments) have longer terms of office than the ministers they serve. A top civil servant may spend 20 to 30 years before reaching an important post, in some cases spending all that time in a single department. This means that civil servants often have a greater knowledge of the working of the Whitehall machinery than their political masters.

Second, Britain reshuffles its Cabinet ministers more often than other European governments. As the EU makes more of an impact on British policy, British ministers will be expected to work more and more closely with their European counterparts. This task will not be made any easier if the personnel is continually changing. Also, compared to British ministers, other European ministers are far more likely to have greater specialist knowledge of the department in which they work. In France, the Netherlands and Norway, ministers must resign their seats when they take office as ministers. Many have come to the post with experience in administration gained at local or regional level. On the other hand, it should be noted that British ministers tend to have more parliamentary experience than their European counterparts.

Resignation issues

According to Woodhouse:

> 'Ministerial resignations are an important element of accountability...justified in a system in which routine accountability is weak.' (Woodhouse, 1993, p.278)

Resignations reassure the public that, beneath the adversarial party politics and the dramatic performances which take place in Parliament, moral values and a sense of responsibility are upheld by those in power.

It should be noted that ministers do not automatically resign when a mistake has been made. Resignation, in fact, may depend on a variety of factors. First, it depends on the Prime Minister's attitude. If the minister concerned is close to the Prime Minister, there may be a timely reshuffle to avoid resignation. New ministers cannot then be blamed for the mistakes of their predecessors. Second, it depends on the position of the minister in the party. If backbenchers are supportive of a minister's stance, the minister is less likely to resign. Third, ministers who are popular in the country or who have powerful friends are less likely to resign. Pyper (1993) suggests that there are:

> 'Five reasonably distinct types of ministerial departure. Resignations or dismissals could result from:
> 1. Changes in government structure and personnel (ie reshuffles).
> 2. Electoral defeat of a minister.
> 3. Miscellaneous personal reasons (including age, health, family factors, career development outside government).
> 4. Factors concerned with the convention of collective responsibility.
> 5. Factors concerned with the doctrine of individual ministerial responsibility.' (Pyper, 1993, p.66)

Collective responsibility is discussed in chapter 12 (section 2.2). The doctrine of individual ministerial responsibility is discussed below.

1.4 Individual ministerial responsibility

The official definition of individual ministerial responsibility is as follows:

> 'The individual responsibility of ministers for the work of their departments means that they are answerable to Parliament for all their department's activities. They bear the consequences of any failure in administration, any injustice to an individual or any aspect of a policy which may be criticised in Parliament, whether personally responsible or not. Since most ministers are members of the House of Commons, they must answer questions and defend themselves against criticism in person. Departmental ministers in the House of Lords are represented in the Commons by someone qualified to speak on their behalf, usually a junior minister.' (HMSO, 1994, p.42)

Pyper (1993 and 1994) argues that the doctrine of individual ministerial responsibility has two strands which he describes as '**role responsibility**' and '**personal responsibility**'. By 'role responsibility' Pyper means that ministers are responsible for four areas which he describes as:

> 'Policy leadership in their departments; managing departments; piloting legislation through its various parliamentary stages; [and] representing departmental interests in Cabinet,

> with pressure groups and with departmental clients.' (Pyper, 1994, p.12)

These are, in other words, areas of responsibility connected with the role played by ministers. On occasion, ministers are forced to resign due to failings in the performance of their role as head of a government department or part of a government department.

By 'personal responsibility' Pyper means that ministers are responsible for their own personal conduct:

> 'Naturally, like all other citizens they are expected to obey the law. Like all other MPs, they are expected to obey the rules and conventions of Parliament, such as those relating to possible conflicts of interest between private and parliamentary activities. As ministers, they are subject to a further set of rules of conduct, most of which are published as *Questions of Procedure for Ministers*. These establish guidelines on issues such as the holding of company shares and directorships. Less tangibly, ministers are also expected to act in accordance with an unwritten moral code.' (Pyper, 1994, p.12)

On occasion, therefore, ministers are forced to resign because of some personal failing which is not necessarily related to their performance as head of a government department or part of a government department.

Personal responsibility

All MPs are under public scrutiny, but this becomes even greater once they become ministers. An irregularity in an MP's private life may bar that MP from being considered for ministerial office in the first place. The media is only too eager to pick up on any event in an MP's past which might suggest that the MP has been dishonest or hypocritical. The following examples illustrate the type of personal behaviour which can lead to resignation.

First, mixing with the wrong people can be fatal as the Home Secretary, Reginald Maudling, found to his cost over the 'Poulson Affair' in 1972. John Poulson, an architect, was found to have bribed public officials. Maudling had conducted business with Poulson in the 1960s. Once this was revealed, whether or not Maudling was guilty of any misdemeanour, he had no choice but to resign. Similarly, Michael Mates, Minister of State for Northern Ireland, was forced to resign in June 1993 after his connections with Asil Nadir were exposed. Nadir jumped bail and returned to Northern Cyprus to avoid answering charges of fraud. Mates admitted supporting Nadir and giving him a gold watch.

Second, a thoughtless action can lead to resignation. In February 1995, for example, the Under Secretary of State for Scotland, Allan Stewart, resigned after brandishing a pickaxe in a confrontation with anti-motorway campaigners.

And third, revelations of a more personal nature can prove to be a minister's undoing. In 1983, Cecil Parkinson was forced to resign after an affair with his former secretary, Sarah Keays (and the birth of their child), became public. Similarly, the media's exposure of Minister of State for the Environment, Tim Yeo's extra-marital affair led to his resignation in January 1994.

The media has often been criticised for playing a role in the downfall of ministers. But, although criticism from the media may damage a minister's reputation, this alone cannot force a minister to resign. Despite that, there is little doubt that resignations for personal misdemeanours would be much less common if the misdemeanours were not widely reported in the media. In other words, it is often only when the media finds out about a personal misdemeanour that it becomes a resignation issue.

Role responsibility

Ministers are expected to be aware of and to be prepared for any eventualities that may arise in the area of government covered by their department (or their part of a department if they are junior ministers). They are responsible not only for the decisions they take, but also for those which they should have taken. An error of judgement may lead to resignation. This is as true with senior ministers as it is with junior ministers. Three examples can be used to illustrate what constitutes a failing in the sphere of role responsibility. First, in 1966, the then Chancellor of the Exchequer, James Callaghan, stated in public that devaluation of the pound was not a solution to the economic difficulties faced by the government. In November 1967, the government decided to devalue the pound and Callaghan immediately offered his resignation. At first the Prime Minister, Harold Wilson, refused the resignation offer, because:

> 'It was the policy of the government, not one minister, to fight to maintain the parity of the pound.' (Wilson, 1971, p.451)

After Callaghan had supervised measures to help achieve stability following the devaluation, he resigned. He was then appointed to the Home Office in a government reshuffle.

Second, when Argentina attacked the Falkland Islands in 1982, the Foreign Secretary, Lord Carrington, the Lord Privy Seal, Humphrey Atkins, and the Minister of State in the Foreign Office, Richard Luce, all resigned. Carrington accepted that his assessment of Argentinian intentions was wrong and it was, therefore, his constitutional duty to resign. John Nott, the Defence Secretary, also offered to resign, but his resignation was not accepted on the grounds that the Department of Defence was not responsible for Falklands policy.

Third, in December 1988, the Under Secretary of State for Health, Edwina Currie, was forced to resign two weeks after making a statement on television claiming that most of Britain's egg production was affected by salmonella. The impact of her claim was an immediate slump in egg sales. This led to an outcry from egg producers and their supporters in Parliament and the government was pressurised into agreeing to compensation costing several million pounds. A combination of media and backbench pressure forced Currie's resignation.

Mismanagement in a minister's department

In theory, since they are political heads of departments, ministers are held responsible for the actions of all subordinates as well as for their own acts:

> 'Viewed simplistically - as it often is - the doctrine of individual ministerial responsibility tells us that it is ministers, not civil servants, who are accountable to Parliament for the work of government departments and, correspondingly, it is ministers who take the blame when things go wrong. It is, however, not difficult to show the superficiality of such assumptions.' (Pyper, 1994, p.13)

Pyper goes on to point out that civil servants are legally accountable to the Public Accounts Committee for the accuracy of departmental accounts and civil servants appear before departmental select committees (although they are not allowed to answer questions about the conduct of individual civil servants). The trend, he suggests, is towards direct civil service accountability to Parliament. He then goes on to argue that the idea that ministers always protect their officials is erroneous. He cites the example of the collapse of the Vehicle and General Insurance company in 1971:

> 'Using the highly tendentious official report...as the basis for his argument, the Secretary of State effectively "passed the buck" to a single civil servant who was publicly named and blamed for the Department of Trade and Industry's failure to act in advance of Vehicle and General's collapse.' (Pyper, 1994, p.13)

As a result, the Secretary of State managed to avoid taking the blame for the actions of his department.

Although it is possible for ministers to avoid taking responsibility for the actions of their officials, mismanagement in a minister's department can still lead to resignation. In 1986, for example, the Secretary of State for Trade and Industry, Leon Brittan, was forced to resign over the Westland Affair when it was revealed that he had authorised one of his officials to leak a letter designed to undermine the reputation of Michael Heseltine (Brittan supported an American takeover of Westland helicopters whilst Heseltine preferred takeover by a European company - see chapter 12, section 2.2 for a fuller account of this event). It should be noted, however, that Brittan resigned because he had acted improperly, not because his official had acted improperly.

Does individual ministerial responsibility really exist?

In practice, the convention of individual ministerial responsibility does not work predictably. Individual ministers may be shielded against the consequences of serious errors by their departments or by collective ministerial responsibility. Whether or not a particular minister is required to resign over a particular issue becomes a political rather than a constitutional question.

If the Prime Minister wishes or party solidarity applies, the issue may be made into a test of confidence in the government as a whole. Norman Lamont came under severe criticism after 'Black Wednesday' when Britain withdrew from the ERM (see chapter 15, section 2.2), but he did not resign because he was shielded by the Prime Minister.

The convention of individual ministerial responsibility is a product of Britain's uncodified constitution (see chapter 4). This makes it difficult to define exactly what it means or to say precisely what ministers' responsibilities are. As a result, therefore, it can be difficult to condemn individual ministers since there are no clear rules against which ministers' performance or behaviour can be judged. Woodhouse, writing in the *Economist* (1 October 1994), agrees with this and points out that in the 19th century ministers could be expected to know everything that went on in their departments, whereas today no minister can expect to know about even a small proportion of the work that is done. This situation, she claims, has been further complicated by the delegation of government tasks to quasi-autonomous agencies. As Pyper points out:

> 'There were fears from the outset that if policies were formulated in the parent department, but implemented by the agencies, this was a recipe for the type of buck passing which had stalled many attempts to enforce accountability in the old nationalised industries, where ministers would decline to take responsibility on the grounds that: "This is a matter of day-to-day management", while members of the board would claim in turn that: "It is really a matter of strategic policy - ask the minister".' (Pyper, 1994, p.14)

Activity 13.2

Item A *Resignations and individual ministerial responsibility*

Nov 1967
James Callaghan
Chancellor
Role responsibility
Devaluation of sterling

July 1972
Reginauld Maulding
Home Secretary
Personal responsibility
Poulson affair

May 1973
Lord Lambton
Under Secretary of State, Defence (RAF)
Personal responsibility
Call girl scandal

May 1973
Earl Jellicoe
Leader of Lords
Personal responsibility
Call girl scandal

Sept 1974
Lord Brayley
Under Secretary of State, Defence (Army)
Personal responsibility
Business scandal

Jan 1982
Nicholas Fairbairn
Solicitor-General
Personal & role responsibility
'Glasgow rape case' and personal life

Apr 1982
Lord Carrington
Foreign Secretary
Role responsibility
Invasion of Falklands

Apr 1982
Humphrey Atkins
Lord Privy Seal
Role responsibility
Invasion of Falklands

Apr 1982
Richard Luce
Minister of State, Foreign Office
Role responsibility
Invasion of Falklands

Oct 1985
Cecil Parkinson
Transport Secretary
Personal responsibility
Adultery - Sara Keays affair

Jan 1986
Leon Brittan
Trade & Industry Secretary
Role responsibility
Westland affair

Jan 1986
Michael Heseltine
Defence Secretary
Role responsibility
Westland affair

Dec 1988
Edwina Currie
Under Secretary of State, Health
Role responsibility
Salmonella in eggs affair

Sept 1990
Patrick Nicholls
Under Secretary of State, Environment
Personal responsibility
Drink driving

Sept 1992
David Mellor
National Heritage Secretary
Personal responsibility
Personal life

May 1993
Norman Lamont
Chancellor
Role & personal responsibility
'Black Wednesday' and personal life

Jun 1993
Michael Mates
Minister of State, Northern Ireland
Personal responsibility
Connections with Asil Nadir

Jan 1994
Tim Yeo
Minister of State, Environment
Personal responsibility
Adultery - illegitimate child

Jan 1994
Lord Caithness
Minister of State, Transport
Personal responsibility
Adultery - wife committed suicide

Oct 1994
Tim Smith
Under Secretary of State, Northern Ireland
Personal responsibility
Cash for questions

Oct 1994
Neil Hamilton
Under Secretary for Corporate affairs
Personal responsibility
Cash for questions

Feb 1995
Allan Stewart
Under Secretary of State, Scotland
Personal responsibility
Brandished pickaxe at demonstrators

Feb 1995
Charles Wardle
Under Secretary of State, Industry and Energy
Role responsibility
Opposed government's immigration policy

Mar 1995
Robert Hughes
Parliamentary Secretary, OPSS
Personal responsibility
Adultery

Adapted from Pyper 1994 and the *Times*, 7 March 1995.

Item B *Shuffling the pack (1)*

Ministers in the Department of the Environment tend not to stay there for long. The current Secretary of State, John Gummer, has stayed longer than most. He has served there for 14 months. Michael Howard only lasted for 13 months before moving to the Home Office. Kenneth Baker only lasted for eight months before moving to Education. Tom King only lasted for six months before moving to Transport. The same trend is found with ministers of state. Whereas, in the last Labour government, Reg Freeson and Denis Howell served five years at Environment, there have been 15 ministers of state since the 1987 election and only two have served for more than two years. Similarly, until 1979 it was not unknown for under secretaries to remain in post for long enough to master their brief. Since then, it has been rare for them to serve a two year term. There have been 23 under secretaries in the Department of Environment since 1983 - and Environment is not untypical. A case can be made for this. Some departures are inevitable and have nothing to do with politics. Others are calculated. Ministers may grow stale if they stay in one place for too long or they may 'go native' (put the views of their civil servants before their party commitments). But, much of the work done by junior ministers is complex. It takes time to learn and those going through the learning process are dependent on civil servant advice.

Adapted from the *Guardian*, 25 July 1994.

Item C *Shuffling the pack (2)*

This cartoon shows John Major (middle) talking to the Foreign Secretary, Douglas Hurd. The man on the right is the new Employment Secretary, Michael Portillo.

This cartoon appeared in *Private Eye* on 29 July 1994.

Item D *Ministerial responsibility (1)*

The idea that there was once a golden age when ministers behaved honourably is derived from the Crichel Down case of 1954. Sir Thomas Dugdale, Secretary of State for Agriculture, resigned after a row about the maladministration of his officials. It appeared that he was taking the blame for what had been done in his name, but without his knowledge. Recent evidence, however, suggests that the real reason for his resignation was the loss of support of his colleagues. That is why ministers resign. They do not usually resign because of rows over policy or allegations about their private lives. Keith Dowding who has studied postwar resignations argues: 'Ministers fight to retain their jobs, spending the last penny of their political capital. By and large, ministers who resign are those whose capital has been exhausted by previous efforts to retain their position.' Recently, the government has drawn a distinction between accountability (which cannot be delegated by ministers) and responsibility (which can). A minister can be challenged in Parliament about the conduct of civil servants and asked to account for their behaviour. But, that does not mean that the minister is responsible for all mistakes made by civil servants. The trouble is that this distinction makes it unclear who should be penalised if mistakes are made. Critics argue that the distinction does not work because ministers do not determine the extent of their responsibilities. What they are asked about in Parliament is the result of external pressures, such as stories in the media.

Adapted from the *Times*, 21 December 1994.

Item E *Ministerial responsibility (2)*

Yesterday, the Home Secretary, Michael Howard, claimed: 'With regard to operational responsibility, there has always been a division between policy matters and operational matters.' Mr Howard has no constitutional authority for this claim. *Questions of Procedure for Ministers* states: 'Each minister is responsible to Parliament for the conduct of his or her department and for the actions carried out by the department in pursuit of government policies or in the discharge of responsibilities laid upon him or her as a minister.' The spectacle of a government minister trying to set new constitutional guidelines to suit the political embarrassment of the day has profound implications.

Adapted from a letter to the *Times*, 12 January 1995.

Questions

1. Why do ministers resign? Use Items A, D and E in your answer.
2. 'The doctrine of individual ministerial responsibility is a myth'. Give arguments for and against this statement using Items A, D and E.
3. Judging from Items B and C what are the benefits and drawbacks of frequent and extensive government reshuffles?

1.5 Ministerial roles

Before 1830, departments were small and all ministers below Cabinet rank were undifferentiated:

> 'They were all alike in their legal, administrative and political subordination to their ministerial chiefs.' (Theakston, 1987, p.1)

By 1830, government business had increased in volume and this led to a gradual change in the structure of departments. From 1914 onwards, departmental work not only increased, but became more complex. This led to duties being broken down into particular areas of responsibility.

The trend of appointing a number of junior ministers with specific responsibilities began in 1964 when Alec Douglas Home was Prime Minister, and has continued ever since. During the 1970s:

> '[It gradually] became the practice to assign to named ministers specific areas of departmental work to oversee, rather than delegating to them miscellaneous duties on an ad hoc basis.' (Theakston, 1987, p.87)

Today, some junior ministers are appointed to a specific job by the Prime Minister. Alternatively, the allocation of a junior minister's duties is left to the minister who heads the department. The job allocated to a junior minister depends on that minister's experience, abilities and the particular circumstances at the time. Areas of responsibility are not fixed and:

> 'There may be frequent adjustments as ministers enter, leave or change their posts and as changing circumstances push issues up or down the political agenda.' (Theakston, 1987, p.87)

In general terms, however, because junior ministers tend to have greater responsibility today than used to be the case, they have moved more into the political limelight. They now defend their particular area of work at Question Time and in the media. On occasion, this greater exposure can lead to greater criticism. For example, in late 1994 Nicholas Scott, Minister for Social Security and Disabled People, was the focus of prolonged attack from pressure groups and certain sections in the media when he was accused of blocking a private member's Bill on disabled people's rights.

Ministerial decision making

Ministers are responsible for the policy initiated in their departments. They must study the different options presented to them by their civil servants and then use their political judgement to decide what policies or options should be decided upon or rejected. Decisions are made on ideological grounds or financial grounds (or both). Ministers are also diplomats who liaise with the public and outside bodies on behalf of their department.

According to Madgwick, much of the work in a department is routine. He compares the role of Cabinet ministers with those of managing directors. Cabinet ministers oversee the work of their departments and are:

> 'Semi-detached, at the top but not in touch, on a cloud rather than a mountain.' (Madgwick, 1991, p.22)

They rely on their officials to keep them up-to-date with what is happening.

The way in which junior ministers handle their role largely depends on their previous experience and personality. For example, a junior minister with business experience is likely to be used to dealing with administrative pressures, whilst a minister with journalistic experience is likely to be familiar with the communication requirements of the job. Sideways movement from one ministerial post to another helps ministers gain a wide range of experience and tests their abilities.

Relationships between ministers

Generally, Cabinet ministers have little say as to who their junior ministers should be. They may inherit an existing team when they move to a department or the Prime Minister may decide to shuffle junior ministers to spread their experience.

Relationships between ministers vary according to the role adopted by the Cabinet minister. Some Cabinet ministers have regular team meetings. Others do not. In the Treasury, for example, although each minister has a separate area of responsibility, the whole team is brought together for the annual Budget. The following two extracts indicate the importance of cultivating good relations between ministers working in the same department. The first was written by William Whitelaw:

> 'I found a fascinating ministry under John Hare whom I came to admire as a most skilful and sensitive minister. He was an ideal minister to serve under as he brought his junior minister in on all discussions and, once he had delegated work, he left you to get on with it without interference. Subsequently, as a minister myself, I have tried to follow that example and it must be the right way to run a government department. It is, alas, more difficult today since government departments are much larger and there are so many more ministers involved with whom to keep in touch.' (Whitelaw, 1990, p.57)

The second extract was written by Peter Walker, who, in 1970, was asked by the Prime Minister, Edward Heath, to set up the new Department of the Environment. Every morning he briefed the whole ministerial team:

> 'These daily meetings did mean that all ministers knew what was happening throughout the whole department. Civil servants could never go to a junior minister and get him to agree to something that the Secretary of State would turn down. It led to more cohesion and enthusiasm. There was another important advantage. PPSs could attend, so I had, in fact, 15 ministers and PPSs going around the Commons explaining why we had adopted this or that policy. In this way, you were able to make a big impact on the parliamentary party where so much strength ultimately lay.' (Walker, 1991, p.76)

Ministers and their departments

Ministers are mainly concerned with major policy decisions. The everyday work of the department is carried out by a parallel hierarchy of civil servants. The civil servants who advise ministers (those at the top of the hierarchy) change their jobs much less frequently than ministers. As a result, a continuity of policy is maintained regardless of how often ministers are shuffled. Civil servants are also able to ensure that there is a smooth transition if there is a complete change of government. Rose argues:

> 'The inertia of ministries provides a relatively stable environment in which the government of the day can introduce innovations selectively. The continuities of ministries is a necessary condition of government persisting from election to election. Ministries, and the civil servants who serve them, are the agents that ensure that the Queen's government is always carried on.' (Rose, 1987, p.5)

Civil servants are supposed to be impartial and neutral advisers. It is not their responsibility to make decisions. Rather, it is their job to consult with a minister over a proposed course of action and to point out both the benefits and drawbacks that might arise (see part 3 below for a detailed discussion of the relationship between ministers and civil servants). Peter Hennessy argues that senior civil servants (the small group at the top of the hierarchy) have an unwritten code of ethics which is passed down from one generation to the next. This code contains three elements:

> 'Firstly, a constant and careful concern for the law. Secondly, a concern for Parliament, its needs and procedures - no lying and misleading. Thirdly, a constant concern for democracy - even the milder forms of destabilisation are out.' (*Independent*, 5 June 1989)

Although those civil servants at the top are highly paid, Hennessy suggests that their main motivation is the desire to be of service to the country and to act on behalf of the electors as well as the government.

Ministers are answerable to Parliament for all the work of their department. Therefore, the job of civil servants is also to ensure that ministers are well briefed. In return, ministers seek to defend the interests of their department.

Pressures on ministers

There are immense pressures on the time of ministers, especially Cabinet ministers. They are expected to run their departments and to perform their constituency duties as MPs. They are also expected to speak in public for both government and party.

Departmental work has increased considerably in recent years and ministers cannot possibly watch over all the day-to-day work carried out by a department. It should be noted, however, that the vast majority of work done by a department is routine and uncontroversial. Ministers need to learn the art of delegation, as Norman Fowler explains:

> 'I regularly started work at 5.30 am when I had just taken over the DHSS [Department of Health and Social Security] and every issue - big, small and minute - appeared to run through my office...Whitehall would feed you red boxes as long as you wanted to eat. If you were not careful, you simply ended up with the interdepartmental prize for letter signing and a reputation for seeing every piece of paper in

circulation at the time. I found it better to devolve.' (Fowler, 1991, pp.318-19)

It is not just the amount of work that brings pressure to bear on ministers, it is also the nature of the work. On his first day as Under Secretary of State in the Department of the Environment, Alan Clark complained that:

> 'The subject matter is turgid: a mass of "schemes" whose purpose, plainly, is not so much to bring relief to those out of work as to devise excuses for removing them from the Register...The Enterprise Allowance Scheme, the Job Release Scheme, the Community Scheme. Convoluted and obscure even at their inception, they have since been so picked over and "modified" by civil servants as to be incomprehensible. I ought to welcome these devices, and must try to master their intricacies. But, my head is bursting.' (Clark, 1993, p.10)

So, as well as lack of time, ministers are constrained by a lack of specialist knowledge. The constant reshuffling of ministers prevents many of them from acquiring any detailed knowledge and understanding of the work of their department. The result, according to Madgwick, is that:

> 'Some ministers stay for two years or more in one office, learn fast and master enough of their subject to be reasonably effective. Others can be no more than visiting amateurs, reading a brief on the way to a meeting, hoping not to be found in error in public.' (Madgwick, 1991, p.42)

A further problem is access to information. Theakston (1987) suggests that less than 1% of a department's work is seen by a minister and that information is rationed on a 'need to know' basis. In some cases, junior ministers do not even know what is going on in their own department outside their own area of work.

There is also constant pressure on ministers from their own party, from the opposition parties, from pressure groups, from other lobbyists, from the media and from members of the public. This pressure can become particularly intense if there is disagreement within the government ranks. The split between the pro-Europeans and Eurosceptics which emerged in the Cabinet in late 1994, for example, added to the pressure on the government at all levels.

Activity 13.3

Item A *Pressures on ministers*

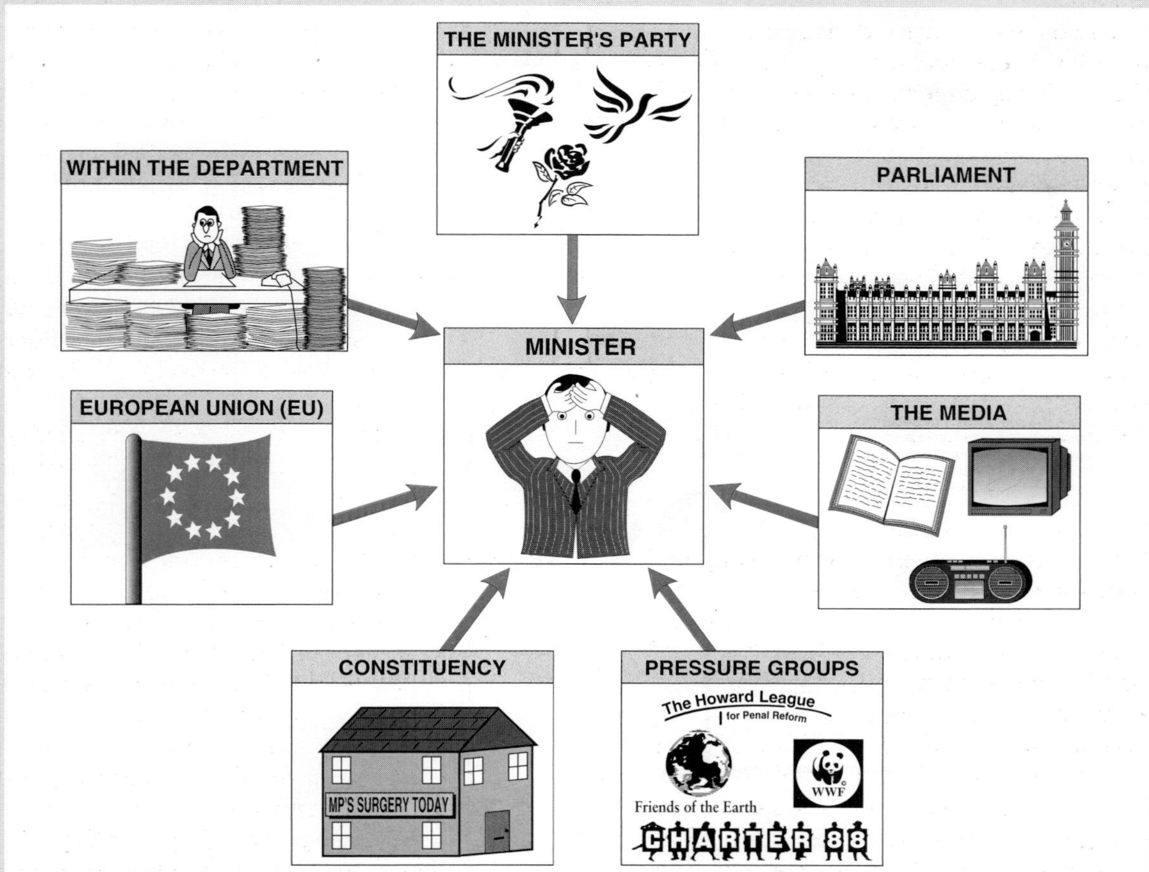

Item B *Policy making in the Department of Transport*

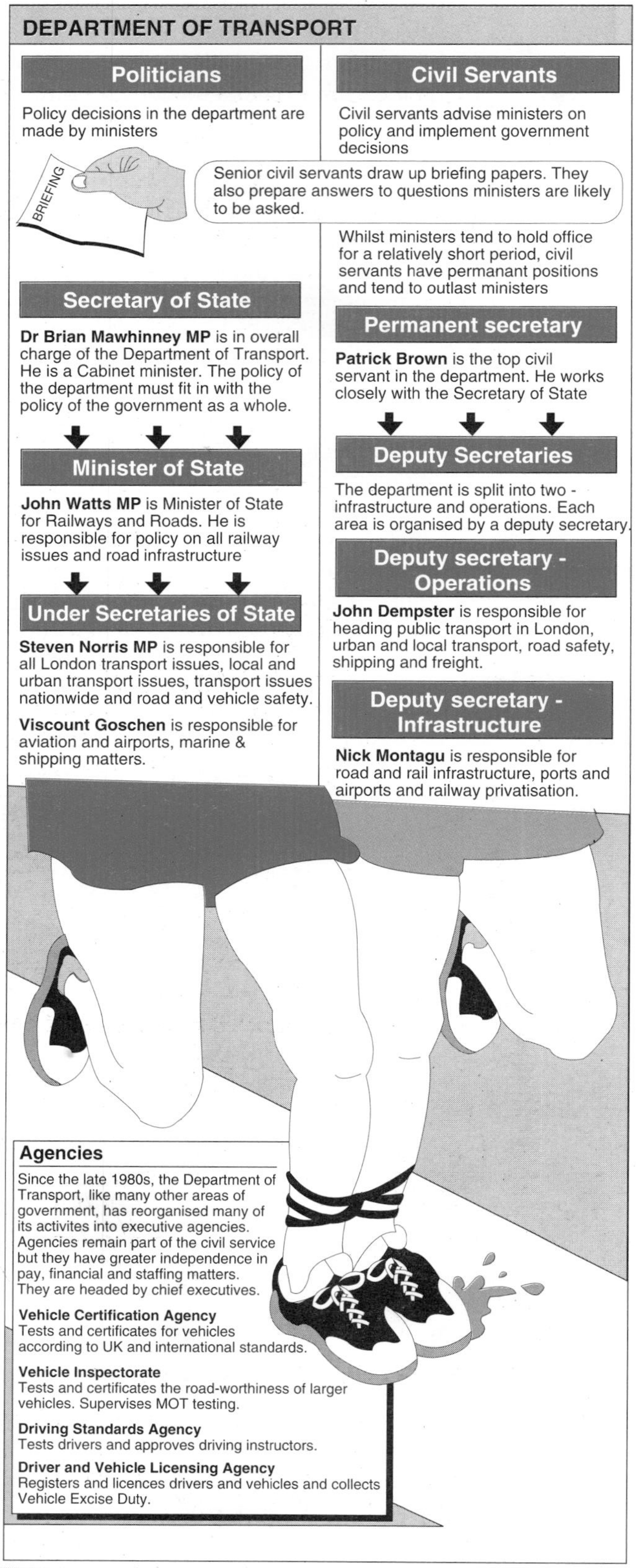

DEPARTMENT OF TRANSPORT
Politicians
Policy decisions in the department are made by ministers
BRIEFING
Civil Servants
Civil servants advise ministers on policy and implement government decisions
Senior civil servants draw up briefing papers. They also prepare answers to questions ministers are likely to be asked.
Whilst ministers tend to hold office for a relatively short period, civil servants have permanant positions and tend to outlast ministers
Secretary of State
Dr Brian Mawhinney MP is in overall charge of the Department of Transport. He is a Cabinet minister. The policy of the department must fit in with the policy of the government as a whole.
Minister of State
John Watts MP is Minister of State for Railways and Roads. He is responsible for policy on all railway issues and road infrastructure
Under Secretaries of State
Steven Norris MP is responsible for all London transport issues, local and urban transport issues, transport issues nationwide and road and vehicle safety.
Viscount Goschen is responsible for aviation and airports, marine & shipping matters.
Permanent secretary
Patrick Brown is the top civil servant in the department. He works closely with the Secretary of State
Deputy Secretaries
The department is split into two - infrastructure and operations. Each area is organised by a deputy secretary.
Deputy secretary - Operations
John Dempster is responsible for heading public transport in London, urban and local transport, road safety, shipping and freight.
Deputy secretary - Infrastructure
Nick Montagu is responsible for road and rail infrastructure, ports and airports and railway privatisation.
Agencies
Since the late 1980s, the Department of Transport, like many other areas of government, has reorganised many of its activites into executive agencies. Agencies remain part of the civil service but they have greater independence in pay, financial and staffing matters. They are headed by chief executives.
Vehicle Certification Agency
Tests and certificates for vehicles according to UK and international standards.
Vehicle Inspectorate
Tests and certificates the road-worthiness of larger vehicles. Supervises MOT testing.
Driving Standards Agency
Tests drivers and approves driving instructors.
Driver and Vehicle Licensing Agency
Registers and licences drivers and vehicles and collects Vehicle Excise Duty.

Adapted from the *Guardian*, 23 June 1992 and the *Times*, 21 July 1994.

Item C *Alan Clark, Minister for Trade*

Alan Clark, who was Minister for Trade between 1986 and 1989, complains that much of ministers' time is wasted in meetings with delegations because there are so few occasions when a minister's mind is altered during a discussion. Yet, he relates how one particular delegation - from the charity Lynx - won him over just after he became Minister for Trade. After meeting the delegation from Lynx, Clark agreed to draw up an order which would force fur traders to label garments made of the skins of animals that had been caught in leg-hold traps. Clark felt so strongly about this measure that he even writes: 'Sometimes I think that all I want is to stay in office here long enough to get my fur legislation on to the statute book.' As a result of his devotion to this cause, Clark was prepared to devote enormous energy and time to it. He met, threatened and cajoled all sorts of people - such as lawyers, ambassadors, senior civil servants from several departments, eskimos, furriers and small shopkeepers. By June 1988, it seemed that the path had been cleared for his legislation to be adopted. But, on 14 June 1988, Clark was summoned to see the Prime Minister. She wanted Clark to drop the scheme. After four and a half minutes, Clark realised he had lost. The meeting was scheduled for 15 minutes, but lasted 55. About three quarters of the way through the meeting Clark said: 'Well, if that's what you want, I will obey you.'

Adapted from Clark, 1993.

Item D *Engagement diaries of junior ministers, 1986*

In 1986, William Waldegrave was Minister of State for the Environment, Country and Local Government. David Trippier was Parliamentary Under Secretary in the Department of Employment.

Tuesday 22 April 1986	**William Waldegrave**
9.20	Arrive Ringway, Manchester (shuttle)
10.20	Arr. Heyside, near Oldham. Launch of Oldham Countryside Voluntary Projects Programme
10.30	Press Call
10.45	Depart for Rochdale
11.10	Arrive Healey Dell: 10th anniversary of local nature reserve
11.30	Press call - stocking of new lagoons, tree planting etc.
11.55	Depart.
12.00 to 12.45	TBA Industrial Products Ltd. Reception and buffet lunch
1.40	Arrive Ringway
2.50	Arrive Heathrow
3.45	Briefing for...
4.00	Meeting with Alistair Goodlad (Parliamentary Under Secretary Energy):
4.45	Briefing for First Order Parliamentary Questions (next day)
5.30	Meeting with Kenneth Baker (Secretary of State) to discuss Chairmanship of the Audit Commission.
6.15	Briefing for First Order Parliamentary Questions
6.30 for 7.00	Two-line whip on opposition day debates: Housing and Transport (House of Commons)
7.15 for 7.45	United and Cecil Club Dinner (House of Commons)
9.30 for 10.00	Two-line whip on opposition day debates

Tuesday 22 April 1986	**David Trippier**
8.00	Wages Bill team (Caxton House)
9.00	Meeting with Peter Morrison (Minister of State, Trade and Industry): management development and training (Department of Trade and Industry)
10.30 to 1.00	Standing Committee: Wages Bill (House of Commons)
2.30	First Order Parliamentary Questions (House of Commons)
3.00	Ministry of Defence Small Firms Group: meeting with Lord Young (Secretary of State), Norman Lamont (MoD Minister of State), Peter Levene (Chief of Defence Procurement)
3.15	Prime Minister's Questions
3.30	Small business lobby: Department of Employment
4.00	MSC presentation on non-advanced further education: Secretary of State and Chris Patten (Minister of State, Education) (Caxton House)
4.30 to 7.00	Standing Committee: Wages Bill (House of Commons)
6.30 for 7.00	Two line whip on opposition day debates (House of Commons)
7.00 for 7.30	British Tissues Dinner: Speech (House of Commons)
9.30 for 10.00	Two line whip on opposition day debates

Questions

1. Suppose you had been asked to give advice to a minister who complained that there were too many pressures pulling in different directions. What advice would you give? Use Items A, C and D in your answer.
2. Using Item B describe the relationship between ministers and their department.
3. What do Items C and D tell us about (a) the role played by ministers and (b) the pressures on ministers?

2 The civil service

Key Issues

1. What is the civil service?
2. What sort of people become civil servants?
3. What role does the civil service play in theory and in practice?
4. How have recent reforms affected the civil service?

2.1 What is the civil service?

The civil service is an administrative system which consists of a body of government officials who are employed in civil occupations. According to a government publication:

> 'Civil servants are servants of the Crown. For all practical purposes, the Crown in this context means, and is represented by, the government of the day...The civil service as such has no

constitutional responsibility separate from the government of the day which it serves as a whole, that is to say Her Majesty's ministers collectively. The duty of an individual civil servant is first and foremost to the minister of the Crown who is in charge of the department concerned. A change of minister, for whatever reason, does not involve a change of staff.' (HMSO, 1994, pp.47-48)

This may be the official view, but, in practice, the role and responsibilities of civil servants are more complex than this suggests (see section 2.4 below for a discussion of the role of civil servants).

Historical background

The earliest recorded civil service existed in China 2,000 years ago under the Ch'in dynasty (221-206 BC). It consisted of a centralised bureaucracy of talented people whose role was to serve the state. Entry into the civil service was by examination. Officials were called 'mandarins', a term still used to describe the small elite at the top of the British civil service today.

According to Hennessy (1989) the term 'civil service' was coined by the East India Company which ran India on behalf of the British government from 1599 to the mid-19th century. The term was introduced to distinguish civilian employees from those serving with the military.

Before the 19th century, a civil service in the modern sense did not exist. The state's administrative system was not regarded as a single service and the number of full-time staff was small (in the 1820s, for example, the total number of civil servants employed by the Home Office was just 17). What appointments there were, were made by nepotism or patronage rather than on merit. Ministers tended to look after their own departmental affairs, whilst officials performed tasks which today would be considered political. Drewry & Butcher note that:

> 'It was not uncommon for civil servants to combine their official tasks with those of ministerial office.' (Drewry & Butcher, 1991, p.127)

It was not until the mid-19th century that an attempt was made to establish an efficient and organised civil service.

The Northcote-Trevelyan Report (1854)

The impetus for civil service reform came from the Treasury. The Chancellor, Gladstone, set up an inquiry in April 1853 under Northcote and Trevelyan. Trevelyan had served in the Indian civil service (set up by the East India Company) and he aimed to bring the British civil service up to the high standard of administration for which the Indian civil service was known. The Northcote-Trevelyan Report was published in 1854. It made five main recommendations:

> '1. Civil service posts should be divided between superior and inferior categories, creating a distinction between intellectual and mechanical tasks.
> 2. Entrants into the service should, in general, be young men who would receive on-the-job training for their duties (it rejected recruiting mature men who had acquired experience elsewhere).
> 3. Recruitment should be through open competitive examination - one for graduates to higher posts, one for junior posts.
> 4. The examination should be, in all cases, a competing literary examination (ie in liberal arts rather than professional or technical subjects).
> 5. Promotion should be on the basis of merit, not favouritism.' (Drewry & Butcher, 1991, p.43)

The report was welcomed by Gladstone, but was opposed by his colleagues and by top civil servants who saw it as a threat to the system of patronage. Although entrance examinations were conducted by the Civil Service Commission set up in May 1855, open competition was not fully established until the Playfair Report was published in 1875.

The Fulton Report (1968)

Although there were a few small inquiries and adjustments to the civil service after 1875, its structure remained virtually unchanged until 1968 when the Fulton Report, commissioned by Prime Minister Harold Wilson was published. This report was commissioned in response to growing concern over the continuing tradition of employing recruits with a generalist rather than a specialist background.

The Fulton Report found that civil servants still came from a narrow background and had little real experience of the outside world. It also found that they were poorly trained, lacked expertise and had few managerial skills. The report made recommendations designed to professionalise the service by making civil servants more accountable. Greenaway notes that Fulton was:

> 'Concerned with three areas of the civil service - its structure and grading, recruitment procedures and in-service training...One of the key recommendations [was the introduction of a] single, unified grading structure...linked to a desire to abolish the dividing lines between the generalist administration and specialist classes.' (Greenaway, 1992, pp.176-7)

The report recommended the setting up of a civil service college to provide training and the introduction of greater mobility both between departments and in the recruitment of specialists from the outside world.

Although some of these changes were made, Fulton's radical plans were never fully implemented. The main reason for this was that it was the civil servants themselves who had to implement the reforms. They only implemented reforms which were acceptable to them (see Table 13.1 below).

le 13.1

Fulton Report on the civil service, 1968

at it found	What it recommended	What happened
Dominant philosophy of he 'amateur'.	Preference for 'relevant' degrees when recruiting.	Preference for 'relevance' rejected.
nsufficient scope given to pecialists.	Specialisation in economic or financial administration or social administration.	Not implemented.
Too few civil servants rained in management	Civil service college (courses to include management training for specialists)	Set up (but most training still done in departments).
Staff management inadequate. Not enough career planning; too much movement from job to job.	Civil service department to be set up.	Established, but abolished in 1981).
'Rigid and prolific departmentalism'	Unified grading, following job evaluation exercise	Some rationalisation.
Not enough contact between the civil service and the community it serves.	Greater mobility between civil service and other employment.	Civil service pension rules modified but little evidence of much effect
Too much secrecy	Inquiry into the Official Secrets Act	Franks Report (1972) on the Official Secrets Act 1911. Not yet implemented.
. Social and educational exclusiveness	(a) Inquiry into methods of recruitment and (b) larger graduate entry.	(a) Davies Report (1969) on 'Method II' (b) Administration Trainee grade set up, and enlarged entry.
. Deficiencies in aspects of departmental structure, relating, for example, to accountability and policy planning	Recommendations such as: (a) 'Hiving off' some departmental functions. (b) Promotion of 'accountable management'. (c) Planning units, headed by senior policy advisers.	(a) Some functions hived off (eg in employment). (b) Continuing debate on accountability. (c) Some planning units, but not on Fulton's model.

Adapted from Drewry & Butcher, 1991.

2.2 The structure of the civil service

Following the Northcote-Trevelyan reforms, the civil service was based on three 'classes' - the **administrative class** (which advised ministers on policy), the **executive class** (which was concerned with the implementation of policy) and the **clerical class** (which carried out detailed routine tasks). By the 1960s, however, these three broad classes had been subdivided into 47 different general classes and 1,400 departmental classes (Greenwood, 1989).

The Fulton Report suggested that classes should be renamed 'grades' since the word 'class' suggests inferior and superior groups. This, it was argued, could inhibit mobility and restrict opportunities for people to advance within the structure. The idea was that there would be a single unified grading system - around 20 grades which covered all jobs from top to bottom. This, it was hoped, would simplify the structure of the service. But, by 1977, there were still 38 general classes and 500 departmental classes.

Today, the non-industrial civil service can still be divided roughly into three groups - service-wide groups, service-wide specialist groups and departmental groups. **Service-wide groups** are made up of generalist administrators who operate in various or all departments. The main service-wide group is the Administration Group (see below). **Service-wide specialist groups** are made up of specialists who operate in various or all departments. These groups have their own grading and qualification systems. Examples are the Economist, Information Officer, Librarian and Statistician Groups. **Departmental groups** are made up of civil servants peculiar to a single department. They also have separate pay and qualification structures. Examples of departmental groups are tax inspectors working for the inland revenue, driving inspectors working for the Department of Transport and prison officers employed by the Home Office. The structure of the civil service can, therefore, be broken down as follows:

> 'About half of all civil servants are engaged in the provision of public services. These include paying sickness benefits and pensions, collecting taxes and contributions, running employment services, staffing prisons and

> providing services to industry and agriculture. Around a quarter are employed in the Ministry of Defence. The rest are divided between: central administrative and policy duties [the Administration Group]; support services; and largely financially self-supporting services, for instance, those provided by the department for National Savings and the Royal Mint...Four fifths of civil servants work outside London.' (HMSO, 1994, p.48)

It should be noted, however, that whilst the basic structure still remains in place, reforms made since the publication of the Ibbs Report in 1988 (see p.389) have affected it.

The Administration Group

By far the biggest service-wide group is the Administration Group:

> 'The Administration Group, the largest group within the service, [was] created in 1972 from the former clerical, executive and lower administrative classes.' (Greenwood, 1989, p.57)

The Administration Group provides policy advice and general administration. At the top of the Administration Group is the 'open structure'. Below it are the lower administrative levels.

The open structure

The top seven grades in the civil service make up the open structure. Before 1979, the open structure consisted of just the top three grades, but this was gradually extended. Grade six was included in 1984 and grade seven was included in 1986. These seven grades run from **permanent secretary** at the top to **principal** in the seventh grade.

Table 13.2 The seven grades in the open structure

Grade 1	First permanent secretary
Grade 1A	Second permanent secretary
Grade 2	Deputy secretary
Grade 3	Under secretary
Grade 4	Executive directing bands
Grade 5	Assistant secretary
Grade 6	Senior principal
Grade 7	Principal

The open structure, therefore, includes those civil servants at the very top of the hierarchy. These civil servants are involved in the policy making process and make up just 5% of the non-industrial civil service as a whole.

As far as the policy making process is concerned, the key advisers to ministers are drawn from grades 1-4. Grade 5 civil servants are responsible for a section of a department's work and may make a significant input into policy making (though their views are normally filtered through more senior officials). Grades 6 and 7 are more concerned with the finer details of potential legislation. For example, they are the civil servants who deal with pressure groups. There are roughly 1,000 civil servants in grades 1-4.

The administrative levels

Those civil servants who work for the Administration Group but are not on grades 1-7 belong to the administrative levels. Their number is, unsurprisingly, much larger than that employed in the open structure. The range of tasks varies from middle management to routine clerical jobs. The administrative levels consist of:

> 'A plethora of categories, groups and classes, many with their own separate pay and grading scales.' (Greenwood, 1989, p.57)

Industrial civil servants

The number of industrial civil servants is small. They make up around 6% of the overall total. Industrial civil servants work in government controlled industrial concerns, such as the navy shipyards in Scotland.

Reforms since 1979

By the time that the first Thatcher government was elected in 1979, it was clear that the Fulton reforms had largely failed. Soon after her election, Margaret Thatcher began to argue that the civil service was too large, wasteful of resources and did not provide value for money. The result was a new attempt to reform the service.

Certainly, the civil service had grown. In 1961, it employed 640,000 people, but by 1979 this had grown to 732,000. On taking up office, however, Thatcher froze civil service recruitment (compulsory redundancies were avoided by not replacing those who retired). Thatcher notes that this policy was not readily accepted by civil servants themselves:

> 'Departments came up with a range of ingenious reasons why this principle should not apply to them. But, one by one they were overruled.' (Thatcher, 1993, p.94)

The drive for reform was managed from Downing Street. Sir Derek Rayner (a leading businessman brought in from the private sector) was given a small unit within the Cabinet Office (the Efficiency Unit) whose job was to scrutinise the civil service from within. As a result of this initiative, the Management Information System for Ministers (MINIS) was introduced into the Department of the Environment in 1980 and this led to the introduction of the Financial Management Initiative (FMI) in 1982. The FMI covered all departments and was the first real attempt at streamlining the civil service. Its aim was to improve efficiency by initiating a change of attitude and introducing new management practices. Civil servants were to become the equivalent of line managers in business by being held directly responsible for particular policies in their departments. They were to be given a clear view of their objectives and encouraged to use their initiative to make the best use of resources available to them.

Margaret Thatcher also argued that a great deal of potential talent in the civil service was being wasted because of the culture of bureaucracy which was fostered by Whitehall. She argued for performance related pay to improve efficiency. But, introduction of performance related pay did not prove easy:

> 'The difficulties of introducing pay rates related to merit proved immense...It took several years and a great deal of pushing and shoving.' (Thatcher, 1993, p.46)

The Next Steps and its agencies

The Rayner reforms were intended to produce long-term changes, but, by 1987, many of the supporters of the new managerialism remained disappointed. Three main criticisms were made. First, experimentation with budgeting and performance related pay had not gone far enough. Second, devolution of responsibility had not been achieved in practice. And third, promotion to the top continued to be from too narrow a base.

These concerns led to the setting up of a new efficiency scrutiny into management practice right across government. This was carried out by Sir Robert Ibbs. Ibbs began work under Margaret Thatcher and continued when John Major became Prime Minister. The Ibbs Report *Improving Management in Government: The Next Steps* was first presented to Margaret Thatcher before the 1987 general election. But, the document's contents were so sensitive that it was kept secret until after that election. It was finally published in February 1988.

The Ibbs Report

The Ibbs Report made three main points. First, it argued that the civil service was too vast both in scale and in size to carry out its role in an efficient manner:

> 'The civil service is too big and too diverse to manage as a single entity...A single organisation of this size which attempts to provide a detailed structure within which to carry out functions as diverse as driver licensing, fisheries protection, the catching of drug smugglers and the processing of parliamentary questions is bound to develop in a way which fits no single operation effectively.' (HMSO, 1988, para.10)

Second, it criticised civil servants for playing safe rather than taking an enterprising outlook. Third, it complained that the civil service was still spending too much and not providing value for money.

The Ibbs report advocated a programme which would lead to substantial changes in the structure of the civil service. Its most important recommendation was that semi-autonomous agencies should be set up:

> 'We recommend that "agencies" be established to carry out the executive functions of government within a policy and resources framework set by a department.' (HMSO, 1988, para.19)

The agencies

The main recommendations made by the Ibbs Report were accepted in February 1988 and, since then, steps have been taken to implement them:

> 'The plan is that, by 1998, 75% of civil service personnel will be employed through executive agencies. And in the longer term - beyond the year 2000 - the aim is to cover 95% of the civil service, leaving around 20-25,000 civil servants employed by the ministries at the central level. (Burch, 1993, p.169)

At first, progress was slow. By the end of March 1990, just 12 agencies employing just over 10,000 staff had been set up. But, since then, the number of agencies has grown rapidly. By 1995, there were more than 90 agencies, employing more than half of all civil servants. These agencies retain links with their government department but have a great deal of autonomy:

> 'Individual agencies are run by chief executives who sign framework agreements which specify the service and delivery targets the agencies must meet. This agreement gives conditions for reporting and accountability between the chief executive, the parent department and the Treasury. Each agreement establishes a corporate plan covering current and future objectives as well as policy...Once the policy objectives and budgetary arrangements are established, the chief executive has overall responsibility for the everyday functions of the agency.' (Dowding, 1993, p.188)

The Citizen's Charter

In response to concerns over the provision of public services, John Major launched the Citizen's Charter in 1991 (see also chapter 3, p.60 and chapter 17, part 1). Half of all civil servants are in contact with the general public and provide a front line service - for example, issuing passports, dealing with benefit claims or collecting income tax. By drawing up charters which describe the sort of service which the public is entitled to and by setting targets, the government aims to make civil servants more accountable to members of the public and to ensure that they provide a better service than that provided in the past.

Contracting out and privatisation

Just as many of the services in local government have been contracted out to private contractors (see chapter 16, section 2.5), so too has the government begun to attempt to introduce market forces into the civil service. This was initiated in a 1991 white paper *Competing for Quality* with the result that:

> 'Where services could not be privatised, competition was to be introduced by means similar to the compulsory competitive tendering imposed on local government. This forced councils to put services such as refuse collection and street cleaning out to tender. Henceforth, government departments and agencies would be required to do the same, to see whether private sector contractors could do their work more cheaply and to a higher standard.' (Willman, 1994, p.66)

Little progress was made before 1992. But, following his election victory in 1992, John Major took action to increase the pace of change. Those critics who argued that the creation of executive agencies was a vehicle for privatisation were proved correct. Some of these agencies have begun to be sold off. A white paper published in December 1993 pointed out that:

> 'With 50 or so executive agencies in the pipeline, around three quarters of civil servants would soon be in agencies. Each agency was operating as a discrete organisation with its own chief executive and board, delivering services under contract to Whitehall. If some agencies had already been privatised or identified for privatisation, others ought to be similarly considered.' (Willman, 1994, p.69)

Activity 13.4

Item A *The non-industrial civil service in 1990*

Grade level	Numbers	% of total	% Women
Open structure			
1-4	1,026	0.2	5%
5	2,800	0.6	11%
6	5,200	1.1	10%
7	16,200	3.3	12%
Administrative levels			
SEO	23,900	4.9	10%
HEO	73,100	14.9	18%
EO	121,000	24.7	40%
AO	154,400	31.6	66%
AA	91,600	18.7	73%

KEY
SEO Senior executive officer
HEO Higher executive officer
EO Executive office
AO Administrative officer
AA Administrative assistant

Men (white) / Women (shaded)

This diagram shows the structure of the non-industrial civil service in 1990.

Item B *Next Steps*

The Next Steps initiative is the most far-reaching reform of the civil service in the 20th century. The term 'Next Steps' is used because it is the successor to a whole range of other changes in the management and financial control of government departments that have taken place since 1979. The creation of agencies which are responsible to ministers for the execution of policy will transform public administration and public policy in the UK. The first agency was the Vehicle Inspectorate launched in August 1988. The largest agency is the Social Security Benefits Agency which employs 63,000 staff and the smallest is Wilton Park, employing 30 staff. The aim of the Next Steps initiative is to improve the efficiency and quality of service delivered by public agencies. Agencies do not decide what these services should be. The Vehicle Inspectorate, for example, performs tests, but only has an advisory role in deciding what the structure and parameters of the tests should be. Transport policy, road safety and the links between vehicle testing, driver licensing, vehicle registration and motorway design all remain the responsibility of the Department of Transport. Similarly, although the Benefits Agency costs £2 billion to run and distributes over £50 billion in benefits, the structure and levels of benefits and the agency's objectives are set by the Department of Social Security - the agency is one adviser amongst many.

Adapted from Thain, 1993.

Item C *Setting up a Next Steps agency*

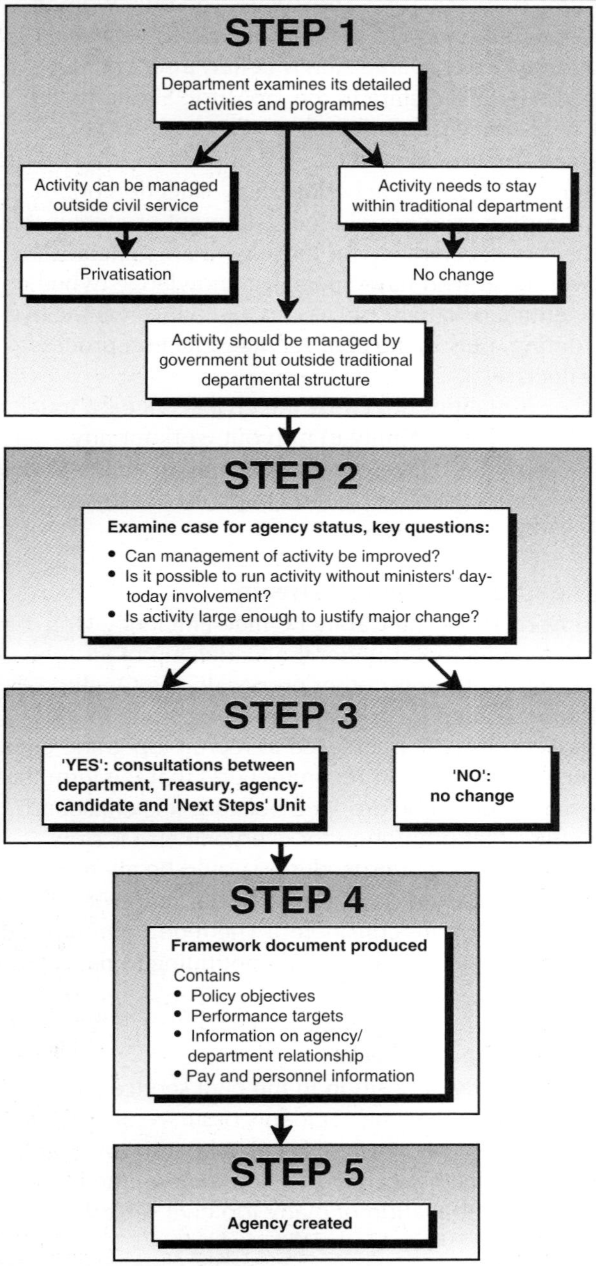
STEP 1
Department examines its detailed activities and programmes
Activity can be managed outside civil service
Activity needs to stay within traditional department
Privatisation
No change
Activity should be managed by government but outside traditional departmental structure
STEP 2
Examine case for agency status, key questions:
• Can management of activity be improved?
• Is it possible to run activity without ministers' day-today involvement?
• Is activity large enough to justify major change?
STEP 3
'YES': consultations between department, Treasury, agency-candidate and 'Next Steps' Unit
'NO': no change
STEP 4
Framework document produced
Contains
• Policy objectives
• Performance targets
• Information on agency/ department relationship
• Pay and personnel information
STEP 5
Agency created

Adapted from Pyper, 1992.

Item D *Whatever Next?*

The revolution which has swept over the civil service in the last few years has largely escaped the attention of the public. More than half of civil servants no longer work for government departments. Instead, these departments employ over 100 Next Step executive agencies which operate at arm's length from the government. This revolution, it can be argued, has brought marked improvements to the service provided by civil servants. For example, social security benefits are now cheaper and quicker to administer and it now takes, on average, just seven days for the Passport Agency to process an application. But, the House of Commons Public Accounts Committee (PAC) is sceptical. It has questioned the ability of some agencies to meet their performance targets and suggests that it is doubtful whether the correct targets were set in the first place. A PAC report on the Vehicle Inspectorate found that, although the Inspectorate's efficiency had improved when measured by a performance index, there were 'significant weaknesses' in the design of the index and its parameters. For example, the index did not measure some aspects of the Inspectorate's operations. The PAC concluded that there was no proof that the Inspectorate had actually improved its performance.

Adapted from the *Independent*, 27 May 1993.

Questions

1. Look at Item A.
   a) Describe the main features of the structure of the civil service in 1990.
   b) How has the structure of the civil service changed since 1979?
2. Judging from Items B-D what is the Next Steps initiative? How does it work? What are its benefits and drawbacks?
3. 'The Next Steps initiative is the most far-reaching reform of the civil service in the 20th century' (Item B). Explain this statement using the information in this section.

2.3 Recruitment

At its peak in 1976, the civil service employed a total of 746,000 people. By 1979, this number had fallen to 732,000. Since 1979, the efforts of Margaret Thatcher and then John Major to slim down the service have resulted in a substantial decrease. By July 1994, the total number of civil servants had fallen to 533,350. In that month, the government announced plans to reduce the number of civil servants by a further 50,000 over the following four years.

Civil servants are recruited to different levels according to their academic qualifications. Those whose only qualification is GCSE passes can apply to be administrative assistants. Those with A levels but no degree can apply to be administrative officers. For graduates, there are two types of entry. First, graduates can apply to join the executive grade (middle management with the prospect of gaining promotion up the hierarchy). Second, they can apply to join the 'fast stream'. If their application is successful, they enter the Administration Group as an administrative trainee at the higher executive officer grade.

The fast stream

As the term implies, the 'fast stream' is the route to the top of the civil service hierarchy. Candidates are appointed only if they succeed in passing the rigorous tests and interviews set by the Civil Service Selection Board (whose methods are based on techniques pioneered by the War Office in the Second World War). As well as tests and interviews, candidates take part in a series of exercises designed to test their ability to handle work they might encounter on a day-to-day basis in a government department - exercises such as writing a tactful letter of apology or producing a policy recommendation in a limited period of time.

Recruitment to the fast stream has been criticised on the grounds that it favours candidates whose background is middle class, public school and Oxbridge. Hennessy notes that this image was reinforced by a 1986 BBC documentary which followed two candidates through the selection process. The result was that:

> '[The] charming and beautiful ex-public schoolgirl [was] admitted to the Foreign Office despite demonstrating appalling ignorance of foreign affairs and the spiky ex-comprehensive schoolboy brimming with passionate views [was] turned down for the home civil service.' (Hennessy, 1989, p.513)

Recruitment figures indicate that this trend remains. Of the 122 administrative trainees recruited in 1991, for example, 35 had degrees from Oxford, 24 from Cambridge, nine from London, three from Durham and two from St Andrews. In other words, 60% of recruits came from these five universities.

It should be noted, however, that a number of defences can be offered for this apparent bias. First, it could be argued that the most able students go to Oxbridge anyway and, therefore, if the civil service is to recruit the most able civil servants it is bound to find most of its recruits there. Second, it is the case that Oxford and Cambridge colleges have a long tradition of encouraging their students to apply for civil service positions. Certainly, the number of applications from Oxbridge is proportionately higher than elsewhere. Third, although Oxbridge provides proportionately more candidates than other universities, the success rate of other universities is statistically higher. For example, 43% of applicants from Oxford reaching the Civil Service Selection Board passed on to the next stage in 1988, compared to 57% of applicants from other universities and polytechnics.

Criticisms of fast stream recruitment have also been made because very few women and even fewer people from ethnic minority groups are selected. Women tend to be over-represented at the bottom of the civil service hierarchy and under-represented at the top. Theakston & Fry (1989) found that out of 304 permanent secretaries appointed between 1900 and 1979, only two had been women (they both held office between 1955 and 1963). The only woman to reach the top tier of the civil service between 1979 and 1995 was Dame Ann Mueller, a second permanent secretary in the Treasury. Similarly, the Civil Service Commissioners' report of 1991-92 shows that not one of the 452 applicants from ethnic minority groups reached the final selection board.

A further criticism of the recruitment process is that there is a preference for those who are generalists over those who have specialist knowledge (whether scientific or otherwise). As an ex-civil servant, Clive Ponting, puts it, the civil service selection process reflects:

> 'Qualities prized by the civil service - a touch of greyness, ability to turn out work for any purpose, no strong beliefs and an ability to fit in amongst other "good chaps" in the service.' (Ponting, 1986, p.73)

The future of the fast stream

In April 1994, the Cabinet Office Efficiency Unit produced a report under the leadership of Sir John Oughton. Amongst other proposals, the Oughton Report argued for adjustments to be made to the procedures which are used to recruit top grade civil servants. The report recommended that the term 'fast stream' should be dropped because it is elitist and implies that promotion for everyone else is slow. Also, recruitment procedures should be altered to ensure that candidates from a wider range of backgrounds are considered. The report emphasised, however, the importance of continuing to recruit the ablest candidates.

Senior appointments

Traditionally, a position in the civil service has meant a job for life (barring accidents or gross misconduct). The former Cabinet minister Cecil Parkinson notes in his memoirs that career development seemed to be the main motivation of many top civil servants (Parkinson 1992). Under the traditional arrangements, promotions at the higher levels were centralised and advancement depended on the opinions of colleagues, ministers and, in some cases, the Prime Minister. Promotion was, in other words, an internal matter. Senior posts were not advertised.

In theory, any civil servant with potential can rise up the hierarchy. Employees entering with A levels, for example, are encouraged to take part-time degrees to improve their prospects. But, Ponting (1986) argues that, in reality, those recruited in the fast stream have a distinct advantage. Once they have been recruited, fast stream appointees are moved from department to department to broaden their experience and to gain an overview of how the Whitehall machinery works.

Training is given on the job. After about 18 months as a HEO(D) - higher executive officer (development) - a fast stream recruit can expect to be promoted to the post of principal, the bottom rung of the open structure. Although anyone within the civil service can apply for promotion into the open structure, in practice, those who enter via the fast stream monopolise appointments.

The way in which senior appointments are made is important because such decisions have an impact both on the character of the civil service and on relationships between civil servants and politicians. Under the traditional arrangements, the formal position was that the Prime Minister approved all appointments at permanent and deputy secretary level on the recommendation of the head of the home civil service. Departmental ministers were consulted before such recommendations were made to the Prime Minister. There were different views about what this meant in practice. For example, in 1986, Sir Robert Armstrong, the head of the home civil service, was asked by the Treasury and Civil Service Committee whether a minister can request a particular person to be appointed. Armstrong replied that:

> 'There will be a balance between that and whatever other considerations arise.' (HMSO 1986, p.26)

A former minister, Patrick Jenkin, told the same committee that he was involved in three permanent secretary appointments. The person appointed in each case was not on the original list submitted by the civil service:

> 'I got my man in every case, with the support of the Prime Minister.' (HMSO 1986, p.132)

The white paper of July 1994

The Oughton Report (see above) made three recommendations which affected senior appointments in particular. First, it recommended that all senior posts should be advertised to attract talent from outside the civil service. Second, it recommended that an equal opportunities adviser should be appointed to gain greater representation from ethnic minorities and women at senior level. And third, it recommended an end to the 'job for life' ethos by means of the introduction of fixed term contracts, together with a system of appraisal.

When the white paper *The Civil Service: Continuity and Change* was published in July 1994, critics claimed that the reforms proposed in the Oughton Report had been watered down. The *Economist* (16 July 1994) even claimed that the mandarins in Whitehall had won a victory by maintaining the status quo. There were two main reasons for this criticism. First, although senior posts were to be advertised, the government made it clear that in the majority of cases senior posts would be held by insiders. William Waldegrave, the Public Services Minister, said:

> 'Most senior posts are likely to be held by insiders as they are in most big firms...open competition need not be used in every case, but it should be considered in every case.' (quoted in the *Independent*, 14 July 1994)

Second, although the white paper recommended that departments should be able to choose their own management structures and have more control over pay levels, fixed term contracts for top civil servants were to be introduced only in an 'appropriate minority' of cases.

Despite these criticisms, however, there is little doubt that the implementation of the proposals made by the white paper will make an impact on senior appointments. The white paper proposes, for example, that nothing short of a:

> 'New senior group will be created, covering 3,500 civil servants (the existing grade 5 and above). They will be appointed by individual, written contracts which, in the main, will not be fixed term but will include specific periods of notice...[and] there will be longer, less rigid, pay ranges for the senior civil service, reflecting the responsibility of the individual.' (*Guardian*, 14 July 1994)

This new senior civil service will, in other words, be placed on performance related contracts with a new, higher pay scale. This higher pay scale is justified on the grounds that senior civil servants will be more vulnerable to losing their jobs than was the case before and that higher rates of pay will attract outside talent to apply for the senior posts which are advertised. As with many other government reforms since 1979, the aim is to introduce private sector business practices into the public sector.

Following the publication of the white paper, a report on the civil service by the all-party Treasury and Civil Service Select Committee was published in November 1994. This report argued that new powers should be given to the revamped Civil Service Commission:

> 'Rather than a senior appointments selection committee, largely drawn from within the service, advising ministers on whether posts should be filled and who is the best person for the job, that role should be given to the Commission. A strengthened and independent Commission...would be "the most effective guarantor of senior appointments based on merit and free from other considerations, including political partisanship".' (*Independent*, 25 November 1994)

The Next Steps initiative and senior appointments

The creation of executive agencies under the Next

Steps initiative has produced a new breed of senior civil servants. The chief executives of the agencies are on fixed term contracts and performance related pay. In addition, according to the *Observer* (22 May 1994), two thirds of these posts are advertised and a number of outsiders have been appointed. For example, Lawrence Haynes was appointed as head of the Highways Agency (responsible for the £23 billion roads programme) in April 1993, after working as a project director at British Aerospace. Although chief executives are nominally paid at rates tied to civil service grades, some receive higher pay than top civil servants. Lawrence Haynes, for example, was employed on a salary of £100,000 (excluding bonuses and other benefits). In 1994, he and three other chief executives were paid more than Sir Robin Butler, the head of the home civil service (who was paid £100,000, but with no bonuses). In total, 11 chief executives were paid more than the maximum set for the equivalent civil service pay scale (*Guardian*, 13 December 1994).

Generalists and specialists

Those in the top seven civil service grades tend to have a generalist rather than a specialist background. For example, civil servants working in the Treasury would not be expected to have an expertise in accounting or economics. The idea is that high fliers have such good brains that they are able to pick up the relevant strands of an argument, whatever the subject area, without needing specialist knowledge themselves. If specific information is required, then it is obtained by consulting with an expert in the field. Indeed, the very fact that most top civil servants are generalists ensures that the views of a range of interest groups and individuals with specific areas of expertise are listened to during the decision making process.

According to Drewry & Butcher (1991), this tradition of generalist administrators is derived from the way in which British representative democracy evolved. In the 19th century, the role of government expanded and ministers began to seek advice from their civil servants (most of whom came from the same social and educational background as themselves). The First World War led to more specialists being involved in government work, but, by then, the tradition had become established.

The Fulton Report argued that generalists were amateurs at worst and all-rounders at best. It suggested that they had too much influence at the top of the civil service. In theory, specialists can now compete equally for senior positions. But, in practice, the top grades of the civil service are still dominated by generalists. Greenwood (1989) argues that the main reason why specialists (civil servants with detailed knowledge and experience in a specific area) find it difficult to gain appointment to the top three grades is that:

> 'Generalists from the Administration Group still have an advantage of getting to the top mainly because the higher policy and administrative content of their work gives them an "edge" in competing for open structure posts.'
> (Greenwood, 1989, p.57)

Activity 13.5

Item A *The mandarins*

Name	Department (Dept.)	Public school	Oxbridge	Outside job?
Patrick Brown	Dept. of Transport	●		1
Sir Terence Burns	Treasury			1
Sir Robin Butler	Cabinet Office	●	●	3
Sir John Chilcot	Nothern Ireland Office	●	●	2
Sir Christopher France	Ministry of Defence		●	2
Sir David Gillmore	Diplomatic Service	●	●	1
Sir Peter Gregson	Dept. of Trade and Industry	●	●	3
Graham Hart	Dept. of Health	●	●	3
Sir Russell Hillhouse	Scottish Office	●		3
Sir Timothy Lankester	Dept. for Education	●	●	1
Sir Thomas Legg	Lord Chancellor's Dept.	●	●	1
Nicholas Monck	Dept. of Employment	●	●	3
Richard Mottram	Office of Public Service and Science			3
Richard Packer	Ministry of Agriculture, Fisheries and Food	●		3
Sir Michael Partridge	Dept. of Social Security	●	●	3
Hayden Phillips	Dept. of National Hertitage		●	3
Michael Scholar	Welsh Office	●	●	1
John Vereker	Overseas Development Administration	●		3
Sir Clive Whitmore	Home Office	●	●	3
Richard Wilson	Dept. of the Environment	●	●	3

Key

1. Has held substantial non-civil service job
2. Has been transferred temporarily to non-civil service job
3. Has never worked in a non-civil service job

All those listed in this table are grade 1 civil servants.

Adapted from the *Economist*, 19 March 1994.

Item B *Ethnic minority groups and the fast stream*

	Number of Applicants			Success rate at first selection stage		Success rate at final selection stage		Overall success rate	
	Total	White	Ethnic minority	White	Ethnic minority	White	Ethnic minority	White	Ethnic minority
Fast stream	5,905	5,435 (92.4)	452 (7.7)	928 (17)	19 (4.2)	109 (11.8)	0 (0)	2	0
Specialist positions at grade 7 and above	2,920	2,547 (87.2)	373 (12.8)	491 (19.3)	65 (17.4)	126 (25.7)	12 (18.5)	49	3.2
	Figures in brackets = % total			Figures in brackets = % total		Figures in brackets = % candidates successful at first stage		Figures = % total	

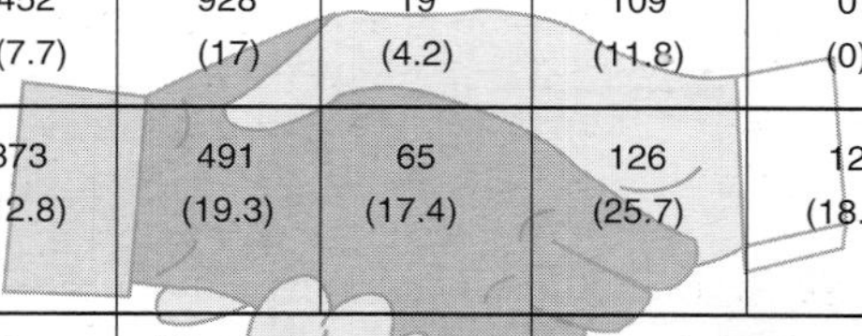

This table shows civil service recruitment in 1992, according to ethnicity.

Adapted from the *CSC*, 1993.

Item C *Women in top grades (1)*

Department	Women as % of grade 1-4 staff
Office of Public Service & Science	23.5
Department of National Heritage	16.7
Home Office	15.6
Regulatory Bodies (eg OFTEL)	15.4
Department of the Environment	14.6
Customs & Excise	14.3
Department of Social Security	14.3
Department of Transport	13.8
Cabinet Office	13.3
Department of Health	10.5
Lord Chancellor's Department	9.1
Department of Employment	9.1
Department of Trade & Industry	9.1
Scottish Office	8.8
Welsh Office	6.7
Legal Departments	6.4
Treasury	6.3
MAFF	6.3
Ministry of Defence	3.3
Central Statistical Office	0.0 (5)
GCHQ	0.0 (6)
Northern Ireland Office	0.0 (7)
Overseas Development	0.0 (11)
Department for Education	0.0 (15)
Inland Revenue	0.0 (24)
Others (small departments)	7.1
Total	**8.9**

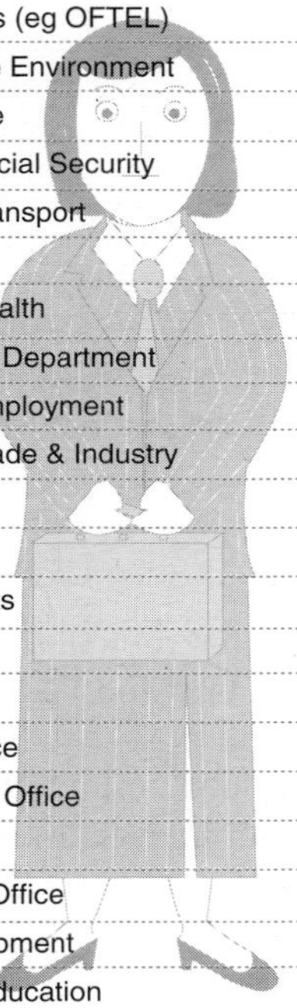

This table shows the number of women in the top grades of the civil service in 1994. Figures in brackets indicate the number of grade 1-4 positions available

Adapted from the *Independent*, 6 November 1994.

Item D *Women in top grades (2)*

Women are not confined to typing, catering and cleaning posts within the civil service. Of course, there are not currently as many women as we would like to see in top civil service posts, but the service has a better record than most organisations in bringing women forward into senior jobs. This has been recognised in independent publications. Our own published records show that 46% of executive officers (the first managerial grade) are women, compared to 29% in 1984. Programmes to ensure that women are offered equal opportunities with men have been running for 10 years. During that time, the number of women in the feeder grades for top jobs has risen dramatically. Whilst 6.6% of posts at grade 5 (just below the top posts) were held by women in 1984, that figure has now risen to 13%. At grade 7, figures have increased from 7.3% to 17.8% in the same period. This is due in part to the practice of offering part-time opportunities at all levels - to enable women to combine careers and family responsibilities. In 1984, just 2.4% of women worked part time. Today this figure has risen to 14%. As a result of this and other initiatives, 15% of top civil service jobs are expected to go to women, on the basis of promotion on merit, by the year 2000.

Adapted from a letter to the *Guardian* written by David Davis, a parliamentary secretary in the Cabinet Office, 14 January 1994.

Item E *Contracting out, July 1994*

This cartoon was published in the *Independent* on 15 July 1994.

Questions

1. a) What does Item A tell us about senior appointments in the civil service?
   b) How, if at all, would you expect senior appointments to change over the next 10 years? Give reasons for your answer.
2. Why do you think there are so few senior civil servants from ethnic minority groups? Use Item B in your answer.
3. 'Since the early 1980s, a great deal of progress has been made by women in the civil service.' Using Items C and D give arguments for and against this view.
4. Describe the context in which the cartoon in Item E was produced. What point is the cartoon making?

2.4 The role of civil servants

Most of the work done in a government department is never seen by the minister in charge. It is carried out by the department's civil servants. In theory at least, the British civil service is apolitical (not political). Appointments are supposedly not made on political grounds, for example, and promotional prospects are not supposed to be affected by a change in government. As Ridley (1986) notes, this is in contrast to some other European countries where key officials are appointed because they are sympathetic to their government's policies. In Britain, the emphasis is on the competence of civil servants. Their role is to provide advice to ministers, regardless of which party is in power:

> 'All civil servants are bound by the civil service pay and conditions service code which demands that they deliver duties of confidentiality and loyal service "for all practical purposes" to the minister of the day. An individual's duty to the courts, Parliament and the public is subsumed in their primary duty to their minister.' (Elizabeth Symons, leader of the top civil servants' union, writing in the *Guardian*, 2 April 1993)

The terms of the civil service pay and conditions service code were clarified by a memorandum written by the head of the home civil service, Sir Robert Armstrong, in 1986. This memorandum was published in the 1986 Treasury and Civil Service Select Committee Report. It outlines the role that civil servants should play:

> 'The determination of policy is the responsibility of the minister...In the determination of policy the civil servant has no constitutional

> responsibility or role distinct from that of the minister. It is the duty of the civil servant...to give the minister honest and impartial advice, without fear or favour, and whether the advice accords with the minister's view or not. Civil servants are in breach of their duty and damage their integrity as servants of the Crown...if they seek to obstruct or delay a decision simply because they do not agree with it. When, having been given all the relevant information and advice, the minister has taken a decision, it is the duty of civil servants loyally to carry out the decision with precisely the same energy and good will, whether they agree with it or not.' (HMSO, 1986, pp.7-8)

There are, then, three main elements in the role played by civil servants. First, civil servants are expected to be **impartial** - that is, they must not be seen to be politically active in any way. It is the role of the government to take decisions and the role of civil servants to implement policy loyally, regardless which party is in power.

Second, civil servants must remain **neutral** - even if they personally disagree with a particular government policy. Senior civil servants who wish to participate in national politics or stand for a party must resign. Civil servants must not express their own opinions in the media or before parliamentary committees.

Third, civil servants should remain **anonymous**. They work behind the scenes and must not discuss what takes place in their department with outside agencies or with the media. In addition, they must not reveal written information. If something is in an official file, it is an official secret (all civil servants working in government departments sign the Official Secrets Act).

Problems with neutrality

It can be argued that the preservation of the confidentiality of discussions and documents is a crucial part of the preservation of a neutral civil service. In theory at least, it is for ministers to decide what the public should or should not know and civil servants to remain silent and neutral, even if they do not agree. The reasoning behind this view is that ministers are held responsible for any errors of judgement that take place in their departments and it is they who take the blame, not the civil servants.

Ridley (1986), however, raises two questions about the neutrality of the civil service. First, is the civil service really as neutral as tradition claims? And second, should the civil service be neutral? A number of recent developments suggest that, in practice, the maintenance of neutrality is much more difficult than the theory suggests.

First, civil servants are servants of the Crown. They should, therefore, act in the interests of the state. But, what if they believe that a government policy is not in the interests of the state? Should they loyally implement such policies without question? And, in particular, what should they do if they believe that a minister is deliberately misleading the public?

An example of the sort of dilemma faced by civil servants was revealed in 1984-85 during the trial of Clive Ponting, a civil servant who worked for the Ministry of Defence during the Falklands War. After the Falklands War, there were allegations that *The General Belgrano* (an Argentinian ship sunk by the British navy during the war) had been sunk for unnecessary political reasons, not on military grounds. The government denied these allegations, but Ponting had information which contradicted the public line taken by the government. He chose to leak this information to a Labour MP on the grounds that the public ought to know what had actually happened. When his identity was discovered subsequently, he was prosecuted for breaking the Official Secrets Act. In his trial, Ponting argued that it was his duty to inform an MP about a major constitutional impropriety. In other words, he placed his duty to the state above his duty to his minister. The judge instructed the jury to find Ponting guilty since it was up to ministers to define what was in the best interests of the state, but the jury acquitted him. After the trial, Ponting wrote:

> 'A number of questions remained unsolved. Why did Parliament not have the right to know this information? Why had the old Official Secrets Act been wheeled out yet again when national security was not involved and the only matter at risk was the political reputation of certain government ministers?...Before the trial there had been much debate about the role and duties of civil servants. Were they just blind servants of ministers, doing only what they were told or could there be circumstances when they might have a higher loyalty either to Parliament or possibly the public interest?' (Ponting, 1985, pp.3-4)

Second, in the 'Arms for Iraq' affair (which came to light in 1992 and is the subject of the Scott Inquiry) the impartiality of civil servants was questioned not because civil servants acted against the wishes of ministers, but because they colluded with them. In particular, there was concern that civil servants not only advised ministers on ways to get round government guidelines forbidding the sale of arms and military equipment to Iraq in the late 1980s, but that they also helped ministers to misinform Parliament and the public:

> 'One reason why we have such an expensive civil service is to ensure that there is a body of independent advisers ready to say "No, minister". The official investigation has only just begun, but already there is worrying evidence

which suggests not just that civil servants were too ready to say "Yes, minister", but even worse, were advising ministers on how they might get round the guidelines and keep public, press and Parliament uninformed. Consider the quote from W.R. Morgan, a DTI official, on discovering that British machine tools were being used by Iraq for military rather than purported civil purposes in January 1988: "There seems to be considerable merit in keeping as quiet as possible about this politically sensitive issue."' (*Guardian* leader, 23 November 1992)

And third, since the 1992 general election, civil servants themselves have begun to make public their disquiet at the increasing political pressure which they feel they are under. This pressure, they argue, makes it harder for them to be impartial. In part, this can be explained by the Conservatives' monopoly of power since 1979. Government matters and party matters, it seems, have sometimes become blurred and there appears to be an increasing tendency for ministers to use civil servants for what used to be considered as party political matters. Civil servants feel reluctant to refuse to help because they are worried that, with all the changes in the civil service, they might lose their job or their prospects for promotion. The following extract is typical:

> 'The administration has been in power for 15 years and it's inevitable that, where black used to meet white, you can get grey areas developing. A few years ago you might have said: "Stop, I can't do that, it breaks all the civil service rules". That's become less and less easy. Nowadays you end up finding ways to break those rules instead. We're not supposed to be party political, but we are. We send out press notices which are fundamentally political. They ought to come from Conservative Central Office.' (Whitehall press officer quoted in the *Observer*, 29 May 1994)

A statutory ethics code?

In response to the criticisms that the civil service's reputation for impartiality was suffering, the all-party Treasury and Civil Service Select Committee recommended in its 1994 report that a statutory code of ethics should be agreed. This code would set out civil servants' duties and ministers' responsibilities. In January 1995, the government announced its support for a code of conduct which:

> 'Will ensure that civil servants can appeal if theyare being asked to act in ways which they believe breach "integrity, honesty, impartiality and objectivity"...The government is to consider putting the code on a statutory basis under a new Civil Service Act if all-party support is forthcoming.' (*Guardian*, 27 January 1995)

In addition to the statutory code, the government agreed to set up an independent appeal procedure which civil servants could use if they felt they were being asked to compromise their neutrality.

Activity 13.6

Item A *The need for an ethics code (1)*

In October 1994, Sir Robin Butler, head of the home civil service and Cabinet Secretary, provided cover for the Prime Minister in two highly political cases. In the first case, two ministers were accused of receiving money and favours from the owner of Harrods. Sir Robin's report into the matter cleared one of the ministers, but both resigned anyway. In the second case, Jonathan Aitken, Chief Secretary to the Treasury, was accused of lying about a free holiday in the Ritz Hotel in Paris. He was also cleared by Sir Robin. In March 1995, Sir Robin, responding to the charge that he had jeopardised his role as impartial head of the civil service, admitted that he had been careless in reporting a key part of his inquiry. He said that he had been unable to conduct a full investigation into the Aitken affair because the Prime Minister needed to show he was taking speedy action. But, suppose an ethics code had been in force and the Prime Minister had asked Sir Robin to play the same role. He could then have said 'no', citing the code's reference to civil servants not being required to act 'in breach of constitutional conventions' (in other words, matters of party political controversy). If Major had then been unwise enough to push the point, Sir Robin would have had a right of appeal to an independent Civil Service Commission. At present, he can appeal only to himself as head of the civil service.

Adapted from the *Economist*, 26 November 1994 and the *Times*, 9 March 1995.

Item B *The need for an ethics code (2)*

Sir Robin Butler, head of the civil service, has admitted that civil servants drafted amendments which were used to kill off six private members' bills in the last two years. Earlier this year, MPs were outraged to discover that civil servants had prepared 70 amendments for use by Conservative backbenchers to kill off the Civil Rights Disabled Persons Bill. One Conservative, Lady Olga Maitland, was forced to apologise after falsely claiming that she had drafted the amendments put down in her name. Sir Robin admitted that civil servants had drafted amendments for the Medicines Information Bill (1993), the Osteopaths Bill (1993), the Right To Know Bill (1993), the Chiropractors Bill (1993), the Energy Conservation Bill (1993) and the Race Relations Bill (1994). But, he refused to reveal whether there had been other occasions on the grounds that he can only reveal civil service involvement where the government itself was willing to acknowledge it. He wrote: 'I cannot indicate whether or not amendments were intended to wreck Bills...There may be an understandable difference of view between supporters of a bill and others on that point.' Sir Robin added that civil servants had been involved in the preparation of amendments for six Bills during the 1974-79 Labour government.

Adapted from the *Guardian*, 12 August 1994.

Item C *The need for an ethics code (3)*

The civil service is in crisis. The Scott Inquiry has revealed that civil servants provided bad advice and colluded in a cover-up. The Commons Public Accounts Committee has revealed that the commercialisation of Whitehall has resulted in mismanagement, incompetence and fraud. A study by ex-civil servant William Plowden finds a loss of confidence and respect between ministers and civil servants. Both are to blame. One result of 15 years in power is arrogance. Ministers not only ignore advice which does not fit into their ideological framework, they discourage officials from even producing it. But, equally, civil servants have been too ready to produce what is wanted, fearing their careers will suffer if they appear obstructive. There is, however, an important difference between pointing out problems and being obstructive. Initially, civil servants should be as blunt and honest as they can be about possible problems - that is what they are paid for. They are only being obstructive if they continue to push their ideas after ministers have rejected them. One indication of how wrong things are is yesterday's report that Sir Robin Butler had written to departments advising them to avoid controversial issues until after the local and European elections. Even if the Prime Minister made this decision, it is not the role of the head of the civil service to issue political instructions. Civil servants will only restore respect if they restore their neutrality.

Adapted from the *Guardian*, 25 April 1994.

Item D *No, minister*

Questions

1. a) Using Items A-C give the case for a statutory ethics code for civil servants.
   b) What provisions should the code include?
2. 'In the last few years, the civil service has become over-politicised.' Is there any evidence in Items A-C to support this statement?
3. Using Item A explain why civil servants might want the right of appeal to an independent Civil Service Commission.
4. Look at Item D.
   a) In what circumstances should a civil servant say 'No, minister'?
   b) What might prevent a civil servant from saying 'No, minister'?

3. Ministers and civil servants

Key Issues

1. What is the ideal relationship between ministers and civil servants?
2. What sort of relationships exist in practice?
3. Have relationships between ministers and civil servants changed?

The ideal relationship

According to Norton (1989), the civil service is a:

> 'Well oiled machine, manned by public servants of integrity and serving loyally successive governments of whatever political persuasion.' (Norton, 1989, p.82)

The role of the minister is to determine the policies of the government. The role of civil servants is to advise ministers on how best to implement those policies which they wish to introduce.

In the ideal world, therefore, both ministers and civil servants are motivated by a sense of public duty and a genuine desire to act in the public interest. Both ministers and civil servants know their place and the role they should play. Civil servants brief ministers impartially and objectively. Ministers listen carefully to what their civil servants have to say and make decisions after weighing up this advice. Civil servants expect the minister in charge of their department to fight courageously for funds during the annual spending round and to defend the actions of the department in public. Ministers expect to be kept informed of what is happening in the department and they expect civil servants to implement, with a good grace, decisions with which they disagree. Although ministers are members of a political party, they would never dream of asking their civil servants to undertake party political matters. Similarly, whatever their personal views, civil servants would never act in a partisan manner.

The real world

In reality, a number of factors affect the relationship between ministers and their civil servants.

First, ministers may have little knowledge of the area covered by their departments. On taking up their new post, they do not see the papers of their predecessors, but are supplied with a briefing document by their officials. From the outset, therefore, there is the chance for civil servants to shape the way in which ministers view their job.

Second, ministers have other commitments - in Parliament and in their constituencies, for example. They, therefore, have less time to devote to decision making than their full-time officials. For this reason, they rely on the experience and administrative expertise of their civil servants. Often, this advice is shaped by the internal culture of the department. Most senior civil servants have been steeped in this internal culture for many years. Headey quotes one permanent secretary who said:

> 'In effect, it was just a question of getting my ministers to take on board policies that we had in hand anyway. Of the six ministers I worked with closely, it would be hard to say that any of them made even a minor contribution to policy.' (quoted in Headey, 1974, p.109)

It should noted, however, that this quote comes from the 1970s, before the civil service reforms instigated by Margaret Thatcher had been enacted.

Third, civil servants outnumber ministers. There are about 10 civil servants for every one minister in the top policy making grades and 40 civil servants to every one minister if all civil servants who make an input into policy making are included. If all these officials take a similar line, this adds weight to the line taken.

Fourth, although civil servants outnumber ministers, there is still a sufficiently small number of permanent secretaries at the top of the hierarchy (about 40 in all) for them to meet together often, both formally and socially. A permanent secretary having 'problems' with a minister might, therefore, be able to persuade a colleague in another government department to persuade a more compliant minister to put pressure on the minister causing the 'problems'. In this way, top civil servants might be able to agree upon and engineer certain policies.

Fifth, ministers spend more time with civil servants than they do with other politicians:

> 'In an average week, a Cabinet minister is likely to see at least two civil servants - his permanent secretary and his private secretary - far more frequently than he sees the Prime Minister or any of his or her party colleagues. The significance of this simple fact should not be underestimated as a source of pressure on ministers to conform to civil service expectations.' (Headey, 1974, p.153)

Sixth, civil servants often outlast ministers and can use various tactics to avoid having to implement a policy they do not like. According to Norton (1989), there are three ways in which civil servants can reverse a minister's decision. First, they can wait for a change of ministers - new ministers may be open to the advice they are offering. Second, they can brief officials in other departments to ensure that their ministers are primed to oppose the minister's decision (as suggested above). And third, they can leak a document to the media in the hope that this will undermine the minister's credibility.

Theakston's models

Theakston (1992) argues that four separate models are used by political scientists to describe the relationship between ministers and civil servants.

First, there is the **formal-constitutional model**. This model defines the civil service as a non-political neutral bureaucracy whose sole aim is to serve loyally the interests of the government of the day. Civil servants make sure that ministers are fully aware of all the constraints and options open to them before making decisions. Once decisions have been taken, civil servants loyally work to implement the policy which has been laid down.

Second, there is the **adversarial model**. This model sees the relationship between ministers and civil servants as a constant struggle for power. Both Richard Crossman and Tony Benn (Labour ministers) claimed that their civil servants were only concerned with preserving the status quo and were less than helpful when it came to implementing the Labour government's policies. Similar criticisms have been expressed by ministers on the New Right.

Third, there is the **village life in the Whitehall community model**. This model sees a cosy relationship in which both sides work together in harmony. The civil servants provide the expertise acquired through long experience in the department, whilst the minister provides the ideological energy.

And fourth, there is the **bureaucratic expansionism model**. This model claims that bureaucrats are self-centred and only interested in expanding their own areas of power - an attitude which leads to waste and inefficiency. Top civil servants are, therefore, more interested in empire building than in what is best for the country. It is up to ministers to find ways of improving efficiency (for example, by introducing competition and market testing). This theory originated in the USA, but has been adopted by the New Right.

In essence, therefore, there are two contrasting views of the relationship between ministers and civil servants. One view is that civil servants are neutral advisers. The other view is that it is civil servants who make the policy, expecting ministers to go along with what the department already has in hand.

Ministers and civil servants in the 1990s

The civil service reforms enacted during the 1980s have taken their toll on the relationship between ministers and civil servants. Willman notes:

> 'The arrival of Mr Major in Downing Street in late 1990 was greeted with relief by many civil servants. They hoped it would bring to an end 11 years of permanent revolution in Whitehall, with privatisations, staff cuts, pay restraint, efficiency drives and institutional reform. They could hardly have been more mistaken. Majorism has intensified the pace of change in the civil service.' (Willman, 1994, p.64)

Before 1979, many commentators complained that the civil service had its own policy goals and was able to manipulate ministers into taking a certain direction. By 1990, however, the relationship between ministers and civil servants had changed. There are a number of reasons for this.

First, a single party had been in power throughout the 1980s. By 1994, Plowden could note:

> 'The promotion of every single occupant of a grade 1 or grade 2 has been approved by Mrs Thatcher or Mr Major. In that sense, they could be said to owe their positions to the Conservatives. Probably every occupant of a grade 3 has reached that position during the Conservative years. No administrator aged 35 or less will have worked for ministers of another party.' (Plowden, 1994, pp.101-2)

This, in itself, is not enough to change the relationship between ministers and civil servants, but, combined with other factors, that has been the net result.

Second, although, according to Plowden (1994), ministers have rarely taken action to secure the appointment of a particular individual in a top position, they manipulate the promotion process and use their influence to prevent the promotion of individuals:

> 'Some individuals, for ill-defined reasons, fail to make progress. Speaking of a senior official whose promotion to permanent secretary was widely felt to have been unduly delayed, a former minister commented, almost in passing, "Yes, his card was marked for some reason, wasn't it?"' (Plowden, 1994, p.101)

The net result is that senior positions are filled with civil servants who are compliant and unlikely to disapprove of ministers' ideological goals.

Third, and perhaps most important, ministers' attitudes towards officials seem to have changed. In any relationship, mutual respect is important. But, many ministers have lost their respect for their officials:

> 'The root of today's problem lies in the Thatcherite attitude towards civil servants. Too many ministers feel that if civil servants were any good, they would not be in Whitehall. Their advice is vitiated by their professional weaknesses. Unadventurous by nature and unenterprising by habit, they exaggerate the difficulties and risks of ministers' proposals rather than concentrating on putting them into practice. A good minister will not be deflected by their ingenious objections. Indeed - this line of thinking continues - a determined minister will not use them as advisers on policy but, as they should be used, as instruments for implementing his/her own original intentions.' (Plowden, 1994, p.103)

The relationship between ministers and civil servants in the 1990s is, in other words, by no means a relationship between equals - ministers are very much in charge. It is, therefore, no surprise to learn that civil servants have been accused of weakness and of lacking impartiality. On the other hand, that does not mean that ministers are all-powerful. Ministers do not have the time or specialist knowledge to determine every last detail. They might set the parameters, but it is the civil servants who do the spade work. By so doing, civil servants are able to exercise some control over the policy making process.

Activity 13.7

Item A

It was 8.56 am on Monday 20 June 1983. The phone rung and Alan Clark (Under Secretary of State at the Department of Employment) overheard Jenny Easterbrook, his private secretary, telling someone that, yes, he had arrived. She then came into Clark's office. 'Have you read the brief on the revised conditions for the Job Splitting Scheme?', she said. 'Yes', replied Clark (he was lying). 'Good', she said (meaning good that she had caught him out), 'because Donald Derx would like to come round to discuss it with you.' When Clark asked when Derx, Deputy Secretary at the Department of Employment would come, he was told that he was due in five minutes (enough time for Clark to skim-read the brief). But Derx arrived in just 80 seconds and proceeded to raise a number of points about the brief. Clark just managed to keep the discussion going by glancing surreptitiously at the brief. In Clark's opinion, the meeting was an ambush. Derx wanted to know at what time Clark arrived in his office and he wanted to find out the extent to which Clark was reading the contents of his ministerial red boxes. The brief under discussion had been hidden a quarter of the way down the box. But, Clark was wise to this trick - he didn't take the papers out in the order in which they were arranged. He had learned that the little photocopied documents marked 'PUSS to see', with Jenny's initials, were the difficult items.

Adapted from Clark, 1993.

Item B *The minister's workload*

Item C *Civil servants and ministers*

Top civil servants have taken the unprecedented step of complaining to Sir Robin Butler, the head of the home civil service, about the conduct of Charles Wardle, the Home Office immigration minister. Sir Robin cannot force the minister to respond to these complaints, but if he finds they are justified, he can raise the matter with the Home Secretary. Civil servants have complained about abrupt and dismissive treatment. They were appalled, for example, that their advice was ignored over the Police and Magistrates Courts Bill and the Criminal Justice Bill (both of which were subsequently torn apart in the House of Lords). One civil servant said officials were 'fed up with being bawled out'. In addition, research projects have been abandoned because their findings conflict with government policy. The latest outburst from Mr Wardle came when a study of 263 refugees living in Britain was presented. This study did not support ministers' view that asylum seekers were generally economic migrants who wanted to live on benefit. Rather, it found that most wanted to and did contribute to Britain's economy and most had fled from political persecution, not poverty. In the last 12 months, two permanent secretaries have quit because, it was alleged, they found work with their Secretaries of State intolerable.

Adapted from the *Independent on Sunday*, 17 July 1994 and the *Guardian*, 23 April 1994.

Item D *What civil servants say*

(i) A grade 2 civil servant who had recently retired said that political pressure was something new. In the past, ministers often asked advisers to rethink, but had respect for their views. This began to change about five years ago. The problem now is that senior civil servants are too close to ministers - so close that they do not or cannot give impartial advice. After 15 years of Conservative rule, civil servants have come to believe that there will never be any change and so they dare not risk their futures by making life difficult for ministers.

(ii) A grade 3 civil servant argued that officials knew that some government decisions (such as the poll tax and the original school curriculum) were unworkable, but they did not dare speak out. Although officials wrote papers explaining the problems with the curriculum, stories were planted in the newspapers saying that civil servants were determined to wreck the government's parent-power plans. These stories were planted by the government.

(iii) A middle ranking official in the Department of Education said that two highly respected officials, John Wiggins and Clive Saville, were worried about the proposals for the reform of teacher training and voiced their concerns. A delegation of Conservative right wingers went to see the minister and demanded that they were moved. They were moved.

Adapted from the *Observer*, 29 May 1994.

Questions

1. a) 'Civil servants have too much power'. Using Items A-D, give arguments for and against this view.
   b) How have relations between ministers and civil servants changed since 1979?
2. Judging from Items A and B how can civil servants manipulate the decisions made by ministers?
3. Using Theakston's models describe the relationship between ministers and civil servants found in Items A and C.
4. 'Morale in the civil service is very low, lower I think than I have ever seen in more than 20 years in Whitehall.' Why do you think a senior civil servant made this comment? Use Item D in your answer.

References

Barnett (1982) Barnett, J., *Inside the Treasury*, Andre Deutsch, 1982.

Bruce-Gardyne (1986) Bruce-Gardyne, J., *Ministers and Mandarins*, Sidgwick and Jackson, 1986.

Burch (1993) Burch, M., 'The Next Steps for Britain's civil service', *Talking Politics*, Vol.5, No.3, summer 1993.

Cabinet (1992) Cabinet Office, *Questions of Procedure for Ministers*, Cabinet Office, 1992.

Clark (1993) Clark, A., *Diaries*, Weidenfeld & Nicolson, 1993.

CSC (1993) *Civil Service Commissioners' Report* 1991-92, HMSO, 1993.

Dowding (1993) Dowding K., 'Government at the centre' in *Dunleavy et al. (1993)*.

Drewry & Butcher (1991) Drewry, G. & Butcher, T., *The Civil Service Today*, Blackwell, 1991.

Dunleavy et al. (1993) Dunleavy P. , Gamble A. , Holliday I. & Peele, G. (eds), *Developments in British Politics 4*, Macmillan, 1993.

Fowler (1991) Fowler, N., *Ministers Decide*, Chapman, 1991.

Greenaway (1992) Greenaway, J., 'The civil service - 20 years of reform' in *Jones & Robins* (1992).

Greenwood (1989) Greenwood, J., 'Managing the civil service - from Fulton to Ibbs', *Talking Politics*, Vol.1, No.2, winter 1988/89.

Headey (1974) Headey, B., *British Cabinet Ministers*, Allen & Unwin, 1974.

Hennessy (1989) Hennessy, P., *Whitehall*, Secker & Warburg, 1989.

HMSO (1986) Seventh Report of the Treasury and Civil Service Committee 1985-86, *Civil Servants and Ministers: Duties and Responsibilities*, HMSO, 1986.

HMSO (1988) Efficiency Unit, *Improving Management in Government: The Next Steps*, report to the Prime Minister, HMSO, 1988.

HMSO (1994) Central Office of Information, *The British System of Government*, HMSO, 1994.

Jones & Robins (1992) Jones, B. & Robins, L. (eds), *Two Decades of British Politics*, Manchester University Press, 1992.

Kavanagh & Seldon (1994) Kavanagh, D. & Seldon, A. (eds), *The Major Effect*, Macmillan, 1994.

Madgwick (1991) Madgwick, P., *British Government: the Central Executive Territory*, Phillip Allan, 1991.

Norton (1989) Norton, P., *The Constitution in Flux*, Blackwell, 1989.

Parkinson (1992) Parkinson, C., *Right of Centre: an Autobiography*, Weidenfeld & Nicolson, 1992.

Plowden (1994) Plowden, W., *Ministers and Mandarins*, Institute for Public Policy Research, 1994.

Ponting (1985) Ponting, C., *The Right to Know*, Sphere, 1985.

Ponting (1986) Ponting, C., *Whitehall: Tragedy and Farce*, Sphere, 1986.

Pyper (1992) Pyper, R., 'A new model civil service?', *Politics Review*, Vol.2, No.2, November 1992.

Pyper (1993) Pyper, R., 'When they have to go...why ministers resign', *Talking Politics*, Vol.5, No.2, winter 1993.

Pyper (1994) Pyper, R., 'Individual ministerial responsibility', *Politics Review*, Vol.4, No.1, September 1994.

Ridley (1986) Ridley, F., 'Political neutrality in the civil service', *Social Studies Review*, Vol.1, No.4, March 1986.

Rose (1987) Rose, R., *Ministers and Ministries*, Clarendon Press, 1987.

Rose (1991) Rose, R., 'Too much reshuffling of the Cabinet pack?', *Institute of Economic Affairs Inquiry*, No.27, 1991.

Thatcher (1993) Thatcher, M., *The Downing Street Years*, HarperCollins, 1993.

Theakston (1987) Theakston, K., *Junior Ministers in British Government*, Basil Blackwell, 1987.

Theakston (1992) Theakston, K., 'Ministers and mandarins', *Talking Politics*, Vol.4, No.2, winter 1991/92.

Theakston & Fry (1989) Theakston K. & Fry, G.K., 'Britain's administrative elite: permanent secretaries 1900-86', *Public Administration*, Vol.67, No.2, summer 1989.

Walker (1991) Walker, P., *Staying Power*, Bloomsbury, 1991.

Whitelaw (1990) Whitelaw, W., *The Whitelaw Memoirs*, Headline, 1990.

Willman (1994) Willman, J., 'The civil service' in *Kavanagh & Seldon* (1994).

Wilson (1971) Wilson, H., *The Labour Government 1964-70: a Personal Record*, Weidenfeld and Nicolson, 1971.

Wood & Wood (1992) Wood, A.H. & Wood, R. (eds), *The Times Guide To The House of Commons 1992*, Times Books, 1992.

Woodhouse (1993) Woodhouse, D., 'When do ministers resign?', *Parliamentary Affairs*, Vol.46, No.3, 1993.

14 Parliament

Introduction

Parliament is the UK's legislative authority. Strictly speaking, it has three elements - the monarch, the House of Lords and the House of Commons - and all three elements must be in agreement before a proposal can become law. The legislative role of the monarch, however, has largely been taken over by government ministers (see chapter 4). Usually, therefore, when people talk about 'Parliament', they are referring to the Palace of Westminster where the House of Commons and the House of Lords are located. Parliament, in this sense, is perhaps the most visible of Britain's political institutions. Its proceedings are reported in the press and broadcast on radio and television. Whether or not Parliament is the focal point of political power in the UK, however, is debatable. Although some commentators argue that the work done by the House of Commons and the House of Lords makes an important contribution to the shaping of legislation, others argue that, in reality, Parliament is little more than a talking shop where ambitious politicians polish their egos and their public speaking skills.

This chapter looks at the role played by the House of Commons and the House of Lords in the decision making process. It traces the development of the two chambers and examines the work they do and the procedures they follow. It also considers arguments for and against reform. By concentrating on these areas, it should be possible to form a judgement about exactly how powerful and how effective Parliament is and how (if at all) its power and effectiveness have changed in recent years.

Chapter summary

Part 1 examines the **evolution, composition and functions** of the **House of Commons**.

Part 2 looks at the development of and work performed by **committees in the House of Commons**. It also discusses the **procedures for debates and questions** in the House.

Part 3 discusses the composition of and work performed by the **House of Lords**. It also considers the arguments for and against **abolishing** the House of Lords.

Part 4 considers the debate about the **effectiveness of Parliament**. What criteria are used to judge Parliament's effectiveness and are these criteria fulfilled?

1 The House of Commons

Key Issues

1. What were the key events in the development of the House of Commons?
2. How does the House of Commons work?
3. What does the House of Commons do?
4. What part does the Commons play in the legislative process?

1.1 The evolution of the House of Commons

The origins of Parliament can be traced right back to the 11th century when Saxon monarchs established the principle that advice should be sought from the 'Witangemot' (the assembly of the wise). The Witangemot was made up of powerful landowners and church leaders. It was the forerunner of Parliament in the sense that proposed laws and new taxes were discussed by its members.

After the Norman invasion of 1066, monarchs took advice from the Great Council of barons. This Council:

> 'Met three or four times a year at the summons of the King to help him decide policies of state, to review the work of the administration, to sit as a high court of justice and to take part in making and amending laws...Medieval kings were expected to meet all royal expenses, private and public, out of their own revenue. If extra resources were needed for an emergency, such as war, the Sovereign would seek to persuade his barons, in the Great Council, to grant an aid.' (HMSO, 1994, pp.10 & 12)

In 1254, Henry III's brother (acting regent whilst the

King was abroad) was unable to raise sufficient funds from the barons and, therefore, summoned two knights from each English shire to the Great Council in the hope that they would be able to raise funds for the King. Ten years later, not only knights but also two leading citizens from each city and borough were summoned. The Great Council, therefore, came to contain two groups - those summoned by name (the barons and clergy - Lords) and those who were representatives of local communities (the knights and leading citizens - Commoners). These two groups formed the basis for what were to become the House of Lords and the House of Commons.

The term 'Parliament', from the French 'parlement' meaning 'speaking', was first used in Britain in 1236 and applied, in general terms, to meetings called for the purpose of discussion. It was only later in the 13th century that the term began to refer to meetings of the Great Council. Later, in the 13th century, monarchs began to call Parliaments regularly. Edward I, for example, held his first general Parliament in 1275 and held 30 Parliaments during his 25 year reign. Commoners, however, were not always summoned to these Parliaments (Edward I summoned them just four times). It was only after 1325 that commoners were summoned regularly.

Two important developments regarding the Commons took place in the 15th century. First:

> 'In 1407 Henry IV pledged that, henceforth, all money grants should be approved by the House of Commons before being considered by the House of Lords.' (HMSO, 1994, p.14)

And second, the Commons began to play an important role in law making:

> 'During the 15th century, [the Commons] gained the right to participate in giving their requests - or Bills - the form of law. The costs of government and war forced the king to turn with increasing frequency to Parliament for supplies. Before supplies were granted, he was often called upon, through petitions, to redress stipulated grievances. Since this usually resulted in some kind of legislation, the law making power, as well as the power to raise taxes, passed into parliamentary hands.' (HMSO, 1994, pp.14-15)

The impact of the English civil war

Conflict between the monarchy and the Commons resulted in civil war in the mid-17th century. Defeat of the royalist forces led to the execution of Charles I (in 1649) and the abolition of the monarchy and the House of Lords (though this was short-lived). British government was dominated by the Lord Protector, Oliver Cromwell. In 1660, two years after Oliver Cromwell died, Charles II returned from exile and was restored to the throne, having given the guarantees the Commons demanded. But, although the monarchy was restored (as was the House of Lords), the relationship between the monarch and the Commons had changed for good. When James II (who succeeded Charles II in 1685) tried to reassert the dominance of the monarchy, he was deposed and replaced by William of Orange (the so-called 'Glorious Revolution' of 1688). William was granted the throne on condition that he agreed to the introduction of a Bill of Rights which limited the royal prerogative. By accepting this Bill of Rights, William effectively ended the monarch's claim to absolute power and accepted the notion of parliamentary government. From this point onwards, the monarch ruled through Parliament. In practice, this meant that the monarch increasingly delegated the task of government to ministers. It is in the 18th century, for example, that the post of Prime Minister and the Cabinet emerged for the first time (although not in the same forms as today - see chapter 12, section 1.1).

The impact of industrialisation

Parliamentary politics in the 18th century was dominated by a political elite. This elite was made up of the aristocracy and large landowners. It did not include those whose wealth was created through industry. One result of the growth of industry in the late 18th century was the development of a commercial middle class. Members of this middle class had economic power but lacked political representation. By the beginning of the 19th century, members of this middle class had begun to demand the vote and, after a long political struggle, the Great Reform Act of 1832 was passed (see chapter 7, p.165). Not only did this Act extend the vote to a large number of middle class men, it also established the principle that those who contributed to the development of society deserved the right to have a say in the complexion of the government. Later in the 19th century, the vote was extended in further Electoral Reform Acts. By 1900, about 70% of men (but no women) could vote.

The development of a mass electorate had a profound effect on Parliament. First, it necessitated the development of the party system. The party apparatus came to dominate parliamentary activity. And second, there was a growing divide between the House of Commons, with its members elected by the mass of the people, and the House of Lords which remained unelected. In the early 20th century, this divide led to a struggle between the two Houses, with the Commons emerging victorious. Not only has the convention developed that the Prime Minister should be chosen from the Commons rather than the Lords, the legislative and financial powers of the House of Lords were restricted by the Parliament Act of 1911 and its ability to delay the passage of legislation was curtailed further in 1949.

1.2 The House of Commons today

Composition of the House

According to a government pamphlet:

> 'The House of Commons is a representative assembly elected by universal adult suffrage, and consists of men and women (Members of Parliament 'MPs') from all sections of the community, regardless of income or occupation. There are 651 seats in the House of Commons: 524 for England, 38 for Wales, 72 for Scotland and 17 for Northern Ireland. Of the 651 MPs, there are at present 59 women, three Asian and three black MPs.' (HMSO, 1994, p.32)

In 1995, it was announced that the number of MPs would rise to 658, due to constituency boundary changes.

Since 1945, the vast majority of MPs have stood for and won an election under a party label. The importance of parties, including the division into governing and opposition parties, is emphasised in the seating arrangements of the House of Commons chamber. Government ministers occupy the front benches on one side of the House. They face the frontbench team of the opposition party (or parties) on the other side. The seating arrangements thus serve to favour a two party system and a confrontational (or 'adversarial') style of party debate. The seating in other Parliaments is organised differently - the European Parliament, for example, is arranged almost in a circle. This makes a symbolic as well as a practical difference to the way in which the proceedings in the European Parliament work.

Parliamentary business

After each general election, a new Parliament begins. This new Parliament has a life of up to five years - the Parliament Act of 1911 stipulates that five years should be the maximum time between general elections. Each Parliament is divided into sessions, with each parliamentary session normally lasting about a year (from November to November). At the start of each session, the Queen's Speech is delivered. This speech is written by the Prime Minister and outlines the legislative proposals which the government intends to put before Parliament during the year ahead. There are annual breaks, when the house is in recess - at Christmas, Easter, Spring Bank and during the summer.

Until 1995, the daily business in the chamber of the House of Commons began at 2.30 pm on Mondays to Thursdays and at 9.30 am on Fridays (it began earlier on Fridays since MPs have to get back to their constituencies for the weekend). The amount of business to be covered, however, meant that the House frequently sat past its official closing time of 10.30 pm. Growing demands from some MPs for reforms in working practices led to the setting up in 1990 of an all-party committee whose report in 1992 called for more rational hours in the House of Commons. In December 1994, MPs voted for an experimental period of reforms as follows:

> '1. A 10.00 pm finish Mondays to Thursdays and 2.30 pm on Fridays.
> 2. A 10.00 am start on Wednesdays.
> 3. Ten Friday sitting days to be dropped from each session.
> 4. A 7.30 pm finish on those Thursdays when the House is not sitting on the following day.
> 5. Long speeches and debates on minor legislation to be curtailed.' (Adapted from Ceefax, 19 December 1994)

The weekly business of the House is arranged by the government and opposition chief whips. The Speaker is informed about which leading MPs from each party would like to address the House during debates. This is termed '**arranging business though the usual channels**'. Other matters may also be agreed 'through the usual channels'. The business for the week ahead is announced by the Leader of the House. The Leader of the House also arranges the Commons' programme for the entire parliamentary session.

The Speaker

The proceedings in the chamber of the House of Commons are chaired by the Speaker or one of the deputy Speakers. Speakers are chosen by their fellow MPs at the start of each new Parliament or when the previous Speaker dies or retires. Although Speakers are elected MPs, they are not permitted to speak on behalf of their constituents in the Commons and they do not take part in debates since they are supposed to be impartial. The Speaker only votes in the House in the event of a tie and, even then, is guided by precedent - by the decisions of Speakers in similar previous cases.

As well as representing the House of Commons on ceremonial and formal occasions, it is the Speaker's job to see that the procedural rules of the House (contained in the standing orders) are followed and to decide which MPs are called upon to speak. In attempting to preserve order there are a number of sanctions at the Speaker's disposal. First, MPs can be directed to withdraw remarks made in 'unparliamentary language'. Second, if these instructions are ignored, MPs can be suspended from the House. Third, in the event of a serious general disorder in the chamber, the Speaker can suspend the entire proceedings. This happened in 1985, for example, when the then Speaker, Bernard Weatherill, suspended proceedings for 20 minutes following continued protests from a group of opposition Labour MPs against the government's refusal to agree to a debate on the dispute in the coal industry.

Activity 14.1

Item A *The layout of the House of Commons*

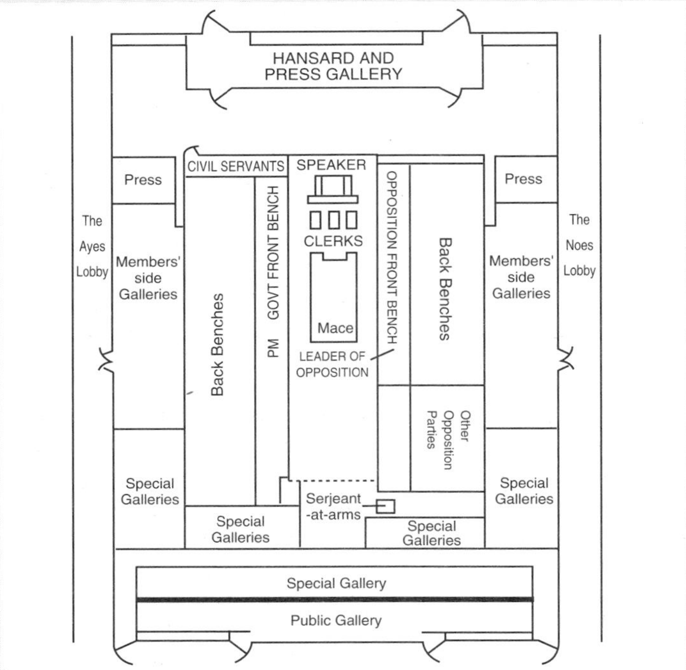
HANSARD AND PRESS GALLERY
Press
CIVIL SERVANTS
SPEAKER
Press
The Ayes Lobby
Members' side Galleries
CLERKS
Mace
GOVT FRONT BENCH
PM
OPPOSITION FRONT BENCH
LEADER OF OPPOSITION
Back Benches
Back Benches
Members' side Galleries
The Noes Lobby
Other Opposition Parties
Special Galleries
Serjeant-at-arms
Special Galleries
Special Galleries
Special Galleries
Special Gallery
Public Gallery

Adapted from Padfield & Byrne, 1987.

Item D *House of Commons timetable*

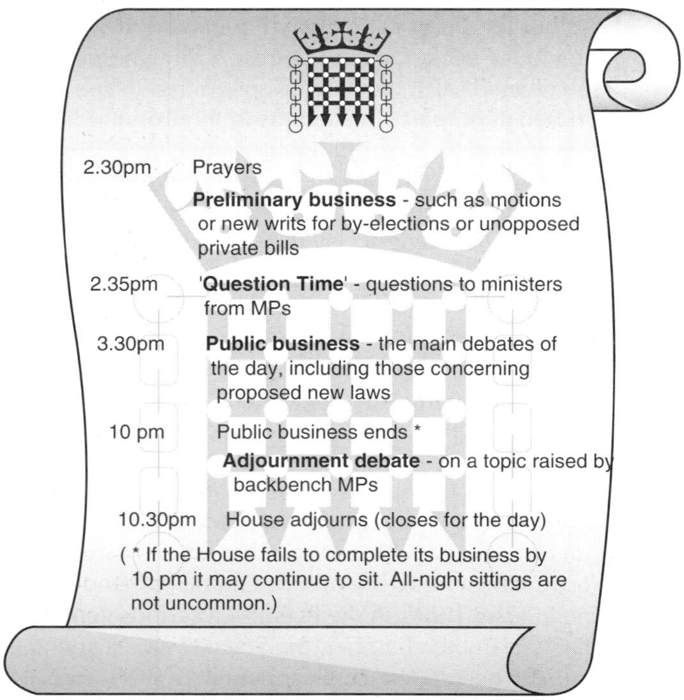
2.30pm Prayers
Preliminary business - such as motions or new writs for by-elections or unopposed private bills
2.35pm 'Question Time' - questions to ministers from MPs
3.30pm **Public business** - the main debates of the day, including those concerning proposed new laws
10 pm Public business ends *
Adjournment debate - on a topic raised by backbench MPs
10.30pm House adjourns (closes for the day)
(* If the House fails to complete its business by 10 pm it may continue to sit. All-night sittings are not uncommon.)

This diagram shows the timetable for a typical day in the Commons before the reforms of December 1994 were introduced.

Item B *The Speaker (1)*

Yesterday, the Labour MP for West Bromwich West, Betty Boothroyd, ended more than 700 years of male tradition by being elected Parliament's first woman Speaker by an overwhelming majority of MPs. More than 70 Conservative MPs were among the 372 votes in her favour. She obtained 134 more than her nearest rival the former Conservative Cabinet minister, Peter Brooke. This was only the sixth time that an open election for a new Speaker had been held. It is the third election this century and the first since 1951. The usual pattern has been to arrange matters behind the scenes. The Prime Minister, John Major, said: 'The holder of the office of Speaker must know when to turn a blind eye and when not. She needs a quick mind and a ready wit. She must be unfailing in her impartiality. She will sometimes need the wisdom of Solomon and, if I am strictly honest, she will sometimes need the patience of Job.'

Adapted from the *Guardian*, 28 April 1992.

Item C *The Speaker (2)*

The Speaker of the House of Commons, Betty Boothroyd, has been attacked by the Labour front bench on the grounds that she has shown bias towards the government. She has been accused of applying the iron fist to her former colleagues, while treating rowdy Conservative MPs with kid gloves. She has also been accused of being overprotective towards an already overpowerful government. Leading Labour MPs argue that the Speaker's pro-Conservative bias was illustrated last week when she twice asked the Prime Minister to withdraw an unparliamentary remark (he claimed that Labour's deputy leader Margaret Beckett had 'peddled an untruth'), but then backed down when he ignored her. The accusation of bias was also being linked to two other decisions made by the Speaker. First, she has banned one Labour MP, Llew Smith, from asking ministers any further questions on the Scott Inquiry (which is examining the 'Arms to Iraq' affair). And second, she has banned another Labour MP, Peter Hain, from tabling any further motions on losses suffered by Conservative MPs who had money invested in the Lloyd's insurance market.

Adapted from the *Observer*, 17 April 1994.

Questions

1. What are the arguments for and against moving the House of Commons to a new, purpose-built, semicircular chamber outside London? Use Item A in your answer.
2. a) Judging from Item B, what are the qualities required by the Speaker? Which qualities are most important?
   b) What difficulties is the Speaker likely to face? Use Item C in your answer.
3. a) Judging from Item D why do you think some MPs were unhappy with the House of Commons' daily timetable?
   b) Explain how the reforms of December 1994 might improve the situation.

1.3 The functions of the House of Commons

Philip Norton notes that:

> 'The functions ascribed to Parliaments...are not static. The form of Parliaments may remain, but what is expected of them will change as political conditions change.' (Norton, 1985, pp.1-2)

It is clear from section 1.1 above that political conditions have certainly changed during Parliament's long history. Relations between Parliament and the monarchy and indeed between the House of Commons and the House of Lords are very different today from what they were in the 19th century or earlier. Perhaps the most important development in the last hundred years is the growth of the power of the executive (the government). Today, it is the government which sets the legislative agenda and, since it is formed from the majority party (or parties) in the Commons, it is usually able to muster a majority in favour of its proposed laws, regardless of the strength of feeling of opposition MPs. But, even if the executive has the upper hand, the House of Commons still performs a number of functions. These can be discussed under the following headings: legitimation, scrutiny and influence, representation, the recruitment of government ministers and law making.

i) Legitimation

As an elected body, the House of Commons can be said to confer legitimacy on the exercise of political power by governments and on public policy in general. Following a general election, the majority party in the House (or coalition of parties, if there is a hung Parliament) forms the government. By supporting the government (primarily by giving their assent to government proposals to change the law), MPs of the governing party (or parties) provide the government with legitimacy. That is why the government is thrown into crisis if it loses a vote in the Commons - the loss of the vote is a loss of legitimacy which can only be restored if a subsequent vote of confidence in the government is passed.

In addition, since assent to legislative proposals is based on majority voting in the Commons, a further dimension to the process of legitimation comes from the House as a whole. This is the (at least tacit) agreement from all sides in the Commons that once parliamentary approval has been given to a change in the law, that new law should be obeyed unless and until Parliament assents to the law being changed again.

ii) Scrutiny and influence

The policy proposals, executive actions and expenditure of governments are all legitimate subjects for examination and criticism by the House of Commons. They are of particular concern to the opposition parties, but a government's own supporters (whose loyalty is needed by the government) are also involved in the process of scrutiny.

(iii) Representation

Each MP represents a particular geographical area in the UK. Although MPs are elected on a party platform, after the election they are expected to represent the interests of all their constituents, regardless of party affiliation. One of the functions of MPs, therefore, is to look after the interests of their constituents in Parliament and to take up their grievances (see chapter 17, part 3). As a whole, the Commons is often seen (realistically or not) as an institution able to give expression to public opinion or sentiment.

(iv) The recruitment of government ministers

The House of Commons is the recruiting ground for the vast majority of government ministers. A few members of government are still chosen from the House of Lords and the Prime Minister is able to bring in individuals from outside Parliament (though they would normally be expected to win a seat in the Commons at a subsequent by-election or to be given a seat in the Lords), but most ministers are selected from among MPs of the governing party in the House of Commons. Many members have ambitions to become government ministers and see their backbench parliamentary role as a preparation for future promotion to office.

(v) Law making

Although there are limited opportunities for backbench MPs to initiate legislative proposals, much of the work done by the House of Commons involves the scrutiny of legislative proposals put forward by the government. As far as the government is concerned, the job of the House of Commons is to give assent to the government's legislative programme. The process of scrutiny prior to assent, however, can provide MPs with the possibility of influencing the content of legislation.

Proposed legislation enters Parliament in the form of Bills. There are two main types of Bill - private and public.

Private Bills play only a minor role in legislation today. They are intended to apply only to a particular area, a specific organisation or a certain section of the population. They are sometimes promoted for large capital projects on behalf of private companies or by public bodies (such as local authorities) as a means of avoiding long and costly public inquiries. Private Bills were popular in the 19th century when local authorities sought means to improve their facilities. Large-scale projects, such as the Manchester Ship Canal and the Birmingham Municipal Bank, were set into motion by private Bills. The Transport and Works Act of 1992 has restricted the scope of private Bills by changing the basis on which statutory authority for major infrastructure developments is granted:

> 'Projects such as railways, tramways, ports, harbours and barrages will, in most cases, no longer come before Parliament for approval by way of a private Bill, but by ministerial orders following, in most cases, public local inquiries conducted by professional departmental inspectors.' (HMSO, 1994, p.75)

The vast majority of Bills passing through Parliament are **public Bills** (they are aimed at the public as a whole). Most public Bills are sponsored by the government and, therefore, referred to as 'government Bills'. But, around 10% of Commons' time is spent on a second type of public Bill - the private member's Bill. Private members' Bills are introduced and promoted by backbench MPs.

Private members' Bills

Since private members' Bills encounter special difficulties in their passage through Parliament, the vast majority fail and do not become law. Out of 441 private members' Bills introduced during the 1983-87 Parliament (including 60 in the House of Lords), for example, only 68 were successful (Adonis, 1993, p.109). Many of those which were successful were either politically uncontentious or received government support.

There are three ways of introducing a private member's Bill into Parliament - the ballot, the 'ten minute rule' procedure and standing order 58. At the start of each parliamentary session, MPs can enter their names in a ballot from which 20 names are drawn, but only 12 Fridays in each session are normally set aside for discussion of 'ballot Bills' and half of these tend to be taken up with the later stages of Bills already in the pipeline. Attendance at the House on Fridays is usually low (many MPs return to their constituencies for the weekend) and the MP promoting a ballot Bill may well see it delayed or pushed off the Commons timetable because an insufficient number of MPs is present in the chamber for a division (vote) to take place. Even so, the chances of success for a ballot Bill are much higher than private members' Bills introduced in other ways.

Under the ten minute rule, an MP is allowed 10 minutes to outline the case for a new piece of legislation. MPs frequently use this procedure to gain publicity for ideas they wish to express rather than in hope of getting new legislation onto the statute book.

MPs have a slightly higher chance of success with the procedure laid down in standing order 58. This allows a Bill to be introduced without debate if a day's notice is given to the Speaker. The vast majority of Bills introduced in this way, however, fail.

Overall, the majority of private members' Bills fail because the government does not provide the support necessary for their successful passage through the House. The main requirement is that of time. Without the provision of extra time by the government, a Bill has little chance of success. Controversial private members' Bills are especially vulnerable to hostile government tactics. For example, filibustering is a technique whereby an opponent of a Bill carries on speaking (often about unrelated matters) simply to use up time and to prevent a vote being taken.

Some private members' Bills, however, do receive government (and even bi-party) support. These Bills are sometimes used as a means of introducing social reforms with which the government does not wish to be directly identified. In the 1960s, for example, reforms to the law on abortion and homosexuality were achieved through private members' Bills. Similarly, in 1994, the age of consent for homosexuals was lowered to 18 after the government supported a private member's Bill.

Pressure groups often target MPs who have been successful in the ballot in the hope that they will introduce a Bill in support of their cause or interest. In the 1983-84 session, for example, the Consumers' Association persuaded the Labour MP, Austin Mitchell (who had come sixth in the ballot), to introduce the Home Buyer's Bill to end solicitors' monopoly on conveyancing. Although the Bill was not successful, the support it attracted in the House encouraged the government to introduce its own proposals (Silk, 1989).

Government Bills

Some types of government Bill are introduced in every parliamentary session - for example the Finance Bill containing the provisions of the Budget. Some are brought in to deal with emergencies (wars or civil strife, for example) or in response to pressure. Others are planned as part of the general process of implementing government policy. Often, such Bills relate to manifesto promises.

Consultation takes place between the sponsoring government department and other departments (especially the Treasury). There may also be consultation with outside organisations. Sometimes, the consultation process involves the publication of a green paper in which the government outlines its ideas, presents policy options and invites comments. The 1993 Ripon Commission report, however, noted that green papers were becoming rare. The trend was to produce less formal 'consultation papers'. In addition to, and sometimes instead of, an initial consultation stage, the government publishes a white paper which states its policy on a particular topic or view. In effect, a white paper is a statement of intended legislation and may be the subject of parliamentary debate. Once the Cabinet decides to go ahead with the proposals, a date is fixed for their introduction into Parliament and a draft Bill is drawn up.

A government Bill is usually given its first reading in the House of Commons, though it can begin in the

Lords. It then goes through further stages - second reading, committee stage, report stage and third reading - before passing to the other House where it goes through a similar series of stages. Once the Bill has received royal assent, it becomes law in the form of an Act of Parliament.

The function of the Commons with regard to law making, therefore, is to debate the proposed legislation, to scrutinise it at the committee stage, to suggest amendments and to agree on its final shape. It should be emphasised, however, that it is the government (on the whole) which decides what matters require legislation and the government is normally able to command a majority in any vote taken in the House. The scope for opposition MPs (and indeed for government backbenchers) to make an impact on legislation which comes before the House is, therefore, limited.

The role of the whips

Each party in the Commons appoints a chief whip and assistant whips. The role of government whips in the legislative process is to ensure that the government maintains its majority in votes taken in the House. The opposition whips organise their supporters to mount an effective challenge to the government.

MPs receive weekly printed instructions from their party whips indicating when they should attend the House to vote. These instructions are also referred to as 'whips'. A **three-line whip** means attendance is essential. A **two-line whip** means that MPs must attend unless arrangements have been made under the 'pairing' system (government and opposition whips can agree for an MP on each side to 'pair' up and be absent at the same time). A **one-line whip** merely requests the attendance of MPs.

Whips can apply pressure to rebellious MPs in a number of ways. Normally a stiff talking to is enough to secure the MP's loyalty. But, if an MP votes against the government in a motion with a three-line whip, the whip may be withdrawn from the MP - the equivalent of being expelled from the party. This is what happened to eight Conservative MPs in November 1994 when they voted against the government Bill increasing Britain's contributions to the EU (this was the first time this century that such a large number of Conservative MPs had been disciplined in this way at one time).

Maintaining party support and party discipline form only part of the managerial role of the party whips (see Alderman, 1995). The government's chief whip attends Cabinet meetings and has the status of a senior minister. The chief whips arrange the weekly business of the House. Whips arrange 'pairs' and allocate offices in Westminster. Also, Whips provide an important means of communication between the party leadership and backbenchers.

Activity 14.2

Item A *The MP, the House and the constituency*

Item B *League for the Introduction of Canine Control (LICC)*

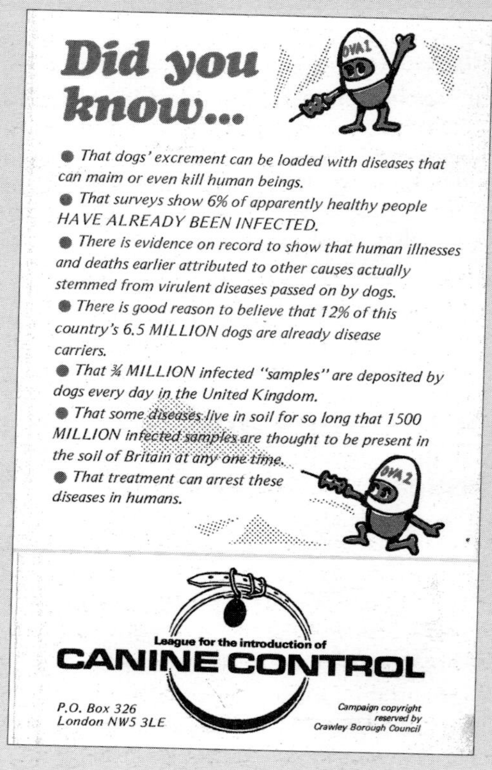

Item C *The passage of a Bill through Parliament*

House of Commons

First reading — The Bill is formally introduced to allow MPs to consider the proposals before the second reading.

Second reading — The aims and main **principles** of the Bill are debated. Voting is whipped on government Bills. Non-controversial Bills may be discussed by a committee instead of the whole House.

Committee stage — The details of the Bill are discussed by a **standing committee** composed of MPs from different parties roughly in proportion to their numbers in the House. The government may attempt to use the 'guillotine'(setting time limits to curtail debate) to ensure completion of this stage.

Report stage — The House considers amendments made at the committee stage and may make further changes.

Third reading — The Bill as a whole is debated. Whipped voting. Usually takes place together with the report stage.

↓

House of Lords

The Bill passes through the same five stages as in the Commons.

If the Lords **accept** the Bill, it is passed for the Royal Assent.

If the Lords **reject** the Bill, it is delayed for a year.

If the Lords **amend** the Bill, it goes back to the Commons, which accepts the changes or the Lords withdraw them.

↓

Royal Assent

In practice, a formality. The Bill then becomes an Act of Parliament.

Item D *A whip*

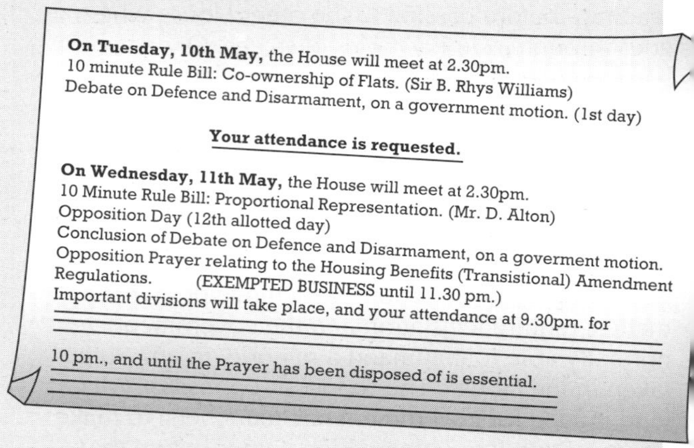
On Tuesday, 10th May, the House will meet at 2.30pm.
10 minute Rule Bill: Co-ownership of Flats. (Sir B. Rhys Williams)
Debate on Defence and Disarmament, on a government motion. (1st day)

Your attendance is requested.

On Wednesday, 11th May, the House will meet at 2.30pm.
10 Minute Rule Bill: Proportional Representation. (Mr. D. Alton)
Opposition Day (12th allotted day)
Conclusion of Debate on Defence and Disarmament, on a goverment motion.
Opposition Prayer relating to the Housing Benefits (Transistional) Amendment Regulations. (EXEMPTED BUSINESS until 11.30 pm.)
Important divisions will take place, and your attendance at 9.30pm. for 10 pm., and until the Prayer has been disposed of is essential.

Item E *The whips' contact network*

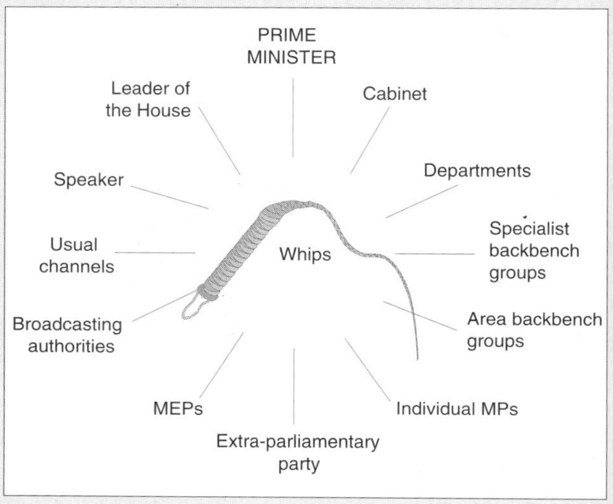

Questions

1. What does Item A tell us about the function of the Commons?
2. a) Suppose a minister agreed to meet LICC (Item B) and to sponsor a Bill imposing heavy fines on dog owners whose pets fouled the pavement. Using Item C describe the process to be undertaken before the Bill became law.
   b) How much influence would backbench and opposition MPs have on the final form of the Bill?
   c) Suppose ministers refused to sponsor such a Bill. Advise LICC on the best way to proceed to achieve legislation.
3. 'The House of Commons' most important function is to participate in the law making process.' Give arguments for and against this view.
4. a) Identify the types of Bills mentioned in Item D.
   b) How does the role of the whips affect the way in which the Commons performs its functions? Use Items D and E in your answer.

2. Committees and procedures

Key Issues

1. What are standing committees and what do they do?
2. What are select committees? How do they differ from standing committees?
3. What are the procedures for debates and questions in the House?

2.1 Committees in the House of Commons

Philip Norton explains that:

'Within the House of Commons there are basically two types of committee: official and unofficial. Each can be further subdivided. The two principal types of official committees are the standing and select committees, though the

House also makes use of a form of hybrid, known as special standing committees. Unofficial committees comprise essentially party committees and all-party groups. The official committees are established by the House under its standing orders. They are subordinate bodies: the House retains the final say on all matters. Unofficial committees are, as the name indicates, not bodies established formally by the House: they are created within the parliamentary parties or by groups of Members.' (Norton, 1991, p.5)

Norton points out that, although the use of committees can be traced back to the 14th century, the current, extensive use of committees in the House of Commons is a recent development. Since 1907, the sending of Bills to standing committees has been normal practice. It is only since 1979, however, that select committees have been appointed to investigate the activities of government departments.

Standing committees

When a Bill has received its second reading, it reaches its committee stage. The Bill is then usually sent to a standing committee for consideration - unless the House decides otherwise (the committee stage of uncontentious Bills or Bills of constitutional importance, such as the Maastricht Bill, are taken on the floor of the House). Standing committees examine the details of a Bill within the confines of the Bill's general principles which were approved at the second reading. The job of standing committees is to debate and consider amendments to the Bill.

Despite their name, standing committees are ad hoc committees. They are set up specifically to examine a particular Bill and are then disbanded. No collective identity (which might lead to a stronger, more investigative, role) is, therefore, likely to develop.

Standing committees' origins lie in the 19th century - two standing committees, each of 60-80 MPs, were established in 1883. The present structure, however, dates from 1907. Since then, the number of committees has increased and the numbers serving on each committee has decreased.

Standing committees do not have distinctive names, but are referred to as standing committee A, B, C and so on. Each standing committee must have between 16 and 50 members (between 18 and 25 is the usual number). Members come from different parties in rough proportion to the party political make-up of the House as a whole. A government with a secure majority can, therefore, normally expect to secure acceptance of its proposals, although during the detailed consideration of a Bill it may wish to make minor amendments.

The Committee of Selection, composed of senior MPs, decides which MPs should sit on each standing committee (after consulting with party whips). The relevant minister and opposition spokesperson is included as a matter of course and members with a special interest or expertise in the subject of the Bill are normally considered. The committee's work is presided over by a senior backbencher appointed by the Speaker from the 'Chairmen's panel' (they are supposed to be impartial). It should be noted that:

> 'The committee meets in a similar adversarial format to the House itself, the government supporters sitting on one side of the committee room and the opposition parties on the other side.' (Norton, 1995, p.23)

Standing committees examine Bills by considering each clause in turn. Amendments can be put forward by any member of the committee, but, unless they are moved by the minister, they usually fail (clauses of government Bills which are voted on tend to be whipped). In order to reduce the time a committee spends on a Bill, the government may seek to apply the guillotine. This involves setting a time limit for debate on each clause. Its use is not restricted to committee stage and it is used particularly for those occasions when it has not been possible to reach agreement with the opposition 'through the usual channels' (see above, p.407).

Standing committees have often been criticised for taking excessive time to carry out their work. A sitting lasts for two to three hours and Norton (1995) records that:

> 'In the 1988-89 session, for example, 27 government Bills were considered at 437 meetings of standing committees. The Broadcasting Bill was considered at 38 sittings and the Environment Protection Bill at 32.' (Norton, 1995, p.23)

The general pattern in standing committees is for opposition members to begin by tabling numerous amendments. These are usually rejected. Since little progress has been made, the government then calls for a guillotine to be imposed. This restricts the opportunity for significant changes to be made.

Standing committees have also been criticised because they operate on adversarial party lines. As a result, the outcome of their deliberations is, generally, predictable. In addition, it is argued that these committees have inadequate information at their disposal since they are not permitted to take evidence from outside bodies or individuals.

In response to these criticisms, Norton (1995) has identified four possible reforms. First, the House of Commons Procedure Committee suggested that Bills should be given a fixed timetable. This would prevent the imposition of the guillotine and allow more balance since each part of the Bill would be given a certain amount of time for scrutiny. Second, the Hansard Society Commission recommended that standing committees should be set up on a permanent basis. A core of permanent members would be supplemented by the cooption of extra members for each Bill. This would allow a body of knowledge to develop and help to reduce the partisan nature of the committees. Third, Norton (1992) has suggested that the committee stage should precede the Bill's second reading. This would allow the committee to consider wider issues since the principles upon which the Bill is based would not have been established. And fourth, the report of the Ripon Commission in 1993 recommended that, where appropriate, standing committees should be able to take on the powers of 'special standing committees' which can spend up to three public sessions questioning witnesses and considering particular aspects of a Bill before carrying out the clause-by-clause examination. The advantage of this would be that committees could obtain adequate information to scrutinise the Bill properly. Also, outside groups would be able to make representations in an open environment, rather than relying on the secret or private contacts that are normally made with government departments during the legislative process.

One further suggestion (see Downs, 1985) is to amalgamate the work of standing committees with that of select committees. Select committees are responsible for scrutinising and reviewing the work of government departments (see below). An amalgamation would result in the committee reviewing the work of a particular department, including the legislation produced by that department.

Select committees

According to a government pamphlet:

> 'Select committees are generally set up to help Parliament with the control of the executive by examining aspects of public policy and administration. They may also undertake more specific responsibilities related to the internal procedures of Parliament. They examine subjects by taking written and oral evidence and, after private deliberation, present a report to the House.' (HMSO, 1994, p.80)

Drewry (1989) explains that select committees were used a great deal before the mid-19th century, but the development of a disciplined party system in Parliament and greater control by the executive led to their decline. A number of non-departmental select committees have a long history, but it is only since 1979 that departmental select committees have been in operation.

Perhaps the most important non-departmental select committee is the Public Accounts Committee, first set up in 1861. This committee, with its large staff of auditors working under the Comptroller and Auditor General, checks the government accounts and attempts to ensure that money has been spent in properly authorised ways. Other non-departmental select committees include the Committee on the Parliamentary Commissioner for Administration (which supervises the work of the 'ombudsman'- see chapter 17, pp.518-20) and the Select Committee on European Legislation (which scrutinises legislation proposed by the European Union). There are also non-departmental select committees which deal with the House's internal affairs (such as the Privileges Committee which meets when a matter of parliamentary privilege is referred to it) or ad hoc committees set up to investigate particular issues.

In 1979, despite ministerial reluctance, MPs voted to set up a number of departmental select committees whose task would be to examine the expenditure, administration and policy of individual government departments and to report back to the House. Initially, 14 departmental select committees were set up. Two more were set up in 1992 and one for Northern Ireland was set up in 1994.

Departmental select committees each have 11 members (except for the Committee on Northern Ireland Affairs which has 13). Members are chosen by the Committee of Selection. Apart from the Committee on Northern Ireland Affairs (which includes five MPs from Northern Irish parties), membership of select committees (as with standing committees) roughly reflects the relative party sizes in the Commons as a whole. Unlike standing committees, however, no government ministers or front bench opposition members are included and no whips attend. Select committees do not tend to operate on the adversarial party lines of standing committees. Party-based differences may still occur, but select committees, generally, aim to produce unanimous reports at the end of their investigations.

Most departmental select committees meet once a week. In theory, they can investigate any issue within the scope of the work of the relevant department, but time places severe limits on what a small group of backbench MPs, who have the support only of a small administrative staff, can achieve. The committees do have, however, the power to send for 'persons, papers and records'. Witnesses can be interviewed (in public unless confidential or security matters are discussed) and specialist advisers can be appointed.

Despite such powers, however, the committees may not obtain the information they require. The tradition of government secrecy makes it difficult to obtain information from ministers and civil servants. Without the express permission of the House as a whole, committees cannot compel ministers or other MPs to attend, although they generally do. More important is the difficulty some committees have in persuading ministers and other witnesses to give straight answers to direct questions. Committees do not have automatic recourse to departmental papers and records (though concern is normally expressed in the House and increasingly by the media if evidence is refused on unreasonable grounds). In addition, the government is not obliged to act upon the recommendations of select committees and there is no guarantee that their reports will even be debated in the House. The government usually responds to reports with a detailed memorandum.

Membership of select committees is, however, more popular than membership of standing committees. In part, this is because MPs believe that the work done by such committees is important (if nothing else, ministers and civil servants are aware that a select committee can investigate any aspect of a department's work and so the committee acts as a deterrent against arbitrary government). In part, it also reflects the media attention which is sometimes given to the work of committees (for example, the 1991-92 Trade and Industry Committee's inquiry into the sale of arms to Iraq). Select committees allow backbenchers to engage in investigative work and, in some cases, this is a substitute for ministerial office.

When departmental select committees were set up in 1979, some people hoped that this would alter the balance between Parliament and the executive. But, given the strength of the party system, the idea that the Commons could in some way control the government is unrealistic. Rather, the effectiveness of select committees should be judged by the extent to which they influence the executive. Norton argues that:

> 'The impact of committees on government policy has been modest. Some policies have been affected by committee reports; many have not. The Prime Minister in 1986 identified 150 recommendations from select committees that the government had accepted in the period from March 1985 to March 1986. However, many of the recommendations were essentially minor and constituted a minority of the recommendations emanating from the committees. Nonetheless, those accepted were proposals that otherwise would probably never have seen the light of day.' (Norton, 1991, p.9)

Concern was also expressed that the setting up of select committees would reduce interest in and attendance at meetings of the full House. These concerns, however, appear to have been largely unfounded. Adonis argues that, if anything, the committees have:

> 'Enhanced the profile and reputation of the House of Commons among policy formers and the media.' (Adonis, 1993, p.170)

Norton agrees that there have been advantages, but points out that the system also has limitations:

> 'The committees have proved of value to the House and to MPs individually. They have acted as a means of specialisation, as deterrents, as agents of open government, as safety valves and as policy influencers. The combination is an impressive one...Against the advantages, one has to put the limitations. The committees stand accused of having inadequate resources, an amateurish approach, limited powers, little linkage with the floor of the House, limited influence and of wilting under the pressure of political interference and of other demands on MPs' time.' (Norton, 1994, pp.29 & 31)

Activity 14.3

Item A *Select committees, March 1995*

Select committees have proved to be remarkably active. In the four sessions of the 1983-87 Parliament, for example, select committees questioned 210 ministers, 1,365 civil servants and 3,579 other witnesses. During that period, they produced 306 reports (over 900 reports have been produced since 1979). The fact that ministers and civil servants can be examined serves as a reminder to other ministers and officials that they might be summoned (the deterrent effect). By examining witnesses and written evidence, the committees have generated more open government. By interviewing outside witnesses, they have become an outlet for pressure group activity (and, therefore, a safety valve). By building up pools of information, they are able to challenge the government's near monopoly on the information presented to the House. Also, their non-partisan approach adds weight to their recommendations. Recent successes include: getting the Chancellor to admit indirect tax increases equalled 7p on income tax (Treasury Select Committee); making top earners squirm (Employment Select Committee); and, triggering reform of the Child Support Agency (Social Security Select Committee).

Adapted from Norton, 1991 and 1994 and the *Guardian*, 22 March 1995.

Item B *The record of standing committees*

Whips who attend standing committees encourage government supporters on the committee to attend, but not to speak. They need to attend to ensure that the government maintains its majority on the committee. But, speeches take up valuable time and the whips want the business to be done as quickly as possible. A study of the standing committees in three parliamentary sessions in the early 1970s showed that only 171 out of 3,510 amendments proposed by private members were agreed to. It should be noted, however, that whilst the Labour government of 1974-79 suffered more than 100 standing committee defeats, this was exceptional. All but two of the other postwar governments have commanded substantial Commons majorities and suffered no more than a handful of inconsequential defeats in the standing committees.

Adapted from Norton, 1986 and Adonis, 1993.

Item C *The standing committee on the Electricity Bill in the 1988-89 parliamentary session*

	Number
Sittings of committee	36
Amendments made to Bill	114
Ministerial amendments carried	113
Amendments moved by Conservative backbenchers	22
Conservative backbench amendments carried	1
Amendments moved by opposition MPs	227
Opposition amendments carried	0
Votes on opposition amendments	37
Voted amendments carried	0
Hours of deliberation in committee	110

Adapted from Adonis, 1993.

Item E *Edwina Currie and the Agriculture Select Committee*

From Mrs EDWINA CURRIE MP

HOUSE OF COMMONS
LONDON, SW1 0AA

6 February 1989

Mr J. Wiggin MP
Chairman
Agriculture Select Committee,

Dear Chairman

I hope you will not mind my writing to you again, in view of Press comments and remarks made by some of the members of the Committee since I last wrote to you.

I have asked to be excused attendance at the Select Committee's current investigation as I can be of no assistance to you, not because I would withhold anything relevant, but because I have no more to tell you than you already know. The Committee has seen the research material to which I had access. My reported comments in December were based on published sources on this topic as on most of the others for which I had ministerial reponsibility. I cannot convey to you any conversations which I had with officials : those must remain confidential. You are to question Ministers and no doubt they will answer you. I have nothing to add; and can be of no assistance to you.

Please may I be allowed to get on with the rest of my life? I am elected to care for the people of South Derbyshire and this intense interest is interfering with my ability to do that. I wish the Committee well in its endeavours and hope that it will not delay its report any further.

With very best wishes

Yours ever
Edwina

In 1986, the junior Health minister Edwina Currie claimed that most of Britain's egg production was infected with salmonella. This claim led to her resignation and an inquiry by the Select Committee on Agriculture. On three occasions, Currie refused to appear before the select committee (the letter above is the third refusal). Two days after the letter above was sent and in the face of growing media criticism, however, she relented and agreed to appear. Since 1979, it has been very rare for witnesses to refuse to appear and those who have refused initially, have later relented. More frequent is witnesses' refusal to answer questions.

Adapted from Shell, 1993.

Item D *Select committees - watchdogs or poodles?*

The former Cabinet minister Michael Jopling described select committees as: 'The most important development in parliamentary procedure in my 30 years in the House. Select committees are giving backbenchers teeth with which to challenge the executive.' This is a verdict with which most MPs would probably agree. There are still criticisms, however. When committee chairs are too effective, for example, they are replaced. This happened to Nicholas Winterton in 1992 after chairing the Health Select Committee for two terms. He was replaced by Marion Roe, a loyalist with a desire for cosy consensus. The problem with select committees is that they are the creation of an executive-dominated system and they lack the resources or the prestige to sustain a rigorous investigative role. Most committees are staffed with former ministers or future ministers plus worthy plodders who lack firepower. Most lack the staff and budgets to be independent from Whitehall. Their range of inquiries has been too narrow and cumbersome (though it is improving) and ministers can simply ignore their findings (as the President of the Board of Trade, Michael Heseltine did when, in 1993, a select committee report recommended that a number of coal mines should not be shut down). Select committees also find it difficult to obtain information from ministers and their officials. Significantly, the head of the civil service, Sir Robin Butler, said that select committees usually reached an amicable agreement with the government over which civil servants should give evidence.

Adapted from the *Guardian*, 22 March 1995.

Questions

1. To what extent and in what ways is the select committee system able to act as a check on the executive? Use Items A, D and E in your answer.
2. Do you agree with the following statements? Use Items A, D and E for your answer.
   (i) Select committees are to be welcomed because of their emphasis on consensus rather than party division.
   (ii) By questioning ministers and civil servants, select committees make the executive more accountable to Parliament.
   (iii) Select committees give backbenchers more power.
   (iv) Select committees lead to more open government.
3. a) Judging from Items B and C why do you think standing committee work is unpopular with (i) opposition MPs and (ii) government backbenchers?
   b) What are the drawbacks with the existing standing committee system? What improvements would you recommend? Use Items B and C in your answer.

2.2 Debates and questions

A large proportion of time in the House of Commons is taken up with debates and the questioning of government ministers. It is in debates and at Prime Minister's Question Time that party political conflict is at its fiercest.

Debates

The House of Commons is a debating chamber and an elaborate set of rules for the conduct of debates has developed over time. Some of the rules are laid down in standing orders (the regulations governing the House of Commons' procedures). Others operate by convention:

> 'The subject for debate starts off as a proposal or motion made by a member. When a motion has been moved, the Speaker proposes the question (in the same terms as the motion) as the subject for debate...In both Houses, members speak from wherever they have been sitting and not from a rostrum (although front bench members usually stand at one of the despatch boxes on the Table of the House). They may not read their speeches (although they may refresh their memories by referring to notes). Generally, no member may speak twice to the same motion, except to clarify some part of a speech that has been misunderstood, or by leave of the House'. (HMSO, 1994, pp.60-61)

Major debates are normally opened and closed either by government ministers or members of the opposition front bench and frontbenchers are, generally, given more time than backbenchers to make their speeches. MPs wishing to make contributions to a debate must first 'catch the Speaker's eye', although this is usually done by notifying the Speaker before the beginning of the debate. Also, by custom, privy councillors are given priority in debates. Privy councillors are mainly existing and former Cabinet ministers or leading members of the opposition parties. Unlike ordinary MPs who are referred to as 'honourable' members, privy councillors are referred to as 'right honourable' members.

Although the purpose of debates is, in theory, to decide upon government policy and administration, a government can usually rely on its majority in the House to gain approval for its actions (see Table 14.1 for the range of debates). The division (vote) at the end of a debate is, therefore, generally a foregone conclusion (it is called a 'division' because MPs divide up into those going into the 'ayes' lobby and those going into the 'noes' lobby). Commons debates are, perhaps, more accurately seen as a device for expressing government, opposition and dissenting views.

Table 14.1 **Debates in the Commons**

1. Debates on white papers

2. Debates on Bills

3. Debates on ministerial statements

4. Debates on reports of parliamentary committees

5. Debates on the Queen's Speech
The Queen's Speech is the annual address to Parliament, written by the Prime Minister, outlining the government's legislative programme for the forthcoming session. The subsequent debate takes place over a number of days and is one of the few occasions during the year when a major Commons speech is delivered by the Prime Minister.

6. Daily adjournment debates
These take place during the final half hour of each day's sitting when an MP can raise almost any subject. These debates are often used to air constituents' grievances or draw attention to matters in which individual backbenchers are personally interested.

7. Government motions
About 20 days per session are devoted to debates on government motions.

8. Opposition days
There are 20 days per session for debates on subjects chosen by the opposition.

9. Motions of no confidence (in the government)
No confidence debates are more likely to be called for by the opposition when the government's majority is small. If defeated, the government must resign or call a general election, but this has occured only once this century - James Callaghan's Labour government was defeated on a no confidence vote in March 1979.

10. Private members' motions
About 10 days per session are reserved for debates on these motions together with the final day before each recess (holiday). These debates are usually poorly attended.

11. Emergency debates
Requests for emergency debates are rarely granted by the Speaker, but opposition requests for them can secure media attention.

Debates vary in quality, but are frequently little more than a series of speeches which make party political points to a sparsely attended chamber. Unless the government has a small majority, most debates have little impact on government policy. Even if the government only has a small majority, it is not often the quality of the points made in a debate which result in government action. For example, in the first few months after the 1992 general election, the government made policy concessions over its plans to close coal mines and over its intended timetable for ratification of the Maastricht Treaty. Both of these concessions were made, however, in response to backbenchers' threats not to vote with the government rather than because of the content or quality of the debates themselves (see Adonis, 1993, p.144).

Occasionally, a debate on a matter of crucial national or international significance can prove to be an exception. In September 1990, for example, Parliament was summoned to meet before the end of the recess so that a debate could be held on the crisis in the Gulf following Iraq's occupation of Kuwait. Immediately after the debate, a Labour frontbencher claimed that this was one of those rare occasions when a parliamentary debate may have influenced the government (in this case, by showing the strength of feeling in the House about the need to maintain international consensus on any future action in the crisis).

Lengthy sessions of this debate were covered live on radio and television, thus bringing the views expressed to a much wider audience. Yet, the broadcasting of the proceedings of the House is of fairly recent origin. Regular radio coverage began in 1978 and television cameras were first allowed into the Commons in 1989 (see chapter 19, section 3.2).

The performance in debates can help to determine the direction of an MP's career. A reputation as a poor performer in the Commons does not help an MP to gain promotion to the front bench, nor does it make it easy for an MP to retain such a position.

In general, as a means of scrutinising the executive or influencing policy, debates have their limitations. But, they may have some effect in forcing the government to explain its policies and to justify its actions. They also bring conflicting political views to the attention of the electorate.

Question Time

Question Time is held in the Commons each day (except Fridays) and lasts for one hour. The Prime Minister answers questions from 15.15 to 15.30 pm on Tuesdays and Thursdays every week. Other government ministers take turns to answer questions (a rota system is used to determine which minister answers at which time):

> 'Questions are usually handed in at the Table Office in writing, but may be sent by post. Usually, at least two days' notice must be given to allow time for an answer to be prepared. If an oral answer is required, the question must be marked with an asterisk; questions without asterisks are answered in writing. An MP may ask up to two oral questions and any number of written questions a day. No more than eight questions requiring oral answers may be tabled by any MP during a period of 10 sitting days. An MP may ask only one oral question of any one minister on any day.' (HMSO, 1994, p.88)

The Table Office (which consists of four clerks under the control of a principal clerk) scrutinise proposed questions to ensure that they conform to the parliamentary rules. They may edit the questions. The admissability of questions is determined by whether they conform to principles established by the rulings made by successive Speakers. They must conform to five broad criteria:

> 'A question must be framed as a genuine question and not as a statement or a speech in the interrogative; it must not seek the interpretation of a statute or legal opinion; it must not ask for information already published or for the confirmation of a rumour or press report; it must not be "tendentious, controversial, ironic, vague, frivolous or repetitive"; and, it must be concerned with a matter for which a minister is officially responsible.' (HMSO, 1994, p.89)

Before each Question Time, ministers work with their civil servants to prepare their responses. In particular, they try to anticipate the **supplementary questions** which follow each initial answer. Each questioner is permitted to ask one supplementary question and the Speaker may then allow further supplementaries from other MPs. Supplementaries from opposition MPs are often, therefore, designed to test the ability and efficiency of the minister. These supplementaries must be confined to matters for which the answering minister has responsibility. Since the Prime Minister has no particular department, initial questions to the Prime Minister are usually 'open' (asking whether the Prime Minister will pay an official visit to a place or list the official engagements for that day). Having asked the open question, questioners can then ask the question they really wanted to ask in the form of a supplementary. The purposes behind questions are summarised in Table 14.2.

Table 14.2 The purposes behind questions asked at Question Time

1. To gain information (but more effective ways, such as writing to the appropriate government department, are usually available).
2. To press for action on an issue.
3. To raise a grievance on behalf of a constituent or group.
4. To give publicity to the aims or interests of a pressure group.
5. To impress constituents, constituency party or party managers.
6. To embarass the government (particularly the leader of the opposition's questions to the Prime Minister).
7. To attempt to show government policy or actions in a favourable light (including the'planted' question, about which the opposition complains from time to time).

For opposition members, therefore, Question Time is an opportunity for political point scoring whilst government ministers and their civil servants tend to regard it as an exercise in damage limitation and reveal as little as possible. Ministers are not obliged to answer questions. If they refuse to answer a question, they do not even have to supply a reason, although they usually do. Referring to the carefully prepared responses of ministers which are provided by civil servants, one backbench MP declared:

> 'Most of the words they say haven't even passed through their own brains.' (quoted in Jordan & Richardson, 1987, p.72)

MPs on both sides, however, agree that, regardless of the limitations, Question Time is an important means of scrutinising the work of ministers:

> 'In an average length session between 1945 and 1985, the number [of oral questions] tabled would not exceed 15,000 and sometimes would be closer to half that figure. Since then, the number tabled in an average session has exceeded 20,000 and is usually closer to 25,000...In some recent sessions, the number [of written questions] tabled has exceeded 45,000...One recent survey of some MPs on both sides of the House found that there was general agreement that questions were important for holding ministers to account...Oral questions were seen as marginally more important than written questions in this context. Written questions were deemed more important than oral questions for obtaining information that would otherwise be difficult to acquire.' (Norton, 1993, p.96-97)

Question Time may not be a mechanism for obtaining detailed, informative and open answers to searching political questions, but it can help to publicise party political positions and conflicts and, as with debates, it has a part to play in securing a degree of ministerial accountability to Parliament.

The cash for questions scandal

In July 1994, the *Sunday Times* revealed that two Conservative MPs, David Tredinnick and Graham Riddick, had each accepted £1,000 in return for tabling a written question to a minister. The *Sunday Times* had set up an undercover operation in which a journalist posed as a businessman and approached 20 MPs - 10 Labour and 10 Conservative. Of these 20 MPs, four Conservatives agreed to ask questions. One asked for the money to be sent to charity, a second agreed to ask a question for nothing, whilst Tredinnick and Riddick asked for the money to be sent to their home addresses.

Technically, Tredinnick and Riddick would have done nothing wrong so long as they declared the payment in the Register of Members' Interests (see chapter 11, pp.228-30) within a month. But, the news that the two MPs had accepted cash for questions caused great public outrage because of the moral issues it raised. This outrage was then fuelled by reports in the *Guardian* in October 1994 that junior ministers Neil Hamilton and Tim Smith had also received money in return for tabling parliamentary questions between 1987 and 1989 (when they were both backbenchers). Smith resigned from the government immediately and Hamilton resigned soon afterwards.

In response to these allegations, an investigation was launched by the Commons Select Committee on Privileges and the government set up a committee on standards in public life under Lord Justice Nolan. The Nolan Committee was given the following brief:

> 'To examine current concerns about the standards of conduct of all holders of public office, including arrangements relating to financial and commercial activities, and to make recommendations as to any changes in present arrangements which might be required to ensure the highest standards of propriety in public life.' (quoted in the *New Statesman and Society*, 4 November 1994)

Activity 14.4

Item A *Cash for questions (1)*

The integrity of MPs ought to be above suspicion, but the willingness to table questions for money taints that integrity. Most people are outraged that such a large sum was paid for such a small favour. The point is that Mr Tredinnick was not offering his valuable expertise (for which he could have legitimately charged), but the exploitation of a privilege granted to him simply because he was an MP. More generally, it is a time for the rules on MPs' interests to be tightened. This is an area where Conservatives are more vulnerable than Labour MPs. Although most Labour MPs are sponsored by trade unions, they do not receive any personal gain from this - the union pays the money to the MP's constituency party. There is no reason to ban all outside payments - since lobbyists will find a way round the rules, as they have in the USA. Rather, the declaration of interests should be more transparent. Before MPs rise to make a speech in a debate in the Commons, they have to declare any relevant interest. The same should apply to written questions. Also, MPs should notify the Register before, not after, they undertake work for payment. Finally, they should be required to declare in the Register how much they have been paid - shame is often a more effective sanction than the law.

Adapted from the *Times*, 12 July 1994.

Item B *Cash for questions (2)*

Reporter:	Hello David. Thanks so much. I got your message on the answerphone when I got back. You tabled questions this evening, did you?
Tredinnick:	Yes.
Reporter:	Fine, brilliant.
Tredinnick:	So you will get an answer on Tuesday.
Reporter:	Right. OK.
Tredinnick:	That's unless they can't get the information in time. It went down as it was written, without change.
Reporter:	I will send you the £1,000 in the post now then.
Tredinnick:	That's very kind of you.
Reporter:	You checked that this is all above board and everything, didn't you?
Tredinnick:	Oh yes, that's fine.
Reporter:	There's no problem about that?
Tredinnick:	I probably will declare an interest, but I don't have to be specific on that and it's confidential between the two of us.
Reporter:	Right. OK, fine. The address I have is the correct address to which to send the cheque?
Tredinnick:	Yes, it's my home address.

Adapted from the *Times*, 12 July 1994.

Item D *Cash for questions (3)*

This cartoon was inspired by news that two Conservative MPs had accepted money in return for tabling questions in the House of Commons. It appeared in the *Guardian* on 12 July 1994.

Item C *Prime Minister's Question Time*

Until 1959, questions to the Prime Minister did not begin unless oral question number 45 on the order paper had been reached. Very often it was not. As a result, in 1959, Harold Macmillan began the practice of answering questions for 15 minutes every Tuesday and Thursday. But, according to the former Prime Minister James Callaghan, standards at Prime Minister's Question Time have fallen in recent times. Speaking to the Commons Procedure Committee on 14 March 1995, he said: 'I rather feel that the bludgeon has replaced the rapier'. Edward Heath agreed with this view and also claimed that questions had never been planted when he was Prime Minister. Margaret Thatcher changed the style of Prime Minister's Questions by allowing the so-called 'open' question. With the help of questions planted by supporters, this made Question Time a propaganda platform. John Major attempted to introduce a more relaxed style, but great anxiety has developed about producing a successful sound bite for the evening news. Both Major and the Labour leader Tony Blair have backed changing the procedures on the grounds that the current slot is so stage managed and rowdy that it is bringing the House into disrepute. In future, Major said, MPs should table questions on any topic 24 hours before Question Time to allow answers to be fully prepared.

Adapted from the *Guardian*, 15 & 16 March and 15 June 1994 and the *Times*, 15 June 1994.

Questions

1. Use Items A and B to explain the point being made in Item D.
2. 'A storm in a tea cup'. Is this a fair reflection of the cash for questions scandal that broke out in 1994? Use Items A, B and D in your answer.
3. Give arguments for and against the view that Prime Minister's Question Time should be reformed. Use Item C in your answer.

3. The House of Lords

Key Issues

1. How does the House of Lords work?
2. What does the House of Lords do?
3. What are the arguments for and against the abolition of the House of Lords?

3.1 The composition and organisation of the Lords.

Nobody is elected to the House of Lords (which is also known as the 'upper House'). The House of Lords is composed of the **Lords Temporal** and the **Lords Spiritual** (Lords are also known as 'peers'). The Lords Spiritual are the 26 bishops of the Church of

England (the number includes the two archbishops). The vast majority of Lords are the Lords Temporal:

> 'Temporal peerages (both hereditary and life) are created by the Sovereign on the advice of the Prime Minister. They are usually granted either in recognition of distinguished service in politics or in other walks of life, or because one of the political parties wishes to have the recipient in the upper House. The House of Lords also provides a place in Parliament for people who offer useful advice, but who do not wish to be involved in party politics. Unlike the House of Commons, there is no fixed number of members in the House of Lords. Relatively few are full-time politicians.' (HMSO, 1994, pp.28-29)

As suggested above, Lords Temporal fall into two categories. By far the largest category is that of hereditary peers (those whose heirs automatically become members of the House of Lords once they reach the age of 21). In March 1995, there were 772 hereditary peers. In addition, there are the life peers (those who are appointed to be members of the House of Lords for life, but whose heirs do not succeed to a peerage). In March 1995, there were 402 life peers. This figure includes 12 Law Lords - 'Lords Appeal in Ordinary'. Law Lords are life peers whose major role is to listen to cases when the House of Lords sits in its capacity as the highest court of appeal. In such cases, only the Law Lords take part.

The total number of peers in March 1995 was, therefore, 1,174. Of these, just 82 were women. It should be noted, however, that 85 peers were not entitled to seats in the Lords (a few hereditary peerages, for example, bequeath no right to a Lords seat) and a further 75 were on leave of absence and, therefore, unable to take part in proceedings during the lifetime of the Parliament. So, a total of 1,007 peers were eligible to attend the proceedings of the House in 1995. Yet, a large number of these peers rarely or never attend the Lords. Average daily attendance, which has increased since 1957 when peers were first able to claim an attendance allowance, was 378 in the 1993-94 parliamentary session (all the above figures come from the House of Lords information department).

Organisation and procedure

There are a number of similarities with the Commons in the way in which the House of Lords is organised. In the chamber, peers supporting the government sit on benches opposite those who support the opposition parties. There is also the distinction between the front and back benches which is found in the Commons. At any one time, a number of peers (usually around 20) are members of the government and it is their task to explain and defend government policy in the Lords. They are shadowed by opposition spokespeople who sit on the opposition front bench.

The business of the House is arranged by the party leaders and party whips **through the usual channels** (see p.407 above). Proceedings, however, are presided over by the Lord Chancellor who acts as a Speaker (the Lord Chancellor is appointed by the Prime Minister and sits in Cabinet). But the Lord Chancellor has a less active role than the Speaker in the Commons. Peers are expected to regulate their own proceedings. They decide themselves who is to speak and when, for example. The Lord Chancellor merely 'puts the question' to the House when a decision is required:

> 'In the House of Lords, the Speaker...has no authority to check or curtail debate. Members of the House of Lords do not address themselves to the Speaker during debates, but to all their fellow members in the House. If two peers rise to speak at the same time during a debate, the House itself, not the Speaker, determines who shall speak.' (HMSO, 1994, p.61)

Guidance on procedural matters comes from the Leader of the House of Lords, a government minister of Cabinet rank.

The activity of the House has grown considerably in the second half of the 20th century. The total number of hours in which the House sat increased from 294 in 1950 to 1,072 in 1990, for example, and over the same period the average daily sitting rose from under three hours to over seven (Rush, 1994). Peers receive no salary for their parliamentary work, but since 1957 they have been able to claim expenses.

Party composition

Although there is a party system in the Lords, including party whips, a major difference between the two Houses of Parliament is the significant number of **crossbenchers** in the Lords. Crossbench peers do not take the whip of the main political parties and, in this sense, are independent. In practice, however, about two thirds of crossbenchers vote with the Conservatives (although crossbench peers do not attend the Lords as regularly as party peers). Party allegiance for any peer, however, is ultimately a voluntary affair. They are not elected and, therefore, do not represent constituents. As a result, the ultimate sanction of withdrawal of the whip for disloyalty lacks the severity it has in the Commons. Despite this, the House does operate on a party basis. Even if, on paper, there is not a Conservative overall majority, in practice, Conservative supporters dominate the House and Conservative governments can expect their legislative programme to have a smoother passage through the Lords than governments formed by other parties.

Powers of the House of Lords

The extension of the franchise through the Reform Acts passed in the 19th century (see chapter 7, section 1.2) increased the authority of the Commons. The Parliament Act of 1911 removed the Lords' veto over public legislation, replacing it with the weaker power of delaying the passage of a Bill for two years. The 1911 Act also effectively removed the Lords' power over money Bills (which give approval for raising taxes, for example). The Parliament Act of 1949 reduced the Lords' power of legislative delay to one parliamentary session. The House of Lords does, however, retain an absolute veto over any proposal to extend the life of a Parliament beyond five years. This gives the Lords some significance as a 'residual guardian of the constitution' (Richards, 1988, p.173).

Functions of the House of Lords

Some of the functions of the House of Lords appear similar to those performed by the Commons, but there are also differences both in the range of activities and how they are carried out.

(i) Legislative role

Although some non-controversial Bills are introduced into the Lords first, conventionally the role of the upper House is to amend and revise Bills sent from the Commons. The more leisurely pace and less partisan nature of the Lords' proceedings allows more time to be spent on a detailed examination of a Bill than in the Commons. As a result, peers can point out problems which may not have been foreseen by the government and they can pass amendments to clauses in Bills before returning them to the Commons for reconsideration. When this happens, however, the government often relies on its overall majority in the Commons to overturn the amendment.

Since it is unelected, the House of Lords rarely rejects a Bill in its entirety. Also, it usually accepts the principle that it should not defeat a government Bill at second reading if the proposed legislation is meeting a manifesto commitment of the governing party. This is known as the '**Salisbury doctrine**' after the Conservative Leader of the Lords, Lord Salisbury, who, in 1945, suggested such a response to the legislative proposals of the newly elected Labour government. Lord Salisbury argued that, since the new Labour government had a clear mandate to introduce its nationalisation and welfare state measures, the Lords should not oppose them at second reading.

(ii) Legitimation

As an elected body, it is the House of Commons which has the chief legitimating role in Parliament. But, according to Rush (1994), the House of Lords also contributes to legitimation in the sense that it also gives formal approval to Bills which pass through it.

(iii) Scrutiny

The House of Lords examines the work of government through questions and select committees. Although the Lords has no structure of departmental select committees on the Commons model, it can and does set up committees to investigate particular policy areas or subjects.

Particularly significant is the Select Committee on the European Communities. Through its five subcommittees, it investigates and reports on those European proposals which appear to raise important questions of policy or principle, or other matters to which the committee feels the House should be alerted. These terms of reference are wider than those for its counterpart in the Commons since the Lords' committee can consider the merits of the proposals before it. The committee and its subcommittees have an administrative and secretarial support staff and can employ specialist advisers to assist in their investigations. The work done by the committee is widely admired by European decision makers and is often cited as a model that other EU members should follow (see Norton, 1995).

In addition, there is a joint committee consisting of members of both Houses which plays a scrutiny role over the form of delegated legislation known as 'statutory instruments':

> 'In order to reduce unnecessary pressure on parliamentary time, primary legislation often gives ministers or other authorities the power to regulate administrative details by means of secondary or 'delegated' legislation, most of which takes the form of Orders in Council, Regulations and Rules known as statutory instruments. These instruments are as much the law of the land as the Act of Parliament from which they are derived...There are about 2,000 statutory instruments each year.' (HMSO, 1994, pp.77-78)

The limited powers of this joint committee, however, has led to the criticism that Parliament's scrutiny over the growing volume and scope of delegated legislation is too weak. Following a proposal in 1992, the upper House set up a Delegated Powers Scrutiny Committee to consider the proposed powers to be delegated to ministers under new Bills. According to Rush, this is:

> 'An important development, extending significantly Parliament's scrutiny of secondary legislation.' (Rush, 1994, p.33)

The House of Lords does have a daily Question Time, but the procedure is different from that in the Commons. For example, it is briefer (30 minutes maximum) and up to four starred questions are answered per day (no more than one question can be tabled by a particular Lord):

> 'Starred questions are so called because they appear on the order paper with an asterisk against them. They are asked in order to obtain specific information, and not with a view to making a speech or raising a debate, although supplementaries may be asked. In addition, 'unstarred' (debatable) questions may be asked at the end of business on any day, when speeches may be made.' (HMSO, 1994, pp.91-92)

(iv) Deliberative function

Debates are held on specific matters of policy or on topical issues, but, although there are whips, party lines are not so rigidly adhered to as in the Commons. The House of Lords has gained a reputation for holding high quality debates - though some commentators are sceptical about this and claim that such a view is held most strongly by the peers themselves who have a vested interest in maintaining their privileged position. Politically, it is not the quality of the debate that is significant, but the extent to which a debate has an effect or influence. Adonis suggests:

> 'Lords debates may not entirely be without influence, but they rarely make an impact which is more than minor and indirect.' (Adonis, 1993, p.216)

(v) Judicial role

Unlike the Commons, the House of Lords has a judicial function. It should be noted, however, that this is a specialised role, divorced from the main proceedings and functions of the House. It is also a role in which the vast majority of peers can take no part. When the House sits as the highest court of appeal, only the Law Lords, including the Lord Chancellor, may take part.

Activity 14.5

Item A *The House of Lords in session*

This photograph shows the House of Lords during a debate.

Item B *The functions of the House of Lords*

(i) The functions of Parliament

Function	Performed by House of Commons	House of Lords	Collectively	Individually
Legitimising	X[a]	x	x	
Representative	X	x	x	x
Financial	X	x	x	
Redressing of grievances	X	x	x	x
Legislative	X	x	x	x
Recruitment of ministers	X	x	x	
Scrutinising and informing	X	x	x	x
Judicial		X	x[b]	

[a] X indicates the more important of the two houses in performing a particular function, x the less important.
b performed exclusively by Law Lords

This table shows the functions performed by Parliament as a whole and the relative importance of each House.

(ii) The functions of the House of Lords

Function	Performed in chamber	in committees
1. Causing sufficient delay to enable the government or the public, or both, to reconsider legislation passed by the House of Commons	X	
2. Examining and revising Bills passed by the House of Commons	X	x
3. Initiating non-controversial legislation	X	x
4. Holding debates on major issues and policies unconstrained by strict party discipline	X	
5. The consolidation of existing legislation	x	X
6. Dealing with private legislation	x	X
7. Dealing with delegated legislation	x	X
8. Scrutinising policy and administration	x	X

X - major role; x - lesser role.

This table shows the functions performed by the House of Lords

Both tables adapted from Rush, 1994.

Item C *The Lords and the abolition of the Greater London Council (GLC)*

During the debate over the 1984 'Paving Bill' which eventually resulted in the abolition of the GLC, the Conservatives claimed that they did not have a majority in the House of Lords. On closer examination, however, this can be shown to be untrue. At the time, there were 943 peers eligible to vote. Only 413 took the Conservative whip, but many peers never attended the House. In the 40 divisions on the Paving Bill, 627 peers voted. The breakdown was as follows:

Conservative	324			Labour	119
Conservative crossbenchers	45	Independent crossbenchers	73	Alliance	66
Totals	369		73		185
					258

This gave, in practice, a Conservative majority in the Lords of 111. The 45 crossbenchers in the Conservative column were peers who claimed to be independent, but sided with the government on every occasion on which they voted. In reality, what happened was that the government encouraged peers who were actually Conservatives not to take the government whip. This then preserved the fiction that the Lords was not dominated by the Conservatives. The only factor which allowed the Conservatives occasionally to be defeated was the better attendance of opposition peers. The Labour party should, therefore, bear in mind that there is a comfortable majority of Conservative peers waiting to be used against the policies of an incoming Labour government.

Adapted from Livingstone, 1987.

Item D *The Lords and the Criminal Justice Bill*

The Home Secretary Michael Howard's law and order programme has become one of the most damaged packages of legislation ever. Attacked in the House of Lords, it has suffered 40 defeats or substantive concessions during its passage through Parliament. Howard admitted: 'The House of Lords has a particular role to play in our constitution and it carried out that role.' Shifting alliances of senior judges, police officers, former Home Secretaries, magistrates and opposition peers have ensured that the legislation suffered a rough ride. The result is that the criminal justice half of the package will not now become law until October 1994. The main triumph in the Lords came in March 1994 when the Lords defeated the government by 133 votes to 107 over the abolition of senior ranks. The government aimed to abolish two senior ranks, but the Lords supported an amendment allowing only one of the ranks to be abolished. This was only the second actual defeat on the Bill for the government in the Lords (the first concerned proposals to reform police disciplinary procedures), but Michael Howard has been forced to make important concessions to avoid further defeats. For example, he was forced to retract his plans to reform elected police authorities after it became clear that he would be defeated on this issue in the Lords.

Adapted from the *Guardian*, 25 March and 19 July 1994.

Item E *Party affiliation in the House of Lords*

Party	No.	%
Con	482	48.8
Lab	166	16.8
Lib Dem	55	5.6
Crossbenchers	304	30.2
Total	1,007	100

Figures from the House of Lords Information Department, March 1995.

Questions

1. a) How do the powers and procedures of the House of Lords differ from those of the Commons? Use Items A-E in your answer.
   b) Give arguments for and against the view that the House of Lords plays an important role in the British political system.
2. a) What do Items C and E tell us about the balance of power within the House of Lords?
   b) What are the political implications of this?
3. 'The real opposition to the government comes not from the opposition parties in the Commons, but from the House of Lords'. Is this a fair statement? Use Item D in your answer.

3.2 Should the Lords be abolished?

The main criticism of the House of Lords is that, as an unelected body which is not accountable to the electorate, it is undemocratic. New peers are appointed on the recommendation of the Prime Minister, giving powers of patronage to the holder of that office. The retention of the hereditary principle, is anachronistic (outdated and, therefore, not appropriate to the modern world) and helps to restrict the social composition of the House (a narrow range of interests still predominates - peers tend to be wealthy, white, privately educated males). Criticism of the undemocratic nature of the House of Lords has brought calls for its reform or its abolition. This section examines the arguments for and against reform or abolition and considers what a reformed second chamber might look like.

Arguments in favour of reform or abolition

The main argument put forward by those who support the reform or abolition of the House of Lords is that heredity and patronage can no longer be justified as the basis for choosing part of the legislature. It is, in other words, a matter of political principle that those chosen to make political decisions should be chosen by the electorate in an election. The main reason for this is that election ensures that representatives are, in some sense, accountable for their actions. Unelected decision makers are accountable to nobody but themselves.

Having decided that the House of Lords needs to be changed as a matter of principle, two questions then arise. First, should the upper House be abolished or reformed? And, second, if a reformed second chamber is to remain, what form should it take?

Those who argue that the House of Lords should simply be abolished (and not replaced) emphasise that Britain would not be alone if it only had a single legislative chamber. A number of other countries, such as Denmark, Israel, New Zealand and Sweden operate in this way. After all, the only formal legislative power exercised by the current House of Lords is the power to delay the passage of a Bill. If the House of Commons is determined that a piece of legislation should reach the statute book, there is nothing that the Lords can do about it in the long term. Given that the House of Lords' main function is to provide a checking mechanism, there is no reason why a similar checking mechanism should not be built into a single chamber system.

Yet, it is the power of delay, coupled with what, in effect, is an in-built Conservative majority in the Lords, which concerns some Labour party opponents of the upper House. They point out that this power of delay could prevent a Labour government from completing its legislative programme in the year before a general election. The way to prevent this happening, they argue, is to abolish the second chamber.

It should also be noted that:

> 'One of the commonest rationales for having a second chamber is in federal systems, in which the lower house is popularly elected in proportion to the distribution of the population and the upper house represents, usually, though not always, on an equal status, the states or constituent parts of the federation. The most well known case is the United States' Senate which consists of 100 members, two from each state, regardless of population or geographical size.' (Rush, 1994, p.35)

Since Britain does not have a federal system, it could be argued, there is, therefore, no need for a second chamber.

Those who argue that the House of Lords should be reformed (rather than abolished) fall into two main groups. One group argues that a second chamber should be retained and should perform pretty much the same functions that are performed by the current House, but its members should be elected (by a system of proportional election, most argue). Since the members of this new elected second chamber would not be Lords, most supporters of this type of reform support the idea that this new chamber should be given a new name (such as 'Senate'). Those in favour of this type of reform argue that it is the only way to ensure that the second chamber is democratically accountable.

The second group argues that what is needed is reform of the existing system. Hereditary peers could be banned from voting, for example, leaving the legislative function of the Lords in the hands of life peers (the majority of whom are distinguished former MPs with a wealth of experience). Alternatively, the House could be made up of a mixture of elected and unelected peers. Supporters of this line argue that this is a pragmatic stance (it has a better chance of being brought into practice than outright abolition or replacing the Lords with an elected second chamber). They also argue that it solves the main problem with the Lords (namely, the hereditary element). Finally, they argue that retention of life peers is beneficial since these peers provide a wealth of experience which would be lacking if all members were elected to the second chamber.

Both sets of reformers, it should be clear, agree that it is necessary to have a second chamber. They argue that the current House of Lords performs a number of important functions which would either not be performed or would be performed inadequately if there was no second chamber:

> 'The additional scrutiny of primary or secondary legislation and of government policy and administration, and the airing of various issues would fall on the Commons or on nobody. In particular, the government would have to find ways of amending its own legislation through better or further scrutiny in the Commons, or subsequently passing amending Bills, or make even greater use of delegated legislation, or leave much legislation in an unamended and unsatisfactory state.' (Rush, 1994, pp.35-36)

It should also be noted that the argument that a second chamber is necessary in a federal state appeals to many reformers. The Liberal Democrats support the introduction of federalism in Britain (and they support an elected second chamber as part of their constitutional package). The Labour party supports devolution in Scotland and Wales and (possibly) regional assemblies in England. Like the Liberal Democrats, Labour also supports the retention of a second chamber. In 1995, it was Labour policy to introduce legislation in the first year of a Labour government to end the voting rights of hereditary peers. A Labour government would also consider the introduction of elections for the second chamber.

Arguments against reform

The main argument put forward by those who support the status quo is that the existing system works and there is a danger that any alternative system would not work as well.

Supporters of the status quo claim that there has been a revival of the Lords since the introduction of life peers in 1958. Norton notes that:

> 'In the 1940s, the House [of Lords] had a membership of over 800, but of those "only about 100 attend regularly and of these about 60 of them take an active part in its business" (Gordon, 1948, p.139). The House rarely met for more than three days a week and on those days would often sit for no more than three hours. Votes were rare and, when they were taken, peers voted on party lines...Limited powers and limited activity led to little interest in the House.' (Norton, 1993, p.26)

Norton goes on to argue that, since the early 1970s, there has been a major revival in the activities performed by the House:

> 'Over the past 20 years, the daily attendance has increased. By the end of the 1980s, the average daily attendance exceeded 300. More than 700 peers attended one or more sittings each year and, of those, more than 500 contributed to debate...The House now sits on more days and, for longer hours, than it did in previous decades. In the 1985-86 session, for example, the House sat after 10 pm on 93 occasions. Votes have also become more frequent, as have government defeats...From 1979 to 1990, the Thatcher government suffered just over 150 defeats at the hands of their Lordships.' (Norton, 1993, p.27)

This revival in the activities performed by the Lords, it is argued, proves that the House of Lords can perform an important role. Indeed, it has been argued that the House of Lords has a number of advantages over the Commons. For example, the House of Lords is able to deal with the details of legislation more thoroughly than the Commons and now has the opportunity to scrutinise delegated legislation. It also examines proposed European legislation more closely than the Commons. The quality of debates and select committee work in the Lords is high. The Lords performs a crucial role as a check on the executive.

During the 1980s and early 1990s, supporters of the status quo became able to use another argument to back up their case. Throughout the 1980s, the Conservatives remained in power. Since Margaret Thatcher and then John Major were able to rely on overall majorities in the Commons, the opposition in the Commons often appeared to be impotent. There was, after all, nothing the Labour party could do to prevent the passage of legislation so long as the Conservative government managed to retain the support of all its MPs. Whilst the opposition in the Commons was unable to inflict parliamentary defeats on the government, the Lords did, occasionally, vote against the government (not that this made much of a difference in the long term since the government could rely on its Commons majority to overturn Lords' amendments). As a result, supporters of the status quo began to argue that the **real** opposition to the government was to be found in the Lords. It was only in the Lords that one party government could be checked and, therefore, maintenance of the existing system was of crucial importance.

Supporters of the status quo, however, do not only use positive arguments to justify the House of Lords' current role. They also use negative arguments, designed to illustrate the drawbacks of alternatives. One argument against the introduction of an elected second chamber is that, at present, the House of Commons derives its seniority and legitimacy, in part, because it is the only elected chamber. If both chambers were elected, then this would detract from the legitimacy of the Commons:

> 'First, the House of Commons is acknowledged as the superior of the two Houses of Parliament precisely because it is the elected chamber; an elected second chamber would secure a significant degree of democratic legitimacy which the House of Lords, at present, inevitably lacks. Second, if elections for the second chamber were held at a different time, possibly on a staggered basis with a proportion of the membership retiring at regular intervals (as with the US Senate), then the more recently elected chamber might claim or be seen to have greater legitimacy because it reflected a more recent expression of public opinion.' (Rush, 1994, pp.36-37)

A second argument is that if the second chamber was elected, it would almost certainly become dominated by the political parties. This would change the nature of the second chamber. At present (the argument goes), there is little partisanship in the Lords and, as a result, mature and rational examination of government proposals and policy is possible. If party politics became more intense, there would be less room for the development of consensus and constructive criticism. A third argument is that if the second chamber was elected, then its members would have constituents. These constituents would put pressure on the members which might conflict with the pressure placed on MPs by their constituents. This could lead to conflict between the two chambers.

The chances of reform

It is unlikely that the House of Lords would be reformed whilst a Conservative government remained in power. Both Labour and the Liberal Democrats, however, have made commitments to reform the Lords. That does not mean that reform of the Lords is inevitable if the Conservatives lose a general election. Attempts to reform the Lords in the past have failed. In 1969, for example, Harold Wilson's Labour government sponsored a Bill which proposed the phasing out of hereditary membership of the House of Lords and its eventual replacement by an entirely nominated membership. This Bill failed because an unusual alliance of Labour backbenchers on the left (who argued that the Bill did not go far enough) and Conservative backbenchers on the right (who argued that the Bill went too far) was able to squash the Bill as it went through its committee stage. Warning of the problems that an incoming Labour government might face, Anthony Lester points out that:

> 'Every effort at constitutional reform that has been attempted has been brought down by the necessity for it to be debated on the floor of the Commons, with endless scope for filibustering.' (*Observer*, 20 November 1994)

Activity 14.6

Item A *Brick's view of the House of Lords*

Item B *Arguments against reform*

In July 1994, Tony Blair announced that he supported early legislation to end the voting rights of hereditary peers. If this proposal was passed, it would mean that voting rights in the House of Lords would be confined to bishops, Law Lords and life peers. William Rees Mogg, a life peer himself, argues that such an arrangement would be unsatisfactory. He points out that life peers are themselves appointed, not elected, and are, therefore, not selected by a democratic procedure. Besides, he argues, the hereditary principle has a number of advantages. First, it produces a sense of national continuity and an attractive randomness 'like that of a jury'. Second, hereditary peers do not owe their position to a party and are, therefore, able to remain detached from party politics. Third, some hereditary peers are people with high abilities. Rees Mogg claims that, during the time he has sat in the Lords, when the House of Lords has disagreed with the House of Commons, it is the House of Lords (with its mixture of life peers and hereditary peers) which has usually been right. The problem is that the House of Commons has the democratic authority which the Lords lacks. As a result, even if the House of Lords is right, it has to allow the Commons to have its way. This problem would not be solved if Labour's proposal was adopted.

Adapted from the *Times*, 7 July 1994.

Item C *Activity in the House of Lords, 1950-94*

Activity	1950	1959-60	1989-90	1993-94	Percentage increase 1950-59	Percentage increase 1959-90
Average daily attendance	86	136	318	378	58	134
Sitting days	100	113	147	142	13	30
Sitting hours	294	450	1,072	971	53	138
Length of sitting (hrs.mins)	2.57	4.00	7.21	6.51	36	84
Sittings after 10pm	1	1	74	64	-	7,300

Adapted from Rush, 1994.

Item D *Arguments for reform*

David McKie argues that Labour has a political as well as a constitutional interest in removing voting rights from hereditary peers. In support of this view, he produces evidence from recent votes in the House of Lords. These figures suggest that hereditary peers are more likely than life peers to support the government. On 5 July 1994, for example, peers voted by 170 to 139 in favour of an anti-government amendment to the Criminal Justice Bill (proposed by a life peer). Whilst life peers voted 111 to 57 in favour, hereditaries voted 82 to 58 against. McKie then goes on to counter the arguments put forward by Rees Mogg (see Item B above). In particular, he objects to the view that the hereditary principle allows some kind of 'randomness'. It is simply not true that hereditary peers are some kind of cross section of British society. Of the 139 hereditary peers who voted for the government on 5 July 1994, for example, just four were women (2.8%), 56 were Old Etonians (40%), most of the rest had been to public school (only four may have attended state schools). Of the minority who listed their interests, 28 listed something like hunting or shooting. The idea, therefore, that the House of Lords produces a representative sample of the population 'like a jury' is absolute nonsense.

Adapted from the *Guardian*, 11 July 1994.

Item E *John Naughton's view of the House of Lords*

A Channel 4 programme broadcast this week gave viewers a glimpse of what really goes on inside the House of Lords. It showed Milords Healey and Howe dressing up like Santa Claus whilst preparing to take their seats in the Lords. There was a great deal of bowing, scraping and the doffing of the sort of hat Napoleon wore in bed. Much is made in some quarters of the ability of the Lords to delay and amend legislation. Lord Teviot, however, is more interested in the catering. 'It's the most marvellous tea here', he gurgled. The film followed Earl Russell's attempts to ambush the government over changes to the benefits system. He tried to rustle up support for an amendment which would give homeless people £10 a week more for food. By delaying the vote until the end of Neil Kinnock's farewell party, he and his allies ensured a large Labour turnout and defeated the government. But then, it was announced that the legislation would be reintroduced in the Commons unamended. You could not have asked for a better case study in the impotence of the Second Chamber.

Adapted from the *Observer*, 22 November 1992.

Item F *Does Britain need a second chamber?*

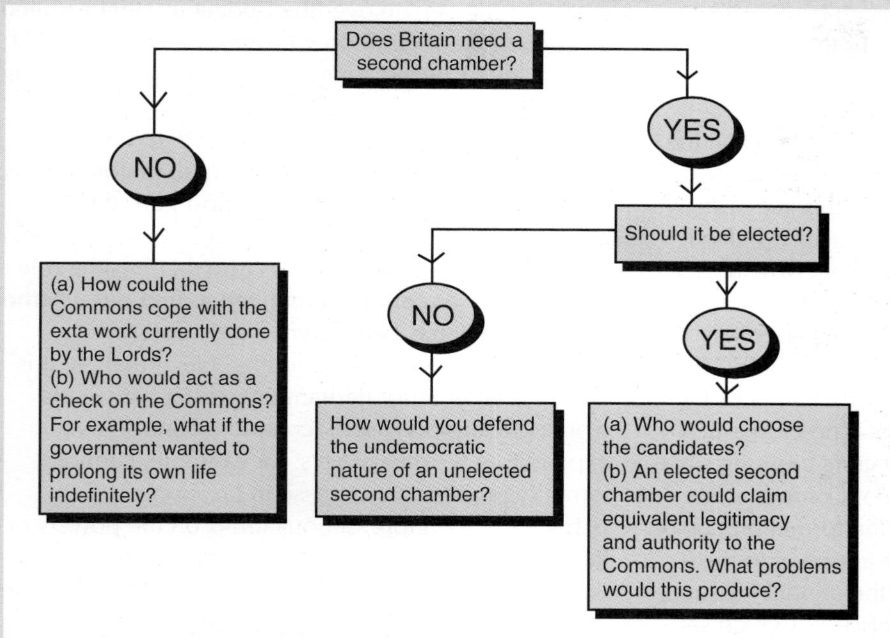

Questions

1. Give arguments for and against the view that the House of Lords should be abolished.
2. Find evidence in Items B-E to support or oppose the point being made by the cartoon in Item A.
3. To what extent does the composition of the House of Lords affect its ability to perform its functions? Use Items B-E in your answer.
4. Follow your preferred pathway through Item F answering the questions you encounter. Explain why you did not choose one of the other pathways.

4. How effective is Parliament?

Key Issues

1. What criteria are used to judge Parliament's effectiveness?
2. Using these criteria, how effective is Parliament?

Limits on the power of Parliament

Whether or not Parliament is judged to be effective depends on what expectations are held about Parliament's role in British politics in the late 20th century. In the 1990s, it is not unusual for Parliament to appear to be bypassed and, therefore, to have less of an essential function than in earlier periods. The growth, specialisation and professionalisation of the civil service, the increased influence of pressure groups on ministers and departments and the impact of the mass media have all contributed to this apparent decline. Given the party system in Parliament, it is certainly unrealistic for Parliament to govern the country or to control the government. But this is nothing new. It is doubtful if Parliament has ever really been in a position to govern the country or control the government. Even in the 'golden age' of Parliament in the early 19th century (before the extension of the franchise led to the development of the party system), Parliament's power was limited. Yet, given these limits on the powers of Parliament, it is still pertinent to consider how effective Parliament is in carrying out its functions - especially its legislative and scrutiny functions.

All proposals to change the law have to be passed by Parliament. Yet, in the main, what this means is that Parliament gives its approval to measures that have been drawn up elsewhere - either by the British government or by the European Union. As far as domestic legislation is concerned, Parliament is, at most, a reviser of Bills that are prepared in Whitehall and given priority by the government.

The operation of the party system means that Parliament functions to maintain the government's majority. Parliament does have the power to throw a government out, but it rarely uses this power. In fact, it can be argued, sustaining a government has become the prime task of Parliament and it is true to say that most members of Parliament (especially in the Commons) act as party politicians most of the time. In other words, most MPs (and peers) who support the government are likely to regard their primary role as supporting the government.

It is also the job of Parliament to scrutinise the executive, and this gives rise to something of a paradox. How can Parliament scrutinise the executive effectively when most of its members see their primary role as maintaining a majority for their government?

One way round this problem is for Parliament to gain a degree of independence from government and, in recent years, there have been signs that this is happening. For example, the work done by select committees (see section 2.1 above) and the readiness of the House of Lords to amend government Bills (in the initial stages of a Bill's passage through Parliament at least - see p.422 above) are both signs that Parliament is willing to investigate and object to the work of government. The upper House has also set up mechanisms to scrutinise European legislation and the work of the EU bureaucracy - though few people would pretend that parliamentary scrutiny in this increasingly important area is anywhere near satisfactory. Indeed, greater European integration in the future (whether economic or political) is likely to decrease the influence and relevance of Parliament (see, Norton, 1995).

Perhaps, however, the limits to parliamentary effectiveness are best illustrated by Parliament's lack of any real say in financial matters. The House of Lords' influence over financial matters has long since disappeared, but does the House of Commons fare any better? There are, of course, the formal processes in the Commons where MPs give approval to the Budget proposals (in the form of the annual Finance Bill) and to the government's 'estimates' (which set out the amounts required for each government department for the following year). On occasion, these formal processes can yield change - for example, the debate over the Budget in 1994 resulted in a government climbdown over an increase in VAT on fuel after Conservative backbenchers voted against the measure. But, such rebellions are unusual and they can only bring a government defeat if the government commands a small overall majority (or is extremely incompetent). For the most part, the government's financial proposals are rubber stamped by Parliament. In addition, it is true that it is the role of the Public Accounts Committee to find out whether public money has been spent wisely and to investigate cases of overspending. Nevertheless, it is the government (not Parliament) which has, in the words of Harold Wilson, 'complete control' over expenditure. Ordinary MPs, for example, cannot formally propose an increase in taxation.

There are, therefore, serious limits on the powers of Parliament. But, how then have these limits determined the ways in which political commentators have judged the effectiveness of Parliament? The following activity explores this question.

Activity 14.6

Item A *Brick's view of the effectiveness of Parliament*

Item B *Peter Richards' view*

Parliament's role is best understood by regarding it not primarily as a check on the executive, but as one of the institutions through which the government operates. It is worth noting, for example, that truly independent MPs (the sort who ousted Neville Chamberlain from the leadership of the Conservative party in 1940) are increasingly rare. Both major parties are increasingly producing career politicians who have professional training and similar outlooks. Such politicians are not content to sit on the back benches and so there is a strong motive not to annoy the leader on whose patronage a ministerial career depends. In addition, the public is becoming aware that Parliament has little influence.

Adapted from Richards, 1988.

Item C *Tam Dalyell's view*

Tam Dalyell records that Richard Crossman, Labour Cabinet minister between 1964 and 1970, argued that the House of Commons lived in a world of wish-fulfillment and illusion. Crossman noted that Parliament was forever demanding emergency statements from ministers. In reality, it did this for no better reason than that Parliament had to feel important. Crossman found this embarrassing.

Adapted from Dalyell, 1989.

Item D Peter Riddell's view

According to those who argue that Parliament is ineffective, the House of Commons is a rubber stamp - a loud, self-indulgent sideshow whose actors are kept in line by the party whips. Peter Riddell, however, argues that the idea that Parliament is ineffective is false. On the contrary, he claims, Parliament remains as central as it ever has been. This conclusion is reached by considering Parliament's role. According to Riddell, Parliament's central role is to set up a government which meets the wishes of the voters (as expressed at general elections) and to put that government's programme into practice. In addition, Parliament has other functions - to provide an outlet for public opinion, to teach and inform society and to legislate, for example. These functions are still performed by Parliament. Even a government with a clear overall majority has to listen to its supporters (and critics), make concessions and respond to demands. Similarly, the government cannot avoid dealing with issues that are raised in Parliament (albeit mainly in the Commons) - the Commons provides an arena in which the issues of concern to the nation are voiced. But, most crucially, political careers are built up and broken down in Parliament. Parliament provides the pool from which members of the government are chosen. It also ensures that the executive is accountable in the sense that ministers are answerable to Parliament for their actions.

Adapted from Riddell, 1989.

Item E Andrew Adonis' view

Andrew Adonis argues that Parliament performs an important scrutiny role which has been strengthened in recent years by the development of the committee system (in both the Commons and the Lords) and by the rise of a new generation of full-time and more independent MPs. He claims that what makes Parliament effective is that, although it does not govern itself, government takes place through Parliament. As a result, parliamentary committees are able to scrutinise the work of government, whilst the televising of parliament means that ordinary voters can themselves scrutinise the behaviour of government and parliamentary activity. Adonis notes that, despite popular cycnicism about politicians, social attitude surveys show a significant increase in people's readiness to attempt to influence decisions and in the perception of their ability to do so. This activity is focused on Parliament and, therefore, suggests that Parliament has an important role to play. Adonis does concede, however, that there is widespread public discontent with the quality of parliamentary representation and government, and that less and less government is taking place through Parliament because of the growing influence of European institutions.

Adapted from Adonis, 1993.

Item F Philip Norton's view

Philip Norton evaluates the effectiveness of Parliament by asking a number of questions. What would the British political system be like if Parliament did not exist? How would the government be chosen? Who or what would represent citizens and confer legitimacy on the actions of government? Who would champion the views of ordinary citizens? What forum would allow for the expression of conflicting views? Norton acknowledges that in answering most of the above questions it is possible to come up with an alternative to Parliament. The press, for example, champions the views of ordinary citizens. The National Audit Office and the media scrutinise the action of government. Ministerial actions can be challenged in court. Conflicting views can be expressed through opinion polls, television debates and referendums. Despite this, Norton argues, what makes Parliament distinctive and indispensable is the fact that it enjoys the popular as well as the formal legitimacy to undertake all these tasks. This legitimacy, he claims has been enhanced by the greater degree of scrutiny undertaken by Parliament over recent years and the greater willingness of MPs to take on greater amounts of constituency casework and a more active role as interrogators of government.

Adapted from Norton 1985 and 1993.

Questions

1. 'Parliament is no longer central to British politics'. Do you agree? Use Items A-F in your answer.
2. Identify points of agreement and disagreement amongst Items A-F.
3. Which of Items B-F support the view expressed in Item A? Explain how you reached your answer.
4. In what ways could Parliament be reformed to ensure that it performed its functions more effectively?

References

Adonis (1993) Adonis, A., *Parliament Today (2nd edn)*, Manchester University Press, 1993.

Alderman (1995) Alderman, K., 'The government whips', *Politics Review*, Vol.4, No.4, April 1995.

Dalyell (1989) Dalyell, T., *Dick Crossman: a Portrait*, Weidenfeld & Nicolson, 1989.

Downs (1985) Downs, S.J., 'Select committees: experiment and establishment' in *Norton (1985)*.

Drewry (1989) Drewry, G., 'The new select committees - nine years on', *Social Studies Review*, Vol.4, No.4, 1989.

Gordon (1948) Gordon, S., *Our Parliament* (3rd edn), Hansard Society, 1948.

HMSO (1994) Central Office of Information, *Parliament*, HMSO, 1994.

Jordan & Richardson (1987) Jordan, A.G. & Richardson, J.J., *British Politics and the Policy Process*, Allen & Unwin, 1987.

Livingstone (1987) Livingstone, K., *If Voting Changed Anything, They'd Abolish It*, Collins, 1987.

Norton (1985) Norton, P. (ed.), *Parliament in the 1980s*, Blackwell, 1985.

Norton (1986) Norton, P., 'Committees in the House of Commons', *Social Studies Review*, Vol.1, No.3, January 1986.

Norton (1991) Norton, P., 'Committees in the House of Commons', *Politics Review*, Vol.1, No.1, September 1991.

Norton (1992) Norton, P., 'A reformed Parliament?', *The House Magazine*, 22 June 1992.

Norton (1993) Norton, P., *Does Parliament Matter?*, Harvester Wheatsheaf, 1993.

Norton (1994) Norton, P., 'Select committees in the House of Commons: watchdogs or poodles?', *Politics Review*, Vol.4, No.2, November 1994.

Norton (1995) Norton, P., 'Standing committees in the House of Commons', *Politics Review*, Vol.4, No.4, April 1995.

Padfield & Byrne (1987) Padfield C.F. & Byrne, A., *British Constitution Made Simple* (7th edn.), Heinemann, 1987.

Richards (1988) Richards, P.G., *Mackintosh's the Government and Politics of Britain* (7th edn), Hutchinson, 1988.

Riddell (1989) Riddell, P., 'In defence of Parliament', *Contemporary Record*, Vol.3.1, Autumn 1989.

Rush (1994) Rush, M., 'The House of Lords, end it or mend it?' in *Wale (1994)*.

Shell (1993) Shell, D., 'Departmental select committees', *Politics Review*, Vol. 2, No. 4, April 1993.

Silk (1989) Silk, P. with Walters, R., *How Parliament Works* (2nd edn), Longman, 1989.

Wale (1994) Wale, W. (ed.), *Developments in Politics*, Vol.5, Causeway Press, 1994.

15 Management of the economy

Introduction

The management of the economy is a central task of modern government. Indeed, it is often the yardstick by which a government is judged. The ability to manage the economy in a way which is perceived as being successful is one of the keys to re-election. Governments, therefore, give a very high priority to the development of economic policies.

Since 1945, public (government) spending has risen dramatically because central government has become responsible for the financing of the welfare state. The National Health Service and Social Security, for example, both require the expenditure of huge sums of public money. Exactly how much money should be raised to be spent on these and on other areas of the economy is a key problem that must be faced by every government. The decisions that are taken affect every person in the country - whether they are taxpayers faced with a larger or smaller tax burden or people who rely on state benefits.

This chapter looks at the economic theories which have dominated postwar economic policy and at the ways in which these economic theories have been translated into practice. It examines the process by which economic decisions are made and the pressures that are exerted on decision makers both from within the governmental system and from outside.

Chapter summary

Part 1 looks at different **economic theories** and how British governments have attempted to translate each theory into practice.

Part 2 analyses the **development of economic policy** since 1985.

Part 3 examines **Britain's economic decline**. When did it start, what caused it and what consequences has it had?

Part 4 focuses on the **way in which economic decisions are made**. What is the role of the **Treasury** and the **Chancellor**? Why is the **Budget** so important? What is the role of the **Bank of England**?

Part 5 discusses **the raising of taxes**. What is the difference between **direct** and **indirect taxation**? Should income tax be higher or lower?

1 Economic theories

Key Issues

1. What is laissez faire economics?
2. How does Keynesian economics differ from laissez faire economics?
3. What is Monetarism?

1.1 Laissez faire economics

The first industrial nation

Britain was the first country to become industrialised. In the short term, this gave Britain an economic advantage. In the longer term, it proved to be a burden.

It is impossible to date the beginning of the industrial revolution precisely. There is no single event that can be said to have sparked it off. Rather, it was a process that gathered momentum as it became established. By 1750, this process was underway. By 1900, Britain was an industrial nation.

The industrial revolution brought immense change to Britain. Perhaps the key development was the growth of mass production which was made possible by the increasing use of mechanisation. The invention of new machines and new methods of powering them encouraged the growth of industry, new modes of transport and new ways of working. A rapid growth of population, linked to changes in agriculture and the growth of industry, resulted in the expansion of towns and cities. This brought a new way of life and new problems.

Industrialisation did not just have an impact domestically. Mass production produced a surplus which could be sold abroad. Britain's trade with other countries grew rapidly. Also, the need to secure new markets overseas (as well other factors such as a mission to 'civilise' newly discovered areas) led to the growth of a huge overseas Empire.

Since Britain was the first country to become industrialised, its manufacturing output in the late 18th and early 19th centuries far exceeded that of other countries. But, as other countries developed industries of their own, their output grew and they were able to compete with and sometimes overtake Britain. This experience - of leading the field and then being caught up and overtaken (by some competitors) - had an important effect on economic thinking in Britain in the 20th century.

A capitalist economy

Industrialisation in Britain was piecemeal. It relied upon individual initiative. New industrial enterprises were set up and owned by private individuals. On the whole, central government did not encourage or attempt to organise economic development. It certainly did not attempt to gain ownership of the new industrial enterprises.

An industrial country whose wealth (ie land, raw materials and businesses) is owned mainly by individuals rather than by the state is a capitalist country. In simple terms, those who own and control the wealth are capitalists whilst the people they employ are workers. Although the capitalists are fewer in number than the workers, they tend to acquire political as well as economic power. As a result, the economic ideology of capitalists often determines the economic policies adopted by governments.

Capitalists have a particular interest in how much the government intervenes in the management of the economy since government regulations often adversely affect the cost of running businesses. For example, a government decision to impose a minimum wage would mean that employers paying very low wages would have to pay out more money to meet this requirement. This would increase their overheads and, perhaps, force them to lay off staff or even to close down. Such a measure is likely to be opposed by capitalists even though it might prove to be beneficial to large numbers of people.

Laissez faire economics

Laissez faire is French for 'leave alone'. Supporters of laissez faire economics oppose government intervention. They want a free market in which the government leaves them alone. Support for a laissez faire approach to economics was first articulated in Adam Smith's *An Enquiry into the Nature and Causes of the Wealth of Nations* which was published in 1766. In this book, Smith argued that producers should not be subject to any restrictions. They should be free to supply products at the price consumers are willing to pay. Provided that competition was fair, he argued, the 'invisible hand' of the market would allocate resources to everyone's advantage.

Supporters of laissez faire, or free market economics, accept that producers are primarily motivated by the desire to make profits. But, they argue, producers employ people, create wealth and distribute it. By employing people, they provide them with a means to live. By creating and distributing wealth they ensure that society as a whole becomes richer.

Laissez faire economics can be applied on a larger scale, too. The question of whether or not the British government should support a policy of free trade with its overseas trading partners has often been the cause of fierce debate.

Free trade versus protectionism

A country practising free trade refuses to protect its economy by imposing quotas limiting the number of goods which can be imported or by charging a tariff (a tax or duty) on goods which are imported into the country. So, suppose that Britain and France were practising free trade. If Britain imported cheese from France, no limit would be imposed on the amount of cheese that France could send over for sale and nor would a tariff be charged when that cheese arrived in Britain. Similarly, British firms producing beer would be able to export as much beer to France as they liked and they would not have to pay a tariff when it arrived in France.

But suppose that British people stopped buying British cheese because they preferred imported French cheese. Should the British government then intervene and protect the jobs of British cheese manufacturers? Supporters of free trade would argue against intervention. They would argue that the market should determine whether or not the British cheese manufacturers should survive. If the government chose to protect British cheese manufacturers by imposing a quota or a tariff, then it is likely that the French would respond by imposing their own quotas and tariffs - on British beer, say. British beer exported to France would then rise in cost (because less could be sold in France and because of the duty paid on it). This would adversely affect the British beer industry. In other words, by intervening the government would artificially protect an uncompetitive industry (the cheese manufacturers) whilst jeopardising the future of a competitive one (the beer industry). Free trade, on the other hand, would ensure that only those companies which are truly efficient and competitive survived.

Supporters of protectionism use the following arguments to justify the imposition of tariffs and quotas. First, tariffs are a good way of raising revenue for the government without burdening voters with greater taxation. Second, the imposition of quotas or tariffs tends to raise the final price of a product (unless the foreign producer absorbs the extra cost). If the final price is higher, then it is easier for domestically produced products to compete. Quotas and tariffs, therefore, help domestic producers to remain viable. Third, a truly free market is a utopian idea. Since the economies of countries are so interlinked, every country in the world would have to agree not to impose any trading restrictions before a truly free market could be achieved. In reality all countries choose to adopt protectionist policies to some extent. Rather than aiming for something that is simply unattainable, it is better to be realistic and to plan accordingly.

The debate between free trade and protectionism presents a choice between two ways of managing the economy. On the one hand, those who support free trade argue for a laissez faire approach. On the other hand, those who support protectionism believe that government has a positive role to play in the management of the economy.

Activity 15.1

Item A *The impact of the industrial revolution, 1750-1960*

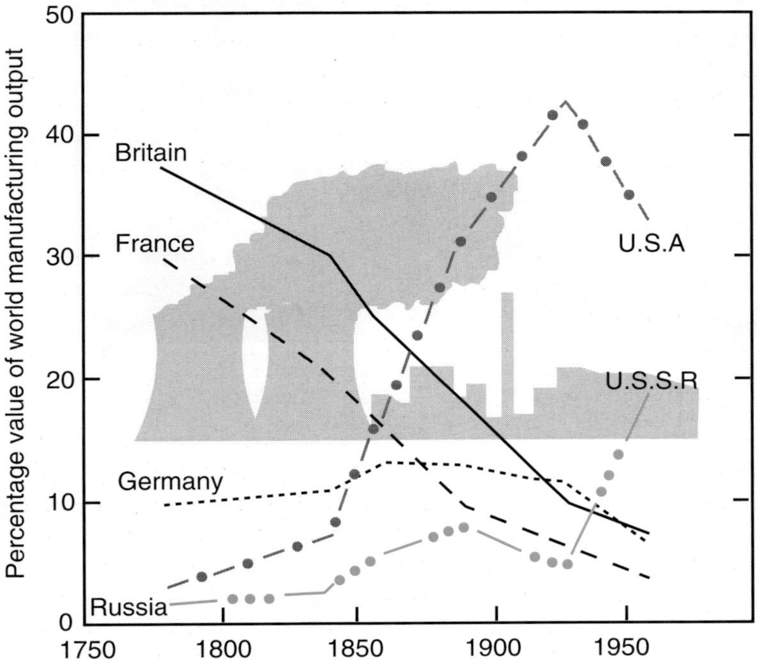

This graph examines the impact of the industrial revolution in various countries. Each line shows a country's share of world manufacturing output between 1750 and 1960.

Adapted from Hobsbawm, 1968.

Item B *Opposition to free trade in the late 19th century*

Thirty years ago Britain had almost a monopoly of the manufacturing industries of the world. It produced everything in excess of its consumption, other nations produced comparatively nothing. The world was obliged to buy from Britain because it could not buy anywhere else. Well, that was 30 years ago. Now France and America and Belgium have our machinery, our workmen and our capital. They are sending us a yearly increasing surplus that is driving our goods out of our own markets. Every year they are closing their markets to our goods. Foreigners see industries dying out under free trade in Britain and springing into life under protection in France, Belgium, Germany and America.

Adapted from Sullivan, 1881.

Item C *German tariffs*

The staunchest free trader cannot afford to overlook the advantages of the German system of protection. English iron and steel, on entering Germany, are handicapped with a duty varying in amount, but reaching to over half a crown per hundred weight for tin plates. This makes it very difficult for us to compete with home produced materials. It, likewise, enables Germans to raise their prices to their compatriots and to screw such a profit from them that they can afford a big reduction on their export prices. So, they cut at their English rivals in two directions. The duty makes our goods too dear to sell in Germany and, at the same time, it makes German goods so cheap in the world market that we are being undercut and ousted from it.

Adapted from Williams, 1896.

Item D *World exports, 1890-1913*

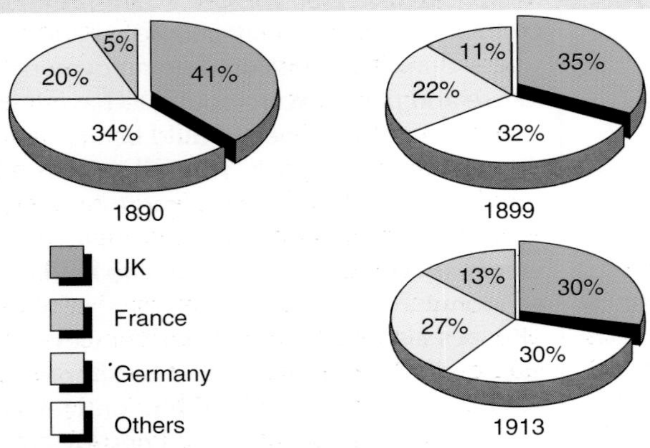

These charts show Britain's percentage share of world exports compared to other countries between 1890 and 1913.

Adapted from Briggs, 1993.

Item E *Pro-free trade poster, 1906*

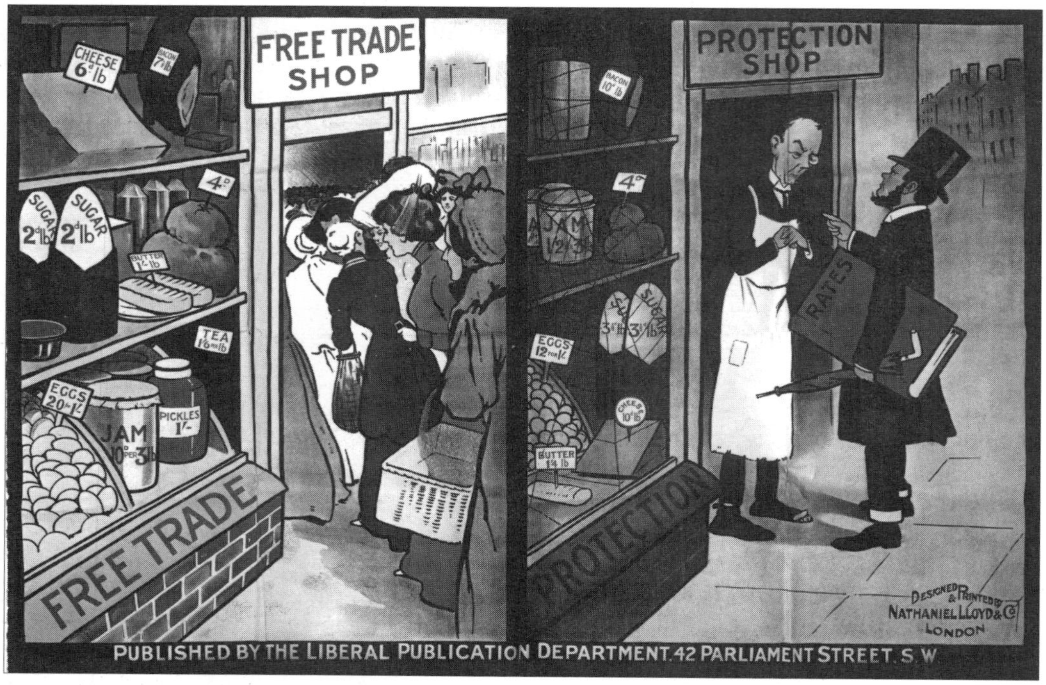

The main issue in the 1906 general election campaign was whether or not to end free trade. The Conservatives argued for a return to protection whilst the Liberals supported free trade. The Liberals won the election.

Item F *In support of free trade*

I observe that your Tory candidate and his friends are opposed to free traders. They make this complaint. We are allowed to buy freely all the products of foreign countries. But, owing to some foreign tariffs, we cannot sell our own products as freely as we wish to do. Let your workmen reflect on the change which free trade has wrought. The price of tea is now less than the duty paid on it in former days. Sugar is not more than one third of its cost.

Adapted from a letter written by John Bright, a Liberal MP and campaigner for Free Trade, 1884.

Questions

1. Using Items A-F give arguments for and against free trade.
2. 'There was more justification for a policy of free trade in 1800 than there was in 1900.' Explain this statement using Items A-F.
3. Judging from Item E how did the Liberals in the 1906 election campaign justify their support for free trade?
4. What lessons might contemporary politicians learn from Items A-F?

1.2 Keynesianism

For much of the postwar period, British economic policy was based on the theories put forward by the economist J.M. Keynes (1883-1946). During the Great Depression of the 1930s, capitalist economies all over the world had slumped and millions of workers had lost their jobs. In 1936, Keynes published his *General Theory of Employment, Interest and Money* which put forward a theoretical framework to explain why the recessions which periodically hit capitalist economies happened and how they could be overcome.

Keynes rejected laissez faire policies which left the market to regulate wages and prices. He argued that, if it was left to itself, the market would stabilise at a point below its full capacity (ie in recession). Since companies tended to lay people off and to reduce wages during a recession, unemployment was bound to rise and people were bound to have less money to spend. As a result, there would be an inevitable fall in demand for new goods. This fall in demand would intensify the recession. Even more people would be laid off and demand would fall still further. In other words, a vicious circle would take hold of the economy.

Keynes also rejected the socialist view that the economy could be stimulated by simple redistribution of wealth to the poor. He argued that redistribution of wealth would destroy any incentive to achieve.

Keynes' solution was to argue that recessions could be overcome by government intervention. The government, he argued, should direct investment into new economic activity. Extra government spending and/or lower taxes would stimulate the economy. Instead of saving during a recession, governments should take the lead and borrow money to invest in new projects. These new projects would provide jobs and create wealth. The people who did these new jobs would have money to spend and, by spending this money, they would stimulate the economy. As a result of this stimulation, demand would increase and the economy would come out of recession.

So, what Keynes proposed was **demand management** in a mixed economy. He proposed a capitalist economy in which the government was prepared to intervene to achieve full employment and planned economic growth. In this mixed economy, if there was a rise in unemployment, the government would, if necessary, increase the budget deficit by investing in new projects and lowering taxes (If a government spends more than it receives in revenue from taxation and other sources, then it is said to have a budget deficit). But, equally, when there was full employment and demand was threatening to rise too much (ie the economy was beginning to overheat) the government would reduce the budget deficit - for example, by raising taxes and thus dampening down demand.

Butskellism

The term 'Butskellism' comes from the amalgamation of the names of two Chancellors of the Exchequer - R.A. Butler, Conservative Chancellor 1951-55 and H. Gaitskell, Labour Chancellor 1950-51. Although from different parties, both Chancellors pursued the same broad **Keynesian** economic policies. Having established a consensus in the early 1950s, governments continued to work within it until the late 1970s. 'Butskellism', therefore, is a term used to describe the management of the economy during the period of the postwar consensus (see also chapter 3, section 1.1).

The fundamental aim of governments during this period was to keep unemployment to a minimum and to maintain and improve the new welfare state through increases in public expenditure. Keynesianism, therefore, became the economic orthodoxy. But, as Grant points out, the application of Keynes' theory was not undiluted:

> 'When discussing Keynesianism in Britain, it is important to remember that what is being referred to is not the undiluted application of Keynes' ideas as set out in his *General Theory*, but rather a particular interpretation of Keynesian ideas by the Treasury. What the Treasury particularly liked about Keynesianism is that it offered the possibility of managing the economy without getting one's hands dirty. By manipulating the level of aggregate demand in the economy by increasing or decreasing taxes, it was seen as possible to influence key economic indicators, notably the trade-off between inflation and unemployment.' (Grant, 1992, p.99)

Keynesian economics in the 1950s and 1960s

During the 1950s and 1960s, unemployment tended to fluctuate between 1% and 2% of the working population. There were never more than one million people unemployed at any one time during this period. And, whilst the unemployment figures remained low, other economic indicators remained favourable. Between 1950 and 1970, the rate of inflation averaged at 4.5% and, until 1969, stayed in single figures (inflation is a general sustained rise in the price level). During the same period, wages grew in real terms by 20% and, although Britain's rate of economic growth was lower than that of many of its rivals in Western Europe, it still remained at 2% a year, on average. In July 1957, the Prime Minister Harold Macmillan felt able to boast:

> 'Let's be frank about it. Most of our people have never had it so good. Go around the country, go to the industrial towns, go to the farms and you will see a state of prosperity such as we have had never in my lifetime - nor indeed ever in the history of the country.' (Speech made at Bedford, 20 July 1957)

The successes Macmillan referred to were achieved by the application of the Keynesian mechanism of demand management.

The Stop-Go cycle

The problem with the system of demand management was that it was impossible to maintain a stable level of low unemployment over the long term. The economy still tended to move from mild boom to mild recession. When unemployment was low, growth was high. But this brought higher inflation and a growing balance of payments deficit. By reducing demand, the balance of payments deficit was reduced and inflation curbed but the economy then moved into mild recession and unemployment grew. A recession encouraged the government to intervene to increase the level of demand. As a result, the whole cycle began again. This process is known as the 'Stop-Go cycle'.

The breakdown of Keynesianism

The Stop-Go cycle was exacerbated in Britain by the existence of a fixed exchange rate in the 1950s and 1960s (an exchange rate is the price at which one currency is convertible into another). A strong pound made imports relatively cheap. As a result, when the economy moved into boom, consumers spent surplus income on imports. This produced an alarming balance of payments deficit which forced the government to intervene and slow down the economy. The problem was alleviated in 1967 when the pound was devalued (with the result that exports became cheaper and imports dearer). It remained, however, until a floating exchange rate was introduced in the 1970s.

It could be argued that the Stop-Go cycle was an inevitable product of the application of Keynesian economics. The goal of Keynesian economics is full employment. When there is full employment, labour is, by definition, in short supply. This pushes up its price. If the price of labour increases, then so does the price of goods. Suppose, for example, an employer grants a 10% wage rise. Then, assuming that all other factors remain constant and assuming that wages make up 50% of the company's costs, the company's costs rise by 5%. These higher costs are then usually passed on to the customer in the form of higher prices. Higher prices lead to demands for higher wages. Higher prices and higher wages on a large scale produce inflation. So, Keynesian policies with their goal of full employment inevitably produce an inflationary spiral.

During the period 1960 to 1979, the link between wage levels and inflation led to increasingly close links between government, management and unions. This was the era of corporatism and tripartite agreements (see chapter 10, part 3). Although both Labour and Conservative governments attempted to negotiate incomes policies in the hope that wage restraint would curb inflation, this proved particularly difficult. Agreements were broken by management and unions alike. Industrial action was a frequent occurrence. The failure to produce a workable incomes policy meant that the inflationary spiral (described above) could not be broken.

When oil prices quadrupled in 1974, a world recession began and the economic growth that had continued since 1945 came to an end. Britain's trade deficit soared to £5,351 million in 1974. The following year inflation reached nearly 25% whilst unemployment grew to almost one million. Over the next five years, unemployment continued to grow whilst inflation remained high. Under Keynesian theory, inflation and wage demands should have come down as unemployment went up. But, that simply did not happen. By the end of the decade, opponents of Keynesianism were able to argue that the theory had failed and it was time to try something new.

Activity 15.2

Item A *Affluent Britain*

In the second half of the 1950s, Britain seemed to be changing fundamentally and for the better. This was due to unprecedented prosperity and full employment. Unemployment had disappeared in the war and remained minimal throughout the 1950s. Better still was the fact that earnings rose faster than prices. There had also been a reduction in the working week. The new affluence was measured in consumer durables. By 1965, 88% of households in Britain had TVs, 39% had fridges and 56% had washing machines. The number of TV licences grew from half a million in 1950 to over 12 million in 1964. In 1951, there were 2.25 million cars on the road. In 1964, this figure had risen to over eight million. Growth in ownership was facilitated by hire purchase and the lowering of purchase tax as well as higher earnings. Home ownership also grew between 1955 and 1964. By 1964, over 40% of the population owned their own homes. In addition, the Conservatives cut income tax five times between 1955 and 1964.

Adapted from Childs, 1992.

Item B *The Stop-Go cycle*

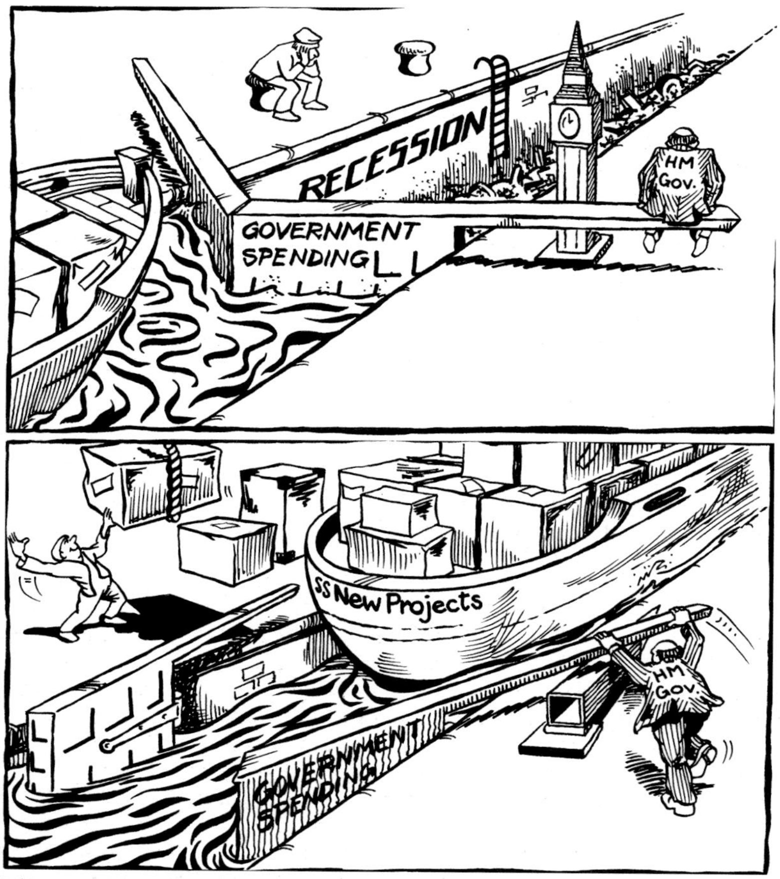

This cartoon shows how the Stop-Go cycle works.

Item C *The mixed economy*

Two parties shared the government of Britain in the 30 years after 1945. The prime aim of both was to restore and expand the British economy by restoring and expanding industry and exports. The focus of debate throughout these years was on whether the government was doing the right or wrong things. This shows how government action and policy had become central. Every government acted within the established system - a capitalist system. By nationalising industries, Labour governments diminished the area of private capitalism and extended the public sector. But, these two sectors remained capitalist in structure and operation. The mixed economy was mixed in different proportions. All governments tried to contribute positively to both the private and public sectors. This contribution was essentially financial. Governments provided money or facilitated credit. Private and nationalised industries used this money to invest, modernise and grow. At the same time, governments saw it as their role to keep wages in check either by bargaining with the unions or by subsidising the cost of living by law. But, government intervention of this kind was inflationary.

Adapted from Calvocoressi, 1978.

Item D *Inflation and unemployment*

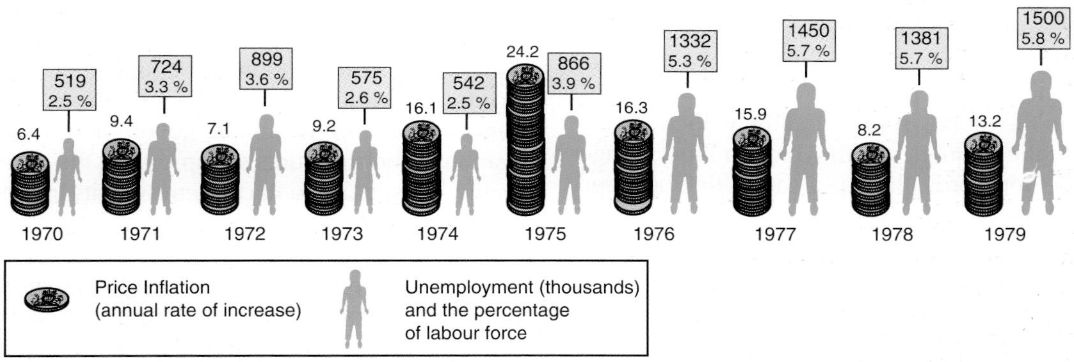

Item E *The limitations of demand management policies (1)*

Assume that the government announces a £500 million increase in civil servant salaries and a £500 million increase in road building. The increase in civil servant salaries will work through the economy relatively quickly. Civil servants will increase their spending within months of receiving their pay increase. But, the road building programme may take years even to start. So, a government needs to be careful to take account of lags in spending when using active fiscal policy (the manipulation of government expenditure) to fill or remove deflationary or inflationary gaps. In the past governments have been accused of destabilising the economy by using active fiscal policy. In 1972, for example, the Chancellor reflated the economy at a time when (arguably) the economy was moving into a boom of its own accord. The combination of extra private and public spending then created an inflationary gap. In addition, active fiscal policy assumes that the Chancellor knows the current state of the economy. But, statistics are notoriously unreliable and have become more so over time. If the balance of payments is in deficit, the Chancellor will not know how much is due to genuine deficit and how much is due to inaccurate recording of statistics. Further, some economists argue that it is impossible to predict changes in variables to the last few per cent. But, many of the variables governments wish to control are small numbers. For instance, the government may wish to reduce economic growth by half. To do so it might have to cut the growth in national income from 3% to 1.5%. But, active fiscal policy is unlikely to be sensitive enough to achieve exactly that 1.5% fall.

Adapted from Anderton, 1991.

Item F *The limitations of demand management policies (2)*

Today, we understand how the economy works. We should be able to avert depressions and prevent massive unemployment. But, we have not done so. There are several reasons for this. First, measures required to control inflation (unlike those to stimulate demand) are unpleasant and painful. It is much easier psychologically and politically to encourage people to do things than to stop them doing what they want to do. By curbing demand, governments are bound to encounter friction, especially in a democracy. Second, in the early postwar years, Britain imported inflation. Because the costs of our imports rose during those years, industries were faced with mounting raw material costs which they passed on to the consumer in higher prices. Wage earners, faced with a higher cost of living, demanded higher pay increases. In this way, the inflationary spiral of rising wages and rising prices began. Third, the object of every economic system is to increase the standard of living as fast as possible. It goes against the grain deliberately to reverse this and to slow down the rate of expansion. Governments are understandably reluctant to do so.

Adapted from Shanks, 1961.

Questions

1. Judging from Item A why do you think there was little criticism of the Keynesian model before the late 1970s?
2. a) Using Items A-C describe how Keynes' economic theory was put into practice.
   b) How did this system differ from the laissez faire approach adopted by earlier governments?
3. a) Using Items D-F describe the limitations of the Keynesian economic model.
   b) Why do you think criticism of Keynesianism grew during the 1970s?

1.3 Monetarism

Monetarism is an economic theory which completely rejects the aims and techniques of economic management proposed by Keynes. Whilst the primary goal of Keynesianism is to maintain full employment, the primary goal of monetarism is to keep inflation under control - even if that means maintaining a high level of unemployment. Whereas Keynesian economists argue that the government should play an active role by managing demand, monetarists argue that the government's only role should be to control the money supply (the money supply is the total amount of money circulating in the economy).

Monetarism is based on the quantity theory of money, one of the oldest economic theories. It dates back at least 500 years. The quantity theory of money states that increases in prices are caused solely by increases in the money supply and the velocity of its circulation (the frequency with which money changes hands). In other words, there is a causal link between the money supply and inflation.

Today, monetarism is most often associated with the economist Milton Friedman. He argued that the economy was not really affected by the level of public expenditure or the level of taxation. Rather, what mattered was the money supply. As he put it in 1968 'inflation is always and everywhere a monetary phenomenon'. Friedman argued that the money supply can be measured and controlled and that it was the government's job to measure and control it. It was his contention that if the government restricted the money supply, inflation would fall.

Applying monetarism in Britain

By the mid-1970s, high inflation was a major problem in Britain and Keynesianism came under attack. There is evidence that the Labour government of 1974-79 began to move away from Keynesianism. For example, in 1976, the Prime Minister, James Callaghan, made a speech at the Labour party conference which seemed to reject the Keynesian approach:

> 'We used to think that you could spend your way out of recession by cutting taxes and boosting government spending. I tell you in all candour that that option no longer exists and in so far as it ever did exist, it only worked on each occasion since the war by injecting a larger dose of inflation into the economy, followed by a higher level of unemployment as the next step.' (quoted in Grant, 1992, p.102)

This speech may have been a turning point away from orthodox Keynesianism, but it was the Conservative government elected in 1979 which openly abandoned the Keynesian goal of full employment. The reduction of inflation, not the reduction of unemployment was the new Conservative government's main goal. Monetarism, not Keynesianism, was the economic tool which would achieve this goal.

In practice, the British experiment with monetarism in the early 1980s was far more than an attempt to control the money supply. The Thatcher governments in the early 1980s favoured a laissez faire economic approach and their support for monetarism was used to justify this. The aim was to reduce government spending and borrowing and to provide the conditions in which the market could regulate itself. Clearly, this went against Keynesian thinking, but it fitted well with monetarism. Monetarists argued that the government's only role was to control the money supply. This suggests that the government should play a minimal role in economic management. In other words, monetarism provided an ideological framework within which the government could dismantle the structures set up during the period of Keynesianism and replace them with its free market solutions.

There were three main strands to British monetarism in the early 1980s. First, each year the government attempted to control the supply of money in the economy. Second, each year the government attempted to reduce the level of government spending. And third, the government actively set out to take away government controls and to create a free market economy.

Measuring money supply

There is no single method of calculating money supply. In Britain, during the early 1980s, two main measures were used by the government to calculate money supply.

M0 is a narrow definition of money supply. It is equal to the notes and coins in circulation together with the balances held by banks with the Bank of England.

M3 is a broad measure of money supply. It is equal to all the notes and coins in circulation plus money in current accounts in banks plus monies in deposit accounts in banks plus private sector holdings of certificates of deposit.

Controlling the money supply

Despite Milton Friedman's confidence that the money supply could be measured and controlled, experience in Britain in the early 1980s shows that this is more difficult in practice than in theory. By means of its **Medium Term Financial Strategy**, the government set annual targets for the rate of monetary growth over four year periods (using M3 as the measure of money supply). These targets were first published with the 1980 budget.

A reduction in money supply was to be achieved by three means. First, the government would set interest rates high enough to lower the demand for money. Second, the government would finance the Public Sector Borrowing Requirement (PSBR) - the budget deficit - without printing money. And third, the government would allow the exchange rate to float - to prevent the buying and selling of foreign currencies from affecting the money supply.

Failure to control the money supply

Unfortunately for the government, these policy instruments were unsuccessful. In the early 1980s, the money supply grew at around twice the rate set by the government. Despite the government's attempts to control it, M3 sterling remained at a higher level between 1979 and 1985 than it had been at any time during the period of the previous Labour government. It is ironic to note that inflation did fall during this period, but it fell while money supply was increasing. Therefore, the monetarists' claim that inflation would only fall if the money supply was restricted was proved false.

In November 1985, the government abandoned M3 sterling as a measure of money supply and replaced it with M0, the narrower measure. Most economists dismissed M0 as an entirely unrealistic measure of true money supply because today's society is relatively cashless (the M0 measurement does not take that into account). The experiment with orthodox monetarism, therefore, was over by 1986. From 1986, control of the money supply was no longer a main priority of the government.

Reducing the level of government spending

The second main strand in the Thatcher governments' monetarist policy was the reduction of government spending. The argument was that if public spending exceeded public income, the result would be an increase in the money supply. Unlike Keynesians, therefore, monetarists were not prepared to stimulate the economy by investing government money if that investment resulted in a deficit. Margaret Thatcher argued that the nation's economy should be run like a household economy.

Until 1979, governments rarely balanced their Budgets. Most years they ran budget deficits by spending more than they received. As a result, governments borrowed money.

In his first Budget, just three weeks after the general election in 1979, Geoffrey Howe, the Chancellor, placed cash limits on the public sector, raised the minimum lending rate to 14%, sold some public assets to help finance the PSBR and switched from direct taxation to taxes on spending (income tax was lowered to 30% whilst VAT was raised). This Budget signalled a move away from Keynesian demand management. Whereas Keynesians would have attempted to keep unemployment down by allowing a deficit, this Budget was designed to reduce the budget deficit even if that meant higher unemployment and a recession in the short term. This policy was tightened in 1981. The 1981 Budget imposed huge increases in indirect tax (for example a 20p per gallon increase on petrol) and a total of £3,500 million was taken out of the PSBR. By the mid-1980s, the government had managed to achieve a budget surplus.

Although the government achieved a budget surplus in the mid-1980s, public spending rose every year from 1979. One reason for this was the huge growth in unemployment. A growth in unemployment means that the Social Security bill increases (since state benefits have to be paid to those out of work). It also means that the government receives less in both direct and indirect taxes. Direct taxes are taxes raised directly from an individual or an organisation. Indirect taxes are taxes on goods or services. Income tax is an example of direct tax. VAT is an example of an indirect tax. When unemployment grows, less income tax is collected since people out of work do not pay it and less indirect tax is collected since unemployed people cannot afford to buy as many goods and services which contain indirect taxes.

Creating a free market economy

The third main strand in the Thatcher governments' monetarist policy was the attempt to create a free market economy. This is closely linked to the policy of reducing government spending. By definition, a free market economy is an economy in which government intervention is minimal.

The election of the Thatcher government in 1979 meant an end to income policies. Wage settlements were to be made by employers and their workers. The market would decide the level of settlements, not the government. The refusal to consider income policies marks a break with the Keynesian past.

In addition, the programme of privatisation, which gained momentum after 1983, marks an important break with the past. Privatisation is attractive to monetarists for two reasons. First, it allows the government to raise money without having to borrow it. Money raised by privatisation, so the argument goes, does not affect the money supply and, therefore, is not inflationary. It should be noted, however, that money raised from privatisation was an important contribution to the budget surpluses of the mid-1980s. Second, privatisation reduces the state's direct involvement in the economy. By selling state owned assets to the private sector, the government reduces the size of the public sector and, therefore, allows market forces to exert more influence over the economy.

Activity 15.3

Item A Conservative economic strategy in the early 1980s

To explain the government's policies, we must turn to the Medium Term Financial Strategy (MTFS) published along with the Budget of 1980. This laid down target ranges for the growth of money supply for several years ahead, declining steadily from 7-11% in 1980-81 to 4-8% in 1983-84. This implies a steady deceleration on the monetary front, the intention being that there would be an accompanying decline in the rate of inflation. But the MTFS also laid down a similar reduction in the Public Sector Borrowing Requirement (PSBR) from 5.5% of GDP in 1978-79 to 1.5% in 1983-84 (GDP or gross domestic product is a measure of the amount of income generated as a result of a country's economic activity. It does not include net property income from abroad). This implied a steady fall in government expenditure relative to tax receipts. If the economy had been expanding, this need not have been a problem because the growth in income would have increased tax receipts and all the government would have had to do was to keep its own expenditure growing at a smaller rate. But, the economy was already moving into recession when the Conservatives took office and so this strategy has come close to pushing the economy into a deflationary whirlpool. Each addition to the unemployment register adds several thousand pounds to the PSBR as a result of extra benefit rates and lost tax revenue. The recession, therefore, raised the PSBR just as the government was trying to reduce it. The only way it could reduce it was to bring forward in each Budget a new package of expenditure cuts and/or tax increases which would inevitably exacerbate the recession.

Adapted from Hall & Jacques, 1983.

Item B Trickle down economics

One of the guiding principles of Britain's Tory governments since 1979 has been that top people should be well rewarded. If incentives were sufficient, executives would perform well and create wealth, the argument ran. The rewards might seem excessive and unfair to ordinary people, but they too would benefit from the 'trickle down' effect. This did not happen. Pay packages of £500,000 per year have become commonplace for company directors yet a fifth of the population is worse off than it was 15 years ago. Far from trickling down, the money has been swilling around the boardroom. Besides, several studies have failed to find any relation between top executives' pay rises and company success. What these studies have found is that those who design and make, refine and improve, market and sell a product - engineers, scientists, television programme makers - are often not those who get the biggest share of profits, the largest company cars or the most generous severance terms. In British companies, the finance director, say, nearly always does better than the chief engineer.

Adapted from the *Independent on Sunday*, 6 March 1994.

Item C Monetary targets 1980-85

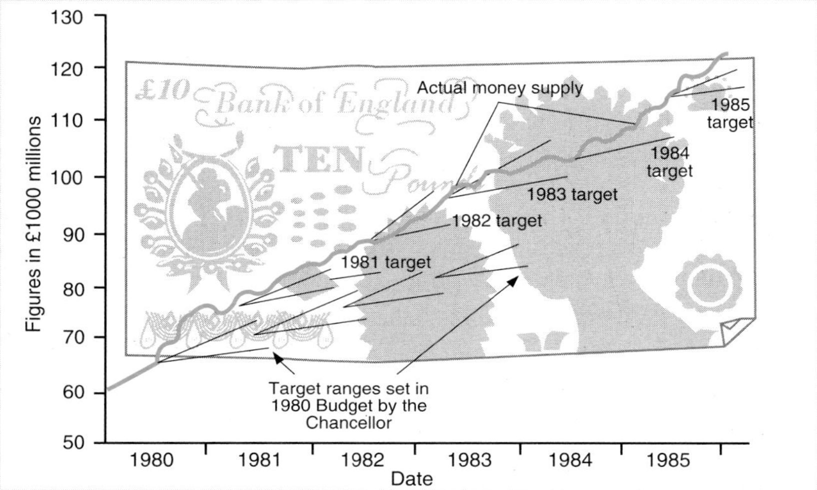

Adapted from the *Guardian*, 24 October 1985.

Item D Inflation rate 1978-92

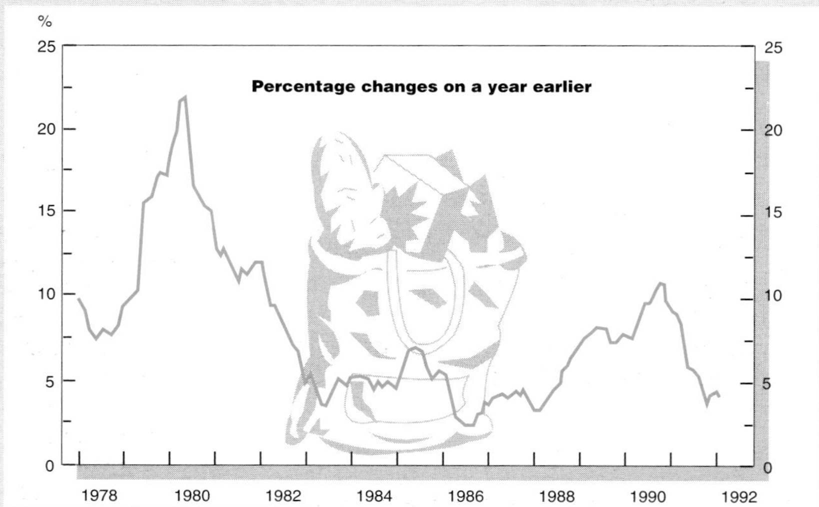

Adapted from Anderton, 1992.

Item E *Unemployment 1971-93*

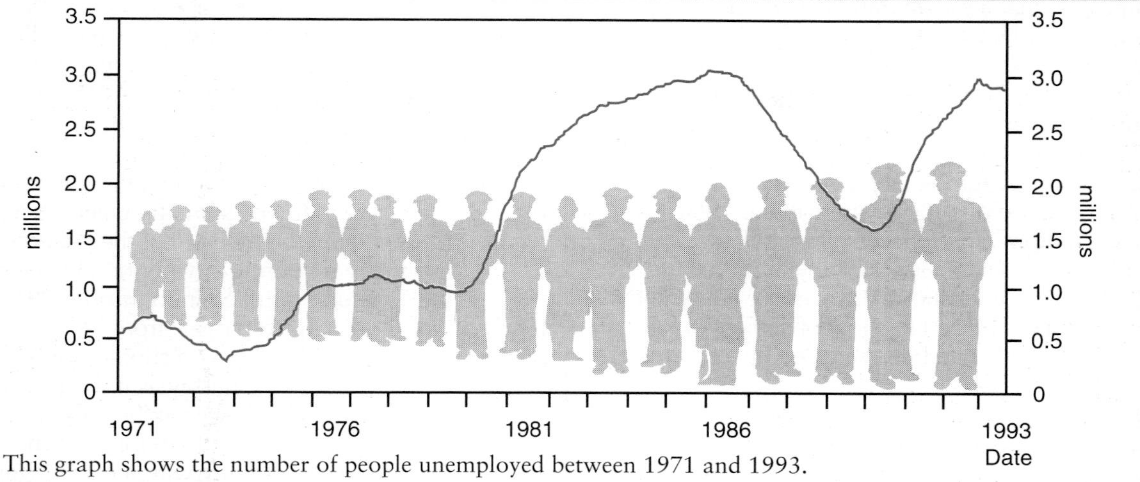

This graph shows the number of people unemployed between 1971 and 1993.

Adapted from HMSO, 1994.

Item F *Government expenditure as a proportion of GDP, 1963-94*

This table shows government expenditure as a proportion of GDP. GDP or gross domestic product is a measure of the amount of income generated as a result of a country's economic activity, excluding net property income from abroad.

Date	% GDP	Date	% GDP
1963-64	36	1985-86	45
1968-69	41.5	1986-87	44
1973-74	43.5	1987-88	41.75
1978-79	44	1988-89	39.25
1979-80	44	1989-90	39.75
1980-81	46.5	1990-91	40.25
1981-82	47.25	1991-92	42
1982-83	47.5	1992-93	44.75
1983-84	46.5	1993-94	45.5
1984-85	47		

Adapted from McKie, 1993 and Anderton, 1994.

Questions

1. Using Items A-F explain how economic management in the early 1980s differed from economic management in the previous 30 years.
2. Judging from Items C-F what were the consequences of the pursuit of a monetarist economic policy in the early 1980s?
3. From the point of view of a monetarist, how successful would you say that the economic management of the economy in the early 1980s was?

2 Management of the economy since 1985

Key Issues

1. What have been the main developments in economic policy since 1985?
2. Did the resignation of Margaret Thatcher lead to a fundamental change in economic policy?
3. Why did Britain leave the ERM and what consequences did this have?

2.1 Economic policy 1985-90

Management of the economy under Margaret Thatcher had four main aims. First, the Thatcher governments aimed to change the structure of ownership by transferring the ownership of industries and services from the state to private individuals. Privatisation, it was argued, would increase efficiency. In addition, privatisation had two other advantages from the government's point of view. It generated a great deal of money for the Treasury (which helped to finance tax cuts). And, the sale of shares to the public encouraged large numbers of ordinary people to become share holders for the first time. By increasing the number of people with a vested interest in the capitalist system, the government hoped to increase the number of Conservative voters. The same idea lay behind the decision to sell off council houses to tenants at reduced rates.

The second aim was to cut public expenditure. At

the heart of the Thatcher view of the economy was the idea that the nation's economy should be managed in the same way that a good housekeeper would manage a household budget. In other words, the Budget should be balanced and the nation should not live on credit.

The third aim was to change the distribution of wealth. By promising and making cuts in income tax rates whilst increasing the level of indirect taxation, the government ensured that the real incomes of the richest 10% of the population grew in the 1980s whilst that of the bottom 10% fell (see part 5 below).

And finally, the Thatcher governments aimed to reduce the level of inflation. This was the government's main aim and it replaced the goal of achieving full employment which had been pursued by all previous postwar governments.

Although the aims of the Thatcher governments remained constant, the policies employed to achieve the aims changed. In the early 1980s, for example, there was a concerted effort to translate monetarist theory into practice. Economic policies were designed to control the money supply in the hope that this would bring down inflation. But, control of the money supply was simply not possible. In October 1985, the Chancellor of the Exchequer, Nigel Lawson, suspended the M3 measure of monetary supply (see section 1.3 above). This, effectively, ended the government's attempt to apply orthodox monetarist policies. In the same speech, however, Lawson made it clear that control of inflation still remained the primary aim of the government:

> 'The acid test of monetary policy is its record in reducing inflation. Those who wish to join the debate about the intricacies of different measures of money and the implications they may have for the future are welcome to do so. But, at the end of the day, the position is clear and unambiguous. The inflation rate is judge and jury.' (Nigel Lawson's Mansion House speech, 17 October 1985)

Rather than using measures of money supply to control inflation, Lawson argued that British monetary policy was constrained by the exchange rate of the pound. Between 1985 and 1989, the main levers with which Lawson attempted to manipulate the economy were the exchange rate and the level of interest rates. Indeed, it was concern about the exchange rate which led to his public argument with Margaret Thatcher. Earlier in the 1980s, Thatcher had favoured a form of alignment with the dollar. Lawson, however, saw greater benefit in a closer relationship with Europe because Europe was much more important for trade than the USA. This led to a public debate about whether or not Britain should join the European Community's ERM - Exchange Rate Mechanism (see section 2.2 below). Lawson favoured participation whilst Thatcher, egged on by her adviser Alan Walters, did not. The resignation of Lawson in 1989 and the ensuing debate over Britain's role in Europe were important ingredients in the chain of events which led to the resignation of Margaret Thatcher in November 1990 (see chapter 3, pp.58-59).

Management of the economy under John Major

John Major replaced Nigel Lawson as Chancellor in 1989 and then, the following year, he replaced Margaret Thatcher as Prime Minister. As Chancellor, Major was careful to distance himself from orthodox monetarism, saying:

> 'That used to be the theory...the government may have followed some time ago. It certainly has not been the theory that the government has followed during any period I have been at the Treasury.' (quoted in Johnson, 1991)

John Major also distanced himself from his predecessor, arguing that Lawson should not have allowed demand to rise as sharply as it did in 1987 and 1988. Major became Chancellor at the tail-end of the boom engineered by Lawson (the boom which was timed to coincide conveniently with the 1987 general election). It was, therefore, important for him not to be held responsible for the decline in economic fortunes which would follow Lawson's so-called 'economic miracle'. He was, perhaps, fortunate that he only presented a single Budget (in 1990). By then, the economy was moving into recession. If the leadership crisis had come later, he might not have been so popular.

As it was, Major succeeded Thatcher as Prime Minister and immediately promised to continue to pursue policies which followed the general direction taken by his predecessor. Under Major, the main goals of economic policy remained a commitment to privatisation, more efficient public services, lower direct taxation and the maintenance of low inflation. That the control of inflation would remain the overriding priority was indicated by the Chancellor, Norman Lamont, in 1991 when he said that growing unemployment and business failures were, 'a price worth paying' for low inflation.

That John Major's government should have the same economic goals as the Thatcher governments is not, perhaps, surprising. John Major was regarded as a loyal Thatcherite who had been groomed by Margaret Thatcher as her successor. Also, most of the members of John Major's Cabinet had served in Margaret Thatcher's Cabinet.

The initial problem faced by the new Prime Minister was to show that he was 'his own man'. This was achieved partly by projecting a 'caring' image and partly by making policy adjustments. Of these policy adjustments perhaps the two most important were the abandonment of the poll tax and the willingness to increase public expenditure even though that meant running up a large budget deficit. Both policy adjustments were taken before the 1992 general election was called. Since the economy remained in recession right up to the 1992 general election and beyond, the scope for government action was limited. Even so, public spending was increased and tax cuts - the traditional Thatcherite pre-election 'sweeteners' - were made in the 1992 Budget.

These measures were sufficient to secure a Conservative victory in the 1992 general election, but the result was the accumulation of a huge budget deficit (£28 billion in 1992-93 and £50 billion in 1993-94). The size of this budget deficit shocked Thatcherite backbenchers and forced the government to raise levels of taxation in the 1993 Budget - a policy reversal which was particularly embarrassing because the Conservative's main message in the 1992 general election campaign had been that the Conservatives would protect tax cuts whilst Labour would increase taxes.

Although this reversal, combined with the government's withdrawal from the ERM (see below, next section) shook the credibility of the Major government, the principles behind the management of the economy remained those which had prevailed in the late 1980s. The government's priority was the maintenance of low inflation. Privatisation, further deregulation and the cutting of public expenditure remained high on the agenda.

Activity 15.4

Item A *The legacy of Thatcherism*

In reality, most people in the government aim to pursue Thatcherism by other means. But, the old Thatcherites can no longer admit this because their heroine has gone and the Majorites cannot admit it because it suits their purposes to describe the 1990s as a new age. Look at the Major government's programme and it is clear where it comes from. The 1993 Act bashing trade unions is the seventh since 1980. British Rail is to be privatised and there is the promise that the privatisation of the Post Office will follow. Before the Thatcher age, it would have been impossible to conduct the debate about welfare cuts which is now under way. Nor is economic policy counter-Thatcherite either. Low income tax is still god, low inflation is still the holy grail and a balanced Budget the target to which other policies are supposed to bend. It has been difficult to keep the economy under control, but that was part of Thatcherism too. The main point is that on these important policies there is no debate. The orthodoxy prevails, especially in the Cabinet. And Major's distinctive contributions are forgettably meagre: a council tax which almost reinvents the rates and a Citizens' Charter which most people regard as a joke.

Adapted from Young, 1993.

Item B *The privatisation of the railways*

This rail is owned by the Fat Controller
This rail is owned by the Thin Stockbroker
6
Michael the 'privatised' tank engine takes his passengers for a ride...

In the 1992 election manifesto, the Conservatives made a committment to end British Rail's state monopoly (see Item C). This has proved a complicated business. Although a Railways Act paved the way for privatisation in 1994 and British Rail was, in effect, split into 80 separate companies, virtually all of these companies remained within the public sector (*Guardian*, 21 September 1994). Bob Horton, the Chairman of Railtrack (one of these new companies) admitted in September 1994 that his hope of complete privatisation before the next general election in 1996-97 was unlikely to be realised.

Item C *Conservative election manifesto, 1992*

1. In the 1990s, the government's task will be to provide an economic environment which encourages enterprise - the mainstream of prosperity. Our aims must be: to achieve price stability; to keep firm control over public spending; to continue to reduce taxes as fast as we prudently can; to make sure that market mechanisms and incentives are allowed to do their job.
2. We will aim to bring home ownership, share ownership and personal pensions within the reach of most families.
3. We will continue our privatisation programme. British Coal will be returned to the private sector. So will the local authority bus companies. We will encourage local authorities to sell their airports. We will end British Rail's state monopoly.

Adapted from the CCO, 1992.

Questions

1. 'Management of the economy was hardly affected by the resignation of Margaret Thatcher.' Explain this statement using Items A-C.
2. a) Judging from Items A and C what were the economic goals of the Major government between 1990 and 1993?
   b) Why do you think the Major government distanced itself from Thatcherism?
3. What does Item B tell us about the management of the economy under John Major?

2.2 Britain and the ERM

The long-term aim of the European Union is to achieve monetary union. This will have occurred when a single European currency has been adopted by all the member countries. The first stage in the process towards monetary union is for member countries to agree to peg their exchange rates within a band of a weighted average of European currencies. This is done by means of the Exchange Rate Mechanism (ERM). The ERM is neither a fixed nor a floating exchange rate system, it combines elements of both. On the one hand, currencies in the ERM are fixed in value against each other. On the other hand, currencies can move up and down within a narrow band against each other and the whole currency bloc can fluctuate freely against other world currencies such as the dollar or the yen. The ERM was created in 1979 by six member countries. Britain joined in October 1990.

Arguments for and against the ERM

The main argument in favour of entry into the ERM is that it provides the best way forward to achieve low inflation rates throughout the European Union. It does this for two main reasons. First, since exchange rates are fixed within a band, countries participating in the ERM do not have the option of devaluing their currency if it becomes uncompetitive. Instead, they have to increase competitiveness by controlling their unit costs and prices. By controlling costs and prices, they ensure that inflation is low. Second, weaker currencies can strengthen their currencies by raising interest rates (high interest rates encourage investors to buy in that currency). High interest rates also lead to low inflation. A further argument in favour of entry into the ERM is that it reduces currency fluctuations which harm confidence and trade.

The main argument against monetary union is that monetary union will lead to a loss of political and economic sovereignty and should, therefore, be opposed. There is little doubt that monetary union would lead to a loss of **political** sovereignty because some power over economic decisions would be transferred from British to European decision making bodies. The Bank of England, for example, would lose power to a new European Central Bank. Equally, under full monetary union, Britain would lose some control over interest rates, exchange rates and its Budget. Sterling would disappear, interest rates would be set by the new European Central Bank and the British government would have limited powers to alter taxes or run up budget deficits. But, even without monetary union, the UK has limited control over policy because foreign trade is so important to its economy. Successive postwar governments have found that they cannot run large-scale budget deficits. As a result, their hands have been tied. It could be argued, therefore, that monetary union would merely formalise an existing arrangement.

The British government and the ERM

Nigel Lawson was a supporter of Britain's entry into the ERM from the outset. In 1979, he wrote an article in *Financial Weekly* supporting Britain's ERM membership. His advice was rejected partly on the grounds that inflation was too high to join. Two years later, when inflation had fallen, he wrote to the Chancellor, Geoffrey Howe, suggesting that the right time to join had arrived. But, his advice was rejected in the Cabinet by those who argued that stability against the dollar was more important than stability against European currencies.

When Lawson became Chancellor he was able to convince Margaret Thatcher that, in principle, Britain should join the ERM. He used two arguments to persuade her. First, he argued that because Britain was a member of the European Union it was important for the Prime Minister to be seen to show some commitment to it. Second, he argued that greater economic stability would result from having a single European currency. But, although agreeing in principle, Thatcher continued to use delaying tactics.

From the end of 1987, Chancellor Lawson and the Treasury let the pound shadow the Deutschmark in preparation for joining the ERM. They sold sterling whenever the pound threatened to go over the three Deutschmark level. But in, March 1988, strong upward pressure on the pound led to this policy being abandoned.

Lawson's resignation in October 1989 was closely linked to the delay in entry into the ERM. Margaret Thatcher's economic adviser, Alan Walters, strongly opposed entry into the ERM and she accepted his, rather than her Chancellor's, advice on this matter. As a result, Lawson had little choice but to resign. Ironically, a year later John Major, Lawson's successor, finally persuaded the government to join the ERM.

The wrong time and the wrong rate?

At the time when Britain joined the ERM, it was experiencing high inflation (7% above that in Germany), it had a high balance of payments deficit (estimated at £15 billion in 1990) and it was steadily moving into recession. It was, in short, a less than ideal moment to join the ERM. At the time, many commentators argued that Britain had joined the ERM at too high an exchange rate. They suggested that since the exchange rate was too high and Britain was moving into recession, it would be difficult for Britain to grow out of recession without having a balance of payments problem (since, once Britain was within the ERM, its exchange rate would be fixed within a band). But, the government decided that a high exchange rate would help in the fight against inflation since British exporters and British firms competing against imports would have to cut costs and lower prices if they wanted to survive. When John Major became Prime Minister, he made it clear that membership of the ERM was the key to his economic strategy. This commitment was explicitly stated during the run up to the general election in April 1992:

> 'Membership of the ERM is now central to our counter-inflation discipline.'
> (CCO, 1992, p.6)

Despite the reservations of some economists about the conditions in which Britain joined the ERM, the pound traded comfortably within its broad bands until July 1992. From July 1992, however, the pound (together with the French Franc and Italian lira) came under intense selling pressure. The foreign exchange markets decided that Germany was overcoming the problems produced by reunification and, therefore, the Deutschmark was not sufficently strong. As a result, they wanted either the Deutschmark to be revalued or the pound, franc and lira to be devalued. Pressure on the pound, franc and lira grew so strong that, by 13 September, the Italian government had decided to devalue the lira by 7%. The revalued lira remained within the ERM. Attention then turned to the pound. There was such strong selling pressure on the pound that, despite spending as much as £10 billion in an effort to avert the crisis (the actual figures have not been revealed), the government was forced to devalue on 16 September ('Black Wednesday'). On the same day, the government decided to leave the ERM. Britain's withdrawal from the ERM was a major blow to European monetary union. In the past, member countries stayed within the ERM even when forced to realign their currencies. Britain was the first member to withdraw from the system.

One reason why the British government decided to leave the ERM was that it was felt that being tied to the ERM had prolonged the recession. Whilst it remained in the ERM, the government was unable to make large interest rate cuts because they would result in the pound falling out of its band. After it decided to leave the ERM, the government was able to cut interest rates without worrying if the level of the pound fell. As a result, the government was able to encourage growth and ease the economy out of recession. A second reason for leaving the ERM was a coolness towards European integration and a desire to appease the Eurosceptics who had threatened to split the Conservative party over the Maastricht Treaty (see chapter 6 section 3.3). But, even though the British government was able to ease Britain out of recession, withdrawal from the ERM was a severe blow to its credibility. It was, after all, just five months before withdrawal that the government had been elected on a platform which stressed that membership of the ERM was central to its economic strategy.

The future of the ERM

According to the Delors plan of 1989 which first set out the timetable for monetary union, stable exchange rates in the ERM were supposed to lead by 1996-97 to completely fixed exchange rates. The Delors plan was incorporated into the Maastricht Treaty (see chapter 6, section 3.2). According to the terms of the Maastricht Treaty, in 1996 the European Commission has to decide whether to launch monetary union in 1997 (seven countries must be willing to proceed). If monetary union is not launched in 1997, a review must take place by mid-1998. Also, assuming that the January 1997 deadline has been met, a single currency will be introduced into those countries which are part of the monetary union in January 1999. Britain's withdrawal from the ERM is an important setback. The British government has stated that it will not consider rejoining the ERM until favourable conditions prevail. It is likely, therefore, that the whole process will be delayed and possibly even jettisoned. The activity which follows examines the crisis in 1992 over the ERM and the advantages and disadvantages of joining the ERM.

Activity 15.5

Item A *Britain in the ERM 1990-1992*

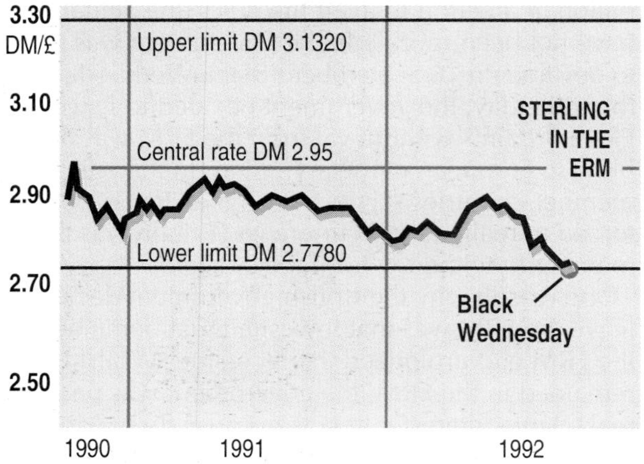

This graph shows the level of the pound against the Deutschmark (DM) during the period in which Britain participated in the ERM.

Adapted from Anderton 1993 and 1994.

Item B *The advantages of the ERM*

The point of membership of the ERM is not that the Bundesbank is able to run UK monetary policy better than the UK. Rather, there are a number of reasons why it is a system worth joining. First, for a mixture of historical, cultural and institutional reasons, Germany is able to maintain a reasonable degree of price stability with less difficulty than other European countries. Therefore, it makes sense to link exchange rates to the Deutschmark. Second, the financial markets attach greater credibility to a monetary policy based on the Deutschmark than they do to one which is not. Without the support of the financial markets, it is hard to make a success of any monetary policy. Third, within the ERM, companies know that if they fail to control their costs they are unlikely to be saved from bankruptcy by devaluation. Membership of the ERM, therefore, encourages companies and individuals to lower their inflationary expectations and act accordingly. And fourth, if one member country refuses to join the ERM, this is likely to be interpreted, however wrongly, as that country wishing to retain the right to devalue.

Adapted from Lawson, 1992.

Item C *Performance of the franc, the pound and the lira, 1992-94*

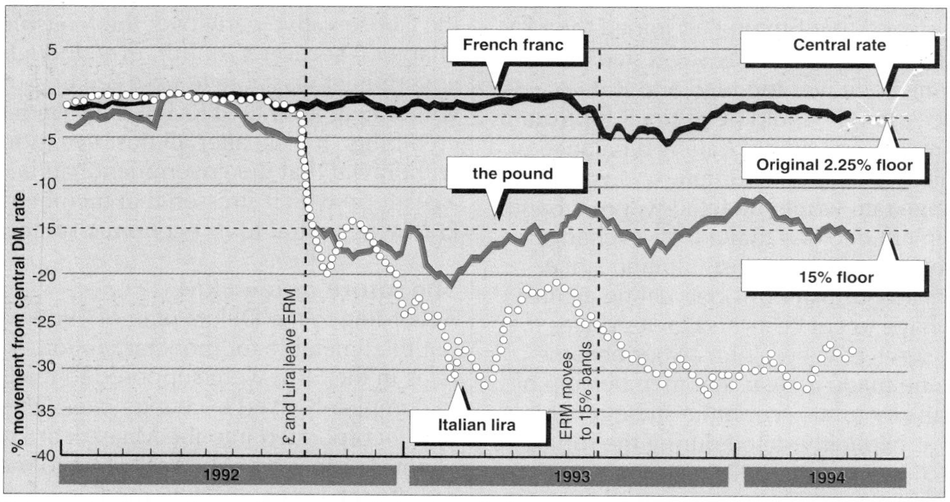

This graph shows the performance of the French franc, the pound and the lira between 1992 and 1994. It shows that for much of 1993 and 1994 the pound remained within a relatively narrow band against the Deutschmark (DM).

Item D *The disadvantages of the ERM*

(i) German reunification and British devaluation have given further proof of how diverse a region Europe is and how it lacks the mechanisms to offset this asymmetry. Europe is far from suitable to be covered by a single currency. There is no doubt of the importance of exchange rate stability in an area so dependent on intra-regional trade. But the lesson to be learned from the turmoil of the ERM is that the European Union is not yet ready for fully fixed exchange rates.

Adapted from a letter to the *Economist*, 20 November 1993.

(ii) What purpose does the European Union serve? Is it desirable to force uniformity on a ragbag of countries who have nothing in common with each other but their borders? Isn't one massive European economy serviced by one single currency vulnerable to bureaucracy, inefficiency, fraud and collapse? The EU serves no purpose. It is possible to negotiate trade agreements without sacrificing sovereignty. Technological advances make it practical and the threat of unfettered multinational companies makes it imperative that all the world's nations have their own currencies and economies.

Adapted from a letter in the *Guardian*, 4 June 1994.

Item E *The Maastricht Treaty*

The Maastricht Treaty was drawn up in 1991 and ratified by all members of the European Union in 1993. This cartoon was published in *Private Eye* on 5 November 1993. It portrays John Major (left) talking to his Foreign Secretary, Douglas Hurd.

Item F *The impact of the ERM crisis*

According to a report by City analysts, the low popularity ratings of John Major's government are a direct result of the loss of credibility suffered after the withdrawal from the ERM in September 1992. Normally, the economic recovery which followed this crisis would have put the Conservatives on 42% in the opinion polls. But, the ERM crisis cost them 16% and not even a new leader would make much of a difference. The analysts say that the Major government is only scoring in the mid-20s% because the crisis: 'allowed an economic recovery, but triggered a political collapse which left the government exposed to scandal, internal division and protests about unpopular decisions over pit closures and VAT.' Even if income tax was cut from 25p to 20p this would only recover 7.5% for the Tories. The report suggests that the economy alone will now be unable to deliver a general election victory for the Conservatives.

Adapted from the *Guardian*, 4 June 1994.

Questions

1. a) Using Item A explain how the ERM is meant to work.
   b) Judging from Items A and C would you expect European monetary union to go ahead in 1997? Give reasons for your answer.
2. Using Items B, D, E and F give the arguments for and against membership of the ERM.
3. a) What point is the cartoon in Item E making about European monetary union?
   b) Suppose the cartoon had been used to illustrate an article on the ERM, write the text to accompany the cartoon.
4. According to Item F the ERM crisis cost the government a 16% drop in popularity. Why do you think this was so?
5. Do you think that European monetary union would be beneficial or harmful to Britain? Give reasons for your answer.

3 Britain's economic decline

Key Issues

1. When did Britain's economic decline begin?
2. How has Britain's economy changed since the 19th century?
3. What are the indications of decline?

When did the economic decline begin?

In 1860, Britain was known as the 'workshop of the world'. It was in Britain that new and exciting ways of work had developed. Britain had a large share of world trade and each year increased its industrial output. Other countries regarded Britain as advanced and modern. Indeed, Britain set the standards by which other countries measured their own development. Britain was truly a major world player.

In the 1990s, Britain is no longer top of the economic league. Although the British economy generally continues to grow in absolute terms, the growth is smaller than that achieved by many of Britain's competitors. Although Britain is still the world leader in some fields (for example, pharmaceuticals), often British industrialists look abroad for inspiration - to the USA, to Germany or to Japan.

Today, few people would deny that Britain has suffered an economic decline. It is, however, difficult to pinpoint exactly when this decline began and what was responsible for it, but two perspectives can be isolated.

First, there is the long-term view. This suggests that, because Britain was the first industrial nation, it was inevitable that other countries would catch up and overtake it in terms of output and trade. By the end of the 19th century, Britain's machinery was old and its ways of work outdated. Other countries had the advantage that their industrial revolutions began later and they could, therefore, select what was best and most up-to-date. This gave them an advantage over Britain. By the turn of the century, Britain had lost the initiative. The First World War disrupted Britain's trading patterns and the Second World War was an enormous financial burden from which Britain was unable to recover.

Second, there is the short-term view. This suggests that Britain has been badly managed since the Second World War. According to this view, Britain had an excellent chance to regain its status as a major world player in 1945, but it failed to take its chance. The setting up of the welfare state and the adoption of Keynesian economic policies led to low growth, inefficiency and poor industrial relations.

Explanations of Britain's decline depend in part on ideological preference. It is no surprise to learn, for example, that supporters of laissez faire economics are particularly critical of Britain's economic performance between 1945 and 1979, whilst opponents of laissez faire economics tend to argue that Britain's decline had begun long before 1945 (before 1945, British governments took a laissez faire approach to economic management).

From industrialisation to de-industrialisation

Economists divide the British economy into three sectors. In the **primary sector** raw materials are extracted and food is grown. This sector, therefore, includes farming and coal mining. In the **secondary sector** raw materials are made into goods. This sector, therefore, includes all manufacturing and construction industries. In the **tertiary sector** services are provided. Transport, banking, education and the health service all fall into this sector.

Britain's wealth in the 19th century was mainly derived from the development of manufacturing industries such as textiles, iron and steel and shipbuilding. These industries required the development of new transport systems (canals and then railways) and the exploitation of natural resources (such as coal). The majority of the working population was employed in manufacturing rather than service industries.

The productivity of those industries upon which British wealth had been based (cotton, iron, shipbuilding and coal) declined during the interwar period. There were two main reasons for this. First, by 1918, British production methods had become relatively old fashioned and uncompetitive. And second, established trading patterns were disrupted by the First World War. Japan, for example, managed to increase its trade with the USA by 700% during the war. Much of this trade was taken from Britain (British trade with the USA was curtailed by the war).

Despite this, the British economy as a whole continued to grow at an average rate of 2% per year during the interwar period. This was due, in part, to the growth of new industries. The production of cars, electrical goods, plastics and chemicals, for example, all increased during the interwar period. It should be noted, however, that these new industries, unlike the older industries, tended to be located in the Midlands and the South of England rather than the North of England, Wales and Scotland. This regional diversity led to talk in the 1930s of a North/South divide. When the world depression hit Britain in the 1930s, the North of England, Wales and Scotland suffered higher unemployment rates than the Midlands and the South of England.

In the late 1930s, preparations for war stimulated manufacturing industries such as steel and aircraft production. Then, the outbreak of war led to full employment and emergency economic measures. During the war, the government intervened in the economy much more than had been the case in peacetime. Government intervention and the feeling of solidarity which came from fighting a common enemy brought a new political climate at the end of the Second World War. It was this new political climate which provided the basis of the postwar consensus.

Central to the postwar consensus was the setting up of the welfare state and the nationalisation of key industries such as coal, steel and electricity. At first, it seemed that there would be a revival in the fortunes of British manufacturing industries. Full employment was achieved and postwar reconstruction brought a great demand for goods. But, by the 1960s, Britain's Western European competitors, the USA and Japan were growing at a much faster rate than Britain. Traditional British industries had become uncompetitive and new technologies were being developed elsewhere. The loss of the Empire (see chapter 6, section 4.1) had economic as well as political consequences. Increasingly, Britain seemed to be falling behind.

By 1950, the share of manufacturing output in Britain's total output was 34% whilst the share of services was 49%. Since then, the share of manufacturing has declined whilst the share of services has increased. In addition, manufacturing has not just declined in relative terms, it has declined in absolute terms. Between 1973 and 1976, manufacturing fell by 6% and, between 1979 and 1981, it fell by 14%. By 1989, manufacturing was only 20% higher than in 1969, whilst during the same period there had been a 70% increase in the output of services.

This process of both relative and absolute decline in manufacturing has been termed **de-industrialisation**. Although there was a trend towards de-industrialisation before 1980, it is only since then that the process has become marked. Its most obvious manifestation is the change in the structure and pattern of employment. As a result of the economic policies pursued in the early 1980s, thousands of businesses were forced to slim down or close down. This resulted in a huge rise in unemployment. Manufacturing industries which faced harsh competition from abroad were especially badly hit. Consequently, the traditional manufacturing regions of Britain (Northern England, Scotland and Wales) have suffered higher rates of unemployment than Southern England which has a greater number of service industries.

The causes of de-industrialisation

De-industrialisation has not only occurred in Britain. Britain remains one of the G7 countries (the G7 are the seven largest industrial economies in the world). Other G7 countries show signs of de-industrialisation (for example, falling employment in the 1980s), though at a slower rate than in Britain. Britain experienced the largest fall in manufacturing amongst the seven countries between 1960 and 1988. Also, Britain was the only country to show a consistent fall in employment over that period (see Activity 15.7, Item E below).

One cause of this fast rate of de-industrialisation is the failure of British manufacturing industry to satisfy domestic demand for manufactured goods. In the 1980s, consumer spending rose by 30% whilst manufacturing rose by only 7.8%. During this same period, imports grew to satisfy this demand whilst exports fell. This suggests that British manufacturing industries failed to compete on the world market.

A second reason for the fast rate of de-industrialisation is the British government's low rate of investment. Since 1960, Britain's level of investment (measured as a percentage of GDP) has been the lowest of all G7 countries. Japan's level of investment has been the highest and its growth has also been the highest.

A third reason for the fast rate of de-industrialisation is the nature and organisation of the workforce. Not only is there a long history of poor industrial relations, the British government has failed to train and educate its workers to the level of other G7 countries. In 1988, for example, Germany was spending $3,500 per trainee, Canada was spending $2,300 and France and Japan were spending $1,000 whilst Britain was spending just $400.

Does de-industrialisation matter?

There are three main reasons why de-industrialisation matters. First, the fast rate of de-industrialisation has resulted in very high unemployment. The growth in service industries has failed to provide sufficient job opportunities for all those who have lost their jobs in manufacturing industries. As a result, there is a growing number of long-term unemployed people, especially in areas where manufacturing industries were traditionally based. This trend has been exacerbated by the introduction of labour-saving devices (increased computerisation and so on) within those manufacturing businesses which have survived.

Second, the fast rate of de-industrialisation has increased Britain's balance of payments difficulties. Countries with a strong manufacturing base are able to achieve a balance of payments surplus. But, in Britain, imports have regularly exceeded exports, thus producing a deficit. Government action to reduce such a deficit (raising taxes or interest rates) dampens demand and encourages a further fall in manufacturing output. The fast rate of de-industrialisation, in other words, produces a downwards spiral.

Third, a growth in manufacturing translates into a growth in living standards. Conversely, low manufacturing output means low growth and a poorer standard of living. Britain's fast rate of de-industrialisation means that, relatively speaking, British people are getting poorer than people living in countries with successful manufacturing industries and high growth rates.

Two activities follow. The first looks at Britain's economic decline in general terms. The second examines Britain's de-industrialisation.

Activity 15.6

Item A *The cotton industry*

(i)

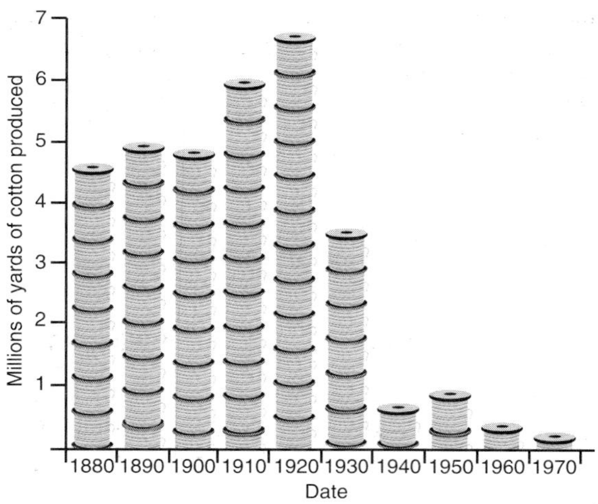

(ii)

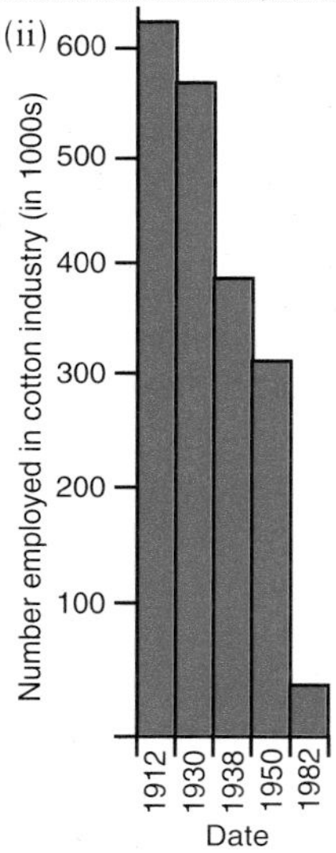

These graphs show the amount of cotton produced in Britain and the number of people employed in the cotton industry.

Adapted from Cook & Stevenson, 1988.

(iii)

I believe that the main reason for the decline was the conservative attitude of the men in charge. Employers, in general, did not face the issue of re-equipment when all the signs were that they should have done. Profits were being made on machinery which was completely out of date. I think they should have installed more modern machinery in the thirties, forties and fifties. Not doing that led to the destruction of the Lancashire cotton industry.

A former manager of a Lancashire cotton mill interviewed in Pagamenta & Overy, 1984.

Item B *Britain between the wars*

Throughout the 1920s, total unemployment in Britain averaged 10-12%. The root problem lay in the structure of British industry. Britain still relied on the old staple industries - mining coal, making iron and steel, building ships and weaving cloth. Where the USA was revolutionising business methods, mechanising factories and investing in research and development, much of Britain carried on as if nothing had changed. The USA developed new markets based, not on the use of coal and steam, but on electricity and oil. The motor car and electrical gadgets for the office and home lent themselves to efficient production with standardised parts, assembly lines and aggressive marketing to produce enormous profits.

Adapted from Dimbleby & Reynolds, 1988.

Item C *The coal industry 1850-1985*

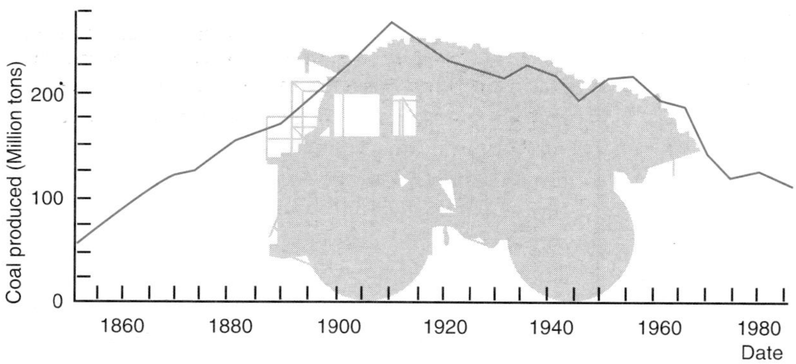

This graph shows the amount of coal produced in Britain between 1850 and 1985.

Adapted from Cook & Stevenson, 1988.

Item D *Unions and management*

It would probably be the fault of the union that the men were being sacked. It usually was. According to the papers, the unions were responsible for all the economic ills of the country. They were too greedy (ie tried to keep up with rising prices), too strong (ie well organised), always on strike (ie only as a last resort), and they were Communists (ie disagreed with management policies). They were criticised for over-manning (ie looking after jobs), underproduction (ie ancient machinery), working to rule (ie doing an 8 hour day) and wanting too much overtime (ie were paid a poor basic rate). All of which reduced profits, discouraged investment and led to redundancies. Which was all the fault of the unions...

Adapted from Hines, 1981.

Item E *The shipbuilding industry*

The growth of South Korea's shipbuilding industry has been spectacular. In 1974, it ranked 70th in the world. Just seven years later, it was second only to Japan. Its premier company Hyundai now boasts one of the world's largest shipyards spreading over five million square metres. It has 45 ships in varying stages of completion. Although it has not escaped the effects of recession, like many other companies in South Korea, Hyundai is jammed to the gills with work. Britain's ailing shipbuilding industry, on the other hand, has shed 23,000 jobs over the past five years and faces further drastic surgery as a result of mounting losses and a continuing lack of orders. British Shipbuilders' Chairman, Sir Robert Atkinson, warned his 65,000 workforce last night: 'We are fighting for our lives.' He says bluntly that men cannot be kept on at yards with no work. Among yards most at risk is Scott Lithgow on the Clyde. This is said to be the world's oldest surviving shipbuilding company formed in 1711. Atkinson said that government cash and protection are needed urgently if yards are to survive against competition from the Far East.

Adapted from the *Sunday Times*, 13 February 1983.

Item F *Car production, 1940-80*

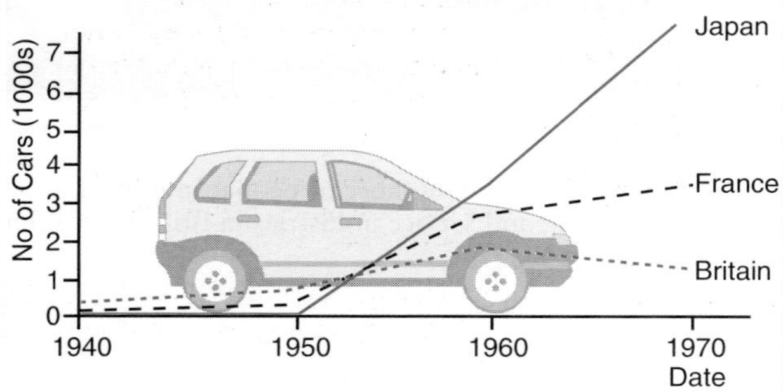

This graph shows the number of cars produced by Britain, France and Japan, 1940-80.

Adapted from Culpin, 1987.

Item G *Britain's share of world trade, 1938-62*

	1938	1950	1951	1959	1962
Britain	22	25	22	17	15
USA	20	27	26	21	20
W. Germany	23*	7	10	19	20
Japan	7	3	4	7	7

* this figure relates to the whole of Germany

This table shows Britain's share of world trade between 1938 and 1962 compared to other leading industrial countries.

Questions

1. a) What evidence is there in Items A-G to suggest that Britain's economic position has declined?
   b) When would you say that this decline started? Explain your answer.
2. What happened to Britain's traditional manufacturing industries (a) between the two world wars and (b) after 1945? What would you expect the short-term and long-term effects of this to be?
3. Who or what is to blame for Britain's economic decline?

Activity 15.7

Item A *UK exports and imports 1955 and 1992*

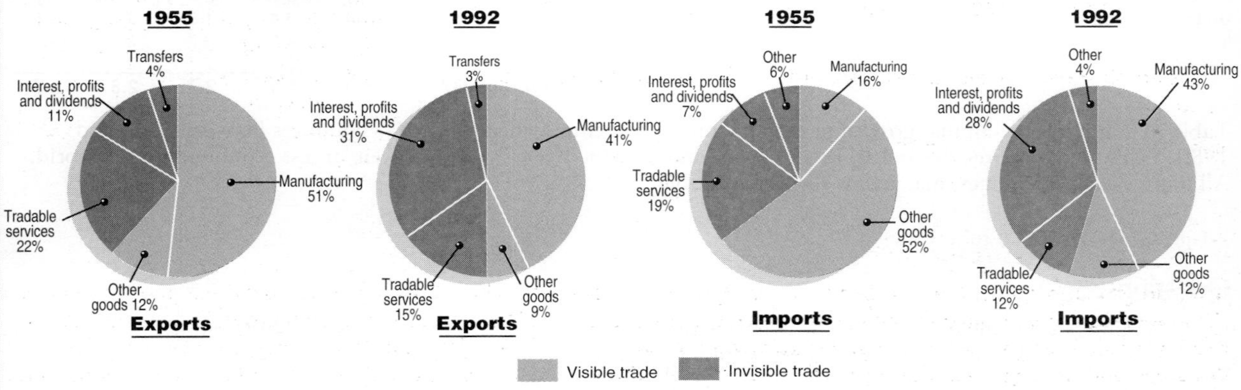

These charts show that, between 1951 and 1992, the contribution to exports made by manufacturing fell from 51% to 41%, whilst the contribution to imports rose from 16% to 43%. This is important because there is little that the government can do to influence the rest of the current account. Interest, profits and dividends are fixed. Other goods are mainly food and raw materials. Tradable services could fill the gap. But, they are only 1/3 of the value of manufacturing.

Adapted from Anderton, 1993.

Item B *Manufacturing and service output, 1950-89*

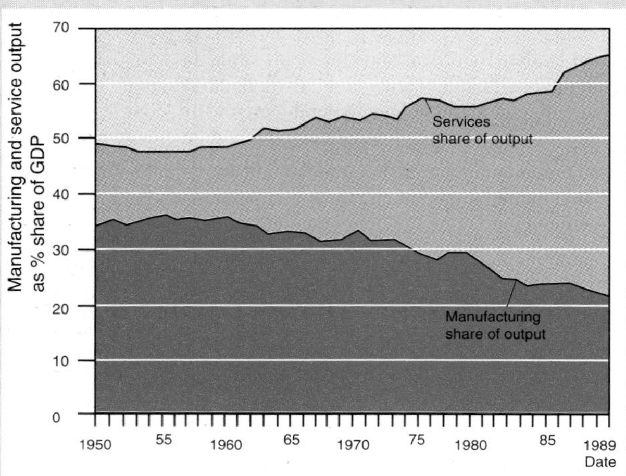

This graph shows manufacturing and service output as a share of GDP.

Adapted from Anderton, 1991.

Item C *Employment in manufacturing and non-manufacturing industry, 1980-92*

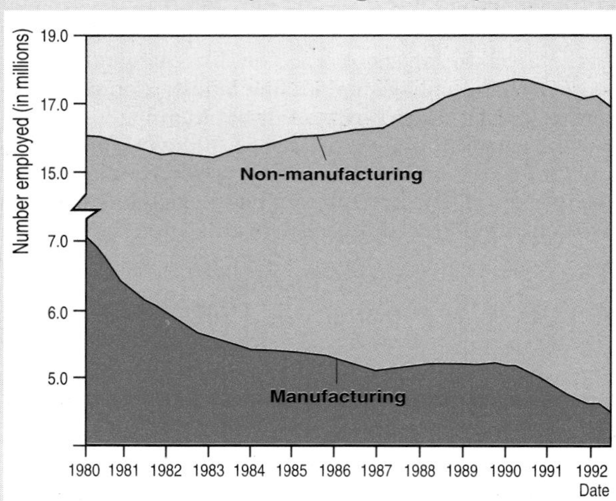

This graph shows the number of people employed in manufacturing and service industries in Britain between 1980 and 1992

Adapted from Chambers, 1993.

Item D *De-industrialisation in the South East*

According to a study published today, the South East of England has become Britain's first de-industrialised region. Services have replaced manufacturing as the backbone of the region's economy. More services are exported than goods. Finance and business have overtaken manufacturing. In the South East, employment trends have changed rapidly. In 1980, manufacturing employed twice as many people as the financial sector. But, by 1989, the financial sector employed 10% more people than manufacturing.

Adapted from the *Financial Times*, 15 January 1990.

Item E *The G7 countries, 1960-88*

(i)

	Manufacturing output as % of GDP			Annual % growth in employment			
	1960	1979	1988	1960-67	1968-73	1974-79	1980-88
United States	28	23	19	1.9	1.0	1.5	0.0
Japan	35	29	29	4.0	2.5	-0.4	0.8
Germany	40	34	31	-0.2	0.9	-1.8	-1.0
France	29	26	21	1.1	1.6	-1.1	-2.0
United Kingdom	**32**	**25**	**21**	**-0.3**	**-1.1**	**-1.2**	**-2.7**
Italy	29	28	23	0.8	0.4	0.3	-1.2
Canada	n.a.	19	17	2.5	2.2	1.9	0.5

(ii)

	Economic growth				
	1960-67	1968-73	1974-79	1980-88	1960-88
United States	4.5	3.2	2.4	2.8	3.3
Japan	10.2	8.7	3.6	4.1	6.5
Germany	4.1	4.9	2.3	1.7	3.1
France	5.4	5.5	2.8	1.9	3.7
United Kingdom	**3.0**	**3.4**	**1.5**	**2.2**	**2.5**
Italy	5.7	4.5	3.7	2.4	4.0
Canada	5.5	5.4	2.7	2.8	4.4
Average G7	**5.0**	**4.4**	**2.7**	**2.8**	**3.7**

Table (i) compares the annual growth in manufacturing and employment in the G7 countries between 1960 and 1980. Table (ii) compares the annual rate of economic growth. The G7 are the seven largest economies in the world. All figures are percentages. n.a. stands for not available.

Adapted from OECD, Historical Statistics.

Questions

1. a) Judging from Items A-D what is the evidence that a process of de-industrialisation has been taking place in Britain since the 1960s?
   b) Can you think of any reasons why this process speeded up in the 1980s?
   c) What have been the consequences of this process?
2. 'De-industrialisation is proceeding at a faster pace in Britain than in other developed economies.'
   a) Explain this statement using Item E .
   b) Explain how this is likely to affect Britain in the long term.
3. Suppose you were invited to advise the government on how to reverse the process of de-industrialisation. What advice would you give?

4 Economic decision making

Key Issues

1. Who makes the key economic decisions?
2. What role do these people play in the decision making process?
3. What factors restrict the scope of the decision makers?
4. How are economic decisions made?

4.1 The key economic decision makers

One of the most important functions of government is to raise money from the public and to decide how this money should be spent. Although all members of the government make decisions which involve the spending of public money, overall responsibility for economic strategy rests with the Chancellor of the Exchequer. The Chancellor is supported by a team of junior ministers and civil servants in the Treasury and by a fellow Cabinet member, the Chief Secretary to the Treasury. In addition, the Chancellor works closely with the Prime Minister. This section looks at the role of the Chancellor and other economic decision makers within the governmental system.

The role of the Chancellor

It is the Chancellor's job to determine how much public money should be raised and how it should be spent. Although the Chancellor does not make such decisions alone, it is upon the Chancellor that final responsibility for these decisions rests. Since economic success, or the perception of it, tends to be translated into electoral success, the Chancellor is, therefore, often regarded as the architect of the government's success or failure.

The Chancellor's most prominent role is the presentation of the annual Budget Statement. In the Budget speech the Chancellor explains how the government intends to raise the money it needs to run public services during the following year. Until 1993, the Budget was announced in early spring (usually March) and public expenditure plans were announced separately in the Autumn Statement. In 1993, this changed. The two statements were joined together and a unified Budget statement was made in November.

In addition to preparing the Budget, the Chancellor is responsible for policy making in the Treasury and for liaising with finance ministers from other countries. According to the former Chancellor Nigel Lawson, British Chancellors have a broader role to play than their counterparts from overseas:

> '[The job of the Chancellor of the Exchequer] is an absorbing one and a difficult one, at times a frustrating one; but it is also a particularly demanding one. We are unusual in Britain in that the Chancellor has responsibility for taxation, for the control of public expenditure and for the whole of monetary policy, including interest rates and the management of sterling. In other countries these jobs are normally divided up. In the United States, for example, the Treasury Secretary is responsible for tax; the Director of the Office of Management and the Budget (OMB) for public expenditure; and the Chairman of the Federal Reserve for the monetary side.' (Lawson, 1992, p.272)

Lawson argues that this concentration of responsibilities is healthy since it allows a coherence of policy. But, it can put the Chancellor under great strain. Denis Healey, Labour Chancellor from 1974 to 1979 recalled that:

> 'It was exceptionally hard and frustrating work. The Chancellor of the Exchequer's is a lonely job, particularly in a period like mine when he was obliged to disappoint the hopes of his party and the aspirations of his colleagues - not to speak of his own.' (Healey, 1989, p.388)

It is, perhaps, worth noting that only two postwar Prime Ministers have made a direct move from Number 11 to Number 10 Downing Street - Harold Macmillan and John Major. Two others served as Chancellors earlier in their career. Winston Churchill was Chancellor in the 1920s and James Callaghan was Chancellor from 1964 to 1967. Callaghan then served as Home Secretary (1967-70) and Foreign Secretary (1974-76) before becoming Prime Minister in 1976.

Since the Chancellor is responsible for the government's overall economic strategy, there is a great deal of scope for influencing policies which are not the direct responsibility of the Treasury. Nigel Lawson admitted that:

> 'If somebody had managed to penetrate security and called on me at a random hour of the working day, he would probably have found me not considering interest rates or exchange rates or government borrowing - the issues so beloved of financial commentators - but playing a substantial role on a Cabinet Committee on a vast range of subjects...The Chancellor, if he proceeds with care and caution, can affect the content and not merely the cost of other ministers' policies and, in a limited number of carefully selected areas, generate the ideas which decisively influence the direction of government policy...This is exemplified by the

long-standing rule that any minister who has a proposal to put before Cabinet must first submit it to the Treasury.' (Lawson, 1992, p.273)

The Budget

The Budget is a political set piece which has developed its own traditions. Under the pre-1993 system, the Chancellor would announce details of the government's spending plans in the Autumn Statement (usually in early November) and then spend the next few months deciding how much money the government would need to raise in taxes to pay for these plans. Between 1982 and 1993, all the Treasury ministers and their advisers would meet at a country house in Kent for the 'Chevening Weekend' early in the new year. This would be a time for reflecting about the major options open to the Chancellor in light of current and forecast economic performance. No final decisions would be taken, but the available choices would be discussed. Jock Bruce-Gardyne recalls some of the choices faced at a Chevening Weekend when he was a junior Treasury minister in the mid-1980s:

> 'Would oil prices, so crucial to our revenues, and the exchange rate for sterling, behave themselves? Could the Budget help us to turn the tide of unemployment? What did the Tory backbenchers expect of us on Budget day and what were the potential points of trouble with the disaffected? How were we to cope with President Reagan's "supply side economic", creating a huge budget deficit and sucking in the savings of the world to finance it? (Bruce-Gardyne, 1986, p.184)

In the two months before Budget day, the Chancellor would go into 'purdah' (an Urdu word for a curtain used to keep women hidden from men). During the period of purdah, the Chancellor would keep a low public profile and refuse to answer any questions on matters relating to the Budget. Even the Cabinet would not be informed of details until the last moment.

Budget day would normally be held in mid-March, just before the beginning of the financial year in April. In the morning, the Chancellor would be photographed holding an old battered Gladstone Budget box. These photographs would invariably appear on the front page of the following day's newspapers.

Following proposals made by the former Chancellor Norman Lamont, after March 1993 the spring Budget and the period of purdah were scrapped and a unified Budget established. It was argued that it made sense to discuss raising and spending public money together and openly so that taxpayers could see clearly how the money they paid in taxes would be spent. But, a number of criticisms have been made of this new system (see Activity 15.8).

Relations between the Chancellor and Prime Minister

According to Nigel Lawson, the relationship between the Chancellor and Prime Minister is of great importance:

> 'A Chancellor who is doing his job properly has few friends. That is one reason why it is of vital importance to the successful conduct of government that there is an extremely close and special relationship between the Chancellor of the day and the Prime Minister. They do not have to be cronies or soul mates, but they do have to be on the same wavelength. This was the case with Margaret Thatcher and myself for very many years. When the harmony came to an end, I took the view that it was impossible to do the job effectively and, therefore, it was better not to do it at all.' (Lawson, 1992, p.273)

Grant (1992) notes that the close relationship between Chancellor and Prime Minister is symbolised by the unlocked connecting door between 10 and 11 Downing Street. He argues that there are three basic types of relationship. First, there are compliant Chancellors who willingly follow the wishes of a strong Prime Minister. Second, there are cases where the Chancellor and Prime Minister have managed to form a partnership of equals. And third, there have been occasions when an independent Chancellor is pressurised by the Prime Minister into reluctantly following a particular line. Whatever the personalities of the individuals, however, prime ministerial participation in economic decision making is now part of the established procedure.

The role of the Treasury

The importance of the Treasury is indicated by the fact that it is the only government department to be represented in the Cabinet by two members (the Chancellor of the Exchequer and the Chief Secretary to the Treasury). Although the Treasury stands at the centre of the economic decision making process it is a small, intimate department with around 350 officials at the rank of principal and above. Like other government departments, the Treasury is hierarchical and is staffed jointly by ministers and civil servants. It is headed by the permanent secretary, one of the most high ranking posts in the civil service.

The Treasury has three main functions. First, it provides senior ministers (notably the Prime Minister and Chancellor) with policy advice concerning the general management of the economy. Second, the Treasury is the key institution in which decisions about the raising and spending of public money are made. Third, together with the Bank of England, the Treasury is responsible for designing policies relating to financial markets and international economic institutions (such as the International Monetary Fund and the European Union).

In practice, this means that the central task of the

Treasury is the preparation of the annual Budget. In addition, the Treasury provides information and advice to ministers on matters such as the control of the money supply, the raising or lowering of interest rates and exchange rates and the management of the government's debt.

Although Treasury officials, like any other civil servants, are supposed to be politically neutral, critics have argued that there is a distinct 'Treasury view' of the British economy and Chancellors are put under pressure to conform to this view. For example, Denis Healey has accused the Treasury of:

> 'Misleading the government, the country and the world for so many years about the true state of public spending in Britain. Indeed, I suspect that Treasury officials were content to overstate public spending in order to put pressure on governments who were reluctant to cut it.' (Healey, 1989, p.402)

The role of the Chief Secretary to the Treasury

The minister in charge of the annual expenditure round is the Chief Secretary to the Treasury. It is the Chief Secretary who conducts the 'bilaterals' - separate meetings with each minister in charge of a government department. It is at these bilaterals that the amount of money to be allocated to a particular department is finally decided.

During the 1980s, senior ministers (notably the Prime Minister, Margaret Thatcher) publicly advocated a reduction in public expenditure. As a result, ministers in charge of government departments came under pressure to cut their department's spending. Understandably, ministers were then torn between the need to make cutbacks and the desire to finance projects which would improve the performance of their department. It was the job of the Chief Secretary to work out where priorities should lie and where cutbacks should be made. It was as Chief Secretary to the Treasury in the 1980s that John Major first came to prominence.

During the 1990s, the reduction in public expenditure has remained a priority. As a result, much still depends on the skill of the Chief Secretary in resolving the rival demands of the Treasury and individual departments. But, having said that, in practice, most public expenditure is committed in advance:

> 'Even if they wished to do so, it would be a mistake to think that departments had complete freedom of manoeuvre to decide their plans for the coming year. About two thirds of all public expenditure consists of programmes, such as social security benefit, which are determined by entitlement or demand. Another 20% consists of long-term commitments, such as payments to finance European Community expenditure, notably the Common Agricultural Policy. This leaves only 10-15% which is open to short-term variation. Most of this expenditure can only be varied quickly at the margin, though in the long run, of course, all expenditure can be varied by altering entitlement to benefits and long-term commitments. (Likierman, 1988, p.42)

Activity 15.8

Item A *The financial year 1992-93*

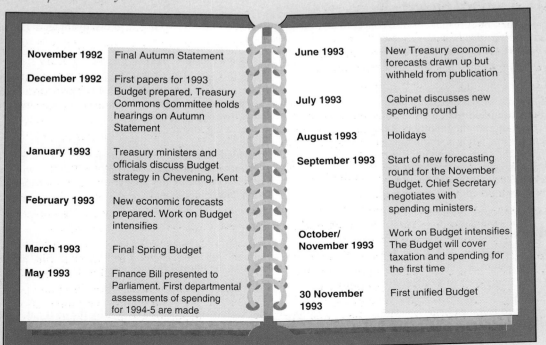

November 1992	Final Autumn Statement
December 1992	First papers for 1993 Budget prepared. Treasury Commons Committee holds hearings on Autumn Statement
January 1993	Treasury ministers and officials discuss Budget strategy in Chevening, Kent
February 1993	New economic forecasts prepared. Work on Budget intensifies
March 1993	Final Spring Budget
May 1993	Finance Bill presented to Parliament. First departmental assessments of spending for 1994-5 are made
June 1993	New Treasury economic forecasts drawn up but withheld from publication
July 1993	Cabinet discusses new spending round
August 1993	Holidays
September 1993	Start of new forecasting round for the November Budget. Chief Secretary negotiates with spending ministers.
October/ November 1993	Work on Budget intensifies. The Budget will cover taxation and spending for the first time
30 November 1993	First unified Budget

Item B *A unified Budget (1)*

A month before the first unified Budget is to be presented, the new system has come under attack. One senior Conservative said that the change could cost the Conservatives the next general election. The government had won the last three elections by holding an election within weeks of announcing income tax cuts in March. Nobody had considered that it would make no sense to call an election in January. Conservative party managers are also worried about the danger of backbench rebellions. In the past, the finance bill was debated in April after the tax changes announced in the Budget were already in place. The new system, however, allows a five month gap that could be exploited by rebels, especially if the economic outlook were to change during that period. Treasury officials are worried about the huge margins of error that might result from making decisions nearly six months before the start of the new financial year. This problem is particularly acute this year because the pace of economic recovery is uncertain. Whilst Treasury officials agree that the Chancellor should announce significant tax increases, they acknowledge that, because evidence of recovery will remain patchy until next year, the political pressures are in the opposite direction.

Adapted from the *Independent*, 28 October 1993.

Item C *A unified Budget (2)*

This cartoon appeared in the *Independent* on 29 November 1993, the day before the Chancellor Kenneth Clarke presented the first unified Budget.

Item D *A unified Budget (3)*

Whilst a unified Budget makes sense conceptually, the proposal suffers from two practical disadvantages. The first is the need to determine how large the PSBR for the year ahead should be and to frame a Budget consistent with this at a time when the margin for uncertainty over the outcome of the PSBR for the current year remains enormous. The second is the immense burden of work the new system will impose on the Chancellor of the day and his top officials in the three month period between his return from the summer holidays in September and the Budget Statement. All the key decisions on both public expenditure and taxation will be concentrated into this period. This is a problem which other countries avoid by having two separate departments headed by two different ministers responsible for the two sides of the Budget. If, in addition, a unified Budget tilts the balance back towards the public spending lobbies (which it could well do even though the intention is clearly the reverse) it could be a big mistake. It is true that in my day a crucial argument for excluding spending decisions from the March Budget was the need to avoid allowing spending ministers two bites of the cherry - one in November with the Autumn statement and a second in March with the Budget. The proposed amalgamation will certainly eliminate that danger. But, it will still require a strong Chancellor who enjoys the full backing of the Prime Minister to overcome the risks inherent in converting the Budget from an event solely concerned with taxation to one shared equally by taxation and spending decisions.

Adapted from Lawson, 1992.

Questions

1. Judging from Items A-D, if you belonged to a pressure group seeking extra money when would be the best time to lobby ministers (a) before there was a unified Budget or (b) after the unified Budget was introduced?
2. a) Using Items A-D write down the advantages and disadvantages of having a unified Budget.
   b) Do the advantages outweigh the disadvantages? Explain your answer.
3. Write an editorial passage to accompany the cartoon in Item C. Explain in the passage why the next day's Budget would be breaking new ground and what might be the consequences of this.

4.2 External influences on economic decision making

In addition to the pressures and advice which come from within the governmental system, economic decision makers have to take account of the views of individuals and institutions outside the governmental system. Although the weight attached to particular pieces of advice varies according to the personality and overall strategy of the decision maker, there are three main sources of pressure and advice outside the governmental system - economic advisers, the Bank of England and international institutions.

Economic advisers

Although the major economic decision makers (the Chancellor and the Prime Minister) receive a great deal of advice from economic advisers working within the governmental system (for example from the hundred or so members of the Government Economic Service who are spread across the government departments), economic advisers outside the governmental system also exert pressure on economic decision making. Financial experts are employed by the mass media to comment on every move made by the Chancellor and often media campaigns are launched to try and alter the direction in which the government's economic strategy is moving. A good example of external economic advisers trying to put pressure on the government was a letter published in the *Times* shortly after Geoffrey Howe's Budget in 1981. This letter protested against the folly of government economic policy and was signed by 364 British economists.

As with pressure groups (see chapter 10, section 1.3), economic advisers who manage to gain insider status have a better chance of influencing the outcome of the decision making process than those with outsider status. It is normal for the Chancellor and the Prime Minister to listen to independent economic advisers (usually academics seconded from universities) whose ideological stance is compatible with their own. On occasions, this can cause problems. When Margaret Thatcher's economic adviser, Professor Alan Walters, publicly disagreed with the view of the Chancellor, Nigel Lawson, in 1989 this led to Lawson's resignation.

Since 1992, the division between independent and non-independent advisers has been blurred. In that year, the Chancellor, Norman Lamont, announced the setting up of a new panel of independent economic forecasters (the 'seven wise men') to advise the Chancellor. This formalised what had previously been an informal relationship.

The Bank of England

The Bank of England is Britain's central bank. Although the Bank is a public body (it was nationalised in 1946 and is, therefore, owned by the government), it retains a degree of independence from government. Its Governor, for example, is nominated by the Prime Minister, but is usually an independent figure. Employees of the Bank are not civil servants. They are recruited independently and paid more than civil servants.

When the Bank was nationalised no clear guidance was given as to what its role should be. As a result, it has performed a wider role than other central banks. The Bank has a number of functions. First, it is responsible for the issue of notes and coins. Second, it supervises Britain's financial system. For example, one of its roles is to prevent fraud and dishonest trading by financial institutions. Third, it advises government on monetary policy and implements the decisions made by government in this area. Fourth, it manages the Exchange Equalisation Account - the account used to buy and sell foreign currency. The Bank's role is to maintain a given level of sterling in the foreign exchange markets. Fifth, it acts as a banker to the government. It manages the National Debt and arranges government loans. And sixth, it acts as a banker to the banking system. All banks have to keep 0.5% of their liabilities with the Bank of England and, if banks are short of cash and other liquid assets, the Bank of England arranges loans for them.

It should be clear from this list of functions that the Bank of England plays a central role in the formulation of economic policy - especially economic policy which depends on the control of the monetary supply. It is no surprise, therefore, to find that Nigel Lawson argues that the role of the Bank grew in importance after 1975:

> 'Constitutionally, the Bank was subordinate to the Treasury and merely carried out in the financial markets the wishes of its political masters. In reality, apart from the critical issue of the level of interest rates, the Bank had considerable discretion. Yet, as monetary concerns assumed greater importance in economic policy after 1975, and still more after 1979, the activities of the Bank became central to the success of government strategy.' (Lawson, 1992, p.83).

It is also, perhaps, no surprise to find that greater government involvement in the control of the money supply was resented by the Bank:

> 'The tension was undoubtedly exacerbated by our making it clear that the Chancellor was now in unequivocal control of monetary policy. The Bank could not be expected to like the new approach, even though it had never at that time taken monetary policy very seriously... Successive Governors concentrated, instead, on reading stern lectures on matters outside their

> responsibility, such as the need to control public spending and to maintain a tight incomes policy.' (Lawson, 1992, p.83)

The tension referred to in this passage arose because it seemed that the Bank's independence was being eroded. Just how independent the Bank of England should be is a question which is frequently debated.

Arguments against an independent Bank of England

At present, if the British government decides to loosen monetary policy, for example by lowering interest rates, it can order the Bank of England to carry out this policy on its behalf. If the Bank of England was independent, then it would not have to follow the policy favoured by the government. It might choose to keep interest rates high, for example, even though the government wanted to lower them. Those who oppose an independent Bank of England argue that elected representatives should have control over economic decisions rather than professional bankers. Elected representatives are accountable to the electorate whilst professional bankers are not.

Because both Margaret Thatcher and John Major have opposed calls for the creation of an independent Bank of England, the journalist Samuel Brittan has argued that this is a sign that Prime Ministers want to be heavily involved in economic policy making (*Financial Times*, 17 June 1993). But, since the perception of economic success is so important electorally, it is perhaps understandable that senior government members are reluctant to allow their grip on economic policy to be loosened.

Arguments for an independent Bank of England

In November 1988, the Chancellor, Nigel Lawson, issued a memorandum to Margaret Thatcher advocating the creation of an independent but accountable Bank of England. Although the proposal was rejected, Lawson returned to it in his resignation speech. Lawson saw three advantages in giving the Bank of England independence. First, monetary policy would be formulated by a body whose sole task was to do just this. Monetary policy would, therefore, be formulated by experts rather than amateur politicians with a political axe to grind. Second, the removal of political pressures would enable greater cooperation between the Bank of England and other central banks. And third, depoliticising the Bank would not only depoliticise interest rates it would increase the Bank's credibility with the market and prevent governments trying to make their policies seem more attractive just before a general election.

According to Samuel Brittan (writing in the *Financial Times*), arguments in favour of an independent Bank gain strength from an examination of what happened in New Zealand. New Zealand's central bank, the Reserve Bank, was granted total independence over the operation of monetary and exchange rate policy in 1990. Since then, the government's role has been to define price stability and to set a target range for inflation. The Governor of the Reserve Bank is given a fixed term contract and is held personally responsible for delivering this inflation rate. For the first three years this was a success:

> 'The Act marked a watershed for New Zealand which has suffered double digit inflation for most of the 20 years since 1970...Growth in GNP [Gross National Product, a measure of national income] has reached 3% in 12 months and is widely expected to stay near this rate.' (*Financial Times*, 23 June 1993)

Not only has the New Zealand economy grown since 1990, Don Brash, Governor of the Reserve Bank, argues that the new arrangement prevents governments from:

> 'Saying one thing to the public about the need to control inflation and at the same time trying to get the mortgage rates down before an election.' (*Financial Times*, 23 June 1993).

International constraints on economic decision making

As economic barriers between countries break down, individual countries have less freedom of manoeuvre. Since 1945, there has been greater economic interdependence and, as a result, economic management in Britain has increasingly been affected by external constraints.

One constraint is the increasing globalisation of financial markets. Modern methods of communication have linked together stock exchanges in different parts of the world and this has made an impact on the economies of individual countries. For example, if Britain is going through a difficult period economically, traders on the London exchanges will be up early to hear how sterling has been faring in Tokyo. Movements in Japan will influence the value of sterling against other currencies on the London market and this, in turn, will affect the price of shares in London. If the pound falls sharply and shares begin to tumble, the British government may have to intervene - for example, by asking the Bank of England to buy sterling or by raising interest rates.

A second constraint is the influence of international economic organisations, notably the International Monetary Fund (IMF). The IMF was set up at the end of the Second World War. Its function is to stabilise exchange rates and to lend money to its members when they need foreign currency. Members pay a regular sum into the pool on the understanding that they can borrow from the pool when they have balance of payments problems. When the IMF makes a loan, however, it does so only if the government requesting the loan meets certain conditions. A request for assistance from the IMF by the Labour government in 1976, for example, led to significant changes in government policy (so that the IMF conditions were met). The Chancellor, Denis Healey, abandoned Keynesian demand management policies and introduced measures designed to control the money supply (see also chapter 3, pp.43-44).

A third constraint is the membership of GATT - the General Agreement of Tariffs and Trade. GATT was set up in 1947. Its aim was to prevent a repetition of the Great Depression (during the 1930s many countries devalued their currencies and set up trade barriers to save and create jobs in their domestic markets. Because many countries did this, the result was a fall in overall trade and a deeper depression). GATT has established a system of rules governing international trade. One rule is that member nations are not allowed to increase the degree of protection given to their domestic producers. A second rule (the most favoured nation clause) is that a country which offers a cut in tariffs to one country has to offer it to all members. To encourage countries to reduce tariffs and quotas, GATT organises a series of negotiations ('rounds'). At the first round of talks in Geneva in 1947, there were just 23 members. At the Uruguay round in 1993, there were 116 members. Each round builds on the work of earlier talks. In the early days, the main job was cutting tariffs. More recently, rules against dumping exports (the sale of a product in an export market at a cheaper price than that charged in the domestic market) have been introduced. Since Britain is a member of GATT, Britain's economic decision makers are obliged to conform to the rules established by GATT.

Similarly, British economic decision makers are constrained by membership of the European Union (EU). The creation of a single internal market in 1992 has led to greater uniformity and standardisation. The need to conform to European standards has restricted individual member states' freedom of manoeuvre. Whilst membership of the EU brings many trading advantages, concern about the extent to which economic decision makers in member states will be able to determine their own economic future is at the heart of the sovereignty debate which has preoccupied many British politicians since the late 1980s.

Activity 15.9

Item A *The Bank of England's range of activities (1)*

Functions of central banks

	Bundesbank (Germany)	Federal Reserve (USA)	Bank of Japan	Bank of France	Bank of England
Independent monetary policy	yes	yes	no	no	no
Government funding	no	no	no	no	yes
Banknote printing	no	no	no	yes	yes
Promotion of financial centre	no	no	no	partial	yes*
Intervention in company/ creditor rows	no	no	no	no	sometimes

* The Bank of England does much to promote the City of London

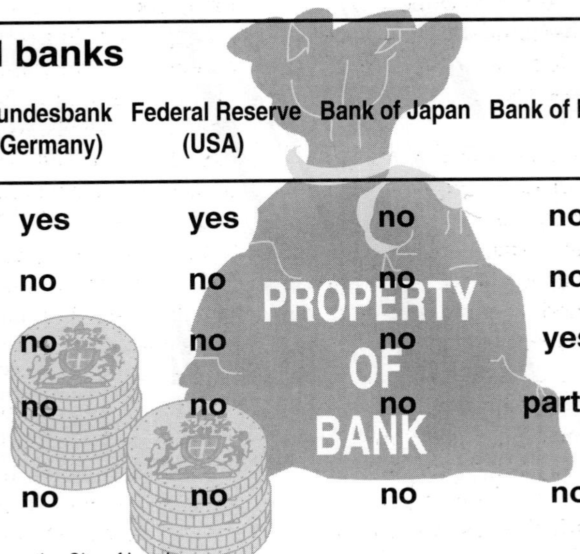

This table compares the functions of the Bank of England with those of central banks in four leading industrial countries.

Adapted from the *Economist*, 28 August 1993.

Item B *The government and the Bank*

This cartoon appeared in the *Guardian* on 16 May 1994. It shows Chancellor Kenneth Clarke cycling with the Old Lady of Threadneedle Street (the Bank of England is also known as the Old Lady of Threadneedle Street).

Item C *Who should control the economy?*

Who should control the economy - the bankers or politicians? The bankers argue that the value of the currency is too important an issue to be left in the hands of the politicians. The politicians say that its very importance means that those who deal with it should be democratically accountable. Today, this debate boils down to an argument between monetarists and Keynesians. Monetarists claim that all that matters is the control of the money supply. Therefore, it is best to contract the job out to bankers who will treat it as a technical problem free from political considerations. The Keynesians, however, believe that government should intervene and manage demand through interest rates, exchange rates and so on to achieve political objectives such as full employment. Whenever the bankers have had the upper hand, the result has been the same - an obsession with zero inflation which has stifled demand and led to recession. That was the case in the 1930s and it is the case today. But, the idea that deciding monetary policy is somehow a politically neutral activity is self- delusion. Prosperity and social cohesion depend on how and in whose interests these decisions are made. Bankers will always represent the interests of their asset holders and, therefore, give priority to those who hold wealth. There can be no starker political choice than whether to run the economy in the interests of the wealthy or the workers. To contract-out to the bankers the power of decision over the central questions of economic management is an affront to and a denial of democracy.

Adapted from the *Guardian*, 5 January 1994.

Item D *Pressures on the Chancellor*

The Governor of the Bank of England and the Chancellor's own economic advisers yesterday made public their advice concerning interest rates and tax policy. Eddie George, Governor of the Bank of England, argued that higher inflation was a greater threat than a slowdown in the recovery. He reiterated his opposition to interest rate cuts. Further warnings came from the Treasury's 'wise men'. Four of the six panel members agreed with George that a further cut was unjustified. At the same time, four of the six urged the Chancellor, Kenneth Clarke, not to reverse the current programme of tax increases. Yet, two days ago, the Chancellor said that tax cuts would be back on the agenda once public finances had been sorted out. John Shepperd, chief economist at Yamaichi International (Europe) said: 'It may not be an independent central bank, but a central bank which goes public with its advice is the next best thing. Eddie is laying down the law and has Clarke boxed into a corner.'

Adapted from the *Times*, 20 May 1994.

Item E *The Bank of England's range of activities (2)*

'Too many pies for the Old Lady'

This cartoon acompanied an article in the *Economist* (28 August 1993) which argued that there were two main advantages to slimming down the Bank of England's range of activities. First, there would be a stronger case for independence in monetary policy. Second, it would mean the Treasury taking over work now being done by the Bank. To do this extra work properly, the Treasury would have to improve its knowledge of financial markets. If it did that, then it would be much warier of running up such large budget deficits.

Questions

1. You have been asked to brief your local MP on the issue of whether or not the Bank of England should be independent. Write a briefing paper which gives the arguments in support of your view and prepares your MP for the counter arguments that might be used by supporters of the opposing point of view.
2. Give arguments for and against the view that the Bank of England should be responsible for monetary policy and nothing else. Use Items A, C and E in your answer.
3. Look at Items B and D. Do you think the cartoonist was right to show the Chancellor driving in the front seat or should it be the other way round? Give reasons for your answer.

5 The debate over taxation

Key Issues

1. What is the difference between direct and indirect taxation?
2. Why is the level of taxation important?
3. Why has taxation been a crucial issue in recent elections?
4. Alternative systems of taxation.

Taxation and general elections

Since the Conservatives gained power in 1979, they have been careful to manipulate the economic cycle so that the Chancellor has been able to announce income tax cuts just before the Prime Minister announces the date of a general election. Most people agree that this is an important reason for the Conservatives' success in general elections. Indeed, in the 1992 general election, the debate over taxation was billed by many commentators as the key issue of the campaign. This section looks at the debate over taxation and examines why it has been so important.

Direct and indirect taxation

Taxes can be raised in two ways - either directly or indirectly. Direct taxation is a tax levied directly on an individual or an organisation. Income tax is one form of direct taxation. Everyone earning more than a minimum amount pays a percentage of their earnings to central government in income tax. The rate of income tax is fixed by the Chancellor and announced in the Budget speech each year. Income tax is the single most important source of revenue for the government. Other examples of direct tax are corporation tax (a tax on company profits), inheritance tax (a tax on the value of assets left by an individual on their death) and capital gains tax (a tax on real capital gains - the difference between the buying price and selling price of an asset after adjustment for inflation. Most goods and services are exempt from this tax. It is paid mainly on stocks and shares). In addition, National Insurance Contributions (NICs) are, in effect, a form of direct taxation (strictly speaking NICs are not taxes because they are a form of insurance premium, but they have come to be seen and used by government as a form of taxation). All workers have to pay NICs to qualify for certain state benefits. Employers also pay NICs for each worker they employ.

Indirect taxation is a tax levied on goods or services. The tax is indirect since it is only paid by those people who buy the goods or use the services which are subject to it. The main indirect tax is VAT (Value Added Tax). This is a tax on expenditure. 'Essential' goods and services such as food and children's clothes are exempt from VAT. All other goods and services are taxed.

Excise duties - such as the taxes levied on alcoholic drinks, tobacco and petrol - are the second main type of indirect tax. The level of excise duty is calculated not by value (as with VAT), but by volume sold.

Since all but 5% of government revenue is gained from taxation, the levels at which the various taxes are set is of crucial importance. Each year the government needs to raise a certain amount of revenue to finance public services and the government's programme. This money is raised from both direct and indirect taxes. The dilemma that faces the government, once it has determined how much money it needs to raise, is what proportion of this money should be raised from direct taxation and what proportion from indirect taxation. The choice made by the government determines to a large extent how the nation's wealth is shared out.

Why is the level of taxation important?

The money that is raised from taxes is spent on public services. The more money that is raised, the more money there is for spending on education, the health service and so on. But, against this, the more money that is raised in taxes, the less money that people have to spend themselves. If the level of direct taxes is high, people's take-home pay is low. If the level of indirect tax is high, goods and services become expensive.

For Keynesians, the level of taxation is important since it helps to determine demand. The raising or lowering of taxes slows down or boosts demand and is, therefore, a tool used to manipulate the economic cycle.

Taxation can also be used to influence consumption patterns. By placing large duties on tobacco and spirits, for example, the government discourages people from buying these products.

Taxation since 1979

Since 1979, successive Conservative governments have attempted to shift the burden from direct to indirect taxes. In the 1979 Budget, the rate of VAT was increased from 8% to 15% and the extra revenue raised was used to finance cuts in income tax (the top rate of income tax was reduced from 83% to 60%). This set the trend. Between 1979 and 1990, the top rate of income tax fell from 83% to 40% and the standard rate fell from 33% to 25%. During the same period, the amount of government income raised from income tax dropped from 31% to 26.6% whilst the amount of government income raised from indirect taxes (excise duties and VAT) rose from 27.9% to 30.6%. This suggests that the tax burden was shifting from direct to indirect taxes. But, during the same period, NICs paid by employees increased as a percentage of tax revenue whilst contributions paid by employers declined. It could be argued, therefore, that part of the reduction in income tax has effectively been paid for by the overall increase in NICs.

As a result of these changes, there has been a change in the distribution of wealth in the country. Between 1985 and 1994 the richest 10% of the population added 6% to their net income whilst middle earners added 0.4% and the poorest 10% have seen their incomes fall by 3% (Balls, 1994). These figures show that changes in taxation have resulted in the poor becoming poorer whilst the rich have become richer. This happens because the lower the income of a family, the greater the proportion of that income which is spent on goods and services which charge indirect taxes. When the Chancellor, Norman Lamont, announced in 1993 that VAT would be charged on domestic fuel, one Conservative backbench MP admitted that the consequence of this would be that:

> 'People on lower incomes will pay a higher proportion of income in tax than those earning more...In the case of food or domestic heating ...such a tax would bear disproportionately on lower income earners.' (*Independent*, 29 November 1993)

Electoral advantage, ideology and taxation

To a large extent, the hands of government are tied (see above p.457). Up to 90% of government expenditure is fixed. Long-term commitments and public services have to be financed and it is the government's responsibility to raise money to pay for them. The question that the party of government has to address is how should this money be raised? The Conservative and Labour parties give fundamentally different answers to this question. The answers which they give are determined by their ideological commitments.

Since 1979, the Conservative party has promoted itself as the party of low taxation and 'sound' economic management. Low taxation (which, in practice, means low rates of direct taxation and high rates of indirect taxation) has been a priority for two main reasons. First, such a policy has electoral appeal. According to Nigel Lawson:

> 'There are large numbers of people in this country who have been conditioned to believe that it sounds better to say that they would like to see more money spent on worthy public services - however doubtful they may be about whether the worthy public services will improve as a result - than that they would like to receive a tax cut. But, when it comes to casting a vote which might determine which of the two takes place, it is a different matter altogether. This was clearly demonstrated, to my complete lack of surprise, by the outcome of the 1987 general election.' (Lawson, 1992, p.377).

And second, low taxation fits with the ideological goals of the Conservative party. Since 1979, the aim of Conservative governments has been to create an economy in which market forces predominate. Since, according to Conservative thought, it is the 'captains of industry' and individual entrepreneurs who are responsible for economic progress, it is considered important to ensure that these individuals are given every incentive to perform well. Low income tax achieves this since it ensures that people have a larger percentage of their earnings to spend as they see fit. In other words, low taxation empowers individuals and allows them suitable rewards for the contribution that they make. This was the message in Geoffrey Howe's Budget speech in 1979 when he said that the Conservatives aimed to cut taxes because:

> 'This is the only way we can restore incentives and make it worthwhile to work.'

Traditionally, the Labour party has favoured a greater emphasis on direct rather than indirect taxation. Direct taxes, it is argued, are fairer because they are determined by the ability to pay. If VAT is added to a product, the same price is paid by a person on income support and a millionaire. It is better to raise public money from those who can afford it. Therefore, it is better to raise public money by taxing the income of the millionaire. As a result, under Labour governments, income tax rates were graduated to ensure that high earners paid high rates of income tax. The effect of this was to redistribute wealth from the rich to the poor.

Although Labour has undoubtedly suffered in general elections because it is perceived as a 'tax and spend' party, this may not be the case in the future. In 1993, the Conservative government was forced to raise taxes in an attempt to reduce the huge budget deficit (over £50 billion). In January 1994, the Labour party was able to provide evidence that, for the first time in 15 years, tax levels under a Conservative government exceeded the tax levels of the last Labour government. Since the main thrust of the Conservatives' 1992 general election campaign had been that a vote for Labour would mean a vote for higher taxes whilst a vote for the Conservatives would not, Labour was able to charge the government with hypocrisy and dent the Conservative party's image as a party of low taxation.

Alternative systems of taxation

One problem with the existing taxation system is that money raised from different taxes all goes into a central pool. Some people argue that it would be better if certain taxes were targeted for specific purposes. For example, the Liberal Democrats, in their 1992 election manifesto, suggested that the money collected from a 1p rise in income tax should be used exclusively to improve education. If this was done, the argument goes, people would be less resentful of paying taxes because they would be able to see that the money they paid was being used for specific, concrete projects and not just being swallowed up by government bureaucracy. Similarly, when President Clinton increased the income tax paid by high earners, the money collected was set aside in a special trust so that people could see exactly how much was collected and what it was used for. By doing this, President Clinton avoided the criticism that he was a typical 'high tax, high spend' Democrat.

A second alternative means of taxation is the ad hoc local tax. At present, local authorities are not able to improve their services by raising extra money by ad hoc or 'one-off' taxes. The advantage of allowing such taxes would be that local people could choose to raise money for specific projects. The think tank Demos argues that such taxes should be levied only if local people vote for them in referendums (Demos, 1993).

Activity 15.10

Item A *Tax will not be a big issue*

The next election is at least two years away, but it will clearly be very different from the last election. Tax, for a start, will not be a big issue. It may generate a lot of noise but it can never again have the impact it had in 1992. This is not because people no longer care about tax. It is because they have learned that nobody's promises are worth believing. The Conservatives raised taxes having promised they would not. John Major then attempted to justify the tax rise by claiming that he could not foretell what would happen in the economy after the election and, therefore, is innocent of electoral deception. The lesson people have learned from this is that tax is liable to be raised by any government.

Adapted from the *Guardian*, 1 February 1994.

Item B *Tax rates 1978-96*

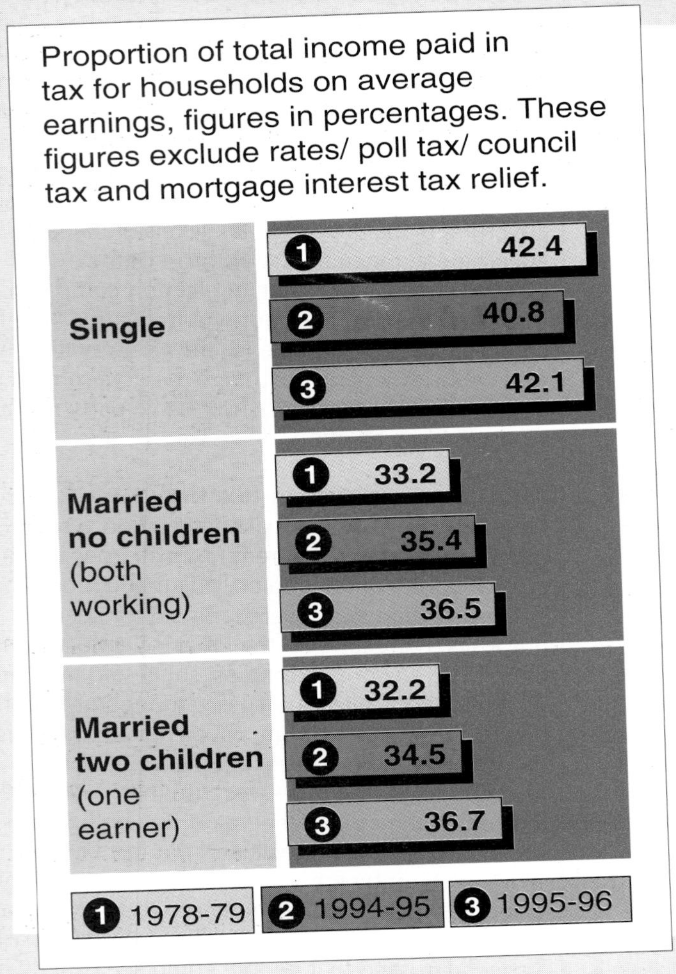

The Conservatives' image as the party of low tax was further eroded last night when the Treasury was forced to publish figures which show that, from April 1995, the average family will pay £22.32 a week - or £1,160 per year - more tax than now. This is particularly embarrassing for John Major who argued during the 1992 election campaign that a Labour victory would mean, 'the average taxpayer paying £1,000 more a year in tax.' The statistics show that the burden of tax as a percentage of earnings for the typical family will rise to 36.2% from April 1995. In the final year of the last Labour government, the figure was 32.2%, according to government figures. Harriet Harman, shadow Chief Secretary to the Treasury said: 'These figures show once and for all that the Conservatives committed a massive fraud on the British people at the last general election. It is not just that these taxes are a breach of promise, they are unfair and they threaten to stifle economic recovery.

Adapted from the *Guardian*, 18 February 1994.

Item C *The impact of tax changes 1985-95*

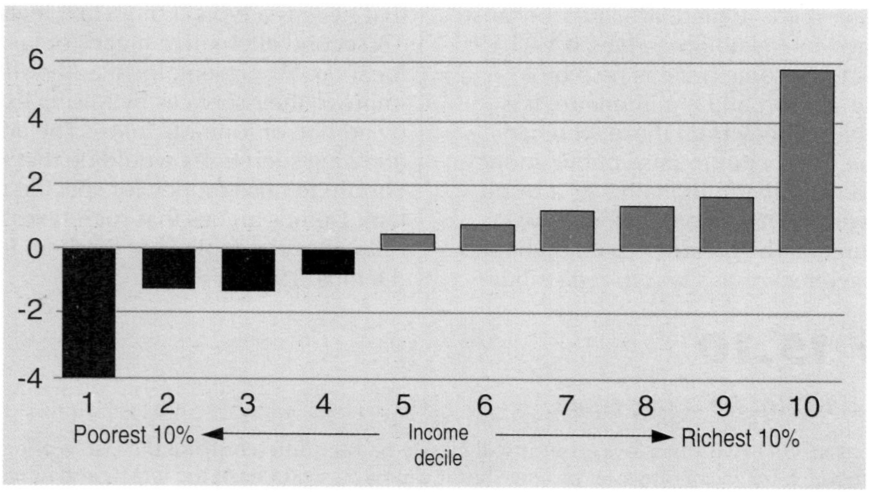

By dividing the British population into 10% blocks according to income (income deciles), it is possible to see how the tax changes made between 1985 and 1995 have affected different groups in society. Each bar in the chart shows the net percentage gain or loss made by that 10% of the population.

Adapted from the *Independent* 9 February 1994.

Item D *Tax will be a big issue*

The Tories have lost all claim to be the party of low taxation. The inevitable consequence of high unemployment, slow growth and increased poverty is that taxes have to rise to pay for this. Nobody should be fooled into thinking that tax policy will cease to be an issue at the next election. Only, next time the options for the electorate will be different from the bogus choice posed by the Tories in 1992. Then, the Tories pretended to be a low tax party. This no longer rings true. Most families are paying more of their income in taxes today (indirect tax plus income tax) than they did in 1979 under Labour. And taxes are not being raised fairly. The British tax system which, in theory, is redistributive has become a powerful weapon to reinforce inequality. The £64,000 question which the Tories must now answer is this. Why is it that only those earning £64,000 or more are paying less tax than they did in 1979?

Adapted from an article by the shadow Chancellor, Gordon Brown, in the *Guardian*, 9 February 1994.

Questions

1. Judging from Items A-D:
   a) Why do you think taxation was an important issue in the 1992 election campaign?
   b) Do you think taxation will be an important issue in future general elections? Give reasons for your answer.
2. What does the information in this section tell us about the way in which the economy has been managed since 1979?
3. What changes (if any) would you make to the current system of taxation? Explain in your answer why you would or would not make changes.

References

Anderton (1991) Anderton, A., *Economics*, Causeway Press, 1991.

Anderton (1992) Anderton, A. *The Economy in Focus 1992/3*, Causeway Press, 1992.

Anderton (1993) Anderton, A., *The Economy in Focus 1993/4*, Causeway Press, 1993.

Anderton (1994) Anderton, A., *The Economy in Focus 1994/5*, Causeway Press, 1994.

Balls (1994) Balls, E., 'The rich get even richer', *New Statesman and Society*, 15 April 1994.

Briggs (1993), Briggs, A. (ed.), *The Golden Age of Empire*, 1993.

Bruce-Gardyne (1986) Bruce-Gardyne, J., *Ministers and Mandarins*, Sidgwick & Jackson, 1986.

Calvocoressi (1978) Calvocoressi, P., *The British Experience 1945-75*, Bodley Head, 1978.

Chambers (1993) Chambers, I (ed.), Hall, D., Jones, R. & Raffo, C., *Business Studies*, Causeway Press, 1993.

Childs (1992) Childs, D., *Britain Since 1945*, Routledge, 1992.

Cook & Stevenson (1988) Cook, C. & Stevenson, J., *Modern British History 1714-1987*, Longman, 1988.

Culpin (1987) Culpin, C., *Making Modern Britain*, Collins, 1987.

Demos (1993) Mulgan, G. & Murray, R., *Reconnecting Taxation*, Demos, 1993.

Dimbleby & Reynolds (1988) Dimbleby, D. & Reynolds, D., *An Ocean Apart*, Hodder, 1988.

Friedman (1968) Friedman, M., *Dollars and Deficits*, 1968

Grant (1992) Grant, W., 'Management of the economy' in *Wale (1992)*.

Hall & Jacques (1983) Hall, S. & Jacques, M. (eds), *The Politics of Thatcherism*, Lawrence & Wishart, 1983.

Healey (1989) Healey, D., *The Time of My Life*, Penguin, 1990.

Heller (1987) Heller, R., *The State of Industry*, BBC, 1987.

Hines (1981) Hines, B., *Looks and Smiles*, Joseph, 1981.

Hobsbawm (1968) Hobsbawm, E., *Industry and Empire*, Pelican, 1968.

HMSO (1994) Central Statistical Office, *Social Trends*, Vol. 24, HMSO, 1994.

Johnson (1991) Johnson, C., *The Economy Under Mrs Thatcher 1979-90*, 1991

Lawson (1992) Lawson, N., *The View from No. 11*, Bantam Press, 1992.

Likierman (1988) Likierman, A., *Public Expenditure,* Penguin, 1988.

May (1987) May, T., *An Economic and Social History of Britain 1760-1970*, Longman, 1987.

McKie (1993) McKie, D. (ed.), *The Guardian Political Almanac 1993/4*, Fourth Estate, 1993.

Pagamenta & Overy (1984) Pagamenta, L. & Overy, R., *All Our Working Lives*, BBC, 1984.

Shanks (1961) Shanks, M., *The Stagnant Society*, Penguin, 1972.

Sullivan (1881) Sullivan, E., *The Nineteenth Century*, August 1881.

Wale (1992) Wale, W. (ed.), *Developments in Politics*, Vol.3, Causeway Press, 1992.

Williams (1896) Williams, E.E., *Made in Germany*, 1896.

Young (1993) Young, H. in *McKie (1993)*.

16 Sub-national government

Introduction

In Britain, politics tends to be seen and understood in national political terms. The focus is on the world of Westminster and Whitehall. But, it is the various agencies of sub-national government (whether local authorities or other bodies) which most often impinge on the lives of ordinary citizens. The services provided by these agencies range from education to refuse collection and from roads to health care. They are, therefore, services which are of vital importance to the whole population. But, it is not only because sub-national government is responsible for a wide range of services that it is important. There is a political principle to consider - the extent to which, in a parliamentary democracy, there is a need for a system of local democracy to counterbalance the power of a centralising state. It is the balance between the demands of centralised power and the needs of local autonomy which is at the heart of a discussion of the role and functions of sub-national government.

In recent years, major changes have taken place in sub-national government. Local government services have been privatised, for example, and local finance has been brought under strict central control. At the same time, there has been a striking growth in the number of unelected bodies (quangos), many of which are responsible for spending public money and making decisions which used to be made by local authorities. Since these changes were initiated by central government and are opposed by many who work in local government, the relationship between central and local government is fraught with a strong sense of crisis.

This chapter looks at the changes that have taken place in sub-national government since the 1970s and considers what impact these changes have made and where sub-national government is heading.

Chapter summary

Part 1 looks at the **organisation and structure of local authorities**. Special attention is paid to the changes that have taken place since 1945.

Part 2 examines **policy and decision making in local authorities**. The range of activities and the functions local authorities perform are considered. Local authority financing is reviewed.

Part 3 considers the changes in **central/local government relations.**

Part 4 charts the growing importance of quasi government with particular emphasis on the **development of quangos**.

1 The structure of local government

Key Issues

1. How did the modern system of local government develop?
2. How did the past shape the present?

1.1 Origins

Although local government can be traced back to Saxon times, strong central control by the monarch was a feature of its early history. The three basic units of local government today date back to the 15th century: the parish (the area served by the local church); the county (or shire); and the town (also known as the borough or burgh).

Before the 19th century, there was little uniformity and little local democracy in Britain. Roughly speaking, there was a two tier system by 1800. At one level, counties were administered by unelected Justices of the Peace (JPs) who were agents of the monarch. JPs delegated duties to officials in the parishes. At a second level, boroughs (towns which had been granted a royal charter) were autonomous local units administered by unelected Mayors or Aldermen. Bribery and corruption were common.

The industrial revolution brought the momentum for change. Rapid urbanisation led to overcrowding, disease, poor housing and crime. These problems led to demands for change, especially from the growing urban middle classes.

Municipal Reform Act 1835
The first phase of reform began with the Municipal Reform Act of 1835. This established elected town councils for the first time, but only applied to 178 boroughs in England and Wales. In many towns, progressive leaders had already campaigned for special Acts of Parliament to deal with problems such as water supply or street lighting. The new elected councils took over these projects. The 1835 Act was important in the long term since it set the standard pattern of local government. It established the principle that elected members should be responsible to those who paid local taxes and gave the council responsibility for maintaining local services.

Local Government Acts
The second phase of reform came with the Local Government Act of 1888. Elected county councils were created and towns with populations above 50,000 became 'county boroughs', independent of the county.

The second Local Government Act of 1894 set up a further tier of local government - urban and rural district councils. District councils had responsibility for health, housing and highways. The 1894 Act also set up 7,000 parish councils.

By 1900, therefore, England and Wales was divided into 82 county boroughs and 58 counties. The county boroughs provided services for larger towns whilst county councils and district councils served other areas. The late 19th century was the 'golden age' of local government. The new councils took over services which had been provided by voluntary agencies on an ad hoc basis (if they had been provided at all). They also bought out public utility companies and began to administer basic services. This system remained unchanged for over 60 years.

London
Any description of the organisation of local government in England should include the warning 'with the exception of London'. The size and extent of the city has meant that a system appropriate for other cities is not workable in London.

The London Government Act of 1889 set up an entirely new London County Council (LCC). This was supplemented in 1899 with a second tier of 28 metropolitan boroughs and 3 county boroughs. By 1901, the LCC covered an area which contained 4.5 million people.

1.2 Changes in organisation since 1945
Although the organisation of local government remained fundamentally unchanged until the 1960s, even before the Second World War the system had come under pressure, mainly because of population growth and demographic change. After 1945, four main criticisms were made. First, there were too many authorities and they were too small to deliver their services efficiently. Second, size varied enormously even amongst authorities of the same type. Borders did not reflect social and economic realities. Third, the two tiers of county and district did not allow accountable, democratic government since the division of functions between the two tiers was piecemeal and often illogical. And fourth, there was no tier to deal with the special problems of major conurbations outside London (especially, Birmingham, Liverpool and Manchester).

The London Government Act, 1963
To examine the problem of local government in London, the Herbert Commission was set up in 1957. It recommended that old boundaries be redrawn and a new two tier system be set up consisting of the Greater London Council (GLC) and 32 new borough councils. The GLC would plan on a London-wide basis and the boroughs would provide services within their locality. These recommendations were accepted by the government and the London Government Act of 1963 came into operation in 1965. The system survived until the mid-1980s.

The Local Government Act, 1972
The Maud Commission was set up in 1966 to investigate local government in England and Wales. The majority report of 1967 supported a unitary solution. England (apart from Birmingham, Liverpool and Manchester) was to be divided into 58 unitary areas in which a single authority would carry out all functions. The three conurbations were to be organised in the same way as London. One member of the Commission did not agree with this and submitted a minority report arguing for two tiers (35 city regions and 135 districts).

The Labour government fell before legislation was passed on these recommendations and the new Conservative government rejected the unitary solution. As a result, the Local Government Act of 1972 provided a two tier system. In the higher tier, the 58 counties of England and Wales became 47 shire counties and 6 metropolitan counties. In the lower tier, 1,249 districts were reduced to 333 rural (shire) districts and 34 metropolitan districts. Whereas metropolitan districts had responsibility for providing important services such as social services and education, in rural (shire) districts, these services were provided by the county council. This Act came into force in 1974. Critics claimed that the changes made local government more remote and less accountable.

The Scottish Local Government Act, 1973
In 1973, a separate Local Government Act was passed for Scotland. This Act also provided a two tier system. It created nine regional councils and three island councils in the higher tier and 53 district councils in the lower tier.

Minor councils
Town, parish and community councils in existence before the Acts of 1963, 1972 and 1973 remained untouched and still survive. There are more than 10,000 of such bodies in operation outside London.

They undertake minor functions and act as a mouthpiece for public opinion.

Abolition of the GLC and metropolitan counties

The Widdicombe Committee was set up in 1985 to examine the practices and procedures governing the conduct of local authority business in Britain with particular reference to the rights and responsibilities of elected councillors and the relationship between councillors and officers. The subtext was that the Conservative government was worried about Labour councillors' activities. Some Labour councils had introduced programmes in the early 1980s which flew in the face of the Thatcher government's ideology - for example, they subsidised the arts and public transport and introduced job creation schemes which favoured women and black people. Although the central government hoped that the Widdicombe committee would find ways of stopping these programmes, the Widdicombe Report, published in 1986, failed to do this.

The government then came up with its own solutions. In 1986, it abolished the GLC and metropolitan counties on the grounds that they were an unnecessary burden on public resources. Ministers argued that these councils performed few functions which could not be performed at district or borough level. These few functions (for example, fire, police and public transport), they argued, would be better performed by new joint boards (composed of representatives from borough and district councils).

Critics accused the government of acting in a partisan manner since all these councils had a Labour majority and the GLC, in particular, had developed a high public profile and a record of support for causes which the Conservative party found unacceptable. Critics also argued that abolition would not really remove a tier of government because many of the functions of metropolitan counties would be transferred to the new joint boards. These new boards would be more remote from the public and, therefore, less accountable. Third, critics pointed out that there was no guarantee that neighbouring districts or boroughs would cooperate (especially if they were dominated by different parties). So, services might suffer. And fourth, they claimed that metropolitan counties made savings through economies of scale. Abolition would neither improve efficiency nor save money.

The abolition of the GLC was followed by the abolition of ILEA (Inner London Education Authority). ILEA had been responsible for organising education in the inner London boroughs. Responsibility was devolved to the individual boroughs.

Activity 16.1

Item A *Self-help*

The spirit of self-help is the root of all genuine growth in the individual. Help from without is often weakening in its effects, but help from within invariably strengthening. Whatever is done for men or groups to a certain extent takes away the stimulus and necessity of doing for themselves. And where men are subjected to over-guidance and over-government, the inevitable tendency is for them to become comparatively helpless.

Adapted from Smiles, 1859.

Item B *Municipal socialism*

The individualist Town Councillor will walk along the municipal pavement, lit by municipal gas and cleansed by municipal brooms with municipal water and seeing by the municipal clock in the municipal market that he is too early to meet his children from the municipal school close by the county lunatic asylum and municipal hospital, will use the national telegraph system to tell them not to walk through the municipal park, but to come by the municipal tramway, to meet him in the municipal reading room by the municipal art gallery, museum and library. 'Socialism, sir', he will say, 'don't waste the time of a practical man by your fantastic absurdities. Self-help, sir, individual self-help, that's what's made our city what it is.'

Adapted from Webb, 1889.

Item C *Southport town hall*

Southport town hall was built in 1852.

Item D *Organisation of local government at the end of the 19th century*

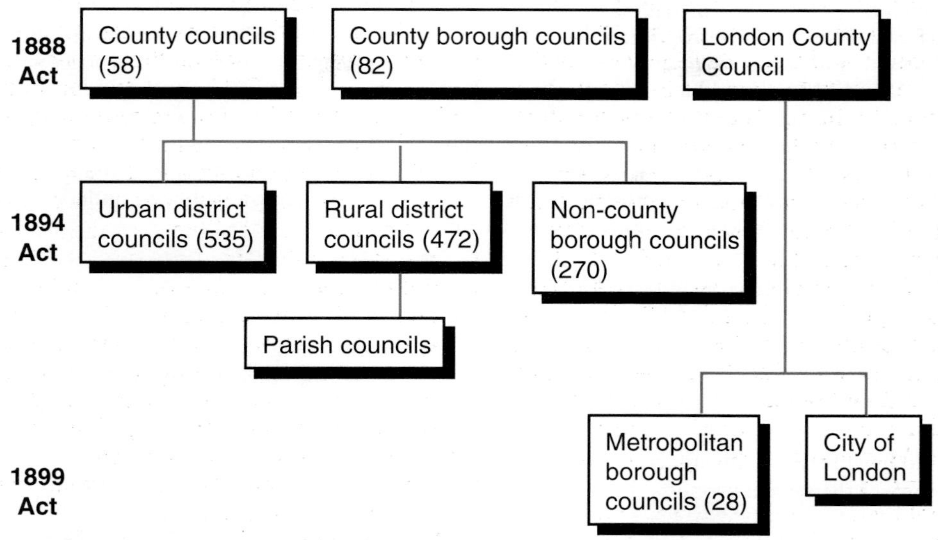

This diagram shows the organisation and structure of local government in England and Wales in 1900. The numbers of each type of council are shown in brackets.

Questions

1. Describe the attitudes towards local government expressed in Items A and B. Why do you think people had such different views of local government?
2. a) Use Items A-D to explain how the organisation of local government changed in the late 19th century.
   b) Why do you think this is known as the 'golden age' of local government?

Activity 16.2

Item A *The (majority) Maud Commission Report*

England should be divided into 61 new local government areas. In 58 of them a single authority should be responsible for all services. In the three very large metropolitan areas around Birmingham, Liverpool and Manchester responsibility for services should be divided between a metropolitan authority whose key functions would be planning, transport and major development and 20 metropolitan district authorities whose key functions would be education, social services, health and housing. These 61 new local government areas should be grouped together with Greater London into eight provinces, each with its own provincial council. The key function of these councils would be to settle provincial strategy and the planning framework within which the main authorities must operate.

Adapted from Maud, 1967.

Item B *Organisation of local government after 1974*

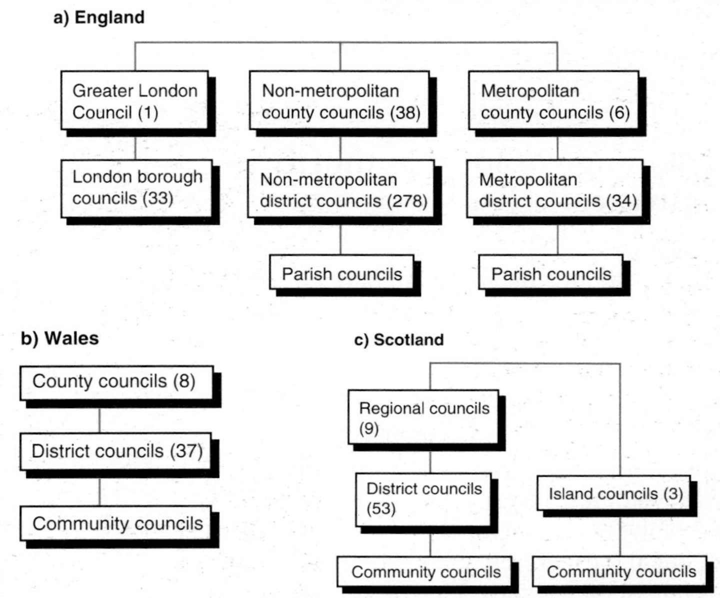

This diagram shows the organisation and structure of local government in England, Wales and Scotland after the Local Government Acts of 1972 and 1973 were passed. Parish and community councils existed in some, but not all, districts. The numbers of each type of council are shown in brackets.

Item C *Streamlining the cities*

The basic principle of earlier reorganisations was that there was a need for a two tier system of local government throughout the country- a lower tier providing essentially local services and an upper tier dealing with a wider area of administration. But the GLC and Metropolitan County Councils (MCCs) have full responsibility for only a limited number of services. In many areas, they share powers with the borough and district councils. A strict interpretation of the role of the GLC and MCCs would leave them with too few real functions. As a result, they search for a 'strategic role' which may have little basis in real needs and which often brings them into conflict with the lower tier authorities. It may also lead them to promote policies which conflict with national policies. The abolition of the GLC and MCCs will streamline local government in the metropolitan areas. It will remove a source of conflict and tension. It will save money after some initial costs. It will also provide a system which is simpler for the public to understand since responsibility for virtually all services will rest with a single authority.

Adapted from HMSO, 1983.

Questions

1. a) Use Item A to draw a diagram showing what the organisation and structure of local government would have been if the Maud proposals had been adopted.
   b) What would have been the advantages and disadvantages of the system proposed by the Maud Commission?
   c) Can you think of any reasons to explain why the Maud proposals were not accepted?
2. a) Draw a diagram similar to that in Item B which shows the current organisation and structure of local government in England and Wales.
   b) What sort of local authority area do you live in?
3. Before the proposals in Item C became law there was consultation with interested groups. Write a consultation paper putting forward the arguments against abolition of the GLC and MCCs.

2 Decision making in local authorities

Key Issues

1. How is policy formulated and how are decisions made in local authorities?
2. What role is played by councillors and council officers?
3. Why have party politics become important in local government?
4. How is local government finance organised?
5. What changes have resulted from privatisation?

2.1 The range of local authority activities

Local government in 1991-92 cost £41.8 billion. This amounted to about a quarter of all public expenditure and a tenth of the UK's gross domestic product (GDP). Local government is a major employer. It employs about one in 10 of the working population.

Councils provide a wide range of services. For example, Manchester City Council's *A-Z Guide* contains information about its services under more than 700 headings. This huge range of activities is a product of the two main functions of local authorities: their political (or representative) function and their administrative (or executive) function.

Political function of local authorities

Local authorities are democratically elected bodies, the only form of representative government in Britain apart from Parliament. They provide an opportunity for people to stand for political office as councillors (see chapter 11, part 1). One of the functions of local authorities, therefore, is to provide a forum in which elected representatives can determine how local affairs should be run. Equally, because the local authority is a democratically elected body, it is (in theory at least) directly accountable to local people.

Administrative function of local authorities

The range of activities carried out by local authorities is determined by law and, therefore, ultimately by Parliament. A number of Acts of Parliament, some of which are specific to local government and some of which are more general, lay down the parameters within which local government can operate. It is the function of local authorities to implement and to administer the decisions made by central government.

For example, metropolitan districts and county councils are obliged by law to provide, without charge, adequate primary and secondary education for all children between the ages of five and 16. Central government determines overall education policy and circulates detailed regulations on educational matters. Local authorities are obliged to comply with these regulations. This is not just the case with education. Most of the activities performed by local authorities are mandatory (compulsory).

Local authorities do have some room for manoeuvre, however. The Local Government Act of

1972 states that councils may do anything which is:

> 'Calculated to facilitate or is conducive or incidental to the discharge of their mandatory activities.'

To use the example of education again, it is not mandatory for local authorities to provide nurseries for children under the age of five. But, under the terms of the 1972 Local Government Act, they may choose to do so.

Although local authorities can choose to carry out additional functions, they may not take action which is not sanctioned by law or which exceeds their lawful authority. If they do, they are deemed to have acted 'ultra vires' (beyond their legitimate powers). When a court finds that a local authority has acted ultra vires, it declares its actions illegal and may punish its councillors or officers.

The council and committees

The full council is the supreme decision making body in a local authority. Elected representatives - councillors - make decisions in the full council. Their decisions are implemented by officers who are full-time council employees. Since it would be impossible to deal with all council business at full council, detailed work is delegated to committees.

Before the Bains Report of 1972, committees liaised between the full council and the relevant local authority departments (departments are teams of officers whose job is to implement policy). So, for example, a county council would delegate matters concerning education to its education committee. The education committee would then be responsible for the county's overall education policy (within the parameters set by central government) and the allocation of resources. Decisions made by the education committee would be implemented by the council's education department.

In 1971, however, the Bains Committee was set up to consider how the new system of local government (which was to be introduced by the 1972 Act) should be managed. The Bains Report recommended a new system of corporate management. The aim was to encourage councillors and officers to focus on the corporate good rather than on their own specific area of interest. To achieve this, the two main innovations were the creation of a principal chief officers' management team under the control of a chief executive and the setting up of a Policy and Resources Committee. It was the job of both of these new structures to take an overview of council policy.

The result of these innovations was a change in the way that the committee system worked. Instead of reporting direct to full council, committees now reported to the Policy and Resources Committee which, in turn, reported to full council. Also, instead of liaising directly with local authority departments, committees now relayed their decisions to the principal chief officers' management team which then passed them on to individual departments.

Case study - Oxford City Council

Oxford is divided into 17 wards (geographical areas). Each ward elects three councillors who sit for four years. Oxford City Council therefore has 51 councillors (for the number of councillors from each political party on the council see section 2.3 below).

The council's work is shared among committees which meet either every month or every two months. There are 12 main committees and, generally, 12 councillors sit on a committee. The Housing Committee, for example, is responsible for managing some 10,000 dwellings in and around the city of Oxford. It also has the statutory duty to deal with sub-standard accommodation, the harrassment of tenants and vulnerable homeless people. In 1993-94, it was responsible for the net expenditure of £4.5 million.

Most of the business of committees is held in public. The main decisions and recommendations of the committees are submitted to the meetings of the full city council. There are 10 meetings of the full city council each year. To support the committees, there is a series of subcommittees, working groups and advisory groups, many of which coopt their members from the community. Most subcommittees are advisory, although a small number have statutory powers. All committees and subcommittees are advised by council officers. The number of councillors from a political party on each committee must, by law, reflect the number of councillors of that party elected to the council as a whole.

Oxford City Council employs about 1,000 people to carry out the day-to-day work of the council. Laws govern the council's responsibilities in areas such as litter collection, traffic management, road maintenance, planning and building control, housing, the environment, and leisure and recreation. But, the level of services and the allocation of resources are the responsibility of the elected councillors.

Case study - Oxfordshire County Council

A total of 70 councillors (or members) sit on Oxfordshire County Council, each member representing a different part of the county. Elections for all seats on the council are held every four years. After the 1993 county council elections, Oxfordshire County Council was hung. No political party had overall control. The Conservatives were the largest party with 25 seats. Labour had 24 seats. The Liberal Democrats had 20 seats. There was one Green party councillor.

Meetings of the full county council take place five times each year. These meetings determine the overall policy and direction to be taken by the county. In particular, the full council agrees the annual budget and takes responsibility for seeking new or amended legislation. Committees and subcommittees are responsible for specific areas of the council's work. The size of each committee varies, but its composition reflects the relative numbers of councillors belonging to each of the political parties on the council as a whole. Some committees also include people coopted because of their particular knowledge or experience. Coopted committee members have speaking and voting rights even though they are not councillors. The Education Committee, for example, includes people representing the teaching profession and the churches.

Committees and their subcommittees consider detailed policy issues. They also review existing policies, examine efficiency and recommend budgets for services. A statement of the business dealt with by each committee is considered at meetings of the full county council.

Meetings of the full council, its committees and sub-committees are normally open to the public. A limited number of subjects, however, are dealt with in private. For example, cases involving named individuals are usually discussed in private.

Activity 16.3

Item A *Local authorities' areas of responsibility (1)*

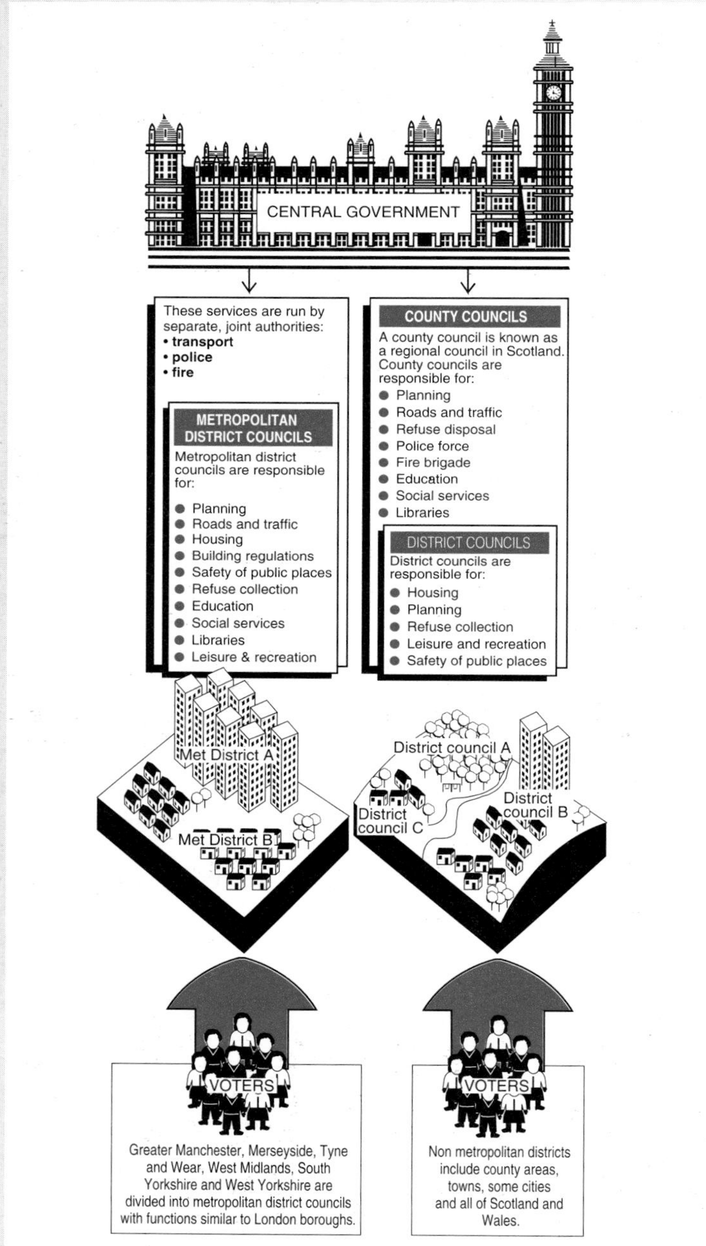

Adapted from the *Guardian*, 5 March 1991.

Item B *Local authorities' areas of responsibility (2)*

Item C *Management structure before the Bains Report*

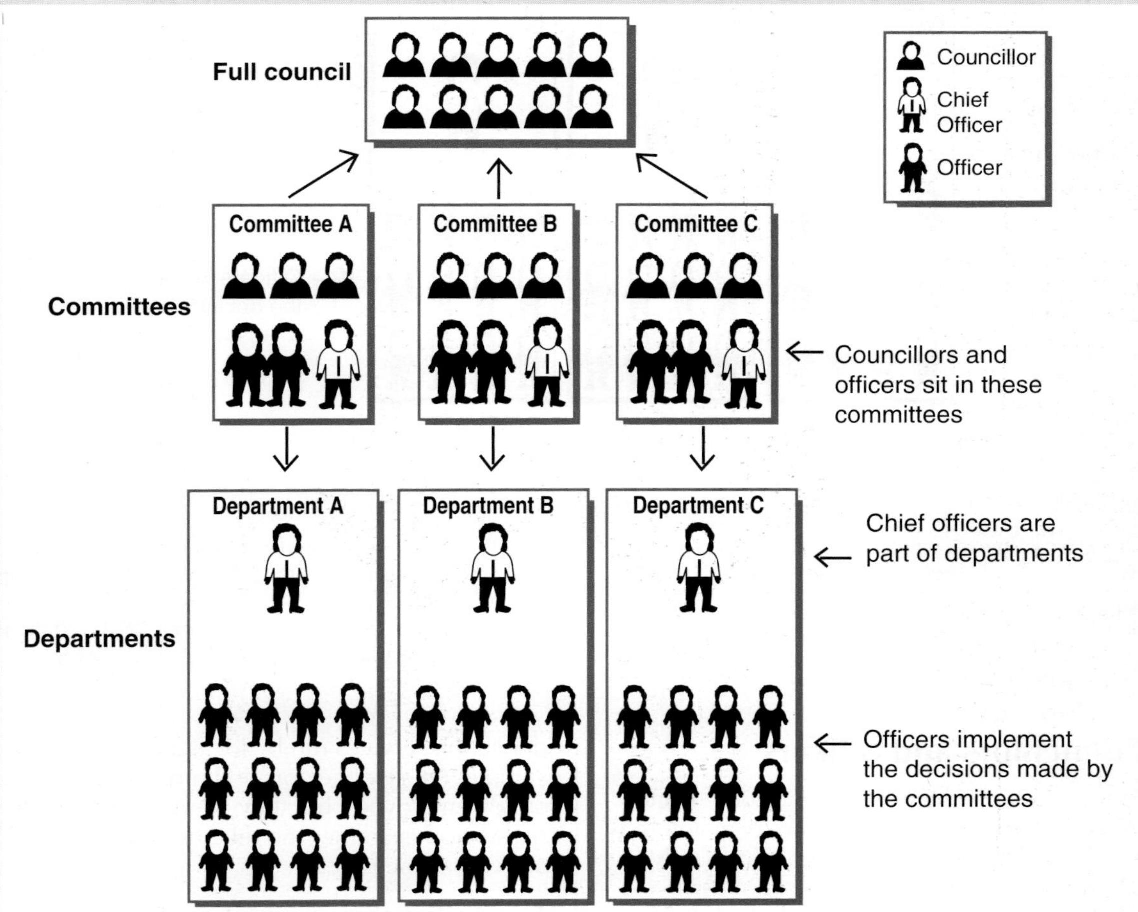

This diagram shows the management structure which existed in local authorities before 1972.

Item C *Management structure after the Bains Report*

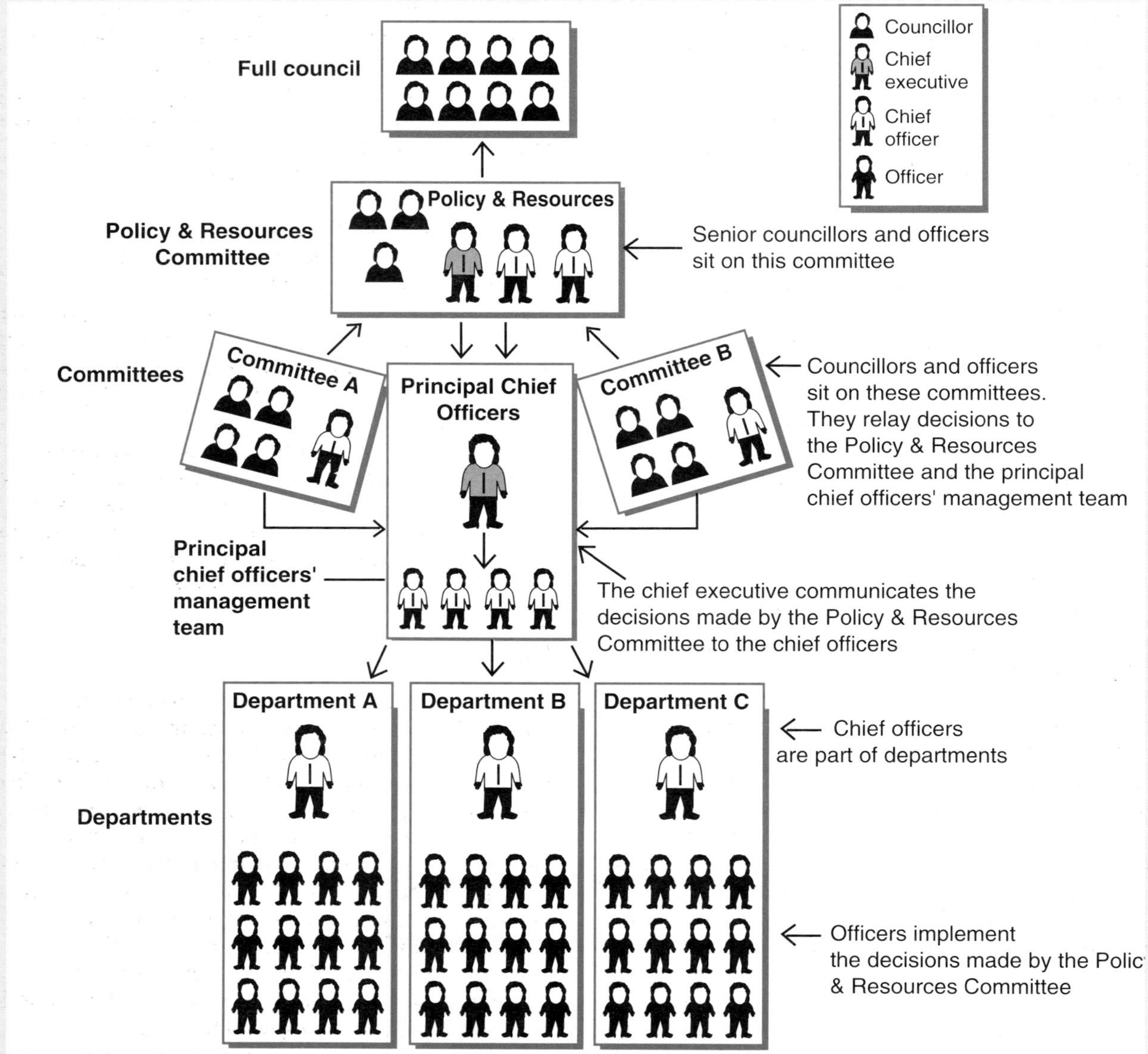

This diagram shows the management structure which existed in local authorities after 1972.

Questions

1. Judging from Item A what are the main differences between the three types of local authority?
2. Suppose the man in Item B lived where you live. Which departments in which type of council would be responsible for solving the problems he faced?
3. a) What do Items C and D tell us about the way in which decision making in local authorities changed after 1972?
   b) Where was power located before 1972? Where is it located now? Give reasons for your answer.

2.2 Councillors and officers

In the UK as a whole, there are over 25,000 elected councillors and more than 2.3 million local authority employees. Of these 2.3 million employees, only 500,000 can be described as local government officers (professional, technical and clerical staff). Council officers are, in other words, bureaucrats, whilst the remaining 1.8 million council employees operate the services run by local authorities (for example, refuse collectors and most teachers are council employees, but they are not council officers). This section examines the relationship between councillors and officers.

The traditional view and its variants

The traditional or formal view of the relationship between councillors and officers is that councillors make policy and officers implement it. So, power rests with the elected councillors.

An alternative view is that administration actually involves policy making. Since officers have technical and professional expertise which councillors lack, they help to set the agenda and give advice. Since they help to set the agenda and give advice, they play an important role in determining policy outcomes.

Since the traditional view is contradicted by its alternative, it is, perhaps, no surprise to find that a third view has developed. According to this view, developing and administering policy is a joint activity of both officers and councillors. This view was supported by the Bains Committee (see above, section 2.1). The Bains Report stated that:

> 'If local government is to have any chance of achieving a corporate approach to its affairs, members [elected councillors] and officers must both recognise that neither can regard any area of the authority's work and administration as exclusively theirs.' (Bains, 1972)

Elite Theory

During the late 1970s, some political commentators argued that local government had fallen into the hands of an elite made up of senior officers and senior councillors (for example, Cockburn, 1977 and Saunders, 1979). This elite, it was claimed, was a direct result of the Local Government Acts of 1972 and 1973. Reorganisation of local government meant the adoption of new management structures. These new structures had produced an elite.

According to this theory, before the Acts of 1972 and 1973, a loose assembly of council committees had determined policy which was then administered by a large number of small departments. Reorganisation after the Bains Report of 1972 brought streamlining and a hierarchical structure. The principal chief officers management team became, in effect, a board of directors under a single head (the chief executive). Only senior councillors sat on the new Policy and Resources Committee. The net result was that power became concentrated in the hands of a small group - the chief executive, the senior officers and the senior councillors.

The pluralist model

Elite theory has been criticised on the grounds that it is too simplistic. Supporters of the pluralist model argue that the relationship between officers and councillors is such that the balance of power is varied and changes according to the issues, the personalities, the strength of the political parties and the particular local authority.

Councillors, it is argued, are rarely united in their objectives. Alliances, therefore, develop between certain councillors and officers who then compete against other councillors and officers over particular policies. This is especially likely to happen when members of one committee have to compete with another committee for funds.

Second, attention must be paid to the ruling party group as a whole rather than just the senior councillors. Junior or 'backbench' councillors can exert influence through the party caucus meetings where policy priorities are discussed. If the party caucus meetings decide on a particular policy, senior as well as junior councillors must pursue this policy. On occasions, therefore, senior councillors may be overruled.

Third, policy disagreement and rivalry can exist both between departments and even within departments of the council. So, it is misleading to suggest that the officers are a homogenous group with a uniform view. For example, the interests of officers working in the Treasury department are unlikely to be the same as those working in a spending department like Housing.

Fourth, the fact that individual councillors represent a particular geographical area should not be ignored. Although the constraint of party discipline makes it difficult for councillors to take an independent line, there are occasions when ward interests predominate and party discipline is broken or modified.

Decision making

At full council meetings, the main business is to finalise the council's policy on all matters which have been through committees. Councillors have their last chance to make changes after examining reports from the main committees. The full council has four choices when it has examined the committee minutes. First, it may receive a committee minute. This means it approves the action taken. Second, it may accept a recommendation as it is. Third, it may change a minute in some way before accepting it. Fourth, where a minute records a decision taken by the committee on behalf of the full council, the council can rule that it is not happy with the decision and send the matter back to the committee for further consideration.

At committee or subcommittee meetings, the main business is to consider reports from the officers. Normally, these contain recommendatioins for action. After considering the officers' reports, committees or subcommittees have three choices. First, they may accept the officers' recommendations or advice as they are. Second, they may change them in some way. Third, they may decide to do something different.

At both full council meetings and at committee meetings, decisions are reached by councillors suggesting a course of action. For example, a councillor might propose that an officer's recommendation is accepted by the whole meeting. Other councillors might then propose amendments. When all the amendments have been dealt with, the proposal as it then stands is voted on.

Is the role of chief officers parallel to that of senior civil servants?

At first sight, it might seem that the relationship between local government chief officers and councillors is similar to that between senior civil servants and Cabinet ministers (see chapter 13, part 3). After all, the role of senior local authority officers, like that of senior civil servants, is to provide policy advice and to implement the decisions made by elected representatives. Also, like civil servants, officers are supposed to be politically neutral. But, on closer inspection, two important differences appear.

First, unlike the generalist civil servants at Whitehall (see chapter 13, p.394) local government officers are specialists. Their technical knowledge is extensive, usually much greater than that of councillors. On the other hand, councillors, unlike Cabinet ministers, are part-time, amateur politicians.

Second, unlike senior civil servants, chief officers are often publicly identified with particular policies and projects and they are sometimes prepared to make public statements in support of such policies and projects. For example, many chief education officers in the 1970s supported the adoption of a comprehensive system of education and they publicly encouraged local councils to convert their schools to that system. Most senior civil servants would avoid such publicity.

The relationship between local government officers and councillors

In theory, the relationship between officers and councillors is symbiotic. The councillors need the officers to develop and implement policy, whilst the officers need the councillors to provide their actions with political legitimacy. Neither could survive without the other. In practice, a number of factors combine to determine which of the two has the upper hand.

First, the technical knowledge of local government officers undoubtedly affects their relationship with councillors. There is a danger of the full-time professionals (the officers) dominating the part-time, amateurs (the councillors) who are often elected with low turnouts and who rely on electoral fortune to retain their position. The professionals, after all, know what can and cannot be achieved and that knowledge could easily be translated into power. But, officers do not always have their own way. For example, if one party has a majority on the council, then it is likely that there is a clear policy manifesto and a mandate from the electorate. Councillors from the majority party can expect officers to implement their programme (so long as none of their commitments are ultra vires) whether they approve of the policies or not.

Second, the political climate can be an important factor. For example, in the 1980s, the New Urban Left (Labour-controlled local councils with radical political ideas) set out to challenge central government by developing a new approach to local politics. Councillors began to use the corporate structures set up after the Bains Report to advance their political causes. Officers were required to provide support for these policies. By the mid-1980s, according to the Widdicombe Report (which, amongst other things, was instructed to examine the relationship between councillors and officers), councillors became more dominant in local government than they had been before because they became clearer about their political objectives (Widdicombe, 1986).

A third factor is the intervention of central government. The long-term aim of Conservative governments since 1979 has been to change the role of local authorities. Councils, it has been suggested, should no longer provide services. Rather, they should be **enabling authorities**, bodies which regulate the services provided by outside organisations. Legislation enacted by central government since the mid-1980s has begun this process, and it is a process which will undoubtedly change the relationship between officers and councillors. One theory is that there will be the opportunity for councillors to reassert their authority because officers will no longer be responsible for delivering services. Councillors will, therefore, no longer be so reliant on officers' technical expertise. A second theory suggests that the power of officers will be enhanced because the awarding of contracts will increasingly be seen as a technical matter and, therefore, not the prerogative of councillors.

Fourth, attention should be paid to hung councils where no party has overall control. The number of these councils has grown since the mid-1980s, creating a new balance of power. Since many of these newly hung councils had been used to a long period of majority party control, the new arrangements upset the long established officer/councillor relationships. Since no single party has control, inter-party deals have to be struck. Officers find that they are responsible, in a very real way, to all political parties and not just to a ruling group. As a result, officers need to cultivate the vote of all councillors. They can no longer rely upon a ruling group to rubber stamp decisions already agreed in private. However, although the creation of some hung councils has resulted in more open and democratic decision making, in others, confusion has allowed officers to gain greater control over the decision making process.

Activity 16.4 (below) examines the decision making process in local authorities and considers where power lies.

Activity 16.4

Item A *Decision making*

As with most organisations, the way in which local authorities actually make decisions is as much dictated by discussions behind the scenes as it is by the formal process of a committee's deliberations. Each council has its own way of working and within each council the different departments may have quite individual styles in the way that they handle business. In some cases, a committee may discuss an item without there being a preconceived view on it. On other occasions, the decision will have been made long before the matter was placed on the committee agenda. Sometimes, the views of the officers are all important, whereas at other times individual councillors dominate decision making. When a single party is in control it will usually hold all the important positions - such as chair of all the committees. Under the Local Government Housing Act of 1989, councillors from all political parties represented on the council must be appointed to committees in the same proportion to the number of seats they won in the election. By controlling the chairs of committees and by virtue of their strength in numbers on the committees, the party in control can exercise considerable power.

Adapted from Hutt, 1990.

Item B *Committees and departments*

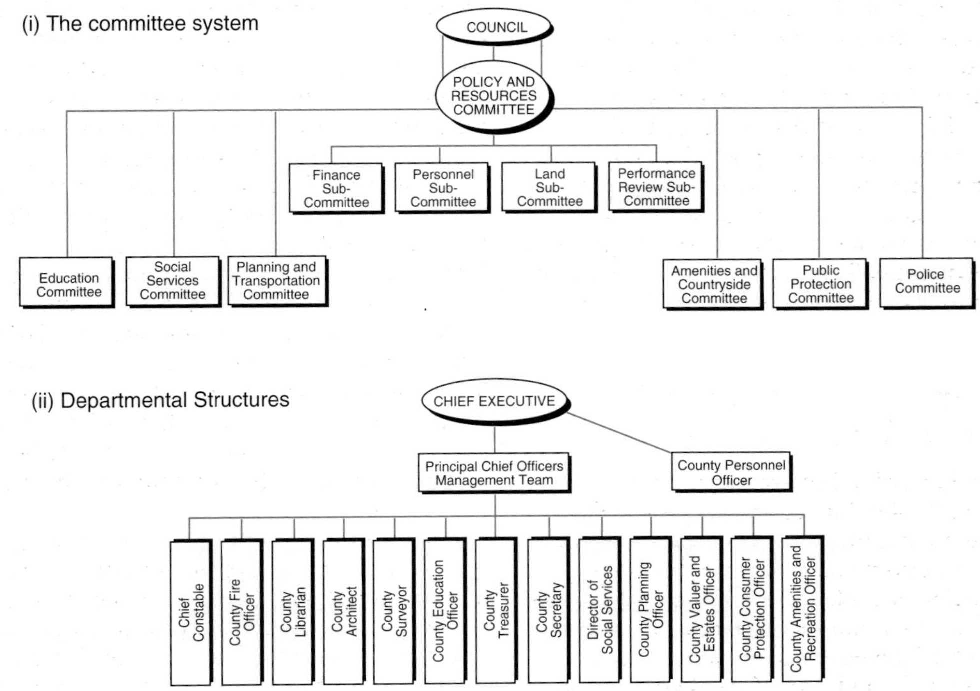

This diagram shows the committee and departmental structures in a typical county council.

Adapted from Stoker, 1990.

Item C *Councillors, officers and the public*

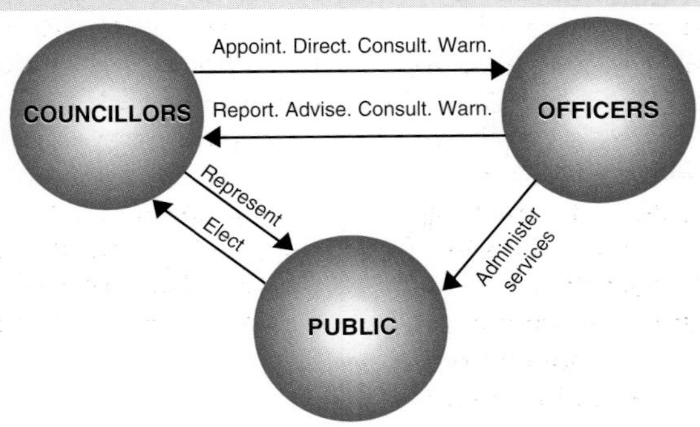

This diagram shows the relationship between councillors, officers and the public.

Adapted from Roberts, 1986.

Item D *The role of senior local government officers*

The various roles of senior officers can be categorised under three headings. First, they are the professional managers of local authority service departments. As such, they have day-to-day responsibility for major budgets and a large staff. Second, they are advisers responsible for ensuring that the council and its committees are informed of the facts, the law and all other relevant considerations before they make decisions. They are also responsible for proposing and advising on policy options. Third, they are arbitrators who stand outside the political conflicts between councillors and ensure that council business is conducted fairly. Skilled officers are able to carry out all three roles. But some officers are only able to concentrate on one or two of their roles. For example, officers who place very strong stress on their professional judgement and on their legal duty to serve the council might fail to satisfy the need to advise the majority party leadership. This might result in pressure for the appointment of officers sympathetic to the majority party's political views. On the other hand, officers who spend too much time with the majority party leadership might neglect their duties as professional managers and fail to retain the confidence of the minority parties.

Adapted from Widdicombe , 1986.

Item E *The role of the chief executive*

Although there is no legal requirement to do so, in practice over 90% of councils in Britain appoint a chief executive. The Widdicombe Committee recommended that the post of chief executive become a statutory requirement. The government agrees that it is desirable to strengthen the position of officers in certain important respects. But, it considers that the idea of a statutory chief executive suffers from three main drawbacks. First, this would give to the chief executive functions which are inappropriate for an officer. For example, it would give a chief executive the power to decide whether a councillor needs to see a document or attend a meeting. If the chief executive were to sit in judgement on an elected member this would widely be seen as being undemocratic. Second, it would impose a uniform pattern of organisation, at the highest level, on all authorities even though their responsibilities and resources vary enormously. Organisational flexibility is valued by authorities. Third, it would require a detailed definition of the role of the chief executive in relation to both members and other chief officers. In the absence of general consensus, the government doubts the practicality of this. The government considers that a chief executive can have a vital role to play in exercising overall responsibility for coordinating policy advice and for ensuring that decisions are carried out. But, it also considers that the case for a statutory requirement has not been made out.

Adapted from HMSO, 1988.

Questions

1. A press release issued by a county council announces that a decision has been made to reduce the amount of money available for discretionary grants to support students. Using Items A-E explain how this might have been initiated, discussed, decided upon and implemented.
2. Look in your local newspaper for a piece of news which mentions a decision made by a local council. Find out as much as you can about this decision and write a piece explaining the various steps taken before this piece of news was released.
3. a) Does Item C illustrate the traditional view of the relationship between officers and councillors or one of its variants? Explain your answer.
   b) Redraw the diagram to illustrate one of the other theoretical models mentioned in this section.
4. a) Using Items A-E explain where power lies in the decision making process in local authorities.
   b) How important is the role of (i) the chief executive and (ii) chief officers?

2.3 Party politics and local government
(see also chapter 11, section 1.1)

Local government is now dominated by party politics. Some commentators argue that this is a new phenomenon (see, for example, Barber, 1978). Others claim that it is a return to the political climate in which local government operated before the Second World War (see, for example, Stoker, 1988 and Alexander, 1985). Those who subscribe to the latter theory claim that during the period 1945 to 1970, local authority officers managed to depoliticise local government.

The growth of party politics

There is good evidence to suggest that party politics has grown in importance since 1970. The Maud Report of 1967 found that 50% of local authorities were under independent control whereas the Widdicombe Report of 1986 found that just 16% of local councils (mainly in rural areas) were dominated by independent councillors.

As the number of independent councillors has declined, so the number of councillors standing on a party ticket has increased. According to the Widdicombe Report, 83% of councillors in 1985 stood on a party ticket. The result of this is an inevitable growth in party discipline, party caucuses and party voting, both at full council meetings and on committees.

This trend has continued since the Widdicombe Report. Local government is increasingly conducted on party lines with the majority party (or sometimes a coalition) forming a government and the minority parties forming an opposition. The make-up of committees is determined by the overall strength of the parties in the council as a whole. Issues are, increasingly, defined in party political terms.

Whilst this pattern has been quite common in the cities for a number of years, it is a recent phenomenon in the shire counties. In particular, the growth of the Liberal vote since the early 1980s means that all three main parties now have a real opportunity of exercising power. After the 1993 county council elections, 28 out of 47 county councils were left with no overall control. Of the remainder, Labour controlled 14 county councils, the Liberals controlled three and the Conservatives and independents controlled one each. In a council where no overall control exists, effective party discipline is essential if alliances are to be forged between parties which seek to share power.

In 1995, Labour had 10,867 councillors, the Conservatives 4,982 and the Liberal Democrats 5,035 (*Guardian*, 6 May 1995). The Conservatives put up fewer candidates than usual in the 1995 local government elections because of the unpopularity of the Conservative central government. Some of their candidates chose to stand as independents in an attempt to avoid defeat at the polls.

Party politics in Oxford City Council

After the 1995 election, Oxford City Council had a Labour majority. There were 38 Labour councillors, four Conservative councillors and eight Liberal Democrat councillors. Just one of the 51 councillors did not belong to one of the three main parties (a Green councillor).

Since it has a majority, the Labour group can be sure of winning all the votes taken at full council meetings and at committees. A Labour councillor holds the position of leader of the council. Also, Labour councillors are chairs and vice chairs of all the council committees.

A large number of Labour councillors would have to defy the party whip and vote with the opposition to defeat the ruling group on any issue. But, Labour councillors are unlikely to do this since they would risk being expelled from the Labour group in the council and even from the Labour party.

The Labour group meets regularly to determine what view the group should take on particular issues. There are often heated discussions at these meetings with different points of views being advanced. Once a majority position is established, however, all Labour councillors are expected to follow the agreed line. This agreed line is also expected to be in accord with nationwide local Labour party thinking. The Labour party organises nationwide local government conferences which are attended by local councillors.

There is a close link between the Labour group and the DLP (District Labour Party). Observers from the DLP (which represents all Labour party members living in the area of the City Council) attend the Labour group meetings. Their role is to inform Labour councillors of views expressed by members of the DLP and to report back to the DLP the decisions made by the Labour councillors. The relationship between the two bodies is similar to the relationship between the Labour party at national level and the PLP (parliamentary Labour party). The Labour party's election manifesto for the Oxford City Council elections is debated by the DLP and has to be approved by that body. Although the choice of candidate to fight council seats is made by local party branches, it has to be endorsed by the DLP.

The benefits and drawbacks of party involvement

Greater party involvement in local government is supported on the following grounds. First, it helps to define the issues placed before the electorate. Parties stand on a manifesto which clearly distinguishes their different policies. Second, policies tend to be based on principles rather than personalities. This leads to greater consistency. Third, there is greater coherence because of party discipline. Fourth, more seats are contested and there is a slightly higher turnout at elections. Fifth, there is greater accountability because the electorate is able to comment on a party's performance by re-electing it or voting it out of office. Sixth, there is better coordination between local and national politics. Seventh, the democratic structure of parties allows party members to participate in decision making, so, as a result, political participation increases.

Greater party involvement in local government has been criticised for the following reasons. First, party involvement is not desirable because most local issues are not party political. Second, real decisions are no longer taken in council chambers but in party meetings. Third, the electorate votes on party lines rather than on the quality of candidates. Fourth, local issues are neglected because party concerns predominate. Fifth, council decisions are made in an adversarial climate (two hostile groups debate angrily) - this is neither the most effective nor the most efficient way to make decisions. Sixth, wholesale reversal of policies takes place when party control changes hands. Seventh, decisions are made by party activists rather than by democratically elected councillors. Eighth, independent councillors find it much harder to be elected because they do not have a party machine behind them.

The nationalisation of local politics

In addition to the growth of party politics, some commentators claim that there has been a growing 'nationalisation' of local politics (see, for example, Schofield, 1977). By this, they mean that local government is perceived less in local terms and more in terms of national government and national political issues. For example, local elections are seen as judgements on the performance of parties nationally rather than as a test of local opinion or as a judgement on the performance of local politicians.

Some doubts, however, have been expressed about the extent of the 'nationalisation' of local politics. The Widdicombe Report of 1986, for example, claimed that local matters can still determine local election results, especially at ward level. Research for the Report indicated that 56% of those interviewed claimed to be influenced more by local issues than by national issues in local elections. Also, 39% of those interviewed claimed that the quality of the individual was more important than the party in local elections and 20% voted for different parties in local elections and national elections.

The findings of the Widdicombe Report were confirmed by Rallings & Thrasher in 1990. They claimed that:

> 'There may be strong undercurrents reflecting national trends, [but] local voting contains many examples of parties doing better or worse than expected, of candidates having a personal following, and of electorates who distinguish themselves either by their significant involvement or their massive indifference.' (Rallings & Thrasher, 1990, p. 166)

Activity 16.5

Item A *Party control of local authorities, 1965-94*

(i) Councils by party

Party	1979	1989	1994
Con	262	169	80
Lab	79	163	156
Lib Dem	1	1	44
Other	39	12	6
Independent	57	32	19
No overall control	77	127	144

This table shows the number of councils controlled by parties and independents between 1979 and 1994.

(ii) Independent councils and councillors, 1965 and 1988

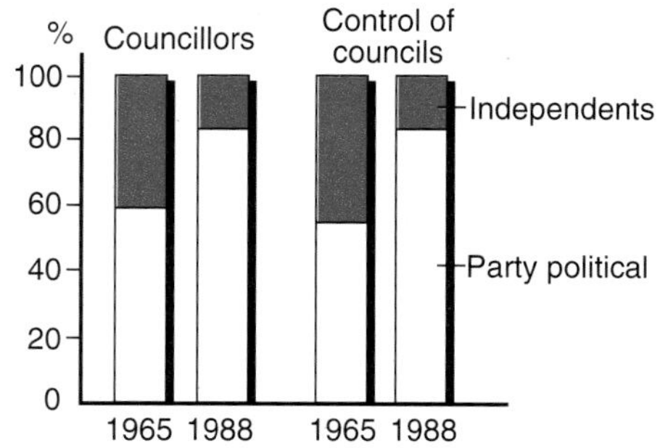

This graph shows the proportion of councils and councillors elected on a party or an independent ticket in 1965 and 1988.

Adapted from Chandler, 1991 and the *Guardian*, 6 May 1994.

Adapted from Byrne, 1990.

Item B *Hung councils*

The local elections on 6 May saw the number of hung county councils more than double from 12 to 28. Councillors have had to sort out how these authorities should be managed and whether to work with their opponents. The overall pattern is mixed and complex, but one major shift is already clear: a dramatic increase in the number to be run jointly by Labour and the Liberal Democrats. Some are happy with the term 'joint administration'. Others prefer 'working arrangement' or 'understanding'. Nobody likes the word 'pact' or 'coalition'. But, whatever term is used, the two parties will be cooperating in the exercise of power. Before the election, the only explicitly Lab/Lib Dem county was Berkshire. In six others, the two groups have now reached agreement on sharing the executive posts of leader and committee chairs and also on pressing ahead with common policies. Compare this to 1985 when the elections left 23 hung counties in England, but not one such deal was struck. 'We laid the two manifestos out on the table', says Peter Pinfield, Labour group leader in Hereford and Worcester, 'and to be dead honest, there was very little difference between them.' Under the 'no administration' system which has existed in Avon and Oxfordshire, everything is decided on an issue-by-issue basis. Committee chairs are stripped of power and are usually elected on a rotational basis. Each party picks a spokesperson for each committee and the resulting panel takes decisions between meetings. A set of conventions governs parity of access to officers and information. Such councils can function efficiently and Labour policy often gets through with Liberal Democrat support. But, it can also lead to inconsistency.

Adapted from Rosenbaum, 1993.

Item C *Political control by type of authority*

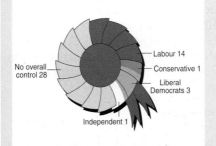

The big cities

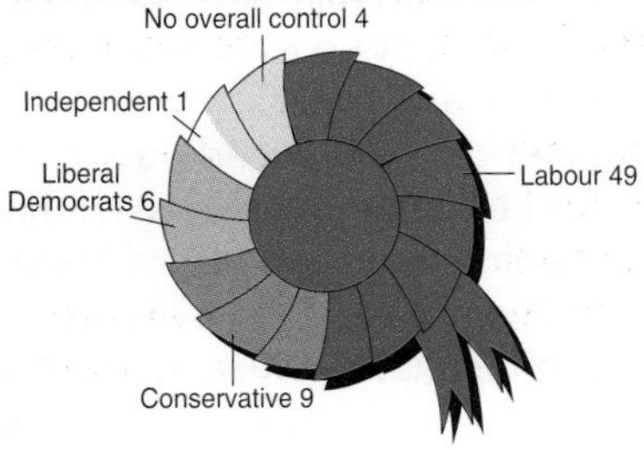

County councils

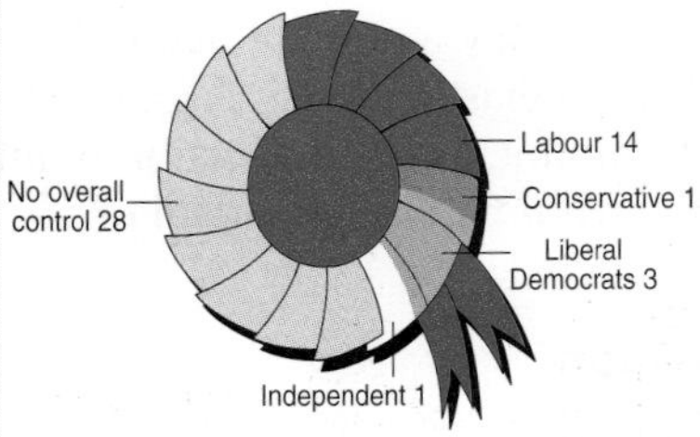

District councils

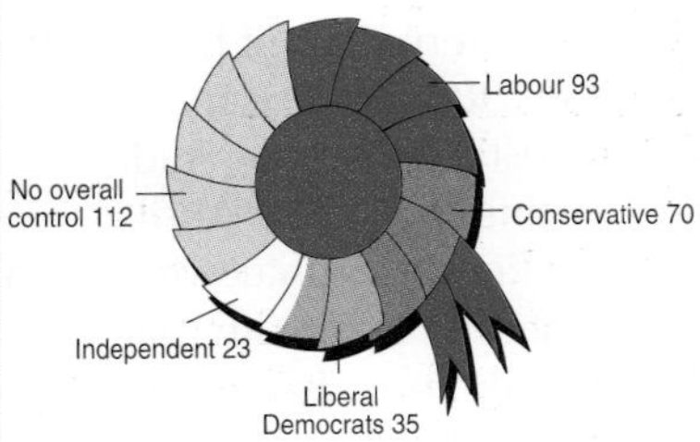

These diagrams show the political control of local authorities in 1994. The figures are from the Association of District Councils, County Councils and Metropolitan Authorities.

Item D *Selling council houses to buy votes*

As chair of Wandsworth Council's property sales committee in the mid-1980s, Peter Bingle admitted: 'My aim is to reduce the number of council properties in Wandsworth from 35,000 to 20,000 and to make Battersea a Conservative constituency.' The 1987 general election duly saw the defeat of Battersea's sitting Labour MP. Bingle told the *Guardian* afterwards: 'I don't think any of us has ever tried to hide the fact that we have sought not just to run Wandsworth more efficently, but to change Wandsworth into a Conservative borough. There have been too many Tory councils just trying to "manage the service". We have done that but we have always remembered that we are primarily Conservative politicians. We are one of the few Tory councils that has actually realised the political potential of running a town hall.'

Adapted from Creighton, 1994.

Item E *The blurring of roles*

Local government auditors are busy investigating the housing policies of Westminster and Wandsworth councils. Their aim is to decide what was proper and what was not. It is alleged that Conservative councillors plotted to ensure that their party would be re-elected by selling council houses in strategically selected wards (wards with only a fragile Conservative majority). What startled me was the realisation that full-time council officials now seem to sit in on discussions at which the ruling party decides how to get re-elected. The clear dividing line that once existed between elected members, belonging to a political party, and appointed officers, from the town clerk or chief executive downward, has been blurred.

Adapted from Cole, 1994.

Questions

1. Judging from Item A what evidence is there of greater party political control of local government since 1970? Why do you think this has happened?

2. Look at Items B and C.
   a) What type of local authority is most likely to have no overall control?
   b) Does it matter whether a council has a party with an overall majority? Give reasons for your answer.

3. Judging from Items C-E should the electorate be concerned about the growing involvement of party politics in local government?

4. Do you agree with Peter Bingle (Item D) that local councillors' foremost allegiance should be to their political party? Give arguments for and against this view.

2.4 Local finance - background information

Local government costs a great deal of money. This money comes from a number of sources. First, fees and charges are made for some local authority services. Car parking charges, swimming pool entrance fees and council house rents are all examples. Second, councils also raise money to pay for local services through local taxation. Since 1993, this local taxation has been the council tax - a tax based on property. Third, councils receive money from business rates paid by the owners of offices, shops and factories in the area. Fourth, councils receive central government grants which are earmarked for specific services. And fifth, councils can acquire money by borrowing for capital expenditure (for example, for building schools or houses). Loans are raised from banks, from finance houses and from central government's Public Works Loan Board.

The money raised by local authorities is used to provide a range of services (see above, section 2.1).

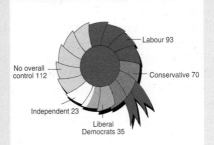

This money is spent both on running the service (current expenditure) and on buildings, roads and equipment (capital expenditure). A significant part of current expenditure is the salaries of council employees. Teachers, social workers and trading standards officers are all examples of people employed by a local authority. The actual cost of running the council (the cost of meetings, councillors' allowances and so on) is a very small proportion of the total.

Raising finance 1945-76

Between 1945 and 1976, the main political parties agreed that local authority spending was an important and worthwhile expense. There was all-party support for the welfare reforms introduced after the Second World War. These reforms gave local authorities an expanded role which was financed by larger central government grants. In addition, local authorities raised money locally through the rates - a local property tax.

During this period, local authorities were free to decide upon the quantity and quality of the local services they provided so long as they met their statutory obligations. According to one commentator, the main restraint on spending was:

> 'The extent to which local electors would vote for councillors who increased rate demands.' (Chandler, 1991, p.60).

Tighter restraint after 1976

The oil crisis of the mid-1970s led to a balance of payments problem. The Labour government elected in 1976 was forced to approach the International Monetary Fund (IMF) for a loan (see chapter 3, pp. 43-44). One of the stipulations made by the IMF when providing this loan was that public expenditure should be cut. The result was that central government had to reduce the amount of money granted to local government. As the minister responsible for local government, Anthony Crosland, put it in 1975:

> 'We have come to terms with the harsh reality of the situation which we inherited. The party's over.' (Crosland, 1983, p.295)

The Thatcher governments which followed in the 1980s had no interest in lifting the financial restraints imposed by the Labour government. They saw local government as an unnecessary evil. According to John Kingdom, the New Right thought that local expenditure:

> 'Created a dependency culture, a postwar funk in which wasteful councils elected by non-ratepaying voters, served by empire building bureaucrats dispensed lavish patronage to working class scroungers.' (Kingdom, 1991, p.174).

Government grants

Between 1979 and 1990, central government grants as a proportion of local authority expenditure fell from 58% to 42% with a corresponding increase in the burden on local taxpayers. Also, within budgets, the overall proportions spent on the different services changed. Less money was spent on education, for example, and more on law and order.

To ensure that local authorities reduced public spending, the first Thatcher government passed the Local Government Planning and Land Act of 1980. This fundamentally changed the system by which grants were allocated to local authorities. From 1980, grants were allocated on the basis of an assessment prepared by the Department of the Environment. At first this was known as the Grant Related Expenditure Assessment (GREA). It is now called the Standard Spending Assessment (SSA). This assessment determines how much money a council needs to provide its services at the existing level. A grant is then paid up to that amount. The introduction of this system gave central government a great deal of control over local finances.

The Audit Commission

Tighter financial control was also achieved through the activities of the Audit Commission. An audit is an investigation of financial accounts to check whether money has been spent legally and efficiently and in line with stated policies. Local authorities had always been subject to an annual external audit by impartial district auditors. But, after 1984, the Local Government Finance Act established the Audit Commission to take over this work. The Audit Commission has a chief officer appointed by central government. Its brief is not only to ensure that councils spend money legally, but also to ensure that they achieve value for money in commercial terms. Many local authorities have seen the Audit Commission as a device to ensure more control from the centre.

Local taxation since 1945

The rates

Until the late 1980s, local authorities raised revenue by means of a property tax - the rates. The rates were an ancient form of taxation, first introduced in 1601, to raise money for the new poor law. The advantage of the rating system was that it was easy to administer and difficult to avoid. Money was raised by charging an annual rate for each piece of property in the locality. The size of the fee was determined by the size and standard of the property. Businesses paid a special business rate on their property.

The rates had a number of disadvantages. First, the rates hit poorest people hardest. The poor paid a larger proportion of their income in rates than the wealthy.

Second, the rates were not related to ability to pay but to the size and standard of the property. Third, the tax took no account of how much use was made of the services provided by the local authority. A single property of low ratable value might house five people who made use of local services a great deal, whereas a property of high ratable value might house a single person who made very little use of local services. Fourth, there was no incentive to improve properties because improvements led to higher rates being charged. And finally, only about half the total number of households in the UK paid rates. The other half received rebates.

From the time when Margaret Thatcher was shadow Environment Minister in the mid-1970s, she supported the abolition of the rates. It was not until the mid-1980s, however, that this became a serious proposition. By then, Conservative think tanks were arguing that many of those who voted in local elections did so without having to consider the rates burden since they did not have to pay it themselves. This, they argued, was particularly hard on businesses. Businesses paid over 50% of rates, but were given no right of representation.

The reduction of central government finance after 1976 forced many local authorities to put up the rates so that services could be maintained. When the Thatcher government introduced the Grant Related Expenditure Assessment in 1980, councils began to use 'creative accountancy' to avoid the impact of central government's squeeze on their resources. In response to this, further Acts of Parliament were passed in the 1980s. These Acts increased central government's control over local government finance and plugged the loopholes which councils had exploited. Especially contentious was the introduction of 'rate-capping' in 1984. Rate-capping permitted central government to control the expenditure of overspending councils by setting upper limits on the amount they could spend and limiting the amount they could raise in rates. This led to 18 councils being rate-capped in 1985-86 and another 12 in 1986-87. Despite the protests against rate-capping, all except Liverpool and Lambeth councils eventually complied with the law. Liverpool budgeted to overspend and refused to reduce services. As a result, 49 councillors were surcharged and disqualified from office for five years.

The poll tax or Community Charge

The Conservatives were anxious to produce an alternative to the rates and in 1985-86 decided to opt for the 'Community Charge'. This tax was to be based on residence. Almost all adult residents, some 35 million people, would have to pay this tax - about double the number who had paid the rates. The government claimed that this was the best alternative to the rates because it meant that all adult consumers of local authority services would pay something towards them and this would increase local accountability. Although the tax was not based on the electoral register, it rapidly became known as the poll tax.

The poll tax plans met with significant opposition. Before the new tax had been introduced, critics raised the following objections. First, the tax was regressive (individuals in an area would pay the same amount regardless of income). Second, many people, and especially those families with adult families living at home, would find that their poll tax bills were much bigger than the rates. Third, it would be expensive and complicated to collect the tax because it would involve tracing people rather than property.

As well as reforming the domestic rates, the government also changed the rating system for businesses (the non-domestic rate). Local businesses would no longer pay rates set by councils. They would pay a uniform business rate set by central government.

The poll tax was initially introduced in Scotland in April 1989 and in England and Wales a year later. It soon became the focus of a huge protest movement. A mass campaign of non-payment was launched. This was based on two principles - that people could not afford to pay and that some should not have to pay. By the end of the 1990-91 financial year, £1 billion (nearly 10% of poll tax revenue) remained uncollected in England and Wales (*Guardian*, 7 March 1991). This compared to an average collection of 98% under the rates. Poll tax-capping of 21 Labour controlled authorities in 1990 and a further 17 in 1991 added to the criticism of the tax. The capping negated the argument that the poll tax would bring greater local accountability.

The deep unpopularity of the tax led the government to announce in March 1991 that it would be abolished.

The council tax

Announcing the abolition of the poll tax in March 1991, Michael Heseltine, Secretary of State for the Environment, said that he would introduce:

> 'A new local tax under which there will be a single bill for each household comprising two essential elements, the number of adults living there and the value of the property.' (*Guardian*, 22 March 1991)

He insisted that the new local tax would be fair and linked to the ability to pay, but it would include the poll tax principle that most people would make some contribution for the use of services.

The change was seen as a major climbdown by the government and a reversal of Thatcherite policies. The council tax came into operation in April 1993. The title of the tax was carefully chosen so that those facing new bills would be conscious that they were paying for local authority services. But the tax itself only accounts for about 15% of local government expenditure.

It should be noted that the business rates (the national non-domestic rates) are still set and distributed by central government. All the money raised from businesses is collected into a national pool. Central government decides how much each district and county council should receive from that pool.

Alternative systems

While the council tax has not earned the unpopularity of the poll tax, the question of finding a satisfactory solution for local authority finance remains.

In 1976, the Layfield Report recommended a local income tax which would be a supplement to the rates. The Liberal Democrats support a local income tax as a means of local government finance. The Labour party, on the other hand, has suggested a return to the rates system, but related to people's ability to pay. A local sales tax has also been suggested. But, this would be difficult to implement because neighbouring authorities might levy it at different rates.

Another idea is to transfer some local government expenditure to central government (for example, education). This would reduce the local burden. It has even been suggested that no local taxes be levied locally. Rather, local government should be entirely funded by central government.

Activity 16.6

Item A *Income for 1994-95: Lancashire County Council and West Lancs District Council*

WEST LANCS DISTRICT COUNCIL INCOME 1994-95

Income	Amount	%
1 Revenue support grant	£3,895,624	35
2 National non-domestic rates	£3,545,288	32
3 Council tax	£2,795,205	25
4 Balances	£543,393	5
5 Interest	£388,130	3

LANCASHIRE COUNTY COUNCIL INCOME 1994-95

Income	Amount	%
1 Revenue support grant	£435 million	45
2 National non-domestic rates	£267 million	28
3 Council tax	£239 million	25
4 Balances	£18 million	2

Adapted from information provided by West Lancs District Council Finance Department and a leaflet produced by Lancashire County Council in 1994.

Item B *What councils spent their budgets on in 1981-82 and 1991-92*

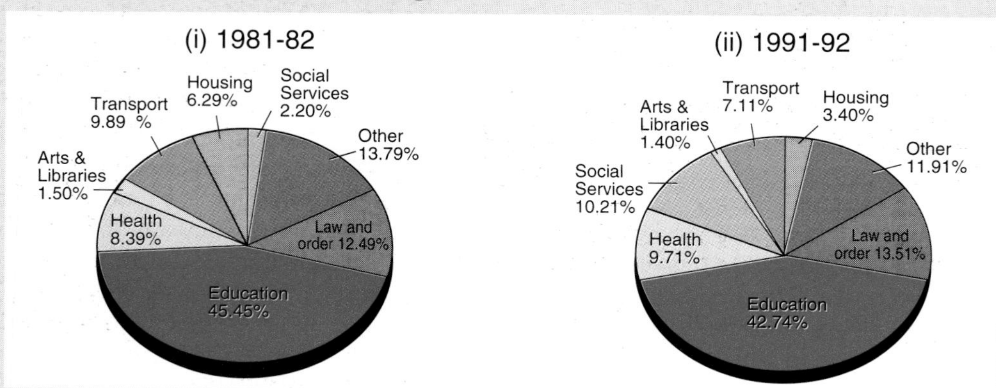

Adapted from information from the Institute of Public Finance and Accountancy.

Item C *Changes in council spending, 1981-1994*

All figures are percentages

	Government grants	Business rates	Domestic rates
1981-82	56	25	20
1982-83	53	26	21
1983-84	54	26	19
1984-85	54	26	20
1985-86	54	28	21
1986-87	50	28	22
1987-88	49	28	23
1988-89	46	28	25
1989-90	44	29	26
1990-91	42	29	28
1991-92	52	31	16
1992-93	54	29	17
1993-94	56	27	16

This table shows the percentage of local government expenditure met by central government grants, non-domestic rates and domestic rates. In 1990, domestic rates were replaced by the poll tax. In 1993, the council tax replaced the poll tax.

Adapted from McKie, 1993.

Item F *Anti-poll tax poster*

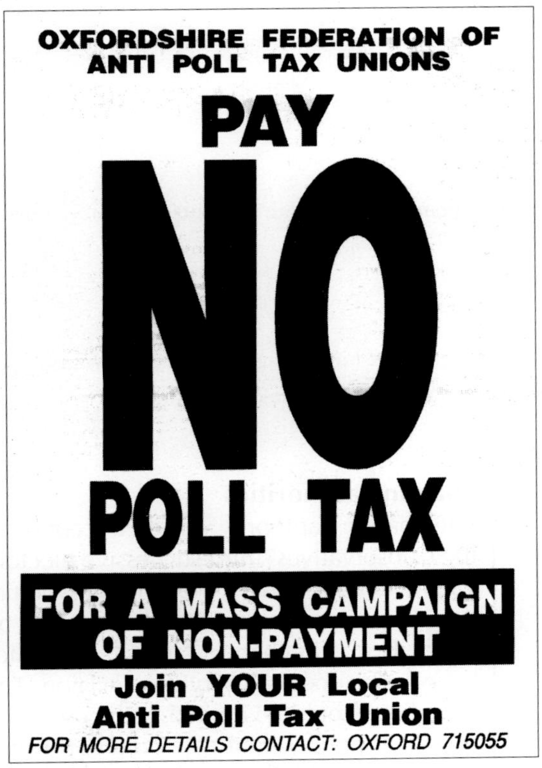

This poster was produced for the Oxfordshire Federation of Anti Poll Tax Unions in 1989.

Item D *The poll tax*

Every voter now faced with paying their share of council expenditure will have a powerful incentive to consider the possible costs of their candidate's policies before they cast their vote. Officials will have to take account of the effect of their recommendations on the public they deal with. Councillors will have to consider the impact of their decisions on their voters. Accountability and responsibility will reappear in many communities where, in recent years, both have been lacking. This will create substantial pressure on authorities to reduce their expenditure.

Adapted from ASI, 1989.

Item E *The council tax*

The council tax is a local tax set by local authorities to pay for local services. There will be one bill per dwelling whether it is a house, bungalow, flat, maisonette, mobile home or house boat and whether it is owned or rented. The amount of tax to be paid by each household is based on the relative value of their property compared to others in the area. Discounts will be paid where one adult lives alone or where people have very low incomes or disabilities. The value of each property is assessed not by the local council, but by the Valuation Office Agency (part of the Inland Revenue). Properties are placed into one of the eight council tax valuation bands, depending on their estimated sale price. The value of each property is based on its estimated sale price on 1 April 1991, taking account of any significant changes between then and 1 April 1993 (such as an extension). The fact that homes may be worth more or less today does not, in itself, mean that have been put in the wrong band.

Adapted from a leaflet produced by the Department of the Environment, September 1992.

Item G *How the council tax is used*

£1.13 A Day If Your Home Is In Band C

Oxfordshire County Council needs to raise £94m from Council Taxpayers in Oxfordshire in 1993-94. That works out at £1.13 a day for a home in Band C. This is how it is made up.

66p **EDUCATION**
- 74,658 children attending 315 nursery, primary, secondary and special schools.
- 3,983 teachers.
- 34 youth centres and projects working with 10,000 young people.
- 600 discretionary further and higher education awards for students over 18.
- 23,396 people enrolled on courses at 29 community and adult education centres.

18p **SOCIAL SERVICES**
- 71 residential places for children.
- 1,035 residential places for elderly people in 22 homes, and 200 day-centre places.
- 290 children cared for by foster parents.
- Home-care service assisting about 4,300 people at home.

9p **POLICE**
- Towards the cost of policing Oxfordshire.

7p **HIGHWAYS**
- 3,841 kilometres of roads, 851 road bridges, 41,545 street lights maintained.
- 170 bus routes subsidised.

4p **FIRE SERVICE**
- 51 vehicles from 24 fire stations which answered about 9,300 calls for assistance in 1992.
- 235 full-time, 276 part-time firefighters.
- 37 fire-prevention officers. About 12,000 inspections of buildings and planning applications, lectures and other visits carried out in 1992.

3p **LEISURE AND ARTS**
- 45 public libraries and nine mobile libraries issuing 5.4m books, cassettes, videos and discs a year.
- Six museums visited by 270,000 people a year.
- Support to 72 arts and community organisations.
- Management of 3,790 kilometres of public rights of way.
- Heritage services including Centre for Oxfordshire Studies, County Archives and County Archaeological Services.

1p **WASTE REGULATION, RECYCLING & DISPOSAL**
- Regulation of all waste-handling activities.
- 220,000 tonnes of household waste and over 260,000 tonnes of commercial and industrial waste disposed of or recycled at County sites.

1p **PLANNING**
- Structure Plan, local transportation planning, control of mineral extraction.

1p **TRADING STANDARDS**
- Protecting consumers and reputable traders by enforcing 70 Acts and 800 regulations covering the supply of a wide range of goods and services.

3p **MISCELLANEOUS SERVICES**
- A wide range including probation, courts, emergency planning and flood defence.

What Is Capping?

If the government thinks a council's spending is 'excessive', it can step in and make that council spend less. For 1993-94 the government said the County Council would be capped if it spent more than £319m.

This cap is 1.75% more than the County Council spent in 1992-93 and just 1.9% above the government's 'standard level' for 1993-94.

The government calculates a 'standard level of service' for each council, using a very complicated system. For 1993-94, the government's 'standard level' for the County Council is £313m.

What Do Houses In Other Bands Pay?

The most that your household will be asked to pay for County services per day is:

Band A	£0.85	**Band E**	£1.56
Band B	£0.99	**Band F**	£1.84
Band C	£1.13	**Band G**	£2.13
Band D	£1.28	**Band H**	£2.55

Working For Oxfordshire

15,762 people work for Oxfordshire County Council. 7,239 of them are full-time and 8,523 part-time. This is the equivalent of 11,372 full-time employees, which is how the figures below are shown.

December 1991		December 1992
7,000	Education	6,280
2,410	Social Services	2,560
288	Environmental	283
322	Leisure and Arts	334
290	Fire Service	290
47	Trading Standards	43
206	Planning & Property Services	78
118	County Treasurer	115
72	Chief Executive	70
68	Central & Other Services	65
28	Trainees	21
10,849		10,139
1,350	Commercial Services	1,233
12,199	TOTAL	11,372

The 1992 Education figure above excludes 947 staff in further education colleges. These colleges will be removed from local authority control in April 1993. Contracting out by the Planning and Property Services Department has reduced their figures by 128. Cleaning, caretaking, catering and maintenance of grounds and highways are carried out by four Direct Service Organisations, combined in the Commercial Services Department. Figures exclude any vacant posts.

Like To Know More?

- **At your local library.** Check the OXCIS free information point. Ask for the *Revenue Budget 1993-94* and other booklets which are available for reference.
- **By telephone or letter.** Contact the Chief Executive's Office (tel Oxford 815352) or the Public Relations Unit (tel Oxford 815060) for general information including a list of councillors.
- **By attending Council meetings at County Hall.** You are welcome to attend and in some cases make your points to the meeting.

Published by Oxfordshire County Council County Hall Oxford OX1 1ND (Tel Oxford 792422)

Printed on recycled paper

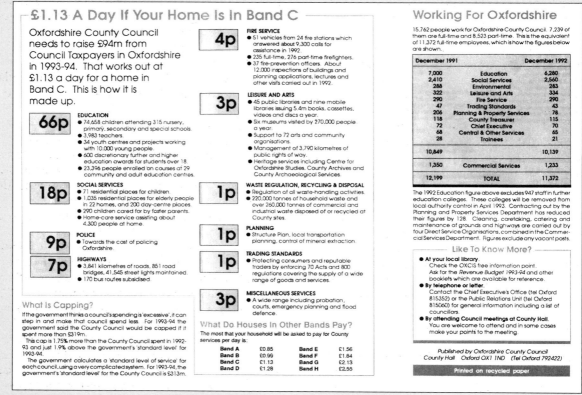

A leaflet produced by Oxfordshire County Council, 1993.

Questions

1. Look at Items A-C.
   a) Explain how the system of local government finance works.
   b) How has local government expenditure changed since 1981?
   c) Do you think that councillors should be responsible for spending such large amounts of money? Give arguments for and against.
2. Look at Items D-G.
   a) Why do you think the poll tax was introduced?
   b) How does the council tax differ from the poll tax?
   c) Why do you think there was a mass campaign against the poll tax but not against the council tax?
3. Judging from Items E and G what are the advantages and disadvantages of the council tax?

2.5 The privatisation of local government

Until the election of the first Thatcher government in 1979, it was taken for granted that local authorities would provide services themselves. Since then, however, there has been increasing pressure on local authorities to introduce market mechanisms - to 'privatise' their services. The long-term aim is clear. Conservative governments have been working towards a fundamental change in the role played by local authorities. If they achieve this, local authorities will no longer provide services. Rather, they will be **enabling authorities**, bodies which regulate the services provided by outside organisations.

Enabling authorities

The enabling authority was a concept developed after the Conservatives' third successive electoral victory in 1987. Nicholas Ridley, the minister who first promoted the idea, suggested in 1988 that the role played by councils should change. No longer should councils have a monopoly on service provision. Their spending should be limited to the provision of essential services contracted out to private firms. Councils should give up ownership of leisure centres, recreation grounds, retail centres, factory units, workshop and land. Instead of actually providing services, it should be the role of councils to identify markets, to devise strategies to meet consumer demands and to monitor services once they had been contracted out.

So, no longer would a local authority run its own refuse collection service. Instead, the council's job would be to find out what refuse services were required by local citizens and then to contract a private refuse collection company to undertake the work. The company contracted would be the company that could do the work at the lowest possible cost whilst maintaining the standards required by the council. Having contracted out the work, it would then be the job of the council to monitor the delivery of the service. If standards were not maintained, then the council would be able to refuse to renew the contract or to impose penalties.

Privatisation

The creation of the enabling authority depends upon the widespread privatisation of local government services. Privatisation is advocated for two main reasons. First, it is claimed that privatisation increases efficiency. A common criticism of local government, especially in the late 1970s, was that it was over-bureaucratic, inflexible and inefficient. By allowing private firms to bid for public service contracts, it was argued, local people would get better value for money.

Second, it is claimed that privatisation increases direct accountability to the consumers of services. According to this view, local government public service provision operates not in the interest of those who receive the service, but in the interest of those who administer it. Private sector provision, on the other hand, is more genuinely controlled by the public. Private companies have to satisfy public taste or they will not survive. Privatisation, therefore, increases accountability because, although not everyone participates in local elections, everyone is a consumer. Consumer pressure determines whether a company succeeds or fails.

During the 1980s and early 1990s, the privatisation of local authority services has taken a number of different forms.

The sale of assets

One of the consequences of the setting up of the welfare state after 1945 was a change in local government responsibilities. Before 1945, local authorities had been responsible for the provision of public utilities such as water, gas and electricity. After 1945, these public utilities were nationalised and transferred from local authority control into the hands of public corporations.

Having lost control in some areas, local authorities gained responsibility for a new range of social and welfare services - such as education and housing. In the 20 years after 1945, education and housing expenditure dominated local government budgets. Whereas education and housing amounted to 35% of local authority expenditure in the 1940s, it had increased to 60% in the 1950s. By 1961, there were 4.2 million council houses and flats, 27% of all households.

Although the sale of council houses had been permitted since before the Second World War, most council tenants could not afford to buy their houses. The Housing Act of 1980, however, offered tenants a major discount if they agreed to buy their council house within a certain period (long-term tenants could receive a discount of as much as 60% of the market price of the house). The result was the sale of over a million council houses by 1987.

The Conservative party had promised council tenants the 'right to buy' in their 1979 election manifesto. This was not just a ploy to win the votes of council tenants. The policy reflected the Conservatives' belief in owner occupation and their concern about public spending. By selling council houses, they argued, public expenditure would be reduced since the new owners would be responsible for their upkeep.

The revenue received from the sale of council houses has been used to finance new house building, though councils are only allowed to reinvest a proportion of it in new buildings. At first, this proportion was 50%. Later, it was reduced to 20%. As a result, much of the money raised from council house sales is locked up by central government controls on capital spending.

Council houses are not the only local government assets to be sold off since 1979. Local authority land has also been sold off. Perhaps the most notorious example of this was Westminster Council's decision in 1987 to sell three cemeteries for 15 pence. After the ombudsman declared that 'maladministration causing injustice' had taken place, the council bought back the cemeteries in 1992 for £5 million.

The imposition of market mechanisms

Market mechanisms have been imposed on local authorities in two ways. First, some services have been 'deregulated'. An example of this is the provision of bus services. Until 1980, strict licensing of bus transport meant that, in practice, private operators found it hard to compete with bus companies run by local authorities. Changes in legislation in 1980 made it easier for private companies to obtain licences. This broke the public monopoly. Then, the Transport Act of 1985 forced public sector operators to form private companies and to operate in line with market criteria. The National Bus Company was broken up and privatised. Routes were deregulated so that a single route might have buses from several companies running on it. On such a route, different companies could charge different fares for the same distance. The market would determine how many buses would run how often and which companies would survive to operate them.

Second, compulsory competitive tendering (CCT) has been introduced. Rather than simply employing their own staff to provide services, councils have been forced to allow private companies to bid for contracts. To facilitate this, council employees have to be detached from the local authority's main management structure and set up as free standing companies (direct service organisations). If a private company makes a bid which is lower or in some way better than that made by the council's direct service organisation, then the council is expected to award the contract to that private company. The 1980 Local Government and Land Act required CCT in the areas of highways and building construction and maintenance. The Local Government Act of 1988 extended this requirement to refuse collection, street cleaning, catering, cleaning buildings and vehicle maintenance. The Local Government Act of 1992 extended this requirement still further to professional, financial and technical services.

Evidence suggests that between 75% and 80% of contracts are awarded to councils' direct service organisations (Wilson, 1993). CCT has been criticised because when local authority workers have won contracts, they have often found that their pay and working conditions have suffered. Also, the quality of work provided by private companies is not always of a sufficiently high standard.

Greater provision of services outside local authority control

In a number of areas, central government has encouraged the transfer of services from local authority control to the private sector. In education, for example, Grant Maintained Schools have opted out of the local authority system. Instead, they are controlled and financed directly by central government. Similarly, central government has encouraged private housing corporations at the expense of local authority council housing. In addition, under the terms of the Community Care Act which came into operation in April 1993, local authorities are expected to dispose of most of their own residential homes, day care centres and other facilities to the private and voluntary sectors. As a result, the function of the local authority will be to award contracts to the private and voluntary providers of the services.

The impact of privatisation

The changes brought about by privatisation have varied widely. Some 'flagship' Conservative controlled councils, such as Wandsworth and Westminster, have embarked enthusiastically on privatisation drives. In an interview in 1987, for example, Wandsworth council leader, Paul Beresford, described his strategy as:

> 'The efficient management of services; to cut waste; to ensure high quality; to test all council services, where possible, against the private sector; to contract out where appropriate; and to promote a vigorous sales policy involving (a) the sale of land and buildings where such action proves economically efficient and (b) the sale of houses to families on low incomes, thus breaking up enormous housing estates and providing a stimulus to the maintenance of such housing.'

Similarly, when the Conservatives briefly took over control of Bradford in the late 1980s, they introduced competitive tendering across a wide range of council services, they ended council provision of a number of services and they increased council house rents.

In local authorities controlled by Labour or the Liberal Democrats, however, considerable efforts have been made to minimise the impact of privatisation. Even in some Conservative controlled councils, the changes have not been excessive.

Activity 16.7

Item A *Refuse collection*

This photo shows a dustcart owned by West Lancs District Council. Since 1988 council employees have had to compete with private companies.

Item B *Arguments in favour of CCT*

Allowing the private sector to compete to provide local authority services can bring significant improvements in value for money either because the in-house workforce improves its efficiency (to match the competition) or because the private firm which wins the contract can beat the in-house staff on price and/or quality. Some local authorities have led the way in using the private sector to deliver services to the consumer. These authorities are free to concentrate on planning the future direction of service delivery, setting quality standards and monitoring the service to ensure that the standard required is achieved. But, a number of other authorities have persisted in retaining all work in-house. We have, therefore, had to introduce compulsory competitive tendering for a significant number of services, to ensure that local taxpayers in all areas share in the benefits which competition brings. Much remains to be done. The government is looking urgently at ways of extending competition further. We intend to ensure that private firms have a fair chance to compete for local authority work. The government already has powers to prevent the local authority's own workforce carrying out certain activities where it fails to meet its financial obligations or seeks to gain an unfair advantage over the private sector by other means. This could also be appropriate where an authority demonstrably fails to provide an acceptable level of service.

Adapted from the Citizen's Charter, 1991.

Item C *Arguments against CCT*

The main arguments against the extension of compulsory competitive tendering in local government are as follows. First, the costs of setting up CCT are high both in terms of time and in terms of money. Second, recurrent costs will be increased. Inspectors will have to be recruited, extra work will be generated for lawyers and costly court cases are likely. Third, there is the likelihood that redundancies will result from CCT. Fourth, downward pressure on wages and conditions of service will occur. The experience of 1980-88 shows that this is likely. Fifth, there are high risks of lower standards of service provision. Damage may be done before penalty clauses can have a real impact on a rogue contractor. Sixth, services will be run for profit, not to meet social needs. Flexibility will be lost. Seventh, elected councillors will come close to losing control over key areas of local authority work. And, finally, the character of the 'competition' in CCT is inherently unfair.

Adapted from Pyper, 1990.

Item D *The privatisation of services in Wandsworth*

A MESSAGE TO ALL RESDIENTS OF WANDSWORTH

WANDSWORTH BOROUGH COUNCIL WANTS TO SELL OFF VARIOUS COUNCIL SERVICES TO PRIVATE CONTRACTORS, STARTING ALMOST IMMEDIATELY WITH STREET CLEANING

It is claimed that this move will mean major savings for ratepayers and greater efficiency. Is this really so? We think that the people of Wandsworth have a right to know the full facts.

- The Council has cut a quarter of all street cleaning jobs in the last two years. This has led to a marked deterioration in the cleaniness of the Borough's streets.
- The street cleaners have already negotiated a new scheme with less men, which gives Cllr. Chope all the £250,000 savings he wanted, and which satisfies Technical Services Officers operationally.
- The Direct Labour Scheme is cheaper than the majority of contractors who have tendered. The Direct Labour force knows the Borough.
- With the exception of one man, the whole of the street cleaning force have refused severance pay and an interview with the private contractors - because they know (and the government body ACAS has confirmed) that wages in the contract cleaning industry are some of the lowest in the country, and industrial relations practises are appalling.
- Should the council contract-out for political reasons, it will still have to make work for the 90-odd street cleaners by redeploying them. A massive hidden cost to the ratepayer of up to £1/2 million each year.
- There are a substantial number of disabled people employed as street cleaners. The Conservative party's local election manifesto specifically referred to improving the numbers of disabled employed by the council, but selling their jobs breaks that promise as private contractors have given no promises to employ these people.
- Wandsworth have already burnt their fingers once recently with private contractors. Last year the job of cutting grass at Old People's and Children's Homes in the Borough was put out to a firm. Performance slumped and there were many complaints - now the council is asking its own workforce to put in a bid for the contract!

A CONTRACTOR IS ONLY INTERESTED IN THE PROFIT TO BE MADE - SURELY THIS SHOULD NOT BE THE MAIN MOTIVE IN RUNNING A PUBLIC SERVICE?

WHAT EFFECTIVE CONTROL WILL THE COUNCIL HAVE ONCE THE VEHICLES AND EQUIPMENT ARE SOLD OFF? WHAT HAPPENS IF A CONTRACTOR GOES BANKRUPT? AND IF YOU ARE NOT SATISFIED WITH THE STANDARDS - YOU CAN'T GET RID OF A COMPANY WITH A LONG CONTRACT BY VOTING FOR A DIFFERENT PARTY...

DON'T BE FOOLED BY THESE FOOLISH PLANS - TELL THE COUNCIL THAT YOU THINK LOCAL SERVICES SHOULD BE LOCALLY CONTROLLED AND RUN IN THE PUBLIC INTEREST.

This leaflet was produced in 1983.

Questions

1. Judging from Items A-D would you say that CCT was a positive or a negative development? Give reasons for your answer.
2. Look at Item A. Find out who is responsible for refuse disposal at your home. How would you judge whether this service is efficient?
3. a) Judging from Items B and C what role does the government expect local authorities to play in the future?
   b) What attitude would you expect (i) councillors (ii) council employees and (iii) members of local businesses to have towards these developments?
4. Using Items A-D give arguments for and against the view that privatisation of local authority services increases their efficiency.

3 Central/local government relations

Key Issues

1. Is there a need for a system of local government?
2. What changes have taken place in central/local relations?
3. What are the likely future directions?

Is there a need for local government?

Between the mid-19th century and the 1980s, few people seriously challenged the need for local government. As in many other areas, however, the breakdown of the postwar consensus stimulated a new debate about existing local government arrangements. Opponents of local government argued that local authorities were inefficient and unrepresentative, whilst supporters claimed that the powers of local authorities were being eroded by central government. The question of whether, and if so why, local government is necessary has increasingly been debated. The arguments on both sides can be summarised as follows.

In theory, of course, there is no absolute need to have a system of local government. Services could be delivered locally, but administered and controlled by central government. This happens today with social security. Social security is delivered locally through offices located all over the country, but control rests with the Department of Social Security in London. All services provided by local government could be organised in this way. Some critics of local government favour this approach. They point out that there is a great deal of variation in the standard, range and quality of services which are offered by local authorities. If all services were controlled from the centre, they argue, then provision would be uniform throughout the country.

Other reasons for doing away with local government are as follows. First, some local authorities are inefficient. The services they provide cost more than the same services provided by other local authorities. Abolition of local government would increase efficiency. Second, local government itself is a cost. Meetings of councillors and the full range of support services they require does not come cheap. Third, local government can be narrow and introspective. Local authorities are often concerned only with local issues. How these local issues fit into the national picture or even how they relate to what is happening just over the authority's border is simply ignored. Central government is better able to plan. Fourth, since local government has become dominated by political parties, narrow party self-interest has become the crucial determinant of policy decisions. Fifth, there is a marked lack of interest in local democracy. This is reflected in the low turnout in local elections and in the public's lack of knowledge about councils' functions. The public only cares about the efficient delivery of services, it does not care about local democratic control. Sixth, local councillors are amateur politicians who lack the detailed knowledge to run complex modern bureaucracies. Seventh, there is such wide central government control that the scope for local autonomy is so small that it is hardly worth bothering with a system of local government. And eighth, since local government reorganisation in 1974, local government has become remote to many people.

Supporters of local government have countered these criticisms with the following arguments. First, all but the smallest democratic states have systems of local government. The tendency elsewhere is to increase, not to erode, the powers of local government. The setting up of a tier of local government in Spain, for example, was seen as an important step in the transition from Franco's fascism to democracy. Second, local government is an efficient method of administering certain services since local authorities are run by local people who know local needs. What works in one area may not work in a different area, so it is better to retain local control. Control exerted from the centre tends to be rigid and inflexible. Third, there is no indisputable evidence to suggest that services could be provided more cheaply without local government. Fourth, local authorities are multi-purpose bodies and can, therefore, ensure policy coordination across a range of departments. They are not necessarily narrow or introspective. Fifth, local authorities can experiment with ideas because they have a degree of independence. An individual authority can introduce a pilot scheme, which, if successful, may be adopted elsewhere. Sixth, local government encourages democracy because local representatives run councils and local people are given the opportunity to vote in local elections. Low turnout is not a good reason for doing away with local democracy. It could be a sign that people are generally happy with the way local affairs are run. Also, local government reflects the different political balance of different parts of the country. The North of England, for example, is a Labour stronghold. But, during the 1980s, Conservative victories in general elections meant that the majority view of the North of England was not represented by central government. It was represented at local level, however. Seventh, local authorities can be seen as a barrier or defence against an all-powerful central government. Eighth, an important function of local government is to hold public servants accountable.

Activity 16.8

Item A *Central/local government relations*

After more than a decade of fighting against local councils, there are plans in Whitehall to bury the hatchet. A number of ministers agree with the view that too much power was stripped from local government in the 1980s. In particular, they are worried that the centre has too much control over funding. The government's tough line, it is argued, especially the powers to cap excessive local authority budgets, has paid dividends by making the vast majority of councils more aware of their financial responsibilities. This new sense of responsibility should be rewarded. In return for the restoration of some powers, councils would be required to put one third of their members up for election annually. This, it is claimed, would act as a brake on local tax increases.

Adapted from the *Daily Telegraph*, 28 March 1994.

Item B *Local government re-organisation*

This cartoon appeared in the *Guardian* on 19 January 1994.

Item C *In support of unitary authorities*

Changing the structure of local government will not solve all the problems. It is desirable, however, that people can identify one authority which secures services for their area. Having a single tier should reduce bureaucracy and improve the coordination of services, increasing quality and reducing costs. This will be the case even if the county council and district councils in a county are efficient now. Such a structure is also important for proper financial accountability. People must know who is responsible for setting a budget and achieving value for money in services in their area. Introducing unitary authorities would also offer the opportunity of relating the structure of local government more closely to the communities with which people identify. This should increase interest in local affairs and make for more responsive and representative local government. The government certainly does not intend that county or district councils be abolished wholesale. In some places, it may be best for existing authorities to be merged. In others, the best approach may be to create or recreate quite different authorities. In some areas, there could be a case for two tiers.

Adapted from HMSO, 1991.

Item D *Against unitary authorities*

For once, it is not financial cutbacks which are responsible for the threat to Somerset's nine mobile and 35 static libraries, though they have certainly made their mark. This time it is the restructuring of local government which may undo much of the hard work put into the county's bookshelves. Under the government's plans for unitary authorities, Somerset is to be divided into three. Accordingly, the management of the county's library service will follow suit. But, if the county's libraries are split into three separate bodies, the book stock available to local people will be immediately diluted by two thirds. It will be too costly, impracticable and bureaucratic to rotate books from one end of the county to another. The money spent on administration will increase threefold. Nor is this impending disaster restricted to the South West. Librarians throughout the country know that small units will never be able to afford the more expensive and specialist material good libraries need. Few units will have the infrastructure for static branches, let alone mobiles.

Adapted from an article by Joanna Coles in the *Guardian*, 8 April 1994.

Item E *Proposed changes to local government*

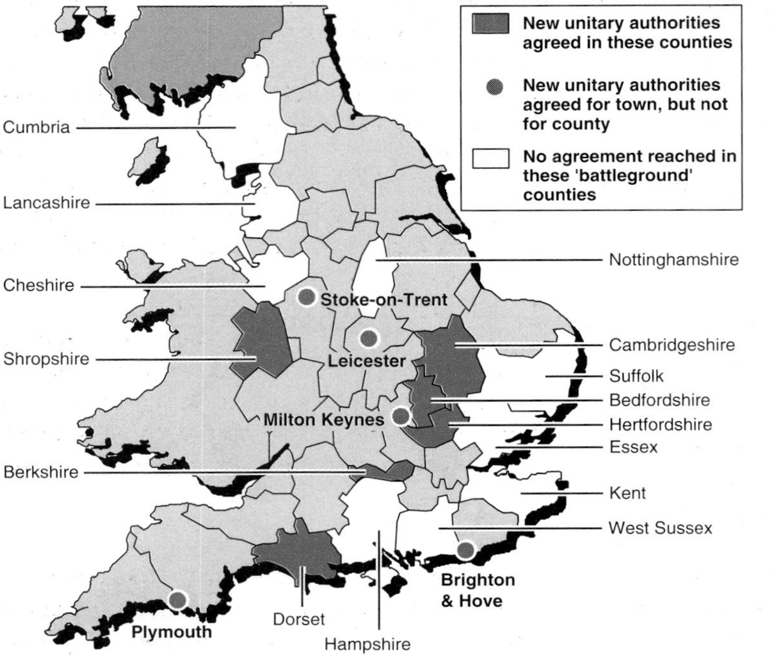

This map shows how councillors in different areas responded to the idea of unitary authorities. The government hoped for consensus from local politicians, but it did not materialise. In at least nine 'battleground' counties, county councillors wanted to keep the two tier structure while district councillors wanted new unitary authorities.

Adapted from the *Financial Times*, 25 February 1994.

Questions

1. Describe how the relationship between central and local government is viewed in Items A and B. In what ways do the viewpoints differ?
2. Judging from Items B-E would you expect local government reorganisation to improve central-local government relations? Give reasons for your answer.
3. What does Item D tell us about the impact of the government's local government review?
4. 'Unitary authorities will result in better local government.' Using Items C-E, give arguments for and against this view.

4 Quasi government

Key Issues

1. What is quasi government?
2. Why has the number of public corporations declined since 1979?
3. Why has the number of quangos grown since 1979?
4. What are the consequences of the growing number of quangos?

Quasi government

When people use the term 'public sector' they are usually referring to the areas of the economy which are financed by central government and to the agencies through which decisions made by central government are implemented. Local authorities make up one branch of the public sector. The civil service makes up another. But, local authorities and the civil service are not the only agencies to be financed by central government. Nor are they the only organisations to implement decisions taken by central government. The public sector has a third main branch. This branch can be described as **quasi government** or **government at arm's length**.

The main characteristic of quasi governmental organisations is that they are run by governmental appointees, not by elected representatives. They are described as quasi governmental organisations because, although they are not actually branches of the government, their role is to perform a specific function or range of functions laid down by central government.

Since quasi governmental organisations are set up on a statutory basis and since they are run by government appointees, they retain close ties with central government. But, since ministers have no control over their day-to-day running and since those who run them are not elected, they differ from the other agencies in the public sector. The key difference is their lack of accountability. The actions performed by local authorities are the responsibility of elected representatives who are directly accountable to the electorate. Similarly, the actions performed by civil servants are the responsibility of ministers who are accountable to Parliament and ultimately to the electorate. The actions of quasi governmental organisations, however, are the responsibility of those who are appointed to run the organisation. They are accountable neither to an electorate nor to a minister. It is this lack of democratic accountability that is at the bottom of criticism of quasi governmental organisations.

Although different political commentators use different classifications, most would agree that there are two main types of quasi governmental organisation - public corporations and quangos.

Public corporations

Public corporations are organisations set up by statute to run services or industries on behalf of the government. All public corporations have a written constitution which lays down their terms of reference. This constitution can only be modified by Act of Parliament. Each public corporation is run by a board appointed by the minister in charge of the department responsible for sponsoring the corporation. The minister has the right to approve capital investment programmes, the right to information and the power to issue directions of a 'general character' in relation to matters which affect the public interest. The day-to-day running of the corporation, however, is left to the board. Although the assets of public corporations are owned by the state, public corporations trade and are expected to derive the greater part of their revenue from customers.

Case study - the BBC

An example of a public corporation is the BBC. Initially, the BBC was a private company (the British Broadcasting Company). But, late in 1926, the company ceased to exist. It was replaced by the British Broadcasting Corporation which was created by Royal Charter. The BBC is financed largely through licence fees paid by consumers and run by a board of directors nominated by the Prime Minister. Formally, this board of directors is politically independent. But, the Prime Minister (through patronage) and other members of the government (by making public statements) may influence its policies informally.

The BBC was one of a small number of public corporations set up before the Second World War. This number grew rapidly once the Labour government elected in 1945 began its programme of nationalisation. Between 1945 and the 1980s, much of British industry was nationalised and, therefore, run by public corporations. According to a report published in 1976, nationalised industries are public corporations with four characteristics. First, there are no private shareholders. Assets are publicly owned. Second, members of the board are appointed by a Secretary of State. Third, the board members are not civil servants. And fourth, these public corporations are mainly engaged in industrial or other trading activities (NEDO, 1976).

By the late 1970s, however, Conservative party policy had turned against public corporations. Two main criticisms were made. First, many public corporations had monopoly status which reduced efficiency. Second, relations between ministers and boards were unsatisfactory. Since ministers could intervene in the 'national interest', they could prevent corporations succeeding commercially. The Conservative solution in the 1980s was to privatise more than 20 public corporations, including key services such as the Central Electricity Generating Board, British Telecom, British Gas and the water authorities. This policy has continued in the 1990s with the privatisation of British Rail, for example. Once privatised, these industries and services move out of the public sector and it becomes much harder for central government to regulate their activities.

Quangos

According to some commentators, quango is an acronym for **q**uasi **a**utonomous **n**on-**g**overnmental **o**rganisation. Others replace the **n**on with **n**ational or argue that the term quango should be replaced with QGA (quasi governmental agency).

Commentators do not just disagree about what the term 'quango' stands for. They also disagree about what it means. Some use the term loosely to mean any organisation set up and funded by central government but not run by civil servants or local authorities (under this definition, public corporations are quangos). Others are more specific. They suggest that quangos are unelected agencies that have one thing in common - they are all responsible for spending public money (this definition excludes public corporations since they are responsible for providing a service or running an industry not for spending public money). It is in this latter sense that the term is used below.

The procedures used to recruit and appoint personnel to quangos are discussed in detail in chapter 11, part 5.

The Pliatzky Report, 1980

According to the 1980 Pliatzky Report on Non-Departmental Public Bodies (another name for quangos), there are three different types of quangos - those with an executive function, those with an advisory function and tribunals (Pliatzky, 1980).

Executive quangos tend to be permanent bodies with large staffs whose role is to regulate a particular area of the law, to disseminate information or to distribute funds. The Commission for Racial Equality (CRE) is one example. The function of the CRE is to monitor race relations and to work for 'a just society which gives everyone an equal chance to learn, work and live free from discrimination and prejudice and from the fear of racial harassment'

(CRE mission statement). It has an annual budget of c.£14 million and a staff in its five regional offices and headquarters of around 200. A second example is the Higher Education Funding Council (HEFC). The function of the HEFC is to advise on the distribution of public funds to institutions of higher education. According to the *Independent on Sunday* (10 April 1994) the HEFC was responsible in 1992-93 for distributing £2.6 billion to English Universities. In that year, it had running costs of £11 million. The council consists of 14 members appointed by the Education Secretary. None is elected. Meetings of the council are closed to the public.

The function of **advisory quangos** is to examine specific problems and to make recommendations. Some are permanent bodies, others are set up on a temporary basis. The Overseas Projects Board is an example of a permanent advisory quango. This board, made up of 16 representatives of British companies and an academic, helps the government to formulate export policy and helps to coordinate joint British bids for projects in the Third World by providing 'expert advice' to the Department of Trade and Industry (*Independent on Sunday*, 20 February 1994). There are many hundreds of similar advisory quangos working on all aspects of government policy.

The function of the third category of quangos, **tribunals**, is to arbitrate between people who feel aggrieved and government officials. Some tribunals operate on a permanent basis - such as supplementary benefits appeal tribunals and rent tribunals. Others are set up to address a particular complaint. The work of tribunals is considered in greater detail in chapter 17, part 3.

The quango explosion

When Margaret Thatcher was elected in 1979, she made a pledge to reduce the number of quangos on the grounds that they were an unnecessary layer of bureaucracy. She said in 1980:

> 'There will always be pressure for new bodies. We shall be robust in resisting them.'

But, although the number of public corporations was decimated during the 1980s, there is evidence to suggest that, far from reducing the number of quangos, the Thatcher administration sowed the seeds for what has been described as 'the quango explosion'.

It is not easy to establish exactly how many quangos there are, not least because some exist only temporarily. According to figures from the Cabinet Office, in 1979 there were 2,167 non departmental public bodies (the government does not officially recognise the term 'quangos'). By April 1992, this number had fallen to 1,412. These figures, however, fail to take into account the huge changes in the public sector that were initiated in the late 1980s. These changes can be summarised as follows.

First, changes in the organisation of the National Health Service have led to the creation of quangos. The new trust hospitals are run by quangos - boards of directors who are appointed not elected. Also, district health authority boards no longer include local authority representatives and so they have become quangos.

Second, reforms of the education system have resulted in the creation of quangos. Quangos such as the Higher Education Funding Council have been set up to distribute funds, whilst there are plans for the governing bodies of schools which opt out of local government control no longer to include local authority representatives. If this happens, then these schools will be run by quangos.

Third, quangos have taken over what used to be the function of local authorities. For example, between 1980 and 1988, 10 Urban Development Corporations (UDCs) were set up with budgets ranging from £26 million to £160 million. These UDCs are responsible for regenerating a targeted area by investing in the environment, housing and local business. The boards which run UDCs are not elected. They are nominated by the Secretary of State for the Environment. Similarly, training programmes have been removed from local government control and placed into the hands of quangos - TECs (Training and Enterprise Councils) in England and Wales and LECs (Local Enterprise Councils) in Scotland.

And fourth, privatisation has led to the development of a new type of regulatory quango. Quangos such as Oftel, Ofgas and Ofwat have been set up to ensure that the privatised essential services carry out their functions and operate economically.

If these changes are taken into account, the real number of quangos in 1994 was 5,521, about three times as many quangos as the government officially acknowledges. If the government-appointed advisory bodies and Next Step agencies (see chapter 13 p.389) are added to the list, the number rises to 6,708 (Weir & Hall, 1994).

Central government and quangos

Placing responsibility into the hands of quangos has a number of advantages for central government. First, there are political advantages for ministers. Often it is in the interest of ministers not to be directly responsible for performing tasks. By delegating tasks to quangos, they can distance themselves from controversial issues and avoid awkward questions in Parliament. Also, ministers are responsible for appointing people to sit on quangos. They can, therefore, choose people who will support their political objectives and ensure, by this means, that government decisions are implemented in the way in which members of the government desire. Second, quangos may be a more efficient way of administering governmental decisions. Quangos have a free hand to fulfill their remit. They are not bound by the conventions and ways of work normally followed by civil servants. They have the time and resources to concentrate on tasks which might not gain so much attention in a government department. Specialists rather than generalist civil servants can be appointed to undertake tasks. Third, quangos provide an alternative to elected local government. Conservative governments since 1979 have been hostile to elected local government and have made a concerted effort to control it. By farming out responsibilities to quangos, central government has increased control over local affairs from the centre and it has diminished the powers and responsibilities of local authorities. Quangos have, therefore, helped central government to achieve one of its strategic aims.

Public money administered by quangos

According to figures from the Cabinet Office, during the period 1979-92, the amount of public money administered by non departmental public bodies rose from £6,150 million per year to £13,750 million per year. But, following an independent survey of quangos (including those not counted in the official figures) carried out by the Democratic Audit (a research project funded by the Joseph Rowntree Charitable Trust), it has been established that, actually, quangos have been responsible for spending a great deal more public money than the official figures suggest. In 1993, for example, it was found that quangos were responsible for spending £46.6 billion of taxpayers money - nearly one third of total public spending (Weir & Hall,1994). When this figure was made public in May 1994, it shocked many people since previous estimates had suggested that quangos were responsible for spending a quarter of all public spending at most.

Sefras

Over the last few years, a new type of quango has come into existence - the Sefra. Sefra stands for **s**elf-**f**inancing **r**egulatory **a**gency. These agencies do not just have powers of regulation over industries, they are expected to pay their own way by levying charges. According to Christopher Booker:

> 'There are hundreds of thousands of businesses in this country which can only operate by permission of a Sefra. These have the power to 'authorise' anything from running a chemical plant to the discharging of water into a river, from the manufacture of a drug to running an insurance company, from storing electronic data to the right to take a fishing boat to sea. All this must be paid for by way of licences or authorisation charges, fees for inspections and the imposition of penalties for non-compliance.'
> (*Daily Telegraph*, 7 March 1994)

An example of a Sefra is the Medicines Control Agency (MCA) which controls the quality, safety and efficacy of drugs prescribed by doctors. Until 1991, this was the responsibility of civil servants working for the Department of Health. But as a result of the Next Steps programme (see chapter 13, section 2.2), responsibility was transferred to the newly formed MCA. The MCA is required to finance its own activities from charges levied on the drugs producers. In the year after it came into operation, the profits raised by the MCA rose from £9 million to £18 million. This was good news for those who worked for the MCA. Their salaries rose by up to 60%. But, it was not such good news for the drugs producers who had to pay for this. Other examples of Sefras are the Driver and Vehicle Licensing Agency, the Data Protection Agency and the Child Support Agency.

The argument in favour of Sefras is that they save taxpayers' money because they are self-financing. But, the extra financial burden they place on the companies they regulate has two effects. First, some companies are forced out of business by the additional costs. And second, the extra costs are passed back to customers (who are taxpayers) indirectly as higher prices for goods or services.

Consequences of the growth of quangos

The growing number and influence of quangos has brought two major criticisms. The first is that quangos are beyond democratic control. The second is that quangos have been set up for party political purposes.

The first criticism has been expressed as follows:

> 'Just over 100 years ago, the counties of England were governed by the magistrates, the Justices of the Peace who not only administered justice, but every quarter met together in quarter sessions to determine how the county should be run, how its roads should be built, how its police should be run. But, 100 years ago, we took power away from them and we gave it to elected representatives. We removed the lay elite and replaced it by councillors. Now just 100 years on, we're doing exactly the opposite: we're taking power away from the elected representatives and giving it to a new lay elite, a group of appointed people who now run an increasing range of services. They run health, they run Training and Enterprise Councils, they increasingly run parts of education, and they are what I call the unknown government of the country, because nobody really knows how they are appointed. If you ask a member of the public who is a member of the Health Authority nobody will know. You cannot hold the government to account if people do not know who is running that government.'
> (John Stewart quoted in Jones, 1994, p.105)

The second criticism is linked to the first. Between

1979 and 1992, the Conservative party won four general elections and, therefore, had continuous control of central government. During the same period, however, many local councils were controlled by other political parties. In many areas, the number of Conservative councillors fell. Understandably, local councils controlled by other parties had different priorities to councils controlled by the Conservative party. So, although the Conservatives had power centrally, they did not have power locally in many parts of Britain. This, it is alleged, was frustrating for Conservative strategists and explains why so many of local councils' responsibilities have been stripped away and handed over to quangos. According to one commentator:

> 'Local government seems destined to become a residual safety net, dealing with services which no one else can be bothered to provide, such as special schools and housing for the deprived, and purely local services such as street cleaning and refuse collection. Councillors will come to resemble the boards of guardians which administered the Poor Law before the welfare state came into existence.' (Vernon Bogdanor in the *Observer*, 20 March 1994)

Although firm evidence to support the view that quangos have been set up for party political purposes is difficult to establish, circumstantial evidence certainly exists, as the following extract shows:

> 'One member [of the Further Education Funding Council] is Les Lawrence, a Conservative councillor and education spokesman in Birmingham. Neither he nor his party has been in power in Birmingham since 1984, but there he is on the Funding Council in control of a £2.62 billion budget - almost twice as much as the budget in Britain's second biggest city.' (*Independent on Sunday*, 3 April 1994)

Activity 16.8

Item A *Relentless advance of 'quangocracy'*

Neither the local nor the national politicians seem to be in charge as the great machinery of state progressively falls into the hands of unelected, unaccountable quangos. Nothing less than the future of our nation is at stake as a once democratic society is falling into the hands of faceless bureaucracy. It is time our politicians recognised this growing threat and clawed back power from these monsters, restoring it to elected bodies at the lowest level at which decisions can be taken.

Adapted from the *Daily Mail*, 25 March 1994.

Item B *The transfer of services to quangos*

Speaking last year, William Waldegrave, the Minister for Open Government, declared that the transfer of services from local government yielded a democratic gain because public services became directly accountable to their 'customers'. Grant Maintained Schools, for example, would increase parental choice and be responsive to consumers in the same way that the supply of cars or compact discs responds to demand. But, there is a fundamental flaw in this argument. Neither in Britain nor in any other democracy has a market for education, police services, inner city developments or training arisen spontaneously as it has for cars and compact discs. Any market in public services, therefore, must be an artificial one that is created and regulated by government.

Adapted from an article by Vernon Bogdanor in the *Observer*, 20 March 1994.

Item C *The transfer of public spending to quangos*

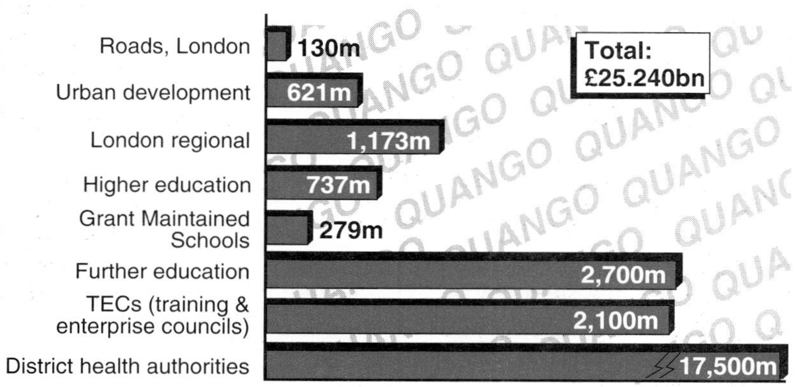

This diagram shows how much public money was transferred from local authorities to quangos in £million in 1992-93.

Adapted from the *Guardian*, 19 November 1993.

Item D *Government by quango*

This cartoon appeared in the *Guardian* on 19 November 1993.

Item E *Quangowatch*

Quangowatch

A guide to those unelected quasi-autonomous non-governmental organisations that run our lives

No 5: The Welsh Development Agency

What does it do? Attracts investment to Wales, clears derelict land and encourages the growth of local businesses.
Budget: £170m (about £70m from public funds).
Who appoints its board? The Welsh Secretary.
Controversy one: Its chairman was Gwyn Jones, a businessmen, appointed by Peter Walker, a former Welsh Secretary, after meeting him at a Conservative fund-raising lunch. He resigned from his £40,610, part-time job last June ahead of a Commons Public Accounts Committee report that condemned the agency for: giving out illegal redundancy payments costing £1.4m; allowing free private motoring for board members; appointing a discharged bankrupt as marketing director who was later jailed; and flying directors on Concorde. Dr Jones, who was told to repay the agency £3,379, was made chairman of the Welsh Broadcasting Council (salary £15,140) and a BBC governor.
Controversy two: Philip Head, WDA's £71,000 a year chief executive, resigned after the report. He was made head of property for another quango, the Further Education Funding Council of England (salary £46,000).
Are things getting better? Last month staff passed a motion of censure against management for not following a recommendation of Sir John Caines, a former permanent secretary in the Department of Education, that senior jobs in the agency should be advertised rather than given out in secret.
Accountability. No directly elected members. Press and public do not have access to meetings and papers.
Send details of any quango you feel may be behaving improperly to Quangowatch, the Independent on Sunday, 40 City Road, London EC1Y 2DB.

Quangowatch was a weekly series which appeared in the *Independent on Sunday* in 1994.

Questions

1. a) Why do you think the number of public corporations has declined since 1979 whilst the number of quangos has grown?
   b) What are the advantages and disadvantages of government by quango?
2. Explain the fears of the author of Item A using Items B and C.
3. What does Item D tell us about quangos? Why do you think the cartoonist chose these images?
4. a) Write an article criticising the growth of quangos based on Item E.
   b) How might a member of Welsh Development Agency's governing board reply to your criticisms?

References

Alexander (1985) Alexander, A., *Borough Government and Politics: Reading 1835-1985*, Allen & Unwin, 1985.

ASI (1989) *Wiser Counsels: the Reform of Local Government,* Adam Smith institute, 1989

Bains (1972) Bains, M.A., *The New Local Authorities*, HMSO, 1972.

Barber (1978) Barber, M.P., *Local Government*, MacDonald and Evans, 1978.

Byrne (1990) Byrne, T., *Local Government in Britain*, Penguin, 1990.

Chandler (1991) Chandler, J., *Local Government Today*, Manchester University Press, 1991.

Cockburn (1977) Cockburn, C., *The Local State*, Pluto Press, 1977.

Cole (1994) Cole, J., 'Sitting tenants who need evicting', *New Statesman and Society*, 21 January 1994.

Creighton (1994) Creighton, S., 'Sell, sell, sell', *New Statesman and Society*, 21 January 1994.

Crosland (1983) Crosland, S., *Tony Crosland*, Coronet, 1983.

HMSO (1983) Department of the Environment, *Streamlining the Cities,* HMSO, 1983.

HMSO (1988) Department of the Environment, *The Conduct of Local Authority Business: the Government's Response to the Report of the Widdicombe Committee of Enquiry*, Cmnd 433, HMSO, 1988.

HMSO (1991) Department of the Environment, *The Structure of Local Government in England*, HMSO, 1991.

Hutt (1990) Hutt, J., *Opening the Town Hall Door*, Bedford Square Press, 1990.

Jones (1994) Jones, B., 'The unknown government: government by quango', *Talking Politics,* Vol.6, No.2, winter 1994.

Kingdom (1991) Kingdom, J., *Local Government and Politics in Britain,* Philip Allan, 1991.

Maud (1967) Maud, J., *Management of Local Government*, HMSO, 1967.

McKie (1993) McKie, D. (ed.), *The Guardian Political Almanac 1993/4*, Fourth Estate, 1993.

NEDO (1976) McIntosh, R., *A Study of the UK Nationalised Industries*, National Economic Development Organisation Report, HMSO, 1976.

Pliatzky (1980) Pliatzky, L., *Report on Non-Departmental Public Bodies*, Cmnd 7797, HMSO, 1980.
Pyper (1990) Pyper, R., 'Compulsory Competitive Tendering', *Social Studies Review*, Vol.5, No.5, May 1990.

Rallings & Thrasher (1990) Rallings, C. & Thrasher, M., 'Local elections the changing scene', *Social Studies Review*, Vol.5, No.4, March 1990.

Roberts (1986) Roberts D., *Politics a New Approach*, Causeway Press, 1986.

Rosenbaum (1993) Rosenbaum, M., 'Pact to the future', *New Statesman and Society*, 28 May 1993.

Saunders (1979) Saunders, P., *Urban Politics*, Hutchinson, 1979.

Smiles (1859) Smiles, S., *Self Help*, Penguin, 1986.

Schofield (1977) Schofield, M., 'The nationalisation of local politics', *New Society*, 28 April 1977.

Stoker (1988) Stoker, G., *The Politics of Local Government*, Macmillan, 1988.

Stoker (1990) Stoker, G., 'Local government' in *Wale (1990).*

Wale (1990) Wale, W. (ed.), *Developments in Politics*, Vol.1, Causeway Press, 1990.

Webb (1889) Webb, S., *Socialism in England*, Gower, 1987.

Weir & Hall (1994) Weir, S. & Hall, W., *Ego Trip*, Democratic Audit, The Charter 88 Trust, 1994.

Widdicombe (1986) Widdicombe, D., *The Conduct of Local Authority Business*, Cmnd 9797, HMSO, 1986.

Wilson (1993) Wilson, D., 'Central-local government relationships', *Talking Politics*, Vol.5, No.3, summer 1993.

Part 5

Citizenship

17 Citizenship and redress of grievances

Introduction

Suppose you overheard the following statement: 'Britain is a free country. Everybody has rights here. That's why it is a privilege to be a British citizen.' Is it a statement you would agree with? Is it true?

The statement makes reference to two terms which are at the heart of this chapter - 'citizenship' and 'rights'. Most people living in the UK are British citizens. That means that most people living in the UK have certain rights. They have the right to vote in elections, for example, the right to free education from the ages of five to 16 and the right to say or to write whatever they like (so long as they do not break the laws of libel or slander). But, what exactly are rights? Where do they come from and what has shaped them? How do they relate to the concept of citizenship? This chapter begins by considering these questions.

In the ideal world, citizens would never have any problem exercising their rights. In the real world, however, citizens often feel that their rights have been denied or infringed. Whilst some disputes are settled amicably, many are not. When a dispute cannot be settled amicably or when citizens have grievances which they feel should be redressed, it may be necessary for an independent judgement to be made on the merits of the case put by each side. This chapter also, therefore, examines the legal, non-legal and quasi legal mechanisms which exist in the UK for the purpose of settling disputes and redressing grievances.

Chapter summary

Part 1 examines what is meant by the term '**citizenship**'. What **rights and liberties** are enjoyed by British citizens? What has been the impact of the **Citizens' Charter**?

Part 2 looks at the **administration of justice** in the UK. How does the **legal system** work? Who becomes a judge? How **independent** is the judiciary?

Part 3 focuses on the **quasi-judiciary**. What is it? What role is played by **administrative tribunals**, **judicial inquiries** and **ombudsmen**?

Part 4 considers the proposals that have been put forward for **judicial reform**. What are the arguments for and against a **Bill of Rights**? What other reforms have been suggested and why?

1 Citizenship

Key Issues

1. What is citizenship?
2. What rights and liberties are enjoyed by British citizens?
3. What has been the impact of the Citizens' Charter?

Citizenship

A citizen is any member of a state who is formally recognised as a citizen by that state. The concept of citizenship is, therefore, legalistic. Citizens are individuals who have some sort of legal status within a state - they have been granted certain rights by the state and are expected to perform certain duties. The precise range and balance between the rights conferred on citizens and the duties they are expected to perform varies from time to time and from state to state. In times of warfare, for example, the duties a state expects its citizens to perform may be very great and the rights and liberties enjoyed by citizens may be very few. When peace returns, however, the situation may be reversed. The precise balance between rights, liberties and duties is a matter to be resolved, either by negotiation or through conflict, by the citizens living in a particular society at a particular time.

Where exactly do political rights come from?

This is a question which has concerned political philosophers for many centuries. Whilst no single satisfactory answer has been found, the distinction is often made between natural rights and positive rights.

a) Natural rights

Political theorists who acknowledge that there are natural rights argue that certain rights are universally applicable to all societies. The origin of these rights, it is generally argued, is to be found in the essential nature of human beings or in laws given by God. The classic statement of this theory is to be found in the writing of John Locke who argued in his *Second Treatise on Government* of 1690 that before the creation of political societies, human beings existed in a state of nature in which God-given natural laws and rights existed. These laws and rights were to be the basis of political societies when they were eventually created. Locke claimed that life, liberty and property were natural rights.

b) Positive rights

Despite the attraction of natural rights theories, a number of problems arise. It is difficult to prove that a state of nature ever existed, for example, or that rights are derived from God. It is also difficult to work out which rights are natural and which are not. As a result, some political philosophers have abandoned the idea of natural rights altogether in favour of a theory which asserts that the only rights which exist are positive rights granted by a state to its citizens. This avoids the problems associated with natural rights theories, but it raises questions about why citizens should be given rights, which (if any) rights they should be given and how extensive these rights should be.

The development of rights and liberties in the UK

Unlike in the USA and many other states, the rights and liberties of British citizens are not set out in a single constitutional document. Rather, the rights and liberties of British citizens are part of the British uncodified constitution (see chapter 4). Many of these rights and liberties are the product of custom and convention, but a considerable number are also contained in written documents - Acts of Parliament. Many of the rights and liberties contained in these Acts are the result of the struggles waged by people and their representatives against the absolute power of their rulers. The key events were as follows.

In 1215, King John was forced to sign the Magna Carta. This was the first time in the UK that the power of an absolute ruler had been limited by law. The Magna Carta established that laws made by the monarch were to be within the common law (see chapter 4, p.70), the monarch could only levy certain taxes with the permission of the council and no person could be imprisoned except by a process of law involving the lawful judgement of their peers.

In 1679, the Habeas Corpus Act was passed. This Act insisted that people should be told the reason for their arrest and should be informed of the charges against them. A person who was arrested had to be brought before a court and charged with a specific offence within three days. This Act was particularly important since it limited the arbitrary power of rulers.

In 1689, the Bill of Rights was passed. Unlike such Bills in other countries, however, the British Bill of Rights had no special status - it was an ordinary Act of Parliament. Nonetheless, it did increase the rights enjoyed by citizens. The Bill guaranteed the supremacy of Parliament over the monarch and ensured that the monarch could not impose taxation without giving representation to the people's grievances as expressed through their representatives in Parliament. The Bill also guaranteed freedom of speech and the right of citizens to petition both the monarch and Parliament.

Subsequently, a number of Acts were passed extending the rights and liberties of British citizens. The right to worship freely, for example, was established by a number of Acts such as the Catholic Emancipation Act of 1829 (which allowed Catholics to stand for Parliament for the first time). Slavery was abolished in 1833. Sex Discrimination Acts were passed in 1975 and 1987. A Race Relations Act was passed in 1976. The Data Protection Act was passed in 1984. In addition to these pieces of domestic legislation, two international agreements have a bearing on rights in the UK. The first is the United Nations Declaration of Human Rights, agreed in 1948. The Declaration sets out a number of general rights which governments are meant to grant to their citizens and more detailed guidelines stipulating specific rights and types of treatment. The second is the European Convention on Human Rights, signed in 1950. This treaty not only set out the rights which all citizens in Europe could expect, it also established a Commission of Human Rights and a European Court of Human Rights to enforce the Convention (see below, p.511).

As a result of the above developments, British citizens enjoy the following basic rights and liberties:

1. Freedom of movement.
2. Freedom from arbitrary arrest or unjustified police searches.
3. Freedom of conscience in matters of religion and politics.
4. Freedom of expression.
5. Freedom of association, including the right to protest peacefully.
6. Social freedoms - such as the right to marry, divorce, procure abortions or enjoy homosexual relations.
6. The right to vote and to stand for election.
7. The right to a fair trial.
8. The right not to be coerced or tortured by

agents of the state.
9. The right not to be subjected to surveillance without due legal process.
10. The right to own property.

Citizenship in the UK in the 1990s

Since the late 1980s, a debate about what citizenship is and what it should be has risen up the political agenda. There are two main reasons for this. First, there has been a campaign by the Conservative government under John Major to promote the idea of 'active citizenship'. And second, concern has been expressed by pressure groups and opposition parties that legislation passed in the 1980s and early 1990s has resulted in the removal of or restriction of British citizens' basic rights and liberties. These two factors have combined to ensure that citizenship remains high on the political agenda.

a) Active citizenship

The idea of active citizenship came out of the Conservatives' experience of government in the 1980s. According to Oliver:

> 'By the end of the 1980s, the Conservative government had itself become disillusioned with the potential for government to solve problems with any real or lasting success.' (Oliver, 1993, p.26)

Since, Oliver argues, governmental policies had, for example, failed to solve the problem of rising crime and rising public spending levels, the government began to look for solutions to these problems which did not involve governmental intervention. One solution was to suggest that responsibility for society's problems did not lie with the government, but with the whole community. Every British citizen, in other words, had a duty to take an active part in solving society's problems:

> 'Active citizens, according to the Conservative view, would themselves take responsibilities for some of the things that needed doing in society, rather than expect the state to do them: charitable and voluntary work, housing associations, neighbourhood watch schemes and the like are seen as alternatives to expensive and often unsuccessful state provision.' (Oliver, 1993, p.26)

Not only did this fit with the predominant ideology in the Conservative party, it also presented the government with a means of deflecting criticism.

To promote the idea of active citizenship, John Major launched the Citizen's Charter initiative in the summer of 1991.

The Citizen's Charter

The dilemma faced by Conservative governments in the 1980s and early 1990s was that they wanted to reduce public spending and yet, at the same time, they wanted to be able to claim that high standards were being maintained in public services. One way out of this dilemma was to find ways of improving standards in public services which were not costly. It was this thinking which was behind the launch of the Citizen's Charter initiative in July 1991.

John Major first mentioned the idea of a charter initiative in a speech made on 23 March 1991. In this speech, he said:

> 'People who depend on public services - patients, passengers, parents, pupils, benefit claimants - all must know where they stand and what service they have a right to expect. Where necessary, [we will] look for ways of introducing financial sanctions, involving direct compensation to the public or direct loss to the budgets of those who fall down on the job.'

According to Farnham, the stated aims of the Citizen's Charter initiative are as follows:

> 'To raise the quality of provision of the public services; to increase "consumer" choice for those using them; to increase competition within them; to raise standards of public service performance; and to give "value for money within a tax bill the nation can afford".' (Farnham, 1992, p.75)

Since the initiative was launched, public services have been required to set themselves performance targets which are laid out in separate charters. These charters are available to the public. By the beginning of 1995, over 40 service specific charters had been published. Independent inspectorates have been set up to monitor the performance of these services and there is redress for those citizens who claim, with justification, that the service provided has not reached the standards laid out in its charter. In addition, a Charter Mark Scheme has been set up to give recognition to successful public services.

In general, the charters do not increase citizens' legal rights, but they do explain what people's legal rights are. The importance placed on the initiative by John Major's government is suggested by the following comment:

> 'The Charter programme will be at the heart of government policy in the 1990s. Quality of service to the public and the new pride it will give to the public servants who provide it will be a central theme.' (Citizen's Charter, 1991)

b) Liberties under attack

The second reason for the prominence given to citizenship in the mid-1990s is the concern expressed by some pressure groups and opposition parties that, since 1979, Conservative governments have eroded and even destroyed basic rights which used to be enjoyed by citizens.

At heart, this concern is derived from the nature of the British constitution. Since Parliament is sovereign, Parliament can pass laws which take away (or add to) any or all of the rights enjoyed by citizens.

This means that the rights and responsibilities enjoyed by British citizens are entirely dependent on the government of the day. Citizens have no right of appeal if the government chooses to take away a right or liberty which they hold dear. This, it is argued, is especially unsatisfactory when a single party has been in power for a prolonged period, especially when that party's share of the vote never rose above 45% of the total population.

There were a number of occasions in the 1980s when opponents to the government were outraged by the government's erosion of civil liberties. During the miners' strike of 1984-85, for example, the police prevented miners (or those suspected of being miners) from travelling freely around the country. In 1985, the government banned employees at the Government Communications Headquarters (GCHQ) from belonging to trade unions. And, in 1990, many protesters at an anti-poll tax demonstration in London complained that they were being denied their right to protest peacefully in public. According to the pressure group Liberty (which campaigns on a wide range of civil rights issues), however, the greatest threat to civil liberty since the Second World War is the Criminal Justice Act of 1994 (see below, Activity 17.1, Item C and chapter 18 pp.553-54).

Activity 17.1

Item A *The British Rail Passengers' Charter*

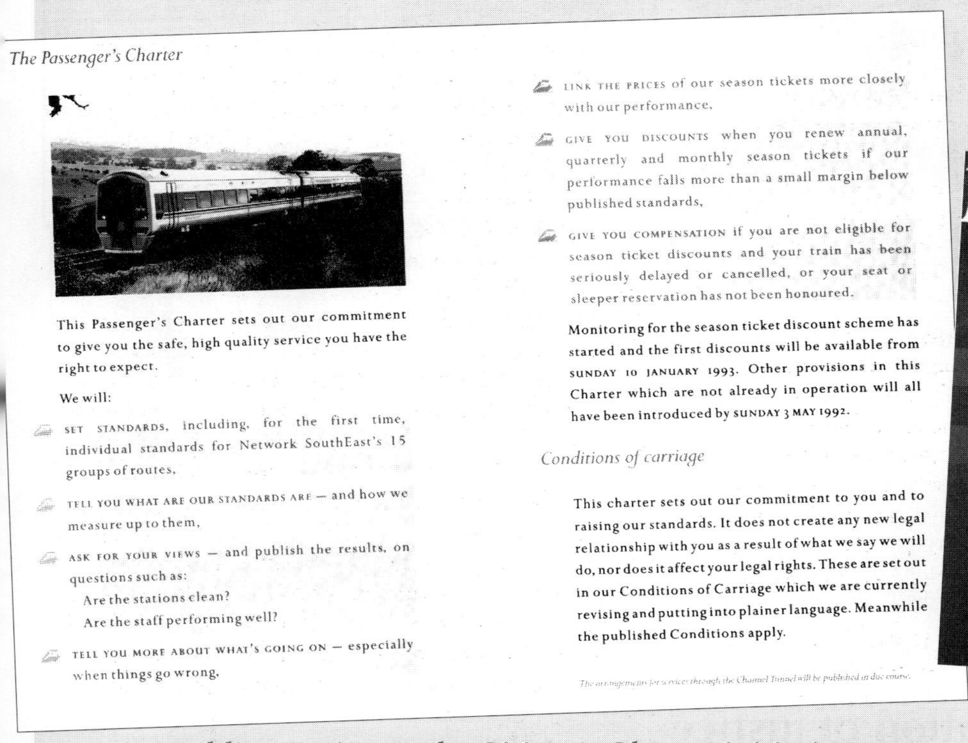

The Passenger's Charter

This Passenger's Charter sets out our commitment to give you the safe, high quality service you have the right to expect.

We will:

- SET STANDARDS, including, for the first time, individual standards for Network SouthEast's 15 groups of routes,
- TELL YOU WHAT ARE OUR STANDARDS ARE — and how we measure up to them,
- ASK FOR YOUR VIEWS — and publish the results, on questions such as:
  Are the stations clean?
  Are the staff performing well?
- TELL YOU MORE ABOUT WHAT'S GOING ON — especially when things go wrong,
- LINK THE PRICES of our season tickets more closely with our performance,
- GIVE YOU DISCOUNTS when you renew annual, quarterly and monthly season tickets if our performance falls more than a small margin below published standards,
- GIVE YOU COMPENSATION if you are not eligible for season ticket discounts and your train has been seriously delayed or cancelled, or your seat or sleeper reservation has not been honoured.

Monitoring for the season ticket discount scheme has started and the first discounts will be available from SUNDAY 10 JANUARY 1993. Other provisions in this Charter which are not already in operation will all have been introduced by SUNDAY 3 MAY 1992.

Conditions of carriage

This charter sets out our commitment to you and to raising our standards. It does not create any new legal relationship with you as a result of what we say we will do, nor does it affect your legal rights. These are set out in our Conditions of Carriage which we are currently revising and putting into plainer language. Meanwhile the published Conditions apply.

The arrangements for services through the Channel Tunnel will be published in due course.

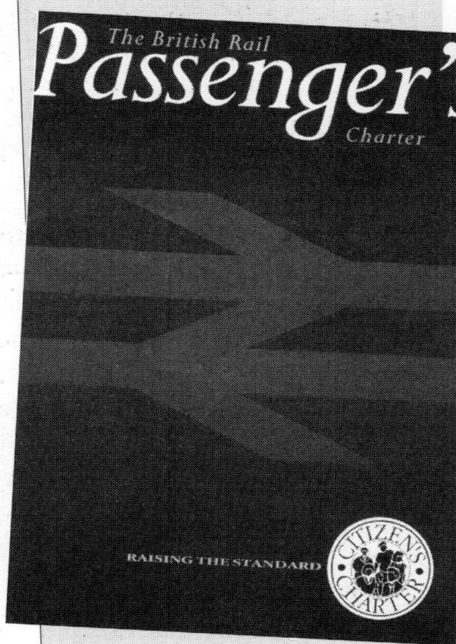

Item B *Public reaction to the Citizen's Charter initiative*

(i) The Citizen's Charterline for complaints over public services is to be scrapped today because hardly anybody is bothering to ring up. Charterline was launched in 1993, but the pilot scheme has taken only 25 calls a day at a cost of £68 for each inquiry. Lines were open for 12 hours a day, five days a week and on Saturday mornings. Complaints could be made in five languages.

Adapted from the *Guardian*, 6 May 1994.

(ii) A poll published on 18 October 1994 suggested that two out of three people regard the Citizen's Charter initiative as a 'public relations exercise'. Just 2% of respondents had used one or more of the 40 charters set up to improve public services. This poll appears to confirm the widely perceived doubts about the initiative's impact. Only 33% of those questioned had seen a copy of any of the charters, 10% had read them and only 1.6% were satisfied with them. To counter this scepticism, John Major announced two new proposals. First, members of the public would be able to nominate organisations for a Charter Mark award. And second, two further awards would go to the best staff suggestion for better services and the best customer suggestion. He said of these proposals: 'They have a common purpose: to recognise the contribution of the individual citizen and the individual public servant...to produce better services.'

Adapted from the *Guardian*, 18 October 1994.

Item C *The Criminal Justice Act*

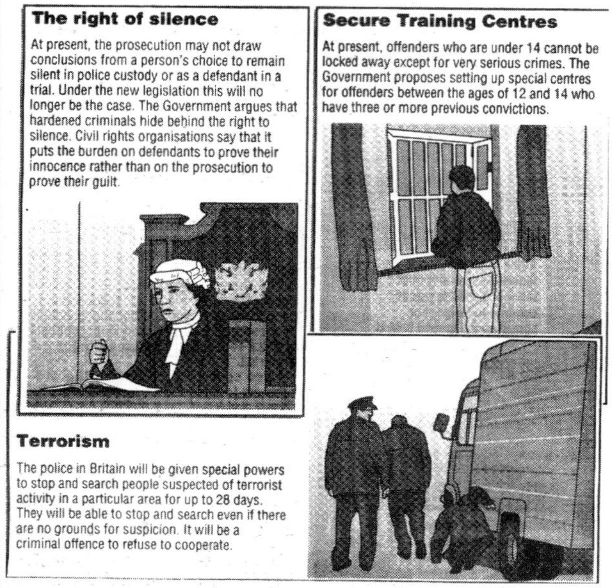

The right of silence
At present, the prosecution may not draw conclusions from a person's choice to remain silent in police custody or as a defendant in a trial. Under the new legislation this will no longer be the case. The Government argues that hardened criminals hide behind the right to silence. Civil rights organisations say that it puts the burden on defendants to prove their innocence rather than on the prosecution to prove their guilt.
Secure Training Centres
At present, offenders who are under 14 cannot be locked away except for very serious crimes. The Government proposes setting up special centres for offenders between the ages of 12 and 14 who have three or more previous convictions.
Terrorism
The police in Britain will be given special powers to stop and search people suspected of terrorist activity in a particular area for up to 28 days. They will be able to stop and search even if there are no grounds for suspicion. It will be a criminal offence to refuse to cooperate.

Travellers
Local authorities will no longer have to provide travellers with sites. It will now be a criminal offence for them to camp after a local authority has asked them to leave. It also becomes a criminal offence not to leave land when asked to do so by a senior police officer if there has been damage to land or if there are more than 6 vehicles on the land.
Ravers
If an outdoor festival or rave has not been licensed the police can stop it. It will be a criminal offence (with a maximum sentence of three months) if a person refuses to leave the site of such an event. Police will also be able to arrest someone whom they believe is going to one within a 5-mile radius.
OCCUPIED BY THE SQUATTERS
WE INTEND TO STAY
Squatters
It will become a criminal offence with a sentence of up to six months to occupy a squat for more than 24 hours after a landlord has gained an eviction order. It will also be possible for landlords or their representatives to force entry into squats to gain repossession. Appeals can only be made after the eviction.
Hunt saboteurs/peaceful protest/road blocks
A new offence of "aggravated trespass" will be introduced. Trespassers will now be committing a criminal offence if they are intending to disrupt a legal activity. This measure has been introduced to outlaw hunt saboteurs, but might easily apply to other forms of protest such as demonstrations against road-building, trade union pickets or demonstrations outside foreign embassies. The Bill also bans assemblies which are held on land without the permission of the owner and gives the police the power to stop people they suspect of travelling to such an assembly.

This diagram was published in the *Guardian* on 12 July 1994, before the Criminal Justice Bill became law (it became law in November 1994). It highlights a number of the implications of provisions in the Bill.

Questions

1. Use Items A-C to describe the role which the government expects citizens to play in the 1990s.
2. a) Using Item A, explain what the Passenger's Charter is supposed to achieve.
   b) Why do you think the Citizen's Charter initiative has failed to excite the popular imagination? Use Item B in your answer.
3. Judging from Item C, in what ways is the Criminal Justice Act a threat to civil liberty?

2 The administration of justice

Key Issues

1. How does the legal system work in the UK?
2. Who becomes a judge?
3. How independent is the judiciary?

2.1 The legal system in the UK

A key characteristic of citizenship is that citizens are subject to and protected by the laws of the state. When citizens are accused of breaking the law or when disputes arise between citizens which cannot be solved by mutual agreement, it may be necessary for the matter to be settled in court. In the UK, this is complicated by the fact that there are three separate legal systems in operation - one which operates in England and Wales, a second which operates in Scotland and a third which operates in Northern Ireland. To some extent, therefore, the justice that British citizens receive depends on where they live or where they commit their crime.

It is a characteristic common to all three legal systems that they distinguish between criminal law and civil law. Criminal law is concerned with behaviour which is disapproved of by the state and has, therefore, been made illegal by statute. Since criminal offences are regarded as offences against the state, most cases in England and Wales are brought by the Crown Prosecution Service on the state's behalf. People accused of theft or murder, for example, are tried in criminal courts. Those found guilty may be punished in a variety of ways, depending on their past behaviour and the seriousness of the offence. Punishment ranges from fines and community service to long-term imprisonment. Civil law, on the other hand, is concerned with the relationships between individuals and groups. It deals with disputes which arise over matters such as the making of contracts or wills, accusations of libel and slander or the custody of children after divorce. Individuals (or organisations) who lose a case in a civil court are not punished in the same way as in a criminal case. Rather, they are ordered to recompense the other party in some way - for example, by paying damages or by handing over the rights to property or the custody of children. As a consequence of their different objectives, the criminal and civil systems operate within different court structures, though these structures come together at the highest level.

The legal system in England and Wales

The legal system in England and Wales is organised hierarchically. Superior courts hear more serious cases and re-examine, on appeal, cases which were first brought to the lower courts.

The civil courts

At the bottom of the hierarchy are the 270 **county courts**. These deal with relatively minor civil actions and, therefore, deal with the majority of civil actions. County courts are able to make judgements about disputes over contracts to the value of less than £5,000, repossessions of property by building societies, disputes between tenants and landlords, most cases involving wills and legacies and most matrimonial matters (especially divorce cases). County courts are presided over by Circuit judges (in June 1995, there were 514 Circuit judges in total). Circuit judges must have worked as a barrister for at least 10 years. They are appointed by the Lord Chancellor.

The next step up the hierarchy is the **High Court**. Confusingly, the High Court is not one court, but three. It is made up of three divisions which have jurisdiction over separate, though occasionally overlapping, areas of law. The largest division is the **Divisional Court of the Queen's Bench Division** (the King's Bench when the monarch is male). This division hears cases which are referred from county courts either because the amount of money involved is too large or because the dispute involves a complex point of law. In addition, it plays the important role of judging writs of Habeas Corpus (deciding whether a person has been unlawfully detained). This court is also responsible for reviewing administrative decisions made by public bodies such as local authorities, government departments and health authorities. The second largest division is the **Family Division**. This has responsibility for adjudicating on all matters relating to the family and the legal side of people's personal relations. The smallest division is the **Chancery Division**. This is responsible for considering issues involving taxation and wills, issues which are often complex and involve large sums of money. Proceedings in the High Court are presided over by one or more High Court judges (in June 1995, there were 95 High Court judges in total). They are appointed by the Lord Chancellor to judge cases in one of the three divisions. High Court judges are officially responsible to the Crown.

Above the High Court is the **Civil Division of the Court of Appeal**. This court is responsible for adjudicating when the High Court gives permission for a case to go to appeal or when those in dispute successfully request such a right from the Appeal Court itself. The Master of the Rolls presides over this court. Judgements are made by the Lord Justices of Appeal (in June 1995, there were 32 Lord Justices of Appeal in total). They do not hear witnesses except in exceptional circumstances. The three judges who preside over each appeal make their decisions on the basis of documents and the arguments of barristers. Their interpretations of law set precedents which the lower courts must follow.

At the apex of both the civil and the criminal legal systems is the **House of Lords**. Cases which reach the House of Lords are heard by the Law Lords or 'Lords of Appeal in Ordinary' as they are officially known:

> 'The Law Lords consist of...senior judges made life peers and salaried with a duty to sit on the appeals committees of the House of Lords.'
> (Davis, 1995, p.64)

Normally, two Scottish members are included. Current and past Lord Chancellors may sit in judgement in the House of Lords. The Law Lords only accept cases referred to them by the Court of Appeal. They sit in judgement in a House of Lords committee room, without wigs or robes, and deliver their decision not as a judgement, but after a vote on whether the appeal should be accepted or dismissed. Each appeal, of which there are around 1,500 a year, is heard by five Law Lords. In June 1995, there were 12 Law Lords in total.

The criminal courts

At the bottom of the hierarchy lie the **magistrates courts**. These courts have two roles. First, they pass judgement on the 96% of criminal cases which are not 'indictable' (not serious enough to be tried in a Crown Court). Second, they are responsible for the committal proceedings of those cases which are indictable and will go to the Crown Court if the magistrate decides that the evidence appears strong enough. There are around 700 magistrates courts in England and Wales. They are presided over by lay magistrates or 'JPs' (Justices of the Peace), as they are also known. JPs are members of the public who are trained but not legally qualified. They sit in court part-time. In June 1995, there were 30,008 JPs. In areas with a heavy workload, legally qualified, full-time stipendiary magistrates provide lay magistrates with assistance. In June 1995, there were 51 metropolitan stipendiary magistrates, 36 provincial stipendiary magistrates and 103 acting stipendiary magistrates. The post of stipendiary magistrate was created in the late 18th century to give a professional gloss to the magistracy at a time when it was falling into disrepute.

The main responsibility of magistrates is to pass sentence upon minor offences. Most people brought before magistrates courts plead guilty. In cases where a not guilty plea is registered, three magistrates have to weigh the evidence and make a decision. Occasionally, a magistrate's court will refer a case to the Crown Court for sentence because Crown Courts are able to impose stiffer sentences than magistrates' courts. As well as committal, trial and sentencing, magistrates are also responsible for remanding or bailing defendants and for granting or withholding licences from pubs, betting shops and casinos.

All serious crimes are tried in a **Crown Court**. The Crown Courts were established in 1972 to replace the outdated quarter sessions and assize courts. Offences such as murder, rape, manslaughter and robbery are tried in the Crown Court. Where defendants plead not guilty, they are entitled to a jury trial. In this case, the role of the judge is confined to advising the jury on points of law and providing a summing up of the evidence presented and the legal situation relating to it. If the jury finds a defendant guilty, it is the responsibility of the judge to pass sentence.

Less serious cases are heard by a Recorder. Recorders are part-time judges drawn from the ranks of the barristers. In June 1995, there were 927 Recorders and 334 Assistant Recorders. More serious offences are heard in front of a Circuit judge and the most serious offences are heard in front of a High Court judge. There are 94 Crown Court centres in England and Wales. The best known is the Central Criminal Court or Old Bailey in London. Like most other Crown Court centres, the Old Bailey contains several court rooms.

Appeals against both sentences and convictions in the magistrates court go to the Crown Court. Appeals against Crown Court decisions go to the **Criminal Division of the Court of Appeal** and then, with the permission of the Appeal Court to the **House of Lords**. Behind this apparently simple procedure lies a process for criminal appeals which has been much criticised. The Appeal Court is obliged to allow an appeal where the conviction appears unsafe or unsatisfactory, where there was a wrong judgement on any question of law or where there was a material irregularity in the trial process (Griffith, 1991, p.190). If an appeal is allowed, the Appeal Court may either order a retrial or acquit the accused. Criticisms have been made of the Appeal Court judges in cases involving the Guildford Four and Birmingham Six whose convictions for IRA bombings were unsafe (the Guildford Four were acquitted in 1989 and the Birmingham Six in 1991). It has been argued that the Appeal judges initially interpreted the grounds on which an appeal could be allowed too narrowly, thus condemning these people to spend more than 15 years in prison even though they had committed no crime. Acquittal does not have to come via the Court of Appeal, however. The Home Secretary can recommend to the monarch that a pardon be granted or that part or all of a sentence be removed.

The legal system in Scotland

Unlike Wales, Scotland did not become part of the United Kingdom through conquest. As a result, it was able to preserve a degree of independence from the rest of the UK. One example of this independence is its legal system.

The system of criminal justice in Scotland differs in organisation and procedure from the English system. For legal purposes, Scotland is divided into districts. All criminal investigations in a particular district are overseen by an officer called the procurator fiscal. The procurator fiscal can request the police to make further enquiries before allowing a prosecution to go ahead and has the right to interview witnesses. Procurators fiscal make the final decision about whether a case should go to court. They perform, therefore, the same function as that performed by the Crown Prosecution Service in England and Wales. In overall charge of the procurators fiscal is the Crown Agent, based in Edinburgh. The Crown Agent oversees the work of procurators fiscal and helps them to decide whether to prosecute in difficult cases. The Crown Agent is responsible to the Lord Advocate, the senior criminal lawyer in Scotland.

Minor criminal cases in Scotland are tried in **district** or **sheriff courts** (the name varies). More serious cases are tried at the **High Court of Justiciary**. There is, in other words, no intermediate level of court, equivalent to the Crown Court. In Scotland, all appeals are heard by the High Court of Justiciary in front of three judges. No further appeal to the House of Lords is permitted.

The relationship between judge and jury in Scotland is different from that in England and Wales. The judge decides on questions of law, whilst the jury decides on matters of fact. Juries in Scotland contain 15 people (compared to 12 in England and Wales). At the conclusion of trials, juries in Scotland are able to give the verdict of 'not proven' as well as that of 'guilty' or 'not guilty'.

The civil court system in Scotland also differs in organisation and procedure from the English system. Most civil litigation in Scotland is dealt with by the sheriff courts (the same courts that deal with criminal litigation). With very few exceptions, there is no upper limit on the value of contracts dealt with by the sheriff courts. There is the right to appeal in some cases from the sheriff to the sheriff principal (the head of the judiciary in each sheriffdom) and in other cases from the sheriff to the **Court of Session**.

The Court of Session is the supreme civil court in Scotland. There is, however, the right of appeal from the Court of Session to the **House of Lords**. A leading principle of the Court of Session is that the cases are first decided by judges sitting alone and are then reviewed by several judges. The total number of judges is 25, of whom 17 (the Lords Ordinary) mainly decide cases in the first instance. This branch is called the Outer House. The eight other judges are divided into two divisions of four judges each. This branch is called the Inner House. The main business of each division of the Inner House is to review the decisions of the Lords Ordinary or inferior courts which have appealed to it (SOID, 1993). Despite these differences in organisation and procedure, the two systems are not that far apart. Madgwick & Woodhouse note, for example, that:

> 'Scotland's legal system has its own historic identity, though it is not so different that a Scottish lawyer like Lord MacKay cannot be Lord Chancellor in the British government...The House of Lords in London is the final court of appeal for the United Kingdom and the precedents it creates have a general application. Moreover, all law emanates from the same source: the Parliament at Westminster.'
> (Madgwick & Woodhouse, 1995, p.304)

The European dimension

Two courts outside the UK now play an important part in its legal system. They have entirely distinct functions, but are frequently confused.

The first is the **European Court of Justice**, the highest court of the European Union which sits in Luxembourg (see also, chapter 6, section 2.1). In matters relating to EU law, the European Court of Justice is the most senior court and, in its areas of competence, its judgements override even those of the House of Lords.

The second is the **European Court of Human Rights** which sits in Strasbourg. This court was established by the European Convention on Human Rights. Appeals can be made to this court if people believe their rights under the European Convention have been violated. Two conditions, however, are placed on such appeals. First, the appellant (the person making the appeal) must have exhausted all the procedures for justice in their own country. Second, appeals cannot be made directly. They go to court via the Commission of Human Rights. The Commission first decides whether the case is admissible and, if it is, tries to achieve an agreed settlement before referring it to court. Of all the signatories to the convention, the greatest number of cases to go to court have come from the UK - 14 since 1955. Of these, all but two judgements went against the government.

Activity 17.2

Item A *The legal system in England and Wales*

(i) The criminal courts

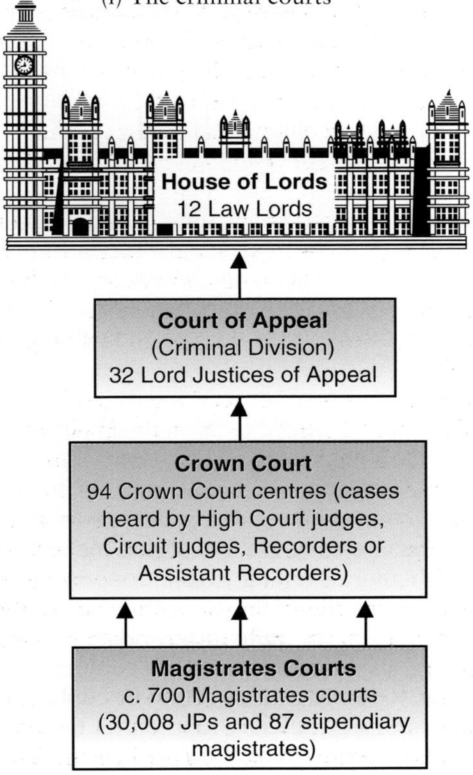

(ii) The civil courts

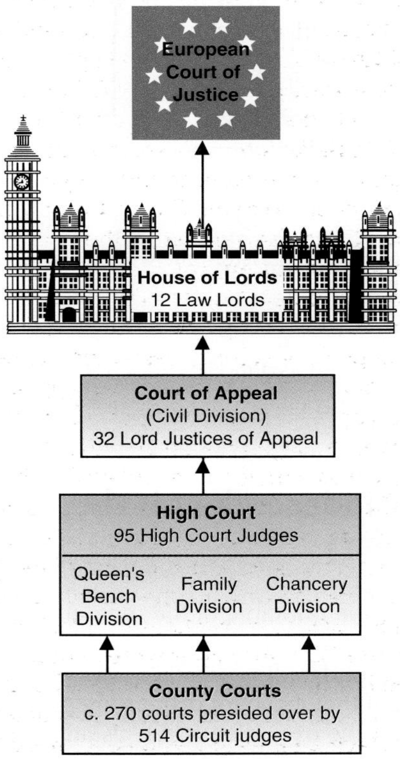

Item B *The Jury system (1)*

Unlike judges, a jury can ignore the facts, overlook statute and brush precedents aside. The main benefit of the jury system is not its capacity to apply the law, but to make decisions that are wrong in law but right in common sense. This can be illustrated by three recent trials. The first was the conviction of Private Lee Clegg. He was given a life sentence for shooting and killing a joyrider who sped through the roadblock he was guarding whilst on duty in Northern Ireland. When Clegg was given a life sentence, there was public outrage. Clegg was tried and sentenced in a court without a jury. The second trial was that of retired miner Ted Newbery who had shot a thief prowling outside his garden shed. Although a jury acquitted him of any criminal wrongdoing, in a trial without a jury he was sued successfully for damages by the thief. Again, the nation was outraged. The third trial was that of Ben Lyon, an ex-soldier aged 73. He was acquitted of attempted murder and unlawful wounding after he had shot in the face someone he suspected of stealing old railway lines near his allotment. Lyon was acquitted by a jury, much to the public's delight. The point is that the closer you look at the facts in the cases of Clegg and Newbery, the harder it becomes to argue that a wrong decision was reached. No judge is likely to ignore law, precedent and legal reasoning and make judgements on the basis of what is perceived to be the popular point of view. No judge should be asked to. Only a jury can be relied upon for the necessary, vulgar indifference to the facts.

Adapted from the *Times*, 30 January 1995.

Item C *The Jury system (2)*

"The jury will ignore that last remark..."

Questions

1. What factors might determine whether justice is done in the legal system in England and Wales? Use Items A-C in your answer.
2. a) Using Item A write a paragraph explaining the principles which lie behind the legal system in England and Wales.
   b) Using Item A as a model, draw a diagram of the Scottish legal system.
3. Discuss the advantages and disadvantages of the jury system in the administration of justice. Use Items B and C in your answer.

2.2 How independent is the judiciary?

According to the principle of the separation of powers (see chapter 4, p.69), the judicial task of law enforcement (of deciding whether laws have been broken and, if they have, of dispensing punishment) is separate from the executive and legislative tasks of devising and making laws. It is, therefore, the role of judges (known collectively as 'the judiciary') to examine cases where citizens or organisations are accused of breaking the law and to make judgements about whether or not they have done so. In theory at least, the principle of the separation of powers means that the judiciary is quite independent of the executive. Its judgements are not subject, for example, to ministerial direction or control. Equally, it is the role of the judiciary to interpret the law as it stands, not to determine what the law should be. How far this theory is borne out in practice, however, depends upon a number of factors - such as who is given the right to judge cases, how they are appointed and the extent to which one judgement affects others. In addition, as Davis points out, the British judiciary does much more than simply judge cases in court:

> 'Take the Law Lords for example...Since they are peers, they can contribute to the debates and votes in the House of Lords sitting as a legislature. Senior judges make public speeches or publish articles which contribute to the debate on controversial government policies, particularly those which affect them directly... Similarly, it is common practice to appoint judges to lead inquiries into controversial or difficult matters and for their conclusions to be taken into account in legislation.' (Davis, 1995, p.64)

It should also be noted that the Lord Chancellor straddles all three branches of the government as a member of the Cabinet (part of the executive), a member of the House of Lords (part of the legislature) and head of the judiciary.

Who are the judges?

When you picture in your mind a judge, what do you see? Do you see a young, black woman who speaks with a strong regional accent or an old, white male whose accent suggests an expensive public school and a university education at Oxford or Cambridge? If your mind conjures up the latter image, then, according to a survey published by *Labour Research* in October 1994, that image is not far from the truth. *Labour Research* examined the background of 641 judges and found that:

> 'Britain's judges remain elderly, white and overwhelmingly male...The most senior judges are even more likely to have public school and Oxbridge education backgrounds than was the case seven years ago. (*Labour Research*, October 1994, p.10)

One reason for this is the nature of their selection. Until October 1994, all judges were appointed by the Lord Chancellor or the Lord Chancellor's office. Since October 1994, vacant positions for junior judges (those below the level of High Court judge) have been advertised, but only Recorders (part-time judges) are eligible to fill the posts. It should be noted that Recorders are appointed by the Lord Chancellor's office in the first place, and so competition for appointment at the level of junior judge is still by no means open to all who work in the legal professions.

According to a pamphlet produced by the Lord Chancellor's Department in 1986, the following selection criteria are used:

> 'The Lord Chancellor's policy is to appoint to every judicial post the candidate who appears best qualified to fill and perform its duties, regardless of party, sex, religion or ethnic origin. Professional ability, experience, standing and integrity alone are the criteria, with the requirements that the candidate must be physically capable of carrying out the duties, and not disqualified by any personal unsuitability.' (LCD, 1986)

Despite this policy, the *Labour Research* survey found that just 4.6% of judges were female and only two judges (out of the 641 to take part in the survey) were black. One reason for this may be that the selection process remains largely informal. The process is secret, but it is known that the records of the Lord Chancellor's staff and the Lord Chancellor's private consultations with High Court judges are crucial. Obviously, those already appointed as judges are more likely to recommend people like themselves as worthy successors.

The appointment system has given rise to concerns about the independence of the judiciary, especially the senior judges. These concerns have become more pronounced in recent years because of the Conservative party's prolonged grip on power. At the most senior level, appointments are overtly political. They are made by the Lord Chancellor and the Prime Minister. When the two main parties alternated in government, it could be argued that, over time, political appointments which favoured one party or another would balance themselves out. This argument has become less convincing as time has gone on.

A second concern about the impartiality and fairness of the judiciary concerns their social background. Senior judges are drawn from the ranks of barristers. Traditionally, those training to become barristers have required a private income in order to survive the first few years of practice. Although it is less true than used to be the case, becoming a barrister is an expensive process which excludes large sections of the population. The result is that most barristers and, therefore, most judges come from a small section of society, move in rarefied circles, and share the values of the privileged few. Not only did the *Labour Research* survey find that 80% of judges attended a public school and 87% went to Oxford or Cambridge Universities, it found that judges tend to enjoy the lifestyle of the upper classes. When asked what they did when they were not in court, for example, 25 judges (including a Law Lord and three Appeal judges) said they enjoyed hunting and shooting and 66 judges said they belonged to two of the top gentleman's clubs. People who move in such circles live in a world far removed from that in which most people live.

This combination of professional and social characteristics, it can be argued, inevitably affects the outlook of judges and, therefore, affects the way in which they do their job. At the very least, it is likely that most judges are profoundly conservative. That is not to say that many are active proponents of the Conservative party (though, according to *Labour Research*, eight judges stood as parliamentary candidates for the Conservative party). Rather, it suggests that given the need to decide between the new and radical or the ancient, tried and tested, many judges opt for the latter. This has raised serious questions about the genuine impartiality of judges, especially in cases of judicial review (see below) where political judgements quite often have to be made.

Common law (see also, chapter 4, p.70)

According to constitutional theory, it is the role of the judge to interpret the law, not to make it. Two factors, however, combine to produce a conflict between constitutional theory and legal practice. The first factor is the convention of precedent. This stipulates that the decisions made by a higher court are binding upon lower courts. Second, the essence of a legal case consists of the application of and interpretation of a general set of rules (the law) in particular cases:

> 'The law consists of general rules (rules which relate to all persons or to wide categories of persons). These general rules (laws) are laid down by the legislature. Laws are then given effect through policies chosen and enforced by the executive. Like the laws to which they relate, such policies apply in general, rather than specific, terms.' (Davis, 1995, p.63)

By applying the general rule to a particular case, therefore, the court decides on the meaning of the law in a particular instance. This, combined with the convention of precedence, determines that what a senior court says the law means in a particular circumstance is binding on all lower courts in cases which involve the same law in similar circumstances. In essence, therefore, the court and specifically the judges in senior courts, are actually making the law through their interpretations of what Parliament has laid down.

Two schools of thought exist among leading judicial practitioners and thinkers about how the duty to interpret the law and the binding power of precedent should be used. Suppose for example that a senior judge was called upon to judge a race relations case. Should the judge interpret the law to ensure that the law reflects current public thinking on this issue or should the judgement go beyond current thinking in the hope of altering the consensus? According to Lord Devlin, the judiciary should be creative, but not dynamic. It is, in other words, not the role of the judge to make what is, effectively, new law, nor should judges act as social reformers. Lord Denning, however, represents the alternative school of thought. He argued that it was the role of the judge to achieve justice. If this meant overturning precedent or interpreting legislation very widely, that indeed was the proper role of the senior judge. Supporters of this 'dynamic' judicial role argue that if the law is not clear, then what Parliament intended to do should be taken into account. Intention, however, is difficult to establish and this perspective, therefore, gives the senior judiciary a vastly extended role in shaping laws.

According to Griffith, however, whether or not judges choose to adopt a dynamic role is not that important:

> 'More important are their reactions to the moral, political and social issues in the cases that come before them.' (Griffith, 1991, p.261)

If this is the case, then the factors which determine how senior judges apply the law are those discussed under the heading 'Who are the judges?' - the fact that they tend to come from a narrow segment of society and most have conservative views.

Judicial review

The courts are not only responsible for interpreting the precise meaning of an Act of Parliament, they are also responsible for reviewing the actions of public agents (including ministers) to find out whether their actions are ultra vires (beyond their powers). The government can be brought to court on the same grounds as an ordinary person or organisation. So, when a person or organisation feels aggrieved at the actions of some minister, government department or local authority action, then they can apply for a judicial review:

> 'Judicial review is a direct challenge to the lawfulness of the government's action and clearly involves the courts in judgements which have political fall-out.' (Davis, 1995, p.66)

For a judicial review to take place, the aggrieved individual or organisation must apply for a judicial review at the High Court. The right to judicial review is not automatic. Only when leave to proceed has been granted can a case be heard in front of two or three judges in the Divisional Court of the Queen's Bench Division. Leave is granted for one of three reasons. First, a judicial review is allowed if it seems that there is sufficient evidence to suggest that a public authority may have exceeded its statutory power (ie an act performed by a public agent may have been ultra vires). Second, a judicial review is allowed if it appears that a public body has acted 'irrationally' (in a highly 'unreasonable' way):

> 'The reasonableness test is highly uncertain and is sometimes objected to because the discretion it gives to judges is apparently unprincipled or difficult to predict...A problem is that it seems to involve at least two broad thresholds of illegality and it is not always easy to predict which test the courts will use in any particular circumstance. One threshold involves a requirement that only relevant factors should be taken into account by the decision maker. This clearly gives the courts wide scope to intervene if they want to and involves them in deciding what was the purpose or policy underlying an Act of Parliament. The second threshold requires that an applicant for judicial review establish that a decision is 'outrageous' in its defiance of logic or of accepted moral standards...Here, rather than identifying in detail the relevant matters, judges will accept a decision so long as it is coherent and

supported by reasons.' (Davis, 1995, p.67)

Third, a judicial review is granted when there appears to have been procedural impropriety (where actions taken by a public body have contravened 'natural justice'). In this case, 'natural justice' means that in carrying out their procedures, public bodies must be free from bias and act fairly (Griffith, 1991, p.125).

If leave to apply for judicial review is granted and the judges find against the public agent, five possible remedies are available to the Court. First, the Court may quash decisions made by public agents who have been acting outside their lawful jurisdiction. A planning authority, for example, which made a decision to reject a planned building for reasons not specified in the legislation which gave it the authority to act, could be ordered to change its decision. Second, a tribunal can be prevented from considering matters outside its authority. Third, a public body can be compelled to perform a specified function by law - for example, a local authority can be compelled to provide schooling. Fourth, any public body can be ordered not to carry out or to stop carrying out an action which the Court decides is unlawful. In other words, the Court can issue an injunction. Injunctions played a major part in the miners' strike of 1984-85. Judges ruled that the strike was illegal as no ballot had been held and issued injunctions against the NUM. And fifth, the judges can choose to clarify the legal position in a particular case. This is a stronger remedy than it might appear since any public body acting against a newly clarified legal position would certainly have judgement made against them in future legal action. Davis points out that:

> 'Systematic study in recent years has shown that judicial review is an expanding tool with which to challenge official decisions. It is a tool which has become available to citizens, businesses, pressure groups and public authorities. However, it is also clear that the impact of judicial review is variable. Judicial activity is focused on particular issues such as immigration and housing. Some departments, such as agriculture, are involved in very few cases.' (Davis, 1995, p.68)

This increasing use of judicial review has been criticised for a number of reasons. First, the growing number of cases suggests that there is an increasing willingness of the judiciary to intervene in the day-to-day business of government (see Griffith, 1991, p.63). Second, judicial review is a complex and expensive process and, therefore, unavailable to many individuals or groups. Third, some critics have questioned whether unelected judges from an elite social background should be responsible for scrutinising and ruling upon the legality of the actions of elected governments and local authorities. Fourth, the question has been raised as to whether judges, regardless of their background, are sufficiently well trained to take legal decisions in a highly politicised environment. And fifth, it is debatable whether principles valid in court are appropriate for such matters.

What cannot be doubted is that the process of judicial review necessarily involves judges in decisions of a political nature. The greater use of judicial review may be evidence that people are making greater use of the legal remedies available to them when they feel that their rights are being infringed or it may be that there has been a growth of the abuse of rights by public bodies.

Activity 17.3

Item A *The background of the judiciary*

(i) Judges by gender, 1995

Judges	Men	Women	Total
House of Lords	12	0	12
Appeal Court	31	1	32
High Court	89	6	95
Circuit Judges	483	31	514
Recorders	872	55	927
Assistant Recorders	284	50	334

This table shows the number of male and female judges in June 1995.

Adapted from figures provided by the Lord Chancellor's Department, June 1995.

(ii) Judges by education and age, 1994

Judges	Public School (%)	Oxbridge (%)	Average age (Years)
House of Lords	91 (90)	82 (80)	65.7 (65.7)
Appeal Court	77 (83)	87 (86)	63.4 (63.4)
High Court	80 (62)	80 (78)	58 (63)
All Judges	80 (70)	87 (80)	–

Figures in brackets show the equivalent figures in a survey carried out in 1987

This table shows the age and educational background of judges in June 1995.

Adapted from Labour Research, October 1994.

Item B *Who are the judges?*

Item C *The common law*

Let it not be thought that I am against the doctrine of precedent. I am not. All that I am against is its too rigid application, a rigidity which insists that a bad precedent must necessarily be followed. I would treat it as you would a path through the woods. You must certainly follow it so as to reach your end, but you must not let the path become too overgrown. You must cut out the dead wood and trim the side branches, else you will find yourself lost in thickets and brambles. My plea is simply to keep the path of justice clear of obstructions which would impede it.

Lord Denning quoted in Berlins & Dyer, 1989 (adapted).

Item D *Number of judicial reviews*

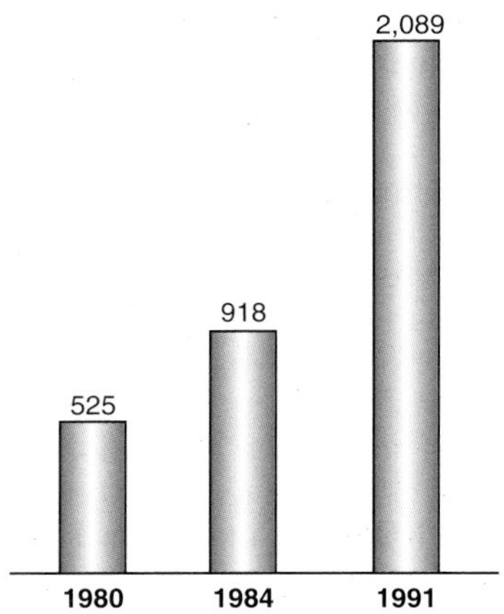

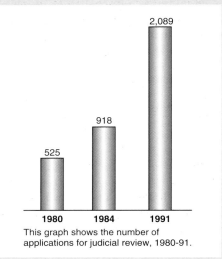

This graph shows the number of applications for judicial review, 1980-91.

Adapted from Madgwick & Woodhouse, 1995.

Item E *How independent is the judiciary?*

When, in 1994, Somerset County Council's decision to ban deer hunting on its land was challenged, the judge ruled that since the land was held under section 122 of the Local Government Act 1974 which stipulated that the land be used 'for the benefit, improvement and development' of the area, decisions had to be made for reasons which were objectively necessary for the preservation or development of the land. The ban was, therefore, unlawful because the motive for it was that the majority of council members disliked deer hunting. This case continues a trend established in the 1980s. The House of Lords, for example, ruled against Leicester City Council when it tried to prevent Leicester Rugby Club from using its pitches because some players had toured South Africa. Similarly, the courts held that Lewisham Borough Council's boycott of Shell (because of its links with apartheid South Africa) was illegal. And the courts ruled that it was illegal for local authorities to refuse to stock newspapers published by News International during a printers' strike. Conspiracy theorists should note a case in 1987 (Beddowes v Hammersmith) where a Conservative council sold part of a council estate and placed the properties on the unsold part under covenants which made them unsuitable for council lettings. This was done just before local elections which the Conservatives correctly thought they would lose. In the Court of Appeal, a majority ruled that the policy was a reasonable exercise of the council's power. Only one of the judges, who gave a dissenting opinion, noted an alleged improper motive, namely that the Conservative councillors aimed to prevent the incoming Labour council from keeping the houses in public control.

Adapted from Davis, 1995.

Questions

1. Consider the extent to which British judges undertake a political role and assess their suitability to do so. Use Items A-E in your answer.
2. Is there any evidence in Item A to support the point made by Item B?
3. a) According to Item C what role should be played by the judiciary?
   b) Does this role fit with the principle of the separation of the powers? Explain your answer.
4. 'The increasing use of judicial review means an increasingly political role for judges.' Explain this statement using Items D and E.

3 The quasi-judicial system

Key Issues

1. What are administrative tribunals and how effective are they?
2. When and why are judicial inquiries set up?
3. What role do MPs and the Ombudsman play in enabling citizens to gain redress for their grievances?

Administrative justice

When citizens have a grievance about an administrative action (an action taken by the government), it is not usually practical to go to court - it is usually far too expensive. Rather, a number of other channels have developed to enable the citizen to obtain redress from the state. Since these channels are not part of the mainstream judicial system, they can be described as 'quasi judicial'.

In some countries, a separate system of administrative courts exists specifically to hear complaints about the actions taken by the government. In the UK, however, such cases are dealt with in one of three ways - by administrative tribunals, by the setting up of a judicial inquiry or by the involvement of the citizen's local MP.

Administrative tribunals

Although the system of tribunals is not new, their proliferation and the growth in their importance is a development which has taken place since 1945. This reflects the development of the welfare state - the state plays a more active role than it played before 1945. Madgwick & Woodhouse note that:

> 'There are now about 2,000 tribunals, not all statutory and not all actually called "tribunal", concerned with the adjudication of disputes between the state and the citizen in the administration of regulatory legislation and welfare provision...Matters dealt with include disputes over tax assessments, compensation for the compulsory purchase of land, the grant of welfare benefits and pensions, appeals related to disability allowances, mental health and immigration. Tribunals are also used extensively to resolve employment and landlord/tenant disputes, which may or may not involve government agencies.' (Madgwick & Woodhouse, 1995, p.291)

The development of tribunals was unstructured. As the role of the state expanded, so did the number of complaints about government actions and, therefore, the number of tribunals. The Franks Committee of 1957, however, criticised the existing system and made a number of recommendations:

> 'Franks' contribution was, in effect, to confirm that the tribunals were neither part of the administrative process nor quite courts of law; rather, their function lay in what might be called administrative adjudication. Hence their work must bear the characteristics of the judicial process - openness, fairness and impartiality.' (Madgwick & Woodhouse, 1995, p.291)

Each tribunal differs in its membership and procedures, but the proceedings are carried out in accordance with legal principles. In general, tribunals are less formal, less costly and less time-consuming than the courts. Tribunals are normally composed of a chair who has legal training (usually a solicitor) and two lay members. The lay members generally have experience in the area with which the tribunal is concerned. Since tribunals are mainly set up by statute, they are the responsibility of ministers and tribunal members are often appointed by ministers. Although, therefore, those who sit on tribunals are supposedly independent, they may have a vested interest in opposing grievances. Hearings are held in public, and the decisions made by the tribunal are binding. The reasoning behind a decision may be made public, but there is no obligation to make it public. As a result, the decisions made by tribunals cannot form the basis for a body of law, as happens in the courts. Appeals are only possible on points of law and some tribunals do not allow appeals in any circumstances - for example, NHS and immigration tribunals. The panel can award compensation if the grievance is judged to be justified. Alternatively, matters can be settled between the disputing parties before the hearing is held.

Inquiries

Some Acts of Parliament, especially those which deal with town and country planning, make provision for a public inquiry to be held before a final decision is made. Legislation which provides for a new motorway to be built, for example, might make provision for a public inquiry to be held into the route which it should follow. Public inquiries are set up by ministers. Normally, an inspector is appointed by the minister to conduct the inquiry. This inspector then invites those with an interest to appear before the inquiry as witnesses. The report produced by the inquiry is published and reasons are given for the inquiry's recommendations. Public inquiries, it should be noted, do not make a final decision. They advise the minister. The minister is obliged to consider the advice of the inquiry, but may choose to ignore it.

Where a major question relating to the conduct of ministers, MPs, public officials or some combination of these arises, the Prime Minister may set up an inquiry headed by a senior judge. The purpose of such an inquiry is to investigate the alleged wrongdoings and to make recommendations to ensure that such misdeeds do not occur again. Such an inquiry can be one of two types. First, it might be a Tribunal of Inquiry (also known as a statutory tribunal), a body established under the 1921 Tribunals of Inquiry Act. Statutory tribunals have substantial powers - they can, for example, demand statements and evidence from witnesses. Their procedures, however, tend to be ponderous. Each party, for example, has the right to be represented by a lawyer who, in turn, has the right to cross examine every other party. This takes time and is expensive. Referring to the statutory tribunal which looked into the Crown Agents affair (a financial scandal which affected a central government agency in the 1970s), the barrister Anthony Lester complains:

> 'The inquiry took years and years, cost the taxpayer millions of pounds and was completely obsolete by the time that the report was published.' (*Guardian*, 14 January 1994)

Alternatively, the inquiry might be a judicial inquiry. Judicial inquiries do not have the power to demand statements and evidence from witnesses and, unlike statutory tribunals, they report to a specific government department. They are less formal than statutory tribunals, with witnesses speaking for themselves, rather than being represented by lawyers. An example of a judicial inquiry is the Scott Inquiry which was set up after the collapse of the Matrix Churchill trial in November 1992. During this trial, it emerged that ministers had suppressed important evidence by signing Public Interest Immunity certificates (which prevented government documents becoming available to the defence). When the former minister, Alan Clark, admitted during the trial that the government had been aware that the machine tools exported to Iraq by Matrix Churchill would be used in weapon production, there was the suspicion that ministers had been involved in a cover-up. It was this which led to the setting up of the inquiry:

> 'Following the trial's collapse, the Prime Minister announced that a judicial inquiry headed by Lord Justice Scott would investigate the entire issue of exporting defence equipment and "dual use goods" to Iraq between 1984 and 1990 and the attempt by ministers to conceal crucial evidence from the defence by declaring Public Interest Immunity.' (Adams & Pyper, 1995, p.89)

The scale of the inquiry can be demonstrated by the following statistics. The inquiry sat for over 400 hours in open session and for 50 hours in closed session. In addition, it took written evidence from 160 witnesses and scrutinised over 200,000 pages of documentation.

Inquiries headed by senior judges can be an important means of investigating actions taken by government. If the judge is scrupulous, those being investigated have much to fear if they were guilty of improper action. If, however, the judge refuses to rock the boat, the issues and responsibilities can become clouded. As in other areas in which senior judges are involved, much depends on their individual views and competence.

The role of MPs

In many cases, the constituency MP is the person to call upon if a right seems to have been infringed or a grievance requires redress. Whether the local MP will agree to take on a case, however, depends on a number of factors. First, the MP has to decide whether the matter is important enough to raise. Second, MPs are extremely busy and may have insufficient time to take on new cases or to pursue the cases they have taken on with sufficient vigour to ensure that a positive outcome is achieved. Third, party discipline in Parliament is strong and MPs on both sides may be discouraged from raising issues which might cause embarrassment to their party. Fourth, MPs have only limited office, research and secretarial facilities. And fifth, MPs vary enormously in terms of interests and ability.

Once they have agreed to take on a case, MPs can take action in a number of ways in support of their constituent. First, if the problem is local, the MP can write to the person or organisation concerned. Second, if the problem relates to central government, the MP can write to the minister concerned and request assistance. Third, the MP can issue a written or an oral question to a relevant government minister (the government minister is obliged to answer such questions). And fourth, the MP can request that the Parliamentary Commissioner for Administration, also known as the 'ombudsman', investigates the complaint. The term 'ombudsman' is Scandinavian, meaning 'complaints person'.

The Parliamentary Commissioner for Administration (PCA)

Since administrative tribunals have grown up on an ad hoc basis (see above), there are areas of public administration where no tribunal exists to hear complaints. To bridge this gap and to create a mechanism for dealing with complaints of maladministration, a PCA was first appointed in

1967. It is the job of the PCA to investigate complaints of maladministration which occur in the departments of central government. In 1987, the range of bodies included within the PCA's jurisdiction was extended to include the Equal Opportunities Commission, Sports Council, Legal Aid Board, Charity Commission, Royal Mint and Scottish Tourist Board. The PCA is supported by a staff of around 55.

Since 1967, ombudsmen have been established for Northern Ireland (1969), the Health Service (1973), local government (1974) and Scottish local government (1975). Some sectors of private industry have also established ombudsmen schemes, but these should not be confused with the statutory schemes.

Members of the public cannot refer cases directly to the PCA. They must be passed on through an MP. Once a complaint is received, it is acted upon only if no other form of redress exists and if the complaint satisfies the provisions of the 1967 Act, namely that a person has good reason to claim 'to have sustained injustice in consequence of maladministration' (section 5.1). A major problem is that 'maladministration' is not defined in the Act, though De Smith & Brazier claim that the PCA now defines maladministration as:

> 'Corruption, bias, unfair discrimination, harshness, misleading a member of the public as to his rights, failing to notify him properly of his rights or to explain the reasons for a decision, general high handedness, using powers for a wrong purpose, failing to consider relevant materials, taking irrelevant material into account, losing or failing to reply to correspondence, delaying unreasonably before making a tax refund or presenting a tax demand or dealing with an application for a grant or licence and so on.' (De Smith & Brazier, 1989, p.649)

Thompson (1993) notes that only about 20% of cases referred to the PCA are investigated, though Madgwick & Woodhouse (1995) point out that over half the complaints were rejected because they did not concern administrative actions.

Once an investigation does begin, the PCA has wide powers. Although hearings are in private, the PCA can compel witnesses to attend and can inspect relevant files and papers. After the investigation, the PCA submits a report to a House of Commons select committee. The report is also published. If maladministration has taken place, the PCA recommends an appropriate remedy. Although the government department found to be guilty of maladministration is not obliged to accept the PCA's recommendation, it is under strong pressure to do so. In most cases, an apology or financial compensation is offered. In some cases, changes to administrative procedures are implemented.

A number of criticisms have been made of the way in which the ombudsman system works. First, it is claimed that the PCA is under-used. This may be because complaints have to be channelled through MPs and because they must be placed in writing - a difficult and time consuming task. Second, the large number of rejected complaints is a cause for concern. The PCA has to be satisfied that both maladministration and injustice have occurred before a complaint is considered. Some critics argue that this should be considered in the course of an investigation, not as a condition of its beginning. And third, critics argue that the PCA ought to be given powers to enforce the recommendations made in reports. Although the recommendations are usually adopted, the gravity of the investigation is reduced because the recommendations are not enforceable.

Despite these criticisms, however, the system has its advantages. Madgwick & Woodhouse, for example, point out that:

> 'The very presence of the Commissioner with his authority to conduct in-depth investigations has made departments think more carefully about their administration; and for those citizens who have a grievance, the Commissioner provides a free means of seeking redress.' (Madgwick & Woodhouse, 1995, p.289)

Activity 17.4

Item A *The Barlow Clowes affair*

In 1988, around 18,000 people who had invested in the company Barlow Clowes found that their investments had failed because funds had been misappropriated by Peter Clowes. Since the company was licensed by the Department of Trade and Industry (DTI), several hundred of these investors approached the PCA, alleging that the DTI had been negligent in fulfilling its regulatory function. The PCA, Anthony Barrowclough, joined the claims together into one action and found that there had been 'significant maladministration' on five counts and that the DTI was liable for compensation. The Secretary of State at the DTI, Nicholas Ridley, refused to accept that there had been maladministration, saying: 'In the government's view, the department's handling of the case was within the acceptable range of standards reasonably to be expected of a regulator.' The PCA, however, was not willing to be disregarded and replied that: 'The grounds for questioning my findings have left me unconvinced.' In the end, the government paid £150 million compensation because of the 'exceptional circumstances' and in deference to the PCA. This compensation may not have been paid if pressure had not been applied by Conservative backbenchers whose constituents were affected.

Adapted from Madgwick & Woodhouse, 1995.

Item B *Complaints received and investigations completed by the PCA*

(i) Complaints received by the PCA

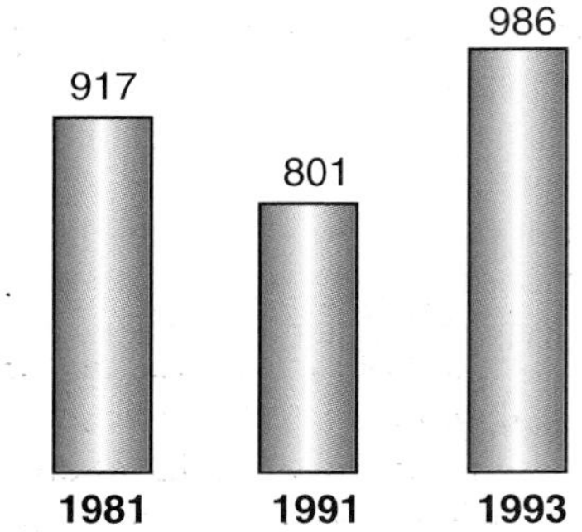

This graph shows the number of complaints received by the PCA, 1981-93.

(ii) Investigations completed by the PCA, 1967-91

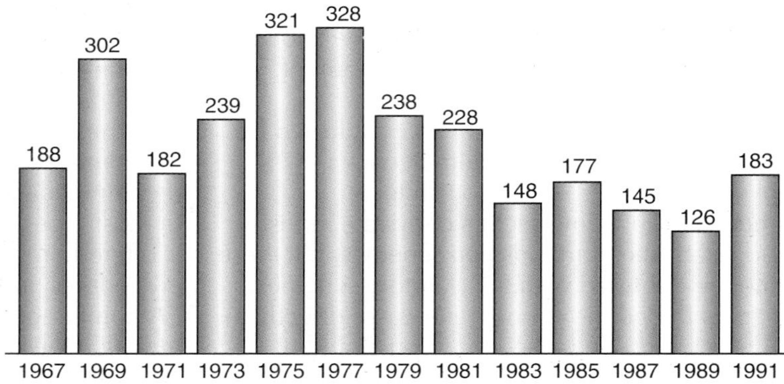

This graph shows the number of investigations completed by the PCA, 1967-91.

Item C *The PCA*

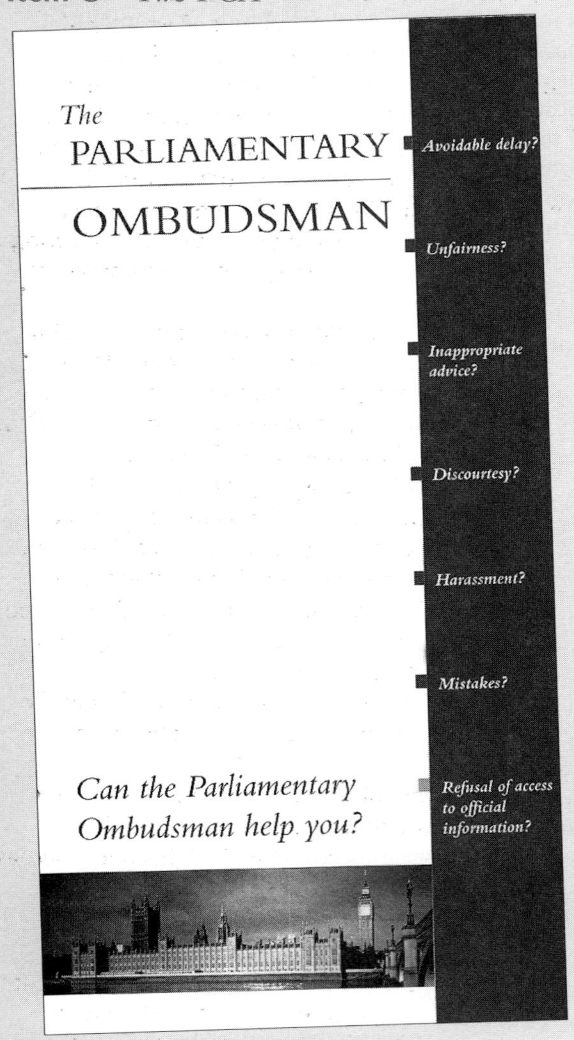

The PARLIAMENTARY OMBUDSMAN
Avoidable delay?
Unfairness?
Inappropriate advice?
Discourtesy?
Harassment?
Mistakes?
Refusal of access to official information?
Can the Parliamentary Ombudsman help you?

This leaflet was produced in 1995.

Item D *The May Inquiry*

Within hours of the release of the Guildford Four in October 1989, the Home Secretary announced that a judicial inquiry was be set up under the retired High Court Judge, Sir John May. The inquiry's final report has at last been published, but people hoping those involved would be called to account will be disappointed. Although the Guildford Four were convicted on false confessions, the report expresses no view about the manner in which the confessions were obtained. It mildly criticises the Surrey police for arresting a crucial witness with the clear intention of persuading him to change his story. It does not criticise the forensic scientist who changed his evidence at the suggestion of the police and the Director of Public Prosecutions (DPP). It finds the DPP not guilty of suppressing crucial evidence, even though it agrees the evidence should have been disclosed. It does not criticise the Metropolitan police for failing to investigate a claim made by a member of an IRA unit in December 1975 that he and his colleagues were responsible for the bombing. It does not criticise the Appeal judges for failing to grant a retrial when it was clear that important new evidence had emerged. Someone somewhere had decided these were small lives that could be thrown away in order to preserve great reputations. That is the scandal the May Inquiry ought to have unearthed. After an inquiry lasting nearly five years and costing several million pounds of taxpayers' money not a single police officer, forensic scientist or lawyer, let alone a judge, has been convicted of anything.

Adapted from an article by Chris Mullin, a Labour MP who campaigned for the release of the Guildford Four, *Guardian*, 1 July 1994.

Questions

1. 'An energetic MP with a determination to fight for justice is all that a constituent with a grievance really requires.' Do you agree with this statement? Use Items A-D in your answer.
2. 'A toothless tiger'. Assess this judgement of the powers of the PCA using Items A-C.
3. What are the benefits and drawbacks of judicial inquiries? Use Item D in your answer.
4. Would you agree that the various methods for the redress of citizens' grievances in the UK are inaccessible and weak? Give reasons for your answer.

4 Judicial reform

Key Issues

1. What is a Bill of Rights?
2. What arguments have been used for and against the introduction of a Bill of Rights?
3. What other judicial reforms have been proposed and why?

A Bill of Rights

According to current British constitutional theory, there is no difference between constitutional laws and ordinary laws. Any law can be repealed or replaced at any time using normal parliamentary procedures. There is, in other words, an absence of any procedural protection or 'entrenchment' of constitutional legislation. In this respect, the UK differs from many other liberal democracies. In the USA and in most EU countries, for example, some basic rights are entrenched in the constitution. At present, this is not the case in the UK. British citizens have the freedom to act in any way which is not prevented by law. This is very different from having certain rights and liberties guaranteed by law.

A Bill of Rights, therefore, is usually a special law which sets out the basic rights and freedoms to be shared by every citizen. It is a special law because it is entrenched in the constitution and has a different status from other laws. It would be much more difficult for Parliament to repeal an entrenched Bill of Rights, for example, than an ordinary law. Clearly, if such a law was passed in the UK, it would have important constitutional implications.

It should be noted, however, that a Bill of Rights does not have to be an entrenched law. It would be possible to pass a Bill of Rights with the same status as any other law. This law would still set out the basic rights and freedoms to be shared by every citizen, but it would be possible for Parliament to amend or change it in the usual way.

The Bill of Rights passed in 1689 (see chapter 12, p.344 & chapter 14, p.406) is not a Bill of Rights in the sense described above since it curbs the powers of the monarch, it does not set out the basic rights and freedoms to be shared by every citizen.

Arguments in favour of a Bill of Rights

The main argument in favour of the introduction of a new Bill of Rights is that, at present, the rights, liberties and responsibilities of British citizens are not clearly laid out in law. A Bill of Rights would remedy this by making it clear to both citizens and to government exactly where their rights and obligations lay. According to the barrister Anthony Lester (1991), this is particularly important in the UK since, over the years, British governments (both Labour and Conservative) have been responsible for a large number of human rights violations. Certainly, the British government has been found guilty of breaching the European Convention on Human Rights more often than any other signatory. Whilst Lester is careful to place the blame on both Labour and Conservative governments, other critics have suggested that the violation of rights has become more pronounced in recent years, especially during the Conservatives' long tenure of government after 1979:

> 'Rights are now high on the political agenda. The last 12 years have demonstrated the potential dangers inherent in Britain's overcentralised political system in a devastating catalogue of rights abuses. The Local Government Act, GCHQ, *Spycatcher*, the broadcasting ban, countless miscarriages of justice, Zircon, deportations, shoot to kill, the coal strike - all have provided instances of individuals' or groups' rights being diminished, abused or simply ignored, and the list is in no way definitive.' (Allen, 1993, p.1)

A Bill of Rights, these critics argue, would limit the power of government and provide a check on its actions.

A second argument is that a Bill of Rights would provide citizens with the information and the mechanism to gain redress if their rights and liberties were violated. At present, people's rights are determined by reference to a mixture of statutes, conventions, European laws and international treaties. Where judges are called upon to adjudicate in such cases, they often discover that the law is ambiguous. A Bill of Rights would clarify the legal position.

A third argument is that a Bill of Rights would act as a deterrent to any government thinking of undermining people's rights for reasons of political expediency or to deal with a short-term crisis. In addition, a Bill of Rights would discourage those accidental decisions which undermine rights because administrative convenience is placed before the protection of liberty. It would do this since liberties would be clearly defined and any breach of them could be challenged in court.

A fourth argument in favour of a Bill of Rights is that it would provide a good basis for civic education. It could form the focus for programmes to ensure that every citizen knew their rights, respected those of others and knew how to act if their rights were violated.

In addition, supporters of a Bill of Rights argue against opponents who claim that the introduction of such a Bill is impractical. They point out that such Bills work effectively in other liberal democracies. Indeed, they argue that the introduction of such a Bill enhances the democratic ethos of such countries and would do the same in the UK.

Arguments against a Bill of Rights

Philip Norton sums up the arguments against a Bill of Rights as follows:

> 'A judicially enforceable Bill of Rights, by which I mean a Bill of Rights enjoying some degree of entrenchment, is undesirable, unnecessary, unachievable, and - even if it were achievable - offers the unattainable.' (Norton, 1993, p.149)

He argues that a Bill of Rights is undesirable for two main reasons. First, a Bill of Rights would inevitably reflect the prevailing values of the time. As a result, it would become dated. Because of its entrenchment, it would be difficult to modify the Bill without a major constitutional upheaval. And second, since judges would be called upon to decide if the Bill of Rights had been infringed in individual cases, judges would be forced to take on a much more overtly political role than is the case at present. Political decisions (he argues) should rest with Parliament not with the judiciary. Another way of putting this is to claim that a Bill of Rights is dangerous because it would undermine parliamentary sovereignty, currently the main source of the British constitution.

Opponents of a Bill of Rights also use the following arguments. First, a Bill of Rights is unnecessary. According to this view, citizens' rights in the UK are already well protected and good methods for redress already exist. There is no need, therefore, to change the existing system. Second, the introduction of an entrenched Bill of Rights would upset the balance of the British constitution which is uncodified and flexible (see chapter 4). A Bill of Rights, so the argument goes, would introduce an unfamiliar (entrenched) element into the constitution. This would simply be unworkable because it would fit ill with the institutions surrounding it. Following this line, opponents of a Bill of Rights often then go on to claim that because a Bill of Right would be unworkable on its own, supporters of such a Bill are actually using it as a kind of Trojan Horse to smuggle in full-scale constitutional reform. In other words, the proposal to introduce a Bill of Rights should be opposed because, by blocking that proposal, it is also possible to block major constitutional reform (see chapter 4, part 5). Third, the adoption of a Bill of Rights would lead to endless litigation, much of it unreasonable and futile. The result would be that the courts would be clogged up for years on end. Fourth, there would be problems if judges were given the role of interpreting and enforcing such a Bill. To have at the heart of the system people who come from a narrow and elite background might well lead to a Bill of Rights being interpreted in a narrow and biased fashion. And fifth, there is no consensus about what rights should be included in a Bill of Rights, so it would be difficult to produce a Bill which satisfied the majority without alienating a minority.

Norton concludes by suggesting:

> 'A Bill of Rights is held aloft as a remedy for many perceived problems in society. In scope and number, they exceed what a Bill of Rights could ever hope to remedy. By building up a Bill of Rights into something it cannot be, and elsewhere has not been, the potential for disappointment is immense, serving to threaten the legitimacy of the system of government far more than exists under our present arrangements.' (Norton, 1993, p.151)

Other proposed judicial reforms

In October 1989, the Court of Appeal overturned the convictions of the 'Guildford Four' (three men and a woman who had been jailed in 1975 after being found guilty of bombing a pub in Guildford). These convictions were overturned on the grounds that the evidence against them had been based on police lies and false confessions. The release of the Guildford Four was of great importance. In the words of Paul Foot:

> 'The Guildford case broke the dam. Month after month, wrongful convictions were set aside: the Birmingham Six, the Broadwater Three, the Cardiff Three, the Swansea Two, the East Ham Two, Judy Ward, Stefan Kisko, the Taylor sisters, Eddie Browning. All had been convicted of murder and all were, in the proper sense, victims of miscarriages of justice - they didn't do it.' (*Guardian*, 4 July 1994)

This steady stream of miscarriages of justice in the early 1990s severely shook the public's faith in the judicial system and led some politicians and commentators to propose reforms both to the way in which the police gather evidence (see chapter 18) and to the judicial system.

At the top of the judicial system, one proposal is to replace the Lord Chancellor's Department with a Department of Justice. This has been suggested because, although the Lord Chancellor is one of the most powerful positions in the British government, at present it is also one of the least accountable. The Lord Chancellor, for example, is not accountable to any committee in the House of Commons. Labour MP Graham Allen suggests that:

> 'A Department of Justice should be considered in place of the Lord Chancellor's Department, with a Legal Affairs Select Committee through which it would be answerable to Parliament in the same way as every other government department - enabling effective democratic scrutiny of British legal policy for the very first time.' (Allen, 1993a, p.2)

Allen suggests that the new department be headed by a Secretary of State for Justice who is appointed in the same way as any other member of the Cabinet. Allen notes that the Secretary of State for Health does not have to be a doctor and so there is no reason why the minister responsible for the administration of the law should be a lawyer. A second proposal is to replace the House of Lords with a Supreme Court. There are two main arguments in favour of this. First, the House of Lords is old-fashioned. The Law Lords are drawn from an extremely narrow section of society and (so the argument goes) are, therefore, unable to make impartial decisions. And second, a Supreme Court would strengthen the separation of the powers and, thereby, provide a new and potentially powerful safeguard for citizens' rights. At present, reformers note, the House of Lords forms part of the legislature and its members are selected by two members of the executive (the Lord Chancellor and the Prime Minister). Since this is the case, it is small wonder that decisions so often favour the interests of government. If a Supreme Court was set up with the powers currently wielded by the Law Lords and with judges appointed by a commission which was independent of the executive, these problems would be solved.

A third proposal is that judges should be elected. This, it is argued, would ensure that a range of people from wider backgrounds would be encouraged to enter the legal profession. In addition, the need to secure election would make judges more responsive to public opinion and less isolated from mainstream society. Such changes would also inject an element of public choice into a key area of the UK's constitutional arrangements. On the other hand, the introduction of elections might encourage judges to make decisions which were popular rather than just. Also, the insecurity of elected office might deter some people from seeking election. An alternative to outright election is to set up an open judicial commission which contains lay as well as professional representatives. This commission would be responsible for the appointment of judges. Judges would then retain their position unless they made gross errors of judgement.

Calls for reform not only concern the top levels of the judicial system. A major problem with the British judicial system is its cost. Solicitors are expensive to hire, but in most court cases it is necessary to hire a barrister (who is more expensive to hire than a solicitor). The system is such that legal action is, generally, only a realistic option for the very rich, big organisations or those on legal aid (legal aid is granted to people who cannot afford to pay their legal fees. It is only granted to certain people for certain cases, however). According to Toynbee & Ward:

> 'As the Lord Chancellor struggles to contain the ballooning legal aid bill, he is like a sailor trying to control the tide from his boat. Unless the whole legal system is reformed, there is a danger that rationing and rationalising legal aid will simply take us further down the path where there is one legal system for the rich and another for the rest.' (*Independent*, 18 May 1995)

The problem, they argue, is exacerbated because barristers have fought hard to prevent solicitors representing clients in court. At present, the cost of barristers' near monopoly on representation in court is very high. In 1994, for example, 100 barristers each cost more than £100,000 in legal aid fees. Toynbee & Ward estimate that if the Crown Prosecution Service could use its own solicitors in court rather than barristers, it would save around £70 million per year. They add that it is from the ranks of barristers that judges are drawn. If judges come from a narrow section of society, it is because a large proportion of barristers come from a narrow section of society. As a result, they conclude, barristers should be abolished.

Activity 17.5

Item A *Ten ways to reform the legal system*

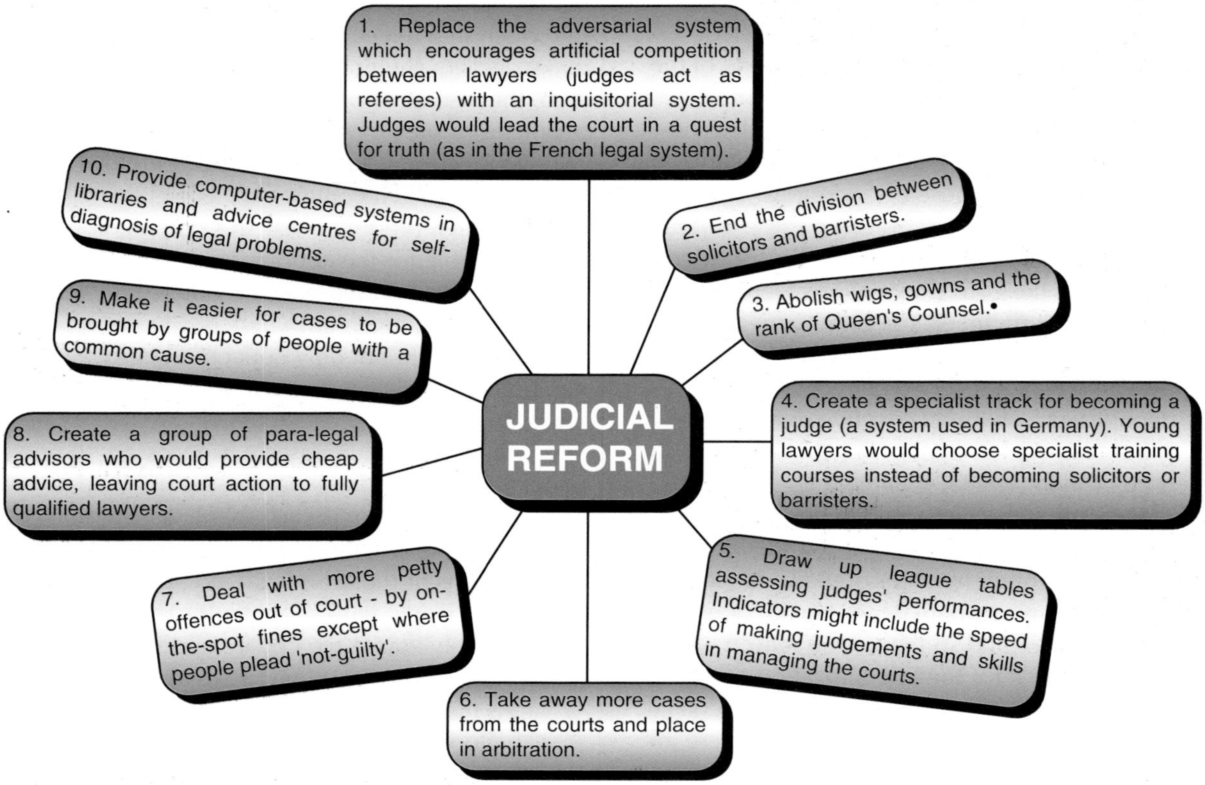

JUDICIAL REFORM
1. Replace the adversarial system which encourages artificial competition between lawyers (judges act as referees) with an inquisitorial system. Judges would lead the court in a quest for truth (as in the French legal system).
2. End the division between solicitors and barristers.
3. Abolish wigs, gowns and the rank of Queen's Counsel.•
4. Create a specialist track for becoming a judge (a system used in Germany). Young lawyers would choose specialist training courses instead of becoming solicitors or barristers.
5. Draw up league tables assessing judges' performances. Indicators might include the speed of making judgements and skills in managing the courts.
6. Take away more cases from the courts and place in arbitration.
7. Deal with more petty offences out of court - by on-the-spot fines except where people plead 'not-guilty'.
8. Create a group of para-legal advisors who would provide cheap advice, leaving court action to fully qualified lawyers.
9. Make it easier for cases to be brought by groups of people with a common cause.
10. Provide computer-based systems in libraries and advice centres for self-diagnosis of legal problems.

* Those barristers whose work meets with the approval of the Lord Chancellor may be promoted to the rank of Queen's Counsel (QC). This is an honarary title, but it ensures that QCs are able to charge much higher fees than other barristers.

Adapted from the *Independent*, 18 May 1995.

Item B *A Bill of Rights - for and against*

(i) A Bill of Rights - for

(1) If we have rights, there is no reason why they should not be written down to protect citizens

(2) At present, it is too costly and time consuming for most people to seek justice through the British courts and then to go to the European Court of Human Rights.

(3) Judges already play a role in interpreting laws.

(4) Our rights should not depend on who wins a general election.

(5) It might be difficult to implement, but that is no reason not to do it.

(ii) A Bill of Rights - against

(1) The current system works well. People can go to court if they believe their rights have been violated.

(2) Parliament, not judges, should make political decisions.

(3) Rights legislation is often vague. A loosely drafted law would give judges too much power.

(4) The British constitution has no means of entrenching a law. A future government could simply repeal a Bill of Rights.

(5) Who should decide what rights to include? What if large minorities disagree with parts of the Bill?

Item C *Liberty and a Bill of Rights*

This leaflet was produced by Liberty in 1995. Liberty is an organisation which campaigns for an extension of citizens' rights in the UK and takes up cases where citizens allege their rights have been violated.

Questions

1. a) Is there any need to reform the judicial system?
   b) Which (if any) of the reforms in Item A should be adopted? Give reasons for your answer.

2. 'A Bill of Rights would raise expectations, but fail to bring the benefits its supporters desire.' Is this a fair comment? Use Items B and C in your answer.

3. Judging from what you know of the three main parties, which (if any) would you expect to support a Bill of Rights? Give reasons for your answer.

4. How would the passing of a Bill of Rights make the work of Liberty (Item C) easier?

References

Adams & Pyper (1995) Adams, J. & Pyper, R., 'A guide to the Scott Inquiry: truths, half truths and nothing like the truth', *Talking Politics*, Vol.7, No.2, winter 1994/95.

Allen (1993) Allen, G., 'A Bill of Rights', *Labour and the Constitution*, Issue No.1, consultation paper produced by Graham Allen MP, February 1993.

Allen (1993a) Allen, G., 'Reform of the judiciary', *Labour and the Constitution*, Issue No.2, consultation paper produced by Graham Allen MP, March 1993.

Berlins & Dyer (1989) Berlins, M. & Dyer, C., *The Law Machine*, Penguin, 1989.

Citizen's Charter (1991) *The Citizen's Charter: Raising the Standard*, HMSO, 1991.

Davis (1995) Davis, H., 'The judiciary' in *Lancaster* (1995).

De Smith & Brazier (1989) De Smith, S. & Brazier, R., *Constitutional and Administrative Law* (6th edn), Penguin, 1989.

Farnham (1992) Farnham, D., 'The Citizen's Charter: improving the quality of the public services or furthering market values?', *Talking Politics*, Vol.4, No.2, winter 1991/92.

Griffith (1991) Griffith, J.A.G., *The Politics of the Judiciary*, Fontana, 1991.

Lancaster (1995) Lancaster, S. (ed.), *Developments in Politics*, Vol.6, Causeway Press, 1995.

Lester (1991) Lester, A., *A Bill of Rights for Britain*, Charter 88 pamphlet, 1991.

LCD (1986) *Judicial Appointments*, Lord Chancellor's Department, 1986.

Madgwick & Woodhouse (1995) Madgwick, P. & Woodhouse, D., *The Law and Politics of the Constitution*, Harvester Wheatsheaf, 1995.

Norton (1993) Norton, P., 'The case against a Bill of Rights', *Talking Politics*, Vol.5, No.3, summer 1993.

Oliver (1993) Oliver, D., 'Citizenship in the 1990s', *Politics Review*, Vol.3, No.1, September 1993.

SOID (1993) Scottish Office Information Directorate, *Scottish Courts (factsheet 9)*, The Scottish Office, October 1993.

Thompson (1993) Thompson, K., 'The role of the ombudsmen', *Talking Politics*, Vol.6, No.1, autumn 1993.

18 Law and order

Introduction

From *Dixon of Dock Green*, through *The Sweeny* and *Inspector Morse*, to *The Bill*, British TV audiences have shown a fascination with the work of the police force. But, this fascination is not confined to fiction. Opinion polls have shown time and again that most people put the issue of law and order high on their political agenda. A majority supports the allocation of greater resources to the police force in the hope that this will lead to the conviction of more offenders. Most people also support harsher regimes for those convicted of crime. Generally, there has been greater concern with law and order than with our rights and liberties. But, the maintenance of a free society involves the preservation of a precarious balance between the demands for individual freedom and the limits placed upon that freedom by the rule of law and the powers given to the forces responsible for enforcing that law.

This chapter examines the reasons why order - and the law to enforce it - are necessary in society. It considers the basis upon which law and order are either accepted or imposed and the major controversies which surround the role of the police and other law enforcement agencies in modern Britain. These are crucial issues since they impinge upon every aspect of our lives and upon our conception of the society in which we live.

Chapter summary

Part 1 examines some **key political theories** on freedom, law and order.

Part 2 describes the controversy surrounding the **breakdown of legitimacy in Britain**. It includes a section on the breakdown of order in **Northern Ireland**.

Part 3 looks at the **organisation of the police force**. What are the recent trends in policing? To whom are the police accountable?

Part 4 investigates the **role of other law enforcement agencies** - the armed forces and the security services.

Part 5 discusses the **policies of the main political parties** on law and order.

1 Law, order and society

Key Issues

1. What have political theorists had to say concerning the relationship between society, freedom, law and order?
2. How is order maintained in society?

Classical political thought and the need for social order

In many respects, the very idea of society implies a notion of order. To speak of society is to talk of a group of people who have come together to work and to live. This implies some kind of voluntary or compulsory organisation and, therefore, a degree of order. If this order is agreed upon wholly voluntarily, there will be no need for law or for people to impose order. But, where people dissent or break the voluntarily agreed rules, laws and law enforcers are required. In these circumstances, the question of establishing a balance between the freedom to be given to the individual, the level of dissent and deviation to be permitted and the place of the law and its enforcers in society inevitably arises.

Plato on law and order

Questions relating to law and order have been the subject of philosophical speculation for many centuries. As early as the fourth century BC, for example, the nature of the 'just' society and the degree of freedom and order required to establish it were discussed in *The Republic* by Plato, the Greek philosopher.

Plato maintained that each person has a skill which makes them suited to a particular type of activity. So, for example, some people are suited to being traders or artisans, some to being soldiers and some to being rulers. *The Republic* describes an ideal state ruled by philosophers - the people whom Plato believed are best suited to govern (see Plato, 1987).

These philosophers are the best rulers for two reasons. First, they have the knowledge necessary for the task. Second, their knowledge ensures that they always make laws for the common good. Plato's *Republic* envisages a society made up of three tiers - at the top, the philosophers who rule, below them, the auxiliaries (soldiers) who defend the Republic and, at the bottom, the mass of people. In this ideal state, the auxiliaries have the power to defend and enforce the laws made by the philosophers. The mass of people are expected to obey these laws because they are made for the common good.

In theory, such a government is entirely benevolent - the leaders know what is in the best interest of society and act accordingly. In such circumstances, there could be no justification for dissent. Indeed, the very survival of society depends upon obedience to the law.

Plato, who lived through a period of political instability himself, believed that strict censorship and severe penalties were necessary if order was to be maintained. He placed a low priority on individual freedom. It is these factors which have led some modern philosophers to argue that, by emphasising the common good (as opposed to the individual's good) and by supporting tough measures (such as strict censorship), Plato advocated a form of totalitarianism (see, for example, Popper, 1945).

Hobbes on law and order

For different reasons, the English philosopher Thomas Hobbes (1588-1679) also argued that the maintenance of order was paramount in the ideal state. Hobbes' book, *The Leviathan* was published in 1651, two years after the execution of Charles I. Like Plato, therefore, Hobbes lived through a period of great political instability (the English civil war).

In *The Leviathan,* Hobbes asked himself why the first societies had been formed. To find an answer to this question, he attempted to examine what sort of lives people led before they formed societies. This examination was by no means a scientific study, however. It was based on a set of philosophical assumptions. Hobbes assumed that people lived in a 'state of nature' before they formed societies. In this state of nature people were completely selfish. They only pursued their own interests. If it suited them, they would rob or kill their neighbours. As a result, people's lives were completely insecure. According to Hobbes, it was to combat this insecurity that people decided to come and live together in societies.

Since societies were formed to provide security, it is no surprise to find that Hobbes' ideal society was to be ruled by a sovereign with absolute power. This sovereign could compel obedience to the law and thus guarantee the security of all. As far as Hobbes was concerned, the key role of government was to ensure order - order was a far more valuable good than individual freedom (Hobbes, 1651).

Rousseau on law and order

The French philosopher Jean Jacques Rousseau (1712-78) also examined the life of people in a 'state of nature'. But in his *Social Contract* of 1762 Rousseau drew entirely different conclusions from Hobbes.

Rousseau maintained that in the state of nature people lived cooperative lives. They only lost their natural freedom when they began to live in societies. Rousseau said:

> 'Man is born free, but is everywhere in chains.' (Rousseau, 1762, p.49)

By this, he meant that when people are born they are in a **natural** state. It is only because they are brought up to live in societies that they lose their **natural freedom** - societies' rules and regulations are like chains.

Rousseau drew a distinction between the **particular will** (the will of individuals) and the **general will** (the will of society as a whole). True freedom, he argued, was being able to rise above the desires of the particular will. People should do what is best for society as a whole, not necessarily what is best for them as individuals. In terms of law and order, Rousseau is clearly arguing, therefore, that people should obey laws which are for the good of society even if they are not for their own personal good. By arguing that the general will should be supreme, Rousseau claimed that he was putting freedom above order. But, in reality, it is clear that he had as little time for individual freedom as did either Plato or Hobbes.

Marx on law and order

Karl Marx (1818-83) offered an alternative perspective. He argued that the institutions responsible for making law and enforcing order work in the interests of the economically dominant class. In capitalist societies, this class is the bourgeoisie (the people who own land and businesses). Governments in capitalist societies are dominated by members of the bourgeoisie. They make laws and enforce order to ensure their continued rule.

Marx argued that capitalist society is inherently unstable because the rule of the bourgeoisie necessarily means the exploitation of the other major class in capitalist society - the proletariat (the workers). Exploitation, he suggested, would inevitably lead to discontent. Members of the proletariat would challenge the right of the bourgeoisie to rule. There would be a class struggle.

Marx was convinced that, eventually, the proletariat

would win this struggle and overthrow the capitalist system. Once the capitalist system had been overthrown, the state would 'wither away' and a classless society would be established. As there would no longer be a class struggle, there would be no need for coercive structures to enforce order. In the classless society, therefore, individual freedom and order would be guaranteed for all.

The liberal tradition and law and order

Although the ideas of Karl Marx made an impact throughout the world, it is the liberal tradition which has had a greater role in British political debate. The liberal tradition owes much to John Locke (1632-1704) and John Stuart Mill (1806-73). These and other liberal philosophers argued that the individual should have as much freedom as is compatible with the freedom of everybody else. This belief in individual freedom led liberals to argue that governments should be accountable to the population through representative democracy. The law and forces of coercion should intervene in the life of the individual only in circumstances where this is essential on the grounds that the actions of the individual are harmful to other people (see, for example, Mill, 1859).

Conclusions

Two key problems emerge from these considerations. First, where exactly should the line be drawn between order and freedom? Second, how should those who impose order be made accountable to the people they regulate? The different answers given to these questions lie at the heart of the current debates concerning law and order, the role of the police and rising rates of crime and urban disorder.

Activity 18.1

Item A *Crime in England and Wales, 1979-92*

Police force areas	1979 Offences per 100,000 population	1979 % cleared up	1992 Offences per 100,000 population	1992 % cleared up
Avon & Somerset	3,616	43	12,214	17
Bedfordshire	5,293	48	11,019	20
Cambridgeshire	4,050	47	9,843	27
Cheshire	3,053	58	7,944	29
Cleveland	5,769	51	14,510	32
Cumbria	3,858	56	8,739	37
Derbyshire	3,914	50	8,943	22
Devon & Cornwall	3,006	46	7,571	18
Dorset	3,769	46	7,864	32
Durham	4,150	52	10,362	30
Essex	3,708	42	7,703	29
Gloucestershire	3,095	51	11,310	24
Greater Manchester	6,052	45	14,149	35
Hampshire	3,941	46	8,934	26
Hertfordshire	4,430	54	6,916	26
Humberside	5,238	45	14,678	23

Adapted from McKie, 1993.

Item C *The balance between freedom and restraint*

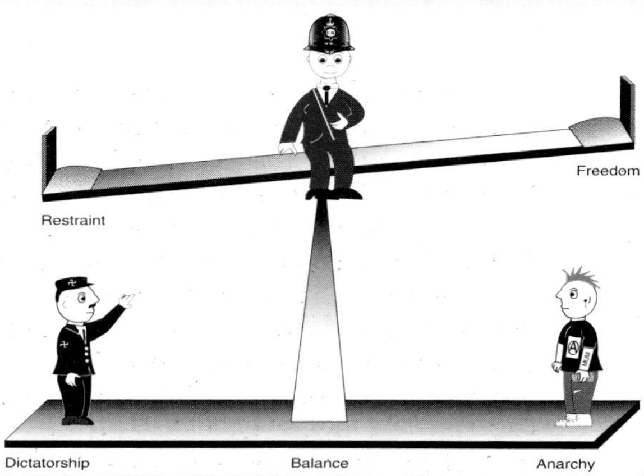

Adapted from Bradley & Clark, 1983.

Item B *Recorded crime in 1993*

Recorded crime in England and Wales fell by 1% in 1993 to 5.5 million offences. Ministers are, however, treating this news with caution. This is the first fall in recorded crime since 1988 when crime dropped by 5%. But, that drop was followed by four years in which crime rose by 40%. A similar fall in 1983 was followed by a rise of 19% in the next four years. Despite the drop in the overall number of offences, the rise in violent crime accelerated slightly. It increased by 4% in 1993 to 295,000 offences. This accounts for 5% of the total number of offences. There were 671 murders in 1993, 16 less than 1992. Attempted murders, however, were up by 99, to 667. The largest increases in violent crime were in rape which rose by 500 cases (12%) to 4,631 recorded attacks and robbery which was up by 10% to 58,274 offences. Robberies include muggings as well as attacks on banks and building societies. The figures for individual police forces show that recorded crime fell in 25 out of the 43 police areas in England and Wales with the largest fall in the City of London with its anti-terrorist 'ring of steel'. Police clear-up rates continued to decline from 26% of offences in 1992 to 25% in 1993.

Adapted from the *Guardian*, 20 January 1994.

Item D *The Leviathan*

This picture was designed to illustrate Thomas Hobbes' *Leviathan.*

Item E *Russian poster*

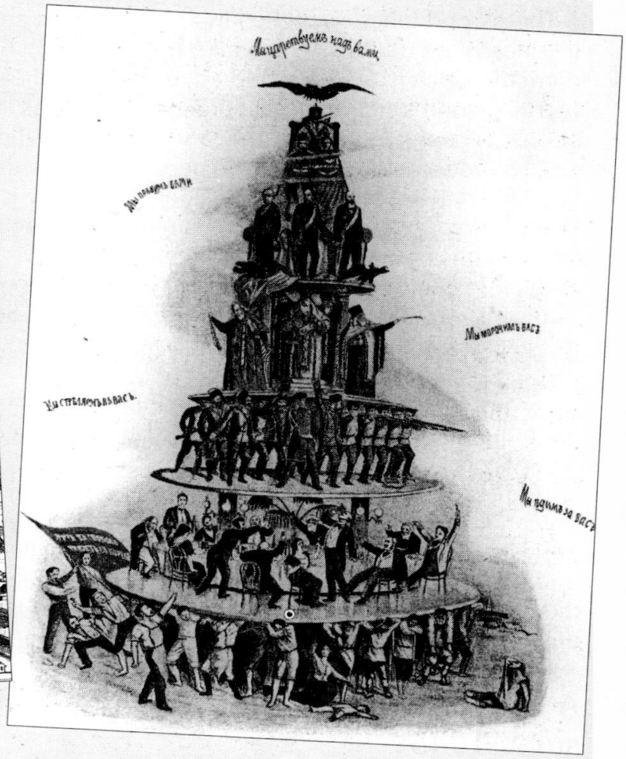

A cartoon produced in Russia in 1900. From the top the captions read: 'We reign over you'; 'We govern you'; 'We mystify you'; 'We shoot you'; 'We eat for you'.

Questions

1. Suppose that (a) Plato (b) Hobbes (c) Rousseau (d) Marx and (e) a liberal philosopher were able to look at Items A and B. What explanation would one of them have given for the problems faced by law enforcers in Britain? What solution would another have called for? Write a paragraph from the point of view of each philosopher.
2. a) What does Item C tell us about the difficulties democratic governments face when making laws?
   b) Where do you think (i) Plato (ii) Hobbes (iii) Rousseau (iv) Marx and (v) a liberal philosopher would have set the 'balance' on the diagram? Draw your own diagram showing where each philosopher would set the balance and explain why you have chosen those positions.
3. Explain the point being made by Item D. What does it tell us about Hobbes' *Leviathan*?
4. Which philosopher's viewpoint is being expressed in Item E? Explain how you know.

2 Law and order in Britain since 1945

Key Issues

1. What is legitimacy?
2. What are the arguments for and against the view that Britain has experienced a decline in legitimacy since 1945?
3. How does the disorder in Northern Ireland relate to this debate?

2.1 Legitimacy and the law

The law and the institutions which enforce it are intended to fulfill two functions. The first is to arbitrate between people who are in dispute and to enforce the outcome. An example of this was the libel action brought by actress Gillian Taylforth and her partner, Geoff Knights, against the *Sun* newspaper in January 1994. The *Sun* printed a story alleging that Gillian Taylforth and Geoff Knights had been caught by a policeman having oral sex in their car. They denied the story and took the *Sun* to court. The court's function was to decide which of the two sides was telling the truth. If the jury had agreed that Gillian Taylforth and Geoff Knights were telling the truth, then the court would have forced the *Sun* to pay compensation. But, the jury's verdict was that the *Sun* had been telling the truth. As a result, Gillian

Taylforth and Geoff Knights were faced with costs of £500,000.

The second function of the law is to lay down and to enforce the rules by which all members of a particular society are expected to abide. At the heart of this second function lies a paradox. So long as people accept that the law, the law makers and the law enforcers are legitimate, the need to enforce the law rarely arises. If a person considers that a law is fair (legitimate), then that person is unlikely to break the law. It is only when the legitimacy of the law and the institutions which make and enforce it come into question that people actually break the law. So, the paradox is this: only when the law fails does the need to enforce it arise.

In most circumstances, only a small proportion of the population breaks the law. As a result, the forces of law and order are able to catch and prosecute transgressors - thereby punishing actual, and deterring potential, lawbreakers. But, if the legitimacy of the law, the law makers and the law enforcers is called into question by a large proportion of the population, the result is an ever increasing willingness to break the law and to tolerate those engaged in so doing.

A breakdown of legitimacy in Britain since 1945?

Looking at the postwar period in Western Europe, some writers have noted a range of trends and events which could signify a decline in the legitimacy of the regimes which govern these countries. Indeed, such has been the depth and breadth of this apparent decline that some writers have been led to discuss a 'legitimation crisis' (for example, Habermas, 1973).

A breakdown in legitimacy - Habermas' view

When examining developments in modern industrial societies, Habermas uses a definition of legitimation which goes beyond the simple idea that legitimation means a willing acceptance of the authority of those who rule. This passive definition must be rejected, he argues. It should be replaced with a more active definition. Legitimacy should be seen as the means by which a justification is provided for a whole range of social actions, institutions and arrangements.

Take, for example, relations between men and women. The traditional arrangement was that men were breadwinners whilst women looked after the home. For many years, the legitimacy of this traditional relationship was provided by reference to the work of God or nature. People justified the role of women by arguing either that it was God's will that they should stay at home or that, by nature, women were weaker than men and, therefore, not suited to undertake the work done by men. It was, in other words, by exploiting people's religious sensibilities and by using a pseudo-scientific rationale that legitimacy for the traditional arrangement was secured.

These arguments, however, no longer have popular appeal. Britain is a predominantly secular society. Most women now work. Although some people still subscribe to the traditional view that a woman's place is in the home, very many do not. The traditional justification has collapsed. The idea, therefore, lacks legitimacy.

Habermas argues that when traditional justifications collapse, people turn to the government to provide solutions to the difficulties caused by the collapse. In general, however, governments have failed to provide long-term solutions. This gives the impression that governments are ineffective or out of touch with the wishes of the people. Indeed, it seems that the political system itself is inadequate. The result is a legitimation crisis. Once governments lack legitimacy, this lack of legitimacy threatens the stability of the political system.

Arguments in support of Habermas' theory

Writers sympathetic to Habermas' thesis can point to a number of examples in the political, economic and social sphere which demonstrate the way in which Western European governments' failure to solve problems has undermined the legitimacy of the political system.

Perhaps the most obvious example is the student disturbances of 1968-69. Especially in France, but also in Britain, students directly challenged the authority of the government and thus attempted to undermine its legitimacy. Although the students' movement failed to achieve its political goals (not least because of the use of force by the government), social change followed in its wake. The growing popularity of anti-establishment values and the development of a youth subculture since the 1960s, could be interpreted as a fundamental, if temporary, breakdown in legitimacy.

Further evidence in support of Habermas' theory might be derived from the outbreaks of civil disobedience in Britain which have happened periodically since 1970. Opposition to the government's Industrial Relations Act in 1971 and 1974, the inner city riots which took place in the early 1980s and the mass campaign against the poll tax between 1988 and 1990 all indicate a breakdown in legitimacy. It is significant that both the Industrial Relations Act and the poll tax were eventually abolished. In both cases, the government realised that their unpopularity was undermining the legitimacy of the government as a whole.

In addition to the specific examples mentioned above, the rise in crime since 1945 may suggest a more general collapse of legitimacy. In 1951, there was just one notifiable criminal offence per hundred people in England and Wales. This had risen to two by 1961, to six by 1981 and to 10 by 1991. Although these figures may reflect changing police procedures or a greater willingness to report crimes, it does seem that there has been a growing willingness to break the law. As was argued above, people only break the law when that law lacks legitimacy. A rise in crime, therefore, suggests a breakdown in legitimacy.

Arguments against a legitimation crisis

The belief that a legitimation crisis exists is based upon two fundamental claims. The first claim is that, at some point since 1945, there has been a significant collapse in people's willingness to give loyal support to the law and to those who make and enforce it. The second claim is that this represents, both in scale and severity, a new political and social development. Both these claims can be challenged.

A problem with the first claim is that of identifying precisely when the crisis point occurred. Different authors suggest different times - immediately after the Second World War, in the late 1960s, in the late 1970s or in the early 1990s (see, for example, Leys, 1983). It is difficult to talk about a crisis when the crisis point cannot be identified with any accuracy.

Also, the very idea that a collapse in legitimacy has taken place is open to question. It has been argued, for example, that the student disturbances in 1968-69 were short-lived, lacked support from large sections of the population and, in reality, posed no genuine threat to the political system (Childs, 1992). Similarly, it has been argued that, although the Industrial Relations Act and poll tax did produce a great deal of opposition, this was not a sign of a general collapse in legitimacy. Rather, these protests were examples of the successful operation of the democratic political system (Leys, 1983). Moreover, the rising crime rates do not mean there is a crisis. The rise has been gradual and the explanation for this is more complex than the legitimacy theory would allow.

The trouble with the second claim is that it assumes a significant change in behaviour since 1945. But, whatever indicator is chosen, problems of at least comparable severity to those experienced in postwar Britain can be found much earlier in British history. For example, some supporters of the legitimation crisis theory argue that the inner city riots in the early 1980s are evidence of a breakdown of legitimacy. But, as John Benyon points out, the Gordon riots of 1780 and the Captain Swing outbreak of 1830-31 are two of many examples of serious lawbreaking and civil unrest on a scale comparable to the modern riots. Yet, these disturbances took place over 100 years ago (Benyon, 1986).

Conclusion

Although it is difficult to find incontrovertible evidence that a 'legitimation crisis' has arisen since 1945, it is clear that at least some sections of society have little confidence in the law and those who enforce it. Rising crime figures and sporadic occurrences of civil unrest produce a climate in which the public and the media express concern about the balance between freedom and order in society. It is this concern which fuels much of the current debate on law and order.

Activity 18.2

Item A *The number of offences committed per 100 people, 1951-92*

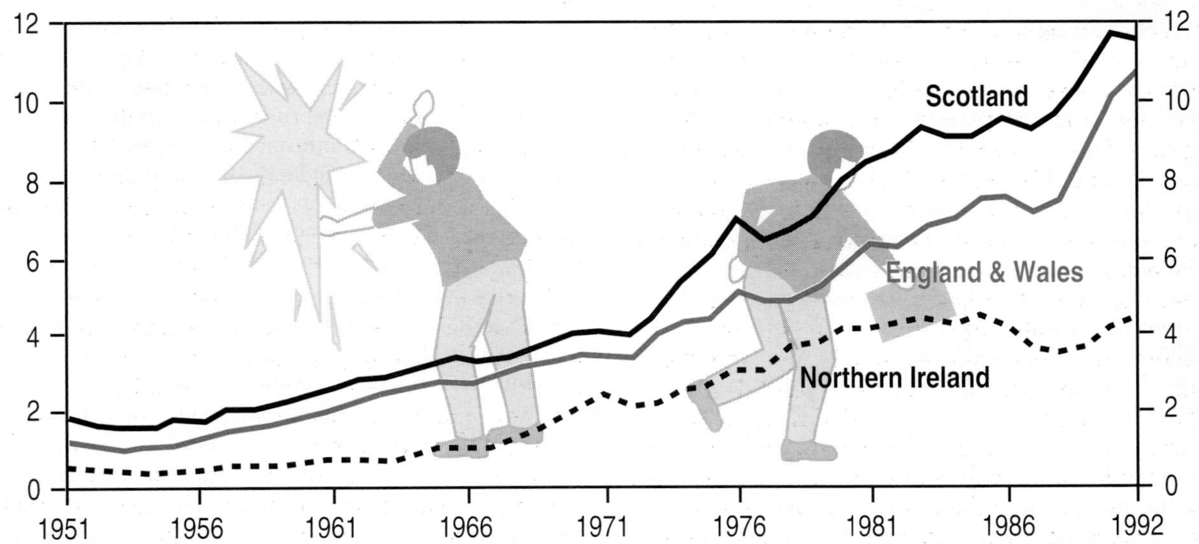

This graph shows the number of notifiable criminal offences committed per 100 people in England and Wales, Scotland and Northern Ireland between 1951 and 1992.

Adapted from *HMSO*, 1994.

Item B *Violent crime*

Seen objectively against the background and problems of 50 million people, crime is not even among the more serious of our difficulties. In 1976, there were only 565 homicides in England and Wales, including deaths from terrorism, and 548 of these led to arrests.

Comment made by Sir Robert Mark, Metropolitan Police Commissioner, 1981.

Number and type of homicides in United Kingdom, 1982 and 1992

	Male victims		Female victims	
	1982	1992	1982	1992
Sharp instrument	31	39	32	27
Beating	13	20	10	20
Shooting	19	18	4	8
Blunt instrument	10	8	13	9
Strangulation	7	5	31	22
Burning	6	3	2	6
Other	14	7	8	9
Total number of offences	431	590	312	280

Adapted from *HMSO, 1994.*

Item C *Recorded crime*

In October 1992, the Home Office published two sets of figures on crime in Britain. The first was based on crimes reported to the police. The second was a survey based on interviews with more than 10,000 people about their experience of crime. The survey revealed that there were nearly three times as many crimes committed as were reported to the police. It indicated that c.15 million crimes had been committed in the year before June 1992. Just over 5.5 million notifiable offences were recorded by the police. The difference between the two figures owes much to the fact that many minor offences are not considered to be worth reporting to the police - for example, minor thefts and assaults. Other reasons include the belief that the police could do nothing to help and the belief that the police were not interested. Some people took the law into their own hands and dealt directly with offenders themselves.

Adapted from Denscombe, 1993.

Item D *Anti-poll tax demonstration (1)*

This photograph shows a demonstration against the poll tax in 1990.

Item E *Anti-poll tax demonstration (2)*

The trouble began in Whitehall. The police didn't know what they were doing. Their horses were galloping around and the foot police looked just as likely to get trampled as we were. Then I saw what to me was a wonderful sight. Union jacks from in front of an MOD building were pulled down and set alight. The crowd was jubilant at the sight of the union jack burning by Downing Street. We walked on to Trafalgar Square and joined the crowd. Some time later the police began to charge the crowd. People began to panic and this led to fights with the police. We cheered every time a blood spattered policeman was helped to safety. Bigger, better missiles began to fly. The crowd was delirious, maniacal smiles all round. Suddenly, I found a rock in my hand and hurled it at the police line. Power surged through me. I was beyond any law the police could impose. To dismiss this riot as politically inspired or as 'criminal' misses the point by a mile. While it's seen as such, the police won't come to terms with the fact they're distrusted. It wasn't even about the poll tax. It was a young person's riot, a spontaneous outburst. I did what I did because I could.

Adapted from *New Statesman and Society*, 6 April 1990.

Questions

1. Using Items A-E give the arguments for and against the view that a 'legitimation crisis' has developed since 1945.
2. 'There are a lot of bad statistics in this world but there are few that are more unreliable than crime statistics' (Ken Clarke, February 1993). Explain how the information in Items A-C could be used either to support or to oppose the view that crime has reached crisis proportions in Britain.
3. Judging from Items D and E would you say that the poll tax riots were 'part of the successful operation of the democratic political system'? Explain your answer
4. a) What does Item E tell us about attitudes towards the law and law enforcers?
   b) How do you think governments should respond to such attitudes?

2.2 Northern Ireland

The breakdown of legitimacy

When legitimacy breaks down completely, very often the result is violent conflict. This is what happened in Northern Ireland from the late 1960s until the agreement of a ceasefire by the paramilitary groups in August 1994.

The breakdown in legitimacy occurred after the growth of the Civil Rights movement in 1968. This movement aimed to win civil rights for Catholics by mass demonstration. Civil Rights marches were non-violent, but Protestants saw them as a challenge to their dominance. The result was a series of violent clashes. In July and August 1969, following the annual Orange parades, riots broke out. These riots culminated in the 'Battle of the Bogside'. When police tried to take control of the Bogside (a Catholic area in Londonderry) Catholics set up barricades and fought them off declaring the area 'Free Derry'. Since the police were unable to keep order, the British government decided to send in troops. By the end of 1969, 6,000 British troops had been sent to Northern Ireland. This figure grew to 7,500 in 1970 and 16,827 by 1972.

The decision to send in troops was an admission that legitimacy had collapsed. It indicated that normal security measures were no longer sufficient to keep the peace. This collapse in legitimacy was confirmed in 1972 when the Northern Irish government (based in Stormont castle) was suspended and direct rule from Britain began.

Between 1969 and 1994, a violent conflict was fought between loyalist paramilitary groups whose aim is to ensure that Northern Ireland remains part of the UK and that Protestant dominance survives and Republican paramilitary groups whose aim is a united Ireland. Although the majority of people in Northern Ireland may not support the means used by the paramilitary groups, the community is divided along religious, sectarian and class lines. These divisions ensure that it is very difficult to draw up a set of constitutional arrangements which can be accepted as legitimate by all sections of the community.

An example of the sort of dilemma which faces those who try to restore legitimacy is suggested by a survey carried out in 1978. This found that 69% of Catholics regarded their national identity as Irish whilst 67% of Protestants regarded themselves as British. It is clear from this that a substantial proportion of the population would regard any settlement, based either on continued British involvement or on the involvement of the Irish Republic, as illegitimate.

Similarly, class plays a crucial role. A Protestant is more than twice as likely to fall into Class 1 of the Registrar General's classification (the richest class) than a Catholic. A Catholic is nearly twice as likely to fall into Class 5. In 1984, Catholics were twice as likely to be unemployed than Protestants. So, economic grievances and insecurities are enmeshed with religious and national differences. This produces a climate in which the creation of a legitimate law making authority is difficult.

The security forces in Northern Ireland

The job of the security forces in Northern Ireland, as elsewhere, is to ensure that peace is maintained, that people obey the law and that people who break the law are caught and punished. The lack of legitimacy, however, means that a greater degree of coercion is necessary in Northern Ireland than in a state where consent to the law is high. But, what level of coercion is acceptable? The answer to this question depends on several factors. For example, a Protestant from Northern Ireland is likely to give a different answer from a Catholic. A Labour supporter living in mainland Britain may well give a different answer from a Conservative. In addition, the security forces face the problem that the acceptability of the use of force is lower in Northern Ireland since the very law which sanctions the use of force by the security forces is regarded as illegitimate by many people. If the security forces use too much coercion they run the risk of creating further polarisation in the community.

The Royal Ulster Constabulary (RUC)

The RUC was set up in 1922 when Ireland was partitioned. In recognition of the difficulties that were likely to arise in policing the new state, the Northern Irish government encouraged both Catholics and Protestants to join the new organisation. But, because many Catholics refused to accept partition, they were unwilling to join. The result was a police force composed overwhelmingly of Protestants. As late as 1969, the Hunt committee found that only 11% of the RUC's membership was Catholic (Farrell, 1976).

The lack of Catholic recruits meant that the RUC encountered great difficulty in appearing to be an impartial force - particularly after the riots broke out in 1969. By then, the RUC was an organisation which lacked legitimacy with a significant minority of the population (the Catholics). Not only that, but the laws it tried to enforce also lacked legitimacy. For example, the RUC was required to enforce regulations banning marches and demonstrations. If these took place, members of the RUC were ordered to disperse them as swiftly as possible and to detain the leaders. Often this meant the use of excessive force. The result was a vicious circle. The RUC used force to disperse peaceful demonstrators. This alienated and enraged the demonstrators who felt that they had the right to march. Because the demonstrators were alienated and angry they became more inclined to break the law and had less respect for the RUC. So, the actions of the RUC had the opposite effect to that which was intended - they brought an escalation of violence and a speedier breakdown of order.

Internment

The security problems in Northern Ireland led in 1971 to the introduction of internment - a system of detention without trial. Such a practice contradicts a central principle of liberal democracy, namely that no person should be imprisoned without due process of the law. It was argued, however, that this contravention of the usual conventions of British justice was acceptable as a means of restoring order because it would remove the IRA leaders from circulation.

This decision was flawed in two ways. First, internment was perceived by the Catholic population as blatant victimisation. No paramilitary Loyalists were arrested and nor were any of their sympathisers. Second, it was ineffective. Most IRA leaders escaped from Northern Ireland before they could be detained.

The plan backfired. Instead of restoring order, it served to undermine further the legitimacy of the legal system, the law makers and the law enforcers. The immediate consequence was the outbreak of riots. In the four days after the internees were first detained, 22 people died in the rioting.

In the longer term, internment fuelled anger against the security forces and, therefore, hastened the collapse of, rather than the restoration of, legitimacy. After the internees were released they made allegations that they had been beaten and even tortured by the security forces. These allegations led to the British government being taken to the European Court of Human Rights in Strasbourg and being found guilty of 'inhuman and degrading treatment'. The security forces had subjected some internees to an in-depth interrogation method known as 'sensory deprivation'. The aim was to cut off outside stimuli to produce a temporary episode of insanity in which the prisoner was responsive to questioning. To achieve this, prisoners were hooded, kept in isolation and put in a fixed position against a wall. Any movement resulted in a beating from the guards. Prisoners were deprived of sleep and food and subjected to loud and constant background noise. This treatment lasted for up to seven days.

Diplock courts

If internment was one serious consequence of the absence of legitimate law making and law enforcing bodies, the loss of trial by jury in cases involving suspected terrorist violence was another.

Northern Ireland was such a sharply divided society in the early 1970s that it was extremely difficult to find impartial jurors. Also, it was very difficult to persuade witnesses to testify in open court, for fear of reprisals. As a result Lord Diplock was asked to report on judicial arrangements in Northern Ireland and to make proposals for change, if necessary. The Diplock Commission published its report in 1972. Its key recommendation was that trial by jury be suspended and cases involving terrorist violence be tried by a judge. It also recommended that the period of time suspects could be held on remand should be extended. Both recommendations were implemented.

Diplock courts, however, were bitterly criticised on two grounds. First, it was argued that judges could not be impartial - their background and beliefs would preclude the suspect from having a fair trial. Second, convictions were often obtained on the basis of confessions extracted after prolonged interrogation. These confessions, it was argued, were made under duress and, therefore, should not have been admissable as evidence. Like internment, the introduction of Diplock courts did nothing to rebuild legitimacy in Northern Ireland. Diplock courts were abolished in 1975.

Criminalisation

The way in which trials were conducted and the methods used by the RUC in interrogation gave weight to the argument that those convicted of 'terrorist' offences were somehow different from ordinary criminals. At first, such prisoners were given **Special Category status** as political prisoners. This meant they had the right to wear their own clothes, to be excused prison work, to be segregated from other prisoners, to have free association with their colleagues, and to receive unlimited mail.

But, the granting of Special Category status drew attention to the abnormal political conditions existing in Northern Ireland. In 1975, therefore, the Labour government introduced a policy which has continued ever since - the policy of **criminalisation**. The idea behind this was to portray the violence in Northern Ireland as an extreme crime wave. Those who took part in 'terrorist' activity were, therefore, no different from any other group of organised criminals.

The institutional framework for the policy of criminalisation was set up in 1975 when internment was ended and Diplock courts were abolished. It was then announced that, from March 1976, Special Category status was to end. Anyone convicted of a terrorist offence would be considered as a common criminal and would not be granted any special privileges. Since most prisoners who had been granted Special Category status were members of the IRA, it is no surprise that the IRA attempted to resist this measure.

The first prisoner to be denied political status was Ciaran Nugent. He refused to wear a prison uniform and was left with only his blanket to cover him. Others followed his example. Since these prisoners had been deprived of their privileges and were not allowed out of their cells with their blankets, they were, in effect, in solitary confinement. When chamber pots were upset after scuffles with prison warders, the prisoners began to smear excrement on their walls. The 'blanket' protest, therefore, turned into the 'dirty' protest. Then, in October 1980, some of the prisoners went on hunger strike. By the time the hunger strikes finished, ten prisoners had died. But, a political solution was no nearer.

A further attempt to produce a negotiated settlement was initiated in 1985. The Anglo-Irish agreement aimed to stimulate peace talks, but it failed to win over the loyalist political parties and the paramilitaries on both sides. As a result, the violence continued.

Restoring legitimacy 1993-95?

The Anglo-Irish agreement was suspended in 1991 to allow further talks to take place, but, ultimately, these also broke down. In 1993, however, pressure began to build for a new attempt to reconcile the interests of the two communities. John Hume, leader of the SDLP, and Gerry Adams, leader of Sinn Fein, reached an agreement which, although it was not actually published, was felt to provide the basis for a possible cessation of violence by the IRA. The Hume-Adams agreement, together with an upsurge in both loyalist and IRA violence, prompted the British and Irish governments to negotiate what became known as the Downing Street Declaration in December 1993. The Declaration (see chapter 4, section 3.3) was an attempt to reconcile the conflicting interests of nationalists and loyalists and, hence, to find a peaceful means by which legitimate authority could be established in Northern Ireland. The Declaration was followed in August 1994 by an IRA ceasefire which, in turn, was followed by a Loyalist ceasefire. By the beginning of 1995, the British army had been removed from the streets of Northern Ireland during daytime (the beginning of a return to normality) and in March 1995 the first British troops were withdrawn. But, when the British and Irish governments produced a Framework Document in February 1995, it was rejected out of hand by Unionist politicians. This suggests that, although considerable progress has been made, the situation in Northern Ireland remains exceedingly delicate.

Conclusions

The problems experienced in maintaining law and order in Northern Ireland clearly demonstrate the complex relationship between coercion and consent that exists in every society. Where a high level of consent exists, relatively little coercion is required to enforce the law. Once the level of consent breaks down, however, ever greater levels of coercion are necessary. When consent to the political arrangements in a society falls to a very low level or collapses entirely, coercion is the only way of maintaining a basic level of social stability. It should be remembered, however, that this is just one model that can be used to understand the growth of crime and unrest. Other models will be discussed later in the chapter.

Activity 18.3

Item A *Deaths in Northern Ireland, 1969-94*

Date	Civilians	Army/ Police	Total	Date	Civilians	Army/ Total Police	
1969	12	1	13	***1983***	44	33	77
1970	23	2	25	***1984***	36	28	64
1971	115	59	174	***1985***	25	29	54
1972	321	146	467	***1986***	37	24	61
1973	171	79	250	***1987***	66	27	93
1974	166	50	216	***1988***	54	39	93
1975	216	31	247	***1989***	39	23	62
1976	245	52	297	***1990***	49	28	77
1977	69	43	112	***1991***	75	19	94
1978	50	31	81	***1992***	75	9	84
1979	51	62	113	***1993***	70	12	58
1980	50	26	76	***1994****	51	7	58
1981	57	44	101	***1994***	0	0	0
1982	57	40	97				

** 1 Jan - 31 Aug 1994 (IRA ceasefire began on 1 September 1994)*

This table shows the number of people killed in Northern Ireland in 1969 and 1994.

Figures from the *Guardian*, 13 September 1994.

Item B *The turn of the road gang*

We were the 'turn of the road' gang. There were about a dozen of us, all in our mid-teens. We were all Protestants - except for an Italian, and he didn't count. Day in, day out, we'd go and stand outside the chip shop. Now and again, we'd get into a little trouble. First, it was raiding apple orchards. Everybody noticed who went in first and who hung back. Then a few people wanted to break into shops. Two of the best orchard raiders broke into a chemist's shop, 'for the drugs'. They had no idea what they were looking for or what to do with it. My nights of homework paid off. I went to university in England. But, I came back in the holidays. It was the mid-1970s. 'There's going to be a civil war', they told me. Everyone was asking: 'Who will save Ulster?' The answer is the same in any war. On whom does responsibility always fall? Who actually fights? The kind of lads who hang round on corners. And so it turned out. Three of the gang who became Ulster Volunteer Force (UVF) members are serving life sentences now. The pub beside the chip shop, owned by a Catholic, was burned down. The owner of the fruit shop on the other side of the chip shop was shot dead. My friend Tampy had his throat cut and two other members of the gang were assassinated. Looking back, I can see that the lads from the turn of the road were always an easy target.

Adapted from the *Observer*, 11 July 1993.

Item C *A British soldier in Northern Ireland*

My saddest moment in Northern Ireland wasn't being shot at or bombed or attacked by rioting crowds, but the first time I was spat at. That was the biggest shock, just being spat on, by an extremely pretty girl. If you're shot at it's detached. They're doing it for military advantage, to create political pressure or whatever. But, if someone spits at you, it's hate, pure hate, and that's a very strong emotion to inflict on someone.

Adapted from Arthur, 1987.

Item D *The Framework Document, February 1995 (1)*

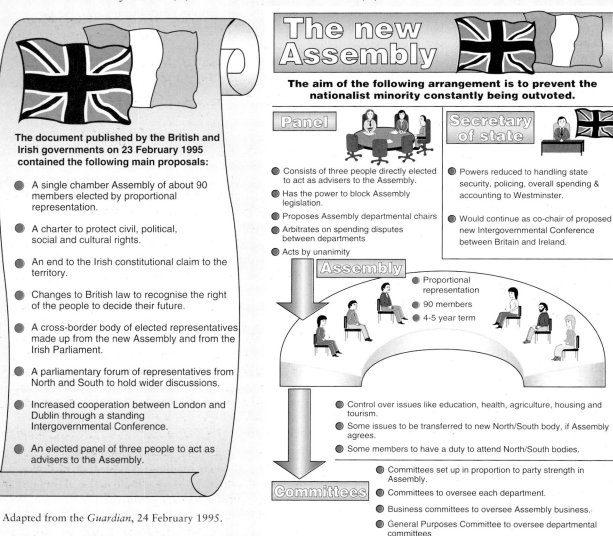

The document published by the British and Irish governments on 23 February 1995 contained the following main proposals:

- A single chamber Assembly of about 90 members elected by proportional representation.
- A charter to protect civil, political, social and cultural rights.
- An end to the Irish constitutional claim to the territory.
- Changes to British law to recognise the right of the people to decide their future.
- A cross-border body of elected representatives made up from the new Assembly and from the Irish Parliament.
- A parliamentary forum of representatives from North and South to hold wider discussions.
- Increased cooperation between London and Dublin through a standing Intergovernmental Conference.
- An elected panel of three people to act as advisers to the Assembly.

Adapted from the *Guardian*, 24 February 1995.

Item E *The Framework Document, February 1995 (2)*

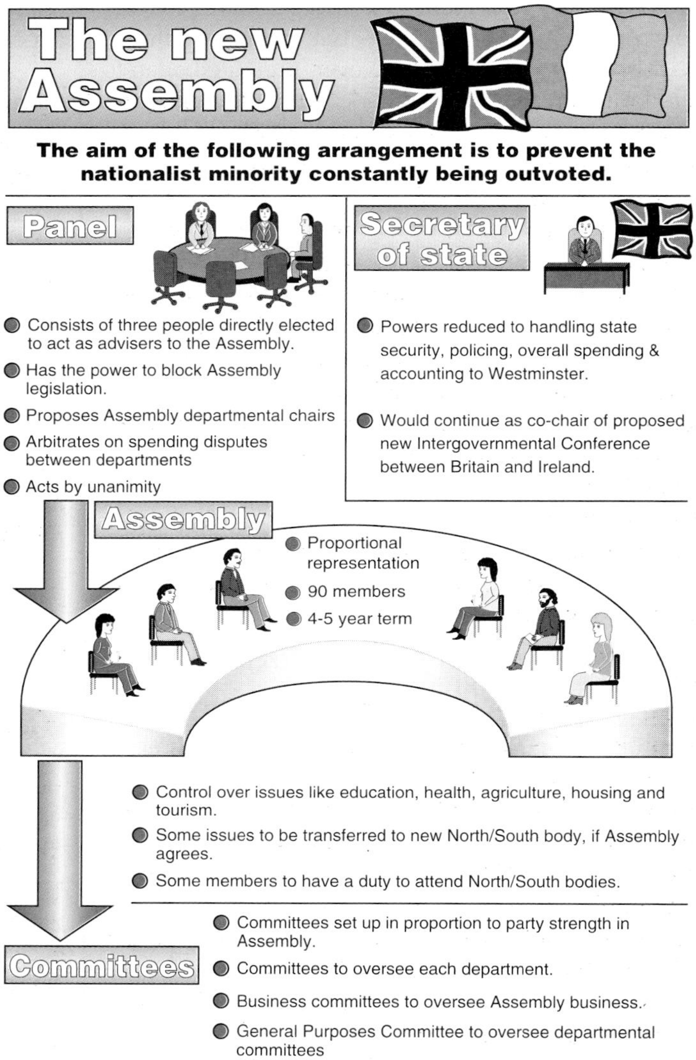

The new Assembly
The aim of the following arrangement is to prevent the nationalist minority constantly being outvoted.
Panel
Consists of three people directly elected to act as advisers to the Assembly.
Has the power to block Assembly legislation.
Proposes Assembly departmental chairs
Arbitrates on spending disputes between departments
Acts by unanimity
Secretary of state
Powers reduced to handling state security, policing, overall spending & accounting to Westminster.
Would continue as co-chair of proposed new Intergovernmental Conference between Britain and Ireland.
Assembly
Proportional representation
90 members
4-5 year term
Control over issues like education, health, agriculture, housing and tourism.
Some issues to be transferred to new North/South body, if Assembly agrees.
Some members to have a duty to attend North/South bodies.
Committees
Committees set up in proportion to party strength in Assembly.
Committees to oversee each department.
Business committees to oversee Assembly business.
General Purposes Committee to oversee departmental committees

Adapted from the *Guardian*, 24 February 1995.

Questions

1. What evidence is there in Items A-C to suggest that legitimacy broke down in Northern Ireland?
2. How do the attitudes expressed in Items B and C help us to explain why legitimacy broke down?
3. a) Judging from Items D and E how might the framework document lead to a restoration of legitimacy in Northern Ireland?
   b) What factors will determine whether or not legitimacy is restored in Northern Ireland?

3 The organisation of the police force

Key Issues

1. How is the police force organised, staffed and funded?
2. What sort of people join the police force?
3. How has policing changed during recent years?

3.1 Historical context

The modern police force dates from the 1829 Metropolitan Police Act, piloted through Parliament by Sir Robert Peel. This Act set up the first professional civilian police force in London. The first police officers wore blue frock coats and top hats and were armed with wooden truncheons. They were known as 'Bobbies' or 'Peelers' after their founder.

Over the next 30 years, other large towns and cities followed the pattern established in London. But, it was not until the County and Borough Police Act was passed in 1856 that a national police force was established. This Act made all police forces subject to Home Office inspection and made grants dependent on efficiency.

The fact that the modern police force developed in a piecemeal fashion goes some way to explaining the stress which is still laid upon the decentralised, local basis of British policing.

Origins of the modern police force

Before the 1829 Metropolitan Police Act, local authorities relied upon two groups to preserve law and order. First, in the event of major civil disturbances such as riots, there was the professional army. But, the intervention of the army often had disastrous results. During the Gordon riots of 1780, for example, 700 people were killed. Second, there were the privately paid (and often corrupt) watchmen and constables. They were appointed by Justices of the Peace (JPs) and were responsible for combatting crime and catching criminals.

A considerable controversy has raged between academics who have tried to explain why a professional police force emerged when it did (see Reiner, 1992, pp. 12-56). Robert Peel himself argued in the House of Commons that rising crime and civil disorder had led to the need for a new force. Recent research, however, indicates that there was neither a rapid rise in crime nor an increase in civil disorder in the years immediately preceding the Act. Some academics have argued that the setting up of the first police force was an inevitable consequence of urbanisation and the growth of capitalism. Others suggest that it was the product of the entrepreneurial zeal of reformers who had become dominant in central government.

The early years

The new police force encountered considerable opposition at first. Many members of the upper and middle classes were worried that their individual freedom and their rapidly developing privileges would be undermined. Sections of the working class, on the other hand, were afraid that the new police force would be used to aid in their oppression.

The extent of this opposition, however, should not be exaggerated. As early as 1838, J. Grant could write:

> 'The large reduction in the amount of crime committed has become sufficient to remove the feelings against the new force and to make it popular with the public.'

By the 1850s, the idea of a professional police force had gained fairly widespread acceptance. By the 1870s, the police enjoyed a high level of legitimacy.

The reason for this rapid rise to acceptability was probably not that the police were required to work in a society with widely shared values and lacking in serious divisions - Britain was rife with such divisions in the 19th century. Rather, the pressure exerted by those opposed to the creation of a professional force ensured that the police adopted an organisation and methods which made them acceptable. For example, the bureaucratic organisation of the police, their subjection to the rule of law, their use of minimal force in dealing with suspects, their politically non-partisan role, their image as a service as well as a force and, above all, their effectiveness all helped to achieve a high level of legitimacy.

By 1960, when a Royal Commission was set up to investigate the police, public and political concern had begun to develop about each of the areas mentioned above. Since then these concerns have continued to trouble the public, politicians, academics and the police themselves.

The activity which follows looks at the ways in which the police force in the 19th century attempted to gain legitimacy.

Activity 18.4

Item A *Police duties, 1830*

June 3, 1830

The police constable is not authorised to arrest anyone without being able to prove that a law has been broken. No constable is to arrest anyone for words only. Language, however violent, towards a police constable is not to be noticed.

August 21, 1830

Constables are to remember that they are required to do their duty with good temper and discretion. Any instance of unnecessary violence by them will be severely punished.

General instructions for constables, issued by the Metropolitan Police Commissioners, 1830.

Item B *A group of police constables*

The new police force's uniform was specially designed to avoid too much of a military look. That is why uniforms were blue (soldiers wore red) and distinctive helmets were designed. Constables were armed with wooden truncheons, except in times of crisis when swords were issued. Officers carried pistols. This photo was taken in the late 19th century.

Item C *Fears about the new police force*

Liberty or death! Britons! Honest men! The time has at last arrived. We assure you that 6,000 cutlasses have been removed from the Tower of London for the use of Peel's bloody gang. These damned police are now to be armed. Englishmen, will you put up with this?

Anonymous leaflet produced in the 1830s.

Questions

1. Using Items A and B explain how the early police force tried to gain legitimacy.
2. Judging from Item C why do you think people were suspicious of the new police force at first? Can you think of any other reasons why they might have been suspicious?
3. How has policing changed since the mid-19th century? In what ways has it stayed the same?

3.2 Police organisation

In a formal sense, policing in England and Wales is a function of local government. England and Wales have 43 separate police forces. With the exception of the Metropolitan Police Force of Greater London (which comes under the direct control of the Home Office), each force is answerable to a police authority.

The police authority

A police authority is a committee whose job is to oversee the work of the police in a particular locality. The duties of police authorities were laid down in the 1964 Police Act. In general terms, it is their duty to secure the maintenance of an adequate and efficient police force for the area. Specifically, they have the power to appoint Chief Constables and to secure their retirement on grounds of efficiency (though a decision is only binding if it receives the approval of the Home Secretary). Also, police authorities expect to receive an annual report from their Chief Constable, though this can be refused if the Chief Constable decides it would be inappropriate to circulate such a document. In cases of dispute, the matter is decided by the Home Secretary.

The make-up of police authorities became a contentious issue when the Home Secretary, Michael Howard, published his Police and Magistrates Courts Bill in 1993. The existing arrangement was for each police authority to be made up of one third JPs and two thirds local councillors. Councillors were given a majority on the committee because they were elected representatives and, therefore, directly accountable to the local electorate. The 1993 Police Bill, however, aimed to change this arrangement in a number of ways. First, the number sitting on a police authority was to be 16, regardless of the size of the locality and local police force. Second, the Home Secretary was to be given the power to appoint a third of members on each police authority. Third, local councillors would no longer have a majority on police authorities. They would have eight of the 16 places. And fourth, the Home Secretary was to be given the power to appoint the police authority's chair.

These proposals faced stiff opposition in the House of Lords in early 1994 and the Home Secretary was forced to make a number of concessions. The plans to give the Home Secretary the power to choose the police authority's chair were dropped. Police authorities, it was finally decided, should normally have 17 members. A majority of members (nine) would be elected councillors. Three would be JPs. The remaining five would be appointed by the Home Secretary.

Chief Constables

The Chief Constables of the 43 forces, together with the Commissioner of the Metropolitan Police, occupy a central position in the organisation of the police force of England and Wales. These officers have complete operational control over their forces (operational matters are the everyday activities of maintaining order, catching criminals and so on) and they are responsible for allocating human and financial resources. Chief Constables are officers of the Crown. It is this which secures their independence from political control since, in theory, they are only responsible to the monarch. An attempt by the Bains committee in 1972 to place Chief Constables in the same position as other local government chief officers was fiercely resisted with complete success. Chief Constables retained their independence.

Police personnel

The number of police officers has risen from 87,000 in 1961 to 142,000 in 1992. But, the force remains overwhelmingly male, white and working class. Between 1961 and 1992, the number of women police officers rose from 3% to 12%. In 1987, there were just 1,105 black officers in England and Wales. By 1992, the number had risen to 1,730. By 1987, the number of graduates had risen to 12% of the force.

The Sheehy Report

The Sheehy Report, published in July 1993, proposed a new career and pay structure for the police force. It was the first inquiry into police responsibilities and rewards to be carried out since 1964. Perhaps the most important break with the past was the proposal that police recruits should no longer expect a job for life.

The report argued that the police force's management structure was 'top heavy' and should be simplified. It also proposed a new salary structure whereby officers could be rewarded financially without necessarily having to seek promotion. A police constable, for example, might earn £20,952 per year whilst a sergeant (the next rank up) might earn £17,214. This would be achieved by the introduction of performance related pay.

In addition, the report argued that the starting rate for constables should be cut and that new recruits should be appointed on fixed-term contracts (initially for 10 years and then renewed for five year periods). It recommended that many existing officers face compulsory severance by 1996 and new disciplinary procedures be introduced.

In an article written in October 1993, Eric Caines, a member of the Sheehy team, explained the reasoning behind some of the recommendations in the Sheehy Report. He said that fixed-term contracts were:

> 'Intended to be no more than a device to ensure that performance appraisal was taken seriously. At best, lip service is paid to performance at

present; at worst, it is not used at all. Similarly, performance related pay was another way of making police managers take seriously the need to monitor how work is done by individual policemen. Only by linking appraisal to a reward or sanction - performance related pay or the non-renewal of fixed-term appointments - will it ever be made effective.' (*Guardian*, 29 October 1993).

In October 1993, the Home Secretary, Michael Howard, announced which of the recommendations in the Sheehy Report would be implemented. These are summarised in Activity 18.5, Item D.

Career structure

Every new recruit in the police force starts at the same level (constable) with the same basic training. Normally, recruits can expect promotion to the rank of sergeant within five years, but there are fast track courses for recruits showing exceptional potential. For example, those who pass a special 12 month course at the Police Staff College at Bramshill are promoted to the rank of sergeant in their third year and can be promoted to the rank of inspector two years later. All promotion is dependent on examination success.

Promotion is strictly hierarchical. Sergeants learn the basic principles of management and deployment of officers and equipment. It is their job to ensure that their officers work efficiently and as a team. The ranks above sergeant are progressively more competitive. The Sheehy Report recommended the abolition of three senior ranks - Deputy Chief Constable, Chief Superintendent and Chief Inspector. This would increase competition for the remaining senior posts.

Funding of the police force

Funding for the police comes from the local police committee (which is allocated money raised from the council tax) and from the Home Office (which uses money raised from general taxation).

Expenditure on the police has increased substantially since the Conservatives came to power in 1979. In 1981, £2,445 million was spent on the police force (4% of total government spending). By 1991, this figure had risen to £6,324 million (6% of total government spending). This increase was used in three ways. First, the number of officers was increased. Second, the force was substantially re-equipped (see section 3.4 below). Third, forces such as Special Branch (which is responsible for the detection of criminally subversive activities against the state) were expanded.

Activity 18.5

Item A *Two Chief Constables*

Since Sir James Anderton quit as Chief Constable last summer, Greater Manchester Police has been headed by David Wilmot, an inconspicous 48 year old Sociology and Politics graduate who believes in consensus and community policing. Wilmot certainly has his work cut out. During Anderton's era, Greater Manchester sported the worst figures in almost every category of crime and policing outside London. Wilmot is keen to emphasise that, since his promotion, detection rates have improved significantly. Anderton thrived on controversy. Who could forget his rants against homosexuality, adultery, Aids sufferers, drug taking and left wing subversion? Wilmot prefers moderation. Anderton saw himself as part of a crusade to sweep the streets of sin and, with it, crime. Wilmot sees himself as a manager, whose duty is to uphold the law, not make it or reinterpret it. Anderton claimed that he might have been answerable to God. Wilmot admits he is answerable to the public.

Adapted from Glinert, 1992.

Item B *Councillors and police officers*

'Nothing to bother about councillor...purely an operational matter'.

Item C *Career opportunities in the police force*

(i) Police structure before the publication of the Sheehy Report

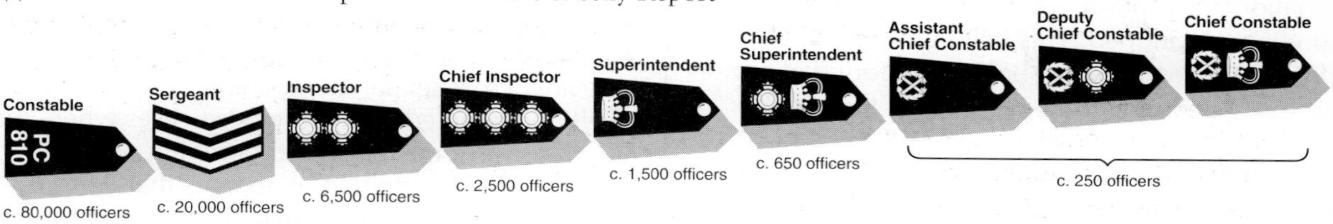

The City of London Police and the Metropolitan Police have a slightly different structure above the rank of Chief Superintendent

(ii) Police structure recommended by the Sheehy Report

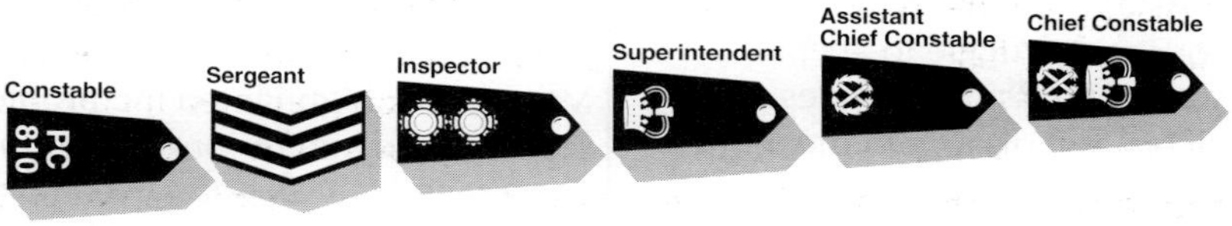

- 3 ranks abolished, 600 officers lost
- Performance related pay for Chief Constables and their assistants
- An end to guaranteed index-linked pay increases for other ranks

These diagrams shows the rank structure of police forces in England and Wales before the publication of the Sheehy Report and as recommended in the Sheehy Report.

Item D *The government's response to the Sheehy Report*

Proposals in Sheehy Report	Home Secretary's reaction to the Sheehy Report
1. ***Abolition of ranks -*** the ranks of Deputy Chief Constable, Chief Superintendent and Chief Inspector should be abolished with 5,000 jobs to go within three years.	1. ***Abolition of ranks -*** Michael Howard agreed to abolish the three ranks. But job losses to be phased: 1,500 jobs to go through natural wastage over 18 months; more later.
2. ***Fixed-term contracts -*** should be introduced for all ranks, renewable every 10 years to end 'jobs for life' culture.	2. ***Fixed-term contracts -*** are to apply to chief officer ranks from July 1994. New disciplinary procedures to sack incompetent officers to be introduced.
3. ***Pensions -*** full pensions should only be available for those who complete 40 years service. Other changes associated with fixed-term appointments should be introduced.	3. ***Pensions -*** are to be reviewed by Police Negotiating Board. Proposals for greater flexibility to be made by April 1994.
4. ***Performance Related Pay -*** Should be introduced with a national 'matrix' indicating how each officer should be assesed.	4. ***Performance Related Pay -*** to be introduced, but not Sheehy's system. Pay to be linked to performance, taking account of experience, skill and circumstances of job. Unsatisfactory performace will lead to reduced pay.
5. ***Starting pay -*** should be cut because it was out of line with market rates for people aged 18-22.	5. ***Starting pay -*** Howard rejected Sheehy's proposal saying that the police should recruit older recruits with wider experience as well as high calibre youngsters.
6. ***Allowances -*** a wide range of allowances, including housing allowance worth £5,000 per year, should be abolished.	6. ***Allowances -*** housing allowance to be abolished for new officers from September 1994 and its value to be frozen for those who receive it now. The future of other allowances to be a matter of discretion of the Chief Constable.
7. ***Overtime -*** should be abolished for all ranks.	7. ***Overtime -*** to be abolished for superintendents and above. Its future for other ranks to be subject to a review.

Adapted from the *Guardian*, 29 October 1993.

Questions

1.a) What do Items A and B tell us about the role of the Chief Constable?

b) Do you think it is right that Chief Constables have complete operational control over their local police force? Give arguments for and against.

2.a) Judging from Items C and D what was the impact of the Sheehy Report?

b) How were the Sheehy Report's recommendations designed to improve efficiency in the police force?

c) Why do you think that the Home Secretary did not accept all of Sheehy's proposals?

d) Would you expect the Sheehy Report and the Home Secretary's response to it to be popular with members of the police force? Explain your answer.

3.3 Cop culture

Policing is a demanding and highly pressured occupation. In response to this, a dominant 'cop culture' has developed. This culture is particularly marked in the lower ranks, but can be found at senior levels too. According to Reiner (1992), this culture has seven key characteristics.

First, many police officers feel that the police force has a mission to fulfill. Policing is seen as a worthwhile occupation since it provides the means of protecting the weak in society and of gaining retribution for victims. As a result, many police officers regard their work as a struggle to keep anarchy at bay. This sense of mission provides an incentive for many officers, but disappointment often leads to cynicism and pessimism. As a result, many police officers have a low opinion of human nature.

Second, police work can breed in officers an excessive level of suspicion. This may be directed against particular social groups, types of people or activities.

Third, because of irregular hours, the demands of work and the authority they are seen to wield, police officers can lead socially isolated lives. Many spend little time socialising with people outside their working environment. This, combined with the reliance on colleagues at work, tends to create a sense of solidarity between officers, particularly those working at the operational level. Conversely, the hierarchical structure of the force may ensure that junior officers lack a sense of solidarity with senior colleagues because they are seen as 'management'.

Fourth, most police officers are politically conservative in both their attitudes and their voting behaviour. In addition, many exhibit a moral conservatism in relation to such issues as homosexuality and drug taking.

Fifth, within the police force there is a 'macho' atmosphere where sexism and sexual boasting are commonplace and physical strength, aggression and daring are seen as highly commendable attributes. The evidence of sexual harrassment in the workplace is well documented. There are even cases where male colleagues have been accused of raping women police officers. In addition, it appears that there is discrimination in both employment and in promotion. Not only is the proportion of women employed as police officers small (12% in 1992), few women reach senior posts. The much publicised case of Alison Halford, Assistant Chief Constable of Merseyside, highlighted the problems faced by women who aim for promotion in the police force. She alleged that she had been discriminated against when she applied for promotion (it was only in 1995 that the first woman was appointed as a Chief Constable). After counter-accusations were made concerning her private life, she retired on the grounds of ill health at the end of August 1992.

Sixth, there is evidence that some police officers are racists. But it should be emphasised that, generally, those who join the police force do not exhibit substantially more racist attitudes than those in the social classes from which they are drawn. A report in 1983 maintained that prejudice was rarely converted into discriminatory behaviour (PSI Report, 1983). The key point is that racism forms part of the overall power structure in British society and this is reflected in the the police force.

Seventh, police culture demonstrates a high level of pragmatism. The practical completion of tasks and the achievement of goals are highly valued. As a result, many police officers are distrustful of innovatory theoretical approaches.

Activity 18.6

Item A *Life in the police force*

Personally, I don't like policemen. I don't think we are very nice people. We're bound to be warped by the horrible incidents in which we're involved. We're bound to get our hands dirty. We make horrible jokes to keep the horror at bay and, yes, we are racist and probably a lot more sexist and ageist too. But, we are also what you, society at large, makes us. And when you attack us, we take it personally. We draw in on ourselves. You force us to see ourselves as different. On holiday, I don't tell people what I do for a living. But, why should I, after 17 years, feel that defensive? All right, so some of us joined to strut about in our uniforms. But most want to do something for the public. Society devalues the work we do.

Adapted from an interview conducted with a senior detective in *New Statesman and Society*, 2 February 1990.

Item B *Racism and the police*

A lot of country lads who join the Met have never seen a black face before. In the same way that the unemployed coloured youth gets fed up with being stopped all the time by horrible policemen, you've got the young poiceman who's fed up with coloured lads who spit at him, verbally abuse him and, if they can, beat him up. It's Catch 22. Even experienced policemen, blokes who have got the same amount of service as me, still don't know how to deal with it properly. One person overreacts, the other overreacts and it builds up. The thing about coloureds is that they're naturally more excitable. They shout and jump about. That's the way they are.

Adapted from an interview with a Metropolitan Police Inspector in Graef, 1989.

Item C *Cop Culture?*

Questions

1. a) What do Items A and B tell us about 'cop culture'?
   b) How good a justification of 'cop culture' is provided by these items?
2. Would you expect the Met Inspector interviewed in Item B to be impartial when dealing with people from ethnic minority groups? Explain your answer.
3. What does the cartoon (Item C) tell us about Cop culture?
4. What measures could be taken to combat sexism and racism in the police force?

3.4 Recent trends in policing

The image of the police officer on the beat, armed only with a truncheon, a whistle to call colleagues and a bicycle for rapid response never provided a complete picture of police work. Today, such an image has little grounding in reality. Over the last 20 years, the police force has employed a variety of new techniques which have transformed the nature of police work.

The impact of technology

The most widespread innovation is the growth in the use of cars both to patrol local areas and to respond speedily to actual or suspected criminal acts. Although there was a campaign in the mid-1970s to get police officers back onto the beat (since, it was felt, valuable personal contact between the police and the public was being lost), the importance of motorised patrols has remained.

A second development is a great improvement in the methods of communication between officers on patrol and between officers and their police station. Better communication enables colleagues to be summoned more quickly to the scene and allows officers to receive intelligence and information held at the station.

A third innovation is the Police National Computer (PNC). This is based in Hendon, near London. The PNC holds information supplied by and accessible to every force in the country. Subjects include missing persons, stolen vehicles and their owners, known criminals and fingerprints. The development of the PNC has enabled police forces which are located far apart to obtain and share information. Though there is nothing sinister about this in the case of, for example, a nationwide murder enquiry, its use becomes questionable when the police are engaged in overtly political activities such as policing the miners' strike in 1984-85. Those who support the cooperation made possible by the PNC maintain that it makes a major contribution to the ability of local forces to apprehend criminals. Its opponents argue that it has been instrumental in allowing the development of a national police force by the back door. They claim that this raises problems of local responsiveness and accountability.

The militarisation of the police

Although it is difficult to prove that Britain is a more violent place today than it was 30 years ago (see above, section 2.1), many people believe that this is, the case. In a sense, the truth of the matter is irrelevant. Because many people believe that there is a rising tide of violence, they are ready to accept measures which, they are told, will combat it. One such measure is the growth of 'militarisation' of the police. Since 1979, the police force has acquired and used a selection of hardware which is more usually associated with the military than with a civil police force. This militarisation has affected the way in which the police fulfill two of their major roles - dealing with crime and maintaining public order.

In the fight against crime, two developments suggest greater militarisation. First, there is evidence of the increasing use of firearms by the police, though it is difficult to appraise this accurately since the method of counting changed in 1983. Before 1983, the number of **occasions** when firearms were issued was counted. After 1983, the number of **operations** in which firearms were issued was counted (firearms may be issued on a number of **occasions** during a single **operation**). Between 1970 and 1972, police were issued with firearms on 5,244 occasions - an average of 1,748 occasions per year. In 1991, firearms were issued for 3,783 operations. These figures show that there has been a substantial increase in the issuing of firearms.

The danger of greater reliance on firearms was demonstrated in 1983 when armed officers shot and seriously wounded Steven Waldorf. Waldorf was entirely innocent of any crime. He was mistaken for a wanted criminal. Since then, training in the use of firearms has changed, but the trend towards greater reliance on armed officers has continued. In March 1995, the Metropolitan Police Commissioner admitted that some police officers in London carried firearms as a matter of course.

A second sign of greater militarisation of the police force was the decision made by Michael Howard, the Home Secretary, in 1993 to allow the experimental introduction of a collapsible two-handed baton. This baton is being considered as a replacement for the traditional truncheon. The new weapon is similar to that used by the American police. The Home Secretary sanctioned this experiment on the grounds that there was a rising number of violent attacks on police officers. Police officers, he argued, therefore needed better protection.

It is in the maintenance of public order, however, that the increased militarisation of the police has been most evident. During the 1970s and 1980s, large numbers of police officers were trained in riot tactics. The use of baton charges in the miners' strike of 1984-85 was particularly militaristic and seen by many as a turning point. Also, during the 1980s, the police began to use new riot gear such as long shields and helmets and they began to arm themselves with CS gas ('tear' gas) and rubber bullets.

The acquisition of this hardware was seen by senior police officers as a necessity if the police were to deal with what was perceived as the growing breakdown of public order. Those concerned about civil rights, however, argue that the deployment of this type of equipment encourages the police to initiate action rather than to react to it. Police officers are, the argument goes, more likely to restrict the legitimate right to picket, demonstrate and march and are more likely to use excessive force if events get out of hand.

Increased police specialisation and centralisation

Since the 1970s, a number of police functions have become the preserve of specialised groups of officers. For example, all forces now have units of officers who are specialists in dealing with terrorism and public order problems.

Specialisation may in itself result in centralisation. This can be demonstrated by reference to Police Special Units (PSUs). PSUs were created after 1974 to ensure that each local police force has a number of officers specially trained in the control of strikes, crowds and demonstrations. Each unit contains 23 officers (an inspector, two sergeants and 20 constables). These officers are engaged on ordinary police duties, but can be mobilised speedily when required. They are also available to deal with problems arising outside their own force.

The National Reporting Centre (NRC)

When a large number of PSUs are mobilised in an emergency, they are coordinated by the National Reporting Centre (NRC) at Scotland Yard in London. The NRC is a large, adapted conference room. It is not a permanent centre. It is only activated when its controllers judge that police forces in more than one area are likely to require reinforcements to deal with major public order events. The most controversial example of such coordination was during the miners' strike of 1984-85. PSUs from all over the country were called to mining areas to maintain order. Some journalists claimed that the NRC became an operational centre during this dispute, though this was vehemently denied by the police officers in charge of the NRC. They claimed that the NRC was:

> 'Purely an efficient convenience for administering the long established mutual aid system between local forces.' (Kettle, 1985, p.27)

Specialist Units

In addition, there are several specialist units within the police force which are entirely centralised. For example, the National Drugs Intelligence Unit, the National Identification Bureau and the Serious Fraud Office. These national police units have increased in importance. For example, the number of officers in Special Branch grew from c.350 in the 1960s to 1,750 in 1984. All these national units are centrally controlled and lack any local accountability.

Amalgamations

There is also a tendency towards amalgamation of police forces. In 1963, there were 117 local police forces in England and Wales. By 1993, this number had fallen to 43. Clearly the connection between a large force covering a large geographical area and the locality it serves is less pronounced. It is also less easy to make a large organisation accountable or responsive.

The implications of centralised control

The growth of centralised control has been justified on the basis of efficiency. Disorder can cross local police authority boundaries and it can escalate to a level beyond the capabilities of the local force.

Because of this, it is argued, a mobile, specialised force is necessary. Also, in the case of serious law breaking, such as that related to drugs or fraud (which may involve complex criminal conspiracies), skilled and specialised officers are more likely to be successful.

Critics of centralisation, however, claim that, even though this argument has some merit, local control prevents the growth of a monolithic centralised force which would be open to direct political manipulation. It preserves some degree of accountability between the local force and the community it is supposed to serve. In addition, local control creates the possibility of diversity and responsiveness to local conditions.

The Police and Criminal Evidence Act 1984 (PACE)

The 1984 Police and Criminal Evidence Act (PACE) was partially based on the report of the Royal Commission on Criminal Procedure published in 1981. PACE has made a major impact on police procedure.

Since PACE came into operation, police officers have a statutory obligation to tape record all interviews and they must be able to produce a complete and contemporaneous account of the entire interview process. Also, since suspects have the right to have a solicitor present, police cannot, on the whole, afford to detain and interrogate anyone unless they have sufficient evidence to win a commital to a magistrates' court. In other words, procedure is designed to prevent the police presenting cases based on a forced confession. Confessions are only permissable as evidence if they are tape recorded and voluntarily made.

It is important to note that the recent spate of acquittals in the Court of Appeal following wrongful convictions based on forced confessions (the Guildford Four, Birmingham Six, Maquire Seven and so on) all stem from the days before PACE.

Activity 18.7

Item A *Policing the miners' strike (1)*

In the first few days of the miners' strike, the NRC (National Reporting Centre) sent some 8,000 men from the Police Support Units to the main target areas. Of these, 1,000 had been mobilised in the first four hours. The first aim was to seal off the Nottinghamshire coalfield. Road blocks were set up, spotter aircraft, helicopters and dog patrols were deployed. A reserve of 3,000 riot trained police stayed in army barracks. During the following days, stories of aggressive and arbitrary police behaviour were commonplace. This initial high profile policing did much to set the tone for the dispute. Orgreave, a coking depot in South Yorkshire, was the scene of a series of set piece battles with the police. The police lined up in military formation - some mounted, some in full riot gear and some in normal uniforms with helmets. They were drawn from 10 counties. Reserves were kept on National Coal Board land while others were deployed against the pickets. Baton charges took place. A Barnsley miner said: 'When the lads resort to the only weapons they've got - throwing stones, Oh it's terrible. But it's OK when they're bashing you about the head with a bit of wood.' The same man explained how the police provoked pickets by holding £10 notes up to the windows of vans and coaches as they passed by.

Adapted from Fine & Millar, 1985.

Item B *Policing the miners' strike (2)*

Item C Policing the miners' strike (3)

This photograph shows one of the battles between the police and strikers at Orgreave in South Yorkshire in June 1984.

Item D *Police and firearms*

Officers are trained never to fire unless their life or somebody else's life is in danger. That means that if some villain has a shotgun and it's pointing at the floor when we come in, we can't shoot. We've got to challenge him, tell him to drop the gun and do as he's told. There was a case when a member of the tactical firearms team was shot. It happened within months of the Waldorf shooting. This chap had a sawn off shotgun in a plastic bag. They challenged him to put the bag down, but he didn't. He put his hand inside, squeezed the trigger and killed a police officer. At the time, the PC didn't know there was a gun in the bag. I'm sure he was thinking: 'This is dangerous, yet I can't do anything unless I see a gun.' I sometimes think that the criticisms of the police after the Waldorf affair were perhaps made in haste. If Waldorf hadn't happened, we might have done something different and that PC would never have died.

Adapted fom an interview with a Chief Inspector in Graef, 1989.

Item E *The number of offences involving firearms*

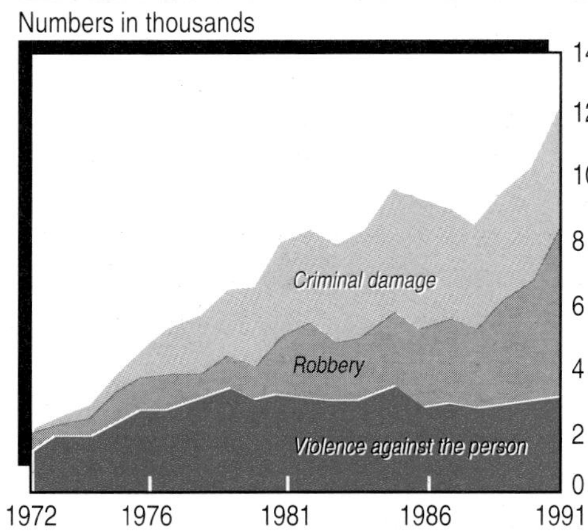

This graph shows the number of offences involving firearms in England and Wales. There was a sixfold increase between 1972 and 1991, but the total number of offences remains 0.25% of all recorded offences.

Adapted from HMSO, 1993.

Questions

1. Using Items A-E examine the arguments for and against the view that greater militarisation and specialisation have fundamentally altered the role of police officers as neutral upholders of the law.
2. Why do you think the miners' strike of 1984-85 has been described as, 'a turning point in the history of postwar policing'? Use Items A-C in your answer.
3. Do you think police officers should carry guns as a matter of course? Give arguments for and against. Use Items D and E in your answer.

3.5 The accountability of the police

An accountable organisation is an organisation whose members are answerable to a person or a body that can exercise some form of power over them. In the case of the police force, two questions arise. First, for what actions **are** the police accountable and for what actions **should** they be accountable? Second, to whom should they be accountable?

Accountability and operational matters

Operational matters are the everyday activities of maintaining order, catching criminals and so on. Chief Constables have full responsibility for these operational matters. Individual police officers are, therefore, accountable to their Chief Constable for the execution of operational duties. But, if the wider problem of to whom, or to what, the police force as a whole is accountable is considered, the matter becomes more complex.

One consideration is that the police force as a whole is accountable to the law. Police officers must act within the law and, like every other citizen, officers who break the law are liable to prosecution through the proceedings of the judicial system. Officers suspected of criminal misconduct, for example, can be prosecuted. Civil actions for cases of wrongful arrest or trespass can be brought. A writ of habeas corpus can be issued to end an illegal detention. Judges can exclude evidence from court cases if they believe that it has been obtained by questionable means.

In practice, however, these legal processes of accountability frequently break down. Until recent cases which undermined the credibility of police evidence, magistrates and juries tended to believe the testimony of police officers, assuming that officers were honest and upright. It has become clear, however, that some officers are willing to perjure themselves in court to gain a conviction. At the successful appeal of the Guildford Four, for example, the Appeal Court judge, Lord Lane, maintained that new evidence showed that Surrey detectives 'must have lied' at the original trial.

In addition, it is often difficult to enforce accountability through the courts. The Department of Public Prosecutions demands higher standards of evidence before prosecuting a police officer than in other cases. For example, in 1986 a group of police officers in a mobile police van stopped and assaulted a group of boys walking along the Holloway Road in London. It was several years before sufficient evidence was gathered to enable prosecutions to be made, partly because of a police cover-up. Eventually, three officers were sent to prison.

A further point should be made in this context. Some judges do not regard it as a proper function of the judiciary to enforce accountability on the police force. For example, Lord Diplock said in 1979:

> 'It is not a part of a judge's function to exercise disciplinary powers over the police.'

Internal disciplinary procedures, 1964-76

The Police Act of 1964 placed a statutory obligation upon Chief Constables to investigate all complaints against police officers made by the public. Officers from other forces could be brought in if the Chief Constable so wished. If, in the opinion of the Chief Constable, an officer had committed a criminal offence, a report was to be sent to the Director of Public Prosecutions (DPP). The DPP would decide whether or not to prosecute.

This system attracted a great deal of criticism because police officers were given the power to investigate complaints against fellow officers and to conduct their own disciplinary procedures.

The Police Complaints Board (PCB)

The first attempt to improve the complaints procedure was the setting up of the Police Complaints Board (PCB) in 1976. Police officers were still responsible for investigating complaints. But, at the conclusion of an internal investigation, the PCB received a copy of the report and was informed by the Deputy Chief Constable whether disciplinary charges, prosecution, or both should be implemented. The PCB then had the power to insist on charges being made if it felt that the report warranted it. In practice, members of the PCB questioned the decisions of Deputy Chief Constables only very rarely. As a result, the PCB failed to gain the trust of those who wanted independent investigations, whilst the police were angry that their professional judgement should be questioned.

Members of the PCB themselves became aware of the problems they faced in providing a credible means of ensuring police accountability. In their 1980 report, they advocated a number of changes to procedure and practice, arguing that a national team of officers should be established on secondment from their regular duties for two or three years. This team would look into serious allegations against police officers, especially those involving assault. The officers in the team would be responsible to a senior lawyer or a judge.

These recommendations were rejected by the government. But, Lord Scarman's report into the 1980 Brixton riots and the House of Commons Home Affairs Select Committee also called for independent investigation of complaints.

The Police Complaints Authority

The 1984 Police and Criminal Evidence Act (PACE) replaced the PCB with the Police Complaints Authority (PCA).

The investigation of complaints remained in the hands of the police, but the PCA was given the power to supervise the investigation either in serious cases leading to death or injury or where it is felt that the public interest could be served by supervision. When carrying out supervision, the PCA can reject any investigating officer it feels is unfit. Also, the PCA has to certify that it is happy with an investigation once it has been completed. Legal representation is guaranteed to police officers who could lose their job or rank as a consequence of the investigation. In cases of minor complaints where both sides agree, the PCA is involved in the informal resolution of the matter.

The lack of an independent investigatory body was a matter of great regret in 1984. Many were convinced that this would prejudice the effectiveness and legitimacy of the new arrangements. But the evidence of the PCA's success or failure is inconclusive. It is generally considered, for example, that procedures for resolving minor complaints have worked well. Many commentators, however, argue that for serious accusations only a fully independent system will secure public confidence in accountability and police confidence in fairness.

Accountability and policy making

There are three channels through which police policy making is made accountable - the Home Secretary, the Chief Constable and the local police authority.

As well as being directly responsible for policing in London, the Home Secretary controls funding and, therefore, has an indirect overall control over policing policy nationally. In theory, the Home Secretary is accountable to the public through Parliament, but the power of ministers tends to frustrate attempts by backbench MPs to question them. As a result, attempts to ensure accountability through Parliament are largely ineffective.

Chief Constables have complete operational control over their forces and are, therefore, responsible for local police policy. Although Chief Constables are answerable to their local police authority, the power of the police authority to examine in detail or to enforce policy changes is very limited. The key point is that in cases of dispute between the police authority and the Chief Constable, the matter is referred to the Home Secretary. From the early 1980s, Home Secretaries have been noticeably unresponsive to the wishes of police authorities. Perhaps the best example of this with regard to policy was the policing of the miners' strike in 1984-85. Police authorities dominated by Labour councillors sought to limit the spending or to alter the manner of policing the strike. The Chief Constables protested to and received support from the Home Secretary. The opposition of the police authorities was ignored. In 1988, the powers of police authorities were further eroded by a Court of Appeal judgement. This gave the Home Secretary authority to override the views of police authorities on matters of equipment and expenditure.

The already tenuous link between local democracy and the police, through which some degree of accountability is supposed to be ensured, has been further undermined by Michael Howard's 1993 Police and Magistrates Courts Bill. This aimed to alter the structure of police authorities by reducing the number of elected councillors and including nominees appointed directly by the Home Secretary (see above, section 3.2). Although Michael Howard was forced to make concessions, the proportion of elected representatives on police authorities was reduced.

Accountability and the use of resources

Local police forces receive their funding in roughly equal proportions from their local authority and central government. Before 1979, the assumption was that accountability would be achieved through the local police authority (Chief Constables would report to the police authority, explaining how resources had been used). But, since 1979, controls have been placed on local government expenditure and conditions have been imposed on central government grants. The result is that financial control over the police has been centralised. There is, therefore, little local accountability.

Although extra resources for the police were made available in the 1980s, they were conditional upon the police force providing value for money. In 1983, a Home Office circular was issued making new money available only if existing resources were being used at full capacity. Tighter regulations followed in 1988 when a circular instructed Chief Constables to specify the precise objectives to be met when the establishment of new posts was requested. In terms of resources, therefore, accountability has not been a priority. If police forces are accountable to anyone, it is to central government. If this is the case, however, it means that the police force is far removed from the public which it serves. The activity which follows examines the accountability of the police force and considers the implications of Michael Howard's 1993 Police and Magistrates Courts Bill.

Activity 18.8

Item A *Michael Howard's Police Bill*

Take a Chief Constable who in another part of Michael Howard's Police and Magistrates Courts Bill is going to be put on a short-term contract. The end of his contract looms and his thoughts turn to the chairman of his local police authority who will have a large hand in deciding to renew it. The chairman, in turn, must consider his own future. The Home Secretary will appoint police authority chairs and wants them to be paid a salary. The chairman's future, therefore, depends on the Home Secretary alone. Meanwhile, a delicate policing situation has arisen: how to handle a political strike, perhaps, or a simmering racial crisis, or even a simple question of priorities between traffic control and the burglary clear-up rate. From where will the pressure bear heaviest on the police chief? From local people and their needs? Or the mighty hand of Whitehall, with the tabloid headlines which are never far behind?

Adapted from the *Guardian*, 14 December 1993.

Item B *The organisation of the police force*

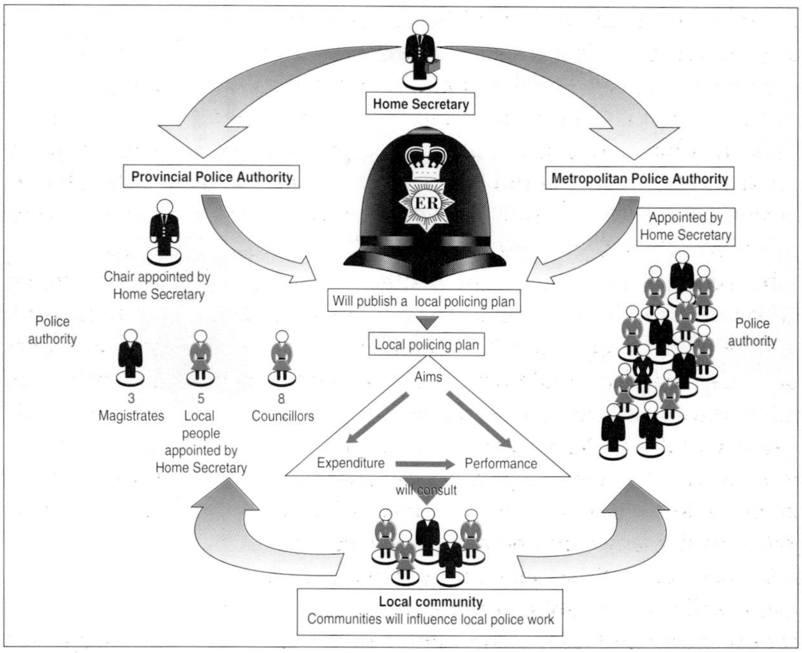

This diagram shows how the police force would have been organised if all of the proposals in Michael Howard's 1993 Police and Magistrates Courts Bill had been implemented.

Item C *U-turn over police authorities*

Rather than face defeat in the Lords, the government yesterday abandoned plans to deprive local councillors of their majority on police authorities. A new amendment to the Police and Magistrates Courts Bill means that the standard size of police authorities will be 17 (not 16 as previously planned). Authorities will be made up of nine councillors, three JPs and five independent members. Councillors will, therefore, have a majority of one seat on the new authorities which are due to begin operating in April 1995. The following procedure will be used to appoint the five independent members. A shortlist of 20 will be drawn up by a selection panel of three. The panel of three will consist of one person chosen by the councillor and JP members of the police authority, one person chosen by the Home Secretary and one person chosen by the other two panel members. The Home Secretary will reduce the shortlist of 20 to 10. The councillor and JP members of the authority will select the five independent members from this list of 10. The government's retreat comes a month after backing down from a proposal that the Home Secretary be empowered to appoint police authority chairs.

Adapted from the *Daily Telegraph*, 2 March 1994.

Item D *Police leader fears coercive national force*

Sir John Smith, President of the Association of Chief Police Officers, warned the Home Secretary, Michael Howard, yesterday that the police were afraid that his Police and Magistrates Courts Bill would result in a coercive national force because Chief Constables would become tools of central government. He warned that the combination of nationally laid down objectives, performance tables and performance related pay paved the way to a coercive style of policing which, in the USA, had led to the Los Angeles riots. The police, he said, had unfairly been accused of being 'Maggie's boot boys' during the miners' strike. 'We acquitted ourselves well in the circumstances', he claimed, 'and were assisted by the ready presence of democratically elected members of the current police authorities. But, imagine if similar events were to happen under these new proposals.'

Adapted from the *Guardian*, 5 February 1994.

Item E *The death of Joy Gardner*

The 1800 page report into the death of the Jamaican deportee, Joy Gardner, received by the Police Complaints Authority yesterday contains conflicting evidence from seven pathologists over how she died. The report has been passed to the Crown Prosecution Service to consider whether charges should be brought against the three officers from Scotland Yard's deportation unit involved in the case. But the conflicting evidence from the pathologists as to whether she died of suffocation, from the gag on her mouth or from a blow to a head may mean that the three suspended police officers will not face criminal charges. Mrs Gardner, aged 40, died on 1 August 1993, four days after an attempt to deport her. She resisted attempts to remove her and collapsed during the struggle.

Adapted from the *Guardian*, 18 February 1994

Item F *Michael Howard and the police, 1994*

The man addressing the police officers is Michael Howard, Home Secretary in 1994.

Questions

1. Look at Items A-D.
   a) To whom would police officers have been accountable if Michael Howard's original proposals had been implemented?
   b) Why do you think there was opposition to these proposals?
2. a) Using Items A-D explain why the composition of police authorities is important.
   b) What are the arguments for and against the creation of a national police force?
3. Using Item E give arguments for and against the view that the current system of dealing with complaints against police officers is satisfactory.
4. Item F is making a serious point about police accountability. What is it?

4. Other law enforcement agencies

Key Issues

1. What organisations, other than the police, play a role in enforcing the law?
2. What is the structure and function of these organisations?
3. To what extent and through what channels are these organisations accountable?
4. Does the operation of these organisations pose a threat to civil liberties?

The armed forces

The armed forces are only ordered to enforce the law as a last resort in exceptional circumstances. But, law enforcement is one of their functions. It is a function which has aroused considerable political controversy.

In 1993, there were 320,000 members of the British armed forces. They were supported by 175,000 civilian staff working for the Ministry of Defence. The main function of the armed forces is to protect Britain from aggression by foreign countries and to fight for British interests abroad.

In constitutional terms, control of the armed forces is vested in the Crown. In practice, this means that government ministers exercise control using the royal prerogative. Ministers in charge of the armed forces are advised by senior civil servants and the Chiefs of Staff of the armed forces. The opinion of these senior advisers has a significant impact on decisions - especially those concerning tactical matters. This means that, at the heart of the decision making process, is a group of unelected and unaccountable people. While this may be entirely justifiable on the basis of efficiency, it fits poorly the requirement that, in a democratic society, people who make decisions should be answerable to those affected by them.

In terms of law enforcement, the armed forces' most prominent role has been played in Northern Ireland. Troops have shared responsibility for security since 1969 (see above, section 2.2). The armed forces have been considered the only force capable of ensuring even a minimal degree of adherence to the law.

But, it is not just in Northern Ireland that members

of the armed forces have been given the duty of enforcing the law. In the 1960s, senior officers were apparently engaged in plots to destabilise the Labour government headed by Harold Wilson. It is even alleged that in certain circumstances they would have staged a coup (Wright, 1987). In addition, rumours circulated during the miners' strike of 1984-85 that the army were used to bolster the number of police officers on picket duty. It is alleged that army personnel wore police uniforms without the customary number given to constables.

A number of problems arise when members of the armed forces become involved in law enforcement. First, members of the armed forces are not subject to the same laws as police officers. Rather, their activities are governed by rules of engagement which determine the levels of force they can employ in particular circumstances. Second, there exists no formal channel through which the accountability of the armed forces can be obtained. Third, members of the armed forces, owing to their training, are more likely to use greater levels of force than police officers.

The security services

The popular image of the officer in the security services comes from fiction. Whether it is the fantastic exploits of James Bond or the more mundane activities of George Smiley (the Secret Service agent created by John Le Carré), the spy is seen to occupy a shadowy world of evil villains and their righteous enemies.

Until the Security Services Act of 1989, there was little public information to contradict this view. Indeed, until then, no government had even publicly admitted that such organisations existed. Since 1989, more information has gradually become available and, in one respect at least, the fictionalised accounts and official statements are in agreement. Both suggest that the security services are a necessity if law and order, democracy, freedom and the British way of life are to be preserved against the wicked activities of spies, terrorists and subversives who can be found both at home and abroad. The ordinary law-abiding citizen, it is implied, has nothing to fear from the activities of the security services.

Although the structure of the security services is a state secret, five organisations can be identified. **Special Branch** which is responsible for the policing of terrorism and subversion within the UK. The **Defence Intelligence Staff** which is responsible for security within the armed forces. **MI5** which is charged with the task of maintaining internal security (secret investigation and monitoring of subversive and terrorist activity within the UK). **MI6** which undertakes the same tasks as MI5 but in respect to activities outside the UK. And **GCHQ** which monitors a wide variety of communications for intelligence purposes.

With all these organisations, a central political question arises. Given the secrecy of the security services, how can sufficient scrutiny and accountability be enforced to ensure that their activities are confined to enforcing the law and investigating those who pose a genuine threat to the state?

The 1989 Security Services Act defines the objective of the service as the:

> 'Protection of national security [against attempts to] undermine parliamentary democracy by political, industrial or violent means.'

The key point, therefore, is the dividing line between what is defined as a threat and what is considered to be legitimate activity. The difficulty is that these are vague, ill-defined ideas.

In extreme cases, no problem arises. Suppose a terrorist organisation was planning to plant bombs in the House of Commons. Most people would agree that such people should be the target of the security forces. But, problems arise in less clearly defined cases. For example, is a trade union which organises a strike against the express wishes of the government subverting national security by industrial means? What about an organisation like the Campaign for Nuclear Disarmament (CND)? In the 1980s, CND campaigned to abolish British nuclear weapons, a policy opposed by the government and most members of the armed forces. Was CND detrimental to national security? CND organisers acted lawfully. But, even though the law had not been broken, did the security forces have the right to intervene on the grounds that national security was under threat? Suppose that many members of CND were also members of the Labour party. Would that give the security services the right to investigate the Labour party as a threat to national security?

The questions raised above are not hypothetical. In *Spycatcher* (which the government attempted to ban), former MI5 officer Peter Wright claimed that plans had been laid to prevent the Labour party winning the October 1974 general election on the grounds that a Labour victory was not considered conducive to national security. This episode reveals two key points. First, it is the security services themselves which define what is and what is not a threat to national security. Second, members of the security forces tend to have a conservative viewpoint. Any activity of the political left, constitutional or otherwise, is viewed as a potential threat.

If the deliberations of the security services were open to public scrutiny, they could be debated and challenged. Because they are secret, however, they are not. As a result, anything that senior security service officers regard as a threat to national security can form the basis of covert action without any check or balance being placed upon such actions. So, granted that some secret service activity is necessary in a democratic society, how is the necessary degree of secrecy to be preserved whilst the freedom to engage in legitimate political activity is maintained?

Activity 18.9

Item A *MI5 comes in from the cold (1)*

MI5 came in from the cold yesterday carrying a glossy prospectus and carefully posed photographs of its director general, Stella Rimington. The object, says Mrs Rimington in a signed introduction to the 36 page brochure, is to dispel some of the more fanciful allegations surrounding the work of the most secret of security services in the Western world. MI5, the brochure tells us, employs 2,000 people (more than at the height of the Cold War). Over half are women. Over half are under the age of 40. Only a quarter are Oxbridge educated. The brochure explains that 70% of MI5's resources are devoted to countering terrorism. Only 5% is now spent looking for political subversives. Last year, MI5 took control of anti-IRA intelligence gathering in mainland Britain. The brochure is the government's reply to media reports about the activities of MI5. The brochure paints a picture of an efficient organisation under the control of the Home Secretary. But, there are significant omissions - no mention, for example, of how much money MI5 spends. Its annual budget is thought to be about £150 million. Shadow Home Secretary, Tony Blair, pointed out that MI5 is still well behind the standards of openness and democratic accountability adopted years ago by most of Britain's allies. He said that the new openness was a welcome step forward, but must be accompanied by a proper independent system of oversight through an all-party parliamentary committee.

Adapted from the *Guardian*, 17 July 1993.

Item B *MI5 comes in from the cold (2)*

Item C *Troops in Northern Ireland*

Questions

1. 'The security services play an important role in law enforcement.' Explain this statement using Items A-C.
2. a) What do Item A and B tell us about the organisation and role of MI5?
   b) Why is the existence of MI5 a problem in a democracy?
   c) Give arguments for and against the idea that publication of MI5's brochure was more than just a publicity stunt.
3. Suppose there was a serious industrial dispute. Explain the likely role and attitude of the security services and the army. What problems might this create in relation to democratic values?

5 Party policy on law and order

Key Issues

1. What are the main parties' policies on law and order?
2. How do these policies differ?

The policies of the Conservative party

Traditionally, the Conservative party has presented itself (and has been presented by the media) as a party which is 'strong' on law and order. This means that any Conservative Home Secretary is under great pressure to take measures to combat rising crime figures. After their fourth election victory in a row in 1992, Conservative ministers could no longer argue with any conviction that rising crime figures resulted from failed Labour policies. So, when in 1993 opinion polls began to show that Labour was gaining support for its ideas on law and order, Conservatives decided to respond.

The Conservative party conference in 1993 pushed the issue of law and order to the top of the political agenda. In his speech to the conference, Michael Howard, the Home Secretary, announced 27 measures which he intended to put in place. The Prime Minister, John Major, made it clear that law and order was to be a central plank in his 'Back to Basics' campaign.

The 1993 Queen's Speech included the commitment by the government to introduce 17 of Michael Howard's 27 measures. Two major pieces of legislation were proposed - the Criminal Justice Bill and the Police and Magistrates Courts Bill. The measures proposed in these Bills are indicative of the current Conservative approach to law and order. They include the following: the end of the use of repeated cautions; the extension of powers to review lenient sentences; plans to build six new private sector prisons; plans to build secure youth training institutions; the end of the right to silence; the granting of the right to the police to take DNA samples from non-intimate parts of the body without consent; changes to bail regulations; the introduction of stop and search for terrorist suspects; new laws for evicting squatters and powers to seize materials relating to child pornography.

The Criminal Justice Act (see also, chapter 17, p.508)

After a difficult passage through Parliament, during which several amendments were made (particularly in the House of Lords), the Criminal Justice Bill finally became law in November 1994. The Criminal Justice Act has a number of key provisions. Most controversially, it altered the traditional right to silence enjoyed by a person accused of a crime. This right was embodied in the caution which police officers were obliged to recite to people arrested on suspicion of committing a crime. The new law allows judges to direct a jury in a criminal trial to take into account the fact that a person chose to remain silent. Also, if a defendant fails to provide the police with information which is later used by the defence, the judge can direct the jury to draw conclusions from this. As a result of these changes, the caution recited by police officers has been changed.

A second key provision of this Act relates to the power of the police to stop and search. Before the Act was passed, that power could only be exercised where there was some suspicion on the part of the police that a crime had been or was about to be committed. Since the Act has been passed, however, the police have been permitted to stop and search where no real suspicion exists, so long as the police action relates to an investigation into a terrorist offence.

The Act also implemented proposals to deal with New Age travellers, squatters, people who attend raves and protestors against hunting, road developments and other such activities. First, it is an offence for travellers to camp on land after a local authority has asked them to leave. It is also an offence for travellers not to leave private land if there has been damage done to the land or if the travellers are in a convoy of more than six vehicles and they have been asked to leave by a senior police officer. Second, a prison sentence of up to six months can be imposed for squatting for more than 24 hours after an eviction order has been gained and landlords (or their representatives) have the right to force an entry into a squat to gain repossession. Third, it is a criminal offence not to leave an unlicensed festival or rave, if asked to do so, and the police can arrest anyone travelling to such an event within a five mile radius of the event. Fourth, a new offence of 'aggravated trespass' has been introduced - trespassers commit a criminal rather than a civil offence if they disrupt a legal activity (for example, a hunt or road building operation) as a result of their trespass. Demonstrations held where the landowner has not given permission are also subject to this law.

Opponents of this Act claim that it significantly undermines civil liberties and confers upon the police a great number of new powers which they may abuse. Supporters of the Act argue that it is necessary to deal with a growing number of problems not addressed by existing legislation.

The measures contained in the Act can be seen to

represent a threefold emphasis in Conservative thinking on crime. First, the measures make the conservative assumption that individuals must be held responsible for their actions. No amount of talk about socio-economic factors can mitigate this personal responsibility. Second, the measures reflect the conservative belief that those who are personally responsible for crime should be punished for their actions, partly in the hope that they and others will be deterred from committing similar crimes in the future, and partly from a belief that wrongdoers should simply be punished. Third, these measures make a moral statement about society's attitude towards crime. The implication is that society regards crime as a wrong that must be severely dealt with.

The policies of the Labour party

Until recently, the Labour party did not place a great deal of emphasis on the issue of law and order. Labour's 1992 manifesto, for example, devoted only a single paragraph to the subject. The rise in crime in the early 1990s and a new approach by Labour's front bench team, however, has led to more energy being devoted to this policy area since early 1993.

Labour's policy on law and order has two strands. First, an emphasis on the socio-economic causes of crime. This has been a constant theme of Labour thought on the subject. And second, a stress upon the rights and duties of the individual as a member of society. This is a new approach to the subject. It was developed by Tony Blair when he was shadow Home Secretary in 1993.

The emphasis on socio-economic causes of crime can be seen in the commitments made in Labour's 1992 manifesto. In this manifesto, the Labour party promised to work in cooperation with local authorities to remove many of the causes of crime, especially crime in inner city local authority housing estates. It promised central government assistance in modernising these estates by improving street lighting, demolishing derelict buildings and fencing in waste land. It also promised to ban the sale of replica guns, to place more officers on the beat and to promote non-custodial sentences. This last point highlights a significant difference between the ideology of the Labour and Conservative parties on this matter. The Conservatives stress the punitive aspects of punishment (hence the prison building programme) whilst Labour stresses the element of rehabilitation and community service in punishment (hence the emphasis on non-custodial sentences).

Since 1993, a new element has been added to Labour's thinking on law and order. A stress has been placed on the duties and responsibilities that individuals have as citizens. Tony Blair has argued that policy should not be determined by consideration of socio-economic factors alone. Individuals have a moral duty to take responsibility for their own actions and for their community as a whole. His ideas are derived from the link he sees between the early Labour party and non-conformist Christianity. The Labour party, he argues, derived its moral basis from non-conformist Christianity. Individual morality, therefore, should be as much a part of Labour's thinking on law and order as it is for Conservatives. Labour's policy on law and order since 1993 can best be summed up by the slogan - 'tough on crime, tough on the causes of crime'.

These developments have gone some way towards closing the gap between Labour and the Conservatives in their ideas about the causes and treatment of crime. But, the two parties still differ about the measures which should be introduced to deal with crime. Labour still emphasises social as well as judicial and penal measures.

The policies of the Liberal Democrats

Liberal Democrat policy on law and order is similar to that adopted by the Labour party. In the *Pocket Guide to Liberal Democrat Policies* their policies are described as follows:

> 'A return to community policing by officers on the beat; community crime prevention strategies such as links between local authorities and the police; the setting up of special police squads to deal with racist attacks; reviews of sentencing policy by a Sentencing Advisory Council; the creation of channels for the rectification of miscarriages of justice; and the avoidance of prison sentences for those found guilty of minor sentences.' (Lib Dems, 1991)

These policies build upon the Liberal Democrats' emphasis on community politics. The premise upon which they are based is as follows: as far as is possible, issues should be dealt with on as local a level as possible.

Conclusions

The main difference between the parties over law and order is their underlying philosophical premises. These philosophical differences, concerning the origins of crime and the nature of individual responsibility, translate into different policy objectives.

Activity 18.10

Item A *Crime link to economy*

For the first time, ministers publicly acknowledged a link between economic deprivation and crime rates yesterday as the number of reported offences reached unprecedented levels. The link between the economy and crime centres on Home Office research completed in 1991. This looked at the effect of recessions on crime by examining consumption levels. As consumption levels dropped in a recession, property crime went up. As society came out of a recession and personal consumption rose, property crime fell. Violent crimes, often associated with alcohol, rose during booms. The Home Office minister, Michael Jack, admitted the link.

Adapted from the *Guardian*, 29 April 1993.

Item B *Recorded crime and unemployment, 1971-91*

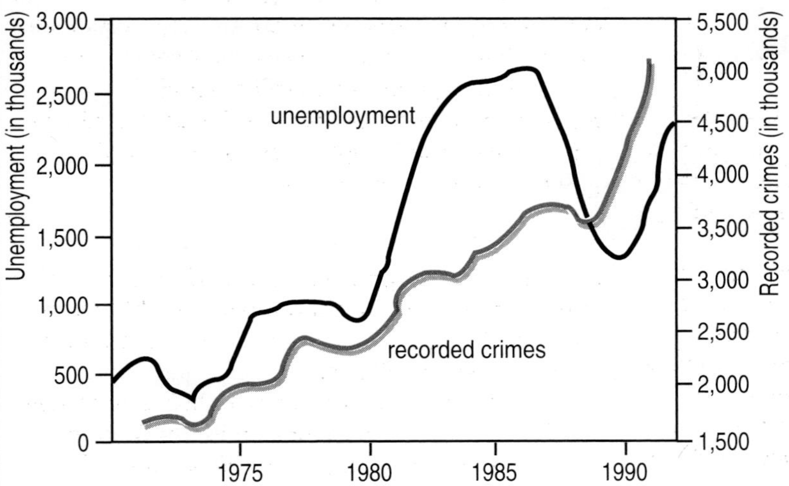

This graph compares the number of people unemployed between 1971 and 1991 to the number of crimes recorded.

Adapted from *New Statesman and Society*, 14 January 1994.

Item C *Tony Blair's view*

Crime is quintessentially a problem the individual cannot tackle alone. Crime demands that communities work as communities to fight it. There is a growing and open determination in the Labour party to make crime a genuine people's issue, a national campaign for better and safer communities. We are moving beyond the old debate which suggested there were only two sides - those who want to punish the criminal and those who point to poor social conditions in which crime breeds. The obvious common sense is that such a choice is false and misleading. People have a right to go about their business without being attacked or abused or having their property stolen. They have a right, society has a duty, to bring those who commit crimes to justice. Equally, the purpose of any system of punishment should not just be to punish and deter but also to rehabilitate, for the good of society as well as the criminal. Above all, any sensible society will recognise that poor education and housing, inadequate or cruel family backgrounds, low employment prospects and drug abuse will affect the likelihood of young people turning to crime. We should be tough on crime and tough on the underlying causes of crime.

Adapted from Blair, 1993.

Item D *Conservative Manifesto, 1992*

The Conservative party has always stood for the protection of the citizen and the defence of the rule of law. Society is entitled to a sense of security and individuals are entitled to peace of mind. Our policies on law and order are designed to protect the people of this country and their way of life. We must continue to ensure that the sentence fits the crime. There should be long sentences for dangerous criminals. There should be fines and a tougher regime outside prison available as an alternative for less serious crime. We must maintain confidence in our legal system. We must tackle crime at its roots. Two thirds of the offences dealt with by our courts are committed by only 7% of those convicted. Most of these constant offenders started down the path of crime while still of school age. Above all, we must remember that it is our police force which is in the front line of battle. To combat crime effectively, the police force needs the full support of the government and public.

Adapted from the Conservative party manifesto, 1992.

Item E *Violent Britain*

Questions

1. Look at Item A. Why do you think Conservatives had been reluctant to link crime with the economy?
2. How would you expect a member of (i) the Conservative party and (ii) the Labour party to explain the figures in Item B?
3. What ideological differences are there between Items C and D?
4. How did the Conservatives attempt to carry out the pledges made in Item D after winning the 1992 election?
5. Look at Item E. How can the problems illustrated by this picture be solved? Answer this question from the perspective of
   (a) a Labour politician
   (b) a Conservative politician
   (c) a Liberal Democrat politician.

References

Arthur (1987) Arthur, M., *Northern Ireland: Soldiers Talking*, Sidgwick & Jackson, 1987.

Benyon (1986) Benyon, J., 'Turmoil in the cities', *Social Studies Review*, Vol.1, No.3, January 1986.

Blair (1993) Blair, T., 'Why crime is a socialist issue', *New Statesman and Society*, 29 January 1993.

Bradley & Clark (1983) Bradley, K.R. & Clark, R.A., *The Legal Framework: Law and the Individual*, Rinehart & Winston, 1983.

Childs (1992) Childs, D., *Britain Since 1945*, Routledge, 1992.

Denscombe (1993) Denscombe, M., *Sociology Update 1993*, Olympus Books UK, 1993.

Farrell (1976) Farrell, J., *The Orange state*, Pluto Press, 1976.

Fine & Millar (1985) Fine, B & Millar, R. (eds), *Policing the Miners' Strike*, Lawrence & Wisehart, 1985.

Glinert (1992) Glinert, E., 'The force of calm after the crusades', *New Statesman and Society*, 17 January 1992.

Graef (1989) Graef, R., *Talking Blues*, Fontana, 1989.

Habermas (1973) Habermas, J., *Legitimation Crises*, Heinemann, 1973.

HMSO (1993) Central Statistical Office, *Social Trends*, Vol.23, HMSO, 1993.

HMSO (1994) Central Statistical Office, *Social Trends* Vol.24, HMSO, 1994.

Hobbes (1651) Hobbes, T., *The Leviathan*, Penguin, 1985.

Kettle (1985) Kettle, M., 'The National Reporting Centre and the 1984 miners' strike in *Fine & Millar (1985)*.

Leys (1983) Leys, C., *Politics in Britain*, Verso, 1983.

Lib Dems (1991) Liberal Democrats, *Pocket Guide to the Party*, Liberal Democrat Publications, 1991.

McKie (1993) McKie, D. (ed.), *The Guardian Political Almanac 1993/4*, Fourth Estate, 1993.

Mill (1859) Mill, J. S., *On Liberty*, Penguin, 1982.

Plato (1987) Plato, *The Republic*, Penguin, 1987.

Popper (1945) Popper, K., *The Open Society and its Enemies*, Vol.1, RKP, 1945.

PSI (1983) Smith, D. J., *'A survey of police officers'*, Policy Studies Institute, 1983.

Reiner (1992) Reiner, R., *The Politics of the Police*, Harvester Wheatsheaf, 1992.

Rousseau (1762) Rousseau, J.J., *The Social Contract*, Penguin, 1968.

Wright (1987) Wright, P., *Spycatcher*, Viking Press, 1987.

19 Political information

Introduction

Most people gain their information about politics through the mass media - television, radio and newspapers. The media decides what is newsworthy and then explores the issues which are thrown up by the news. Furthermore, the media controls the way in which news items are presented. Reports are edited. Speeches are reduced to 'sound bites'. As a result, the media does not just keep people informed about what is happening in the world. It offers a particular interpretation of what is happening.

Because people often have no way of checking the validity of what they see, hear or read, they are, to a large extent, reliant on the mass media to shape their view of the world. If the mass media can shape people's view of the world, then it may be able to influence their political behaviour. This is one of the reasons why the way in which the media works and who controls it are issues of great importance. This chapter considers how much influence the mass media has - both upon the political behaviour of the individual citizen and upon the political culture of the UK.

A frequent criticism of the mass media is that it lacks objectivity and impartiality. Often this criticism comes from politicians. Yet, politicians rely on the mass media to communicate their point of view. This chapter considers the pressures on the different media outlets and asks whether there is any justification for the criticism that the media is subjective and partial. It also considers the extent to which government intervenes to suppress the dissemination of political information. Can restrictions on the freedom of information ever be justified? If so, in what circumstances?

Chapter summary

Part 1 defines the term the '**mass media**' and describes its **historical development**. It considers why the dissemination of political information is important in a democracy.

Part 2 examines the o**wnership and control of the press**. It considers whether there is **political bias in the press**.

Part 3 examines the **ownership and control of radio and television**. The effect of **televising Parliament** is reviewed.

Part 4 asks **how much influence the mass media has**. It looks at the different ways in which this question has been answered and considers the future of the media in Britain.

Part 5 focuses on **secrecy** and whether or not there is a genuine move towards **open government**.

1 The mass media

Key Issues

1. What do we mean by the 'mass media'?
2. How did the mass media develop?
3. Why is political information important in a democracy?

1.1 Development of the mass media

The mass media can be defined as:

> 'The methods and organisations used by specialist social groups to convey messages to large, socially mixed and widely dispersed audiences.' (Trowler, 1988, p.5).

Television, newspapers, radio, cinema, magazines and books are all part of the mass media. But, usually, the term is used to refer to television, the radio and newspapers (the press). The growth of the mass media is a 20th century phenomenon. In 1900, books and newspapers were available, but were too expensive for most people to buy regularly. Radio and cinema had been discovered, but were not widely available. Television had not been invented.

Historical development

The development of the mass media was only possible because of the development of modern technology. As Barratt puts it:

> '[Mass communication] is a product of industrial techniques such as the steam powered

> printing press, cinematography and radio and television broadcasting and receiving equipment.' (Barratt, 1986, p.14)

The development of the mass media is, in other words, a product of the process of industrialisation that took place in Britain in the 19th century. New technology combined with new ways of work and new social conditions to provide the conditions for the growth of the mass media.

The Press

The first media outlet to develop was the newspaper industry. Modern newspapers have been published since the 18th century. The first daily newspaper, the *Courant*, began publication in 1702. The *Times* began publication in 1785. Throughout the 18th and early 19th centuries, however, the content of newspapers was restricted by Parliament. Until 1771, newspapers were forbidden to report parliamentary proceedings and there were frequent bans on the reporting of subjects regarded as 'political'. In addition, a stamp duty was imposed on newspapers in 1725 (a tax which added to the price of each newspaper). This was designed to restrict circulation of the radical press by making their newspapers too expensive for ordinary people. The abolition of stamp duty in 1855 is regarded as a major step on the road to a free press. However, in the 19th century low standards of living and low levels of literacy combined to ensure that it was mainly the better-off members of society who read newspapers.

It was not until the beginning of the 20th century that newspapers actively sought a mass readership. The turning point was the decision of Alfred Harmsworth (Lord Northcliffe), in 1896, to buy the *Daily Mail*. Newspapers in the 19th century looked dull. No pictures were included and the columns were filled with long reports of political speeches in minuscule text. The *Mail* under Harmsworth (Northcliffe) changed all this by using large headlines and pictures, by no longer including long reports of political speeches and by covering sport. These changes appealed to people. The *Mail*'s circulation grew from 200,000 in 1896 to 980,000 in 1900 to 1.48 million in 1920. As the readership grew, so did the revenue generated from printing adverts. The success of the *Mail* (especially its financial success) was noted by the other newspapers and most began to copy the new formula. The new appearance of newspapers combined with their cheap price resulted in a growing readership. By 1920, two newspapers sold over a million copies per day. By 1930, five newspapers sold over a million copies per day. And by 1939, two newspapers sold more than 2 million copies per day.

Radio and the BBC

The period during which newspapers began to attract a mass audience was also the period in which radio became established in most homes. The 1920s have sometimes been described as the 'golden age of wireless' (radio was called 'wireless' in its early years to differentiate it from the telephone). It was in the 1920s that radio first gained a mass audience in Britain. This was facilitated by the ability of radio manufacturers to mass produce cheap radios. The number of radios in Britain rose from 35,000 in 1922 to three million in 1929 to over nine million in 1939.

At first, private companies were allowed to apply to the post office for licences to broadcast radio programmes and to sell radios. By 1922, over 100 companies had submitted applications. The government persuaded these companies to join together into a single organisation - the British Broadcasting Company. This operated as a private company until 1926, when a royal charter changed its status. From 1926 the company became a 'corporation' (see chapter 16, p.497). Its aim was no longer to make a profit, but to provide a public service. To ensure that the British Broadcasting Corporation (BBC) was politically independent, a board of directors, not the government, had control over what was broadcast and the BBC was financed not by adverts, but by a licence fee paid by each owner of a radio.

The first director general of the BBC was John Reith. He had very firm ideas about the sort of values that should be promoted by the BBC. For example, Reith was a Christian and he only allowed religious and 'serious' programmes to be broadcast on Sundays. Also, he refused to allow people with regional accents to present programmes on the radio. Reith said in 1926:

> 'Our responsibility is to carry into the greatest possible number of homes everything that is best in every human department of knowledge, endeavour and achievement, and to avoid the things which are or may be hurtful. It is occasionally said that we are apparently setting out to give the public what we think they need and not what they want. But, few know what they want and very few what they need. There is often no difference.'

Radio remained the main broadcasting medium until the 1950s when television replaced it. Commercial radio was introduced for the first time in the 1970s.

Television

The first demonstration of television was organised by John Logie Baird and took place in London in January 1926. Ten years later, the BBC began to broadcast television programmes. The BBC, however, did not use Baird's system. It used a system based on the cathode ray tube and developed by EMI in 1935. The first television programmes could only be seen in the

London area. By 1939, just 12,000 people owned television sets. Whilst radio broadcasts were used as an important means of imparting information and maintaining morale during the Second World War, television broadcasting shut down when war was declared and did not resume until 1945. It was only in the 1950s that television began to become a mass medium.

The turning point was the broadcast of the Queen's coronation in 1953. In 1950, just 10% of homes had television sets. But, neighbours crowded into homes with televisions to see the coronation and what they saw caught their imagination. By 1963, just ten years after the coronation, 90% of homes had television sets.

Since the 1950s, television technology has improved tremendously and there is a growing choice of programmes and channels. The Independent Television Authority (ITA) was set up in 1954 and commercial television (television funded by revenue from advertising) began to be broadcast in 1955. Colour televisions replaced black and white sets in the 1970s. In the early 1980s, Channel Four was set up to cater for minority interests and, in the late 1980s, cable and satellite television became available. By 1993, over 99% of households had at least one television set. Nearly 10% of homes had three or more colour television sets. Also, by 1993, over 70% of households owned a video recorder and 3.6 million homes could receive satellite television (HMSO, 1995).

Activity 19.1

Item A *Newspapers in the 19th century*

THE NEWS OF THE WORLD.

Item B *Newspapers in the early 20th century*

PURE INDIAN TEA

Weekly Dispatch

ESMOLIN NEURITIS

109TH YEAR

SUNDAY SPECIAL EDITION.

SUNDAY, JULY 31, 1910.

ONE PENNY.

CRIPPEN'S LIFE AT SEA DESCRIBED BY 'WIRELESS.'

DETECTIVE INS. DEW

MRS CRIPPEN (MISS BELLE ELMORE)

H.H. Crippen.

THE DOCTOR'S FIRST WIFE MRS CHARLOTTE CRIPPEN

CAPT KENDALL

CRIPPEN'S LIFE AT SEA DAY BY DAY.

DESCRIBED BY CAPTAIN KENDALL, OF THE MONTROSE.

FULL EXCLUSIVE "WIRELESS" TO "THE DAILY MAIL."

THE BOOKS CRIPPEN READS, AND THE SONG HE LIKED.

WHY HE FAILED TO ANSWER THE NAME "ROBINSON."

MISS LE NEVE

NOTICE.

Item C *Reactions to radio*

I'm only writing to say how much radio means to me and thousands of the same sort. It is a real magic carpet. Before, it was a fortnight at Rhyll and that was all the travelling I did that wasn't on a tram. Now I hear the Boat Race and the Derby and the opening of the Menai bridge. There are football matches some Saturdays and talks by famous men and women who have travelled and can tell us about places.

Adapted from a letter written by an office worker to the *Radio Times*, 12 October 1928.

I have now been a regular listener for ten years - that is from the age of 12. I should like to take this opportunity of thanking the BBC for the part it has played in my education, pleasures and the formation of my tastes and opinions.

Adapted from a letter to the BBC from a listener in 1938.

Item D *The coronation and TV*

It was the coronation that really pushed television forward: the crowning of Queen Elizabeth in 1953 was the first occasion that ever drew the British together to witness an event as an entire nation. On the day, anyone in Britain who had a television set invited their less privileged neighbours in to watch. There were more viewers per set than ever before or since and the audience topped 20 million, exceeding that of radio for the first time. In the year following the coronation, the number of licensed television sets rose by 50% and from that day to this no public event has been complete without television cameras.

Adapted from Dunkley, 1985.

Item E *Television in the 1950s*

This advert was produced in 1953.

Questions

1. a) 'The development of the mass media is a 20th century phenomenon.' Explain this statement using the items in this Activity.
   b) What factors contributed to the development of the mass media?

2. a) Judging from Items A and B how did newspapers change in the early years of the 20th century?
   b) Why do you think their readership grew?

3. a) Using Items C-E explain the popularity of radio and television.
   b) In what ways do you think the spread of radio and television might have changed political life in Britain?

1.2 The impact of the growth of the mass media

The growth of the mass media has brought a new era in the conveying of political information. In effect, it has resulted in the manufacture of a second hand version of reality. By the time a news item appears on the television or in the newspaper, what actually happened at the original event has necessarily been altered by the involvement of media professionals. No matter how long the real event, for example, the news item on television will probably be over within five minutes and it is unlikely to be allotted more than a page in a newspaper. That means that what happened has to be edited down to fit the slot. So, only part of a politician's speech is given verbatim. The remainder of the speech is summarised by the reporter. And, by summarising, the reporter is providing a particular viewpoint or interpretation.

Not only does the media's intervention produce a second-hand version of an event, it also encourages apathy rather than active political participation. Whilst someone who attends a political meeting is able to respond to what is said by asking questions, applauding or heckling, the mass media's audience has limited feedback - letter writing, phone-in programmes and, very occasionally, open access slots. And even with the limited feedback which does exist, audience responses nearly always have to pass through an editing system with the media professionals acting as 'gate-keepers'.

Despite these drawbacks, the various media outlets

have become a major source of information in general and of political information in particular. People receive news of political events and developments much more quickly than they did 50 or 100 years ago. Political information is much more widely available than was ever the case in the past. And people certainly take advantage of the various media outlets which are available - for example, on average in 1993, people in Britain spent just over 25 hours per week watching television and just over 16 hours per week listening to the radio (HMSO, 1995). Whether or not people are better informed about politics, however, is a matter of debate. The media provides entertainment, not just information, and some critics claim that the amount of serious political reporting as a proportion of total media output has diminished (see, for example, Curran & Seaton, 1991).

Political ignorance and the manipulation of information

Hillyard & Percy-Smith argue that:

> 'Effective political participation at all levels depends crucially on access to information. Decisions about which party to support or which policies to endorse, and judgements about the capabilities of decision makers require that people have the facts about those parties, policies and decisions. But, access to information in Britain is severely limited.' (Hillyard & Percy-Smith, 1988, p.111).

Democracy requires the informed participation of the people. Yet, the sum total of many people's political participation is to cast a vote every five years. Between elections, only a minority of people take an active interest in politics. It is, therefore, perhaps no surprise to find that political ignorance is widespread, particularly amongst young people. One survey revealed, for example, that 64% of teenagers agreed with the statement that: **the IRA is a Protestant organisation committed to the cause of maintaining the division of Ireland**. It is difficult to know what sense these teenagers make of the news coverage of events in Northern Ireland and it is a matter of concern that people do not always have the knowledge to make informed political decisions.

The consequences of political ignorance are alarming. They were vividly described in George Orwell's *Nineteen Eighty Four* where the party slogan, 'ignorance is strength', was used by the Ministry of Truth to ensure continuing control by Big Brother (Orwell, 1949). Britain has not reached the depth of manipulated ignorance that George Orwell feared, but his book raises issues about the control and content of the mass media, secrecy and freedom of information that remain important today.

Explanations of political ignorance vary according to ideological stance. Those on the left tend to argue that people in power have a vested interest in maintaining ignorance and trivialising political matters to avoid debate. They claim that conscious efforts are made to limit information and to control what individuals can be told. Those on the right, however, tend to argue that most people have no need to develop a political understanding. Indeed, many people are not capable of so doing. The right claims that politics should be left to those who are really concerned about it.

Taking an historical perspective, it is clear that those in power have sought to limit the amount of political information that is available to ordinary people. What was blatant control of political information in the 18th and 19th centuries has evolved into more varied and, perhaps, more subtle forms of what is now known as 'news management'. Sir Angus Maude, paymaster general in Margaret Thatcher's first government, was responsible for policy on information. He argued:

> 'News management, when it means representing the facts in a way that reflects most favourably on the government, is a perfectly fair process and it is one which has been undertaken by all governments since the beginning of time.' (quoted in Cockerell et al., 1984, p.52)

Information and the 'national interest'

Information is itself rarely neutral. Whether the information is made available, the way in which it is presented, the context of the ideas, the emphasis that is given - all these factors help to dictate what sense is or is not made of political developments. Those who present political information are themselves rarely disinterested observers. In a 'free' society it tends to be assumed that there should be a free trade in ideas. But, this ignores the fact that some individuals, groups or institutions may be in a more powerful position than others to give their definitions of reality.

Governments, in particular, are in a powerful position to provide their version of reality and, in so doing, they often justify their actions by claiming to have acted 'in the national interest'. This claim is frequently made during times of conflict - such as in the middle of a major strike or during a war. During the Falklands War, for example, the government was able (through censorship and tight control over what information should be made publicly available) to present a view of events conducive to its own political position. The government was undoubtedly supported in this by the popular press which launched a tide of jingoism (extreme patriotism). When the BBC, attempting to maintain its reputation for independence, questioned aspects of military policy, it came under attack from the government. On this occasion, the national interest became the same as the government's interest and, therefore, the same as the Conservative party's interest. But, some critics have argued that this confusion between national and partisan interests was not an isolated incident. Robert Harris, for example, in a review of information policy and the media in the Falklands War, concluded:

> 'The instinctive secrecy of the military and the civil service; the prostitution of sections of the press; the lies, the misinformation, the manipulation of public opinion by the authorities; the political intimidation of broadcasters; the ready connivance of the media in their own distortion...all these occur as much in normal peace time in Britain as in war.' (Harris, 1983, p.151)

The role of the mass media

The above discussion suggests that a number of different interpretations of the role which the mass media should and does play are possible. According to Miller (1991), there are three contrasting interpretations - the media's role is either mobilising, libertarian or public service. If the media plays a **mobilising role**, it is subordinate to the state. The government is the guardian of the national interest and the media should promote this national interest. If, on the other hand, the media plays a **libertarian role**, it should have freedom to publish and to broadcast what it likes, with only very few constraints. And third, if the media plays a **public service role**, it has a duty to scrutinise the government, to hold it to account for its actions and to respond to demands from the public.

Activity 19.2

Item A *The impact of the growth of the mass media*

Before the mass media existed, a child growing up in a slowly changing village built his or her model of reality out of images received from a tiny handful of sources - the teacher, the priest, the chief or official and, above all, the family. There was no television or radio in the home to give the child a chance to meet many different kinds of strangers from many different walks of life and even from different countries. Very few people ever saw a foreign city. The result was that people had only a small number of different people to imitate or model themselves on. Their choices were even more limited by the fact that the people they could model themselves on were themselves all of limited experience. The images of the world built up by the village child, therefore, were extremely narrow.

Adapted from Toffler, 1980.

Item B *The sale of Rover to BAe, 1988*

In March 1988, Lord Young, the minister responsible for the privatisation of the Rover car company, arranged for hidden 'sweeteners' (extra cash) to be given to British Aerospace (BAe) to encourage it to buy the company. In November 1988, the National Audit Office revealed that the taxpayer had lost £400 million because of a discrepancy in valuing the company. Nearly two years later, in May 1990, a confidential draft report from the Trade and Industry Committee found that the government had misled Parliament by not revealing the £38 million sweeteners. In June 1990, the European Commission ruled that ministers acted illegally in subsidising the takeover of Rover by BAe. A month later the Commons Committee on Privileges decided that the *Guardian* newspaper should not have published a leaked document which revealed the existence of sweeteners. The committee said: 'The significance of this leak as a potential threat to the relationship between committees and witnesses is aggravated by the character of the material disclosed. The memorandum was classified since it contained information the publication of which the Department of Trade and Industry believed at the time would be detrimental to the national interest.'

Adapted from the *Guardian*, 27 July 1990.

Item C *The number of newspapers available in Britain 1900-92*

	1900	1921	1947	1987	1992
National dailies	21	12	9	11	11
Provincial morning	70	41	28	16	18
Provincial evening	101	89	75	64	76
National/Provincial Sundays	-	21	16	13	9

Adapted from Negrine, 1994.

Item D *Participation in home based leisure activities 1977-90*

	1977	1980	1983	1986	1987	1990
Watching TV	*97*	*98*	*98*	*98*	*99*	*99*
Visiting or entertaining friends or relatives	*91*	*91*	*91*	*94*	*95*	*96*
Listening to radio	*87*	*88*	*87*	*86*	*88*	*89*
Listening to records	*62*	*64*	*63*	*67*	*73*	*76*
Reading books	*54*	*57*	*56*	*59*	*60*	*62*
Gardening	*42*	*43*	*44*	*43*	*46*	*48*
DIY	*35*	*37*	*36*	*39*	*43*	*43*
Needlework or knitting	*29*	*28*	*27*	*27*	*27*	*23*

This table shows the percentage of people participating in each activity in the four weeks before being interviewed.

Adapted from HMSO, 1993.

Item E *Censorship*

A Sinn Fein election mural, Belfast 1989.

In 1989, the Home Secretary announced that television and radio were banned from broadcasting any words spoken by 11 political and paramilitary groups in Northern Ireland, including the political party Sinn Fein. Their words, however, could be spoken by an actor or screened as subtitles. The overall effect of the censorship of these groups was to deny them a voice in the British media and the broader political debate. The broadcasting ban was not lifted until September 1994, after the paramilitary organisations announced a ceasefire.

Adapted from Franklin, 1993.

Questions

1. Judging from the Items A-E, what impact has the growth of the mass media made on people's lives?
2. 'The growth of the mass media has led to the greater availability of political information.' Give arguments for and against this view using Items A- E.
3. Look at Item B. Suppose you were editor of the *Guardian*. Write a letter to the Commons Committee on Privileges explaining why you felt it was right to publish the leaked document.
4. a) Why do you think the government imposed the broadcasting ban (Item E)?
   b) What does it tell us about the government's attitude towards the mass media?

2 The press

Key Issues

1. Who owns the press?
2. Why is ownership important and what role do owners of the press play?
3. What other factors affect newspapers' dissemination of political information?

2.1 Ownership and the press

The press in Britain is privately owned and controlled. It is free to print whatever it likes within the laws of libel and the requirements of official secrecy. This section looks at who owns newspapers and asks why ownership is concentrated into so few hands.

The quality and the tabloid press

A distinction is commonly made between the **quality press** and the **tabloid press** (the tabloid press is sometimes referred to as the 'popular' press). The quality daily press is made up of the *Times, Daily Telegraph, Financial Times, Independent* and *Guardian*. The other dailies are all tabloids. Unlike the tabloid press, the quality press relies more heavily on advertising than sales for its commercial success.

The press barons

When newspapers first gained a mass readership in the early part of the 20th century, they were owned by wealthy individuals who are referred to collectively as 'press barons'. Perhaps the best known of these press barons were the brothers Alfred and Harold Harmsworth who became Lord Northcliffe and Lord Rothermere respectively and William Aitken who became Lord Beaverbrook. It was Alfred Harmsworth who bought the *Daily Mail* in 1896 and transformed its style (see above section 1.1). He, his brother and Beaverbrook dominated the press before the Second World War. And it was not just the style of newspapers that changed under their direction. All three were prepared to impose their own political viewpoints on their newspapers.

Northcliffe, Rothermere and Beaverbrook all had right wing views and this is reflected in the line which their newspapers took. For example, in the 1930s, for a short time, Rothermere decided to support the British Union of Fascists (BUF). As a result, the *Daily Mail* carried headlines such as, 'Give the Blackshirts a helping hand'. When Rothermere changed his mind about the BUF, so did the *Daily Mail*. That newspapers were being used as a vehicle to promote personal political views was freely admitted by Beaverbrook in 1948. Interviewed by the Royal Commission on the Press, he said:

> 'I run the *Daily Express* purely for the purpose of making propaganda, and with no other motive.'

Multinationals

Today, much of the press is owned by multinational, multimedia corporations. These huge companies operate in a number of countries, tend to own a range of media outlets (for example, television stations as well as newspapers) and some have business interests which are nothing to do with the media. For example, News International which owns the *Times, Sunday Times, Sun, News of the World* and *Today* newspapers in Britain also owns major newspapers, magazines and book publishing companies in Australia and the USA as well as Festival Records, 20th Century Fox, Channel Ten (an Australian television station), BSkyB and the Star Network which beams five channels to 45 million viewers in 38 countries in Asia. Other News International interests include computer software, offshore oil and gas and air transport (Franklin, 1994). News International is the creation of Rupert Murdoch. Murdoch is a modern 'press baron'. But, as the above list suggests, his business interests are so wide that he has less time to become actively involved in the day-to-day running of his newspapers than was the case with press barons such as Northcliffe and Rothermere.

This does not mean, however, that Murdoch (or the heads of the other multinationals) never intervene. When Harold Evans, editor of the *Times*, did not follow Murdoch's preferred line, he was dismissed. Evans claimed that Murdoch frequently sent him:

> 'Articles marked **worth reading** which espoused right wing views [and he jabbed] a finger at headlines which he thought could have been more supportive of Mrs Thatcher.' (Evans, 1984, p.296)

Negrine (1994) has pointed out that owners do appoint editors and chief executives. They decide budgets and staffing levels and they put their imprint on the organisations they own. In consequence, editors and journalists work within already defined structures.

Exceptions to multinational control do exist. The *Guardian*, for example, is owned by a Trust which appoints the editor and guarantees editorial independence.

The concentration of ownership

Concentration of ownership of the press is nothing new. In 1908, for example, in addition to the *Daily Mail*, Northcliffe owned the *Daily Mirror*, the *Times*, the *Observer* and the *Dispatch*, as well as several periodicals and evening newspapers (Wagg, 1989). Not only is concentration of ownership of the press nothing new, it has long been a cause for concern as this comment, made by a Labour MP in 1946, makes clear:

> 'For years we have watched this freedom [of the press] being whittled away. We have watched the destruction of great papers. We have watched the combines come in, buying up and killing independent journals and we have seen the honourable profession of journalism degraded by high finance and big business.' (quoted in Hansard, 29 October, 1946)

Ownership of the press in the 1990s is narrower and more concentrated in Britain than anywhere else in the Western world. Grant (1994), for example, notes that, in 1994, 85% of daily and Sunday newspaper circulation was controlled by just seven companies, of which five companies owned and controlled nine out of every 10 newspapers sold. News International alone accounted for one third of all newspapers sold in Britain.

In the early 1980s, there was the suggestion that ownership would diversify because new printing technology was becoming available. But, this idea proved to be unfounded. The start-up costs for a new newspaper are prohibitive. For example, it cost £20 million to launch the *Independent* in 1986. Most of the new newspapers launched in the late 1980s - the *Sunday Correspondent, News on Sunday* and the *Post* - were forced to close down because they were unable to generate high enough sales and sufficient advertising revenue. Others - such as *Today* - were taken over by existing owners. The man who launched *Today*, Eddie Shah, spent £22.5 million in the first 10 weeks before selling it to Rupert Murdoch's News International (Wagg, 1989). Until the launch of the *Independent*, no new national quality daily had been launched for 113 years.

Anti-monopoly legislation has failed to prevent the growing concentration of ownership of the press. News International's takeover of the *Times* in 1981 and *Today* in 1987, for example, were not referred to the Monopoly and Mergers Commission by the government. In 1900, there were 21 national dailies. In 1994, this number had shrunk to 11. And it is not just the national newspapers which are owned by the multinationals. Most regional and local newspapers and even many of the free broadsheets are controlled by the large corporations.

It should be noted, however, that the development of multinational corporations is not just a phenomenon associated with the mass media. The growth of multinationals has resulted in concentrated ownership in many business areas - motor manufacture, for example, is dominated by multinationals like Ford and Volkswagen, whilst multinationals like Matsui and Sony produce electrical goods.

The effect of the market

The press is not just owned to represent the political views of its owners. Newspapers are owned by capitalist organisations and so the creation of profit is an important motivation. Negrine points out that:

> 'It is unlikely that such proprietorial power will be exercised without reference to commercial considerations or market considerations.'
> (Negrine, 1994, p.64)

In other words, newspapers need to make money by selling copies to the general public. And, unless they provide what the public (or at least a sufficiently large section of the public) wants, they will not survive.

Over the past few years, overall sales of daily and Sunday national newspapers have been falling as the public turns to other sources of information. Also, newspapers are in competition with each other. The actions of newspapers, therefore, (and, to some extent, their content) are determined by the need to maintain or improve their market share.

One result of this is that much of what newspapers cover has a minimal political content. This is especially the case with the tabloid press. But even the quality press has reduced its political coverage, especially its coverage of Parliament (see, for example, Straw, 1993).

Activity 19.3

Item A *Circulation & average net sales of British newspapers 1995*

Owner	Titles	Average net sales
United Newspapers	Daily Express Daily Star Sunday Express	1,280,904 738,759 1,411,445
Associated Newspapers	Daily Mail Mail on Sunday	1,780,155 1,952,832
Mirror Group	Daily Mirror Sunday Mirror The People	2,478,109 2,537,856 2,081,498
Hollinger	Daily Telegraph Sunday Telegraph	1,062,775 685,555
Pearson	Financial Times	294,766
Guardian & Manchester Evening News plc	Guardian Observer	400,813 467,017
Newspaper Publishing plc	Independent Independent on Sunday	289,057 322,333
News International	The Sun The Times Today The Sunday Times News of the World	4,069,928 631,448 565,731 1,246,446 4,753,919

This table shows who owns British newspapers and their average net sales between December 1994 and May 1995.

Adapted from figures provided by the Audit Bureau of Circulations, June 1995.

Item B *Owners and editors*

The idea that newspaper owners are no longer interested in imposing their views on their editors (and thus their newspapers) is a myth. More realistic is the comment made by Victor Matthews when Trafalgar House won the auction for the Express Group in 1977 (the Express Group is now owned by United Newspapers). Matthews said: 'By and large, editors will have complete freedom as long as they agree with the policy I have laid down.' The concern that interventions by owners may restrict press freedom and responsible journalism prompted Parliament to insist that Rupert Murdoch, the owner of News International, sign documents guaranteeing editoral independence when he bought the *Times*. These guarantees, however, proved worthless. Murdoch continued to interfere in editorial affairs and eventually sacked the editor Harold Evans. When Evans reminded Murdoch about the guarantees he had made, Murdoch said: 'They're not worth the paper they're written on.'

Adapted from Franklin, 1994.

Item C *The power of the advertisers*

It is not just the owners who control the content of newspapers. The real cost of producing a national newspaper is about four times more than the cover price. So, most of the balance must come from advertising. Sometimes, editors are wary of offending the advertisers. In the 1980s, for example, the *Sunday Times* lost £500,000 worth of advertising from the tobacco company WD & HO Wills because it ran an anti-smoking article. On other occasions, the advertisers may directly influence the newspaper's strategy. In 1987, for example, the *Daily Star* decided to go down-market. Circulation fell and Tesco and other big companies threatened to withdraw their advertising. The paper quickly changed its policy and went up-market again. And it is not just advertisers which exercise control. On occasion, distributors flex their muscles. For example, many newsagents refused to sell the *Sun* in Liverpool after it made derogatory remarks about Liverpudlians when 94 Liverpool football fans were crushed to death at Hillsborough in 1989. Also, for many years, WH Smith refused to stock either *Private Eye* or *Gay News* on the grounds that they were 'abhorrent, though lawful'.

Adapted from Grant, 1994.

Item D *News International*

All these newspapers are owned by News International.

Questions

1. 'The concentration of ownership of the press is a threat to democracy'. Give arguments for and against this statement.
2. Does it matter that ownership of the press in Britain is private? Give reasons for your answer.
3. Judging from Items A-D would you say that modern press barons have too much power? Give reasons for your answer.

2.2 The press and political information

Ownership and market forces are by no means the only factors which determine how newspapers disseminate political information. The newspaper's editorial 'line', the editorial process itself, the aims and attitudes of the journalists and the lines of communication between politicians and journalists all help to determine what appears in a newspaper.

A partisan press?

During the 1992 general election campaign, six daily newspapers with a combined circulation of more than 8.5 million copies per day and five Sunday newspapers with a circulation of 10.1 million per edition urged their readers to vote Conservative. Three daily newspapers with a combined circulation of 4.3 million copies per day and three Sunday newspapers with a combined circulation of 5.5 million per edition urged their readers to vote Labour. And two daily newspapers with a combined circulation of 1.2 million copies per day and two Sunday newspapers with a combined circulation of 0.7 million copies per edition refused to recommend that their readers vote for any particular party. These figures indicate that the press has a pro-Conservative bias. Only one tabloid - the *Daily Mirror* supported and campaigned for the Labour party. All the others (with the exception of the *Daily Star* which did not endorse any party) encouraged their readers to vote Conservative.

Of course, a general election campaign is unusual because it is a time when newspapers feel able to canvass support for their chosen party openly. The rest of the time their support for their chosen party is more subtle. But, whether or not a newspaper is wearing its party allegiance on its sleeve, according to most commentators it will be playing a conservative role (see, for example, Trowler, 1988 and Seabrook, 1987). On the whole, the mainstream press (unsurprisingly) approves of business and the creation of wealth. It tends to condemn excessive trade union power. It supports the monarchy. It is suspicious of feminists, black people, young people, the working class, radicals and protesters. And, it is often fiercely nationalistic.

Political information is not necessarily communicated in 'political' articles. Many of the attitudes described above are the premises upon which general or 'non-political' articles are based. In other words, fundamentally conservative values are dressed up as 'common sense'. For example, an article on the background and career of a rich and famous film star may, on one level, be a 'human interest' story. But, on another level, it may suggest support for the status quo. If it is a 'rag to riches' story, for example, then the message is likely to be 'it could be you', thus encouraging people to dream of fame and fortune. Furthermore, Wagg has argued that the tabloids produce:

> 'Daily doses of undisguised racism and sexism [which make it harder for parties] committed to greater equality, particularly parties of the left, to be elected because they are felt to be peddling 'weird' views on cultural matters.' (Wagg, 1989, p.21)

So, newspapers may use either positive or negative means to achieve the same end, namely support for conservative values.

Although the mainstream newspapers support and encourage conservative values, they do not always support the Conservative party. In the 1992 general election campaign, for example, the *Financial Times* which had traditionally supported the Conservatives, urged its readers to vote Labour and, in 1993, traditional Conservative supporting newspapers - the *Daily Mail, Express, Sun,* and *Sunday Times* - all launched a fierce attack on John Major's government. In addition, in July 1995, the *Daily Mail, Sun, Telegraph* and *Times* all argued that John Major should be replaced as leader of the Conservative party. This, however, does not mean that the press has necessarily swung towards the Labour party. As Kuhn pointed out:

> 'The national press was not so much acting as a conduit for the views of the Labour party and the Liberal Democrats as adopting its own oppositional stance to the government.' (Kuhn, 1994, p.192)

Indeed, Andrew Neil, editor of the *Sunday Times* in 1993, claimed that the newspapers had become the 'real' opposition to the government. By making this claim, he cleverly managed to attack the credibility of the Labour party whilst seeming to make an attack on the government.

There is an argument that newspapers reflect the views of their readers rather than vice versa. The *Sun*, for example, had great difficulty getting established in Scotland. As a result, in January 1992, the Scottish *Sun* argued for an independent Scotland - a policy favoured by the Scottish National party but opposed by the Conservatives. In other words, the Scottish *Sun* trimmed its political message to appeal to its readership. Similarly, in August 1994, Rupert Murdoch surprised many people when he stated that he might be able to support a Labour government under Tony Blair. At the time he said this, opinion polls put Labour over 30% ahead of the Conservatives. It was also at this time that the Conservative government was considering whether to tighten press regulation. Whether or not Murdoch's comment was intended to warn the government not to tighten press regulation, it does suggest that newspapers are, to some extent, sensitive to changes in public opinion.

It should be noted that each day most newspapers cover many of the same stories. What is different is the weight given to a particular news item and the way in which that item is used. What appears with a large headline on the front page of the *Guardian*, for example, might only feature as a small paragraph on page seven of the *Sun* and vice versa. Similarly, an item used as an example of misgovernment in the *Guardian* might be used to illustrate the impotence of the opposition in the *Daily Express*. So, both the editorial process (the selection of items and weighting given to them) and the editorial 'line' (both the overt stance taken in editorials and the underlying values supported by the newspaper) help to determine how political information is presented.

The role of journalists

Whilst editors make strategic decisions, it is journalists who translate raw political information into the articles which the public rely on for their knowledge of the outside world. The way in which journalists perceive their role is, therefore, important since it is likely to determine how they present political information. Two contrasting views are suggested by Franklin:

> 'Sidney Jacobson, editor of the now defunct left wing *Daily Herald*...argued that "relations between the government and the press are bad, getting worse and should, under no circumstances, be allowed to improve". [This suggests] that journalists should be independent and highly critical reporters of the political process and the behaviour of politicians...But this view of journalists' relationship with politicians has always been contested by those who are sceptical about media independence of politicians. Marxists, for example, argue that the media are the servants rather than the masters of politicians. The media do not criticise and challenge politicians but, in various ways, sustain them in power.' (Franklin, 1993, p.1).

The lobby system (see also section 5.3 below)

Journalists use a wide range of sources of political information. Since politicians have a vested interest in gaining publicity for their views, much of this information is brought to the press - for example, politicians hold press conferences and send out press releases. In addition, a great deal of information is gathered simply by placing reporters in the right place - for example, by sending journalists to watch proceedings in the House of Commons or to wait outside Number 10 Downing Street. For further information, journalists are sent to interview people - to get their views 'on the record'.

In addition to these sources of information, however, there is the 'lobby system'. The lobby is a club with strict rules. Those political journalists who are members of the lobby are given special and privileged access to government information at daily meetings with politicians and civil servants. Usually, the information given at these meetings is 'unattributable' - the source of it cannot be mentioned by the journalists. The use of phrases such as 'sources close to the Prime Minister...' indicate that the information has come from the lobby. Any journalist who reveals the source of information given at lobby meetings is banned from attending future meetings of the lobby.

Whilst supporters claim that the lobby is an important means of obtaining information the public otherwise would not receive, the lobby system has been criticised for its secretiveness and because there is scope for manipulation and misinformation. Members of the government, for example, can use the lobby to float ideas which - if they prove unpopular - are then dropped. Since the information about such an idea is given via the lobby, then the member of government responsible for floating it cannot be identified. Critics also argue that the lobby system results in lazy, uncritical journalism since journalists tend to use lobby press releases rather than their own sources of information. Critics also complain that the lobby system allows the Prime Minister to dictate what should be the main news items for the following week. Between 1986 and 1990, the *Independent*, *Guardian* and *Scotsman* refused to participate in the lobby system in protest at the way it was used by Margaret Thatcher and her chief press officer, Bernard Ingham. As a result, these newspapers received no information about the Prime Minister from the Press Secretary's office. Even the most routine enquiries about the Prime Minister's whereabouts were unanswered.

Press regulation

By definition, a 'free' press is not regulated by government or anyone else. A free press should be free to print whatever it likes within the laws of libel and the requirements of official secrecy. There should be no need for regulation.

In practice, the press in Britain is self-regulating. The Press Council - a body made up of representatives from within the newspaper industry - was set up in 1953 to protect press freedom and to promote and ensure responsible journalism by eradicating bias and inaccuracies from press coverage. In 1963, it was given the power to consider complaints about the press or conduct of persons or organisations towards the press. But the Press Council proved incapable of controlling the excesses of the tabloid newspapers, especially with regard to the invasion of privacy, and it ceased activity in 1990. This followed the report of Sir David Calcutt and his colleagues whose inquiry into press regulation was set up by the Home Secretary. The Calcutt Report threatened a statutory regulation body if the press did not achieve effective self-regulation. As a result, the Press Council was replaced in 1991 with the Press Complaints Commission, another self-regulating body. The Press Complaints Commission drew up a code of conduct for the press. But, a review of the work of the Commission by Calcutt, published in 1993, argued that it had been a failure. Sensational coverage of the breakdown of royal marriages and the press coverage of the 1992 general election campaign had not, according to Calcutt, been responsive to voluntary self-regulation (again the issue of invasion of privacy was of greatest concern). The Calcutt review recommended:

> 'The establishment of a regulatory body for the press which among other things, would have the power to fine newspapers which broke the code of conduct and award compensation to claimants.' (quoted in Kuhn, 1994, p.186).

This view was rejected by Lord Wakeham, chair of the Press Complaints Commission. He preferred the press to clean up its own act, though he warned the newspaper industry that media excesses could force the government into press regulation which could be hijacked by backbench MPs and turned into something much more restrictive (*Guardian*, 6 April 1995).

Activity 19.4

Item A *The 1992 general election*

THE Sun

Saturday, April 11, 1992 — 25p

'THREE DEAD' AS IRA HIT CAPITAL

THREE people were feared killed last night after a massive car bomb blasted the City of London.

IT'S THE SUN WOT WON IT

HERE'S HOW PAGE 3 WILL LOOK UNDER KINNOCK!

Warning . . . Pat as our Page 3 girl

PHOTO FINISH

If Kinnock wins today will the last person to leave Britain please turn out the lights

Warning . . . Page 1 on polling day

Big thank-you from MPs

By JOHN KAY and JOHN TROUP

TRIUMPHANT MPs were queueing yesterday to say "Thank You My Sun" for helping John Major back in to Number 10.

SWING

Continued on Page Two

Celebrating . . . roly-poly Page 3 star Pat Priestman at Parliament yesterday

Item B *Public opinion and the Sun*

Do readers reflect the *Sun* or the *Sun* its readers? In trying to answer this question, Robert Worcester has come up with some interesting information. His findings confirm that in April 1992 the nation voted on much the same lines as the *Sun*'s readership - 43% of the electorate voted Conservative compared to 45% of *Sun* readers; 35% voted Labour compared to 36% of *Sun* readers; and, 18% voted Liberal Democrat compared to 15% of *Sun* readers. In 1993, the Conservatives began to lose support in opinion polls and if the *Sun* had continued to support the Tories, it would have been out of step with public opinion. But, it was during 1993 that the *Sun*'s support for the Tories evaporated. By the end of 1993, the paper emerged with a readership whose political mood still closely mirrored the mood of the nation. The nation divided Conservatives 29%, Labour 46% and Liberal Democrat 22%. The *Sun* readership divided Conservatives 29%, Labour 48%, Liberal Democrats 19%. But, that does not mean that the *Sun* is likely to support Labour at the next election - after all, it keeps slipping in the line that though the government is bad, Labour would be worse. The *Sun*'s problem is that by telling us how useless Major's government is now, it will lack credibility when it calls on its readers to vote Tory at the next election.

Adapted from the *Guardian*, 7 March 1994.

Item C *Newspapers and party allegiance*

Title	Party	Circulation	Title	Party	Circulation
Daily Express	Con	1,525,000	**Independent on Sunday**	None	402,000
Daily Mail	Con	1,575,000	**Mail on Sunday**	Con	1,941,000
Daily Mirror	Lab	3,581,000	**News of the World**	Con	4,788,000
Daily Star	None	806,000	**Observer**	Lab	541,000
Daily Telegraph	Con	1,038,000	**The People**	Lab	2,165,000
Financial Times	Lab	290,000	**Sunday Express**	Con	1,666,000
Guardian	Lab	429,000	**Sunday Mirror**	Lab	2,775,000
Independent	None	390,000	**Sport**	None	301,000
Sun	Con	3,571,000	**Sunday Telegraph**	Con	558,000
The Times	Con	386,000	**Sunday Times**	Con	1,167,000
Today	Con	533,000			

This table shows the party preference and circulation of newspapers at the time of the 1992 general election.

Adapted from Seymour Ure, 1993.

Item D *Political bias in the press*

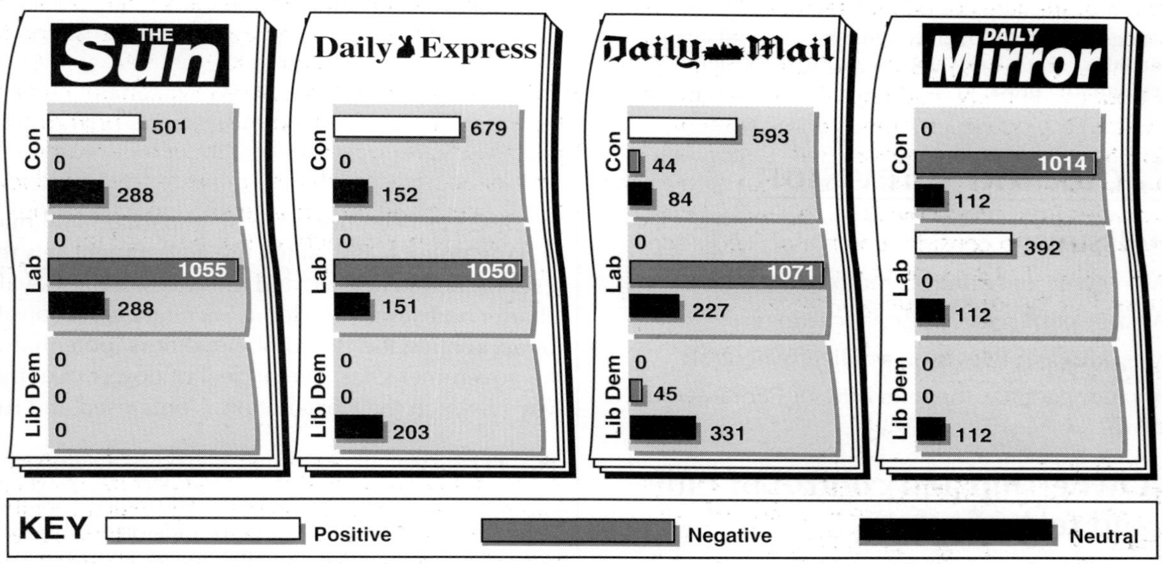

This diagram shows how four national daily newspapers reported political events on 3 and 7 April 1992. Each story was assessed on a scale of one to 10 and the score added to the total in the appropriate column.

Adapted from the *Guardian*, 26 January 1994.

Item E *Press regulation*

Criticism of the Press Complaints Commission has led the government to consider drawing up a new privacy law. This idea is strongly opposed by the press itself. The Association of British Editors attacked the idea, saying that 26 statutes already restrict freedom of speech. The Association published a long list of examples of stories that would not have been published if a privacy law had been passed. These stories include the following: (1) a report that Norman Lamont, the Chancellor, had gone over his credit card limit on 22 occasions and had received legal warning letters (*Sun*, 1992); (2) a report that David Mellor, the Heritage Secretary, accepted a foreign holiday for himself and his wife, paid for by the daughter of a prominent Palestinian (*Sun*, 1992); (3) publication of a personal letter from Michael Mates, Northern Ireland Minister, to Asil Nadir (*Daily Mail*, 1993); (4) a report which revealed that an Italian doctor had impregnated a 58 year old woman with another woman's egg (*Daily Mail*, 1993); (5) a report that an eye surgeon carried out 1,000 operations after being diagnosed as having AIDS (*News of the World*, 1992); (6) coverage, including interviews with parents and teachers, of the Lyme Bay canoeing accident in which four pupils drowned (*Western Morning News*, 1993).

Adapted from the *Guardian*, 24 February 1994.

Item F *Invasions of privacy*

When the *Daily Mirror* published pictures of Princess Diana working out in a gym, it caused a furore. The *Mirror* photos are only the latest in a long line of 'intrusive' pictures and stories - Princess Anne putting up two fingers to the press, Prince Philip's gaffes about 'slanty-eyed orientals', Prince William's 'royal wee' when the camera caught him peeing in the playground, the Fergie toe sucking episode. In his book *Naff Off: Confessions of a Fleet Street Photographer*, former *Express* photographer Victor Blackman tells how he obtained a scoop 30 years ago by sitting for days on top of Westminster cathedral with a zoom lens. From there, he could see into Buckingham Palace grounds, albeit from a distance of half a mile. In due course, he got his pictures of Princess Anne in her Brownie uniform. He sent them in and awaited praise from his editor Edward Pickering. Pickering invited him into his office, but instead of praising him said: 'These pictures are the result of gross intrusion. It's disgraceful and, if it weren't for the fact that you thought you were doing it for the good of the paper, you'd be fired immediately.' He made Blackburn fetch the negatives and burn them. They don't make editors like that any more - and why should they?

Adapted from Platt, 1993.

Questions

1. 'Don't believe what you read.' Would this be good advice to someone who reads a British newspaper? Give reasons for your answer.

2. Does the fact that newspapers openly support and campaign for political parties matter? Use Items A-D in your answer.

3. Using Items E and F give arguments for and against the introduction of a privacy law or other legislation to regulate the press.

4. Obtain three or more newspapers on the same day.
   a) Go through the newspapers and make a list of stories which appear in two or more of the newspapers.
   b) How does the treatment of each story differ in the different newspapers?
   c) What does this tell us about the way in which political information is conveyed?

3 Radio and television

Key Issues

1. Who owns and controls radio and television?
2. What is public service broadcasting?
3. Are radio and television politically neutral?
4. What impact has the televising of Parliament made?

3.1 Ownership and control of radio and television

Radio and television broadcasting is controlled by two bodies - the British Broadcasting Corporation (BBC) and the Independent Television Commission (ITC). The radio and television stations run by the BBC are publicly owned whilst those provided by the ITC are owned by private individuals or by private companies.

The BBC (see also, chapter 16, p. 497)

The BBC is controlled by a Board of Governors, appointed by the Home Secretary. This Board of Governors appoints a director general who has day-to-day control of the Corporation. In 1994, the BBC was responsible for the running of two television stations, five national radio stations and 48 local radio stations. The BBC is funded from the money paid by the public in the form of a licence fee.

Under the terms of the BBC's Royal Charter (first granted in 1926), advertising has been forbidden and the BBC has been bound to be impartial in all matters of party politics. But, since the government sets the level of the licence fee and the terms of the Royal Charter and since the Home Secretary is responsible for appointing the Board of Governors, potentially, the government has a great deal of power over the way in which the Corporation is organised and run.

The ITC

Commercial broadcasting was first established in 1954 when the Independent Television Authority (ITA) was set up. Like the BBC, the ITA (which later became the Independent Broadcasting Authority - IBA) was controlled by a Board of Governors appointed by the Home Secretary. The 1990 Broadcasting Act replaced the IBA with a new body, the Independent Television Commission (ITC). Although, like the IBA, the ITC is controlled by a Board of Governors appointed by the Home Secretary, the ITC has a different role from the IBA. It lacks the IBA's detailed involvement in scheduling, but has wider powers to enforce licence conditions and ownership rules. In commercial broadcasting, therefore, it is the individual companies granted licences which are responsible for the day-to-day running of the stations. Competition for licences (also called franchises) is correspondingly fierce.

In 1995, commercial broadcasting includes ITV (Channel Three), Channel Four, two national and 132 local commercial radio stations. Commercial broadcasting is funded by the revenue raised from advertising. It should be noted that companies granted licences to broadcast by the ITC operate on a commercial basis and, therefore, their aim is to make a profit for their shareholders. It should also be noted that the government's control of commercial broadcasting has been reduced since the advent of satellite television in 1989.

The concentration of ownership

A major concern about the ownership and control of broadcasting in Britain is that it is in the hands of a relatively small number of people from a narrow segment of society. This concern was voiced in a discussion paper published by the European Commission and entitled *Pluralism and Media Concentration in the Internal Market*:

> 'The media sector is characterised by a fairly high level of concentration compared to other sectors and by a complex web of shareholding and media ownership networks centred around a few national operators...The UK is alone in the EU in not having a written constitution from which an obligation to safeguard media pluralism could be deduced.' (quoted in Peak, 1994, pp.14-15)

Since the 1990 Broadcasting Act came into effect, the concentration of ownership has gathered pace as constraints on multiple ownership have been reduced. An obvious example of this is what happened to satellite television in Britain. When it was introduced in 1989, two companies - BSB and Sky - competed for trade. But, in early November 1990, just after the 1990 Broadcasting Act became law, Rupert Murdoch's News International (see section 2.1 above), which owned Sky, announced that it was merging with BSB. BSkyB now has a monopoly in the delivery of satellite television in Britain. A second example is what happened after the ITC awarded Channel Three licences in 1991. These licences, awarded on the basis of competitive tender, permit companies to broadcast in the 15 regions of the ITV network. It should be noted that, under the terms of the 1990 Broadcasting Act, licences must be awarded to the highest bidder amongst those passing a 'quality threshold'. Wagg explains that:

> 'In 1993, the Secretary of State for National Heritage, Peter Brooke, relaxed the rules governing takeovers in the British media, opening the way for major mergers among the ITV companies and for more cross ownership between media. More specifically, Brooke had ruled that any ITV companies could now hold two licences.' (Wagg, 1994, p.102)

The result of this was a greater concentration of ownership:

> 'This resulted in three major takeovers - Carlton TV of Central; Meridian of Anglia and Granada of London Weekend Television. However, there was then a clear imbalance in the size of ITV companies - Yorkshire TV, for example, which had taken over Tyne Tees in 1992 had less than half the audience share of either Carlton or Central, who were now merged. ' (Wagg, 1994, p.102)

In May 1995, the government announced a far-reaching liberalisation of media ownership rules which will permit wider cross-ownership of television, radio and newspapers. However, national newspapers with more than 20% of the market share will be restricted in their ownership of TV licences (*Guardian*, 24 May 1995).

Public service broadcasting

The notion of public service broadcasting is ill defined, but is taken to refer to:

> 'A set of principles, not the character of ownership of broadcasting organisations, and consequently public service broadcasting can inform both publicly and privately owned stations.' (Franklin, 1994, pp.56-7)

This 'set of principles' has evolved from a number of sources - broadcasting legislation, committee and commission reports and the views expressed by various director generals of the BBC - particularly John Reith, the first director general.

According to the Broadcasting Research Unit, the principles can be summarised as follows (BRU, 1985). First, broadcast programmes should be available to the whole population regardless of how remote or inaccessible the places in which people live. Second, programmes should appeal to a broad range of tastes. Third, one main broadcasting organisation should be financed by a licence fee or tax paid for by everyone who uses a television. Fourth, some institutional mechanism must distance broadcasters from vested interests (whether commercial or political) and must protect broadcasters from intrusion upon their activities. Fifth, public service broadcasters should reflect national concerns, interests and culture. Sixth, the emphasis on national concerns should not be at the expense of minority interests. Seventh, broadcasting should be organised in such a way that there is competition to produce quality programming rather than competition for audiences. And finally, the public guidelines for broadcasters should liberate rather than restrict programme makers.

As this list suggests, the ethos of public service broadcasting, potentially at least, rests uneasily with the free market principles developed by the Conservative government since 1979. The BBC and its licence fee have come in for particular attack from the New Right and support for advertising gathered pace in the early 1980s. But, the Peacock Committee, set up by the government, opposed advertising as a means of funding the BBC in 1986. According to

Franklin, the 1990 Broadcasting Act goes some way to challenging the ethos of public service broadcasting by:

> 'Promoting commercial competition, encouraging the proliferation of channels and the fragmentation of the audience, trying to break the "old duopoly" by creating a multi-channel system with an enhanced role for independent producers and...by relegating programme quality to the last, rather than to the first, policy priority.' (Franklin, 1994, p.58).

The Act does, however, give statutory recognition to two regulatory bodies - the Broadcasting Complaints Commission (BCC) and the Broadcasting Standards Council (BSC). The BCC was established to consider and adjudicate complaints received from individuals who feel they have been treated unfairly or suffered an unwarranted infringement of their privacy. The BSC is responsible for drafting a code of conduct for broadcasters offering guidance concerning portrayals of violence, sex and of 'matters of taste and decency generally'.

The government's long awaited white paper on the future of the BBC appeared in 1994. It envisaged that the BBC would continue as the main public service broadcaster, funded by the licence fee until 2001 (when the matter would be reviewed). A new Royal Charter was proposed. This would ensure that the BBC remained as a public corporation for a further 10 years from 1997. With regards to regulation, the white paper suggested the merger of the BCC and BSC (*Guardian*, 7 July 1994).

Are radio and television politically neutral?

The terms of the BBC's Royal Charter and the Television and Broadcasting Acts place a requirement on the BBC and the ITC to maintain political impartiality. This is in contrast to the press where there is no such requirement. The 1990 Broadcasting Act strengthened this requirement by imposing a new code of impartiality - which was included in the Act mainly because of pressure from right wing Conservatives who claimed that broadcasters had flouted existing rules on impartiality. In particular, the Conservatives' Media Monitoring Unit attacked the *Today* programme on Radio Four for anti-government bias. The attacks on the BBC by the Conservative Party were renewed in 1995. A number of ministers criticised BBC interviewers claiming they were biased in their questioning. Jonathan Aitken, Chief Secretary to the Treasury, launched a campaign against what he described as the 'open partisanship' of the BBC, suggesting it should be renamed the 'Blair Broadcasting Corporation' (*Independent on Sunday*, 26 March 1995).

But, critics on the left also claim there is bias - though they argue that it is bias to the right. The Glasgow University Media Group, for example, has produced a series of studies which claim to show bias in the news. They have claimed:

> 'Television news gives a partial view of the world: it offers an open door to the powerful and a closed door to the rest of us. In this way, it violates its own proclaimed principles of fairness and objectivity.' (GUMG, 1982, p.16)

With attacks from the right and from the left, the response of broadcasters has been to suggest that they must be successful in achieving impartiality. Certainly, broadcasters maintain that they offer a wide variety of independent, objective sources of information which provide an essentially balanced presentation. For example, at election times the broadcasters are scrupulous in ensuring that the different political parties are given equal amounts of air time.

On the other hand, it can be argued that broadcasters have to operate with certain basic assumptions:

> 'Broadcasters are operating within a system of parliamentary democracy and must share its assumptions. They should not be expected to give equal weight or to show impartiality which is not due to those who seek to destroy it by violent, unparliamentary or illegal means.' (Annan, 1977, p.268)

This notion of 'due impartiality' means that there can only be objectivity and impartiality within the boundaries of what is generally agreed and acceptable in society. So, for example, members of the IRA should be described as 'terrorists' rather than 'freedom fighters', though their activities should be described as accurately as possible to avoid the danger of propaganda.

The notion of 'due impartiality' also implies that the television and radio should not consistently present one viewpoint to the exclusion of others. A range of views and a variety of opinions should be given - though, over time, there should be a balance of views from those on the left and those on the right who believe in parliamentary democracy. If there is not the variety of different views, then there is the danger that the audience has no alternative sources of information on which to base its understanding.

There is tension about how this should work in practice, especially when contentious events like industrial disputes or military conflicts involving Britain are covered. This tension is compounded by the fact that the government of the day has the power to intervene in broadcasting.

Government intervention

Since the early 1980s, a great deal of concern has been expressed at the extent of the government's intervention in broadcasting and the failure of the Boards of Governors to stand up to pressure from politicians. This concern is derived from a number of sources.

First, the government has the power to make appointments to the Boards of Governors. In recent years, a number of prominent government supporters have been appointed to these boards. One managing director of the BBC said:

> 'The government has tended to put people [on the Board] who are sympathetic to its views in greater numbers than has been the practice in the past. There is a question that the PM is said to ask about every appointee to a public body: is he one of ours? (*Guardian*, 25 August 1985)

Obviously, if the Board of Governors is packed with government supporters, it is less likely to stand up to pressure from ministers.

Second, some authors have suggested that the ITC has refused to renew franchises because a company has been involved in making programmes perceived as having an anti-government bias. In 1988, for example, Thames Television made a programme called *Death On The Rock* which examined the shooting of three members of the IRA in Gibraltar. The IRA members were later found to be unarmed and the programme challenged the official version of the incident. According to Franklin:

> 'Politicians, like elephants it seems, have long memories. Three years later, when Thames Television were refused the renewal of their franchise to broadcast, Peter Kellner described the process of allocating new television licences as "an exercise in ideological vengeance" used by the government "to punish the company that made *Death On The Rock*."' (Franklin, 1993, p.6)

Third, the broadcasting laws allow the Home Secretary ultimate control over all broadcasting content. For example, it was the Home Secretary who, in 1988, announced a ban on the broadcasting of all interviews with or speeches by representatives of 11 Northern Irish organisations, including Sinn Fein (see above, p.563).

Fourth, legislation concerned with state secrecy - such as the Official Secrets Act and the Public Records Act (see section 5 below) can restrict broadcasting output.

And fifth, there are ways in which the government can intervene directly. It can impose direct censorship - as, for example, happened during the Falklands War when no demoralising pictures of wounded British soldiers could be shown until after the war ended. Or, it can make objections about the broadcasting of certain programmes and put pressure on programme schedulers to block them. Franklin notes that:

> 'The 1992 election witnessed unprecedented pressures on broadcasters from politicians. Conservatives continued to complain about bias in election coverage despite the BBC's decision, taken early in the campaign, not to broadcast a documentary about the efficacy of government policy in dealing with the recession.' (Franklin, 1993, p.6)

Activity 19.5

Item A *Ownership*

Under the terms of the Broadcasting Act of 1990, no national newspaper may own more than 20% of a television or radio franchise. No television company may own more than 20% of a national newspaper. Then, there are the impartiality rules. These have to be followed by satellite and cable channels as well as by terrestrial channels. And third, licence holders are forbidden to use their programmes to express the political, religious or otherwise controversial views of the owner. The problem in Britain is excessive restriction, not too little. Keeping newspapers and television apart is technological nonsense. If newspapers are to thrive in the next century, they have to move on to the screen and into the air. Three rules are essential. No one group should be allowed to control more than 25% of terrestrial advertising sales. The impartiality requirement must remain on terrestrial broadcasting channels (because they are few and reach most of the population). And, change in newspaper ownership should automatically be referred to the Monopolies and Mergers Commission. That done, the various players should be left to get on with it. Then, the satellite and cable channels could even be allowed to be as partisan as newspapers are. If 500 channels were available, does it matter if someone thinks they can attract an audience, let alone advertisers and subscribers, by saying 'vote for me' or even 'believe in me'?

Adapted from the *Daily Telegraph*, 23 February 1994.

Item B *Television and newspaper reporting in the 1992 election campaign*

	BBC %	ITN %	Total %
Major & Cons			
Negative	18	30	23
Mixed	19	26	22
Positive	6	5	6
Straight	57	40	49
No. of stories	128	101	229
Kinnock & Labour			
Negative	14	14	14
Mixed	15	23	19
Positive	5	5	5
Straight	66	57	62
No. of stories	127	94	221
Ashdown & Lib Dems			
Negative	4	2	3
Mixed	18	27	22
Positive	6	7	7
Straight	73	64	69
No. of stories	103	83	186

This table shows the tone of stories mentioning party leaders and/or parties in BBC 1's *Nine O'clock News* and ITN's *News at Ten* between 16 March and 9 April 1992. Straight stories are descriptive and contain no evaluations. Figures do not necessarily add up to 100% because they are rounded up or down.

Adapted from Heath et al., 1994.

	Sun %	Mirror %	Daily Mail %	Independent %	Guardian %	Times %	Total %
Major & Cons							
Negative	-	87	-	6	29	9	18
Mixed	-	-	-	19	13	3	8
Positive	55	-	33	-	5	16	12
Straight	45	13	67	75	53	72	62
No. of stories	11	15	21	47	85	111	290
Kinnock & Labour							
Negative	85	-	81	-	2	10	15
Mixed	-	-	5	10	11	11	9
Positive	-	87	-	3	23	10	19
Straight	15	13	14	87	64	68	57
No. of stories	13	15	21	38	84	117	288
Ashdown & Lib Dems							
Negative	50	-	37	-	2	2	4
Mixed	-	25	25	-	16	5	9
Positive	-	-	-	4	16	16	13
Straight	50	75	37	96	66	78	74
No. of stories	6	4	8	26	68	103	215

This table shows the tone of stories mentioning party leaders and/or parties on the front pages of newspapers between 16 March and 9 April 1992. Figures do not necessarily add up to 100% because they are rounded up or down.

Adapted from Health et al., 1994.

Item C *Language and broadcasting*

(i) The language used by broadcasting institutions indicates their implicit viewpoint. For example, in news broadcasts during 1984-85, the National Union of Miners (NUM) always 'claimed' whilst the National Coal Board (NCB), police or government 'said'. 'Claiming' implies a degree of doubt whilst 'saying' implies certainty. Also the very phrase 'miners' strike' is not neutral. It puts the blame firmly, if implicitly, on the miners' shoulders and, therefore, masks the real reasons for the dispute and the government's role in it. Consider for example the following statement on ITN News at Ten on 13 February 1985: 'Electricity loses £2 billion because of the miners' strike'. This implies that the miners are to blame for this loss, not the NCB or the government which was determined to prevent a negotiated settlement.

Adapted from CSE, 1985.

(ii) During the Falklands War, BBC broadcasters insisted that, in the interests of balance and detachment, British soldiers should be referred to as 'British' troops rather than 'our troops' or 'our boys' (phrases which were popular in the tabloid press). This brought angry complaints from Conservative backbenchers and the Prime Minister, Margaret Thatcher, said she shared: 'The deep concern...that the case for our country is not being put with sufficient vigour on certain - I do not say all - programmes.' When *Newsnight* tried to piece together what was happening in the South Atlantic using reports from the USA and Argentina, Thatcher told the Commons: 'Many people are very concerned indeed that the case for our British forces is not being put over fully and effectively. There are times when it seems that we and the Argentines are being treated almost as equals and on an almost equal basis. I can only say that, if this is so, it gives offence and causes great emotion among many people.'

Adapted from Franklin, 1993.

Item D *The government and the governors*

Questions

1. Using the items in this Activity explain how radio and television coverage of political events differs from that of the press.
2. Look at Item A. Would you agree that there are 'excessive restrictions' on the ownership of radio and television stations? Give reasons for your answer.
3. Using Items B-D give the arguments for and against the view that broadcasting is politically biased.
4. During the course of a single evening, listen to a news bulletin broadcast by a BBC radio station and a commercial radio station and watch the news on the BBC and on a commercial television station.
   a) Make a list of stories covered by each bulletin.
   b) How did the treatment of each story differ in the different broadcasts?
   c) How did the treatment of each story differ from the way it would be treated in the press?
   d) Would you say the broadcasts met the criteria laid down for public service broadcasting? Give reasons for your answer.

3.2 Televising the House of Commons

Although radio broadcasts from the House of Commons began in 1975 and the televising of the House of Lords began in 1985, it was not until February 1988 that MPs (in a free vote) voted by a majority of 54 to allow cameras into the House of Commons as an experiment.

By 1988, there was a great deal of pressure on the Commons to introduce television coverage. By then, 58 other countries allowed cameras to televise the proceedings of their legislative bodies. The experiment in the House of Lords had been judged a success. And, recent debates in the House of Commons suggested that it was only a matter of time before a majority in favour could be mustered (in 1980 and 1983, ten minute rule Bills were accepted by a majority, only to fall because of lack of parliamentary time and, in November 1985, a majority of 12 voted against televising the Commons only after a number of MPs in the 'aye' lobby tried to change their vote when they realised that the Prime Minister, Margaret Thatcher, had voted 'no').

Despite the pressure on MPs to introduce the cameras, there was still a large number of opponents. In the debate in February 1988, 231 Conservative MPs and 28 Labour MPs voted against televising the Commons. This does not just reflect the conservative nature of Conservative MPs. It also indicates a genuine fear of misrepresentation on television. It is significant that during the 1980s whilst Labour MPs claimed bitterly about their treatment by the tabloid newspapers, Conservatives complained equally bitterly about the bias of television (especially the BBC). Nevertheless, 116 Conservatives voted for the cameras and, combined with the support of 176 Labour MPs and 26 MPs from the minor parties, this was sufficient to secure a majority.

Arguments for and against televising the Commons

There were five main objections to televising the Commons. First, some MPs argued that the practical and technological difficulties of installing cameras were insurmountable. Second, others claimed that the reputation of the House would be damaged because television would misrepresent and trivialise its proceedings. This was a view favoured by the Prime Minister, Margaret Thatcher, who claimed that radio broadcasting of the Commons had damaged the reputation of the Commons. Third, some were afraid that the reputation of the House would be damaged because the public would see low attendances and boring debates. Fourth, there was concern that television might favour certain photogenic or controversial MPs or it might favour leading politicians or even one or more parties. And fifth, it was suggested that the proceedings of the House would be distorted by television coverage.

Those who favoured televising the Commons argued that it would mean an extension of democracy since the communications gap between MPs and citizens would be closed. They claimed that the House would become more accountable to the public and that an educational role would be performed since members of the public would be alerted to the key issues of the day. Supporters also argued that broadcasting would allow many more people to participate in the political process:

> 'During an experiment in televising the proceedings of the Lords in 1985, ITN compared television to an electronic extension of the public gallery. ITN calculated that if the gallery seated 65 people for the 140 days of the parliamentary session, the *News at Ten* on 3 April 1985, with 12,136,000 viewers watching the debate on unemployment, was equivalent to filling the public gallery for 1,333 years. Such figures represent an unrealistic extrapolation, of course, but they indicate the possibilities for television to enhance accountability and participation.' (Franklin, 1993, p.12)

Control of Commons broadcasting

The broadcasting of the Commons is under control of the Television Select Committee. It was this Select Committee which finally reported in May 1989. Its report was accepted in June 1989 and broadcasting finally began when the new parliamentary session was opened on 21 November 1989. The experimental period of televising lasted from then until July 1990. On 19 July 1990, MPs voted in favour of television broadcasting for the foreseeable future.

The television pictures of the Commons are provided by what was an independent company - Broadcast Communications. This company is now owned by the *Guardian* and *Manchester Evening News* plc (another example of the growing concentration of ownership in the media). At first, the rules concerning what the camera could show were quite strict. No close ups or pictures of MPs being drunk, disorderly or asleep were permitted. At the slightest hint of disorder, all the viewers saw was the Speaker calling for order. The following extract indicates the limitations:

> 'The cameras should normally remain on the member speaking until he has finished; and during questions...the director should only show the member asking a question and the minister replying to it. At other times, cutaway shots to illustrate reaction are not normally to be allowed except to show a member who has been referred to by the member speaking. However, medium angle shots, including over the shoulder shots, are permissable where the director wishes to show both the member who has the floor and other members intervening or seeking to do so.' (HC 141, 1989, paragraph 39.iv)

After the experimental period, however, the rules were relaxed so that wide camera shots were permitted. This allowed for more interesting coverage.

After an initial period of curiosity, the audiences for programmes showing proceedings at length have been small. But, when extracts are used on main news broadcasts, large audiences inevitably do see (albeit briefly) major events in the House.

The effect of televising the Commons

Most observers agree that the behaviour of MPs has been altered by the arrival of the cameras. Not only do MPs tend to dress more smartly and not put their feet up on the seats, they also tend to make their interventions in the House in a more media friendly way by providing sound bites rather than long rambling speeches. There has been some training - for example Harvey Thomas, a Conservative public relations adviser, coached more than 100 Conservative MPs on how to appear concise, interesting and sincere in their contributions. There has also been the growth of practice known as 'doughnutting' - surrounding speaking MPs with a group of attentive supporters to ensure that they appear to have support for their views when they are seen on television. In addition, some MPs intervene in the House or sit next to speakers so that they are seen by their constituents. Franklin notes that during election times:

> 'Whips may try to give air time to backbenchers who have not been "overly active" in their constituencies and need to make a parliamentary showing. Members with seats in very marginal constituencies might similarly receive a publicity fillip by being seen on television questioning the Prime Minister.' (Franklin, 1993, p.19)

In general, television favours the government of the day since parliamentary procedures push the government of the day to the forefront. Much parliamentary time, for example, is taken up with ministers answering questions from other MPs. This gives the impression that the ministers are highly knowledgeable and have great authority, whilst the questioners are minor players. Franklin (1993) notes that there has been an increase in the length of front bench speeches and that techniques have been developed to ensure that ministers appear in a good light at set pieces such as Prime Minister's Questions (for example, friendly questions are put by backbenchers). A further consequence of televising Parliament is that it bolsters the impression that Britain has a two party system. The Liberal Democrats and minor parties gain much less coverage than the Conservatives and Labour, partly because of the layout of the chamber and partly because of procedure.

Activity 19.6

Item A *Televising the House*

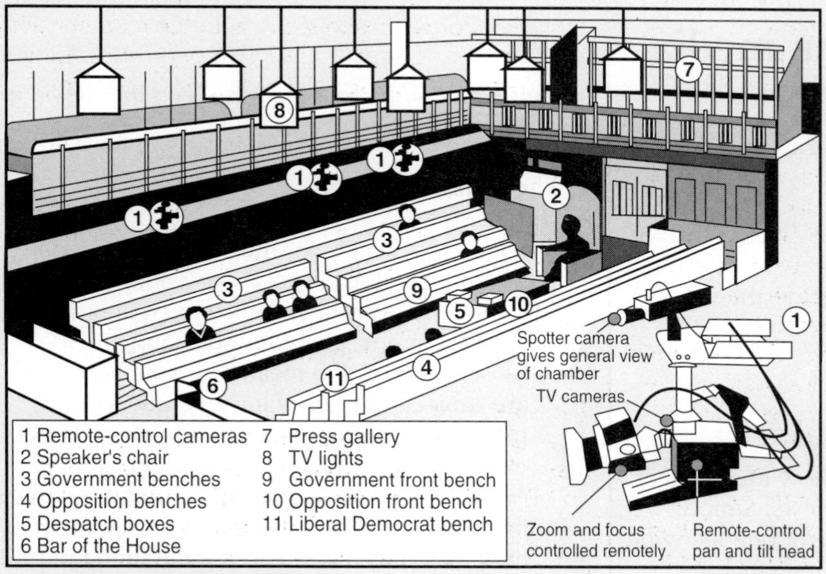

Item B *MP-TV*

What is remarkable about television is how little it has changed the House of Commons. All those MPs who trooped off to charm schools should be demanding their money back. Hair is a bit better combed. Dresses are slightly less dour. But there are still plenty of MPs who do not realise that if they wear checks it will have a strobing effect on television and that constituents are not impressed to see their representative wearing his lunch down his tie. Those who have been good on MP-TV tend to be those who were already good on TV. For example, Labour's Gordon Brown was never a slouch at producing the pithy 20 second quote for the news bulletin. He can now construct a Commons speech of sound bites.

Adapted from the *Guardian*, 11 July 1990.

Item C *Party contributions to broadcast items*

Party	Number of contribution occasions	Total number of contributions	Average no. of contributions per occasion
Conservative	1182	3873	3.27
Labour	885	2274	2.56
Liberal Democrats	230	395	1.71
SDP	18	25	1.38
Plaid Cymru	16	24	1.50
SNP	28	45	1.60
SDLP	19	32	1.68
Ulster Unionist	17	19	1.11
DUP	18	24	1.33

This table shows the results of research undertaken during the trial period of televising the Commons (November 1989 to July 1990). It shows the number of occasions on which a party was able to contribute to parliamentary programmes and the number of contributions made on each occasion.

Item D *Broadcasting and political balance*

The party of government can expect greater television coverage because the government initiates political events. Besides, there is the argument that parties should not receive equal air time because they do not have equal numbers of seats. Rather, they should gain air time proportionate to the size of the party in the Commons. Another way of looking at this issue is to ignore the numbers in each party and to concentrate on the issues. If this was done, what would count would not be which party a speaker came from, but what opinion was articulated. The aim would be to make sure that opinions for and against an issue were covered evenly. There are also regional considerations to be taken into account. During 1989-90, for example, all 58 MPs in the TVS region were Conservatives whilst Scotland and the North of England had large Labour majorities. Should regional programmes reflect the local or national political balance or a mixture of both?

Adapted from Franklin, 1993.

Questions

1. Watch a TV news bulletin in which footage from the Commons is shown and then, the next day, read a newspaper account of the proceedings. What similarities and differences are there?

2. a) Judging from Items A and B how far do you think the cameras affect the behaviour of MPs?
   b) Suppose you were a backbench MP. What would you do to ensure that you appeared on television coverage of the Commons?

3. a) Why is it difficult to achieve political balance when broadcasting from the Commons?
   b) Would you say that balance had been achieved? Use Items C and D and information from the news bulletin you watched in your answer.

4 The influence of the media

Key Issues

1. Why is it difficult to measure the media's influence?
2. How can the media's influence be interpreted?
3. What is the media's role in setting the political agenda?

The media and political understanding

There is much debate about exactly how much effect the media has on people's political views. Simply demonstrating that the media has a right or a left wing bias, for example, does not in itself prove that the media determines how people perceive political events. Although much research has been undertaken to find out how much effect the media has, the results of this research are contradictory and inconclusive.

There are a number of reasons why it is difficult to measure the effect of the media on the individual. First, most people have access to more than one media outlet and so it is difficult to isolate, for example, the effect of reading a particular newspaper compared to the effect of watching the television. Second, there is a range of other influences on people (for example social factors like class, age and education) and these may mitigate or distort the effects of the media. Third, there may be a difference between the short-term effects and the long-term effects of exposure to the media. And fourth, most people's opinions are shaped to some extent by friends and relatives. These 'significant others' may affect the way in which an individual interprets what the media has to say.

Further examination of the influence of the media is undertaken in chapter 9, part 4. There, the impact of the media on voting behaviour is considered.

Theoretical Models

In order to study the way in which the media works in society, a number of different theories have been developed. These theories can be grouped into four models. Each of the four models views the media in a fundamentally different way.

1. The Marxist model

According to Marx & Engels:

> 'The class which has the means of material production at its disposal has control at the same time over the means of mental production, so that thereby, generally speaking, the ideas of those who lack the means of mental production are subject to it...Insofaras [members of the ruling class] rule as a class and determine the extent and compass of an epoch, it is self-evident that they, among other things, regulate the production and distribution of the ideas of their age: thus their ideas are the ruling ideas of the epoch.' (Marx & Engels, 1976, p. 64)

This passage suggests that, ultimately, the power, control and direction of ideas lie with those who own and control the means of production. In a capitalist society, this means the capitalist class and, more specifically, the owners and controllers of the mass media. The owners and controllers of the mass media use the media to project the views of the ruling class and these views come to dominate the thinking of the mass of the population. In other words, the owners and controllers of the mass media exercise ideological domination. Ideological domination is crucial to the survival of capitalism since means of physical coercion are limited.

The Marxist model emphasises the way in which a narrow range of conservative values dominate the messages given out by the media. The media works against change and, therefore, against the interest of the mass of the population. It promotes a false consciousness which prevents people seeing the harsh reality of their place in society.

Miliband argues that it is not just the owners and controllers who are responsible for ideological domination:

> '[Owners and controllers] may confidently rely on editors, journalists, producers and others who work for them to remain well within a well understood ideological spectrum of thought which stretches from mild social democracy at

one end to far right conservatism at the other.'
(Miliband, 1989, p.145)

Equally, it is not only 'political' reporting which projects the ideology of the ruling class. Programmes that are supposedly designed just to entertain have a role to play. They suggest that all is well with the status quo and thus contribute to the promotion of false consciousness.

2. The pluralist model

The pluralist model claims that, contrary to what the Marxists suggest, a large range of ideas is expressed in the media and, because of this variety and diversity, no single view can predominate. Consumers, after all, are free to choose what they watch, listen to or read. Alternative views are always available if people are prepared to buy them. The mass media simply responds to the demands of the market.

According to the pluralist view, the media does have an influence and it is biased, but it exerts its influence by reflecting and reinforcing views that are already held. So, Conservative supporters will find much to agree with if they read the *Daily Telegraph* whilst they may well be outraged by the views expressed in the *Guardian*. Conservative supporters will, therefore, either not read the *Guardian*, or they will read it only to find out what 'the other side' is thinking.

The pluralist model assumes that no one group dominates society. Power is shared by a range of groups. The mass media reflects this diversity and presents the audience with a wide ranging choice. Most people who work in the media tend to subscribe to the pluralist model. For example, Max Aitkin, a former chair of Beaverbrook newspapers, claimed:

> 'Newspapers of today offer the public a complete range of opinion and expression.'
> (quoted in Trowler, 1988, p.39)

The theory is that the media provides what the public wants (not that the public gets what the media gives it). Those who own and control the market are, therefore, serving the market not dictating to it. For example, Alistair Hetherington, former controller of BBC Scotland, argued:

> 'The BBC and ITV enjoy a near monopoly, but they too must try to gauge the interests of their audiences if viewing figures are to be maintained.' (quoted in Trowler, 1988, p.40)

3. The mass manipulation model

This model suggests that the media plays an all-powerful role because the public is incapable of resisting the messages presented by the media. The media itself is seen as monolithic. This model came into existence in the 1930s when, in both Germany and the Soviet Union, it was believed that the media played a key role in indoctrinating the people.

Within this model, there are two alternatives. The left wing version argues that the media is run in the interests of the ruling class to corrupt and deradicalise the proletariat. The right wing version sees the media as a pernicious influence in society, lowering cultural standards, producing a dull uniformity by pandering to the lowest common denominator and encouraging permissiveness. Both versions agree that the media has a great deal of influence and that people can be manipulated and controlled by the media.

4. The consensus model

This model claims that what is produced by the media is produced within the framework of a consensus invented by the media. The media does define and structure reality for consumption by the general public. It, therefore, plays an important role in setting the political agenda. But, the media does this within the parameters of a selective framework which defines what should be included and excluded. Within the consensus, there is a hierarchy with some groups being better placed to meet the expectations raised by the consensus than others. Those groups outside the consensus are portrayed as being marginal or extreme. Critiques from outside the consensus may appear in the media, but they appear spasmodically and are the exception.

According to this model, the media is controlled by powerful groups in society, but direct manipulation by these groups is rare. Much more important are the routine practices of the media professionals and the technical constraints of media production.

The media and the political agenda

It should be clear from the above discussion that the different theoretical models have different ideas about how powerful the media is and therefore how much effect it has on what people think and how they behave. In answer to the question - is it the media or the politicians who set the political agenda? - three contradictory answers have been given.

1. The media sets the agenda

Those who claim that the media sets the political agenda point to examples where a concerted media campaign has led to political action. For example, it is argued that the resignation of David Mellor, the National Heritage Secretary, in September 1992 was the direct consequence of a concerted media campaign following revelations about his private life. Indeed, Mellor himself said that his decision to resign had been made because of 'the constant barrage of stories about me in certain tabloid newspapers.' Equally, it is possible to support this point of view by citing examples of events of importance which are not reported by the media. The fact that they are not reported implies that it is the media which is deciding what is important. In other words, it is setting the agenda. An example of this is the lack of media coverage of the Deregulation Bill which became law in 1994. Although this law gave the government sweeping new powers to alter existing regulations, it was hardly mentioned by the media. One BBC producer (who wishes to remain anonymous) admitted that the reason why the BBC did not provide more coverage of the passage of this Bill was:

> 'Because the programmers did not think that deregulation was a 'sexy' enough issue to interest viewers and listeners. I brought forward proposals for a programme on this subject, but they were rejected .' (interview with the author, May 1994)

Those who support the view that the media sets the political agenda argue that the media operates with a set of news values which informs its judgement as to which stories to cover. So, for example, a bomb which explodes in Britain will be given many times as much coverage as a bomb which explodes in France, say, or China. It should be noted that, even though the television and radio are less partisan than the press:

> 'It has long been argued that newspapers are significant in establishing the national news agenda which is adopted by broadcasters...Both in setting the agenda and establishing the main issues, and also in creating the images of the parties and leading personalities, newspapers play a key role.' (Benyon & Denver, 1990, p.95)

2. The politicians set the agenda

Those who claim that the politicians set the agenda argue that the media is merely the servant of politicians. Franklin points out that:

> '[Politicians] control the funding of public sector television, they make appointments to regulatory bodies, they can intervene directly when programming affects national security, they can censor programmes and, ultimately, it is politicians who drive the legislative process which enables them to restructure the wider environment in which broadcasters and journalists operate.' (Franklin, 1994, p.14)

According to this view, therefore, politicians use the media to their own advantage to promote themselves and their policies and to pass their message on to the general public.

3. Neither the media nor the politicians set the agenda

The third view is that neither the media nor the politicians are the servants or the masters. Instead, there is a symbiotic relationship between them. Each relies on the other and each makes an effort to accommodate the needs of the other. So, politicians hold press conferences or give interviews so that their views will be communicated to the general public. What happens at the press conference or interview provides information which journalists can use in their reports. Without press conferences and interviews, it would be more difficult for politicians to get across their views. Equally, it would be more difficult for journalists to gather news.

Those who subscribe to this view emphasise that neither the media nor politicians are a homogenous group. There is a great deal of difference between what is reported in the *Independent* and what is reported in the *Sun*, for example. Similarly, the Conservative leader has a very different agenda from the Labour leader. As a result, there is no single political agenda, but a number of agendas which surface at different places at different times.

Activity 19.7

Item A *Magazines and the Conservative party leadership election, July 1995*

Item B *Newspaper headlines, 5 July 1995*

The Sun

It's worse than that, he's won

Daily Express

John Major sweeps to historic leadership win

Independent

MAJOR'S BIG GAMBLE PAYS OFF

Mirror

218 vote for the donkey just to save their asses

Today

Er...Um...Ah...I've won, haven't I, dear

These headlines all appeared on 5 July 1995, the day after the result of the Conservative party's leadership election was announced.

Item C *How to end the welfare state*

The dismantling of the welfare state began on Budget day in December 1993. The public outcry, however, was muted. Measures that only a year ago would have been unthinkable had become a reality, yet the usually vocal charities and pressure groups seemed resigned to their fate. They had all been well-prepared to expect the worst. Over the past year, ministers have warned us, via the media, that the welfare state can no longer be sustained if it continues to grow. They have talked about an ageing population (with fewer workers to support pensioners), about those on invalidity benefit who are not really invalids, about the unemployed who don't want to work, about foreigners exploiting our benefits system and about single mothers who have babies to get council houses. The debate on the welfare state is a classic example of how the unthinkable becomes thinkable. The lobby system is used to float ideas (ministers then cannot be named) and information is leaked. Leaks take several forms - the genuine leak by a disenchanted insider, the deliberate leak to test the water and the accidental leak. Throughout 1992, leaks provided the press with information about government plans to cut back benefits.

Adapted from the *Independent on Sunday*, 5 December 1993.

Item D *Government by columnist*

There is nothing new in politicians' complaints that the press has 'power without responsibility'. In recent years, however, there does seem to have been a shift in the balance between politicians and journalists, with journalists gaining influence and prestige. Politics used to be lucrative, especially at ministerial level. By contrast, journalism was ill paid. As recently as 1974, when W.F. Deedes (a former Cabinet minister) became editor of the *Daily Telegraph*, his salary was substantially less than the Prime Minister's at the time. Tweny years on, it is a safe bet that no national newspaper editor is paid less than the Prime Minister's £76,000. Ministers' incomes have declined sharply in real terms while those of political commentators have risen. And it is not just an economic shift. Between 1940 and 1965, the Tories were led by men educated in major public schools. This did not give them superior abilities, but it gave them the self-confidence (or arrogance) of the upper class. And that affected their dealings with the press. In those days, Tory politicians made no pretence that journalists were their social equals and political reporters habitually called ministers 'sir' in private. Once the MP crowed and the correspondent cringed; now it is the other way round.

Adapted from the *Independent on Sunday*, 6 February 1994.

Item E *The Prime Minister's media handler*

In January 1994, John Major appointed a new media handler, Christopher Meyer. Meyer is quite clear about his role. Off the record chats will be avoided. His relationship with journalists will be adversarial. He will play an unusually strong role in setting policy. He will never say 'no comment' and he will never lie. Meyer said: 'The aim is always to take and hold the initiative in public debate'. He has devised what he calls ' the 10 commandments' of dealing with reporters. These are as follows. (1) Be accessible. (2) Be helpful. (3) Be friendly. (4) Do not waffle. (5) Do not lie. (6) Do not have favourites (7) Take journalists seriously (8) If you want coverage, make news. If you cannot make news, make irresistible phrases. (9) Do not waste time complaining if journalists have not reported what you wanted them to report. (10) Always ensure that the basis on which you are briefing is understood and agreed.

Adapted from the *Guardian*, 25 January 1994.

Questions

1. Take one of the theoretical models described in the section above and explain how Items A and B could be used as evidence in support of this model.
2. Which theoretical model or models does Item C support? Give reasons for your answer.
3. a) Judging from Items A-E who sets the political agenda?
   b) What does your answer tell you about the influence of the press?

5 Official information

Key Issues

1. What are the justifications for secrecy in a democracy?
2. What is the government's attitude towards secrecy and openness?
3. What are the mechanisms by which secrecy is maintained?

5.1 Secrecy and the state

According to Hennessy:

> 'Secrecy is the bonding material which holds the rambling structure of central government together. Secrecy is built into the calcium of a British policy maker's bones...It is the very essence of the Establishment view of good government, of private government carried on beyond the reach of the faction of political party, the tunnel vision of pressure group and the impertinent curiosity of the journalist.' (Hennessy, 1989, p.346)

There is, in other words, a strong tradition of secrecy in Britain and this tradition is supported and strengthened by the actions of governments and civil servants.

Those in power and supporters of the status quo advance the following arguments to justify this secrecy. First, they emphasise the need to maintain security. It is claimed that the government needs wide powers to prevent foreign enemies from discovering secrets important to the nation's security. It is also argued that there must be a network of internal security to protect the smooth running and, ultimately, the continued existence of the state. For example, economic and financial information must be kept secret for fear of competition. Second, it is argued that policy issues are generally too complex for the general public to understand and secrecy is needed to prevent them from being misconstrued. Third, it is argued that the wider dissemination of information would be costly and difficult to administer. If there was access to information at every point in the decision making process then government would become inefficient. And fourth, it is argued that the doctrine of ministerial responsibility (see chapter 13, section 1.4) relies upon secrecy. If there was less secrecy, unelected and, therefore, unrepresentative groups might gain power at the expense of elected representatives.

Most critics accept that a certain amount of secrecy is essential if security (both internal and external) is to be maintained. But, they argue, the British government is much too secretive. According to these critics, the three main reasons for this great secretiveness are: Whitehall conservatism; the vested interests of the state security apparatus; and the fact that members of the government and civil servants are hostile to change for fear of jeopardising their own position.

Open and closed government

Governments claim that they represent the national interest. If governments do represent the national interest and they argue that secrecy is a crucial means of defending the state, then (logically speaking) secrecy must be in the interest of everybody living in that nation. This, in effect, was the argument advanced by the British government during the Cold War. Secrecy, so the argument went, was necessary to protect British citizens from the threat posed by Communism, especially Soviet Communism.

Whilst the above argument was used to justify **closed** (secretive) **government**, some people have advocated **open government** - government which minimises the areas of secrecy and maximises the dissemination of information. According to Tony Benn MP, an open government is a more participatory and a more democratic government:

> 'If we accept that the control of information about decisions and how they are arrived at is a prerogative of the government, then we are accepting that democracy cannot be mature enough to allow people to share even the thinking that precedes these decisions.' (Benn, 1979, p.129)

Since the collapse of Communism in Eastern Europe, the perceived threat to national security from abroad has diminished. This has resulted in a new interest in and new demands for open government.

The Campaign for Freedom of Information

The Campaign for Freedom of Information is a pressure group set up in 1984. Since then, this group has managed to win the support of many leading politicians and ex-civil servants. The group plays a watchdog role, checking on the proposals made by government in areas which might involve secrecy. All-party support and the backing of senior civil servants has helped to give the group legitimacy. Supporters of the Campaign for Freedom of Information aim to give the public the right of access to official information except in a few categories of exemption. Their case is strengthened by comparing the position in Britain to examples of freedom of information legislation in other countries - for example, the USA has had a Freedom of Information Act since 1966 and in Sweden it has been a legal right to inspect government documents (apart from those covered by a Secrecy Act) since 1809.

The Campaign for Freedom of Information was set up to put pressure on a government which appeared reluctant to lessen the degree of state secrecy. Indeed, the Prime Minister, Margaret Thatcher, argued against freedom of information on constitutional grounds. In a letter to the Campaign for Freedom of Information she said:

> 'Under our constitution ministers are accountable to Parliament for the work of their departments and that includes the provision of information...A statutory right of access would remove this enormously important area of decision making from ministers and Parliament.' (quoted in Wilson, 1984, pp.134-5)

John Major and open government

Whilst Margaret Thatcher refused to consider more open government, her successor, John Major claimed to take a different view. His government began to promote the idea that government should be more open. This new approach was allied to the development of the new Citizen's Charter (see chapter 17, part 1). The Citizen's Charter, it was claimed, would make available more information on the services provided by government. This idea was taken up in the 1992 Conservative election manifesto:

> 'Government has traditionally been far too reluctant to provide information. This secrecy extends from the processes of Cabinet government to schools which refuse to release exam results. Under the Citizen's Charter, a great deal more information is now being made available on the services provided by government...We will be less secretive about the workings of government. For example, when the Committees of the Cabinet are reconstituted after the election, we will, for the first time, set out their names and membership. We will update and - for the first time - publish the guidance for ministers on procedure.'
> (Conservative Election Manifesto, 1992, p.16)

These manifesto promises were developed in a white paper published in 1993 and entitled *Open Government*. This white paper proposed a new Whitehall code of practice on access to official information. The government claimed that three themes would govern its approach: handling information in a way which promotes informed policy making and debate; providing timely and accessible information to the citizen to explain the government's policies, actions and decisions; and restricting access to information only when there are good reasons for doing so. This code of practice came into force in 1994.

Limitations of government policy on open government

Critics - for example, the Campaign for Freedom of Information - argue that the 1993 white paper and subsequent code of practice are a weak set of instruments which allow ministers a wide measure of discretion. Many areas are exempt from disclosure and the policy making process, internal opinion, discussion and advice all still remain secret. Crucially, the government has given people the right of access to information, not the right to see correspondence, documents or reports. Ironically, few people have complained about official secrecy under Whitehall's *Open Government* code because so few people are aware of it. The Parliamentary Commission for Administration (see pp.518-19), who is responsible for investigating complaints, revealed that after one year of the code's operation there were only 41 complaints, and, of these, only 11 were appropriate for him to investigate. He had expected over 1,000 complaints (*Guardian*, 9 March 1995).

In addition, the credibility of the Conservative government's claim to support open government was undermined by three developments.

First, in March 1994, the Minister for Open Government, William Waldegrave, told a cross-party committee of MPs that, in exceptional circumstances, it was necessary for ministers to tell lies in the House of Commons. He also vigorously defended the use of blocking answers by ministers - the device where half truths or half answers are used in Parliament to avoid spelling out the true picture.

Second, Waldegrave and other ministers gave evidence to the Scott Inquiry which was set up in 1992 to find out about:

> 'The role of ministers in the sale of arms to Iraq and specifically the alleged alterations of the guidelines and misinformation given to the House of Commons.' (Allan et al., 1994, p.41)

Evidence given by ministers at the Scott Inquiry revealed just how secretive the working of government was and it became clear that much crucial information had not been revealed to the House of Commons.

And third, the response of the government to European plans for more open government suggest a continuing desire for secrecy. In January 1994, a new information code drawn up by the Council of Ministers called for the widest possible access to documents. But, attempts to make use of the code have been blocked (*Guardian,* 18 April 1994).

These three developments, combined with the criticisms outlined above, have led critics to argue that the Major government's claims to support more open government are largely rhetorical - a change of style rather than substance.

Activity 19.8

Item A *Open government? (1)*

This cartoon was produced in 1995.

Item B *Open government? (2)*

The Prime Minister, John Major, last night announced an overhaul of Whitehall security. The following new system of protective marking for government information will be introduced next month. Material will be marked **Top Secret** if its disclosure might threaten the internal stability of Britain or its allies, lead to widespread loss of life, cause damage to British or allied forces or to important security operations, or cause severe long term damage to the British economy. Material will be marked **Secret** if its disclosure might raise international tension, damage relations with friendly governments, threaten life, public order or individual liberty, harm security operations or national finances. Material will be marked **Confidential** if its disclosure might damage diplomatic relations, threaten individual liberty, adversely affect the work of British or allied forces or harm national economic interests. Material will be marked **Restricted** if its disclosure might damage diplomatic relations, cause distress to individuals, adversely affect the work of British or allied forces, result in financial loss, facilitate improper gain for individuals or companies, prejudice the investigation of crime or impede the operation of government policies. Documents using any of the headings described above will not be available to the general public. Ministers and civil servants have access depending on their security classification. Under the old system, **Top Secret** was defined as 'causing exceptionally grave damage to the nation'. **Secret** was defined as 'causing serious injury to the nation'. And, **Restricted** was defined as 'being undesirable in the interests of the nation'. The old classification was, therefore, more abstract than the new.

Adapted from the *Daily Telegraph*, 24 March 1994.

Item C *Open government? (3)*

Yesterday was supposed to be the day when, according to the Prime Minister, the 'cobwebs of secrecy' would be swept away. But, although there was enthusiasm from government information officers, there was little extra enlightenment for the public. From yesterday, a code of practice came into operation in government departments under which they promised to respond to reasonable requests for information. The code says that the information will be provided as soon as possible, with a target of 20 working days for simple requests. Where information cannot be provided, the department is obliged to give an explanation. But, the Campaign for Freedom of Information has pointed out that there is a wide range of exemptions. All policy advice to ministers is exempt, including their analysis of factual information, unless the government considers it relevant and important. Even then, it will only be published when policies and decisions are announced. Also, no original documents are to be released under this scheme. As well as the normal exclusions covering information harmful to security, defence and international relations, data which the government does not regard as reliable is to be withheld.

Adapted from the *Guardian*, 6 April 1994.

Item D *The Dimbleby Lecture, 1994*

Those who wish to damage the state will naturally organise themselves and make plans in secret. So, we will have to use secret means to investigate them. With the proper legal authority, we may need to tap their telephones, open their letters or eavesdrop on their conversations to find out their intentions. We may have to observe their movements secretly or recruit members of these organisations as agents to tell us from the inside what is being planned. Then, we have to analyse and assess the information and use our findings to counter the harm which is being considered.

Part of the Dimbleby lecture given by Stella Rimington, head of MI5, in 1994.

Questions

1. What point is being made about official information in Item A?
2. 'Britain is moving towards open government.' Using Items A-D give arguments for and against this statement.
3. Do you think restrictions such as those described in Item B should exist? Give reasons for your answer.
4. Can you think of any reasons why people might oppose the views put forward by Stella Rimington in Item D?

5.2 Official secrets

Governments have a number of official tools which they can use to prevent information reaching the public. These include the Official Secrets Act, the Public Records Act and the Privy Counsellor's oath.

The 1911 Official Secrets Act

The first Official Secrets Act was passed in 1911, after a debate which lasted less than an hour. At the time, there was a great deal of public anxiety about spying.

Section One of the Act made it an offence, punishable by up to 14 years imprisonment, to disclose information which might be of use to an enemy or to engage in conduct which was 'prejudicial to the safety or the interests of the state'.

Section Two of the Act made it an offence, punishable by up to two years imprisonment, for a person employed by the state to pass on any official information to anyone not authorised to receive it. The 'catch all' nature of this section of the Act meant that, theoretically at least, the release of information such as the number of cups of tea drunk in a government department could be an offence.

To many people, it might seem absurd that the release of such information could be regarded as an offence, but not to the official mind and the security conscious. The following extract was submitted as evidence to the Franks Committee on Official Secrecy (see below) by an ex-member of the security branch of a government department:

> 'There is much danger in the thoughtless release of seemingly innocuous information. There is frequent quoting of the hypothetical case of it being an offence against the Act to divulge the number of cups of tea drunk by a specific government department or establishment. Like all tongue in cheek utterances, this one has its element of truth in it, in that, knowing the approximate size of most departments and learning the number of cups of tea consumed by them, it's a simple matter to work out the average number of cups of tea per person per day. If an intelligence officer can find out how many cups of tea are consumed by those departments the strength of which, for good reason, remains classified information, he can then make a fairly good 'guesstimate' of these unknown strengths.' (quoted in the *Sunday Times*, 23 September 1984)

Demands for reform

It has been argued that the demise of the 1911 Official Secrets Act was inevitable after the prosecution of Jonathan Aitken in 1970. Aitken was a journalist who was prosecuted for handling a confidential report which seemed to show that statements by government ministers were inaccurate. The outcry against his prosecution led to the setting up of the Franks Committee on Official Secrecy. The report, published by this committee in 1972, condemned the breadth and uncertainty of the 1911 Act and recommended its repeal (Franks, 1972).

Although the Labour government which came to power in 1974 promised to reform the Official Secrets Act, nothing was done. This was due in part to the attitude of the Home Secretary, Merlyn Rees. Rees said:

> 'To be blunt, the *Guardian* can go on for however long it likes about open government and the reform of the Official Secrets Act, but I can tell you that, in my constituency of 75,000 electors, I would be hard pressed to find many who would be interested in what I was talking about.' (quoted in Chapman & Hunt, 1987, p.32)

A second important trial was the 'ABC trial' of 1977 (so called after the initials of the three defendants Aubrey, Berry and Campbell). Aubrey and Campbell were journalists arrested whilst interviewing Berry, a former corporal in Signals Intelligence, about his work. The trial descended into farce when it became clear that information described as 'secret' by the prosecution was available from public sources. Although the defendants were convicted, their light sentences were taken as a further sign that reform was necessary. Michael has argued:

> 'One effect of the ABC trial was to stiffen Conservative resolve to get a respectable and effective substitute for Section Two of the Official Secrets Act through Parliament as quickly as possible with no nonsense about an accompanying law to require disclosure of anything.' (Michael, 1982, p.57)

This indicates there were two ways of considering reform. Whilst those on the left tended to aim for a much more limited Official Secrets Act and greater freedom of information, those on the right accepted the need for the reform of the Official Secrets Act, but only to make it more effective.

In the 1980s, three further cases with a high public profile added pressure for reform. First, in 1984 Sarah Tisdall, a clerk at the Foreign Office, was prosecuted under the Official Secrets Act for leaking documents to the *Guardian* which showed that Cruise Missiles had arrived at Greenham Common. Tisdall pleaded guilty and was sentenced to six months in prison. Then, in 1985, Clive Ponting was prosecuted under the Official Secrets Act for passing information to a Labour MP about the sinking of the Argentine ship, the *General Belgrano*, during the Falklands War. Ponting believed that the government refused to release this information because it was seeking to save itself from political embarrassment. Unlike Tisdall, Ponting fought his case and he was acquitted by a jury:

> 'Although Ponting was undoubtedly guilty in a narrow technical sense (he had undoubtedly released information without prior authorisation) he was acquitted by the jury which agreed with Ponting's public interest defence: in other words, Ponting argued that his revelation of government deceit and duplicity were in the wider public interest and that the benefits to a democratic society of releasing information were greater than any harm caused.' (Jones et al., 1989, p.106)

The third case was the *Spycatcher* trial of 1987-88. *Spycatcher* was a book written by a former MI5 agent, Peter Wright. The government tried to ban the book's publication in Britain, even though it was available abroad, on the grounds that it breached the oath of confidentiality taken by MI5 employees. But, copies of the book were brought in from abroad because the government had failed to place an import restriction on the book and public readings were held. As a result, the book became the focus for the struggle to gain greater freedom of information. When the House of Lords, sitting as the final court of appeal rejected the government's case, the government moved quickly to introduce new legislation.

The 1989 Official Secrets Act

In 1988, the government introduced a white paper admitting the defects of the existing Official Secrets Act, particularly its excessive scope which had led to its reputation as an:

> 'Oppressive instrument for the suppression of harmless and legitimate discussion.' (Keesings, 1988, July/August)

The new Official Secrets Act, passed in 1989, was designed to prevent any disclosures about security or intelligence matters by making such disclosures a criminal offence for current and past members of the security services, crown servants or government contractors. Anybody found guilty of disclosing damaging information could face up to two years in prison. Disclosure is defined as 'damaging' if it prejudices the capability of the armed forces to carry out their tasks or leads to loss of life, injury, damage of equipment or installation. In addition, disclosure of information about foreign policy, police operations and relations with other countries or international organisations is an offence and civil servants may only disclose information when it is in accordance with their duty (they must not keep documents and must take steps to prevent unauthorised disclosures).

There are two other important elements in the Act. First, under the terms of the new law it is no longer a defence to argue that information is disclosed in the public interest or that it is available abroad. And second, the Act also covers the disclosure of information by journalists. Editors who encourage journalists to publish information they have reason to believe has been divulged without lawful authority are in breach of the law.

Critics of the new Act have argued that it has been designed to close the loopholes in the 1911 Act and, therefore, ensures there is greater secrecy rather than greater freedom of information. Also, the new Act makes conviction more likely since defendants cannot claim that it was in the public interest to reveal information.

The 1958 Public Records Act

Under the British Public Records Act of 1958, government papers are not available to historians, journalists and members of the public until 30 years have elapsed 'or such other period as the Lord Chancellor may provide'. There are 40 categories of government paper that are automatically kept away from public view for longer than 30 years. These 40 categories make up around 5% of all government papers. They include papers containing distressing or embarrassing personal details about living persons; papers containing information received by the government in confidence; state papers on Ireland; and papers which affect the security of the state.

According to a leading barrister and campaigner for greater freedom of information, Geoffrey Robertson, papers kept secret for 50 or 100 years include those produced in 1913 which provide evidence of forcible feeding in reformatory schools, those produced between 1913 and 1916 which provide evidence of experiments on animals with poison gas and those produced in 1939 which provide evidence of the dental service for the police in wartime (Robertson, 1989). Whilst, for example, information on the fire in 1957 at Windscale (the nuclear reactor now called Sellafield) was released in 1988, the evidence from individual witnesses has been withheld for another 30 years.

In a lecture delivered in 1992, Robertson noted that:

> 'The government refused to incorporate into its 1989 reforms of the Official Secrets Act a legal right of access to information collected or generated by civil servants - at a time when such access (through Freedom of Information Acts) has become almost a defining characteristic of democratic government elsewhere in the world...[There is] an urgent need to reform the Public Records Act and to provide a legal right to appeal against over-secretive bureaucratic decisions to close files to public inspection for immeasurable times.' (Charter 88, 1993, p.2)

The Privy Counsellor's oath

One of the earliest recorded mechanisms for ensuring secrecy is the Privy Counsellor's oath. This dates from 1250 and is still used today. The oath is worded as follows:

> 'You will in all things to be moved, treated and debated in Council, faithfully and truly declare your mind and opinion according to your heart and conscience; and will keep secret all matters committed and revealed unto you, or that shall be treated of secretly in Council. And if any of the said treaties or counsels shall touch any of the counsellors, you will not reveal it unto him, but will keep the same until such time as, by the consent of Her (His) Majesty, or the Council, publication shall be made thereof.' (quoted in Hunt, 1992)

Originally, the Privy Council was a group of advisers to the monarch. It was from the Privy Council that Charles II chose the first Cabinet and the modern Cabinet remains, formally, a committee of the Privy Council. Only senior members of government and leading opposition figures are made members of the Privy Council. Membership is for life. All new members of the Privy Council are required to swear the oath quoted above in the presence of the monarch.

Ministers who are Privy Counsellors are more likely to receive papers classified as 'top secret'. Occasionally, members of the opposition who are Privy Counsellors are given secret material on the basis of the Privy Counsellor's oath (on the understanding that they will not divulge the contents). This binds leading opposition figures to secrecy and, therefore, must inhibit democratic debate.

5.3 Unofficial secrets

As well as the formal, legal mechanisms for ensuring secrecy and maintaining closed government, there are also a number of informal mechanisms which work to the same end.

D Notices

Much secrecy and mystery surrounds the operation of D Notices (Defence Notices). D Notices are issued to prevent the publication of articles or the broadcast of programmes harmful to national defence or security. They are issued by the D Notice Committee.

The D Notice Committee was established in 1912, a year after the Official Secrets Act was passed. The committee is composed of four senior civil servants and 11 press and broadcasting representatives. Whilst the full committee usually meets annually, the day-to-day work is carried out by the Secretary (who is usually a Ministry of Defence employee).

D notices have no legal force whatever and merely serve as guidance for the media. According to Robertson (1989), there are eight D Notices in operation, covering areas such as defence plans and equipment, nuclear weaponry, codes and communication interception, the security services, civil defence and the photography of defence installations. For example, D Notice number one on defence plans and equipment covers:

'Information relating to...defence policy or plans...actual service manpower strengths or specialities, categories or trades...future movements or intended destinations of HM ships...current or projected tactics or trials. In case of doubt, you are requested to seek advice through the appropriate government department.' (*New Statesman*, 4 April 1980)

Admiral Higgens, the Secretary to the D Notice Committee in 1992 has described the system as:

'A voluntary advisory service and like pregnancy testing, its consultations are confidential.' (quoted in the *Guardian*, 21 February 1992)

According to a further report in the *Guardian*, Admiral Higgens gave positive advice to editors, urging them not to publish about a dozen times a year. He received about 100 enquiries a year from editors and publishers (*Guardian*, 24 September 1992). Compliance with the Secretary's advice, however, does not guarantee immunity from prosecution under the 1989 Official Secrets Act.

In practice, the media does explore areas covered by D Notices. But, there is evidence that some areas are not explored because of fear of D Notice intervention. The fact that the system is informal has probably been responsible for the lack of outcry or reaction from the media. The D Notice system encourages the media to accept that there are sensitive areas which should not be probed.

The lobby system (see above section 2.2)

Secrecy and control of information is enhanced by the lobby system. The system has evolved into a secretive and informal system of news control suited to the needs of politicians and journalists alike. As Hennessy argues:

'Any system of mass non-attributable briefings is a restrictive practice rigged for the benefit and convenience of the givers and receivers of information and against the interests of the consumer - the reader, the listener, the viewer and the voter.' (Hennessy & Walker, 1987, p.14)

Refusal to answer questions in Parliament

Ministers can refuse to answer questions in the House of Commons or they can choose to give incomplete answers to MPs' questions. The Table Office which receives MPs' questions and decides which can be submitted, holds a list of topics which will not be accepted. This list has developed out of the rulings made by successive Speakers. In 1972, it was revealed that there were 95 taboo subjects (Hillyard & Percy-Smith, 1988). Ministers can refuse to answer any question on the grounds of national security.

The routine operation of government business

The principles of collective Cabinet responsibility (see chapter 12, section 2.2) and individual ministerial responsibility (see chapter 13, section 1.4) help to ensure that secrecy begins at the top. Little is left to chance. *Questions of Procedure for Ministers*, the official guidelines laid down for ministers, explain in some detail how secrecy is maintained and how the public is denied the right to know. The routine operation of government business is, therefore, structured to ensure that closed government, with its veil of secrecy, is the norm.

Activity 19.9

Item A *The Official Secrets Act 1989*

Critics of the Official Secrets Act 1989 have argued that its most serious flaw is that it does not allow a public interest defence. It has also been suggested that, while the 1911 Act was ineffective and unworkable, the 1989 Act might prove to be a more formidable political weapon for a government determined to prevent disclosures. Further, critics have asked why a government not noted for its support of civil liberties or freedom of information would want to liberalise secrecy legislation. Throughout the 1980s, the Campaign for a Freedom of Information Act gained momentum. This would give the public the right of access to official information (except for that in a few exempt categories). Could it be that the 1989 Act has undermined the arguments for more fundamental reforms and distracted attention away from the real problems of UK government secrecy?

Adapted from Hunt, 1992.

Item B *The D Notice system*

According to a Commons Defence Committee report, newspapers simply do not use the D Notices. Some have not consulted them for years. One newspaper had lost its copy of them. The Committee also notes that some categories of sensitive information are not covered by the system, that both foreign and fringe press are excluded and that the wording of the Notices is so broad that it is almost meaningless. The report states that there were four main criticisms of the system. First, it was a form of censorship which could be used by the government to suppress information for political convenience. Second, the freedom of the press was compromised. Third, there was confusion between the D Notice system and the law. And fourth, the system was little used and, therefore, unnecessary. The report notes that the Notices have been little altered in nine years and, in the last six months, there were just 30 minor enquiries to the committee.

Adapted from the *Guardian*, 8 August 1990.

Item C *The lobby system*

This cartoon was drawn to mark the centenary of the founding of the lobby system. The lobby system was founded in 1884.

Item D *Questions of Procedure for Ministers*

According to *Questions of Procedure for Ministers*, all ministers should be concerned to protect both the government's reputation for integrity and the confidentiality of its proceeding. These are the essential basis of collective responsibility. On the first appointment and, in certain cases, on appointment to subsequent ministerial office, ministers will be briefed by members of the Security Service who will explain both the basic threat to our security and the system of protection against it. Premature and unauthorised disclosure of matters under discussion by the Cabinet or its committees damages the reputation of the government and impairs the efficiency of administration. Ministers who share the collective responsibility for the government's programme must be kept generally aware of the development of important aspects of government policy. But, outside this limited circle, knowledge of these matters should be confined to those, whether ministers or officials, who are assisting in the formulation of particular policy.

Adapted from the *New Statesman*, 21 February 1986.

Questions

1. Write an article explaining how the British government is able to maintain secrecy in the 1990s.
2. Was the Official Secrets Act 1989 designed to increase or reduce the government's scope for restricting the dissemination of information? Use Item A in your answer.
3. 'The lobby system and the D Notice system are tools which the government use to gag the press.' Give arguments for and against this statement using Items B and C.
4. What does Item D tell us about the pressure on ministers to be secretive?

References

Allan et al. (1994) Allan, P., Benyon, J & McCormick, B., *Focus on Britain 1994*, Perennial Publications, 1994.

Annan (1977) Annan Committee, *Report of the Committee on the Future of Broadcasting*, Cmnd 6753, HMSO, 1977.

Barratt (1986) Barratt, D., *Media Sociology*, Tavistock, 1986.

Benn (1979) Benn, T., *Arguments for Socialism*, Penguin, 1979.

Benyon & Denver (1990) Benyon J. & Denver, D., 'Mrs Thatcher's electoral success', *Social Studies Review*, Vol. 5, No. 3, January 1990.

BRU (1985) Broadcasting Research Unit, *The Public Service Idea in British Broadcasting - Main Principles*, Broadcasting Research Unit, 1985.

Chapman & Hunt (1987) Chapman, R. & Hunt, M. (eds), *Open Government*, Routledge, 1987.

Charter 88 (1993) Robertson, G., 'The Cure for the British disease', *Violations of Rights in Britain No.4*, Charter 88 Enterprises, 1993.

Cockerell et al. (1984) Cockerell, M., Hennessy, P. & Walker, P., *Sources Close to the Prime Minister: Inside the Hidden World of the News Manipulators*, Macmillan, 1984.

CSE (1985) *Politics and Profit*, monthly newsletter of the Conference of Socialist Economists, June 1985.

Curran & Seaton (1991) Curran, J. & Seaton, J., *Power Without Responsibility*, Routledge, 1991.

Dunkley (1985) Dunkley, C., *Television Today and Tomorrow: Wall-to-Wall Dallas?*, Penguin, 1985.

Evans (1984) Evans, H., *Good Times, Bad Times*, Coronet, 1984.

Franklin (1993) Franklin, B., 'Packaging politics: politicians and the media' in *Haralambos* (1993).

Franklin (1994) Franklin, B., *Packaging Politics*, Edward Arnold, 1994.

Franks (1972) Franks, O., *Departmental Committee on Section 2 of the Official Secrets Act 1911*, Cmnd 5104, HMSO, 1972.

Grant (1994) Grant, M., 'The politics of the British media', *Talking Politics,* Vol.6, No.2, winter 1994.

GUMG (1982) Glasgow University Media Group, *Really Bad News*, Writers & Readers, 1982.

Haralambos (1993) Haralambos, M. (ed.), *Developments in Sociology*, Vol. 10, Causeway Press, 1993.

Harris (1983) Harris, R., *Gotcha. The Media, the Government and the Falklands Crisis*, Faber & Faber, 1983.

HC 141 (1989) *First Report from the Select Committee on Televising of Proceedings of the House*, HC 141, 1988-89, 1989.

Heath et al. (1994) Heath, A., Jowell, R. & Curtice, J., *Labour's last chance?*, Dartmouth, 1994.

Hennessy (1989) Hennessy, P., *Whitehall*, Fontana Press, 1989.

Hennessy & Walker (1987) Hennessy, P. & Walker, D., 'The Lobby' in *Seaton & Pimlott (1987)*.

Hillyard & Percy-Smith (1988) Hillyard, P. & Percy-Smith, J., *The Coercive State*, Fontana, 1988.

HMSO (1993) Central Statistical Office, *Social Trends 23*, HMSO, 1993.

HMSO (1994) Central Statistical Office, *Social Trends 24*, HMSO, 1994.

HMSO (1995) Central Statistical Office, *Social Trends 25*, HMSO, 1995.

Hunt (1992) Hunt, S., 'State secrecy in the UK', *Politics Review*, Vol.1, No.4, April 1992.

Jones et al . (1989) Jones, K., Millard, F. & Twigg, L., 'Government information policy in the 1980s', *Talking Politics*, Vol.1, No.3, summer 1989.

Kuhn (1994) Kuhn, R., 'The Media' in *Allan et al.*, 1994.

Marx & Engels (1976) Marx, K. & Engels, F., *Collected Works*, Laurence and Wishart, 1976.

Michael (1982) Michael, J., *The Politics of Secrecy*, Penguin, 1982.

Miliband (1989) Miliband, R., *Divided Societies*, Oxford University Press, 1989.

Miller (1991) Miller, W.L., *Media and Voters: the Audience, Content and Influence of Press and Television at the 1987 General Election*, Clarendon Press, 1991.

Negrine (1994) Negrine, R. *Politics and the Mass Media in Britain (2nd edn)*, Routledge, 1994.

Orwell (1949) Orwell, G., *Nineteen Eighty Four*, Penguin, 1989

Peak (1994) Peak, S., *The Media Guide*, Fourth Estate, 1994.

Platt (1993) Platt, S., 'A zoom with a view', *New Statesman and Society*, 12 November 1993.

Robertson (1989) Robertson, G., *Freedom, the individual and the Law*, Penguin, 1989.

Seabrook (1987) Seabrook, J., 'What the papers show', *New Society*, 5 June 1987.

Seaton & Pimlott (1987) Seaton, J. & Pimlott, B. (eds), *The Media in British Politics*, Gower, 1987.

Seymour Ure (1993) Seymour Ure, C., 'The media under Major', *Politics Review*, Vol.2, No.3, February 1993.

Straw (1993) Straw, J., *The Decline of Press Reporting of Parliament*, Labour party pamphlet, 1993.

Toffler (1980) Toffler, A., *The Third Wave*, Collins, 1980.

Trowler (1988) Trowler, P., *Investigating the Media*, Unwin Hyman, 1988.

Wagg (1989) Wagg, S., 'Politics and the popular press', *Social Studies Review*, Vol.5, No.1, September 1989.

Wagg (1994) Wagg, S., 'Politics and the media' in *Wale (1994)*.

Wale (1994) Wale, W. (ed.), *Developments in Politics*, Vol.5, Causeway Press, 1994.

Wilson (1984) Wilson, D., *The Secrets File: the Case for Freedom of Information in Britain Today*, Heinemann, 1984.

Index